Make the Connection

For trip planning and local activities, AAA guidebooks are just the beginning.

Open the door to a whole lot more on **AAA.com**. Get extra travel insight, more information and online booking.

Find this symbol for places to look, book and save on AAA.com.

iStockphoto.com_shapecharge

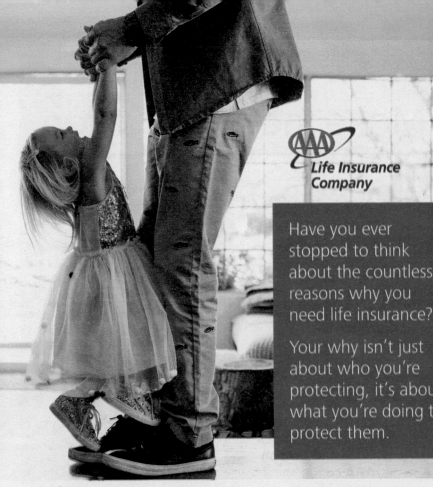

AAA
Life Insurance Company

Have you ever stopped to think about the countless reasons why you need life insurance?

Your why isn't just about who you're protecting, it's about what you're doing to protect them.

Whether it's a new house, a new grandchild or a new life with the one we love, life insurance can cover you for the now and whatever's next.

What's your why?

Get a free quote at AAALife.com

Northern California

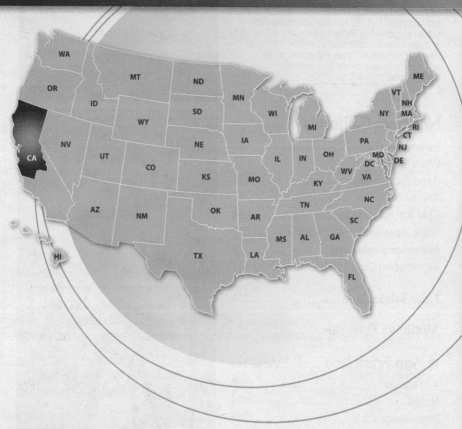

Published by AAA Publishing
1000 AAA Drive, Heathrow, FL 32746-5063
Copyright AAA 2019, All rights reserved

Advertising Rate and Circulation Information: (407) 444-8280

Printed in the USA by Quad/Graphics

This book is printed on paper certified by third-party standards for sustainably managed forestry and production.

Printed on recyclable paper.
Please recycle whenever possible.

Stock #4671

CONTENTS

Get more travel information at AAA.com/travelguides and AAA.com/traveltips

Attractions, hotels, restaurants and other travel experience information are all grouped under the alphabetical listing of the city in which those experiences are physically located—or the nearest recognized city.

Northern California

Featured Information

ESCAPE

SHOP

ENJOY

EARN[1]

3x ✈

points on eligible travel
and AAA purchases

2x 🛒

points on gas, grocery
store, wholesale club
and drugstore purchases

1x ☕

1 point per $1 on all
other purchases

AAA Member Rewards
4000 1234 5678 9123
VALID THRU 00/00
CHRIS L MARTIN
VISA Signature

FROM **EVERYDAY** TO **EXTRAORDINARY**

APPLY TODAY!
Visit your local AAA office or AAA.com/CreditCard

Using Your Guide

AAA TourBook guides are packed with travel insights, maps and listings of places to stay, play, eat and save. For more listings, more details and online booking, visit **AAA.com/travelguides**.

Helping You Make the Connection

Look for this symbol @ throughout the guides for direct links to related content.

A to Z City Listings

Cities and places are listed alphabetically within each state or province. Attractions, hotels and restaurants are listed once — under the city in which they are physically located.

Cities that are considered part of a larger destination city or area have an expanded city header. The header identifies the larger region and cross-references pages that contain shared trip-planning resources:

- Destination map – outline map of the cities that comprise a destination city or area
- Attraction spotting map – regional street map marked with attraction locations
- Hotel/restaurant spotting map and index – regional street map numbered with hotel and restaurant locations identified in an accompanying index

Cities that are not considered part of a larger destination city or area but have a significant number of listings may have these resources within the individual city section:

- Attraction spotting map
- Hotel/restaurant spotting map and index

Location Abbreviations

Directions are from the center of town unless otherwise specified, using these highway abbreviations:

Bus. Rte.=business route
CR=county road
FM=farm to market
FR=forest road
Hwy.=Canadian highway
I=interstate highway
LR=legislative route
R.R.=rural route
SR/PR=state or provincial route
US=federal highway

About Listed Establishments

AAA/CAA Inspected & Approved hotels and restaurants are listed on the basis of merit alone after careful evaluation and approval by full-time, professionally trained AAA inspectors. An establishment's decision to advertise in the TourBook guide has no bearing on its evaluation or rating; nor does inclusion of advertising imply AAA endorsement of products and services.

Information in this guide was believed accurate at the time of publication. However, since changes inevitably occur between annual editions, please contact your AAA travel professional, visit **AAA.com/travelguides** or download the free AAA Mobile app to confirm prices and schedules.

Attraction Listing Icons

[SAVE] AAA Discounts & Rewards® member discount

[🔌] Electric vehicle charging station on premises. Domestic station information provided by the U.S. Department of Energy. Canadian station information provided by Plug'n Drive Ontario.

[GT] Guided Tours available

[▲] Camping facilities

[🍴] Food on premises

[☒] Recreational activities

[🐾] Pet friendly (Call for restrictions/fees.)

[🏕] Picnicking allowed

In select cities only:

[🚇] Mass transit station within 1 mile. Icon is followed by station name and AAA/CAA designated station number within listing.

[GEM] AAA/CAA travel experts may designate an attraction of exceptional interest and quality as a AAA GEM — a *Great Experience for Members®*. See GEM Attraction Index (listed on CONTENTS page) for a complete list of locations.

Consult the online travel guides at **AAA.com/travelguides** or visit AAA Mobile for additional things to do if you have time.

Hotel Listing Icons

May be preceded by CALL and/or SOME UNITS.

Member Information:

[SAVE] Member rates: discounted standard room rate or lowest public rate available at time of booking for dates of stay.

ECO Eco-certified by government or private organization.

Electric vehicle charging station on premises. Domestic station information provided by the U.S. Department of Energy. Canadian station information provided by Plug'n Drive Ontario.

✗ Smoke-free premises

In select cities only:

🚇 Mass transit station within 1 mile. Icon is followed by station name and AAA/CAA designated station number within listing.

Services:

✈ Airport transportation

🐾 Pet friendly (Call for restrictions/fees.)

🍴 Restaurant on premises

🍴→ Restaurant off premises

🍽 Room service for 2 or more meals

🍸 Full bar

🧸 Child care

BIZ Business center

♿ Accessible features (Call property for available services and amenities.)

Activities:

🎰 Full-service casino

🏊 Pool

🏋 Health club or exercise room on premises

In-Room Amenities:

HS High-speed Internet service

$HS High-speed Internet service (Call property for fees.)

🛜 Wireless Internet service

$🛜 Wireless Internet service (Call property for fees.)

🚫🛜 No wireless Internet service

📽 Pay movies

🧊 Refrigerator

🔲 Microwave

☕ Coffeemaker

ᛆ No air conditioning

📺 No TV

☎ No telephones

Restaurant Listing Icons

SAVE AAA Discounts & Rewards® member discount

ECO Eco-certified by government or private organization.

Electric vehicle charging station on premises. Domestic station information provided by the U.S. Department of Energy. Canadian station information provided by Plug'n Drive Ontario.

ᛆ No air conditioning

♿ Accessible features (Call property for available services and amenities.)

◥ Designated smoking section

B Breakfast

L Lunch

D Dinner

24 Open 24 hours

LATE Open after 11 p.m.

🐾 Pet friendly (Call for restrictions/fees.)

In select cities only:

🚇 Mass transit station within 1 mile. Icon is followed by station name and AAA/CAA designated station number within listing.

Map Legend

For attraction and hotel/restaurant spotting maps, refer to the legend below to identify symbols and color coding.

Roads/Highways

Free — Interchange
Toll —

Controlled access
Controlled access toll
Local toll
Primary
Secondary
Local unpaved
Under construction
Tunnel
Pedestrian only
Auto ferry
Passenger ferry
Scenic byway

Areas of Interest

Incorporated city
✈ ✈ Int'l/Regional airport
Park
Recreation sites
Forest
Natural lands
Military
Historic
Native American
Beach
Marsh

Route Shields

Interstate	95	95 Business	Trans-Canada	Primary	Secondary
Federal	Primary 22	Secondary 22	Provincial Autoroute	22	22
State	①	①	Mexico	1	1
County	1	1	Historic	66	

Boundaries

International   Time zone
State   Continental Divide

Points of Interest

⭐ National capital   o Town
★ State/Prov capital   ⛺ Campground
■ AAA/CAA club location   ⚑ Winery
■ Feature of interest   Customs station
⬥ GEM attraction   Historic
⑫ Hotel listing   △ Mountain peak
③ Restaurant listing   Rapid transit
🏛 College/University   Stations   Metromover

Understanding the Diamond Ratings

Hotel and restaurant inspections are unscheduled to ensure our trained professionals encounter the same unbiased experience members do.

Inspected & Approved

- The first step for every hotel and restaurant is to demonstrate they meet expected standards of cleanliness, comfort and hospitality.
- Only hotels and restaurants that pass AAA's rigorous on-site inspection are designated **AAA Inspected & Approved.**

But all AAA Inspected & Approved properties aren't the same: The difference is in the **Diamonds.** Each additional Diamond means greater comfort, amenities and service. Learn more at **AAA.com/Diamonds.**

Hotels

Budget-oriented, offering basic comfort and hospitality.

Affordable, with modestly enhanced facilities, décor and amenities.

Distinguished, multifaceted with enhanced physical attributes, amenities and guest comforts.

Refined, stylish with upscale physical attributes, extensive amenities and high degree of hospitality, service and attention to detail.

Ultimate luxury, sophistication and comfort with extraordinary physical attributes, meticulous personalized service, extensive amenities and impeccable standards of excellence.

Restaurants

Simple, economical food, often quick-serve, in a functional environment.

Familiar food, often cooked to order, served in casual surroundings.

Trendy cuisine, skillfully prepared and served, with expanded beverage options, in an enhanced setting.

Distinctive fine-dining. Creative preparations, skillfully served, often with wine steward, amid upscale ambience.

Leading-edge cuisine of the finest ingredients, uniquely prepared by an acclaimed chef, served by expert service staff led by maître d' in extraordinary surroundings.

Guest Safety

Inspectors view a sampling of rooms during hotel evaluations and, therefore, AAA/CAA cannot guarantee working locks and operational fire safety equipment in every guest unit.

Contacting AAA/CAA About the TourBook Guide

Tell us what you think about the TourBook guides or your experience at a listed hotel, restaurant or attraction. If your visit doesn't meet your expectations, please contact us **during your visit or within 30 days**. Be sure to save your receipts. We also welcome your recommendations on places to inspect.

Use the easy online form at **AAA.com/MemberFeedback,** email memberrelations@national.aaa.com or mail your feedback to: AAA Member Comments, 1000 AAA Dr., Box 61, Heathrow, FL 32746.

Bixby Bridge in Big Sur

Northern California

The Golden State's allure must be powerful: Millions of people can't be wrong. Abundant resources and a stunning landscape help explain the attraction. Northern California, from the regal redwoods near the Oregon border to Monterey Peninsula's jagged coastline, is immensely blessed.

Most Americans who have never been west of the Rockies have heard of Yosemite Valley, Big Sur, Lake Tahoe and Wine Country. Thanks to movies and television, California and all its associations—surfing, environmentalists chaining themselves to condemned trees, pollution, earthquakes—have all entered the popular imagination.

When a fad sweeps the country, odds are that it started in California. The sense of style here is often imitated, the cuisine savored around the world.

Besides physical appeal, perhaps nothing epitomizes the "Left Coast" more than the people and their almost mythical lifestyle.

Napa

Populated by entrepreneurs, visionaries, counterculture radicals, trendsetters and a few eccentrics, the state is fertile ground for innovations and technological breakthroughs. No wonder Americans looking to the future often face west.

The Golden State

Picture a snow-clad mountainside. A man and a woman in ski gear swoosh down an alpine slope. Cut to a sun-washed beach hours later. The same twosome strolls along the shore, water lapping at their feet. Then, at a swank urban bistro that evening they sit across from each other savoring a sumptuous dinner.

Although unusually energetic, the duo described above is realistic. It's the setting that seems unreal. Skiing in the mountains within hours of a walk on a picture-postcard beach? Both within reach of a major city? Does such a place really exist?

The place is real. As you've probably guessed, this could only be California.

From that first cry of "Eureka!" at Sutter's Mill to the chaotic tidal wave of the ensuing gold rush and the tragedy of the San Francisco earthquake decades later, drama has been one of the state's most notable traits.

The California landscape itself is dramatic. Breathtaking only begins to describe Big

Sur's rocky, sea-splashed cliffs, the Sierra Nevada's glacier-sculpted peaks or vineyards flourishing in dappled sunlight.

Vistas impossible to truly capture on film abound in Yosemite National Park. It's difficult to comprehend the colossal escarpments and the height of its waterfalls. And what camera could do justice to the grandeur of Half Dome or El Capitan?

Zoom in on the mountains, valleys and shores and you'll find a fascinating array of plants and animals. Off the coast, migrating whales are the stars while sea lions and playful sea otters make their appearances closer to shore. California's signature flora includes giant redwoods and giant sequoias.

The Original Settlers

Even before the flood of gold rush prospectors, Northern California was home to a cast of characters that included Franciscan missionaries, Spanish ranchers and the Native Americans who had lived here for thousands of years. Then the possibility of instant riches created towns almost overnight, and folks have never stopped being drawn to the spectacle of the place.

The results of their labors take myriad forms: centuries-old Spanish missions that dot the coast; the futuristic glass-and-steel skyscrapers of San Francisco; the lovely beach resort of Carmel-by-the-Sea; and the quaint gold rush towns sprinkled along the western slopes of the Sierra Nevadas.

Recreation

The great outdoors truly is great here. Wetsuited surfers flock to Monterey Bay's chilly waters, especially Santa Cruz's Steamer Lane. And the coastline's inlets and coves are perfect for boating.

San Francisco Bay draws wind surfers, with the Presidio's Crissy Field offering amazing urban views and the chance to sail under the Golden Gate Bridge.

Anglers can rent saltwater fishing gear in many coastal towns; salmon is among the most popular catches. Freshwater fishing and boating are plentiful, too. Lake Tahoe and Shasta Lake draw small fleets of pleasure craft on balmy weekends. In addition to being California's second-largest freshwater lake, Clear Lake near Kelseyville is one of the nation's finest bass repositories.

April to October is best for white-water rafting on California's rushing rivers. The Lower Klamath and the South Fork of the American River are ideal for families, as the excitement of maneuvering rapids is interspersed with the calm of peaceful floats. The more daring should try the North Fork of the American or the Tuolumne River. A bonus of rafting trips is the chance to see great blue herons, ospreys, bald eagles, river otters and deer.

If hiking or backpacking is your sport, consider the California Coastal Trail or the Pacific Crest Trail, both stretching from Mexico to Canada. Check out Mount Tamalpais and Mount Diablo state parks and the Golden Gate National Recreation Area near San Francisco. Also, Marin County, on the north end of the Golden Gate Bridge, offers mountain biking trails.

Hikers at Lake Tahoe should not miss the views from the Tahoe Rim Trail. Then there's Yosemite, which deserves its reputation for amazing scenery. Don't limit yourself to the valley floor; the park's high country, accessible in summer, offers spectacular vistas.

Many parks and recreation areas are great for camping, too. In fact, Tahoe National Forest claims to have 1,400 camping sites.

California boasts some of the nation's finest golfing. Monterey Peninsula courses offer a choice of windswept ocean views or forested valleys; those near Pebble Beach are probably the best known.

When temperatures drop, Californians head outdoors for great skiing and snowboarding. The Lake Tahoe area alone is sprinkled with more than a dozen ski resorts.

Giant sequoia at Mariposa Grove, Yosemite National Park

Historic Timeline

1769	Fathers Junípero Serra and Fermín Lasuén begin building a chain of 21 missions extending from San Diego to Sonoma.
1848	James Marshall discovers gold at Sutter's Mill; the following year fortune seekers rush into California.
1850	California becomes the 31st state.
1890	Yosemite National Park is established.
1906	An earthquake and resulting fires destroy most of San Francisco.
1945	Representatives of 51 countries meet in San Francisco to sign the charter forming the United Nations.
1962	California becomes the most populous state in the nation.
1989	A 7.1 magnitude earthquake centered 51 miles south of San Francisco causes $6 billion in property damage.
1992	An acquittal verdict in the Rodney King beating trial sparks race riots in Los Angeles.
1994	An earthquake centered 20 miles northwest of Los Angeles leaves 22,000 homeless.
2010	With their state facing a fiscal crisis, voters elect former governor Jerry Brown to another term in office.

What To Pack

Temperature Averages Maximum/Minimum	JANUARY	FEBRUARY	MARCH	APRIL	MAY	JUNE	JULY	AUGUST	SEPTEMBER	OCTOBER	NOVEMBER	DECEMBER
Eureka	55 / 41	56 / 42	56 / 42	57 / 44	60 / 48	62 / 51	63 / 53	64 / 53	64 / 51	61 / 48	58 / 44	55 / 41
Fresno	54 / 38	61 / 41	66 / 45	74 / 48	83 / 55	91 / 61	97 / 66	95 / 65	89 / 60	78 / 52	63 / 42	53 / 37
Mendocino	56 / 41	57 / 42	58 / 42	61 / 43	62 / 45	65 / 48	67 / 50	67 / 50	67 / 49	64 / 46	59 / 43	55 / 40
Mount Shasta	44 / 26	48 / 29	52 / 30	59 / 33	67 / 39	76 / 45	83 / 49	83 / 48	76 / 43	64 / 37	50 / 30	44 / 26
San Francisco	56 / 43	59 / 46	61 / 47	64 / 48	67 / 51	70 / 53	71 / 55	72 / 56	73 / 55	70 / 52	62 / 48	56 / 43
Truckee	40 / 14	42 / 17	45 / 21	52 / 25	61 / 31	71 / 37	79 / 41	79 / 41	72 / 35	62 / 28	47 / 21	40 / 15

From the records of The Weather Channel Interactive, Inc.

Good Facts To Know

ABOUT THE STATE

POPULATION: 37,253,956.
AREA: 163,695 square miles; ranks 3rd.
CAPITAL: Sacramento.
HIGHEST POINT: 14,505 ft., Mount Whitney.
LOWEST POINT: -282 ft., Death Valley.
TIME ZONE(S): Pacific. DST.

GAMBLING

MINIMUM AGE FOR GAMBLING: 18 if alcohol is not available; 21 if alcohol is available.

REGULATIONS

TEEN DRIVING LAWS: Teens who have had a license less than 1 year are not permitted to transport non-family members under 20 unless someone over age 25 is in the front seat. Driving is not permitted 11 p.m.-5 a.m. by licensed teens under 17 (except under special circumstances). The minimum age for an unrestricted license is 17. Phone (800) 777-0133 for more information about California driver's license regulations.

SEAT BELT/CHILD RESTRAINT LAWS: Seat belts are required for the driver and all passengers ages 16 and over; passengers ages 8-15 or over 57 inches tall must use an approved child restraint or seat belt. Child restraints are required for children under age 7 or under 57 inches tall and must be in the rear seat if available. AAA recommends the use of seat belts and appropriate child restraints for the driver and all passengers.

DISTRACTED DRIVING LAWS: All drivers are banned from text messaging and using handheld cellphones. Drivers under 18 are prohibited from all cellphone use.

HELMETS FOR MOTORCYCLISTS: Required for all riders.

RADAR DETECTORS: Permitted. Prohibited in commercial vehicles.

MOVE OVER LAW: Driver is required to slow down and vacate the lane nearest stopped police, fire and rescue vehicles using audible or flashing signals. The law also applies to recovery vehicles such as tow trucks, Caltrans vehicles displaying warning lights and waste service vehicles.

FIREARMS LAWS: Vary by state and/or county. Contact Department of Justice, Bureau of Firearms, P.O. Box 820200, Sacramento, CA 94203-0200; phone (916) 227-7527.

SPECIAL REGULATIONS: The State Department of Food and Agriculture inspects all produce, plant materials and wild animals at the borders to see if they are admissible under current quarantine regulations. For California regulations concerning plants phone (916) 654-0312; for regulations concerning animals phone (916) 854-3950. Dogs older than 4 months must have a current rabies vaccination certificate.

HOLIDAYS

HOLIDAYS: Jan. 1 ▪ Martin Luther King Jr. Day, Jan. (3rd Mon.) ▪ Washington's Birthday/Presidents Day, Feb. (3rd Mon.) ▪ Easter ▪ César Chávez Day, Mar. 31 ▪ Memorial Day, May (last Mon.) ▪ July 4 ▪ Labor Day, Sept. (1st Mon.) ▪ Columbus Day, Oct. (2nd Mon.) ▪ Veterans Day, Nov. 11 ▪ Thanksgiving, Nov. (4th Thurs.) ▪ Christmas, Dec. 25.

MONEY

TAXES: California's statewide sales tax is 7.5 percent. Additional local taxes of up to 2 percent may be imposed in some counties; more than one tax may be in effect in some locations. A transient occupancy tax is levied in some counties and cities.

VISITOR INFORMATION

INFORMATION CENTERS: California welcome centers are in Anderson off I-5 Deschutes Road exit on SR 273 ▪ in El Dorado Hills at 2085 Vine St. ▪ in Buena Park off I-5 exit 116 at 6601 Beach Blvd. ▪ in Ontario at the Ontario Mills Premium Mall ▪ in Salinas at 1213 N. Davis Rd. ▪ in Santa Rosa off US 101 Downtown/Third Street exit at the end of Fourth Street ▪ in Auburn off I-80 Foresthill exit on Lincoln Way ▪ in Truckee at 10065 Donner Pass Rd. ▪ in San Francisco at Pier 39 ▪ in Mammoth Lakes at 2510 Hwy. 203 Bus. Rte. ▪ in Merced on W. 16th Street ▪ in Pismo Beach on US 101 at Five Cities Drive ▪ in Barstow off I-15 Lenwood Road exit ▪ in Oxnard off US 101 at Town Center Drive ▪ in Yucca Valley on SR 62 ▪ and in Oceanside off I-5 Coast Highway exit.

ROAD CONDITIONS: Caltrans provides current information about road conditions; phone (800) 427-7623.

FURTHER INFORMATION FOR VISITORS:
Visit California
555 Capitol Mall Dr., Suite 1100
Sacramento, CA 95814
(916) 444-4429
(877) 225-4367 (Tourist Guide info)

NATIONAL FOREST INFORMATION:
Pacific-Southwest Region
USDA Forest Service
1323 Club Dr.
Vallejo, CA 94592
(707) 562-8737
(877) 444-6777 (reservations)

FISHING AND HUNTING REGULATIONS:
California Department of Fish and Wildlife
1416 9th St., 12th Floor
Sacramento, CA 95814
(916) 445-0411

RECREATION INFORMATION:
California State Park System
Department of Parks and Recreation
1416 9th St.
Sacramento, CA 95814
(916) 653-6995
(800) 777-0369

NATIONAL PARKS:
National Park Service
Dept. of Interior
333 Bush St., Suite 500
San Francisco, CA 94104
(415) 623-2100
(877) 444-6777 (reservation center)

Northern California Annual Events

Please call ahead to confirm event details.

 Visit AAA.com/travelguides/events to find
AAA-listed events for every day of the year

WINTER

Dec. - Union Street Holiday Festivities / San
Francisco / 800-310-6563
- Christkindlmarkt / Sacramento
916-442-7360
- Cornish Christmas / Grass
Valley / 530-272-8315

Jan. - Golden Gate Kennel Club Dog Show
Daly City / 415-819-5773
- Whalefest Monterey / Monterey
831-649-6544
- Sea Lions' Arrival / San
Francisco / 415-705-5500

Feb. - AT&T Pebble Beach National Pro-Am
Pebble Beach / 831-649-1533
- Cloverdale Citrus Fair / Cloverdale
707-894-3992
- Tulipmania Festival / San
Francisco / 415-705-5500

SPRING

Mar. - Dublin's St. Patrick's Day Festival
Dublin / 925-556-4500
- Fort Bragg Whale Festival / Fort
Bragg / 707-961-6300
- North Lake Tahoe SnowFest! / Tahoe
City / 530-583-7167

Apr. - Northern California Cherry Blossom
Festival / San
Francisco / 415-563-2313
- San Joaquin Asparagus Festival
Stockton / 916-370-3647
- Red Bluff Round-Up / Red
Bluff / 530-527-5534

May - Stanford Powwow / Palo
Alto / 650-723-4078
- Calaveras County Fair & Jumping
Frog Jubilee / Angels
Camp / 209-736-2561
- Sacramento Music Festival
Sacramento / 916-372-5277

SUMMER

June - North Beach Festival / San
Francisco / 415-989-2220
- Western States Horse Expo
Sacramento / 800-352-2411

July - Gilroy Garlic Festival / Gilroy
408-842-1625
- California State Fair / Sacramento
877-225-3976
- Feast of Lanterns / Pacific
Grove / 831-800-1905

Aug. - Rolex Monterey Motorsports Reunion
Salinas / 831-242-8201
- Lake Tahoe Concours d'Elegance
Wooden Boat Show / Homewood
775-851-4444
- Pebble Beach Concours d'Elegance
Pebble Beach / 831-659-0663

FALL

Sept. - San Francisco Fringe Festival / San
Francisco / 415-931-1094
- California International Airshow
Salinas / 888-845-7469
- Valley of the Moon Vintage Festival
Sonoma / 707-996-2109

Oct. - Sonora Bach Festival / Sonora
209-536-6330
- Grand National Rodeo, Horse and
Livestock Show / Daly
City / 415-404-4111
- Fleet Week / San
Francisco / 415-306-0911

Nov. - Valhalla Holiday Faire / South
Lake Tahoe / 530-541-4975
- Craftsman's Days / Eureka
707-444-3437
- Harvest Festival Original Art & Craft
Show / Sacramento / 800-231-1213

**Love the great outdoors? Find places to camp
at AAA.com/campgrounds**

Julia Pfeiffer Burns State Park, Big Sur

Hog Island Oyster Co., San Francisco

Pinnacles National Park

Mission San Juan Bautista

Lassen Volcanic National Park

◥GEM Index: Great Experience for Members

AAA editor's picks of exceptional note

Mission San Carlos
Borroméo del Río

Muir Woods National
Monument

Devils Postpile
National Monument

Golden Gate Bridge

See Orientation map on p. 24 for corresponding grid coordinates, if applicable.
*Indicates the GEM is temporarily closed.

The California Academy of Sciences
(See p. 279.)

Chinatown *(See p. 276.)*

de Young Museum *(See p. 280.)*

Exploratorium *(See p. 277.)*

Golden Gate Bridge *(See p. 278.)*

Golden Gate Park *(See p. 278.)*

Legion of Honor *(See p. 283.)*

Mission San Francisco de Asis *(See p. 285.)*

San Francisco Museum of Modern Art
(See p. 287.)

San Jose (E-9)

Lick Observatory *(See p. 344.)*

Rosicrucian Egyptian Museum *(See p. 344.)*

Winchester Mystery House *(See p. 345.)*

San Juan Bautista (G-3)

Mission San Juan Bautista *(See p. 357.)*

San Juan Bautista State Historic Park
(See p. 357.)

Santa Clara (E-9)

California's Great America *(See p. 360.)*

Santa Cruz (F-9)

Santa Cruz Beach Boardwalk *(See p. 363.)*

Santa Rosa (A-7)

Safari West *(See p. 370.)*

Sequoia and Kings Canyon National Parks (G-5)

Sequoia and Kings Canyon National Parks
(See p. 375.)

Shasta (C-2)

Shasta State Historic Park *(See p. 378.)*

Sonoma (B-7)

Sonoma State Historic Park *(See p. 381.)*

Tiburon (C-7)

Angel Island Immigration Station *(See p. 394.)*

Vallejo (B-8)

Six Flags Discovery Kingdom *(See p. 400.)*

Weott (C-1)

Avenue of the Giants *(See p. 402.)*

Yosemite National Park (F-4)

Yosemite National Park *(See p. 420.)*

Northern California
Atlas Section

VT 41 REFERENCE PAGE INDICATOR

ROADS/HIGHWAYS
- INTERSTATE
- CONTROLLED ACCESS
- CONTROLLED ACCESS TOLL
- TOLL ROAD
- PRIMARY DIVIDED
- PRIMARY UNDIVIDED
- SECONDARY DIVIDED
- SECONDARY UNDIVIDED
- LOCAL DIVIDED
- LOCAL UNDIVIDED
- UNPAVED ROAD
- UNDER CONSTRUCTION
- TUNNEL
- PEDESTRIAN ONLY
- AUTO FERRY
- PASSENGER FERRY
- SCENIC BYWAY
- 10 DISTANCE BETWEEN MARKERS
- EXIT NUMBER-FREE/TOLL
- INTERCHANGE FULL/PARTIAL
- WELCOME/INFORMATION CENTER
- REST AREA/ SERVICE CENTER

BOUNDARIES
- INTERNATIONAL
- STATE
- COUNTY
- TIME ZONE
- CONTINENTAL DIVIDE

ROAD SHIELDS
- INTERSTATE/BUSINESS
- U.S./STATE/COUNTY
- FOREST/INDIAN
- TRANS- CANADA
- PROVINCIAL AUTOROUTE/ KING'S HIGHWAY
- MEXICO
- HISTORIC ROUTE 66
- REFERENCE PAGE INDICATOR

AREAS OF INTEREST
- INDIAN
- MILITARY
- PARK
- FOREST
- GRASSLANDS
- HISTORIC
- INT'L/REGIONAL AIRPORT
- INCORPORATED CITY

POINTS OF INTEREST
- TOWN
- NATIONAL CAPITAL
- STATE/PROVINCIAL CAPITAL
- AAA/CAA CLUB LOCATION
- FEATURE OF INTEREST
- COLLEGE/UNIVERSITY
- CUSTOMS STATION
- HISTORIC
- LIGHTHOUSE
- MONUMENT/MEMORIAL
- STATE/PROVINCIAL PARK
- NATIONAL WILDLIFE REFUGE
- SKI AREA
- SPORTS COMPLEX
- DAM

CITIES/TOWNS are color-coded by size, showing where to find AAA Inspected and Approved lodgings or restaurants listed in the AAA TourBook guides and on AAA.com:
- ● Red - major destinations and capitals; many listings
- ● Black - destinations; some listings
- ● Grey - no listings

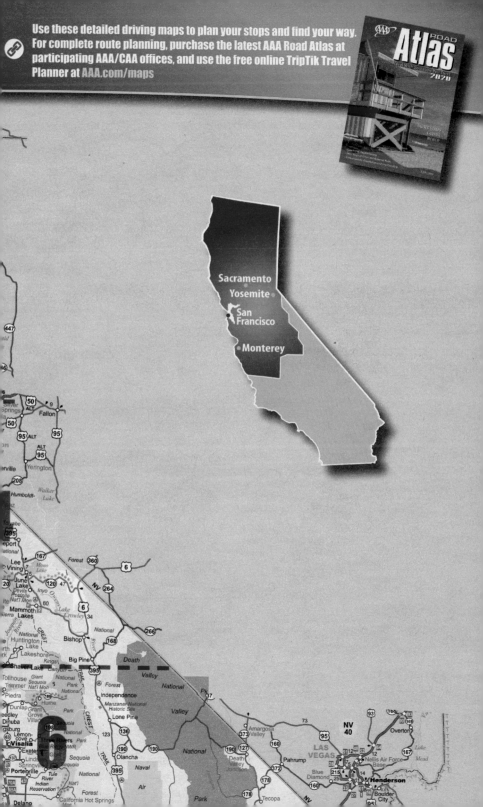

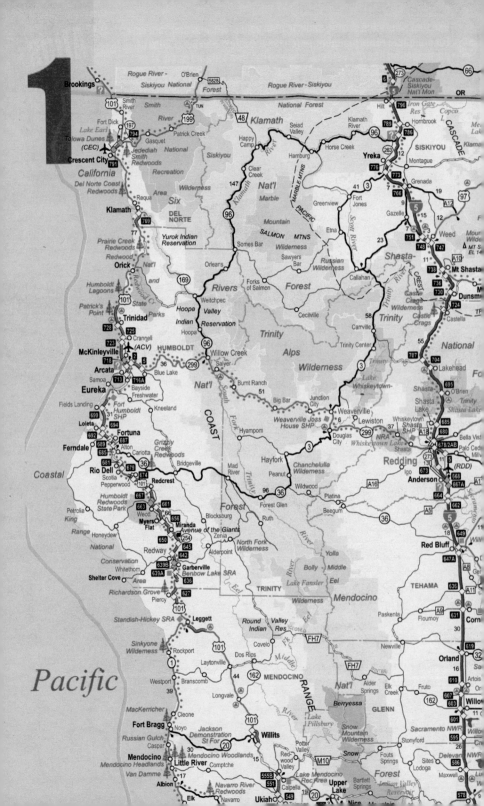

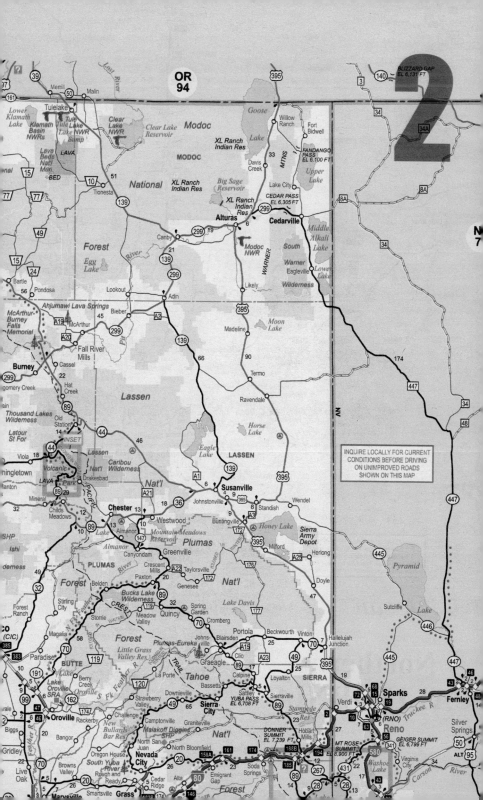

When traveling across the Golden Gate Bridge,
note that tolls can only be paid via the
Bay Area Fastrak System, or as a one-time
payment on-line. Refer to the Bay Area Fastrak
website at www.bayareafastrak.org/ for more information.

Ocean

Northern
CALIFORNIA

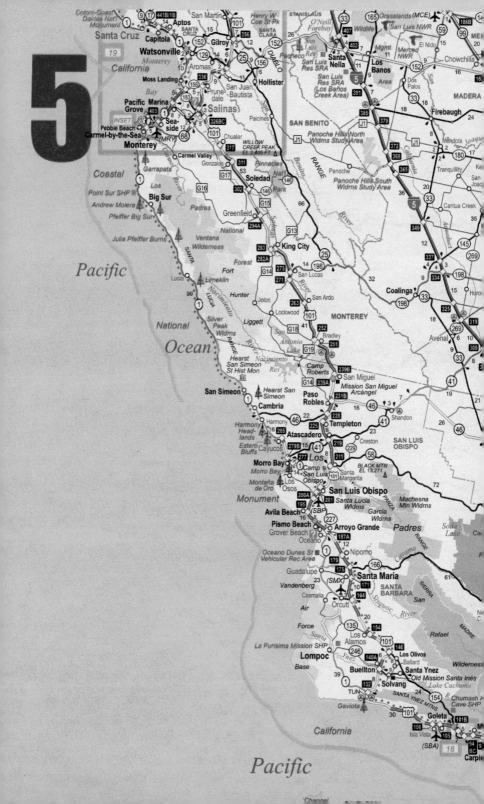

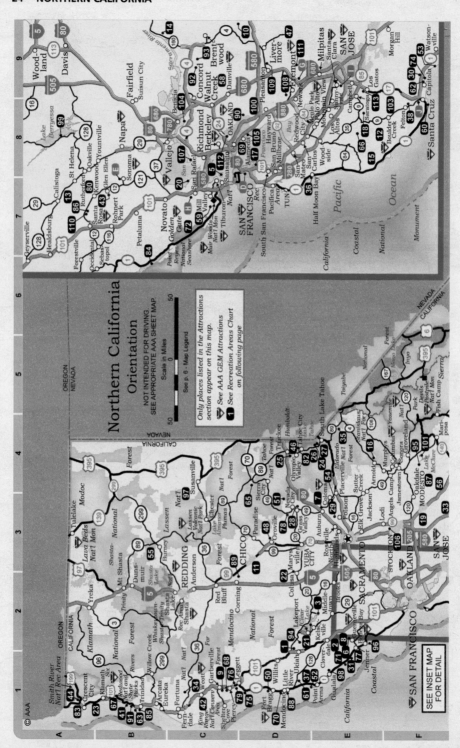

Northern California Orientation

NOT INTENDED FOR DRIVING
SEE APPROPRIATE AAA SHEET MAP

Scale in Miles

See p. 6 - Map Legend

Only places listed in the Attractions section appear on this map.

See AAA GEM Attractions

1 See Recreation Areas Chart on following page

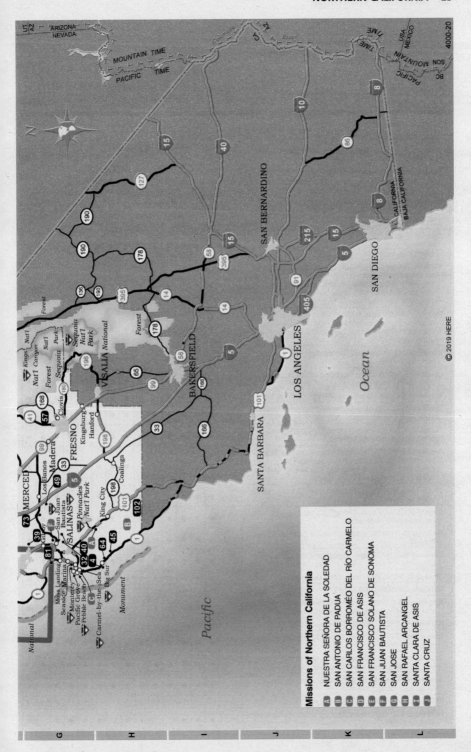

Missions of Northern California

- Ⓐ NUESTRA SEÑORA DE LA SOLEDAD
- Ⓑ SAN ANTONIO DE PADUA
- Ⓒ SAN CARLOS BORROMÉO DEL RÍO CARMELO
- Ⓓ SAN FRANCISCO DE ASIS
- Ⓔ SAN FRANCISCO SOLANO DE SONOMA
- Ⓕ SAN JUAN BAUTISTA
- Ⓖ SAN JOSE
- Ⓗ SAN RAFAEL ARCANGEL
- Ⓘ SANTA CLARA DE ASÍS
- Ⓙ SANTA CRUZ

© 2019 HERE

Recreation Areas Chart

The map location numerals in column 2 show an area's location on the preceding map.

Find thousands of places to camp at AAA.com/campgrounds

	MAP LOCATION	CAMPING	PICNICKING	HIKING TRAILS	BOATING	BOAT RAMP	BOAT RENTAL	FISHING	SWIMMING	PET FRIENDLY	BICYCLE TRAILS	WINTER SPORTS	VISITOR CENTER	LODGE/CABINS	FOOD SERVICE
NATIONAL PARKS (See place listings.)															
Lassen Volcanic (C-3) 106,372 acres.		●	●	●	●			●	●	●		●	●	●	●
Redwood (B-1) 131,983 acres. Kayaking; horse rental, ranger-led activities.		●	●	●				●	●	●	●	●	●		●
Sequoia and Kings Canyon (G-5) 1,351-square miles. Cross-country and downhill skiing, rock climbing, sledding, snowshoeing; horse rental.		●	●	●				●		●		●	●	●	
Yosemite (F-4) 1,189 square miles. Rock climbing; horse rental, raft rental. Motorized vessels prohibited.		●	●	●	●			●	●	●	●	●	●	●	●
NATIONAL FORESTS (See place listings.)															
Eldorado (E-4) 676,780 acres. Central California. Bird-watching, equestrian camping, rock climbing, winter sports; off-highway vehicle trails, horse trails.		●	●	●	●			●	●	●	●	●	●	●	●
Humboldt-Toiyabe (D-4) 6,343,735 acres. Central, western, southern and northern Nevada and eastern California. Cross-country and downhill skiing, heli-skiing, hunting, sledding, snowboarding, snowmobiling, snowshoeing, tubing; horseback riding trails, interpretive trails, scenic byway.		●	●	●	●		●	●	●	●		●	●	●	
Inyo (F-5) 1,944,040 acres. Central California. Cross-country and downhill skiing, hunting, ice-skating, rock climbing, sledding, snowmobiling, snowshoeing, tubing; gondola, horse rental, scenic byway.		●	●	●	●			●	●	●	●	●	●	●	●
Klamath (A-2) 1,726,000 acres. Northern California. Horseback riding; winter sports.		●	●	●	●			●	●	●	●	●	●		●
Lassen (C-3) 1,375,000 acres. Northern California. Horseback riding, hunting, winter sports.		●	●	●	●	●		●	●	●	●	●	●		●
Mendocino (C-2) 886,048 acres. Northwestern California. Hunting.		●	●	●	●			●	●	●	●	●	●		●
Modoc (A-3) 1,654,392 acres. Northeastern California. Horseback riding, hunting, winter sports.		●	●	●	●			●	●	●	●	●	●		●
Plumas (C-3) 1,162,863 acres. Northern California. White-water rafting; horse rental, motorcycle trails.		●	●	●	●	●		●	●	●	●	●	●		●
Sequoia (G-5) 1,139,519 acres. South-central California. Beach-combing, caving, cross-country skiing, horseback riding, hunting, rock climbing, sledding, snowmobiling, snowshoeing, white-water rafting; cabins, horse rental, scenic byway.		●	●	●	●			●	●	●	●	●	●	●	●
Shasta-Trinity (B-3) 2,129,524 acres. Northern California. Hunting; cabins, horse rental.		●	●	●	●	●		●	●	●	●	●	●		●
Sierra (F-5) 1,304,476 acres. Central California. White-water rafting, winter sports; horse rental.		●	●	●	●	●		●	●	●	●	●	●	●	●
Six Rivers (B-1) 990,000 acres. Northwestern California. Hunting, kayaking.		●	●	●	●			●	●	●	●		●		●
Stanislaus (E-4) 898,602 acres. Central California. Winter sports; horse rental.		●	●	●	●	●		●	●	●	●	●	●	●	●
Tahoe (D-4) 797,205 acres. North-central California. Horse rental.		●	●	●	●	●		●	●	●		●	●	●	●
NATIONAL CONSERVATION AREAS															
King Range (C-1) 68,000 acres w. of Garberville. Wildlife viewing, wilderness hiking, hunting, surfing, beachcombing.		●	●	●	●			●	●	●	●		●	●	●
NATIONAL RECREATION AREAS (See place listings.)															
Golden Gate (C-7) 74,000 acres. Bird-watching, golfing, sailing; horse rental.		●	●	●	●			●	●	●	●		●	●	●
Smith River (A-1) 305,337 acres. Historic. Gold panning, hunting, kayaking, rafting, scuba diving; horse trails, scenic byway.		●	●	●	●	●		●	●	●	●		●		●
Whiskeytown-Shasta-Trinity (B-2) 246,087 acres. Kayaking, sailing, scuba diving; horse rental.		●	●	●	●	●		●	●	●	●		●	●	●
NATIONAL SEASHORES (See place listings.)															
Point Reyes (C-6) 65,300 acres. Kayaking, wildlife viewing; horse rental, lighthouse.		●	●	●				●		●	●	●	●		●

Recreation Areas Chart

The map location numerals in column 2 show an area's location on the preceding map.

 Find thousands of places to camp at AAA.com/campgrounds

	MAP LOCATION	CAMPING	PICNICKING	HIKING TRAILS	BOATING	BOAT RAMP	BOAT RENTAL	FISHING	SWIMMING	PET FRIENDLY	BICYCLE TRAILS	WINTER SPORTS	VISITOR CENTER	LODGE/CABINS	FOOD SERVICE
ARMY CORPS OF ENGINEERS															
Lake Mendocino (D-2) 5,000 acres 5 mi. n.w. of Ukiah on SR 20. Nature trails. Disc golf, horseback riding, hunting.	**1**	•	•	•	•	•		•	•	•	•	•	•		
Lake Sonoma (E-2) 17,600 acres 26 mi. n.w. of Santa Rosa on Dry Creek Rd. Horseback riding, hunting; fish hatchery, interpretive trails.	**2**	•	•	•	•	•	•	•	•	•	•		•		•
STATE															
Anderson Marsh (E-2) 1,065 acres .75 mi. n. of Lower Lake on SR 53. Bird-watching; archeological sites, nature trail, tours.	**3**		•	•	•			•		•			•	•	
Andrew Molera (G-3) 4,800 acres 21 mi. s. of Carmel-by-the-Sea on SR 1. Bird-watching, beachcombing, surfing; horse rental.	**4**	•	•	•				•		•					
Angel Island (C-8) 758 acres in San Francisco Bay; ferry from San Francisco or Tiburon. Historic. Beachcombing, kayaking; bicycle rentals, interpretive services, museum, nature trails, tours.	**5**	•	•	•	•	•		•		•	•		•		•
Armstrong Redwoods (E-1) 805 acres 2 mi. n. of Guerneville on Armstrong Woods Rd. Nature trails. Horseback riding.	**6**		•	•						•			•	•	
Auburn (E-3) 30,000 acres 1 mi. s. of Auburn on SR 49. Historic. Gold panning, horseback riding, hunting, rafting, water skiing; farm, marina, pond.	**7**	•	•	•	•	•		•	•	•	•				
Austin Creek (E-2) 4,236 acres 2 mi. n. of Guerneville on Armstrong Woods Rd.	**8**	•	•	•				•							
Benbow Lake (C-1) 1,200 acres 3 mi. s. of Garberville on US 101. Motorboats not permitted. Golfing; tours.	**9**	•	•	•	•	•	•	•	•	•		•			
Bethany Reservoir (D-9) 600 acres 7 mi. n. of I-580 via Altamont Pass, Mountain House and Christensen rds. Surfing, windsurfing.	**10**		•		•	•		•		•	•				
Bidwell/Sacramento River (D-3) 180 acres 5 mi. w. of Chico on River Rd. Canoeing, geocaching, kayaking, rafting, tubing.	**11**	•	•	•	•	•	•	•	•						
Big Basin Redwoods (E-8) 18,000 acres 9 mi. n.w. of Boulder Creek on SR 236. Windsurfing; horse rental, nature trails, tours.	**12**	•	•	•				•	•	•	•		•	•	•
Bothe-Napa Valley (A-7) 1,916 acres 4 mi. n. of St. Helena on SR 29. Bird-watching, geocaching, interpretive programs, wildlife viewing; horse trails. Swimming pool.	**13**	•	•	•					•	•	•		•		
Brannan Island (C-9) 336 acres 3.25 mi. s. of Rio Vista. Water skiing, windsurfing; nature trails, tours, wildlife habitat.	**14**	•	•	•	•	•	•	•	•	•		•			•
Butano (E-8) 2,200 acres 7 mi. s. of Pescadero on Cloverdale Rd. Geocaching, horseback riding, wildlife viewing. Interpretive displays.	**15**	•	•	•					•		•	•	•		
Calaveras Big Trees (E-4) 6,500 acres 4 mi. e. of Arnold on SR 4. Winter sports; beach, interpretive exhibits, nature trails, tours, wildlife site.	**16**	•	•	•				•	•	•	•	•	•	•	
Candlestick Point (D-8) 37 acres in San Francisco e. of US 101 via Candlestick exit. Windsurfing; cultural programs, fishing pier, guided nature walks.	**17**		•	•				•		•	•	•	•		
Castle Rock (E-8) 4,350 acres 2 mi. w. of Los Gatos via SR 9. Rock climbing, wildlife viewing; horse trails, nature trails.	**18**	•		•						•	•				
Caswell Memorial (F-3) 258 acres 6 mi. s.w. of Ripon on Austin Rd. Geocaching. Interpretive displays, wildlife habitat.	**19**	•	•	•				•	•	•	•		•		
China Camp (C-7) 1,640 acres n. of San Rafael via US 101 and N. San Pedro Rd. Geocaching, surfing, windsurfing; guided tours, horse trails, wildlife site.	**20**	•	•	•	•			•	•	•	•		•		•
Clear Lake (D-2) 565 acres 3.5 mi. n. of Kelseyville on Soda Bay Rd. Water skiing, wildflower viewing; nature trails.	**21**	•	•	•	•	•	•	•	•	•			•	•	•
Colusa-Sacramento River (D-2) 67 acres near downtown Colusa on SR 20. Nature trails. Geocaching, horseback riding, wildlife viewing.	**22**	•	•		•	•		•	•	•					

Recreation Areas Chart

The map location numerals in column 2 show an area's location on the preceding map.

Find thousands of places to camp at AAA.com/campgrounds

Area	MAP LOCATION	CAMPING	PICNICKING	HIKING TRAILS	BOATING	BOAT RAMP	BOAT RENTAL	FISHING	SWIMMING	PET FRIENDLY	BICYCLE TRAILS	WINTER SPORTS	VISITOR CENTER	LODGE/CABINS	FOOD SERVICE
Del Norte Coast Redwoods (B-1) 31,400 acres 7 mi. s. of Crescent City on US 101. Interpretive displays, nature trails. Horseback riding, scuba diving, snorkeling, surfing, windsurfing.	23	•	•	•				•		•	•	•	•		
D.L. Bliss (E-4) 1,830 acres on the w. shore of Lake Tahoe on SR 89. Nature trails.	24							•	•	•					
Donner Memorial (D-4) 353 acres 2 mi. w. of Truckee on Donner Pass Rd. Cross-country skiing, windsurfing; nature trails, winter sports.	25	•	•	•	•	•		•	•	•	•	•	•		
Ed Z'Berg-Sugar Pine Point (E-4) 1,975 acres 10 mi. s. of Tahoe City on SR 89. Historic. Cross-country ski trails, guided tours, nature trails; scuba diving, snorkeling.	26	•	•	•	•			•	•	•	•	•	•		
Emerald Bay (E-4) 593 acres on the s.w. shore of Lake Tahoe. Boat-in campsites, guided tours, interpretive displays, museums. Scuba diving, snorkeling.	27	•	•	•				•	•	•	•		•		
Empire Mine (D-3) 845 acres in Grass Valley 1 mi. e. of SR 49 on E. Empire St. Guided tours, historic buildings, horse rental.	28		•	•						•	•		•		
Folsom Lake (E-3) 17,718 acres 2 mi. n.w. of Folsom off US 50. Water skiing, windsurfing; horse rental, nature trails.	29	•	•	•	•	•	•	•	•	•	•	•	•		•
Forest of Nisene Marks (F-9) 9,960 acres 4 mi. n. of Aptos on Aptos Creek Rd. Horse trails, interpretive exhibits.	30	•	•	•						•	•				
Fort Ross (E-1) 3,386 acres 12 mi. n. of Jenner on SR 1. Scuba diving; historic buildings.	31	•	•	•				•					•	•	
Fremont Peak (G-3) 244 acres 11 mi. s. of San Juan Bautista on San Juan Canyon Rd. Guided tours, nature trails; geocaching, wildlife viewing.	32	•	•	•						•			•		
George J. Hatfield (F-3) 47 acres 28 mi. w. of Merced on Kelly Rd.	33	•	•			•		•	•	•					
Grizzly Creek Redwoods (C-1) 390 acres 15 mi. e. of Fortuna on SR 36. Guided tours, interpretive displays, nature trails.	34	•	•	•				•	•	•			•	•	
Grover Hot Springs (E-4) 700 acres 4 mi. w. of Markleeville on Hot Springs Rd. Nature trails.	35	•	•	•					•	•		•			
Half Moon Bay Beach (D-7) 170 acres .5 mi. w. of US 1 on Kelly Ave. in Half Moon Bay. Geocaching, surfing, wildlife viewing, windsurfing, interpretive displays, horse rental.	36	•	•	•				•		•	•				
Hendy Woods (D-1) 690 acres 3 mi. w. of Philo off SR 128. Interpretive programs, nature and horse trails. Geocaching, wildlife viewing.	37	•	•	•					•	•	•		•	•	
Henry Cowell Redwoods (F-8) 4,082 acres 3 mi. e. of Felton on Graham Hill Rd. Guided tours, museum, nature and horse trails.	38	•	•	•				•		•	•		•		•
Henry W. Coe (G-3) 80,000 acres 14 mi. e. of Morgan Hill on E. Dunne Ave. Guided tours, interpretive displays, museum, nature and horse trails.	39	•	•	•				•		•			•		
Hollister Hills (G-3) 6,627 acres 8 mi. s. of Hollister via Cienega Rd. Nature trails, motorcycle trails, trails for four-wheel-drive vehicles.	40	•	•							•	•		•		•
Humboldt Lagoons (B-1) 1,886 acres 4 mi. s. of Orick on US 101. Beachcombing, geocaching, kayaking, paddleboarding, windsurfing.	41	•	•	•	•	•		•	•	•					
Humboldt Redwoods (C-1) 52,000 acres along the Redwoods Hwy. near Weott. Horse rental, nature trails.	42	•	•	•				•	•	•	•		•		
Jack London (B-7) 1,400 acres 1 mi. w. of Glen Ellen on London Ranch Rd. Historic. Horse rental, museum.	43		•	•						•	•		•	•	
Jedediah Smith Redwoods (A-1) 10,000 acres 9 mi. n.e. of Crescent City on US 199. Beach, horse rentals, interpretive displays, nature trails. Geocaching.	44	•	•	•	•	•		•	•	•	•		•		
Julia Pfeiffer Burns (H-3) 3,583 acres 37 mi. s. of Carmel-by-the-Sea on SR 1. Scuba diving, whale-watching.	45	•	•	•						•					
Kings Beach (D-4) 8 acres 12 mi. n.e. of Tahoe City on SR 28. Surfing, windsurfing.	46		•		•	•	•	•	•						

Recreation Areas Chart

The map location numerals in column 2 show an area's location on the preceding map.

Find thousands of places to camp at AAA.com/campgrounds

	MAP LOCATION	CAMPING	PICNICKING	HIKING TRAILS	BOATING	BOAT RAMP	BOAT RENTAL	FISHING	SWIMMING	PET FRIENDLY	BICYCLE TRAILS	WINTER SPORTS	VISITOR CENTER	LODGE/CABINS	FOOD SERVICE
Lake Del Valle (D-9) 4,000 acre park and 750 acre lake on Del Valle Rd. 10 mi. s. of Livermore.	47	•	•	•	•	•	•	•	•	•	•	•	•		
Lake Oroville (D-3) 28,450 acres 6 mi. n.e. of Oroville off SR 70. Water skiing, windsurfing; beach, horse rental, nature trails.	48	•	•	•	•	•	•	•	•	•	•	•	•		•
Los Baños Creek Reservoir (G-4) 10 mi. s.w. of Los Baños via SR 165, Pioneer and Canyon rds. Horse trails.	49	•	•	•	•	•		•	•	•			•		
MacKerricher (D-1) 2,030 acres 3 mi. n. on SR 1. Historic. Bird-watching, geocaching, scuba diving, wind surfing; interpretive exhibits, nature trails, horse rental.	50	•	•	•	•	•		•	•	•	•	•	•		
Malakoff Diggins (D-3) 3,000 acres n.e. of Nevada City on N. Bloomfield Rd. Historic. Nature and horseback riding trails.	51	•	•	•				•		•		•	•	•	
Manchester (E-1) 760 acres 7 mi. n. of Point Arena on SR 1. Scuba diving, snorkeling, surfing, windsurfing; beach.	52	•	•	•				•			•	•			
Manresa Beach (F-9) 83 acres 5 mi. w. of Watsonville off SR 1. Surfing, windsurfing.	53	•	•					•	•	•					
Marshall Gold Discovery (E-4) 274 acres in Coloma on SR 49. Historic. Gold panning, nature trails.	54		•	•	•			•		•		•	•		•
McArthur-Burney Falls Memorial (B-3) 910 acres. Scenic. Geocaching, horseback riding, scuba diving, snorkeling, water skiing; nature trails.	55	•	•	•	•	•	•	•	•	•	•	•	•		
McConnell (F-4) 74 acres 5 mi. e. of Delhi on the Merced River.	56	•	•	•				•	•	•	•				
Millerton Lake (G-4) 6,553 acres 21 mi. n.e. of Fresno via SR 41. Historic. Water skiing, wildlife viewing, windsurfing; horse trails.	57	•	•	•	•	•	•	•	•	•	•	•	•		•
Mount Diablo (C-9) 18,000 acres off I-680 Diablo Rd. exit, then 3 mi. e. to Mount Diablo Scenic Blvd. near Danville. Horse rental, museum.	58	•	•	•						•	•	•	•		
Mount Tamalpais (C-7) 6,300 acres 6 mi. w. of Mill Valley on Panoramic Hwy. Horse rental, nature trails.	59	•	•	•				•			•	•	•		
Natural Bridges State Beach (F-8) 65 acres on West Cliff Dr. in Santa Cruz. Windsurfing; monarch butterfly preserve, nature trails.	60		•	•				•	•		•	•			
Navarro River Redwoods (D-1) 12 acres 6 mi. w. of Navarro on SR 128. Canoeing, kayaking.	61	•	•		•			•	•	•					
New Brighton Beach (F-9) 94 acres off SR 1 New Brighton/Park Ave. exit in Capitola. Surfing, windsurfing; interpretive programs.	62	•	•	•				•	•		•				
Patrick's Point (B-1) 632 acres 5 mi. n. of Trinidad via US 101. Nature trails.	63	•	•	•				•			•	•	•		
Pfeiffer Big Sur (H-3) 964 acres s. of the village of Big Sur on SR 101. Nature trails.	64	•	•	•				•	•	•	•	•	•	•	•
Plumas-Eureka (D-3) 6,749 acres 4 mi. w. of Johnsville on CR A14. Horse rental, nature trails.	65	•	•	•				•		•	•	•	•		
Portola Redwoods (E-8) 2,010 acres 20 mi. s.w. of Palo Alto off SR 35. Geocaching. Interpretive displays, nature trails.	66	•	•	•				•		•	•	•	•		
Prairie Creek Redwoods (B-1) 14,000 acres 6 mi. n. of Orick on US 101. Nature trails.	67	•	•	•				•			•	•	•		
Richardson Grove (C-1) 1,000 acres 8 mi. s. of Garberville on US 101. Nature trails.	68	•	•	•	•			•	•	•	•	•	•		•
Robert W. Crown Memorial State Beach (D-8) 389 acres, including a 2.5-mi. beach, in Alameda at Eighth St. and Otis Dr. Kiteboarding, windsurfing. Bird sanctuary, interpretive programs.	69		•	•	•			•	•	•	•		•		
Russian Gulch (D-1) 1,300 acres 2 mi. n. of Mendocino on US 101. Scuba diving; horse trails.	70	•	•	•				•		•	•	•	•		
Salt Point (E-1) 5,676 acres 24 mi. n. of Jenner on SR 1. Geocaching, scuba diving, snorkeling; horse trails, interpretive displays.	71	•	•	•		•		•		•	•	•	•		
Samuel P. Taylor (C-7) 2,708 acres 15 mi. w. of San Rafael on Sir Francis Drake Blvd. Guided tours, nature and horse trails. Geocaching, wildlife viewing.	72	•	•	•			•	•		•	•	•	•		

Recreation Areas Chart

The map location numerals in column 2 show an area's location on the preceding map.

🔗 **Find thousands of places to camp at AAA.com/campgrounds**

	MAP LOCATION	CAMPING	PICNICKING	HIKING TRAILS	BOATING	BOAT RAMP	BOAT RENTAL	FISHING	SWIMMING	PET FRIENDLY	BICYCLE TRAILS	WINTER SPORTS	VISITOR CENTER	LODGE/CABINS	FOOD SERVICE
San Luis Reservoir (G-3) 26,026 acres 12 mi. w. of Los Baños on SR 152. Water skiing, windsurfing; motorbike area.	73	•	•	•	•	•		•	•	•	•		•		
Seacliff Beach (F-9) 85 acres 5.5 mi. s. of Santa Cruz on SR 1. Fishing pier. Surfing, windsurfing.	74	•	•	•				•	•	•	•	•	•		•
Sinkyone Wilderness (D-1) 7,302 acres 30 mi. w. of Redway on CR 435 (Briceland Rd.). Horse trails. Surfing, windsurfing.	75	•	•	•				•		•			•		
Smithe Redwoods (C-1) 665 acres 4 mi. n. of Leggett on US 101.	76		•					•	•	•			•		
Sonoma Coast (E-1) 5,333 acres n. of Bodega Bay on SR 1. Crabbing, surfing; horse rental.	77	•	•	•	•	•		•	•	•			•		
South Yuba River (D-3) 2,000 acres 8 mi. n.w. of Nevada City on SR 49. Gold panning; guided tours, interpretive displays, nature trail.	78		•	•				•	•	•			•		
Standish-Hickey (D-1) 1,012 acres 2 mi. n. of Leggett on US 101. Nature trail.	79	•	•	•				•	•	•			•		
Sugarloaf Ridge (A-7) 2,700 acres 7 mi. e. of Santa Rosa on SR 12. Horse rental, museums, nature trails, observatory. Geocaching.	80	•	•	•				•	•	•			•		
Sunset Beach (G-3) 324 acres 4 mi. w. of Watsonville via SR 1 and San Andreas Rd. Geocaching, surfing, windsurfing.	81	•	•	•				•	•	•			•		
Tahoe (D-4) 57 acres on Lake Tahoe .25 mi. s. of Tahoe City. Surfing, windsurfing.	82	•	•		•			•	•	•					
Tolowa Dunes (A-1) 5,000 acres n. of Crescent City off US 101. Horse rental.	83		•	•	•	•		•		•			•		
Tomales Bay (B-7) 2,000 acres 4 mi. n. of Inverness on Pierce Point Rd. Clamming, scuba diving, snorkeling, windsurfing; guided tours, nature trails.	84	•	•	•	•			•	•	•			•	•	
Trinidad Beach (B-1) 159 acres 19 mi. n. of Eureka on US 101. Scuba diving, snorkeling, surfing, windsurfing.	85		•	•	•	•	•	•	•	•			•	•	
Trione-Annadel (A-7) 4,913 acres s.e. of Santa Rosa on Channel Dr. Horse rental, tours; wildlife viewing.	86		•	•				•		•			•		
Turlock Lake (F-4) 408 acres 23 mi. e. of Modesto off SR 132. Water skiing.	87	•	•	•	•	•		•	•	•			•		
Van Damme (D-1) 1,831 acres 3 mi. s. of Mendocino on SR 1. Geocaching, scuba diving, surfing, windsurfing; kayak tours, interpretive displays, nature trails.	88	•	•	•				•	•	•			•		
Woodson Bridge (C-3) 428 acres 6 mi. w. of Corning and I-5. Interpretive displays, nature trails. Geocaching, horseback riding, wildlife viewing.	89	•	•	•	•	•		•		•			•		
OTHER															
Anthony Chabot Regional Park (C-8) 4,500 acres e. of Oakland on Redwood Rd. Horse trails.	90	•	•	•						•	•	•			
Big Lagoon (B-1) 50 acres 7 mi. n. of Trinidad on US 101. Kayak and paddleboard rentals.	91	•	•	•	•	•		•	•	•					
Black Diamond Mines Regional Preserve (C-9) 6,286 acres 2.5 mi. s. of Antioch off SR 4 Somersville Rd. exit.	92	•	•	•						•	•	•	•		
Contra Loma (C-9) 776 acres 1 mi. s. of Antioch. Sailboarding, windsurfing.	93		•	•	•			•	•	•	•	•	•		•
Cow Mountain (D-2) 50,000 acres e. of Ukiah on Talmage Rd. Hunting. Horse trails.	94	•	•	•					•	•			•		
Don Pedro Lake (F-4) 12,960 acres n.e. of La Grange on Bond's Flat Rd.	95	•	•	•	•	•		•	•	•		•		•	•
Doran (E-2) 120 acres on Doran Park Rd. s. of Bodega Bay. Canoeing, kayaking.	96	•	•	•	•	•		•	•	•			•		
Eagle Lake (C-3) 22,000 acres 20 mi. n.w. of Susanville.	97	•	•	•	•	•	•	•	•	•		•		•	•
Gualala Point (E-1) 300 acres off SR 1 s. of Gualala. Canoeing, kayaking.	98	•	•	•	•			•		•	•		•		

Recreation Areas Chart

The map location numerals in column 2 show an area's location on the preceding map.

 Find thousands of places to camp at AAA.com/campgrounds

	MAP LOCATION	CAMPING	PICNICKING	HIKING TRAILS	BOATING	BOAT RAMP	BOAT RENTAL	FISHING	SWIMMING	PET FRIENDLY	BICYCLE TRAILS	WINTER SPORTS	VISITOR CENTER	LODGE/CABINS	FOOD SERVICE
Lake Berryessa (A-8) 13,000 acres 20 mi. n.w. of Napa on SR 121.	99	•	•	•	•	•	•	•	•	•	•		•	•	•
Lake Chabot Marina (D-8) 1,500 acres in Castro Valley off Lake Chabot Rd. Horse trails.	100		•	•	•	•	•	•		•	•		•		•
Lake McClure (F-4) 7,100 acres 4 mi. w. of Coulterville on SR 132.	101	•	•		•	•	•	•	•						
Lake San Antonio (H-3) 5,000 acres 40 mi. s. of King City off US 101. Bird-watching; horse rental.	102	•	•		•	•	•	•	•	•			•	•	•
Loch Lomond (F-8) 2,100 acres n. of Ben Lomond.	103		•	•	•	•	•	•	•	•		•	•		•
Martinez Shoreline (C-8) 343 acres in Martinez. Bird-watching; nature trails.	104		•	•	•		•	•	•	•	•				
Martin Luther King Jr. Shoreline (D-8) 1,220 acres in Oakland. Bird-watching; fishing pier.	105		•	•	•			•		•					
Oak Grove Regional Park (F-3) 180 acres off I-5 exit 481 at Eight Mile Rd. in Stockton. Disc golf course, horseshoe pits, nature center, outdoor amphitheater, playground.	106		•	•				•		•			•	•	
Point Pinole Shoreline (C-8) 2,147 acres n.w. of San Pablo. Fishing pier, horse trails.	107		•	•				•	•	•	•				
Quarry Lakes Regional Recreation Area (D-9) 450 acres on three lakes on Isherwood Way in Fremont.	108		•	•	•	•	•	•	•	•	•		•		•
Shadow Cliffs Regional Recreation Area (D-9) 249 acres at Pleasanton. Bird-watching.	109		•	•	•	•	•	•	•	•					•
Spring Lake (A-7) 320 acres e. of Santa Rosa at Newanga Ave.	110	•	•	•	•			•	•	•	•				•
Sunol Wilderness (D-9) 6,858 acres 6 mi. s. of Sunol. Bird-watching, horseback riding. Nature trails.	111	•	•	•						•	•		•	•	
Temescal (C-8) 48 acres in Oakland.	112		•	•					•	•	•				•
Vasona Lake Park and Reservoir (E-8) 151 acres near Los Gatos. Motorboats not permitted.	113		•	•	•	•	•	•		•			•	•	

free to
rock the boat

TripAssist travel insurance allows you to go with the flow. It can free you up to make the most of your vacation. Nothing will hold you back knowing that you and your travel plans are safe.

**Talk to your AAA Travel Agent
today for more information.**

Global Assistance

Allianz ⑪

AHWAHNEE pop. 2,246

- Hotels & Restaurants map & index p. 426
- Part of Yosemite National Park area — see map p. 420

HOMESTEAD COTTAGES   559/683-0495   **17**

♦♦ Cottage. **Address:** 41110 Rd 600 93601

ALAMEDA (D-8) pop. 73,812, elev. 30'

- Hotels & Restaurants map & index p. 176

Fall and winter in Alameda are the best times to observe such sea birds as loons, grebes and ducks at Robert W. Crown Memorial State Beach. Crab Cove, at the north end of the beach, has been designated a marine reserve. Crab Cove Visitor Center, on McKay near Central, features exhibits about shoreline and undersea life and a saltwater aquarium with live bay creatures; phone (510) 544-3187. *See Recreation Areas Chart.*

San Francisco Bay Ferry round-trip service between the Ferry Building terminal, on The Embarcadero at the foot of Market Street in San Francisco (Gate E), and Bay Farm Island, 215 Adelphian Way, is available on weekdays; there is no service Jan. 1, Thanksgiving and Christmas. One-way fare is $7.10 (cash) or $5.30 (Clipper Card); $3.50 (ages 5-18, ages 65+ and the physically impaired).

The Alameda/Oakland Ferry also departs from 2990 Main St. in Alameda, stops at Jack London Square in Oakland and continues to the Ferry Building and Fisherman's Wharf in San Francisco. Seasonal service is available to AT&T Park. Phone (415) 705-8291 for departure time and additional information.

Alameda Chamber of Commerce: 2215-A South Shore Center, Alameda, CA 94501. **Phone:** (510) 522-0414.

PACIFIC PINBALL MUSEUM is at 1510 Webster St. The museum has a collection of 90 historic pinball machines with games dating from 1936 to the present. All machines are playable and are included with the cost of museum admission. Staff members are available to explain the history and science of pinball, relate stories about the game and provide information about how to play the machines.

Time: Allow 1 hour minimum. **Hours:** Tues.-Thurs. 11-9, Fri.-Sat. 11-10, Sun. 11-9. Closed Jan. 1, July 4, Thanksgiving and Christmas. **Cost:** $15; $7.50 (ages 2-16). **Phone:** (510) 769-1349. GT

HAMPTON INN & SUITES BY HILTON ALAMEDA-OAKLAND AIRPORT   510/521-4500   **35**

♦♦♦♦ SAVE Hotel. **Address:** 1700 Harbor Bay Pkwy 94502

AAA Benefit: Members save up to 15%!

HAWTHORN SUITES BY WYNDHAM-OAKLAND/ALAMEDA   510/522-1000   **34**

♦♦♦♦ Hotel. **Address:** 1628 Webster St 94501

WHERE TO EAT

EAST OCEAN SEAFOOD RESTAURANT   510/865-3381   **35**

♦♦ Chinese Dim Sum. Casual Dining. **Address:** 1713 Webster St 94501

PASTA PELICAN   510/864-7427   **34**

♦♦ Italian. Casual Dining. **Address:** 2455 Mariner Square Dr 94501

SPEISEKAMMER   510/522-1300   **36**

♦♦ German. Casual Dining. **Address:** 2424 Lincoln Ave 94501

ALBION pop. 168

- Part of Wine Country area — see map p. 405

ALBION RIVER INN   707/937-1919

♦♦♦ Country Inn. **Address:** 3790 N SR 1 95410

WHERE TO EAT

ALBION RIVER INN RESTAURANT   707/937-1919

♦♦♦ California. Fine Dining. **Address:** 3790 N SR 1 95410

ALTURAS pop. 2,827, elev. 4,366'

RIM ROCK MOTEL   530/233-5455

♦ **Motel**

Address: 22760 US 395 96101 **Location:** Jct US 295 and SR 299, 0.7 mi ne. **Facility:** 33 units, some two bedrooms and efficiencies. 1 story, exterior corridors. **Activities:** picnic facilities.

SAVE CALL ⬇ 📶 ✕ 🅿 🍽 🖥 / SOME UNITS HS

TRAILSIDE INN   530/233-4111

♦♦ Motel. **Address:** 343 N Main St 96101

WHERE TO EAT

ANTONIO'S CUCINA ITALIANA   530/233-5600

♦♦ Italian. Casual Dining. **Address:** 220 S Main St 96101

LAZY B GRILL   530/233-2426

♦ Burgers. Quick Serve. **Address:** 303 Hwy 395 E 96101

AMERICAN CANYON pop. 19,454

• Part of Wine Country area — see map p. 405

DOUBLETREE BY HILTON HOTEL & SPA NAPA VALLEY-AMERICAN CANYON   707/674-2100

Hotel

DOUBLETREE
BY HILTON

AAA Benefit:
Members save up to 15%!

Address: 3600 Broadway St 94503 **Location:** I-80 exit 36 (American Canyon Rd), 3.1 mi w, then 0.5 mi n on SR 29 (Broadway St). **Facility:** 132 units. 2 stories, interior corridors. **Amenities:** safes. **Dining:** Table 29 Bistro & Bar, see separate listing. **Pool:** heated outdoor. **Activities:** hot tub, exercise room, spa. **Guest Services:** valet laundry.

FAIRFIELD INN & SUITES BY MARRIOTT NAPA AMERICAN CANYON   707/643-3800

Hotel. **Address:** 3800 Broadway St 94503

AAA Benefit:
Members save 5% or more!

HOLIDAY INN EXPRESS & SUITES-NAPA VALLEY AMERICAN CANYON   707/552-8100

Hotel. **Address:** 5001 Main St 94503

WHERE TO EAT

RISTORANTE LA STRADA   707/226-3027
Italian. Casual Dining. **Address:** 6240 Napa Vallejo Hwy (SR 29) 94503

TABLE 29 BISTRO & BAR   707/674-2100
American. Casual Dining. **Address:** 3600 Broadway St 94503

ANDERSON (C-2) pop. 9,932, elev. 430'

Anderson was named for Elias Anderson, who owned the area's largest land grant; today part of that grant is Anderson River Park, with entrances off Rupert Road (north) and Dodson Lane (south). It offers soccer and baseball fields, a playground, a boat ramp, picnicking areas and hiking trails.

Anderson Chamber of Commerce: 2375 North St., P.O. Box 1144, Anderson, CA 96007. **Phone:** (530) 365-8095.

BEST WESTERN ANDERSON INN   530/365-2753

Hotel

Best Western.

AAA Benefit:
Members save up to 15% and earn bonus points!

Address: 2688 Gateway Dr 96007 **Location:** I-5 exit 668 (Central Anderson/Lassen Nat'l Park) northbound, just e on Balls Ferry Rd, then just s; exit southbound, just e, just s on McMurry Dr, just e on Balls Ferry Rd, then just s. **Facility:** 40 units. 2 stories (no elevator), exterior corridors. **Pool:** outdoor. **Featured Amenity:** full hot breakfast.

GAIA HOTEL & SPA REDDING, AN ASCEND HOTEL COLLECTION MEMBER   530/365-7077

Hotel

Address: 4125 Riverside Pl 96007 **Location:** I-5 exit 670 (Riverside Ave), just e, then just n. **Facility:** 120 units, some cottages. 2 stories (no elevator), exterior corridors. **Terms:** check-in 4 pm. **Dining:** Woodside Grill, see separate listing. **Pool:** heated outdoor. **Activities:** hot tub, exercise room, spa. **Guest Services:** valet laundry.

WHERE TO EAT

WOODSIDE GRILL   530/365-7077
American. Casual Dining. **Address:** 4125 Riverside Pl 96007

ANGELS CAMP (F-4) pop. 2,400, elev. 1,379'

Named after shopkeeper Henry Angel, who started a trading post at this site in 1848, Angels Camp was a popular spot for gold miners. Early diggers uncovered riches, and within 1 year approximately 4,000 miners populated the town to try their luck. Angels Camp sits atop numerous tunnels, which proved to be successful mines.

Angels Camp inspired Mark Twain to write his famous short story "The Celebrated Jumping Frog of Calaveras County"—his first published success. The tall tale is remembered each year in May during the Calaveras County Fair and Jumping Frog Jubilee, held, appropriately enough, at the Frogtown Fairgrounds. Fifty frogs compete in the grand finals in an attempt to break the world record, currently held by Rosie the Ribeter.

Calaveras Visitors Bureau: 1192 S. Main St., P.O. Box 637, Angels Camp, CA 95222-0637. **Phone:** (209) 736-0049 or (800) 225-3764.

Self-guiding tours: A packet that includes walking tour maps and information about the town's historic district, as well as other areas in Calaveras County, is available from the visitors bureau.

RECREATIONAL ACTIVITIES
White-water Rafting
• **O.A.R.S. River Trips** is 1.7 mi. s. on SR 49. **Hours:** Daily Apr.-Oct. **Phone:** (209) 736-4677 or (800) 346-6277.

BEST WESTERN CEDAR INN & SUITES   209/736-4000

Hotel

Best Western.

AAA Benefit:
Members save up to 15% and earn bonus points!

Address: 444 S Main St 95222 **Location:** On SR 49; center. **Facility:** 41 units, some two bedrooms. 2 stories (no elevator), interior/exterior corridors. **Pool:** outdoor. **Activities:** hot tub, exercise room. **Guest Services:** coin laundry. **Featured Amenity:** continental breakfast.

TRAVELODGE ANGELS CAMP
209-736-4242

Hotel

Address: 600 N Main St 95222 **Location:** On SR 49; north end of town. **Facility:** 55 units. 2 stories (no elevator), exterior corridors. **Pool:** outdoor. **Guest Services:** coin laundry. **Featured Amenity: continental breakfast.**

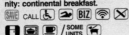

CAMPS RESTAURANT AT GREENHORN CREEK
209-736-8181
American. Casual Dining. **Address:** 676 McCauley Ranch Rd 95222

CRUSCO'S
209-736-1440
Italian. Casual Dining. **Address:** 1240 S Main St 95222

MIKE'S PIZZA
209-736-9246
Pizza. Quick Serve. **Address:** 294 S Main St 95222

APTOS pop. 6,220
• Hotels & Restaurants map & index p. 365

BEST WESTERN SEACLIFF INN
831/688-7300   **38**

Hotel

Best Western

AAA Benefit: Members save up to 15% and earn bonus points!

Address: 7500 Old Dominion Ct 95003 **Location:** SR 1 exit State Park Dr, just e. **Facility:** 148 units. 2 stories (no elevator), interior/exterior corridors. **Terms:** check-in 4 pm. **Dining:** Severino's Grill, see separate listing, entertainment. **Pool:** heated outdoor. **Activities:** hot tub, exercise room. **Guest Services:** valet and coin laundry. **Featured Amenity: breakfast buffet.**

RIO SANDS HOTEL
831/688-3207   **39**

Motel

Address: 116 Aptos Beach Dr 95003 **Location:** SR 1 exit Rio Del Mar Blvd, 1.5 mi sw. **Facility:** 51 units, some kitchens. 2 stories (no elevator), interior/exterior corridors. **Terms:** check-in 4 pm. **Pool:** heated outdoor. **Activities:** hot tub, beach access, trails. **Featured Amenity: continental breakfast.**

SEASCAPE BEACH RESORT
831/688-6800   **40**

Resort Condominium

Address: One Seascape Resort Dr 95003 **Location:** Oceanfront. 1 mi w of SR 1 exit San Andreas Rd, n on Seascape Blvd. **Facility:** This resort property, on a hillside overlooking the Pacific Ocean, offers units with gas fireplaces and balconies or patios. Complimentary use of the local gym is included in the room rate. 235 units, some two bedrooms, efficiencies, kitchens and condominiums. 3 stories (no elevator), exterior corridors. **Terms:** check-in 4 pm. **Amenities:** video games. *Some:* safes. **Pool:** heated outdoor. **Activities:** hot tub, tennis, bicycles, trails, massage. **Guest Services:** complimentary and valet laundry, area transportation.

APTOS ST. BBQ
831/662-1721   **23**
American. Quick Serve. **Address:** 8059 Aptos St 95003

CAFE BITTERSWEET
831/662-9799   **24**
American. Casual Dining. **Address:** 787 Rio Del Mar Blvd 95003

PALAPAS RESTAURANT & CANTINA
831/662-9000   **25**
Mexican. Casual Dining. **Address:** 21 Seascape Village 95003

SEVERINO'S GRILL
831/688-8987   **22**
American. Casual Dining. **Address:** 7500 Old Dominion Ct 95003

ARCATA (B-1) pop. 17,231, elev. 33'
• Hotels p. 36 • Restaurants p. 36

Founded in 1858 as a mining supply center, Arcata also was where author Bret Harte once worked as a journalist and miner; he made the town the setting for some of his stories of mining camp life. Arcata also is home to Humboldt State University.

Southwest of town on Humboldt Bay is the 307-acre Arcata Marsh and Wildlife Sanctuary, a former industrial area and county landfill transformed into a breeding ground for more than 300 species of birds. Some 4.5 miles of foot trails wind past seven wetland habitats. The annual spring migration of marbled godwits and other shorebirds is observed during the Godwit Days Migratory Bird Festival, a 7-day April event featuring lectures, boat excursions and more than 100 observation field trips.

Arcata Chamber of Commerce: 1635 Heindon Rd., Arcata, CA 95521-5816. **Phone:** (707) 822-3619.

Self-guiding tours: The chamber of commerce has maps showing points of interest in Humboldt County, a walking tour of Victorian houses and Redwood Park, a city park within the Arcata Community Forest.

BEST WESTERN ARCATA INN   707/826-0313

Motel

  Best Western. **AAA Benefit:** Members save up to 15% and earn bonus points!

Address: 4827 Valley West Blvd 95521 **Location:** US 101 exit Giuntoli Ln/Janes Rd, just e, then just s. **Facility:** 61 units. 2 stories (no elevator), exterior corridors. **Terms:** check-in 4 pm. **Pool:** heated indoor. **Activities:** hot tub. **Guest Services:** coin laundry. **Featured Amenity:** breakfast buffet.

/ SOME UNITS

DAYS INN & SUITES ARCATA   707/826-2827
Motel. **Address:** 4701 Valley West Blvd 95521

HAMPTON INN & SUITES   707/822-5896
Hotel. **Address:** 4750 Valley West Blvd 95521

AAA Benefit: Members save up to 15%!

WHERE TO EAT

FOLIE DOUCE   707/822-1042
California. Fine Dining. **Address:** 1551 G St 95521

KEBAB CAFE   707/826-2121
Greek. Casual Dining. **Address:** 5000 Valley West Blvd, Suite 19 95521

ORIENTAL BUFFET   707/822-2286
Chinese. Buffet Style. **Address:** 5000 Valley W Blvd, Suite 11 95521

PLAZA GRILL   707/826-0860
California. Casual Dining. **Address:** 791 8th St 95521

RITA'S MARGARITA'S & MEXICAN GRILL   707/822-1010
Mexican. Casual Dining. **Address:** 855 8th St 95521

SLICE OF HUMBOLDT PIE   707/630-5100
American. Quick Serve. **Address:** 828 I St 95521

TONI'S 24 HOUR RESTAURANT   707/822-0091
American. Quick Serve. **Address:** 1901 Heindon Rd 95521

ARNOLD (E-4) pop. 3,843, elev. 4,000'

CALAVERAS BIG TREES STATE PARK is 4 mi. e. on SR 4. Within its 6,500 acres are impressive stands of Sierra redwoods and giant sequoias. Hiking trails wind through the groves of trees. Interpretive programs are offered in summer; in winter conditions are favorable for snowshoeing and cross-country skiing.

The park's most iconic tree was the Pioneer Cabin Tree, a massive giant sequoia more than a thousand years old. A tunnel was carved through the base of the tree's trunk more than a century ago; cars and riders on horseback passed through it over the years, but in more recent decades only hikers

were permitted. Cutting a tunnel into a living sequoia damages the tree over time, and in January 2017 a powerful winter storm felled the landmark and tourist attraction. *See Recreation Areas Chart.* **Hours:** Daily dawn-dusk. **Cost:** Day use fee $10-$12 per private vehicle; $9-$11 (ages 62+ per private vehicle). **Phone:** (209) 795-2334.

SIERRA NEVADA LOGGING MUSEUM is at 2148 Dunbar Rd. in the logging community of White Pines. Overlooking White Pines Lake, it preserves the logging histories of 18 counties in the Sierra Nevada range, beginning with the 1848 discovery of gold. Indoor displays emphasize the 1930s logging era and feature working models of a sawmill, an incredibly steep logging incline that was just outside Yosemite, lumber camps, photographs, dioramas, tools and a depiction of a family cabin from a camp.

Outdoors visitors can see historic logging artifacts, including a restored 1929 Shay logging locomotive, a steam donkey, logging arches, a large collection of chain saws, tractors and a grader. **Time:** Allow 1 hour minimum. **Hours:** Thurs.-Sun. noon-4, Apr.-Nov. (weather permitting); by appointment rest of year. **Cost:** Free. **Phone:** (209) 795-6782, or (209) 795-1226 in the off-season.

ARNOLD BLACK BEAR INN   209/795-8999
Bed & Breakfast. **Address:** 1343 Oak Cir 95223

ARNOLD MEADOWMONT LODGE   209/795-1394
Motel. **Address:** 2011 Hwy 4 95223

WHERE TO EAT

SNOWSHOE BREWING COMPANY   209/795-2272
American. Brewpub. **Address:** 2050 CA-4 95223

AUBURN (E-3) pop. 13,330, elev. 1,255'

Take a trip back in time exploring Historic Old Auburn; among the many restored 19th-century buildings are a firehouse and the oldest continuously operating post office in California. Then peruse the array of Placer County-grown fruits and vegetables at the Foothill Farmers Market, which sets up in the Old Town Courthouse parking lot at Auburn-Folsom Road and Lincoln Way. It's open Saturdays 8-noon, year-round.

Placer County Visitor Bureau: 1103 High St., Auburn, CA 95603. **Phone:** (530) 887-2111 or (866) 752-2371.

BEST WESTERN GOLDEN KEY   530/885-8611

Hotel

Best Western. **AAA Benefit:** Members save up to 15% and earn bonus points!

Address: 13450 Lincoln Way 95603 **Location:** I-80 exit 121 (Foresthill Rd/Auburn Ravine Rd), just e, then just n. **Facility:** 68 units. 2 stories (no elevator), exterior corridors. **Pool:** outdoor. **Activities:** hot tub. **Guest Services:** coin laundry. **Featured Amenity:** continental breakfast.

HOLIDAY INN AUBURN   530/887-8787

♦♦♦ Hotel. **Address:** 120 Grass Valley Hwy 95603

AUBURN ALEHOUSE   530/885-2537

♦♦ American. Casual Dining. **Address:** 289 Washington St 95603

AWFUL ANNIE'S   530/888-9857

♦♦ American. Casual Dining. **Address:** 13460 Lincoln Way 95603

DINGUS MCGEE'S   530/878-1000

♦♦ Steak Seafood. Casual Dining. **Address:** 14500 Musso Rd 95603

JOE CARIBE BISTRO & CAFE   530/823-5333

♦♦ Caribbean. Casual Dining. **Address:** 13470 Lincoln Way 95603

MONKEY CAT RESTAURANT & BAR   530/888-8492

♦♦♦ American. Casual Dining. **Address:** 805 Lincoln Way 95603

OLD TOWN PIZZA   530/888-7600

♦♦ Pizza. Casual Dining. **Address:** 150 Sacramento St 95603

BELMONT pop. 25,835

• Hotels & Restaurants map & index p. 316
• Part of San Francisco area — see map p. 243

HOLIDAY INN EXPRESS HOTEL & SUITES
   650/654-4000 68

♦♦♦ Hotel. **Address:** 1650 El Camino Real 94002

HOTEL BELMONT   650/593-3495 67

♦♦ Motel. **Address:** 560 El Camino Real 94002

HYATT HOUSE BELMONT/REDWOOD SHORES
   650/591-8600 66

♦♦♦♦
Extended Stay Hotel

HYATT house™ **AAA Benefit:** Members save up to 10%!

Address: 400 Concourse Dr 94002 **Location:** US 101 exit 412 (Ralston Ave), just e, then 0.3 mi n on Island Pkwy. **Facility:** 132 kitchen units, some two bedrooms. 3 stories (no elevator), exterior corridors. **Pool:** heated outdoor. **Activities:** exercise room. **Guest Services:** valet and coin laundry, area transportation. **Featured Amenity:** breakfast buffet.

GODFATHER'S BURGER LOUNGE   650/637-9257 62

♦♦ Burgers. Casual Dining. **Address:** 1500 El Camino Real 94002

VIVACE RISTORANTE   650/637-0611 61

♦♦♦ Italian. Casual Dining. **Address:** 1910 Ralston Ave 94002

BENICIA (C-8) pop. 26,997, elev. 33'
• Restaurants p. 38

Named after the wife of Mariano Guadalupe Vallejo, one of its founders, Benicia is the location of California's oldest standing capitol building. It was the site of an Army arsenal and barracks as well as the Pacific Mail Steamship Co. before becoming the state's third capital in 1853. Several well-preserved houses date back to the early years of statehood.

The oldest Masonic lodge in the state stands at 110 West J St. Saint Paul's Episcopal Church, 120 East J St., was one of the first Episcopal cathedrals in northern California. Scandinavian shipwrights who worked on the church created a ceiling that resembles an inverted ship's hull, a design adapted from Norwegian stave churches.

Other historic structures include the four sandstone buildings comprising the Benicia Historical Museum, 2060 Camel Rd. Built in the mid-1850s, they contain exhibits about Benicia history and the U.S. Army arsenal. The last of the beasts from the Army's camel corps were auctioned off at the arsenal in 1864, following a brief attempt at using them as draft animals in the deserts of the Southwest.

Benicia Chamber of Commerce and Visitor Center: 601 First St., Suite 100, Benicia, CA 94510-3211. **Phone:** (707) 745-2120.

Self-guiding tours: The chamber of commerce distributes a visitor's guide that includes information about self-guiding walking tours of historic Benicia.

BENICIA CAPITOL STATE HISTORIC PARK, First and West G sts., preserves the Greek Revival building that served as the third state capitol for just over a year beginning Feb. 4, 1853. It is restored and furnished in period. The Fischer-Hanlon House, adjacent to the park at 135 West G St., is a renovated gold rush hotel that also contains period furnishings; it can only be visited on a guided tour.

Time: Allow 30 minutes minimum. **Hours:** Park open Thurs. noon-4, Fri.-Sun. 10-5. Closed Jan. 1, Thanksgiving and Christmas. Phone ahead to confirm schedule. **Cost:** $3 (includes Fischer-Hanlon House, when open); $2 (ages 6-17). Reservations are required for guided tours of the capitol and for tours of the Fischer-Hanlon House. **Phone:** (707) 745-3385.

BEST WESTERN PLUS HERITAGE INN   707/746-0401

♦♦♦ **Hotel**

Best Western PLUS. **AAA Benefit:** Members save up to 15% and earn bonus points!

Address: 1955 E 2nd St 94510 **Location:** I-780 exit Central Benicia/E 2nd St, just ne. **Facility:** 96 units, some efficiencies. 3 stories, interior corridors. **Pool:** outdoor. **Activities:** hot tub, exercise room. **Guest Services:** valet and coin laundry. **Featured Amenity:** continental breakfast.

HOLIDAY INN EXPRESS   707/297-6873
 Hotel. **Address:** 1375 E 5th St 94510

WHERE TO EAT

FIRST ST CAFE & CATERING   707/745-1400
American. Casual Dining. **Address:** 440 First St 94510

LUCCA BAR & GRILL   707/745-0943
American. Casual Dining. **Address:** 439 First St 94510

SAILOR JACK'S   707/746-8500
Seafood. Casual Dining. **Address:** 123 First St 94510

BEN LOMOND pop. 6,234

JAYE'S TIMBERLANE RESORT   831/336-5479

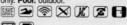
Cottage

Address: 8705 Hwy 9 95005 **Location:** SR 9, 0.5 mi s. **Facility:** 10 cottages. 1 story, exterior corridors. *Bath:* shower only. **Pool:** outdoor.

QUALITY INN & SUITES SANTA CRUZ MOUNTAINS
                                          831/336-2292

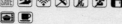
Motel

Address: 9733 Hwy 9 95005 **Location:** SR 9, 0.3 mi n; on San Lorenzo River. **Facility:** 25 units, some cottages. 2 stories (no elevator), exterior corridors. **Pool:** outdoor. **Activities:** picnic facilities. **Guest Services:** valet laundry. **Featured Amenity:** full hot breakfast.

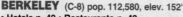

BERKELEY (C-8) pop. 112,580, elev. 152'

• Hotels p. 42 • Restaurants p. 43
• Hotels & Restaurants map & index p. 176

Eclectic, inquiring and experimental are all words that apply to Berkeley—and it's no surprise, given the city's reputation as one of the nation's leading academic enclaves. The David Brower Center, downtown at 2150 Allston Way, epitomizes this progressive atmosphere. The LEED Platinum mixed-use building utilizes the latest in energy-saving technologies, and more than half of the materials used in its construction were recycled. There are usually thought-provoking art installations on display in the building's public areas.

Like San Francisco, Berkeley spreads over a series of hills that are called, not surprisingly, the Berkeley Hills. Residential neighborhoods cover their western slopes, which overlook San Francisco, the Golden Gate Bridge and the northeastern portion of San Francisco Bay. Streets twist and turn according to the contours of the land, and the higher you ascend the more impressive the views become.

Grizzly Peak Boulevard, which can be reached from the head of Spruce Street or from other points along the city's northeastern edge, winds along the crest of the hills. This scenic drive provides access to Tilden Regional Park and offers panoramic views of the bay, bridges and San Francisco.

And also like San Francisco, Berkeley has a network of pedestrian paths and stairways. Some of these "pathways" are simply steps built into the sidewalk that make it easier to climb a steep section of hill; others are public paths in between houses. And fortunately for walkers and urban explorers, most of them are located in lovely old neighborhoods full of trees, gardens, architecturally diverse homes and frequently glorious vistas.

One of the most picturesque of these stairways is Orchard Lane. (To get to Orchard Lane from the UC campus, walk east on Bancroft Way to the Bancroft Steps, take the Bancroft Steps up to Prospect Street, continue to Panoramic Way, turn right and watch for the sign on the left-hand side of the street.) The formal pedestrian residence to the Panoramic Hill residential neighborhood, it was built in 1909 in the grand classical style, linking houses near and along it with the university and downtown Berkeley. The stone steps, pillars, balustrades and benches all have a weathered beauty, heightened by an overhanging bower of trees. At the top of the stairway you can catch a glimpse of San Francisco Bay in the distance.

Short Cut Path is another attractive stone stairway that begins at a parking lot on the grounds of the Claremont Club & Spa. This sprawling complex is situated on a hillside and looks every inch the handsomely appointed resort. Built in 1915, the Claremont has long been a favorite honeymoon destination as well as a weekend getaway for well-heeled Bay Area residents. If you're not a guest, you can still stroll around the attractively landscaped grounds.

Many of Berkeley's paths and stairways are hard to find, even if you're a resident, and while they're all named, some of them are not signed. If you intend to do a little exploring, it's well worth obtaining the detailed map produced by the Berkeley Path Wanderers Association. The map can be purchased online or by mail for $10.45; write the Berkeley Path Wanderers Association, 1442A Walnut St., Box 269, Berkeley, CA 94709.

Golden Gate Fields, 1100 Eastshore Hwy., offers horse racing Thursday through Sunday (with simulcast racing on Wednesday) on a seasonal schedule; for race times and other information phone (510) 559-7300.

Berkeley Marina, at the foot of University Avenue, is a base for a small charter boat fleet. Off Spinnaker Way, north of the west end of University Avenue, is César Chávez Park, built on the site of a former landfill. The park's bayfront walking trail traverses shoreline and wetland areas while offering spectacular views of the Golden Gate, San

(See map & index p. 176.)

Francisco-Oakland and Richmond bay bridges as well as Alcatraz and Angel islands.

The park is also the site of the acclaimed Berkeley Kite Festival at the end of July. This family-oriented event features kite-making classes and a candy drop for kids, while adults will appreciate the ingenuity and expertise that go into the creation of custom-made, house-sized Flying Creature kites. If you can't make the festival, the park's bayside location provides optimum kite-flying conditions much of the year.

The Tilden Park Golf Course, off Golf Course Road within Tilden Regional Park, is nestled in the Berkeley Hills above the UC-Berkeley campus. The championship layout features rolling fairways in a peacefully wooded setting. To book a tee time phone (510) 848-7373.

Sidewalk creativity and a sweet tooth are both satisfied at the family-friendly Chocolate & Chalk Art Festival, held in August. The sidewalks along North Shattuck Avenue, 6 blocks north of downtown Berkeley in the "Gourmet Ghetto" district, are open to artists young and old, professional and amateur, with a cash prize awarded to the best drawing. Food booths offer such concoctions as habañero chocolate gelato and Caribbean chocolate soup, and activities for kids include face painters and street performers. For event information phone (510) 548-5335.

Visit Berkeley: 2030 Addison St., Suite 102, Berkeley, CA 94704. **Phone:** (510) 549-7040 or (800) 847-4823.

Shopping: For those who prefer an afternoon shopping excursion to be an experience—strolling outdoors in an attractive setting, places to stop for coffee or a bite to eat—Fourth Street is where it's at. The tree-lined blocks between Virginia Street and Hearst Avenue offer chain retailers beloved by the upwardly mobile (Apple Store, Anthropologie, Crate & Barrel Outlet, Sur La Table) as well as specialty boutiques.

Creative types will dig the collection of stationery, craft supplies, pens and paperweights at Castle in the Air. The store also sells puppets, masks and unusual toys. The furniture at CB2 is more expensive than IKEA but similar in its utilitarian yet hip aesthetic. The Gardener is somewhat of a misnomer, since the emphasis at this artsy store is more on quirky home accessories (think Indian prayer bells, decorative baskets and candles). The merchandise is pricey, but it's a fun spot to browse.

The blocks of Telegraph Avenue extending south from the University of California Berkeley campus are filled with head shops, funky boutiques and cheap eateries catering to cash-strapped students. Vendors set up at street corners selling incense and jewelry. The street exudes energy and authenticity; in addition to wandering packs of students, homeless street people and panhandlers you may also run into a Nobel Prize-winning professor.

Stop by Amoeba Music (2455 Telegraph Ave.) for a taste of Berkeley's counterculture heyday. This branch isn't nearly as big as the one on Haight Street in San Francisco, but the selection of CDs and vinyl is just as wide-ranging. Be sure and check out the awesome exterior wall murals. Moe's Books (2476 Telegraph Ave.) is a Berkeley institution, one of the Bay Area's few remaining independent bookstores. Another institution is Top Dog (just off Telegraph at 2534 Durant Ave.), which has long gotten raves for its frankfurters, sausages and extra-spicy Russian mustard. And as befits a joint frequented by students, it stays open late (until 3 a.m. on Friday and Saturday).

Shattuck and University avenues are lined with mostly run-of-the-mill shops and stores, although a few distinctive ones stand out. The aroma of incense permeates the Little Tibet Gift Shop (2037 University Ave.), where you'll find clothing, Himalayan jewelry, books and music. Downtown Berkeley is, however, in the midst of a major transformation, with the relocation of the Berkeley Art Museum and Pacific Film Archive, new transit-centric condo development and tech start-ups run by graduates of UC Berkeley graduate schools.

The stretch of Shattuck Avenue in North Berkeley is known as the "Gourmet Ghetto" for its eclectic eateries and bakeries. The best-known restaurant—and one that pioneered California's local and sustainable food movement when it opened in 1971—is Chez Panisse, co-founded by restaurateur, chef and author Alice Waters.

The Cheese Board Collective (1504 and 1512 Shattuck Ave.) is very Berkeley, both in its offerings (gourmet cheeses, hand-crafted breads, rolls, muffins, scones and fruit tarts) and the fact that it's a worker-owned business. And fans of mocha lattes and other caffeinated concoctions should pay a visit to the original outpost of Bay Area institution Peet's Coffee & Tea (2124 Vine St., between Shattuck and Walnut Street).

The Elmwood Shopping District, centered at the intersection of College and Ashby avenues (several blocks south of the university), is a neighborhood conglomeration of eateries along with a scattering of clothing and specialty stores.

(See map & index p. 176.)

And if you need a quick sugar and carb fix, the glazed apple fritters at Dream Fluff Donuts (2637 Ashby Ave.) absolutely rule. This friendly, family-run shop also dishes up good, diner-style breakfasts.

Nightlife: Berkeley has always nurtured creative juices, and an evening at the theater is a rewarding way to experience the flow. The Tony award-winning Berkeley Repertory Theatre (2025 Addison St.) presents a season of seven productions on two stages; works are a mix of modern classics and more recent plays. In recent years Berkeley Rep has premiered such high-profile events as the first stage adaptation of "American Idiot," Green Day's punk rock musical. Phone (510) 647-2949 for the box office.

The Aurora Theatre Company stages seven thought-provoking productions annually at the Aurora Theatre (2081 Addison St.), an intimate black box space that immerses the audience in what's happening on stage. Phone (510) 843-4822 for ticket information.

The 1,400-seat UC Theatre (2036 University Ave.) was long downtown Berkeley's pride and joy. Opened in 1917, it was known for presenting revivals of classic old films and for late-night showings of the 1970s cult favorite "The Rocky Horror Picture Show" before closing for good in 2001. Renovated and refurbished, it reopened in January 2016. For schedule and performance information phone (510) 356-4000.

Traditional roots music takes the stage at the Freight & Salvage Coffeehouse (2020 Addison St.), an all-ages venue that presents live entertainment most nights of the year. The Freight also offers live-streaming access to their shows. Phone (510) 644-2020, ext. 120, for schedule and ticket information.

Everything from zydeco and blues to Afro-Brazilian funk and Grateful Dead cover bands can be heard at the Ashkenaz Music & Dance Community Center (1317 San Pablo Ave.). This family-friendly venue has a big dance floor and a very NorCal hippie vibe. Phone (510) 525-5054.

If you're searching for a relaxed spot to play darts or board games over a couple of micro-brewed beers and several bowls of $1 popcorn, look no further than The Albatross Pub (1822 San Pablo Ave.). There's a toasty fireplace for chilly nights as well as jazz, bluegrass and other musical performers on Wednesday and Saturday evenings. Sunday trivia night begins promptly at 8:30 p.m. Phone (510) 843-2473.

BERKELEY ROSE GARDEN, Euclid Ave. at Bayview Pl., contains more than 3,000 rose bushes representing 250 varieties of the flower. The main blooming season is May through September; the roses are at their peak in May and June. A terraced amphitheater and arbor overlook the bay and Golden Gate Bridge. Also available are tennis courts and scenic hiking trails. **Hours:** Daily dawn-dusk.

The garden may be closed during special occasions; phone ahead. **Cost:** Free. **Phone:** (510) 981-5150. ⛩

HABITOT CHILDREN'S MUSEUM is downtown at 2065 Kittredge St.; there are entrances on both Kittredge St. and Shattuck Ave. This hands-on museum geared toward children 7 and under has themed exhibits where infants, toddlers and small children can learn while they play. Kids can float a ball down a stream, get messy in the art studio, shop in a grocery, order and serve food at a café, and maneuver through a floor-to-ceiling tunnel-like maze.

Time: Allow 1 hour minimum. **Hours:** Mon.-Thurs. 9:30-12:30, Fri.-Sun. 9:30-4:30, Oct.-Mar. (also 12:30-4:30 on Martin Luther King Jr. Day, Presidents Day and Columbus Day); Mon.-Thurs. 9:30-12:30, Fri.-Sat. 9:30-4:30, rest of year. Closed Jan. 1, Easter, Memorial Day, July 4, Labor Day, Thanksgiving, Christmas Eve and Christmas. **Cost:** Admission Fri.-Sun. $12; $11 (ages 60+ and the physically impaired); free (ages 0-12 months). Admission Mon.-Thurs. $10; $9 (ages 60+ and the physically impaired); free (ages 0-12 months). **Phone:** (510) 647-1111. 🏛 Downtown Berkeley, 13

TILDEN REGIONAL PARK has several entrances off Grizzly Peak Blvd. This extensive park, located in northeastern Berkeley, offers something for everyone. More than 10 miles of hiking trails crisscross the 740-acre Tilden Nature Area, where the native and introduced plant communities include grasslands, oak groves and stands of eucalyptus.

A boardwalk leads to Jewel Lake, a former reservoir in a peaceful setting good for wildlife observation. Near the lake is the Environmental Education Center (EEC), which has exhibits about the Wildcat Creek watershed and a schedule of park activities. Bring lettuce and celery to feed the goats, sheep, rabbits, pigs and other animals that live at Little Farm.

Lake Anza, in a pretty, tree-shaded setting, has a small beach for swimming and sunbathing. The park also has a Herschell Spillman merry-go-round complete with vintage wooden carousel animals. A miniature steam train takes visitors on a ride through the park's redwood groves.

Hours: Park open daily 5 a.m.-10 p.m. Environmental Education Center open Tues.-Sun. 10-5. Train rides Mon.-Fri. 11-5, Sat.-Sun. 11-6, mid-June through Labor Day; Sat.-Sun. 11-6, rest of year. Merry-go-round Mon.-Fri. 11-5, Sat.-Sun. 11-6, mid-May through Labor Day; Wed.-Sun. 11-5, rest of year. Park closed holidays, except July 4 and Labor Day. Environmental center closed Jan. 1, Thanksgiving, day after Thanksgiving, Christmas Eve, Christmas and Dec. 31.

Cost: Park free. Swimming at Lake Anza $3.50; $2.50 (ages 1-15 and 62+). Train ride $3; free (ages

(See map & index p. 176.)

0-1); $12 (family, includes five rides). Merry-go-round $3 per ride, or seven rides for $15. **Phone:** (510) 544-2233 for the Environmental Education Center, (510) 548-6100 for the train, or (888) 327-2757 for the park. 🍴 ⊠ 🐾 ⛱

Botanic Garden entrance is at Wildcat Canyon Dr. and South Park Rd. within Tilden Regional Park. This jewel of a garden is devoted entirely to California natives. These trees, shrubs and flowering plants come from a diverse spectrum of habitats—rugged mountains, arid foothills, desert, coastal dunes, Pacific rain forest. Represented within the garden's 10 acres are nearly all of the state's varieties of conifers and oaks as well as extensive collections of shrubs, grasses and bulbs.

There is something to appreciate in every season. In January the distinctive red bark of the manzanita, an evergreen shrub or small tree, is complemented by pretty pink flowers. Rhododendrons, California poppies and other wildflowers bloom in spring, perennials during the summer months. Cottonwoods, hawthorn, willows and vine maples provide fall foliage color.

Unusual plants include Humboldt's lily, which flaunts deep orange trumpets speckled with oval-shaped brown spots, and woolly blue curls, an evergreen shrub that produces fuzzy spikes of purple flowers. Many California natives are adapted to survive in semi-arid or desert climates; the garden's redwood grove, on the other hand, is a cool, damp, hushed retreat, the tall trees forming a deep canopy of shade. It's a perfect spot for a few quiet moments of contemplation. **Hours:** Daily 8:30-5:30, June-Sept.; 8:30-5, rest of year. Closed Jan. 1, Thanksgiving and Christmas. **Cost:** Free. **Phone:** (510) 544-3169. GT

UNIVERSITY OF CALIFORNIA BERKELEY is e. of Oxford St. between Hearst St. and Bancroft Way. More than 42,000 students attend the university, which not only occupies a beautiful 1,232-acre campus but is often in the vanguard of any nationwide campus movement, whether it be political, artistic or philosophic.

South Hall, built in 1873, is California's oldest university building. Regarded as one of the nation's leading public universities, Berkeley is known for its quality undergraduate and graduate programs.

Zellerbach Hall, just north of Bancroft Way near the Cesar Chavez Student Center, is the home venue for Cal Performances, a major performing arts presenter. A variety of events—from chamber, orchestral music and jazz concerts to recitals, dance performances and theatrical presentations—take place during the September-through-May season. For schedule and ticket information phone (510) 642-9988.

The University of California Golden Bears football team takes to the gridiron at California Memorial Stadium, and the university's men's and women's basketball teams play at Haas Pavilion.

The UC Berkeley Koret Visitor Center is located at 2227 Piedmont Ave., on Goldman Plaza at California Memorial Stadium. Guided campus walking tours depart from the center; check the online calendar for schedules and more information.

Hours: UC Berkeley Visitor Center open Mon.-Fri. 8:30-4:30, Sat.-Sun. 9-1. Closed holidays and during special events. Walking tours depart from the center daily; an online reservation is required. On football home game days tours depart from the Campanile (Sather Tower) in the center of the campus. **Phone:** (510) 642-5215 for the visitor center, (510) 642-3277 for the athletic department, or (800) 462-3277 for ticket information. 🚇 Downtown Berkeley, 13

Berkeley Art Museum and Pacific Film Archive (BAMPFA) is downtown at 2155 Center St. The collection at the Berkeley Art Museum comprises more than 19,000 works of art and 17,500 films and videos. Representing a diversity of global cultures and historical periods, the art collection has particular strengths in Asian, modern and international contemporary art.

The theater at the Pacific Film Archive Library & Film Study Center, located within the art museum, screens a variety of classic, international and avant-garde films throughout the year.

Hours: Wed.-Sun. 11-7 (also Fri.-Sat. 7-9 p.m.). **Cost:** Galleries $12; $10 (ages 65+, non-UC Berkeley students with ID and the physically impaired); free (UC Berkeley students, faculty and staff and also ages 0-18 plus one adult and to all on the first Thurs. of the month). Theater admission $12; $8 (ages 0-18 and 65+, UC Berkeley faculty and staff members, non-UC Berkeley students with ID and the physically impaired); $7 (UC Berkeley students); $5 (additional same-day feature). **Phone:** (510) 642-0808. 🍴 🚇 Downtown Berkeley, 13

Campanile (Sather Tower) is at the center of the University of California Berkeley campus. Built in 1914, it is 307 feet tall and contains a 61-bell carillon that chimes on the hour and plays music. An elevator and staircase take visitors to the observation deck, which offers expansive views (on clear days) of nearby Oakland and more distant San Francisco and the Golden Gate Bridge.

Hours: Music is played daily at 7:50 a.m., noon and 6 p.m., during the school year; schedule varies rest of year. Recitals lasting 45 minutes are performed Sun. at 2. Elevator operates Mon.-Fri. 10-3:45, Sat. 10-4:45, Sun. 10-1:30 and 3-4:45. Closed university holidays. **Cost:** Elevator fee $3; $2 (ages 3-17, ages 65+ and Cal Alumni Association members with ID); free (ages 0-2 and UC Berkeley students, faculty and staff). **Phone:** (510) 642-5215. 🚇 Downtown Berkeley, 13

(See map & index p. 176.)

Lawrence Hall of Science, Centennial Dr. in the hills above the University of California Berkeley campus, is a public science center that includes hands-on exhibits, a planetarium, a 3D theater and an outdoor science park.

Time: Allow 2 hours minimum. **Hours:** Science hall open Wed.-Sun. and holidays 10-5. Phone for planetarium and 3D show schedules. Closed July 4, Thanksgiving and Christmas. **Cost:** $12; $10 (ages 3-18 and 62+). Planetarium and 3D shows cost an additional $4. **Phone:** (510) 642-5132.

Phoebe A. Hearst Museum of Anthropology is in Kroeber Hall on Bancroft Way (at College Ave.). It has exhibits about ethnology, archeology and anthropology. The nearly 4 million items in the museum's collections encompass objects from six continents, with strengths in ancient Egypt, Peru, California and Africa. People Made These Things: Connecting With the Makers of Our World is on exhibit in the newly renovated Kroeber Hall Gallery. **Hours:** Wed., Fri. and Sun. 11-5, Sat. 10-6, Thurs. 11-8. Closed university holidays. **Cost:** $6; $3 (ages 65+ and non-UC Berkeley students with ID); free (ages 0-17 and UC Berkeley students, faculty, and staff with ID). **Phone:** (510) 643-1191. ⊡ Downtown Berkeley, 13

UC Botanical Garden is at 200 Centennial Dr., about midway between UC Berkeley Memorial Stadium and the Lawrence Hall of Science. This scientific research and display garden has a collection of plants from around the world, grouped according to origin in nine major geographic regions. One of the most interesting sections is New World Desert, which contains a variety of cacti, succulents and other desert dwellers.

Another fascinating collection, Southern Africa, explodes with color in spring when such perennials as Cape cowslips, Cape marigolds and proteas are in bloom. The California collection showcases the state's diversity of native flora, including a redwood forest and such wildflowers as the California poppy (the California state flower), which blooms from February through June.

There's also a garden with rose cultivars from the 19th and early 20th centuries, a Chinese medicinal herb garden, and greenhouses containing cacti, tropicals, orchids, ferns and carnivorous plants. The hillside location, surrounded by woodlands, is serene and lovely.

Time: Allow 1 hour minimum. **Hours:** Daily 9-5. One-hour tours are given Thurs.–Sun. and the first Wed. of the month at 1:30. Last admission is 30 minutes before closing. Closed Jan. 1, Martin Luther King Jr. Day, Thanksgiving, Christmas Eve, Christmas, Dec. 31 and the first Tues. of the month. **Cost:** $12; $10 (ages 65+ and students with ID); $7 (ages 7-17); free (first Wed. of the month). **Parking:** $1 per hour. **Phone:** (510) 643-2755.

CLAREMONT CLUB & SPA, A FAIRMONT HOTEL
510/843-3000 **24**

Historic Hotel

Address: 41 Tunnel Rd 94705 **Location:** SR 24 exit SR 13, 0.8 mi n; I-80 exit 11 (University Ave), just e, 1.5 mi s on San Pablo Ave, 2.6 mi e on Ashby Ave, then just e. **Facility:** Located in Berkeley Hills, this newly renovated, converted 1915 Victorian castle is a popular spot for honeymooners as well as a weekend getaway for the locals. 276 units, some two bedrooms. 9 stories, interior corridors. **Parking:** on-site (fee) and valet. **Terms:** check-in 4 pm. **Amenities:** safes. **Pool:** heated outdoor. **Activities:** sauna, hot tub, steamroom, tennis, recreation programs, kids club, bicycles, trails, health club, spa. **Guest Services:** valet laundry.

[SAVE] [icons] CALL [icons] [BIZ]
[HS] [icons] / SOME UNITS [icons]

DOUBLETREE BY HILTON BERKELEY MARINA
510/548-7920 **19**

Hotel

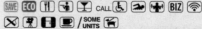

AAA Benefit: Members save up to 15%!

Address: 200 Marina Blvd 94710 **Location:** Waterfront. I-80 exit 11 (University Ave), 0.5 mi w; on Berkeley Marina. **Facility:** 378 units. 1-4 stories, interior corridors. **Parking:** on-site (fee) and valet. **Terms:** check-in 4 pm. **Amenities:** safes. **Pool:** heated indoor. **Activities:** sauna, hot tub, bicycles, trails, exercise room. **Guest Services:** valet and coin laundry, area transportation.

[SAVE] [ECO] [icons] CALL [icons] [BIZ] [icons]
[icons] / SOME UNITS [icons]

GRADUATE BERKELEY
510/845-8981 **23**

Historic Boutique Hotel

Address: 2600 Durant Ave 94704 **Location:** I-80 exit 11 (University Ave), 2 mi e to Oxford St, 0.3 mi s, then 0.5 mi e; jct Bowditch St. ⊡ Downtown Berkeley, 13. **Facility:** Featuring contemporary appointments with a bit of retro, the rooms at this property have locally inspired artwork that is a nod to the university. 144 units. 6 stories, interior corridors. **Parking:** on-site (fee). **Amenities:** safes. **Activities:** exercise room. **Guest Services:** valet laundry.

[SAVE] [ECO] [icons] CALL [icons] [BIZ]
[HS] [icons]
/ SOME UNITS [icons]

HOLIDAY INN EXPRESS HOTEL & SUITES
510/548-1700 **20**

♦♦♦ Hotel. **Address:** 1175 University Ave 94702

HOTEL SHATTUCK PLAZA
510/845-7300 **22**

Historic Boutique Hotel

Address: 2086 Allston Way 94704 **Location:** I-80 exit 11 (University Ave), 2 mi e, just s on Shattuck Ave, then just w. ⊡ Downtown Berkeley, 13. **Facility:** Opened in 1910, this was the first hotel built in Berkeley. Beautifully restored with a retro-contemporary décor, the property features original chandeliers and marble flooring in the lobby area. 199 units. 5 stories, interior corridors. **Parking:** street only. **Amenities:** safes. **Activities:** exercise room. **Guest Services:** valet laundry.

[SAVE] [ECO] [icons] CALL [icons]
[icons] [BIZ] [HS] [icons]
/ SOME UNITS [icons]

(See map & index p. 176.)

TRAVELODGE BERKELEY   510/843-4262   **21**
🔻🔻 Hotel. **Address:** 1820 University Ave 94703

WHERE TO EAT

BERKELEY SOCIAL CLUB   510/900-5858   **18**
🔻🔻 Korean Fusion. Casual Dining. **Address:** 2050 University Ave 94704

BETTE'S OCEANVIEW DINER   510/644-3230   **15**
🔻🔻 American. Casual Dining. **Address:** 1807 4th St 94710

THE CHEESE BOARD COLLECTIVE   510/549-3183   **13**
🔻 Pizza Vegetarian. Quick Serve. **Address:** 1512 Shattuck Ave 94709

CHEZ PANISSE   510/548-5525   **14**
🔻🔻🔻 Regional American. Fine Dining. **Address:** 1517 Shattuck Ave 94709

GATHER   510/809-0400   **20**
🔻🔻🔻 California. Casual Dining. **Address:** 2200 Oxford St 94704

IPPUKU   510/665-1969   **19**
🔻🔻 Japanese Small Plates. Casual Dining. **Address:** 2130 Center St 94704

IYASARE   510/845-8100   **16**
🔻🔻🔻 Japanese Small Plates. Casual Dining. **Address:** 1830 Fourth St 94710

KIRALA RESTAURANT   510/549-3486   **22**
🔻🔻 Japanese Sushi. Casual Dining. **Address:** 2100 Ward St 94705

SKATES ON THE BAY   510/549-1900   **17**
🔻🔻🔻 American. Fine Dining. **Address:** 100 Seawall Dr 94710

SPOON KOREAN BISTRO   510/704-9555   **23**
🔻🔻 Korean. Casual Dining. **Address:** 933 Ashby Ave 94710

VIK'S CHAAT CORNER   510/644-4432   **21**
🔻 Indian. Quick Serve. **Address:** 2390 4th St 94710

BIG SUR (H-3) elev. 155'
• Hotels p. 44 • Restaurants p. 44

The name Big Sur is derived from the Spanish *el sur grande,* which means "the big south." It's a reference to terrain comprising sheer cliffs that loom above the ocean; to the foothills of the rugged Santa Lucia Mountains, rising up less than 10 miles inland; and to the wooded valleys between them. This entire wilderness region was basically inaccessible until the 1937 opening of SR 1, also referred to as California Highway 1 and the Pacific Coast Highway. The road paved the way for tourism.

The village of Big Sur is scenically strung out along SR 1 south of Andrew Molera State Park *(see Recreation Areas Chart),* at one of the few points where the roadway veers inland and tunnels though a beautiful stand of redwoods. More commonly, though, Big Sur refers to the magnificently rugged—and blessedly pristine—90-mile-long stretch of California coast that runs from Carmel-by-the-Sea *(see place listing p. 54)* south to San Simeon.

Two-lane SR 1 snakes along the Big Sur coast in a seemingly endless series of sinuous S-curves, rarely out of sight of the ocean. Even though there's a guardrail along the side, a couple of bends are dizzyingly close to a sheer drop-off. Needless to say, you don't speed on this highway—but who would want to?

Better yet, there's an almost complete absence of man-made distractions. There are no billboards. No strip centers. No fast-food outlets. No gas stations (just gas pumps at a couple of roadside establishments in Big Sur village). In other words, no visual blight gets in the way of nature's glory.

Numerous strategically located pull-off parking areas allow you to stand at the very edge of a cliff top and position yourself for what is almost guaranteed to be a memorable photo. Just point and click; nature takes care of the rest. The elevation of the highway varies from near sea level to nearly 1,000 feet above. But most of the vista points are high above the Pacific, and the panoramic views of headlands extending for miles along the coastline—against a backdrop of steel-blue ocean—are simply breathtaking.

A variety of plants cling for dear life to the cliff edges. Rocks are carpeted with ice plants, a succulent ground cover with fleshy, deep green leaves and pink, yellow and white flowers that look like small daisies. Wildflowers bloom in seasonal bursts of color. It's nature at its wildest that resembles a manicured rock garden.

One necessary man-made concession to travel is the suspension bridge, and there are several of them along the highway. Shutterbugs can clamber down an ice plant-covered sand dune to get a shot of the Rocky Creek Bridge. A bit farther south is the larger Bixby Bridge, arching above waves crashing against the rocks far below.

In addition to a wealth of spectacular scenery, Big Sur has an artsy, quintessentially Californian vibe; spas, healing centers and art galleries line SR 1 in the vicinity of Big Sur village. Henry Miller was a resident for 18 years, Jack Kerouac sang Big Sur's praises in a novel and Hollywood weighed in with "The Sandpiper," a 1965 movie starring Richard Burton and Elizabeth Taylor that featured Taylor playing a caftan-clad Big Sur artist.

Nepenthe, 48510 SR 1, totally embodies this bohemian spirit. The three-level complex perches on a hillside landscaped with pretty gardens. Both Café Kevah and the Nepenthe restaurant above it have outdoor terraces with umbrella-shaded tables and to-die-for views of green hills rolling down to the Pacific. Either one is a perfect spot to just chill for an hour or so.

Phoenix, on the lower level, is one of those gift shops that sells things you don't really need but have to have: Navajo jewelry, wall hangings, meditation CDs, art books, stone Buddha sculptures and "vertical gardens," miniature succulents planted in flat, shallow wood containers that can be hung on a wall. The shop's cozy back patio, overlooking the ocean with a soundtrack of tinkling wind chimes, feels like a little corner of paradise.

Point Sur State Historic Park faces SR 1 about 19 miles south of Rio Road in Carmel-by-the-Sea and a quarter mile north of the Point Sur Naval Facility. The park includes Point Sur Lighthouse *(see attraction listing)* and its seven lightstation buildings as well as an interpretive center.

There are campsites at Limekiln State Park, on SR 1 56 miles south of Carmel-by-the-Sea and 2 miles south of Lucia. The park, in the midst of a redwood forest, offers breathtaking views of the Big Sur coast; for information phone (805) 434-1996.

JULIA PFEIFFER BURNS STATE PARK is about 10 mi. s. of Pfeiffer Big Sur State Park on SR 1; watch for the turn-off and prominent entrance sign. Don't confuse Julia Pfeiffer Burns with the similar-sounding park to the north. Named for an early 20th-century pioneer who had an abiding love for the rugged Big Sur backcountry, this 4-square-mile park offers groves of redwood, tan oak and madrone trees as well as dramatic coastal views from the higher elevations of the hiking trails east of SR 1.

The park's unquestionable highlight is McWay Falls. From the parking area, take the signed Waterfall Trail; the approximately quarter-mile path follows McWay Creek, goes through a tunnel that burrows under SR 1 and emerges at a boardwalk that leads to the 80-foot drop, which you'll hear before you see. A slender ribbon of water plunges down to a rocky cove, with an ocean backdrop that is (at least on a sunny day) stunningly turquoise. Since the waterfall is fed by underground springs, it flows year-round. There's no access to the beach below, but the view from the boardwalk's elevated perspective is picture-perfect, and even more so during the spring months when the hillside tumbling down to the cove is blanketed with wildflowers.

The boardwalk continues past the falls for a short distance before ending at the ruins of the Waterfall House, where there's another awesome view—framed by eucalyptus trees—looking north along the Big Sur coastline. Sunsets at this spot are spectacular. In December and January the end of the trail is a good vantage point to spot gray whales migrating south to breeding grounds off the Baja California coast. *See Recreation Areas Chart.*

Note: McWay Falls can by seen from Waterfall Trail, but the part of the trail that approaches the falls is closed. **Time:** Allow 2 hours minimum. **Hours:** Daily 8 a.m.-dusk. **Cost:** $10 (per car). **Phone:** (831) 667-1112.

PFEIFFER BIG SUR STATE PARK, s. on SR 1, encompasses 964 acres of coastal redwood and chaparral on the Big Sur River. Hiking trails wind through groves of redwoods and other conifers, stands of oaks, maples, alders and willows, and open meadows where black-tail deer might be spotted. Rangers conduct naturalist and campfire programs Memorial Day weekend through Labor Day. Year-round overnight camping is permitted. *See Recreation Areas Chart.*

Note: Although it partially reopened in May 2017, much of the park remains closed due to ongoing impacts caused by the Soberanes fire in 2016 and flooding from heavy rains in early 2017. Check the Caltrans website for traffic conditions and phone ahead for the latest park updates. **Hours:** Daily 30 min. prior to dawn-30 min. after dusk. **Cost:** Day use $10 per private vehicle; $9 (ages 62+ per private vehicle). **Phone:** (831) 667-2315, or (800) 444-7275 for camping reservations.

POINT SUR LIGHTHOUSE tours meet at the farm gate along the w. side of SR 1, .25 mi. n. of the Point Sur Naval Facility. Docents lead 3-hour walking tours, beginning with a .5-mile uphill walk, which includes two stairways, to the stone lighthouse. Whale, pelican and peregrine falcon sightings are possible on the trek, as are glimpses of spring wildflowers and panoramic views of the Big Sur coast.

The lighthouse is automated and is part of Point Sur State Historic Park. The restored lightstation buildings were both home and workplace to lightkeepers and their families from 1889 to 1974. Visitors can climb to the top of the lighthouse tower to see the light itself and to walk around the tower's catwalk.

Note: Wear comfortable walking shoes and layered clothing; the weather can be quite cold and windy. Strollers are not permitted. **Hours:** Tours are given on a first-come, first-served basis Wed. and Sat. at 10 and 2, Sun. at 10, Apr.-Oct.; Wed. at 1, Sat.-Sun. at 10, rest of year. Moonlight tours are offered on select evenings Apr.-Sept. Phone ahead for moonlight tour schedule. Tours may be canceled due to weather conditions or road closures; phone ahead to confirm. **Cost:** Daytime tours $12; $5 (ages 6-17). Moonlight tours $20; $10 (ages 6-17). **Phone:** (831) 625-4419.

VENTANA BIG SUR, AN ALILA HOTEL   831/667-2331

Hotel

Address: 48123 Hwy 1 93920 **Location:** Off SR 1, 0.3 mi e. **Facility:** This attractively decorated property and richly appointed spa keeps in theme with the rustic nature of Big Sur. Enjoy spectacular views of the Pacific Coast or the surrounding forest. 59 units, some cottages. 2 stories (no elevator), exterior corridors. **Terms:** check-in 4 pm, age restrictions may apply. **Amenities:** safes. **Pool:** heated outdoor. **Activities:** sauna, hot tub, recreation programs, trails, exercise room, spa. **Guest Services:** valet laundry, area transportation.

WHERE TO EAT

THE RESTAURANT AT BIG SUR LODGE   831/667-3109
American. Casual Dining. **Address:** 47225 Hwy 1 93920

BODEGA BAY (E-2) pop. 1,077, elev. 59'
• Restaurants p. 47
• Part of Wine Country area — see map p. 405

This Sonoma coast community is perhaps best known for its association with Alfred Hitchcock's

1963 thriller "The Birds," although practically all of the landmarks associated with the film are now gone. One that remains is the Tides Wharf Restaurant, although it's unrecognizable (due to several subsequent expansions and renovations) from the movie scene when Tippi Hedren burst in calling for help after the frightening attack on school children by a marauding flock of seagulls.

Fortunately today's birds are much better mannered, and you'll still encounter the same picturesque views of coastal hills and the gleaming Pacific that featured prominently in Hitchcock's film—before the mayhem began, that is. Nearby Sonoma Coast State Park encompasses an exceptionally scenic stretch of northern California coastline.

The biggest event of the year is the Bodega Bay Fisherman's Festival in April. It began as a celebration of the start of salmon fishing season, and the annual Blessing of the Fleet is still one of the festival's highlights. Despite the decline of the local fishing industry, this traditional blessing, bestowed on a parade of decorated boats, both honors and acknowledges those individuals who farm the sea for a livelihood. Food vendors dish up local favorites like barbecued oysters, and craft booths, a golf tournament, live entertainment, wine tastings and lots of activities for kids add to the fun. It all takes place at Westside Regional Park, on Westshore Road (at the north end of the bay, past the Spud Point Marina).

Sonoma Coast Visitors Center: 850 SR 1, Bodega Bay, CA 94923. **Phone:** (707) 875-3866.

SONOMA COAST STATE PARK extends along and off SR 1 from Bodega Bay n. to Jenner, at the mouth of the Russian River. This stretch of Sonoma County coast embraces rugged headlands and a craggy shoreline pocked with secluded coves and natural arches rising from the waters just offshore. The park has approximately 17 miles of beaches, separated by rocky bluffs and headlands, that can be accessed from more than a dozen parking pull-offs along SR 1.

The entire coastline is ruggedly beautiful, but Coleman and Gleason beaches have particularly scenic backdrops. At Goat Rock, near the northern end of the park at the mouth of the Russian River, there's an easily accessible sandy beach that also is home to a colony of harbor seals. From Duncans Landing, steps lead down to the beach at Duncans Cove. The spring wildflower displays in this area are beautiful.

Between Goat Rock Beach and Duncans Landing is Shell Beach, favored by beachcombers and tide pool enthusiasts and also known as a prime fishing spot. Another popular summer destination for surf fishing and beachcombing is Salmon Creek Beach, just north of Bodega Head. *See Recreation Areas Chart.*

Note: As is the case at most northern California coast beaches, strong rip currents, heavy surf and sudden ground swells make swimming dangerous, even at the shoreline. Enter the water at your own risk, as lifeguards are not always available. Dogs are not permitted on beaches or trails, and must otherwise be leashed. **Hours:** Park open daily dawn-dusk. **Cost:** Day use fee for developed sections $8 per private vehicle; $7 (ages 62+ per private vehicle). Designated beach parking pull-offs along SR 1 free. **Phone:** (707) 875-3483 or (707) 865-2391.

Bodega Head is within Sonoma Coast State Park; from SR 1 take Eastshore Rd. to Westshore Rd., then Westshore Rd. to the parking area. This is the rocky headland that forms the entrance into Bodega Harbor. The harbor side has a popular crabbing area along the jetty. Rocky cliffs overlook Campbell Cove, and steps lead down to a small sand beach where waves crash against the rocks. All of Bodega Head is a state marine reserve and protected conservation area.

Be sure to hike the Bodega Head Trail, a loop trail that encircles the headland. The views of Bodega Harbor, and particularly of the ocean and sheer cliff walls descending vertically to the water far below, are absolutely spectacular. From December through April, this elevated vantage point is also a good place from which to spot migrating gray whales. The hardy ground cover of native shrubs and grasses is brightened in spring with displays of yellow and blue lupine, Indian paintbrush and other wildflowers.

Note: At points the trail goes right to the very edge of clifftops that plunge straight down to the water; while the views are amazing, approach these spots at your own risk. The shale rock formations are unstable and unsafe for climbing; stay on marked trails and heed warning signs. **Time:** Allow 1 hour minimum. **Hours:** Daily dawn-dusk. **Cost:** Bodega Head parking access free. **Phone:** (707) 875-3483.

BODEGA BAY INN   707/875-3388

Contemporary Country Inn

Address: 1588 Eastshore Rd 94923
Location: SR 1, just w. **Facility:** 7 units. 2 stories (no elevator), interior corridors. **Activities:** trails.

BODEGA BAY LODGE   707/875-3525
Hotel. **Address:** 103 Coast Hwy 1 94923

▼ *See AAA listing p. 47* ▼

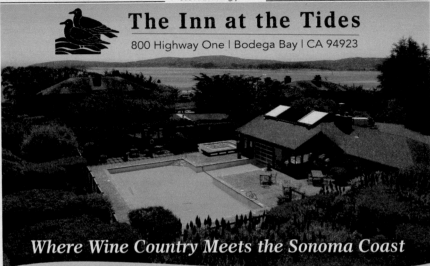

INN AT THE TIDES

Hotel

707/875-2751

Address: 800 Hwy 1 94923 **Location:** Center. **Facility:** 86 units. 2 stories (no elevator), exterior corridors. **Terms:** check-in 4 pm. **Dining:** 2 restaurants. **Pool:** heated outdoor. **Activities:** sauna, hot tub, exercise room, massage. **Guest Services:** coin laundry. **Featured Amenity: full hot breakfast.** *(See ad p. 46.)*

/ SOME UNITS

WHERE TO EAT

FISHERMAN'S COVE DELI BAIT GIFTS   707/377-4238
Seafood. Quick Serve. **Address:** 1850 Bay Flat Rd 94923

GINOCHIO'S KITCHEN   707/377-4359
American. Quick Serve. **Address:** 1410 Bay Flat Rd 94923

LUCAS WHARF RESTAURANT   707/875-3522
Seafood. Casual Dining. **Address:** 595 SR 1 94923

SPUD POINT CRAB COMPANY   707/875-9472
Seafood. Quick Serve. **Address:** 1860 Westshore Rd 94923

TERRAPIN CREEK CAFE & RESTAURANT   707/875-2700
American. Casual Dining. **Address:** 1580 Eastshore Rd 94923

BOULDER CREEK (F-8) pop. 4,923, elev. 493'

BIG BASIN REDWOODS STATE PARK is 9 mi. n.w. on SR 236. Covering more than 18,000 acres, the park was established in 1902 as California's first state park. Some of the trees it protects, including a stand of coast redwoods, have attained a diameter of 18 feet and a height of 330 feet.

Trails for hikers and equestrians, waterfalls and a chance to spot wildlife such as deer, raccoons, egrets and herons draw nature lovers. Among the 80 miles of trails is the Redwood Trail, an easy, half-mile nature hike leading to some of the park's tallest trees; the trail begins near the park headquarters. A natural history museum is on the grounds. Camping supplies and naturalist services are available June through October. *See Recreation Areas Chart.*

Note: Portions of the park are closed due to storm damage; phone for updates. Natural history museum is under renovations. **Time:** Allow 2 hours minimum. **Hours:** Park open daily 6 a.m.-dusk. Museum open daily 9-5. **Cost:** Day use $10 per private vehicle; $9 (ages 62+ per private vehicle). **Phone:** (831) 338-8860.

MERRYBROOK LODGE   831/338-6813

Cottage

Address: 13420 Big Basin Way 95006 **Location:** Just n on SR 236. **Facility:** 9 cottages. 1 story, exterior corridors. *Bath:* shower only. **Activities:** picnic facilities.

/ SOME UNITS

WHERE TO EAT

BOULDER CREEK PIZZA & PUB   831/338-2141
Pizza. Casual Dining. **Address:** 13200 Central Ave (Hwy 9), Suite B 95006

BRENTWOOD (C-9) pop. 51,481, elev. 79'
• Restaurants p. 48

• Restaurants p. 48

This Contra Costa County city, located about 55 miles east of San Francisco, is known for Brentwood Harvest Time from April through September, which collectively brings more than 150,000 visitors to the region's numerous U-pick farms and roadside produce stands. The Brentwood Harvest Time Festival in mid-July celebrates the agricultural bounty with a farmers market, gourmet food trucks, cooking and agricultural demonstrations, wine tastings, miniature tractor races and live entertainment.

Brentwood is located near the Sacramento-San Joaquin River Delta region, and the area offers lots of opportunities for boating, fishing and water recreation. The Brentwood Family Aquatic Complex, 195 Griffith Ln., caters to families with two waterslides, a lap pool and plenty of grassy areas to spread out a picnic; phone (925) 516-5430. Older kids can show off their maneuvers at the adjacent skate park, which can also be used by inline skaters.

At Round Valley Regional Preserve, 19450 Marsh Creek Rd., you can hike a 5-mile loop trail that traverses grasslands dotted with clumps of oak trees and offers panoramic views of rolling hills. The preserve is at its greenest following winter rains; the spring months are also the best time to see wildflowers. Summer temperatures can top 100 degrees; hikers should use sunscreen, wear a hat and bring plenty of drinking water.

Shopping: The Streets of Brentwood, 2455 Sand Creek Rd., is an outdoor shopping complex featuring about 30 chain retailers (think Hollister Co., Justice, Talbots and Victoria's Secret), restaurants and a 14-screen multiplex.

BEST WESTERN BRENTWOOD INN   925/634-6400

Hotel

 Best Western

AAA Benefit: Members save up to 15% and earn bonus points!

Address: 8820 Brentwood Blvd 94513 **Location:** SR 4 exit Balfour Rd, 2.7 mi e, then just s. **Facility:** 50 units. 2 stories, interior corridors. **Pool:** outdoor. **Activities:** exercise room. **Guest Services:** valet laundry. **Featured Amenity:** breakfast buffet.

HAMPTON INN BRENTWOOD   925/513-1299
Hotel. **Address:** 7605 Brentwood Blvd 94513

AAA Benefit: Members save up to 15%!

WHERE TO EAT

DINO'S SANDWICH SHOP   925/684-7248
 Sandwiches. Quick Serve. **Address:** 729 1st St 94513

ZEPHYR GRILL & BAR   925/418-4708
American. Casual Dining. **Address:** 613 1st St 94513

BRISBANE pop. 4,282

- **Hotels & Restaurants map & index p. 316**
- **Part of San Francisco area — see map p. 243**

**DOUBLETREE BY HILTON SAN FRANCISCO AIRPORT
NORTH**   415/467-4400   **19**

Hotel

DOUBLETREE
BY HILTON

AAA Benefit:
Members save up to
15%!

Address: 5000 Sierra Point Pkwy 94005 **Location:** US 101 exit Sierra Point Pkwy, just e. **Facility:** 210 units. 8 stories, interior corridors. **Amenities:** safes. **Pool:** heated indoor. **Activities:** hot tub, trails, exercise room. **Guest Services:** valet and coin laundry.

/ SOME
UNITS

**HOMEWOOD SUITES BY HILTON SAN FRANCISCO
AIRPORT-NORTH**   650/589-1600   **20**
Extended Stay Hotel.
Address: 2000 Shoreline Ct 94005

AAA Benefit:
Members save up to
15%!

WHERE TO EAT

7 MILE HOUSE   415/467-2343   **13**
American. Casual Dining. **Address:** 2800 Bayshore Blvd 94005

BROOKS (E-2) elev. 341'

The stretch of SR 16 that runs from Brooks north to where the highway dead-ends at SR 20 at Wilbur Springs is a particularly scenic drive. The road passes beautiful hillsides and follows a creek as it travels through the Capay Valley; driving time is approximately 2 hours.

CACHE CREEK CASINO RESORT   530/796-3118

Resort Hotel

Address: 14455 State Hwy 16 95606 **Location:** I-505 exit 21 (SR 16/Esparto), 12.4 mi w. **Facility:** This upscale property offers beautiful, sweeping views of the Capay Valley. Cabanas, complete with LCD TVs, are offered as well as a relaxing poolside water feature. 200 units. 4 stories, interior corridors. **Parking:** on-site and valet. **Terms:** check-in 4 pm. **Amenities:** safes. **Dining:** Asian Kitchen, C2 Steak & Seafood, Canyon Cafe, Chang Shou, Harvest Buffet, see separate listings, nightclub. **Pool:** heated outdoor. **Activities:** hot tub, cabanas, regulation golf, spa. **Guest Services:** valet laundry.

WHERE TO EAT

ASIAN KITCHEN   530/796-3118
Asian. Quick Serve. **Address:** 14455 State Hwy 16 95606

C2 STEAK & SEAFOOD   530/796-3118
Steak Seafood. Fine Dining. **Address:** 14455 State Hwy 16 95606

CANYON CAFE   530/796-3118
American. Casual Dining. **Address:** 14455 State Hwy 16 95606

CHANG SHOU   530/796-3118
Asian. Casual Dining. **Address:** 14455 State Hwy 16 95606

HARVEST BUFFET   530/796-3118
International. Casual Dining. **Address:** 14455 State Hwy 16 95606

BURLINGAME pop. 28,806, elev. 39'

- **Hotels & Restaurants map & index p. 316**
- **Part of San Francisco area — see map p. 243**

BAY LANDING HOTEL   650/259-9000   **43**
Hotel. **Address:** 1550 Bayshore Hwy 94010

CROWNE PLAZA SAN FRANCISCO AIRPORT
    650/342-9200   **46**

Hotel

Address: 1177 Airport Blvd 94010 **Location:** US 101 exit Broadway-Burlingame or Old Bayshore Hwy, just e. **Facility:** 309 units. 10 stories, interior corridors. **Parking:** on-site (fee). **Pool:** heated indoor. **Activities:** hot tub, trails, exercise room. **Guest Services:** valet laundry, area transportation.

/ SOME
UNITS

DOUBLETREE BY HILTON HOTEL SAN FRANCISCO AIRPORT
    650/344-5500   **48**
Hotel. **Address:** 835 Airport Blvd 94010

AAA Benefit:
Members save up to
15%!

**EMBASSY SUITES SAN FRANCISCO AIRPORT -
WATERFRONT**   650/342-4600   **47**
Hotel. **Address:** 150 Anza Blvd 94010

AAA Benefit:
Members save up to
15%!

**HAMPTON INN & SUITES SAN FRANCISCO
AIRPORT-BURLINGAME**   650/697-5736   **42**

Hotel

Hampton
BY HILTON

AAA Benefit:
Members save up to
15%!

Address: 1755 Bayshore Hwy 94010 **Location:** US 101 exit Millbrae Ave, just e. Millbrae, 54. **Facility:** 78 units. 4 stories, interior corridors. **Activities:** exercise room. **Guest Services:** valet and coin laundry. **Featured Amenity:** breakfast buffet.

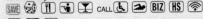

(See map & index p. 316.)

HILTON GARDEN INN SAN FRANCISCO AIRPORT/BURLINGAME
650/347-7800 **49**

  Hotel. **Address:** 765 Airport Blvd 94010

AAA Benefit: Members save up to 15%!

HILTON SAN FRANCISCO AIRPORT BAYFRONT
650/340-8500 **50**

Hotel

 Hilton HOTELS & RESORTS

AAA Benefit: Members save up to 15%!

Address: 600 Airport Blvd 94010 **Location:** US 101 exit Broadway-Burlingame or Anza Blvd, 0.3 mi e. **Facility:** 400 units. 15 stories, interior corridors. **Parking:** on-site (fee) and valet. **Amenities:** safes. **Pool:** heated indoor. **Activities:** trails, exercise room. **Guest Services:** valet laundry, area transportation.

HOLIDAY INN EXPRESS SAN FRANCISCO AIRPORT SOUTH
650/347-2381 **45**

Hotel

Address: 1250 Bayshore Hwy 94010 **Location:** US 101 exit Broadway-Burlingame or Bayshore Hwy, just e. **Facility:** 146 units. 3 stories, interior corridors. **Parking:** on-site (fee). **Amenities:** safes. **Pool:** outdoor. **Activities:** exercise room. **Guest Services:** valet and coin laundry. **Featured Amenity:** continental breakfast.

HYATT REGENCY SAN FRANCISCO AIRPORT
650/347-1234 **44**

Hotel

HYATT REGENCY **AAA Benefit:** Members save up to 10%!

Address: 1333 Bayshore Hwy 94010 **Location:** US 101 exit Broadway-Burlingame, just e. **Facility:** 789 units. 9 stories, interior corridors. **Parking:** on-site (fee) and valet. **Amenities:** safes. **Pool:** heated outdoor. **Activities:** hot tub, exercise room, massage. **Guest Services:** valet laundry, boarding pass kiosk, area transportation.

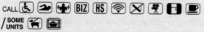

SAN FRANCISCO AIRPORT MARRIOTT WATERFRONT
650/692-9100 **41**

Hotel

 MARRIOTT

AAA Benefit: Members save 5% or more!

Address: 1800 Old Bayshore Hwy 94010 **Location:** Waterfront. US 101 exit Millbrae Ave, just e. 🚉 Millbrae, 54. **Facility:** 688 units. 11 stories, interior corridors. **Parking:** on-site (fee) and valet. **Terms:** check-in 4 pm. **Amenities:** safes. **Pool:** heated indoor. **Activities:** sauna, hot tub, bicycles, trails, exercise room. **Guest Services:** valet and coin laundry, boarding pass kiosk, area transportation.

WHERE TO EAT

CAFE FIGARO 650/344-8277 **30**
 Italian. Casual Dining. **Address:** 1318 Broadway 94010

LIMON ROTISSERIE 650/727-0050 **34**
 Peruvian Small Plates. Casual Dining. **Address:** 1101 Burlingame Ave 94010

MINGALABA RESTAURANT 650/343-5130 **35**
 Burmese. Casual Dining. **Address:** 1213 Burlingame Ave 94010

NEW ENGLAND LOBSTER MARKET & EATERY
650/443-1559 **29**
Seafood. Quick Serve. **Address:** 824 Cowan Rd 94010

PIZZERIA DELFINA 650/288-1041 **37**
Italian Pizza. Casual Dining. **Address:** 1444 Burlingame Ave 94010

SALTYARD RESTAURANT AND BAR 650/342-7355 **33**
American. Casual Dining. **Address:** 322 Lorton Ave 94010

SAPORE ITALIANO 650/348-3277 **38**
Italian. Casual Dining. **Address:** 1447 Burlingame Ave 94010

SESAME KOREAN CUISINE 650/347-4348 **31**
Korean. Casual Dining. **Address:** 1355 Broadway 94010

STEELHEAD BREWING CO. 650/344-6050 **32**
American. Brewpub. **Address:** 333 California Dr 94010

TRAPEZE 650/344-4242 **36**
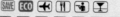 Continental. Casual Dining. **Address:** 266 Lorton Ave 94010

🔗 # Use the free travel planning tools
at AAA.com/maps

BURNEY (B-3) pop. 3,154, elev. 3,173'

Named for an early English settler killed in a Native American raid in 1857, Burney's location between Lassen National Forest and Mount Shasta makes it popular with campers and anglers.

Burney Chamber of Commerce: 36789 Main St., Burney, CA 96013. **Phone:** (530) 335-2111.

MCARTHUR-BURNEY FALLS MEMORIAL STATE PARK, 5 mi. e. on SR 299, then 6 mi. n. on SR 89, features a 129-foot spring-fed waterfall that flows down several levels over moss-covered lava rock in a lush forest setting. *See Recreation Areas Chart.* **Hours:** Daily dawn-dusk. **Cost:** Day use $8 per private vehicle; $7 (ages 62+ per private vehicle). **Phone:** (530) 335-2777.

CHARM MOTEL   530/335-3300

Motel

Address: 37363 Main St 96013 **Location:** 0.5 mi ne on SR 299; jct Roff Way. **Facility:** 42 units, some two bedrooms and kitchens. 2 stories (no elevator), exterior corridors. **Guest Services:** coin laundry. **Featured Amenity: continental breakfast.**

GREEN GABLES MOTEL   530/335-3300

Motel

Address: 37385 Main St 96013 **Location:** 0.5 mi ne on SR 299; jct Roff Way. **Facility:** 27 units, some two bedrooms and kitchens. 1 story, exterior corridors. **Guest Services:** coin laundry. **Featured Amenity: continental breakfast.**

SHASTA PINES MOTEL   530/335-2201

Motel

Address: 37386 Main St 96013 **Location:** 0.5 mi ne on SR 299; jct Roff Way. **Facility:** 30 units. 1-2 stories (no elevator), exterior corridors. **Activities:** picnic facilities. **Featured Amenity: continental breakfast.**

WHERE TO EAT

ART'S OUTPOST   530/335-2835

Steak Seafood. Casual Dining. **Address:** 37392 Main St 96013

CALIFORNIA COASTAL NATIONAL MONUMENT (D-5, I-2)

Consisting of thousands of islands, rocks, exposed reefs and pinnacles extending up to 12 miles

out from the shore off California's entire 1,100-mile coastline, California Coastal National Monument was established to preserve these uninhabited outcroppings.

The diverse geological formations found within the national monument's fragile coastal ecosystem provide feeding and nesting grounds for many sea birds, including gulls, bald eagles, peregrine falcons, pigeon guillemots, common murres and cormorants. Two threatened species, southern sea otters and Steller sea lions, as well as California sea lions and Guadalupe fur seals are examples of marine mammals that find shelter and breeding habitats within the monument's boundaries. For such birds as brown pelicans, a threatened species, the monument serves as a roosting ground.

Visitor centers for the offshore sanctuaries are being established along the California coast in conjunction with existing marine conservation organizations. The first to open, the Coastal Discovery Center at William Randolph Hearst Memorial State Beach in San Simeon, has interactive exhibits that provide information about the ocean environment. For additional information phone (831) 582-2200 or (805) 927-6575 for the Coastal Discovery Center.

CALISTOGA (A-7) pop. 5,155, elev. 362'

- Restaurants p. 52
- Hotels & Restaurants map & index p. 412
- Part of Wine Country area — see map p. 405

It's obvious that Calistoga, at the Napa Valley's northern end, is all about wine—the tasting rooms of well-respected vintners are within close proximity. However, wellness and water are two other highly regarded Calistoga commodities, a fact that becomes readily apparent as you stroll through this delightful town. Indeed, you may have already sampled the bottled mineral water produced by Calistoga Water Company.

In the late 1800s the railroad transported visitors to Calistoga by the droves to bask in the reputedly therapeutic natural mineral springs, which continue to draw health enthusiasts as well as the curious. Spas dotted along Calistoga's early 1900s main drag, Lincoln Avenue, pipe in the bubbling "medicinal" waters of the hot springs to pamper customers with relaxing treatments—some facilities have outdoor pools. Many establishments post signs out front enticing passersby to take a bath in steaming mud, a concoction prepared from ingredients like mineral water, clay, volcanic ash and peat moss.

If soaking in a tub of mud isn't your thing, explore the Western-influenced downtown's art galleries and funky shops displaying wares that lean toward the artsy and earthy. Or observe geothermal activity in the form of Old Faithful Geyser, which reliably erupts about every half-hour, providing a perfect photo op.

(See map & index p. 412.)

North of town is an extinct volcano, Mount St. Helena. Robert Louis Stevenson State Park, 7 miles north via SR 29, offers plenty of opportunities for hiking and biking.

Hit the road and go for a drive. Calistoga is the southern end of an approximately 95-mile stretch of SR 128 that runs northwest. Past Cloverdale it enters the Anderson Valley and then skirts Navarro River Redwoods State Park before ending at SR 1, the Pacific Coast Highway, a couple of miles south of the oceanside hamlet of Albion. In the opposite direction, SR 29 runs south from Calistoga through the equally scenic heart of the Napa Valley to the town of Napa.

Calistoga Chamber of Commerce and Visitor's Center: 1133 Washington St., Calistoga, CA 94515. **Phone:** (707) 942-6333 or (866) 306-5588.

SHARPSTEEN MUSEUM, 1311 Washington St., displays artifacts, photographs and dioramas depicting 19th-century Calistoga; a scale model of Calistoga Hot Springs Resort is included. Attached to the museum is one of the resort's 1860s cottages. In addition to the permanent exhibits, which include an interactive geothermal display, is a rotating exhibit that changes every 3 months. Docents conduct tours on request. **Hours:** Daily 11-4. Closed Thanksgiving and Christmas. **Cost:** Donations. Reservations are required for tours. **Phone:** (707) 942-5911.

WINERIES

- **Castello di Amorosa** is 3 mi. s.e. at 4045 N. St. Helena Hwy., between Petersen Dr. and Maple Ln. **Hours:** Tastings daily 9:30-6, Mar.-Oct.; 10-5, rest of year. Castle tours are offered daily; schedule varies. Various specialty guided tours also are offered; reservations are required and are strongly recommended as tours can fill up quickly. Closed Christmas. **Phone:** (707) 967-6272. GT

- **Sterling Vineyards** is between SR 29 and Silverado Tr. at 1111 Dunaweal Ln. **Hours:** Mon.-Fri. 10:30-5, Sat.-Sun. 10-5, in summer; Mon.-Fri. 10:30-4:30, Sat.-Sun. 10-5, rest of year. Closed Jan. 1, Thanksgiving and Christmas. **Phone:** (707) 942-3300 or (800) 726-6136. GT

AURORA PARK COTTAGES   707/942-6733   10
 Cottage. **Address:** 1807 Foothill Blvd 94515

THE BERGSON   707/942-5755   14

Boutique Hotel

Address: 1010 Foothill Blvd 94515 **Location:** On SR 29, just s of jct Lincoln Ave. **Facility:** Designer fabrics and finishes complete the interiors of this property, which is made up of three Georgian-style houses. The lobby features relaxing furniture and a fireplace. 22 units. 2 stories (no elevator), interior/exterior corridors. **Featured Amenity:** continental breakfast.

SAVE ⊞ ⏱ CALL ⛍ ➰ 🛜 ✕ ▣ / SOME UNITS ▤

BEST WESTERN PLUS STEVENSON MANOR
707/942-1112   5

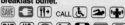

Hotel

Best Western PLUS. **AAA Benefit:** Members save up to 15% and earn bonus points!

Address: 1830 Lincoln Ave 94515 **Location:** 0.5 mi n on SR 29. **Facility:** 34 units. 2 stories, exterior corridors. **Terms:** check-in 4 pm. **Pool:** heated outdoor. **Activities:** sauna, hot tub, steamroom, exercise room. **Guest Services:** coin laundry. **Featured Amenity:** breakfast buffet.

SAVE ⊞ ⏱ CALL ⛍ ➰ 🛠
BIZ HS 🛜 ✕ ▣ ▦ ▤

BRANNAN COTTAGE INN   707/942-4200   8
♦♦♦ Historic Boutique Hotel. **Address:** 109 Wappo Ave 94515

CALISTOGA MOTOR LODGE AND SPA
707/942-0991   1

Motel

Address: 1880 Lincoln Ave 94515 **Location:** 0.7 mi n on SR 29. **Facility:** 50 units. 1 story, exterior corridors. **Terms:** check-in 4 pm. **Amenities:** safes. **Pool:** heated outdoor. **Activities:** hot tub, cabanas, lawn sports, massage.

SAVE CALL ⛍ ➰ 🛜 ✕ ▣
 ▤ / SOME UNITS ▥

CALISTOGA RANCH, AN AUBERGE RESORT
707/254-2800   15
♦♦♦♦ Boutique Resort Hotel. **Address:** 580 Lommel Rd 94515

CARLIN'S COTTAGE COURT   707/942-9102   4
♦♦ Cottage. **Address:** 1623 Lake St 94515

CHELSEA GARDEN INN   707/942-0948   9
♦♦ Bed & Breakfast. **Address:** 1443 2nd St 94515

COTTAGE GROVE INN   707/942-8400   7
♦♦♦ Cottage. **Address:** 1711 Lincoln Ave 94515

EUROSPA & INN   707/942-6829   13

Motel

Address: 1202 Pine St 94515 **Location:** Just s of Lincoln Ave; at Myrtle St. **Facility:** 13 units. 1 story, exterior corridors. **Pool:** heated outdoor. **Activities:** hot tub, spa.

SAVE ⏱ CALL ⛍ ➰ 🛜 ✕
▣ ▦ ▤

GOLDEN HAVEN HOT SPRINGS   707/942-8000   3
♦♦ Hotel. **Address:** 1713 Lake St 94515

(See map & index p. 412.)

MOUNT VIEW HOTEL & SPA 707/942-6877

Historic Hotel

Address: 1457 Lincoln Ave 94515 **Location:** On SR 29; center. **Facility:** A private courtyard, mineral hot tub and large outdoor pool all invite you to relax at this 1917 historic hotel that offers unique and contemporary rooms. The serene spa offers seven treatment rooms. 33 units, some cottages. 2 stories (no elevator), interior/exterior corridors. **Parking:** on-site and street. **Terms:** check-in 4 pm. **Amenities:** safes. **Dining:** 2 restaurants, also, Johnny's, see separate listing. **Pool:** heated outdoor. **Activities:** sauna, hot tub, spa. **Featured Amenity:** continental breakfast.

ROMAN SPA HOT SPRINGS RESORT
707/942-4441

Hotel

Address: 1300 Washington St 94515 **Location:** Just n of Lincoln Ave. **Facility:** 60 units, some kitchens. 2 stories (no elevator), exterior corridors. **Amenities:** *Some:* safes. **Pool:** heated outdoor. **Activities:** sauna, hot tub, picnic facilities, spa. **Guest Services:** coin laundry. *(See ad this page.)*

SOLAGE 707/226-0800

Resort Hotel

Address: 755 Silverado Tr 94515 **Location:** Jct SR 29, 0.5 mi se. **Facility:** With an impressive setting along the Silverado Trail, this upscale modern resort boasts expansive views, fine dining and a luxurious spa featuring mud and mineral water therapies. 89 units. 1 story, exterior corridors. **Parking:** on-site and valet. **Terms:** check-in 4 pm. **Amenities:** safes. **Pool:** heated outdoor. **Activities:** hot tub, steamroom, cabanas, recreation programs, bicycles, lawn sports, trails, health club, spa. **Guest Services:** valet laundry.

UPVALLEY INN & HOT SPRINGS, AN ASCEND HOTEL COLLECTION MEMBER 707/942-9400

Hotel

Address: 1865 Lincoln Ave 94515 **Location:** 0.5 mi n on SR 29. **Facility:** 55 units. 2 stories (no elevator), exterior corridors. *Bath:* shower only. **Pool:** heated outdoor. **Activities:** sauna, steamroom.

ALL SEASONS BISTRO 707/942-9111
American. Casual Dining. **Address:** 1400 Lincoln Ave 94515

▼ See AAA listing this page ▼

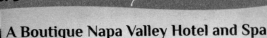

(See map & index p. 412.)

CAFE SARAFORNIA   707/942-0555   **6**
🍷 Breakfast. Casual Dining. **Address:** 1413 Lincoln Ave 94515

EVANGELINE   707/341-3131   **5**
🍷🍷 French. Fine Dining. **Address:** 1226 Washington St 94515

HYDRO BAR & GRILL   707/942-9777   **7**
🍷🍷 American. Gastropub. **Address:** 1403 Lincoln Ave 94515

JOHNNY'S   707/942-5938   **4**
🍷🍷 California. Sports Bar. **Address:** 1457 Lincoln Ave 94515

LINCOLN AVENUE BREWERY CALISTOGA
                               707/403-5028   **12**
🍷🍷 American. Brewpub. **Address:** 1473 Lincoln Ave 94515

LOVINA   707/942-6500   **11**
🍷🍷 American. Casual Dining. **Address:** 1107 Cedar St 94515

PALISADES DELI CAFE   707/942-0145   **3**
🍷 Deli. Quick Serve. **Address:** 1458 Lincoln Ave 94515

SAM'S SOCIAL CLUB   707/942-4913   **1**
🍷🍷🍷 Pacific Northwest. Casual Dining. **Address:** 1712 Lincoln Ave 94515

SUSHI MAMBO   707/942-4699   **2**
🍷🍷 Japanese. Casual Dining. **Address:** 1631 Lincoln Ave 94515

CAMPBELL (E-9) pop. 39,349, elev. 196'
• Hotels & Restaurants map & index p. 348

CAMPBELL HISTORICAL MUSEUM & THE AINSLEY HOUSE are at the corner of N. Central Ave. and Civic Center Dr. at 51 N. Central Ave. Campbell's rich agricultural history is depicted in the museum. Hands-on exhibits focus on the canneries that were the city's lifeblood, home life and recreation enjoyed during free time. A preliminary 5-minute videotape gives insights into the city's past.

The 1925, Tudor-style Ainsley House, just across the green, is lavishly furnished in accordance with the status of its owners, an English-born canning pioneer and his wife. Many furnishings are original to the house. A video presentation precedes the guided tour.

Allow 30 minutes minimum each for house and museum. **Hours:** Museum and house open Thurs.-Sun. noon-4, early Mar.-Dec. 22. Museum hours may vary; phone to confirm schedule. Last house tour begins at 3:15. Closed major holidays. **Cost:** Museum $2; free (ages 0-6). House tour $8; $6 (ages 55+); $4 (ages 7-17). Combination ticket $9; $7 (ages 55+); $5 (ages 7-17). Admission for house tours increases during holiday seasons. **Phone:** (408) 866-2119.

COURTYARD BY MARRIOTT SAN JOSE/CAMPBELL
                               408/626-9590   **89**
🍷🍷🍷 SAVE Hotel. **Address:** 655 Creekside Way 95008
AAA Benefit: Members save 5% or more!

DOUBLETREE BY HILTON-CAMPBELL PRUNEYARD PLAZA
                               408/559-4300   **90**
🍷🍷🍷 SAVE Hotel. **Address:** 1995 S Bascom Ave 95008
AAA Benefit: Members save up to 15%!

LARKSPUR LANDING CAMPBELL   408/364-1514   **88**
◆◆ Hotel
Address: 550 W Hamilton Ave 95008 **Location:** SR 17 exit Hamilton Ave, 1 mi w. **Facility:** 117 efficiencies. 4 stories, interior corridors. **Activities:** hot tub, exercise room. **Guest Services:** complimentary and valet laundry. **Featured Amenity:** continental breakfast.
[SAVE] [ECO] CALL [⟲] [♨] [BIZ] [HS]
[📶] [✕] [🔋] [📷] [📂]
/ SOME UNITS [🐾]

RESIDENCE INN BY MARRIOTT-SAN JOSE/CAMPBELL
                               408/559-1551   **92**
🍷🍷🍷 SAVE Extended Stay Hotel. **Address:** 2761 S Bascom Ave 95008
AAA Benefit: Members save 5% or more!

TOWNEPLACE SUITES BY MARRIOTT-SAN JOSE/CAMPBELL
                               408/370-4510   **91**
🍷🍷🍷 SAVE Extended Stay Hotel. **Address:** 700 E Campbell Ave 95008
AAA Benefit: Members save 5% or more!

WHERE TO EAT

AL CASTELLO RISTORANTE   408/369-9820   **47**
🍷🍷 Italian. Casual Dining. **Address:** 3155 S Bascom Ave, Suite B 95008

BLUE LINE PIZZA   408/378-2800   **44**
🍷🍷 Pizza. Casual Dining. **Address:** 415 E Campbell Ave 95008

GRILL 'EM STEAKHOUSE   408/371-8729   **46**
🍷🍷 Steak. Casual Dining. **Address:** 2509 S Bascom Ave 95008

NASCHMARKT RESTAURANT   408/378-0335   **45**
🍷🍷🍷 Austrian. Casual Dining. **Address:** 384 E Campbell Ave 95008

PACIFIC CATCH   408/879-9091   **43**
🍷🍷🍷 Seafood. Casual Dining. **Address:** 1875 S Bascom Ave 95008

CAPITOLA (F-9) pop. 9,918, elev. 50'
• Hotels p. 54 • Restaurants p. 54
• Hotels & Restaurants map & index p. 365

Capitola, a seaside community on the north shore of Monterey Bay, claims to be California's oldest beach resort. The town, founded in 1874, faces New Brighton State Beach *(see Recreation Areas Chart)*. The city is located on a scenic stretch of SR 1 that extends from San Francisco south to San Luis Obispo.

Capitola-Soquel Chamber of Commerce: 716-G Capitola Ave., Capitola, CA 95010. **Phone:** (831) 475-6522 or (800) 474-6522.

(See map & index p. 365.)

BEST WESTERN PLUS CAPITOLA BY-THE-SEA INN & SUITES   831-477-0607 **34**

Hotel

Best Western PLUS

AAA Benefit: Members save up to 15% and earn bonus points!

Address: 1435 41st Ave 95010 **Location:** SR 1 exit 41st Ave, 0.8 mi w. **Facility:** 58 units, some two bedrooms. 3 stories, interior corridors. **Pool:** heated outdoor. **Activities:** hot tub, exercise room. **Guest Services:** coin laundry. **Featured Amenity:** continental breakfast.

FAIRFIELD INN & SUITES BY MARRIOTT SANTA CRUZ-CAPITOLA   831/427-2900 **35**

 Hotel. **Address:** 1255 41st Ave 95010

AAA Benefit: Members save 5% or more!

THE INN AT DEPOT HILL   831/462-3376 **33**

 Bed & Breakfast. **Address:** 250 Monterey Ave 95010

QUALITY INN & SUITES   831/462-3004 **32**

Hotel

Address: 720 Hill St 95010 **Location:** SR 1 exit Bay Ave, just w. **Facility:** 55 units. 2 stories (no elevator), interior/exterior corridors. **Amenities:** safes. **Pool:** outdoor. **Guest Services:** coin laundry. **Featured Amenity:** full hot breakfast.

WHERE TO EAT

PARADISE BEACH GRILLE   831/476-4900 **19**

 Island Fusion. Casual Dining. **Address:** 215 Esplanade 95010

SHADOWBROOK RESTAURANT   831/475-1511 **18**

 Regional American. Fine Dining. **Address:** 1750 Wharf Rd 95010

CARMEL-BY-THE-SEA (G-3) pop. 3,722, elev. 20'

• **Hotels p. 56** • **Restaurants p. 57**
• **Hotels & Restaurants map & index p. 144**
• **Part of Monterey Peninsula area — see map p. 141**

Carmel-by-the-Sea (simply Carmel to residents and admirers) was established in 1904 by a group of artists and writers as a bucolic retreat. As the settlement grew, its founders fought the encroachment of paved streets, gas and electricity. Although modern life's necessities eventually took over, stringent zoning ordinances have helped preserve Carmel's village flavor.

To really experience the exceptional beauty of this seaside town up close and personal, stroll the length of the very aptly named Scenic Road. Scarcely a mile in length, its name is an almost comic understatement. On one side of the street is a wide expanse of white-sand beach edged by clear turquoise water. Picturesque rocks are covered with a thick green carpet of ice plants, and gracefully arching Monterey pines frame the views. On the other side are homes that collectively comprise some of Monterey Bay's most desirable real estate. Several sets of steps along the length of Scenic Road lead down to the beach.

Note: The north end of Scenic Road can be accessed via Ocean Avenue west off SR 1. Parking along the street is hard to come by at any time, and all but impossible on weekends. If you're driving, the south end veers left and becomes Carmelo Street; after about half a mile, turn right on Santa Lucia Street, then right again on Rio Street to return to SR 1.

By far the best way to explore Carmel, though, is on foot—an amble along the beach followed by ducking into art galleries, boutiques and antique shops, many of which are secluded behind courtyard walls. There really isn't a prevailing architectural style; Carmel's impossibly charming little bungalows, complete with picture-perfect gardens, do exhibit a degree of Spanish influence but tend to embody the whims of their owners.

The nonprofit Center for Photographic Art (CPA) is located in the Sunset Center at San Carlos Street and 9th Avenue, where Friends of Photography first opened its doors in 1967, and remains one of the oldest continuously operating photography members' organizations in America. Bimonthly exhibitions of fine art photography by both established and emerging artists showcase a wide technical, thematic and stylistic range. Lectures and workshops featuring guest artists, curators and educators are also offered. The gallery is open Wed.-Sun. noon-4; admission is free. Phone (831) 625-5181.

The Forest Theater Guild presents a series of summer performances under the stars at the Outdoor Forest Theatre, a block south of Ocean Avenue at Santa Rita Street and Mountain View Avenue. The outdoor theater, founded in 1910, is situated in a lush setting of pine trees in the heart of Carmel. Many theatergoers bring along a bountiful picnic supper. For schedule and ticket information phone (831) 626-1681.

The sound of baroque orchestral and choral music perfectly complements Carmel's exquisite natural beauty during the 3-week Carmel Bach Festival in July. The festival's centerpiece is the concert series that takes place in the Sunset Center Theater on San Carlos Street. Chamber music concerts are given in churches and other venues throughout town. For schedule and ticket information phone (831) 624-1521.

Carmel is located just off the delightfully scenic stretch of SR 1 that extends from San Francisco south to San Luis Obispo. Just north of town is the southern entrance to 17-Mile Drive, yet another beautiful oceanfront route that links Carmel and Pacific Grove (see Pebble Beach p. 194).

(See map & index p. 144.)

Downtown parking meter time limits are strictly enforced. If you can find an empty space, a city lot on Third Street at Torres Street offers free, unlimited parking; enter from Third.

Carmel Visitor Center: Carmel Plaza, Suite 219A, P.O. Box 4444, Carmel, CA 93921. **Phone:** (831) 624-2522.

Self-guiding tours: A brochure describing a walking tour of downtown Carmel's courtyards is available at the visitor center.

Shopping: Carmel's compact business center is filled with shops and galleries that display the work of local artists. The Barnyard, SR 1 and Carmel Valley Road with access from Carmel Rancho Boulevard, is as popular for its garden setting and country atmosphere as for its more than 50 galleries and specialty shops. The Crossroads, east of SR 1 and Father Serra's Carmel Mission on Rio Road, offers nearly 100 boutiques and specialty shops.

INSIDER INFO:
California Missions

To secure its northern territorial claims in the New World, Spain ordered the creation of a series of Franciscan missions in California. Begun under the leadership of Father Junípero Serra, who died in 1784, 21 missions were established between 1769 and 1823, spaced about a day's journey apart along the northern extension of El Camino Real, the Royal Road.

Each mission had its own herd of cattle, fields and vegetable gardens, which were tended by native converts. For furniture, clothing, tools and other implements, the missions traded their surplus of meal, wine, oil, hemp, hides and tallow. Their attempts to "civilize" the indigenous population yielded mixed results: For the thousands of Indians brought under the wing of the church, thousands of others died at the hands of the Spanish or from their diseases. But the missions succeeded in other regards: Around them and their accompanying presidios, or military posts, grew the first permanent settlements in California.

After winning its independence from Spain and during the secularization, Mexico removed control of the missions from the Franciscans and subdivided much of their land among the Mexican soldiers and settlers. During the ensuing years, neglect and earthquakes took their toll; many of the missions were severely damaged or destroyed. Subsequent restoration and reconstruction have revitalized these historic structures, and today US 101 roughly traces the route of the old El Camino Real.

MISSION SAN CARLOS BORROMÉO DEL RÍO CARMELO, at 3080 Rio Rd., is called Carmel Mission. Established by Father Junípero Serra at Monterey in 1770 and moved to its present site the following year, the mission was Father Serra's residence and headquarters until his death in 1784. He is buried beneath the church floor in front of the altar.

Relics of the mission's early days and some of Father Serra's books and documents are displayed. The courtyard gardens and Moorish bell tower are of interest, and a museum contains exhibits about the mission. A fiesta usually is held the last Sunday in September.

Time: Allow 1 hour minimum. **Hours:** Daily 9:30-7, Memorial Day-Labor Day; daily 9:30-5, day after Labor Day to mid-Apr.; Mon.-Thurs. 9:30-5, Fri.-Sun. 9:30-7, rest of year. Closed Jan. 1, Easter, Thanksgiving, Christmas Eve, Christmas and day after Christmas. **Cost:** $9.50; $7 (ages 62+); $5 (ages 7-17). **Phone:** (831) 624-1271.

POINT LOBOS STATE NATURAL RESERVE, 3 mi. s. on SR 1, is a magnificent example of the central California coast at its grandest: jutting headlands, irregular coves and rolling meadows formed over millions of years through the ceaseless interaction of land and water. The reserve encompasses some 550 acres of rugged seacoast and another 775 acres that are offshore. Pick up a brochure that includes a trail map at the entrance station.

If you don't have a lot of time, the South Shore Trail is an easy, scenic walk. The trail follows the ocean's edge past wave-splashed rocks and cliffs blanketed with ice plants, bluff lettuce and seaside daisy, all of which are adapted to the coastal climate. Toward the southern end of the trail stone steps descend to Hidden Beach, a little cove with pebbly sand where you can sit on a rock and meditate to the soothing sound of the waves. Succulents find a foothold in the crevices of rock walls, and in April and May wildflowers brighten the meadows.

Past Hidden Beach, Bird Island Trail winds through coastal scrub high above two gorgeous white-sand beaches, China Cove and Gibson Beach. At China Cove the water ranges from deep blue to turquoise to jade green, and cliffside gardens frame the views. This beautiful spot is favored by

(See map & index p. 144.)

artists. The steps leading down to the cove are closed until further notice due to erosion.

A bit farther on is Gibson Beach, a wide stretch of sand accessible via a long staircase; wading is permitted, but the water is cold all year. Bird Island is a spring and summer breeding ground for Brandt's cormorants. Harbor seals and sea otters are often spotted basking on rocks just above the water.

The Cypress Grove Trail, which begins at the Sea Lion Point parking area, winds through a grove of Monterey cypresses and has spectacular views of coastline rocks, with the Pacific an ever-changing palette of blue and turquoise hues. The gnarled trees display the effects of relentless wind and salt spray; they survive by thrusting their roots deep into cracks in the rocks. On these shaded, north-facing slopes you'll also see tree branches covered in velvety growths of algae with an orange color that comes from carotene, the same pigment found in carrots.

The North Shore Trail offers a wonderful hike through the woods, with frequent views from overlooks of the coves below. Follow the trail all the way to Cannery Point, where there are spectacular views looking out to Carmel Bay.

Whalers Cabin, built by Chinese fishermen in the 1850s, and an adjacent museum document the late 19th-century whaling industry at Point Lobos, where an abalone cannery and granite quarry also once operated. Diving in Whalers Cove is permitted by permit only. Guided nature walks are offered regularly; a daily schedule is posted at the entrance station.

Note: Stay on designated paths and within the wire guides along trails. Avoid touching the leaves or dried stems of poison oak, which grows almost everywhere; it has glossy green leaves divided into three leaflets. Pets are not permitted within the reserve.

Time: Allow 2 hours minimum. **Hours:** Daily 8-7, during daylight saving time; 8 a.m.-30 minutes after sunset, rest of year. Hours may be extended in summer. Last admission is 30 minutes before closing. Information station and Whalers Cabin museum open daily 9-5; phone ahead to confirm. **Cost:** $10 per private vehicle; $9 (ages 62+ per private vehicle); $5 (physically impaired per private vehicle); free (if entering on foot). Parking areas within the reserve fill up quickly during the summer months. **Phone:** (831) 624-4909, or (831) 624-8413 for diving reservations. 🏧

TOR HOUSE is on Carmel Point at 26304 Ocean View Ave. Perched on a rugged promontory overlooking a dramatic coastline, the 1918 home provided the creative backdrop for poet Robinson Jeffers, who received such guests as Charlie Chaplin, George Gershwin and Edna St. Vincent Millay. *Tor* is Celtic for an outcropping of rock. Docents guide visitors through the house, the English gardens and Hawk Tower, which Jeffers built himself by transporting stones from the beach.

Time: Allow 1 hour, 30 minutes minimum. **Hours:** Tours are given Fri.-Sat. on the hour 10-3. A maximum of six people is allowed on each tour. **Cost:** $10; $5 (full-time students with ID). Under 12 are not permitted. Cash or checks only. Reservations are required. **Phone:** (831) 624-1813.

BEST WESTERN CARMEL'S TOWN HOUSE LODGE
831/624-1261

Motel

AAA Benefit: Members save up to 15% and earn bonus points!

Address: San Carlos St & 5th Ave 93921 **Location:** 2 blks n of Ocean Ave. **Facility:** 28 units. 2 stories (no elevator), exterior corridors. **Amenities:** safes. **Pool:** heated outdoor. **Featured Amenity:** continental breakfast.

BRIARWOOD INN
831/626-9056 69

Bed & Breakfast

Address: San Carlos St 93921 **Location:** 2 blks n of Ocean Ave; between 4th and 5th aves. **Facility:** Most rooms have a fireplace and some have a wet bar. A garden beautifies the well-maintained grounds. 17 units, some two bedrooms and kitchens. 1-2 stories (no elevator), exterior corridors. **Parking:** on-site and street.

CANDLE LIGHT INN   831/624-6451 71
Hotel. **Address:** San Carlos Ave 93921

CARMEL BAY VIEW INN   831/624-1831 76
Hotel. **Address:** Junipero Ave 93921

CARMEL FIREPLACE INN BED & BREAKFAST
831/624-4862 68

Bed & Breakfast

Address: San Carlos St & 4th Ave 93921 **Location:** 2 blks n of Ocean Ave. **Facility:** 18 units. 2 stories (no elevator), exterior corridors. **Parking:** on-site and street. **Activities:** massage.

CARMEL GARDEN INN   831/624-6926 70
Bed & Breakfast. **Address:** 4th Ave & Torres St 93921

CARMEL GREEN LANTERN INN 831/624-4392 79
Bed & Breakfast. **Address:** Casanova St & 7th Ave 93921

(See map & index p. 144.)

CARMEL INN & SUITES
831/624-1900 **75**

♦♦♦ Motel

Address: Junipero Ave & 5th Ave 93921 **Location:** 2 blks n of Ocean Ave. **Facility:** 20 units. 2 stories (no elevator), exterior corridors. **Parking:** on-site and street. **Featured Amenity: continental breakfast.**

SAVE ⊞ 🛜 ✕ 🎦 🛏 🖵 / SOME UNITS 🖾

CARMEL LODGE
831/624-1255 **73**
♦♦ Motel. **Address:** San Carlos St & 5th Ave 93921

CARMEL MISSION INN
831/624-1841 **84**
♦♦♦ Hotel. **Address:** 3665 Rio Rd 93923

CARMEL OAKS INN & SUITES CLARION COLLECTION
831/624-5547 **74**

♦♦♦ Motel

Address: 5th Ave & Mission St 93921 **Location:** 2 blks n of Ocean Ave. **Facility:** 17 units. 2 stories (no elevator), exterior corridors. **Featured Amenity: continental breakfast.**

SAVE ⊞ CALL 🔌 🛜 ✕ 🎦 🛏 🖵 / SOME UNITS 🖾

CARRIAGE HOUSE INN
831/625-2585 **83**
♦♦♦♦ Bed & Breakfast. **Address:** Junipero Ave between 7th & 8th Ave 93921

COACHMAN'S INN
831/624-6421 **82**
♦♦♦ Hotel. **Address:** San Carlos St & 7th Ave 93921

COMFORT INN CARMEL BY THE SEA
831/622-7090 **78**

♦♦♦♦ Motel

Address: Torres St & Ocean Ave 93921 **Location:** Corner of Ocean Ave and Torres St. **Facility:** 19 units. 2 stories (no elevator), exterior corridors. **Parking:** on-site and street. **Amenities:** safes. **Featured Amenity: full hot breakfast.**

SAVE ⊞ 🛜 ✕ 🎦 🛏 🖾 🖵

CYPRESS INN
831/624-3871 **80**
♦♦♦ Classic Hotel. **Address:** Lincoln St & 7th Ave 93921

HOFSAS HOUSE
831/624-2745 **66**

♦♦♦ Hotel

Address: 2 NW of 4th Ave on San Carlos St 93921 **Location:** 3 blks n of Ocean Ave; between 3rd and 4th aves. **Facility:** 38 units, some kitchens. 4 stories (no elevator), exterior corridors. **Pool:** heated outdoor. **Activities:** sauna. **Featured Amenity: continental breakfast.**

SAVE ⛵ 🛜 ✕ 🎦 🖵 / SOME UNITS 🥗 🛏 🖾

HYATT CARMEL HIGHLANDS
831/620-1234 **85**

♦♦♦♦ Hotel

HYATT **AAA Benefit:** Members save up to 10%!

Address: 120 Highlands Dr 93923 **Location:** 4.5 mi s on SR 1. Located in Carmel Highlands. **Facility:** 48 units, some kitchens. 2-3 stories (no elevator), exterior corridors. **Parking:** on-site and valet. **Terms:** check-in 4 pm. **Amenities:** safes. **Dining:** California Market at Pacific's Edge, see separate listing. **Pool:** heated outdoor. **Activities:** hot tub, bicycles, picnic facilities, exercise room, massage. **Guest Services:** valet laundry.

SAVE 🔌 ⊞ 🎦 ☂ 🎦 CALL 🔌 ⛵ 🛜 BIZ HS 🛜 ✕ 🎭 🛏 🖵 / SOME UNITS 🖾

PINE INN
831/624-3851 **77**
♦♦♦ Historic Hotel. **Address:** Ocean Ave & Monte Verde St 93921

SVENDSGAARD'S INN
831/624-1511 **67**
♦♦♦ Hotel. **Address:** San Carlos St & 4th Ave 93921

TICKLE PINK INN
831/624-1244 **86**

♦♦♦♦ Hotel

Address: 155 Highland Dr 93923 **Location:** Oceanfront. 4 mi s on SR 1. Located in Carmel Highlands. **Facility:** Sweeping views of the Pacific coast are a highlight of this hillside inn, which offers beautifully appointed guest rooms, most with a balcony and some with a fireplace. 35 units, some cottages. 2-3 stories (no elevator), exterior corridors. **Amenities:** safes. **Activities:** hot tub. **Featured Amenity: breakfast buffet.** *(See ad p. 58.)*

SAVE ⊞ BIZ 🛜 ✕ 🛏 🖵 / SOME UNITS 🎦 🖾

WAYSIDE INN
831/624-5336 **81**
♦♦♦ Hotel. **Address:** Mission St & 7th Ave 93921

WHERE TO EAT

ANTON & MICHEL
831/624-2406 **47**
♦♦♦ Continental. Fine Dining. **Address:** Mission St at 7th Ave 93921

AUBERGINE AT L'AUBERGE
831/624-8578 **45**
♦♦♦♦ New European. Fine Dining. **Address:** Monte Verde St & 7th Ave 93921

BAJA CANTINA
831/625-2252
♦♦ Mexican. Casual Dining. **Address:** 7166 Carmel Valley Rd 93923

CALIFORNIA MARKET AT PACIFIC'S EDGE
831/622-5445 **52**
♦♦♦ Regional American. Fine Dining. **Address:** 120 Highlands Dr 93923

CASANOVA
831/625-0501 **40**
♦♦♦ French. Fine Dining. **Address:** 5th Ave between Mission St & San Carlos St 93922

CHINA DELIGHT
831/625-3367 **51**
♦♦ Chinese. Casual Dining. **Address:** 145 Crossroads Blvd 93923

CULTURA COMIDA Y BEBIDA
831/250-7005 **42**
♦♦♦ New Mexican. Casual Dining. **Address:** 100 Dolores St 93921

TICKLE PINK INN®
at Carmel Highlands

simple moments

MAKE SPECIAL MEMORIES

FEATURES & AMENITIES FOR OUR GUESTS

Spectacular ocean views from
private balconies

Bottle of champagne upon arrival

Evening wine & cheese reception

Deluxe continental breakfast &
fresh-baked pastries

Outdoor hot tub & in-room spas*

In-room wood-burning fireplaces*

Available in select rooms

(See map & index p. 144.)

FLYING FISH GRILL   831/625-1962   (46)
♥♥ Japanese Seafood. Casual Dining. **Address:** Carmel Plaza 93921

FROM SCRATCH RESTAURANT   831/625-2448   (49)
♥♥ American. Casual Dining. **Address:** 3626 The Barnyard 93923

HOG'S BREATH INN CARMEL   831/625-1044   (41)
♥♥ American. Casual Dining. **Address:** San Carlos St between 5th Ave & 6th Ave 93921

IL FORNAIO   831/622-5100   (44)
♥♥♥ Italian. Fine Dining. **Address:** Ocean Ave & Monte Verde St 93921

KATY'S PLACE   831/624-0199   (43)
♥♥ Breakfast. Casual Dining. **Address:** Mission St 93921

LUGANO SWISS BISTRO   831/626-3779   (48)
♥♥ Swiss. Casual Dining. **Address:** 3670 The Barnyard 93923

RIO GRILL   831/625-5436   (50)
♥♥♥ California. Fine Dining. **Address:** 101 Crossroads Blvd 93923

CARMEL VALLEY
- **Hotels & Restaurants map & index p. 144**
- **Part of Monterey Peninsula area — see map p. 141**

BERNARDUS LODGE & SPA   831/658-3400   (90)
♥♥♥♥♥
Boutique Resort Hotel
Address: 415 W Carmel Valley Rd 93924 **Location:** 9.5 mi e of SR 1; just e of Los Laureles Grade. **Facility:** Surrounded by stunning views of the vineyards and mountains, the hotel's gorgeous guest rooms include radiant heated floors in the bathrooms. Mercedes to rent-complimentary for four hours are offered. 73 units. 2 stories (no elevator), exterior corridors. **Parking:** on-site and valet. **Terms:** check-in 4 pm. **Amenities:** safes. **Pool:** heated outdoor. **Activities:** sauna, hot tub, steamroom, tennis, lawn sports, trails, exercise room, spa. **Guest Services:** valet laundry.

CARMEL VALLEY RANCH   831/625-9500   (89)
♥♥♥♥
Resort Hotel

Address: One Old Ranch Rd 93923 **Location:** 6.3 mi e of SR 1 via Carmel Valley Rd to Robinson Canyon Rd exit, follow signs. **Facility:** This beautiful property lis ocated on a hillside overlooking the Santa Lucia Mountains, golf course and vineyards. The large rooms evoke an elegant yet residential vibe. Some offer a private balcony. 181 units, some two bedrooms and efficiencies. 1 story, exterior corridors. **Terms:** check-in 4 pm. **Amenities:** safes. **Dining:** 3 restaurants. **Pool:** heated outdoor. **Activities:** hot tub, steamroom, cabanas, regulation golf, tennis, recreation programs, kids club, playground, lawn sports, trails, health club, spa. **Guest Services:** valet laundry. Affiliated with Joie de Vivre Hotels & Resorts.

CONTENTA INN   831/659-2298   (92)
♥♥ Motel. **Address:** 20 Via Contenta 93924

HIDDEN VALLEY INN   831/659-5361   (91)
♥♥ Motel. **Address:** 102 W Carmel Valley Rd 93924

HOLMAN RANCH TAVERN   831/659-2774   (55)
♥♥ Steak. Casual Dining. **Address:** 16 E Carmel Valley Rd 93924

CARNELIAN BAY pop. 524
- **Hotels & Restaurants map & index p. 114**
- **Part of Lake Tahoe Area — see map p. 111**

GAR WOODS GRILL & PIER   530/546-3366   (28)
♥♥♥
American Fine Dining $18-$48
AAA Inspector Notes: A varied menu featuring pasta, fresh seafood and steaks is presented with a lakefront view on Tahoe's north shore. Take a seat on the heated deck where favorites include burgers and fish tacos. Valet boat parking is available at the 130-foot pier. **Features:** full bar, patio dining, Sunday brunch, happy hour. **Reservations:** suggested. **Address:** 5000 N Lake Blvd 96140 **Location:** SR 28, 6 mi e of SR 89.   L D CALL ⟁ ⟍

CASTRO VALLEY pop. 61,388
- **Hotels & Restaurants map & index p. 176**

COMFORT INN CASTRO VALLEY   510/538-9501   (52)
♥♥ Hotel. **Address:** 2532 Castro Valley Blvd 94546

HOLIDAY INN EXPRESS CASTRO VALLEY   510/889-9300   (53)
♥♥ Hotel. **Address:** 2419 Castro Valley Blvd 94546

LUCCAS ITALIAN DELICATESSEN   510/537-2222   (52)
♥ Deli. Quick Serve. **Address:** 3121 Castro Valley Blvd 94546

TOFU HOUSE   510/247-8889   (51)
♥♥ Korean. Casual Dining. **Address:** 2788 Castro Valley Blvd 94546

CEDARVILLE pop. 514

SUNRISE MOTEL AND RV PARK   530/279-2161
♥
Motel

Address: 62271 Hwy 299 W 96104 **Location:** Jct US 395 and SR 299, 16.6 mi w. Located in a quiet area. **Facility:** 15 units, some houses. 1 story, exterior corridors. **Activities:** picnic facilities. **Guest Services:** coin laundry.

CHESTER (C-3) pop. 2,144, elev. 4,528'
- **Hotels p. 60 • Restaurants p. 60**

Nearby Lake Almanor was formed when a dam was built on the north fork of the Feather River in 1914. When full, the reservoir covers 52 square miles and is a popular recreation area, offering swimming, boating, water skiing, fishing, hiking and camping. Winter visitors come for cross-country skiing and snowmobiling. Resorts, vacation homes and campgrounds nestle among the pines along the lakeshore.

Lake Almanor Chamber of Commerce and Visitor's Bureau: 328 Main St., #6, P.O. Box 1198, Chester, CA 96020. **Phone:** (530) 258-2426.

BEST WESTERN ROSE QUARTZ INN
530/258-2002

Hotel

Best Western. AAA Benefit: Members save up to 15% and earn bonus points!

Address: 306 Main St 96020 **Location:** 0.3 mi w of center on SR 36. **Facility:** 65 units, some kitchens. 2 stories, interior/exterior corridors. **Activities:** hot tub, picnic facilities, exercise room. **Featured Amenity:** continental breakfast.

THE BIDWELL HOUSE
530/258-3338

Bed & Breakfast

Address: 1 Main St 96020 **Location:** 0.6 mi n of center on SR 36. **Facility:** This renovated, comfortable and charming 1901 farmhouse is nestled at the east edge of town near Lake Almanor. There is a fireplace in the living area and wood-burning fireplaces in three guest rooms. 14 units, some cottages. 2 stories (no elevator), interior/exterior corridors. **Bath:** some shared. **Activities:** lawn sports. **Featured Amenity:** full hot breakfast.

WHERE TO EAT

KOPPER KETTLE CAFE
530/258-2698
American. Casual Dining. **Address:** 243 Main St 96020

CHICO (D-3) pop. 86,187, elev. 200'

Bidwell Park, a 3,618-acre city park spanning an area from downtown to the foothills of the Sierra Nevada, offers hiking and bicycling trails, a pool, a playground and various sports facilities as well as Chico Creek Nature Center. The original acreage was a gift to the city in 1905 from Annie Bidwell, wife of Chico's founder.

Chico Chamber of Commerce & Visitor Bureau: 441 Main St., Suite 150, Chico, CA 95928. **Phone:** (530) 891-5556 or (800) 852-8570.

BIDWELL MANSION STATE HISTORIC PARK, 525 The Esplanade, preserves a three-story, 26-room Victorian residence built 1865-68 for city founder Gen. John Bidwell and his wife Annie. Guests entertained at the brick mansion covered in pink stucco included such well-known figures as Susan B. Anthony, President Rutherford B. Hayes, John Muir and Gen. William Tecumseh Sherman.

Time: Allow 1 hour minimum. **Hours:** Guided tours are given on the hour Sat.-Mon. 11-4. Closed Jan. 1 and Christmas. Phone ahead to confirm schedule. **Cost:** $6; $3 (ages 5-17). **Phone:** (530) 895-6144.

SIERRA NEVADA BREWING CO. is w. of SR 99 at 1075 E. 20th St. Ninety-minute guided tours of the brewery explain how the company's ales and lagers are produced, from their beginnings in the brewhouse, through the fermentation process to the keg or bottle. Public tours include a 30-minute educational tasting. **Hours:** Self-guiding tours Sun.-Thurs. 10-6, Fri.-Sat. 10-7. Guided tours are offered Mon.-Thurs. on the hour 11-4; Fri.-Sat. at 11 and noon, then every half-hour 12:30-5; Sun. at 11 and noon and then every half-hour 12:30-4. Other tours are offered; phone for schedule. **Cost:** Free. **Phone:** (530) 893-3520.

BEST WESTERN HERITAGE INN - CHICO
530/894-8600

Hotel

Best Western. AAA Benefit: Members save up to 15% and earn bonus points!

Address: 25 Heritage Ln 95926 **Location:** SR 99 exit 387A (Mangrove Ave/Cohasset Rd), just n. **Facility:** 97 units. 3 stories, interior corridors. **Pool:** outdoor. **Activities:** hot tub, exercise room. **Guest Services:** valet laundry.

COURTYARD BY MARRIOTT CHICO
530/894-6699
Hotel. **Address:** 2481 Carmichael Dr 95928

AAA Benefit: Members save 5% or more!

HOTEL DIAMOND
530/893-3100

Boutique Hotel

Address: 220 W 4th St 95928 **Location:** SR 99 exit 385 (SR 32), 1.2 mi sw to Salem St, just nw to 4th St, then just ne; jct Broadway St; downtown. **Facility:** A boutique-style hotel, this renovated 1904 building is adorned with antiques, original hardwood plank flooring and upscale touches. A few guest rooms include a balcony and fireplace. 43 units. 4 stories, interior corridors. **Amenities:** safes. **Activities:** massage. **Guest Services:** valet laundry. **Featured Amenity:** full hot breakfast.

OXFORD SUITES CHICO
530/899-9090

Hotel

Address: 2035 Business Ln 95928 **Location:** SR 99 exit 384 (E 20th St), just e, then just s. **Facility:** 184 units, some two bedrooms, efficiencies and kitchens. 4 stories, interior corridors. **Terms:** check-in 4 pm. **Pool:** heated outdoor. **Activities:** sauna, hot tub, steamroom, exercise room. **Guest Services:** valet and coin laundry, area transportation. **Featured Amenity:** breakfast buffet.

SUPER 8 530/345-2533

Hotel

Address: 655 Manzanita Ct 95926 **Location:** SR 99 exit 387A (Mangrove Ave/Cohasset Rd), just s, then just e. **Facility:** 51 units. 3 stories (no elevator), interior corridors. **Pool:** outdoor. **Guest Services:** coin laundry. **Featured Amenity: continental breakfast.**

SAVE ⏱ CALL ⬤ 🚗 BIZ 🛜 ⬛ 🖥 💻 / SOME UNITS 🐾

WHERE TO EAT

5TH STREET STEAKHOUSE 530/891-6328
Steak. Fine Dining. **Address:** 345 W 5th St 95926

CASA RAMOS 530/894-0119
Mexican. Casual Dining. **Address:** 216 East Ave 95926

CHRISTIAN MICHAELS RISTORANTE 530/894-4005
California. Fine Dining. **Address:** 192 E 3rd St 95928

HAPPY GARDEN RESTAURANT 530/893-2574
Chinese. Casual Dining. **Address:** 180 Cohasset Rd 95926

NASH'S RESTAURANT 530/896-1147
Regional California. Casual Dining. **Address:** 1717 Esplanade 95926

THE RAWBAR RESTAURANT & SUSHI 530/897-0626
Asian Sushi. Casual Dining. **Address:** 346 Broadway St 95928

RED TAVERN 530/894-3463
Mediterranean. Casual Dining. **Address:** 1250 Esplanade 95926

SICILIAN CAFE 530/345-2233
Southern Italian. Casual Dining. **Address:** 1020 Main St 95928

SIERRA NEVADA TAP ROOM & RESTAURANT 530/345-2739
American. Casual Dining. **Address:** 1075 E 20th St 95928

TIN ROOF BAKERY & CAFE 530/892-2893
Breads/Pastries. Quick Serve. **Address:** 627 Broadway St, Suite 170 95928

TRES HOMBRES LONG BAR & GRILL 530/342-0425
Mexican. Casual Dining. **Address:** 100 Broadway St 95928

CHOWCHILLA pop. 18,720, elev. 239'

DAYS INN GATEWAY TO YOSEMITE 559/665-4821
Motel. **Address:** 220 E Robertson Blvd 93610

HOLIDAY INN EXPRESS & SUITES GATEWAY TO YOSEMITE
559/665-3300
Hotel. **Address:** 309 Prosperity Blvd 93610

CLEARLAKE pop. 15,250
• Part of Wine Country area — see map p. 405

BEST WESTERN EL GRANDE INN 707/994-2000

Hotel

BW Best Western.

AAA Benefit: Members save up to 15% and earn bonus points!

Address: 15135 Lakeshore Dr 95422 **Location:** SR 53 exit Lakeshore Dr, just w. **Facility:** 68 units. 4 stories, interior corridors. **Pool:** heated indoor. **Activities:** hot tub, exercise room.

SAVE ⏱ 🍸 CALL ⬤ 🚗 👪 BIZ 🛜 ⬛ 🖥 💻 / SOME UNITS HS

WHERE TO EAT

CACTUS GRILL 707/994-0905
Mexican. Casual Dining. **Address:** 3900 Baylis Ave 95422

MAIN STREET BAR & GRILL 707/994-6450
American. Casual Dining. **Address:** 14084 Lakeshore Dr 95422

CLEARLAKE OAKS pop. 2,359
• Part of Wine Country area — see map p. 405

LAKE POINT LODGE 707/998-4350

Motel

Address: 13470 E Hwy 20 95423 **Location:** Jct SR 20 and 53, 2.7 mi w. **Facility:** 40 units. 2 stories (no elevator), exterior corridors. **Pool:** outdoor. **Guest Services:** coin laundry. **Featured Amenity: continental breakfast.**

SAVE ⏱ 🚗 🛜 ⬛ 🖥 💻 / SOME UNITS 🐾

WHERE TO EAT

HAPPY GARDEN RESTAURANT & BAR 707/998-0398
Chinese. Casual Dining. **Address:** 13440 E Hwy 20 95423

CLOVERDALE (E-2) pop. 8,618, elev. 335'
• Hotels p. 62 • Restaurants p. 62
• Part of Wine Country area — see map p. 405

CLOVERDALE HISTORY CENTER AND HISTORIC GOULD-SHAW HOUSE are at 215 N. Cloverdale Blvd. The 1864 Gothic Revival Gould-Shaw House features Victorian and Craftsman furnishings, period clothing and linens, other items from the late 19th and early 20th centuries, and a Victorian cottage garden. The History Center contains permanent and rotating exhibits, including a "mud wagon" that once carried passengers from Cloverdale to the Geysers Resort.

A research center has photographs, newspaper articles and other historical data about Cloverdale and the surrounding area. **Time:** Allow 1 hour minimum. **Hours:** Wed.-Thurs. 11-3, Fri. 1-3, Sat. 10-2, Sun. noon-4; also by appointment. Phone ahead to confirm schedule. **Cost:** Donations. **Phone:** (707) 894-2067.

CLOVERDALE WINE COUNTRY INN & SUITES 707/894-7500
 Hotel. **Address:** 324 S Cloverdale Blvd 95425

OLD CROCKER INN 707/894-4000
Historic Bed & Breakfast. **Address:** 1126 Old Crocker Inn Rd 95425

SUPER 8 CLOVERDALE 707/894-9288

Hotel

Address: 1147 S Cloverdale Blvd 95425 **Location:** US 101 exit S Cloverdale Blvd, just w at top of off ramp, just n on S Cloverdale Blvd, then just w on Treadway Dr; in shopping center. **Facility:** 43 units. 2 stories (no elevator), interior corridors. **Pool:** outdoor. **Activities:** hot tub, exercise room. **Guest Services:** coin laundry. **Featured Amenity:** continental breakfast.

WHERE TO EAT

101 THAI WAY 707/894-9999
Thai. Casual Dining. **Address:** 1198 S Cloverdale Blvd, Suite C 95425

RAILROAD STATION BAR AND GRILL 707/894-4779
American. Casual Dining. **Address:** 236 S Cloverdale Blvd 95425

RUTH MCGOWAN'S BREWPUB 707/894-9610
American. Casual Dining. **Address:** 131 E 1st St 95425

CLOVIS (G-4) pop. 95,631, elev. 361'
• **Hotels & Restaurants map & index p. 89**

The town of Clovis was named after Clovis Cole, the area's largest grain grower, who donated land for a rail station in the late 19th century. The city was incorporated in 1912. Lumbering was the initial economic mainstay, though fruit farming also became important. Many buildings date to the early 1900s, and today the Old Town section of Clovis is a reflection of the city as it was at the turn of the 20th century.

Clovis Tourist Information & Visitors Center: 399 Clovis Ave., Clovis, CA 93612. **Phone:** (559) 324-2084 or (877) 725-6847.

Self-guiding tours: Brochures featuring information about Clovis' antique district and describing walking tours of the historic district are available at the visitors center.

Shopping: A cluster of antique shops and malls can be found in Old Town, along Pollasky Avenue between Fifth and Fourth streets. Sierra Vista Mall at Clovis and Shaw avenues has more than 70 stores and restaurants, including anchors Sears and Target.

WILD WATER ADVENTURE PARK, 11413 E. Shaw Ave., is a 52-acre water park offering 38 water slides; a Blue Wave pool that holds almost 1 million gallons of water; Orca Lagoon; a large swimming pool; three fishing lakes; and toddler-friendly play at Adventure Bay and Buccaneer Landing.

Glass items and alcohol are not permitted. **Hours:** Open Memorial Day weekend-Labor Day. Hours vary throughout the season; phone ahead for hours of operation on specific days. **Cost:** Admission Sat. $36.99; $28.99 (age 4 to 48 inches tall); $17.99 (ages 62+). Admission Sun.-Fri. $33.99; $25.99 (age 4 to 48 inches tall); $17.99 (ages 62+). Discounted rates are available after 4 p.m. Single tube rental $8; double tube $10. Life jackets free. A refundable deposit is required for tube and life jacket rentals. **Parking:** $5-$20. **Phone:** (559) 299-9453.

BEST WESTERN CLOVIS COLE 559/299-1547 **23**

Hotel

 Best Western. **AAA Benefit:** Members save up to 15% and earn bonus points!

Address: 415 Clovis Ave 93612 **Location:** SR 168 exit Herndon Ave E, 1 mi s. **Facility:** 58 units. 3 stories, interior corridors. **Pool:** outdoor. **Activities:** hot tub, exercise room. **Guest Services:** coin laundry. **Featured Amenity:** full hot breakfast.

COMFORT SUITES 559/299-9992 **22**

Hotel

Address: 143 Clovis Ave 93612 **Location:** SR 168 exit Herndon Ave E, 0.6 mi s. **Facility:** 54 units. 4 stories, interior corridors. **Pool:** heated outdoor. **Activities:** trails, exercise room. **Guest Services:** valet and coin laundry. **Featured Amenity:** continental breakfast.

FAIRFIELD INN & SUITES BY MARRIOTT-FRESNO/CLOVIS 559/323-8080 **21**

Hotel

Fairfield. **AAA Benefit:** Members save 5% or more!

Address: 50 N Clovis Ave 93612 **Location:** SR 168 exit Herndon Ave E, just s. **Facility:** 85 units. 3 stories, interior corridors. **Pool:** heated outdoor. **Activities:** hot tub, exercise room. **Guest Services:** valet and coin laundry. **Featured Amenity:** breakfast buffet.

HAMPTON INN & SUITES CLOVIS-AIRPORT NORTH 559/348-0000 **28**

 Hotel. **Address:** 855 Gettysburg Ave 93612

AAA Benefit: Members save up to 15%!

(See map & index p. 89.)

HILTON GARDEN INN CLOVIS   559/299-2203   **26**
WWW SAVE Hotel. **Address:** 520 W Shaw Ave 93612

AAA Benefit: Members save up to 15%!

HOLIDAY INN EXPRESS HOTEL & SUITES   559/297-0555   **25**
WWW Hotel. **Address:** 650 W Shaw Ave 93612

HOMEWOOD SUITES BY HILTON FRESNO AIRPORT/CLOVIS, CA   559/292-4004   **27**
WWW SAVE Extended Stay Hotel. **Address:** 835 Gettysburg Ave 93612

AAA Benefit: Members save up to 15%!

LA QUINTA INN & SUITES BY WYNDHAM CLOVIS OLD TOWN   559/291-9000   **24**
WWW Hotel. **Address:** 1508 Clovis Ave 93612

WHERE TO EAT

ANDIAMO RISTORANTE ITALIANO   559/298-3196   **24**
WW Italian. Casual Dining. **Address:** 1275 Shaw Ave, Suite 120 93612

HOUSE OF JUJU   559/298-3090   **22**
WW Burgers. Casual Dining. **Address:** 565 Pollasky Ave 93612

LUNA PIZZERIA AND ITALIAN RESTAURANT   559/299-4141   **21**
WW Italian. Casual Dining. **Address:** 349 Pollasky Ave 93612

THE MAD DUCK NEIGHBORHOOD GRILL & TAPHOUSE   559/298-3825   **20**
WW American. Casual Dining. **Address:** 765 W Herndon Ave 93612

PHO 2006   559/322-8922   **23**
WW Vietnamese. Casual Dining. **Address:** 1468 Clovis Ave 93612

COALINGA (H-4) pop. 13,380, elev. 671'

Coalinga began as a loading point for coal shipments transported by the Southern Pacific Railroad Co. Eventually "Coaling Station A" became a permanent oil-boomer settlement and the name was abbreviated.

Coalinga Area Chamber of Commerce: 265 W. Elm Ave., Coalinga, CA 93210. **Phone:** (559) 935-2948.

BEST WESTERN BIG COUNTRY INN   559/935-0866

Motel

 Best Western **AAA Benefit:** Members save up to 15% and earn bonus points!

Address: 25020 W Dorris Ave 93210 **Location:** I-5 exit 334, just nw. **Facility:** 48 units. 1 story, exterior corridors. **Amenities:** safes. **Pool:** outdoor. **Guest Services:** coin laundry. **Featured Amenity:** breakfast buffet.

BEST WESTERN PLUS COALINGA INN   559/934-0101

WWWW
Hotel

 Best Western PLUS **AAA Benefit:** Members save up to 15% and earn bonus points!

Address: 1786 Jayne Ave 93210 **Location:** I-5 exit 325 (Jayne Ave), 9.5 mi w. **Facility:** 70 units. 3 stories, interior corridors. **Pool:** outdoor. **Activities:** exercise room. **Guest Services:** coin laundry.

THE INN AT HARRIS RANCH   559/935-0717

WWW
Hotel

Address: 24505 W Dorris Ave 93210 **Location:** I-5 exit 334, just e. **Facility:** 153 units. 2-3 stories, interior/exterior corridors. **Dining:** Harris Ranch Steak House, Ranch Kitchen, see separate listings. **Pool:** heated outdoor. **Activities:** hot tub, exercise room. **Guest Services:** coin laundry.

WHERE TO EAT

HARRIS RANCH STEAK HOUSE   559/935-0717
WWW Steak. Fine Dining. **Address:** 24505 W Dorris Ave 93210

RANCH KITCHEN   559/935-0717
WW American. Casual Dining. **Address:** 24505 W Dorris Ave 93210

COARSEGOLD pop. 1,840
• **Part of Yosemite National Park area — see map p. 420**

CHUKCHANSI GOLD RESORT & CASINO   559/692-5200

WWW
Hotel

Address: 711 Lucky Ln 93614 **Location:** 5 mi s on SR 41, just e. **Facility:** No matter what your interests, you'll find plenty to do at this hotel. Start the day with a morning swim in the indoor/outdoor pool or a treatment at the luxurious spa. 402 units. 5-11 stories, interior corridors. **Parking:** on-site and valet. **Amenities:** safes. **Dining:** 2 restaurants. **Pool:** heated outdoor, heated indoor. **Activities:** hot tub, game room, exercise room, spa. **Guest Services:** valet laundry.

COLOMA (E-3) pop. 529, elev. 750'

In January 1848, near Capt. John Sutter's sawmill on the American River, James Marshall discovered the first yellow flecks of metal that launched the great California gold rush. By the summer more than 2,000 miners were sifting for gold along the river near Sutter's mill, and Coloma, the first of the gold rush towns, was born. Finds grew scarce within a few years, and the once thriving city of 10,000 dwindled to the quiet village it is today.

INSIDER INFO:
The Mother Lode

Mexican miners called it "La Veta Madre"—the Mother Lode—a rich vein of gold lacing the western slopes of the Sierra Nevada for 120 miles. The name eventually came to denote the entire band of territory extending roughly from Mariposa to Sierra City, where the gleaming metal was mined during the frenetic years of the California gold rush.

The discovery of gold near Coloma in 1848 lured thousands of prospectors to the Mother Lode. Tales of nuggets littering the hillsides were not entirely unfounded during the early years of the gold rush, and the possibility of unearthing a mammoth find, like the 195-pound nugget found near Carson Hill, stoked the get-rich-quick dreams of many a '49er.

Nearly 550 mining towns proliferated in the Mother Lode; fewer than half remain today. Like the fortunes of many of the miners, the towns rose and fell precipitately and often were simply abandoned when the miners moved on to more profitable stakes. A few, such as Sonora, Placerville, Auburn and Grass Valley, weathered the diminishing reserves to become prosperous small cities. Others survive as little more than intriguing names on a map.

Aptly numbered SR 49 traverses the length of the Mother Lode country. The facades of the surviving buildings, the historical parks along the route and the ghost towns and empty mines scattered throughout the hills still retain a sense of the atmosphere from this colorful period.

MARSHALL GOLD DISCOVERY STATE HISTORIC PARK is on SR 49. The 274-acre park preserves the site where James W. Marshall's discovery of gold began the California gold rush. In partnership with John Sutter to construct a sawmill, Marshall chose a site adjacent to the American River and a stand of pine trees. It was there, on Jan. 24, 1848, that Marshall noticed the glint of gold in the tailrace of the sawmill.

A statue of Marshall, marking his grave site, points toward the site of his discovery, a half-mile away. The gold rush era and its historical impact are depicted through museum exhibits, mining memorabilia and interpretive programs. Staff provide daily history talks at a replica of Sutter's mill, which stands near the river not far from the site of the original structure. Also part of the park is the 1860 cabin in which Marshall lived. *See Recreation Areas Chart.*

Panning for gold is allowed in designated areas, using hands and pans only, and fishing is permitted in season. **Time:** Allow 1 hour minimum. **Hours:** Park open daily 8-8, Memorial Day weekend-Labor Day; 8-6, Mar. 1-Fri. before Memorial Day weekend and day after Labor Day-Oct. 31; 8-5, rest of year. Museum open daily 10-5, Mar.-Oct.; 10-4, rest of year. Closed Jan. 1, Thanksgiving and Christmas. **Cost:** Day use $8 per private vehicle; $7 (ages 62+ per private vehicle). Museum included in day use fee. Gold panning $7. **Phone:** (530) 622-3470.

COLUMBIA (F-4) pop. 2,297, elev. 2,143'

In the foothills of the Sierra Nevada, Columbia was one of the largest and most important mining towns along the Mother Lode. Between 1850 and 1870 local placer mines yielded $87 million in gold.

Columbia Chamber of Commerce: P.O. Box 1824, Columbia, CA 95310. **Phone:** (209) 536-1672.

COLUMBIA STATE HISTORIC PARK, covering 12 square blocks in the old business district, depicts a typical boomtown of the 1850s. Never completely deserted, the settlement has been partially restored to its appearance in gold rush days. Among the more than 30 restored buildings in the town are a schoolhouse, bank, newspaper building, barbershop, saloons, the Wells Fargo Express Co. building, shops, the Fallon Hotel and the City Hotel, which still houses guests.

A 22-minute DVD presentation weaves information about the original town settlement with how important a permanent source of water was to gold rush towns. The Columbia Diggins 1852, a 4-day living-history re-enactment, is held in late May, and plays are presented year-round in the restored Fallon House Theater. Townsite tours, stagecoach rides and gold panning also are available.

Hours: Park, museum and most stores open daily 10-4; phone to confirm winter hours. DVD presentation daily on the half-hour. Townsite tours daily at 11, mid-June through Labor Day; Sat.-Sun. at 11, rest of year. Plays are presented Wed.-Thurs. at 2, Fri.-Sat. at 7 p.m. (also some Sat. and Sun. at 2 if the production is a musical), except during breaks between one closing and another opening. Stagecoach rides Mon.-Thurs. 10-4, Fri.-Sun. 10-5, Memorial Day-Labor Day; Fri.-Sun. 11-4, Mar. 1-day before Memorial Day and day after Labor Day-Oct. 31; Sat.-Sun. 11-4, rest of year (weather permitting). Phone ahead to confirm stagecoach schedule.

Cost: Park free. Plays $32-$47. Stagecoach fare (inside) $7; $6 (ages 4-12 and 60+). Fare $10 to ride on top (minimum age 8). Gold panning $5-$12. **Phone:** (209) 588-9128 for park information, (209) 532-3120 for play information, (209) 532-3184 for the museum, (209) 532-9693 for gold panning information, or (209) 984-3125 for the stagecoach.

COLUSA (D-2) pop. 5,971, elev. 61'

West of Colusa, more than 4,500 acres of seasonal marsh, permanent ponds, watergrass habitats and uplands shelter large flocks of ducks and geese during fall and winter; the best viewing opportunities are in November and again in mid-January. A 3-mile, self-guiding driving tour route and 1-mile walking trail lead through part of the Colusa National Wildlife Refuge; phone (530) 934-2801 for additional information.

RIVER VALLEY LODGE   530/458-8844

Resort Hotel

Address: 3770 Hwy 45 95932 **Location:** I-5 exit 586 (Maxwell Rd), 8.0 mi e, then 1.7 mi s on SR 45. **Facility:** With modern décor and attractive furnishings in a Native American theme, the hotel features an abundance of wood accents giving the property a rustic feel. Some rooms include fireplaces. 55 units. 3 stories, interior corridors. **Parking:** on-site and valet. **Terms:** check-in 4 pm. **Amenities:** safes. **Dining:** 2 restaurants. **Pool:** heated outdoor. **Activities:** sauna, health club.

CONCORD (C-9) pop. 122,067, elev. 80'

Guided tours take visitors onto an active military base to see the Port Chicago Naval Magazine National Memorial, erected to honor the 320 military personnel and civilians (more than 200 of whom were African-Americans) killed on July 17, 1944, in the largest homeland disaster during World War II. The incident, which occurred when a full munitions ship exploded during loading operations, was one of the catalysts that spurred the U.S. military to look into racial justice and equality after World War II. Reservations are required 2 weeks in advance; phone (925) 228-8860 for information.

SIX FLAGS HURRICANE HARBOR is .3 mi. e. off I-680 Willow Pass Rd. exit, then n. on Waterworld Pkwy. The water park offers body slides, a lazy river, a wave pool, raft rides, thrill attractions and children's play areas in a lush tropical setting.

Hours: Daily 10:30-6, mid-June to mid Aug.; hours vary Sat.-Sun., mid-May to mid-June and mid-Aug. to late Sept. **Cost:** $38.99; $28.99 (under 48 inches tall and ages 60+); free (ages 0-2). **Parking:** $15. **Phone:** (925) 609-1364.

BEST WESTERN HERITAGE INN   925/686-4466

Hotel

 Best Western.

AAA Benefit: Members save up to 15% and earn bonus points!

Address: 4600 Clayton Rd 94521 **Location:** I-680 exit 48 (Treat Blvd/Geary Rd), 4.8 mi ne, then 0.4 mi e. **Facility:** 128 units, some efficiencies. 2 stories (no elevator), exterior corridors. **Pool:** outdoor. **Activities:** exercise room.

HILTON CONCORD   925/827-2000

Hotel

Hilton HOTELS & RESORTS

AAA Benefit: Members save up to 15%!

Address: 1970 Diamond Blvd 94520 **Location:** I-680 exit 51 (Willow Pass Rd), just e, then just nw. **Facility:** 329 units. 11 stories, interior corridors. **Parking:** on-site (fee) and valet. **Amenities:** safes. **Dining:** Plate & Vine, see separate listing. **Pool:** heated outdoor. **Activities:** hot tub, exercise room. **Guest Services:** valet laundry, area transportation.

WHERE TO EAT

BUTTERCUP DINER & BAR   925/521-9224
Comfort Food. Casual Dining. **Address:** 4301 Clayton Rd 94521

LAZY DOG RESTAURANT & BAR   925/849-1221
American. Casual Dining. **Address:** 1961 Diamond Blvd 94520

MIKUNI 925/265-7660
 Japanese Sushi. Casual Dining. **Address:** 2075 Diamond Blvd 94520

PLATE & VINE 925/827-2000
 California. Casual Dining. **Address:** 1970 Diamond Blvd 94520

CORNING (C-2) pop. 7,663, elev. 279'

Spanish missionaries introduced olive trees to California in the late 18th century, and they were planted in the Corning area beginning in the 1890s. By the 1920s there were seven olive canneries in town, and this self-proclaimed "Olive City" located at the northern end of the Sacramento Valley still packages a significant percentage of the nation's olive crop.

Corning Chamber of Commerce: 1110 Solano St., Corning, CA 96021. **Phone:** (530) 824-5550.

BEST WESTERN PLUS CORNING INN 530/824-5200

Hotel

Best Western PLUS
AAA Benefit: Members save up to 15% and earn bonus points!

Address: 910 Hwy 99 W 96021 **Location:** I-5 exit 631 (Central Corning), just se. **Facility:** 58 units. 2 stories, interior corridors. **Pool:** heated indoor. **Activities:** hot tub, exercise room. **Guest Services:** coin laundry. **Featured Amenity: full hot breakfast.**

ECONOMY INN 530/824-4322
 Motel. **Address:** 945 S Hwy 99 W 96021

THE LODGE 530/824-3220
Hotel. **Address:** 2665 Everett Freeman Way 96021

▼ See AAA listing p. 67 ▼

WHERE TO EAT

CASA RAMOS 530/824-3123
Mexican. Casual Dining. **Address:** 636 Edith Ave 96021

OLIVE PIT CAFE 530/824-4667
American. Quick Serve. **Address:** 2156 Solano St 96021

TIMBERS STEAKHOUSE 530/528-3500
Steak. Casual Dining. **Address:** 2655 Everett Freeman Way 96021

CORTE MADERA pop. 9,253
• Part of San Francisco area — see map p. 243

BEST WESTERN CORTE MADERA INN 415/924-1502

Hotel

BW Best Western
AAA Benefit: Members save up to 15% and earn bonus points!

Address: 56 Madera Blvd 94925 **Location:** US 101 exit Madera Blvd southbound, just w; exit Tamalpais Rd/Paradise Dr northbound, just w, then 0.3 mi n. **Facility:** 110 units. 2 stories (no elevator), exterior corridors. **Terms:** check-in 4 pm. **Pool:** indoor. **Activities:** hot tub, picnic facilities, trails, exercise room, massage. **Guest Services:** valet and coin laundry, area transportation.

Booth or table?

AAA.com/travelguides/restaurants

MARIN SUITES HOTEL
415/924-3608

Hotel

Address: 45 Tamal Vista Blvd 94925 **Location:** US 101 exit Lucky Dr southbound, just w on Fifer Ave, then 0.4 mi s; exit Tamalpais Rd/Paradise Dr northbound, 0.5 mi n on Madera Blvd (which becomes Tamal Vista Blvd). **Facility:** 101 units, some two bedrooms and kitchens. 3 stories, exterior corridors. **Terms:** check-in 4 pm. **Amenities:** safes. **Pool:** heated outdoor. **Activities:** sauna, hot tub, picnic facilities, exercise room. **Guest Services:** coin laundry. *(See ad p. 66.)*

CRESCENT CITY (A-1) pop. 7,643, elev. 44'

Founded in 1853 as a gold-mining supply center, Crescent City edges a harbor defined by a crescent-shaped beach. Point St. George, just above the harbor, protects the city from strong north winds; it was on Point St. George Reef that the side-wheeler *Brother Jonathan* wrecked on July 30, 1865. Brother Jonathan Cemetery, 9th Street and Pebble Beach Drive, contains the graves of many victims.

Lake Earl Wildlife Area, 5 miles north at the junction of Northcrest Drive and Old Mill Road, is a 6,100-acre wildlife habitat offering wildlife observation, boating, hiking, waterfowl hunting and fishing.

Crescent City is at the southern end of a scenic 42-mile stretch of US 199 that heads northeast through Smith River National Recreation Area to the Oregon border. It's also convenient to Jedediah Smith Redwoods and Del Norte Coast Redwoods state parks, both part of Redwood National and State Parks *(see place listing p. 210).* A visitor center inside the Redwood National and State Parks Headquarters, near the downtown waterfront at 1111 2nd St., has maps and brochures describing both parks; phone (707) 464-6101.

Crescent City-Del Norte County Chamber of Commerce: 1001 Front St., Crescent City, CA 95531. **Phone:** (707) 464-3174 or (800) 343-8300.

DEL NORTE COUNTY HISTORICAL SOCIETY MUSEUM, 577 H St. at jct. 6th St., is in the building built in 1926 and used until 1963 as the County Hall of Records and the county jail. It features a fine collection of Tolowa and Yurok baskets, musical instruments, logging and mining tools and equipment as well as vintage clothing and furniture. The second floor has some of the jail's original cells, which now house exhibits.

An annex contains the first order Fresnel lens from the St. George Reef Lighthouse and artifacts from an 1856 shipwreck and the 1964 tsunami that destroyed much of the city. **Time:** Allow 1 hour minimum. **Hours:** Mon.-Sat. 10-4, May-Sept.; Mon. and Sat. 10-4, rest of year. Phone ahead to confirm schedule. **Cost:** $3; $1 (ages 5-17). **Phone:** (707) 464-3922.

BEST WESTERN PLUS NORTHWOODS INN
707/464-9771

Hotel

Best Western PLUS **AAA Benefit:** Members save up to 15% and earn bonus points!

Address: 655 US Hwy 101 S 95531 **Location:** On US 101. Opposite harbor. **Facility:** 100 units. 2-3 stories (no elevator), interior/exterior corridors. **Amenities:** safes. **Dining:** Oceans 675 by Northwoods, see separate listing. **Pool:** heated indoor. **Activities:** sauna, hot tub, exercise room. **Guest Services:** coin laundry. **Featured Amenity:** breakfast buffet.

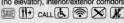

CURLY REDWOOD LODGE
707/464-2137

Vintage Motel

Address: 701 US Hwy 101 S/Redwood Hwy 95531 **Location:** On US 101. Opposite harbor. **Facility:** It is said the wood used to build this lodge came entirely from one curly redwood tree. This blast-from-the-past vintage 1957 lodging is located opposite the harbor, offering fresh air off the ocean. 36 units. 2 stories (no elevator), interior/exterior corridors.

LIGHTHOUSE INN
707/464-3993

Hotel. **Address:** 681 Hwy 101 S 95531

QUALITY INN & SUITES
707/464-3885

Hotel

Address: 100 Walton St 95531 **Location:** Just w of US 101. **Facility:** 46 units, some kitchens. 2 stories (no elevator), exterior corridors. **Activities:** exercise room. **Guest Services:** coin laundry. **Featured Amenity:** breakfast buffet.

WESTWARD INN
707/464-6106

Motel. **Address:** 725 Hwy 101 N 95531

CHART ROOM RESTAURANT
707/464-5993

Seafood. Casual Dining. **Address:** 130 Anchor Way 95531

CRISTINA'S MEXICAN RESTAURANT
707/464-9213

Mexican. Casual Dining. **Address:** 237 Price Mall 95531

THE GOOD HARVEST CAFE
707/465-6028

American. Casual Dining. **Address:** 575 Hwy 101 S 95531

MARLO'S GREEK AND ITALIAN RESTAURANT   707/465-8388

Greek. Casual Dining. **Address:** 632 M St 95531

OCEANS 675 BY NORTHWOODS
707/465-5656

American. Casual Dining. **Address:** 675 US Hwy 101 S 95531

PERLITA'S AUTHENTIC MEXICAN
707/465-6770

Mexican. Casual Dining. **Address:** 297 US 101 95531

VITA CUCINA BAKERY AND GOURMET FOODS   707/464-1076

◆ American. Quick Serve. **Address:** 1270 Front St 95531

WING WAH RESTAURANT   707/465-3935

◆◆ Chinese. Casual Dining. **Address:** 383 M St 95531

CUPERTINO   pop. 58,302
• Hotels & Restaurants map & index p. 348

ALOFT CUPERTINO   408/766-7000   **79**

◆◆◆ SAVE Hotel. **Address:** 10165 N De Anza Blvd 95014

AAA Benefit: Members save 5% or more!

COURTYARD BY MARRIOTT SAN JOSE CUPERTINO
408/252-9100   **78**

◆◆◆ SAVE Hotel. **Address:** 10605 N Wolfe Rd 95014

AAA Benefit: Members save 5% or more!

CUPERTINO HOTEL   408/996-7700   **76**

Hotel

Address: 10889 N De Anza Blvd 95014 **Location:** I-280 exit Sunnyvale-Saratoga Rd, just n. **Facility:** 128 units. 4 stories, interior/exterior corridors. **Terms:** check-in 4 pm. **Pool:** heated outdoor. **Activities:** hot tub. **Guest Services:** valet laundry. **Featured Amenity:** breakfast buffet.

HILTON GARDEN INN CUPERTINO   408/777-8787   **77**

Hotel

AAA Benefit: Members save up to 15%!

Address: 10741 N Wolfe Rd 95014 **Location:** I-280 exit Wolfe Rd N, w on Pruneridge Rd. **Facility:** 164 units. 5 stories, interior corridors. **Amenities:** Some: safes. **Pool:** heated outdoor. **Activities:** hot tub, exercise room. **Guest Services:** valet and coin laundry, area transportation. **Featured Amenity:** full hot breakfast.

HYATT HOUSE SAN JOSE CUPERTINO
669/220-3800   **80**

◆◆◆
Extended Stay
Hotel

 AAA Benefit: Members save up to 10%!

Address: 10380 Perimeter Rd 95014 **Location:** I-280 exit Wolf Rd S, just w, then just s. **Facility:** 148 units, some efficiencies and kitchens. 5 stories, interior corridors. **Amenities:** safes. **Pool:** heated outdoor. **Activities:** exercise room. **Guest Services:** valet and coin laundry.

/ SOME UNITS

JUNIPER HOTEL CUPERTINO, CURIO COLLECTION BY HILTON   408/253-8900   **81**

◆◆◆◆
Hotel

 CURIO A COLLECTION BY HILTON

AAA Benefit: Members save up to 15%!

Address: 10050 S De Anza Blvd 95014 **Location:** I-280 exit De Anza Blvd, 0.7 mi s. **Facility:** This beautifully appointed hotel is conveniently located in the heart of the Silicon Valley. Each guest room is elegantly appointed with premium mattresses and bed linens and offer a 55-inch TV. 224 units. 9 stories, interior corridors. **Parking:** on-site and valet. **Amenities:** safes. **Dining:** Parkview, see separate listing. **Activities:** bicycles, exercise room, massage. **Guest Services:** valet laundry, area transportation.

RESIDENCE INN BY MARRIOTT SAN JOSE CUPERTINO
408/777-0188   **82**

◆◆◆ SAVE Extended Stay Hotel. **Address:** 19429 Stevens Creek Blvd 95014

AAA Benefit: Members save 5% or more!

WHERE TO EAT

ALEXANDER'S STEAKHOUSE   408/446-2222   **35**

◆◆◆
Steak
Fine Dining
$12-$165

AAA Inspector Notes: This casually elegant steakhouse is known for its Prime cuts of Certified Angus Beef that is dry aged at the restaurant. A Japanese flair is influenced into the menu items. The open grill kitchen allows guests to watch the chefs prepare their unique creations. Their specialty is Wagyu (Japanese beef) from various prefectures, such as Miyazaki, Gunma and Kagoshima. The texture and richness is nothing like western beef. **Features:** full bar. **Reservations:** suggested. **Address:** 19379 Stevens Creek Blvd 95014 **Location:** I-280 exit 9, 0.6 mi w.   L   D   CALL

ARMADILLO WILLY'S BAR-B-QUE   408/252-7427

◆ Barbecue. Quick Serve. **Address:** 10100 S De Anza Blvd 95014

THE BLUE PHEASANT RESTAURANT   408/255-3300   **32**

◆◆ American. Casual Dining. **Address:** 22100 Stevens Creek Blvd 95014

FONTANA'S ITALIAN RESTAURANT   408/725-0188   **33**

◆◆ Italian. Fine Dining. **Address:** 20840 Stevens Creek Blvd 95014

LITTLE SHEEP MONGOLIAN HOT POT   408/996-9919   **36**

◆◆ Mongolian. Casual Dining. **Address:** 19062 Stevens Creek Blvd 95014

PARKVIEW   408/873-1000   **34**

◆◆ American. Casual Dining. **Address:** 10030 S De Anza Blvd 95014

DALY CITY   pop. 101,123
• Hotels & Restaurants map & index p. 316
• Part of San Francisco area — see map p. 243

HAMPTON INN BY HILTON SAN FRANCISCO/DALY CITY
650/755-7500   **16**

◆◆◆ SAVE Hotel. **Address:** 2700 Junipero Serra Blvd 94015

AAA Benefit: Members save up to 15%!

(See map & index p. 316.)

WHERE TO EAT

KOI PALACE RESTAURANT   650/992-9000 ⑩
♦♦ Chinese Dim Sum. Casual Dining. **Address:** 365 Gellert
Blvd 94015

DANVILLE (C-9) pop. 42,039, elev. 368'
• Hotels p. 70 • Restaurants p. 70
• Hotels & Restaurants map & index p. 176

Historic buildings connect Danville to its Old West
past. A mute witness to history is a massive oak tree
that stands on Diablo Road, estimated to be some 300
years old. The Iron Horse Regional Trail, a rails-to-trails
conversion that is a popular jogging, biking and walking
route, passes behind the restored Southern Pacific
Railroad Depot. The trail begins in Concord and winds
almost 25 miles to the Contra Costa county line in San
Ramon.

Scenic views of Mount Diablo, visible throughout
Danville, are what brought playwright Eugene
O'Neill to the area. His home in the Las Trampas
foothills can be toured by reservation. Mount Diablo
State Park, popular with hikers and for the views
from its summit, is east on Diablo Road.

The Danville Certified Farmers Market sets up Saturday mornings 9-1 year-round in the parking lot next to
The Museum of the San Ramon Valley, at Railroad and
W. Prospect avenues. Regional farmers sell organic
and nonorganic fruits and vegetables, eggs, cut flowers
and bedding plants, and vendors offer specialty products from fresh-baked breads to olive oil.

Danville Area Chamber of Commerce: 117-E
Town and Country Dr., Danville, CA 94526. **Phone:**
(925) 837-4400.

EUGENE O'NEILL NATIONAL HISTORIC SITE is
reached by a shuttle from a designated pick-up
point; information is provided when reservations are
made. Guided 2.5-hour tours are given of Tao
House, the Pulitzer- and Nobel Prize-winning playwright's home from 1937 to 1944. This sanctuary is
where he wrote his most successful plays—"The
Iceman Cometh," "Long Day's Journey Into Night"
and "A Moon for the Misbegotten." The tour provides insights into O'Neill's life, his marriage to wife
Carlotta and his contributions to American theater.

Time: Allow 2 hours, 30 minutes minimum. **Hours:**
Guided tours are given Wed.-Fri. and Sun. at 10 and 2.
Self-guiding tours are offered Sat.; shuttles depart from
The Museum of the San Ramon Valley, 205 Railroad
Ave., at 10:15, 12:15 and 2:15. Closed Jan. 1, Thanks-
giving and Christmas. **Cost:** Free. Reservations are re-
quired 1 to 2 weeks in advance for guided tours.
Reservations are not required for self-guiding tours.
Phone: (925) 838-0249.

⬥ **MOUNT DIABLO STATE PARK** is off I-680
Diablo Rd. exit, then 3 mi. e. to Mount Diablo
Scenic Blvd. and the South Gate entrance station.
At 3,849 feet, Mount Diablo isn't all that impressive
from an elevation standpoint. But because this
mountain is surrounded by broad, flat valleys, the
view from its summit is remarkable—under the best
conditions you can see almost 200 miles away, a
40,000-square-mile region that includes the Sacramento Valley, parts of the Sierra Nevada mountain
range and up to 35 California counties.

The views from Diablo's upper reaches are best
during winter and early spring, especially after a
storm has cleared the air. The sky is frequently hazy
during the hot and dry summer months.

The 8-mile drive on South Gate Road to the
summit is rewarding. As you ascend the mountain,
pull off the twisty, two-lane road for panoramic views
of rolling hills, some cloaked in a blanket of tawny
grasses and others dotted with oak trees. Spring
(especially April and May) is the best time to see
yellow cow parsnips, pink shooting stars and other
wildflowers that fill the meadows with color. Resident
wildlife includes deer, rabbits and coyotes. The road
has many sharp turns and also is used by cyclists;
obey the speed limit and exercise caution.

There are hiking trails throughout the park. Only
the fit should attempt the 6.5-mile Grand Loop Trail.
This loose gravel trail encircles Diablo's summit, has
a 1,700-foot elevation gain and includes some hair-
raisingly narrow portions that wind along cliff faces.
Rock City, accessed via South Gate Road (watch for
signs to the parking area), has narrow, crisscrossing
walking paths that lead past unusual sandstone
formations—many of them pocked with small
caves—and meander through forested meadows.

In addition to hiking, outdoor activities include nature photography, horseback riding and camping.
There are historical exhibits at the Mitchell Canyon
Interpretive Center in nearby Clayton. See Recreation Areas Chart.

Dogs are allowed only in developed areas (picnic
sites, campgrounds, paved roads) and must be on a
leash at all times. **Time:** Allow 2 hours minimum.
Hours: Park open daily 8-dusk. Mitchell Canyon Interpretive Center open Sat.-Sun. and some holidays
8-4, in summer; 10-2, in winter. **Cost:** Day use fee
$10 per private vehicle; $9 (ages 62+ per private vehicle). **Phone:** (925) 837-2525. ▲ ⊞

Summit Museum, at the top of Mount Diablo in
Mount Diablo State Park, is in a historic 1930s stone
building that is also the park's visitor center. Exhibits
depict the park's natural and cultural history, and a
rock wall and accompanying video recount geological forces that formed the mountain. A diorama
with audio features presents an overview of park
ecosystems. Key features are shown on a model of
the mountain. There also are high-quality displays of
artwork and photos.

A circular stairway leads to an observation tower with
a deck that provides panoramic 360-degree views; marine fossils embedded in the building's sandstone walls
can be seen on the way up. **Time:** Allow 1 hour
minimum. **Hours:** Daily 10-4. Phone ahead to confirm
schedule. **Cost:** Free. **Phone:** (925) 837-6119.

(See map & index p. 176.)

BEST WESTERN DANVILLE SYCAMORE INN
925/855-8888

Hotel

Best Western **AAA Benefit:** Members save up to 15% and earn bonus points!

Address: 803 Camino Ramon 94526 **Location:** I-680 exit 38 (Sycamore Valley Rd), just e, then just s. **Facility:** 62 units. 2 stories (no elevator), interior/exterior corridors. **Pool:** heated outdoor. **Featured Amenity:** continental breakfast.

[icons]

 WHERE TO EAT

BLACKHAWK GRILLE 925/736-4295
American. Fine Dining. **Address:** 3540 Blackhawk Plaza Cir 94506

EL NIDO MEXICAN RESTAURANT & CATERING
925/820-5330 **(39)**
Mexican. Casual Dining. **Address:** 107 A Town and Country Dr 94526

ESIN RESTAURANT & BAR 925/314-0974 **(40)**
Mediterranean. Casual Dining. **Address:** 750 Camino Ramon 94526

DAVIS (A-9) pop. 65,622, elev. 50'

Progressive Davis has been awarded several energy conservation awards as a result of its foresight and commitment to preserving native habitats. But one thing that's unusual about the 400-acre City of Davis Wetlands is that it depends on storm water and treated wastewater runoff to maintain a wetlands environment. This area attracts migrating waterfowl and songbirds, and the open spaces are great for wildlife viewing, hiking and biking. The site is off CR 28H, about a mile past the Davis Wastewater Pollution Control Plant; phone (530) 757-5686. The wetlands may be closed due to construction on the access road; phone for updates.

Another wetland habitat is the 16,000-acre Yolo Bypass Wildlife Area, at the east end of CR 32B. You can either hike this area or view the scenery from a car window courtesy of a loop road; phone (530) 757-2461. The city also offers more than 100 miles of bike paths and more than 500 acres of parks, scenic greenbelts and open recreational space.

The University of California Davis has an enrollment of approximately 30,000 students. Free, 90-minute guided walking tours are given weekdays at 9 and 1 and Saturdays at 11; they depart from the Walter A. Buehler Alumni and Visitors Center. Reservations are required and should be made at least 1 week in advance; phone (530) 752-8111.

The Jan Shrem and Maria Manetti Shrem Museum of Art, on Old Davis Road at Alumni Lane (near the university welcome center), display fine art including works by UC Davis faculty and alumni. Phone (530) 752-8500.

The Davis Farmers Market is held Saturday mornings 8-1, year-round. On Wednesdays from 4:30-8:30, mid-March to late October, a festival atmosphere prevails at "Picnic in the Park." The event features international food vendors, a wine and beer garden, live performances from local musicians, a carousel, a portable fountain and play areas for children. To get to the market from I-80, take the Downtown Davis exit to Richards Boulevard, turn left on 1st Street, then turn right on C Street; the market is between 4th and 5th streets.

Davis Chamber of Commerce: 604 Third St., Davis, CA 95616. **Phone:** (530) 756-5160.

AGGIE INN, AN ASCEND HOTEL COLLECTION MEMBER
530/756-0352
Hotel. **Address:** 245 1st St 95616

BEST WESTERN PLUS PALM COURT HOTEL
530/753-7100

Boutique Hotel

Best Western PLUS **AAA Benefit:** Members save up to 15% and earn bonus points!

Address: 234 D St 95616 **Location:** I-80 exit 72B (Richards Blvd) westbound; exit 72 eastbound, just nw, w on 1st St, then just n; corner of 3rd and D sts; downtown. **Facility:** In the heart of downtown and within walking distance of art galleries, restaurants and retail, this property features attractive décor in its atrium-style areas. 27 units. 3 stories, interior corridors. **Activities:** exercise room.

[icons]

BEST WESTERN UNIVERSITY LODGE 530/756-7890

Motel

Best Western **AAA Benefit:** Members save up to 15% and earn bonus points!

Address: 123 B St 95616 **Location:** I-80 exit 72B (Richards Blvd) westbound; exit 72 eastbound, just nw to 1st St, just w to B St, then just n; at 2nd and B sts. **Facility:** 52 units. 2 stories (no elevator), exterior corridors. **Amenities:** safes. **Activities:** hot tub, exercise room. **Featured Amenity:** continental breakfast.

[icons]

HILTON GARDEN INN DAVIS DOWNTOWN 530/753-3600
Hotel. **Address:** 110 F St 95616

AAA Benefit: Members save up to 15%!

HOLIDAY INN EXPRESS & SUITES - DAVIS UNIVERSITY AREA
530/297-1500
Hotel. **Address:** 1640 Research Park Dr 95618

HYATT PLACE UC DAVIS   530/756-9500

Hotel

AAA Benefit: Members save up to 10%!

Address: 173 Old Davis Rd Ext 95616 **Location:** I-80 exit 71 (UC Davis), 0.6 mi ne; just n of jct Alumni Ln; follow signs for Mondavi Center. **Facility:** 127 units. 4 stories, interior corridors. **Parking:** on-site (fee). **Pool:** heated outdoor. **Activities:** exercise room. **Guest Services:** valet laundry. **Featured Amenity:** breakfast buffet.

WHERE TO EAT

BURGERS AND BREW   530/750-3600
Burgers. Quick Serve. **Address:** 403 3rd St 95616

CAFE BERNARDO   530/750-5101
New American. Quick Serve. **Address:** 234 D St 95616

CREPEVILLE   530/750-2400
Breakfast. Quick Serve. **Address:** 330 3rd St 95616

MIKUNI JAPANESE RESTAURANT & SUSHI BAR
530/756-2111
Japanese Sushi. Casual Dining. **Address:** 500 1st St, Suite 11 95616

OSTERIA FASULO   530/758-1324
Italian. Casual Dining. **Address:** 2657 Portage Bay E 95616

PAESANOS   530/758-8646
Italian Pizza. Casual Dining. **Address:** 139 G St 95616

SAM'S MEDITERRANEAN CUISINE   530/758-2855
Greek. Quick Serve. **Address:** 301 B St 95616

SEASONS RESTAURANT   530/750-1801
American. Casual Dining. **Address:** 102 F St 95616

DEVILS POSTPILE NATIONAL MONUMENT (F-5)

Near Mammoth Lakes and surrounded by Inyo National Forest, Devils Postpile National Monument lies at an elevation of 7,560 feet in the eastern Sierra Nevada. The highlight of this 800-acre monument is a sheer wall of symmetrical basaltic columns more than 60 feet high. The formation is a remnant of a basalt flow worn smooth on top by glacial action. A trail leads to the top where the surface resembles a tile inlay.

The Middle Fork of the San Joaquin River drops more than 100 feet at Rainbow Falls, 2 miles by trail from the Devils Postpile formation. Fishing is permitted; anyone over 15 must have a California license. Hunting is prohibited.

The monument is reached via SR 203, which leads west from US 395 and Mammoth Visitor Center to the Mammoth Mountain Ski Area and Adventure Center parking lot, then by shuttle bus to the Postpile ranger station. The shuttle, which runs 7 a.m.-7 p.m., also departs from the Village at Mammoth in Mammoth Lakes. A half-mile trail leads to the Postpile. Except for vehicles with camping permits, the physically impaired, overnight resort guests or trailers carrying horses or other livestock, private vehicles are not allowed beyond Minaret Vista (just beyond the ski area parking lot) during the day, mid-June through the Wednesday after Labor Day.

Rangers conduct interpretive walks and programs mid-June through the Wednesday after Labor Day (weather permitting). Leashed pets are permitted in the monument and on shuttle buses. Pets must wear muzzles on the buses. Monument open May-Oct. (weather permitting). Ranger station open daily 9-5, mid-June through the Wednesday after Labor Day. Shuttle bus tickets $8; $4 (ages 3-15). Three-day pass $16; $8 (ages 3-15). Passes for exempt vehicles $10 (single day); $20 (3 days). A Federal Recreation Pass is only valid for vehicles that are exceptions to the shuttle bus or for camping discounts, if applicable. Phone (760) 934-2289.

DIXON pop. 18,351

BEST WESTERN PLUS INN DIXON   707/678-1400

Hotel

Best Western PLUS.

AAA Benefit: Members save up to 15% and earn bonus points!

Address: 1345 Commercial Way 95620 **Location:** I-80 exit 64 (Pitt School Rd), just s, just e on Stratford Ave, then just n. **Facility:** 101 units, some efficiencies. 2 stories (no elevator), interior/exterior corridors. **Pool:** outdoor. **Activities:** sauna, hot tub, steamroom, exercise room. **Guest Services:** coin laundry. **Featured Amenity:** breakfast buffet.

COUNTRY INN & SUITES BY RADISSON, DIXON, CA-UC DAVIS AREA   707/676-5000
Hotel. **Address:** 155 Dorset Dr 95620

WHERE TO EAT

CATTLEMENS   707/678-5518
Steak. Casual Dining. **Address:** 250 Dorset Ct 95620

LA COCINA MEXICANA RESTAURANT   707/693-1102
Mexican. Casual Dining. **Address:** 105 E Dorset Dr 95620

SOLANO BAKING CO   707/678-0959
Breads/Pastries. Quick Serve. **Address:** 1160 Pitt School Rd 95620

DUBLIN pop. 46,036
• Restaurants p. 72

ALOFT DUBLIN-PLEASANTON   925/248-8500
Hotel. **Address:** 4075 Grafton St 94568

AAA Benefit: Members save 5% or more!

HOLIDAY INN DUBLIN   925/828-7750
Hotel. **Address:** 6680 Regional St 94568

HYATT PLACE DUBLIN/PLEASANTON   925/828-9006

WWW
Hotel

☰ HYATT PLACE· **AAA Benefit:** Members save up to 10%!

Address: 4950 Hacienda Dr 94568 **Location:** I-580 exit 46 (Hacienda Dr), just n; in Hacienda Crossing Shopping Center. ☰ Dublin-Pleasanton, 34. **Facility:** 127 units. 6 stories, interior corridors. **Parking:** on-site (fee). **Pool:** heated outdoor. **Activities:** exercise room. **Guest Services:** valet laundry. **Featured Amenity:** breakfast buffet.

SAVE 🍴 CALL 🚫 🏊 🐾 BIZ
📶 ✕ 🎥 🛏 🖥 / SOME UNITS 🐾 🚪

WHERE TO EAT

AMAKARA   925/803-8485
WW Japanese. Casual Dining. **Address:** 7222 Regional St 94568

ARMADILLO WILLY'S BAR-B-QUE   925/833-0400
W Barbecue. Quick Serve. **Address:** 4480 Tassajara Rd 94568

CASA OROZCO   925/828-5464
WW Mexican. Casual Dining. **Address:** 7995 Amador Valley Blvd 94568

DUNSMUIR (B-2) pop. 1,650, elev. 2,289'

Dunsmuir is an old railroad town just south of Mount Shasta. The Sacramento River, which runs through town, offers excellent fly fishing. Other recreational opportunities in the area include camping, hiking and skiing.

Dunsmuir Chamber of Commerce and Visitor's Center: 5915 Dunsmuir Ave., Suite 100, P.O. Box 122, Dunsmuir, CA 96025. **Phone:** (530) 235-2177 or (800) 386-7684.

DUNSMUIR INN & SUITES /   530/235-4395
W Motel. **Address:** 5400 Dunsmuir Ave 96025

TRAVELODGE DUNSMUIR   530/235-4100
WW Hotel. **Address:** 4000 Siskiyou Ave 96025

WHERE TO EAT

CORNERSTONE BAKERY & CAFE   530/235-4677
WW American. Casual Dining. **Address:** 5759 Dunsmuir Ave 96025

YAKS   530/678-3517
WW American. Casual Dining. **Address:** 4917 Dunsmuir Ave 96025

EAST PALO ALTO pop. 28,155
• Hotels & Restaurants map & index p. 190

FOUR SEASONS HOTEL SILICON VALLEY AT EAST PALO ALTO   650/566-1200 22
WWW WWW Contemporary Hotel. **Address:** 2050 University Ave 94303

WHERE TO EAT

QUATTRO RESTAURANT & BAR   650/470-2889 21
WWW WWW Italian. Fine Dining. **Address:** 2050 University Ave 94303

EL CERRITO pop. 23,549

HOTEL MIRA VISTA-BERKELEY NORTH   510/232-0900
WW Hotel. **Address:** 6009 Potrero Ave 94530

EL DORADO HILLS pop. 42,108
• Hotels & Restaurants map & index p. 224

36 HANDLES   916/941-3606 71
WW American. Brewpub. **Address:** 1010 White Rock Rd 95762

AJI JAPANESE BISTRO   916/941-9181 64
WW Japanese. Casual Dining. **Address:** 4361 Town Center Blvd, Suite 111 95762

BAMIYAN AFGHAN RESTAURANT   916/941-8787 70
WW Afghan. Casual Dining. **Address:** 1121 White Rock Rd, Suite 101 95762

BELLA BRU CAFÉ   916/933-5454 63
W American. Quick Serve. **Address:** 3941 Park Dr, #70 95762

C. KNIGHT'S STEAKHOUSE   916/235-1730 67
WWW Steak. Fine Dining. **Address:** 2085 Vine St 95762

KOCHI SUSHI & JAPANESE BAR AND GRILL   916/933-8899 62
WW Japanese. Sushi. Casual Dining. **Address:** 2205 Francisco Dr 95762

MILESTONE RESTAURANT   916/934-0790 66
WW New American. Casual Dining. **Address:** 4359 Town Center Blvd 95762

PETE'S RESTAURANT & BREWHOUSE   916/933-3400 65
WW American. Casual Dining. **Address:** 2023 Vine St 95762

SELLAND'S MARKET CAFE   916/932-5025 69
WW American. Quick Serve. **Address:** 4370 Town Center Blvd, Suite 120 95762

ELDORADO NATIONAL FOREST (E-4)

Elevations in the forest range from 3,382 ft. in the foothills to 9,983 ft. at Pyramid Peak. Refer to AAA maps for additional elevation information.

Bounded on the west by the Mother Lode Country and on the east by Lake Tahoe, Eldorado National Forest encompasses 676,780 acres in the rugged, lake-strewn Sierra Nevada. US 50 and SR 88 provide access to most of the forest's recreational facilities. Carson Pass Highway (SR 88) is a 58-mile scenic route through the forest.

Although the forest is most popular in spring and summer, three downhill ski areas and trails for cross-country skiing and snowmobiling attract winter visitors as well. Segments of the Pacific Crest National Scenic Trail pass through the forest; snow renders some sections impassable until mid-June or July. Hikers wishing to camp on the trail should obtain campfire permits. Permits also are required for day use and overnight stays in the Desolation Wilderness and Mokelumne Wilderness.

Maps for off-road vehicle use are available at national forest offices; for information phone (530) 644-2349. For additional information contact the Forest Supervisor, Eldorado National Forest, 100 Forni Rd., Placerville, CA 95667; phone (530) 622-5061. *See Recreation Areas Chart.*

ELK
• **Part of Wine Country area — see map p. 405**

ELK COVE INN & SPA   707/877-3321
 Country Inn. **Address:** 6300 S Hwy 1 95432

ELK GROVE (E-3) pop. 153,015, elev. 49'

Elk Grove is not only a suburb of sprawling Sacramento but—because of its relative proximity to the Greater Bay Area—a community from which people commute to jobs in San Francisco. Spend a lazy afternoon at Miwok Park, 9344 Village Tree Dr. This local green space has plenty of shade trees as well as a variety of play areas for kids.

In late July, the 4-day Strauss Festival of Elk Grove presents evening orchestral performances choreographed to the music of Austrian composer Johann Strauss. Each performance ends with a display of fireworks. This family-oriented event takes place on Strauss Island in Elk Grove Regional Park, 9950 Elk Grove-Florin Rd. (take the Elk Grove Boulevard exit from either I-5 or SR 99 and follow signs). For festival information phone (916) 714-2527.

FAIRFIELD INN & SUITES BY MARRIOTT SACRAMENTO ELK GROVE   916/681-5400

Hotel
 AAA Benefit: Members save 5% or more!

Address: 8058 Orchard Loop Ln 95624 **Location:** SR 99 exit 289 (Cosumnes River Blvd/Calvine Rd), just se. **Facility:** 76 units. 3 stories, interior corridors. **Pool:** heated indoor. **Activities:** hot tub, exercise room. **Guest Services:** complimentary and valet laundry, boarding pass kiosk.

HAMPTON INN & SUITES SACRAMENTO/ELK GROVE LAGUNA I-5   916/683-9545

Hotel
 AAA Benefit: Members save up to 15%!

Address: 2305 Longport Ct 95758 **Location:** I-5 exit 508 (Laguna Blvd), 0.5 mi e, just s on Harbour Point Dr, then just w. **Facility:** 110 units. 4 stories, interior corridors. **Pool:** heated outdoor. **Activities:** hot tub, exercise room. **Guest Services:** valet and coin laundry. **Featured Amenity:** full hot breakfast.

HILTON GARDEN INN SACRAMENTO/ELK GROVE
916/691-1900

Hotel
 **AAA Benefit:** Members save up to 15%!

Address: 9241 Laguna Springs Dr 95757 **Location:** SR 99 exit 287 (Laguna Blvd), just w, then just s. Located at Laguna Pointe Business Park. **Facility:** 116 units. 4 stories, interior corridors. **Pool:** heated outdoor. **Activities:** hot tub, exercise room. **Guest Services:** valet and coin laundry.

HOLIDAY INN EXPRESS & SUITES   916/478-4000
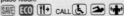 Hotel. **Address:** 2460 Maritime Dr 95758

HOLIDAY INN EXPRESS HOTEL & SUITES   916/478-9000
 Hotel. **Address:** 9175 W Stockton Blvd 95758

WHERE TO EAT

BOULEVARD BISTRO   916/685-2220
Regional American. Casual Dining. **Address:** 8941 Elk Grove Blvd 95624

BRICK HOUSE RESTAURANT & LOUNGE   916/714-0840
American. Casual Dining. **Address:** 9027 Elk Grove Blvd, Suite 100 95624

CHICAGO FIRE   916/667-8370
Pizza. Casual Dining. **Address:** 7101 Laguna Blvd 95757

LEATHERBY'S FAMILY CREAMERY   916/691-3334
American. Casual Dining. **Address:** 8238 Laguna Blvd 95758

MIKUNI JAPANESE RESTAURANT & SUSHI BAR
916/714-2112
Japanese Sushi. Casual Dining. **Address:** 8525 Bond Rd 95624

PAESANOS   916/690-8646
Italian. Casual Dining. **Address:** 8519 Bond Rd, #101 95624

THAI CHILI   916/714-3519
Thai. Casual Dining. **Address:** 8696 Elk Grove Blvd, Suite 5 95624

TODO UN POCO   916/684-7774

🔱🔱 International. Casual Dining. **Address:** 9080 Laguna Main St, Suite 1A 95758

EMERYVILLE pop. 10,080
• **Hotels & Restaurants map & index p. 176**

COURTYARD BY MARRIOTT EMERYVILLE
                                            510/652-8777 **31**

🔱🔱🔱 SAVE Hotel. **Address:** 5555 Shellmound St 94608

| **AAA Benefit:** Members save 5% or more! |

FOUR POINTS BY SHERATON-SAN FRANCISCO BAY BRIDGE
                                            510/547-7888 **29**

🔱🔱🔱 SAVE Hotel. **Address:** 1603 Powell St 94608

| **AAA Benefit:** Members save 5% or more! |

HILTON GARDEN INN SAN FRANCISCO OAKLAND/ BAYBRIDGE   510/658-9300 **28**

🔱🔱🔱
Hotel

Hilton Garden Inn **AAA Benefit:** Members save up to 15%!

Address: 1800 Powell St 94608 **Location:** I-80 exit 9 (Powell St), just w. **Facility:** 278 units. 13 stories, interior corridors. **Parking:** on-site (fee). **Activities:** hot tub, trails, exercise room. **Guest Services:** valet and coin laundry, area transportation.

SAVE ECO 🍴 🍽 CALL ♿ 🛗
BIZ HS 📶 ✕ 📷 🔌 📇
🍵

HYATT HOUSE EMERYVILLE/SAN FRANCISCO BAY AREA   510/601-5880 **27**

🔱🔱🔱
Extended Stay Hotel

H HYATT house™ **AAA Benefit:** Members save up to 10%!

Address: 5800 Shellmound St 94608 **Location:** I-80 exit 9 (Powell St), just e, just n on Christie Ave, then just e on Shellmound Way. Adjacent to train tracks. **Facility:** 234 units, some efficiencies. 12 stories, interior corridors. **Parking:** on-site (fee). **Pool:** heated outdoor. **Activities:** hot tub, exercise room. **Guest Services:** valet and coin laundry, area transportation. **Featured Amenity:** breakfast buffet.

SAVE 🍴 🍽 CALL ♿ 🛶 🛗 BIZ 📶 ✕ 🔌
📇 📇 /SOME UNITS 🐾

HYATT PLACE EMERYVILLE/SAN FRANCISCO BAY AREA
                                            510/285-9232 **30**

🔱🔱🔱 Hotel. **Address:** 5700 Bay St 94608

WHERE TO EAT

P.F. CHANG'S CHINA BISTRO   510/879-0990 **27**
🔱🔱🔱 Chinese. Fine Dining. **Address:** 5633 Bay St 94608

RUDY'S CAN'T FAIL CAFE   510/594-1221 **28**
🔱🔱 American. Casual Dining. **Address:** 4081 Hollis St 94608

SHIBA RAMEN   510/985-8309 **26**
🔱 Japanese Noodles. Quick Serve. **Address:** 5959 Shellmound St 94608

EUREKA (B-1) pop. 27,191, elev. 44'

The chief port between San Francisco and the Columbia River, which defines much of the Washington/Oregon border, Eureka has a distinct maritime feel courtesy of its location on Humboldt Bay. Ornate Victorian dwellings like the Carson Mansion at 2nd and M streets (not open to the public) reflect the days when lumber barons prospered.

Old Town Eureka runs the length of First, Second and Third streets between C and M streets. This historic district of renovated 19th-century buildings has specialty shops, restaurants and art galleries to explore.

Humboldt Bay yields catches of crab, salmon, shrimp, albacore and bottom fish. Fishing fleets dock just across the Samoa Bridge at Woodley Island Marina, where a copper-clad redwood statue of a fisherman commemorates fishermen lost at sea. Humboldt Bay Maritime Museum, adjacent to the Samoa Cookhouse, displays marine artifacts and photographs of an earlier Eureka; phone (707) 444-9440.

Established in the late 1800s as a large lumber camp chowhouse, the Samoa Cookhouse Museum, 908 Vance Ave., displays equipment, utensils and memorabilia from the lumber and logging industry in the restaurant's museum and dining rooms; phone (707) 442-1659.

Eureka-Humboldt Visitors Bureau: 322 First St., Eureka, CA 95501. **Phone:** (707) 443-5097 or (800) 346-3482.

Self-guiding tours: Information describing some 100 vintage homes is available from the Greater Eureka Chamber of Commerce, 2112 Broadway, Eureka, CA 95501-2189; phone (707) 442-3738.

BLUE OX HISTORIC VILLAGE is at 1 X St., 4 blks. n. of US 101. Visitors can learn about Victorian craftsmanship as they watch products being made on 19th-century equipment. After a detailed introduction and demonstration, the self-guiding tour includes a full-production wood shop, a blacksmith shop, a ceramics studio, a print shop, a re-created logging skid camp, a rose garden, an aviary and a visit with farm animals.

Visitors also can observe artisans as they work. Casual dress and low-heeled shoes are advised. **Time:** Allow 2 hours minimum. **Hours:** Mon.-Fri. 9-5, Sat. 9-4, May-Nov.; Mon.-Fri. 9-5, rest of year. **Cost:** $12; $11 (ages 13-17 and 65+); $7 (ages 6-12). **Phone:** (707) 444-3437 or (800) 248-4259.

HUMBOLDT BAY HARBOR CRUISE departs from the foot of C St. The MV *Madaket*, an original 1910 ferry, takes visitors on a 75-minute narrated history cruise around Humboldt Bay. Bring a sweater or jacket. Cocktail, eco and July 4th cruises also are available. **Hours:** Harbor cruise departs Wed.-Sat. at 1, 2:30 and 4, Sun.-Tues. at 1 and 2:30, mid-May to early Oct. **Cost:** Harbor cruise $22; $18 (ages 13-17 and 55+); $12 (ages 5-12). **Phone:** (707) 445-1910.

BEST WESTERN PLUS BAYSHORE INN
707/268-8005

Hotel

Best Western PLUS

AAA Benefit: Members save up to 15% and earn bonus points!

Address: 3500 Broadway 95503 **Location:** Jct US 101 and Truesdale St; south end of town. Adjacent to Bayshore Mall. **Facility:** 129 units, some two bedrooms and kitchens. 2-3 stories, exterior corridors. **Terms:** check-in 4 pm. **Dining:** 2 restaurants. **Pool:** heated outdoor. **Activities:** sauna, hot tub, exercise room. **Guest Services:** coin laundry. **Featured Amenity:** breakfast buffet.

BEST WESTERN PLUS HUMBOLDT BAY INN
707/443-2234

Motel

Best Western PLUS

AAA Benefit: Members save up to 15% and earn bonus points!

Address: 232 W 5th St 95501 **Location:** On US 101, just w of Commercial St. **Facility:** 103 units. 2 stories (no elevator), exterior corridors. **Amenities:** Some: safes. **Pool:** heated outdoor. **Activities:** hot tub, exercise room. **Guest Services:** valet and coin laundry, area transportation. **Featured Amenity:** continental breakfast. *(See ad on p. 76.)*

CLARION HOTEL BY HUMBOLDT BAY　707/442-3261
Hotel. **Address:** 2223 4th St 95501

COMFORT INN HUMBOLDT BAY　707/444-2019
Hotel. **Address:** 4260 Broadway 95503

EUREKA TOWN HOUSE MOTEL　707/443-4536
Motel. **Address:** 933 4th St 95501

HOLIDAY INN EXPRESS & SUITES EUREKA　707-269-0682
Hotel. **Address:** 815 W Wabash Ave 95501

QUALITY INN EUREKA　707/443-1601
Motel. **Address:** 1209 4th St 95501

RED LION HOTEL EUREKA　707/445-0844
Hotel. **Address:** 1929 4th St 95501

WHERE TO EAT

THE BANANA HUT HAWAIIAN BBQ　707/444-3447
Hawaiian. Casual Dining. **Address:** 621 5th St 95501

BAYFRONT RESTAURANT　707/443-7489
Japanese. Casual Dining. **Address:** 1 F St 95501

BRICK & FIRE　707/268-8959
Mediterranean. Casual Dining. **Address:** 1630 F St 95501

CAFE MARINA
707/443-2233

Seafood
Casual Dining
$9-$28

AAA Inspector Notes: The menu is built around fresh local seafood. The oysters and clams are favorites of the locals. The casual dining room, as well as the seasonal patio, overlooks the marina. Many days you can watch the sea lions swimming among the boats. **Features:** full bar, patio dining. **Address:** 601 Startare Dr 95501 **Location:** On Woodley Island; w on SR 255 from jct US 101.

B L D CALL

CAFE NOONER　707/443-4663
International. Casual Dining. **Address:** 409 Opera Alley 95501

FIVE ELEVEN　707/268-3852
American. Casual Dining. **Address:** 511 2nd St 95501

GALLAGHER'S IRISH PUB AND RESTAURANT　707/442-1177
Irish. Gastropub. **Address:** 139 2nd St 95501

LE MONDE RESTAURANT　707/798-6499
French Fusion. Casual Dining. **Address:** 2850 F St 95501

LOS BAGELS　707/442-8525
Breads/Pastries Coffee/Tea. Quick Serve. **Address:** 403 2nd St 95501

STAY CONNECTED

GET THE APP

AAA.com/mobile
CAA.ca/mobile

LOST COAST BREWERY AND CAFE 707/445-4480
 American. Casual Dining. **Address:** 617 4th St 95501

OBERON GRILL 707/443-3663
American. Casual Dining. **Address:** 516 2nd St 95501

PAUL'S LIVE FROM NEW YORK 707/442-5800
Pizza. Casual Dining. **Address:** 604 F St 95501

PORTER STREET BBQ 707/443-1700
Barbecue. Quick Serve. **Address:** 605 Broadway St 95501

RESTAURANT 301 707/444-8062
American. Fine Dining. **Address:** 301 L St 95501

THE SEA GRILL 707/443-7187
Seafood. Casual Dining. **Address:** 316 E St 95501

SHAMUS T BONES 707/407-3550
Steak Barbecue. Casual Dining. **Address:** 1911 Truesdale St 95503

STARS HAMBURGERS 707/445-2061
Burgers. Quick Serve. **Address:** 2009 Harrison Ave 95501

TRES CHILES POCOSOS 707/268-8255
Mexican. Casual Dining. **Address:** 3502 Broadway St 95503

FAIRFIELD (B-8) pop. 105,321, elev. 15'

Fairfield, founded in 1903, is located southeast of the Vaca Mountains. The Travis Air Force Base Heritage Center features aircraft, photographs, uniforms and memorabilia pertaining to the base's history and its role in providing troop airlift to the Pacific region. Public access is limited due to security restrictions; phone (707) 424-5883.

Fairfield-Suisun Chamber of Commerce: 1111 Webster St., Fairfield, CA 94533. **Phone:** (707) 425-4625.

Shopping: JCPenney and Macy's are the anchor stores at Solano Town Center, off I-80 exit 45 at Travis Boulevard and Pennsylvania Avenue.

BEST WESTERN CORDELIA INN 707/864-2029

Hotel

 Best Western **AAA Benefit:** Members save up to 15% and earn bonus points!

Address: 4373 Central Pl 94534 **Location:** I-80 exit 41 (Suisun Valley Rd/Pittman Rd) eastbound, just ne; exit 41 (Green Valley Rd/Suisun Valley Rd) westbound, follow signs (stay right) for Suisun Valley Rd, go over the overpass (Pittman Rd), then just ne. Located in a quiet area. **Facility:** 60 units. 2 stories (no elevator), exterior corridors. **Pool:** outdoor. **Activities:** hot tub. **Featured Amenity:** continental breakfast.

FAIRFIELD INN & SUITES BY MARRIOTT FAIRFIELD NAPA VALLEY AREA 707/864-6672

Hotel

 Fairfield **AAA Benefit:** Members save 5% or more!

Address: 315 Pittman Rd 94534 **Location:** I-80 exit 41 (Suisun Valley Rd/Pittman Rd) eastbound, just sw; exit 41 (Green Valley Rd/Suisun Valley Rd) westbound, follow signs (stay right) for Suisun Valley Rd, go over the overpass (Pittman Rd), then just sw. **Facility:** 68 units. 4 stories, interior corridors. **Pool:** heated indoor. **Activities:** hot tub, exercise room. **Guest Services:** valet and coin laundry. **Featured Amenity:** breakfast buffet.

HILTON GARDEN INN FAIRFIELD 707/426-6900
Hotel. **Address:** 2200 Gateway Ct 94533
AAA Benefit: Members save up to 15%!

HOMEWOOD SUITES BY HILTON FAIRFIELD-NAPA VALLEY AREA 707/863-0300
Extended Stay Hotel. **Address:** 4755 Business Center Dr 94534
AAA Benefit: Members save up to 15%!

STAYBRIDGE SUITES FAIRFIELD-NAPA VALLEY AREA 707/863-0900
Extended Stay Hotel. **Address:** 4775 Business Center Dr 94534

WHERE TO EAT

HUCKLEBERRY'S 707/427-3800
Breakfast. Casual Dining. **Address:** 3101 Travis Blvd 94534

LUIGI'S 707/428-7102
Sandwiches. Quick Serve. **Address:** 721 Texas St 94533

MANKAS STEAKHOUSE 707/425-3207
Steak. Fine Dining. **Address:** 2522 Mankas Corner Rd 94534

PALM THAI BISTRO 707/864-8777
Thai. Casual Dining. **Address:** 5089 Business Center Dr 94534

STICKY RICE CHINESE BISTRO & BAR 707/863-7500
Chinese. Casual Dining. **Address:** 5030 Business Center Dr, Suite 100 94534

FELTON (F-8) pop. 4,057, elev. 286'

One of the tallest covered bridges in the United States—and the only one made of redwood—can be found in Felton. The city lies on a scenic stretch of SR 9 that extends from Los Gatos to Santa Cruz.

Just east of the city on SR 9 is Henry Cowell Redwoods State Park (see Recreation Areas Chart), where Redwood Grove Trail, an easy .75-mile hike, winds among the giant trees. The trail can be accessed from the park's nature center; for additional information phone (831) 335-4598.

(See map & index p. 365.)

ROARING CAMP STEAM TRAIN is .5 mi. s.e. on Graham Hill Rd. The Redwood Forest Steam Train, a vintage steam locomotive, runs south from Roaring Camp Station pulling open-air and passenger cars along a 6-mile, 75-minute round-trip route through the redwoods of the Santa Cruz Mountains. The conductor discusses forest ecology and local history while you enjoy gorgeous scenery. A barbecue lunch is offered on summer weekends.

Hours: Redwood Forest Steam Train departures daily at 11, 12:30 and 2, early June-late Aug. (also Sat.-Sun. at 3:30, July 2-Labor Day); Mon.-Fri. at 11, Sat.-Sun. at 11, 12:30 and 2, Apr. 30-early June (also at 3:30 during Memorial Day weekend) and day after Labor Day-late Oct. Closed Christmas. Phone ahead to confirm schedule. **Cost:** $29; $22 (ages 2-12); free (ages 0-1 on parent's lap). **Parking:** $10 per private vehicle. **Phone:** (831) 335-4400 for recorded information or (831) 335-4484.

Santa Cruz Beach Train departs Roaring Camp Station for a 3-hour round-trip excursion to the Santa Cruz Beach Boardwalk *(see attraction listing in Santa Cruz p. 363).* Vintage passenger coaches and open-air excursion cars travel through Henry Cowell Redwoods State Park and along the San Lorenzo River gorge. Conductors point out scenic highlights and provide information about the history of the railway line, which was established in 1875.

Hours: Departures daily at 10:15, 12:15 and 2:15, mid-June to mid-Aug.; Sat.-Sun. at 10:15 and 2:15, late Mar. to mid-June and mid-Aug. to late Sept. Phone ahead to confirm schedule. **Cost:** $31; $25 (ages 2-12); free (ages 0-1 on parent's lap). **Parking:** $10 per private vehicle. **Phone:** (831) 335-4484.

FERN RIVER RESORT   831/335-4412 25
▼▼ Cottage. **Address:** 5250 Hwy 9 95018

FERNDALE (C-1) pop. 1,371, elev. 30'

Ferndale, in the lower Eel River Valley along the northern California coast, was settled in 1852 by Vermonters Seth and Stephen Shaw, but it was Danish pioneers who established the town's dairying industry in the 1870s, producing the butter that Ferndale has been identified with ever since.

The ornate Victorian houses known as "butterfat palaces," built by Danish and Portuguese dairymen, reflect the town's past and present. In fact, due to preservation efforts the entire town is designated a state historical landmark. Fern Cottage, 3 miles west on Ocean Avenue, is an 1866 farmhouse containing 19th-century items; phone (707) 786-4835.

South of town via Bluff Street is Russ Park, which features 3 miles of nature trails looping through a 110-acre tract of coastal forest. The park is a popular spot for bird-watchers.

The Ferndale Repertory Theatre, 447 Main St., offers several productions each year, including contemporary American, musical and classic plays; phone (707) 786-5483.

Ferndale Chamber of Commerce: P.O. Box 325, Ferndale, CA 95536-0325. **Phone:** (707) 786-4477.

Self-guiding tours: A souvenir newspaper with information about attractions, events, and walking and driving tours can be obtained at various shops on Main Street.

GINGERBREAD MANSION INN   707/786-4000

Historic Bed & Breakfast

Address: 4000 Berding St 95536 **Location:** Jct Brown and Berding sts, just e of Main St. **Facility:** This extremely well-cared-for 1890s Victorian mansion will take you back in time, yet its upscale features will make you feel at home and relaxed. Afternoon tea and wine is included! 11 units. 3 stories (no elevator), interior corridors. **Parking:** street only. **Activities:** massage. **Guest Services:** complimentary laundry. **Featured Amenity:** full hot breakfast.

VICTORIAN INN   707/786-4949
▼▼▼ Historic Country Inn. **Address:** 400 Ocean Ave 95536

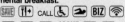
WHERE TO EAT

POPPA JOE'S   707/786-4180
▼▼ American. Casual Dining. **Address:** 409 Main St 95536

VI RESTAURANT   707/786-4950
▼▼▼ American. Casual Dining. **Address:** 400 Ocean Ave 95536

FIREBAUGH pop. 7,549

BEST WESTERN APRICOT INN   559/659-1444

Hotel

(BW) **Best Western.** **AAA Benefit:** Members save up to 15% and earn bonus points!

Address: 46290 W Panoche Rd 93622 **Location:** I-5 exit 368, just nw. **Facility:** 74 units. 2 stories (no elevator), exterior corridors. **Amenities:** *Some:* safes. **Pool:** outdoor. **Guest Services:** coin laundry. **Featured Amenity:** continental breakfast.

FISH CAMP (F-5) pop. 59, elev. 4,990'
• Hotels & Restaurants map & index p. 426
• Part of Yosemite National Park area — see map p. 420

YOSEMITE MOUNTAIN SUGAR PINE RAILROAD is 2 mi. s. on SR 41. One-hour narrated sightseeing tours are offered aboard passenger cars pulled by either restored, vintage Shay steam locomotives or gas-powered Jenny railcars. The narrow-gauge runs through a scenic portion of the Sierra National

(See map & index p. 426.)

Forest. The Moonlight Special excursion features an evening ride, a barbecue dinner and entertainment. Gold panning in authentic sluice boxes is available at the station.

Hours: Shay steam locomotive runs daily, mid-Apr. through Oct. 31 (also some fall and winter holidays), weather permitting; departure times vary. Jenny railcars run daily every half-hour during business hours, mid-Mar. through Oct. 31, and on a limited schedule in winter; check the website or phone for schedule details. Jenny railcar schedule varies when steam train is in operation. Moonlight Special runs Wed. and Sat. evenings during the summer months.

Cost: Steam train fare $27; $15 (ages 3-12). Jenny railcar fare $19; $9.50 (ages 3-12). Moonlight Special fare $63; $36 (ages 3-12). Gold panning $10. Advance reservations are recommended for the Moonlight Special. **Phone:** (559) 683-7273.

THE COTTAGES AT TENAYA LODGE

559/683-6555 **10**

▼▼▼
Hotel

Address: 1122 Hwy 41 93623 **Location:** 2 mi from Yosemite National Park South Gate. **Facility:** 53 cottages. 1-2 stories (no elevator), exterior corridors. **Terms:** check-in 4 pm. **Amenities:** safes. **Dining:** Timberloft Pizzeria, see separate listing. **Pool:** heated outdoor, heated indoor. **Activities:** sauna, hot tub, steamroom, sledding, ice skating, recreation programs, kids club, bicycles, game room, lawn sports, exercise room, spa. **Guest Services:** valet and coin laundry. **Featured Amenity: breakfast buffet.**

TENAYA LODGE AT YOSEMITE

559/683-6555 **9**

▼▼▼▼
Hotel

Address: 1122 Hwy 41 93623 **Location:** 2 mi from Yosemite National Park South Gate. **Facility:** On landscaped grounds surrounded by a national forest, this lodge is convenient to many activities for all seasons. The enormous lobby with its large stone fireplace is a great place to relax. 3-4 stories, interior corridors. **Parking:** on-site and valet. **Terms:** check-in 4 pm. **Amenities:** safes. **Dining:** Jackalope's Bar & Grill, see separate listing. **Pool:** heated outdoor, heated indoor. **Activities:** sauna, hot tub, steamroom, sledding, ice skating, recreation programs, kids club, bicycles, game room, lawn sports, exercise room, spa. **Guest Services:** valet and coin laundry. **Featured Amenity: breakfast buffet.**

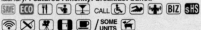

🔗 **For exclusive AAA member savings and benefits:**

AAA.com/hertz

JACKALOPE'S BAR & GRILL 559/683-6555 **9**
▼▼ American. Casual Dining. **Address:** 1122 Hwy 41 93623

TIMBERLOFT PIZZERIA 559/692-8985 **8**
▼ Pizza. Casual Dining. **Address:** 1122 Hwy 41 93623

FOLSOM (E-3) pop. 72,203, elev. 218'
• Hotels p. 80 • Restaurants p. 80
• Hotels & Restaurants map & index p. 224

This former gold-mining town dates from the 1860s, and the restored buildings and houses lining Sutter Street hint at its heyday. The chamber of commerce occupies the old Southern Pacific Depot building at 200 Wool St., where a Southern Pacific railcar, boxcar and caboose are on display. Alongside the cars is the Ashland Freight Depot, believed to be the oldest still-standing station west of the Mississippi River.

A self-guiding tour at Gekkeikan Sake shows how sake is brewed. The facility, at 1136 Sibley St., has a koi pond and a small Japanese garden and also offers tastings of its products; phone (916) 985-3111.

Two miles north of town is the massive granite Folsom State Prison. A museum contains photographs and other items that describe the prison's history. Animal exhibits at the Folsom City Zoo Sanctuary, 403 Stafford St. in Folsom City Park, include black bears, tigers, macaques, pigs, horses and donkeys. For zoo information phone (916) 351-3527. The park offers picnic facilities, a children's play area and a railway.

Jedediah Smith Memorial Trail, also called the American River Bike Trail, is a 32-mile-long paved path paralleling the American River between Folsom and Sacramento. Access points along US 50 provide spots for picnicking, biking, in-line skating, fishing, boating and rafting.

Folsom Chamber of Commerce: 200 Wool St., Folsom, CA 95630. **Phone:** (916) 985-2698.

Shopping: Folsom Premium Outlets, 13000 Folsom Blvd., has more than 80 factory-direct and specialty stores.

FOLSOM POWERHOUSE STATE HISTORIC PARK, on the American River at 9980 Greenback Ln., performed the first long-distance transmission of hydroelectric power to Sacramento in 1895. Now a national landmark as well as a state historic park, it is part of Folsom Lake State Recreation Area *(see Recreation Areas Chart)* and includes an interpretive center. Guided tours of the dam are available. **Hours:** Grounds daily 6 a.m.-9 p.m. Interpretive center open and tours given Wed.-Sun. noon-4. Closed major holidays. **Cost:** Tours free. **Parking:** $10. **Phone:** (916) 985-4843 to arrange powerhouse tours.

(See map & index p. 224.)

COURTYARD BY MARRIOTT SACRAMENTO-FOLSOM
916/984-7624 **58**
♦♦♦ SAVE Hotel. **Address:** 2575
Iron Point Rd 95630

> **AAA Benefit:**
> Members save 5%
> or more!

FAIRFIELD INN & SUITES BY MARRIOTT
SACRAMENTO-FOLSOM
916/984-0100 **60**
♦♦♦ SAVE Hotel. **Address:** 1755
Cavitt Dr 95630

> **AAA Benefit:**
> Members save 5%
> or more!

HILTON GARDEN INN
916/353-1717 **56**
♦♦♦ SAVE Hotel. **Address:** 221 Iron
Point Rd 95630

> **AAA Benefit:**
> Members save up to
> 15%!

LAKE NATOMA INN HOTEL & CONFERENCE CENTER
916/351-1500 **54**
♦♦♦
Hotel

Address: 702 Gold Lake Dr 95630 **Location:** US 50 exit Folsom Blvd, 3 mi n, then 0.5 mi e on Riley St; behind The Lakes Specialty Shopping Center. Adjacent to the American River. **Facility:** 136 units. 4 stories, interior corridors. **Amenities:** safes. **Pool:** heated outdoor. **Activities:** hot tub, trails, exercise room. **Guest Services:** valet laundry.

LARKSPUR LANDING FOLSOM
916/355-1616 **55**
♦♦♦
Extended Stay
Contemporary
Hotel

Address: 121 Iron Point Rd 95630 **Location:** US 50 exit 23 (Folsom Blvd), 0.5 mi n to Iron Point Rd, then just e. **Facility:** 84 efficiencies. 4 stories, interior corridors. **Activities:** hot tub, exercise room. **Guest Services:** complimentary and valet laundry. **Featured Amenity:** continental breakfast.

RESIDENCE INN BY MARRIOTT
916/983-7289 **59**
fyi SAVE Extended Stay Hotel. Under
major renovation, call for details. **Last
Rated:** ♦♦♦ **Address:** 2555 Iron
Point Rd 95630

> **AAA Benefit:**
> Members save 5%
> or more!

STAYBRIDGE SUITES SACRAMENTO-FOLSOM
916/983-7885 **57**
♦♦♦ Extended Stay Hotel. **Address:** 1745 Cavitt Dr 95630

WHERE TO EAT

BACCHUS HOUSE WINE BAR & BISTRO 916/984-7500 **84**
♦♦♦ American. Casual Dining. **Address:** 1004 E Bidwell St, Suite 100 95630

BACK WINE BAR & BISTRO 916/986-9100 **95**
♦♦♦ Small Plates. Casual Dining. **Address:** 230 Palladio Pkwy, Suite 1201 95630

BLUE NAMI 916/983-3388 **92**
♦♦ Japanese Sushi. Casual Dining. **Address:** 330 Palladio Pkwy, Suite 2045 95630

BRISAS DO SUL BRAZILIAN STEAK HOUSE
916/883-2747 **90**
♦♦♦ Brazilian Steak. Casual Dining. **Address:** 380 Palladio Pkwy 95630

BUCKHORN BBQ 916/496-9649 **94**
♦♦ Barbecue. Casual Dining. **Address:** 250 Palladio Pkwy 95630

CASA RAMOS MEXICAN RESTAURANT 916/355-1600 **88**
♦♦ Mexican. Casual Dining. **Address:** 400 Iron Point Rd 95630

CHICAGO FIRE 916/353-0140 **80**
♦♦ Pizza. Casual Dining. **Address:** 614 Sutter St, Suite C 95630

CHICAGO FIRE 916/984-0140 **91**
♦♦ Pizza. Casual Dining. **Address:** 310 Palladio Pkwy 95630

THE FAT RABBIT PUBLIC HOUSE 916/985-3289 **83**
♦♦ Irish. Casual Dining. **Address:** 825 Sutter St 95630

HECKLE ALEHOUSE & EATERY 916/790-8883 **76**
♦ Comfort Food. Casual Dining. **Address:** 705 Gold Lake Dr 95630

KAREN'S BAKERY CAFE & CATERING 916/985-2665 **79**
♦♦ Breads/Pastries Sandwiches. Quick Serve. **Address:** 705 Gold Lake Dr, Suite 340 95630

LAND OCEAN NEW AMERICAN GRILL 916/983-7000 **87**
♦♦♦ Steak Seafood. Fine Dining. **Address:** 2720 E Bidwell St 95630

LAZY DOG RESTAURANT & BAR 916/378-4660 **93**
♦♦ American. Casual Dining. **Address:** 300 Palladio Pkwy 95630

MANDERES 916/986-9655 **85**
♦♦ American. Casual Dining. **Address:** 1004 E Bidwell St 95630

MEXQUITE MEXICAN CUISINE & TEQUILA LOUNGE
916/984-8607 **77**
♦♦ Mexican. Casual Dining. **Address:** 25095 Blue Ravine Rd 95630

MIKUNI JAPANESE RESTAURANT & SUSHI BAR
916/934-5250 **96**
♦♦ Japanese Sushi. Casual Dining. **Address:** 185 Placerville Rd 95630

PETE'S RESTAURANT & BREWHOUSE 916/988-8812 **74**
♦♦ Pizza. Casual Dining. **Address:** 6608 Folsom-Auburn Rd 95630

PIZZERIA CLASSICO 916/351-1430 **81**
♦♦ Pizza. Casual Dining. **Address:** 702 Sutter St, Suite A 95630

SCOTT'S SEAFOOD GRILL & BAR 916/989-6711 **75**
♦♦♦ Seafood. Casual Dining. **Address:** 9611 Greenback Ln 95630

SUTTER STREET GRILL 916/985-4323 **82**
♦♦ American. Casual Dining. **Address:** 811 Sutter St 95630

SUTTER STREET STEAKHOUSE 916/351-9100 **78**
♦♦♦ Steak. Fine Dining. **Address:** 604 Sutter St 95630

THAI PARADISE 916/984-8988 **89**
♦♦ Thai. Casual Dining. **Address:** 2770 E Bidwell St 95630

VISCONTI'S RISTORANTE 916/983-5181 **86**
♦♦ Italian. Casual Dining. **Address:** 2700 E Bidwell St, Suite 700 95630

FORESTVILLE (A-6) pop. 3,293, elev. 3,228'
• Part of Wine Country area — see map p. 405

While Sonoma County is well known for its vineyards, just as celebrated are the farms that produce a bounty of fruits and vegetables. In the early 20th century apples, particularly Gravenstein apples, were planted more extensively than grapes. Although many apple orchards were cut down to clear land for grapevines, enough survived to ensure that the tasty and nutritious fruit remains one of the Russian River Valley's commercially important agricultural products.

Pies made with organic Gravenstein apples are just one of the yummy specialties you can purchase at Kozlowski Farms, 5566 Gravenstein Hwy. (SR 116). Carmen and Tony Kozlowski purchased their apple farm in 1949, and the second generation of Kozlowskis runs the farm—one of the first in the county to be certified organic—as well as the family specialty food business.

Visitors are welcome at the farm, where you can dip spoons into jams, salad dressings and barbecue sauces in a "tasting room." In addition to pies and fruit tarts, the retail store sells a huge variety of gourmet products—from sugar-free red raspberry jam and apple butter to apricot mango preserves and pomegranate jelly—as well as Russian River Valley Pinot Noir wines. The store is open daily 9-5; closed Jan. 1, Easter, Thanksgiving and Christmas. Phone (800) 473-2767.

FARMHOUSE RESTAURANT   707/887-3300
♥♥♥♥ New American. Fine Dining. **Address:** 7871 River Rd 95436

RUSSIAN RIVER PUB   707/887-7932
♥♥ Burgers Sandwiches. Casual Dining. **Address:** 11829 River Rd 95436

FORT BRAGG (D-1) pop. 7,273, elev. 80'
• Hotels p. 82 • Restaurants p. 84
• Part of Wine Country area — see map p. 405

Fort Bragg was established in 1857 to oversee the Mendocino Indian Reservation; when the reservation was moved, the fort was abandoned and the settlement grew into a lumber and port town. Fishing and whale-watching cruises depart from Port Noyo, a small commercial fishing port at the south end of town. SR 1, the Pacific Coast Highway, is especially scenic as it winds through Mendocino County.

Mendocino Coast Chamber of Commerce: 217 S. Main St., P.O. Box 1141, Fort Bragg, CA 95437. **Phone:** (707) 961-6300.

THE GUEST HOUSE MUSEUM, 343 N. Main St., is the 1892 three-story Victorian home built by the city's first mayor, who also was the founder of the Union Lumber Co. It became the company's "guest house" in 1912. Local history is depicted inside, while outside are locomotives and steam donkeys, a type of engine used in the logging industry. The nearby Fort Building is the only structure remaining from the town's 1857-64 military post; it contains a model of the original structure and historical artifacts.

Hours: Tues.-Fri. 11-2, Sat.-Sun. 10-4, Mon. 1-3, June-Oct.; Thurs.-Sun. 11-2, rest of year. Schedule is dependent on volunteer availability; phone ahead to confirm schedule. Closed Jan. 1, Labor Day, Thanksgiving and Christmas. **Cost:** Donations. **Phone:** (707) 964-4251.

MACKERRICHER STATE PARK is 3 mi. n. via MacKerricher Park Rd. to Mill Creek Rd. The park extends approximately 9 miles along the Pacific. The southern portion comprises a series of rocky headlands separated by small coves; the northern half consists of sandy, gently sloping beaches.

An overpass leading to the Laguna Point boardwalk crosses freshwater Lake Cleone. This haul road once carried steam-driven trains to the Union Lumber Company mill in Fort Bragg; today walkers, joggers, cyclists and horseback riders use it. The boardwalk runs along the shoreline for about a mile. Harbor seals bask in the sun on rocks near the point, and from mid-December to early April the boardwalk overlooks are prime spots for spotting gray whales as they migrate from the Bering Sea south to Baja California.

A forest of Bishop pine and Douglas fir grows in the vicinity of the lake and park campgrounds, and a variety of coastal plants like sand verbena and beach morning glory blanket the dunes along the beaches. The Ten Mile Beach Trail from Laguna Point to Ten Mile River offers hikers the opportunity to explore headlands, wetlands, tide pools, sand dunes and meadows. *See Recreation Areas Chart.*

Time: Allow 1 hour minimum. **Hours:** Daily dawn-10 p.m. **Cost:** Free. **Phone:** (707) 964-8898.
🏕 ⊗ 🎣 🏕

MENDOCINO COAST BOTANICAL GARDENS is 1 mi. s. on SR 1. This 47-acre facility is one of the few gardens located directly on an ocean shore. A half-mile stroll begins at a manicured perennial garden. Pathways wind past succulents, camellias, rhododendrons, rose and dahlia gardens, and a coastal forest of pines, magnolias and ferns that leads to bluffs overlooking the Pacific.

This is a seasonal garden, with something to delight the eye at any time of year. Dahlias, heritage roses and perennials are at their peak in summer. Summer and fall is harvest time at the demonstration vegetable and herb garden. More than 150 kinds of wild mushrooms appear beginning in late fall. Mature camellia shrubs are in bloom from fall throughout the winter.

You'll see unusual plants from all over the world like Faber's fir, native to western China. This conifer produces cones that are a lovely blue-purple color. Honeywort, a drought-tolerant, herbaceous annual, is also called the blue shrimp plant for the appearance of its tubular purple flowers (which have a honey-like aroma) and blue flower bracts.

Rhododendrons are the gardens' signature plant; the climate is optimal for cultivation, and there are species from around the world as well as varieties hybridized by local rhododendron enthusiasts. They range from shrubs to 20-foot-tall trees, with exquisite flowers in many different colors. The rhodies are in bloom from early April to mid-May; spring is also the time when coastal bluffs are dotted with California poppies and other wildflowers.

The seaside Cliff House off the Coastal Bluff Trail is a great spot to contemplate the ocean, especially for whale watching during winter and spring. A retail nursery on the premises sells a variety of native plants. Art in the Gardens, the first Saturday in August, features art exhibits, food, wine and music with the gardens' summer beauty as a backdrop. Each November the Festival of Lights transforms the gardens into a winter wonderland of luminescent displays.

Time: Allow 2 hours minimum. **Hours:** Daily 9-5, Mar.-Oct.; 9-4, rest of year. Closed first Sat. in Aug. (except for those attending the Art in the Gardens fundraiser), the Sat. after Labor Day, Thanksgiving and Christmas. **Cost:** $15; $12 (ages 65+); $8 (ages 6-14); free (ages 0-5 and active military with ID). Electric carts are available for a fee (except in wet weather). **Phone:** (707) 964-4352.

BEACHCOMBER MOTEL AND SPA BY THE SEA
707/964-2402
 Motel. **Address:** 1111 N Main St 95437 *(See ad p. 83.)*

BEACH HOUSE INN   707/961-1700
 Motel. **Address:** 100 Pudding Creek Rd 95437 *(See ad p. 83.)*

BEST WESTERN VISTA MANOR LODGE   707/964-4776

Motel

 AAA Benefit: Members save up to 15% and earn bonus points!

Address: 1100 N Main St 95437 **Location:** 1 mi n on SR 1. **Facility:** 55 units, some cottages. 2 stories (no elevator), exterior corridors. **Pool:** heated indoor. **Featured Amenity: continental breakfast.**

COUNTRY INN BED & BREAKFAST   707/964-3737
Bed & Breakfast. **Address:** 632 N Main St 95437

EMERALD DOLPHIN INN & MINI GOLF   707/964-6699

Hotel

Address: 1211 S Main St 95437 **Location:** On SR 1; at Harbor View Dr. **Facility:** 43 units. 2 stories (no elevator), exterior corridors. **Amenities:** safes. **Activities:** miniature golf, game room, massage. **Featured Amenity: continental breakfast.**

HARBOR LITE LODGE   707/964-0221
Motel. **Address:** 120 N Harbor Dr 95437

HOLIDAY INN EXPRESS   707/964-1100

Hotel

Address: 250 Hwy 20 95437 **Location:** On SR 20, just e of jct SR 1. **Facility:** 54 units. 3 stories, interior/exterior corridors. **Pool:** heated indoor. **Activities:** hot tub, exercise room. **Featured Amenity: full hot breakfast.**

NORTH CLIFF HOTEL   707/962-2500
Hotel. **Address:** 1005 S Main St 95437

SUPER 8 FORT BRAGG   707/964-4003
Motel. **Address:** 888 S Main St 95437

AAA.com/maps—Dream, plan, go
with AAA travel planning tools

SURF & SAND LODGE   707/964-9383

 Motel. **Address:** 1131 N Main St 95437 *(See ad this page.)*

CUCINA VERONA   707/964-6844
 Northern Italian. Casual Dining. **Address:** 124 E Laurel St 95437

D'AURELIOS   707/964-4227
 Italian. Casual Dining. **Address:** 438 S Franklin St 95437

DAVID'S RESTAURANT AND DELICATESSEN   707/964-1946
 American. Casual Dining. **Address:** 163 Boatyard Dr 95437

DJANGO'S ROUGH BAR AND GRILL   707/962-0100
 Seafood. Gastropub. **Address:** 32096 N Harbor Dr 95437

EGGHEADS RESTAURANT   707/964-5005
 Breakfast Sandwiches. Casual Dining. **Address:** 326 N Main St 95437

MAYAN FUSION RESTAURANT   707/961-0211
 Latin American Fusion. Casual Dining. **Address:** 418 N Main St 95437

NORTH COAST BREWING CO. TAPROOM & GRILL   707/964-3400
 American. Casual Dining. **Address:** 444 N Main St 95437

NOYO RIVER GRILL   707/962-9050
 American. Casual Dining. **Address:** 32150 N Harbor Dr 95437

PIACI PUB & PIZZERIA   707/961-1133
 Italian Pizza. Casual Dining. **Address:** 120 W Redwood Ave 95437

SEA VALLEY CAFE   707/200-4744
 Asian Fusion. Casual Dining. **Address:** 301 N Main St 95437

SILVER'S AT THE WHARF   707/964-4283
 Seafood. Casual Dining. **Address:** 32260 N Harbor Dr 95437

FORTUNA (C-1) pop. 11,926, elev. 51'

Established in 1875 and named Springville after the numerous springs in the surrounding hills, Fortuna was renamed Slide and finally Fortuna by its "fortunate" citizens. Fortuna is within the Redwood Empire, a name referring to the string of majestically scenic coastal counties extending from San Francisco Bay north to the Oregon border.

Fortuna Chamber of Commerce: 735 14th St., Fortuna, CA 95540. **Phone:** (707) 725-3959 or (800) 426-8166.

CHAPMAN'S GEM AND MINERAL SHOP AND MUSEUM, 4 mi. s. off US 101, has displays of fossils, gems, minerals, petrified wood and Native American artifacts. **Time:** Allow 30 minutes minimum. **Hours:** Daily 10-5. Closed Jan. 1, Easter, Thanksgiving and Christmas. **Cost:** Donations. **Phone:** (707) 725-2714.

AAA.com/campgrounds—

For overnights under the stars

BEST WESTERN COUNTRY INN
707/725-6822

Motel

 Best Western. **AAA Benefit:** Members save up to 15% and earn bonus points!

Address: 2025 Riverwalk Dr 95540 **Location:** US 101 exit 687 (Kenmar Rd), just w. **Facility:** 67 units, some two bedrooms. 2 stories (no elevator), exterior corridors. **Terms:** check-in 4 pm. **Pool:** heated outdoor, heated indoor. **Activities:** hot tub. **Guest Services:** coin laundry. **Featured Amenity: breakfast buffet.**

FORTUNA SUPER 8
707/725-2888
Motel. **Address:** 1805 Alamar Way 95540

THE REDWOOD FORTUNA RIVERWALK HOTEL
707/725-5500
Hotel. **Address:** 1859 Alamar Way 95540

WHERE TO EAT

EEL RIVER BREWING COMPANY
707/725-2739
American. Casual Dining. **Address:** 1777 Alamar Way 95540

LA COSTA MEXICAN RESTAURANT
707/725-9416
Mexican. Casual Dining. **Address:** 664 S Fortuna Blvd 95540

REDWOOD CAFE
707/725-3998
American. Casual Dining. **Address:** 1206 Main St 95540

TACO LOCO
707/725-5546
Mexican. Quick Serve. **Address:** 955 Main St 95540

FOSTER CITY pop. 30,567
• **Hotels & Restaurants map & index p. 316**
• **Part of San Francisco area — see map p. 243**

COURTYARD BY MARRIOTT SAN MATEO FOSTER CITY
650/377-0600 **55**

Hotel

COURTYARD **AAA Benefit:** Members save 5% or more!

Address: 550 Shell Blvd 94404 **Location:** SR 92 exit Foster City Blvd S; se of jct US 101 and SR 92. **Facility:** 147 units. 3 stories, interior corridors. **Pool:** heated indoor. **Activities:** hot tub, exercise room. **Guest Services:** valet and coin laundry, boarding pass kiosk.

CROWNE PLAZA HOTEL FOSTER CITY-SAN MATEO
650/570-5700 **53**
Hotel. **Address:** 1221 Chess Dr 94404

TOWNEPLACE SUITES BY MARRIOTT SAN MATEO - FOSTER CITY
650/539-4600 **54**
Extended Stay Hotel. **Address:** 1299 Chess Dr 94404

AAA Benefit: Members save 5% or more!

WHERE TO EAT

ABC SEAFOOD RESTAURANT
650/328-2288 **41**
Cantonese Dim Sum. Casual Dining. **Address:** 973 E Hillsdale Blvd 94404

FREMONT (D-9) pop. 214,089, elev. 53'
• **Hotels p. 86** • **Restaurants p. 86**

Spanish priests and native Ohlone Indians founded a mission in the Fremont area in 1797. Pioneer John Fremont, for whom the city is named, was apparently so taken with the mission that he offered to buy the adjacent property on which to build his house. The gold rush transformed the mission-based trade and agricultural outpost into a boisterous supply stop for miners, and the use of salt to extract silver from the Comstock Lode led to the development of salt production facilities along San Francisco Bay.

The presence of artesian springs spurred the development of resort facilities. Essanay Studio began a 4-year production stint in 1912, and Charlie Chaplin filmed "The Tramp" here in 1915.

Fremont Chamber of Commerce: 39488 Stevenson Pl., Suite 100, Fremont, CA 94539. **Phone:** (510) 795-2244.

DON EDWARDS SAN FRANCISCO BAY NATIONAL WILDLIFE REFUGE, on Marshlands Rd., was the country's first urban national wildlife refuge. Named for a congressman who spearheaded efforts to preserve the bay's wetlands, it covers some 30,000 acres at the southern end of San Francisco Bay. The area is a sanctuary for endangered species and for migratory shorebirds and waterfowl negotiating the Pacific Flyway. More than 280 bird species take advantage of mudflat, salt marsh, salt pond and vernal pool habitats.

The visitor center near the Dumbarton Bridge has wildlife exhibits and offers views of tidal sloughs and salt marshes. Two of the more popular trails are the Tidelands Trail and the LaRiviere Marsh Trail; the best time to spot wildlife is October through April.

Naturalists conduct programs and guided walks on weekends. The visitor center has schedules as well as information and regulations regarding fishing, hunting and boating within the refuge. **Hours:** Trails daily dawn-dusk. Visitor center open Wed.-Sat. 11-4:30. Closed federal holidays. **Cost:** Free. **Phone:** (510) 792-0222, ext. 363.

MISSION SAN JOSE CHAPEL AND MUSEUM, 43300 Mission Blvd., was founded in 1797 by Father Fermín Francisco de Lasuén. The original adobe structure was destroyed by an 1868 earthquake. The interior of the reconstructed church, based on church inventories from the 1830s, is unusually elegant, containing crystal chandeliers, murals, religious paintings and a gold leaf altar. Several statues, the baptismal font and the mission bells remain from the original structure.

The mission contains a small museum, which displays old paintings, photographs, mission period artifacts and exhibits about the Ohlone Indians and the mission restoration. **Hours:** Daily 10-5. Closed Jan. 1, Easter, Thanksgiving and Christmas. **Cost:** $5; $3 (students with ID). **Phone:** (510) 657-1797.

BEST WESTERN PLUS GARDEN COURT INN
510/792-4300

Hotel

 Best Western PLUS.

AAA Benefit: Members save up to 15% and earn bonus points!

Address: 5400 Mowry Ave 94538 **Location:** I-880 exit 17 (Mowry Ave), just se. **Facility:** 123 units. 3 stories, interior corridors. **Pool:** outdoor. **Activities:** hot tub, exercise room. **Featured Amenity:** breakfast buffet.

COURTYARD BY MARRIOTT FREMONT SILICON VALLEY
510/656-1800

Hotel. **Address:** 47000 Lakeview Blvd 94538

AAA Benefit: Members save 5% or more!

FREMONT MARRIOTT SILICON VALLEY
510/413-3700

Hotel. **Address:** 46100 Landing Pkwy 94538

AAA Benefit: Members save 5% or more!

HAMPTON INN BY HILTON FREMONT/SILICON VALLEY
510/498-1900

Hotel. **Address:** 46500 Landing Pkwy 94538

AAA Benefit: Members save up to 15%!

HOLIDAY INN EXPRESS & SUITES FREMONT MILPITAS
510/651-7373

Hotel. **Address:** 42200 Albrae St 94538

HYATT PLACE FREMONT/SILICON VALLEY
510/623-6000

Hotel

HYATT PLACE

AAA Benefit: Members save up to 10%!

Address: 3101 W Warren Ave 94538 **Location:** I-880 exit 12 (Warren Ave), just nw. **Facility:** 151 units. 7 stories, interior corridors. **Pool:** heated outdoor. **Activities:** exercise room. **Guest Services:** valet laundry, area transportation. **Featured Amenity:** breakfast buffet.

LA QUINTA INN & SUITES BY WYNDHAM FREMONT/SILICON VALLEY
510/445-0808

Hotel. **Address:** 46200 Landing Pkwy 94538

RESIDENCE INN BY MARRIOTT FREMONT SILICON VALLEY
510/794-5900

Extended Stay Hotel. **Address:** 5400 Farwell Pl 94536

AAA Benefit: Members save 5% or more!

BRONCO BILLY'S PIZZA 510/792-1070

Pizza. Casual Dining. **Address:** 37651 Niles Blvd 94536

FALAFEL, ETC. 510/795-7170

Middle Eastern. Quick Serve. **Address:** 39200 Fremont Blvd 94538

THE GREATROOM 510/413-3700

American. Casual Dining. **Address:** 46100 Landing Pkwy 94538

MARKET BROILER GRILLE 510/791-8675

Seafood. Casual Dining. **Address:** 43406 Christy St 94538

MINERVA'S RESTAURANT & CATERING 510/793-9602

American. Casual Dining. **Address:** 37463 Fremont Blvd 94536

P.F. CHANG'S CHINA BISTRO 510/657-1400

Chinese. Fine Dining. **Address:** 43316 Christy St 94538

SAKI'S SPIN-A-YARN STEAKHOUSE 510/656-9141

American. Fine Dining. **Address:** 45915 Warm Springs Blvd 94539

SIMPLY THAI 2 510/573-0083

Thai. Casual Dining. **Address:** 43844 Pacific Commons Blvd 94538

WORLD GOURMET BUFFET RESTAURANT 510/490-6888

Chinese. Buffet Style. **Address:** 6010 Stevenson Blvd 94538

FRESNO (G-4) pop. 494,665, elev. 294'
• Hotels p. 91 • Restaurants p. 92
• Hotels & Restaurants map & index p. 89

Fresno has been a melting pot of cultures from its earliest years, beginning with Chinese railroad workers and Scandinavian settlers, later joined by Germans, Japanese, Armenians and Latinos. Many of these early immigrants initially came to work the land. More than a million acres in the San Joaquin Valley are irrigated, producing cotton, grapes, oranges, other fruits and vegetables that collectively make Fresno County one of the nation's agricultural leaders.

The Tower District is the city's pre-eminent arts and nightlife neighborhood. Centered at the intersection of Olive and Wishon avenues, it's filled with shops, restaurants, nightclubs, theaters and art galleries. The district takes its name from the Tower Theatre, 815 E. Olive Ave., a former movie palace-turned-performing arts center. This Art Deco jewel presents concerts, films, comedians and traveling shows; for schedule information and ticket reservations phone the box office at (559) 485-9050.

The Kearney Mansion Museum, 7160 W. Kearney Blvd. in Kearney Park, contains many original furnishings and wall coverings. Guided tours are offered Saturday and Sunday; phone (559) 441-0862. Also of historical interest is the 1889 Meux Home Museum, 1007 R St. at Tulare Street. Guided tours are also offered Friday through Sunday; phone (559) 233-8007.

Within Woodward Park, on N. Friant Road along the San Joaquin River, is the Shinzen Friendship Garden *(see attraction listing)*. The park also has an equestrian trail, an amphitheater, children's playgrounds, picnic areas, a lake and ponds, and 5 miles of multipurpose trails that offer good opportunities for bird-watching.

The Pacific Coast League Fresno Grizzlies play Triple-A baseball at Chukchansi Park, downtown at 1800 Tulare St. It has an enviable backdrop courtesy of the distant Sierra Nevada mountains. The United Soccer League Fresno Fuego play home games at the stadium as well. Phone (559) 320-8497.

The Fresno County Blossom Trail, southeast of the city, is a 62-mile, self-guiding drive trip route that winds among stone fruit orchards, groves of citrus and almond trees, and vineyards. The best time to see the fruit and nut trees in full bloom is late February through mid-March; the fruit ripens in the summer months. Drip irrigation hoses ensure that the trees not only survive but thrive in a region that receives an average annual precipitation of less than 15 inches. For more information contact the Fresno County Office of Tourism; phone (559) 600-4271.

One of the points of interest along the Blossom Trail is Selma, 15 miles south of Fresno. An agricultural powerhouse in its own right despite being a much smaller city, this San Joaquin Valley community was founded in 1880. Early settlers grew wheat, but they soon switched to the cultivation of fruit trees, which—with the aid of irrigation—grow exceptionally well in the sandy soil and Mediterranean climate.

Selma became known as the "Home of the Peach," and grapes were also successful; by the mid-20th century the town was producing more than 90 percent of the world's raisin crop and had a new nickname: "Raisin Capital of the World." Sun-Maid Growers of California, one of a dozen area raisin packers, has a retail store in nearby Kingsburg at 13525 S. Bethel Ave.; phone (559) 897-6363.

Fresno/Clovis Convention & Visitors Bureau: 1180 E. Shaw Ave., Suite 201, Fresno, CA 93710. **Phone:** (559) 981-5500.

Shopping: Fashion Fair Mall, 1 block east of SR 41 on Shaw Avenue between Fresno and First streets, has JCPenney, Macy's and more than 140 specialty stores. Fig Garden Village, at Palm and Shaw avenues, features about 40 specialty shops including Banana Republic, Chico's, J. Crew, Pottery Barn and Williams-Sonoma, as well as about a dozen casual eateries.

River Park, N. Blackstone Avenue near SR 41 (Yosemite Freeway), is a shopping village with stores, restaurants and entertainment in three sections, all centered around a landscaped courtyard. Shops include Ann Taylor LOFT, buybuy Baby, Macy's and REI.

ISLAND WATERPARK is w. off SR 99 Shaw Ave. exit at 6099 W. Barstow Ave. The park has waterslides, including a three-story drop slide; a lazy river; a wave pool; and a children's area. Locker, tube and cabana rentals are available.

Time: Allow 1 hour minimum. **Hours:** Park opens Sun.-Fri. at 11, Sat. at 10:30, mid-June to late Aug.; schedule varies mid-May to mid-June and late Aug. to mid-Sept. Closing times vary; phone ahead. After-dark hours for ages 21+ Fri.-Sat. 8 p.m.-midnight. Phone ahead to confirm schedule. **Cost:** $32.99; $23.99 (under 48 inches tall, ages 62+ and to all after 3 p.m.); free (ages 0-2). After-dark admission $22.99. **Parking:** $5. **Phone:** (559) 277-6800. 🍴

ROEDING PARK is e. of SR 99 via the Olive Ave. or Belmont Ave. exits. In addition to recreational facilities, it contains the Fresno Chaffee Zoo, the Rotary Storyland and Playland, and the Japanese-American War Memorial. **Time:** Allow 1 hour, 30 minutes minimum. **Hours:** Daily 7 a.m.-10 p.m., Apr.-Oct.; 7-7, rest of year. **Cost:** $5 per private vehicle; $3 (ages 65+ per private vehicle); $7 (holidays). **Phone:** (559) 621-2900.

Fresno Chaffee Zoo, on Belmont Ave. in Roeding Park, houses mammals, birds and reptiles in a setting of dense vegetation and winding pathways. The computerized Reptile House modifies temperature, humidity and light cycles to mimic the native environment of each species. South American plants and animals share the Rain Forest habitat.

(See map & index p. 89.)

Hours: Gates open daily at 8:30 a.m.; closing times range from 4 to 7 depending on the time of year. Closed Christmas. Phone ahead to confirm schedule. **Cost:** Zoo admission $10; $5.50 (ages 2-11 and 62+). Under 16 must be with an adult. Park admission $5 per private vehicle; $3 (ages 65+ per private vehicle); $7 (holidays). **Phone:** (559) 498-5910. 🍴

SHINZEN FRIENDSHIP GARDEN is in Woodward Park, which is bordered by SR 41 (Yosemite Frwy.), N. Friant Rd. and E. Audubon Dr. The park entrance is on Audubon Dr., just w. of Friant Rd. This serene 5-acre garden was established to honor Fresno's sister city of Kochi, Japan.

Divided into sectors according to the four seasons, the garden has plantings representative of each time of year. The garden features a lake, koi pond, stream beds and waterfalls, traditional Japanese bridges, a grove of ume (Japanese apricot) trees and a teahouse. Paved pathways wind among pines, evergreens and seasonally blooming azaleas, camellias and flowering crab apple, cherry and tulip trees. Guided tours are available; advance reservations are required.

Time: Allow 1 hour minimum. **Hours:** Mon.-Fri. 4-7, Sat.-Sun. and holidays 10-7, Apr.-Sept.; Sat.-Sun. and holidays 10-5, rest of year. **Cost:** Park admission $5 per private vehicle; $3 (ages 65+ per private vehicle); $7 (holidays). Garden $5; $1 (ages 4-14, ages 65+ and students with ID); $7 (family, up to five people). **Phone:** (559) 840-1264.

SIMONIAN FARMS OLD TOWN is at 2629 S. Clovis Ave. Family owned and operated, the business started as a fruit stand in 1901, which is now adjacent to the museum and sells farm-direct fruits and vegetables as well as local wine, honey and specialty foods. The facades of a general store, church, gas station, diner, post office, barber shop and livery stable preserve the history of the Central Valley, and the museum contains a time line depicting regional history. Antique tractors and farm equipment are on display outside.

Family-oriented activities include an animated Route 66 shooting gallery and gold mining. Kids can check out the many varieties of nostalgic candy, old-fashioned soda pop and Fresno State University ice cream by the scoop while parents enjoy wine tastings. **Time:** Allow 45 minutes minimum. **Hours:** Daily 9-6. Closed Jan. 1, Thanksgiving and Christmas. **Cost:** Free. **Phone:** (559) 237-2294. 🍴 ⛲

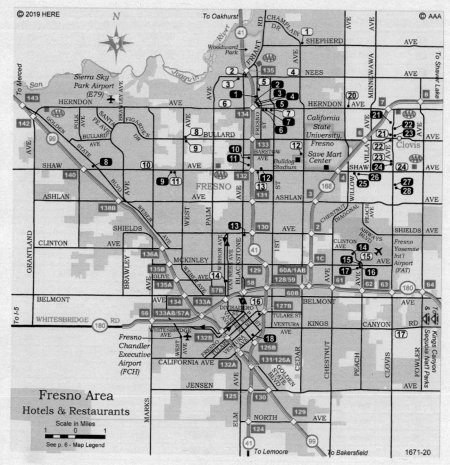

© 2019 HERE

© AAA

Fresno Area
Hotels & Restaurants

Scale in Miles
1   0   1

See p. 6 - Map Legend

1671-20

Fresno Area

This index helps you "spot" where approved hotels and restaurants are located on the corresponding detailed maps. Restaurant price range is a combination of lunch and/or dinner. Turn to the listing page for more information and consult display ads for special promotions.

🔗 **For more details, rates and reservations: AAA.com/travelguides/hotels**

FRESNO

Map Page	Hotels	Diamond Rated	Member Savings	Page
1 this page	**Hyatt Place Fresno**	💎💎💎	✔	91
2 this page	TownePlace Suites by Marriott	💎💎💎	✔	92
3 this page	Holiday Inn Express-River Park	💎💎💎		91
4 this page	**La Quinta Inn & Suites by Wyndham Fresno Riverpark**	💎💎💎	✔	91
5 this page	Hampton Inn & Suites Fresno	💎💎💎	✔	91
6 this page	SpringHill Suites by Marriott Fresno	💎💎💎	✔	92
7 this page	Homewood Suites by Hilton	💎💎💎	✔	91
8 this page	La Quinta Inn by Wyndham Fresno Northwest	💎💎💎		92
9 this page	Hotel Piccadilly	💎💎		91
10 this page	Residence Inn by Marriott	💎💎💎	✔	92

FRESNO (cont'd)

Map Page	Hotels (cont'd)	Diamond Rated	Member Savings	Page
11 p. 89	Courtyard by Marriott-Shaw Ave	◆◆◆	✔	91
12 p. 89	Best Western Plus Fresno Inn	◆◆◆	✔	91
13 p. 89	Best Western Village Inn	◆◆	✔	91
14 p. 89	Wyndham Garden Fresno Airport	◆◆◆		92
15 p. 89	Piccadilly Inn Airport	◆◆	✔	92
16 p. 89	Best Western Plus Fresno Airport Hotel	◆◆◆	✔	91
17 p. 89	Fairfield by Marriott Fresno Yosemite International Airport	◆◆◆	✔	91
18 p. 89	DoubleTree by Hilton Fresno Convention Center	◆◆◆	✔	91

Map Page	Restaurants	Diamond Rated	Cuisine	Price Range	Page
1 p. 89	Yosemite Ranch Steak, Seafood & Roast House	◆◆	Steak Seafood	$16-$50	92
2 p. 89	Westwoods BBQ & Spice Co	◆◆	Barbecue	$11-$15	92
3 p. 89	Pismo's Coastal Grill	◆◆	Seafood	$14-$46	92
4 p. 89	Batter Up Pancakes	◆◆	Breakfast	$8-$18	92
5 p. 89	Sal's Mexican Restaurant	◆◆	Mexican	$7-$18	92
6 p. 89	Red Apple Cafe	◆◆	Breakfast	$9-$14	92
7 p. 89	Thai Royal Orchid	◆◆	Thai	$7-$15	92
8 p. 89	Max's Bistro and Bar	◆◆◆	California	$12-$36	92
9 p. 89	Manhattan Steakhouse and Bar	◆◆◆	American	$13-$25	92
10 p. 89	Diana's Restaurant	◆◆	Armenian	$9-$16	92
11 p. 89	The Annex Kitchen	◆◆◆	Italian	$13-$40	92
12 p. 89	Tacos Marquitos	◆	Mexican	$7-$9	92
13 p. 89	Huong Lan	◆◆	Vietnamese	$6-$14	92
14 p. 89	Veni Vidi Vici	◆◆	New American	$26-$37	92
15 p. 89	Steak & Anchor	◆◆	Steak	$11-$38	92
16 p. 89	Mediterranean Grill and Cafe	◆◆	Mediterranean	$7-$13	92
17 p. 89	Javier's	◆◆	Mexican	$8-$13	92

CLOVIS

Map Page	Hotels	Diamond Rated	Member Savings	Page
21 p. 89	Fairfield Inn & Suites by Marriott-Fresno/Clovis	◆◆◆	✔	62
22 p. 89	Comfort Suites	◆◆◆	✔	62
23 p. 89	Best Western Clovis Cole	◆◆	✔	62
24 p. 89	La Quinta Inn & Suites by Wyndham Clovis Old Town	◆◆◆		63
25 p. 89	Holiday Inn Express Hotel & Suites	◆◆◆		63
26 p. 89	Hilton Garden Inn Clovis	◆◆◆	✔	63
27 p. 89	Homewood Suites by Hilton Fresno Airport/Clovis, CA	◆◆◆	✔	63
28 p. 89	Hampton Inn & Suites Clovis-Airport North	◆◆◆	✔	62

Map Page	Restaurants	Diamond Rated	Cuisine	Price Range	Page
20 p. 89	The Mad Duck Neighborhood Grill & Taphouse	◆◆	American	$10-$15	63
21 p. 89	Luna Pizzeria and Italian Restaurant	◆◆	Italian	$10-$23	63
22 p. 89	House of JuJu	◆◆	Burgers	$6-$14	63
23 p. 89	Pho 2006	◆◆	Vietnamese	$9-$15	63
24 p. 89	Andiamo Ristorante Italiano	◆◆	Italian	$8-$30	63

BEST WESTERN PLUS FRESNO AIRPORT HOTEL
559/251-5200

 Hotel

AAA Benefit: Members save up to 15% and earn bonus points!

Address: 1551 N Peach Ave 93727 **Location:** SR 180 exit Peach Ave, 0.8 mi n. Across from the Fresno Airport. **Facility:** 106 units. 4 stories, interior corridors. **Pool:** outdoor. **Activities:** hot tub, picnic facilities, exercise room. **Guest Services:** coin laundry, area transportation. **Featured Amenity: breakfast buffet.**

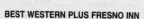

BEST WESTERN PLUS FRESNO INN
559/229-5811

 Hotel

AAA Benefit: Members save up to 15% and earn bonus points!

Address: 480 E Shaw Ave 93710 **Location:** SR 41 exit Shaw Ave, just e; jct Fresno St. **Facility:** 55 units. 3 stories, interior corridors. **Pool:** outdoor. **Activities:** exercise room. **Guest Services:** coin laundry. **Featured Amenity: breakfast buffet.**

BEST WESTERN VILLAGE INN
559/226-2110

 Hotel

AAA Benefit: Members save up to 15% and earn bonus points!

Address: 3110 N Blackstone Ave 93703 **Location:** SR 41 exit 130 (Shields Ave), just w; jct Shields and Blackstone aves. **Facility:** 151 units. 2 stories (no elevator), interior corridors. **Pool:** outdoor. **Featured Amenity: breakfast buffet.**

COURTYARD BY MARRIOTT-SHAW AVE   559/221-6000
Hotel. **Address:** 140 E Shaw Ave 93710

AAA Benefit: Members save 5% or more!

DOUBLETREE BY HILTON FRESNO CONVENTION CENTER
559/268-1000

 Hotel

 DOUBLETREE BY HILTON

AAA Benefit: Members save up to 15%!

Address: 2233 Ventura St 93721 **Location:** SR 99 exit Ventura St, 0.5 mi e. Adjacent to convention center. **Facility:** 321 units. 8 stories, interior corridors. **Terms:** check-in 3:30 pm. **Amenities:** safes. **Pool:** heated outdoor. **Activities:** hot tub, exercise room. **Guest Services:** valet laundry, area transportation.

FAIRFIELD BY MARRIOTT FRESNO YOSEMITE INTERNATIONAL AIRPORT   559/825-5200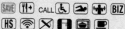
Hotel. **Address:** 1535 N Peach Ave 93727

AAA Benefit: Members save 5% or more!

HAMPTON INN & SUITES FRESNO   559/447-5900
Hotel. **Address:** 327 E Fir Ave 93720

AAA Benefit: Members save up to 15%!

HOLIDAY INN EXPRESS-RIVER PARK   559/577-1350
Hotel. **Address:** 7115 N Howard St 93720

HOMEWOOD SUITES BY HILTON   559/440-0801
Extended Stay Hotel. **Address:** 6820 N Fresno St 93710

AAA Benefit: Members save up to 15%!

HOTEL PICCADILLY   559/348-5520
Hotel. **Address:** 2305 W Shaw Ave 93711

HYATT PLACE FRESNO
559/899-0400

 Hotel

HYATT PLACE

AAA Benefit: Members save up to 10%!

Address: 7333 N Fresno St 93720 **Location:** SR 41 exit Herndon Ave, just e, then 0.5 mi n. **Facility:** 126 units. 5 stories, interior corridors. **Pool:** heated indoor. **Activities:** exercise room. **Guest Services:** valet and coin laundry.

LA QUINTA INN & SUITES BY WYNDHAM FRESNO RIVERPARK
559/449-0928

 Hotel

Address: 330 E Fir Ave 93720 **Location:** SR 41 exit Herndon Ave, just e, just n on Fresno St, then just w. **Facility:** 56 units. 4 stories, interior corridors. **Pool:** heated outdoor. **Activities:** hot tub, exercise room. **Guest Services:** coin laundry. **Featured Amenity: breakfast buffet.**

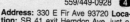

Rest assured:

AAA.com/travelguides/hotels

(See map & index p. 89.)

LA QUINTA INN BY WYNDHAM FRESNO NORTHWEST
559/275-3700 **8**
♦♦♦♦ Hotel. **Address:** 5077 N Cornelia Ave 93722

PICCADILLY INN AIRPORT   559/375-7760 **15**

♦♦ Hotel

Address: 5115 E McKinley Ave 93727 **Location:** SR 180 exit Peach Ave, 1 mi n, then just w. **Facility:** 185 units. 2 stories (no elevator), interior corridors. **Dining:** Steak & Anchor, see separate listing. **Pool:** outdoor. **Activities:** hot tub, exercise room. **Guest Services:** valet and coin laundry, area transportation. **Featured Amenity:** full hot breakfast.

[SAVE] ⊱ 🍴 🛁 🍽 CALL ♿ 🏊 🛗 BIZ 📶 ✕ 🔌 🖥

RESIDENCE INN BY MARRIOTT   559/222-8900 **10**
♦♦♦ [SAVE] Extended Stay Hotel.
Address: 5322 N Diana St 93710

> **AAA Benefit:**
> Members save 5% or more!

SPRINGHILL SUITES BY MARRIOTT FRESNO
559/431-0004 **6**
♦♦♦♦ [SAVE] Hotel. **Address:** 6844 N Fresno St 93710

> **AAA Benefit:**
> Members save 5% or more!

TOWNEPLACE SUITES BY MARRIOTT   559/435-4600 **2**
♦♦♦ [SAVE] Extended Stay Hotel.
Address: 7127 N Fresno St 93720

> **AAA Benefit:**
> Members save 5% or more!

WYNDHAM GARDEN FRESNO AIRPORT   559/252-3611 **14**
♦♦♦ Hotel. **Address:** 5090 E Clinton Way 93727

WHERE TO EAT

THE ANNEX KITCHEN   559/248-8512 **11**
♦♦♦ Italian. Casual Dining. **Address:** 2257 W Shaw Ave 93711

BATTER UP PANCAKES   559/440-1221 **4**
♦♦ Breakfast. Casual Dining. **Address:** 8029 N Cedar Ave 93720

DIANA'S RESTAURANT   559/277-9500 **10**
♦♦ Armenian. Casual Dining. **Address:** 3050 W Shaw Ave, Suite 106 93711

HUONG LAN   559/221-8000 **13**
♦♦ Vietnamese. Casual Dining. **Address:** 4965 N Fresno St 93726

JAVIER'S   559/252-4511 **17**
♦♦ Mexican. Casual Dining. **Address:** 5680 E Kings Canyon 93727

MANHATTAN STEAKHOUSE AND BAR   559/449-1731 **9**
♦♦♦ American. Fine Dining. **Address:** 1731 W Bullard Ave 93711

MAX'S BISTRO AND BAR   559/439-6900 **8**
♦♦♦ California. Fine Dining. **Address:** 1784 W Bullard Ave 93711

MEDITERRANEAN GRILL AND CAFE   559/441-7050 **16**
♦♦ Mediterranean. Casual Dining. **Address:** 1031 U St 93721

PISMO'S COASTAL GRILL   559/439-9463 **3**
♦♦ Seafood. Casual Dining. **Address:** 7937 N Blackstone Ave 93711

RED APPLE CAFE   559/261-1505 **6**
♦♦ Breakfast. Casual Dining. **Address:** 488 W Herndon Ave 93650

SAL'S MEXICAN RESTAURANT   559/438-3030 **5**
♦♦ Mexican. Casual Dining. **Address:** 7476 N Fresno St 93720

STEAK & ANCHOR   559/375-7760 **15**
♦♦ Steak. Fine Dining. **Address:** 5115 E McKinley Ave 93727

TACOS MARQUITOS   559/447-5569 **12**
♦ Mexican. Quick Serve. **Address:** 1772 E Barstow Ave 93710

TAHOE JOE'S FAMOUS STEAKHOUSE   559/299-9740
♦♦ Steak Seafood. Casual Dining. **Address:** 7006 N Cedar Ave 93720

THAI ROYAL ORCHID   559/431-0132 **7**
♦♦ Thai. Casual Dining. **Address:** 6735 N First St 93710

VENI VIDI VICI   559/266-5510 **14**
♦♦ New American. Casual Dining. **Address:** 1116 N Fulton St 93728

WESTWOODS BBQ & SPICE CO   559/449-9227 **2**
♦♦ Barbecue. Casual Dining. **Address:** 8042 N Blackstone Ave 93720

YOSEMITE RANCH STEAK, SEAFOOD & ROAST HOUSE
559/434-4403 **1**
♦♦ Steak Seafood. Casual Dining. **Address:** 1520 E Champlain Dr 93720

GALT pop. 23,647, elev. 52'

BEST WESTERN GALT INN   209/745-9500

[fyi] Hotel

> **AAA Benefit:** Members save up to 15% and earn bonus points!

Under major renovation, call for details. **Last Rated:** ♦♦ **Address:** 620 N Lincoln Way 95632 **Location:** SR 99 exit 275A (Simmerhorn Rd) northbound, just nw, then just n; exit 275B (Pringle Ave) southbound, just sw. **Facility:** 44 units. 2 stories (no elevator), interior corridors. **Pool:** outdoor. **Activities:** hot tub, exercise room. **Guest Services:** coin laundry. **Featured Amenity:** continental breakfast.

[SAVE] CALL ♿ 🏊 🛗 BIZ HS 📶 ✕ 🔌 🖥 🖥

COMFORT INN & SUITES   209/744-7800
♦♦♦ Hotel. **Address:** 10380 Twin Cities Rd 95632

WHERE TO EAT

WHOLEY RAVIOLI ITALIAN RISTORANTE   209/745-5109
 Italian. Casual Dining. **Address:** 1067 C St, Suite 132
95632

GARBERVILLE (C-1) pop. 913, elev. 535'
• Restaurants p. 95

Situated on a terrace adjacent to the South Fork Eel River, Garberville was founded in the late 19th century as a trading center for sheep ranchers. In the 1970s it gained the dubious reputation of being the unofficial world capital for the cultivation of sinsemilla, a highly potent form of marijuana. One contributing factor is the region's weather, more reliably sunny and largely free of the fog that lingers along the coast and in the redwood country to the north. Summer highs here frequently reach 90 and occasionally top 100 degrees.

Southern Humboldt Community Park, off US 101 exit 639B to 934 Sprowl Creek Rd., has multiuse trails that loop through a 431-acre tract of grassland, farmland, upland forest and redwood groves. The park is considered a model of sustainable food production, forest management and watershed restoration.

Within Richardson Grove State Park, 8 miles south on US 101, are significant stands of old-growth redwoods, including several trees that exceed 340 feet in height. Nine miles of hiking trails traverse the groves. The park visitor center, located in the historic Richardson Grove Lodge, has natural history exhibits and provides information about summer nature programs and guided walks; phone (707) 247-3318. *See Recreation Areas Chart.*

One-Log House, on US 101 near the park entrance, was hollowed out of a single redwood tree more than 2,100 years old. Thirty-two feet long and about 11 feet wide, it houses a gift shop with historical photos and a collection of antique drag saws.

BENBOW HISTORIC INN   707/923-2124

Classic Historic Resort Hotel

Address: 445 Lake Benbow Dr 95542 **Location:** US 101 exit 636 (Benbow Lake Rd), just w. **Facility:** A cup of tea with scones in the afternoon is tradition at this 1920's built, English Tudor-style inn. In room complimentary sherry is also provided to guests. Rooms are furnished in period pieces. 65 two-bedroom units. 3 stories, interior/exterior corridors. **Dining:** Benbow Inn Restaurant, see separate listing. **Pool:** heated outdoor. **Activities:** hot tub, regulation golf, recreation programs in summer, bicycles, playground, game room. **Guest Services:** coin laundry.

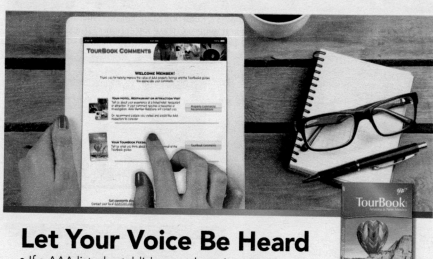

▼ *See AAA listing p. 95* ▼

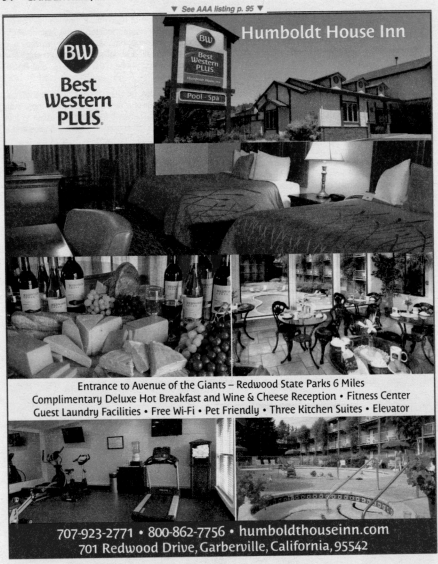

Humboldt House Inn

Entrance to Avenue of the Giants – Redwood State Parks 6 Miles
Complimentary Deluxe Hot Breakfast and Wine & Cheese Reception • Fitness Center
Guest Laundry Facilities • Free Wi-Fi • Pet Friendly • Three Kitchen Suites • Elevator

707-923-2771 • 800-862-7756 • humboldthouseinn.com
701 Redwood Drive, Garberville, California, 95542

BEST WESTERN PLUS HUMBOLDT HOUSE INN
707-923-2771

Motel

AAA Benefit: Members save up to 15% and earn bonus points!

Address: 701 Redwood Dr 95542 **Location:** US 101 exit Garberville, just e. **Facility:** 76 units, some two bedrooms and kitchens. 2-3 stories, exterior corridors. **Terms:** check-in 4 pm. **Pool:** heated outdoor. **Activities:** hot tub, exercise room. **Guest Services:** coin laundry. **Featured Amenity: full hot breakfast.** *(See ad p. 94.)*

WHERE TO EAT

BENBOW INN RESTAURANT
707/923-2124

Regional California Fine Dining
$27-$46

AAA Inspector Notes: *Historic.* Listed as a national historic landmark, this restaurant is an oasis for pleasant dining and great food made from fresh ingredients. Brunch is served daily until 3 p.m. Wine selections are plentiful. **Features:** full bar, patio dining, happy hour. **Reservations:** suggested. **Address:** 445 Lake Benbow Dr 95542 **Location:** US 101 exit 636 (Benbow Lake Rd), just w; in Benbow Historic Inn.

BON BISTRO & BAKERY
707/923-2509

American. Quick Serve. **Address:** 867 Redwood Dr 95542

CECIL'S NEW ORLEANS BISTRO
707/923-7007

Creole. Casual Dining. **Address:** 773 Redwood Dr 95542

GEYSERVILLE (A-6) pop. 862, elev. 209'
• Part of Wine Country area — see map p. 405

Despite the name, there aren't any geysers in the vicinity of Geyserville—steaming hot springs and fumaroles were discovered in the area in the mid-19th century, and these natural phenomena were mistaken for geysers.

"Downtown," along Geyserville Avenue, the main thoroughfare, earns such overused adjectives as quaint and rustic due to a scattering of eclectic shops and eateries as well as Locals (21023 Geyserville Ave.), a popular tasting room featuring the award-winning products of 10 regional wineries. A handful of cozy Victorian-style B&Bs make convenient home bases for exploring some of the approximately 50 wineries in the nearby Alexander and Dry Creek valleys.

Outdoor enthusiasts head to nearby Lake Sonoma for kayaking, fishing and canoeing. Bike tours travel the Alexander Valley's rolling hills, passing bucolic pasturelands laced with grapevines. And although visitors usually venture to "big city" neighbor Healdsburg for provisions, it's always fun to stop by the Jimtown Store (6706 SR 128). This quintessential country store, decorated with vintage Americana, offers a heaping helping of nostalgia along with plenty of fixings for a gourmet picnic lunch.

WINERIES

• **Clos du Bois** is at 19410 Geyserville Ave. **Hours:** Tastings daily 10-4:30. Tours daily at 10 and 2, Apr.-Oct. Marlstone Experience (includes tour and tasting) Sun.-Fri. at noon, Apr.-Oct.; reservations are required. Closed major holidays. **Phone:** (800) 222-3189. GT

• **Francis Ford Coppola Winery** is w. off US 101 Independence Ln. exit to 300 Via Archimedes. **Hours:** Tastings daily 11-6. A variety of tours are offered daily; check the website for schedule and tour details. **Phone:** (707) 857-1400 or (707) 857-1471. GT

GEYSERVILLE INN
707/857-4343

Hotel

Address: 21714 Geyserville Ave 95441 **Location:** US 101 exit E Canyon Rd, just s. **Facility:** 42 units, some two bedrooms. 2 stories (no elevator), interior/exterior corridors. **Terms:** check-in 4 pm. **Pool:** outdoor. **Activities:** hot tub, lawn sports.

WHERE TO EAT

DIAVOLA PIZZERIA & SALUMERIA
707/814-0111

Italian. Casual Dining. **Address:** 21021 Geyserville Ave 95441

GILROY (G-3) pop. 48,821, elev. 194'
• Hotels p. 96 • Restaurants p. 96

Garlic was first commercially grown in Gilroy by immigrant Japanese farmers following World War I, and today this town a little more than an hour's drive south of San Francisco is a major garlic processor. Beloved by cooks and the bane of vampires, this aromatic relative of the onion is a $100-million-a-year industry in the self-proclaimed "Garlic Capital of the World." At the annual Garlic Festival, held in July, it's showcased in every imaginable edible form.

A local wine industry begun by Italian immigrant families has been productive on a small scale since the era of the *ranchos*. Favorable weather and soil conditions also nurture the seed industry.

Historic turn-of-the-20th-century buildings, many of them along Monterey Street downtown, include the 1897 I.O.O.F. Children's Home for California and the 1906 City Hall. The Carnegie Library building on the corner of Fifth and Church streets houses the Gilroy Historical Museum, which displays vintage photos and regional artifacts; phone (408) 846-0446.

Gilroy Welcome Center: 8155-6 Arroyo Cir., Building A, Gilroy, CA 95020. **Phone:** (408) 842-6436.

Self-guiding tours: The welcome center and the Gilroy Historical Museum both offer a walking tour pamphlet of Gilroy's historic district for $1. Oenophiles can follow the Santa Clara Valley Wine Trail to approximately a dozen wineries; a map can be downloaded from the Gilroy Welcome Center website.

Shopping: Gilroy Premium Outlets, 681 Leavesley Rd., has more than 145 stores, including Ann Taylor, Banana Republic, Eddie Bauer, Gap, Levi's, Polo Ralph Lauren and Tommy Hilfiger. Browse for antiques in historic downtown Gilroy along a five-block stretch of Monterey Street.

GILROY GARDENS FAMILY THEME PARK is w. on SR 152 (Hecker Pass Hwy. W.) to just past Burchell Rd., following signs. This 28-acre theme park is centered around trees and horticulture but also has more than 40 rides, gardens and attractions geared to families with young children. For kids there are several roller coasters, a monorail, a rock maze, a 1927 carousel, antique car rides, a water play area and pitch-and-win games. Be sure to check out the "circus trees," topiaries that have been grafted together to form interesting shapes.

Hours: Park open Mon.-Fri. 11-5, Sat.-Sun. 10-6, early June to mid-Aug.; Fri. 11-5, Sat.-Sun. 10-6, early Apr.-early June and mid-Aug. to late Sept.; Sat.-Sun. 10-5, late Sept.-late Nov.; varied hours in Dec. Phone ahead to confirm schedule. **Cost:** $58; $48 (ages 3-11 and 63+). **Parking:** $15. **Phone:** (408) 840-7100.

BEST WESTERN PLUS FOREST PARK INN
408/848-5144

Hotel

Best Western PLUS.
AAA Benefit: Members save up to 15% and earn bonus points!

Address: 375 Leavesley Rd 95020 **Location:** US 101 exit Leavesley Rd, just w. **Facility:** 122 units, some two bedrooms. 3 stories, interior corridors. **Pool:** heated outdoor. **Activities:** hot tub, tennis, exercise room. **Guest Services:** valet and coin laundry. **Featured Amenity:** breakfast buffet.

/ SOME UNITS

GILROY INN
408/847-0688

Motel

Address: 611 Leavesley Rd 95020 **Location:** US 101 exit Leavesley Rd, just e. **Facility:** 44 units. 2 stories (no elevator), exterior corridors. **Guest Services:** coin laundry.

HILTON GARDEN INN GILROY
408/840-7000
 Hotel. **Address:** 6070 Monterey Rd 95020

AAA Benefit: Members save up to 15%!

QUALITY INN & SUITES
408/847-5500

Hotel

Address: 8430 Murray Ave 95020 **Location:** US 101 exit Leavesley Rd, just w. **Facility:** 47 units. 2 stories (no elevator), exterior corridors. **Pool:** outdoor. **Activities:** hot tub. **Guest Services:** coin laundry. **Featured Amenity:** breakfast buffet.

/ SOME UNITS

WHERE TO EAT

CIELITO LINDO RESTAURANT   408/842-7724
Mexican. Casual Dining. **Address:** 7460 Monterey St 95020

GLEN ELLEN (B-7) pop. 784, elev. 230'
• Hotels & Restaurants map & index p. 412
• Part of Wine Country area — see map p. 405

It's refreshing that Glen Ellen hasn't changed that much since the early 20th century, when author Jack London settled here to build his dream ranch and estate. "Sonoma" is the term Native Americans used to describe the sight of the moon rising from a backdrop of rolling hills, a vista that inspired missionary Father Jose Altimira to give it the name "Valley of the Moon." London also penned a novel by the same name.

Today's travelers head to this charming enclave's trendy eateries that specialize in gourmet fare paired with local wines. Glen Ellen makes a convenient base from which to explore Sonoma's most popular wineries; some offer concerts, food pairings and other activities in addition to the usual tastings. You can view fine art at the Imagery Estate Winery (14335 SR 12) or learn about organic farming at the Benziger Family Winery (1883 London Ranch Rd.).

Taste the divine Zinfandel-flavored ganache at Wine Country Chocolates (14301 Arnold Dr.), then pick up items for a savory picnic lunch at the Village Market (13751 Arnold Dr.) and take your portable feast to one of the area wineries with picnic facilities. Sonoma Valley Regional Park, 13630 Sonoma Hwy., is particularly lovely when colorful wildflowers bloom in the spring.

Jack London State Historic Park is the site of a popular summer concert series. Broadway Under the Stars features Broadway and Hollywood stars who take the stage at the Transcendence Theatre to perform in a musical extravaganza. The evening begins with picnicking on the lawn alongside the park's sprawling vineyards, complete with food from local vendors and pours from Sonoma Valley wineries. Shows are presented from mid-June to early September; for schedule and ticket information phone (877) 424-1414.

JACK LONDON STATE HISTORIC PARK is 1 mi. w. on London Ranch Rd. Within the 1,400-acre park is the author's former ranch as well as his grave.

(See map & index p. 412.)

The two-story museum, House of Happy Walls, contains London's personal papers and belongings. Mementos of his travels include South Pacific art objects. The burned ruins of Wolf House, the 26-room mansion London had built but never lived in, are nearby. The original cottage, where he died in 1916, contains period furnishings. *See Recreation Areas Chart.*

Off-road vehicles are not permitted. Leashed dogs are permitted in historic area only. **Time:** Allow 1 hour, 30 minutes minimum. **Hours:** Park open daily 9:30-5. Museum open daily 10-5. Cottage open daily noon-4. Closed Christmas. **Cost:** Park (includes museum) $10 per private vehicle; $5 per person arriving by other means. Cottage $4; $2 (ages 13-18 and 62+). **Phone:** (707) 938-5216.

WINERIES

- **Benziger Family Winery** is at 1883 London Ranch Rd. **Hours:** Daily 10-5. Tram tours of the biodynamic estate are given daily every half-hour 11-11:30 and 12:30-3:30; reservations are recommended. Behind-the-scenes tours with tastings are offered daily at 10:15, 11:15, 1:15 and 2:15; reservations are required. Closed Jan. 1, Easter, Thanksgiving and Christmas. **Phone:** (707) 935-3000. **GT**

GAIGE HOUSE + RYOKAN   707/935-0237   **33**
▼▼▼ Historic Boutique Bed & Breakfast. **Address:** 13540 Arnold Dr 95442

JACK LONDON LODGE   707/938-8510   **34**
▼▼ Hotel. **Address:** 13740 Arnold Dr 95442

WHERE TO EAT

GLEN ELLEN STAR   707/343-1384   **37**
▼▼▼ American. Casual Dining. **Address:** 13648 Arnold Dr 95442

YETI RESTAURANT   707/996-9930   **38**
▼▼ Indian. Casual Dining. **Address:** 14301 Arnold Dr, Suite 19 95442

GOLDEN GATE NATIONAL RECREATION AREA (C-7)
- Part of San Francisco area — see map p. 243

Encompassing both the rolling coastal hill country north of the Golden Gate Bridge and the diverse urban parklands strung around San Francisco's northern and western edges, Golden Gate National Recreation Area (GGNRA) covers approximately 74,000 acres of land and water.

The Marin Headlands looming above the northern end of the Golden Gate Bridge contrast dramatically with the densely packed city across the water. Smooth, grassy ridges slope down through valleys to a craggy shoreline scalloped with sandy coves. Abandoned gun emplacements stud the hillsides above the bridge and offer dramatic perspectives for viewing the bridge and Golden Gate, the strait that forms the entrance to San Francisco Bay.

Northward from the Marin Headlands are Mount Tamalpais State Park and Muir Woods National Monument *(see place listing p. 161).* Beyond the state park, the Olema Valley section of GGNRA abuts Point Reyes National Seashore *(see place listing p. 200).*

About 100 miles of hiking and riding trails traverse the pastoral countryside between Point Reyes and Golden Gate Strait. Hikers should stay on the trails, as the hillsides are often laced with poison oak. Dress in layers so you can adapt to the changeable weather (cool ocean winds and frequent fog, especially in the summer months). Swimming is permitted at Stinson Beach, China Beach, Muir Beach and Aquatic Park. Backcountry campsites require reservations. Fishing spots and picnic facilities are scattered throughout these parklands.

Muir Beach Overlook, a small cliffside park off SR 1 west of Muir Woods National Monument (watch for the signed turnoff) offers dramatic views of coastal cliffs along the Pacific Ocean shoreline. From the parking area a wood-fenced pathway winds to the very edge of a clifftop, where a small viewing platform stands high above the water. On sunny days the views north and south along the coast are spectacular.

Also within the park are the remains of several base-end stations, where soldiers stationed with artillery units along the coast once observed ship distance, speed and direction. The stations were important in the aftermath of the bombing of Pearl Harbor, but with the widespread advent of radar their function became obsolete.

The Marine Mammal Center, in the Marin Headlands at 2000 Bunker Rd., rescues and rehabilitates marine animals native to this section of California coast; phone (415) 289-7325 for information regarding hours of operation. *See attraction listing in Sausalito p. 373.*

Fort Baker, on the east side of US 101 just across San Francisco Bay via the Golden Gate Bridge, was once filled with artillery fortifications. It is now a popular recreational area offering hiking, bicycling, fishing and picnicking as well as splendid views of the bay and Angel Island. To reach Fort Baker, cross the Golden Gate Bridge northbound, take exit 442 (Alexander Avenue) off US 101 and follow signs.

From the vantage point of Battery Spencer there's a dramatic perspective of the Golden Gate Bridge from above. To get there, take exit 442/Alexander Avenue, keep left at the fork following signs for US 101 south to San Francisco, turn left at Sausalito Lateral Road, then turn right onto Conzelman Road; a parking area is a short way up the crest of the hill on the left. The name refers to the concrete military installations—deactivated during World War II and now crumbling and rusted—that were designed to protect San Francisco Bay from attack.

From the parking area a path leads uphill to the Hendrik Point overlook; at this lofty perch you're at tower height with the bridge looking down at the roadbed, itself some 220 feet above the water. The views of the bridge, Angel Island, the San Francisco skyline and the Marin Headlands are spectacular on both sunny and foggy days (fog frequently rolls in on summer afternoons), and this is a favorite spot for photographers. **Note:** It's often very windy at the overlook, so watch your footing. Finding a space in the small parking area can also be problematic.

Fort Funston, where hang gliders launch themselves from beachside cliffs, is at the southern end of the recreation area. The long, windswept stretch of Ocean Beach links Fort Funston with the Cliff House, the adjacent Sutro Baths site and Lands End *(see attraction listing in San Francisco p. 282)*, all of which occupy the city's northwestern corner. The Coastal Trail follows Lands End to China and Baker beaches and the abandoned coastal batteries just south of the Golden Gate Bridge.

The Golden Gate Promenade extends 3.5 miles along the shore of San Francisco Bay and connects Fort Point, below the southern end of the Golden Gate Bridge, with Crissy Field and Fort Mason. Alcatraz Island *(see attraction listing in San Francisco p. 268)* also is part of the recreation area. The information center at Fort Mason is open Mon.-Fri. 8:30-4:30. For further information write the Information Center, Golden Gate National Recreation Area, Building 201, Fort Mason, San Francisco, CA 94123; phone (415) 561-4700. *See Recreation Areas Chart.*

BAY AREA DISCOVERY MUSEUM is off US 101 at 557 McReynolds Rd., at the n. end of Golden Gate Bridge. The hands-on children's museum features both indoor exhibitions and outdoor activities. Crawling through an underwater sea tunnel, creating natural art and fishing off a boat or pier are some of the activities offered. Tot Spot is an animal habitat environment for ages 6 months to 3 years.

Hours: Daily 9-5, mid-June through Labor Day; Tues.-Fri. 9-4, Sat.-Sun. 9-5, rest of year. Closed Jan. 1, Easter, July 4, Thanksgiving, Christmas Eve, Christmas Day and 2 weeks in Sept. Phone ahead to confirm schedule. **Cost:** $14.95; $13.95 (ages 6-11 months and 65+); free (ages 0-5 months). **Phone:** (415) 339-3900. ⓘ

FORT POINT NATIONAL HISTORIC SITE is at the s. end of the Golden Gate Bridge, off Long Ave. at the end of Marine Dr. Built by the U.S. Army between 1853 and 1861, Fort Point is similar in design to Fort Sumter, S.C. Although it once was the principal defense bastion on the West Coast, no battle ever occurred at Fort Point.

This vantage point offers an expansive, ground-level view of the Golden Gate Bridge. Walk out on the fishing pier across from the Warming Hut for views of the bay and Angel and Alcatraz islands. The Warming Hut has a selection of books and eco-friendly gifts as well as a café. You also can watch video presentations about the history of the fort and bridge construction.

To get to the Golden Gate Bridge's southeast plaza, walk along Marine Drive a short distance until you see the sign for the steps that ascend a hill. The climb is steep but fairly short (four-tenths of a mile), and there's a perspective of the bridge at the halfway point that you won't see anywhere else.

There are restrooms in the building behind the Warming Hut. Free, guided 30-minute tours of the brick masonry fortification and cannon-loading demonstrations are given. Candlelight tours are conducted Saturday evenings November through February; reservations are required. **Note:** During security alerts the fort may be closed. **Hours:** Fort Point open Fri.-Sun. 10-5. Warming Hut open daily 9-5; hours may be extended in summer. Closed Jan. 1, Thanksgiving and Christmas. Phone ahead to confirm schedule. **Cost:** Free. **Phone:** (415) 556-1693.

PRESIDIO OF SAN FRANCISCO, in the n.w. part of the city, was an active military garrison almost continuously for 218 years; it closed as an Army post in 1994. Within the 1,480-acre site are historic military barracks as well as wooded areas, beaches, and expansive bay and ocean vistas.

The Presidio's boundaries encompass Fort Point, San Francisco National Cemetery, Fort Winfield Scott, Crissy Field, The Walt Disney Family Museum and film and animation giant Lucasfilm Ltd. Maps outlining 11 miles of hiking and bicycling trails are available at the visitor center at 210 Lincoln Blvd.

Hours: Visitor center open daily 10-5. Closed Jan. 1, Thanksgiving and Christmas. **Cost:** Park and guided tours free. **Phone:** (415) 561-4323 or TTY (415) 561-4314. Ⓖ️ⓣ

The Society of California Pioneers Museum and Research Library is at 101 Montgomery St. in the Presidio of San Francisco. Changing exhibits in Pioneer Hall highlight California's 19th-century history and heritage. The society's collections, amassed by pioneer families and their descendants, include 19th- and early 20th-century paintings, artifacts, photographs and manuscripts.

The Alice Phelan Sullivan Research Library contains more than 10,000 books, manuscripts, maps, journals and autobiographical materials pertaining to the state's early history. Its holdings include pioneer diaries that belonged to John A. Sutter and Henry W. Bigler, primary sources that document the discovery of gold in California. Educational programs and events are offered regularly.

Hours: Wed.-Sat. 10-5. Access to the research library is by appointment. Closed major holidays. **Cost:** Free. **Phone:** (415) 957-1849.

The Walt Disney Family Museum is at 104 Montgomery St. in the Presidio of San Francisco. The inspirational life story of Walt Disney—the man who raised animation to an art form—is told in 10 extensive galleries on the site of this former military base.

The museum features contemporary, interactive exhibits narrated in Walt's own voice, featuring early drawings, cartoons, movies, music, more than 200 video screens and a spectacular model of Disneyland. Over 250 of Walt's awards and accolades are on display in the museum lobby, including his honorary Academy Award for *Snow White and the Seven Dwarfs,* customized to feature one large and seven small Oscar statuettes.

Enjoy monthly screenings of classic Disney films, special talks, as well as immersive animation classes and workshops for all ages, available throughout the year in the museum's state-of-the-art learning center.

Time: Allow 2 hours minimum. **Hours:** Wed.-Mon. 10-6. Last admission is at 4:45. Closes at 4 on Christmas Eve and Dec. 31. Closed Jan. 1, Thanksgiving and Christmas. **Cost:** $25; $20 (ages 65+ and students with ID); $15 (ages 6-17). **Phone:** (415) 345-6800. ⊓⌐

GRASS VALLEY (D-3) pop. 12,860, elev. 2,420'

In 1850 settler George Knight stubbed his toe on a piece of quartz laced with gold and put Grass Valley on the map. Aided by advanced mining techniques that first were developed and used in this region, Grass Valley ultimately became the richest gold-mining town in California. Unlike most gold rush towns, it survived the mining heyday; today high-tech manufacturing and tourism anchor the economy.

Greater Grass Valley Chamber of Commerce: 128 E. Main St., Grass Valley, CA 95945. **Phone:** (530) 273-4667.

EMPIRE MINE STATE HISTORIC PARK, 1 mi. e. of SR 49 at 10791 E. Empire St., produced nearly 6 million ounces of gold during its operation. Within the park are 10 miles of hiking trails and a mine with 367 miles of passageways. Restored buildings include the owner's cottage, clubhouse, a smithy, hoist and compression houses and a machine shop. Living-history tours, with guides in period garb; a scale model of the underground workings of the mine; and guided tours of the cottage, mine yard and gardens are offered. *See Recreation Areas Chart.*

Picnic facilities are in the parking area; food is not permitted inside the park. **Time:** Allow 30 minutes minimum. **Hours:** Park open daily 10-5. Trails open daily dawn-dusk. Cottage and mine yard tours are given daily (weather permitting). Living-history and garden tours are given Sat.-Sun. in summer. Closed Jan. 1, Thanksgiving and Christmas. Phone ahead to confirm schedule. **Cost:** $7; $3 (ages 6-16). Most

tours free; living-history cottage tours cost $2. **Phone:** (530) 273-8522. 📷 🏛

BEST WESTERN GOLD COUNTRY INN   530/273-1393

♦♦♦ **Motel**   BW **Best Western.**   **AAA Benefit:** Members save up to 15% and earn bonus points!

Address: 972 Sutton Way 95945 **Location:** SR 20 and 49 exit 183B (Brunswick Rd), just e, then just n; midway between Grass Valley and Nevada City. **Facility:** 84 units, some two bedrooms. 1-2 stories (no elevator), exterior corridors. **Pool:** outdoor. **Activities:** hot tub, exercise room. **Guest Services:** coin laundry. **Featured Amenity:** continental breakfast.

[SAVE] 🍽 CALL ♿ 🛏 🖥 [BIZ] 📶 🗄 🖨 💳 / SOME UNITS 🐾 [HS]

GOLD MINERS INN, AN ASCEND HOTEL COLLECTION MEMBER   530/477-1700
♦♦♦ Hotel. **Address:** 121 Bank St 95945

GRASS VALLEY COURTYARD SUITES & CONFERENCE CENTER   530/272-7696
♦♦♦ Hotel. **Address:** 210 N Auburn St 95945

WHERE TO EAT

CIRINO'S AT MAIN STREET   530/477-6000
♦♦ Mediterranean. Casual Dining. **Address:** 213 W Main St 95945

DIEGO'S RESTAURANT   530/477-1460
♦♦ Latin American. Casual Dining. **Address:** 217 Colfax Ave 95945

MARSHALL'S PASTIES   530/272-2844
♦ English. Quick Serve. **Address:** 203 Mill St 95945

PAULETTE'S COUNTRY KITCHEN   530/273-4008
♦♦ American. Casual Dining. **Address:** 875 Sutton Way 95945

PENNY'S DINER   530/477-5673
♦♦ Breakfast. Casual Dining. **Address:** 2072 Nevada City Hwy 95945

RISTORANTE ALLORO CUCINA ITALIANA   530/273-3555
♦♦ Italian. Casual Dining. **Address:** 124 Bank St 95945

SOUTH PINE CAFE   530/274-0261
♦♦ Breakfast. Casual Dining. **Address:** 102 Richardson St 95945

TOFANELLI'S GOLD COUNTRY BISTRO   530/272-1468
♦♦ American. Casual Dining. **Address:** 302 W Main St 95945

GROVELAND (F-4) pop. 601, elev. 2,846'
• Hotels p. 100 • Restaurants p. 100
• Hotels & Restaurants map & index p. 426
• Part of Yosemite National Park area — see map p. 420

This gold rush-era boom town went through a pair of menacing-sounding names—Savage's Diggings and Garrote—before citizens agreed on a more benign moniker.

(See map & index p. 426.)

GROVELAND YOSEMITE GATEWAY MUSEUM is at 18990 Main St. (SR 120), in the same building as the country library and adjacent to Mary Lavaroni Park. Displays depict area history from the 1849 gold rush era to the Hetch Hetchy railroad period, as well as flora and fauna native to the Sierra foothills. A theater features DVD programs about local history and pioneer families as well as Yosemite National Park. **Time:** Allow 1 hour minimum. **Hours:** Sun.-Thurs. 1-4:30, Fri.-Sat. 10-4:30. Closed Jan. 1, Easter, Thanksgiving, Christmas Eve, Christmas and Dec. 31. **Cost:** Free. **Phone:** (209) 962-0300.

RUSH CREEK LODGE AT YOSEMITE   209/379-2373 **6**
▼▼▼ Hotel. **Address:** 34001 CA 120 95321

YOSEMITE ROSE BED & BREAKFAST   209/962-6548 **4**
▼▼▼ Bed & Breakfast. **Address:** 22830 Ferretti Rd 95321

YOSEMITE WESTGATE LODGE   209/962-5281 **5**
▼▼ Motel. **Address:** 7633 Hwy 120 95321

WHERE TO EAT

BUCK MEADOWS RESTAURANT   209/962-5181 **4**
▼▼ American. Casual Dining. **Address:** 7647 State Hwy 120 95321

TAVERN AT RUSH CREEK LODGE   209/379-2373 **5**
▼▼ American. Casual Dining. **Address:** 34001 CA 120 95321

GUALALA (E-1) elev. 67'
• Part of Wine Country area — see map p. 405

Amiable little Gualala (wa-LA-la) means "where the water meets," a nod to its location along the Pacific and above the mouth of the Gualala River. Scenic coastal beauty, recreational opportunities like abalone diving and kayaking, and a thriving artists' community make it a popular weekend destination for San Francisco Bay Area residents.

Redwood Coast Chamber of Commerce/Visitor's Center: 39150 S. SR 1, P.O. Box 199, Gualala, CA 95445. **Phone:** (707) 884-1080 or (800) 778-5252.

GUALALA COUNTRY INN   707/884-4343
▼▼▼ Motel. **Address:** 47975 Center St 95445

NORTH COAST COUNTRY INN   707/884-4537
▼▼▼ Bed & Breakfast. **Address:** 34591 S Hwy 1 95445

WHERE TO EAT

ST ORRES   707/884-3335
▼▼▼▼ California. Fine Dining. **Address:** 36601 S Hwy 1 95445

TRINKS CAFE   707/884-1713
▼ American. Quick Serve. **Address:** 39140 CA-1 95445

GUERNEVILLE (E-2) pop. 4,534, elev. 56'
• Part of Wine Country area — see map p. 405

Lumber mills flourished during Guerneville's early years. Railroads were built to ship wood from the town, and agricultural endeavors were undertaken on the cleared land.

The Russian River Chamber of Commerce and Visitor Information Center: 16209 First St., P.O. Box 331, Guerneville, CA 95446. **Phone:** (707) 869-9000 or (877) 644-9001.

▼ **ARMSTRONG REDWOODS STATE NATURAL RESERVE** is 2 mi. n. on Armstrong Woods Rd. Ohio native Col. James B. Armstrong was one of the very few 19th-century lumber barons who appreciated the majesty as well as the commercial potential of coastal California's redwood groves. He settled in Sonoma County in 1874 and began purchasing land north of Guerneville covered with dense redwood forest, in part to control the amount of acreage that was being reduced to tree stumps (inspiring Guerneville's original name, Stumptown).

Thanks to Armstrong's foresight, visitors are able to enjoy the beauty of these incredible trees. Although other walking trails thread through the reserve, the Redwood Discovery Trail that begins at the visitor center includes the high points. The natural setting is every bit as impressive as what you'll see at Muir Woods National Monument, but Armstrong Woods is less well-known and not nearly as crowded, which makes the experience even more magical.

Notable specimens, all marked, include the Parson Jones Tree, at 310 feet the tallest in the grove, and the Colonel Armstrong Tree, estimated to be more than 1,400 years old. There are few birds and wildlife species in the moist, deep-shade environment of a redwood forest, but you might spot creatures like the banana slug, which lives on the forest floor and has a shape and coloration that resembles the tropical fruit. *See Recreation Areas Chart.*

Except for service animals, dogs are permitted only on paved roads and must be on leash. **Time:** Allow 1 hour minimum. **Hours:** Daily 8 a.m.-1 hour after sunset. **Cost:** Day use fee $10 per private vehicle; $7 (ages 62+ per private vehicle). **Phone:** (707) 869-2015.

COTTAGES ON RIVER ROAD   707/869-3848
▼▼ Cottage. **Address:** 14880 River Rd 95446

FERNGROVE COTTAGES   707/869-8105
▼▼ Cottage. **Address:** 16650 River Rd 95446

WEST SONOMA INN & SPA   707/869-2874
▼▼ Cottage. **Address:** 14100 Brookside Ln 95446

WHERE TO EAT

BIG BOTTOM MARKET   707/604-7295
▼ Deli. Quick Serve. **Address:** 16228 Main St 95446

BOON EAT + DRINK   707/869-0780
♥♥ California. Casual Dining. **Address:** 16248 Main St 95446

HALF MOON BAY (D-8) pop. 11,324, elev. 69'

- **Hotels & Restaurants map & index p. 316**
- **Part of San Francisco area — see map p. 243**

Half Moon Bay is situated along a scenic stretch of SR 1 that extends from San Francisco south to San Luis Obispo. The rugged coastline is bordered by sandy beaches perfect for walking and beachcombing. This is a popular launching spot for sightseeing, fishing and whale-watching cruises.

The Half Moon Bay Farmers Market sets up at Shoreline Station, 225 Cabrillo Hwy. S., Saturdays 9-1 from May through December. This small farmers market specializes in seasonal organic produce grown by local farmers. You can also shop for honey, cheeses, fresh fish, artisanal bread and homemade baked goods. Half Moon Bay is known for its wholesale plant nurseries, and the stands displaying beautiful bunches of cut flowers attest to that fact.

Half Moon Bay Coastside Chamber of Commerce and Visitors Bureau: 235 Main St., Half Moon Bay, CA 94019. **Phone:** (650) 726-8380.

BEACH HOUSE HOTEL   650/712-0220   **91**
♥♥♥ Hotel. **Address:** 4100 N Cabrillo Hwy 94019

BEST WESTERN PLUS-CAMERON'S INN
     650/713-5151   **98**

♥♥♥
Hotel

Best Western PLUS. **AAA Benefit:** Members save up to 15% and earn bonus points!

Address: 1410 S Cabrillo Hwy 94019 **Location:** Jct SR 92, 1.3 mi s. **Facility:** 46 units. 2 stories, interior corridors. **Activities:** trails, exercise room. **Guest Services:** coin laundry.

COASTSIDE INN HALF MOON BAY   650/726-3400   **95**
♥♥ Hotel. **Address:** 230 S Cabrillo Hwy 94019

CYPRESS INN ON MIRAMAR BEACH   650/726-6002   **93**
♥♥♥ Bed & Breakfast. **Address:** 407 Mirada Rd 94019

HALF MOON BAY LODGE   650/726-9000   **100**
♥♥♥ Hotel. **Address:** 2400 Cabrillo Hwy S 94019

HARBOR VIEW INN
     650/726-2329   **90**

♥♥
Motel

Address: 51 Ave Alhambra 94018 **Location:** SR 1 exit Capistrano Ave, just e; 4 mi n of jct SR 92. Located in El Granada. **Facility:** 17 units. 2 stories (no elevator), exterior corridors. *Bath:* shower only. **Featured Amenity:** continental breakfast.

MILL ROSE INN   650/726-8750   **96**
♥♥♥♥ Boutique Bed & Breakfast. **Address:** 615 Mill St 94019

NANTUCKET WHALE INN   650/726-1616   **97**
♥♥♥ Bed & Breakfast. **Address:** 779 Main St 94019

THE OCEANFRONT HOTEL   650/726-6642   **92**
♥♥♥ Hotel. **Address:** 211 Mirada Rd 94019

QUALITY INN   650/712-1999   **94**
♥♥ Hotel. **Address:** 2930 N Cabrillo Hwy 94019

THE RITZ-CARLTON, HALF MOON BAY
     650/712-7000   **99**

♥♥♥♥♥
Resort Hotel

THE RITZ-CARLTON   **AAA Benefit:** Unequaled service at special member savings!

Address: 1 Miramontes Point Rd 94019 **Location:** 2.5 mi s of jct SR 1 (Cabrillo Hwy S) and 92, 0.8 mi w. **Facility:** On a high bluff that juts into the Pacific Ocean, this seaside resort is surrounded by gorgeous golf courses. The rooms feature upscale artwork, beautiful furnishings and luxurious bedding. 261 units, some two bedrooms. 6 stories, interior corridors. **Parking:** valet only. **Terms:** check-in 4 pm. **Amenities:** safes. **Dining:** 2 restaurants, also, Navio, see separate listing. **Pool:** heated indoor. **Activities:** sauna, hot tub, steamroom, regulation golf, tennis, recreation programs, kids club, bicycles, trails, health club, spa. **Guest Services:** valet laundry.

WHERE TO EAT

ASIAN KINGS KITCHEN   650/560-9898   **85**
♥ Chinese. Casual Dining. **Address:** 3048 N Cabrillo Hwy 94019

CAFFE MEZZALUNA   650/560-0137   **81**
♥ Italian Sandwiches Desserts. Quick Serve. **Address:** 240 Capistrano Rd 94019

HALF MOON BAY BREWING COMPANY   650/728-2739   **82**
♥♥ American. Brewpub. **Address:** 390 Capistrano Rd 94018

HALF MOON BAY JOE'S   650/560-9250   **94**
♥♥ American. Casual Dining. **Address:** 2380 Cabrillo Hwy S 94019

IT'S ITALIA   650/726-4444   **91**
♥♥♥ Italian. Fine Dining. **Address:** 401 Main St. 94019

JERSEY JOE'S COASTSIDE   650/726-4043   **88**
♥ Sandwiches. Quick Serve. **Address:** 40 Stone Pine Rd 94019

MAVERICKS CREPERIE   650/713-5298   **87**
♥ American. Quick Serve. **Address:** 146 San Mateo Rd 94019

MEZZALUNA ITALIAN RESTAURANT   650/728-8108   **80**
♥♥ Italian. Casual Dining. **Address:** 459 Prospect Way 94019

MIRAMAR BEACH RESTAURANT
     650/726-9053   **84**

♥♥
California Seafood Casual Dining $17-$39

AAA Inspector Notes: *Historic.* Inside this historic restaurant, guests' attention is drawn to the spectacular view of the ocean and many surrounding photographs of Half Moon Bay's past. Fresh seafood, fine steak and their famous seafood chowder are featured. **Features:** full bar, patio dining, Sunday brunch, happy hour. **Reservations:** suggested. **Address:** 131 Mirada Rd 94019 **Location:** 2.7 mi n of jct SR 92 and 1, then w.

(See map & index p. 316.)

NAVIO   650/712-7040 93
◈◈ ◈◈ Northern California. Fine Dining. **Address:** 1 Miramontes Point Rd 94019

PASTA MOON RISTORANTE   650/726-5125 89
◈◈◈
Italian
Casual Dining
$14-$40
AAA Inspector Notes: Daily specials and homemade soups are among selections at this restaurant that emphasize fresh ingredients and unusual preparation. The pasta selection is fantastic, and is made fresh daily. The menu also offers a variety of pizza and salad options. **Features:** full bar, patio dining, happy hour. **Reservations:** suggested. **Address:** 315 Main St 94019 **Location:** Just s of SR 92; east of SR 1. **Parking:** street only. L D 🅰️

SAM'S CHOWDER HOUSE   650/712-0245 83
◈◈
Seafood
Casual Dining
$13-$33
AAA Inspector Notes: This casual eatery with outdoor dining, offers panoramic views of the Pacific Ocean. Menu favorites include the lobster roll sandwich or the petrale sole with quinoa, and potato cake with a caper lemon butter sauce. **Features:** full bar, patio dining. **Address:** 4210 N Cabrillo Hwy 94019 **Location:** 3.5 mi n of jct SR 92. L D

SPICE ME THAI CUISINE   650/560-0076 92
◈◈ Thai. Casual Dining. **Address:** 500 Purissma St 94019

SUSHI MAIN STREET   650/726-6336 90
◈◈ Japanese Sushi. Casual Dining. **Address:** 696 Mill St 94019

VIA UNO CUCINA ITALIANA BAR   650/560-8858 86
◈◈◈ Italian. Casual Dining. **Address:** 2810 Cabrillo Hwy N 94019

HANFORD (H-5) pop. 53,967, elev. 248'

Founded in 1882 in the San Joaquin Valley, Hanford was named for a Southern Pacific Railroad paymaster who became a power in the community. He paid millions of dollars of workers' wages in gold.

Hanford was once the site of one of the largest Chinese communities in California. Among the highlights of China Alley, a remnant of the former community, is a Taoist temple with an upstairs museum exhibiting a variety of everyday artifacts used by Hanford's Chinese residents. Courthouse Square, the center of historic Hanford, includes a renovated carousel and many specialty shops.

Hanford Chamber of Commerce: 113 Court St., Suite 104, Hanford, CA 93230. **Phone:** (559) 582-0483.

Self-guiding tours: Maps for tours of historic Hanford are available from the chamber of commerce.

KINGS ART CENTER is at 605 N. Douty St. The 10 gallery shows mounted each year feature media such as photography, watercolors, prints, oil paintings, pottery, sculpture and textiles. **Time:** Allow 1 hour minimum. **Hours:** Wed.-Fri. 11-4, Sat.-Sun. noon-3. Closed major holidays. **Cost:** Donations. **Phone:** (559) 584-1065.

BEST WESTERN HANFORD INN   559/583-7300
◈◈ ◈◈
Motel

🅱️ **Best Western.**
AAA Benefit: Members save up to 15% and earn bonus points!

Address: 755 Cadillac Ln 93230 **Location:** SR 198 exit 86 (11th Ave) eastbound, just s, then just w; exit 87A (Redington St) westbound, 0.4 mi w on 4th St, just s on 11th Ave, then just w. **Facility:** 40 units. 2 stories (no elevator), exterior corridors. **Pool:** outdoor. **Guest Services:** coin laundry. **Featured Amenity:** continental breakfast.

SAVE ▮▮ CALL ♿ 🛒 BIZ 📶
✕ 🅿️ 🖥️ 🖨️

HOME2 SUITES BY HILTON, HANFORD LEMOORE   559/587-9957
◈◈◈ SAVE Extended Stay Hotel.
Address: 1589 Glendale Ave 93230

AAA Benefit: Members save up to 15%!

SEQUOIA INN   559/582-0338
◈◈◈
Hotel

Address: 1655 Mall Dr 93230 **Location:** SR 198 exit 85 (12th Ave), just n, then just e. **Facility:** 56 units. 3 stories, interior corridors. **Terms:** check-in 4 pm. **Pool:** outdoor. **Activities:** hot tub, exercise room. **Guest Services:** coin laundry. **Featured Amenity:** continental breakfast.

SAVE ▮▮ CALL ♿ 🛒 👪 HS
📶 ✕ 🅿️ 🖥️ 🖨️
/SOME
/UNITS 🐾

WHERE TO EAT

SUPERIOR DAIRY PRODUCT CO INC   559/582-0481
◈ American. Quick Serve. **Address:** 325 N Douty St 93230

ZAYTOONA   559/584-5290
◈◈ Mediterranean. Casual Dining. **Address:** 129 W 7th St 93230

HAYWARD (D-8) pop. 144,186, elev. 111'
• Hotels & Restaurants map & index p. 176

JAPANESE GARDENS, 22373 N. Third St. off Crescent Ave., encompasses 3.3 acres of trees native to Japan and California, along with stones and plants arranged in traditional Japanese style. A small pond contains koi and goldfish, and there's also a gazebo. **Hours:** Daily 8:30-4. Closed Christmas. **Cost:** Free. **Phone:** (510) 881-6700. 🚌 Castro Valley, 32

(See map & index p. 176.)

BEST WESTERN PLUS INN OF HAYWARD
510/785-8700

Hotel

Best Western PLUS

AAA Benefit: Members save up to 15% and earn bonus points!

Address: 360 W A St 94541 **Location:** I-880 exit 29 (A St), just e. **Facility:** 91 units. 2-3 stories, interior/exterior corridors. **Pool:** outdoor. **Activities:** hot tub, exercise room. **Guest Services:** valet laundry. **Featured Amenity:** breakfast buffet.

FAIRFIELD INN & SUITES BY MARRIOTT OAKLAND HAYWARD
510/782-5000

Hotel. **Address:** 25921 Industrial Blvd 94545

AAA Benefit: Members save 5% or more!

HAMPTON INN BY HILTON OAKLAND/HAYWARD
510/247-1555

Hotel. **Address:** 24137 Mission Blvd 94544

AAA Benefit: Members save up to 15%!

LA QUINTA INN & SUITES BY WYNDHAM OAKLAND - HAYWARD
510/732-6300

Hotel. **Address:** 20777 Hesperian Blvd 94541

QUALITY INN
510/538-4466

Motel. **Address:** 24997 Mission Blvd 94544

WHERE TO EAT

ACQUA E' FARINA RISTORANTE   510/888-1568   (65)
Italian. Casual Dining. **Address:** 22622 Main St 94541

BUFFALO BILL'S BREWERY   510/886-9823   (64)
American. Brewpub. **Address:** 1082 B St 94541

CANNERY CAFE   510/581-0223   (63)
American. Quick Serve. **Address:** 22380 Foothill Blvd 94541

HEALDSBURG (A-7) pop. 11,254, elev. 106'
- **Restaurants p. 104**
- **Part of Wine Country area — see map p. 405**

Healdsburg is one of those northern California towns that just radiates charm. For one thing it's a shopper's delight, packed with trendy boutiques, art galleries and antique shops. The compact downtown area is perfect for strolling, dog walking, people-watching at an outdoor café or partaking of the libations at any number of coffee houses and wine bars. During the weekend, shady Healdsburg Plaza is usually the center of activity, and you're quite likely to come across an art show, free concert or antique sale.

Those in search of culinary excellence make the trek to experience such upscale restaurants as Dry Creek Kitchen and Spoonbar. Sample the vintages

of the neighboring Dry Creek, Alexander and Russian River valleys at one of the tasting rooms bordering the plaza. Or get out and explore some of these renowned vineyards, many of which are open to visitors for tastings and tours. Access Westside Road, just off Healdsburg Avenue, and head west—the winding route is exceptionally scenic, passing rolling hills and gorgeous countryside.

The Russian River flows through town, providing invigorating recreation for canoeists and kayakers as well as an excuse to relax for the casual day-tripper. Healdsburg Veterans Memorial Beach, 13839 Healdsburg Ave., has picnic facilities as well as a man-made swimming beach along the river. Biking through the surrounding wine country is a perfect way to combine exercise and bucolic scenery.

The Raven Performing Arts Theater, 115 North St., presents everything from plays and musical and comedy acts to fashion shows. For schedule information phone (707) 433-6335.

Healdsburg Chamber of Commerce and Visitors Bureau: 217 Healdsburg Ave., Healdsburg, CA 95448. **Phone:** (707) 433-6935.

Self-guiding tours: Maps outlining tours of local historic buildings as well as a winery map are available at the chamber of commerce and visitors bureau.

WINERIES
- **Chalk Hill Estate** is s. of downtown off US 101 (Shiloh Rd. exit) at 10300 Chalk Hill Rd. **Hours:** Daily 10-5. Ninety-minute estate tours are given by appointment daily at 11. Closed major holidays and for occasional special events. **Cost:** Tasting fee $20-$30 per person. Estate tour $50 per person. Appointments are preferred. **Phone:** (707) 657-4837.
- **J Vineyards & Winery** is at 11447 Old Redwood Hwy. **Hours:** Daily 11-5. Tours are offered at 11:30 and 2:30 (weather permitting). **Cost:** Tour fee $30 per person. **Phone:** (888) 594-6326.
- **Rodney Strong Vineyards** is 3 mi. s. off US 101 at 11455 Old Redwood Hwy. **Hours:** Daily 10-5 (reduced hours on Christmas Eve and Dec. 31). Tours are given daily at 11 and 2, except during concerts (weather and staff availability permitting). Closed Jan. 1, Easter, Thanksgiving and Christmas. Phone ahead to confirm schedule. **Phone:** (707) 431-1533 or (800) 678-4763. (GT)
- **Simi Winery** is off US 101 Dry Creek Rd. exit, e. to Healdsburg Ave., then 1 mi. n. to 16275 Healdsburg Ave. **Hours:** Daily 10-5. Guided tours are given at 11 and 2. Closed Jan. 1, Easter, Thanksgiving, Christmas Eve and Christmas. **Phone:** (800) 746-4880. (GT)

BELLA VILLA MESSINA   707/433-6655
Bed & Breakfast. **Address:** 316 Burgundy Rd 95448

BEST WESTERN DRY CREEK INN
707/433-0300

Hotel

 Best Western. **AAA Benefit:** Members save up to 15% and earn bonus points!

Address: 198 Dry Creek Rd 95448 **Location:** US 101 exit Dry Creek Rd, just se. **Facility:** 163 units. 3 stories, exterior corridors. **Terms:** check-in 4 pm. **Amenities:** safes. **Pool:** heated outdoor. **Activities:** sauna, hot tub, steamroom, exercise room. **Guest Services:** complimentary laundry. **Featured Amenity: breakfast buffet.**

HEALDSBURG INN ON THE PLAZA 707/433-6991
Bed & Breakfast. **Address:** 112 Matheson St 95448

HONOR MANSION A RESORT INN 707/433-4277
Historic Bed & Breakfast. **Address:** 891 Grove St 95448

HOTEL TRIO
707/433-4000

Hotel

 MARRIOTT **AAA Benefit:** Members save 5% or more!

Address: 110 Dry Creek 95448 **Location:** US 101 exit Dry Creek Rd, just se. **Facility:** 122 kitchen units. 4 stories, interior corridors. **Parking:** on-site and valet. **Amenities:** safes. **Pool:** heated outdoor. **Activities:** bicycles, trails, exercise room. **Guest Services:** valet and coin laundry, area transportation. **Featured Amenity: breakfast buffet.**

MADRONA MANOR WINE COUNTRY INN & RESTAURANT
707/433-4231
Historic Country Inn. **Address:** 1001 Westside Rd 95448

WHERE TO EAT

AGAVE MEXICAN RESTAURANT 707/433-2411
Mexican. Casual Dining. **Address:** 1063 Vine St 95448

BEAR REPUBLIC BREWING CO 707/433-2337
American. Casual Dining. **Address:** 345 Healdsburg Ave 95448

BRAVAS BAR DE TAPAS 707/433-7700
Spanish Small Plates. Casual Dining. **Address:** 420 Center St 95448

DRY CREEK KITCHEN 707/431-0330
California. Fine Dining. **Address:** 317 Healdsburg Ave 95448

EL FAROLITO 707/433-2807
Mexican. Casual Dining. **Address:** 128 Plaza St 95448

MADRONA MANOR WINE COUNTRY INN & RESTAURANT
707/433-4231
Regional American. Fine Dining. **Address:** 1001 Westside Rd 95448

SPOONBAR 707/433-7222
California. Casual Dining. **Address:** 219 Healdsburg Ave 95448

WILLI'S SEAFOOD & RAW BAR 707/433-9191
Small Plates Seafood. Casual Dining. **Address:** 403 Healdsburg Ave 95448

HOLLISTER pop. 34,928

CASA DE FRUTA INN 408/842-9316
Hotel. **Address:** 10031 Pacheco Pass Hwy 95023

FAIRFIELD INN & SUITES BY MARRIOTT HOLLISTER
831/634-1101
Hotel. **Address:** 390 Gateway Dr 95023   **AAA Benefit:** Members save 5% or more!

SURESTAY HOTEL BY BEST WESTERN HOLLISTER
831/637-9248
Motel. **Address:** 660 San Felipe Rd 95023

WHERE TO EAT

CASA DE FRUTA RESTAURANT 408/842-7282
American. Casual Dining. **Address:** 10031 Pacheco Pass Hwy 95023

HOPLAND pop. 756, elev. 488'
• Part of Wine Country area — see map p. 405

PIAZZA DE CAMPOVIDA 707/744-1977
Italian Pizza. Gastropub. **Address:** 13441 S Hwy 101 95449

HUMBOLDT-TOIYABE NATIONAL FOREST (C-4)

Elevations in the forest range from 3,714 ft. in Younts Spring to 12,374 ft. at Dunderberg (Castle) Peak. Refer to AAA maps for additional elevation information.

Scattered across divisions in central, northern, western and southern Nevada and in eastern California, Humboldt-Toiyabe National Forest is the second largest national forest in the country, totaling 6,343,735 acres. Ranges in north-central Nevada include the Independence, Santa Rosa, Ruby, White Pine, Jarbidge, Schell Creek and Quinn Canyon. Part of the forest lies along the rugged Monitor, Toquima, Toiyabe, Shoshone and Paradise ranges of central Nevada and along the eastern slopes of the Sierra Nevada and the Spring Mountains near Las Vegas.

Jarbidge Wilderness is north of Elko, Nev.; no motorized vehicles are allowed, but six trails suitable for hiking and horseback riding traverse the area. The Ruby Mountains Wilderness, southeast of Elko, offers backpacking and other recreational opportunities within 90,000 acres of alpine lakes, glaciated canyons and rugged mountains. Other wilderness areas include Currant Mountain, East Humboldt, Grant Range, Mount Moriah, Quinn Canyon and Santa Rosa-Paradise Peak.

Four national hiking trails are within the forest. The Pacific Crest National Scenic Trail traverses 74 miles of forest land; the Toiyabe Crest National Recreation Trail runs 67 miles along the Toiyabe Range;

the Ruby Crest National Recreation Trail travels 33 miles across the Ruby Mountains; and the Mount Charleston National Recreation Trail ascends the 11,918-foot summit of Charleston Peak. Due to unpredictable weather conditions, hiking on these trails is best attempted June through October; high elevations can receive snow during any month of the year. Always confirm conditions with the Forest Supervisor's office.

Recreational activities within the forest include backpacking and hiking on nearly 1,000 miles of trails, as well as fishing, hunting, camping and picnicking. Several mountain biking trails have been developed near Austin in central Nevada. Winter sports areas are at Lee Canyon and Mount Rose. Winter sports such as heli-skiing, snowmobiling and cross-country skiing are popular. Other areas noted for visual and recreational appeal are Lake Tahoe, the Sierra Nevada near Bridgeport, Calif., and Mount Rose.

The National Forest Adventure Pass is required in some of the campgrounds in the Humboldt-Toiyabe National Forest. For further information contact the Forest Supervisor, Humboldt-Toiyabe National Forest, 1200 Franklin Way, Sparks, NV 89431; phone (775) 331-6444. *See Recreation Areas Chart.*

LAMOILLE CANYON SCENIC AREA is in Humboldt-Toiyabe National Forest, 20 mi. s.e. of Elko, Nev., via SR 227. A paved, two-lane scenic drive, overshadowed by towering cliffs, winds 12 miles along the canyon. Several overlooks with posted information enable visitors to observe the past effects of glacial activity. Wildflowers bloom abundantly in spring throughout the canyon's meadows. Rest areas are available May-Oct. **Phone:** (775) 738-5171. ▲ 🛆

INYO NATIONAL FOREST (F-5)

Elevations in the forest range from 3,700 ft. in Owens Valley to 14,505 ft. at the summit of Mount Whitney. Refer to AAA maps for additional elevation information.

Inyo National Forest parallels US 6 and US 395 for 165 miles between the eastern California towns of Inyokern and Lee Vining. The forest contains Mount Whitney—at 14,505 feet, the highest point in the contiguous United States—as well as portions of the Pacific Crest Trail and the John Muir Trail. Inyo National Forest shares in managing nine wilderness areas, including the Ansel Adams and John Muir wildernesses. Between US 6 and the Nevada border, the White Mountains rise to 14,246 feet and hold the Ancient Bristlecone Pine Forest, with the oldest living trees on the planet; the Bristlecone visitor center is open to the public from mid-June through late October (weather permitting). Most of the Sierra's highest peaks are visible to the west from US 395.

Vehicle travel is restricted in Devils Postpile National Monument and the Reds Meadow area of the forest: Only vehicles with camping or disabled parking permits, and a few other exceptions, are allowed beyond the Minaret Vista turnoff between 7:30 a.m. and 5:30 p.m., mid-June through Sept. 30. All others are required to use a shuttle bus that operates during the restricted times.

The 2-hour round-trip makes 10 stops, including the Devils Postpile ranger station, where trails lead to recreation areas. Shuttles, which operate mid-June to mid-September, depart the Mammoth Mountain Adventure Center every 20-30 minutes beginning at 7 a.m. The last return shuttle departs Reds Meadow at 7:45 p.m. A shuttle day pass is $7; $4 (ages 3-15). A shuttle 3-day pass is $14; $8 (ages 3-15). Phone (760) 872-1901. The daily entrance fee for vehicles is $10 per private vehicle or $20 for a 3-day pass. Permits are required for overnight access to the Ansel Adams and John Muir wildernesses.

Mammoth and June mountains have ski areas that are popular in winter, while mountain biking, hiking, camping, fishing and backpacking are the main summertime diversions. Gondola rides to the top of Mammoth Mountain provide outstanding views and access to hiking and mountain biking trails. Rides are available daily 9-3:30, mid-June through late Sept. (weather and wind permitting). Fare $25; $20 (ages 13-22 and 65-79); $12 (ages 5-12); free (up to two children ages 5-12 per paying adult and ages 80+). Phone (760) 934-2571 or (800) 626-6684.

Minaret Vista, at 9,175 feet, offers a sweeping view of the Ritter Range. A store and café, as well as saddle and pack horses, are available at Reds Meadow. An interagency welcome center on Main Street in Mammoth Lakes is open year-round; closed Jan. 1, Thanksgiving and Christmas. Phone (760) 924-5500.

Roads throughout the remainder of the forest provide scenic drives. The Eastern Sierra Interagency Visitor Center is south of Lone Pine at the junction of US 395 and SR 136. Phone (760) 876-6222 or TTY (760) 876-6228.

For additional information contact the Superintendent, Inyo National Forest, 351 Pacu Ln., Suite 200, Bishop, CA 93514; phone (760) 873-2400 or TTY (760) 873-2538. For wilderness information phone (760) 873-2483. Campground and wilderness permit reservations can be obtained online through www.recreation.gov. *See Recreation Areas Chart.*

INSIDER INFO:
High-Altitude Health

Temples throbbing, gasping for breath and nauseated, you barely notice the scudding clouds or the spectacular view.

You might be suffering from Acute Mountain Sickness (AMS). Usually striking at around 8,000 feet (2,450 m) in altitude, AMS is your body's way of coping with the reduced oxygen and humidity of high altitudes. Among the symptoms are headaches, shortness of breath, loss of appetite, insomnia and lethargy. Some people complain of temporary weight gain or swelling in the face, hands and feet.

You can reduce the effect of high altitude by being in top condition. If you smoke or suffer from heart or lung ailments, consult your physician before your trip. Certain drugs will intensify the symptoms. To avoid Acute Mountain Sickness, adjust to elevations slowly; a gradual ascent with a couple days of acclimatization is best if you have time. For example, if you are planning a trip to the Rocky Mountains of Colorado, you might want to spend the first night in a lower altitude city such as Denver as opposed to heading directly to an environment with extreme elevations.

On the way up, eat light, nutritious meals and stay hydrated by drinking a large amount of water, taking care to avoid caffeine, alcohol and salt. In addition, your doctor may be able to prescribe medication that can offset the effects of high-altitude.

If you develop AMS, you should stop ascending; you will recover in a few days. If the AMS is mild, a quick descent will end the suffering immediately.

Other high-altitude health problems include sunburn and hypothermia. Dress in layers to protect yourself from the intense sun and wide fluctuations in temperature.

Finally, after you lounge in the sauna or whirlpool bath at your lodgings, remember to stand up carefully, for the heat has relaxed your blood vessels and lowered your blood pressure.

BISHOP CREEK CANYON is 16 mi. w. of Bishop, Calif., on SR 168. Lined by 1,000-foot granite cliffs, the canyon is popular with anglers from late April to mid-November at spots like North Lake, South Lake, Lake Sabrina, Intake II and Bishop Creek. Marked hiking trails traverse this idyllic wilderness region. **Hours:** Daily 24 hours. **Cost:** Free. **Phone:** (760) 873-8405 for the chamber or (888) 395-3952.

JACKSON (E-4) pop. 4,651, elev. 1,200'

Jackson's downtown and vintage Victorian homes are reminders of its gold rush heritage; it was founded in 1848. North of town are several mine headframes; one shaft is approximately 6,000 feet deep. Kennedy Gold Mine Tours allows visitors to view buildings and other structures associated with a mining site that closed in 1942. The tours are offered on weekends and holidays from March through October; for additional information phone (209) 223-9542.

Amador County Chamber of Commerce: 115 Main St., P.O. Box 596, Jackson, CA 95642. **Phone:** (209) 223-0350.

BEST WESTERN AMADOR INN   209/223-0211

Hotel

AAA Benefit: Members save up to 15% and earn bonus points!

Address: 200 S Hwy 49 95642 **Location:** Just se of jct SR 49 and 88. **Facility:** 117 units, some kitchens. 2 stories (no elevator), interior corridors. **Pool:** outdoor. **Guest Services:** coin laundry. **Featured Amenity: breakfast buffet.**

HOLIDAY INN EXPRESS HOTEL & SUITES
209/257-1500

Hotel

Address: 101 Clinton Rd 95642 **Location:** 0.7 mi se of jct SR 49 and 88; jct SR 49 and Clinton Rd. Adjacent to Jackson Cinemas. **Facility:** 51 units. 2 stories, interior corridors. **Pool:** heated outdoor. **Activities:** hot tub, exercise room. **Guest Services:** coin laundry. **Featured Amenity: breakfast buffet.**

JACKSON RANCHERIA CASINO RESORT 209/223-1677

Hotel

Address: 12222 New York Ranch Rd 95642 **Location:** 2.5 mi e of jct SR 49 and 88, 1.8 mi n on Dalton Rd. **Facility:** This modern hotel offers full gaming activities at the adjacent casino and a spacious lobby with a fireplace. Some guest rooms feature balconies. 86 units. 4 stories, interior corridors. **Parking:** on-site and valet. **Amenities:** safes. **Dining:** 2 restaurants. **Pool:** heated outdoor. **Activities:** hot tub, game room, exercise room.

WHERE TO EAT

BRICKHOUSE BREWS   209/223-3580
American. Casual Dining. **Address:** 140 Main St 95642

ROSEBUD'S CAFE   209/257-0227
Breakfast. Casual Dining. **Address:** 26 Main St 95642

STRINGS ITALIAN CAFE   209/223-7874
Italian. Casual Dining. **Address:** 11976 SR 88 95642

JAMESTOWN (F-4) pop. 3,433, elev. 1,405'

The first gold discovery in Tuolumne County was made near Jamestown in 1848. "Jimtown," as it once was called, has served as a backdrop for such movies as "High Noon" and "Butch Cassidy and the Sundance Kid." Several buildings in town date to the 1870s. Many of the balconied buildings in the town's business district, which date from the 1860s and '70s, now house galleries, boutiques and shops.

CALIFORNIA GOLD PANNING is .5 mi. s. on SR 49/108, then .5 mi. w. to 17712 Harvard Mine Rd.

Gold panning and sluicing on Woods Creek in the historic Harvard Mine District are taught by seasoned prospectors who relate the history and stories of the gold-mining camp. Participants can see what the early miners experienced back in the 1800s.

A change of clothing is recommended for children. **Time:** Allow 2 hours minimum. **Hours:** Open by appointment. Closed Christmas. **Cost:** Two hours of panning and sluicing with an instructor for up to five people $180. Experienced miner fee (no instruction given) $25 for 5 hours. Equipment rental is available; phone for rates. Other packages also are offered. Reservations are required. **Phone:** (209) 916-5166. GT

COUNTRY INN SONORA   209/984-0315
Motel. **Address:** 18730 Hwy 108 95327

NATIONAL HOTEL & RESTAURANT   209/984-3446
Historic Boutique Country Inn. **Address:** 18183 Main St 95327

WHERE TO EAT

NATIONAL HOTEL RESTAURANT   209/984-3446
Continental. Casual Dining. **Address:** 18183 Main St 95327

JENNER (E-2) pop. 136, elev. 12'
• Part of Wine Country area — see map p. 405

Jenner Visitor Center: 10439 SR 1, Jenner, CA 95450. **Phone:** (707) 865-9757.

FORT ROSS STATE HISTORIC PARK, 12 mi. n. on SR 1, is the site of an otter hunting base and trading post established in 1812 by The Russian American Company. In addition to trading supplies with missions, members of the Alaskan Native Force stationed at the post hunted otters and other fur-bearing mammals and facilitated the transport of food supplies to more remote settlements in what is now the state of Alaska.

Restored or reconstructed buildings within the stockade include the chapel, officers' barracks, the Kuskov House, two blockhouses and the reconstructed Magazin. Also within the compound is the Rotchev House, a National Historic Landmark and the oldest original surviving structure between San Francisco and the Alaskan border.

The park visitor center has a museum and bookstore. Visitors also can watch a film about the history of the site. Cultural Heritage Day takes place the last Saturday in July. Russian Orthodox services are held Memorial Day, July 4 and the last Saturday in July. Check the website for information about other special events. *See Recreation Areas Chart.*

Dogs are permitting in parking areas only. **Time:** Allow 1 hour minimum. **Hours:** Grounds open daily dawn-dusk. Fort and visitor center hours vary seasonally; phone ahead to confirm schedule. Interpretive talks are given when staff is available. Closed Thanksgiving and Christmas. **Cost:** $8 per private

vehicle; $7 (ages 62+ per private vehicle). Phone for Cultural Heritage Day admission. **Phone:** (707) 847-3286 for information, or (707) 847-3437 for the museum.

TIMBER COVE RESORT   707/847-3231
Hotel. **Address:** 21780 N Coast Hwy 95450

WHERE TO EAT

RIVER'S END   707/865-2484
California. Fine Dining. **Address:** 11048 Hwy 1 95450

KELSEYVILLE (E-2) pop. 3,353, elev. 1,386'
• Part of Wine Country area — see map p. 405

Known as the "Bartlett Pear Capital of the World," Kelseyville is the agricultural center of Lake County. Pear and walnut orchards share the surrounding valley with vineyards.

CLEAR LAKE STATE PARK is 3 mi. n.e. at 5300 Soda Bay Rd. The lake, California's largest freshwater body of water, is a popular spot for all forms of water-based recreation. Fishing, for bass in particular, is particularly good, and a nature trail passes through the site of a former Pomo Indian village. The visitor center has wildlife dioramas and exhibits depicting the lake environment both on land and in water. A theater presents videos, films and demonstrations. *See Recreation Areas Chart.*

Time: Allow 1 hour minimum. **Hours:** Daily dawn-dusk. Visitor center open Sat. 10-4, Sun. 10-1, Memorial Day-Labor Day. Phone ahead to confirm visitor center schedule. **Cost:** Park $8 per private vehicle; $7 (ages 62+ per private vehicle). **Phone:** (707) 279-4293 or (707) 279-2267.

KENWOOD (A-7) pop. 1,028, elev. 415'
• Part of Wine Country area — see map p. 405

Located at the northern end of the Sonoma Valley, Kenwood is known for wineries, good restaurants and outstanding Northern California scenery. Day trippers passing through town should definitely check out Swede's Feeds (9140 Sonoma Hwy.). Opened in 1975 as a feed store operating out of a former gas station, this one-of-a-kind emporium sells—in addition to pet food and garden supplies— pottery, patio furniture and handmade outdoor art. Many of these creations utilize recycled machine parts, wooden barrels and other utilitarian objects. The multistory birdhouses are particularly impressive. Swede's is open Mon. and Wed.-Fri. 10-6, Sat. 10-5, Sun. 11-4; phone (707) 833-5050.

Sample area wines at the Manzanita Creek Tasting Room, 8910 Sonoma Hwy. (in the Kenwood Village Center). The tree-shaded garden courtyard is also a pleasant spot for a picnic lunch. A tasting flight of five wines is refundable with a purchase; reservations are not required for groups of 10 or fewer guests. It's open Thurs.-Mon. noon-6, Tues.-Wed. 3-6; phone (707) 927-4225.

WINERIES

- **Kunde Family Winery** is at 9825 Sonoma Hwy. (SR 12). **Hours:** Tastings daily 10:30-5. Free guided tours of wine aging caves are offered on the hour 11-3. Paid tours of the Kunde Estate also are offered. Closed Jan. 1, Easter, Thanksgiving and Christmas. **Phone:** (707) 282-1537.

KETTLEMAN CITY pop. 1,439

BEST WESTERN KETTLEMAN CITY INN & SUITES
559/386-0804

Motel

 AAA Benefit: Members save up to 15% and earn bonus points!

Address: 33410 Powers Dr 93239 **Location:** I-5 exit 309 (SR 41), just n, just w on Bernard Dr, then just s. **Facility:** 72 units. 2 stories (no elevator), exterior corridors. **Pool:** outdoor. **Guest Services:** coin laundry. **Featured Amenity:** continental breakfast.

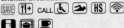

 WHERE TO EAT

WILD JACK'S TEX MEX BBQ   559/386-9750
Barbecue. Quick Serve. **Address:** 33300 Bernard Dr 93239

KING CITY (H-3) pop. 12,874, elev. 330'

King City takes its name from pioneer Charles H. King, who bought 13,000 acres of land in 1884 and founded King Ranch. The town was incorporated in 1911. Crops grown in the surrounding region range from broccoli, lettuce and wine grapes to barley and beans.

King City Chamber of Commerce & Agriculture: 200 Broadway St., Suite 40, King City, CA 93930. **Phone:** (831) 385-3814.

DAYS INN
831/385-5921

Motel

Address: 1130 Broadway St 93930 **Location:** US 101 exit Broadway St, just e. **Facility:** 46 units, some efficiencies. 2 stories (no elevator), exterior corridors. **Pool:** outdoor. **Featured Amenity:** continental breakfast.

KEEFER'S INN   831/385-4843
Motel. **Address:** 615 Canal St 93930

QUALITY INN
831/385-6733

Hotel

Address: 1190 Broadway St 93930 **Location:** US 101 exit Broadway St, just e. **Facility:** 47 units. 2 stories (no elevator), exterior corridors. **Amenities:** safes. **Pool:** heated outdoor.

 WHERE TO EAT

THE CORK & PLOUGH   831/386-9491
American. Casual Dining. **Address:** 200 Broadway St 93930

KINGS BEACH pop. 3,796

- Hotels & Restaurants map & index p. 114
- Part of Lake Tahoe Area — see map p. 111

LANZA'S ITALIAN RESTAURANT   530/546-2434 (10)
Italian. Casual Dining. **Address:** 7739 N Lake Blvd 96143

SPINDLESHANKS AMERICAN BISTRO & WINE BAR
530/546-2191 (11)
American. Casual Dining. **Address:** 400 Brassie Ave 96143

KINGSBURG (G-5) pop. 11,382, elev. 297'

Kingsburg was established in 1875 by the Southern Pacific Railroad. A wave of Swedish emigrants in the late 19th century influenced the local architecture; a number of restored buildings date back to the early 1900s and feature steep, wood-shingled roofs, dormer windows and half-timbers.

Raisin grapes and other fruits are grown in the San Joaquin Valley's fertile soil; Sun-Maid Growers maintains a processing facility in Kingsburg. In keeping with its heritage, the town water tower takes the shape of a giant coffee pot, colorfully decorated in a traditional Swedish motif. This local landmark is illuminated at night.

Kingsburg District Chamber of Commerce: 1475 Draper St., Kingsburg, CA 93631. **Phone:** (559) 897-1111.

FAIRFIELD BY MARRIOTT SELMA-KINGSBURG   559/897-8840
♦♦♦ [SAVE] Hotel. **Address:** 216 Ventura Ct 93631

AAA Benefit: Members save 5% or more!

KINGS CANYON NATIONAL PARK—See Sequoia and Kings Canyon National Parks p. 375

KLAMATH (B-1) pop. 779, elev. 29'

Above the Klamath River on aptly named Bear Bridge, two golden bear statues welcome visitors to the city. Originally painted gray, the bears were re-painted gold in the early 1960s by a group of residents intending to give them a face-lift. State government officials had the bears painted gray again, assuming the new color was the work of vandals; when they realized that well-meaning citizens were responsible, the bears went back to gold.

Klamath Chamber of Commerce: P.O. Box 476, Klamath, CA 95548. **Phone:** (800) 200-2335.

KLAMATH RIVER JET BOAT TOURS departs from 17635 US 101S. Two-hour, 45-mile round-trip narrated jet boat excursions on the Klamath River provide an opportunity to see bears, deer, ospreys, eagles and other wildlife in their natural habitat as well as learn about the history of the river. The captain makes several stops to allow for photographs.

Time: Allow 2 hours minimum. **Hours:** Departures require a minimum of 10 adults. Tours depart daily at 10, 1 and 4, May 1-Oct. 15 (weather permitting). Phone ahead to confirm schedule. **Cost:** $47; $42 (ages 65+ and military with ID); $37 (ages 12-17); $27 (ages 4-11). Reservations are recommended. **Phone:** (707) 482-7775 or (800) 887-5387.

TREES OF MYSTERY is 4 mi. n. on US 101. A .8-mile, groomed interpretive trail leads through a magnificent redwood forest and showcases a number of oddly formed trees, some nearly 2,000 years old

and 300 feet tall. A section of the trail called the Trail of Tall Tales features chainsaw-carved redwood sculptures depicting the legend of Paul Bunyan.

The End of the Trail Museum displays crafts, beadwork and shell ornaments made by members of the Yurok, Karok and Tolowa tribes of northern California. The museum's six rooms also contain Kachina dolls, objects made from cedar wood and exhibits focusing on Native American history. The SkyTrail, a six-passenger gondola, transports visitors through the forest canopy.

Hours: Complex open daily 8-7, June-Aug.; 8:30-6:30, Sept.-Oct.; 9-5, rest of year. Museum opens half an hour later and closes half an hour earlier. Last admission 1 hour, 30 minutes before closing. Closed Christmas. Phone ahead to confirm schedule. **Cost:** $16; $12 (ages 60+); $8 (ages 6-12). Museum free. **Phone:** (707) 482-2251 or (800) 638-3389. 🍴 🏨

HOLIDAY INN EXPRESS-KLAMATH   707/482-1777
♦♦♦ Hotel. **Address:** 171 Klamath Blvd 95548

MOTEL TREES   707/482-3152

♦♦ Motel

Address: 15495 Hwy 101 N 95548 **Location:** On US 101, 4.5 mi n of Klamath. Opposite Trees of Mystery. **Facility:** 23 units, some two bedrooms. 1 story, exterior corridors. **Bath:** shower only.

[SAVE] 🍴 📶 🧺 🛏 🗄 🖥 | SOME UNITS 🐕

KLAMATH NATIONAL FOREST (A-2)

Elevations in the forest range from 523 ft. at Somes Bar to 8,563 ft. at Caribou Mountain. Refer to AAA maps for additional elevation information.

Covering about 1,726,000 acres in northern California with a small segment also extending into Oregon, Klamath National Forest is characterized by rugged forested ridges, rushing rivers and high mountain lakes and streams. Much of this scenic area is included in the Marble Mountain Wilderness and Trinity Alps Wilderness, which are accessible only by trail. Vehicular traffic is prohibited in wilderness areas. Hunting, fishing and white-water rafting opportunities are available.

Good fishing spots abound, and the forest is a prime location for anglers in search of steelhead and salmon. Trout fishing is popular in creeks and high mountain lakes. Outdoor enthusiasts also can camp, hike, horseback ride, ski and snowmobile.

Marble Mountain Guest Ranch, 92520 SR 96, offers a family-oriented dude ranch experience that combines cowboy-style trail riding and other traditional ranch activities with whitewater rafting, kayaking, fly fishing and jet boating on the Lower Klamath River. From Eureka, take SR 299 east to Willow Creek, then SR 96 north past Somes Bar to Siskiyou County mile post 7.6. Drive time from Eureka is about 2 1/2 hours. The ranch is open to visitors from April through November; phone (530) 469-3322 or (800) 552-6284.

Klamath River Highway and forest roads and trails provide access to the region. For information contact the Forest Supervisor, Klamath National Forest, 1711 S. Main St., Yreka, CA 96097-9549; phone (530) 842-6131. *See Recreation Areas Chart.*

LAFAYETTE pop. 23,893
• **Hotels & Restaurants map & index p. 176**

THE PARK BISTRO & BAR   925/283-7108 (31)
💎💎💎 American. Fine Dining. **Address:** 3287 Mt. Diablo Blvd 94549

LAKEPORT (D-2) pop. 4,753, elev. 1,343'
• **Part of Wine Country area — see map p. 405**

On the western shore of Clear Lake *(see Recreation Areas Chart)*, one of California's largest, Lakeport is known for excellent fishing (especially bass) and water recreation.

Lake County Chamber of Commerce & Visitors Center: 875 Lakeport Blvd., Lakeport, CA 95453. **Phone:** (707) 263-5092 or (866) 525-3767.

KONOCTI VISTA CASINO RESORT & MARINA   707/262-1900
💎💎 Motel. **Address:** 2755 Mission Rancheria Rd 95453

LAKEPORT ENGLISH INN   707/263-4317
💎💎💎 Bed & Breakfast. **Address:** 675 N Main St 95453

RODEWAY INN & SUITES SKYLARK SHORES RESORT
                                          707/263-6151
💎💎 Motel. **Address:** 1120 N Main St 95453

WHERE TO EAT

PARK PLACE RESTAURANT   707/263-0444
💎💎 American. Casual Dining. **Address:** 50 3rd St 95453

LAKE TAHOE AREA

Lake Tahoe was named "big water" by the Washoe Indians. According to Washoe legend, it was created during the pursuit of an innocent Native American man by an Evil Spirit. In an attempt to ward off the Evil Spirit, the Great Spirit bestowed upon the pursued man a branch of leaves, promising that each leaf dropped would magically produce a body of water that would impede the Evil Spirit's chase. The man, however, dropped the entire branch in fright, thus creating the giant lake.

It is estimated that Lake Tahoe holds enough water to cover the entire state of California to a depth of 14 inches. Its average depth is 989 feet; the deepest point is 1,645 feet, making Tahoe the third-deepest lake in North America. The water is remarkably clear, deep blue and also 97 percent pure—nearly the same level as distilled water. The first 12 feet below the surface can warm to 68 F in summer, while depths below 700 feet remain at a constant temperature of 39 F.

Twelve miles wide and 22 miles long, this "lake in the sky" straddles the California/Nevada line at an elevation of 6,229 feet. It lies in a valley between the main Sierra Nevada range and an eastern offshoot, the Carson Range. The mountains, which are snow-capped except in late summer, rise more than 4,000 feet above Tahoe's resort-lined shore. Most of the surrounding region is covered by the Eldorado, Humboldt-Toiyabe and Tahoe national forests.

Immigrants and miners were lured to the rugged Sierras by tales of fortunes made during the California gold rush. The discovery of the Comstock Lode increased traffic and depleted the Tahoe Basin's natural resources to a dangerously low level. Between 1860 and 1890 lumber was needed for fuel and to support the web of mines constructed beneath Virginia City, Nev. The subsequent decline of the Comstock Lode spared many thousands of trees.

By the early 20th century Lake Tahoe was a retreat for the rich, with luxury lakeside hotels springing up along its shores. After roads were paved during the 1920s and '30s, the lakeshore was no longer an enclave only for the wealthy.

The landscape is often snow-covered in winter, and skiing and snowboarding enthusiasts head to well-known areas like Diamond Peak, Heavenly and Squaw Valley Alpine Meadows. Despite cold winters, however, the lake never freezes over due to the constant flow of water from the bottom to the surface. Popular summer recreational activities include mountain biking, hiking, fishing, golfing, kayaking, windsurfing, canoeing, horseback riding, snorkeling, water skiing, boating and swimming.

This map shows cities in the Lake Tahoe Area where you will find attractions, hotels and restaurants. Cities are listed alphabetically in this book on the following pages.

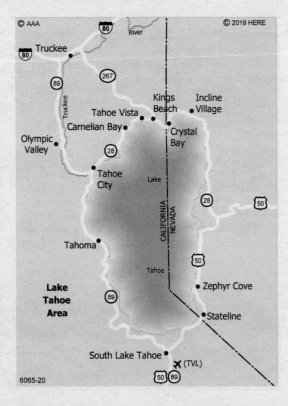

The Tahoe Rim Trail, a 165-mile loop running along the ridges and peaks surrounding Lake Tahoe, offers a splendid panorama of the lake, California's High Sierra and Nevada's Great Basin as well as a route used in summer by hikers and horseback riders and in winter for snowshoeing. Mountain biking is allowed in certain areas. For additional information contact the Tahoe Rim Trail Association; phone (775) 298-4485.

The headquarters of the U.S. Forest Service-Lake Tahoe Basin Management Unit provides year-round information about wilderness permits and forest activities, including camping and hiking in summer and cross-country skiing in winter. The headquarters is open Mon.-Fri. 8-4:30 (weather permitting). For information contact Lake Tahoe Basin Management Unit, 35 College Dr., South Lake Tahoe, CA 96150; phone (530) 543-2600, or TTY (530) 543-0956.

The Taylor Creek Visitor Center *(see attraction listing p. 384)*, on SR 89 between Camp Richardson and Emerald Bay in South Lake Tahoe, Calif., is operated by the U.S. Forest Service; phone (530) 543-2674.

The two main approaches to the Tahoe region are the North Shore via I-80 and the South Shore via US 50. The towns are smaller and the setting more rural along the North Shore, roughly the 14 miles between Tahoe City, Calif., and Incline Village, Nev. Major South Shore tourist destinations like South Lake Tahoe and Stateline, Nev., offer plenty of casinos, shopping and local restaurants.

Two-lane US 50 and SR 28 together encompass the lake; the total circumference is 72 miles. Scenic overlooks off this loop, such as Inspiration Point (near Vikingsholm), offer expansive lake and mountain vistas. SR 89 in the vicinity of Emerald Bay occasionally closes during heavy snowfalls. Road and weather updates are available from the California Department of Transportation (Caltrans); phone (916) 654-2852.

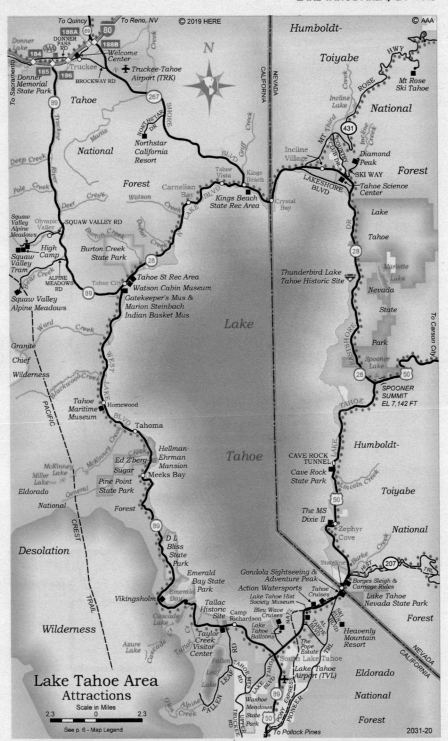

© 2019 HERE   © AAA

To Quincy   To Reno, NV

Humboldt-

Toiyabe

Donner Lake

To Sacramento

Donner Memorial State Park

Welcome Center

Truckee

DONNER PASS RD

BROCKWAY RD

Truckee-Tahoe Airport (TRK)

Mt Rose Ski Tahoe

ROSE HWY

Incline Lake

National

Tahoe

NORTHSTAR DR

Northstar California Resort

Incline Village

431

Diamond Peak

Forest

National

Tahoe Vista

SKI WAY

LAKESHORE BLVD

Tahoe Science Center

Carnelian Bay

Kings Beach

Kings Beach State Rec Area

Crystal Bay

Forest

Squaw Valley Alpine Meadows

SQUAW VALLEY RD

Olympic Valley

Burton Creek State Park

Lake

High Camp

Squaw Valley Tram

ALPINE MEADOWS RD

Tahoe City

Tahoe St Rec Area

Watson Cabin Museum

Gatekeeper's Mus & Marion Steinbach Indian Basket Mus

Thunderbird Lake Tahoe Historic Site

Tahoe

Mariette Lake

Nevada

Squaw Valley Alpine Meadows

State

Spooner Lake

To Carson City

Granite Chief Wilderness

Lake

Park

PACIFIC

Tahoe Maritime Museum

Homewood

SPOONER SUMMIT EL 7,142 FT

Tahoma

50

Tahoe

Hellman-Ehrman Mansion

Humboldt-

Ed Z'berg Sugar Pine Point State Park

Meeks Bay

CAVE ROCK TUNNEL

Cave Rock State Park

Toiyabe

McKinney Lake

Miller Lake

Eldorado

National

Forest

The MS Dixie II

Zephyr Cove

National

CREST

89

D L Bliss State Park

Desolation

Emerald Bay State Park

Gondola Sightseeing & Adventure Peak

Action Watersports

Stateline

207

Borges Sleigh & Carriage Rides

Wilderness

Vikingsholm

Tahoe Cruises

Lake Tahoe Hist Society Museum

Bleu Wave Cruises

Lake Tahoe Nevada State Park

Forest

TRAIL

Tallac Historic Site

Camp Richardson

Lake Tahoe Balloons

Heavenly Mountain Resort

Azure Lake

Taylor Creek Visitor Center

The Pope Estate

South Lake Tahoe

Eldorado

Alpine Lake

Washoe Meadows State Park

Lake Tahoe Airport (TVL)

National

NEVADA

CALIFORNIA

Lake Tahoe Area
Attractions

Scale in Miles

2.3   0   2.3

See p. 6 - Map Legend

To Pollock Pines

2031-20

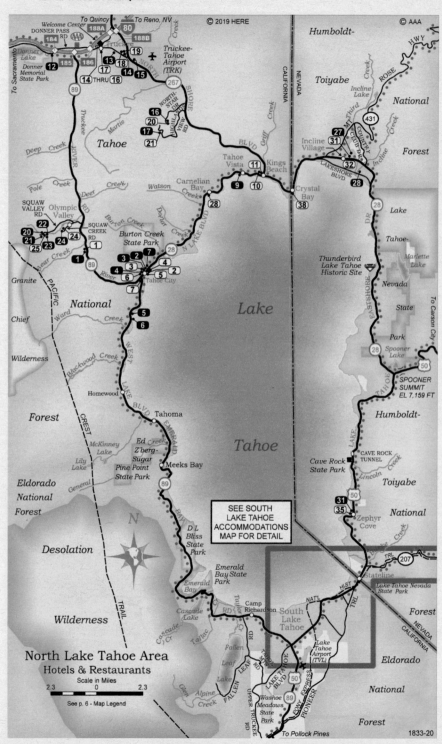

North Lake Tahoe Area
Hotels & Restaurants
Scale in Miles
2.3   2.3
See p. 6 - Map Legend

SEE SOUTH
LAKE TAHOE
ACCOMMODATIONS
MAP FOR DETAIL

© 2019 HERE

© AAA

1833-20

North Lake Tahoe Area

This index helps you "spot" where approved hotels and restaurants are located on the corresponding detailed maps. Restaurant price range is a combination of lunch and/or dinner. Turn to the listing page for more information and consult display ads for special promotions.

 For more details, rates and reservations: AAA.com/travelguides/hotels

TAHOE CITY

Map Page	Hotels	Diamond Rated	Member Savings	Page
1 p. 114	River Ranch Lodge	◈◈		392
2 p. 114	**Pepper Tree Inn**	◈◈	✔	392
3 p. 114	Mother Nature's Inn	◈◈		392
4 p. 114	**Americas Best Value Inn Lake Tahoe/Tahoe City**	◈	✔	392
5 p. 114	Cottage Inn at Lake Tahoe	◈◈◈		392
6 p. 114	Sunnyside Restaurant & Lodge	◈◈◈		392
7 p. 114	Basecamp Tahoe City	◈◈		392

Map Page	Restaurants	Diamond Rated	Cuisine	Price Range	Page
① p. 114	River Ranch Lodge Restaurant	◈◈	American	$14-$34	393
② p. 114	Wolfdale's	◈◈◈	Fusion	$12-$60	393
③ p. 114	Rosie's Cafe	◈◈	American	$10-$20	393
④ p. 114	Jake's on the Lake	◈◈	Seafood	$9-$32	393
⑤ p. 114	Christy Hill Restaurant	◈◈◈	American	$27-$42	393
⑥ p. 114	The Blue Agave Mexican Restaurant & Cantina	◈◈	Mexican	$8-$26	393
⑦ p. 114	Bridgetender Tavern & Grill	◈◈	American	$6-$12	393

TAHOE VISTA

Map Page	Hotel	Diamond Rated	Member Savings	Page
9 p. 114	Mourelatos Lakeshore Resort	◈◈		393

TRUCKEE

Map Page	Hotels	Diamond Rated	Member Savings	Page
12 p. 114	**Truckee Donner Lodge**	◈◈	✔	396
13 p. 114	The Cedar House Sport Hotel	◈◈◈		396
14 p. 114	**Best Western Plus Truckee Tahoe Hotel**	◈◈◈	✔	396
15 p. 114	Hampton Inn & Suites Tahoe-Truckee	◈◈◈	✔	396
16 p. 114	Tahoe Mountain Lodging	◈◈◈		396
17 p. 114	**The Ritz-Carlton, Lake Tahoe**	◈◈◈◈◈	✔	396

Map Page	Restaurants	Diamond Rated	Cuisine	Price Range	Page
⑭ p. 114	Truckee Tavern and Grill	◈◈◈	California	$16-$40	396
⑮ p. 114	**Bar of America**	◈◈	American	$18-$47	396
⑯ p. 114	Jax at the Tracks	◈◈	American	$10-$26	396
⑰ p. 114	Cottonwood Restaurant & Bar	◈◈◈	American	$14-$36	396
⑱ p. 114	Fifty Fifty Brewing Co.	◈◈	American	$11-$29	396
⑲ p. 114	Thai Delicacy	◈◈	Thai	$11-$18	396
⑳ p. 114	Rubicon Pizza Company	◈◈	Italian Pizza	$13-$25	396
㉑ p. 114	Manzanita	◈◈◈	California	$25-$58	396

OLYMPIC VALLEY

Map Page	Hotels	Diamond Rated	Member Savings	Page
20 p. 114	PlumpJack Squaw Valley Inn	◈◈◈		184
21 p. 114	Squaw Valley Lodge	◈◈		185
22 p. 114	The Village at Squaw Valley	◈◈◈		185
23 p. 114	Red Wolf Lodge at Squaw Valley	◈◈		184
24 p. 114	**Resort at Squaw Creek**	◈◈◈◈	✔	185

Map Page	Restaurants	Diamond Rated	Cuisine	Price Range	Page
24 p. 114	Six Peaks Grill	◈◈◈	American	$24-$70	185
25 p. 114	Fireside Pizza Company	◈◈	Italian Pizza	$13-$26	185

INCLINE VILLAGE, NV

Map Page	Hotels	Diamond Rated	Member Savings	Page
27 p. 114	Club Tahoe Resort	◈◈		120
28 p. 114	**Hyatt Regency Lake Tahoe Resort, Spa and Casino**	◈◈◈◈	✔	120

Map Page	Restaurants	Diamond Rated	Cuisine	Price Range	Page
31 p. 114	Azzara's Italian Restaurant	◈◈	Italian	$13-$29	120
32 p. 114	T's Mesquite Rotisserie	◈	Tex-Mex	$3-$12	120

ZEPHYR COVE, NV

Map Page	Hotel	Diamond Rated	Member Savings	Page
31 p. 114	**Zephyr Cove Resort**	◈◈	✔	121

Map Page	Restaurant	Diamond Rated	Cuisine	Price Range	Page
35 p. 114	Zephyr Cove Lodge Restaurant	◈◈	American	$14-$44	121

KINGS BEACH

Map Page	Restaurants	Diamond Rated	Cuisine	Price Range	Page
10 p. 114	Lanza's Italian Restaurant	◈◈	Italian	$15-$26	108
11 p. 114	Spindleshanks American Bistro & Wine Bar	◈◈	American	$17-$38	108

CARNELIAN BAY

Map Page	Restaurant	Diamond Rated	Cuisine	Price Range	Page
28 p. 114	**Gar Woods Grill & Pier**	◈◈◈	American	$18-$48	59

CRYSTAL BAY, NV

Map Page	Restaurant	Diamond Rated	Cuisine	Price Range	Page
38 p. 114	Crystal Bay Steak & Lobster House	◈◈◈	Steak	$24-$84	119

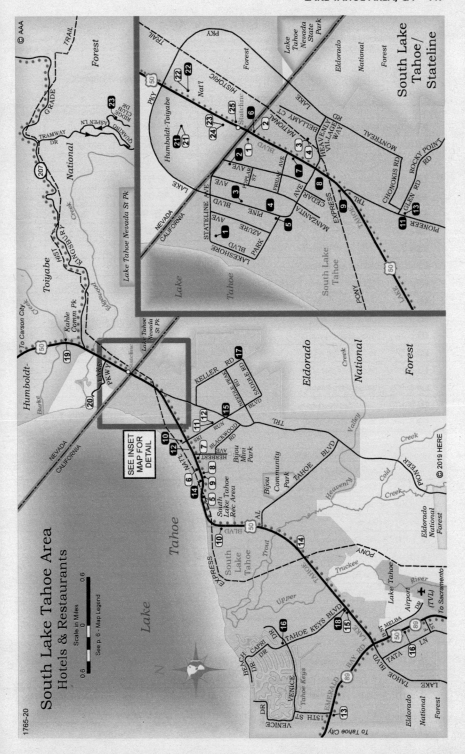

South Lake Tahoe Area
Hotels & Restaurants

South Lake Tahoe/Stateline

South Lake Tahoe Area

This index helps you "spot" where approved hotels and restaurants are located on the corresponding detailed maps. Restaurant price range is a combination of lunch and/or dinner. Turn to the listing page for more information and consult display ads for special promotions.

 For more details, rates and reservations: AAA.com/travelguides/hotels

SOUTH LAKE TAHOE

Map Page	Hotels	Diamond Rated	Member Savings	Page
1 p. 117	The Landing	◈◈◈◈		385
2 p. 117	**Basecamp Hotel**	◈◈	✔	385
3 p. 117	The Coachman Hotel	◈◈		385
4 p. 117	Alpenrose Inn	◈◈		385
5 p. 117	Station House Inn	◈◈		385
6 p. 117	**Lake Tahoe Resort Hotel**	◈◈◈	✔	385
7 p. 117	Stardust Lodge	◈◈		385
8 p. 117	Hotel Becket Trademark Collection by Wyndham	◈◈		385
9 p. 117	**Holiday Inn Express**	◈◈◈	✔	385
10 p. 117	Lake Tahoe Vacation Resort - A Diamond Resort	◈◈◈		385
11 p. 117	Americana Village	◈◈		385
12 p. 117	Tahoe Beach & Ski Club	◈◈		385
13 p. 117	The Lodge at Lake Tahoe	◈◈		385
14 p. 117	Beach Retreat & Lodge at Tahoe	◈◈		385
15 p. 117	Heavenly Valley Lodge	◈◈		385
16 p. 117	**Tahoe Keys Resort**	◈◈	✔	385
17 p. 117	Tahoe Seasons Resort	◈◈		385
18 p. 117	Tahoe Valley Lodge	◈◈		385

Map Page	Restaurants	Diamond Rated	Cuisine	Price Range	Page
1 p. 117	McP's Taphouse Grill	◈◈	Irish	$13-$23	386
2 p. 117	Echo Restaurant & Lounge	◈◈	American	$9-$27	385
3 p. 117	Base Camp Pizza Co.	◈◈	Pizza	$10-$25	385
4 p. 117	Kalani's	◈◈◈	Hawaiian	$12-$42	386
5 p. 117	Freshies Restaurant & Bar	◈◈	Hawaiian	$9-$28	385
6 p. 117	Heidi's Pancake House	◈◈	American	$8-$20	385
7 p. 117	The Brewery at Lake Tahoe	◈◈	American	$12-$28	385
8 p. 117	**Tep's Villa Roma**	◈◈	Italian	$13-$22	386
9 p. 117	A Cup of Cherries	◈◈	American	$6-$16	385
10 p. 117	Sprouts Natural Foods Cafe	◈	Natural/Organic	$8-$12	386
11 p. 117	Nepheles	◈◈◈	California	$26-$38	386
12 p. 117	Cafe Fiore Ristorante Italiano	◈◈◈	Italian	$24-$43	385
13 p. 117	Evans American Gourmet Cafe	◈◈◈	American	$29-$42	385
14 p. 117	Off The Hook Sushi	◈◈	Sushi	$8-$29	386
15 p. 117	Artemis Mediterranean Grill	◈◈	Mediterranean	$7-$24	385
16 p. 117	Lake Tahoe Pizza Company	◈◈	Pizza	$6-$24	386

STATELINE, NV

Map Page	Hotels	Diamond Rated	Member Savings	Page
㉑ p. 117	Hard Rock Hotel & Casino Lake Tahoe	◇◇◇		120
㉒ p. 117	**MontBleu Resort Casino & Spa**	◇◇◇	✔	120
㉓ p. 117	The Ridge Tahoe	◇◇◇		121

Map Page	Restaurants	Diamond Rated	Cuisine	Price Range	Page
⑲ p. 117	Tahoe Hot Pot	◇◇	Korean Soup	$7-$30	121
⑳ p. 117	Brooks' Bar & Deck	◇◇	American	$14-$44	121
㉑ p. 117	Park Prime	◇◇◇	Steak	$29-$55	121
㉒ p. 117	**Ciera Steak & Chop House**	◇◇◇◇	Steak	$30-$140	121
㉓ p. 117	Sage Room Steak House	◇◇◇	Steak	$35-$89	121
㉔ p. 117	19 Kitchen Bar	◇◇◇	Continental	$20-$82	121
㉕ p. 117	Friday's Station Steak & Seafood Grill	◇◇◇	Steak	$31-$95	121

Nearby Nevada

CRYSTAL BAY   pop. 305
- **Hotels & Restaurants map & index p. 114**
- **Part of Lake Tahoe Area — see map p. 111**

CRYSTAL BAY STEAK & LOBSTER HOUSE
775/833-6333   ㊳
◇◇◇ Steak. Fine Dining. **Address:** 14 State Route 28 89402

INCLINE VILLAGE   pop. 8,777, elev. 6,404'
- **Hotels p. 120 • Restaurants p. 120**
- **Hotels & Restaurants map & index p. 114**
- **Part of Lake Tahoe Area — see map p. 111**

Incline Village, the second largest community in the North Lake Tahoe area and the largest on the Nevada shore, spreads back toward the mountains from the lake's northeastern corner. The town takes its name from the Great Incline Tramway, built in 1874 to transport logs to the crest of the Carson Range; from there a flume sluiced them down to the Washoe Valley.

This was Tahoe's quietest corner before development took off in the 1960s; today it's a popular resort town. Lakeshore Drive, a 3-mile stretch that parallels Tahoe Boulevard (SR 28), runs along the lake past pricey-looking homes and condo developments shaded by lush growths of pines and conifers. Businesses and restaurants line busy Tahoe Boulevard.

Perhaps the most spectacularly scenic way to enter Incline Village is via SR 431, better known as the Mount Rose Highway. From downtown Reno, access US 395 South and get off at exit 59 (Damonte Ranch Parkway), following the directional signs to the beginning of this designated scenic route. The road immediately narrows from four lanes to two, and the flat Washoe Valley is left behind for the gently rolling, sagebrush-dotted Sierra Nevada foothills once the climb into the mountains begins.

The Mount Rose Highway doesn't actually ascend Mount Rose; it negotiates the rugged Carson Range of the Sierras, and Mount Rose, at 10,776 feet, is one of several impressively lofty mountain peaks in this wilderness region. The road quickly gains elevation in a series of serpentine bends, with designated pull-offs offering dizzying views of the valley far below.

A different vista reveals itself around each curve. Snow often covers the mountainsides—at this elevation, July and August are just about the only snow-free months of the year. It glints under the brilliant blue sky like diamonds, adding a fairy-tale beauty to the scene.

Mount Rose Summit, at an elevation of just over 8,900 feet, is the point where the highway crests the Sierras. After that the descent toward Incline Village and Lake Tahoe begins via another series of hairpin curves. The initial view of Lake Tahoe, a distant, sapphire-blue mirage framed by tall pine trees, is a stunner. The highway ends at SR 28; follow the roundabout to the second turn and head into Incline Village.

A right turn on Village Boulevard will take you down to Lakeshore Drive; turn left and watch for the entrance to Incline Beach (967 Lakeshore Dr.), a little park right along the shore. The pebbly beach here is often delightfully uncrowded, and the aromatic scent of pine fills the air. The water is calm—only the slightest ripple of a wave breaking at the shoreline—and amazingly clear. The reason? Nearly half of the precipitation falling on the Lake Tahoe Basin lands directly into the lake. The remaining rain and snowfall drains through soils of decomposed granite, which creates a filtering system. This magnificent outdoor setting is a lovely place to spend a peaceful hour.

South of town SR 28 runs through Lake Tahoe-Nevada State Park, which extends from the lake to the summit of the Carson Range. Hidden Beach and Sand Harbor State Park are popular spots known for their large, rounded boulder formations. The highway then climbs above the lake, offering sweeping views westward.

Sand Harbor State Park is the scene for the ▽ Lake Tahoe Shakespeare Festival, which runs early July to late August.

(See map & index p. 114.)

Incline Village Crystal Bay Visitors Bureau: 969 Tahoe Blvd., Incline Village, NV 89451. **Phone:** (775) 832-1606 or (800) 468-2463.

TAHOE SCIENCE CENTER is at 291 Country Club Dr. on the Sierra Nevada College campus. Located on the first floor of the Tahoe Center for Environmental Sciences building, the science center features interactive science exhibits, including one about Lake Tahoe. Visitors can step aboard a virtual research vessel to see how water quality is studied, check out a virtual lab with microscopic zooplankton, and manipulate topography in an interactive sandbox to see how watersheds work. Video presentations include 3-D movies (each 16 minutes) "Lake Tahoe in Depth" and "Mapping Change," which takes a look at Sierra forests, as well as 3-D visualization models of Lake Tahoe and Earth.

The center showcases sustainable design, construction and landscaping. Tours of the LEED Platinum-certified building are available by reservation.

Time: Allow 1 hour, 15 minutes minimum. **Hours:** Building open Mon.-Fri. 8-5. Science center Tues.-Sat. 1-5, Memorial Day-Labor Day; Tues.-Fri. 1-5, rest of year. Guided tours are available; phone ahead for schedule. **Cost:** Free. **Phone:** (775) 881-7566. GT

THUNDERBIRD LAKE TAHOE HISTORIC SITE tours depart from the Incline Village Crystal Bay Visitors Bureau at 969 Tahoe Blvd. (SR 28). A shuttle bus takes visitors to this magnificent estate built in 1936 by George Whittell, an eccentric San Francisco millionaire. The prominent family's fortune was accumulated from gold rush-era banking, real estate and railroads. The somewhat reclusive Whittell developed a fancy for exotic animals and frequently brought his pet lion Bill and Mingo the elephant to his summer retreat.

A picturesque example of the "old Tahoe" style of architecture, the stone lodge was designed to blend into its secluded setting overlooking the lake. The heavily forested site on the eastern shore of Lake Tahoe affords amazing views. In addition to the Tudor Revival lodge, the 6-acre property encompasses a gatehouse, three cottages, a card house, a boathouse, three garages, a lighthouse and a barn for Whittell's elephant.

The 75-minute guided tour includes the light-house room; the old lodge; the servants' quarters; and a 600-foot tunnel leading to the boathouse, home to Whittell's 1939, 55-foot mahogany-hulled yacht *Thunderbird*. After hearing a few card-house poker stories, visitors enjoy the gardens and fountains. Exceptional iron, stone and woodwork can be seen throughout the estate.

Note: The tour requires being able to walk on uneven ground and climb steps. **Time:** Allow 1 hour, 30 minutes minimum. **Hours:** Tours are given Tues.-Sat. at 9:30, 11, 12:30 and 2, late July to mid-Sept.;

Tues. and Fri.-Sat. at 9:30, 11, 12:30 and 2, mid-May through late June and mid-Sept. to mid-Oct. Guests should arrive at the visitor center 30 minutes prior to departure. Phone ahead to confirm schedule. **Cost:** $45; $19 (ages 6-12). Under 6 are not permitted. Reservations are required. **Phone:** (800) 468-2463 for tour reservations. GT

CLUB TAHOE RESORT   775/831-5750   **27**
♦♦ Vacation Rental Condominium. **Address:** 914 Northwood Blvd 89451

HYATT REGENCY LAKE TAHOE RESORT, SPA AND CASINO   775/832-1234   **28**

Resort Hotel

HYATT REGENCY · **AAA Benefit:** Members save up to 10%!

Address: 111 Country Club Dr 89450 **Location:** 0.4 mi w of SR 28, toward lake via Country Club Dr; 2 mi s of Mt. Rose Hwy. **Facility:** Nestled in the pines, this resort offers extensive recreational facilities and manicured grounds. Some rooms front a private Lake Tahoe beach, others overlook the pools. 422 units, some cottages. 3-12 stories, interior corridors. **Parking:** on-site (fee) and valet. **Terms:** check-in 4 pm. **Amenities:** safes. **Dining:** 4 restaurants, entertainment. **Pool:** heated outdoor. **Activities:** hot tub, limited beach access, motor boats, self-propelled boats, fishing, recreation programs in summer, kids club, bicycles, playground, game room, lawn sports, picnic facilities, health club, spa. **Guest Services:** valet laundry, boarding pass kiosk, rental car service, area transportation.

SAVE ECO 🐾 🍴 📶 🍸 🏋 🏊 🚼 BIZ SHS 📶 ✉ 🔌 🖥 / SOME UNITS 🐾 🏖

WHERE TO EAT

AZZARA'S ITALIAN RESTAURANT   775/831-0346   **31**
♦♦ Italian. Casual Dining. **Address:** 930 Tahoe Blvd 89450

T'S MESQUITE ROTISSERIE   775/831-2832   **32**
♦ Tex-Mex. Quick Serve. **Address:** 901 Tahoe Blvd 89451

STATELINE pop. 842, elev. 6,283'

• Hotels & Restaurants map & index p. 114, 117
• Part of Lake Tahoe Area — see map p. 111

Tahoe Chamber: 169 US 50, 3rd floor, P.O. Box 7139, Stateline, NV 89449. **Phone:** (775) 588-1728.

HARD ROCK HOTEL & CASINO LAKE TAHOE   775/588-1010   **21**
♦♦♦ Hotel. **Address:** 50 US 50 89449

MONTBLEU RESORT CASINO & SPA
                             775/588-3515   **22**

Hotel

Address: 55 Lake Tahoe Blvd (US 50) 89449 **Location:** 0.4 mi sw of jct SR 207. **Facility:** The vibrant rooms, many with views, boast a contemporary Tahoe décor with dark furnishings and red accents. The huge indoor pool area is a big hit, along with the bright bustling casino and lounge. 438 units. 15 stories, interior corridors. **Parking:** on-site and valet. **Terms:** check-in 4 pm. **Amenities:** safes. **Dining:** 3 restaurants, also, Ciera Steak & Chop House, see separate listing, nightclub, entertainment. **Pool:** heated indoor. **Activities:** sauna, hot tub, game room, health club, spa. **Guest Services:** valet laundry.

SAVE 🐾 🍴 📶 🍸 CALL 🦽 🏊 🚼 BIZ 📶 🖥 / SOME UNITS 🔌

(See maps & indexes p. 114, 117.)

THE RIDGE TAHOE   775/588-3553 (23)
♦♦♦ Vacation Rental Condominium. **Address:** 400 Ridge Club Dr 89449

19 KITCHEN BAR   775/588-2411 (24)
♦♦♦ Continental. Fine Dining. **Address:** 18 US 50 89449

BROOKS' BAR & DECK   775/588-6183 (20)
♦♦ American. Casual Dining. **Address:** 100 Lake Pkwy 89449

CIERA STEAK & CHOP HOUSE   775/588-3515 (22)

♦♦♦♦

Steak
Fine Dining
$30-$140

AAA Inspector Notes: High-grade steaks and seafood are prepared in an upscale setting that is elegant, yet comfortable. Rich wood accents and private, expansive booths add to the appeal of the dining room. Desserts are delicious, and an extensive wine list has many enticing options. **Features:** full bar. **Reservations:** suggested. **Address:** 55 Lake Tahoe Blvd (US 50) 89449 **Location:** 0.4 mi sw of jct SR 207; in MontBleu Resort Casino & Spa. **Parking:** onsite and valet. [D]

FRIDAY'S STATION STEAK & SEAFOOD GRILL
                                        775/588-6611 (25)
♦♦♦ Steak. Casual Dining. **Address:** 15 Hwy 50 89449

PARK PRIME   775/589-7680 (21)
♦♦♦ Steak. Fine Dining. **Address:** 50 US 50 89449

SAGE ROOM STEAK HOUSE   775/588-2411 (23)
♦♦♦ Steak. Casual Dining. **Address:** 18 US 50 89449

TAHOE HOT POT   775/586-8883 (19)
♦♦ Korean Soup. Casual Dining. **Address:** 177 US-50 89449

ZEPHYR COVE pop. 565, elev. 6,348'
• Hotels & Restaurants map & index p. 114
• Part of Lake Tahoe Area — see map p. 111

ZEPHYR COVE RESORT   775/589-4980 (31)

♦♦
Cabin

Address: 760 Hwy 50 89448 **Location:** 4 mi n of Stateline, NV. **Facility:** 32 units, some cabins. 1-2 stories (no elevator), interior/exterior corridors. **Dining:** Zephyr Cove Lodge Restaurant, see separate listing. **Activities:** beach access, marina, fishing, snowmobiling. **Guest Services:** coin laundry.

    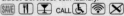   

ZEPHYR COVE LODGE RESTAURANT   775/589-4968 (35)
♦♦ American. Casual Dining. **Address:** 760 Hwy 50 89448

This ends the Lake Tahoe Area section and resumes the alphabetical city listings for Northern California.

LARKSPUR pop. 11,926
• Part of San Francisco area — see map p. 243

COURTYARD BY MARRIOTT LARKSPUR   415/925-1800
♦♦♦ [SAVE] Hotel. **Address:** 2500 Larkspur Landing Cir 94939

AAA Benefit:
Members save 5% or more!

BELCAMPO MEAT CO.   415/448-5810
♦♦ American. Casual Dining. **Address:** 2405 Larkspur Landing Cir, Bldg 4 94939

FARMSHOP   415/755-6700
♦♦ California. Casual Dining. **Address:** 2233 Larkspur Landing Circle 94939

FUKUSUKE   415/924-8848
♦♦ Japanese. Casual Dining. **Address:** 578 Magnolia Ave 94939

LEFT BANK   415/927-3331
♦♦♦ French. Casual Dining. **Address:** 507 Magnolia Ave 94939

PIZZERIA PICCO   415/945-8900
♦♦ Pizza. Casual Dining. **Address:** 316 Magnolia Ave 94939

LASSEN NATIONAL FOREST (C-3)

Elevations in the forest range from 800 ft. near Butte Meadows to 8,172 ft. at West Prospect Peak. Refer to AAA maps for additional elevation information.

Covering approximately 1,375,000 acres surrounding Lassen Volcanic National Park, Lassen National Forest includes numerous lakes formed by ancient volcanic action.

Several highways, forest roads and trails allow access to the region. The Caribou, Thousand Lakes and Ishi wilderness areas allow backpacking. Campfire permits are required, except in campgrounds with developed facilities. Obtain permits in person at any Forest Service, Bureau of Land Management or California Department of Forestry Office. Visitors enjoy hunting, fishing, cross-country skiing and snowmobiling.

The Subway Cave lava tube, about .1 mile north of SR 44 off SR 89, winds 1,300 feet through a lava flow that covered the Hat Creek Valley nearly 20,000 years ago. Carry a jacket and a reliable lantern or flashlight while exploring the .3-mile self-guiding interpretive trail through this cave. The temperature in the cave is 46 degrees Fahrenheit year-round.

Lake Almanor, one of the largest man-made bodies of water in California, and Eagle Lake, the second largest natural lake in California, offer fishing, sailing, water skiing and swimming. Eagle Lake and Hat Creek offer trout fishing. Recreation sites usually are open mid-May to mid-October (weather permitting); the season is shorter at higher elevations. For more information contact the Supervisor's Office, Lassen National Forest, 2550 Riverside Dr., Susanville, CA 96130; phone (530) 257-2151. *See Recreation Areas Chart.*

LASSEN VOLCANIC NATIONAL PARK (C-3)

Elevations in the park range from 5,650 ft. at Warner Valley to 10,457 ft. at Lassen Peak. Refer to AAA maps for additional elevation information.

Accessible via SR 36, 9 miles east of Mineral, Lassen Volcanic National Park covers 106,372 acres in northeastern California where the Cascades join the Sierra Nevada. In addition to Lassen Peak (10,457 ft.) and Cinder Cone (6,907 ft.), the park boasts Prospect Peak (8,338 ft.) and Mount Harkness (8,048 ft.), two shield volcanoes topped by cinder cones with trails leading to their summits. Other features include smaller volcanoes and lava flows, fumaroles, boiling springs, boiling lakes and mudpots.

For a period of several thousand years Lassen Peak was quiescent; then in the spring of 1914 a series of relatively small eruptions began. After reaching its peak in 1915, the activity continued until about 1921.

A plug dome volcano, Lassen Peak once protruded from the north flank of ancestral Mount Tehama. This great stratovolcano was destroyed by glaciers, hydrothermal activity and erosion by East and West Sulphur creeks and other water. Park Highway winds around Lassen Peak, affording views of the volcano and evidence of its destructive might.

In the southern half of the park gurgling mudpots and roaring fumaroles contribute to the unusual atmosphere. The eastern sector encompasses a splendid chain of lakes, extending from Juniper Lake at the northern base of Mount Harkness to Butte Lake near the eastern base of Prospect Peak.

SRs 36 and 44 border the park and provide scenic forest and mountain views. Park Highway traverses the park 30 miles from north to south.

General Information and Activities

Although the park is open all year, heavy snows render most sections inaccessible from late October to mid-June. Winter roads are maintained from the northern gate to Loomis Ranger Station (about 1 mile) and from the southwest gate to the southwest area. Although this is a backcountry experience with no ski lift, cross-country skiing is usually possible from early December to late spring. Mountain bikes are not permitted on trails in the park.

Some of the park's many lakes and streams contain trout. A state fishing license is required, and catch limits and regulations are posted. Wilderness permits issued by the park are required for backcountry camping; phone the park headquarters for information. Gates are open 24 hours daily, but the hours they are attended vary. Motorists entering the park when the stations are unattended must self-register their entrance.

Maps, information and bulletins can be obtained at the visitor center year-round or at Loomis Museum in the summer. Interpretive and evening programs, guided nature walks and self-guiding trails are available during the summer; snowshoe walks are offered in winter.

Kohm Yah-mah-nee Visitor Center, the park's main visitor facility, is on SR 89 near the southwest entrance. Kohm Yah-mah-nee, the Mountain Maidu name for Lassen Peak, translates as "Snow Mountain." A 21-minute film provides an overview about the park, and exhibit panels focus on its geology and natural and cultural history. The visitor center is open daily 9-5, Apr.-Oct.; Wed.-Sun., rest of year. Closed Thanksgiving and Christmas. The visitor center vestibule is open daily 24 hours. Phone (530) 595-4480. *See Recreation Areas Chart.*

Note: Stay on established trails at all times in boiling springs and thermal areas; small children should be kept under strict control. Ground crusts that appear safe can be dangerously thin.

ADMISSION to the park is $30 per private vehicle (mid-Apr. through Nov. 30), $25 per person per motorcycle, $15 per person arriving by other means and to all Dec. 1 to mid-Apr.) Entrance fees are good for 7 days, with a receipt.

PETS are permitted in the park only if they are on a leash, crated or otherwise physically restrained at all times. Pets are not allowed on trails or in buildings.

ADDRESS inquiries to the Superintendent, Lassen Volcanic National Park, Box 100, Mineral, CA 96063. Phone (530) 595-4480.

BUMPASS HELL TRAIL, about .5 mi. beyond Emerald Lake, leads 1.5 mi. off Park Highway to Bumpass Hell, a large area of spectacular boiling springs, mudpots, boiling pools and other types of hydrothermal activity. Boardwalks lead to up-close views of these features.

BUTTE LAKE is 6 mi. off SR 44 in the n.e. corner of the park. A marked trail with wayside exhibits leads to the Cinder Cone summit; interpretive leaflets are available. The trail is 2 miles one way.

CINDER CONE is accessible from a trail beginning at Butte Lake. The Cinder Cone volcano is known for its lava flow, called the Fantastic Lava Beds, and multicolored volcanic ash and cinders. It is possible that some lava flows occurred as recently as 1660.

LASSEN PEAK TRAIL leaves the main park road less than 1 mi. beyond Lake Helen and travels 2.5

miles to the top of the volcano. The round trip requires 4 to 5 hours.

PARK HIGHWAY (SR 89), between the s.w. entrance and Manzanita Lake, is a 30-mile drive. A road guide to points of interest along the north-south route is available for a fee at the park's contact stations. Due to heavy snowfall, most of the road is impassable late Oct. to mid-June.

Chaos Crags and Chaos Jumbles are 2 mi. s. from the park's n.w. boundary. The Chaos Crags are lava plugs believed to have been pushed up more than 1,000 years ago; subsequent falling rocks formed the Chaos Jumbles. The small coniferous trees in the Chaos Jumbles—some more than 300 years old—constitute the Dwarf Forest.

Devastated Area begins about 2.5 mi. n. of Summit Lake. It was stripped of all vegetation by hot blasts, avalanches and mudflows from the May 1915 eruptions of Lassen Peak. Natural reforestation is taking place. Another eruption remnant is Hot Rock, a large black lava rock near the north end of the area.

Diamond Peak is reached via Park Highway, which winds up the remains of old Mount Tehama beginning at a point 2 mi. n. of the Sulphur Works. The road, which encompasses Diamond Peak, offers a glimpse of steam vents below in Little Hot Springs Valley.

Kings Creek Meadows (7,400 ft.) are 4.5 mi. n. from the summit. A 1.5-mile hiking trail leads to beautiful Kings Creek Falls. Both the cascades and falls are visible from the left side of the creek downstream.

Loomis Museum, .5 mi. beyond the n.w. entrance station, is named for B.F. Loomis, who photographed the early 20th-century eruptions and was a proponent of the park's establishment. The museum has a contact station where park information, exhibits, books and wilderness maps can be obtained and visitor assistance is available. **Hours:** Daily 9-5, mid-June through Oct. 31; Fri.-Sun. 9-5, late May to mid-June. Closed major holidays, except in summer. Phone ahead to confirm schedule. **Cost:** Free. **Phone:** (530) 595-6140.

Sulphur Works Hydrothermal Area, about 1 mi. n. of the s.w. entrance station, has steam vents and mudpots. Stay on the trails in these areas at all times. Ground that appears safe might be dangerously thin.

Summit Lake, 5 mi. n.e. of Kings Creek Meadows, has two lakeside campgrounds. They are convenient to hiking, fishing and points of interest.

WARNER VALLEY, in the s. part of the park, is reached by road from Chester or by trail from Summit Lake to Drakesbad. Marked trails lead to Boiling Springs Lake and Devils Kitchen, a large area of boiling pools and other volcanic features.

LATHROP pop. 18,023

HAMPTON INN & SUITES   209/982-5070
 Hotel. **Address:** 103 E Louise Ave 95330

AAA Benefit: Members save up to 15%!

LAVA BEDS NATIONAL MONUMENT (B-3)

In northeastern California, Lava Beds National Monument is reachable from SR 139, following the brown highway signs from Tulelake (the southern entrance road to the monument is paved but in poor repair). Lava Beds National Monument was created from molten lava spewed centuries ago from Medicine Lake volcano. When the lava cooled, the monument's rugged terrain was formed. The 46,500-acre area is characterized by cinder cones, deep chasms and more than 450 lava tube caves of various sizes.

Some of the caves contain permanent ice. The Modoc Indians used the volcanic formations as fortifications 1872-73 during the only major Indian war fought in California. Visitors can explore a lava tube cave on their own or on a ranger-guided tour offered during the summer. Mushpot, a lighted cave, is accessible from the visitor center parking lot. Flashlights for cave exploration are available at the visitor center. Campfire programs are presented in summer.

Hiking trails, some less than a mile in length, lead to other caves, pictographs and petroglyphs, the fire lookout, crater rims, overlooks and battlefield sites. The visitor center has trail brochures.

Camping is allowed, but no lodgings, supplies, gas or oil are available. Pets on leash are permitted in certain areas of the park, but not on the trails. The monument is open all year, and although there are no specified visiting hours, those planning to camp should arrive before 5 p.m. The geology and history of the area are interpreted at a visitor center.

Visitor Center open daily 9-5:30, June-Aug.; 9-4:30, Sept.-Nov. and Mar.-May; 10-4, rest of year. Closed Christmas. Admission $25 per private vehicle; $20 per motorcycle; $15 per person arriving by other means. Cash only. For more information contact the Superintendent's Office, Lava Beds National Monument, P.O. Box 1240, Tulelake, CA 96134; phone (530) 667-8113.

LEGGETT (D-1) pop. 122, elev. 984'
• Part of Wine Country area — see map p. 405

Leggett is at the crossroads of US 101 (the Redwood Highway) and SR 1 (the Pacific Coast Highway). About 10 miles inland from the Pacific, this extravagantly scenic location is also the gateway to Humboldt County's magnificent redwood groves.

REDWOODS RIVER RESORT   707/925-6249
Cabin. **Address:** 75000 Hwy 101 95585

STONEGATE VILLAS 707/925-6226
 Motel. **Address:** 65260 Drive Thru Tree Rd 95585

LEMOORE pop. 24,531

BEST WESTERN INN & SUITES LEMOORE
559/924-3200

Motel

 Best Western. **AAA Benefit:** Members save up to 15% and earn bonus points!

Address: 820 E Bush St 93245 **Location:** SR 198 exit 81 (Houston Ave), 0.8 mi nw. **Facility:** 100 units. 2 stories (no elevator), exterior corridors. **Pool:** outdoor. **Activities:** exercise room. **Guest Services:** valet and coin laundry. **Featured Amenity: continental breakfast.**

WHERE TO EAT

THE VINEYARD RESTAURANT 559/924-1988
 American. Casual Dining. **Address:** 819 E Bush St 93245

LINCOLN pop. 42,819, elev. 167'

HOLIDAY INN EXPRESS HOTEL & SUITES 916/644-3440
Hotel. **Address:** 155 Ferrari Ranch Rd 95648

THUNDER VALLEY CASINO RESORT 916/408-7777

Resort Hotel

Address: 1200 Athens Ave 95648 **Location:** SR 65 exit Sunset Blvd, 0.4 mi w, 1.5 mi n on Industrial Ave, then just w. **Facility:** This upscale lodging features a large gaming area, several restaurants and spacious suites. A shuttle services several cities; call hotel for the current schedule. 408 units, some two bedrooms. 12 stories, interior corridors. **Parking:** on-site and valet. **Terms:** check-in 4 pm. **Amenities:** safes. **Dining:** 5 restaurants, also, High Steaks Steakhouse, Red Lantern, Thunder Cafe, see separate listings. **Pool:** heated outdoor. **Activities:** sauna, hot tub, steamroom, cabanas, regulation golf, exercise room, spa. **Guest Services:** valet laundry.

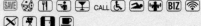

WHERE TO EAT

CASA RAMOS 916/409-0766
Mexican. Casual Dining. **Address:** 925 S State Hwy 65 95648

HIGH STEAKS STEAKHOUSE 916/408-8327

Steak Fine Dining $29-$70

AAA Inspector Notes: This upscale, refined restaurant serves Prime dry-aged, hand-cut steaks along with several seafood selections. Creative, tableside presentations enhance the dining experience. Stop in Sunday-Thursday for late night happy hour on the patio where live music is featured on Wednesdays. **Features:** full bar, patio dining, happy hour. **Reservations:** suggested. **Address:** 1200 Athens Ave 95648 **Location:** SR 65 exit Sunset Blvd, just w, just nw on Placer Corp Dr, 1.3 mi n on Industrial Ave, then just w; in Thunder Valley Casino Resort. **Parking:** on-site and valet.

D CALL

ORCHID THAI CUISINE & BAR 916/543-9988
Thai. Casual Dining. **Address:** 835 Twelve Bridges Dr, Suite 100 95648

RED LANTERN 916/408-8315
Chinese. Casual Dining. **Address:** 1200 Athens Ave 95648

THUNDER CAFE 916/408-8328
American. Casual Dining. **Address:** 1200 Athens Ave 95648

LITTLE RIVER (D-1) pop. 117, elev. 90'
• **Part of Wine Country area — see map p. 405**

Established as a lumber and shipbuilding settlement in the mid-19th century, Little River is a popular base for divers exploring Pacific coast waters. This picturesque hamlet is along an exceptionally scenic stretch of SR 1.

GLENDEVEN INN AND LODGE 707/937-0083
Bed & Breakfast. **Address:** 8205 N Hwy 1 95456

THE INN AT COBBLER'S WALK MENDOCINO 707/937-0088
Bed & Breakfast. **Address:** 8200 N Hwy 1 95456

LITTLE RIVER INN 707/937-5942
Country Inn. **Address:** 7901 N Hwy 1 95456

WHERE TO EAT

LITTLE RIVER INN RESTAURANT 707/937-5942
California. Fine Dining. **Address:** 7901 N SR 1 95456

LIVERMORE (D-9) pop. 80,968, elev. 486'

Livermore is located in the scenic Livermore Valley, an area characterized by vineyards and cattle ranches. Sycamore trees—some more than 2 centuries old—grow along the banks of the Arroyo del Valle.

Livermore Valley Chamber of Commerce: 2157 First St., Livermore, CA 94550-4543. **Phone:** (925) 447-1606.

LAWRENCE LIVERMORE NATIONAL LABORATORY'S DISCOVERY CENTER, off Greenville Rd. about 2.2 mi. s. of I-580 at East Gate entrance, presents a broad-based display of the scientific technology developed at the laboratory and highlights the lab's research in defense, homeland security, biotechnology and new energy sources. Guided tours of the main site last 3 hours. Tours of Site 300, a 7,000-acre experimental test facility south of Tracy, also are offered.

Time: Allow 30 minutes minimum. **Hours:** Center open Tues.-Fri. 1-4. Guided tours of the main site are given Tues. at 8:30 a.m. Site 300 tours are given by appointment when staff is available. Tour reservations must be made at least 2 weeks in advance and are subject to availability. Closed major holidays. **Cost:** Free. Under 18 are not permitted on Tues. or on Site 300 tours. **Phone:** (925) 423-3272 for the discovery center, or (925) 422-4599 for tour reservations.

BEST WESTERN PLUS VINEYARD INN   925/456-5422

Hotel

AAA Benefit: Members save up to 15% and earn bonus points!

Address: 7600 Southfront Rd 94551 **Location:** I-580 exit 57 (N Greenville Rd), just s, then just w; jct Mountain Vista Pkwy. **Facility:** 66 units. 3 stories, interior corridors. **Pool:** heated outdoor. **Activities:** exercise room. **Guest Services:** coin laundry. **Featured Amenity:** continental breakfast.

COURTYARD BY MARRIOTT-LIVERMORE   925/243-1000

Hotel. **Address:** 2929 Constitution Dr 94551

AAA Benefit: Members save 5% or more!

HAMPTON INN   925/606-6400

Hotel. **Address:** 2850 Constitution Dr 94551

AAA Benefit: Members save up to 15%!

HAWTHORN SUITES BY WYNDHAM   925/606-6060

Hotel. **Address:** 1700 N Livermore Ave 94551

HILTON GARDEN INN LIVERMORE   925/292-2000

Hotel. **Address:** 2801 Constitution Dr 94550

AAA Benefit: Members save up to 15%!

HOLIDAY INN EXPRESS HOTEL & SUITES-LIVERMORE
     925/961-9600

Hotel. **Address:** 3000 Constitution Dr 94551

HOME2 SUITES BY HILTON   925/960-1242

Extended Stay Hotel. **Address:** 2625 Constitution Dr 94551

AAA Benefit: Members save up to 15%!

LA QUINTA INN BY WYNDHAM LIVERMORE   925/373-9600

Hotel. **Address:** 7700 Southfront Rd 94551

RESIDENCE INN BY MARRIOTT   925/373-1800

Extended Stay Hotel. **Address:** 1000 Airway Blvd 94551

AAA Benefit: Members save 5% or more!

WHERE TO EAT

CAMPO DI BOCCE OF LIVERMORE   925/249-9800

Italian. Casual Dining. **Address:** 175 E Vineyard Ave 94550

CASA OROZCO   925/449-3045

Mexican. Casual Dining. **Address:** 325 S L St 94550

CATTLEMENS   925/447-1224

Steak. Casual Dining. **Address:** 2882 Kitty Hawk Rd 94551

DEMITRI'S TAVERNA   925/373-0306

Greek. Casual Dining. **Address:** 2235 1st St 94550

DENICA'S REAL FOOD KITCHEN   925/447-9500

American. Quick Serve. **Address:** 2259 Las Positas Rd 94551

FIRST STREET ALEHOUSE   925/371-6588

American. Brewpub. **Address:** 2106 First St 94550

THE RESTAURANT AT WENTE VINEYARDS   925/456-2450

California. Fine Dining. **Address:** 5050 Arroyo Rd 94550

THE RIATA DINER AND TAVERN   925/294-9170

American. Casual Dining. **Address:** 190 S J St 94550

TERRA MIA   925/456-3333

Italian. Casual Dining. **Address:** 4040 East Ave 94550

UNCLE YU'S AT THE VINEYARD   925/449-7000

Chinese. Fine Dining. **Address:** 39 S Livermore Ave, Suite 125 94550

LODI (F-3) pop. 62,134, elev. 52'
• Restaurants p. 126

Lodi is a major wine-producing center, with more than 80 wineries located within a short distance. The sea of vineyards is responsible for the city's self-proclaimed nickname "Zinfandel Capital of the World." The Lodi appellation, comparable to France's Chateauneuf du Pape, is noted for old vine Zinfandel, Merlot, Cabernet Sauvignon, Chardonnay and Sauvignon blanc. The Lodi Wine & Visitor Center, 2545 W. Turner Rd., showcases the grape, and the grounds include an educational demonstration vineyard. Phone (209) 365-0621.

Nearby Lodi Lake Park offers water skiing, boating, swimming and hiking.

Autumn provides an opportunity to witness the yearly arrival of thousands of sandhill cranes as they complete a migratory journey south from Alaska along the Pacific Flyway. The birds spend the winter months at the Isenberg Sandhill Crane Reserve; they can be observed from lookout points along Woodbridge Road, which runs through the reserve's south site. Guided tours are given several times a month from October through February; for schedule information phone (209) 234-3435.

Visit Lodi Conference & Visitors Bureau: 25 N. School St., Lodi, CA 95240. **Phone:** (209) 365-1195 or (800) 798-1810.

BEST WESTERN I-5 INN & SUITES   209/367-3000

Hotel

AAA Benefit: Members save up to 15% and earn bonus points!

Address: 6411 W Banner St 95242 **Location:** I-5 exit 485 (SR 12), just e, then just s. **Facility:** 57 units. 4 stories, interior corridors. **Pool:** heated indoor. **Activities:** hot tub, exercise room. **Guest Services:** coin laundry. **Featured Amenity:** breakfast buffet.

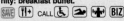

DAYS INN & SUITES   209/369-8484

Hotel. **Address:** 710 S Cherokee Ln 95240

HAMPTON INN & SUITES
209-369-2700

Hotel

 AAA Benefit: Members save up to 15%!

Address: 1337 S Beckman Rd 95240 **Location:** SR 99 exit Kettleman Ln, just e, then just n. **Facility:** 101 units. 4 stories, interior corridors. **Pool:** heated outdoor. **Activities:** hot tub, exercise room. **Guest Services:** valet and coin laundry. **Featured Amenity: breakfast buffet.**

SAVE CALL (wheelchair) (coffee) (gym) BIZ (wifi)
(X) (microwave) /SOME UNITS (refrigerator) (hairdryer)

HOLIDAY INN EXPRESS
209-210-0150
Hotel. **Address:** 1337 E Kettleman Ln 95240

WINE & ROSES HOTEL SPA AND RESTAURANT
209-334-6988
Boutique Hotel. **Address:** 2505 W Turner Rd 95242

WHERE TO EAT

THE FARM CAFE AT MICHAEL DAVID WINERY 209-368-7384
American. Casual Dining. **Address:** 4580 Hwy 12 95242

LODI BEER COMPANY
209-368-9931
American. Brewpub. **Address:** 105 S School St 95240

PIETRO'S TRATTORIA
209-368-0613
Italian. Casual Dining. **Address:** 317 E Kettleman Ln 95240

THAI SPICES
209-369-8424
Thai. Casual Dining. **Address:** 2401 W Turner Rd 95242

TOWNE HOUSE RESTAURANT
209-371-6160
American. Fine Dining. **Address:** 2505 W Turner Rd 95242

LOLETA pop. 783, elev. 46'

BEAR RIVER CASINO RESORT
707/733-9644
Contemporary Resort Hotel. **Address:** 11 Bear Paws Way 95551

LOS ALTOS (E-8) pop. 28,976, elev. 165'
• Hotels & Restaurants map & index p. 190

The Los Altos area was on the route of a 1775-76 expedition led by Spanish commander Juan Bautista de Anza from Mexico into Alta (Upper) California. The purpose of this overland journey was to establish a Spanish presence, including a presidio and mission, near the Bay of San Francisco. In the early 20th century the city became a railroad link between Palo Alto and Los Gatos, which spurred development.

Each July the city celebrates the 🍷 Los Altos Arts and Wine Festival. The 2-day juried event, held downtown, features arts and crafts created by more than 400 artisans, concerts, children's activities, and booths offering food and wine from local merchants and vineyards.

Los Altos Chamber of Commerce: 321 University Ave., Los Altos, CA 94022. **Phone:** (650) 948-1455.

COURTYARD BY MARRIOTT-PALO ALTO/LOS ALTOS
650/941-9900 38
SAVE Hotel. **Address:** 4320 El Camino Real 94022

AAA Benefit: Members save 5% or more!

RESIDENCE INN BY MARRIOTT-PALO ALTO/LOS ALTOS
650/559-7890 39
SAVE Extended Stay Hotel. **Address:** 4460 El Camino Real 94022

AAA Benefit: Members save 5% or more!

WHERE TO EAT

ARMADILLO WILLY'S BAR-B-QUE
650/941-2922
Barbecue. Quick Serve. **Address:** 1031 N San Antonio Rd 94022

SUMIKA
650/917-1822 31
Japanese. Casual Dining. **Address:** 236 Central Plaza 94022

LOS BAÑOS (G-3) pop. 35,972, elev. 120'

Los Baños is named for Los Baños Creek, once a popular bathing spot for missionaries. Cotton, rice and alfalfa were introduced in the mid-19th century, and agriculture remains the leading industry.

Los Baños Chamber of Commerce: 932 Sixth St., Los Baños, CA 93635. **Phone:** (209) 826-2495.

BEST WESTERN EXECUTIVE INN
209/827-0954

Hotel

 Best Western. **AAA Benefit:** Members save up to 15% and earn bonus points!

Address: 301 W Pacheco Blvd 93635 **Location:** 1.2 mi w of jct SR 152 and 165. **Facility:** 56 units. 3 stories, interior corridors. **Pool:** outdoor. **Activities:** hot tub. **Guest Services:** coin laundry. **Featured Amenity: continental breakfast.**

SAVE (food) CALL (wheelchair) (coffee) BIZ (wifi)

(X) (hairdryer) (refrigerator) (microwave) /SOME UNITS (pet)

WHERE TO EAT

EDDIE'S FAMOUS CAFE
209/826-2379
Breakfast. Casual Dining. **Address:** 401 W Pacheco Blvd 93635

ESPANA'S SOUTHWEST BAR & GRILL
209/826-4041
Mexican. Casual Dining. **Address:** 1460 E Pacheco Blvd 93635

M & M ITALIAN RESTAURANT & LOUNGE
209/827-1666
Italian. Casual Dining. **Address:** 400 W Pacheco Blvd 93635

LOS GATOS (E-9) pop. 29,413, elev. 385'
• Hotels & Restaurants map & index p. 348

Two mountain ranges tower above Los Gatos: El Sombroso (the shadowing one) and El Sereno (the night watchman). The town was founded in the late 1860s on a portion of an 1840 Spanish land grant. The original grant was known as *La Rinconada de*

(See map & index p. 348.)

los Gatos (corner of the cats), a name derived from the many mountain lions and wildcats that then inhabited the nearby hills.

Los Gatos Creek Trail is a popular multiuse pathway that runs for 9 miles from Los Gatos through Campbell *(see place listing p. 53)* and on to San Jose *(see place listing p. 341)*. The trail, which follows Los Gatos Creek, is used by walkers, runners, hikers, bicyclists and nature lovers. Los Gatos is the northern end of a scenic 38-mile stretch of SR 17 that runs south to Santa Cruz.

Los Gatos Chamber of Commerce: 10 Station Way, Los Gatos, CA 95030. **Phone:** (408) 354-9300.

Self-guiding tours: Maps for a self-guiding walking tour of historic sites in Los Gatos are available at the chamber of commerce.

Shopping: Old Town, on University Avenue, has about a dozen chain retailers and a couple of restaurants in an attractively landscaped setting of Spanish-style architecture and topiary trees.

NEW MUSEUM LOS GATOS (NUMU) is at 106 E. Main St. Interactive exhibits focus on art in the digital age, exploring such subjects as the history of "selfies." Other exhibits preserve local South Bay history. Temporary exhibits feature the work of area artists. **Time:** Allow 30 minutes minimum. **Hours:** Wed. 1-5, Thurs.-Sun. 11-5 (also Thurs. 5-8 p.m.). One-hour, docent-led guided tours are given Sat. at 1. Closed Jan. 1, Easter, Thanksgiving, Christmas and Dec. 31. **Cost:** $10; $6 (ages 65+, students and military with ID); free (ages 0-17). Guided tour fee $2 per person. **Phone:** (408) 354-2646. [GT] [🎫]

OAK MEADOW PARK are at University Ave. and Blossom Hill Rd. Oak Meadow Park offers a playground, sports field, 1910 English carousel and a lake stocked for fishing. Vasona Lake County Park has a playground and facilities for fishing, picnicking and boating. Boat rentals also are available *(see Recreation Areas Chart)*.

Hours: Daily 8 a.m.-half-hour after sunset. **Cost:** Free. Carousel $2 per ride; free (ages 0-2). **Parking:** $6; free (ages 62+, Los Gatos residents and physically impaired individuals). **Phone:** (408) 399-5770 for Oak Meadow Park, or (408) 356-2729 for Vasona Lake Park.

Billy Jones Wildcat Railroad, in Oak Meadow Park, is a restored 1905 steam train, although a diesel train occasionally is featured. The scenic 1-mile trip passes over Los Gatos Creek and proceeds through Vasona Lake Park. **Hours:** Train departs daily 10:30-4:30, early June to mid-Aug.; Sat.-Sun. 10:30-4:30, mid-Mar. to early June and mid-Aug. through-Oct. 31; Sat.-Sun. 11-3, rest of year (weather permitting). **Cost:** $3 per ride; free (physically impaired individuals and ages 0-2 with paying adult). **Phone:** (408) 395-7433.

BEST WESTERN THE INN OF LOS GATOS   408/356-9191   [95]

  Motel

 Best Western. **AAA Benefit:** Members save up to 15% and earn bonus points!

 Address: 55 Saratoga Los Gatos Rd 95032 **Location:** SR 17 exit E Saratoga Los Gatos Rd, just e. Located in a quiet area. **Facility:** 48 units. 2 stories, exterior corridors. **Amenities:** safes. **Pool:** outdoor. **Activities:** exercise room. **Guest Services:** coin laundry. **Featured Amenity:** breakfast buffet.

[SAVE] [🍴] [🏊] [🏋] [📶] [✕] [♿] [📺]

HOTEL LOS GATOS   408/335-1700   [96]
▼▼▼ Boutique Hotel. **Address:** 210 E Main St 95030

WHERE TO EAT

THE BYWATER   408/560-9639   [50]
▼▼ Cajun Seafood. Casual Dining. **Address:** 532 N Santa Cruz Ave 95030

MANRESA   408/354-4330   [53]
▼▼▼▼ New American. Fine Dining. **Address:** 320 Village Ln 95030

OAK & RYE   408/395-4441   [52]
▼▼ Pizza. Casual Dining. **Address:** 303 N Santa Cruz Ave 95030

OPA! AUTHENTIC GREEK CUISINE   408/399-7417   [54]
▼▼ Greek. Casual Dining. **Address:** 27 N Santa Cruz Ave 95030

PEDRO'S RESTAURANT & CANTINA   408/354-7570   [51]
▼▼ Mexican. Casual Dining. **Address:** 316 N Santa Cruz Ave 95030

MADERA (G-4) pop. 61,416, elev. 272'
• Restaurants p. 128

The Spanish term for "wood" or "lumber," Madera was founded in 1876 by the California Lumber Co. From that year until 1931 a wooden water flume floated cut timber 63 miles from forests in the Sierra Nevada to the railhead at this central California city.

Today, though, it's all about vino. The Madera Wine Trail connects a dozen or so wineries in the vicinity and north along SR 41 to Oakhurst. Madera County is one of the nation's oldest grape-growing regions, and the Madera Vintners Association sponsors wine trail events in February, May and November. For more information phone (800) 613-0709.

HAMPTON INN & SUITES BY HILTON MADERA   559/661-0910
▼▼▼ [SAVE] Hotel. **Address:** 3254 Airport Dr 93637   **AAA Benefit:** Members save up to 15%!

HOLIDAY INN EXPRESS   559/661-7400
▼▼▼ Hotel. **Address:** 2290 Market Place Dr 93637

LA QUINTA INN & SUITES BY WYNDHAM MADERA   559/831-0730
▼▼▼ Hotel. **Address:** 317 N G St 93637

SPRINGHILL SUITES BY MARRIOTT   559/664-9800

Hotel

SPRINGHILL SUITES
MARRIOTT

AAA Benefit: Members save 5% or more!

Address: 1219 E Almond Ave 93637 **Location:** SR 99 exit 152 (Almond Ave) southbound, just w; exit 153A (Gateway Dr) northbound, make U-turn, then just se. **Facility:** 88 units. 3 stories, interior corridors. **Pool:** heated outdoor. **Activities:** hot tub, exercise room. **Guest Services:** valet and coin laundry. **Featured Amenity:** breakfast buffet.

WHERE TO EAT

KEBAB GRILL   559/664-1100
Mediterranean. Quick Serve. **Address:** 300 N Gateway, Suite 106 93637

SAL'S MEXICAN RESTAURANT   559/673-7257
Mexican. Casual Dining. **Address:** 2001 W Cleveland Ave, Suite F 93637

THE VINEYARD RESTAURANT & BAR   559/674-0923
American. Casual Dining. **Address:** 605 S I St 93637

MANTECA pop. 67,096

BEST WESTERN PLUS EXECUTIVE INN & SUITES
209/825-1415

Hotel

Best Western PLUS

AAA Benefit: Members save up to 15% and earn bonus points!

Address: 1415 E Yosemite Ave 95336 **Location:** SR 99 exit 242, just w. **Facility:** 99 units. 3 stories, interior/exterior corridors. **Amenities:** *Some:* safes. **Pool:** outdoor. **Activities:** hot tub, exercise room. **Guest Services:** coin laundry. **Featured Amenity:** breakfast buffet.

/ SOME UNITS

HAMPTON INN & SUITES   209/823-1926
 Hotel. **Address:** 1461 Bass Pro Dr 95336

AAA Benefit: Members save up to 15%!

HOLIDAY INN EXPRESS HOTEL & SUITES
209/239-5600

Hotel

Address: 179 Commerce Ave 95336 **Location:** Jct SR 99 and 120 exit Yosemite Ave, just sw. **Facility:** 72 units. 3 stories, interior corridors. **Pool:** outdoor. **Activities:** hot tub, exercise room. **Guest Services:** valet and coin laundry.

WHERE TO EAT

ERNIE'S FOOD & SPIRITS   209/239-3351
Steak. Fine Dining. **Address:** 1351 N Main St 95336

MOM'S THAI HOUSE   209/665-7890
Thai. Casual Dining. **Address:** 439 N Main St 95336

MARINA (G-3) pop. 19,718, elev. 43'
• Part of Monterey Peninsula area — see map p. 141

Most travelers zip right past Marina en route to Monterey, Pacific Grove, Pebble Beach or Carmel, the Monterey Peninsula's primary tourist destinations. That doesn't mean you should skip Fort Ord Dunes State Park, however. A 1,500-foot trail leads to a 4-mile stretch of beach tailor made for ambling and exploring. Then take a stroll along the boardwalk to a blufftop platform offering panoramic views of Monterey Bay. From SR 1 take the Light Fighter Drive exit and bear right; turn left onto 2nd Avenue, left onto Divarty Street, then right onto 1st Avenue and follow signs to the park entrance.

In addition to plenty of sandy expanses, the persistent winds at Marina State Beach (SR 1 Reservation Road exit) create ideal conditions for surfers, kite flyers and hang gliders. Dolphins can often be spotted leaping above the waves beyond the shoreline. This beach is also a popular local spot for sunset watching.

BEST WESTERN BEACH DUNES INN   831/883-0300

Hotel

Best Western.

AAA Benefit: Members save up to 15% and earn bonus points!

Address: 3290 Dunes Dr 93933 **Location:** SR 1 exit Reservation Rd, just nw. **Facility:** 84 units. 2 stories (no elevator), exterior corridors. **Activities:** hot tub, playground. **Guest Services:** coin laundry. **Featured Amenity:** continental breakfast.

/ SOME UNITS

HOLIDAY INN EXPRESS & SUITES MARINA-STATE BEACH AREA   831/884-2500
Hotel. **Address:** 189 Seaside Cir 93933

HOWARD JOHNSON BY WYNDHAM MARINA AT MONTEREY BAY   831/883-8500
Motel. **Address:** 416 Reservation Rd 93933

THE SANCTUARY BEACH RESORT - MONTEREY BAY
831/883-9478

Hotel

Address: 3295 Dunes Dr 93933 **Location:** SR 1 exit Reservation Rd, just nw. **Facility:** 60 units. 2 stories (no elevator), exterior corridors. **Terms:** check-in 4 pm. **Amenities:** safes. **Dining:** Salt Wood Kitchen & Oysterette, see separate listing. **Pool:** heated outdoor. **Activities:** hot tub, limited beach access, bicycles, spa. **Guest Services:** valet laundry.

/ SOME UNITS

SALT WOOD KITCHEN & OYSTERETTE   831/883-5535

💎💎💎 California Seafood. Casual Dining. **Address:** 3295 Dunes Rd 93933

MARIPOSA (F-4) pop. 2,173, elev. 1,953'

- Hotels & Restaurants map & index p. 426
- Part of Yosemite National Park area — see map p. 420

An old mining town, Mariposa is at the southern end of the Mother Lode country, a gold-mining district that once covered the lower western edge of the Sierra Nevada from Sierra City in the north to Mariposa in the south. SR 49 now traverses this region.

Originally called Logtown, Mariposa was renamed after the Spanish word for butterfly. Gold mining has long been supplanted by tourism; nearby Yosemite Valley attracts hordes of visitors each year, especially during the summer.

Yosemite Mariposa County Tourism Bureau: 5065 SR 140, P.O. Box 967, Mariposa, CA 95338. **Phone:** (209) 966-7081 or (866) 425-3366.

CALIFORNIA STATE MINING AND MINERAL MUSEUM is 1.8 mi. s. on SR 49, at the main entrance to the county fairgrounds. It contains a collection of minerals, gold, diamonds and other gems, including examples of benitoite, the California state gemstone. A highlight is the Fricot Nugget, a nearly 14-pound chunk of crystalline gold discovered in the American River in 1864. Other exhibits include models of an assay office and stamp mill (a machine that crushed quartz) and a full-scale replica of a mine. The museum also presents rotating exhibitions of gem and mineral specimens from other institutions and private collections.

Time: Allow 1 hour minimum. **Hours:** Thurs.-Sun. 10-5, May-Sept.; 10-4, rest of year. Closed Jan. 1, Thanksgiving and Christmas. Phone ahead to confirm schedule. **Cost:** $4; free (ages 0-12). **Phone:** (209) 742-7625.

MARIPOSA MUSEUM AND HISTORY CENTER INC., SR 140 at 12th and Jessie sts., contains a re-created 1850s street, including a five-stamp mill, horse-drawn vehicles and mining and printing equipment. Featured are replicas of a schoolroom, a Native American village, a miner's cabin, a print shop, a sheriff's office, a saloon and an apothecary as well as the restored house of the 1860s county treasurer.

Time: Allow 1 hour minimum. **Hours:** Daily 10-4. Closed Jan. 1, Easter, Thanksgiving, Christmas Eve, Christmas and Dec. 31. **Cost:** $5; free (ages 0-18, first responders and military with ID). **Phone:** (209) 966-2924.

BEST WESTERN PLUS YOSEMITE WAY STATION MOTEL   209/966-7545 🔟4️⃣

Hotel

AAA Benefit: Members save up to 15% and earn bonus points!

Address: 4999 Hwy 140 95338 **Location:** SR 140 at SR 49 S. **Facility:** 78 units. 3 stories (no elevator), exterior corridors. **Terms:** check-in 4 pm. **Pool:** outdoor. **Activities:** hot tub, exercise room. **Guest Services:** coin laundry. **Featured Amenity: full hot breakfast.**

SAVE 🛏️ CALL 👨‍🦽 🏊 ✚ BIZ
📶 ✖️ 🗄️ 🖨️ 💻 / SOME UNITS 🐾

QUALITY INN YOSEMITE VALLEY GATEWAY   209/966-4344 1️⃣3️⃣

Hotel

Address: 4994 Bullion St 95338 **Location:** Jct SR 49 and 4th St, just e. **Facility:** 59 units, some efficiencies. 2-3 stories (no elevator), exterior corridors. **Terms:** check-in 4 pm. **Pool:** outdoor. **Activities:** hot tub. **Guest Services:** coin laundry. **Featured Amenity: full hot breakfast.** *(See ad p. 130.)*

SAVE 🛏️ CALL 👨‍🦽 🏊 BIZ
📶 ✖️ 🗄️ 💻 / SOME UNITS 🐾

1850 RESTAURANT   209/966-2229 1️⃣2️⃣

💎💎 Traditional American. Casual Dining. **Address:** 5114 Hwy 140 95338

CASTILLO'S MEXICAN RESTAURANT   209/742-4413 1️⃣6️⃣

💎💎 Mexican. Casual Dining. **Address:** 4995 5th St 95338

CHARLES STREET DINNER HOUSE   209/966-2366 1️⃣4️⃣

💎💎 American. Casual Dining. **Address:** Hwy 140 & 7th St 95338

JANTZ BAKERY   209/742-4545 1️⃣3️⃣

💎 Breads/Pastries. Quick Serve. **Address:** 5067 Hwy 140 95338

SAVOURY'S   209/966-7677 1️⃣5️⃣

💎💎💎 American. Fine Dining. **Address:** 5034 Hwy 140 95338

▼ See AAA listing p. 129 ▼

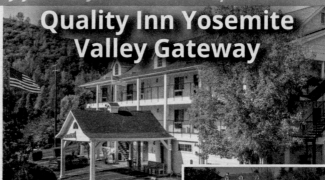

Make the Connction

AAA guidebooks are just the beginning. Open the door to a whole lot more on AAA.com. Get extra travel insight, more information and online booking.

Find this symbol for places to look, book and save on AAA.com.

iStockphoto.com_shapecharge

MARTINEZ pop. 35,824, elev. 23'

BEST WESTERN JOHN MUIR INN 925/229-1010

Hotel

Best Western.
AAA Benefit: Members save up to 15% and earn bonus points!

Address: 445 Muir Station Rd 94553 **Location:** Jct I-680 and SR 4, 2.3 mi w on SR 4 exit 10 (Pine St/Center Ave), then just s. Across from Muir Station Shopping Center. **Facility:** 112 units, some efficiencies. 3 stories, interior corridors. **Pool:** outdoor. **Activities:** hot tub, exercise room. **Guest Services:** valet and coin laundry. **Featured Amenity:** breakfast buffet.

MUIR LODGE MOTEL 925/228-3308
Motel. **Address:** 3930 Alhambra Ave 94553

WHERE TO EAT

LEMONGRASS BISTRO 925/387-0388
Thai. Casual Dining. **Address:** 501 Main St 94553

MARYSVILLE (D-3) pop. 12,072, elev. 63'

Marysville was named for Mary Murphy Covillaud, an early settler and Donner Party survivor. Central to Marysville is Ellis Lake, named for W.T. Ellis, a prosperous town merchant in the early 1900s. John McLaren, the designer of San Francisco's Golden Gate Park, converted a swampy area into this popular recreational outlet. The boulevard along the shore testifies to the merchant's efforts to beautify the lake. Paddleboats are available seasonally.

Riverfront Park, along the Feather River, is beneath the 5th and 10th street bridges, which link Marysville and Yuba City. Recreational facilities include a boat-launching dock, picnic area, playgrounds, soccer fields, baseball fields and motorbike trails. The park also has a concert bowl with grassy slopes for seating.

The Toyota Amphitheatre, on Forty Mile Road in nearby Wheatland, features name entertainment during the summer; phone (530) 743-5200 for information.

COMFORT SUITES 530/742-9200
Hotel. **Address:** 1034 N Beale Rd 95901

WHERE TO EAT

THE BRICK COFFEE HOUSE CAFE 530/743-5283
American. Quick Serve. **Address:** 316 D St 95901

MCCLOUD pop. 1,101, elev. 3,281'

MCCLOUD GUEST HOUSE 530/964-3160
Historic Bed & Breakfast. **Address:** 606 W Colombero Dr 96057

MCCLOUD HOTEL 530/964-2822
Historic Boutique Bed & Breakfast. **Address:** 408 Main St 96057

MCCLOUD MERCANTILE HOTEL 530/964-2330
Historic Bed & Breakfast. **Address:** 241 Main St 96057

MCCLOUD RIVER INN BED & BREAKFAST 530/964-2130
Historic Bed & Breakfast. **Address:** 325 Lawndale Ct 96057

WHERE TO EAT

WHITE MOUNTAIN CAFE 530/964-2005
Breakfast Sandwiches. Casual Dining. **Address:** 245 Main St 96057

MCKINLEYVILLE pop. 15,177

HOLIDAY INN EXPRESS HOTEL & SUITES 707/840-9305
Hotel. **Address:** 3107 Concord Dr 95519

MENDOCINO (D-1) pop. 894, elev. 90'
• Hotels p. 133 • Restaurants p. 133
• Part of Wine Country area — see map p. 405

Beguilingly picturesque Mendocino—unlike Carmel-by-the-Sea, Monterey, Santa Cruz and other touristy coastal California communities—is pretty much off the beaten path. It's about a 3-hour drive north of San Francisco, which gives this little jewel box of a community an air of slightly quirky exclusivity.

The natural setting, perched above the Pacific and surrounded on three sides by the rocky bluffs of Mendocino Headlands State Park, is glorious. And it's pretty easy to get your bearings, since there are only a handful of streets in this historic village. The Ford House Visitor Center at 45035 Main St. is a good first stop.

Architecturally speaking, the word most often used to describe Mendocino's homes and commercial buildings is Victorian, as many of the first settlers arrived in the 1850s, making their fortunes in the timber industry. Almost every house is graced with a well-tended flower garden, and several have a wooden water tower, a feature recalling an era when outhouses were the norm and the chief transportation mode was horseback.

You'll see New England Salt Box, Gothic Revival and Italianate styles. Specific guidelines govern everything from the choice of exterior building materials to such decorative architectural accents as bargeboard (the carved projecting boards placed against the incline of a gable), oriel windows (a bay window located on a building's second story) and dripstones (molding placed over the top of windows and doorways to shield them from rain).

Several shops have false fronts, a vertical extension of the front of a building beyond the roofline. The style was popular in the 19th-century West as a means of giving hastily constructed buildings in frontier towns a sense of visual continuity.

This is perhaps the most popular travel destination on the northern California coast for San Francisco Bay Area residents, especially on sunny summer weekends. As a result Mendocino has many B&B properties, most of them falling into the delightfully charming variety. And if you're a fan of the long-running '80s TV series "Murder, She Wrote" and everything around you looks vaguely familiar, there's a reason; Mendocino stood in for fictional Cabot Cove, Maine, the scene of star Angela Lansbury's sleuthing.

Despite relative inaccessibility—or perhaps because of it—the area's natural beauty began attracting artists in the 1950s, and Mendocino remains a haven for those with a creative bent. The Mendocino Art Center, 45200 Little Lake St., is a highly regarded educational institution that offers more than 200 retreat-style workshops each year. The center's galleries feature changing monthly exhibitions spotlighting local and national artists; phone (707) 937-5818 or (800) 653-3328.

Nearby destinations are equally alluring. About 12 miles south of Mendocino, SR 128 branches off SR 1 and travels through the heart of the Anderson Valley. The first 10 or so miles tunnel through the majestic stand of second-growth trees that make up Navarro River Redwoods State Park (see Recreation Areas Chart). Tall and arrow straight, they create a densely shady environment pierced by shafts of sunlight.

Once past the redwoods SR 128 takes a circuitously winding route through the valley, which once was the site of sawmills and timber-cutting operations. Today it's dotted with vineyards, including several that produce award-winning wines. You also can sample outstanding micro brews in the tasting room at the Anderson Valley Brewing Company in Boonville, 17700 SR 253 (Boonville-Ukiah Road). The drive southeast to Cloverdale is especially scenic in the spring, when apple trees are blossoming and the countryside is lush from winter rains.

A 60-mile drive up the Mendocino County coastline via SR 1, the Pacific Coast Highway, offers more scenic riches in return for the knuckle-whitening aspects involved in negotiating stretches of this often-serpentine roadway. Begin the journey at the small town of Gualala (see place listing p. 100); originally a lumber settlement, it offers browsing potential in the form of art galleries and boutiques housed in a mix of 19th-century and contemporary buildings. North of Gualala is Point Arena (see place listing p. 200), one of several spots along this stretch of coast where it's possible to observe migrating gray whales during the winter months.

At Elk there's a clifftop cluster of country inns, restaurants and shops that feature the work of local artisans. Albion, the next town up the coast, is the site of the last wooden bridge constructed along the Pacific Coast Highway, in 1944. Like neighboring Mendocino, the architectural legacy in Little River (see place listing p. 124) reflects the heritage of the town's original New England settlers.

KELLEY HOUSE MUSEUM, 45007 Albion St., is in a restored dwelling dating from 1861. The archive contains thousands of photographs, family records, maps, documents and historic objects. Guided walking tours of historic Mendocino are offered on weekends; self-guided audio walking tours are available during office hours. **Hours:** Museum open Fri.-Mon. 11-3. Research office open Mon.-Fri. 11-4. Walking tours Sat.-Sun. at 11. **Cost:** Museum by donation. Walking tours $10. **Phone:** (707) 937-5791.

MENDOCINO HEADLANDS STATE PARK surrounds Mendocino on three sides between SR 1 and the ocean. The southern section features bluffs rising abruptly from a rocky shoreline up to a rugged, windswept promontory threaded with walking trails. These headlands not only offer panoramic ocean views but an opportunity to spot gray whales during their winter migration between Alaska and Mexico's Baja Peninsula. The big creatures head south in December and make the return trip north between February and April.

A flight of stone steps leads down to Portuguese Beach, a secluded little spot for picnicking and sunbathing during low tide. Hiking and fishing are popular day-use activities. **Note:** The headlands in the southern portion of the park have sheer drop-offs, and it can be quite windy at times; stick to the marked trails and stay away from the bluff edges. **Time:** Allow 1 hour minimum. **Hours:** Daily dawn-dusk. **Cost:** Free. **Phone:** (707) 937-5804.

Ford House Visitor Center and Museum is at 45035 Main St. The Ford House was built in 1854 for the bride of Jerome B. Ford, one of the town's founders. It is now a visitor center where you can pick up maps and brochures. Exhibits depict the mid-19th-century era when this coastal area was settled. A focal point is a scale model of the town as it appeared in 1890. **Time:** Allow 30 minutes minimum. **Hours:** Daily 11-4. Docent-led tours of the historical home are given daily. Guided whale walks along the Mendocino headlands are offered in March, depending on staff availability. **Cost:** Donations. **Phone:** (707) 937-5397.

POINT CABRILLO LIGHT STATION STATE HISTORIC PARK is 2 mi. n. on SR 1, then 1.3 mi. n. on Point Cabrillo Dr., following signs. On the grounds of this 300-acre park are eight restored buildings and 3.5 miles of hiking trails. The lighthouse, a half-mile walk from the parking lot, dates from 1909 and has an original Third Order Fresnel lens. An exhibit chronicles the 1850 shipwreck of the San Francisco-bound Frolic. One of the restored lightkeeper's homes is now a museum; two additional restored houses and two utility buildings repurposed as cottages function as vacation rentals.

Time: Allow 1 hour, 30 minutes minimum. **Hours:** Preserve open daily dawn-dusk. Lighthouse and museum open daily 10-5, May-Sept.; 11-4, rest of year. **Cost:** Donations. **Phone:** (707) 937-6122.

RUSSIAN GULCH STATE PARK is 2 mi. n.; the signed turnoff is on the ocean side of SR 1. The gulch is a Coastal Range canyon verdant with second-generation redwoods, Douglas fir and California laurel. Growing beneath the trees are ferns, azaleas and rhododendrons, the latter two blooming in April and May. Crisscrossing trails lead to numerous scenic views of the ocean, framed by craggy coastal headlands. Another scenic component is the Frederick W. Panhorst Bridge, which rises 100 feet from the mouth of Russian Gulch.

The park's most unusual geological feature is the Devil's Punchbowl, formed by waves that carved an inland tunnel, leaving a sinkhole some 100 feet across and 60 feet deep. A protective fence surrounds the hole; carefully look over the top and you'll see ocean water below gushing through the cave opening into the bowl before being forcefully sucked out again. At high tide the crashing waves produce a loud rumbling sound.

The Fern Canyon Trail is a wonderful woodland walk, especially lush in the spring (after winter rains) when wild blackberry bushes and horsetail grow along it in an exuberant tangle and delicate blue forget-me-nots are in bloom. The first 1.5 miles run along a stream and are paved and level. A short distance past a picnic area and the signed junction with the North Trail (which leads back to the park campground) is the signed beginning of the Falls Loop Trail. It continues another three-quarters of a mile, ascending via trail, wooden steps and footbridges to a waterfall. Here you can either backtrack to the trailhead or continue on the loop trail; the complete loop is about 5 miles and takes a couple of hours to hike. *See Recreation Areas Chart.*

Time: Allow 2 hours minimum. **Hours:** Daily dawn-dusk. **Cost:** Day use fee $8 per private vehicle; $7 (ages 62+ per private vehicle). **Phone:** (707) 937-5804.

RECREATIONAL ACTIVITIES
Canoeing
- **Catch a Canoe & Bicycles, Too!** is at SR 1 and Comptche-Ukiah Rd., at the Stanford Inn by the Sea. **Hours:** Daily 9-5. **Phone:** (707) 937-0273.

AGATE COVE INN   707/937-0551
Cottage. **Address:** 11201 N Lansing St 95460

BREWERY GULCH INN   707/937-4752

Bed & Breakfast

Address: 9401 N Hwy 1 95460 **Location:** 1.3 mi s of Mendocino Village, just e. **Facility:** Vintage redwood was salvaged for use in the construction of this Craftsman-style inn situated on a bluff with views of Smuggler's Cove. Lush gardens and dense foliage give it a retreat-like ambience. 10 units. 2 stories (no elevator), interior corridors. **Terms:** age restrictions may apply. **Activities:** trails, massage. **Featured Amenity:** full hot breakfast.

HEADLANDS INN BED & BREAKFAST   707/937-4431
Historic Bed & Breakfast. **Address:** 10453 Howard St 95460

SEA ROCK BED & BREAKFAST INN   707/937-0926
Cottage. **Address:** 11101 Lansing St 95460

STANFORD INN BY THE SEA ECO-RESORT
                                           707/937-5615

Resort
Country Inn

Address: 44850 Comptche-Ukiah Rd 95460 **Location:** SR 1 exit Comptche-Ukiah Rd, just e. **Facility:** Magnificent grounds, a rustic setting and many rooms with ocean views and wood-burning fireplaces add to this lodge's appeal. Walk along the ivy covered decks on your way to the indoor saline pool. 41 units, some cottages. 2-3 stories (no elevator), exterior corridors. **Terms:** check-in 4 pm. **Dining:** The Ravens', see separate listing. **Pool:** heated indoor. **Activities:** sauna, hot tub, self-propelled boats, recreation programs, bicycles, trails, exercise room, spa. **Guest Services:** valet laundry. **Featured Amenity:** breakfast buffet.

WHERE TO EAT

CAFE BEAUJOLAIS   707/937-5614
California. Fine Dining. **Address:** 961 Ukiah St 95460

FRANKIE'S PIZZA AND ICE CREAM   707/937-2436
Pizza. Quick Serve. **Address:** 44951 Ukiah St 95460

THE GARDEN ROOM   707/937-0511
American. Casual Dining. **Address:** 45080 Main St 95460

GOODLIFE CAFE AND BAKERY   707/937-0836
Natural/Organic Breads/Pastries. Quick Serve. **Address:** 10483 Lancing St 95460

LUNA TRATTORIA   707/962-3093
Northern Italian. Casual Dining. **Address:** 955 Ukiah St 95460

MACCALLUM HOUSE RESTAURANT   707/937-6759
California. Fine Dining. **Address:** 45020 Albion St 95460

THE RAVENS'   707/937-5615

Vegan
Fine Dining
$15-$27

AAA Inspector Notes: Known for its delectable hearty cuisine and seasonally changing vegan menu, this restaurant gets most of its produce from its own private gardens. The spectacular views will keep you entertained while enjoying entrées like sea palm and root vegetable strudel or tamales with butternut squash and mild green chiles. The chips and fresh salsa has a great mix of salty and spicy. There is also a nice selection of wine and spirits to accompany your meal. **Features:** full bar, Sunday brunch, happy hour. **Reservations:** suggested. **Address:** 44850 Comptche-Ukiah Rd 95460 **Location:** SR 1 exit Comptche-Ukiah Rd, just e; in Stanford Inn by the Sea Eco-Resort.

MENDOCINO NATIONAL FOREST (C-2)

Elevations in the forest range from 1,000 ft. at Elk Creek to 8,110 ft. at the summit of Mount Linn. Refer to AAA maps for additional elevation information.

In the North Coast Mountain Range north of San Francisco, Mendocino National Forest encompasses 913,306 acres. Hang gliding and motorcycling areas are available. Roads and trails afford access to scenic points. Many roads within the forest are unsurfaced; driving can be hazardous, especially in the dusty, dry months.

Yolla Bolly-Middle Eel Wilderness at the north end of the forest and Snow Mountain Wilderness in the south provide peaceful settings for horseback riding and hiking. Wilderness entry permits are not required, but users should sign the registry at trailheads.

The Red Bluff Recreation Area, 488 acres adjacent to the Sacramento River 2 miles from Red Bluff *(see place listing p. 203)*, has such diverse habitats as forests, wetlands and woodlands. In addition to hiking trails and summer fishing, the area also is known for its bird-watching opportunities. The Sacramento River Discovery Center, 1000 Sale Ln. in Red Bluff, has interpretive displays about the river's watershed; phone (530) 527-1196.

Campfire permits are required in some areas; check with the Forest Supervisor, Mendocino National Forest, 825 N. Humboldt Ave., Willows, CA 95988, or a district office. For information phone (530) 934-3316, or TTY (530) 934-7724. *See Recreation Areas Chart.*

MENLO PARK (E-8) pop. 32,026, elev. 70'
• Hotels & Restaurants map & index p. 190

ALLIED ARTS GUILD, off SR 82 at the end of Cambridge Ave. on Arbor Rd., occupies 3.5 acres of land originally granted by the King of Spain to the Commandant of the Presidio de San Francisco in the early 19th century. This complex of buildings has a decidedly Spanish architectural style. The courtyards, gardens, fountains, murals and frescoes all create a simpatico backdrop for the working artists in residence. **Hours:** Mon.-Sat. 10-5. **Cost:** Free. **Phone:** (650) 322-2405. ⦅¶⦆

BEST WESTERN PLUS RIVIERA　　650/321-8772　⓳

Best Western PLUS
Hotel

AAA Benefit: Members save up to 15% and earn bonus points!

Address: 15 El Camino Real 94025 **Location:** On SR 82. Adjacent to Stanford University. **Facility:** 37 units. 2 stories, exterior corridors. **Pool:** outdoor. **Activities:** sauna, hot tub, exercise room. **Guest Services:** valet and coin laundry. **Featured Amenity:** breakfast buffet.

⦅SAVE⦆ ⦅¶⦆ CALL ⦅&⦆ ⦅≈⦆ ⦅♥⦆ ⦅BIZ⦆
⦅HS⦆ ⦅≋⦆ ⦅✕⦆ ⦅▯⦆ ⦅◻⦆ ⦅▯⦆

MENLO PARK INN　　　　　　　650/326-7530　⓱
◈◈ Motel. **Address:** 1315 El Camino Real 94025

RED COTTAGE INN & SUITES　　650/326-9010　⓯
◈◈◈ Motel. **Address:** 1704 El Camino Real 94025

**⊘ AAA.com/maps—Dream, plan,
go with AAA travel planning tools**

RESIDENCE INN BY MARRIOTT PALO ALTO MENLO PARK　　　　　650/327-2000　⓰

◈◈◈◈
Extended Stay Contemporary Hotel

Residence INN. **AAA Benefit:** Members save 5% or more!

Address: 555 Glenwood Ave 94025 **Location:** US 101 exit 406 (SR 84 E/Marsh Rd), 1.1 mi w on Marsh Rd, 0.6 mi s on Middlefield Rd, then 0.5 mi w. **Facility:** 138 efficiencies, some two bedrooms. 3 stories, interior/exterior corridors. **Parking:** on-site (fee). **Terms:** check-in 4 pm. **Amenities:** safes. **Activities:** picnic facilities, trails, exercise room. **Guest Services:** complimentary and valet laundry. **Featured Amenity:** breakfast buffet.

⦅SAVE⦆ ⦅¶⦆ CALL ⦅&⦆ ⦅♥⦆ ⦅BIZ⦆ ⦅≋⦆ ⦅✕⦆ ⦅▯⦆ ⦅◻⦆ ⦅▯⦆
/ SOME / UNITS ⦅🐾⦆ ⦅HS⦆

STANFORD PARK HOTEL　　　　650/322-1234　⓲

◈◈◈◈
Boutique Hotel

Address: 100 El Camino Real 94025 **Location:** On SR 82, 0.5 mi ne of Stanford University. Train tracks run behind property. **Facility:** Signature palm trees dotting the manicured grounds add a retreat feel to this classically elegant lodging. Fireplaces are featured in some guest rooms while others have vaulted ceilings. 162 units. 4 stories, interior corridors. **Parking:** on-site (fee) and valet. **Amenities:** safes. **Pool:** heated outdoor. **Activities:** sauna, hot tub, bicycles, trails, exercise room. **Guest Services:** valet laundry, area transportation.

⦅SAVE⦆ ⦅ECO⦆ ⦅▣⦆ ⦅¶⦆ ⦅♥⦆ ⦅Y⦆ CALL ⦅&⦆ ⦅≈⦆ ⦅♥⦆ ⦅BIZ⦆
⦅HS⦆ ⦅≋⦆ ⦅✕⦆ ⦅▯⦆ ⦅◻⦆

WHERE TO EAT

CARPACCIO　　　　　　　　　650/322-1211　⓲
◈◈ Italian. Casual Dining. **Address:** 1120 Crane St 94025

LEFT BANK　　　　　　　　　　650/473-6543　⓱
◈◈◈ French. Casual Dining. **Address:** 635 Santa Cruz Ave 94025

MERCED (F-4) pop. 78,958, elev. 167'

Merced, in the agricultural San Joaquin Valley, is the principal western gateway to Yosemite National Park for travelers from the north.

Merced National Wildlife Refuge is 16 miles southwest. Water sports are offered 7 miles northeast at Lake Yosemite. Lillian, a capuchin monkey, is one of the animal residents at Applegate Park Zoo, 25th and R streets, which also has children's rides; phone (209) 725-3337.

Merced Visitor Services: 710 W. 16th St., Merced, CA 95340. **Phone:** (209) 724-8104 or (800) 446-5353.

Self-guiding tours: The conference and visitors bureau distributes a guide to historic Merced as well as a blossom guide.

MERCED COUNTY COURTHOUSE MUSEUM, 21st and N sts., is in the Old County Courthouse, one of the oldest buildings in the state. The 1875 three-story Italianate structure, which resembles the state Capitol building, houses exhibits about Merced County history and the Central Valley pioneers who settled the area. Permanent exhibits include a turn-of-the-20th-century classroom, a courtroom, a Chinese temple and a blacksmith shop. **Time:** Allow 2 hours minimum. **Hours:** Wed.-Sun. 1-4. Closed major holidays. **Cost:** Free. **Phone:** (209) 723-2401.

BEST WESTERN INN 209/723-2163

 Hotel

 AAA Benefit: Members save up to 15% and earn bonus points!

Address: 1033 Motel Dr 95341 **Location:** SR 99 exit SR 140, just e. then just s. Adjacent to freeway. **Facility:** 42 units. 2 stories (no elevator), exterior corridors. **Pool:** outdoor. **Activities:** exercise room. **Guest Services:** coin laundry. **Featured Amenity:** full hot breakfast.

COURTYARD BY MARRIOTT 209/725-1221

Hotel. **Address:** 750 Motel Dr 95340

AAA Benefit: Members save 5% or more!

HAMPTON INN & SUITES-MERCED 209/386-1210

Hotel

Hampton **AAA Benefit:** Members save up to 15%!

Address: 225 S Parsons Ave 95340 **Location:** SR 99 exit 186A (E Childs Ave), just e. then just s. **Facility:** 83 units. 3 stories, interior corridors. **Pool:** outdoor. **Activities:** hot tub, exercise room. **Guest Services:** coin laundry. **Featured Amenity:** breakfast buffet.

HOLIDAY INN EXPRESS HOTEL & SUITES 209/384-3700

Hotel. **Address:** 151 S Parsons Ave 95341

TOWNEPLACE SUITES BY MARRIOTT MERCED 209/384-1024

Extended Stay Hotel. **Address:** 229 S Parsons Ave 95341

AAA Benefit: Members save 5% or more!

WHERE TO EAT

FIVE TEN BISTRO 209/381-0280

Continental. Casual Dining. **Address:** 510 W Main St 95340

TONI'S COURTYARD CAFE & BAKERY 209/384-2580

American. Casual Dining. **Address:** 516 W 18th St 95340

MIDDLETOWN (E-2) pop. 1,323, elev. 1,105'
• Part of Wine Country area — see map p. 405

WINERIES

• **Langtry Estate & Vineyards** is at 21000 Butts Canyon Rd. **Hours:** Tastings and tours Fri.-Sun. 10-5. Hours may be extended in summer; phone ahead to confirm schedule. **Phone:** (707) 995-7521. [GT]

TWIN PINE CASINO & HOTEL 707/987-0297

Contemporary Hotel

Address: 22223 Hwy 29 at Rancheria Rd 95461 **Location:** Jct SR 175 and 29, 1.6 mi s. **Facility:** 59 units. 3 stories, interior corridors. **Amenities:** safes. **Activities:** exercise room.

WHERE TO EAT

PERRY'S DELICATESSEN AND CATERING 707/987-2416

Deli. Quick Serve. **Address:** 21308 Calistoga St, #A 95461

MILLBRAE (D-8) pop. 21,532, elev. 33'
• Restaurants p. 136
• Hotels & Restaurants map & index p. 316
• Part of San Francisco area — see map p. 243

This San Francisco Bay Area bedroom community benefits economically from proximity to one of the country's most popular travel destinations, and it's practically next door to bustling San Francisco International Airport. I-280 and US 101 offer easy access to points south like Stanford University, Levi's Stadium (new home of the San Francisco 49ers) and Silicon Valley communities. I-280 also intersects with east-west routes that will take you to the ocean side of the San Francisco Peninsula and the scenic glories of SR 1, the Pacific Coast highway.

ALOFT SAN FRANCISCO AIRPORT 650/443-5500 **36**

Hotel

aloft **AAA Benefit:** Members save 5% or more!

Address: 401 E Millbrae Ave 94030 **Location:** US 101 exit Millbrae Ave, just e. Millbrae, 54. **Facility:** 271 units. 6 stories, interior corridors. **Bath:** shower only. **Parking:** on-site (fee). **Amenities:** safes. **Pool:** heated indoor. **Activities:** trails, exercise room. **Guest Services:** valet and coin laundry.

THE DYLAN AT SFO 650/697-7373 **38**

Hotel. **Address:** 110 S El Camino Real 94030

(See map & index p. 316.)

EL RANCHO INN, BW SIGNATURE COLLECTION
650/588-8500 **34**

Hotel

AAA Benefit:
Members save up to 15% and earn bonus points!

Address: 1100 El Camino Real 94030 **Location:** US 101 exit Millbrae Ave, 0.3 mi sw, then 0.8 mi n on SR 82. San Francisco Int'l Airport, 53. **Facility:** 219 units, some two bedrooms. 2 stories (no elevator), exterior corridors. **Dining:** Terrace Cafe, see separate listing. **Pool:** heated outdoor. **Activities:** hot tub, exercise room. **Guest Services:** valet and coin laundry. **Featured Amenity:** breakfast buffet.

 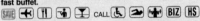 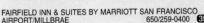

FAIRFIELD INN & SUITES BY MARRIOTT SAN FRANCISCO AIRPORT/MILLBRAE
650/259-0400 **35**

 Hotel. **Address:** 250 El Camino Real 94030

AAA Benefit:
Members save 5% or more!

MILLWOOD INN & SUITES
650/583-3935 **33**

Motel

Address: 1375 El Camino Real 94030 **Location:** 0.3 mi sw of US 101 exit Millbrae Ave, 1 mi n on SR 82. San Francisco Int'l Airport, 53. **Facility:** 34 units, some two bedrooms. 1-2 stories (no elevator), interior/exterior corridors. **Amenities:** safes. **Activities:** exercise room. **Guest Services:** valet and coin laundry. **Featured Amenity:** breakfast buffet.

THE WESTIN SAN FRANCISCO AIRPORT
650/692-3500 **37**

Hotel

AAA Benefit:
Members save 5% or more!

Address: 1 Old Bayshore Hwy 94030 **Location:** US 101 exit Millbrae Ave, just e. Located in a busy commercial area. Millbrae, 54. **Facility:** 397 units. 7 stories, interior corridors. **Parking:** onsite (fee) and valet. **Amenities:** safes. **Pool:** heated indoor. **Activities:** hot tub, trails, exercise room. **Guest Services:** valet laundry, area transportation.

WHERE TO EAT

HONG KONG FLOWER LOUNGE RESTAURANT
650/692-6666 **26**

Chinese Dim Sum. Casual Dining. **Address:** 51 Millbrae Ave 94030

LA COLLINA RISTORANTE
650/652-9655 **25**

Italian. Casual Dining. **Address:** 355 El Camino Real 94030

TERRACE CAFE
650/742-5588 **24**

American. Casual Dining. **Address:** 1100 El Camino Real 94030

MILL VALLEY (C-7) pop. 13,903, elev. 70'
• Part of San Francisco area — see map p. 243

Mill Valley, at the foot of Mount Tamalpais, is an affluent residential Marin County community. Standing in Old Mill Park, at Old Mill Street and Throckmorton Avenue, is the heavy redwood frame of a sawmill. Set in the midst of a redwood grove, this pretty, shady, creekside park also has an amphitheater where performances by the Marin Theatre Company are given in the summer.

Hikers can climb a stone stairway in the park to access the Dipsea Trail trailhead. The trail stretches about 7 miles to Stinson Beach, dipping up and down as it winds through the coastal hills of Mount Tamalpais State Park toward the ocean.

Mill Valley Chamber of Commerce & Visitor Center: 85 Throckmorton Ave., Mill Valley, CA 94941. **Phone:** (415) 388-9700.

MOUNT TAMALPAIS STATE PARK, 6 mi. w. on Panoramic Hwy., encompasses 6,300 acres of picturesque coastal hill country dominated by triple-peaked Mount Tamalpais; the mountain's profile from the south is said to resemble a sleeping Native American girl. Hiking and bicycling trails and a winding road lead to spectacular vistas at the summit, where there is a visitor center.

Theatrical productions known as the Mountain Play are presented in the Sidney B. Cushing Memorial Amphitheatre, 801 Panoramic Hwy., also known as the Mountain Theater. It was constructed out of rock by the Civilian Conservation Corps in the 1930s, although performances have taken place in the amphitheater since 1913. *See Recreation Areas Chart.*

Note: At press time sections of SR 1 were closed due to storm damage; phone ahead to confirm access and route information. **Hours:** Park open daily 7-dusk. Visitor center open Sat.-Sun. and holidays, Apr.-Oct.; hours vary. Visitor center schedule varies rest of year. Ranger station open daily 8-5, Mar.-Aug.; hours may vary. Ranger station schedule varies rest of year. Plays are presented mid-May to mid-June. Phone ahead to confirm schedule. **Cost:** Day use $8 per private vehicle; $7 (ages 62+ per private vehicle). **Phone:** (415) 388-2070 for the state park, or (415) 383-1100 for play and amphitheater information.

HOLIDAY INN EXPRESS MILL VALLEY/SAN FRANCISCO AREA
415/332-5700

Hotel. **Address:** 160 Shoreline Hwy 94941

MILL VALLEY INN
415/389-6608

Boutique Hotel. **Address:** 165 Throckmorton Ave 94941

WHERE TO EAT

THE BUCKEYE ROADHOUSE 415/331-2600
 American. Casual Dining. **Address:** 15 Shoreline Hwy 94941

MILPITAS (E-9) pop. 66,790, elev. 20'
- Restaurants p. 138
- Hotels & Restaurants map & index p. 348

This affluent area just south of San Francisco Bay lies between I-680 and I-880. You'll find industrial parks as well as more than 20 parks for rest and recreation.

Shopping: Great Mall, a former Ford plant, is at 447 Great Mall Dr. and features dozens of outlet stores.

BEST WESTERN PLUS BROOKSIDE INN
408/263-5566 **31**

Hotel

AAA Benefit: Members save up to 15% and earn bonus points!

Address: 400 Valley Way 95035 **Location:** I-880 exit Calaveras Blvd (SR 237), just e. **Facility:** 79 units. 2 stories, interior/exterior corridors. **Pool:** heated outdoor. **Activities:** sauna, steamroom, exercise room. **Guest Services:** valet and coin laundry. **Featured Amenity:** breakfast buffet.

CROWNE PLAZA SAN JOSE-SILICON VALLEY
408/321-9500 **32**

Hotel
Address: 777 Bellew Dr 95035 **Location:** SR 237 exit McCarthy Blvd, just s, then just e. **Facility:** 304 units, some two bedrooms. 10 stories, interior corridors. **Pool:** heated outdoor. **Activities:** hot tub, trails, exercise room. **Guest Services:** valet and coin laundry, rental car service, area transportation.

EMBASSY SUITES BY HILTON MILPITAS SILICON VALLEY
408/942-0400 **28**

Hotel
AAA Benefit: Members save up to 15%!
Address: 901 E Calaveras Blvd 95035 **Location:** I-680 exit Calaveras Blvd (SR 237), just w. **Facility:** 266 units. 9 stories, interior corridors. **Parking:** on-site (fee). **Terms:** check-in 4 pm. **Pool:** heated indoor. **Activities:** hot tub, trails, exercise room. **Guest Services:** valet and coin laundry. **Featured Amenity:** full hot breakfast.

HILTON GARDEN INN-SAN JOSE/MILPITAS
408/719-1313 **29**
 Hotel. **Address:** 30 Ranch Dr 95035
AAA Benefit: Members save up to 15%!

LARKSPUR LANDING MILPITAS
408/719-1212 **30**

Extended Stay Hotel
Address: 40 Ranch Dr 95035 **Location:** SR 237 exit McCarthy Blvd, just n. **Facility:** 124 efficiencies. 4 stories, interior corridors. **Activities:** hot tub, limited exercise equipment. **Guest Services:** complimentary and valet laundry, area transportation. **Featured Amenity:** continental breakfast.

MILPITAS COURTYARD BY MARRIOTT
408/719-1966 **34**
 Hotel. **Address:** 1480 Falcon Dr 95035
AAA Benefit: Members save 5% or more!

RESIDENCE INN BY MARRIOTT MILPITAS SILICON VALLEY
408/941-9222 **27**
Extended Stay Hotel. **Address:** 1501 California Cir 95035
AAA Benefit: Members save 5% or more!

SHERATON SAN JOSE HOTEL
408/943-0600 **35**
Hotel
AAA Benefit: Members save 5% or more!
Address: 1801 Barber Ln 95035 **Location:** 4 mi n of San Jose International Airport; 0.3 mi nw of I-880 and Montague Expwy. **Facility:** 229 units. 2-9 stories, interior/exterior corridors. **Parking:** on-site (fee). **Amenities:** safes. **Pool:** heated outdoor. **Activities:** trails, exercise room. **Guest Services:** valet laundry.

TOWNEPLACE SUITES BY MARRIOTT MILPITAS
408/719-1959 **33**
Extended Stay Hotel. **Address:** 1428 Falcon Dr 95035
AAA Benefit: Members save 5% or more!

AAA.com/campgrounds—
For overnights under
the stars

(See map & index p. 348.)

EL TORITO   408/946-8012

 Mexican. Casual Dining. **Address:** 477 E Calaveras Blvd 95035

JANG SU JANG   408/262-3434 

 Korean Barbecue. Casual Dining. **Address:** 269 W Calaveras Blvd 95035

MIRANDA pop. 520

MIRANDA GARDENS RESORT   707/943-3011

Cottage

Address: 6766 Ave of the Giants 95553 **Location:** US 101 exit 650, 0.3 mi e on Maple Hills Rd, then 1.5 mi nw. Located in a quiet village area. **Facility:** 16 cottages, some kitchens. 1 story, exterior corridors. **Pool:** heated outdoor. **Activities:** playground. **Featured Amenity:** continental breakfast.

MI-WUK VILLAGE pop. 941

CHRISTMAS TREE INN   209/586-1005

Motel

Address: 24685 Hwy 108 95346 **Location:** On SR 108, 15 mi e of Sonora. **Facility:** 16 units. 2 stories (no elevator), exterior corridors. **Pool:** outdoor. **Activities:** hot tub.

MODESTO (F-3) pop. 201,165, elev. 88'

This northern San Joaquin Valley city along the Tuolumne River is near California's geographic center. Modesto offers access to Sonora Pass in Stanislaus National Forest, the Mother Lode Country and the Big Oak Flat route to Yosemite National Park.

The Great Valley Museum has habitat displays pertaining to California's Central Valley, a native plant garden and live animal exhibits. It's located in the Science Community Center building, 2201 Blue Gum Ave., on the Modesto Junior College West Campus. Phone (209) 575-6196.

George Lucas Plaza, at Downey Street, McHenry Avenue and 17th and J streets, salutes native son and filmmaker George Lucas, whose 1973 film "American Graffiti" was an evocative, music-filled reverie recalling the times he spent cruising the streets of his hometown in the early 1960s. A statue in the plaza depicts two teenagers leaning against a '57 Chevrolet.

Modesto Convention and Visitors Bureau: 1000 L St., Modesto, CA 95354. **Phone:** (209) 526-5588 or (888) 640-8467.

Shopping: Vintage Faire Mall, off the SR 99 Standiford/Beckwith exit between Sisk and Dale roads, has anchors JCPenney, Macy's and Sears plus some 125 other stores.

MCHENRY MANSION is at the jct. of 15th and I sts. Built in 1883 by a prominent local rancher and banker, the Victorian Italianate mansion is decorated in period to look as it did while occupied by Robert McHenry and his wife Matilda. Three rooms on the second floor reflect turn-of-the-20th-century style, a time when their son lived in the mansion. Guided tours begin at the visitors center with a DVD presentation. **Time:** Allow 1 hour minimum. **Hours:** Sun.-Fri. 12:30-4. Closed major holidays. **Cost:** Donations. **Phone:** (209) 549-0428.

BAYMONT INN & SUITES MODESTO SALIDA   209/543-9000

 Motel. **Address:** 4100 Salida Blvd 95358

BEST WESTERN PALM COURT INN   209/521-9000

Hotel

 Best Western. **AAA Benefit:** Members save up to 15% and earn bonus points!

Address: 2001 W Orangeburg Ave 95350 **Location:** SR 99 exit 229 (Briggsmore Ave), just e, then just s. **Facility:** 112 units. 2 stories (no elevator), exterior corridors. **Pool:** outdoor. **Activities:** hot tub, exercise room. **Guest Services:** coin laundry. **Featured Amenity:** breakfast buffet.

BEST WESTERN TOWN HOUSE LODGE   209/524-7261

Hotel

 Best Western. **AAA Benefit:** Members save up to 15% and earn bonus points!

Address: 909 16th St 95354 **Location:** Between I and J sts; downtown. **Facility:** 55 units. 2 stories (no elevator), exterior corridors. **Pool:** outdoor. **Activities:** hot tub. **Featured Amenity:** breakfast buffet.

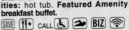

DOUBLETREE BY HILTON HOTEL MODESTO
209-526-6000

  Hotel

 AAA Benefit:
Members save up to 15%!

 Address: 1150 9th St 95354 **Location:** SR 99 exit 226 (Central Modesto) northbound; exit 226B (Maze Blvd) southbound, 0.7 mi ne; between K and L sts. Located at Convention Center Plaza. **Facility:** 260 units. 10 stories, interior corridors. **Parking:** on-site (fee) and valet. **Amenities:** safes. **Dining:** Maxi's, see separate listing. **Pool:** heated outdoor. **Activities:** hot tub, exercise room.
Guest Services: valet laundry.

HOLIDAY INN EXPRESS HOTEL & SUITES
209-543-9009
Hotel. **Address:** 4300 Bangs Ave 95356

RESIDENCE INN BY MARRIOTT
209-382-8850
Extended Stay Hotel. **Address:** 2901 Healthcare Way 95356

AAA Benefit: Members save 5% or more!

SPRINGHILL SUITES BY MARRIOTT MODESTO
209-526-2157

 Hotel

SPRINGHILL SUITES MARRIOTT **AAA Benefit:**
Members save 5% or more!

 Address: 1901 W Orangeburg Ave 95350 **Location:** SR 99 exit 229 (Briggsmore Ave), just e, then just s. **Facility:** 111 units. 3 stories, interior corridors. **Pool:** heated outdoor. **Activities:** hot tub, exercise room. **Guest Services:** valet and coin laundry. **Featured Amenity:** breakfast buffet.

WHERE TO EAT

BELLA ITALIA RISTORANTE & PIZZERIA
209-577-1094
Italian. Casual Dining. **Address:** 2625 Coffee Rd, Suite K 95355

DAMIAN'S RESTAURANT
209-526-3800
Mexican. Casual Dining. **Address:** 2075 W Orangeburg Ave 95350

GALLETTO RISTORANTE
209-523-4500
Italian. Fine Dining. **Address:** 1101 J St 95354

MAXI'S
209-525-3075
American. Casual Dining. **Address:** 1150 9th St 95354

TAHOE JOE'S FAMOUS STEAKHOUSE
209-545-6885
Steak. Casual Dining. **Address:** 3801 Pelandale Ave 95356

VELVET CREAMERY RESTAURANT
209-527-2662
American. Casual Dining. **Address:** 3250 Dale Rd 95356

MODOC NATIONAL FOREST (A-3)

Elevations in the forest range from 4,500 ft. at Devils Gardens to 9,892 ft. at Eagle Peak. Refer to AAA maps for additional elevation information.

Encompassing much of the state's remote northeastern corner, Modoc National Forest's 1,654,392 acres were covered millions of years ago by an immense lava flow. Although geologically the area is known as the Modoc Plateau, it doesn't look like a plateau. The region is distinguished by basins, mountains, lakes and meadows. And despite the relatively dry climate, the plateau supports some of the country's most significant wetlands.

The forest is home to more than 300 species of wildlife, including Rocky Mountain mule deer, pronghorn antelopes, bald and golden eagles and wild horses. The Pacific Flyway for migratory birds crosses directly over the forest.

Volcanism has left many marks on the forest's terrain, and some of the most dramatic examples are in the Medicine Lake highlands. There are such unusual features as Glass Mountain, a huge flow of obsidian, and the Burnt Lava Flow, which is a jumble of black lava interspersed with islands of timber. Medicine Lake itself fills an old volcanic crater and is popular for boating and swimming.

On the forest's eastern boundary, the Warner Mountains are a rolling upland that drops steeply on its eastern edge. Most of the range is above 5,000 feet, and some of the peaks reach an altitude over 9,000 feet in the 70,385-acre South Warner Wilderness, which includes Modoc's highest mountain, Eagle Peak. The forest has 118 miles of trails, accessible by eight trailheads, suited for hikers and horseback riders. Carrying a topography map is advised. Fishing is prime in many reservoirs. Cross-country skiing is a popular wintertime diversion.

Maps, brochures and information about recreational opportunities are available at the district ranger stations and the forest headquarters in Alturas. For more information write the Forest Supervisor, Modoc National Forest, 225 W. 8th St., Alturas, CA 96101; phone (530) 233-5811, or TDD (530) 233-8708. *See Recreation Areas Chart.*

MONTEREY PENINSULA

Although Spanish explorer Juan Rodriguez Cabrillo, the first European to enter Monterey Bay, came within sight of the bay's pine forest-edged beaches in 1542, he was unable to reach land due to high seas. It would be another 60 years before Sebastián Vizcaíno explored the bay and named it for the Count of Monte Rey, viceroy of Mexico. Vizcaíno also named a nearby valley after his patron saint, Our Lady of Carmel.

The remote area was officially claimed for Spain but was not settled until Franciscan priest Junípero Serra and Spanish governor Gaspar de Portolá arrived in 1770 to build a mission and establish a seat of government, respectively. Fishing and whaling provided livelihoods, but by the 1880s tourism began developing. The ocean beckoned once again, however, when sardine harvesting led to the birth of Monterey's Cannery Row during the 1920s.

The peninsula's striking natural beauty restored tourism to the economic forefront after the collapse of the sardine industry. In addition to the obvious attractions of dramatic coastline, beaches and Pacific surf, the Monterey Peninsula also is blessed with gently rolling hills, streams and lush woodlands. It's a mecca for golf aficionados; the AT&T Pebble Beach National Pro-Am, held in early February, is one of the highlights of the professional circuit. And it is offering increasing competition to the Napa and Sonoma valleys courtesy of vineyards, wineries and tasting rooms that offer samples of award-winning products.

Those seeking more active pursuits should check out the Monterey Peninsula Recreational Trail, a walking, jogging and biking path that runs along the coast for 18 miles from Pacific Grove to Castroville. Following the Southern Pacific Railroad line, it passes Monterey's famed Cannery Row and Fisherman's Wharf areas and the impressive sand dunes at Monterey State Beach, and also offers countless scenic vistas of the rocky Pacific shoreline.

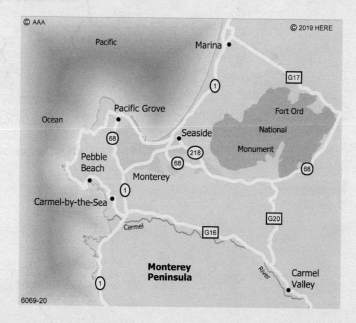

This map shows cities in the Monterey Peninsula where you will find attractions, hotels and restaurants. Cities are listed alphabetically in this book on the following pages.

© 2019 HERE

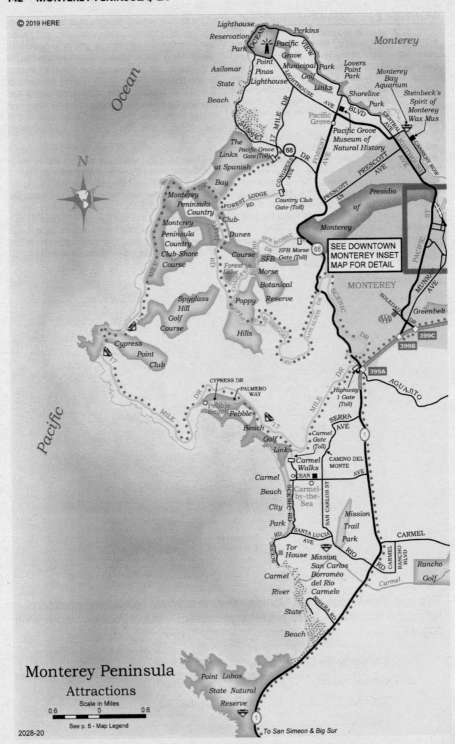

Monterey Peninsula
Attractions

Scale in Miles

0.6   0.6

See p. 6 - Map Legend

2028-20

To San Simeon & Big Sur

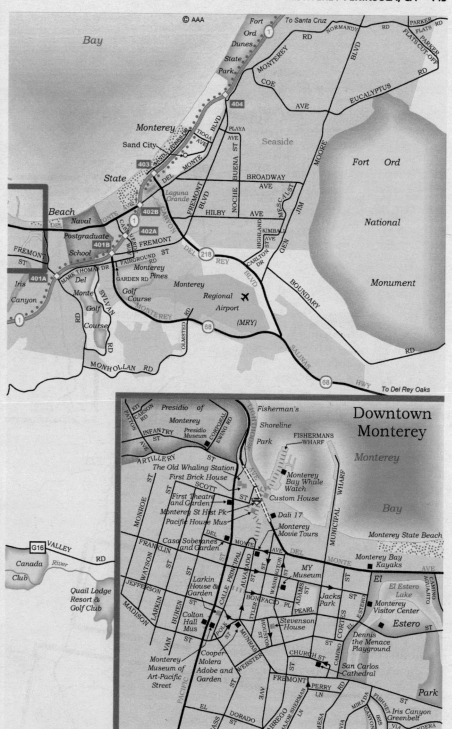

© AAA

Bay

To Santa Cruz

Fort
Ord
Dunes
State
Park.

PARKER
FLATS RD

FLATS CUT OFF

PARKER

NORMANDY

MONTEREY

RD

COE

AVE

EUCALYPTUS

404

Monterey

TIOGA
AVE

PLAYA
AVE

Seaside

Fort   Ord

Sand City

DEL   MONTE   BLVD

BUENA   BLVD

NOCHE

MOORE

National

State

403

Laguna
Grande

FREMONT   BLVD

BROADWAY
AVE

MES CAL ST

JIM

GEN

Monument

Beach

Naval
Postgraduate
School

402B

402A

401B

CASA
VERDE WAY

HILBY   AVE

AVE

HIGHLAND

KIMBALL
AVE

CARLTON DR

BOUNDARY

DEL

FREMONT

FREMONT
ST

1

401A

Iris

Canyon

MARK THOMAS DR

FAIRGROUND
RD

GARDEN RD

Monterey
Pines

DEL   REY

218

BLVD

Del
Monte
Golf
Course

SYLVAN   RD

Golf
Course

Monterey

Monterey
Regional
Airport
(MRY)

✈

OLMSTED
RD

68

SALINAS

RD

1

MONHOLLAN   RD

68   HWY

To Del Rey Oaks

Downtown Monterey

Presidio of
Monterey

KIT
CARSON
RD

PATTON
AVE

INFANTRY
ST

Presidio
Museum

CORPORAL
EWING RD

ARTILLERY   ST

Fisherman's

Shoreline
Park

FISHERMANS
WHARF

Monterey

The Old Whaling Station
First Brick House

SCOTT   ST

Monterey
Bay Whale
Watch

First Theatre
and Garden
Monterey St Hist Pk
Pacific House Mus

Custom House

Dali 17

MONROE   ST

Monterey
Movie Tours

Bay

MUNICIPAL   WHARF

Monterey State Beach

G16   VALLEY

Canada
Club

River

RD

Quail Lodge
Resort &
Golf Club

FRANKLIN   ST

WATSON   ST

Casa Soberanes
and Garden

DEL

MONTE   AVE

Monterey Bay
Kayaks

El Estero
Lake

El

DEL

MONTE

AVE

CAMINO
AGUAJITO

JEFFERSON   ST

Larkin
House &
Garden

CALLE PRINCIPAL

ALVARADO

WASHINGTON   ST

MY
Museum

ADAMS   ST

EL ESTERO   ST

Monterey
Visitor Center

Estero

MADISON   ST

LARKIN   ST

VAN   BUREN   ST

Colton
Hall
Mus

POLK   ST

BONIFACIO   PL

HOUSTON

PEARL

Jacks
Park

ST

CAMINO   CORTES

Dennis
the Menace
Playground

MUNRAS

Stevenson
House

WEBSTER   ST

Monterey
Museum of
Art-Pacific
Street

Cooper
Molera
Adobe and
Garden

PACIFIC   ST

ABREGO   ST

CHURCH   ST

San Carlos
Cathedral

FREMONT   ST

PERRY
LN

Park

Iris Canyon
Greenbelt

EL   DORADO   ST

CASS   ST

MAJOR SHERMAN   LN

MESA

VIA
MIRADA

FISHNET
RD

IRIS

CANYON RD

VIA LAVANDERA

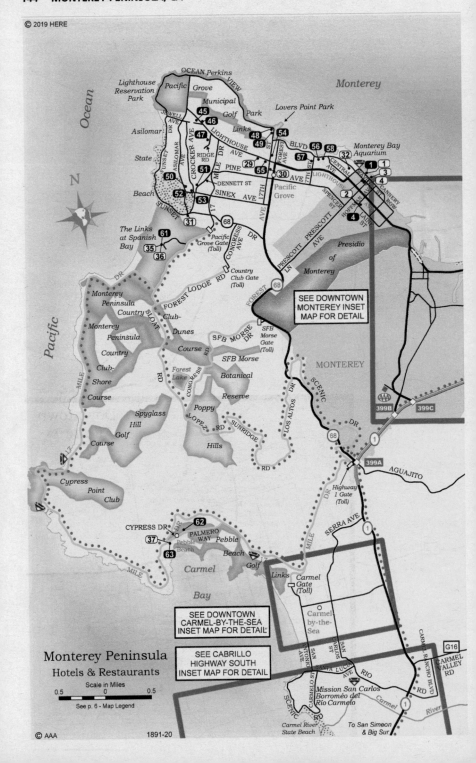

Monterey Peninsula
Hotels & Restaurants

Scale in Miles

0.5   0   0.5

See p. 6 - Map Legend

1891-20

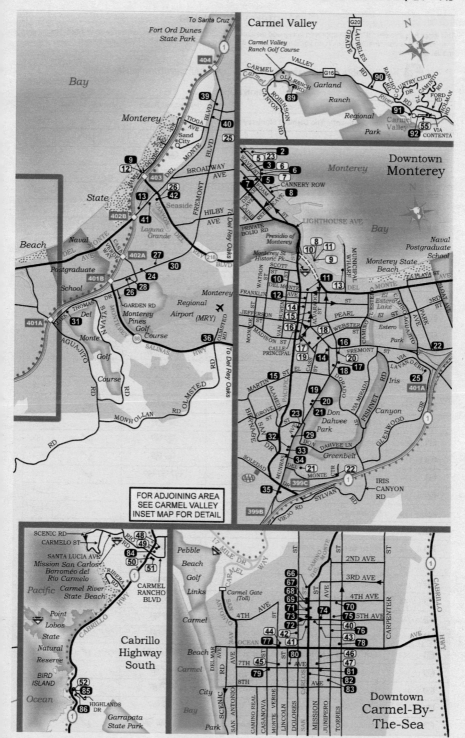

Monterey Peninsula

This index helps you "spot" where approved hotels and restaurants are located on the corresponding detailed maps. Restaurant price range is a combination of lunch and/or dinner. Turn to the listing page for more information and consult display ads for special promotions.

 For more details, rates and reservations: AAA.com/travelguides/hotels

MONTEREY

Map Page	Hotels	Diamond Rated	Member Savings	Page
1 p. 144	**InterContinental The Clement Monterey**	◆◆◆◆	✔	155
2 p. 144	**Spindrift Inn**	◆◆◆	✔	157
3 p. 144	Wave Street Inn	◆◆		157
4 p. 144	The Jabberwock Bed & Breakfast Inn	◆◆◆		155
5 p. 144	**Best Western Plus Victorian Inn**	◆◆◆	✔	154
6 p. 144	**Monterey Plaza Hotel & Spa**	◆◆◆◆	✔	155
7 p. 144	**Holiday Inn Express-Cannery Row**	◆◆◆	✔	155
8 p. 144	**Monterey Bay Inn**	◆◆◆	✔	155
9 p. 144	**Monterey Tides**	◆◆◆	✔	157
10 p. 144	Hotel Pacific	◆◆◆		155
11 p. 144	**Portola Hotel & Spa** *(See ad p. 156.)*	◆◆◆◆	✔	157
12 p. 144	**Monterey Marriott**	◆◆◆	✔	155
13 p. 144	**Hampton Inn Monterey**	◆◆◆	✔	154
14 p. 144	**Casa Munras Garden Hotel & Spa**	◆◆◆	✔	154
15 p. 144	Old Monterey Inn	◆◆◆		157
16 p. 144	Hotel Abrego	◆◆◆		155
17 p. 144	**Best Western Plus Monterey Inn**	◆◆◆	✔	154
18 p. 144	Days Inn-Downtown Monterey	◆◆		154
19 p. 144	**Munras Inn**	◆◆	✔	157
20 p. 144	**Arbor Inn Monterey**	◆◆	✔	154
21 p. 144	**Best Western Park Crest Inn**	◆◆◆	✔	154
22 p. 144	Stage Coach Lodge	◆◆		157
23 p. 144	Monterey Surf Inn	◆◆		157
24 p. 144	**Best Western De Anza Inn**	◆◆	✔	154
25 p. 144	**Hilton Garden Inn Monterey**	◆◆◆	✔	155
26 p. 144	Comfort Inn-Monterey Bay	◆◆		154
27 p. 144	Lone Oak Lodge	◆◆		155
28 p. 144	Ramada By Wyndham Monterey	◆◆		157
29 p. 144	The Inn at 1252 Monterey	◆◆		155
30 p. 144	Pacific Inn Monterey	◆◆		157
31 p. 144	**Hyatt Regency Monterey Hotel & Spa**	◆◆◆	✔	155
32 p. 144	Padre Oaks	◆◆		157
33 p. 144	Days Inn Monterey-Fisherman's Wharf Aquarium	◆◆		154
34 p. 144	Super 8 Monterey/Carmel	◆◆		157
35 p. 144	**Comfort Inn Monterey Peninsula Airport**	◆◆◆	✔	154

Map Page	Restaurants	Diamond Rated	Cuisine	Price Range	Page
① p. 144	The C Restaurant + Bar	◆◆◆	California Seafood	$12-$58	157
② p. 144	**Whaling Station Steakhouse**	◆◆◆	Steak	$26-$65	158
③ p. 144	**The Fish Hopper**	◆◆◆	Seafood	$20-$50	157
④ p. 144	**The Sardine Factory**	◆◆◆◆	Seafood	$29-$59	158
⑤ p. 144	Cooper's Pub	◆◆	American	$12-$20	157
⑥ p. 144	Chart House	◆◆◆	Seafood Steak	$27-$58 SAVE	157
⑦ p. 144	**Schooners Coastal Kitchen & Bar**	◆◆◆	American	$12-$52	158
⑧ p. 144	Cafe Fina	◆◆	Seafood	$17-$65	157
⑨ p. 144	**Domenico's on The Wharf**	◆◆◆	Seafood	$12-$65	157
⑩ p. 144	**Old Fisherman's Grotto**	◆◆◆	Seafood	$20-$95	158
⑪ p. 144	Abalonetti Seafood	◆◆	Seafood	$10-$25	157
⑫ p. 144	Vizcaino Waterfront Food + Drink	◆◆	Spanish	$15-$39	158
⑬ p. 144	Sandbar & Grill	◆◆	Seafood	$13-$37	158
⑭ p. 144	Montrio Bistro	◆◆◆	Regional American	$17-$33	157
⑮ p. 144	**Rosine's**	◆◆	American	$11-$26	158
⑯ p. 144	Lallapalooza Restaurant	◆◆◆	American	$13-$45	157
⑱ p. 144	Ike's Love & Sandwiches	◆	Sandwiches	$11-$13	157
⑲ p. 144	Parker-Lusseau Pastries	◆	Breads/Pastries	$6-$9	158
⑳ p. 144	Bistro Abrego	◆◆	American	$12-$20	157
㉑ p. 144	P.F. Chang's China Bistro	◆◆◆	Chinese	$10-$26	158
㉒ p. 144	Lalla Grill	◆◆	California	$11-$33	157

SEASIDE

Map Page	Hotels	Diamond Rated	Member Savings	Page
㊴ p. 144	Seaside Inn	◆◆		374
㊵ p. 144	Sandcastle Inn	◆◆		374
㊶ p. 144	Holiday Inn Express at Monterey Bay Seaside	◆◆◆		374
㊷ p. 144	Embassy Suites by Hilton Monterey Bay	◆◆◆	✔	374

Map Page	Restaurants	Diamond Rated	Cuisine	Price Range	Page
㉕ p. 144	Stammtisch Restaurant	◆◆	German	$5-$30	374
㉖ p. 144	Silver Tide Bar and Grill	◆◆	American	$14-$26	374

PACIFIC GROVE

Map Page	Hotels	Diamond Rated	Member Savings	Page
㊺ p. 144	**Monarch Resort**	◆◆	✔	188
㊻ p. 144	Sea Breeze Inn & Cottages	◆◆		188
㊼ p. 144	Butterfly Grove Inn	◆◆		188
㊽ p. 144	**Borg's Ocean Front Motel**	◆	✔	188
㊾ p. 144	**Lovers Point Inn**	◆◆	✔	188
㊿ p. 144	Pacific Gardens Inn	◆◆		188
(51) p. 144	**Best Western The Inn & Suites Pacific Grove**	◆◆	✔	187
(52) p. 144	Asilomar Conference Grounds	◆◆		187
(53) p. 144	Deer Haven Inn	◆◆		188

PACIFIC GROVE (cont'd)

Map Page	Hotels (cont'd)	Diamond Rated	Member Savings	Page
54 p. 144	Centrella Inn	◆◆		188
55 p. 144	Gosby House Inn	◆◆◆		188
56 p. 144	Green Gables Inn	◆◆◆		188
57 p. 144	Old St. Angela Inn	◆◆◆		188
58 p. 144	Martine Inn	◆◆◆		188

Map Page	Restaurants	Diamond Rated	Cuisine	Price Range	Page
29 p. 144	Passionfish	◆◆◆	California Seafood	$10-$29	188
30 p. 144	Fandango	◆◆	Continental	$10-$36	188
31 p. 144	Fishwife	◆◆	Seafood	$10-$40	188
32 p. 144	First Awakenings	◆◆	American	$9-$15	188

PEBBLE BEACH

Map Page	Hotels	Diamond Rated	Member Savings	Page
61 p. 144	The Inn at Spanish Bay	◆◆◆◆		195
62 p. 144	Casa Palmero	◆◆◆◆		195
63 p. 144	The Lodge at Pebble Beach	◆◆◆◆		195

Map Page	Restaurants	Diamond Rated	Cuisine	Price Range	Page
35 p. 144	Peppoli at Pebble Beach	◆◆◆	Italian	$20-$55	195
36 p. 144	Roy's	◆◆◆	Pacific Rim Fusion	$9-$85	195
37 p. 144	Stillwater Bar & Grill	◆◆◆	Seafood	$18-$65	195

CARMEL-BY-THE-SEA

Map Page	Hotels	Diamond Rated	Member Savings	Page
66 p. 144	**Hofsas House**	◆◆	✔	57
67 p. 144	Svendsgaard's Inn	◆◆◆		57
68 p. 144	**Carmel Fireplace Inn Bed & Breakfast**	◆◆	✔	56
69 p. 144	**Briarwood Inn**	◆◆◆	✔	56
70 p. 144	Carmel Garden Inn	◆◆◆		56
71 p. 144	Candle Light Inn	◆◆		56
72 p. 144	**Best Western Carmel's Town House Lodge**	◆◆◆	✔	56
73 p. 144	Carmel Lodge	◆◆		57
74 p. 144	**Carmel Oaks Inn & Suites Clarion Collection**	◆◆	✔	57
75 p. 144	**Carmel Inn & Suites**	◆◆	✔	57
76 p. 144	Carmel Bay View Inn	◆◆		56
77 p. 144	Pine Inn	◆◆◆		57
78 p. 144	**Comfort Inn Carmel By The Sea**	◆◆◆	✔	57
79 p. 144	Carmel Green Lantern Inn	◆◆		56
80 p. 144	Cypress Inn	◆◆◆		57
81 p. 144	Wayside Inn	◆◆◆		57
82 p. 144	Coachman's Inn	◆◆◆		57
83 p. 144	Carriage House Inn	◆◆◆◆		57
84 p. 144	Carmel Mission Inn	◆◆◆		57

CARMEL-BY-THE-SEA (cont'd)

Map Page	Hotels (cont'd)	Diamond Rated	Member Savings	Page
85 p. 144	**Hyatt Carmel Highlands**	◈◈◈	✔	57
86 p. 144	**Tickle Pink Inn** *(See ad p. 58.)*	◈◈◈◈	✔	57

Map Page	Restaurants	Diamond Rated	Cuisine	Price Range	Page
40 p. 144	Casanova	◈◈◈	French	$15-$44	57
41 p. 144	Hog's Breath Inn Carmel	◈◈	American	$12-$38	59
42 p. 144	Cultura comida y bebida	◈◈◈	New Mexican	$12-$90	57
43 p. 144	Katy's Place	◈◈	Breakfast	$12-$24	59
44 p. 144	Il Fornaio	◈◈◈	Italian	$17-$40	59
45 p. 144	Aubergine at L'Auberge	◈◈◈◈	New European	$150	57
46 p. 144	Flying Fish Grill	◈◈	Japanese Seafood	$25-$40	59
47 p. 144	Anton & Michel	◈◈◈	Continental	$16-$33	57
48 p. 144	Lugano Swiss Bistro	◈◈	Swiss	$10-$35	59
49 p. 144	From Scratch Restaurant	◈◈	American	$10-$15	59
50 p. 144	Rio Grill	◈◈◈	California	$10-$42	59
51 p. 144	China Delight	◈◈	Chinese	$9-$29	57
52 p. 144	California Market at Pacific's Edge	◈◈◈	Regional American	$15-$58	57

CARMEL VALLEY

Map Page	Hotels	Diamond Rated	Member Savings	Page
89 p. 144	**Carmel Valley Ranch**	◈◈◈◈	✔	59
90 p. 144	**Bernardus Lodge & Spa**	◈◈◈◈	✔	59
91 p. 144	Hidden Valley Inn	◈◈		59
92 p. 144	Contenta Inn	◈◈		59

Map Page	Restaurant	Diamond Rated	Cuisine	Price Range	Page
55 p. 144	Holman Ranch Tavern	◈◈	Steak	$15-$60	59

MONTEREY (G-3) pop. 27,810, elev. 60'
• Hotels p. 154 • Restaurants p. 157
• Hotels & Restaurants map & index p. 144
• Part of Monterey Peninsula area — see map p. 141

Monterey has a historical pedigree as rich as any city in California. Combine that with a lovely waterfront setting along deep blue Monterey Bay and a wealth of attractions—from gorgeous gardens and historic homes to whale-watching cruises and a world-class aquarium—and you have a travel destination as alluring as any in the Golden State.

The Monterey Peninsula was visited by Europeans as early as 1602, when Sebastián Vizcaíno named a location along the bay in honor of the Spanish Count of Monte Rey, under whose orders the explorer was sailing. But it wasn't until 1770 that Gaspar de Portolá, founding governor of Alta California, and Franciscan father Junípero Serra established a mission and presidio (military post) here. In 1776 Monterey was proclaimed the capital of both Baja (lower) and Alta (upper) California.

When Mexico gained independence from Spain in 1822, Monterey became the Mexican capital. Cattle ranches sprang up as land formerly owned by the Catholic church was redistributed, and many Americans—dubbed "Yanquis"—settled in the area and became Mexican citizens.

The Treaty of Guadalupe Hidalgo, signed in 1848, made all of Alta California part of the United States. Monterey lost much of its political clout after that, but at the same time it was becoming an important whaling center, which brought an influx of Japanese, Chinese, Portuguese and Italian fishermen. These immigrants gave the town a robust, seafaring atmosphere that you can still feel today, even though the commercial fishing industry is a thing of the past.

By the 1920s harvesting sardines had become a major industry, and the plants built to process this oily member of the herring family were collectively known as Cannery Row, the colorful and boisterous locale of John Steinbeck's novels "Cannery Row" and "Sweet Thursday." The local sardine population declined rapidly in the 1940s under mysterious circumstances (water pollution and changes in offshore currents are two possible explanations), and soon after that Cannery Row became a ghost town of empty warehouses.

Since then it's been tourism that drives Monterey. Trendy art galleries, boutiques and restaurants long ago replaced smelly fish factories along Cannery Row. And on whale-watching cruises Monterey Bay's rich marine life is observed, not hunted. A bevy of handicraft boutiques lure shoppers to Fisherman's Wharf, another touristy hangout. One of the wharf's cultural mainstays is the Bruce Ariss Wharf Theater, which stages a mix of musicals, comedies and dramatic plays; phone (831) 649-2332 for schedule and ticket information.

Off Lighthouse Avenue within the Presidio of Monterey is the Defense Language Institute Foreign Language Center, where military interpreters for the Department of Defense are trained. This is the site of the original military fortification established in 1770 by Gaspar de Portolá and father Junípero Serra. Lower Presidio Historic Park is open to the public.

Standing within the park is the Sloat Monument, a stone monument that commemorates Commodore John Drake Sloat's capture of Monterey in July 1846 during the Mexican-American War. The 30-foot-tall monument features a bas-relief sculpture of Sloat facing Monterey Bay and is topped by a pouncing eagle; troops stationed at the presidio humorously referred to the monument as "Big Bird." The hillside location is a prime spot for watching the fireworks show that caps off the city's annual July 4th celebrations.

Tourists and locals alike flock to the Old Monterey Farmers Market, which sets up along three blocks of Alvarado Street between Del Monte Avenue and Pearl Street. The market is a cornucopia of organic fruit and vegetable stands selling the bounty of agricultural areas like Watsonville and the Salinas and Sacramento valleys. Baker's Alley has luscious pastries, cookies, muffins and European breads, and prepared food vendors whip up everything from Korean barbecue to naan curry wraps. Arts and crafts vendors sell trinkets and treasures from all over the world. Local musicians also add a lively touch to what is a real community gathering. The market is open Tuesdays 4-8 p.m. from May through September, 4-7 the rest of the year; phone (831) 655-2607.

Whalefest Monterey is not only a celebration of the annual migration of gray whales but is dedicated to educating the public about local organizations involved in marine life conservation and preservation of the Monterey Bay National Marine Sanctuary. In addition to lectures by noted marine scientists and showings of award-winning documentaries, activities include whale-watching trips, live music and a 60-foot model of a gray whale that kids can climb on. The 2-day event takes place in late January at Fisherman's Wharf.

Vintage race and sports cars take the spotlight at the 🏁 Rolex Monterey Motorsports Reunion, part of a mid-August long weekend devoted to classic cars. Held at the Mazda Raceway Laguna Seca, this event draws more than 500 participants, who compete in 14 races grouped according to vehicle type. A highlight is the paddock area, where visitors can speak with the drivers and get an up-close look at cars that span every era of motor sports racing history.

The Monterey International Pop Festival, held in June 1967—the "Summer of Love"—put Monterey on the pop music map in a big way; it's remembered for iconic performances by the Who, Jimi Hendrix and Janis Joplin, as well as introducing Otis Redding and Ravi Shankar to the largest audiences of their careers. Monterey Pop was the first widely promoted and attended American rock festival and embodied the California counterculture vibe that

(See map & index p. 144.)

reached its peak in San Francisco. It also set the stage for the much bigger Woodstock festival 2 years later.

Monterey Pop took place at the Monterey County Fairgrounds, which is the site of the 3-day Monterey Jazz Festival the third week in September. Masters share the stage with up-and-coming artists at an event that year after year attracts the world's best jazz musicians. The fairgrounds are located at 2004 Fairground Rd. (off SR 1 via Casa Verde Way); for schedule and ticket information phone (831) 373-3366 or (888) 248-6499.

Monterey County Convention and Visitors Bureau: 401 Camino El Estero, Monterey, CA 93940. **Phone:** (888) 221-1010.

Self-guiding tours: Maps of the 2-mile Monterey Path of History walking tour, which includes gardens, adobe buildings and historic sites, are available from the visitor center at Camino el Estero (between Del Monte Avenue and Fremont Street) and at Monterey State Historic Park.

Shopping: The two most popular places in Monterey to stroll and window shop are Cannery Row and Fisherman's Wharf. Cannery Row has more choices—everything from name-brand retailers to art galleries to funky boutiques. All things shark-themed can be found at Sharky's Shirts. For quality casual apparel, check out California Classics. Souvenir hunters should make a beeline to Mackerel Jack's Trading Company, which is chock-full of affordable mementos (postcards, fridge magnets, sweatshirts). More souvenirs—think T-shirts and coffee mugs—can be found at Harbor House Gifts.

Besides being a place to score a free sample of clam chowder, Fisherman's Wharf has a couple of candy shops. At Carousel Candies your sweet tooth will get a workout courtesy of hot caramel popcorn, handmade candy apples and specialty chocolates. Or you could just watch while workers stretch salt water taffy into long, pliant ropes.

The open-air Del Monte Center, at SR 1 and Munras Avenue, has about 85 shops and restaurants, including anchor store Macy's. If you're a fan of mall chain stores—Banana Republic, Hot Topic, Williams-Sonoma and the like—you'll find them here.

 17-MILE DRIVE—see Pebble Beach p. 194.

COLTON HALL MUSEUM, in the civic center on Pacific St. facing Friendly Plaza, is in the building where the first Constitution of California was debated, written and signed by delegates in 1849. Now a museum dedicated to its history, the building originally served as the town hall and school and was the largest public hall west of the Rockies. Adjoining Colton Hall, which was completed in 1849, is the Old Monterey Jail, built in 1854. **Time:** Allow 30 minutes minimum. **Hours:** Daily 10-4, late Jan. to mid-Nov.;

Sun. and Tues. noon-3, rest of year. Phone for research appointments. Closed Jan. 1, Thanksgiving and Christmas. **Cost:** Donations. **Phone:** (831) 646-5640.

DALI 17 is at 5 Custom House Plaza in Stanton Center. On display are more than 570 works—mostly lithographs, but also etchings, sculptures, tapestries and photographs—by Spanish surrealist artist Salvador Dali. Dali and his wife Gala lived in the Monterey and Pebble Beach areas between 1941 and 1948, and the museum's name also references Pebble Beach's famed 17-Mile Drive.

Hours: Sun.-Thurs. 10-5, Fri. 10-6, Sat. 10-7, May-Oct.; Sun.-Thurs. 10-5, Fri.-Sat. 10-6, rest of year. **Cost:** $20; $16 (ages 65+, students with ID and military with ID); $10 (ages 6-17). **Phone:** (831) 372-2608.

MONTEREY BAY AQUARIUM is at 886 Cannery Row. This acclaimed facility houses more than 35,000 animals and plants on two levels of expansive galleries and exhibits. The Open Sea, the aquarium's largest exhibit, explores the open ocean; visitors standing in front of a 90-foot window will see tuna and hammerhead sharks speeding past, sardines swarming in huge, glittering schools and sea turtles swimming lazily by.

The Ocean's Edge galleries introduce visitors to the central California coast's varied shoreline habitats. The impressive features include a three-story living kelp forest, a walk-through aviary inhabited by shore birds and an indoor/outdoor coastal stream habitat.

Tentacles is one of the most extensive exhibitions ever devoted to these endlessly bizarre and fascinating creatures. Tentacles gives visitors a look at such rarely seen animals as the cuttlefish and the intriguingly named, strikingly striped wunderpus, a species of octopus. Tentacles also features multimedia interactive exhibits and cephalopod-related art.

Viva Baja! features animals that inhabit the coastal regions of the Baja California Peninsula, including green morays, desert tortoises and brilliantly colored Cortez rainbow wrasses. The Splash Zone & Penguins galleries depict a coral reef as well as reef and rocky shore habitats. Residents include African penguins and seahorses, clownfish and California moray eels.

Don't forget the outdoor tide pools, where you can observe crustaceans and other animals that have adapted to a specialized environment characterized by constant fluctuations in currents, water temperature and salinity as well as the dangers of exposure during low tide.

Feeding demonstrations take place daily at the sea otter, kelp forest and penguin exhibits. Tour programs require an additional fee and include a surface SCUBA experience for kids, a behind-the-scenes tour and family-oriented activities.

(See map & index p. 144.)

Note: The aquarium can get very crowded on weekends and when it first opens. To avoid crowds, plan a visit for later in the day. **Time:** Allow 3 hours minimum. **Hours:** Daily 10-5, (9:30-6 during summer and holiday periods). Hours are subject to change; check the website to confirm schedule. Closed Christmas. **Cost:** $49.95; $39.95 (ages 13-17 and 65+ and college students with ID); $29.95 (ages 3-12). Separate fee for behind-the-scenes tour (ages 6+) $15. **Note:** The AAA Discounts & Rewards pricing applies to advance purchases from AAA branches in Northern California, Nevada and Utah. **Parking:** Parking at the Cannery Row garage on Irving Avenue between Foam and Wave streets is $15 (flat rate); $5 after 4 p.m. **Phone:** (831) 648-4800, or (866) 963-9645 for advance tickets. 🍴

MONTEREY BAY WHALE WATCH departs from 84 Fisherman's Wharf. A marine biologist/naturalist is on board to describe the behavior of various marine animals seen on the trip. Depending on the season, visitors have the opportunity to spot gray, humpback and blue whales as well as orcas, dolphins, porpoises, sea otters, seals, sea lions and sea birds.

Visitors are advised to dress warmly and bring sunscreen. Photography is permitted. Allow a half-day minimum. **Hours:** Full-day (12-hour) trips for ages 12+ depart at 7:30 on select days July-Nov. All-day (8-hour) trips for ages 12+ depart daily at 8, mid-Apr. to mid-May. Four- to 5-hour morning trips depart daily at 9, early Apr. to mid-Dec. Three- to 4-hour afternoon trips depart daily at 2, early Apr. through Nov. 30; Sat.-Sun. at 2, Dec. 1 to mid-Dec. Three-hour evening trips depart Sat.-Sun. in June and daily in July at 5:30. Three-hour winter and spring trips depart daily at 10 and 1:30 (also some weekends and holidays at 7 a.m.), mid-Dec. to mid-Apr. Closed Thanksgiving and Christmas. Phone ahead to confirm schedule.

Cost: Full-day trips $155. All-day trips $115. Four- to 5-hour morning trips $49; $39 (ages 4-12); $15 (ages 0-3). Three- to 4-hour afternoon trips and 3-hour evening trips $45; $29 (ages 4-12); $15 (ages 0-3). Three-hour winter and spring trips $44; $29 (ages 4-12); $15 (ages 0-3). Guests should arrive 30 minutes prior to departure. Reservations are required. **Phone:** (831) 375-4658.

MONTEREY MOVIE TOURS departs from in front of Cibo's Restaurant, 301 Alvarado St. (at the jct. of Del Monte Ave.). The 3-hour scenic motor-coach tour of the Monterey Peninsula showcases the history and beauty of the area and is augmented by showing scenes from movies such as "Play Misty for Me," "Star Trek IV—The Voyage Home," "A Summer Place" and "Turner and Hooch" at the locations where they were filmed.

The guide provides narration about the filming passengers view the scenes on overhead monitors. The tour includes three photo stops along nearby 17-Mile Drive in Pebble Beach. **Time:** Allow 3 hours

minimum. **Hours:** Tours depart daily at 1 (boarding begins at 12:30). Closed Easter, Thanksgiving and Christmas. **Cost:** $55; $50 (ages 65+); $35 (ages 3-15). Reservations are required. **Phone:** (831) 372-6278 or (800) 343-6437.

◤GEM **MONTEREY STATE HISTORIC PARK** is at 20 Custom House Plaza. The 7-acre site, with additional adobes located throughout the downtown area, preserves the historical and architectural heritage of old Monterey. Nearby is the site where Sebastián Vizcaíno landed in 1602—and Father Junípero Serra 167 years later. Monterey served as California's capital under Spanish and Mexican rule, and it was here that the U.S. flag was first officially raised in California on July 7, 1846.

Guided 50-minute walking tours, departing from the Custom House Plaza, allow visitors to see the park as well as buildings and residences from California's early history. Private guided tours of the historic house interiors, individually or in combination, may be booked in advance for groups of up to 14 guests; the house gardens are open to the public.

Hours: Gardens open daily 9-5, May-Sept.; 10-4, rest of year. Guided walking tours are given weekly; phone ahead for times. Closed Jan. 1, Thanksgiving and Christmas. **Cost:** Park and gardens free. Staff-led tours $10; free (ages 0-12). **Phone:** (831) 649-2907.

Casa Soberanes and Garden is at the jct. of Pacific St. and Del Monte Ave., within Monterey State Historic Park. It was built in 1842 and occupied by members of the Soberanes family from 1860 to 1922. Known for its blue entrance gate and garden walkways, this well-preserved adobe house contains period antiques from New England and China as well as Mexican folk art. **Hours:** Garden open daily 9-5, May-Sept.; 10-4, rest of year. **Phone:** (831) 649-7118, or (831) 649-7172 for information about private guided house tours.

Cooper-Molera Adobe and Garden is at the jct. of Polk and Alvarado sts. and Munras Ave., within Monterey State Historic Park. This restored Victorian home belonged to a Yankee sea captain, rancher and adventurer who married the sister of Gen. Mariano Vallejo. Also on the grounds are a barn, vegetable and fruit gardens and a history display. **Hours:** Garden open daily 9-5, May-Sept.; 10-4, rest of year. **Phone:** (831) 649-7118, or (831) 649-7172 for information about private guided house tours.

Custom House, on Custom House Plaza at Fisherman's Wharf, is within Monterey State Historic Park. This is the oldest standing government building in California; its north section was constructed around 1827. When Commodore John Drake Sloat raised the American flag over the building in 1846, approximately 600,000 square miles became part of the United States. Inside are displays of replica trade goods from the 1840s.

(See map & index p. 144.)

A cactus garden is on the grounds, which also offer scenic views of Monterey Harbor. **Hours:** Daily 10-4. **Cost:** Free. **Phone:** (831) 649-7118.

First Brick House is within Monterey State Historic Park, adjacent to the Old Whaling Station. The structure, built by settler Gallant Dickenson in 1847, marks one of the first uses in California of fired clay bricks for building purposes; the new material was stronger, more durable and more water-repellent than traditional sun-dried mud bricks. Dickenson left for the Sierra foothills in search gold rush riches before finishing his home. Inside are displays about Monterey history. **Note:** At press time the house was closed for renovation; phone for updates. **Hours:** Fri.-Sun. and Mon. holidays 10-4. **Cost:** Free. **Phone:** (831) 649-7118.

First Theatre and Garden, Pacific and Scott sts. within Monterey State Historic Park, once was a lodging house for sailors as well as the first venue in town to charge admission for a theatrical performance. The 1846 building contains early California historical artifacts. Succulents and cypress trees grace the garden.

Note: The garden remains open to visitors, but tours of the theater have been discontinued for the foreseeable future. Phone ahead for information regarding a possible reopening. **Hours:** Garden daily 9-5, May-Sept.; 10-4, rest of year. **Cost:** Garden free. **Phone:** (831) 649-7118.

Larkin House and Garden is at Pacific and Jefferson sts., within Monterey State Historic Park. The house's combination of Mexican Colonial and New England architectural features reflects the New England origins of its builder, merchant Thomas Oliver Larkin. The 1835 two-story adobe house served as the American consulate from 1843 to 1846.

The rooms contain early 19th-century antiques from many parts of the world as well as a number of notable 18th-century American-made furniture pieces. The garden was planted by Larkin's granddaughter. Tours include the adjacent Sherman Quarters.

Hours: Garden open daily 9-5. House tours by appointment only. **Cost:** $5. **Phone:** (831) 649-7172 for information about private guided house tours, or (831) 649-7118 for information about private guided house tours.

The Old Whaling Station is within Monterey State Historic Park in Heritage Harbor, adjacent to the pedestrian bridge. This adobe was built in 1847 by Scottish adventurer David Wight for his family, and was later the headquarters of the Old Monterey Whaling Co. Whale vertebrae were used to create the pathway in front of the building, one of only a few such pathways in the U.S. A garden is at the rear of the property. **Hours:** Tues.-Fri. 10-2. Garden open daily. Phone ahead to confirm schedule. **Phone:** (831) 375-5356.

Pacific House Museum is on Custom House Plaza, within Monterey State Historic Park. The 1847 adobe building, built as a U.S. Army storage facility, is a museum with interactive displays depicting the history of Monterey during its days as the capital of Spanish and Mexican California. On the second floor, the Monterey Museum of the American Indian features Native American baskets and pottery. Behind the building is an attractive courtyard called the Memory Garden. **Hours:** Thurs.-Sun. and Mon. holidays 10-4. Phone ahead to confirm schedule. **Cost:** Free. **Phone:** (831) 649-7118.

Stevenson House is at 530 Houston St., within Monterey State Historic Park. Robert Louis Stevenson spent the fall of 1879 in this two-story former rooming house, then known as the French Hotel. Several rooms in the 19th-century adobe house contain Stevenson's personal belongings. **Hours:** House open Sat. 1-4, Apr.-Oct. and by private tour. Phone ahead to confirm schedule. **Cost:** Free. **Phone:** (831) 649-7118, or (831) 649-7172 for information about private tours.

MY MUSEUM is at 425 Washington St., just e. of Fisherman's Wharf. It offers a variety of hands-on exhibits for children. Young visitors can create sandcastles with special "sandcastle" blocks at the MY Day at the Beach exhibit (3 and under only); strengthen hand-eye coordination at MY Go-Fore Golf; or help a nurse administer a shot in MY Hospital. They also can visit MY Healthy Farm or dress up and pretend at MY Theater.

Time: Allow 1 hour minimum. **Hours:** Tues.-Sat. 10-5, Sun. noon-5. Closed major holidays. **Cost:** $8; free (ages 0-1). **Phone:** (831) 649-6444.

NATIONAL STEINBECK CENTER—see attraction listing in Salinas p. 238.

SAN CARLOS CATHEDRAL, at 500 Church St., also is known as Royal Presidio Chapel. Founded in 1770 to be the mission church of the port, San Carlos Cathedral became the church for the Spanish colonists and soldiers instead, as the mission was moved to Carmel the following year. The present church has been in continuous use since 1795. A museum has historical and church-related items.

Hours: Cathedral open Mon.-Sat. 7-4, Sun. 7 until after the last mass. Museum open Wed. 10-noon, Fri. 10-3, Sat. 10-2, Sun. 1-3 (also second and fourth Mon. of the month 10-noon and 1:15-3:15). Phone ahead to confirm schedule. **Cost:** Donations. **Phone:** (831) 373-2628. GT

STEINBECK'S SPIRIT OF MONTEREY WAX MUSEUM, 700 Cannery Row in the Monterey Cannery Building, displays more than 100 wax figures associated with Monterey's often-turbulent history. **Time:** Allow 30 minutes minimum. **Hours:** Daily 9-9. Closing times may vary; phone ahead to confirm schedule. **Cost:** $9.95; $7.95 (ages 13-17 and 60+); $5.95 (ages 6-12). **Phone:** (831) 655-7743.

(See map & index p. 144.)

RECREATIONAL ACTIVITIES
Kayaking
- **Monterey Bay Kayaks** is at 693 Del Monte Ave. **Hours:** Daily 9-7, Memorial Day weekend-Labor Day weekend; 8:30-6, Mar. 1-day before Memorial Day weekend and day after Labor Day through mid-Oct.; 8:30-5, rest of year. Closed Christmas. Phone ahead to confirm schedule. **Phone:** (831) 373-5357 or (800) 649-5357.

ARBOR INN MONTEREY   831/372-3381

Hotel

Address: 1058 Munras Ave 93940 **Location:** SR 1 exit Munras Ave, 0.5 mi w. **Facility:** 55 units. 2 stories (no elevator), exterior corridors.

BEST WESTERN DE ANZA INN   831/646-8300

Hotel

BW Best Western. **AAA Benefit:** Members save up to 15% and earn bonus points!

Address: 2141 N Fremont St 93940 **Location:** SR 1 exit Fremont St or Casa Verde Way, 0.4 mi e. **Facility:** 43 units, some two bedrooms. 3 stories, interior corridors. **Amenities:** safes. **Pool:** heated outdoor. **Activities:** hot tub. **Featured Amenity: continental breakfast.**

BEST WESTERN PARK CREST INN   831/372-4576

Hotel

BW Best Western. **AAA Benefit:** Members save up to 15% and earn bonus points!

Address: 1100 Munras Ave 93940 **Location:** SR 1 exit Soledad Dr/Munras Ave, 0.5 mi w. **Facility:** 53 units. 2 stories (no elevator), exterior corridors. **Pool:** heated outdoor. **Activities:** hot tub, trails. **Featured Amenity: full hot breakfast.**

BEST WESTERN PLUS MONTEREY INN
831/373-5345

Hotel

BW Best Western PLUS. **AAA Benefit:** Members save up to 15% and earn bonus points!

Address: 825 Abrego St 93940 **Location:** SR 1 exit Soledad Dr/Munras Ave, 0.7 mi w. **Facility:** 80 units. 3 stories, interior corridors. **Pool:** outdoor. **Activities:** hot tub. **Guest Services:** valet laundry. **Featured Amenity: breakfast buffet.**

BEST WESTERN PLUS VICTORIAN INN
831/373-8000

Hotel

BW Best Western PLUS. **AAA Benefit:** Members save up to 15% and earn bonus points!

Address: 487 Foam St 93940 **Location:** SR 1 exit Monterey, 3.4 mi w. **Facility:** 70 units. 3 stories, interior/exterior corridors. **Parking:** on-site (fee). **Terms:** check-in 4 pm. **Amenities:** safes. **Activities:** trails. **Guest Services:** valet laundry. **Featured Amenity: continental breakfast.**

CASA MUNRAS GARDEN HOTEL & SPA
831/375-2411

Hotel

Address: 700 Munras Ave 93940 **Location:** SR 1 exit Soledad Dr/Munras Ave, 0.8 mi w. **Facility:** 163 units. 1-2 stories (no elevator), interior/exterior corridors. **Parking:** on-site (fee). **Terms:** check-in 4 pm. **Amenities:** safes. **Pool:** heated outdoor. **Activities:** bicycles, exercise room, spa. **Guest Services:** valet laundry.

COMFORT INN-MONTEREY BAY   831/373-3081
Hotel. **Address:** 2050 N Fremont St 93940

COMFORT INN MONTEREY PENINSULA AIRPORT
831/372-2945

Motel

Address: 1200 Olmstead Rd 93940 **Location:** SR 1 exit Airport-Salinas, 1.5 mi e on SR 68. Across from airport. **Facility:** 46 units. 2 stories (no elevator), exterior corridors. **Guest Services:** valet laundry. **Featured Amenity: full hot breakfast.**

DAYS INN-DOWNTOWN MONTEREY   831/649-6332
Motel. **Address:** 850 Abrego St 93940

DAYS INN MONTEREY-FISHERMAN'S WHARF AQUARIUM
831/375-2168
Motel. **Address:** 1288 Munras Ave 93940

HAMPTON INN MONTEREY   831/373-7100

Hotel

Hampton by Hilton **AAA Benefit:** Members save up to 15%!

Address: 2401 Del Monte Ave 93940 **Location:** SR 1 exit Del Rey Oaks, just e. **Facility:** 49 units. 3 stories, interior corridors. **Amenities:** safes. **Guest Services:** valet laundry. **Featured Amenity: breakfast buffet.**

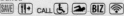

(See map & index p. 144.)

HILTON GARDEN INN MONTEREY 831/373-6141 **25**

Hotel

AAA Benefit: Members save up to 15%!

Address: 1000 Aguajito Rd 93940 **Location:** SR 1 exit Aguajito Rd or Fisherman's Wharf, just w. **Facility:** 204 units. 3 stories, interior corridors. **Parking:** on-site (fee). **Terms:** check-in 4 pm. **Pool:** heated outdoor. **Activities:** hot tub, exercise room. **Guest Services:** valet and coin laundry.

HOLIDAY INN EXPRESS-CANNERY ROW
831/372-1800 **7**

Hotel

Address: 443 Wave St 93940 **Location:** SR 1 exit Monterey, 3 mi w. **Facility:** 43 units. 3 stories, interior/exterior corridors. **Amenities:** safes. **Activities:** trails. **Guest Services:** valet laundry. **Featured Amenity: full hot breakfast.**

HOTEL ABREGO 831/372-7551 **16**
Hotel. **Address:** 755 Abrego St 93940

HOTEL PACIFIC 831/373-5700 **10**
Hotel. **Address:** 300 Pacific St 93940

HYATT REGENCY MONTEREY HOTEL & SPA
831/372-1234 **31**

Hotel

HYATT REGENCY

AAA Benefit: Members save up to 10%!

Address: 1 Old Golf Course Rd 93940 **Location:** SR 1 exit Aguajito Rd northbound; exit Monterey southbound, just e. **Facility:** 550 units. 2-4 stories (no elevator), interior/exterior corridors. **Parking:** on-site (fee) and valet. **Terms:** check-in 4 pm. **Amenities:** safes. **Dining:** 3 restaurants. **Pool:** heated outdoor. **Activities:** hot tub, cabanas, regulation golf, tennis, trails, exercise room, spa. **Guest Services:** valet laundry.

THE INN AT 1252 MONTEREY 831/372-2908 **29**
Hotel. **Address:** 1252 Munras Ave 93940

🔗 Find AAA Inspected & Approved campgrounds at

AAA.com/campgrounds

INTERCONTINENTAL THE CLEMENT MONTEREY
831/375-4500 **1**

Hotel

Address: 750 Cannery Row 93940 **Location:** Oceanfront. Between Prescott and David aves. **Facility:** Located right on the water overlooking Monterey Bay and the Pacific Ocean, this hotel is attractively appointed in both the public areas and guest rooms, many of which have a fireplace. 208 units. 4 stories, interior corridors. **Parking:** on-site (fee) and valet. **Terms:** check-in 4 pm. **Amenities:** safes. **Dining:** The C Restaurant + Bar, see separate listing. **Pool:** heated outdoor. **Activities:** hot tub, exercise room, spa. **Guest Services:** valet laundry.

THE JABBERWOCK BED & BREAKFAST INN
831/372-4777 **4**
Bed & Breakfast. **Address:** 598 Laine St 93940

LONE OAK LODGE 831/372-4924 **27**
Motel. **Address:** 2221 N Fremont St 93940

MONTEREY BAY INN 831/373-6242 **8**

Hotel

Address: 242 Cannery Row 93940 **Location:** Oceanfront. SR 1 exit Monterey, 3.5 mi w. **Facility:** 49 units. 4 stories, interior corridors. **Parking:** on-site (fee). **Terms:** check-in 4 pm. **Amenities:** safes. **Activities:** hot tub, trails, massage. **Guest Services:** valet laundry. **Featured Amenity: continental breakfast.**

MONTEREY MARRIOTT 831/649-4234 **12**

Hotel

MARRIOTT

AAA Benefit: Members save 5% or more!

Address: 350 Calle Principal 93940 **Location:** SR 1 exit Del Monte Ave or Soledad Dr/Munras Ave, 2 mi w. Opposite conference center. **Facility:** 341 units. 10 stories, interior corridors. **Parking:** valet only. **Terms:** check-in 4 pm. **Pool:** heated outdoor. **Activities:** hot tub, trails, exercise room. **Guest Services:** valet and coin laundry, boarding pass kiosk.

MONTEREY PLAZA HOTEL & SPA 831/646-1700 **6**

Hotel

Address: 400 Cannery Row 93940 **Location:** Oceanfront. SR 1 exit Del Monte Ave or Soledad Dr/Munras Ave, 3 mi w. **Facility:** On historic Cannery Row overlooking Monterey Bay and the Pacific Ocean, this property offers many units with balconies and bay views. The hotel is beautifully appointed in rich wood tones throughout. 290 units. 3-5 stories, interior corridors. **Parking:** valet only. **Terms:** check-in 4 pm. **Amenities:** safes. **Dining:** Schooners Coastal Kitchen & Bar, see separate listing. **Activities:** hot tub, bicycles, trails, exercise room, spa. **Guest Services:** valet laundry, area transportation.

▼ See AAA listing p. 157 ▼

(See map & index p. 144.)

MONTEREY SURF INN   831/372-5821   **23**
WW Motel. **Address:** 1200 Munras Ave 93940

MONTEREY TIDES   831/394-3321   **9**

WWW
Hotel

Address: 2600 Sand Dunes Dr 93940 **Location:** Oceanfront. SR 1 exit Del Rey Oaks, just w. **Facility:** 196 units. 4 stories, exterior corridors. **Terms:** check-in 4 pm. **Amenities:** safes. **Dining:** Vizcaino Waterfront Food + Drink, see separate listing. **Pool:** heated outdoor. **Activities:** hot tub, bicycles, trails, exercise room. **Guest Services:** valet laundry.

MUNRAS INN   831/646-9696   **19**

WW
Hotel

Address: 1010 Munras Ave 93940 **Location:** SR 1 exit Soledad Dr/Munras Ave, 0.7 mi w. **Facility:** 29 units. 2 stories (no elevator), interior/exterior corridors. **Featured Amenity: continental breakfast.**

OLD MONTEREY INN   831/375-8284   **15**
WWWW Historic Bed & Breakfast. **Address:** 500 Martin St 93940

PACIFIC INN MONTEREY   831/373-2445   **30**
WW Motel. **Address:** 2332 N Fremont St 93940

PADRE OAKS   831/373-3741   **32**
WW Motel. **Address:** 1278 Munras Ave 93940

PORTOLA HOTEL & SPA   831/649-4511   **11**

WWWW
Hotel

Address: 2 Portola Plaza 93940 **Location:** 2 mi w of SR 1 exit Del Monte or Munras aves; downtown. **Facility:** Located adjacent to the Wharf, the Convention Center and the historic downtown area, this property offers spectacular vista views of Monterey Bay. The rooms are a good size with smaller bathrooms. 379 units. 1-7 stories, interior corridors. **Parking:** on-site (fee) and valet. **Terms:** check-in 4 pm. **Amenities:** safes. **Dining:** 3 restaurants. **Pool:** heated outdoor. **Activities:** hot tub, cabanas, trails, exercise room, spa. **Guest Services:** valet laundry, boarding pass kiosk. (See ad p. 156.)

RAMADA BY WYNDHAM MONTEREY   831/375-9511   **28**
WW Hotel. **Address:** 2058 N Fremont St 93940

SPINDRIFT INN   831/646-8900   **2**

WWW
Hotel

Address: 652 Cannery Row 93940 **Location:** Oceanfront. SR 1 exit Monterey, 3.7 mi w. **Facility:** 45 units. 4 stories, interior corridors. **Parking:** valet only. **Terms:** check-in 4 pm. **Amenities:** safes. **Activities:** beach access, trails. **Guest Services:** valet laundry. **Featured Amenity:** continental breakfast.

STAGE COACH LODGE   831/373-3632   **22**
WW Motel. **Address:** 1111 10th St 93940

SUPER 8 MONTEREY/CARMEL   831/373-3203   **34**
WW Motel. **Address:** 1300 Munras Ave 93940

WAVE STREET INN   831/375-2299   **3**
WW Hotel. **Address:** 571 Wave St 93940

WHERE TO EAT

ABALONETTI SEAFOOD   831/373-1851   **11**
WW Seafood. Casual Dining. **Address:** 57 Fishermans Wharf 93940

BISTRO ABREGO   831/372-7551   **20**
WW American. Casual Dining. **Address:** 755 Abrego St 93940

CAFE FINA   831/372-5200   **8**
WW Seafood. Fine Dining. **Address:** 47 Fishermans Wharf #1 93940

CHART HOUSE   831/372-3362   **6**
WWW SAVE Seafood Steak. Fine Dining. **Address:** 444 Cannery Row 93940

COOPER'S PUB   831/373-1353   **5**
WW American. Casual Dining. **Address:** 653 Cannery Row 93940

THE C RESTAURANT + BAR   831/375-4800   **1**
WWW California Seafood. Casual Dining. **Address:** 750 Cannery Row 93940

DOMENICO'S ON THE WHARF   831/372-3655   **9**

WWWW
Seafood
Fine Dining
$12-$65

AAA Inspector Notes: Don't let the touristy facade fool you! This restaurant features floor-to-ceiling windows overlooking the marina and Monterey Bay and a menu stocked full of seafood options including locally sourced items, such as prawns from the Bay and items brought in from Alaska. Pasta and steak dishes are also available, but I recommend the signature cioppino. **Features:** full bar, patio dining, early bird specials, happy hour. **Reservations:** suggested. **Address:** 50 Fisherman's Wharf #1 93940 **Location:** On Fisherman's Wharf. **Parking:** on-site (fee).

EL TORITO   831/373-0611
WW Mexican. Casual Dining. **Address:** 600 Cannery Row 93940

THE FISH HOPPER   831/372-8543   **3**

WWW
Seafood
Casual Dining
$20-$50

AAA Inspector Notes: Over the water on Monterey Bay and Cannery Row, the menu at this spot offers a wide selection of fresh seafood items. Be sure to try the halibut or tilapia with a macadamia nut crust if it is available. Dine inside or on the cozy dining deck. **Features:** full bar. **Reservations:** suggested. **Address:** 700 Cannery Row 93940 **Location:** On Cannery Row. **Parking:** street only.

IKE'S LOVE & SANDWICHES   831/643-0900   **18**
W Sandwiches. Quick Serve. **Address:** 570 Munras Ave, Suite 70 93940

LALLA GRILL   831/324-4632   **22**
WW California. Casual Dining. **Address:** 1400 Del Monte Shopping Center 93940

LALLAPALOOZA RESTAURANT   831/645-9036   **16**
WWW American. Casual Dining. **Address:** 474 Alvarado St 93940

MONTRIO BISTRO   831/648-8880   **14**
WWW Regional American. Fine Dining. **Address:** 414 Calle Principal 93940

(See map & index p. 144.)

OLD FISHERMAN'S GROTTO   831/375-4604

Seafood
Casual Dining
$20-$95

AAA Inspector Notes: This restaurant features spectacular views of the Monterey Bay and a menu that will please everyone. Highlights include fresh seafood, specialty salads and sandwiches, grilled meats and pasta dishes. Service is warm and friendly. Be sure to save room for one of the special desserts. **Features:** full bar. **Reservations:** suggested. **Address:** 39 Fisherman's Wharf 93940 **Location:** On Fisherman's Wharf. **Parking:** on-site (fee). L D CALL

Sustainable Seafood, Fresh Pasta, Certified Angus Beef

PARKER-LUSSEAU PASTRIES   831/641-9188   (19)
Breads/Pastries. Quick Serve. **Address:** 539 Hartnell St 93940

P.F. CHANG'S CHINA BISTRO   831/375-0143   (21)
Chinese. Fine Dining. **Address:** 1200 Del Monte Center 93940

ROSINE'S   831/375-1400   (15)

American
Casual Dining
$11-$26

AAA Inspector Notes: Breakfast is a specialty at this family-owned-and-operated restaurant, a favorite of the local and downtown crowd for many years. Hearty fare includes homemade soups, melt sandwiches and flatbreads, plus American and Italian-inspired main courses. Save room for a slice of the humongous homemade cakes and pies. **Address:** 434 Alvarado St 93940 **Location:** At Bonifacio St; downtown. **Parking:** street only.

B L D CALL

SANDBAR & GRILL   831/373-2818   (13)
Seafood. Casual Dining. **Address:** Wharf #2, Suite 16 93940

THE SARDINE FACTORY   831/373-3775   (4)

Seafood
Fine Dining
$29-$59

AAA Inspector Notes: Opening in 1968, this restaurant has an impressive history serving celebrities and dignitaries from around the world. The menu showcases preparations of fresh seafood, steaks and pasta, all with a commitment to serving the highest quality, sustainable products in an elegant ambience. **Features:** full bar, early bird specials, happy hour. **Reservations:** suggested. **Address:** 701 Wave St 93940 **Location:** At Prescott Ave; in Cannery Row.

D CALL

SCHOONERS COASTAL KITCHEN & BAR
831/372-2628   (7)

American
Casual Dining
$12-$52

AAA Inspector Notes: Situated on the water, this downstairs pub-style bistro affords beautiful views of the Pacific Ocean and Monterey Bay. The menu carries on this appreciation for the sea in its offerings of fresh fish. The atmosphere is friendly and upbeat. **Features:** full bar, patio dining, happy hour. **Address:** 400 Cannery Row 93940 **Location:** SR 1 exit Del Monte Ave or Soledad Dr/Munras Ave, 3 mi w; in Monterey Plaza Hotel & Spa. **Parking:** on-site and street. B L D CALL

TARPY'S ROADHOUSE   831/647-1444
Regional American. Fine Dining. **Address:** 2999 Monterey Salinas Hwy 93940

VIZCAINO WATERFRONT FOOD + DRINK   831/394-3321   (12)
Spanish. Casual Dining. **Address:** 2600 Sand Dunes Dr 93940

WHALING STATION STEAKHOUSE   831/373-3778   (2)
Steak
Fine Dining
$26-$65

AAA Inspector Notes: Tuscan décor gives this dining room an upscale feel. Prime beef and fresh seafood are prepared over a mesquite-wood broiler. The menu also offers a variety of pasta dishes with special homemade sauces. The steaks are not to be missed. **Features:** full bar, happy hour. **Reservations:** suggested. **Address:** 763 Wave St 93940 **Location:** In Cannery Row area; between Irving and Prescott aves. D

MONTE RIO pop. 1,152
• Part of Wine Country area — see map p. 405

INN ON THE RUSSIAN RIVER   707/865-1143
Motel. **Address:** 20292 Hwy 116 95462

NORTHWOOD LODGE & RESORT   707/865-1655
Motel

Address: 19455 Hwy 116 95462 **Location:** On SR 116, 0.8 mi ne. **Facility:** 26 units, some cottages. 1 story, exterior corridors. **Pool:** heated outdoor. **Activities:** picnic facilities. **Guest Services:** coin laundry.

MORGAN HILL (F-9) pop. 37,882, elev. 345'

Before the arrival of Spanish soldiers and priests in 1776, this area was home to the peaceful Costanoan Indians. The first English-speaking community sprang up around a prosperous estate known as Morgan Hill's Ranch in 1845 and was incorporated in 1906. Morgan Hill is at the southern end of the agriculturally rich Santa Clara Valley, where the French prune was developed.

About 14 miles east of the city via E. Dunne Avenue is Henry W. Coe State Park, its 87,000 acres encompassing varied terrain punctuated by ridges and canyons. The park has more than 250 miles of hiking trails and is home to a variety of indigenous plants and animals, including the elusive mountain lion. Within the park are the headwaters of Coyote Creek; recreational activities include camping, picnicking, fishing, mountain biking and horseback riding. *See Recreation Areas Chart.*

Morgan Hill Chamber of Commerce: 17485 Monterey Rd., Suite 105, Morgan Hill, CA 95037-0786. **Phone:** (408) 779-9444.

COMFORT INN & SUITES MORGAN HILL   408/778-3400
Hotel

Address: 16225 Condit Rd 95037 **Location:** US 101 exit Tennant Ave, just e, then just n. **Facility:** 54 units. 3 stories, interior corridors. **Pool:** outdoor. **Activities:** sauna, hot tub, exercise room. **Guest Services:** coin laundry.

 SAVE CALL BIZ HS

COURTYARD BY MARRIOTT SAN JOSE SOUTH/MORGAN HILL
408/782-6034
♥♥♥♥ SAVE Hotel. **Address:** 18610 Madrone Pkwy 95037

AAA Benefit:
Members save 5% or more!

HAMPTON INN SAN JOSE SOUTH-MORGAN HILL
408/779-7666
♥♥♥♥ SAVE Hotel. **Address:** 16115 Condit Rd 95037

AAA Benefit:
Members save up to 15%!

HOLIDAY INN EXPRESS HOTEL & SUITES SAN JOSE/MORGAN HILL
408/776-7676
♥♥♥♥ Hotel. **Address:** 17035 Condit Rd 95037

LA QUINTA INN & SUITES BY WYNDHAM MORGAN HILL-SAN JOSE SOUTH
669/888-3700
♥♥♥♥ Hotel. **Address:** 17043 Condit Rd 95037

WHERE TO EAT

LADERA GRILL
408/201-9200
♥♥♥ American. Fine Dining. **Address:** 17305 Monterey Rd, Suite 110 95037

LA HACIENDA MEXICAN RESTAURANT
408/778-7002
♥♥ Mexican. Casual Dining. **Address:** 16825 Condit Dr 95037

SINALOA CAFE
408/779-9740
♥♥ Mexican. Casual Dining. **Address:** 17535 Monterey Rd 95037

TRAIL DUST BARBEQUE
408/997-9072
♥♥ Barbecue. Casual Dining. **Address:** 17240 Monterey Rd 95037

MOSS LANDING (G-3) pop. 204, elev. 10'

ELKHORN SLOUGH SAFARI NATURE BOAT TOURS departs from "A" dock in the Moss Landing Harbor, go 1 blk. w. off SR 1 onto Moss Landing Rd., n. onto Sandholdt Rd., then e. into the harbor parking lot. Two-hour cruises on a 27-foot pontoon boat explore the 7-mile Elkhorn Slough estuary. Led by a naturalist, the tours provide opportunities for sighting sea otters, harbor seals, terns, grebes and other species of waterfowl and shorebirds. The captain and naturalist provide information about slough ecology and natural history; photographs circulated during the trip help identify wildlife.

Time: Allow 2 hours, 30 minutes minimum. **Hours:** Departures daily; times vary depending on the tide and the migration of species. Closed Thanksgiving and Christmas. Phone ahead to confirm schedule. **Cost:** $38; $35 (ages 65+) $28 (ages 3-12). Under 3 not permitted on tours. Reservations are required at least 1-2 weeks in advance and can be made online or by phone. **Parking:** $8 in harbor lot. **Phone:** (831) 633-5555.

SANCTUARY CRUISES departs from "A" dock in Moss Landing Harbor; go 1 blk. w. off SR 1 on Moss Landing Rd., n. onto Sandholdt Rd., then e. into the main harbor parking lot. Two- to 3.5-hour whale-watching cruises led by knowledgeable captains and naturalists offer opportunities to spot and learn

about humpbacks, orcas, gray whales, dolphins, blue whales, sea otters, sea lions, harbor seals and other creatures (depending on the season) in Monterey Bay.

Children under 5 are not permitted on morning trips; children under 8 are not permitted on afternoon cruises. **Time:** Allow 4 hours minimum. **Hours:** Daily departures vary with the season; phone for schedule. Closed Christmas. **Cost:** $45-$55. Reservations are recommended. **Parking:** $8 in harbor lot. **Phone:** (831) 917-1042.

CAPTAIN'S INN AT MOSS LANDING
831/633-5550
♥♥♥ Bed & Breakfast. **Address:** 8122 Moss Landing Rd 95039

MOUNTAIN VIEW (E-8) pop. 74,066, elev. 97'
• Hotels p. 160 • Restaurants p. 161
• Hotels & Restaurants map & index p. 190

Located as it is in the heart of Silicon Valley, Mountain View is a center of high-tech industry. On a more natural note is Shoreline Park, a regional recreation area off the US 101 Shoreline Boulevard exit near San Francisco Bay. In addition to being a sanctuary for wildlife and more than 150 species of birds (including many migratory birds that pass through from October through February on their way south), the park offers 7 miles of jogging, hiking and bicycling trails, a saltwater lake for windsurfing and sailing, level expanses for kite flying and an 18-hole golf course.

Major music stars appear at the Shoreline Amphitheatre, 1 Amphitheatre Pkwy.; for event information phone the box office at (650) 967-4040.

Mountain View Chamber of Commerce: 580 Castro St., Mountain View, CA 94041. **Phone:** (650) 968-8378.

COMPUTER HISTORY MUSEUM is just n. off US 101 Shoreline Blvd. exit at 1401 N. Shoreline Blvd. Appropriately located in Silicon Valley, the museum is dedicated to the preservation and celebration of computing history.

Revolution: The First 2000 Years of Computing chronicles the spectacular history of computing, from mysterious ancient devices to technologies of the future. You can also fly through the fantastic world of Azeroth, learn Photoshop from the pros, and speed-text your way to victory in the museum's newest interactive exhibition Make Software Change the World. **Time:** Allow 1 hour minimum. **Hours:** Tues.-Sun. 10-5 (also Fri. 5-9), late June-Aug. 31; Wed.-Sun. 10-5 (also Fri. 5-9), rest of year. **Cost:** $17.50; $13.50 (ages 65+ and students and military with ID); free (ages 0-10). **Phone:** (650) 810-1010.
🔁

MOFFETT FIELD MUSEUM is off US 101 (NASA/Moffett Field exit). Enter at the NASA main gate's far left lane and proceed via S. Akron Dr. to Severyns Ave.; the museum is on Severyns Ave. in

(See map & index p. 190.)

Building 126, adjacent to Hangar One. Originally a home for Navy airships, Moffett Field was an Army Air Corps training base in 1940. Blimps returned to the base during World War II, when it became a Naval Air Station.

Exhibits include dioramas, memorabilia and airship replicas as well as artifacts pertaining to the field's history. Visitors can see Hangar One, the huge structure that housed the Navy's airships.

Note: Photo ID is required to gain access through the NASA gate. **Time:** Allow 1 hour, 30 minutes minimum. **Hours:** Wed.-Sat. 10-3. Closed Jan. 1, Thanksgiving and Christmas. Phone ahead to confirm schedule. **Cost:** $8; $5 (ages 65+ and the physically impaired); $3 (ages 13-17); free (ages 0-12 and military with ID). **Phone:** (650) 964-4024.

NASA AMES RESEARCH CENTER is off US 101 (Moffett Field exit). This NASA field center conducts research on information technology, astrobiology and aeronautics. The NASA Ames Visitor Center, at the research center's main gate, features a moon rock, a Mercury spacecraft, space suits and interactive displays highlighting a variety of NASA missions to the moon and Mars. Also displayed is a mock-up of a laboratory aboard the International Space Station.

The Immersive Theater's 14-foot-tall, 36-foot-wide screen features high-definition videos showing Mars missions and simulated flights through the Milky Way galaxy and beyond, as well as numerous scientific contributions made by NASA Ames researchers. **Hours:** Exploration Center open Tues.-Fri. 10-4, Sat.-Sun. noon-4. Closed major holidays. **Cost:** Free. **Phone:** (650) 604-6497.

BEST WESTERN CRESTVIEW HOTEL & SUITES
650/966-8848 **35**

Hotel

Best Western.
AAA Benefit: Members save up to 15% and earn bonus points!

Address: 901 E El Camino Real 94040 **Location:** On SR 82, 0.5 mi e of SR 85. **Facility:** 64 units, some two bedrooms and efficiencies. 3 stories, interior corridors. **Amenities:** safes. **Activities:** exercise room. **Guest Services:** valet and coin laundry.

EXTENDED STAY AMERICA-SAN JOSE, MOUNTAIN VIEW
650/962-1500 **31**
Extended Stay Hotel. **Address:** 190 E El Camino Real 94040

HAMPTON INN & SUITES BY HILTON MOUNTAIN VIEW/SILICON VALLEY
650/988-0300 **26**

Hotel
Hampton

AAA Benefit: Members save up to 15%!

Address: 390 Moffett Blvd 94043 **Location:** US 101 exit Moffett Blvd W, 0.8 mi w. **Facility:** 109 units. 3 stories, interior corridors. **Amenities:** safes. **Activities:** hot tub, exercise room. **Guest Services:** valet laundry. **Featured Amenity:** full hot breakfast.

HILTON GARDEN INN MOUNTAIN VIEW 650/964-1700 **33**
Hotel. **Address:** 840 E El Camino Real 94040
AAA Benefit: Members save up to 15%!

HOLIDAY INN EXPRESS MOUNTAIN VIEW - S PALO ALTO
650/967-7888 **28**
Hotel. **Address:** 1561 W El Camino Real 94040

HOTEL AVANTE
650/940-1000 **34**

Hotel

Address: 860 E El Camino Real 94040 **Location:** US 101 exit 398B (SR 85/Cupertino); exit SR 82 S (Sunnyvale), 0.5 mi e. **Facility:** 91 units. 4 stories, interior corridors. **Terms:** check-in 4 pm. **Pool:** heated outdoor. **Activities:** hot tub, exercise room. **Guest Services:** valet laundry. Affiliated with Joie de Vivre Hotels & Resorts.

HOTEL STRATA
650/967-6957 **29**

Boutique Contemporary Hotel

Address: 93 W El Camino Real 94040 **Location:** US 101 exit SR 237 northbound, 3 mi e, then just n on SR 82; exit SR 85 southbound, 0.5 mi s to Grant Rd exit, then just n on SR 82. **Facility:** Rooms have conveniently located outlets at various areas and pullout desks for working in bed. Bathrooms have floors warmed with radiant heat and bathtubs with three types of shower heads. 58 units, some efficiencies and kitchens. 2 stories (no elevator), interior/exterior corridors. **Amenities:** safes. **Activities:** bicycles, exercise room. **Guest Services:** valet and coin laundry, area transportation. **Featured Amenity:** full hot breakfast.

HOTEL VUE 650/965-0585 **30**
Hotel. **Address:** 64 W El Camino Real 94040

HOTEL ZICO 650/969-8200 **32**
Boutique Contemporary Hotel. **Address:** 200 E El Camino Real 94040

RESIDENCE INN BY MARRIOTT-PALO ALTO/MOUNTAIN VIEW
650/940-1300 **27**
Extended Stay Hotel. **Address:** 1854 W El Camino Real 94040
AAA Benefit: Members save 5% or more!

(See map & index p. 190.)

WHERE TO EAT

CASCAL   650/940-9500 (27)
ŵŵŵ Latin American Small Plates. Casual Dining. **Address:**
400 Castro St 94041

RISTORANTE DON GIOVANNI   650/961-9749 (25)
ŵŵŵ Italian. Casual Dining. **Address:** 235 Castro St 94041

SCRATCH   650/237-3132 (28)
ŵŵŵ American. Casual Dining. **Address:** 401 Castro St
94041

SHALALA   650/965-8001 (26)
ŵŵ Japanese. Casual Dining. **Address:** 698 W Dana St
94041

TIED HOUSE BREWERY & CAFE   650/965-2739 (24)
ŵŵ American. Brewpub. **Address:** 954 Villa St 94041

MOUNT SHASTA (B-2) pop. 3,394, elev. 3,554'

A small city named for a tall mountain, Mount Shasta is the northern gateway (via scenic SR 89) to Whiskeytown-Shasta-Trinity National Recreation Area *(see place listing p. 402)*, Shasta-Trinity National Forests *(see place listing p. 379)* and nearby Lake Siskiyou.

Mount Shasta Chamber of Commerce and Visitors Bureau: 300 Pine St., Mount Shasta, CA 96067. **Phone:** (530) 926-4865.

BEST WESTERN PLUS TREE HOUSE   530/926-3101

Hotel

Best Western PLUS

AAA Benefit: Members save up to 15% and earn bonus points!

Address: 111 Morgan Way 96067 **Location:** I-5 exit 738 (Central Mount Shasta), just e. **Facility:** 98 units, some efficiencies. 2-3 stories (no elevator), interior/exterior corridors. **Dining:** 2 restaurants, also, Tree House Restaurant, see separate listing. **Pool:** heated indoor. **Activities:** hot tub, exercise room. **Guest Services:** coin laundry.

COLD CREEK INN   530/926-9851
ŵ Motel. **Address:** 724 N Mount Shasta Blvd 96067

MOUNT SHASTA RESORT   530/926-3030

Cottage

Address: 1000 Siskiyou Lake Blvd 96067 **Location:** Waterfront. I-5 exit 738 (Central Mount Shasta), 0.4 mi w on Lake St (which becomes Hatchery Ln), just s on S Old Stage Rd; at split follow sign for resort, 1.4 mi s on W A Barr Rd, then just se. **Facility:** This lodge offers well-appointed attached cottages and inviting chalets in a secluded setting, some with a private deck, skylight and gas fireplace. Expect spacious and very comfortable rooms. 65 cottages, some two bedrooms and kitchens. 1 story, exterior corridors. **Terms:** check-in 4 pm. **Dining:** Highland House Restaurant, see separate listing. **Activities:** regulation golf, tennis, spa. **Guest Services:** coin laundry.

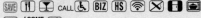

WHERE TO EAT

CASA RAMOS   530/926-0250
ŵŵ Mexican. Casual Dining. **Address:** 1136 S Mount Shasta Blvd 96067

HIGHLAND HOUSE RESTAURANT   530/926-3030
ŵŵ American. Casual Dining. **Address:** 1000 Siskiyou Lake Blvd 96067

SEVEN SUNS COFFEE & CAFE   530/926-9701
ŵ Coffee/Tea. Quick Serve. **Address:** 1011 S Mount Shasta Blvd 96067

TREE HOUSE RESTAURANT   530/926-3101
ŵ American. Casual Dining. **Address:** 111 Morgan Way 96067

◆GEM MUIR WOODS NATIONAL MONUMENT (D-7)

• Part of San Francisco area — see map p. 243

Muir Woods National Monument, 12 miles north of the Golden Gate Bridge on the southwestern slope of Mount Tamalpais, can be reached via US 101 and SR 1. Named for Scottish-born American conservationist and Sierra Club founder John Muir, 560-acre Muir Woods preserves a stand of Sequoia sempervirens, or coast redwoods—trees that once blanketed coastal valleys in much of northern California. A very tall evergreen (some specimens reach more than 250 feet in height), the coast redwood also can live to be more than 1,000 years old.

Muir Woods is a world unto itself. Situated along a canyon floor—part of a coastal valley traversed by Redwood Creek—it's a refuge of cool dampness and deep shade. Animals and birds are elusive (environmental conditions contribute to a lack of food), and there's a serene silence. This region never experienced the depredations of logging, so living redwoods of all ages thrive among dead giants still standing, rotting logs and an exuberant undergrowth of trees, ferns and other plants adapted to the moist, low-light conditions.

Although coast redwoods dominate, Douglas fir, maple, oak and bay laurel also thrive. Paved trails for hiking and exploring range from a half-mile to 2 miles long. One loop trail is divided into half-hour, 1-hour and 90-minute segments, all providing plenty of opportunities to marvel at the giant redwoods. If you don't feel like going on a long hike, Cathedral Grove, a short walk from the entrance, has some particularly large trees and a hushed quiet that seems to envelop the forest. Longer trails cross over into adjoining Mount Tamalpais State Park, near Mill Valley.

Picnicking and camping are not permitted, and bicycles and pets are not allowed. Vehicles longer than 35 feet are not permitted on steep, winding SR 1, the main route to Muir Woods, and adverse weather conditions can cause delays.

Public transportation does not stop at Muir Woods, but various tour companies offer sightseeing trips that include transportation. Marin Transit provides shuttle service from Sausalito and Marin City to Muir Woods daily, late June to mid-Aug.;

Sat.-Sun. and holidays, early Apr.-late June and mid-Aug. to late Oct. Round-trip fare $5; free (ages 0-15). For additional information phone (415) 226-0855.

Food is available. Walking trails open daily 8-8, mid-Mar. to mid-Sept.; 8-7, mid-Sept. to mid-Oct.; 8-6, late Jan. to mid-Mar. and mid-Oct. to early Nov.; 8-5, rest of year. Visitor center opens at 8 and closes 30 minutes before Muir Woods.

Note: Muir Woods can get very crowded during the summer months and on weekends at any time of year, and you may end up having to park along the approach road and hike to the entrance. To avoid crowds and secure a parking space, plan on arriving early (before 10) or after 3. The park is cool, shaded and damp year-round; rainy weather is a possibility from November through May.

Admission $15; free (ages 0-15). For additional information contact the Site Supervisor, Muir Woods National Monument, 1 Muir Woods Rd., Mill Valley, CA 94941-2696; phone (415) 388-2595, or TTY (415) 556-2766.

MURPHYS (F-4) pop. 2,213, elev. 2,171'

WINERIES
• **Ironstone Vineyards** is 1 mi. s. at 1894 Six Mile Rd. **Hours:** Tastings daily 11-5. Tours are given Wed.-Sun.; phone for schedule. Closed Jan. 1, Thanksgiving and Christmas. **Cost:** Tasting $5. **Phone:** (209) 728-1251. GT

DUNBAR HOUSE BED & BREAKFAST INN AND EVENT CENTER   209/728-2897

Bed & Breakfast

Address: 271 Jones St 95247 **Location:** SR 4 exit Main St; in historic downtown. **Facility:** Featuring a wraparound porch, private patio areas and guest rooms with historic style, this property is walking distance to unique gift, food and wine shops, including downtown wine tasting rooms. 6 units. 2 stories (no elevator), interior corridors. **Featured Amenity: full hot breakfast.**

SAVE 🔌 🍴 📶 ✕ 🔋 🖥

MURPHYS INN MOTEL   209/728-1818
Hotel. **Address:** 76 Main St 95247

MURPHYS SUITES   209/728-2121
Hotel. **Address:** 134 Hwy 4 95247

ALCHEMY MARKET & WINE BAR   209/728-0700
American. Casual Dining. **Address:** 191 Main St 95247

ARIA   209/728-9250
Breads/Pastries. Quick Serve. **Address:** 458 Main St 95247

EL JARDIN   209/728-8300
Mexican. Casual Dining. **Address:** 484 E Hwy 4 95247

GROUNDS RESTAURANT   209/728-8663
American. Casual Dining. **Address:** 402 Main St 95247

ROB'S PLACE   209/813-7003
New American. Casual Dining. **Address:** 140 Main St 95247

V RESTAURANT & BAR   209/728-0107
American. Casual Dining. **Address:** 402 Main St 95247

MYERS FLAT pop. 146

MYERS INN   707/943-3259
Bed & Breakfast. **Address:** 12913 Ave of the Giants 95554

NAPA (B-8) pop. 76,915, elev. 17'
• Hotels p. 165 • Restaurants p. 167
• Hotels & Restaurants map & index p. 412
• Part of Wine Country area — see map p. 405

Napa is located in one of California's most famous wine-producing regions, the Napa Valley. This area was a center of gold rush activity in the 1850s. Grapevine cuttings supplied by priests from the missions at Sonoma and San Rafael were the start of what grew into a major industry, and today the valley is a leader in the production of American table wines.

Napa is at the southern end of a scenic 28-mile stretch of SR 29, which heads northwest through the valley to Calistoga. The two-lane road passes acres of vineyards and more than 40 wineries. The Silverado Trail, running parallel to SR 29 to the east, provides stunning views of the valley and the Napa River. There are additional wineries along this less-traveled route.

Downtown Napa is filled with turn-of-the-20th-century houses and buildings in architectural styles from Art Deco, Classic Revival and Italianate to Spanish Colonial and Victorian Gothic. Some 2,500 of these buildings are on the National Historical Registry. The restored Napa Valley Opera House, 1030 Main St., is a local landmark that was built in 1880 and features two theaters. Phone (707) 226-7372 for information and schedules.

(See map & index p. 412.)

Celebrate the grape at Festival Napa Valley, which takes places over 10 days in mid-July. Festivalgoers can sample wines from some 100 area wineries and savor the culinary offerings of celebrated local restaurants. More than 60 planned events include lunches, dinners and concerts. For information about purchasing event passes, phone the box office at (707) 346-5052; for general festival information, phone (888) 337-6272.

TravelBrains' "Napa Valley Tour Guide" features a 154-page illustrated guidebook with profiles of more than 60 wineries, a wine journal and descriptions of the valley's winery towns. Included are a CD and self-guiding audio tour of 11 wineries and five historic locations, plus background information about Napa's wine heritage and history. The guide is available for $24.95; phone (603) 471-0127 or (888) 458-6475.

In August 2014 the valley was rocked by a magnitude 6.0 quake, the strongest to affect the Greater Bay Area region since the Loma Prieta earthquake in 1989. The South Napa Earthquake was felt as far north as Ukiah and as far south as Salinas. Some historic buildings in Napa, including the Napa County Courthouse, were heavily damaged, and countless Twitter images documented the first major California earthquake to occur in the social media age.

Napa Valley Welcome Center: 600 Main St., Napa, CA 94559. **Phone:** (707) 251-5895.

Self-guiding tours: Maps of wineries and the historic downtown area are available from the welcome center.

Shopping: Napa Premium Outlets, west of SR 29 at 629 Factory Stores Dr., has 50 stores, including Ann Taylor, Brooks Brothers, Calvin Klein and Michael Kors.

INSIDER INFO:
Wine Country

Spotlight's Wine Country Guide, a 100-page monthly magazine, provides detailed California Wine Country information. It is available at winery tasting rooms and selected lodgings in Lake, Lower Mendocino, Napa and Sonoma counties, as well as at the concierge desk in some San Francisco and Greater Bay Area hotels. A companion Wine Country map also is available free of charge. The guide can be accessed online.

NAPA VALLEY WINE TRAIN station is located at 1275 McKinstry St. in the heart of downtown. This 3-hour, 36-mile round-trip journey heads through the Napa Valley to St. Helena and back. Step aboard a restored, 100-year-old vintage Pullman dining car or the 1952 Vista Dome car and embark on a scenic trip winding past vineyards and wineries. Guests pre-purchasing a Winery Tour option can transfer to specific wineries at scheduled stops along the way.

A delicious part of the experience is the food; there are three onboard kitchens and a staff of chefs who whip up gourmet meals—with, naturally, selections from an extensive wine list. Service is top notch, and there's also a tasting bar stocked with Napa Valley wines. Summer lunch trips aboard the Silverado Car are alfresco courtesy of open windows.

Romantics will want to pledge their devotion to each other at the Love Lock Bridge, a small pedestrian foot bridge connecting the station to the train's boarding platform. It's dedicated to lovers, who are invited to seal their affection by personalizing a small padlock with initials, names or a date, attaching it to a fence and then tossing the key beneath the bridge. The tradition of "locking" two souls together is believed to have originated in China.

Visitors coming from San Francisco can take advantage of car-free transportation via the San Francisco Connection package. On weekdays passengers depart from the Ferry Building at the foot of Market Street, travel across the bay by ferry to Vallejo and then transfer to a private motorcoach for the trip to Napa; on weekends the trip is by bus. Reservations must be made at least a day in advance.

Time: Allow 3 hours minimum. **Hours:** Lunch trains depart daily at 11:30, Mar.-Nov.; Fri.-Sun. at 11:30, rest of year. Dinner trains depart Fri.-Sun. at 6:30 p.m., May-Sept.; Fri.-Sat. at 6:30 p.m., in Oct.; Sat. at 6:30 p.m., Jan.-Apr. and in Dec. Check-in is 1 hour prior to departure; boarding commences 30 minutes prior to departure. Phone ahead to confirm schedule. **Cost:** Vista Dome lunch fare starts at $221 per person. Vista Dome dinner fare starts at $241 per person. Gourmet Express lunch or dinner fare starts at $146 per person. Winery Tours start at $206 per person. Prepayment is required. San Francisco Connection transportation fare $60 (available only with lunch trains); reservations are required and must be made at least a day in advance. **Phone:** (707) 253-2111 or (800) 427-4124. *(See ad p. 164.)*

WINERIES

- **Artesa Vineyards & Winery** is at 1345 Henry Rd. **Hours:** Daily 10-5. Last pour is 30 minutes before closing. Guided tours with tasting are given daily at 11 and 2. **Cost:** $40; $20 (designated drivers and pregnant women). **Phone:** (707) 224-1668 for general information, or (707) 254-2140 for the tasting room. GT

- **Domaine Carneros** is 4 mi. s.w. just off SR 121/12 (Carneros Hwy.) at 1240 Duhig Rd. **Hours:** Daily 10-5:30. Tours are given daily at 11, 1 and 3. Closed Jan. 1, Thanksgiving and Christmas. **Cost:** $50. Reservations are required for tastings and tours. **Phone:** (707) 257-0101 or (800) 716-2788. GT

(See map & index p. 412.)

- **Stags' Leap Winery** is approximately 7 mi. n. on Silverado Trail from the jct. with Trancas to 6150 Silverado Tr. (look for the small white sign with black-numbered addresses); turn right onto the private road, cross over the cattle guard and keep to the right, following signs to Stags' Leap. Parking is beyond the stone Manor House. **Hours:** Guided 90-minute tasting tours are offered daily at 10, 10:30, 2 and 2:30 by advance reservation only. Closed Jan. 1, Easter, Thanksgiving, Christmas Eve, Christmas and Dec. 31. **Cost:** Guided tour fee $65 per person. Under 21 (including infants and children) are not permitted. **Phone:** (707) 257-5790 for guided tour reservations. GT

1801 FIRST INN 707/224-3739 52
 Historic Bed & Breakfast. **Address:** 1801 1st St 94559

ANDAZ NAPA 707/687-1234 55

Boutique Contemporary Hotel

AAA Benefit: Members save up to 10%!

Address: 1450 1st St 94559 **Location:** SR 29 exit SR 221, 2.6 mi n on SR 221, 1.2 mi nw on Soscol Ave, then just w. **Facility:** Designed utilizing locally sourced products when possible, this intimate, luxury contemporary lodging is located in the historic downtown area adjacent to shops and restaurants. 141 units. 5 stories, interior corridors. **Terms:** check-in 4 pm. **Amenities:** safes. **Activities:** massage. **Guest Services:** valet laundry.

  / SOME UNITS

ARCHER HOTEL NAPA 707/690-9800 54

Hotel

Address: 1230 First St 94559 **Location:** Between Coombs and Randolph sts; center. **Facility:** Understated luxury awaits in the heart of downtown Napa. Enjoy plush bedding, welcome and evening amenities, and a spectacular lobby. Also offered are a rooftop pool, bar, fitness center and spa. 183 units. 5 stories, interior corridors. **Parking:** valet and street only. **Amenities:** safes. **Pool:** heated outdoor. **Activities:** lawn sports, exercise room, spa. **Guest Services:** valet laundry.

 / SOME UNITS

BEL ABRI 707/253-2100 49

Bed & Breakfast

Address: 837 California Blvd 94559 **Location:** SR 29 exit 1st St, just se. **Facility:** Centered in the Napa Valley, this modern B&B offers spacious and attractively appointed guest units. Most have a gas fireplace; some feature a patio. 14 units. 3 stories, interior corridors. **Featured Amenity:** continental breakfast.

BEST WESTERN PLUS ELM HOUSE INN 707/255-1831 50

Boutique Hotel

 Best Western PLUS

AAA Benefit: Members save up to 15% and earn bonus points!

Address: 800 California Blvd 94559 **Location:** SR 29 exit 1st St, 1 1/2 blks s. **Facility:** In a quiet residential location just outside of downtown, the hotel's guest rooms are charming and stylish. Enjoy homemade cookies and milk in the evenings. 22 units. 2-3 stories, interior/exterior corridors. **Activities:** hot tub. **Guest Services:** valet and coin laundry. **Featured Amenity: continental breakfast.**

BEST WESTERN PLUS INN AT THE VINES 707/257-1930 62

Hotel

 Best Western PLUS

AAA Benefit: Members save up to 15% and earn bonus points!

Address: 100 Soscol Ave 94559 **Location:** Jct SR 121 (W Imola Ave) and Soscol Ave. **Facility:** 69 units, some efficiencies. 2-3 stories, interior/exterior corridors. **Terms:** check-in 4 pm. **Pool:** heated outdoor. **Activities:** hot tub, exercise room. **Guest Services:** valet and coin laundry.

/ SOME UNITS HS

BLACKBIRD INN 707/226-2450 53
 Bed & Breakfast. **Address:** 1755 1st St 94559

CARNEROS RESORT AND SPA 707/299-4900 63
Resort Hotel. **Address:** 4048 Sonoma Hwy 94559

CEDAR GABLES INN 707/224-7969 57
Historic Bed & Breakfast. **Address:** 486 Coombs St 94559

CHURCHILL MANOR 707/253-7733 58
Historic Bed & Breakfast. **Address:** 485 Brown St 94559

EMBASSY SUITES BY HILTON NAPA VALLEY 707/253-9540 46

Hotel

EMBASSY SUITES by Hilton

AAA Benefit: Members save up to 15%!

Address: 1075 California Blvd 94559 **Location:** SR 29 exit 1st St, just ne. **Facility:** 205 units. 3 stories, interior/exterior corridors. **Parking:** on-site (fee). **Terms:** check-in 4 pm. **Pool:** heated outdoor, heated indoor. **Activities:** hot tub, bicycles, exercise room. **Guest Services:** valet and coin laundry. **Featured Amenity: full hot breakfast.**

 / SOME UNITS

(See map & index p. 412.)

HAMPTON INN & SUITES NAPA   707/255-4000 **61**
▼▼▼ SAVE Hotel. **Address:** 945 Hartle Ct 94559

AAA Benefit: Members save up to 15%!

HAWTHORN SUITES BY WYNDHAM   707/226-1878 **59**

▼▼▼
Hotel

Address: 314 Soscol Ave 94559 **Location:** SR 29 exit Imola Ave, 1 mi e, then 0.5 mi n. **Facility:** 60 units. 3 stories, exterior corridors. **Pool:** heated indoor. **Activities:** hot tub, exercise room. **Guest Services:** valet laundry. **Featured Amenity: full hot breakfast.**

SAVE ▮◆ CALL ⓺ ⌁ ✚ BIZ
HS ⌁ ✕ ▮ ▭ ▯

HILTON GARDEN INN-NAPA   707/252-0444 **43**
▼▼▼ SAVE Hotel. **Address:** 3585 Solano Ave 94558

AAA Benefit: Members save up to 15%!

HOTEL INDIGO - NAPA VALLEY   707/253-9300 **40**
▼▼▼▼ Hotel. **Address:** 4195 Solano Ave 94558

THE INN ON FIRST   707/253-1331 **51**

▼▼▼
Bed & Breakfast

Address: 1938 1st St 94559 **Location:** SR 29 exit 1st St, just n on California Blvd, just e via Clay St, just s on Warren St, then just w. **Facility:** Located near downtown, this stately four-square Craftsman home dates from 1905 and features upscale guest rooms with fireplaces and oversize jetted tubs. On arrival, homemade truffles are in the room! 10 units. 2 stories (no elevator), interior/exterior corridors. **Terms:** check-in 3:30 pm. **Guest Services:** valet laundry. **Featured Amenity: full hot breakfast.**

SAVE ECO ▮◆ CALL ⓺ BIZ ⌁ ✕ ⍙ ▭
/ SOME UNITS ✚ ▮

THE MERITAGE RESORT AND SPA   707/251-1900 **65**

▼▼▼ ▼▼▼
Resort Hotel

Address: 875 Bordeaux Way 94558 **Location:** 0.5 mi n of jct SR 29 and 121; SR 121 N, follow Downtown Napa/Lake Berryessa, w on Napa Valley Corporate Way, then just s. **Facility:** This resort is surrounded by acres of grape vineyards, and the interior is beautifully appointed in rich, warm colors. Relax by the fireplace inside or at a poolside firepit outside. 322 units, some two bedrooms, efficiencies and kitchens. 3 stories, interior corridors. **Parking:** on-site (fee) and valet. **Terms:** check-in 4 pm. **Amenities:** safes. **Dining:** 2 restaurants, also, Siena, see separate listing. **Pool:** heated outdoor. **Activities:** hot tub, cabanas, bicycles, trails, exercise room, spa. **Guest Services:** valet laundry, area transportation.

SAVE ▮ ⍙ ⍟ CALL ⓺ ⌁ ✚ BIZ sHS s⌁
✕ ▮ ▭ / SOME UNITS ⍙

THE NAPA INN   707/257-1444 **48**
▼▼▼ Historic Bed & Breakfast. **Address:** 1137 Warren St 94559

NAPA RIVER INN   707/251-8500 **56**
▼▼▼ Historic Hotel. **Address:** 500 Main St 94559

NAPA VALLEY MARRIOTT HOTEL & SPA   707/253-8600 **44**
▼▼▼ SAVE Hotel. **Address:** 3425 Solano Ave 94558

AAA Benefit: Members save 5% or more!

NAPA WINERY INN   707/257-7220 **42**

▼▼▼
Hotel

Address: 1998 Trower Ave 94558 **Location:** SR 29 exit Trower Ave, just e. **Facility:** 59 units. 3 stories, interior corridors. **Pool:** outdoor. **Activities:** hot tub. **Guest Services:** valet laundry. **Featured Amenity: full hot breakfast.**

SAVE ▮◆ CALL ⓺ ⌁ BIZ ⌁
✕ ▮ ▭ / SOME UNITS ✚ ▭

RIVER TERRACE INN   707/320-9000 **45**

▼▼▼
Hotel

Address: 1600 Soscol Ave 94559 **Location:** Waterfront. Just e on River Terrace Dr; 0.5 mi ne of downtown. Adjacent to Napa River. **Facility:** 114 units. 3 stories, interior corridors. **Parking:** on-site (fee) and street. **Amenities:** safes. **Activities:** bicycles, trails, exercise room, massage. **Guest Services:** valet laundry.

SAVE ⊟ ▮ ⍙ CALL ⓺ ✚
BIZ ⌁ ✕ ▮ ▭

SILVERADO RESORT AND SPA   707/257-0200 **41**

▼▼▼ ▼▼▼
Resort Hotel

Address: 1600 Atlas Peak Rd 94558 **Location:** SR 121 (Silverado Trail-Monticello Rd), 0.8 mi nw on Atlas Peak Rd, then just e. **Facility:** Located in a quiet area with dramatic views of surrounding mountains, this sprawling complex has its own golf course, tennis center, salon and spa where you can indulge, relax and rejuvenate. 370 units, some three bedrooms, efficiencies and kitchens. 2 stories (no elevator), exterior corridors. **Parking:** on-site and valet. **Terms:** check-in 4 pm. **Amenities:** safes. **Pool:** outdoor, heated outdoor. **Activities:** hot tub, regulation golf, tennis, recreation programs in season, bicycles, lawn sports, health club, spa. **Guest Services:** valet and coin laundry. Affiliated with Dolce Hotels and Resorts.

SAVE ⊟ ▮ CALL ⓺ ⌁ ✚ BIZ s⌁
✕ ▮ ▭ / SOME UNITS ▭

SPRINGHILL SUITES BY MARRIOTT NAPA VALLEY
707/253-1900

▼▼▼
Hotel

SPRINGHILL SUITES MARRIOTT

AAA Benefit: Members save 5% or more!

Address: 101 Gateway Rd E 94558 **Location:** SR 29 exit Airport Blvd, just w, just n on Devlin Rd, then just e. **Facility:** 100 units. 3 stories, interior corridors. **Terms:** check-in 4 pm. **Pool:** heated outdoor. **Activities:** hot tub, cabanas, exercise room. **Guest Services:** valet and coin laundry. **Featured Amenity: breakfast buffet.**

SAVE CALL ⓺ ⌁ ✚ BIZ HS
⌁ ✕ ▮ ▭ ▯

(See map & index p. 412.)

VISTA COLLINA RESORT   707/251-1900 **64**

Resort Hotel

Address: 850 Bordeaux Way 94558 **Location:** 0.5 mi n on SR 221 from jct SR 12/29, just w on Napa Valley Corporate Way, then just s. **Facility:** This resort has a lot to offer! Enjoy a glass of wine by the fire pit or consider renting a cabana poolside. Luxuriously soft bedding makes for an amazing night's sleep in this quiet area of Napa. 145 units, some efficiencies. 3-4 stories, interior corridors. **Parking:** on-site and valet. **Terms:** check-in 4 pm. **Amenities:** safes. **Dining:** Siena, see separate listing. **Pool:** heated outdoor. **Activities:** hot tub, cabanas, lawn sports, exercise room, spa. **Guest Services:** valet laundry, area transportation.

THE WESTIN VERASA NAPA   707/257-1800 **47**

Contemporary Hotel

WESTIN
HOTELS & RESORTS

AAA Benefit: Members save 5% or more!

Address: 1314 McKinstry St 94559 **Location:** Waterfront. Jct Soscol Ave; behind the Napa Valley Wine Train parking area. **Facility:** This beautiful, contemporary property is located on the riverbank. Some of the more unusual amenities include an outdoor heated saltwater pool and bocce courts. 180 units, some two bedrooms, efficiencies and kitchens. 3 stories, interior corridors. **Parking:** valet and street only. **Terms:** check-in 4 pm. **Amenities:** safes. **Dining:** La Toque, see separate listing. **Pool:** heated outdoor. **Activities:** hot tub, bicycles, trails, exercise room, massage. **Guest Services:** complimentary and valet laundry.

WINE VALLEY LODGE   707/224-7911 **60**

Motel. **Address:** 200 S Coombs St 94559

WHERE TO EAT

ALEXIS BAKING COMPANY AND CAFE   707/258-1827 **70**
Breakfast. Casual Dining. **Address:** 1517 Third St 94559

ANGELE   707/252-8115 **73**
French. Fine Dining. **Address:** 540 Main St 94559

AZZURRO PIZZERIA E ENOTECA   707/255-5552 **48**
Italian Pizza. Casual Dining. **Address:** 1260 Main St 94559

BISTRO DON GIOVANNI   707/224-3300 **41**
Italian. Casual Dining. **Address:** 4110 Howard Ln 94558

BOON FLY CAFE   707/299-4900 **74**
California. Casual Dining. **Address:** 4048 Sonoma Hwy 94559

BOUNTY HUNTER   707/226-3976 **57**
Barbecue. Casual Dining. **Address:** 975 1st St 94559

CA' MOMI OSTERIA   707/224-6664 **58**
Italian. Casual Dining. **Address:** 1141 1st St 94559

C CASA   707/226-7700 **52**
New Mexican. Quick Serve. **Address:** 610 First St 94559

CELADON   707/254-9690 **71**
American. Fine Dining. **Address:** 500 Main St, Suite G 94559

CHARLIE PALMER STEAK NAPA   707/819-2500 **59**
Steak. Fine Dining. **Address:** 1260 First St 94559

COLE'S CHOP HOUSE   707/224-6328 **55**
Steak. Casual Dining. **Address:** 1122 Main St 94559

EIKO'S   707/501-4444 **61**
Japanese Sushi. Casual Dining. **Address:** 1385 Napa Town Center 94559

GALPAO GAUCHO BRAZILIAN STEAKHOUSE   707/255-5121 **42**
Brazilian Steak. Casual Dining. **Address:** 1990 Trower Ave 94558

GOTT'S ROADSIDE   707/224-6900 **54**
Burgers. Quick Serve. **Address:** 644 1st St 94559

GRACE'S TABLE   707/226-6200 **68**
California Comfort Food. Casual Dining. **Address:** 1400 2nd St 94559

HERITAGE EATS   707/226-3287 **43**
International Sandwiches. Quick Serve. **Address:** 3824 Bel Aire Plaza 94558

HOG ISLAND OYSTER BAR NAPA   707/251-8113 **51**
Seafood. Casual Dining. **Address:** 610 1st St 94559

KITCHEN DOOR   707/226-1560 **53**
New American. Casual Dining. **Address:** 610 1st Street, Suite 24 94559

LA TAQUIZA FISH TACOS   707/224-2320 **44**
Mexican. Quick Serve. **Address:** 2007 Redwood Rd 94558

LA TOQUE   707/257-5157 **45**
New French. Fine Dining. **Address:** 1314 McKinstry St 94559

MANGO ON MAIN   707/253-8880 **49**
Thai. Casual Dining. **Address:** 1142 Main St 94559

MORIMOTO NAPA   707/252-1600 **69**
Japanese. Casual Dining. **Address:** 610 Main St 94559

NAPA GENERAL STORE   707/259-0762 **72**
American. Casual Dining. **Address:** 540 Main St 94559

NAPA VALLEY BISTRO   707/666-2383 **47**
New American. Casual Dining. **Address:** 975 Clinton St 94559

NAPA VALLEY WINE TRAIN   707/253-2111 **46**

Continental Fine Dining
$141-$161

AAA Inspector Notes: Diners can sit back and relax in restored turn-of-the-20th-century Pullman cars for a three-hour, 36-mile excursion through scenic wine country. The vista dome car enhances the dining experience. Prix-fixe menus list several tempting entrée choices. Dinner is offered Friday through Sunday and lunch 7 days a week during April - October. During off months, lunch and dinner are offered on select days. **Features:** full bar. **Reservations:** required. **Address:** 1275 McKinstry St 94559 **Location:** SR 29 exit 1st St, 0.8 mi e, then 4 blks n on Soscol Ave. *(See ad p. 164.)*

NAPKINS BAR & GRILL   707/224-0607 **65**
American. Casual Dining. **Address:** 1001 2nd St 94558

NORMAN ROSE TAVERN   707/258-1516 **62**
Comfort Food. Casual Dining. **Address:** 1401 1st St 94559

(See map & index p. 412.)

OENOTRI   707/252-1022   64
♥♥♥ Italian. Casual Dining. **Address:** 1425 1st St 94559

RISTORANTE ALLEGRIA   707/254-8006   56
♥♥♥ Italian. Casual Dining. **Address:** 1026 First St 94559

SIENA   707/251-1950   75
♥♥♥ American. Casual Dining. **Address:** 875 Bordeaux Way 94558

SMALL WORLD CAFE & RESTAURANT   707/224-7743   60
♥ Middle Eastern. Quick Serve. **Address:** 932 Coombs St 94559

STONE BREWING - NAPA   707/252-2337   67
♥♥ California. Brewpub. **Address:** 903 3rd St 94559

TARLA MEDITERRANEAN BAR AND GRILL
                                 707/255-5599   63
♥♥ Mediterranean. Casual Dining. **Address:** 1480 1st St 94559

TORC   707/252-3292   50
♥♥ California. Fine Dining. **Address:** 1140 Main St 94559

ZUZU   707/224-8555   66
♥♥ Spanish. Casual Dining. **Address:** 829 Main St 94559

NEVADA CITY (D-3) pop. 3,068, elev. 2,525'

In the High Sierra foothills, Nevada City has been a gold-mining center since the mid-19th century. It also is the seat of Nevada County; during the gold rush era the county's lode and placer mines yielded more than half of California's production of gold.

The Nevada Theatre, 401 Broad St., opened in July 1865 and is said to be California's oldest theater. It presents movies and live performances; for schedule information phone (530) 265-6161.

The Nevada County Narrow Gauge Railroad Museum, 5 Kidder Ct., has exhibits about local transportation, including a steam automobile and artifacts related to the area's narrow gauge railroad, which operated from 1876 to 1942. Exhibits include railroad memorabilia, rolling stock and the narrow gauge line's Engine 5; phone (530) 470-0902.

Firehouse No. 1 Museum, 214 Main St., displays pioneer relics, Native American and Donner party artifacts and a collection of Chinese artifacts that includes an altar from an 1870s Chinese joss house as well as a Quan Yin altar, named after the goddess of compassion and mercy; phone (530) 265-3937.

Hiking and mountain biking trails in the surrounding area range from easy to strenuous. Trails along the South Yuba River Canyon follow streams, pass historic sites and offer plenty of scenic vistas. About 8 miles northwest on SR 49 is South Yuba River State Park, popular with kayakers and noted for spring wildflowers and a 251-foot-long, single-span covered bridge (off Pleasant Valley Road near Bridgeport). *See Recreation Areas Chart.*

Nevada City Chamber of Commerce: 132 Main St., Nevada City, CA 95959. **Phone:** (530) 265-2692 or (800) 655-6569.

Self-guiding tours: Thirteen points of interest in Nevada City's downtown historic district are described in a walking tour brochure provided by the chamber of commerce.

MALAKOFF DIGGINS STATE HISTORIC PARK is 26 mi. n.e. Take SR 49 n. 11 mi., then e. onto Tyler-Foote Crossing Rd. (the road changes names several times; the last mile is unpaved). This was the world's largest hydraulic gold mine before it ceased operation in 1884.

The park museum has exhibits and a 20-minute videotape explaining hydraulic mining methods and describing the miners' way of life. Highlights include a restored church, 1860s general store, drugstore, barber shop, livery stable and house. The homecoming celebration is held in mid-June. *See Recreation Areas Chart.*

Dogs are not permitted in buildings or on some trails. **Time:** Allow 1 hour minimum. **Hours:** Historic park daily dawn-dusk. Museum open daily 10-5, May-Sept. Tours of the townsite are available at 1:30 when the museum is open. Phone ahead to confirm schedule. **Cost:** $8 per private vehicle; $7 (ages 62+ per private vehicle). Reservations for camping are required. **Phone:** (530) 265-2740 for information and cabin reservations. 🅰 🔀 🅰 🅰

EMMA NEVADA HOUSE   530/265-4415
♥♥♥ Historic Bed & Breakfast. **Address:** 528 E Broad St 95959

MADISON HOUSE   530/470-6127
♥♥♥ Bed & Breakfast. **Address:** 427 Broad St 95959

PIETY HILL COTTAGES MOTEL AND B&B   530/265-2245
♥♥ Cottage. **Address:** 523 Sacramento St 95959

WHERE TO EAT

LEFTY'S GRILL   530/265-5838
♥♥ Pizza Burgers. Casual Dining. **Address:** 101 Broad St 95959

NEW MOON CAFE   530/265-6399
♥♥♥ American. Casual Dining. **Address:** 203 York St 95959

SOPA THAI CUISINE   530/470-0101
♥♥ Thai. Casual Dining. **Address:** 312-316 Commercial St 95959

SOUTH PINE CAFE   530/265-0260
♥♥ Breakfast. Casual Dining. **Address:** 110 S Pine St 95959

NEWARK (D-9) pop. 42,573, elev. 20'

This East Bay city is right off I-880, which provides access to San Jose and Silicon Valley communities. The Dumbarton Bridge (SR 84), southernmost of the bridges spanning San Francisco Bay, provides a direct link to Palo Alto and Stanford University. The toll charge (westbound traffic only) is $5 and can be paid by cash or electronically through a FasTrak account.

The Don Edwards San Francisco Bay National Wildlife Refuge is a protected ecological area with habitats ranging from beaches and sand dunes to salt marsh. Within the refuge is Coyote Hills Regional Park, where marshlands and rolling, grass-covered hills lend themselves to outdoor activities like hiking, biking and bird-watching. The park's visitor center has educational exhibits and a picnic area. It's open Wed.-Sun. 10-4; phone (510) 544-3220.

ALOFT SILICON VALLEY   510/494-8800

🏵🏵🏵 SAVE Hotel. **Address:** 8200 Gateway Blvd 94560

AAA Benefit: Members save 5% or more!

CHASE SUITE HOTEL   510/795-1200

🏵🏵 Extended Stay Contemporary Hotel. **Address:** 39150 Cedar Blvd 94560

COURTYARD BY MARRIOTT NEWARK/SILICON VALLEY
                                                    510/792-5200

🏵🏵🏵 SAVE Hotel. **Address:** 34905 Newark Blvd 94560

AAA Benefit: Members save 5% or more!

DOUBLETREE BY HILTON NEWARK/FREMONT   510/490-8390

🏵🏵🏵 SAVE Hotel. **Address:** 39900 Balentine Dr 94560

AAA Benefit: Members save up to 15%!

HOMEWOOD SUITES BY HILTON   510/791-7700

🏵🏵🏵 SAVE Extended Stay Hotel. **Address:** 39270 Cedar Blvd 94560

AAA Benefit: Members save up to 15%!

RESIDENCE INN BY MARRIOTT NEWARK/SILICON VALLEY
                                                    510/739-6000

🏵🏵🏵 SAVE Extended Stay Hotel. **Address:** 35466 Dumbarton Ct 94560

AAA Benefit: Members save 5% or more!

TOWNEPLACE SUITES NEWARK, SILICON VALLEY
                                                    510/657-4600

🏵🏵🏵 SAVE Extended Stay Hotel. **Address:** 39802 Cedar Blvd 94560

AAA Benefit: Members save 5% or more!

WHERE TO EAT

BOONIEPEPPER ISLANDER GRILL   510/790-3839

🏵 Island. Quick Serve. **Address:** 6180 Jarvis Ave 94560

CAMPANELLA MODERN ITALIAN CUISINE   510/794-9900

🏵🏵🏵 Italian. Casual Dining. **Address:** 34903 Newark Blvd 94560

NICE pop. 2,731
• Part of Wine Country area — see map p. 405

FEATHERBED RAILROAD CO.   707/274-8378

🏵🏵 Bed & Breakfast. **Address:** 2870 Lakeshore Blvd 95464

ROBINSON RANCHERIA RESORT & CASINO   707/262-3700

🏵🏵 Hotel. **Address:** 1545 E Hwy 20 95464

NORTH HIGHLANDS (E-3) pop. 42,694, elev. 100'

AEROSPACE MUSEUM OF CALIFORNIA is w. off Watt Ave. at 3200 Freedom Park Dr., in McClellan Business Park. On display are more than 40 iconic military and civilian space rockets, aerospace exhibits and engines. The museum also features a number of interactive educational programs. Visitors get an up-close look at aircraft such as a fully restored 1938 PT-19, a WWII C-47 that supported the Normandy D-Day invasion, and a NASA Saturn IV First and Second State Rocket. Engines on display include a few models built prior to World War I, the first jet engine and the J-58 jet engine that powered the SR-71 Blackbird to three times the speed of sound. Six non-motion flight simulators and a motion ride simulator offer some nerve-tingling thrills.

Time: Allow 1 hour, 30 minutes minimum. **Hours:** Mon.-Sun. 10-4, Oct.-Apr.; Tues.-Sun. 10-4, June-Sep. Closed Jan. 1, Easter, July 4, Thanksgiving, Christmas Eve and Christmas. **Cost:** $15; $10 (ages 4-17 and 65+); free (ages 0-3 and active military with ID). A separate admission may be charged for special exhibits and events. **Phone:** (916) 643-3192.

NOVATO (B-7) pop. 51,904, elev. 18'
• Restaurants p. 170

North of San Francisco on US 101, Novato has one foot in the past and one in the present: It was named for a chief of the Coast Miwok Indians and also is a leading producer of CDs. The Novato History Museum, 815 DeLong Ave., occupies the house of the town's first postmaster. Exhibits include vintage photographs and historical artifacts related to the city's early days; artifacts depicting life in Novato from its earliest days; phone (415) 897-4320.

Novato Chamber of Commerce: 807 DeLong Ave., Novato, CA 94945. **Phone:** (415) 897-1164.

BEST WESTERN PLUS NOVATO OAKS INN
                                                    415/883-4400

🏵🏵🏵 Hotel

 Best Western PLUS

AAA Benefit: Members save up to 15% and earn bonus points!

Address: 215 Alameda Del Prado 94949 **Location:** US 101 exit Alameda Del Prado southbound; exit Hamilton Field northbound. **Facility:** 108 units. 3 stories, interior corridors. **Terms:** check-in 4 pm. **Dining:** Wild Fox Restaurant, see separate listing. **Pool:** outdoor. **Activities:** hot tub, picnic facilities, trails, exercise room. **Guest Services:** valet and coin laundry, area transportation. **Featured Amenity:** continental breakfast.

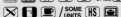

COURTYARD BY MARRIOTT NOVATO MARIN/SONOMA
415/883-8950
▼▼▼ [SAVE] Hotel. **Address:** 1400 N Hamilton Pkwy 94949

AAA Benefit: Members save 5% or more!

THE INN MARIN AND SUITES, AN ASCEND HOTEL COLLECTION MEMBER
415/883-5952
▼▼▼ Motel. **Address:** 250 Entrada Dr 94949

WHERE TO EAT

BATIKA INDIA BISTRO
415/895-5757
▼▼ Indian. Casual Dining. **Address:** 868 Grant Ave 94945

BOCA PIZZERIA
415/883-2302
▼▼ Italian. Casual Dining. **Address:** 454 Ignacio Blvd 94949

DRAGON CAFE
415/883-4595
▼▼ Chinese. Casual Dining. **Address:** 528 Alameda del Prado 94949

HILLTOP 1892
415/893-1892
▼▼ American. Fine Dining. **Address:** 850 Lamont Ave 94945

MOYLAN'S BREWERY & RESTAURANT
415/898-4677
▼▼ American. Casual Dining. **Address:** 15 Rowland Way 94945

TOAST RESTAURANT
415/382-1144
▼▼ American. Casual Dining. **Address:** 5800 Nave Dr 94949

WILD FOX RESTAURANT
415/883-9125
▼▼▼ American. Casual Dining. **Address:** 225 Alameda Del Prado 94949

OAKDALE (F-3) pop. 20,675, elev. 155'

Located in a region known for its Western heritage as well as a number of ranches, Oakdale bills itself—with tongue slightly in cheek—as "The Cowboy Capital of the World." Just east of town, Woodward Reservoir offers both local wranglers and visitors a chance to unwind; swimming, fishing, sailing, water skiing, camping and picnicking can be enjoyed.

At Oakdale Cheese & Specialties, 10040 SR 120, you can observe employees making Gouda cheese several days a week; at other times the process can be seen via a video presentation. Phone (209) 848-3139.

Oakdale Tourism & Visitors Bureau: 214 E. F St., #209, Oakdale, CA 95361. **Phone:** (209) 345-9264.

BEST WESTERN PLUS RAMA INN & SUITES
209/845-2500

Hotel

Best Western PLUS **AAA Benefit:** Members save up to 15% and earn bonus points!

Address: 1450 East F St 95361 **Location:** 1 mi e of jct SR 108 and 120. **Facility:** 47 units. 3 stories, interior corridors. **Pool:** heated indoor. **Activities:** sauna, hot tub, exercise room. **Guest Services:** valet and coin laundry. **Featured Amenity:** breakfast buffet.

[SAVE] [†|†] CALL [♿] [≥] [♟] [BIZ]
[HS] [☎] [✕] [▮] [▭] [▢]

HOLIDAY INN EXPRESS
209/847-9121
▼▼▼ Hotel

Address: 828 East F St 95361 **Location:** 0.8 mi e of SR 108 and 120. **Facility:** 52 units. 2 stories, interior corridors. **Pool:** outdoor. **Activities:** exercise room. **Guest Services:** valet and coin laundry. **Featured Amenity:** continental breakfast.
[SAVE] [†|†] CALL [♿] [≥] [♟] [BIZ]
[HS] [☎] [✕] [▮] [▭] [▢]

WHERE TO EAT

CAHOOTS CORNER CAFE
209/848-0955
▼▼ Breakfast. Casual Dining. **Address:** 110 E F St 95361

OAKHURST pop. 2,829, elev. 2,289'
• **Hotels & Restaurants map & index p. 426**
• **Part of Yosemite National Park area — see map p. 420**

BEST WESTERN PLUS YOSEMITE GATEWAY INN
559/683-2378 **21**

Hotel

Best Western PLUS **AAA Benefit:** Members save up to 15% and earn bonus points!

Address: 40530 Hwy 41 93644 **Location:** SR 41 and 49, 0.8 mi n. **Facility:** 133 units, some kitchens. 2 stories (no elevator), exterior corridors. **Dining:** Oakhurst Grill, see separate listing. **Pool:** heated outdoor, heated indoor. **Activities:** hot tub, playground, picnic facilities, exercise room. **Guest Services:** valet and coin laundry.

[SAVE] [†|†] [🍽] CALL [♿] [≥] [♟]
[BIZ] [☎] [✕] [▮] [▭] [▢] /SOME UNITS [▨] [HS]

CHÂTEAU DU SUREAU
559/683-6860 **23**
▼▼▼▼ ▼▼▼ Country Inn

Address: 48688 Victoria Ln 93644 **Location:** Just w of jct SR 41 and 49. **Facility:** Nine acres of terraced gardens give this romantic and Provence-inspired castle an atmosphere of grandiosity. An exquisite two-bedroom villa featuring an in-ground sunken jetted tub is also available. 11 units, some houses. 1-2 stories (no elevator), interior/exterior corridors. **Parking:** valet only. **Dining:** Erna's Elderberry House Restaurant, see separate listing. **Pool:** outdoor. **Activities:** spa. **Guest Services:** valet laundry. **Featured Amenity:** full hot breakfast.

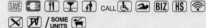
[SAVE] [▬] [†|†] [🍽] [♟] CALL [♿] [≥] [BIZ] [HS] [☎]
[✕] [✍] /SOME UNITS [▨]

COMFORT INN YOSEMITE AREA
559/683-8282 **22**
▼▼ Motel

Address: 40489 Hwy 41 93644 **Location:** SR 41 and 49, 0.6 mi n. **Facility:** 117 units, some two bedrooms. 2 stories (no elevator), exterior corridors. **Pool:** outdoor. **Activities:** hot tub. **Featured Amenity:** full hot breakfast.

[SAVE] [†|†] CALL [♿] [≥] [BIZ] [☎]
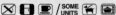

[✕] [▮] [▭] /SOME UNITS [▨] [▨]

(See map & index p. 426.)

HOUNDS TOOTH INN   559/642-6600 **20**

♥♥ ♦
Bed & Breakfast

Address: 42071 Hwy 41 93644 **Location:** Jct SR 41 and 49, 2.5 mi n. **Facility:** 13 units. 2 stories (no elevator), interior/exterior corridors. **Featured Amenity:** full hot breakfast.

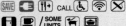
WHERE TO EAT

DICICCO'S ITALIAN RESTAURANT   559/641-5588 **21**
♥♥ Italian. Casual Dining. **Address:** 40282 Hwy 41 93644

EL CID   559/683-6668 **19**
♥♥ Mexican. Casual Dining. **Address:** 41939 Hwy 41 93644

ERNA'S ELDERBERRY HOUSE RESTAURANT
                                      559/683-6800 **22**

**French
Fine Dining
$145**

AAA Inspector Notes: Elegant décor, fresh flowers and the finest table settings are among special touches that enable this dining room to exude warm country French ambience. European influences punctuate inventive preparations of French cuisine. The menu changes daily, based on the freshest local ingredients available. Scrumptious vegetarian and vegan dishes are available. Service is impeccable. **Features:** full bar. **Reservations:** suggested. Semiformal attire. **Address:** 48688 Victoria Ln 93644 **Location:** Just w of jct SR 41 and 49; in Château du Sureau. **D**

OAKHURST GRILL   559/641-2477 **20**
♥♥ American. Casual Dining. **Address:** 40530 Hwy 41 93644

OAKLAND (F-2) pop. 390,724, elev. 42'
- **Hotels p. 182 • Restaurants p. 183**
- **Hotels & Restaurants map & index p. 176**

Oakland may stand in San Francisco's shadow, at least figuratively (it's tough going toe to toe against the City by the Bay). But this major port and manufacturing center stretching along the mainland side of San Francisco Bay has managed to carve out a persona distinct from its older, more illustrious neighbor across the water.

Named for the oak trees that once grew along the grassy coastal plain edging the bay's east side, Oakland was established in 1852 as a point of debarkation for transbay ferry service from San Francisco. It became the terminus of the Transcontinental Railroad in 1869, which brought further growth. Little damaged by the devastating 1906 earthquake, the city—like Berkeley—received displaced refugees from San Francisco.

The biggest impetus to growth came with the opening of the San Francisco-Oakland Bay Bridge in 1936, which provided a vital transportation link. Tens of thousands of San Francisco-bound East Bay commuters depend on the bridge to get to work Monday through Friday, and on weekends San Franciscans head out of the city in droves. Morning and evening rush hour backups are the rule rather than the exception. The toll (westbound only) is $4-$6.

Oakland is a manufacturing powerhouse, which doesn't lend itself to glossily hyped tourist charm. The views from the vantage point of the I-880 freeway tend to be on the gritty side, but that doesn't mean that scenic allure is lacking. And the weather tends to be warmer and sunnier than in San Francisco, and much less prone to capricious summer fog.

Skyline Boulevard follows the rim of the Oakland Hills through the upscale Montclair neighborhood and a series of parklands. Architecturally distinctive homes perch on steep hillsides, and on clear days the East Bay vistas are spectacular.

Regional parks offer rolling hills, lovely vistas and forested areas laced with trails, plus plenty of opportunities for picnicking, hiking, fishing, swimming and horseback riding. They include Anthony Chabot *(see Recreation Areas Chart)*, Claremont Canyon Regional Preserve, Huckleberry Botanic Regional Preserve, Martin Luther King Jr. Shoreline *(see Recreation Areas Chart)*, Miller/Knox, Redwood, Robert Sibley Volcanic Regional Preserve and Temescal *(see Recreation Areas Chart)*. Facilities vary from park to park; for more information phone (510) 238-7275 (Office of Parks & Recreation).

Woodminster Amphitheater, on Joaquin Miller Road in Joaquin Miller Park, is an open-air theater built by the federal WPA program during the mid-20th century. Performances, mostly Broadway musicals, are scheduled from early July to early September; for event and schedule information phone (510) 531-9597.

The Alexander Zuckermann Bike Path is the first leg of a shore-to-shore route from Oakland to San Francisco. Access to the path is from three entrance points: Shellmound Street in Emeryville (at the entrance to the Ikea shopping center), the corner of Maritime Street and Burma Road and on Yerba Buena Island.

From the Shellmound entrance it's about a 2-mile ride to the east span of the Bay Bridge; from the Maritime Street entrance, about 1.75 miles. Cyclists can then ride over the water about 2 miles to Yerba Buena Island. In addition to the lanes (two for biking, one for walking) there are benches and viewing areas called belvederes. For more information contact Bike East Bay; phone (510) 845-7433.

Bret Harte Boardwalk, on 5th Street between Jefferson and Clay streets, is next to the site of the author's boyhood home. A block of renovated Victorian houses and barns house shops and restaurants. Visitor information centers are located at 11th Street and Broadway and at Jack London Square, Broadway and Embarcadero.

Daily round-trip ferries provide a transportation link between Oakland's Jack London Square and San Francisco. The Alameda-Oakland Ferry transports passengers to the Ferry Building, at the foot of Market Street on The Embarcadero, to Pier 41 and seasonally to Oracle Park in San Francisco, as well as to Angel Island in the summer. For schedule and fare information phone (877) 643-3779.

The Oakland-Alameda County Coliseum and Oracle Arena, both off I-880 at the 66th Avenue or Hegenberger Road exits, are where the city's three

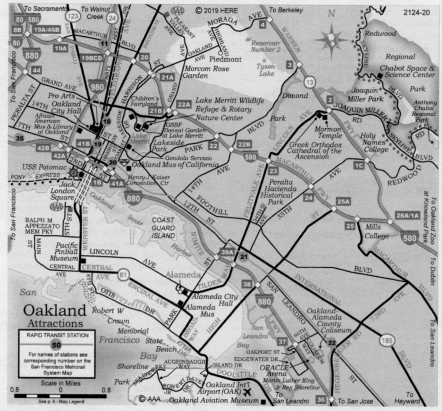

© 2019 HERE — 2124-20

Oakland Attractions

RAPID TRANSIT STATION

50

For names of stations see corresponding number on the San Francisco Metrorail System Map

See p. 6 - Map Legend

Scale in Miles

0.8   0   0.8

© AAA

(See map & index p. 176.)

professional sports teams play. The Oakland-Alameda County Coliseum is the home of the Oakland A's (baseball). The Golden State Warriors (basketball) play at Oracle Arena, adjacent to the stadium; the arena also is utilized for concerts, wrestling events and circus performances. Phone (510) 569-2121 for either facility.

Visit Oakland: 481 Water St., Oakland, CA 94607. **Phone:** (510) 839-9000.

Shopping: The Grand Avenue/Lakeshore district in downtown Oakland offers pleasant sidewalk strolling in the vicinity of scenic Lake Merritt. Foodies and amateur cooks in particular will love the Oaktown Spice Shop (546 Grand Ave.). They carry everything from fresh herbs to pickling spices to curries to hot sauces, and also can whip up a variety of hand-mixed blends. The exotic smells alone will draw you in.

The intoxicating aroma of chocolate permeates Michael Mischer Chocolates (3352 Grand Ave.). You won't find run-of-the-mill candy here; this gourmet chocolate shop specializes in truffles and other decadent treats.

Lakeshore Avenue is a shorter but denser stretch, which makes it a good area to window shop or people-watch. Hip women's designer fashions fill Maribel (3251 Lakeshore Ave.), where fashionistas can also hunt for locally made jewelry, funky sunglasses and other accessories.

Nightlife: Heinold's First and Last Chance Saloon (48 Webster St. in Jack London Square) is an Oakland institution—built from the timbers of a whaling ship, opened in 1883 and looking much the same today as it did way back when. Young schoolboy Jack London studied at the dockside bar and later returned to his favorite table to gain inspiration for such novels as "The Sea Wolf" and "Call of the Wild." The floor even tilts a bit (the 1906 San Francisco earthquake caused the pilings beneath the saloon to sink into the mud). It's an old-school joint loaded with character and memories.

Also at the square is Yoshi's Oakland (510 Embarcadero West). The lineup of jazz musicians at this intimate club is equally impressive, and the sound quality is superb.

The Fox Theater (1807 Telegraph Ave.) has a multi-tiered, beautifully restored interior and an eclectic lineup of entertainment. Street parking is a challenge, but the 19th Street BART station is just a block away; make sure you check the departure time of the final train when planning your evening. For concert information phone (510) 302-2250.

(See map & index p. 176.)

GREEK ORTHODOX CATHEDRAL OF THE ASCENSION, 4700 Lincoln Ave., overlooks downtown Oakland and the bay. Designed in the Byzantine style, the copper-domed church houses colorful mosaics and icons of Christ and the disciples. It is crowned with a 12-foot cross set with light-catching Baccarat crystals. A 3-day Greek festival is held in mid-May. **Time:** Allow 1 hour minimum. **Hours:** Mon.-Fri. 9-noon and 1-4. Closed major holidays. **Cost:** Free. **Phone:** (510) 531-3400.

LAKESIDE PARK is along the n. shore of Lake Merritt, a saltwater tidal lake in the center of the city. Boat rentals, sailing lessons and bowling greens are available. A tour boat also cruises the lake. The Camron-Stanford House, an 1876 Victorian, was home to several prominent Oakland families and formerly housed the Oakland Museum.

Hours: Park open daily during daylight hours. Guided tours of the Camron-Stanford House are given Sun. at 1, 2 and 3. **Cost:** Park free. A fee is charged for Camron-Stanford House tours. **Parking:** $2-$10 (Mon.-Fri.); $5 (Sat.-Sun. and holidays). **Phone:** (510) 238-2196 for tour boat information and reservations, or (510) 874-7802 for the Camron-Stanford House. 🚗 🚇 19th Street/Oakland, 18

Children's Fairyland, jct. Grand and Bellevue aves., depicts fairy tales and nursery rhymes and has children's rides. Puppet shows also are given.

Time: Allow 2 hours minimum. **Hours:** Mon.-Fri. 10-4, Sat.-Sun. 10-5, mid-June through Labor Day; Wed.-Sun. 10-4, Apr. 1 to mid-June and day after Labor Day-late Oct.; Fri.-Sun. 10-4, rest of year. Puppet shows are presented at 11, 2 and 4. Schedule during Fairy Winterland in mid-Dec. daily noon-7; puppet shows presented at 2, 4 and 6 p.m. Closed Jan. 1 and Christmas. **Cost:** $10; free (ages 0-1). **Parking:** $2-$10 (Mon.-Fri.); $5 (Sat.-Sun. and holidays). **Phone:** (510) 238-6876 or (510) 452-2259. 🚇 19th Street/Oakland, 18

Gondola Servizio departs from the boathouse next to the Lake Chalet Seafood Bar and Grill, 1520 Lakeside Dr. Thirty- and 50-minute sightseeing excursions in handmade Venetian gondolas cruise Lake Merritt. **Hours:** Cruises depart daily year-round. Departure times vary; phone ahead for schedule information. **Cost:** Fares start at $60 per couple. Reservations are required. **Phone:** (510) 663-6603. 🚇 Lake Merritt, 20

GSBF Bonsai Garden at Lake Merritt is in Lakeside Park on Bellevue Ave., near the Lakeside Park Demonstration Garden. The intricate art of bonsai is on display. A curved pathway leads visitors to approximately 90 plantings, including the first bonsai brought into the United States during the time of Abraham Lincoln's presidency and a bonsai that was on display at the 1915 Pan Pacific Exposition. Docents can provide background information.

Time: Allow 1 hour minimum. **Hours:** Tues.-Fri. 11-3, Sat. 10-4, Sun. noon-4 (weather permitting). Closed Jan. 1, Thanksgiving and Christmas. Phone ahead to confirm schedule. **Cost:** Donations. **Parking:** $2-$10 (Mon.-Fri.); $5 (Sat.-Sun. and holidays). **Phone:** (510) 763-8409. 🚇 19th Street/Oakland, 18

Lake Merritt Wildlife Refuge and Rotary Nature Center, Bellevue Ave. and Perkins St., has seasonal displays of birds, mammals and reptiles. During migratory seasons hundreds of wild geese, herons, egrets and ducks pass through the wildlife refuge outside the museum; founded in 1870, this is said to be the first established refuge in North America. The nature center also contains a native plant garden. **Note:** At press time the nature center was closed for renovation; phone for updates. **Time:** Allow 30 minutes minimum. **Hours:** Mon.-Fri. 10-5, Sat.-Sun. 10-4:30. **Cost:** Free. **Phone:** (510) 238-3739. 🚇 19th Street/Oakland, 18

Lakeside Park Demonstration Gardens, 666 Bellevue Ave., has a variety of displays, including Japanese, Polynesian, cactus, dahlia, palm, fuchsia, California native, herb and fragrance gardens. Seasonal plant displays and flower shows also are presented. **Time:** Allow 2 hours minimum. **Hours:** Daily 9-5. **Cost:** Free. **Parking:** $2-$10 (Mon.-Fri.); $5 (Sat.-Sun. and holidays). **Phone:** (510) 238-2197. 🚇 19th Street/Oakland, 18

MORCOM ROSE GARDEN is 1 blk. w. of Grand Ave. at 700 Jean St.; additional street parking is available on Olive Ave. It features 8 acres of gardens, reflecting pools and trees, with various varieties in bloom from May through November; the peak season is May through September. **Hours:** Daily dawn-dusk. The garden may be closed for weddings on weekends, May-Oct. Phone ahead to confirm schedule. **Cost:** Free. **Phone:** (510) 238-7275.

MORMON TEMPLE is at 4770 Lincoln Ave. The location of this architecturally impressive church offers a panoramic vista of both downtown Oakland and distant San Francisco across the bay. Guided 25-minute tours of the gardens and visitor center include a 12-minute video presentation about the temple. A family history center is located below the visitor center. Non-members are not permitted to enter the temple interior.

Time: Allow 1 hour minimum. **Hours:** Grounds open 8 a.m.-10 p.m. Visitor center open daily 9-9. Last tour departs 30 minutes before closing. **Cost:** Free. **Phone:** (510) 531-3200, or (510) 531-1475 for the visitor center. 🍴

OAKLAND MUSEUM OF CALIFORNIA (OMCA), 10th and Oak sts., brings art, history and natural science collections under one roof to tell the story of California's character and identity, from its extraordinary natural landscapes, to successive waves of migration, to its unique culture of creativity and innovation.

Exhibits in the Gallery of California Natural Sciences focus on seven places throughout California

(See map & index p. 176.)

that represent the state's ecological diversity while exploring contemporary environmental issues and conservation-based solutions.

The Gallery of California History preserves the past from pre-Spanish colonization to the present, with an emphasis on such events as earthquakes, the 1960s counterculture, technology and the diverse groups of people who have collectively influenced the state's development.

The Gallery of California Art features paintings, sculpture, photography, decorative arts and conceptual media works. Highlights include mid- and late 19th-century California landscape paintings, gold rush-era daguerreotypes, furniture and California ceramics.

Time: Allow 1 hour, 30 minutes minimum. **Hours:** Wed.-Fri. 11-5 (also Fri. 5-9), Sat.-Sun. 10-6. Closed Jan. 1, July 4, Thanksgiving and Christmas. **Cost:** $16; $11 (ages 65+ and students with ID); $7 (ages 9-17). An additional $5 fee is charged for special exhibitions. **Parking:** $3 per hour with validation; $7 flat rate Fri. 5-9. **Phone:** (510) 318-8400. GT ⑪ ⑭ ⑱ Lake Merritt, 20

USS *POTOMAC* is at 540 Water St. in Jack London Square, berthed next to the Lightship *Relief.* Dockside tours of President Franklin Delano Roosevelt's "Floating White House" last 45 minutes and allow visitors to see the restored 165-foot vessel—modified to accommodate FDR's physical limitations—that once hosted European heads of state. Two- and 3-hour history cruises on the presidential yacht travel into San Francisco Bay. Tours are preceded by a 15-minute video presentation in the visitor center.

Allow 1 hour minimum for dockside tours; 2 hours, 30 minutes minimum for history cruises; and 3 hours 30 minutes for special history cruises with lunch. **Hours:** Dockside tours given Wed., Fri. and Sun. 11-2:30, mid-Jan. through mid-Dec. Sightseeing cruises depart on select Thursdays and Saturdays, May-Oct.; phone for schedule. Phone for Special Sightseeing History Cruise schedule. **Cost:** Dockside tours $10; $8 (ages 60+); free (ages 0-12). Sightseeing History cruise $55; $50 (ages 60+); $35 (ages 6-12). Special Sightseeing History cruise (includes lunch) $75; $70 (ages 60+) $50 (ages 3-12). Reservations for history cruises can be booked online and are recommended. **Phone:** (510) 627-1215. ⑱ 12th St. Oakland City Center, 19

Make the Connction

For trip planning and local activities, AAA guidebooks are just the beginning.

Open the door to a whole lot more on **AAA.com**. Get extra travel insight, more information and online booking.

Find this symbol for places to look, book and save on AAA.com.

iStockphoto.com_shapecharge

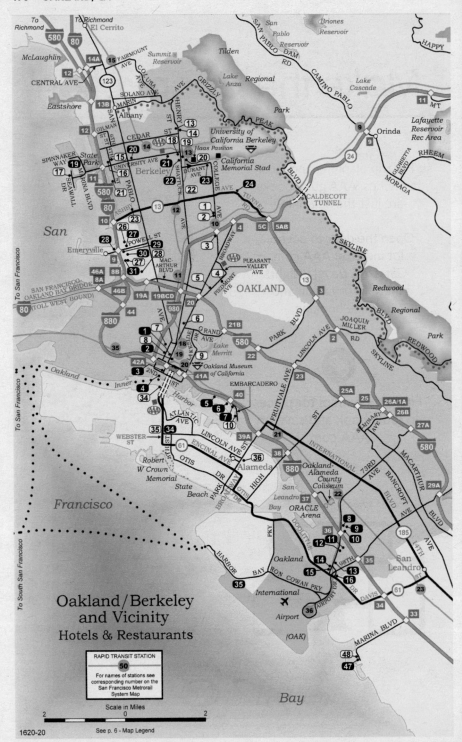

Oakland/Berkeley
and Vicinity
Hotels & Restaurants

RAPID TRANSIT STATION
50
For names of stations see
corresponding number on the
San Francisco Metrorail
System Map

Scale in Miles
2   0   2

1620-20   See p. 6 - Map Legend

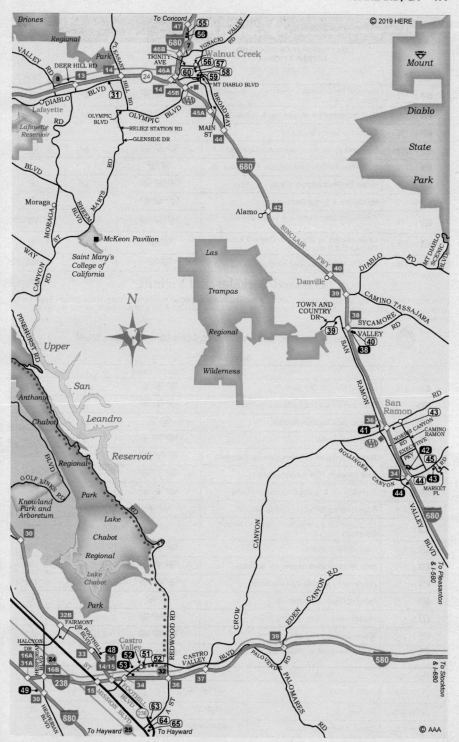

© 2019 HERE

© AAA

✈ Airport Hotels

Map Page	METROPOLITAN OAKLAND INTERNATIONAL (Maximum driving distance from airport: 3.4 mi)	Diamond Rated	Member Savings	Page
35 p. 176	Hampton Inn & Suites by Hilton Alameda-Oakland Airport, 3.4 mi	🔷🔷🔷	✔	33
11 p. 176	**Best Western Plus Airport Inn & Suites, 2.3 mi**	🔷🔷🔷	✔	182
10 p. 176	Comfort Inn & Suites, 3.2 mi	🔷🔷🔷		182
12 p. 176	Courtyard by Marriott-Oakland Airport, 2.2 mi	🔷🔷🔷	✔	182
8 p. 176	Days Hotel by Wyndham Oakland Airport, 3.4 mi	🔷🔷		182
15 p. 176	**Hilton Oakland Airport, 1.9 mi**	🔷🔷🔷	✔	182
14 p. 176	Holiday Inn & Suites Oakland Airport, 1.8 mi	🔷🔷🔷		182
16 p. 176	Holiday Inn Express Hotel & Suites Oakland Airport, 1.5 mi	🔷🔷🔷		182
9 p. 176	**La Quinta Inn by Wyndham Oakland Airport Coliseum, 3.1 mi**	🔷🔷	✔	182
13 p. 176	Oakland Airport Executive Hotel, 1.8 mi	🔷🔷		182

Oakland/Berkeley and Vicinity

This index helps you "spot" where approved hotels and restaurants are located on the corresponding detailed maps. Restaurant price range is a combination of lunch and/or dinner. Turn to the listing page for more information and consult display ads for special promotions.

 For more details, rates and reservations: AAA.com/travelguides/hotels

OAKLAND

Map Page	Hotels	Diamond Rated	Member Savings	Page
1 p. 176	Oakland Marriott City Center	🔷🔷🔷	✔	182
2 p. 176	Courtyard by Marriott Oakland Downtown	🔷🔷🔷	✔	182
3 p. 176	**Z Hotel Jack London Square**	🔷🔷	✔	183
4 p. 176	**Waterfront Hotel**	🔷🔷🔷	✔	182
5 p. 176	Homewood Suites by Hilton Oakland Waterfront	🔷🔷🔷	✔	182
6 p. 176	**Best Western Plus Bayside Hotel**	🔷🔷🔷	✔	182
7 p. 176	Executive Inn & Suites Embarcadero Cove	🔷🔷🔷		182
8 p. 176	Days Hotel by Wyndham Oakland Airport	🔷🔷		182
9 p. 176	**La Quinta Inn by Wyndham Oakland Airport Coliseum**	🔷🔷	✔	182
10 p. 176	Comfort Inn & Suites	🔷🔷🔷		182
11 p. 176	**Best Western Plus Airport Inn & Suites**	🔷🔷🔷	✔	182
12 p. 176	Courtyard by Marriott-Oakland Airport	🔷🔷🔷	✔	182
13 p. 176	Oakland Airport Executive Hotel	🔷🔷		182
14 p. 176	Holiday Inn & Suites Oakland Airport	🔷🔷🔷		182
15 p. 176	**Hilton Oakland Airport**	🔷🔷🔷	✔	182
16 p. 176	Holiday Inn Express Hotel & Suites Oakland Airport	🔷🔷🔷		182

Map Page	Restaurants	Diamond Rated	Cuisine	Price Range	Page
① p. 176	Wood Tavern	🔷🔷🔷	Regional American	$13-$38	183
② p. 176	Southie	🔷🔷	American	$11-$18	183
③ p. 176	Oliveto Cafe & Restaurant	🔷🔷🔷	Italian	$16-$37	183

Map Page	Restaurants (cont'd)	Diamond Rated	Cuisine	Price Range	Page
④ p. 176	Fentons Creamery	◆◆	American	$8-$18	183
⑤ p. 176	Commis Restaurant	◆◆◆◆	New American	$175	183
⑥ p. 176	Calavera Mexican Kitchen & Agave Bar	◆◆	Mexican	$15-$33	183
⑦ p. 176	Uncle Willie's BBQ and Fish	◆	Barbecue	$9-$31	183
⑧ p. 176	Siam Bay	◆◆	Thai	$9-$16	183
⑨ p. 176	Lake Chalet Seafood Bar & Grill	◆◆◆	American	$8-$32	183
⑩ p. 176	Quinn's Lighthouse Restaurant & Pub	◆◆	Seafood	$14-$35	183

BERKELEY

Map Page	Hotels	Diamond Rated	Member Savings	Page
⑲ p. 176	**DoubleTree by Hilton Berkeley Marina**	◆◆◆	✔	42
⑳ p. 176	Holiday Inn Express Hotel & Suites	◆◆◆		42
㉑ p. 176	Travelodge Berkeley	◆◆		43
㉒ p. 176	**Hotel Shattuck Plaza**	◆◆◆	✔	42
㉓ p. 176	**Graduate Berkeley**	◆◆◆	✔	42
㉔ p. 176	**Claremont Club & Spa, A Fairmont Hotel**	◆◆◆◆	✔	42

Map Page	Restaurants	Diamond Rated	Cuisine	Price Range	Page
⑬ p. 176	The Cheese Board Collective	◆	Pizza Vegetarian	$3-$20	43
⑭ p. 176	Chez Panisse	◆◆◆	Regional American	$10-$125	43
⑮ p. 176	Bette's Oceanview Diner	◆◆	American	$8-$17	43
⑯ p. 176	Iyasare	◆◆◆	Japanese Small Plates	$12-$28	43
⑰ p. 176	Skates on the Bay	◆◆◆	American	$15-$49	43
⑱ p. 176	Berkeley Social Club	◆◆	Korean Fusion	$14-$24	43
⑲ p. 176	Ippuku	◆◆	Japanese Small Plates	$5-$19	43
⑳ p. 176	Gather	◆◆◆	California	$10-$29	43
㉑ p. 176	Vik's Chaat Corner	◆	Indian	$8-$15	43
㉒ p. 176	Kirala Restaurant	◆◆	Japanese Sushi	$10-$34	43
㉓ p. 176	Spoon Korean Bistro	◆◆	Korean	$8-$16	43

EMERYVILLE

Map Page	Hotels	Diamond Rated	Member Savings	Page
㉗ p. 176	**Hyatt House Emeryville/San Francisco Bay Area**	◆◆◆	✔	74
㉘ p. 176	**Hilton Garden Inn San Francisco Oakland/Baybridge**	◆◆◆	✔	74
㉙ p. 176	Four Points by Sheraton-San Francisco Bay Bridge	◆◆◆	✔	74
㉚ p. 176	Hyatt Place Emeryville/San Francisco Bay Area	◆◆◆		74
㉛ p. 176	Courtyard by Marriott Emeryville	◆◆◆	✔	74

Map Page	Restaurants	Diamond Rated	Cuisine	Price Range	Page
㉖ p. 176	Shiba Ramen	◆	Japanese Noodles	$11-$15	74
㉗ p. 176	P.F. Chang's China Bistro	◆◆◆	Chinese	$9-$28	74
㉘ p. 176	Rudy's Can't Fail Cafe	◆◆	American	$6-$18	74

ALAMEDA

Map Page	Hotels	Diamond Rated	Member Savings	Page
34 p. 176	Hawthorn Suites by Wyndham-Oakland/Alameda	◆◆◆		33
35 p. 176	Hampton Inn & Suites by Hilton Alameda-Oakland Airport	◆◆◆	✔	33

Map Page	Restaurants	Diamond Rated	Cuisine	Price Range	Page
34 p. 176	Pasta Pelican	◆◆	Italian	$11-$30	33
35 p. 176	East Ocean Seafood Restaurant	◆◆	Chinese Dim Sum	$10-$68	33
36 p. 176	Speisekammer	◆◆	German	$12-$25	33

DANVILLE

Map Page	Hotel	Diamond Rated	Member Savings	Page
38 p. 176	**Best Western Danville Sycamore Inn**	◆◆	✔	70

Map Page	Restaurants	Diamond Rated	Cuisine	Price Range	Page
39 p. 176	El Nido Mexican Restaurant & Catering	◆◆	Mexican	$9-$29	70
40 p. 176	Esin Restaurant & Bar	◆◆◆	Mediterranean	$18-$48	70

SAN RAMON

Map Page	Hotels	Diamond Rated	Member Savings	Page
41 p. 176	**Hyatt House San Ramon**	◆◆◆	✔	360
42 p. 176	**San Ramon Marriott**	◆◆◆	✔	360
43 p. 176	Residence Inn by Marriott	◆◆◆	✔	360
44 p. 176	**Courtyard by Marriott San Ramon**	◆◆◆	✔	359

Map Page	Restaurants	Diamond Rated	Cuisine	Price Range	Page
43 p. 176	Zachary's Chicago Pizza	◆◆	Pizza	$5-$32	360
44 p. 176	Bishop Grill	◆◆	American	$12-$29	360
45 p. 176	The Hopyard American Alehouse & Grill	◆◆	American	$11-$18	360

SAN LEANDRO

Map Page	Hotels	Diamond Rated	Member Savings	Page
47 p. 176	The Marina Inn on San Francisco Bay	◆◆◆		357
48 p. 176	**Budget Inn**	◆◆	✔	357
49 p. 176	Hilton Garden Inn Oakland/San Leandro	◆◆◆	✔	357

Map Page	Restaurant	Diamond Rated	Cuisine	Price Range	Page
48 p. 176	Horatio's	◆◆◆	American	$15-$56	357

CASTRO VALLEY

Map Page	Hotels	Diamond Rated	Member Savings	Page
52 p. 176	Comfort Inn Castro Valley	◆◆		59
53 p. 176	Holiday Inn Express Castro Valley	◆◆◆		59

Map Page	Restaurants	Diamond Rated	Cuisine	Price Range	Page
51 p. 176	Tofu House	◆◆	Korean	$10-$23	59
52 p. 176	Luccas Italian Delicatessen	◆	Deli	$11-$16	59

WALNUT CREEK

Map Page	Hotel	Diamond Rated	Member Savings	Page
56 p. 176	Walnut Creek Marriott	◆◆◆	✔	401

Map Page	Restaurants	Diamond Rated	Cuisine	Price Range	Page
55 p. 176	Atrio	◆◆◆	American	$14-$36	401

Map Page	Restaurants (cont'd)	Diamond Rated	Cuisine	Price Range	Page
56 p. 176	Massimo Ristorante	◆◆◆	Northern Italian	$10-$43	401
57 p. 176	Broderick Roadhouse	◆◆	American	$12-$16	401
58 p. 176	Telefèric Barcelona	◆◆	Spanish	$13-$34	401
59 p. 176	Il Fornaio	◆◆◆	Italian	$10-$35	401
60 p. 176	Va de Vi Bistro & Wine Bar	◆◆◆	International Small Plates	$11-$17	401

LAFAYETTE

Map Page	Restaurant	Diamond Rated	Cuisine	Price Range	Page
31 p. 176	The Park Bistro & Bar	◆◆◆	American	$10-$42	110

HAYWARD

Map Page	Restaurants	Diamond Rated	Cuisine	Price Range	Page
63 p. 176	Cannery Cafe	◆	American	$5-$10	103
64 p. 176	Buffalo Bill's Brewery	◆◆	American	$10-$13	103
65 p. 176	Acqua E' Farina Ristorante	◆◆◆	Italian	$10-$34	103

(See map & index p. 176.)

BEST WESTERN PLUS AIRPORT INN & SUITES
510/633-0500

Hotel

Best Western PLUS.

AAA Benefit: Members save up to 15% and earn bonus points!

Address: 170 Hegenberger Loop 94621 **Location:** I-880 exit 36 (Hegenberger Rd), just w, then just sw. **Facility:** 76 units. 3 stories, interior corridors. **Pool:** heated indoor. **Activities:** hot tub, exercise room. **Guest Services:** coin laundry, area transportation. **Featured Amenity: breakfast buffet.**

BEST WESTERN PLUS BAYSIDE HOTEL
510/356-2450

Hotel

Best Western PLUS.

AAA Benefit: Members save up to 15% and earn bonus points!

Address: 1717 Embarcadero 94606 **Location:** Waterfront. I-880 exit 40 (16th Ave/Embarcadero) southbound, just nw; exit 40 (5th Ave/Embarcadero) northbound. **Facility:** 81 units. 3 stories, interior corridors. **Amenities:** safes. **Activities:** trails, exercise room. **Guest Services:** valet and coin laundry, area transportation. **Featured Amenity: breakfast buffet.**

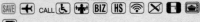

COMFORT INN & SUITES   510/568-1500
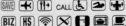 Hotel. **Address:** 8452 Edes Ave 94621

COURTYARD BY MARRIOTT-OAKLAND AIRPORT
510/568-7600
Hotel. **Address:** 350 Hegenberger Rd 94621

AAA Benefit: Members save 5% or more!

COURTYARD BY MARRIOTT OAKLAND DOWNTOWN
510/625-8282
Hotel. **Address:** 988 Broadway 94607

AAA Benefit: Members save 5% or more!

DAYS HOTEL BY WYNDHAM OAKLAND AIRPORT
510/568-1880
Hotel. **Address:** 8350 Edes Ave 94621

EXECUTIVE INN & SUITES EMBARCADERO COVE
510/536-6633

Hotel

Address: 1755 Embarcadero St 94606 **Location:** Waterfront. I-880 exit 40 (16th Ave/Embarcadero) southbound, just sw; exit 40 (5th Ave/Embarcadero) northbound, just sw. **Facility:** 143 units. 3 stories, interior corridors. **Amenities:** safes. **Pool:** heated outdoor. **Activities:** hot tub, trails, exercise room. **Guest Services:** valet and coin laundry, area transportation.

HILTON OAKLAND AIRPORT
510/635-5000

Hotel

Hilton HOTELS & RESORTS

AAA Benefit: Members save up to 15%!

Address: 1 Hegenberger Rd 94621 **Location:** I-880 exit 36 (Hegenberger Rd), 0.9 mi w. **Facility:** 360 units. 3 stories, interior corridors. **Parking:** on-site (fee). **Amenities:** safes. **Pool:** heated outdoor. **Activities:** exercise room. **Guest Services:** valet and coin laundry.

HOLIDAY INN & SUITES OAKLAND AIRPORT
510/638-7777
Hotel. **Address:** 77 Hegenberger Rd 94621

HOLIDAY INN EXPRESS HOTEL & SUITES OAKLAND
AIRPORT   510/569-4400
Hotel. **Address:** 66 Airport Access Rd 94603

HOMEWOOD SUITES BY HILTON OAKLAND WATERFRONT
510/663-2700
Extended Stay Hotel.
Address: 1103 Embarcadero 94606

AAA Benefit: Members save up to 15%!

LA QUINTA INN BY WYNDHAM OAKLAND AIRPORT COLISEUM
510/632-8900

Hotel

Address: 8465 Enterprise Way 94621 **Location:** I-880 exit 36 (Hegenberger Rd), just e. Coliseum/Oakland Airport, 22. **Facility:** 148 units. 3 stories, interior corridors. **Pool:** outdoor. **Activities:** hot tub, exercise room. **Guest Services:** valet and coin laundry, area transportation. **Featured Amenity: full hot breakfast.**

OAKLAND AIRPORT EXECUTIVE HOTEL   510/635-5300
Hotel. **Address:** 150 Hegenberger Rd 94621

OAKLAND MARRIOTT CITY CENTER   510/451-4000
Hotel. **Address:** 1001 Broadway 94607

AAA Benefit: Members save 5% or more!

WATERFRONT HOTEL
510/836-3800

Hotel

Address: 10 Washington St 94607 **Location:** Waterfront. I-880 exit Broadway, 0.5 mi nw. Located in Jack London Square. 12th St. Oakland City Center, 19. **Facility:** 145 units. 3-5 stories, interior corridors. **Parking:** valet only. **Amenities:** safes. **Pool:** heated outdoor. **Activities:** sauna, bicycles, trails, exercise room. **Guest Services:** valet laundry, area transportation. Affiliated with Joie de Vivre Hotels & Resorts.

(See map & index p. 176.)

Z HOTEL JACK LONDON SQUARE   510/452-4565   3

▼▼
Hotel

Address: 233 Broadway 94607 **Location:** I-880 exit Broadway, just w. Located at entrance to Jack London Square. 🅿 12th St. Oakland City Center, 19. **Facility:** 100 units. 3 stories, interior/exterior corridors. **Parking:** on-site (fee). **Pool:** heated outdoor. **Activities:** exercise room. **Guest Services:** valet and coin laundry.

[SAVE] [🍴] [🛎] [🍸] CALL [👤] [🚗]
[🔧] [BIZ] [📶] [✕] [💻]
/ SOME UNITS [🔒] [🖥] [🚌]

WHERE TO EAT

BUTTERCUP DINER & BAR
▼▼ Comfort Food. Casual Dining.
LOCATIONS:
Address: 229 Broadway 94607 **Phone:** 510/444-2976
Address: 1000 Cotton St 94606 **Phone:** 510/535-1640

CALAVERA MEXICAN KITCHEN & AGAVE BAR
510/338-3273   6
▼▼ Mexican. Casual Dining. **Address:** 2337 Broadway 94612

COMMIS RESTAURANT   510/653-3902   5
▼▼▼▼ New American. Fine Dining. **Address:** 3859 Piedmont Ave 94611

FENTONS CREAMERY   510/658-7000   4
▼▼ American. Casual Dining. **Address:** 4226 Piedmont Ave 94611

LAKE CHALET SEAFOOD BAR & GRILL   510/208-5253   9
▼▼▼ American. Fine Dining. **Address:** 1520 Lakeside Dr 94612

OLIVETO CAFE & RESTAURANT   510/547-5356   3
▼▼▼ Italian. Fine Dining. **Address:** 5655 College Ave 94618

QUINN'S LIGHTHOUSE RESTAURANT & PUB
510/536-2050   10
▼▼ Seafood. Casual Dining. **Address:** 1951 Embarcadero 94606

SIAM BAY   510/452-1499   8
▼▼ Thai. Casual Dining. **Address:** 1009 Clay St 94607

SOUTHIE   510/654-0100   2
▼▼ American. Casual Dining. **Address:** 6311 College Ave 94618

UNCLE WILLIE'S BBQ AND FISH   510/465-9200   7
▼ Barbecue. Quick Serve. **Address:** 614 14th St 94612

WOOD TAVERN   510/654-6607   1
▼▼▼ Regional American. Fine Dining. **Address:** 6317 College Ave 94618

OAKLEY   pop. 35,432

BEST WESTERN PLUS DELTA INN & SUITES
925/755-1222

▼▼▼
Hotel

[BW] Best Western PLUS.

AAA Benefit: Members save up to 15% and earn bonus points!

Address: 5549 Bridgehead Rd 94561 **Location:** SR 160 exit 1A (Main St), just e, then just n. **Facility:** 80 units. 3 stories, interior corridors. **Pool:** outdoor. **Activities:** hot tub, exercise room. **Guest Services:** valet and coin laundry. **Featured Amenity:** breakfast buffet.

[SAVE] [🍴] CALL [👤] [🚗] [🔧] [BIZ]
[HS] [📶] [✕] [🔒] [🖥] [💻]
/ SOME UNITS [🐾]

OAKVILLE   (A-8) pop. 71, elev. 155'
• Part of Wine Country area — see map p. 405

During the 1860s Oakville, named for the surrounding area's dense groves of oaks, was a sleepy little railroad stop where steam trains were replenished with water. The Napa Valley Wine Train *(see attraction listing in Napa p. 163)* chugs through town along the same stretch.

In addition to the railroad, the 1860s also brought the first vineyard to Oakville when settler H.W. Crabb purchased acreage near the Napa River. Crabb's efforts prevailed despite battling insect pests and diseases; today the University of California at Davis owns a vineyard in town called Oakville Station, where ongoing experiments to refine viticultural practices are conducted.

A warm, sunny climate and rich soil provide ideal growing conditions for the cabernet grape. Wineries are located along SR 29 (the St. Helena Highway). A few miles south of Oakville at 7856 St. Helena Hwy. (at the junction with the Oakville Crossroad) is the Oakville Grocery, a long-established gourmet food market in the heart of the Napa Valley. This is the perfect place to pick up picnic goodies, sample local specialties from nearby farms and indulge in a caffeinated concoction from the espresso bar.

Take the Oakville Crossroad east until it runs into the Silverado Trail, where there are more wineries within the Oakville appellation; along the way you'll see the white water tower of Silver Oak Cellars looming over expansive vineyards. Take Oakville Grade Road west and you'll enter the Oakville Grade, which geographically links the Napa and Sonoma valleys. This winding mountain drive offers spectacular panoramas but requires caution and should only be driven during daylight hours.

WINERIES

• **Robert Mondavi Winery** is .5 mi. n. on SR 29. **Hours:** Tastings daily 10-5. Various tours are offered daily; phone ahead for details. Closed Jan. 1, Easter, Thanksgiving, Christmas Eve and Christmas. **Phone:** (888) 766-6328. [GT]

OCCIDENTAL (B-6) pop. 1,115, elev. 594'
• Part of Wine Country area — see map p. 405

Occidental, about an hour's drive north of San Francisco, is a mere blip of a town: essentially a two-block main street with a couple of side streets and a sprinkling of homes perched on tree-covered hillsides. It sits at the approximate midpoint of the Bohemian Highway, a 10-mile stretch of winding two-lane road that connects Freestone (at the southern end) and Monte Rio (at the northern end). Snaking past bucolic pastures, around craggy rock formations and through dense woods, the Bohemian Highway—like so many other off-the-beaten-path roadways in this part of California—is a delightfully scenic drive that begs to be taken at a leisurely pace.

This out-of-the-way solitude is one of Occidental's biggest pluses. It's pretty, it's quiet and it's supremely relaxing. Restaurants and shops? There are literally a handful, but that's not really why people come here. Occidental is mainly a place to get away from it all and enjoy the great outdoors, in particular the many recreational opportunities offered by the nearby Russian River.

Another pretty scenic drive is Coleman Valley Road. If you're heading into Occidental from the south, just take a left at the only stop sign in town. Another winding, two-lane route, this is a quintessential country drive. One minute you're passing cows standing in emerald-green meadows; the next you're rounding a tight S-curve while tunneling through deep shade and dense forest. Oak trees spread their horizontal branches in open fields, and there are panoramic vistas of rolling coastal foothills.

The road tops a ridge, offering a glimpse of the Pacific in the distance, then descends to the coast. Coleman Valley Road ends at SR 1 and Coleman Beach, one of many public access points along the spectacular Sonoma County coastline. Here you can pull off, park and stretch your legs while gazing out at rugged, rocky headlands and steel-blue water before making the return trip back to Occidental.

Many Bay Area residents make regular weekend pilgrimages to Wild Flour Bread, on Bohemian Highway at the intersection with SR 12 (Bodega Highway). The bakery's artisanal breads, scones, sticky buns and other fresh-baked treats are that good. It's open Friday through Monday; phone (707) 874-2938.

RECREATIONAL ACTIVITIES
Ziplines
• **Sonoma Canopy Tours** is at 6250 Bohemian Hwy. **Hours:** Guided tours are offered year round, rain or shine. Tour dates and hours are seasonal and availability can vary; phone ahead to confirm schedule. Closed Jan. 1, Easter, Thanksgiving and Christmas. **Cost:** Reservations are required. **Phone:** (888) 494-7868.

OCCIDENTAL LODGE   707/874-3623
▼▼ Motel. **Address:** 3610 Bohemian Hwy 95465

WHERE TO EAT

HOWARD STATION CAFE   707/874-2838
▼▼ American. Casual Dining. **Address:** 3611 Bohemian Hwy 95465

OLYMPIC VALLEY (D-4) elev. 6,079'
• Hotels & Restaurants map & index p. 114
• Part of Lake Tahoe Area — see map p. 111

SQUAW VALLEY TRAM is at 1960 Squaw Valley Rd. at Squaw Valley's base village. The tram provides a full aerial view of Lake Tahoe and Squaw Valley, site of the 1960 Winter Olympics and a year-round recreation area, as it ascends to the 8,200-foot High Camp, the trailhead of the Pacific Crest Trail. In addition to hiking, visitors can roller skate, swim and shop. A museum at the summit commemorates the games.

Hours: Tram operates daily 10:40-4:20, late May-late Aug.; Sat.-Sun. 10:40-4:20, in Sept. Schedule varies during the winter ski season. Phone ahead to confirm schedule. **Cost:** Tram $46; $25 (ages 5-17). Advance purchase (24 hours ahead) $36; $20 (ages 5-17). **Phone:** (800) 403-0206. ▣ ⊞

High Camp, at the upper terminus of the Squaw Valley Tram, boasts panoramic views of Lake Tahoe and the High Sierra and is where many beginner runs start. After riding the tram up the mountain to an elevation of 8,200 feet, visitors can take advantage of several recreational options, including swimming and roller skating. In addition, the Olympic Museum features memorabilia from the 1960 Winter Olympics.

Time: Allow 3 hours minimum. **Hours:** High Camp open Sun.-Thurs. 11-5, Fri.-Sat. 11-6, early June-late Sept. Museum open daily; phone ahead for schedule. **Cost:** Tram (includes Olympic Exhibition) $39; $25 (ages 13-22 and 65+); $10 (ages 5-12); free (ages 0-4 and active duty military with ID). There are additional fees for swimming and roller skating. An all-access pass and combination tickets also are available; phone ahead for prices and age restrictions. **Phone:** (800) 403-0206. ▣ ⊞ ⊠

PLUMPJACK SQUAW VALLEY INN   530/583-1576   **20**
▼▼▼ Boutique Contemporary Hotel. **Address:** 1920 Squaw Valley Rd 96146

RED WOLF LODGE AT SQUAW VALLEY   530/583-7226   **23**
▼▼ Hotel. **Address:** 2000 Village East Rd 96146

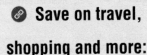

(See map & index p. 114.)

RESORT AT SQUAW CREEK   530/583-6300

Resort Hotel **Address:** 400 Squaw Creek Rd 96146 **Location:** I-80 exit SR 89, 8.3 mi s, 0.6 mi sw on Squaw Valley Rd, then just w; in Olympic Valley. Located at Squaw Valley Ski area. **Facility:** In a spectacular mountain setting, the property's extensive recreational activities are available in both summer and winter, including the resort's 18-hole golf course. 355 units, some two bedrooms, efficiencies and kitchens. 9 stories, interior corridors. **Parking:** on-site and valet. **Terms:** check-in 4 pm. **Amenities:** safes. **Dining:** 5 restaurants, also, Six Peaks Grill, see separate listing. **Pool:** heated outdoor. **Activities:** sauna, hot tub, steamroom, fishing, regulation golf, tennis, downhill & cross country skiing, sledding, ice skating, recreation programs, kids club, bicycles, game room, health club, spa. **Guest Services:** valet and coin laundry, area transportation. Affiliated with Destination Hotels.

SQUAW VALLEY LODGE   530/583-5500 ㉑
Resort Condominium. **Address:** 201 Squaw Peak Rd 96146

THE VILLAGE AT SQUAW VALLEY   530/584-1000 ㉒
Resort Condominium. **Address:** 1750 Village East Rd 96146

WHERE TO EAT

FIRESIDE PIZZA COMPANY   530/584-6150 ㉕
Italian Pizza. Casual Dining. **Address:** 1985 Squaw Valley Rd 96146

SIX PEAKS GRILL   530/583-6300 ㉔
American. Casual Dining. **Address:** 400 Squaw Creek Rd 96146

ORICK pop. 357, elev. 34'

ELK MEADOW CABINS   707/488-2222
Vacation Rental Cabin. **Address:** 7 Valley Green Camp Rd 95555

ORLAND pop. 7,291

ORLAND INN   530/865-7632

Motel **Address:** 1052 South St 95963 **Location:** I-5 exit 618 (CR 16/South St), just ne; in Stony Creek Square Shopping Center. **Facility:** 40 units. 2 stories (no elevator), exterior corridors. **Pool:** outdoor. **Featured Amenity:** continental breakfast.

WHERE TO EAT

FARWOOD BAR & GRILL   530/865-9900
American. Casual Dining. **Address:** 705 5th St 95963

I-5 CAFE AND CREAMERY   530/865-3000
Breakfast. Casual Dining. **Address:** 1165 Hoff Way 95963

OROVILLE (D-3) pop. 15,546, elev. 174'
• Hotels p. 186 • Restaurants p. 186

Cherokee Indians migrated to Oroville from Georgia in the 1850s to work in gold mines north of town. In 1870 alone, hydraulic mining operations at the site yielded $5 million in gold. Later diamonds were discovered; the Cherokee Diamond Mine opened in 1873 and went on to produce some 300 diamonds of industrial quality.

The diamond reserves were soon depleted, however, and the nearby town of Cherokee—like so many other mining towns in California—was forgotten. Ruins of brick stores and foundations identified by markers are all that remain in this ghost town on Cherokee Road, 10 miles north of Oroville via SR 70, the Feather River Scenic Byway.

The foothills east of Oroville were once North America's northernmost commercial citrus-growing district, producing navel and Satsuma mandarin oranges. The Mother Orange Tree at 400 Glen View Dr., planted in 1856, was designated a California Historical Landmark in 2006.

A good time to explore the Oroville area is from late March through mid-May, when wildflowers—particularly poppies and lupine—are in glorious bloom on Table Mountain, just north of the city. Lake Oroville *(see Recreation Areas Chart)* is popular with houseboat owners; recreational activities include sailing, jet skiing, water skiing and camping. Kayakers and canoers navigate the Feather River, while anglers fish for salmon, sturgeon, bass and steelhead.

Oroville Area Chamber of Commerce: 1789 Montgomery St., Oroville, CA 95965. **Phone:** (530) 538-2542 or (800) 655-4653.

LAKE OROVILLE VISITOR CENTER is 7 mi. n.e. of SR 162 to Kelly Ridge, then 1.5 mi. n. The center, overlooking Lake Oroville and Oroville Dam, displays exhibits depicting wildlife, the gold rush era, state water projects, the Beckwourth Trail across the Sierra Nevada and the Maidu Indians. Videos about the area are shown on request. **Time:** Allow 1 hour minimum. **Hours:** Daily 9-5. Closed Jan. 1, Thanksgiving and Christmas. **Cost:** Free. **Phone:** (530) 538-2219.

LOTT HOME MUSEUM is between 3rd and 4th aves. at 1067 Montgomery St., in Sank Park. Built in 1856 and occupied by a prominent local lawyer and his bride, the house is furnished in period; approximately 80 percent of the furnishing are original. The grounds include a Victorian garden. **Hours:** House open Sun.-Mon. and Fri. 11:30-3:30 and by appointment, Feb. 1 to mid-Dec. Grounds open Mon.-Sat. 9-9, Sun. 9-8:30. **Cost:** House $3; free (ages 0-12). Grounds free. **Phone:** (530) 538-2497. GT 🔗

OROVILLE CHINESE TEMPLE COMPLEX & MUSEUM is at 1500 Broderick St. The complex—thought to be the largest in the West that has remained intact from the gold rush era—contains three working temples dating from 1863, complete with original furnishings and an herb shop. Across the garden courtyard are three rooms displaying tapestries, puppets, clothing and other everyday items once used by Chinese immigrants living in the area. **Time:** Allow 1 hour minimum. **Hours:** Daily noon-4, Feb. 1 to mid-Dec. **Cost:** $3; free (ages 0-11). **Phone:** (530) 538-2496.

GOLD COUNTRY CASINO RESORT 530/538-4560

Hotel

Address: 4020 Olive Hwy 95966 **Location:** SR 70 exit 46 (SR 162/Oroville Dam Blvd), 1.6 mi e to Olive Hwy (SR 162), then 2.3 mi e. **Facility:** This hotel features renovated and spacious guest rooms, some with valley views, deep soaking tubs or hot tubs. A few units include a private balcony. 87 units. 6 stories, interior corridors. **Parking:** on-site and valet. **Pool:** heated outdoor. **Activities:** hot tub, exercise room. **Guest Services:** valet and coin laundry.

HOLIDAY INN EXPRESS & SUITES-LAKE OROVILLE
530/534-5566

Hotel. **Address:** 550 Oro Dam Blvd 95965

THE LODGE AT FEATHER FALLS CASINO
530/533-3885

Hotel

Address: 4 Alverda Dr 95966 **Location:** SR 70 exit Ophir Rd, 3.2 mi e. **Facility:** This tastefully decorated property with upscale enhancements offers a fireplace in the lobby and easy access to the adjacent casino. A few guest rooms include a wet bar. 84 units. 3 stories, interior corridors. **Terms:** check-in 4 pm. **Amenities:** *Some:* safes. **Dining:** Feather Falls Casino Brewing Company, see separate listing. **Pool:** heated outdoor, heated indoor. **Activities:** sauna, hot tub, exercise room.

WHERE TO EAT

FEATHER FALLS CASINO BREWING COMPANY
530/533-3885

American. Casual Dining. **Address:** 3 Alverda Dr 95966

MINER'S ALLEY BREWING COMPANY 530/693-4388

American. Casual Dining. **Address:** 2053 Montgomery St 95965

PACIFICA (D-7) pop. 37,234, elev. 60'
• Hotels & Restaurants map & index p. 316
• Part of San Francisco area — see map p. 243

This beach community, just a stone's throw from San Francisco, is a popular getaway for anglers, hikers, surfers and mountain bikers. The ocean views can't be beat, especially from the vantage point of Pacifica Pier, downtown off Beach Boulevard. This "L"-shaped pier extends 1,140 feet into the Pacific and has a reputation as one of the best fishing piers in California for salmon and striped bass (a state license isn't required to fish here). The day following a winter storm usually brings crashing

waves and opportunities for dramatic photos. This is also a great spot for sunset watching. The pier occasionally closes during rough weather.

The bluff-top perspective from Mori Point, part of Golden Gate National Recreation Area, offers outstanding panoramic views of the ocean and coastline, especially on clear, fog-free days. From the parking area at the intersection of Beach Boulevard and Clarendon Avenue (a short distance south of Pacifica Pier), a wide dirt trail runs along the beach to Bootlegger's Steps. Climb the steps to reach the flat expanse at the top. From Mori Point other trails follow the coastal headlands south, providing access to Rockaway Beach and Linda Mar Beach. **Note:** Stay on the marked trails if you explore this area, as the cliffs are fragile and unsafe for climbing.

One thing the northern California coast is famous for is fog, and the Pacific Coast Fogfest celebrates one of the meteorological mainstays of Pacifica's maritime climate. It's also a celebration of sun, sand and surf, plus arts and crafts and food and beverage booths, a parade and marching band competition, and plenty of live music. The fun takes place the last full weekend in September, when the weather is usually—and ironically—sunny and fog-free.

Francisco Sanchez, an *alcalde* (administrative magistrate) of San Francisco under the Spanish government, was awarded land in this area in return for his service to Mexico. Sanchez occupied an adobe built in the 1840s; the preserved two-story house, a half-mile east of SR 1 at 1000 Linda Mar Blvd., stands within Sanchez Adobe County Park and contains period furniture, artifacts and clothing. Tours are offered; phone (650) 359-1462.

Pacifica Chamber of Commerce and Visitors Center: 225 Rockaway Beach Ave., Suite 1, Pacifica, CA 94044. **Phone:** (650) 355-4122.

HOLIDAY INN EXPRESS HOTEL & SUITES
650/355-5000

Hotel

Address: 519 Nick Gust Way 94044 **Location:** SR 1 exit Rockaway Beach Ave, just w. **Facility:** 38 units. 2 stories, interior corridors. **Guest Services:** coin laundry. **Featured Amenity:** full hot breakfast.

WHERE TO EAT

LOVEY'S TEA SHOPPE 650/359-1245

Specialty. Casual Dining. **Address:** 4430 Pacific Coast Hwy 94044

PUERTO 27 PERUVIAN KITCHEN & PISCO BAR
650/733-7343

Peruvian. Casual Dining. **Address:** 525 Crespi Dr 94044

SALADA BEACH CAFE 650/557-1356

American. Quick Serve. **Address:** 220 Paloma Ave 94044

PACIFIC GROVE (G-3) pop. 15,041, elev. 55'

Back in 1875 this delightfully picturesque community was a Methodist summer camp, with tents huddled under Monterey pines. The last chautauqua was held in 1926, but many historic buildings remain and Pacific Grove's residential neighborhoods are filled with charming Victorian-style houses, many with lovingly tended flower gardens.

Just north of Monterey, Pacific Grove is the northern starting point for the popular and spectacularly scenic 17-Mile Drive (see Pebble Beach p. 194). Ocean View Boulevard, which runs along the water in the center of town, is perfect for an early morning stroll. A paved walking path winds along the rocky shoreline past clumps of spiny, fleshy-leaved aloes and green carpets of ice plants all the way to Point Pinos.

Well-groomed Lover's Point Park, at Grand Avenue and Ocean View Boulevard, is a great place to do your morning stretching, have a picnic on the grass or just while away a sunny afternoon on a bench gazing out over the water. You can clamber around the rocks at the point but watch your footing, as it's easy to slip. Because of its east-facing location, Lover's Point is one of a handful of spots along the California coast where the suns rises rather than sets over water.

A stairway leads down to Lover's Point Beach, a small patch of sand with waves that are usually gentle enough for wading and paddleboarding. There's a beach volleyball court, a couple of picnic tables and a snack bar that's open seasonally. Low tide exposes tide pools where you can spot crabs, sea anemones and other marine dwellers.

From Lover's Point Park, walk or bike the Monterey Peninsula Recreational Trail. It runs from Pacific Grove and Monterey all the way to Castroville. The former Southern Pacific Railroad right of way has separate pedestrian and biking lanes and offers plenty of scenic bay views.

The Pacific Grove Farmers Market sets up on Central Avenue between Forest and Grand avenues on Monday afternoons from 3 to 7 (3-6 during the winter months). Vendors at this small market offer organic produce, honey and specialty foods.

Within the Monarch Grove Sanctuary, 1 block west of Lighthouse Avenue and 17-Mile Drive on Ridge Road, is an area where visitors have the opportunity to spot orange-and-black monarch butterflies. The location is a stop on the monarch's seasonal migration route. The butterflies gather between October and mid-February. Contact the sanctuary for information about the likeliest times to see them; phone (831) 648-5716.

A long-running Pacific Grove tradition is the Good Old Days Celebration weekend, which takes place along Central Avenue in early or mid-April. This family-oriented event features an arts and crafts show, a parade, games and contests for kids, kiddie rides, live entertainment and lots of food vendors. Central Avenue also is the site of the Holiday Parade of Lights in late November or early December, a parade complete with marching bands, lighted and holiday-themed floats, dance teams and an appearance by Santa Claus.

Pacific Grove Chamber of Commerce Information Center: 100 Central Ave., Pacific Grove, CA 93950. **Phone:** (831) 324-4668.

Self-guiding tours: Walking tour brochures with information about Pacific Grove's Victorian homes and historic buildings are available at the information center.

Shopping: American Tin Cannery Premium Outlets, 125 Ocean View Blvd., includes factory-direct and specialty stores.

PACIFIC GROVE MUSEUM OF NATURAL HISTORY,
165 Forest Ave., spotlights the natural history of California's central coast and includes exhibits about birds and wildlife, plants, geology and cultural history. **Time:** Allow 1 hour minimum. **Hours:** Tues.-Sun. 10-5. Closed major holidays. **Cost:** $8.95; $5.95 (ages 4-18 and students and military with ID; free (ages 0-3 and Monterey County residents). **Phone:** (831) 648-5716.

POINT PINOS LIGHTHOUSE
is at 80 Asilomar Blvd., off Lighthouse Ave. Standing at the northern tip of the Monterey Peninsula, it has been guiding ships since 1855 and is the oldest continuously operating lighthouse on the Pacific Coast.

The brick lighthouse tower is part of a stone, Cape Cod-style lightkeeper's house; the different levels are connected by a spiral staircase. There are displays of buoys and Fresnel lenses and exhibits focusing on notable shipwrecks. **Time:** Allow 1 hour minimum. **Hours:** Thurs.-Mon. 1-4. Closed Jan. 1, Thanksgiving and Christmas. **Cost:** Donations. **Phone:** (831) 648-3176.

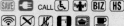

(See map & index p. 144.)

BORG'S OCEAN FRONT MOTEL 831/375-2406 48

Motel

Address: 635 Ocean View Blvd 93950 **Location:** At Lover's Point. **Facility:** 60 units, some two bedrooms. 2 stories (no elevator), exterior corridors. **Activities:** beach access.

BUTTERFLY GROVE INN 831/250-8191 47
Motel. **Address:** 1073 Lighthouse Ave 93950

CENTRELLA INN 831/372-3372 54
Bed & Breakfast. **Address:** 612 Central Ave 93950

DEER HAVEN INN 831/373-7784 53
Motel. **Address:** 750 Crocker Ave 93950

GOSBY HOUSE INN 831/375-1287 55
Bed & Breakfast. **Address:** 643 Lighthouse Ave 93950

GREEN GABLES INN 831/375-2095 56
Bed & Breakfast. **Address:** 301 Ocean View Blvd 93950

LOVERS POINT INN 831/373-4771 49

Hotel

Address: 625 Ocean View Blvd 93950 **Location:** At Lover's Point. **Facility:** 50 units. 3 stories, exterior corridors. **Terms:** check-in 4 pm. **Activities:** beach access, trails. **Featured Amenity: continental breakfast.**

MARTINE INN 831/373-3388 58
Bed & Breakfast. **Address:** 255 Ocean View Blvd 93950

MONARCH RESORT 831/646-8885 45

Hotel

Address: 1111 Lighthouse Ave 93950 **Location:** Just w of Seventeen Mile Dr. **Facility:** 50 units, some efficiencies. 2 stories, interior corridors. **Terms:** check-in 4 pm. **Pool:** outdoor. **Activities:** sauna, hot tub, recreation programs. **Featured Amenity: continental breakfast.**

/ SOME UNITS

OLD ST. ANGELA INN 831/372-3246 57
Bed & Breakfast. **Address:** 321 Central Ave 93950

PACIFIC GARDENS INN 831/646-9414 50
Hotel. **Address:** 701 Asilomar Ave 93950

SEA BREEZE INN & COTTAGES 831/372-7771 46
Motel. **Address:** 1100 Lighthouse Ave 93950

WHERE TO EAT

FANDANGO 831/372-3456 30

Continental
Casual Dining
$10-$36

AAA Inspector Notes: A weatherbeaten exterior here conceals a charming interior of individually appointed dining rooms with a Mediterranean feel. The most popular items are the osso buco and paella. **Features:** full bar, Sunday brunch. **Reservations:** suggested. **Address:** 223 17th St 93950 **Location:** Center.

FIRST AWAKENINGS 831/372-1125 32
American. Casual Dining. **Address:** 125 Ocean View Blvd 93950

FISHWIFE 831/375-7107 31
Seafood. Casual Dining. **Address:** 1996 1/2 Sunset Dr 93950

PASSIONFISH 831/655-3311 29
California Seafood. Fine Dining. **Address:** 701 Lighthouse Ave 93950

PALO ALTO (E-8) pop. 64,403, elev. 23'
• Hotels p. 193 • Restaurants p. 194
• Hotels & Restaurants map & index p. 190

Palo Alto (Spanish for "tall tree") is at the southeastern end of a scenic 31-mile stretch of I-280 heading northwest to San Francisco. It was named for a double-trunked redwood tree, a landmark used by travelers and explorers as early as 1769. A likeness of the tree appears on the seal of Stanford University. The opening of the university in 1891 provided the impetus for Palo Alto's growth, and the livelihoods of both city and university have remained closely intertwined.

The Eucalyptus Grove at Stanford is the site each Mother's Day weekend of the Stanford Powwow, a 3-day celebration of Native American culture. Clad in colorful costumes, tribal members perform exhibition dances and compete in dance contests.

Stanford's SLAC National Accelerator Laboratory is on Sand Hill Road. The research facility, which includes what is said to be the world's longest building, is a U.S. Department of Energy national laboratory. Ninety-minute guided tours of the lab include a visit to the 2-mile linear accelerator. Tours are offered twice per month, typically on a Friday at 1 and 2:30, and are open to ages 12+ with advance online registration. Phone (650) 926-4931 for information.

Palo Alto Chamber of Commerce: 355 Alma St., Palo Alto, CA 94301. **Phone:** (650) 324-3121.

Shopping: Bloomingdale's, Macy's, Neiman Marcus and Nordstrom are the anchor stores at Stanford Shopping Center, on Sand Hill Road adjacent to Stanford University. This upscale, open-air mall includes some 140 retailers, restaurants and services in a setting beautified by lots of blooming plants, ornamental shrubs and whimsical sculptures.

STANFORD UNIVERSITY is about 1 mi. w. off Sand Hill Rd. The campus sprawls on 8,180 acres originally known as the Palo Alto Stock Farm, a former

(See map & index p. 190.)

family estate of Leland and Jane Stanford. Frederick Law Olmstead created the general concept for the grounds, dotted with oak and eucalyptus trees, and the unifying architectural theme: Romanesque and California Mission Revival architecture reflected in sandstone buildings featuring arched arcades and red-tiled roofs.

One-hour walking tours of the campus depart from the Stanford Visitor Center at 295 Galvez St. **Hours:** Tours are given daily at 11 and 3:15, except some holidays and breaks between academic quarters, including the last two weeks of Dec. Phone ahead to confirm schedule. **Cost:** Free. **Phone:** (650) 723-2560. ♿

Cantor Arts Center at Stanford University is just off Palm Dr. at Lomita Dr. and Museum Way. The center's 24 galleries display art from around the world, from Africa to the Americas to Asia and from classical to contemporary. Works from ancient Egypt, China and Greece as well as the 21st century span 5,000 years of art history and a diversity of cultures.

Three galleries are dedicated to sculpture by Auguste Rodin; casts of his famous "The Thinker," "Age of Bronze" and "The Kiss" are crowd-pleasers. The outdoor Rodin Sculpture Garden displays larger-than-life-size bronze figures. Adam and Eve flank "The Gates of Hell," the artist's greatest masterpiece, which also includes many smaller figures.

Other highlights are works by Do Ho Suh, Stephanie Syjuco and Titus Kaphar as well as Ansel Adams, Albert Bierstadt, Andy Goldsworthy, Georgia O'Keeffe, Pablo Picasso and Richard Serra. Stanford family memorabilia and changing exhibits also are featured.

Time: Allow 2 hours minimum. **Hours:** Wed.-Mon. 11-5 (also Thurs. 5-8). Guided tours are given daily, and family programs are offered on the second Sun. of the month; check website for schedule. Highlight tours are given Wed.-Sun. at 1. Closed Thanksgiving and Christmas. **Cost:** Free. **Parking:** Parking is metered; free after 4 p.m. and all day on weekends. **Phone:** (650) 723-4177 or TTY (650) 723-1216. 🍴

Hoover Tower, on Serra Mall, houses the Hoover Institution on War, Revolution and Peace, a public policy research center devoted to the study of world conflict. The institution was founded in 1919 by Herbert Hoover, a member of the university's first class, who would later become the nation's 31st president.

The 285-foot-tall tower is topped by a 48-bell carillon. The building and an observation deck can be visited. **Time:** Allow 30 minutes minimum. **Hours:** Open daily 10-4. Closed major holidays and some school breaks. Phone ahead or refer to the website to confirm schedule. **Cost:** Observation deck $4; $3 (ages 0-12 and 65+); free (Stanford ID holders). **Phone:** (650) 723-2053.

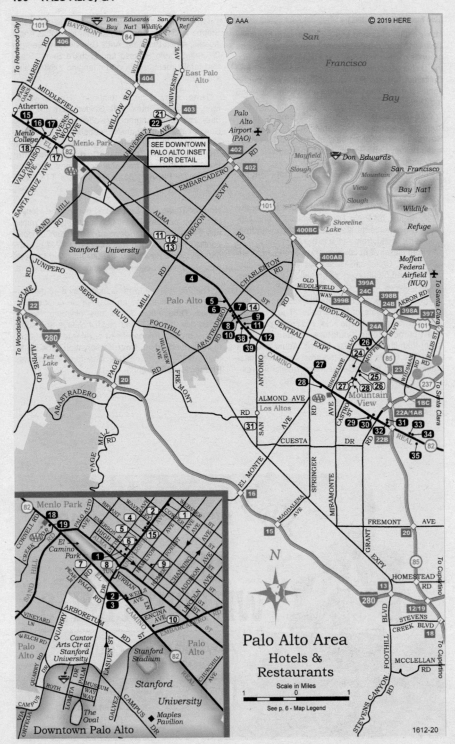

Palo Alto Area
Hotels &
Restaurants

Scale in Miles

See p. 6 - Map Legend

Downtown Palo Alto

1612-20

Palo Alto Area

This index helps you "spot" where approved hotels and restaurants are located on the corresponding detailed maps. Restaurant price range is a combination of lunch and/or dinner. Turn to the listing page for more information and consult display ads for special promotions.

 For more details, rates and reservations: AAA.com/travelguides/hotels

PALO ALTO

Map Page	Hotels	Diamond Rated	Member Savings	Page
1 p. 190	Hotel Keen	♦♦♦		193
2 p. 190	**Sheraton Palo Alto Hotel**	♦♦♦	✔	193
3 p. 190	**The Westin Palo Alto**	♦♦♦♦	✔	193
4 p. 190	**Creekside Inn**	♦♦♦	✔	193
5 p. 190	**The Zen Hotel**	♦♦♦	✔	194
6 p. 190	Hilton Garden Inn Palo Alto	♦♦♦	✔	193
7 p. 190	**Americas Best Value Inn - Sky Ranch Inn**	♦♦	✔	193
8 p. 190	**The Palo Alto Inn**	♦♦	✔	193
9 p. 190	**Dinah's Garden Hotel**	♦♦♦	✔	193
10 p. 190	Crowne Plaza Cabana Hotel	♦♦♦		193
11 p. 190	Homewood Suites Palo Alto by Hilton	♦♦♦	✔	193
12 p. 190	**Country Inn Motel**	♦♦	✔	193

Map Page	Restaurants	Diamond Rated	Cuisine	Price Range	Page
① p. 190	Tamarine Restaurant	♦♦♦	Vietnamese	$19-$34	194
② p. 190	Paris Baguette	♦	Breads/Pastries Desserts	$11-$30	194
④ p. 190	La Strada Ristorante Italiano	♦♦♦	Italian	$12-$25	194
⑤ p. 190	Oren's Hummus Shop	♦♦	Middle Eastern	$9-$18	194
⑥ p. 190	Evvia Estiatorio	♦♦♦	Greek	$18-$51	194
⑦ p. 190	P.F. Chang's China Bistro	♦♦♦	Chinese	$9-$25	194
⑧ p. 190	Lemonade	♦	California	$11-$30	194
⑨ p. 190	Pizzeria Delfina	♦♦	Italian Pizza	$14-$25	194
⑩ p. 190	Howie's Artisan Pizza	♦♦	Pizza	$9-$19	194
⑪ p. 190	Sundance The Steakhouse	♦♦♦	Steak	$17-$64	194
⑫ p. 190	Baume	♦♦♦♦	New French	$365	194
⑬ p. 190	La Bodeguita del Medio	♦♦	Cuban	$12-$28	194
⑭ p. 190	**The Sea by Alexander's Steakhouse**	♦♦♦♦	Seafood	$43-$75	194
⑮ p. 190	Joya Restaurant & Lounge	♦♦♦	Latin American	$9-$50	194

MENLO PARK

Map Page	Hotels	Diamond Rated	Member Savings	Page
15 p. 190	Red Cottage Inn & Suites	♦♦♦		134
16 p. 190	**Residence Inn by Marriott Palo Alto Menlo Park**	♦♦♦	✔	134
17 p. 190	Menlo Park Inn	♦♦		134
18 p. 190	**Stanford Park Hotel**	♦♦♦♦	✔	134
19 p. 190	**Best Western Plus Riviera**	♦♦♦	✔	134

Map Page	Restaurants	Diamond Rated	Cuisine	Price Range	Page
⑰ p. 190	Left Bank	♦♦♦	French	$13-$34	134

Map Page	Restaurants (cont'd)	Diamond Rated	Cuisine	Price Range	Page
⑱ p. 190	Carpaccio	◈◈◈	Italian	$13-$49	134

EAST PALO ALTO

Map Page	Hotel	Diamond Rated	Member Savings	Page
㉒ p. 190	Four Seasons Hotel Silicon Valley at East Palo Alto	◈◈◈◈		72

Map Page	Restaurant	Diamond Rated	Cuisine	Price Range	Page
㉑ p. 190	Quattro Restaurant & Bar	◈◈◈◈	Italian	$20-$49	72

MOUNTAIN VIEW

Map Page	Hotels	Diamond Rated	Member Savings	Page
㉖ p. 190	**Hampton Inn & Suites by Hilton Mountain View/Silicon Valley**	◈◈◈	✔	160
㉗ p. 190	Residence Inn by Marriott-Palo Alto/Mountain View	◈◈◈	✔	160
㉘ p. 190	Holiday Inn Express Mountain View - S Palo Alto	◈◈◈		160
㉙ p. 190	**Hotel Strata**	◈◈◈	✔	160
㉚ p. 190	Hotel Vue	◈◈		160
㉛ p. 190	Extended Stay America-San Jose, Mountain View	◈◈		160
㉜ p. 190	Hotel Zico	◈◈		160
㉝ p. 190	Hilton Garden Inn Mountain View	◈◈◈	✔	160
㉞ p. 190	**Hotel Avante**	◈◈◈	✔	160
㉟ p. 190	**Best Western Crestview Hotel & Suites**	◈◈◈	✔	160

Map Page	Restaurants	Diamond Rated	Cuisine	Price Range	Page
㉔ p. 190	Tied House Brewery & Cafe	◈◈	American	$12-$24	161
㉕ p. 190	Ristorante Don Giovanni	◈◈◈	Italian	$10-$35	161
㉖ p. 190	Shalala	◈◈	Japanese	$8-$13	161
㉗ p. 190	Cascal	◈◈◈	Latin American Small Plates	$9-$31	161
㉘ p. 190	Scratch	◈◈◈	American	$12-$29	161

LOS ALTOS

Map Page	Hotels	Diamond Rated	Member Savings	Page
㊳ p. 190	Courtyard by Marriott-Palo Alto/Los Altos	◈◈◈	✔	126
㊴ p. 190	Residence Inn by Marriott-Palo Alto/Los Altos	◈◈◈	✔	126

Map Page	Restaurant	Diamond Rated	Cuisine	Price Range	Page
㉛ p. 190	Sumika	◈◈	Japanese	$9-$46	126

(See map & index p. 190.)

AMERICAS BEST VALUE INN - SKY RANCH INN
650/493-7221 **7**

Motel

Address: 4234 El Camino Real 94306
Location: US 101 exit San Antonio Rd, 2 mi w to SR 82, then 1 mi n. **Facility:** 28 units. 1-2 stories (no elevator), exterior corridors.

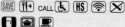

COUNTRY INN MOTEL
650/948-9154 **12**

Motel

Address: 4345 El Camino Real 94306
Location: US 101 exit San Antonio Rd, 2 mi w to SR 82, then just n. **Facility:** 27 units, some kitchens. 1-2 stories (no elevator), exterior corridors. **Pool:** heated outdoor. **Activities:** picnic facilities. **Featured Amenity: continental breakfast.**

CREEKSIDE INN
650/493-2411 **4**

Hotel

Address: 3400 El Camino Real 94306
Location: On SR 82, 0.3 mi s of Oregon Expwy/Page Mill Rd. **Facility:** 136 units, some efficiencies. 2-4 stories, interior/exterior corridors. **Amenities:** safes. **Pool:** heated outdoor. **Activities:** exercise room. **Guest Services:** valet and coin laundry, area transportation. **Featured Amenity: continental breakfast.**

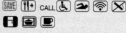

CROWNE PLAZA CABANA HOTEL
650/857-0787 **10**

Hotel. **Address:** 4290 El Camino Real 94306

DINAH'S GARDEN HOTEL
650/493-2844 **9**

Classic Hotel

Address: 4261 El Camino Real 94306
Location: US 101 exit San Antonio Rd, 2 mi s, then 0.4 mi n on SR 82. **Facility:** Beautifully landscaped gardens and waterways surround this property featuring unique pieces of art and a gazebo. The rooms vary in their own style, but all are large and feature luxurious beds. 129 units, some two bedrooms, efficiencies and kitchens. 1-3 stories, interior/exterior corridors. **Amenities:** safes. **Dining:** The Sea by Alexander's Steakhouse, see separate listing. **Pool:** heated outdoor. **Activities:** picnic facilities, exercise room. **Guest Services:** valet laundry, area transportation.

HILTON GARDEN INN PALO ALTO
650/843-0795 **6**

Contemporary Hotel. **Address:** 4216 El Camino Real 94306

AAA Benefit: Members save up to 15%!

HOMEWOOD SUITES PALO ALTO BY HILTON
650/559-8700 **11**

Extended Stay Contemporary Hotel. **Address:** 4329 El Camino Real 94306

AAA Benefit: Members save up to 15%!

HOTEL KEEN
650/327-2775 **1**

Hotel. **Address:** 425 High St 94301

THE PALO ALTO INN
650/493-4222 **8**

Hotel

Address: 4238 El Camino Real 94306
Location: US 101 exit San Antonio Rd, 2 mi w to SR 82, then 1 mi n. **Facility:** 24 units. 2 stories (no elevator), exterior corridors. **Amenities:** safes. **Guest Services:** coin laundry. **Featured Amenity: continental breakfast.**

SHERATON PALO ALTO HOTEL
650/328-2800 **2**

Hotel

SHERATON

AAA Benefit: Members save 5% or more!

Address: 625 El Camino Real 94301
Location: US 101 exit 402 (Embarcadero Rd/Oregon Expwy), 1.8 mi w, then just n on SR 82. Opposite Stanford University. **Facility:** 346 units. 4 stories, interior corridors. **Parking:** on-site (fee) and valet. **Amenities:** safes. **Pool:** heated outdoor. **Activities:** trails, exercise room. **Guest Services:** valet and coin laundry.

THE WESTIN PALO ALTO
650/321-4422 **3**

Hotel

WESTIN
HOTELS & RESORTS

AAA Benefit: Members save 5% or more!

Address: 675 El Camino Real 94301
Location: US 101 exit 402 (Embarcadero Rd/Oregon Expwy), 1.8 mi w, then just n on SR 82. Opposite Stanford University. **Facility:** Contemporary yet classic, this compact property's pool is situated in the gorgeously appointed courtyard. The rooms offer luxurious bedding and bathrooms with impressive dual fixture showers. 184 units. 5 stories, interior corridors. **Parking:** on-site (fee) and valet. **Amenities:** video games, safes. **Pool:** heated outdoor. **Activities:** hot tub, bicycles, trails, exercise room, massage. **Guest Services:** valet laundry, rental car service, area transportation.

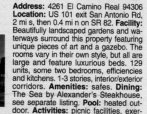

(See map & index p. 190.)

THE ZEN HOTEL
650/493-4492

Boutique Motel

Address: 4164 El Camino Real 94306 **Location:** US 101 exit Oregon Expwy/Page Mill Rd, 2 mi w to SR 82; at Maybell Ave. **Facility:** A contemporary and serene exterior accentuated by bamboo trees and Japanese maple greets you as you drive into the parking courtyard. Guest rooms feature modern décor and amenities. 37 units, some two bedrooms, efficiencies and kitchens. 1-2 stories (no elevator), exterior corridors. **Amenities:** safes. **Activities:** exercise room. **Guest Services:** valet and coin laundry. **Featured Amenity:** breakfast buffet.

[SAVE] [T+] CALL [&] [+] [BIZ] [wifi] [X] [] []
/ SOME UNITS []

WHERE TO EAT

BAUME 650/328-8899 (12)
New French. Fine Dining. **Address:** 201 S California Ave 94306

EVVIA ESTIATORIO 650/326-0983 (6)
Greek. Casual Dining. **Address:** 420 Emerson St 94301

THE FISH MARKET & TOP OF THE MARKET 650/493-9188
Seafood. Casual Dining. **Address:** 3150 El Camino Real 94306

HOWIE'S ARTISAN PIZZA 650/327-4992 (10)
Pizza. Casual Dining. **Address:** 855 El Camino Real, Suite 60 94301

JOYA RESTAURANT & LOUNGE 650/853-9800 (15)
Latin American. Casual Dining. **Address:** 339 University Ave 94301

LA BODEGUITA DEL MEDIO 650/326-7762 (13)
Cuban. Casual Dining. **Address:** 463 S California Ave 94306

LA STRADA RISTORANTE ITALIANO 650/324-8300 (4)
Italian. Casual Dining. **Address:** 335 University Ave 94301

LEMONADE 650/524-5028 (8)
California. Quick Serve. **Address:** 151 University Ave 94301

OREN'S HUMMUS SHOP 650/752-6492 (5)
Middle Eastern. Casual Dining. **Address:** 261 University Ave 94301

PARIS BAGUETTE 650/838-0404 (2)
Breads/Pastries Desserts. Quick Serve. **Address:** 383 University Ave 94301

P.F. CHANG'S CHINA BISTRO 650/330-1782 (7)
Chinese. Fine Dining. **Address:** 900 Stanford Shopping Center, Bldg W 94304

PIZZERIA DELFINA 650/353-2208 (9)
Italian Pizza. Casual Dining. **Address:** 651 Emerson St 94301

THE SEA BY ALEXANDER'S STEAKHOUSE
650/213-1111 (14)

Seafood Fine Dining
$43-$75

AAA Inspector Notes: This restaurant showcases unique dishes sure to please and surprise. Seafood items may include black sea bass with blue crab or grilled Maine lobster with shiitake mushrooms. Other menu choices include Wagyu beef and Prime tenderloin. The desserts, such as the delicious butterscotch crème brulee, are a work of art and should not be missed. The ambience is an enticing mix of upscale and fun. **Features:** full bar. **Reservations:** suggested. **Address:** 4269 El Camino Real 94306 **Location:** US 101 exit San Antonio Rd, 2 mi s, then 0.4 mi n on SR 82; adjacent to Dinah's Garden Hotel. **Parking:** on-site and valet.

[D] CALL [&]

SUNDANCE THE STEAKHOUSE 650/321-6798 (11)
Steak. Fine Dining. **Address:** 1921 El Camino Real 94306

TAMARINE RESTAURANT 650/325-8500 (1)
Vietnamese. Fine Dining. **Address:** 546 University Ave 94301

PARADISE (D-3) pop. 26,218, elev. 1,708'

It was gold that brought prospectors in search of their fortunes to this area in the foothills of the Sierra Nevada during California's gold rush. Although a 54-pound nugget was found nearby, the frenzy for gold eventually died down. Many miners stayed, however, establishing farms, orchards, sawmills and shops. Activities for visitors include nature trail hiking and biking, boating, fishing, gold panning and back-road excursions to old mining sites.

Paradise Ridge Chamber of Commerce and Visitors Bureau: 5550 Skyway 1, Paradise, CA 95969. **Phone:** (530) 877-9356.

PATTERSON pop. 20,413

BEST WESTERN PLUS VILLA DEL LAGO INN
209/892-5300

[fyi] **Hotel**

Best Western PLUS **AAA Benefit:** Members save up to 15% and earn bonus points!

Under major renovation, call for details. Last Rated: Address: 2959 Speno Dr 95363 **Location:** I-5 exit 434 (Sperry Ave), just ne. **Facility:** 82 units. 3 stories, interior corridors. **Pool:** outdoor. **Activities:** sauna, hot tub, exercise room. **Guest Services:** valet and coin laundry.

[SAVE] CALL [&] [] [+] [BIZ] [wifi]
[X] [] [] [] / SOME UNITS []

PEBBLE BEACH (G-2) elev. 12'
• Hotels & Restaurants map & index p. 144
• Part of Monterey Peninsula area — see map p. 141

17-MILE DRIVE can be entered through several gates off SRs 1 and 68; the Pacific Grove gate at Sunset Dr. and SR 68 and the Carmel gate on San Antonio Ave. are the n. and s. entrances, respectively. This winding road hugs the Monterey Peninsula coast as it traverses the private

(See map & index p. 144.)

gated community of Pebble Beach. Grandly scenic, it has plenty of places to pull off, park and admire the panoramic ocean views up close. You can also walk down to the beach from some of the parking areas.

Point Joe, where early seafarers often ran aground due to the erroneous belief that it was the entrance to Monterey Bay, is a good spot to take in the beauty of the rocky shoreline. Another good photo op is Bird Rock; just offshore, it's a favored gathering place for sea gulls and shore birds and also is occasionally visited by harbor seals and California sea lions.

The route's most famous landmark is the Lone Cypress. This solitary Monterey cypress, estimated to be more than 250 years old, stands atop a rocky outcrop that juts into the ocean. Monterey cypresses once had a much wider range but now grow in the wild at only two sheltered seaside locations—here and within Point Lobos State Natural Reserve *(see attraction listing p. 55)*. A bit farther on is Pescadero Point, where there are thick green carpets of fleshy-leaved ice plants, rounded rocks and lovely views of deep blue water.

Golf courses along the route—all but one of them private—include The Links at Spanish Bay, Spyglass Hill and the Pebble Beach Golf Links, where the final round of the ▽ AT&T Pebble Beach National Pro-Am is played in early February. The par-3 14th hole of the Dunes Course at the Monterey Peninsula Country Club is a stunner. Golfers aim for a pin that is literally at the ocean's edge; overshoot the green and your ball will end up in the drink or irretrievably lost in the craggy shoreline rocks.

Bicycles are permitted during daylight hours when no major sporting event is scheduled; no motorcycles or motorbikes are allowed. Bicyclists must enter through the Pacific Grove gate on weekends, holidays and during events. **Time:** Allow 2 hours minimum. **Hours:** Road open to visitors daily dawn-30 minutes before dusk. **Cost:** Toll charge $10.50 per car (cash only), which includes a map/brochure showing points of interest along the route. The fee is subtracted if visitors eat at a Pebble Beach restaurant and provide the toll receipt; the restaurant bill must total more than $35. **Phone:** (800) 654-9300.

CASA PALMERO   831/622-6650   62
▽▽ ▽▽ Resort Hotel. **Address:** 1518 Cypress Dr 93953

THE INN AT SPANISH BAY   831/647-7500   61
▽▽ ▽▽ Resort Hotel. **Address:** 2700 Seventeen Mile Dr 93953

THE LODGE AT PEBBLE BEACH   831/624-3811   63
▽▽ ▽▽ Resort Hotel. **Address:** 1700 Seventeen Mile Dr 93953

WHERE TO EAT

PEPPOLI AT PEBBLE BEACH   831/647-7433   35
▽▽▽ Italian. Fine Dining. **Address:** 2700 Seventeen Mile Dr 93953

ROY'S   831/647-7423   36
▽▽▽ Pacific Rim Fusion. Fine Dining. **Address:** 2700 Seventeen Mile Dr 93953

STILLWATER BAR & GRILL   831/625-8524   37
▽▽▽ Seafood. Dinner Theatre. **Address:** 1700 Seventeen Mile Dr 93953

PETALUMA (B-7) pop. 57,941, elev. 12'
• Hotels p. 196 • Restaurants p. 196
• Part of Wine Country area — see map p. 405

Three of California's oldest and best-preserved historic districts are in Petaluma. The Oakhill-Brewster Historic District, north and west of downtown, and the "A" Street Historic District, south and east of downtown, contain many carefully preserved 19th-century Victorian homes. The Petaluma Historic Commercial District, encompassing much of downtown, includes well-known landmarks like the Philip Sweed House (301 Keokuk St.), the United States Post Office (4th and D streets) and the Phoenix Theatre (201 Washington St.).

The Petaluma Adobe in Petaluma Adobe State Historic Park is one of the country's oldest adobe buildings. Experience this architectural legacy by taking one of the free, 1-hour guided walking tours organized by the Petaluma Historical Museum and led by a costumed docent. The tours are conducted on most Saturdays from May through October; for more information phone (707) 778-4398.

Farms, artisan food producers and wineries in this rich agricultural region offer a variety of tours, tastings and activities, from picking your own organic apples and tomatoes to bakery tours and garden walks. For information about area ranches and farm trails contact the Petaluma Visitor Center.

Petaluma and vicinity have appeared in such movies as "American Graffiti," "Peggy Sue Got Married" and "Mumford." Just 32 miles north of the Golden Gate Bridge, the city makes a convenient base to explore Sonoma County's wineries, towering redwoods and dramatic Pacific coastline, which includes Point Reyes National Seashore.

Stroll through Shollenberger Park, just off the S. McDowell Boulevard extension along the Petaluma River; many species of birds, animals, fish and plants can be seen at this wetlands preserve. The visitor center has a brochure as well as a list of bird species you might spot.

Petaluma Visitor Center: 210 Lakeville St., Petaluma, CA 94952. **Phone:** (707) 769-0429 or (877) 273-8258.

Self-guiding tours: Maps and brochures detailing a driving tour and a self-guiding walking tour of historic residential and commercial areas, film sites, heritage trees and wetland preserve areas can be obtained at the visitor center.

Shopping: Banana Republic, Gap, Nike, Saks Fifth Avenue OFF 5th, Tommy Hilfiger and Van Heusen are some of the 60 outlet stores to be found at Petaluma Village Premium Outlets, 2200 Petaluma Blvd. N.

GARDEN VALLEY RANCH is at 498 Pepper Rd. Self-guiding tours of this 10-acre ranch, which specializes in roses, include such areas of interest as the Fragrance Garden, Pond Garden, Shade Garden and flower borders. Rose arbors and a koi pond accent the property; the roses bloom May through October.

Time: Allow 1 hour minimum. **Hours:** Wed.-Sun. 10-4, mid-Jan. through Oct. 31. **Cost:** $5; free (ages 0-15). **Phone:** (707) 795-0919.

PETALUMA ADOBE STATE HISTORIC PARK, .7 mi. e. on Adobe Rd., preserves the large adobe ranch headquarters built by General Mariano Vallejo about 1836. Exhibits include furnished rooms, weaving tools, outdoor ovens, live animals and interpretive displays.

Time: Allow 1 hour minimum. **Hours:** Daily 10-5. Building closes at 4:30. Closed Jan. 1, Thanksgiving and Christmas. Phone ahead to confirm schedule. **Cost:** $3 (includes house); $2 (ages 6-17). **Phone:** (707) 762-4871.

BEST WESTERN PETALUMA INN   707/763-0994

Motel

 Best Western

AAA Benefit: Members save up to 15% and earn bonus points!

Address: 200 S McDowell Blvd 94954 **Location:** US 101 exit Washington St, just e. **Facility:** 73 units. 2 stories (no elevator), exterior corridors. **Pool:** heated outdoor. **Guest Services:** coin laundry. **Featured Amenity: continental breakfast.**

HAMPTON INN PETALUMA   707/397-0000

Hotel. **Address:** 450 Jefferson St 94952

AAA Benefit: Members save up to 15%!

SHERATON SONOMA COUNTY-PETALUMA   707/283-2888

Hotel. **Address:** 745 Baywood Dr 94954

AAA Benefit: Members save 5% or more!

WHERE TO EAT

BEYOND THE GLORY SPORTS BAR & GRILL   707/971-8366
American. Casual Dining. **Address:** 1371 McDowell Blvd 94954

CUCINA PARADISO   707/782-1130
Italian. Casual Dining. **Address:** 114 Petaluma Blvd N 94952

DELLA FATTORIA DOWNTOWN CAFE   707/763-0161
California. Casual Dining. **Address:** 141 Petaluma Blvd N 94952

PALMS GRILL   707/763-3333
American. Casual Dining. **Address:** 100 S McDowell Blvd 94954

SUGO TRATTORIA   707/782-9298
Italian. Casual Dining. **Address:** 5 Petaluma Blvd S 94952

PIERCY (C-1) elev. 622'
• Part of Wine Country area — see map p. 405

CAMPBELL BROS. CONFUSION HILL is 3 mi. s. on US 101. Designated a California State Point of Historical Interest, it's an experience in contradictory optical and physical sensations occurring in an apparently confused gravitational or magnetic field. In addition to the gravity house, a 1.25-mile, 30-minute round-trip miniature mountain train ride follows a route from redwood grove to hilltop and back, with the engineer providing information about the unique characteristics of coastal redwoods and pointing out historical logging artifacts along the way.

Time: Allow 1 hour minimum. **Hours:** Gravity house open daily 9-6, May-Sept.; 9-5, rest of year. Train rides require a minimum of four paying passengers and are on a first-come, first-served basis. Train operates daily 10:30-5 (weather permitting), Memorial Day weekend-Labor Day. **Cost:** Gravity house $5; $4 (ages 4-12). Train ride $10; $7.50 (ages 4-12). **Phone:** (707) 925-6456.

PINNACLES NATIONAL PARK (G-3)

Entered from the east via SR 146, 35 miles south of Hollister via SR 25, or 35 miles north of King City via CR G13, the park also can be approached from the west via SR 146, off US 101 in Soledad. Pinnacles National Park embraces about 24,000 acres of precipitous bluffs, spires and crags of colorful volcanic rock and a series of caves underneath the formations. The forces of heat, cold, water and wind have worn the contours of the rocky terrain.

The east entrance to the park is open daily 24 hours. The Pinnacles Visitor Center, in the campground at the east entrance to the park, is open daily 9:30-5, with possible extended hours in summer; phone (831) 389-4485. Bear Gulch Nature Center, accessible by car from the east entrance, is open daily 10-4, June-Dec.; Sat.-Sun. 10-4, rest of year (when staff is available). The west entrance, open 7:30 a.m.-8 p.m., has a ranger station; the entrance road is winding and narrow. Trailers and motor homes are advised to use the east entrance. No roads connect the east and west districts.

Pinnacles is strictly a hiking park, although some major formations can be seen from the roadway. The best viewing by car is from the west side. Hiking trails range from easy 1-mile treks to strenuous hikes of more than 10 miles. It also is popular with rock climbers, whose favorite spots include the Balconies and High Peaks.

The park is bisected from north to south by a 1,000-foot-high ridge. Most of the spire-shaped formations, some more than 600 feet high, are located on or alongside the ridge. This central backbone has been cut in two places by streams; huge fragments of rock have fallen into the resulting deep clefts, creating caves. Bear Gulch Cave and Balconies Cave require visitors to carry flashlights. Bear Gulch Cave is generally closed mid-May to mid-July and may be partially closed at other times; phone ahead for schedule.

Note: Neither pets nor bicycles are permitted on the trails. In parking lots, roads and picnic areas, pets must be kept leashed and under physical control; they cannot be left unattended in vehicles. Beware of poison oak.

In addition to geological and scenic interest, the park has an abundant deer and bird population and offers a vibrant display of spring wildflowers. The plant and animal species are characteristic of a coast range chaparral ecosystem. Picnic facilities are available. Admission is $30 per private vehicle, $25 per motorcyle or $15 per person for walk-in visitors (fees are valid for 7 days). Parking areas fill up early on weekends and during spring, the busiest season. Phone (831) 389-4486.

PINOLE pop. 18,390

DAYS INN PINOLE/NORTH BERKELEY   510/222-9400
▼▼ Motel. **Address:** 2600 Appian Way 94564

PITTSBURG pop. 63,264

HAMPTON INN & SUITES   925/473-1300
▼▼▼▼ (SAVE) Hotel. **Address:** 1201
California Ave 94565   **AAA Benefit:**
                             Members save up to
                             15%!

PLACERVILLE (E-4) pop. 10,389, elev. 1,860'
• **Hotels & Restaurants map & index p. 224**

Originally called Dry Diggin's, Placerville became so prosperous—and lawless—that criminals were hanged in pairs. This practice gave rise to a new name for the rough-and-tumble settlement, Hangtown. Located less than 10 miles from the site of the first gold discovery in California, Placerville's past is still evident in the restored late 19th-century architecture along downtown's Main Street.

The Fountain & Tallman Museum, 524 Main St., is in a building dating from 1852, the oldest in Placerville. It originally served as the settlement's soda works, providing bottled water to gold rush miners. Exhibits depict Placerville's early history as a mining outpost; phone (530) 626-0773.

El Dorado County Chamber of Commerce: 542 Main St., Placerville, CA 95667. **Phone:** (530) 621-5885 or (800) 457-6279.

EL DORADO COUNTY HISTORICAL MUSEUM is just n. of US 50 at 104 Placerville Dr., within the El Dorado County Fairgrounds. Exhibits feature ranching, logging, farming and mining equipment, a re-created country store, Studebaker wagons, a Shay locomotive and other railroad rolling stock. Changing exhibits also are presented, and a research library is on site.

Time: Allow 1 hour minimum. **Hours:** Wed.-Sat. 10-4, Sun. noon-4. Research library open Tues. 9-3 or by appointment. Closed Jan. 1, Thanksgiving, Christmas Eve and Christmas. **Cost:** Donations. **Phone:** (530) 621-5865.

HANGTOWN'S GOLD BUG PARK & MINE is 1 mi. n. off the US 50 Bedford Ave. exit, within Gold Bug Park. On the east side of the Mother Lode vein, the Gold Bug mine has wood floors and a 352-foot horizontal drift. Also in the 62-acre park are Hattie's Museum, which displays mining equipment, and the Hendy Stamp Mill and Museum, which shows how gold was extracted from quartz. Visitors can take a self-guiding tour using an audio wand, go hiking and pan for gemstones.

Time: Allow 30 minutes minimum. **Hours:** Mine, museum and stamp mill open daily 10-4, Apr.-Oct.; Sat.-Sun. noon-4, rest of year. **Cost:** $7; $4 (ages 3-17). Under 18 must be with an adult. Gem panning $2 per hour. Reservations are required for guided tours. **Phone:** (530) 642-5207. (GT) (AA)

BEST WESTERN PLUS PLACERVILLE INN
                                        530/622-9100

Hotel

(BW) Best Western PLUS   **AAA Benefit:** Members save up to 15% and earn bonus points!

Address: 6850 Green Leaf Dr 95667 **Location:** US 50 exit 44A (Missouri Flat Rd S), just sw. **Facility:** 105 units. 3 stories (no elevator), interior/exterior corridors. **Amenities:** safes. **Pool:** outdoor. **Activities:** hot tub, exercise room. **Guest Services:** coin laundry. **Featured Amenity:** full hot breakfast.

(SAVE) (11+) CALL (&) (≈) (+) (BIZ)
(⌐) (⊠) (🔒) (📷) (📺)

/ SOME UNITS (🐾)

EDEN VALE INN   530/621-0901 (51)
▼▼ ▼▼ Bed & Breakfast. **Address:** 1780 Springvale Rd 95667

WHERE TO EAT

CASA RAMOS   530/622-2303
▼▼ Mexican. Casual Dining. **Address:** 6840 Green Leaf Dr 95667

CASCADA   530/344-7757
▼▼ Mexican Fusion. Casual Dining. **Address:** 384 Main St 95667

HEYDAY CAFE   530/626-9700
▼▼ New American. Casual Dining. **Address:** 325 Main St 95667

INDEPENDENT RESTAURANT & BAR   530/344-7645
▼▼ New American. Casual Dining. **Address:** 629 Main St, Suite 102 95667

(See map & index p. 224.)

SWEETIE PIE'S   530/642-0128

 Breads/Pastries. Casual Dining. **Address:** 577 Main St 95667

PLEASANT HILL pop. 33,152

COURTYARD BY MARRIOTT-PLEASANT HILL   925/691-1444

 Hotel. **Address:** 2250 Contra Costa Blvd 94523

AAA Benefit: Members save 5% or more!

HYATT HOUSE PLEASANT HILL   925/934-3343

Extended Stay Hotel

HYATT house™

AAA Benefit: Members save up to 10%!

Address: 2611 Contra Costa Blvd 94523 **Location:** I-680 exit Monument Blvd southbound, just w, then just s. **Facility:** 142 efficiencies, some two bedrooms. 4 stories, interior corridors. **Pool:** heated outdoor. **Activities:** hot tub, exercise room. **Guest Services:** valet and coin laundry, area transportation. **Featured Amenity:** breakfast buffet.

RESIDENCE INN BY MARRIOTT-PLEASANT HILL   925/689-1010

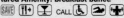 Extended Stay Hotel. **Address:** 700 Ellinwood Way 94523

AAA Benefit: Members save 5% or more!

WHERE TO EAT

BACK FORTY TEXAS BBQ ROADHOUSE AND SALOON   925/935-1440

 Barbecue. Casual Dining. **Address:** 100 Coggins Dr 94523

EL AGUILA MEXICAN CUISINE   925/682-4444

 Mexican. Casual Dining. **Address:** 1300 Contra Costa Blvd 94523

ZACHARY'S CHICAGO PIZZA   925/602-7000

 Pizza. Casual Dining. **Address:** 140 Crescent Dr 94523

PLEASANTON (D-9) pop. 70,285, elev. 352'

Downtown Pleasanton has a number of restored old buildings and houses. Stop by the Museum on Main at 603 Main St. for a crash course in regional history; phone (925) 462-2766. One of the nation's oldest racetracks is at the Alameda County Fairgrounds, off Pleasanton Avenue; it was built in 1858 by the sons of a Spanish don, Augustin Bernal. The presence of limestone in the soil is credited with making this an exceptionally fine track. For upcoming events information phone the events hotline at (925) 426-7559.

Shadow Cliffs Regional Recreation Area, on the outskirts of town, was developed from an abandoned gravel quarry. A lake in the park offers swimming, boating and fishing. *See Recreation Areas Chart.*

Pleasanton Chamber of Commerce: 777 Peters Ave., Pleasanton, CA 94566. **Phone:** (925) 846-5858.

BEST WESTERN PLUS PLEASANTON INN   925/463-1300

Hotel

 Best Western PLUS.

AAA Benefit: Members save up to 15% and earn bonus points!

Address: 5375 Owens Ct 94588 **Location:** I-580 exit 45 (Hopyard Rd/Dougherty Rd), just s on Hopyard Rd, just e on Owens Dr, then just n. Adjacent to freeway. ⊕ Dublin-Pleasanton, 34. **Facility:** 97 units. 3 stories, exterior corridors. **Pool:** outdoor. **Activities:** hot tub, exercise room. **Guest Services:** valet laundry. **Featured Amenity:** full hot breakfast.

COURTYARD BY MARRIOTT PLEASANTON   925/463-1414

Hotel

COURTYARD

AAA Benefit: Members save 5% or more!

Address: 5059 Hopyard Rd 94588 **Location:** I-580 exit 45 (Hopyard Rd/Dougherty Rd), 0.5 mi s; just n of jct Stoneridge Dr. ⊕ Dublin-Pleasanton, 34. **Facility:** 145 units. 3 stories, interior corridors. **Parking:** on-site (fee). **Pool:** heated outdoor. **Activities:** exercise room. **Guest Services:** valet and coin laundry, boarding pass kiosk.

DOUBLETREE BY HILTON PLEASANTON AT THE CLUB 925/463-8000

 Hotel. **Address:** 7050 Johnson Dr 94588

AAA Benefit: Members save up to 15%!

FOUR POINTS BY SHERATON   925/460-8800

Hotel

FOUR POINTS BY SHERATON

AAA Benefit: Members save 5% or more!

Address: 5115 Hopyard Rd 94588 **Location:** I-580 exit 45 (Hopyard Rd/Dougherty Rd), just s; between Owens and Gibraltar drs. ⊕ Dublin-Pleasanton, 34. **Facility:** 214 units. 2 stories (no elevator), interior corridors. **Parking:** on-site (fee). **Dining:** Faz, see separate listing. **Pool:** heated outdoor. **Activities:** hot tub, bicycles, exercise room. **Guest Services:** valet laundry, area transportation.

HYATT HOUSE PLEASANTON
925/730-0070

Extended Stay Hotel

AAA Benefit: Members save up to 10%!

Address: 4545 Chabot Dr 94588 **Location:** I-580 exit 45 (Hopyard Rd/Dougherty Rd), 1 mi s on Hopyard Rd, just e on Stoneridge Dr, then just s. Located in a business park. Dublin-Pleasanton, 34. **Facility:** 128 kitchen units, some two bedrooms. 3 stories (no elevator), exterior corridors. **Pool:** heated outdoor. **Activities:** hot tub, exercise room. **Guest Services:** valet and coin laundry, area transportation. **Featured Amenity:** breakfast buffet.

LARKSPUR LANDING PLEASANTON
925/463-1212

Hotel

Address: 5535 Johnson Dr 94588 **Location:** I-580 exit 45 (Hopyard Rd/Dougherty Rd), just s on Hopyard Rd, just w on Owens Dr, then just n. Dublin-Pleasanton, 34. **Facility:** 123 efficiencies, some two bedrooms. 4 stories, interior corridors. **Activities:** exercise room. **Guest Services:** complimentary and valet laundry, area transportation. **Featured Amenity:** continental breakfast.

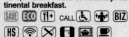

PLEASANTON MARRIOTT
925/847-6000

Hotel

AAA Benefit: Members save 5% or more!

Address: 11950 Dublin Canyon Rd 94588 **Location:** I-580 exit 44A (San Ramon Rd/Foothill Rd), just s, then just w. West Dublin & Pleasanton, 33. **Facility:** 245 units. 6 stories, interior corridors. **Amenities:** safes. **Pool:** heated outdoor. **Activities:** hot tub, exercise room. **Guest Services:** valet laundry, boarding pass kiosk, area transportation.

RESIDENCE INN BY MARRIOTT
925/227-0500

(fyi)

Extended Stay Hotel

Residence INN. AAA Benefit: Members save 5% or more!

Under major renovation, call for details. **Last Rated:** ♥♥♥ **Address:** 11920 Dublin Canyon Rd 94588 **Location:** I-580 exit 44A (San Ramon Rd/Foothill Rd), just s, then just w. West Dublin & Pleasanton, 33. **Facility:** 135 units, some two bedrooms, efficiencies and kitchens. 2-3 stories, interior corridors. **Terms:** check-in 4 pm. **Pool:** heated outdoor. **Activities:** hot tub, exercise room. **Guest Services:** valet and coin laundry, area transportation. **Featured Amenity:** full hot breakfast.

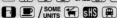

THE ROSE HOTEL   925/846-8802

♥♥♥♥ Hotel. **Address:** 807 Main St 94566

WHERE TO EAT

ANDY & YU'S   925/750-8888

♥♥♥ Chinese. Casual Dining. **Address:** 348 St Mary St 94566

BLUE AGAVE CLUB   925/417-1224

♥♥ Mexican. Casual Dining. **Address:** 625 Main St 94566

DE LA TORRE'S TRATTORIA   925/484-3878

♥♥ Italian. Casual Dining. **Address:** 6025 W Las Positas Blvd 94588

FAZ   925/460-0444

♥♥ Mediterranean. Casual Dining. **Address:** 5121 Hopyard Rd 94588

THE HOPYARD AMERICAN ALEHOUSE & GRILL   925/426-9600

♥♥ American. Casual Dining. **Address:** 3015-H Hopyard Rd 94588

THE HUNAN CHEF CHINESE RESTAURANT   925/484-0480

♥♥ Chinese. Casual Dining. **Address:** 4285 Valley Ave 94566

PLAYERS RESTAURANT   925/463-8000

♥♥ American. Casual Dining. **Address:** 7050 Johnson Dr 94588

SENRO SUSHI   925/600-8040

♥♥ Japanese Sushi. Casual Dining. **Address:** 30 W Neal St 94566

STRIZZI'S   925/484-9600

♥♥ Italian. Casual Dining. **Address:** 649 Main St 94566

PLUMAS NATIONAL FOREST (C-3)

Elevations in the forest range from 1,000 ft. at Feather River Canyon to 8,372 ft. at the summit of Mount Ingalls. Refer to AAA maps for additional elevation information.

Plumas National Forest covers 1,162,863 acres in northern California, straddling the transition zone between two of the West's great mountain ranges, the Sierra Nevada and the Cascades. Although the Sierra block disappears under the younger volcanic rock of the Cascades on the forest's northern boundary near Lake Almanor, it is difficult to tell where one range ends and the other begins.

The mountains of the northern Sierra Nevada, which make up most of the forest lands, are neither as high nor as spectacular as those south of Lake Tahoe. Yet within these mountains are a history of hidden treasure and a wealth of scenery.

The forest's principal gem is the Feather River watershed. The Feather River has carved numerous canyons and ravines full of cascades and white water. Portions of the Middle Fork of the river and three of its tributaries have been designated Feather Falls Scenic Area. The centerpiece of this 15,000-acre scenic area is 640-foot Feather Falls, which is just above Lake Oroville and is the highest of the numerous waterfalls on the 93-mile-long Middle Fork of the Feather River—a designated wild and scenic river. Water from this forest creates the headwaters for the California state water system.

Because of the rugged terrain and dangerous rapids, canoeing and tubing are recommended only in the recreation zone. Hiking trails and campgrounds are located along the river. Near the headwaters of the South Fork is Little Grass Valley Lake Recreation Area, which offers swimming, fishing and camping.

An extensive network of roads crisscrosses the national forest. Routes such as the Feather River National Scenic Byway, which crosses the lowest pass in the Sierra Nevada, are a legacy of the gold rush era when towns like Rich Bar, Pulga and La Porte were flourishing mining camps. Anglers and hikers have replaced miners, frequenting such popular areas as Bucks Lake, Lake Davis, Frenchman Lake and Antelope Lake. Seventy-one miles of the Pacific Crest Trail run through the national forest.

Information about campgrounds and recreational opportunities is available at the District Ranger stations and the Forest Headquarters in Quincy. Maps and guides to the Pacific Crest Trail and the Feather Falls Scenic Area also are available at the headquarters. For more information contact Plumas National Forest, 159 Lawrence St., Quincy, CA 95971; phone (530) 283-2050. *See Recreation Areas Chart.*

PLYMOUTH pop. 1,005, elev. 1,086'

SHENANDOAH INN   209/245-4491
♥♥ Hotel. **Address:** 17674 Village Dr 95669

WHERE TO EAT

TASTE   209/245-3463
♥♥♥ California. Fine Dining. **Address:** 9402 Main St 95669

POINT ARENA (E-1) pop. 449, elev. 220'
• Part of Wine Country area — see map p. 405

B. BRYAN PRESERVE is in the center of town at 130 Riverside Dr. This 100-acre private reserve is a refuge for hoofed mammals native to Africa, many of them on the endangered species list. Zebras, giraffes and antelopes roam in large, open fields in a near-natural environment, offering an opportunity to view them at close range. An introductory talk precedes the guided tour. Visitors also can feed baby animals housed in a barn.

Fog and wind can descend on the area unexpectedly and within minutes; bring a jacket and wear comfortable walking shoes. The terrain may be muddy during winter months. **Time:** Allow 1 hour, 30 minutes minimum. **Hours:** Tours daily at 9:30 and 4, Mar.-Oct.; 9:30 and 3:30, rest of year. **Cost:** Guided tour fee $35; $20 (ages 0-10). Advance reservations are required and must be guaranteed with a credit card; payment by cash is preferred. **Phone:** (707) 882-2297.

BOWLING BALL BEACH is about 2.5 mi. s., accessible via the parking area at jct. SR 1 and Schooner Gulch Rd. The small paved lot, on the ocean side of SR 1, is easy to miss and is marked with a sign saying "Park facing south only." You can follow two dirt trails to the ocean; the trail at the south end of the lot leads to Schooner Gulch Beach, while the trail at the north end provides access to Bowling Ball Beach.

Getting to Bowling Ball Beach is a bit of an adventure. At the end of the north trail is a 10 to 15-foot, nearly vertical descent to the beach by way of wood steps anchored to a cliffside by cables. After climbing down these steps you must carefully cross a mishmash of logs and rocks, some solidly buried in the sand and others loosely anchored in water (watch your step). You then walk north (toward the right) along the beach. The bowling ball rocks are a quarter of a mile or so from the wood steps, about a 10-minute walk.

These round, smooth stones are situated in what appear to be diagonal rows and present a curious sight along the otherwise empty beach. Geologically speaking, they are known as concretions—hard, compact masses of sedimentary rock that often are spherical in shape. The rocks are submerged at high tide; check the tide schedule for Point Arena online before setting out on this trip and plan to arrive during low tide.

In addition to beachcombing—at low tide the beach is wide and flat—there also are spectacular panoramic views from the bluffs overlooking Schooner Gulch Beach (accessible via the north trail).

Use caution when pulling out of the parking lot, as blind curves can obscure approaching vehicles; if you intend to drive north when leaving, head south first and turn around rather than trying to make a U-turn out of the lot, or park along the inland side of SR 1 near the Schooner Gulch Road intersection.

Note: The steps descending to the beach at the end of the northern trail remain closed due to erosion. They are scheduled to be repaired, but the reopening date is unknown; phone ahead for updates. Visitors can take the southern trail to Schooner Gulch Beach and then walk north toward Bowling Ball Beach; depending on the time of year it may be necessary to negotiate around piles of driftwood. **Time:** Allow 1 hour minimum. **Hours:** Daily during daylight hours. **Cost:** Free. **Phone:** (707) 937-5804.

POINT REYES NATIONAL SEASHORE
(C-6)
• Part of San Francisco area — see map p. 243

Just 22 miles north of San Francisco in Marin County, Point Reyes National Seashore is noted not only for a wealth of scenic vistas but for its remarkable biological diversity. This protected reserve has it all: ocean waves crashing against rocky headlands; mile after mile of wide, sandy beaches; open grasslands and brush-covered hillsides; freshwater lakes and saltwater estuaries; dense woodlands aromatic with the scent of pine.

The national seashore's 71,000 acres are along and west of SR 1. The Point Reyes peninsula is a well-defined geological area that was created by a rift zone of the San Andreas Fault; a portion of the peninsula lies below sea level, forming Tomales Bay.

Grass-tufted dunes line the wild coastal beaches; some are wide open while others are more secluded, edging tucked-away coves backed by rocky cliffs. Inland are rolling hills, lush meadows and Inverness Ridge, cloaked with towering stands of Douglas fir. Nearly 450 species of birds have been spotted within Point Reyes. The approximately 80 resident wildlife species range from diminutive (the California tortoiseshell butterfly) to impressively large (the northern elephant seal).

Point Reyes also is a protected haven for tule elk, one of two subspecies of elk native to California. The mammals were on the brink of extinction in the 1870s before a conservation-minded rancher had the foresight to protect a surviving herd on his ranch near Bakersfield. Subsequent preservation efforts were successful, and today free-ranging tule elk can be seen in such wilderness areas as the Tomales Point grasslands.

The park headquarters is at Bear Valley, half a mile west of Olema, the hamlet that is Point Reyes' unofficial gateway. The Bear Valley Visitor Center on Bear Valley Road provides information about Point Reyes facilities and has exhibits depicting the park's ecosystems and cultural heritage, including a seismograph and a touch table. Reservations for backcountry camping and beach fire permits can be obtained here. Many trailheads for park hikes are located nearby. The center is open Mon.-Fri. 10-4:30, Sat.-Sun. and holidays 9-4:30, with reduced hours in winter. Closed Christmas. Phone (415) 464-5100.

Near the park headquarters are three points of interest: the Morgan Horse Ranch, a working ranch with exhibits about the breed; Kule Loklo, a replica of a Coast Miwok Indian village; and Pierce Ranch, a former dairy ranch with self-guiding trail exhibits. At the end of Mesa Road is Point Blue's Palomarin Field Station. Bird-banding demonstrations are given Tuesday through Sunday mornings from sunrise to noon, May 1 through Thanksgiving; Wednesday, Saturday and Sunday mornings, rest of year.

The Earthquake Trail begins at the Bear Valley Picnic Area, across from the visitor center. This short paved loop explores an area within the San Andreas Fault zone. Interpretive signs describe the geological forces at work, and a section of fence that moved 16 feet from its original location during the 1906 San Francisco earthquake is a sobering example of their power. You might also spot the occasional mule deer drinking from a creek that runs along part of the trail.

The Lighthouse Visitor Center, at the end of Sir Frances Drake Boulevard, has exhibits about wildflowers, whales, seals, birds and maritime history. From the parking lot it is a .4-mile, mostly uphill walk to the building. Open Fri.-Mon. 10-4:30. Closed Christmas. Phone (415) 669-1534.

The Kenneth C. Patrick Visitor Center, off Sir Frances Drake Boulevard at Drakes Beach, is open Sat.-Sun. and holidays 9:30-4:30, Dec. 26 through mid-Apr. (staffing permitting). Phone (415) 669-1250 for updated information.

Point Reyes Lighthouse shares the rocky headland with the Lighthouse Visitor Center. Visitors must descend 300 narrow steps from an observation deck to reach the oceanfront beacon, built in 1870. The lens room is open Fri.-Mon. 2:30-4 (weather and staffing permitting). The stairs to the lighthouse are closed if sustained winds exceed 40 mph.

Hiking, beachcombing and bird-watching are all outstanding. Nearly 150 miles of hiking and horseback riding trails fan out from Bear Valley. Some 35 miles of trails also are open to bicyclists; trail maps are available at the visitor centers. Pets are not permitted on any trails (with the exception of the Kehoe Beach Trail) or at campgrounds. Leashed pets are permitted at Kehoe Beach (north of the Kehoe Beach Trail), Limantour Beach (southeast of the parking lot, adjacent to Coast Camp) and at Point Reyes/Great Beach (from the North Beach parking lot to the south).

Hikes within Point Reyes National Seashore vary from easy jaunts of less than a mile to strenuous treks that can take all day, depending on the terrain. The Woodpecker Trail is a short loop that explores Bear Valley's forest and meadow habitats, with interpretive signs describing plant and animal life. The trail begins at the Bear Valley trailhead (south end of the Bear Valley parking lot).

The 1.6-mile Chimney Rock Trail offers spectacular views of Drakes Bay and the ocean, with rocky cliffs dropping off steeply to the water below. The spring wildflower display is renowned, and from January through May it's possible to spot migrating gray whales. This hike is challenging if the weather is foggy or windy. It begins at the Chimney Rock trailhead near the Point Reyes Lighthouse (a 45-minute drive from the Bear Valley Visitor Center).

Abbott's Lagoon is a 2-mile stroll through open grasslands and coastal scrub. Spring wildflowers are plentiful and bird-watching is excellent, particularly in the fall and winter. The trailhead is a 25-minute drive from the Bear Valley Visitor Center via Sir Francis Drake Boulevard and Pierce Point Road.

Point Reyes beaches are spread out over a wide area, and getting from one to another can take upward of half an hour. If you're just visiting for the afternoon or the day, focus on one or two beaches; staff at the Bear Valley Visitor Center can offer suggestions.

Limantour Beach is a long, narrow spit of sand where numerous shorebirds feed at the water's edge and in the nearby wetlands. Harbor seals bob in the gentle surf or bask in the sun. McClures Beach, reached by a short, steep downhill hike, is backed by a small cove with a jumble of rocks at either end; the crashing surf here is dramatic. Great Beach, also known as Point Reyes Beach, is an 11-mile expanse of pristine, undeveloped shoreline where the surf can also be heavy.

Note: At these and other beaches, especially those that face the open ocean, exercise caution when venturing near the water. "Sneaker waves"—unexpectedly large waves that can reach much farther up the beach—have the ability to catch people in rip currents and quickly pull them out to deep water.

Various ranger-led programs take place throughout the year, and there are four hike-in campgrounds. Permits can be obtained at the Bear Valley Visitor Center; phone (877) 444-6777 for camping reservations. Camping is $20 per night for up to six people; reservations are highly recommended on weekends and in summer. Hikers and campers should carry a canteen, since the stream water is not potable.

The national seashore is open all year. All sites are closed Christmas. Admission is free. For additional information contact the Superintendent, Point Reyes National Seashore, 1 Bear Valley Rd., Point Reyes, CA 94956; phone (415) 464-5100. *See Recreation Areas Chart.*

POLLOCK PINES pop. 6,871

BEST WESTERN STAGECOACH INN   530/644-2029

Motel

Best Western.

AAA Benefit: Members save up to 15% and earn bonus points!

Address: 5940 Pony Express Tr 95726 **Location:** US 50 exit 57 (Pollock Pines) eastbound, just n, then 1 mi e; exit Sly Park Rd westbound, just n, then 1 mi w. **Facility:** 26 units. 2 stories (no elevator), exterior corridors. **Terms:** check-in 4 pm. **Pool:** heated outdoor. **Featured Amenity:** breakfast buffet.

 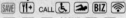

RANCHO CORDOVA pop. 64,776, elev. 90'
• Hotels & Restaurants map & index p. 224

BEST WESTERN PLUS RANCHO CORDOVA INN
916/631-7500

Hotel

Best Western PLUS.

AAA Benefit: Members save up to 15% and earn bonus points!

Address: 10713 White Rock Rd 95670 **Location:** US 50 exit 17 (Zinfandel Dr), just s, then just w. **Facility:** 105 units. 3 stories, interior/exterior corridors. **Pool:** heated outdoor. **Activities:** exercise room. **Guest Services:** valet and coin laundry. **Featured Amenity:** breakfast buffet.

COURTYARD BY MARRIOTT SACRAMENTO/RANCHO CORDOVA   916/638-3800
Hotel. **Address:** 10683 White Rock Rd 95670

AAA Benefit: Members save 5% or more!

DOUBLETREE SUITES BY HILTON SACRAMENTO-RANCHO CORDOVA   916/638-4141

Hotel

DOUBLETREE BY HILTON

AAA Benefit: Members save up to 15%!

Address: 11260 Point East Dr 95742 **Location:** US 50 exit 18 (Sunrise Blvd), just s, e on Folsom Blvd, then just n. Located near light rail. **Facility:** 158 units, some two bedrooms. 3 stories, interior corridors. **Amenities:** safes. **Pool:** heated outdoor. **Activities:** hot tub, exercise room. **Guest Services:** valet laundry, area transportation.

FAIRFIELD INN & SUITES BY MARRIOTT   916/858-8680
Hotel. **Address:** 10745 Gold Center Dr 95670

AAA Benefit: Members save 5% or more!

HAMPTON INN BY HILTON   916/638-4800
Hotel. **Address:** 10755 Gold Center Dr 95670

AAA Benefit: Members save up to 15%!

HOLIDAY INN RANCHO CORDOVA   916/635-4040

Hotel

Address: 11269 Point East Dr 95742 **Location:** US 50 exit 18 (Sunrise Blvd), just s, e on Folsom Blvd, then just n. Located near light rail. **Facility:** 119 units. 3 stories, interior corridors. **Pool:** outdoor. **Activities:** sauna, hot tub, exercise room. **Guest Services:** complimentary and valet laundry.

(See map & index p. 224.)

HYATT PLACE SACRAMENTO/RANCHO CORDOVA
916/635-4799 **73**

Hotel

HYATT PLACE

AAA Benefit: Members save up to 10%!

Address: 10744 Gold Center Dr 95670 **Location:** U5 50 exit 17 (Zinfandel Dr), just s, just e on White Rock Rd, just n on Prospect Park Dr, then just w. **Facility:** 127 units. 6 stories, interior corridors. **Pool:** heated outdoor. **Activities:** exercise room. **Guest Services:** valet laundry, area transportation. **Featured Amenity:** breakfast buffet. (See ad p. 234.)

SAVE ▯▯ ▯ CALL ▯ ▯ ▯ BIZ 🛜 ✕ ▯ ▯ ▯ / SOME UNITS ▯ HS

RESIDENCE INN BY MARRIOTT
916/851-1550 **70**

▼▼▼ SAVE Extended Stay Hotel.
Address: 2779 Prospect Park Dr 95670

AAA Benefit: Members save 5% or more!

SACRAMENTO MARRIOTT RANCHO CORDOVA
916/638-1100 **69**

Hotel

MARRIOTT

AAA Benefit: Members save 5% or more!

Address: 11211 Point East Dr 95742 **Location:** US 50 exit 18 (Sunrise Blvd), just s, then just e. **Facility:** 265 units. 11 stories, interior corridors. **Pool:** heated outdoor. **Activities:** hot tub, exercise room. **Guest Services:** complimentary and valet laundry, boarding pass kiosk. (See ad p. 233.)

SAVE ECO ▯▯ ▯ ▯ CALL ▯ ▯ ▯ BIZ 🛜 ✕ ▯ ▯ ▯ / SOME UNITS SHS

WHERE TO EAT

BROOKFIELDS 916/638-2046 **100**
▼▼ American. Casual Dining. **Address:** 11135 Folsom Blvd 95670

CATTLEMENS 916/985-3030
▼▼ Steak. Casual Dining. **Address:** 12409 Folsom Blvd 95670

FAMOUS BURGERS 916/476-6192 **102**
▼ Burgers. Quick Serve. **Address:** 3101 Zinfandel Dr 95670

GRILLS & GREENS 916/853-2265 **101**
▼ Mediterranean. Quick Serve. **Address:** 3040 Sunrise Blvd 95742

IL FORNO CLASSICO 916/858-0651 **99**
▼▼ Italian. Casual Dining. **Address:** 2121 Golden Centre Ln 95670

RED BLUFF (C-2) pop. 14,076, elev. 304'
• Restaurants p. 204

Named for the red-hued sand and gravel cliffs characteristic of the surrounding area, Red Bluff is a gateway to Lassen Volcanic National Park (see place listing p. 122).

The area's Western heritage is remembered each April at the ▼ Red Bluff Round-Up. In addition to a traditional rodeo, attendees enjoy a parade, wild horse races, a chili cook-off and live entertainment.

Red Bluff-Tehama County Chamber of Commerce: 100 Main St., P.O. Box 850, Red Bluff, CA 96080. **Phone:** (530) 527-6220.

SALMON VIEWING PLAZA, .1 mi. e. of I-5 exit 649 on SR 36, then 2 mi. s. on Sale Ln., is at Diversion Dam on the Sacramento River. Underwater television cameras monitor the fish ladders. There is no viewing mid-September to mid-May. The plaza has exhibits about salmon as well as camping, picnicking and boat-launching facilities.

Hours: Viewing plaza open daily 6 a.m.-8 p.m., mid-May through Aug. 31. River ramp closed in Aug. **Cost:** Free. **Phone:** (530) 527-3043, (530) 527-2813 for camping information, or (530) 527-1196 for the Discovery Center. ▲ ▯

WILLIAM B. IDE ADOBE STATE HISTORIC PARK, 1 mi. n. on Adobe Rd., has an 1850 adobe that is a memorial to the founder and president of the short-lived California Republic. In 1846 rumors that Mexican authorities were about to expel American settlers compelled Ide to join a band of settlers in the Bear Flag Revolt. Subsequently, California became an independent country with Ide as its president for 24 days until the Mexican War began and the area was occupied by U.S. troops.

Hours: Park open daily dawn-dusk. Visitor center open Fri.-Sun. 10-4 when staff is available. Phone ahead to confirm schedule. **Cost:** Day use $6 per private vehicle; $5 (ages 62+ per private vehicle). **Phone:** (530) 529-8599. ▯

BEST WESTERN ANTELOPE INN
530/527-8882

Hotel

 Best Western.

AAA Benefit: Members save up to 15% and earn bonus points!

Address: 203 Antelope Blvd 96080 **Location:** I-5 exit 649 (SR 36), just e. **Facility:** 65 units. 2 stories (no elevator), interior corridors. **Pool:** outdoor. **Activities:** exercise room. **Guest Services:** coin laundry. **Featured Amenity:** full hot breakfast.

SAVE ▯ ▯▯ CALL ▯ ▯ ▯ BIZ 🛜 ✕ ▯ ▯ ▯ / SOME UNITS ▯ HS

COMFORT INN 530/529-7060
▼▼ Hotel. **Address:** 90 Sale Ln 96080

HAMPTON INN & SUITES   530/529-4178

Hotel

AAA Benefit:
Members save up to
15%!

Address: 520 Adobe Rd 96080 **Location:** I-5 exit 650 (Adobe Rd), just w. **Facility:** 97 units. 3 stories, interior corridors. **Pool:** heated outdoor. **Activities:** exercise room. **Guest Services:** coin laundry. **Featured Amenity:** breakfast buffet.

[SAVE] CALL [&] [↗] [♿] [BIZ] [📶]
[✕] [🛏] [📺] [💻] /SOME UNITS [HS]

HOLIDAY INN EXPRESS & SUITES RED BLUFF-SOUTH
REDDING AREA   530/528-1600
[♦♦♦] Hotel. **Address:** 2810 Main St 96080

WHERE TO EAT

CASA RAMOS   530/527-2684
[♦][♦] Mexican. Casual Dining. **Address:** 2001 N Main St 96080

CHINA DOLL CHINESE RESTAURANT   530/529-1981
[♦][♦] Chinese. Casual Dining. **Address:** 182 Main St 96080

FROM THE HEARTH CAFE-RED BLUFF   530/727-0616
[♦] American. Quick Serve. **Address:** 638 Washington St 96080

GREEN BARN STEAKHOUSE   530/527-3161
[♦][♦] Steak Seafood. Casual Dining. **Address:** 5 Chestnut Ave 96080

LOS MARIACHIS   530/529-5154
[♦][♦] Mexican. Casual Dining. **Address:** 604 Main St 96080

LUIGI'S PIZZA AND PASTA   530/527-9227
[♦] Pizza. Quick Serve. **Address:** 75 Belle Mill Rd 96080

NEW ASIAN RESTAURANT   530/529-9888
[♦][♦] Chinese. Casual Dining. **Address:** 628 Main St 96080

REDCREST pop. 89

REDCREST RESORT   707/722-4208

[♦♦]
Cabin

Address: 26459 Ave of the Giants 95569 **Location:** US 101 exit 667 (Redcrest), just e, then just n. **Facility:** 11 cabins. 1 story, exterior corridors. *Bath:* shower only. **Terms:** check-in 4 pm. **Amenities:** safes. **Activities:** hot tub, playground, lawn sports.

 [SAVE] [📶] [✕] [🎿] [🅿] [🛏] [📺]
[💻] /SOME UNITS [🔥]

REDDING (C-2) pop. 89,861, elev. 560'
• Hotels p. 206 • Restaurants p. 208

Redding, in the center of a year-round recreation area, provides scenic access via I-5 to the surrounding Shasta-Trinity National Forests *(see place listing p. 379)* and Whiskeytown-Shasta-Trinity National Recreation Area *(see place listing p. 402).*

The Sundial Bridge at Turtle Bay crosses the Sacramento River in the center of town and serves as both a local landmark and as a connector to hiking and bicycling trails, including the Sacramento River National Recreation Trail, an 11-mile path that runs along both sides of the Sacramento River. There are scenic views of the river from benches along the shady trail. Trail users might catch a glimpse of beavers, otters, turtles and deer.

Clear Creek Greenway, 5 miles south on Market Street (SR 273) and then west on Clear Creek Road, is a 6-mile network of gravel trails used by hikers, bikers and horseback riders. Trailheads are located at Gold Dredge, Honeybee, Clear Creek Gorge and Horsetown Clear Creek Preserve. At Clear Creek Gorge a short hike around the rim trail leads to great views into the canyon; an overlook and salmon viewing platform enables visitors to view the fall run of Chinook salmon spawning in the creek below, which reaches its peak in October and November. Phone (530) 224-2100.

Redding Convention & Visitors Bureau: 1448 Pine St., Redding, CA 96001. **Phone:** (530) 225-4100 or (800) 874-7562. *(See ad p. 205.)*

SHASTA DAM—see Shasta Lake p. 378.

[GEM] **SHASTA STATE HISTORIC PARK**—see Shasta p. 378.

[GEM] **TURTLE BAY EXPLORATION PARK** is off SR 44W (Sundial Bridge Dr.), then n. to the park entrance. This 300-acre interpretive park explores the region's people, cultures and natural resources. The glass-decked Sundial Bridge connects the park's two campuses.

In addition to the Turtle Bay Museum, Paul Bunyan's Forest Camp and Parrot Playhouse, there's an aquarium, an arboretum, botanical gardens, animal exhibits and shows, a boardwalk and changing exhibits. On site is the Monolith, the remains of the aggregate plant that processed gravel used to make concrete for the construction of nearby Shasta Dam in the early 1940s. Segway tours of the park are offered as well.

Hours: Complex open Mon.-Fri. 9-5, Sat.-Sun. 10-5, May 1-early Sept.; Wed.-Fri. 9-4, Sat.-Sun. 10-4, rest of year. Closed Jan. 1, Thanksgiving and Christmas. Phone ahead to confirm schedule. **Cost:** $16.50 (includes arboretum, gardens, forest camp, museum and Parrot Playhouse); $12.50 (ages 4-15 and 65+); $6.50 (ages 65+ on Wed.); free (ages 0-3 and active military and up to five family members with ID). Reduced admission ($5 off) daily 3:30-closing. Admission on the 5th and 10th of the month when the park is open $10; $5 (ages 4-15 and 65+). An additional fee may be charged for special exhibits. **Phone:** (530) 243-8850. [🍴] [⊞]

McConnell Arboretum & Botanical Gardens is accessible from Turtle Bay Exploration Park's east entrance at the north plaza of the Sundial Bridge and from the west entrance of the park off Arboretum Dr. The 200-acre arboretum features 1.5 miles of trails through an oak savanna and a riparian forest, while the 20-acre botanical gardens consist of 12 areas, including gardens representing the Mediterranean basin, California, Australia, South Africa and Chile.

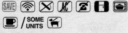

Among the other gardens are an area especially for children and one devoted to medicinal plants. **Hours:** Daily 8-dusk. Closed Jan. 1, Thanksgiving and Christmas. **Cost:** Included with Turtle Bay Exploration Park fee. Free admission for arboretum and gardens only.

Parrot Playhouse is in the Paul Bunyan's Forest Camp section of Turtle Bay Exploration Park. This walk-through aviary is inhabited by Australian lorikeets that perch on your arms, head and hands in exchange for a sip from a cup of nectar. An attendant is on hand to answer questions about these colorful, playful members of the parrot family and will also provide a towel for cleanup if you happen to get hit by droppings released by one of the free-flying birds. **Hours:** Mon.-Fri. 9:30-11:45 and 1-park closing; Sat.-Sun. 10:30-11:45 and 1-park closing. Closed Jan. 1, Thanksgiving, Christmas and Mon.-Tues. during the winter months. **Cost:** Included with Turtle Bay Park admission. Nectar $1 per cup. **Phone:** (530) 243-8850.

Paul Bunyan's Forest Camp, in Turtle Bay Exploration Park, has a working model of the Sacramento River, play equipment for children, ecology and logging displays, a maze, live animal exhibits and a forest trail. **Hours:** Mon.-Fri. 9-5, Sat.-Sun. 10-5, May 1-early Sept.; Wed.-Fri. 9-4, Sat.-Sun. 10-4, rest of year. Closed Jan. 1, Thanksgiving and Christmas. **Cost:** Included with Turtle Bay Exploration Park admission.

Sundial Bridge at Turtle Bay spans the Sacramento River, linking Turtle Bay Exploration Park's two campuses. Designed by noted Spanish architect and engineer Santiago Calatrava, the artistic sundial design features a glass deck that is illuminated at night. The steel, glass and granite suspension bridge, 700 feet long, is for pedestrian traffic only and has public plazas at each end. The bridge pylon and cables create changing shapes, shadows and angles depending on the viewpoint. **Hours:** Daily 24 hours. **Cost:** Free.

Turtle Bay Museum, in Turtle Bay Exploration Park, has exhibits that examine the relationship between man and nature. At the Visible River visitors can view native fish species from an underwater perspective. Historical dioramas, Native American displays, science experiments and art exhibits also explore the man/nature theme. **Hours:** Mon.-Fri. 9-5, Sat.-Sun. 10-5, May 1-early Sept.; Wed.-Fri. 9-4, Sat.-Sun. 10-4, rest of year. Closed Jan. 1, Thanksgiving and Christmas. **Cost:** Included with Turtle Bay Exploration Park admission.

🔗 **For complete hotel, dining and attraction listings: AAA.com/travelguides**

BEST WESTERN PLUS HILLTOP INN   530/221-6100

 Hotel

Best Western PLUS **AAA Benefit:** Members save up to 15% and earn bonus points!

Address: 2300 Hilltop Dr 96002 **Location:** I-5 exit 677 (Cypress Ave), just e, then just n. **Facility:** 114 units. 2 stories, exterior corridors. **Terms:** check-in 4 pm. **Dining:** C.R. Gibbs American Grill, see separate listing. **Pool:** heated outdoor. **Activities:** hot tub, exercise room. **Guest Services:** valet and coin laundry.

BEST WESTERN PLUS TWIN VIEW INN & SUITES
530/241-5500

 Hotel

Best Western PLUS **AAA Benefit:** Members save up to 15% and earn bonus points!

Address: 1080 Twin View Blvd 96003 **Location:** I-5 exit 681 (Twin View Blvd), just w. **Facility:** 79 units. 2 stories, interior corridors. **Pool:** outdoor. **Activities:** hot tub, exercise room. **Guest Services:** valet and coin laundry. **Featured Amenity:** breakfast buffet.

BRIDGE BAY AT SHASTA LAKE LODGE   530/275-3021
Motel. **Address:** 10300 Bridge Bay Rd 96003

COMFORT INN   530/221-4472

 Hotel

Address: 850 Mistletoe Ln 96002 **Location:** I-5 exit 677 (Cypress Ave), 0.8 mi n on Hilltop Dr, then just e. **Facility:** 70 units. 3 stories, interior corridors. **Pool:** outdoor. **Activities:** hot tub, exercise room. **Guest Services:** coin laundry. **Featured Amenity:** breakfast buffet.

COMFORT SUITES REDDING   530/246-8100

 Hotel

Address: 1195 Grand Ave 96003 **Location:** I-5 exit 681 (Twin View Blvd) northbound; exit 681B southbound, just w, then just n. **Facility:** 63 units. 3 stories, interior corridors. **Pool:** heated indoor. **Activities:** hot tub, exercise room. **Guest Services:** valet and coin laundry. **Featured Amenity:** full hot breakfast.

FAIRFIELD INN & SUITES BY MARRIOTT   530/243-3200
Hotel. **Address:** 5164 Caterpillar Rd 96003

AAA Benefit: Members save 5% or more!

HAMPTON INN & SUITES

530/224-1001

 Hotel

 AAA Benefit: Members save up to 15%!

Address: 2160 Larkspur Ln 96002 **Location:** I-5 exit 677 (Cypress Ave), just e, then just n. **Facility:** 80 units. 3 stories, interior corridors. **Pool:** heated outdoor. **Activities:** hot tub, exercise room. **Guest Services:** valet and coin laundry. **Featured Amenity:** full hot breakfast.

HILTON GARDEN INN REDDING

530/226-5111

 Hotel

 AAA Benefit: Members save up to 15%!

Address: 5050 Bechelli Ln 96002 **Location:** I-5 exit 675 (Bonnyview Rd), just w. **Facility:** 93 units. 3 stories, interior corridors. **Pool:** heated outdoor. **Activities:** hot tub, exercise room. **Guest Services:** valet and coin laundry, area transportation. *(See ad this page.)*

 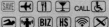

HOLIDAY INN HOTEL AND CONVENTION CENTER

530/221-7500

 Hotel. **Address:** 1900 Hilltop Dr 96002

OXFORD SUITES REDDING

530/221-0100

 Hotel

Address: 1967 Hilltop Dr 96002 **Location:** I-5 exit 677 (Cypress Ave), just e, then just n. **Facility:** 140 units, some efficiencies. 3-4 stories, interior/exterior corridors. **Terms:** check-in 4 pm. **Pool:** heated outdoor. **Activities:** hot tub, exercise room. **Guest Services:** valet and coin laundry. **Featured Amenity:** breakfast buffet.

/ SOME UNITS

SHERATON REDDING HOTEL AT SUNDIAL BRIDGE

530/364-2800

Hotel. **Address:** 820 Sundial Bridge Dr 96001

AAA Benefit: Members save 5% or more!

SUPER 8 MOTEL REDDING

530/221-8881

Motel. **Address:** 5175 Churn Creek Rd 96002

SURESTAY PLUS HOTEL BY BEST WESTERN REDDING

530/722-9100

Hotel. **Address:** 2600 Larkspur Ln 96002

▼ *See AAA listing this page* ▼

TOWNEPLACE SUITES BY MARRIOTT   530/223-0690

Extended Stay Hotel

TOWNEPLACE SUITES MARRIOTT

AAA Benefit: Members save 5% or more!

Address: 2180 Larkspur Ln 96002 **Location:** I-5 exit 677 (Cypress Ave), just e, just n on Hilltop Dr, just e on Industrial St, then just n. **Facility:** 101 units, some two bedrooms, efficiencies and kitchens. 4 stories, interior corridors. **Pool:** heated outdoor. **Activities:** exercise room. **Guest Services:** valet and coin laundry. **Featured Amenity: breakfast buffet.**

[SAVE] [▮▮▮] CALL [⬤] [⬤] [✦] [BIZ]
[HS] [📶] [✕] [⬤] [⬤] [⬤] /SOME UNITS [⬤]

TRAVELODGE BY WYNDHAM REDDING   530/243-5291

Hotel

Address: 540 N Market St 96003 **Location:** I-5 exit 680 (Lake Blvd) northbound, 0.5 mi w to Market St, then 0.5 mi s; exit Market St southbound, 2 mi s. **Facility:** 42 units, some two bedrooms and kitchens. 2 stories (no elevator), exterior corridors. **Pool:** heated outdoor. **Activities:** hot tub, exercise room. **Guest Services:** coin laundry. **Featured Amenity: full hot breakfast.**

[SAVE] [▮▮▮] CALL [⬤] [⬤] [✦] [BIZ]
[📶] [✕] [⬤] [⬤] [⬤]
/SOME UNITS [⬤]

WIN RIVER RESORT & CASINO   530/245-9500

Resort Hotel

Address: 2100 Redding Rancheria Rd 96001 **Location:** I-5 exit 675, 0.3 mi w, 1.9 mi s, then 1.6 w. **Facility:** At this property located just outside of town, a large burden basket at the entrance welcomes visitors. You will find a variety of spacious room types decorated in soothing colors and native artwork. 84 units. 3 stories, interior corridors. **Parking:** on-site and valet. **Amenities:** safes. **Dining:** 2 restaurants. **Pool:** heated outdoor. **Activities:** sauna, hot tub, steamroom, recreation programs, game room, trails, exercise room, spa. **Guest Services:** valet laundry, area transportation.

[SAVE] [🍳] [✈] [▮▮] [🍽] [Y] CALL [⬤] [⬤] [✦] [HS]
[📶] [✕] [📷] [⬤] [⬤]

WHERE TO EAT

CASA RAMOS   530/224-7223
Mexican. Casual Dining. **Address:** 995 Hilltop Dr 96003

CATTLEMENS   530/221-6295
Steak. Casual Dining. **Address:** 2184 Hilltop Dr 96002

CICADA CANTINA   530/638-4979
New Mexican. Casual Dining. **Address:** 1691 Hilltop Dr 96002

THE COOKHOUSE AT BRIDGE BAY   530/275-3021
American. Casual Dining. **Address:** 10300 Bridge Bay Rd 96003

C.R. GIBBS AMERICAN GRILL   530/221-2335

American Casual Dining $13-$21

AAA Inspector Notes: Tasty entrées such as salmon, fish and chips and prime rib along with brick-oven pizza, sandwiches and a few lighter items are served at this restaurant. Recommended for dessert is the chocolate wedge that is big enough for two people to share. Patio dining is available in season. **Features:** full bar, patio dining, happy hour. **Address:** 2300 Hilltop Dr 96002 **Location:** I-5 exit 677 (Cypress Ave), just e, then just n; in Best Western Plus Hilltop Inn. [L] [D] CALL [⬤]

DEJA VU RESTAURANT   530/244-4272
American. Casual Dining. **Address:** 1590 California St 96001

THE HABIT BURGER GRILL   530/223-1027
Burgers. Quick Serve. **Address:** 1020 E Cypress Ave 96002

JANYA'S THAI CUISINE   530/243-7682
Thai. Casual Dining. **Address:** 630 N Market St 96003

MARKET STREET STEAKHOUSE   530/241-1777
Steak Seafood. Casual Dining. **Address:** 1777 Market St 96001

MAZATLAN GRILL AND MEXICAN RESTAURANT   530/223-2454
Mexican. Casual Dining. **Address:** 1630 Hilltop Dr 96002

MOONSTONE BISTRO   530/241-3663
American. Casual Dining. **Address:** 3425 Placer St 96001

NELLO'S PLACE   530/223-1636
Italian. Casual Dining. **Address:** 3055 Bechelli Ln 96002

PUERTO VALLARTA   530/244-2941
Mexican. Casual Dining. **Address:** 2315 Eureka Way 96001

TRENDY'S   530/768-1499
American. Casual Dining. **Address:** 1730 Gold St 96001

VIEW 202 RESTAURANT & LOUNGE   530/226-8439
American. Casual Dining. **Address:** 202 Hemsted Dr 96002

REDWOOD CITY (D-8) pop. 76,815, elev. 15'
• Hotels & Restaurants map & index p. 316

The Lathrop House, downtown in the county government center at 627 Hamilton St., was moved to its present site in 1905 and survived the 1906 earthquake. The restored 1863 house is an example of early Gothic Revival architecture and is furnished in period. It is open to the public on the second Wednesday and third Saturday of the month from 11-3 (closed in August). Contact the chamber of commerce for additional information.

Redwood City-San Mateo County Chamber of Commerce: 1450 Veterans Blvd., Suite 125, Redwood City, CA 94063. **Phone:** (650) 364-1722.

ATHERTON PARK INN & SUITES   650/366-2000 **86**
Hotel. **Address:** 2834 El Camino Real 94061

(See map & index p. 316.)

BEST WESTERN INN
650-366-3808

Motel

AAA Benefit: Members save up to 15% and earn bonus points!

Address: 316 El Camino Real 94062 **Location:** US 101 exit Whipple Ave, 0.5 mi w to SR 82, then 0.3 mi n. **Facility:** 31 units. 2 stories (no elevator), exterior corridors. **Pool:** outdoor. **Guest Services:** valet laundry. **Featured Amenity:** continental breakfast.

BEST WESTERN PLUS EXECUTIVE SUITES
650-366-5794 87

Motel

Best Western PLUS AAA Benefit: Members save up to 15% and earn bonus points!

Address: 25 5th Ave 94063 **Location:** US 101 exit SR 84, 1 mi w, 1.5 mi s on SR 82, then just e. **Facility:** 29 units. 2 stories (no elevator), exterior corridors. **Activities:** exercise room. **Guest Services:** valet and coin laundry. **Featured Amenity:** full hot breakfast.

COMFORT INN BY CHOICE HOTELS
650/599-9636 83

Hotel

Address: 1818 El Camino Real 94063 **Location:** US 101 exit Whipple Ave, 0.5 mi w to SR 82, then 1 mi s. **Facility:** 51 units. 2 stories, interior corridors. **Pool:** heated outdoor. **Activities:** sauna. **Guest Services:** valet laundry. **Featured Amenity:** continental breakfast.

COURTYARD BY MARRIOTT REDWOOD CITY
650/216-9435 80
Hotel. **Address:** 600 Blair Island Rd 94063

AAA Benefit: Members save 5% or more!

GOOD NITE INN REDWOOD CITY
650/635-5500 79
Hotel. **Address:** 485 Veterans Blvd 94063

HOLIDAY INN EXPRESS REDWOOD CITY CENTRAL
650/299-0909 84
Hotel. **Address:** 1836 El Camino Real 94063

PACIFIC INN REDWOOD CITY
650/368-1495 85
Motel. **Address:** 2610 El Camino Real 94061

PULLMAN SAN FRANCISCO BAY HOTEL
650/598-9000 77

Hotel

Address: 223 Twin Dolphin Dr 94065 **Location:** US 101 exit Ralston Ave E, 0.5 mi s; jct Shoreline Dr. **Facility:** The hotel's attractive lobby includes a restaurant and lounge overlooking the lagoon. The updated guest rooms are spacious and some provide views of the bay. 421 units. 8 stories, interior corridors. **Parking:** on-site (fee) and valet. **Amenities:** safes. **Pool:** heated outdoor. **Activities:** trails, exercise room. **Guest Services:** valet laundry, boarding pass kiosk.

REDWOOD CREEK INN
650/369-1731 82
Motel. **Address:** 1090 El Camino Real 94063

TOWNEPLACE SUITES BY MARRIOTT REDWOOD CITY/ REDWOOD SHORES
650/593-4100 78
Extended Stay Hotel. **Address:** 1000 Twin Dolphin Dr 94065

AAA Benefit: Members save 5% or more!

WHERE TO EAT

CRU WINE BAR & MERCHANT CAFE
650/362-3535 74
American. Casual Dining. **Address:** 900 Middlefield Rd 94063

DONATO ENOTECA
650/701-1000 75
Italian. Casual Dining. **Address:** 1041 Middlefield Rd 94063

HARRY'S HOFBRAU
650/366-3733 77
American. Buffet Style. **Address:** 1909 El Camino Real 94063

MILAGROS CANTINA RESTAURANT
650/369-4730 76
Mexican. Casual Dining. **Address:** 1099 Middlefield Rd 94061

PORTOBELLO GRILL
650/575-1003 73
New American. Fine Dining. **Address:** 875 Middlefield Rd 94063

VESTA
650/362-5052 72
Pizza Small Plates. Casual Dining. **Address:** 2022 Broadway 94063

Save on travel, shopping, dining and more: AAA.com/discounts

REDWOOD NATIONAL AND STATE PARKS (B-1)

Elevations in the park range from sea level at Crescent City to 3,262 ft. at an unnamed peak. Refer to AAA maps for additional elevation information.

Along the northern California coast between Crescent City and Orick, 302 miles north of San Francisco on US 101, Redwood National and State Parks encompasses 131,983 acres. Within its boundaries are the 60,286 combined acres of Del Norte Coast, Jedediah Smith and Prairie Creek Redwoods state parks *(see Recreation Areas Chart)*. In addition to dense forests of coast redwoods, the park embraces marshland, beaches, rugged coastline, rivers, streams, prairies and oak woodlands.

General Information and Activities

The beaches are open all year, but visitors should use caution when swimming or surfing. The coastline in Northern California is a dangerous combination of steeply descending beaches, heavy undertows, very cold water and jagged, rocky shoals. Visitors walking along the beaches should be aware of the time of high tide and keep an eye out for the unusually large, strong waves known as "sneaker waves."

Coastal Drive, reached from US 101 exit 768 (Klamath Beach Road), is an 8-mile parade of spectacular coastal scenery. Lost Man Creek Road passes through a beautiful redwood forest and offers access to 10-mile Lost Man Creek Trail. Just a couple miles west of Crescent City, an unpaved stretch of Howland Hill Road showcases the towering old-growth redwoods in Jedediah Smith Redwoods State Park. There are numerous pullouts and trailheads along the way, including the Boy Scout Tree Trail and Stout Grove. These scenic byways are not suitable for RV or trailer travel.

Paved scenic routes include Requa Road, which leads 4 miles up a steep grade from US 101 to the Klamath River Overlook, 600 feet above the Pacific Ocean. Enderts Beach Road connects US 101 near Crescent City with the dramatic vistas of Crescent Beach Overlook. Both overlooks provide particularly good opportunities for whale-watching. Newton B. Drury Scenic Parkway through Prairie Creek Redwood State Park is a scenic alternate to US 101.

Note: Due to storm damage, access to Enderts Beach was closed at press time; phone for updates.

Some public roads also serve adjoining private forest lands; logging truck traffic and other private activities take place along some of the routes.

Trails traverse some 37 miles of wild and untouched coastline along rock promontories that protrude into the ocean, offering vistas of sea lion colonies and migrating whales. Birds inhabit bluffs, lagoons and offshore rocks; bird-watching is particularly rewarding during waterfowl migrations. More than 170 miles of trails provide access to magnificent redwood groves, coastal areas and upland prairies.

The Coastal Trail extends 43.4 miles, nearly the entire length of the parks, through a variety of spectacular landscapes. Hikers will navigate bluffs and pass through grasslands and along deserted beaches, with frequent stretches descending into dim glades created by coast redwood forests. The trail can be accessed at various places within the park, including the Crescent Beach Overlook at the end of Enderts Beach Road; from Damnation Creek Trail in Del Norte Coast Redwoods State Park; and from near Fern Canyon, at the end of Davison Road in Prairie Creek Redwoods State Park.

The park also contains 44.8 miles of horseback riding trails and 33 miles of bicycle trails. Park staff conduct free guided walks, evening programs and other activities from mid-June through Labor Day.

Developed campgrounds are within the state parks and along US 101 (the Redwood Highway). Reservations through ReserveCalifornia are recommended in summer. There also are five primitive walk-in campsites in the national park, although space is limited; permits are free but required. Freshwater and surf fishing are permitted; a California fishing license is required. *See Recreation Areas Chart.*

The Crescent City Information Center is located at Redwood National and State Parks Headquarters, 1111 2nd St. near the Crescent City waterfront; phone (707) 465-7335.

ADMISSION to the national park is free. The state parks charge day use and overnight fees for developed picnicking and camping areas.

PETS must be kept under physical restraint while in the park and are prohibited on most trails. Campers are required to have proof of rabies shots for pets.

ADDRESS inquiries to the Superintendents, Redwood National and State Parks, 1111 2nd St., Crescent City, CA 95531-4198. Phone (707) 465-7335.

CRESCENT BEACH OVERLOOK is within Redwood National Park about 5 mi. s. of Crescent City via US 101 and Enderts Beach Rd. The overlook provides a stunning vantage point high above the Pacific. A half-mile-long trail leads down the bluffs to sandy Enderts Beach and also connects to the Coastal Trail. **Hours:** Daily dawn-dusk. **Cost:** Free.

DEL NORTE COAST REDWOODS STATE PARK, 7 mi. s. of Crescent City on US 101, contains 15 memorial redwood groves within its 31,400 acres. The trees extend down steep slopes almost to the ocean shore at Damnation Creek. In this damp and shady environment the resident wildlife is primarily smaller animals like red squirrels, brown bats, newts, frogs and Western garter snakes. Salamanders and slugs thrive in the most conditions and rich, deep soil.

The Damnation Creek Trail, accessible from a turnout off US 101 at mile marker 16, offers a truly memorable wilderness hiking experience. The trail descends 1,000 feet via switchbacks through majestic, primeval redwood forest, ending at a rocky, starkly beautiful beach. *See Recreation Areas Chart.*

Note: The bridge on Damnation Creek Trail, located 1.75 miles in from the trail parking lot, is closed until further notice. Visitors can still hike the trail as far as the bridge, but there is no access to the beach. Phone ahead for updated reopening information. **Hours:** Daily dawn-dusk. **Cost:** $8 (per private vehicle); $7 (ages 62+ per private vehicle). **Phone:** (707) 465-7335. 🅰 ⊠ 🐎 ⛏

ELK MEADOW DAY USE AREA is in Redwood National Park 2 mi. n. of Orick, just off US 101 on Davison Rd. Named for the Roosevelt elk frequently seen grazing here, this area was allowed to return to a more natural state after being the site of a logging company. The 2.5-mile-long Trillium Falls Loop provides access to small but picturesque Trillium Falls. Beyond the day use area, Davison Road enters Prairie Creek Redwoods State Park and is unpaved; trailers are prohibited along this section. **Hours:** Daily 24 hours. **Cost:** Free.

JEDEDIAH SMITH REDWOODS STATE PARK is 9 mi. e. of Crescent City on US 199. Named for 19th-century fur trapper Jedediah Strong Smith, the state park includes a section of the lovely Smith River in addition to preserving thousands of acres of ancient redwoods. Trails accessible from turnouts on US 199 include the Hiouchi Trail and Hatton Loop.

Visitors can reach Stout Memorial Grove via Howland Hill Road, an unimproved stage route not suitable for RVs or trailers. *See Recreation Areas Chart.* **Hours:** Daily dawn-dusk. **Cost:** Day use $8 per private vehicle at developed parking lots; $7 (ages 62+ per private vehicle). **Phone:** (707) 465-7335. 🅰 ⊠ 🐎 ⛏

Hiouchi Information Center is on US 199, just outside the eastern entrance to Jedediah Smith Redwoods State Park. The center features exhibits about area wildlife and the coast redwood forest. **Hours:** Daily 9-5, mid-June to early Sept.; 9-4, rest of year. **Phone:** (707) 458-3294.

Jedediah Smith Visitor Center is off US 199 just inside the eastern entrance to Jedediah Smith Redwoods State Park. Within the Jedediah Smith Campground, on the opposite side of US 199 from the Hiouchi Information Center, this center offers a few displays about the area's flora and fauna. Trails lead from the center to the Smith River, and in summer hikers can cross the seasonal footbridge and follow trails along Mill Creek and into Stout Memorial Grove. **Hours:** Daily 9-5, Memorial Day-Labor Day; hours may be extended when staffing permits. Phone ahead to confirm schedule. **Cost:** Free. **Phone:** (707) 458-3496.

LADY BIRD JOHNSON GROVE is 1 mi. n. of Orick, then 3 mi. e. on Bald Hills Rd. following signs. The grove features a 1-mile, self-guiding loop trail through a mature grove of coastal redwoods that passes a plaque marking the site where Lady Bird Johnson dedicated the park in 1968. A lush understory of rhododendrons and sword ferns grows here. **Note:** Bald Hills Road has many sharp turns; motor homes and trailers are not recommended. **Time:** Allow 1 hour minimum. **Hours:** Daily 24 hours. **Cost:** Free.

PRAIRIE CREEK REDWOODS STATE PARK is 6 mi. n. of Orick on US 101. A coastal redwood park consisting of 14,000 acres, it protects one of the last wild herds of native Roosevelt elks. Davison Road, off US 101, is a narrow, unpaved route between the base of Gold Bluffs and Gold Bluffs Beach; elk are frequently seen along the road, which leads to picturesque Fern Canyon.

The beach was the site of gold-mining operations in the 1850s. Guided nature hikes and campfire programs are conducted June 1-Labor Day. *See Recreation Areas Chart.* **Hours:** Daily 24 hours. **Cost:** Day use $8 per private vehicle; $7 (ages 62+ per private vehicle). **Phone:** (707) 488-2039. 🅰 ⊠ ⛏

Fern Canyon is off US 101 at the end of Davison Rd. in Prairie Creek Redwoods State Park. This gorge features 30-foot-high walls covered with delicate five-fingered and sword ferns. Water seeping from the walls keeps the luxuriant foliage moist and green throughout the year. A loop trail leads along one side and down into the canyon, although runoff sometimes floods the chasm's floor. The 4.5-mile James Irvine Trail connects Fern Canyon to the Prairie Creek Visitor Center.

Note: Trailers are prohibited on the narrow, unpaved road to the canyon. **Hours:** Daily dawn-dusk. **Cost:** Included in Prairie Creek Redwoods State Park admission. **Phone:** (707) 488-2039.

Newton B. Drury Scenic Parkway is off US 101 6 mi. n. of Orick in Prairie Creek Redwoods State Park. The parkway, connected to US 101 at either end via interchanges, offers a beautifully scenic, 10-mile drive through an old-growth redwood forest, with huge trees often abutting the pavement. Several hiking trails as well as the Prairie Creek Visitor Center can be accessed from the parkway. From Big Tree Wayside, a short trail leads to a coast redwood more than 300 feet tall and estimated to be 1,500 years old. **Hours:** Daily 24 hours. **Cost:** Free.

Prairie Creek Visitor Center is off US 101 exit 753 near the southern end of Newton B. Drury Scenic Pkwy. Natural history exhibits focus on the coastal redwood environment. Several trailheads are located behind the center, including those for the James Irvine Trail to Fern Canyon and the Prairie Creek Trail to the Big Tree Wayside. **Hours:** Daily 9-5, in summer; Wed.-Sun. 9-4, rest of year. Closed

Jan. 1, Thanksgiving and Christmas. Phone ahead to confirm schedule. **Cost:** Free. **Phone:** (707) 488-2039.

THOMAS H. KUCHEL VISITOR CENTER is on US 101 w. of Orick, near the southern end of Redwood National Park. The center features displays about the national park, including one describing the restoration of land that has been extensively logged. A small theater shows videos about the coast redwoods, and a short interpretive trail leads through wetlands to the beach. **Hours:** Daily 9-5, May-Oct.; 9-4, rest of year. Closed Jan. 1, Thanksgiving and Christmas. **Cost:** Free. **Phone:** (707) 465-7765.

REEDLEY pop. 24,194, elev. 348'

EDGEWATER INN 559/637-7777

♦♦ **Motel**

Address: 1977 W Manning Ave 93654 **Location:** SR 99 exit 121 (Manning Ave), 11 mi e. **Facility:** 48 units, some two bedrooms. 2 stories (no elevator), exterior corridors. **Pool:** outdoor. **Activities:** hot tub. **Guest Services:** coin laundry.

SAVE CALL ⟨⟩ 🏊 📶 🅱 🖼 🖵 / SOME UNITS 🐾

RICHMOND (C-8) pop. 103,701, elev. 46'

ROSIE THE RIVETER/WWII HOME FRONT NATIONAL HISTORICAL PARK visitor center is at 1414 Harbour Way South; from I-80 eastbound, merge onto I-580 West after the Gilman St. off ramp, take the Harbour Way South exit, turn right onto Cutting Blvd., then turn right onto Harbour Way South and continue for .8 mi. to the secured parking area for the Ford Assembly Building, where a security guard will direct you to visitor parking.

The park commemorates the City of Richmond's significant role in the nation's World War II home front effort; 747 cargo vessels were built in the four shipyards run by the Kaiser Company. Exhibits and films in the Visitor Education Center tell the human stories behind a massive war effort that impacted the daily lives of many people.

One mile from the visitor center along the SF Bay Trail in Marina Bay Park is the Rosie the Riveter Memorial, a public art sculpture the length of a World War II Liberty cargo ship. **Hours:** Park open daily dawn-dusk. Visitor Education Center daily 10-5. Center closed Jan. 1, Thanksgiving and Christmas. **Cost:** Free.

SS *Red Oak Victory* is within Rosie the Riveter/WWII Home Front National Historical Park, 1.5 mi. s. off the I-580 Canal Blvd. exit, following signs to 1337 Canal Blvd., Berth 6A. (**Note:** This is an active port area with heavy industrial equipment; the speed limit is 5 mph.) Launched in 1944, this 455-foot-long cargo ship is the only vessel built at the shipyard that is being restored. It served during World War II, the Korean War and in Vietnam.

The ship not only functions as a maritime museum providing an overview of the wartime efforts of everyday citizens but is also a testament to the production skills of industrialist Henry J. Kaiser. Kaiser established Richmond's Kaiser Shipyards, which built cargo ships known as Liberty ships for the war effort, and gained world renown for adapting efficient construction techniques that enabled the vessels to be completed in an average time of just 45 days. Docent-led tours provide access to the main deck, officer's mess hall, captain's office and stateroom, chart room, the engine and boiler chamber and the inside hold.

Note: Ship access requires being able to walk up a steep ramp and climb stairs. **Time:** Allow 1 hour minimum. **Hours:** Ship access Tues., Thurs. and Sat.-Sun. 10-4. Last tour departs 1 hour before closing. Closed major holidays. Phone ahead to confirm schedule. **Cost:** Boarding fee $10; free (ages 0-6). Guided tour additional $5-$10. **Phone:** (510) 237-2933. GT

COURTYARD BY MARRIOTT RICHMOND/BERKELEY
510/262-0700

  Hotel. **Address:** 3150
Garrity Way 94806

AAA Benefit:
Members save 5%
or more!

HOTEL MAC
510/235-0010

Historic Country Inn. **Address:** 10 Cottage Ave 94801

WHERE TO EAT

HOTEL MAC RESTAURANT
510/233-0576

Continental. Fine Dining. **Address:** 50 Washington Ave 94801

RIO DELL pop. 3,368

HUMBOLDT GABLES MOTEL
707/764-5609

Motel

Address: 40 W Davis St 95562 **Location:** US 101 exit 680 (Davis St), 0.5 mi w. **Facility:** 16 units. 1 story, exterior corridors. **Guest Services:** coin laundry.

RIPON pop. 14,297

LA QUINTA INN & SUITES BY WYNDHAM MANTECA - RIPON
209/599-8999

Hotel

Address: 1524 Colony Rd 95366 **Location:** SR 99 exit 237B (Jack Tone Rd), just n, then just e. **Facility:** 60 units. 3 stories, interior corridors. **Pool:** outdoor. **Activities:** sauna, hot tub, steamroom, exercise room. **Guest Services:** coin laundry. **Featured Amenity:** full hot breakfast.

ROCKLIN pop. 56,974
• Hotels & Restaurants map & index p. 224

COMFORT INN & SUITES ROCKLIN-ROSEVILLE
916/624-4500 **27**

Hotel. **Address:** 4420 Rocklin Rd 95677

HOLIDAY INN EXPRESS
916/315-1300 **28**

Hotel. **Address:** 6830 Five Star Blvd 95677

STAYBRIDGE SUITES
916/781-7500 **26**

Extended Stay Hotel. **Address:** 6664 Lonetree Blvd 95765

WHERE TO EAT

ANATOLIAN TABLE TURKISH CUISINE & PATISSERIE
916/772-3020 **30**

Turkish. Casual Dining. **Address:** 6504 Lonetree Blvd 95765

THE CHEF'S TABLE
916/771-5656 **34**

American. Casual Dining. **Address:** 6843 Lonetree Blvd, Suite 103 95765

CRAZY SUSHI
916/771-4300 **35**

Japanese Sushi. Casual Dining. **Address:** 6696 Lonetree Blvd, Suite 700 95765

LUCILLE'S SMOKEHOUSE BAR-B-QUE & CATERING
916/780-7427 **32**

Barbecue. Casual Dining. **Address:** 6628 Lonetree Blvd 95765

POTTERY WORLD CAFE
916/624-8080 **37**

American. Casual Dining. **Address:** 4419 Granite Dr 95677

RUBINO'S RISTORANTE
916/624-3401 **38**

Italian. Casual Dining. **Address:** 5015 Pacific St 95677

SKIPOLINI'S PIZZA & PASTA
916/789-1818 **33**

Italian. Casual Dining. **Address:** 6600 Lonetree Blvd 95765

STUDIO MOVIE GRILL
916/238-9000 **36**

American. Casual Dining. **Address:** 5140 Commons Dr 95677

THAI CHILI RESTAURANT
916/780-6555 **31**

Thai. Casual Dining. **Address:** 2164 Sunset Blvd, Suite 200 95765

ROHNERT PARK (B-7) pop. 40,971, elev. 105'
• Restaurants p. 214
• Part of Wine Country area — see map p. 405

About 50 miles north of San Francisco, this Sonoma County city benefits from its geographical proximity to Wine Country; more than three dozen wineries are within an hour's drive.

DOUBLETREE BY HILTON SONOMA WINE COUNTRY
707/584-5466

Hotel

DOUBLETREE
BY HILTON

AAA Benefit:
Members save up to 15%!

Address: One Doubletree Dr 94928 **Location:** US 101 exit Golf Course Dr; 3 mi s of Santa Rosa. **Facility:** 245 units. 3 stories, interior corridors. **Parking:** on-site (fee). **Amenities:** safes. **Dining:** Bacchus Restaurant & Wine Bar, see separate listing. **Pool:** heated outdoor. **Activities:** hot tub, tennis, trails, exercise room. **Guest Services:** valet and coin laundry.

HAMPTON INN & SUITES
707/586-8700

 Hotel. **Address:** 6248
Redwood Dr 94928

AAA Benefit:
Members save up to 15%!

OXFORD SUITES SONOMA COUNTY - ROHNERT PARK
707/584-0333

Hotel

Address: 67 Golf Course Dr W 94928 **Location:** US 101 exit 484, just w. **Facility:** 163 units, some efficiencies. 5 stories, interior corridors. **Terms:** check-in 4 pm. **Amenities:** safes. **Pool:** heated outdoor. **Activities:** sauna, hot tub, steamroom, lawn sports, exercise room. **Guest Services:** valet and coin laundry, area transportation.

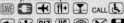
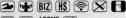

SONOMA WINEGROWER'S INN   707/584-7435
◆◆ Motel. **Address:** 6500 Redwood Dr 94928

AMY'S DRIVE THRU   707/755-3629
◆ American. Quick Serve. **Address:** 55 Golf Course Dr W 94928

BACCHUS RESTAURANT & WINE BAR   707/586-4679
◆◆ California. Casual Dining. **Address:** 1 Doubletree Dr 94928

HANA JAPANESE RESTAURANT   707/586-0270
◆◆ Japanese Sushi. Casual Dining. **Address:** 101 Golf Course Dr 94928

ROSEVILLE (E-3) pop. 118,788, elev. 160'
• Hotels & Restaurants map & index p. 224

GOLFLAND SUNSPLASH is e. off I-80 Atlantic St./Eureka Rd. exit, then just s. to 1893 Taylor Rd. The water park is part of a larger complex that also includes miniature golf, laser tag, go-carts and an arcade with more than 200 video games.

The water park includes 17 slides in addition to a wave pool, a lazy river and two children's pool areas. Among park favorites are the Master Blaster water coaster, The Stealth, Double Dare, Thunder Falls and Stormrider. Lockers and cabanas can be rented.

Note: Height and weight requirements may apply for some slides. **Time:** Allow 4 hours minimum. **Hours:** Water park daily 11-6, early June to mid-Aug.; Sat.-Sun. 11-6, Memorial Day weekend-early June and mid-Aug. through Labor Day. Nite Slides Mon.-Sat. 5:30-10:30 p.m., mid-June through Labor Day. Hours for other attractions vary. Phone ahead to confirm schedule. **Cost:** Waterpark $31.99; $25.99 (age 3-47 inches tall and ages 60+); $22.99 (Nite Slides Fri.-Sat.); $20.99 (twilight admission after 3 p.m.); $19.99 (Nite Slides Mon.-Thurs.); $2 (32 inches tall and under). **Phone:** (916) 784-1273.
🍴

MAIDU MUSEUM & HISTORIC SITE is at 1970 Johnson Ranch Dr. The museum, designed to resemble a Native American roundhouse, has exhibits, artifacts and displays showcasing Maiduan Indian culture.

A nature trail winds through the site, which was a Nisenan settlement for thousands of years until the mid-1800s. Along the trail visitors can see native plants; sandstone outcroppings carved with petroglyphs; and areas where the rocky ground is filled with mortar holes, which were used to process food. An art gallery features contemporary Native American art.

Time: Allow 2 hours minimum. **Hours:** Mon.-Thurs. 9-4, Sat. 9-1 (also third Sat. of the month 6:30-8:30 p.m.). Guided tours are given Sat. at 10 a.m. **Cost:** $5; $4 (students with ID and ages 55+); $2 (Mon.-Fri. 2-4); $16 (family of four); free (ages 0-4 and military with ID). **Phone:** (916) 774-5934.
GT

BEST WESTERN PLUS ORCHID HOTEL & SUITES
916/784-2222 **44**

Hotel

Best Western PLUS

AAA Benefit: Members save up to 15% and earn bonus points!

Address: 130 N Sunrise Ave 95661 **Location:** I-80 exit 103A (E Douglas Blvd) eastbound; exit 103 westbound, just e, then just n. **Facility:** 174 units, some two bedrooms. 3 stories, interior/exterior corridors. **Pool:** outdoor. **Activities:** hot tub, exercise room. **Guest Services:** coin laundry. **Featured Amenity: breakfast buffet.**

BEST WESTERN ROSEVILLE INN   916/782-4434 **43**

◆◆ Motel

Best Western.

AAA Benefit: Members save up to 15% and earn bonus points!

Address: 220 Harding Blvd 95678 **Location:** I-80 exit 103 (Douglas Blvd) westbound; exit 103B eastbound, just w, then just n. **Facility:** 134 units. 2 stories (no elevator), exterior corridors. **Pool:** outdoor. **Activities:** exercise room. **Guest Services:** coin laundry. **Featured Amenity:** breakfast buffet.

COURTYARD BY MARRIOTT   916/772-5555 **39**
◆◆◆ SAVE Hotel. **Address:** 1920 Taylor Rd 95661
AAA Benefit: Members save 5% or more!

COURTYARD BY MARRIOTT GALLERIA   916/772-3404 **36**
◆◆◆ SAVE Hotel. **Address:** 301 Creekside Ridge Ct 95678
AAA Benefit: Members save 5% or more!

FAIRFIELD BY MARRIOTT   916/772-3500 **41**
◆◆ SAVE Hotel. **Address:** 1910 Taylor Rd 95661
AAA Benefit: Members save 5% or more!

HAMPTON INN & SUITES ROSEVILLE   916/772-9900 **45**
◆◆◆ SAVE Hotel. **Address:** 110 N Sunrise Ave 95661
AAA Benefit: Members save up to 15%!

HILTON GARDEN INN ROSEVILLE   916/773-7171 **38**
◆◆◆ SAVE Hotel. **Address:** 1951 Taylor Rd 95661
AAA Benefit: Members save up to 15%!

HOLIDAY INN EXPRESS - ROSEVILLE GALLERIA
916/774-6060 **42**
◆◆◆ Hotel. **Address:** 1398 E Roseville Pkwy 95661

(See map & index p. 224.)

HOME2 SUITES BY HILTON ROSEVILLE SACRAMENTO
916/773-2200

◆◆◆◆ SAVE Extended Stay Hotel. **Address:** 1900 Freedom Way 95678

AAA Benefit: Members save up to 15%!

HYATT PLACE SACRAMENTO/ROSEVILLE
916/781-6400 **35**

◆◆◆ **Hotel**

☰HYATT PLACE· **AAA Benefit:** Members save up to 10%!

Address: 220 Conference Center Dr 95678 **Location:** I-80 exit 105A (Atlantic St/Eureka Rd), just e on Eureka Rd, 0.4 mi ne on Taylor Rd, 1.1 mi w on E Roseville Pkwy, just n on Gibson Dr, then just e. Adjacent to Westfield Galleria Mall. **Facility:** 151 units. 6 stories, interior corridors. **Amenities:** Some: safes. **Pool:** heated outdoor. **Activities:** hot tub, exercise room. **Guest Services:** valet laundry. **Featured Amenity:** breakfast buffet.

SAVE ⏶ ⏷ CALL ⬤ ⬤ ⬤ BIZ 📶 ✕ 🚪
▭ /SOME UNITS 🐾 HS

LARKSPUR LANDING ROSEVILLE 916/773-1717 **40**

◆◆◆ **Extended Stay Hotel**

Address: 1931 Taylor Rd 95661 **Location:** I-80 exit 105A (Atlantic St/Eureka Rd), just e on Eureka Rd, then 0.4 mi n. **Facility:** 90 efficiencies. 3 stories, interior corridors. **Activities:** exercise room. **Guest Services:** complimentary and valet laundry, area transportation. **Featured Amenity:** continental breakfast.

SAVE ECO ⬤ CALL ⬤ ⬤ BIZ
HS 📶 ✕ 🚪 ▭ ▭
/SOME UNITS 🐾

RESIDENCE INN BY MARRIOTT 916/772-5500 **37**

◆◆◆◆ SAVE Extended Stay Hotel. **Address:** 1930 Taylor Rd 95661

AAA Benefit: Members save 5% or more!

RESIDENCE INN BY MARRIOTT ROCKLIN ROSEVILLE
916/780-1850 **34**

◆◆◆◆ SAVE Extended Stay Hotel. **Address:** 1850 Freedom Way Dr 95678

AAA Benefit: Members save 5% or more!

SPRINGHILL SUITES BY MARRIOTT ROSEVILLE
916/782-2989 **31**

◆◆◆◆ SAVE Hotel. **Address:** 10593 Fairway Dr 95678

AAA Benefit: Members save 5% or more!

TOWNEPLACE SUITES BY MARRIOTT ROSEVILLE
916/782-2232 **33**

◆◆◆◆ SAVE Extended Stay Hotel. **Address:** 10569 Fairway Dr 95678

AAA Benefit: Members save 5% or more!

WHERE TO EAT

BLUE NAMI TASTE OF JAPAN 916/787-1177 **52**

◆◆ Japanese Sushi. Casual Dining. **Address:** 1465 Eureka Rd, Suite 120 95661

BOUDIN BAKERY & CAFE 916/782-1849

◆ Breakfast Sandwiches. Quick Serve. **Address:** 1017 Galleria Blvd, Suite 100 95678

BROOKFIELDS 916/784-3399 **48**

◆ American. Casual Dining. **Address:** 1817 Taylor Rd 95661

CATTLEMENS 916/782-5587

◆◆ Steak. Casual Dining. **Address:** 2000 Taylor Rd 95678

CHICAGO FIRE 916/771-2020 **49**

◆ Italian Pizza. Casual Dining. **Address:** 500 N Sunrise Ave 95661

COSTA VIDA FRESH MEXICAN GRILL 916/773-9283 **53**

◆ Mexican. Quick Serve. **Address:** 1475 Eureka Rd, Suite 100 95661

FAT'S ASIA BISTRO & DIM SUM BAR 916/787-3287 **55**

◆◆◆ Asian. Casual Dining. **Address:** 1500 Eureka Rd 95661

FINS MARKET & GRILL 916/783-5200 **58**

◆◆ Seafood. Casual Dining. **Address:** 8680 Sierra College Blvd 95661

IL FORNAIO 916/788-1200 **43**

◆◆◆ Italian. Fine Dining. **Address:** 1179 Galleria Blvd 95678

ISLANDS FINE BURGERS & DRINKS 916/772-5044 **45**

◆◆ Burgers. Casual Dining. **Address:** 1902 Taylor Rd 95661

JOHNNY GARLIC'S 916/789-2000 **42**

◆◆ American. Casual Dining. **Address:** 10505 Fairway Dr 95678

LA HUACA 916/771-2558 **59**

◆◆ Peruvian. Casual Dining. **Address:** 9213 Sierra College Blvd, Suite 140 95661

LA PROVENCE RESTAURANT & TERRACE
916/789-2002 **41**

◆◆◆ Regional French. Fine Dining. **Address:** 110 Diamond Creek Pl 95747

MIKUNI JAPANESE RESTAURANT & SUSHI BAR
916/797-2112

◆◆ Japanese Sushi. Casual Dining. **Address:** 1565 Eureka Rd 95661

MIKUNI KAIZEN 916/780-2119

◆◆ Japanese Sushi. Casual Dining. **Address:** 1017 Galleria Blvd, Suite 160 95678

PAUL MARTIN'S AMERICAN GRILL 916/783-3600 **51**

◆◆◆ American. Casual Dining. **Address:** 1455 Eureka Rd, Suite 100 95661

THE PLACE 916/742-5447 **50**

◆◆ Italian. Casual Dining. **Address:** 221 Vernon St 95678

RANGE KITCHEN & TAP 916/865-4317 **47**

◆◆ American. Casual Dining. **Address:** 1420 E Roseville Pkwy 95661

RUEN THAI 916/774-1499 **54**

◆◆ Thai. Casual Dining. **Address:** 1470 Eureka Rd 95661

THE SQUEEZE INN 916/783-2874 **56**

◆ Burgers. Quick Serve. **Address:** 106 N Sunrise Ave, Suite C1 95661

TAHOE JOE'S FAMOUS STEAKHOUSE 916/797-9220

◆◆ Steak Seafood. Casual Dining. **Address:** 1905 Taylor Rd 95661

THAI BASIL RESTAURANT 916/782-8424 **57**

◆◆ Thai. Casual Dining. **Address:** 1613 Douglas Blvd 95661

(See map & index p. 224.)

ZOCALO   916/788-0303 (44)
♥♥ Mexican. Casual Dining. **Address:** 1182 Roseville Pkwy 95678

RUTHERFORD (A-8) pop. 164, elev. 170'
• **Hotels & Restaurants map & index p. 412**
• **Part of Wine Country area — see map p. 405**

WINERIES
• **Inglenook** is off SR 29 at 1991 St. Helena Hwy. **Hours:** Daily 10-5. A variety of tastings and tours are offered. Reservations are required for most tours; phone ahead for information. Closed Jan. 1, Easter, Thanksgiving and Christmas. **Phone:** (707) 968-1100, or (707) 968-1161 for reservations. [GT]

• **Mumm Napa Valley Winery** is at 8445 Silverado Tr. **Hours:** Daily 10-6. Last seating is 15 minutes before closing. Guided tours are given daily at 10, 11, 1 and 3. Closed major holidays. **Phone:** (707) 967-7700 or (800) 686-6272. [GT]

• **Rutherford Hill Winery** is e. off Silverado Tr. at the end of Rutherford Hill Rd. **Hours:** Tastings daily 10-5. Guided tours are given Mon.-Fri. at 11:30, 1:30 and 3:30, Sat.-Sun. at 11, 12:30, 2 and 3:30. Closed Jan. 1, Easter, Thanksgiving and Christmas. **Phone:** (707) 963-1871. [GT]

• **St. Supéry Estate Vineyards and Winery** is off SR 29 at 8440 St. Helena Hwy. **Hours:** Tastings and tours offered daily by appointment only. **Phone:** (707) 963-4507. [GT] [🎁]

AUBERGE DU SOLEIL   707/963-1211 (37)
♥♥♥♥♥ Hotel. **Address:** 180 Rutherford Hill Rd 94573

WHERE TO EAT

RUTHERFORD GRILL   707/963-1792 (26)
♥♥♥♥ American. Casual Dining. **Address:** 1180 Rutherford Rd 94573

SACRAMENTO (E-3) pop. 466,488, elev. 30'
• **Hotels p. 230 • Restaurants p. 232**
• **Attractions map p. 218**
• **Hotels & Restaurants map & index p. 221, 224**

It was 1839 when Capt. John Sutter—a Swiss emigrant and the beneficiary of a 50,000-acre land grant from the Mexican government—settled at the confluence of the American and Sacramento rivers. Sacramento was platted on Sutter's property in 1848—the same year that James Marshall's discovery of gold near the South Fork of the American River inaugurated the great California gold rush.

Sacramento quickly became a major supply center for the northern Mother Lode country. But right off the bat there were challenges—two floods and two fires in the early 1850s that leveled some two-thirds of the new settlement. It was nevertheless chosen as the state capital in 1854 and retained that status despite subsequent challenges from city leaders in Berkeley, San Jose and Monterey.

In 1856 the first railroad in California connected Sacramento with Folsom, and in 1860 it became the western terminus of the Pony Express line from St. Joseph, Mo. The transcontinental railroad was completed in 1869. Once agriculture was established in the fertile Sacramento Valley, continued prosperity was assured. A deepwater channel to San Francisco Bay was completed in 1963, making the city a major inland port in addition to an important highway, rail and river hub.

The NBA's Sacramento Kings inaugurated their 2016-17 season at the Golden 1 Center, downtown at 547 L St. The brand-new venue opened on Oct. 4, 2016; for more information phone (888) 915-4647.

The 4-day ♥ Sacramento Music Festival over the long Memorial Day weekend is one heck of a street party. The music—played by bands on outdoor stages in the Old Sacramento historic district and in the ballrooms of surrounding hotels—ranges from jazz to big band swing, blues to zydeco and rockabilly to bluegrass. Other activities include a Saturday morning parade and a salute to servicemen and women on Memorial Day. For schedule and ticket information phone (916) 444-2004.

Close to a million people make their way to the Cal Expo fairgrounds in July for the 17-day ♥ California State Fair. In addition to traditional midway rides and games of chance, the fair also boasts big-name entertainment on three stages, competitions in everything from fine arts to livestock, a Kids Park, horse racing, extreme sports, wildlife exhibits, monster truck rides and more. The fairgrounds are on SR 99/Capital City Freeway (Cal Expo exit); for schedule, ticket and parking information phone (916) 263-3247 or (877) 225-3976.

Horse-drawn wagons? The Pony Express? Wild West shootouts? Sacramento relives the past—at least for the 4 days leading up to Labor Day—during the ♥ Gold Rush Days festival. Some 200 tons of trucked-in dirt add a little 19th-century authenticity to Old Sacramento streets. Costumed interpreters give shooting and cooking demonstrations, and street musicians enliven the atmosphere. The diverse cultures that settled the Sacramento Valley are spotlighted at Ethnic Village. For festival information phone (916) 808-7777.

Downtown Sacramento is the end point of the 32-mile Jedediah Smith Memorial Trail, which winds its way west from Folsom (see place listing p. 79). Also known as the American River Bike Trail, the pathway is used by hikers, bikers, in-line skaters and those just out for a stroll. Sacramento also is the northern point of a scenic 33-mile stretch of SR 160 that proceeds south to Isleton, following the Sacramento River.

The Sacramento-San Joaquin River Delta, a region located roughly between the cities of Sacramento, Stockton, Tracy and Pittsburg, was reclaimed in the mid-19th century thanks in large part to the efforts of Chinese railroad workers, who raised levees along the

(See maps & indexes p. 221, 224.)

Sacramento River and then took up farming. Waterways dotted with hundreds of islands meander through this tract of rich agricultural land, and the people who live here often get around by houseboat. Marinas are plentiful; popular recreational pursuits include fishing, camping and picnicking.

Miniscule Locke, off I-5 about 30 miles south of San Francisco, is a unique delta country destination that was designated a National Historic District in 1990. It was founded and constructed by Chinese laborers in 1915, during an era when "yellow peril" laws in California and elsewhere in the country heavily restricted the rights of Asian immigrants. At its peak in the 1940s Locke bustled with bakeries, herb shops, fish markets and boarding houses—as well as gambling halls, speakeasies, opium dens and brothels. Today one of the only reminders of this working-class community's origins is the Sun-Yat-Sen Memorial, off Main Street at the north end of town.

Boat sheds line the west side of River Road, which runs atop the broad left bank levee of the Sacramento River. A road leads along the base of the levee down to one-way Main Street, a narrow lane crowded with two-story weathered frame buildings that are practically leaning with age. It's one of the town's top things to see.

If you find yourself in this hamlet that time seems to have passed by, stop in at the Dai Loy Museum, 13952 Main St. The building was a gambling hall from 1916 to 1950, and it pretty much still looks like that—faded photos, displays about town history, vintage gaming tables and old brandy bottles. Staff members also can arrange guided Locke walking tours. The museum is open Sat.-Sun. 11-5; phone (916) 776-1661.

Al's Place, 13943 Main St. (more commonly known as Al the Wop's), is a local hangout also patronized by bikers and day-tripping tourists. It oozes dive bar authenticity, from the bar to the creaky, slightly slanted wood floor. Regulars swear by the dinner specialty, a grilled steak served with mushrooms—and peanut butter.

Sacramento Convention and Visitors Bureau: 1608 I St., Sacramento, CA 95814. **Phone:** (916) 808-7777 or (800) 292-2334.

Self-guiding tours: Maps and brochures detailing walking tours of Old Sacramento are available at the Old Sacramento Visitor Center, 1002 2nd St.; phone (916) 442-7644.

Shopping: Regional malls include Arden Fair, I-80 and Arden Way, and Westfield Galleria at Roseville, off I-80 (SR 65 exit); anchor stores at both are JC-Penney, Macy's and Nordstrom. The anchors at Sunrise Mall, Sunrise Boulevard and Greenback Lane, are JCPenney and Macy's. There's another Macy's downtown at 414 K St.

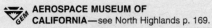 **AEROSPACE MUSEUM OF CALIFORNIA**—see North Highlands p. 169.

CALIFORNIA AUTOMOBILE MUSEUM, 2200 Front St., displays more than 150 vintage automobiles. The development of the automobile is depicted via representations of varied models and makes, from the primitive vehicles of the early 20th century to cosmetic adaptations (tail fins), styles (muscle and race cars) and the future (alternative-power vehicles). Car-related memorabilia and artifacts also are displayed.

Time: Allow 30 minutes minimum. **Hours:** Wed.-Mon. 10-5 (also third Thurs. of the month 5-8). Last tour begins 1 hour before closing. Closed Jan. 1, Thanksgiving and Christmas. **Cost:** $10; $9 (ages 65+ and students and military with ID); $4 (ages 5-17). **Phone:** (916) 442-6802. GT

CALIFORNIA STATE CAPITOL MUSEUM is bounded by 10th, 15th, L and N sts. This "museum," a 12-block expanse in downtown Sacramento, encompasses not just the building where the state's legislature meets, but also the gardens, monuments and statues in Capitol Park and the adjacent State Library. **Hours:** Daily 9-5. Closed Jan. 1, Thanksgiving and Christmas. **Cost:** Free. **Phone:** (916) 324-0333.

Capitol Park is bounded by 10th, 15th, L and N sts. This 40-acre park surrounding the State Capitol has gardens, including the World Peace Rose Garden, and trees and plantings from around the world. Memorials and statues commemorating significant events in state history include a statue of Father Junípero Serra, the Civil War Memorial Grove, the California Veterans Memorial, California Vietnam Veterans Memorial and the Firefighters Memorial.

A brochure describing a walking tour of the park is available at the State Capitol. Phone for information about guided tours of the park. **Hours:** Open daily dawn-dusk. **Cost:** Free. **Phone:** (916) 324-0333.

State Capitol, on 10th St. between L and N sts., was built between 1860 and 1874 and architecturally resembles the United States Capitol. The main building contains art exhibits, murals and statuary. Marble floors and the rotunda dome are highlights; murals depicting important events in California's history are at the base of the rotunda.

One-hour guided tours cover the renovated main building; the legislative chambers, where representatives' desks date from the 1860s; and several offices of state officials, including a 1906 re-creation of the governor's office suite. Limited gallery seating is available on a first-come, first-served basis when the legislature is in session. A 10-minute video presentation is shown in the basement theater.

Time: Allow 1 hour minimum. **Hours:** Guided tour offered daily on the hour 9-4. The legislature is in session early Jan. to mid-Sept. in odd-numbered years and early Jan.-Nov. 30 in even-numbered years. Closed Jan. 1, Thanksgiving and Christmas.

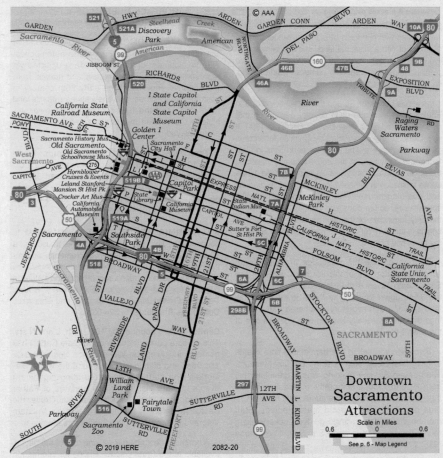

Downtown
Sacramento
Attractions

Scale in Miles
0.6   0   0.6

See p. 6 - Map Legend

© 2019 HERE   2082-20

(See maps & indexes p. 221, 224.)

Cost: Free. Children must be with an adult. **Phone:** (916) 324-0333. 🍴

State Library, 914 Capitol Mall, has a handsome neoclassic granite exterior with a 100-foot mural by California artist Maynard Dixon. A second building at 900 N St. houses the state history section, which includes an interesting collection of early state newspapers. **Hours:** Both buildings open Mon.-Fri. 9:30-4. Closed major holidays. **Cost:** Free. **Phone:** (916) 654-0261.

▼ **CROCKER ART MUSEUM** is off I-5 (J St. exit), s. on 3rd St., then just w. to 216 O St. It was founded in 1885 and is said to be the longest continuously operating art museum west of the Mississippi River. The 1872 building originally served as the gallery for the art collections of Judge Edwin B. Crocker and his wife Margaret. The museum houses art from the prehistoric to the present, with an emphasis on California art, European old masters drawings and international ceramics.

The original, Italianate-style gallery building displays Asian art, European paintings and international ceramics. On view in the expansive wings of the contemporary Teel Family Pavilion are works by American and Californian artists and art from Africa and Oceania. Several halls are devoted to changing exhibitions.

Note: Backpacks and baby back carriers are not permitted; paid lockers are available for storage. **Time:** Allow 2 hours minimum. **Hours:** Tues.-Sun. 10-5 (also Thurs. 5-9). Closed Jan. 1, Thanksgiving and Christmas. **Cost:** $12; $8 (ages 65+, military and college students with ID); $6 (ages 6-17); donations (third Sun. of the month). **Phone:** (916) 808-7000. GT 🍴

GOVERNOR'S MANSION STATE HISTORIC PARK is at 1526 H St. Within the park is the Governor's Mansion, occupied by 13 California governors and their families between 1903 and 1967. Furnishings and decorative accents inside this Second Empire Italianate mansion, built in 1877 for a hardware merchant, reflect the changing tastes and styles of the governors and first ladies who occupied it. The grounds contain flowers, shrubs and trees, including some trees planted the year the mansion was constructed.

(See maps & indexes p. 221, 224.)

Note: The Governor's Mansion remains closed for renovations; phone ahead for updated reopening information. **Phone:** (916) 323-3047.

LELAND STANFORD MANSION STATE HISTORIC PARK is at 800 N St. Built in 1856 and recently restored, the house served three governors during the 1860s. As a pro-Union Civil War governor and president of the Central Pacific Railroad, Leland Stanford negotiated deals to help complete the transcontinental railroad.

Stanford had the mansard-roofed mansion expanded in 1872. He died in 1893, and the house was used as an orphanage and a home for girls from the turn of the 20th century until 1986. It now serves a dual purpose: as a museum recalling an elegant 19th-century past and as a site for state meetings and receptions.

Time: Allow 1 hour minimum. **Hours:** Guided tours are given daily on the hour 10-4. Tour times may be limited when the legislature is in session; phone ahead to confirm schedule. Closed Jan. 1, Thanksgiving and Christmas. **Cost:** Free. **Phone:** (916) 324-0575.

OLD SACRAMENTO is a four-block, 28-acre section of downtown delineated by the Capitol Mall, I St., 2nd St. and the Sacramento River. This was the city's commercial district during the gold rush era. Cobblestone streets and wood sidewalks lend a touch of yesteryear to this vibrant commercial district, which includes Old Sacramento State Historic Park as well as museums, shops and restaurants.

The 1853 B.F. Hastings Building at 2nd and I streets once housed a Wells, Fargo & Co. office, marked the western end of the Pony Express route and, for a time, housed California's Supreme Court; today it's a visitor and interpretive center. The Wells Fargo History Museum within the building displays a Wells Fargo agent's office, a scale model of a Wells Fargo stagecoach, a 19th-century copy machine, a working telegraph and a scale used for weighing gold.

Hours: Guided walking tours of the historic park are offered Mar.-Sept.; by appointment rest of year. Wells Fargo History Museum open daily 10-5 (also 5-6 in summer). **Cost:** Wells Fargo History Museum free. **Phone:** (916) 442-7644 for the visitor center, or (916) 440-4263 for the Wells Fargo History Museum.

California State Railroad Museum is at 125 I St. at jct. 2nd St., part of Old Sacramento. The impressive three-level building houses 21 vintage locomotives and railcars along with temporary interactive exhibits, toy trains and a 20-minute film presentation documenting the history of American railroading.

Sacramento Southern Railroad steam and diesel trains (which one you get depends on the weekend) transport visitors along the Sacramento River levees on a 6-mile (45-minute round-trip) sightseeing journey weekends from April through September. Trains depart from the Central Pacific Freight Depot in Old Sacramento, on Front Street between J and K streets.

Time: Allow 2 hours minimum. **Hours:** Museum open daily 10-5. Last admission 30 minutes before closing. Trains operate Sat.-Sun. on the hour 11-4, Apr.-Sept. Closed Jan. 1, Thanksgiving and Christmas. **Cost:** Museum $12; $6 (ages 6-17). Train fare $12; $6 (ages 6-17). First-class train fare $24; $16 (ages 6-17). **Phone:** (916) 323-9280. GT

Huntington, Hopkins & Company Hardware Store is at street level in the Big Four Building at 111 I St. This representation of a small-town 19th-century hardware store has such period items as lanterns hanging from the ceiling, crates stacked on the floor, and an assortment of vintage tools and implements. Docents provide historical information and explain how some of the older tools were used. A back room displays additional tools and machinery.

The store also has a retail operation that sells hard-to-find items like oil lamps and old-fashioned toys. **Time:** Allow 30 minutes minimum. **Hours:** Thurs.-Sun. 10-4. Closed Jan. 1, Thanksgiving and Christmas. Phone ahead to confirm schedule. **Cost:** Free. **Phone:** (916) 323-7234.

Old Sacramento Schoolhouse Museum is at 1200 Front St. at jct. L St. Designed to resemble an 1884 one-room schoolhouse that served students in Yolo County, the exhibits include a potbellied stove and both original and replica furniture and fixtures. **Hours:** Daily 11-4. Closed Jan. 1, Easter, Thanksgiving and Christmas. Phone ahead to confirm schedule. **Cost:** Free. **Phone:** (916) 483-8818.

Old Sacramento Underground Tours depart from the Sacramento History Museum at 101 I St. Sacramento's streets were raised in the 1860s and '70s to guard against flooding. As a result, participants on these 1-hour, partially underground walking tours will see disappearing windows and doors, alleyways and retaining walls. In addition to historic buildings and excavated building foundations, historic photos and items excavated from beneath the buildings are shown.

Note: Participants should arrive 10-15 minutes before the start of the tour to pick up their tickets. Wear comfortable walking shoes. The tour includes walking over uneven surfaces and in areas with low ceilings. Photography is not allowed underground. **Time:** Allow 1 hour, 15 minutes minimum. **Hours:** Tours are given daily. During the peak summer season, three tours depart Mon.-Wed.; the first departure is at 11 a.m. Six tours depart Thurs.-Fri.; the first departure is at 11 a.m. Sat. tours depart every half-hour 10:30-3. Sun. tours depart every half-hour 10:30-2:30. Phone ahead to confirm schedule. **Cost:** Includes admission to Sacramento History Museum $18; $12 (ages 6-17). Reservations are recommended. **Phone:** (916) 808-7059.

(See maps & indexes p. 221, 224.)

Sacramento History Museum, 101 I St., occupies a structure designed to resemble the 1854 City Hall & Waterworks Building. The museum documents Sacramento history, beginning with the lobby exhibit Gold, Greed & Speculation: The Beginnings of Sacramento City. City founders, rivers, the gold rush and agriculture are among the topics covered. Original artifacts and interactive exhibits include a historic print shop, gold troughs, agricultural machinery and a Wells Fargo delivery wagon. **Time:** Allow 30 minutes minimum. **Hours:** Daily 10-5. Last admission 30 minutes before closing. Closed Jan. 1, Thanksgiving, Christmas Eve and Christmas. **Cost:** $8; $5 (ages 6-17). **Phone:** (916) 808-7059.

SACRAMENTO ZOO is off I-5 exit 516 (Sutterville Rd.) to 3930 West Land Park Dr., at jct. 16th Ave. This attractively landscaped zoo exhibits a variety of animals, including giraffes, chimpanzees, orangutans, lions, Sumatran tigers, jaguars, snow leopards, Grevy's zebras, lemurs and giant anteaters. Blue tree monitors, ball pythons and Tokey geckos are among the residents in the Reptile House.

Asian Forest includes a red panda exhibit. Among the resident bird species are hornbills and flamingos. Giraffes can be viewed from a platform deck, and twice-daily giraffe encounters allow visitors to feed these gentle giants. There's also a carousel that features 32 hand-crafted animals. A small train traverses the grounds. Zoo Backyard has picnic facilities and a children's play area.

Time: Allow 2 hours minimum. **Hours:** Daily 9-4, Feb.-Oct.; 10-4, rest of year. Hours may vary for some exhibits; phone ahead. Closed Thanksgiving and Christmas. **Cost:** $14.95; $13.95 (ages 65+); $9.95 (ages 2-11). Carousel ride $3. Train ride $4; free (ages 0-11 months). Giraffe encounter $5. Combination ticket with Fairytale Town Mon.-Fri. $19.45; $18.70 (ages 65+); $14.45 (ages 2-11). Combination ticket Sat.-Sun. and holidays $20.45; $19.70 (ages 65+); $15.45 (ages 2-11). **Parking:** Free and on-street throughout Land Park. **Phone:** (916) 808-5888, or (916) 808-5885 (after-hours information hotline).

SUTTER'S FORT STATE HISTORIC PARK, 27th and L sts., was the first European outpost in the interior of California. Established by Swiss immigrant John Sutter after the receipt of a 48,000-acre land grant from the Mexican government, the fort's walls were 2.5 feet thick and between 15 and 18 feet tall. The settlement was initially known as New Helvetia (New Switzerland).

After the discovery of gold, Sutter's lands were virtually taken over by prospectors and he eventually left California. The restored, 1839 adobe fort contains pioneer and gold rush artifacts. **Time:** Allow 1 hour minimum. **Hours:** Daily 10-5. Hours may vary during special events; phone ahead. Closed Jan. 1, Thanksgiving and Christmas. **Cost:** $5; $3 (ages 6-17). Admission may increase by $2 per person during special events. **Phone:** (916) 445-4422.

State Indian Museum is at 2618 K St., on the grounds of Sutter's Fort. It focuses on California's Native American cultures through displays of feather baskets, jewelry, clothing and art. **Hours:** Daily 10-5. Closed Jan. 1, Thanksgiving and Christmas. **Cost:** $5; $3 (ages 6-17). **Phone:** (916) 324-0971.

WILLIAM LAND PARK, bounded by Freeport and Riverside blvds., 13th Ave. and Sutterville Rd., encompasses 600 acres, including picnic facilities, a public golf course and a grove of cherry trees. **Phone:** (916) 277-1207 for golf information.

Fairytale Town is at 3901 Land Park Dr., across from the Sacramento Zoo. The park has play sets based on themes from popular children's nursery rhymes and fairy tales. Kids also can view or meet farm animals. Various programs and events are conducted seasonally.

Hours: Daily 9-5, Mar.-Oct.; Thurs.-Sun. 10-5 (also Martin Luther King Jr. Day, Lincoln's Birthday and Presidents Day), rest of year (weather permitting). During Winter Wonderland in mid-Dec. hours are 1-7; phone for details. Last admission 1 hour before closing. Closed Jan. 1, July 4, Thanksgiving and Christmas. **Cost:** Admission Mon.-Fri. $5; free (ages 0-1). Admission Sat.-Sun. and holidays $6; free (ages 0-1). Combination ticket with Sacramento Zoo Mon.-Fri. $19.70; $18.70 (ages 65+); $14.70 (ages 2-11). Combination ticket Sat.-Sun. $20.70; $19.70 (ages 65+); $15.70 (ages 2-11). Adults must be accompanied by a child. **Phone:** (916) 808-7462 for program and event information, or (916) 808-5233 (after-hours information hotline).

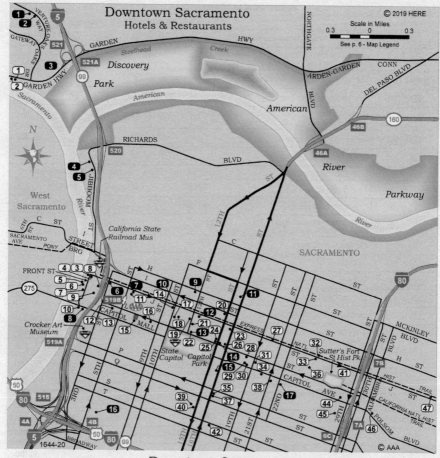

Downtown Sacramento
Hotels & Restaurants

© 2019 HERE

This index helps you "spot" where approved hotels and restaurants are located on the corresponding detailed maps. Restaurant price range is a combination of lunch and/or dinner. Turn to the listing page for more information and consult display ads for special promotions.

 For more details, rates and reservations: AAA.com/travelguides/hotels

DOWNTOWN SACRAMENTO

Map Page	Hotels	Diamond Rated	Member Savings	Page
1 this page	SpringHill Suites by Marriott-Sacramento Airport Natomas	◈◈◈	✔	232
2 this page	Hilton Garden Inn Sacramento/South Natomas	◈◈◈	✔	231
3 this page	**Courtyard by Marriott Sacramento Airport/ Natomas**	◈◈◈	✔	231
4 this page	Days Inn-Sacramento Downtown	◈◈		231
5 this page	**Best Western Sandman** *(See ad p. 230.)*	◈◈	✔	230
6 this page	Holiday Inn Sacramento Downtown Arena	◈◈◈		231
7 this page	**Kimpton Sawyer Hotel**	◈◈◈◈	✔	231
8 this page	**Embassy Suites by Hilton Sacramento-Riverfront Promenade**	◈◈◈	✔	231
9 this page	**Best Western Plus Sutter House**	◈◈◈	✔	230

DOWNTOWN SACRAMENTO (cont'd)

Map Page	Hotels (cont'd)	Diamond Rated	Member Savings	Page
⑩ p. 221	**The Citizen Hotel, Autograph Collection**	◇◇◇	✔	231
⑪ p. 221	Holiday Inn Express Sacramento Convention Center	fyi		231
⑫ p. 221	**Sheraton Grand Sacramento Hotel**	◇◇◇	✔	231
⑬ p. 221	**Hyatt Regency Sacramento**	◇◇◇◇	✔	231
⑭ p. 221	Residence Inn by Marriott- Sacramento Downtown at Capitol Park	◇◇◇	✔	231
⑯ p. 221	Inn and Spa at Parkside	◇◇◇		231
⑰ p. 221	Amber House Inn Of Midtown	◇◇◇		230

Map Page	Restaurants	Diamond Rated	Cuisine	Price Range	Page
① p. 221	Pearl on the River	◇◇	American	$14-$35	232
② p. 221	Crawdad's on the River	◇◇	Cajun	$13-$30	232
③ p. 221	Pilothouse Restaurant Aboard the Delta King	◇◇◇	Continental	$13-$39	232
④ p. 221	Fat City Bar & Cafe	◇◇	American	$12-$26	232
⑤ p. 221	Delta Bar & Grill	◇◇	American	$12-$34	232
⑥ p. 221	Suspects Mystery Dinner Theatre	◇◇	American	$40	232
⑦ p. 221	Rio City Cafe	◇◇	California	$13-$40	232
⑧ p. 221	La Terraza Mexican Restaurant	◇◇	Mexican	$10-$22	232
⑨ p. 221	The Firehouse Restaurant	◇◇◇◇	Continental	$14-$55	232
⑩ p. 221	Tower Bridge Bistro	◇◇◇	American	$11-$48	233
⑪ p. 221	Echo & Rig	◇◇◇	Steak	$14-$41	232
⑫ p. 221	Foundation Restaurant & Bar	◇◇	American	$10-$25	232
⑬ p. 221	Il Fornaio	◇◇◇	Italian	$11-$38	232
⑭ p. 221	Grange Restaurant & Bar	◇◇◇	American	$15-$49	232
⑮ p. 221	Morton's The Steakhouse	◇◇◇	Steak Seafood	$37-$67	232
⑯ p. 221	Frank Fat's	◇◇	Chinese	$12-$36	232
⑰ p. 221	Pizza Rock	◇◇	Pizza	$11-$34	232
⑱ p. 221	Mother Restaurant	◇◇	Vegetarian	$9-$18	232
⑲ p. 221	Ella Dining Room and Bar	◇◇◇	American	$15-$48	232
⑳ p. 221	Zen Sushi	◇◇	Japanese Sushi	$8-$21	233
㉑ p. 221	Tequila Museo Mayahuel	◇◇◇	New Mexican	$13-$30	232
㉒ p. 221	**Dawson's Steakhouse**	◇◇◇	American	$20-$45	232
㉓ p. 221	Mikuni Japanese Restaurant & Sushi Bar	◇◇	Japanese Sushi	$11-$22	232
㉔ p. 221	Cafeteria 15L	◇◇	American	$12-$23	232
㉕ p. 221	Ma Jong's Asian Diner	◇	Asian	$9-$10	232
㉖ p. 221	Firestone Public House	◇◇	American	$12-$25	232
㉗ p. 221	Pete's Restaurant & Brewhouse	◇◇	Italian	$9-$29	232
㉘ p. 221	Aioli Bodega Espanola	◇◇◇	Spanish	$10-$31	232
㉙ p. 221	Zocalo	◇◇	Mexican	$12-$24	233
㉚ p. 221	The Press Bistro	◇◇◇	Mediterranean	$20-$29	232
㉛ p. 221	Mulvaney's Building & Loan	◇◇◇	New American	$8-$38	232

Map Page	Restaurants (cont'd)	Diamond Rated	Cuisine	Price Range	Page
㉜ p. 221	Thai Basil	◆◆	Thai	$10-$23	233
㉝ p. 221	Chicago Fire	◆◆	Pizza	$7-$30	232
㉞ p. 221	The Waterboy Restaurant	◆◆◆	French	$15-$35	233
㉟ p. 221	Magpie Cafe	◆◆	California	$10-$40	232
㊱ p. 221	Tres Hermanas	◆◆	Northern Mexican	$11-$14	233
㊲ p. 221	Orchid Thai Restaurant and Bar	◆◆	Thai	$11-$20	232
㊳ p. 221	Bombay Bar and Grill	◆◆	Indian	$10-$21	232
㊴ p. 221	Burgers and Brew	◆◆	Burgers	$7-$12	232
㊵ p. 221	Iron Horse Tavern	◆◆	American	$10-$19	232
㊶ p. 221	Centro Cocina Mexicana	◆◆	Mexican	$14-$19	232
㊷ p. 221	Hook and Ladder Manufacturing Company	◆◆	American	$12-$31	232
㊸ p. 221	Biba	◆◆◆	Italian	$17-$45	232
㊹ p. 221	Paragary's	◆◆◆	California	$11-$29	232
㊺ p. 221	Kru	◆◆	Japanese Sushi	$11-$29	232
㊻ p. 221	La Trattoria Bohemia	◆◆	Czechoslovakian	$11-$23	232

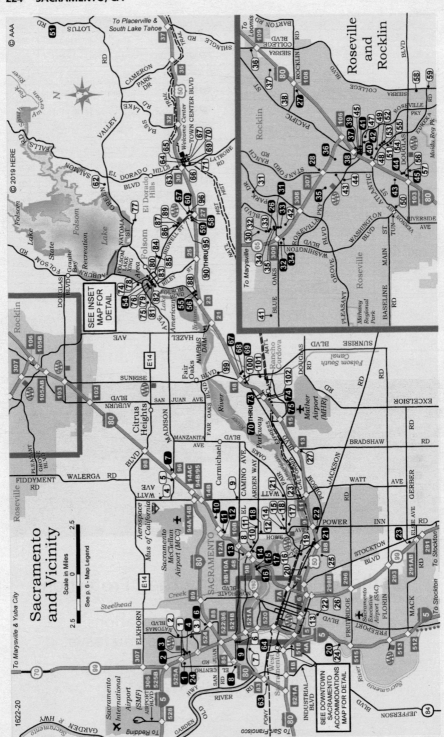

✈ Airport Hotels

Map Page	SACRAMENTO INTERNATIONAL (Maximum driving distance from airport: 6/7 mi)	Diamond Rated	Member Savings	Page
① p. 224	Four Points by Sheraton Sacramento International Airport, 6.1 mi	💎💎💎	✔	234
④ p. 224	Hampton Inn & Suites Sacramento-Airport/Natomas, 6.6 mi	💎💎💎	✔	234
㉔ p. 224	Hilton Garden Inn Sacramento Airport Natomas, 6/7 mi	💎💎💎	✔	234
③ p. 224	Holiday Inn Express & Suites-Sacramento Airport/Natomas, 6.5 mi	💎💎💎	✔	235
② p. 224	Homewood Suites by Hilton Sacramento Airport, 6.5 mi	💎💎💎	✔	235

Sacramento and Vicinity

This index helps you "spot" where approved hotels and restaurants are located on the corresponding detailed maps. Restaurant price range is a combination of lunch and/or dinner. Turn to the listing page for more information and consult display ads for special promotions.

 For more details, rates and reservations: AAA.com/travelguides/hotels

SACRAMENTO

Map Page	Hotels	Diamond Rated	Member Savings	Page
① p. 224	Four Points by Sheraton Sacramento International Airport	💎💎💎	✔	234
② p. 224	Homewood Suites by Hilton Sacramento Airport	💎💎💎	✔	235
③ p. 224	Holiday Inn Express & Suites-Sacramento Airport/Natomas	💎💎💎	✔	235
④ p. 224	Hampton Inn & Suites Sacramento-Airport/Natomas	💎💎💎	✔	234
⑥ p. 224	Staybridge Suites Sacramento Airport/Natomas	💎💎💎		235
⑦ p. 224	Crowne Plaza Sacramento	💎💎💎		233
⑧ p. 224	Fairfield Inn & Suites by Marriott Sacramento Airport Natomas	💎💎💎	✔	234
⑨ p. 224	Residence Inn by Marriott-Sacramento Airport Natomas	💎💎💎	✔	235
⑩ p. 224	Ramada Sacramento	💎💎		235
⑪ p. 224	Hampton Inn & Suites	💎💎💎	✔	234
⑫ p. 224	Holiday Inn Express & Suites Sacramento Cal Expo	💎💎💎		235
⑬ p. 224	Hilton Sacramento Arden West	💎💎💎	✔	235
⑭ p. 224	DoubleTree by Hilton Sacramento	💎💎💎	✔	233
⑮ p. 224	TownePlace Suites by Marriott Sacramento Cal Expo	💎💎💎	✔	235
⑯ p. 224	Fairfield by Marriott Sacramento Cal Expo	💎💎💎	✔	234
⑰ p. 224	Courtyard by Marriott Sacramento Cal Expo	💎💎💎	✔	233
⑱ p. 224	Residence Inn by Marriott Sacramento Cal Expo	💎💎💎	✔	235
⑳ p. 224	The Westin Sacramento	💎💎💎💎	✔	235
㉑ p. 224	Hampton Inn & Suites at Sacramento State	💎💎💎	✔	234
㉒ p. 224	Comfort Inn & Suites	💎💎💎		233
㉓ p. 224	Best Western John Jay Inn	💎💎	✔	233
㉔ p. 224	Hilton Garden Inn Sacramento Airport Natomas	💎💎💎	✔	234

Map Page	Restaurants	Diamond Rated	Cuisine	Price Range	Page
① p. 224	Malabar	💎💎	American	$12-$37	236

Map Page	Restaurants (cont'd)	Diamond Rated	Cuisine	Price Range	Page
2 p. 224	Bella Bru Cafe	◆◆	American	$13-$26	235
3 p. 224	Bangkok Garden Thai Cuisine	◆◆	Thai	$9-$15	235
4 p. 224	House of Thai Rice and Noodle	◆◆	Thai	$9-$14	236
5 p. 224	Brookfields Restaurant	◆◆	American	$8-$20	235
6 p. 224	Ruchi Indian Cuisine Sacramento	◆◆	Indian	$10-$16	236
7 p. 224	The Virgin Sturgeon Restaurant-Marina	◆◆	American	$10-$26	236
8 p. 224	Seasons 52 Fresh Grill	◆◆◆	New American	$10-$32	236
9 p. 224	Sam's Hof Brau	◆	Comfort Food Sandwiches	$7-$13	236
10 p. 224	Taro's by Mikuni	◆◆	Japanese Sushi	$13-$23	236
11 p. 224	Leatherby's Family Creamery	◆◆	American	$8-$17	236
12 p. 224	**The Kitchen Restaurant**	◆◆◆◆◆	American	$135	236
13 p. 224	Andy Nguyen's Vegetarian Restaurant	◆◆	Vegetarian	$11-$15	235
14 p. 224	Wildwood Kitchen & Bar	◆◆◆	American	$12-$18	236
15 p. 224	Piatti Ristorante & Bar	◆◆◆	Italian	$15-$38	236
16 p. 224	Selland's Market - Cafe	◆◆	American	$7-$18	236
17 p. 224	Ettore's European Bakery & Restaurant	◆◆	American	$11-$28	236
18 p. 224	Boudin SF	◆	American	$8-$11	235
19 p. 224	Opa! Opa!	◆	Greek	$7-$14	236
20 p. 224	OneSpeed	◆◆	Pizza	$15-$22	236
21 p. 224	Cafe Vinoteca	◆◆	Italian	$12-$15	235
22 p. 224	Freeport Bakery	◆	Breads/Pastries	$4-$10	236
23 p. 224	Rivers Edge Cafe	◆◆	Breakfast	$10-$16	236
24 p. 224	Scott's Seafood Grill & Bar	◆◆◆	Seafood	$14-$44	236
25 p. 224	Bacon & Butter	◆◆	Breakfast	$6-$18	235
26 p. 224	El Novillero Restaurant	◆◆	Mexican	$9-$19	236
27 p. 224	Perko's Cafe & Grill	◆◆	American	$8-$20	236

ROCKLIN

Map Page	Hotels	Diamond Rated	Member Savings	Page
26 p. 224	Staybridge Suites	◆◆◆		213
27 p. 224	Comfort Inn & Suites Rocklin-Roseville	◆◆◆		213
28 p. 224	Holiday Inn Express	◆◆◆		213

Map Page	Restaurants	Diamond Rated	Cuisine	Price Range	Page
30 p. 224	Anatolian Table Turkish Cuisine & Patisserie	◆◆	Turkish	$9-$28	213
31 p. 224	Thai Chili Restaurant	◆◆	Thai	$12-$15	213
32 p. 224	Lucille's Smokehouse Bar-B-Que & Catering	◆◆	Barbecue	$13-$29	213
33 p. 224	Skipolini's Pizza & Pasta	◆◆	Italian	$9-$34	213
34 p. 224	The Chef's Table	◆◆	American	$15-$33	213
35 p. 224	Crazy Sushi	◆◆	Japanese Sushi	$10-$24	213
36 p. 224	Studio Movie Grill	◆◆	American	$11-$15	213

Map Page	Restaurants (cont'd)	Diamond Rated	Cuisine	Price Range	Page
37 p. 224	Pottery World Cafe	💎💎	American	$7-$20	213
38 p. 224	Rubino's Ristorante	💎💎	Italian	$8-$30	213

ROSEVILLE

Map Page	Hotels	Diamond Rated	Member Savings	Page
31 p. 224	SpringHill Suites by Marriott Roseville	💎💎💎	✔	215
32 p. 224	Home2 Suites By Hilton Roseville Sacramento	💎💎💎	✔	215
33 p. 224	TownePlace Suites by Marriott Roseville	💎💎💎	✔	215
34 p. 224	Residence Inn by Marriott Rocklin Roseville	💎💎💎	✔	215
35 p. 224	**Hyatt Place Sacramento/Roseville**	💎💎💎	✔	215
36 p. 224	Courtyard by Marriott Galleria	💎💎💎	✔	214
37 p. 224	Residence Inn by Marriott	💎💎💎	✔	215
38 p. 224	Hilton Garden Inn Roseville	💎💎💎	✔	214
39 p. 224	Courtyard by Marriott	💎💎💎	✔	214
40 p. 224	**Larkspur Landing Roseville**	💎💎💎	✔	215
41 p. 224	Fairfield by Marriott	💎💎	✔	214
42 p. 224	Holiday Inn Express - Roseville Galleria	💎💎💎		214
43 p. 224	**Best Western Roseville Inn**	💎💎	✔	214
44 p. 224	**Best Western Plus Orchid Hotel & Suites**	💎💎	✔	214
45 p. 224	Hampton Inn & Suites Roseville	💎💎💎	✔	214

Map Page	Restaurants	Diamond Rated	Cuisine	Price Range	Page
41 p. 224	La Provence Restaurant & Terrace	💎💎💎	Regional French	$12-$55	215
42 p. 224	Johnny Garlic's	💎💎	American	$10-$27	215
43 p. 224	Il Fornaio	💎💎💎	Italian	$11-$38	215
44 p. 224	Zocalo	💎💎	Mexican	$13-$24	216
45 p. 224	Islands fine burgers & drinks	💎💎	Burgers	$9-$14	215
47 p. 224	RANGE kitchen & tap	💎💎	American	$11-$24	215
48 p. 224	Brookfields	💎💎	American	$9-$20	215
49 p. 224	Chicago Fire	💎💎	Italian Pizza	$6-$29	215
50 p. 224	The Place	💎💎	Italian	$10-$26	215
51 p. 224	Paul Martin's American Grill	💎💎💎	American	$13-$25	215
52 p. 224	Blue Nami Taste of Japan	💎💎	Japanese Sushi	$11-$25	215
53 p. 224	Costa Vida Fresh Mexican Grill	💎	Mexican	$8-$50	215
54 p. 224	Ruen Thai	💎💎	Thai	$8-$14	215
55 p. 224	Fat's Asia Bistro & Dim Sum Bar	💎💎💎	Asian	$13-$22	215
56 p. 224	The Squeeze Inn	💎	Burgers	$4-$7	215
57 p. 224	Thai Basil Restaurant	💎💎	Thai	$9-$18	215
58 p. 224	Fins Market & Grill	💎💎	Seafood	$10-$26	215
59 p. 224	La Huaca	💎💎	Peruvian	$10-$25	215

PLACERVILLE

Map Page	Hotel	Diamond Rated	Member Savings	Page
51 p. 224	Eden Vale Inn	💎💎💎💎		197

FOLSOM

Map Page	Hotels	Diamond Rated	Member Savings	Page
54 p. 224	**Lake Natoma Inn Hotel & Conference Center**	♦♦♦	✔	80
55 p. 224	**Larkspur Landing Folsom**	♦♦♦	✔	80
56 p. 224	Hilton Garden Inn	♦♦♦	✔	80
57 p. 224	Staybridge Suites Sacramento-Folsom	♦♦♦		80
58 p. 224	Courtyard by Marriott Sacramento-Folsom	♦♦♦	✔	80
59 p. 224	Residence Inn by Marriott	fyi	✔	80
60 p. 224	Fairfield Inn & Suites by Marriott Sacramento-Folsom	♦♦♦	✔	80

Map Page	Restaurants	Diamond Rated	Cuisine	Price Range	Page
74 p. 224	Pete's Restaurant & Brewhouse	♦♦	Pizza	$10-$29	80
75 p. 224	Scott's Seafood Grill & Bar	♦♦♦	Seafood	$14-$55	80
76 p. 224	Heckle Alehouse & Eatery	♦	Comfort Food	$8-$13	80
77 p. 224	Mexquite Mexican Cuisine & Tequila Lounge	♦♦	Mexican	$9-$18	80
78 p. 224	Sutter Street Steakhouse	♦♦♦	Steak	$22-$40	80
79 p. 224	Karen's Bakery Cafe & Catering	♦♦	Breads/Pastries Sandwiches	$12-$17	80
80 p. 224	Chicago Fire	♦♦	Pizza	$4-$27	80
81 p. 224	Pizzeria Classico	♦♦	Pizza	$12-$31	80
82 p. 224	Sutter Street Grill	♦♦	American	$6-$18	80
83 p. 224	The Fat Rabbit Public House	♦♦	Irish	$8-$13	80
84 p. 224	Bacchus House Wine Bar & Bistro	♦♦♦	American	$11-$32	80
85 p. 224	Manderes	♦♦	American	$11-$32	80
86 p. 224	Visconti's Ristorante	♦♦	Italian	$10-$24	80
87 p. 224	Land Ocean New American Grill	♦♦♦	Steak Seafood	$13-$41	80
88 p. 224	Casa Ramos Mexican Restaurant	♦♦	Mexican	$9-$24	80
89 p. 224	Thai Paradise	♦♦	Thai	$11-$19	80
90 p. 224	Brisas Do Sul Brazilian Steak House	♦♦♦	Brazilian Steak	$38-$59	80
91 p. 224	Chicago Fire	♦♦	Pizza	$8-$27	80
92 p. 224	Blue Nami	♦♦	Japanese Sushi	$9-$25	80
93 p. 224	Lazy Dog Restaurant & Bar	♦♦	American	$9-$29	80
94 p. 224	Buckhorn BBQ	♦♦	Barbecue	$9-$27	80
95 p. 224	Back Wine Bar & Bistro	♦♦♦	Small Plates	$10-$28	80
96 p. 224	Mikuni Japanese Restaurant & Sushi Bar	♦♦	Japanese Sushi	$12-$26	80

WEST SACRAMENTO

Map Page	Hotels	Diamond Rated	Member Savings	Page
63 p. 224	Hampton Inn & Suites by Hilton-West Sacramento	♦♦♦	✔	402
64 p. 224	Rodeway Inn Capitol	♦♦		402

RANCHO CORDOVA

Map Page	Hotels	Diamond Rated	Member Savings	Page
67 p. 224	**Holiday Inn Rancho Cordova**	♦♦♦	✔	202
68 p. 224	**DoubleTree Suites by Hilton Sacramento-Rancho Cordova**	♦♦♦	✔	202

RANCHO CORDOVA (cont'd)

Map Page	Hotels (cont'd)	Diamond Rated	Member Savings	Page
69 p. 224	Sacramento Marriott Rancho Cordova *(See ad p. 233.)*	◈◈◈	✔	203
70 p. 224	Residence Inn by Marriott	◈◈◈	✔	203
71 p. 224	Hampton Inn by Hilton	◈◈◈	✔	202
72 p. 224	Fairfield Inn & Suites by Marriott	◈◈◈	✔	202
73 p. 224	Hyatt Place Sacramento/Rancho Cordova *(See ad p. 234.)*	◈◈◈	✔	203
74 p. 224	Best Western Plus Rancho Cordova Inn	◈◈◈	✔	202
75 p. 224	Courtyard by Marriott Sacramento/Rancho Cordova	◈◈◈	✔	202

Map Page	Restaurants	Diamond Rated	Cuisine	Price Range	Page
99 p. 224	Il Forno Classico	◈◈	Italian	$15-$34	203
100 p. 224	Brookfields	◈◈	American	$10-$23	203
101 p. 224	Grills & Greens	◈	Mediterranean	$7-$16	203
102 p. 224	Famous Burgers	◈	Burgers	$6-$10	203

EL DORADO HILLS

Map Page	Restaurants	Diamond Rated	Cuisine	Price Range	Page
62 p. 224	Kochi Sushi & Japanese Bar and Grill	◈◈	Japanese Sushi	$9-$27	72
63 p. 224	Bella Bru Café	◈	American	$10-$20	72
64 p. 224	Aji Japanese Bistro	◈◈	Japanese	$10-$39	72
65 p. 224	Pete's Restaurant & Brewhouse	◈◈	American	$10-$29	72
66 p. 224	Milestone Restaurant	◈◈	New American	$12-$37	72
67 p. 224	C. Knight's Steakhouse	◈◈◈	Steak	$21-$59	72
69 p. 224	Selland's Market Cafe	◈◈	American	$8-$18	72
70 p. 224	Bamiyan Afghan Restaurant	◈◈	Afghan	$6-$39	72
71 p. 224	36 Handles	◈◈	American	$7-$21	72

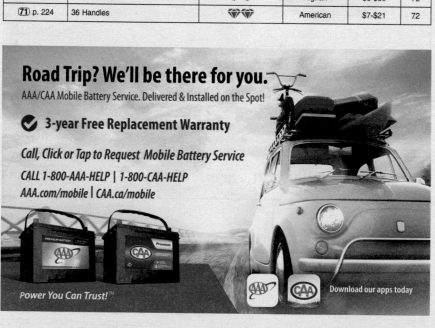

DOWNTOWN SACRAMENTO
- Restaurants p. 232
- Hotels & Restaurants map & index p. 221

AMBER HOUSE INN OF MIDTOWN   916/444-8085
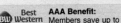 Bed & Breakfast. **Address:** 1315 22nd St 95816

BEST WESTERN PLUS SUTTER HOUSE
916/441-1314 **9**

Hotel

Best Western PLUS.
AAA Benefit: Members save up to 15% and earn bonus points!

Address: 1100 H St 95814 **Location:** 4 blks from state capitol; between 11th and 12th sts. **Facility:** 93 units. 3 stories, interior/exterior corridors. **Pool:** outdoor. **Activities:** exercise room. **Guest Services:** valet laundry. **Featured Amenity:** continental breakfast.

BEST WESTERN SANDMAN   916/443-6515 **5**

Hotel

Best Western.
AAA Benefit: Members save up to 15% and earn bonus points!

Address: 236 Jibboom St 95811 **Location:** I-5 exit 520 (Richards Blvd), just sw. **Facility:** 112 units. 2 stories (no elevator), exterior corridors. **Terms:** check-in 4 pm. **Pool:** heated outdoor. **Activities:** hot tub, exercise room. **Guest Services:** valet and coin laundry, area transportation. **Featured Amenity:** breakfast buffet. (See ad this page.)

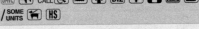

▼ See AAA listing this page ▼

🔗 **For more details, rates and reservations:**

AAA.com/travelguides/hotels

(See map & index p. 221.)

THE CITIZEN HOTEL, AUTOGRAPH COLLECTION
916/447-2700   **10**

Boutique Hotel

AUTOGRAPH COLLECTION HOTELS

AAA Benefit: Members save 5% or more!

Address: 926 J St 95814 **Location:** I-5 exit J St (Old Sacramento), 0.6 mi e; jct 10th St. **Facility:** This historic 1924 hotel, featuring upscale accommodations, is close to the state capitol and convention center. Many rooms offer views of the capitol. 196 units. 14 stories, interior corridors. **Parking:** valet only. **Amenities:** safes. **Dining:** Grange Restaurant & Bar, see separate listing. **Activities:** exercise room. **Guest Services:** valet laundry, boarding pass kiosk.

COURTYARD BY MARRIOTT SACRAMENTO AIRPORT/ NATOMAS
916/922-1120   **3**

Hotel

COURTYARD

AAA Benefit: Members save 5% or more!

Address: 2101 River Plaza Dr 95833 **Location:** I-5 exit 521A (Garden Hwy), just w, just n on Gateway Oaks Dr, then just e. **Facility:** 149 units. 4 stories, interior corridors. **Parking:** on-site (fee). **Pool:** heated outdoor. **Activities:** exercise room. **Guest Services:** valet and coin laundry, boarding pass kiosk.

DAYS INN-SACRAMENTO DOWNTOWN   916/443-4811   **4**
Motel. **Address:** 228 Jibboom St 95814

EMBASSY SUITES BY HILTON SACRAMENTO-RIVERFRONT PROMENADE
916/326-5000   **8**

Hotel

EMBASSY SUITES by HILTON

AAA Benefit: Members save up to 15%!

Address: 100 Capitol Mall 95814 **Location:** Waterfront. I-5 exit J St (Old Sacramento), just s on 3rd St, then just w. Located on Sacramento River; adjacent to Old Sacramento. **Facility:** 242 units. 8 stories, interior corridors. **Parking:** valet only. **Terms:** check-in 4 pm. **Amenities:** safes. **Dining:** Tower Bridge Bistro, see separate listing. **Pool:** heated indoor. **Activities:** hot tub, exercise room. **Guest Services:** valet and coin laundry, boarding pass kiosk, area transportation. **Featured Amenity:** full hot breakfast.

HILTON GARDEN INN SACRAMENTO/SOUTH NATOMAS
916/568-5400   **2**
Hotel. **Address:** 2540 Venture Oaks Way 95833

AAA Benefit: Members save up to 15%!

HOLIDAY INN EXPRESS SACRAMENTO CONVENTION CENTER   916/444-4436   **11**
fyi Hotel. Under major renovation, call for details. **Last Rated:** **Address:** 728 16th St 95814

HOLIDAY INN SACRAMENTO DOWNTOWN ARENA
916/446-0100   **6**
Hotel. **Address:** 300 J St 95814

HYATT REGENCY SACRAMENTO   916/443-1234   **13**

Hotel

HYATT REGENCY

AAA Benefit: Members save up to 10%!

Address: 1209 L St 95814 **Location:** 1/2 blk from state capitol; jct 12th and L sts. Located near convention center. **Facility:** Upscale appointments adorn the spacious lobby and common areas of this centrally located hotel. An attractive patio area features several outdoor fireplaces with seating areas. 505 units. 15 stories, interior corridors. **Parking:** on-site (fee) and valet. **Amenities:** safes. **Dining:** Dawson's Steakhouse, see separate listing. **Pool:** heated outdoor. **Activities:** hot tub, cabanas, exercise room, spa. **Guest Services:** valet laundry, boarding pass kiosk.

INN AND SPA AT PARKSIDE   916/658-1818   **16**
Bed & Breakfast. **Address:** 2116 6th St 95818

KIMPTON SAWYER HOTEL   916/545-7100   **7**

Hotel

Address: 500 J St 95814 **Location:** Between 5th and 7th sts. Adjacent to Golden 1 Center. **Facility:** This new hotel offers special amenities like a stocked mini-bar including snacks, in-room yoga mats, and multiple food and beverage outlets including one with bowling lanes, a pool table and karaoke! 250 units. 11 stories, interior corridors. **Parking:** on-site (fee) and valet. **Amenities:** safes. **Dining:** 2 restaurants. **Pool:** heated outdoor. **Activities:** bicycles, exercise room. **Guest Services:** valet laundry.

RESIDENCE INN BY MARRIOTT- SACRAMENTO DOWNTOWN AT CAPITOL PARK   916/443-0500   **14**
Extended Stay Hotel. **Address:** 1121 15th St 95814

AAA Benefit: Members save 5% or more!

SHERATON GRAND SACRAMENTO HOTEL
916/447-1700   **12**

Hotel

SHERATON

AAA Benefit: Members save 5% or more!

Address: 1230 J St 95814 **Location:** I-5 exit J St (Old Sacramento), 1 mi e; between 12th and 13th sts. Adjacent to Sacramento Convention Center. **Facility:** 503 units. 27 stories, interior corridors. **Parking:** on-site (fee) and valet. **Amenities:** safes. **Pool:** heated outdoor. **Activities:** exercise room. **Guest Services:** valet laundry.

(See map & index p. 221.)

SPRINGHILL SUITES BY MARRIOTT-SACRAMENTO AIRPORT NATOMAS   916/925-2280 **1**
▼▼ SAVE Hotel. **Address:** 2555 Venture Oaks Way 95833

AAA Benefit:
Members save 5% or more!

WHERE TO EAT

AIOLI BODEGA ESPANOLA   916/447-9440 **28**
▼▼▼ Spanish. Casual Dining. **Address:** 1800 L St 95811

BIBA   916/455-2422 **44**
▼▼▼ Italian. Fine Dining. **Address:** 2801 Capitol Ave 95816

BOMBAY BAR AND GRILL   916/441-7100 **38**
▼▼ Indian. Casual Dining. **Address:** 1315 21st St 95811

BURGERS AND BREW   916/442-0900 **39**
▼▼ Burgers. Quick Serve. **Address:** 1409 R St 95811

CAFETERIA 15L   916/492-1960 **24**
▼▼ American. Casual Dining. **Address:** 1116 15th St 95814

CENTRO COCINA MEXICANA   916/442-2552 **41**
▼▼ Mexican. Casual Dining. **Address:** 2730 J St 95816

CHICAGO FIRE   916/443-0440 **33**
▼▼ Pizza. Casual Dining. **Address:** 2416 J St 95816

CRAWDAD'S ON THE RIVER   916/929-2268 **2**
▼▼ Cajun. Casual Dining. **Address:** 1375 Garden Hwy 95831

DAWSON'S STEAKHOUSE   916/321-3600 **22**

▼▼▼▼
American Fine Dining $20-$45

AAA Inspector Notes: This upscale restaurant offers classic steakhouse fare. For diners with hearty appetites a recommended signature cut is the 16-ounce, 28-day dry-aged Kansas City strip. The chocolate soufflé will end your meal on a sweet note. Some menu items are available in smaller portion sizes. **Reservations:** suggested. **Address:** L St 95814 **Location:** 1/2 blk from state capitol, at 12th and L sts; in Hyatt Regency Sacramento. **Parking:** on-site (fee) and valet. D CALL &

DELTA BAR & GRILL   916/444-5464 **5**
▼▼ American. Casual Dining. **Address:** 1000 Front St 95814

ECHO & RIG   916/619-8939 **11**
▼▼▼ Steak. Fine Dining. **Address:** 500 NW J St, Suite 150 95814

ELLA DINING ROOM AND BAR   916/443-3772 **19**
▼▼▼ American. Fine Dining. **Address:** 1131 K St 95814

FAT CITY BAR & CAFE   916/446-6768 **4**
▼▼ American. Casual Dining. **Address:** 1001 Front St 95814

THE FIREHOUSE RESTAURANT   916/442-4772 **9**
▼▼▼▼ Continental. Fine Dining. **Address:** 1112 2nd St 95814

FIRESTONE PUBLIC HOUSE   916/446-0888 **26**
▼▼ American. Casual Dining. **Address:** 1132 16th St 95814

FOUNDATION RESTAURANT & BAR   916/321-9522 **12**
▼▼ American. Casual Dining. **Address:** 400 L St 95814

FRANK FAT'S   916/442-7092 **16**
▼▼ Chinese. Casual Dining. **Address:** 806 L St 95814

GRANGE RESTAURANT & BAR   916/492-4450 **14**
▼▼▼ American. Casual Dining. **Address:** 926 J St 95814

HOOK AND LADDER MANUFACTURING COMPANY   916/442-4885 **42**
▼▼ American. Casual Dining. **Address:** 1630 S St 95811

IL FORNAIO   916/446-4100 **13**
▼▼▼ Italian. Fine Dining. **Address:** 400 Capitol Mall 95814

IRON HORSE TAVERN   916/448-4488 **40**
▼▼ American. Casual Dining. **Address:** 1800 15th St 95811

KRU   916/551-1559 **46**
▼▼ Japanese Sushi. Casual Dining. **Address:** 3135 Folsom Blvd 95816

LA TERRAZA MEXICAN RESTAURANT   916/440-0874 **8**
◆ Mexican. Casual Dining. **Address:** 1027 2nd St 95814

LA TRATTORIA BOHEMIA   916/455-7803 **47**
◆ Czechoslovakian. Casual Dining. **Address:** 3649 J St 95816

MAGPIE CAFE   916/452-7594 **35**
▼▼ California. Casual Dining. **Address:** 1601 16th St 95814

MA JONG'S ASIAN DINER   916/442-7555 **25**
▼ Asian. Quick Serve. **Address:** 1431 L St 95814

MIKUNI JAPANESE RESTAURANT & SUSHI BAR   916/447-2112 **23**
▼▼ Japanese Sushi. Casual Dining. **Address:** 1530 J St 95814

MORTON'S THE STEAKHOUSE   916/442-5091 **15**
▼▼▼ Steak Seafood. Fine Dining. **Address:** 621 Capitol Mall, Suite 100 95814

MOTHER RESTAURANT   916/594-9812 **18**
▼▼ Vegetarian. Quick Serve. **Address:** 1023 K St 95814

MULVANEY'S BUILDING & LOAN   916/441-6022 **31**
▼▼▼ New American. Fine Dining. **Address:** 1215 19th St, Suite 100 95811

ORCHID THAI RESTAURANT AND BAR   916/476-3681 **37**
▼▼ Thai. Casual Dining. **Address:** 1609 16th St 95814

PARAGARY'S   916/457-5737 **45**
▼▼▼ California. Casual Dining. **Address:** 1401 28th St 95816

PEARL ON THE RIVER   916/567-3275 **1**
▼▼ American. Casual Dining. **Address:** 1379 Garden Hwy 95833

PETE'S RESTAURANT & BREWHOUSE   916/442-6770 **27**
▼▼ Italian. Casual Dining. **Address:** 2001 J St 95814

PILOTHOUSE RESTAURANT ABOARD THE DELTA KING   916/441-4440 **3**
▼▼▼ Continental. Fine Dining. **Address:** 1000 Front St 95814

PIZZA ROCK   916/737-5777 **17**
▼▼ Pizza. Casual Dining. **Address:** 1020 K St 95814

THE PRESS BISTRO   916/444-2566 **30**
▼▼▼ Mediterranean. Casual Dining. **Address:** 1809 Capitol Ave 95811

RIO CITY CAFE   916/442-8226 **7**
▼▼ California. Casual Dining. **Address:** 1110 Front St 95814

SUSPECTS MYSTERY DINNER THEATRE   916/443-3600 **6**
▼▼ American. Dinner Theatre. **Address:** 1000 Front St 95814

TEQUILA MUSEO MAYAHUEL   916/441-7200 **21**
▼▼▼ New Mexican. Casual Dining. **Address:** 1200 K St, Suite 3 95814

(See map & index p. 221.)

THAI BASIL   916/442-7690
 Thai. Casual Dining. **Address:** 2431 J St 95816

TOWER BRIDGE BISTRO   916/326-5050 ⑩
 American. Casual Dining. **Address:** 100 Capitol Mall 95814

TRES HERMANAS   916/443-6919 ㊱
Northern Mexican. Casual Dining. **Address:** 2416 K St 95816

THE WATERBOY RESTAURANT   916/498-9891 ㉞
French. Fine Dining. **Address:** 2000 Capitol Ave 95811

ZEN SUSHI   916/446-9628 ⑳
Japanese Sushi. Casual Dining. **Address:** 900 15th St 95814

ZOCALO   916/441-0303 ㉙
Mexican. Casual Dining. **Address:** 1801 Capitol Ave 95811

SACRAMENTO

- Restaurants p. 235
- Hotels & Restaurants map & index p. 224

BEST WESTERN JOHN JAY INN   916/689-4425 ㉓

Hotel

AAA Benefit: Members save up to 15% and earn bonus points!

Address: 15 Massie Ct 95823 **Location:** SR 99 exit Stockton Blvd/Mack Rd northbound, 0.8 mi n on Stockton Blvd, then just w; exit 291A (Mack Rd E) southbound, just e, then just n on Stockton Blvd, then just w. **Facility:** 58 units. 3 stories, interior corridors. **Pool:** outdoor. **Activities:** hot tub. **Guest Services:** coin laundry. **Featured Amenity:** continental breakfast.

COMFORT INN & SUITES   916/379-0400 ㉒
Hotel. **Address:** 21 Howe Ave 95826

COURTYARD BY MARRIOTT SACRAMENTO CAL EXPO   916/929-7900 ⑰

Hotel

COURTYARD **AAA Benefit:** Members save 5% or more!

Address: 1782 Tribute Rd 95815 **Location:** Business Rt I-80 exit 9A (Exposition Blvd), just sw. **Facility:** 152 units. 3 stories, interior corridors. **Pool:** outdoor. **Activities:** hot tub, exercise room. **Guest Services:** valet and coin laundry, area transportation.

CROWNE PLAZA SACRAMENTO   916/338-5800 ⑦
Hotel. **Address:** 5321 Date Ave 95841

DOUBLETREE BY HILTON SACRAMENTO   916/929-8855 ⑭

Hotel

DOUBLETREE BY HILTON **AAA Benefit:** Members save up to 15%!

Address: 2001 Point West Way 95815 **Location:** Business Rt I-80 (Capital City Frwy) exit Arden Way, just e. Across from Arden Fair Mall. **Facility:** 448 units. 3-4 stories, interior corridors. **Parking:** on-site (fee). **Terms:** check-in 4 pm. **Pool:** outdoor. **Activities:** hot tub, exercise room. **Guest Services:** valet laundry, area transportation.

▼ See AAA listing p. 203 ▼

(See map & index p. 224.)

FAIRFIELD BY MARRIOTT SACRAMENTO CAL EXPO 916/920-5300 16

Hotel

Fairfield **AAA Benefit:** Members save 5% or more!

Address: 1780 Tribute Rd 95815 **Location:** Business Rt I-80 exit 9A (Exposition Blvd), just sw. **Facility:** 75 units. 3 stories, interior corridors. **Pool:** outdoor. **Activities:** hot tub, exercise room. **Guest Services:** valet and coin laundry, area transportation. **Featured Amenity:** breakfast buffet.

SAVE ECO CALL BIZ / SOME UNITS

FAIRFIELD INN & SUITES BY MARRIOTT SACRAMENTO AIRPORT NATOMAS 916/923-7472 8

Hotel

Fairfield **AAA Benefit:** Members save 5% or more!

Address: 2730 El Centro Rd 95833 **Location:** I-80 exit 85 (W El Camino Ave), just w, just s on El Centro Rd, then just e on Tomato Patch Ln. **Facility:** 93 units. 3 stories, interior corridors. **Pool:** heated outdoor. **Activities:** hot tub, exercise room. **Guest Services:** valet and coin laundry, area transportation. **Featured Amenity:** breakfast buffet.

SAVE CALL BIZ HS / SOME UNITS

FOUR POINTS BY SHERATON SACRAMENTO INTERNATIONAL AIRPORT 916/263-9000 1

SAVE Hotel. **Address:** 4900 Duckhorn Dr 95834

AAA Benefit: Members save 5% or more!

HAMPTON INN & SUITES 916/927-2222 11

SAVE Hotel. **Address:** 2230 Auburn Blvd 95821

AAA Benefit: Members save up to 15%!

HAMPTON INN & SUITES AT SACRAMENTO STATE 916/451-1135 21

SAVE Hotel. **Address:** 1875 65th St 95819

AAA Benefit: Members save up to 15%!

HAMPTON INN & SUITES SACRAMENTO-AIRPORT/NATOMAS 916/928-5700 4

Hotel

Hampton by HILTON **AAA Benefit:** Members save up to 15%!

Address: 3021 Advantage Way 95834 **Location:** I-5 exit 525A (Del Paso Rd), just e, just s on East Commerce Way, then just w. **Facility:** 100 units. 3 stories, interior corridors. **Pool:** heated outdoor. **Activities:** hot tub, exercise room. **Guest Services:** valet and coin laundry.

SAVE CALL BIZ

HILTON GARDEN INN SACRAMENTO AIRPORT NATOMAS 916/579-7000 24

SAVE Hotel. **Address:** 20 Advantage Ct 95834

AAA Benefit: Members save up to 15%!

▼ *See AAA listing p. 203* ▼

(See map & index p. 224.)

HILTON SACRAMENTO ARDEN WEST
916/922-4700 **13**

Hotel

Hilton
HOTELS & RESORTS

AAA Benefit: Members save up to 15%!

Address: 2200 Harvard St 95815 **Location:** Business Rt I-80 (Capital City Frwy) exit Arden Way, just w, then just n. Located near Arden Fair Mall. **Facility:** 335 units. 12 stories, interior corridors. **Parking:** on-site (fee). **Amenities:** safes. **Dining:** 2 restaurants. **Pool:** heated outdoor. **Activities:** hot tub, exercise room. **Guest Services:** valet laundry, area transportation.

HOLIDAY INN EXPRESS & SUITES-SACRAMENTO AIRPORT/NATOMAS
916/928-9400 **3**

Hotel

Address: 2981 Advantage Way 95834 **Location:** I-5 exit 525A (Del Paso Rd), just e, just s on East Commerce Way, then just w. **Facility:** 100 units. 3 stories, interior corridors. **Amenities:** safes. **Pool:** heated outdoor. **Activities:** hot tub, exercise room. **Guest Services:** valet and coin laundry.

HOLIDAY INN EXPRESS & SUITES SACRAMENTO CAL EXPO
916/923-1100 **12**

 Hotel. **Address:** 2224 Auburn Blvd 95821

HOMEWOOD SUITES BY HILTON SACRAMENTO AIRPORT
916/263-9510 **2**

Extended Stay Hotel

HOMEWOOD SUITES BY HILTON

AAA Benefit: Members save up to 15%!

Address: 3001 Advantage Way 95834 **Location:** I-5 exit 525A (Del Paso Rd), just e, just s on East Commerce Way, then just w. **Facility:** 123 efficiencies, some two bedrooms. 3 stories, interior corridors. **Pool:** heated outdoor. **Activities:** hot tub, exercise room. **Guest Services:** valet and coin laundry.

GET THE APP
Download today.
Connect every day.
AAA.com/mobile
CAA.ca/mobile

RAMADA SACRAMENTO
916/664-3780 **10**

 Hotel. **Address:** 2600 Auburn Blvd 95821

RESIDENCE INN BY MARRIOTT-SACRAMENTO AIRPORT NATOMAS
916/649-1300 **9**

Extended Stay Hotel

Residence INN. **AAA Benefit:** Members save 5% or more!

Address: 2618 Gateway Oaks Dr 95833 **Location:** I-5 exit 521B (W El Camino Ave) northbound, just w, then just s on Gateway Oaks Dr; I-80 exit W El Camino Ave, 1.5 mi e, then just s on Gateway Oaks Dr. **Facility:** 126 units, some two bedrooms, efficiencies and kitchens. 2 stories (no elevator), exterior corridors. **Pool:** heated outdoor. **Activities:** hot tub, exercise room. **Guest Services:** valet and coin laundry. **Featured Amenity:** breakfast buffet.

RESIDENCE INN BY MARRIOTT SACRAMENTO CAL EXPO
916/920-9111 **18**

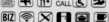 Extended Stay Hotel. **Address:** 1530 Howe Ave 95825

AAA Benefit: Members save 5% or more!

STAYBRIDGE SUITES SACRAMENTO AIRPORT/NATOMAS
916/575-7907 **6**

 Extended Stay Hotel. **Address:** 140 Promenade Cir 95834

TOWNEPLACE SUITES BY MARRIOTT SACRAMENTO CAL EXPO
916/920-5400 **15**

 Extended Stay Hotel. **Address:** 1784 Tribute Rd 95815

AAA Benefit: Members save 5% or more!

THE WESTIN SACRAMENTO
916/443-8400 **20**

 Boutique Hotel. **Address:** 4800 Riverside Blvd 95822

AAA Benefit: Members save 5% or more!

WHERE TO EAT

ANDY NGUYEN'S VEGETARIAN RESTAURANT
916/736-1157 **13**
Vegetarian. Casual Dining. **Address:** 2007 Broadway 95818

BACON & BUTTER
916/346-4445 **25**
Breakfast. Casual Dining. **Address:** 5913 Broadway 95820

BANGKOK GARDEN THAI CUISINE
916/263-9600 **3**
Thai. Casual Dining. **Address:** 2069 Arena Blvd 95834

BELLA BRU CAFE
916/928-1770 **2**
American. Casual Dining. **Address:** 4680 Natomas Blvd 95835

BOUDIN SF
916/973-1849 **18**
American. Quick Serve. **Address:** 2573 Fair Oaks Blvd 95825

BROOKFIELDS RESTAURANT
916/332-0108 **5**
American. Casual Dining. **Address:** 4343 Madison Ave 95842

CAFE VINOTECA
916/487-1331 **21**
Italian. Casual Dining. **Address:** 3535 Fair Oaks Blvd 95864

(See map & index p. 224.)

EL NOVILLERO RESTAURANT   916/456-4287 26
💎💎 Mexican. Casual Dining. **Address:** 4216 Franklin Blvd 95820

ETTORE'S EUROPEAN BAKERY & RESTAURANT
                                 916/482-0708 17
💎💎 American. Casual Dining. **Address:** 2376 Fair Oaks Blvd 95825

FREEPORT BAKERY   916/442-4256 22
💎 Breads/Pastries. Quick Serve. **Address:** 2966 Freeport Blvd 95818

HOUSE OF THAI RICE AND NOODLE   916/333-2591 4
💎💎 Thai. Casual Dining. **Address:** 5738 Watt Ave 95660

THE KITCHEN RESTAURANT   916/568-7171 12

💎💎💎💎💎
American Fine Dining
$135

AAA Inspector Notes: While offering table or counter seating, sitting close to the exhibition kitchen allows diners to interact with chefs as they prepare a seasonal five-course menu featuring locally sourced ingredients prepared into unique and savory creations. There is an "intermission" mid-evening, allowing guests to peruse the kitchen and stop by several appetizer stations within the kitchen and outdoor patio area to sample creative small plates. There is one seating per evening, by reservation only. **Features:** full bar. **Reservations:** required. **Address:** 2225 Hurley Way 95825 **Location:** US 50 exit Howe Ave, 2.5 mi n; Business Rt I-80 exit Howe Ave, 2 mi s; just e of jct Howe Ave. D CALL ♿

LEATHERBY'S FAMILY CREAMERY   916/920-8382 11
💎💎 American. Casual Dining. **Address:** 2333 Arden Way 95825

MALABAR   916/574-9074 1
💎💎 American. Casual Dining. **Address:** 2960 Del Paso Rd 95834

ONESPEED   916/706-1748 20
💎💎 Pizza. Casual Dining. **Address:** 4818 Folsom Blvd 95819

OPA! OPA!   916/451-4000 19
💎 Greek. Quick Serve. **Address:** 5644 J St 95825

PERKO'S CAFE & GRILL   916/362-3274 27
💎💎 American. Casual Dining. **Address:** 9647 Micron Ave 95827

PIATTI RISTORANTE & BAR   916/649-8885 15
💎💎💎 Italian. Casual Dining. **Address:** 571 Pavilions Ln 95825

RIVERS EDGE CAFE   916/362-2221 23
💎💎 Breakfast. Casual Dining. **Address:** 8740 La Riviera Dr 95826

RUCHI INDIAN CUISINE SACRAMENTO 916/927-2600 6
💎💎 Indian. Casual Dining. **Address:** 2600 Gateway Oaks Dr 95833

SAM'S HOF BRAU   916/482-2175 9
💎 Comfort Food Sandwiches. Quick Serve. **Address:** 2500 Watt Ave 95825

SCOTT'S SEAFOOD GRILL & BAR   916/379-5959 24
💎💎💎 Seafood. Casual Dining. **Address:** 4800 Riverside Blvd 95822

SEASONS 52 FRESH GRILL   916/922-5252 8
💎💎💎 New American. Fine Dining. **Address:** 1689 Arden Way, Suite 1065 95815

SELLAND'S MARKET - CAFE   916/736-3333 16
💎💎 American. Casual Dining. **Address:** 5340 H St 95819

TARO'S BY MIKUNI   916/564-2114 10
💎💎 Japanese Sushi. Casual Dining. **Address:** 1735 Arden Way, Suite 200 95815

THE VIRGIN STURGEON RESTAURANT-MARINA
                                 916/921-2694 7
💎💎 American. Casual Dining. **Address:** 1577 Garden Hwy 95833

WILDWOOD KITCHEN & BAR   916/922-2858 14
💎💎💎 American. Casual Dining. **Address:** 556 Pavilions Ln 95825

ST. HELENA (A-7) pop. 5,814, elev. 255'
- Hotels & Restaurants map & index p. 412
- Part of Wine Country area — see map p. 405

One of the Napa Valley's most delightful destinations, St. Helena is located on a scenic stretch of SR 29 running from Napa north to Calistoga. It shares its name with 4,342-foot-tall Mount St. Helena, a prominent landmark to the north.

Settlers began planting vineyards in the 1860s, and from its earliest days St. Helena was the central valley's commercial center and an important shipping point. Two of the area's many wineries—Beringer Vineyards and the Charles Krug Winery—are California Historical Landmarks.

The St. Helena Farmers Market is one of the valley's oldest and largest. It offers a cornucopia of seasonal organic fruits and vegetables, including a number of heirloom varieties. In addition to produce vendors sell products like fresh seafood, herbal teas and honey as well as jewelry and pottery created by local artisans. It sets up Friday mornings 7:30-noon, May through October, at Crane Park, about a mile south of downtown via Main Street/SR 29 to Grayson Avenue; the market entrance is adjacent to St. Helena High School.

Locally handmade items include the candles produced at the Hurd Beeswax Candle Factory, 345 La-Fata St. No molds are used; each candle is individually hand-twisted to the desired shape. The on-site store is open by appointment only; phone (707) 963-7211. Sunshine Foods, 1115 Main St., is packed to the rafters with specialty items, an awesome selection of locally produced cheeses and a deli that makes specialty sandwiches to go—everything you need for a picnic lunch to accompany a day of winery visits.

The Culinary Institute of America has a campus in St. Helena, housed in the imposing Greystone Cellars building at 2555 Main St. (accessible from SR 29). Cooking demonstrations are given regularly, and there are herb and organic gardens on the grounds. For more information phone (707) 967-1100.

St. Helena Chamber of Commerce: 657 Main St., St. Helena, CA 94574. **Phone:** (707) 963-4456.

WINERIES
- **Beringer Vineyards** is at 2000 Main St. **Hours:** Daily 10-5:30, June 1 through mid-Oct.; 10-5, rest of year. Various tours are conducted throughout the day; phone ahead for schedule. Closed Jan. 1, Thanksgiving and Christmas. **Phone:** (707) 302-7592. GT

- **Charles Krug Winery** is at 2800 Main St. (SR 29). **Hours:** Daily 10:30-5. Ninety-minute tours of the winery and hospitality center are given by appointment. Closed Jan. 1, Easter, July 4, Thanksgiving, Christmas Eve, Christmas and Dec. 31. **Cost:** Tasting fee $15-$45 per person. Tour and tasting $75 per person. **Phone:** (707) 967-2229 or (800) 682-5784. GT

- **Franciscan Estate** is s. on St. Helena Hwy. (SR 29) at jct. Galleron Rd. **Hours:** Tastings daily 10-5. Guided tours are available by appointment. Closed major holidays. **Phone:** (707) 967-3830. GT

EL BONITA MOTEL   707/963-3216   23
👑👑 Motel. **Address:** 195 Main St 94574

HARVEST INN   707/963-9463   24
👑👑👑👑 Hotel. **Address:** One Main St 94574

HOTEL ST. HELENA   707/963-4388   21
👑👑 Historic Hotel. **Address:** 1309 Main St 94574

MEADOWOOD NAPA VALLEY   707/967-1200   20
👑👑👑👑 **Address:** 900 Meadowood Ln 94574
Resort Hotel **Location:** From SR 29, 0.8 mi e on Pope St, 0.4 mi n on Silverado Tr, then just e. **Facility:** A true haven, this 250-acre private and lush reserve wraps around the upscale cottage-style rooms. All accommodations have fireplaces and decks. There are so many activities here and so little time! 99 units, some two and three bedrooms. 2 stories (no elevator), exterior corridors. **Parking:** on-site and valet. **Terms:** check-in 4 pm. **Amenities:** safes. **Dining:** The Grill at Meadowood, The Restaurant at Meadowood, see separate listings. **Pool:** heated outdoor. **Activities:** sauna, hot tub, steamroom, regulation golf, tennis, recreation programs, bicycles, lawn sports, trails, exercise room, spa. **Guest Services:** valet laundry, area transportation.

SPANISH VILLA INN   707/963-7483   18
👑👑👑 Bed & Breakfast. **Address:** 474 Glass Mt. Rd 94574

VINEYARD COUNTRY INN   707/963-1000   22
👑👑👑 Bed & Breakfast. **Address:** 201 Main St 94574

WINE COUNTRY INN   707/963-7077   19
👑👑👑 Hotel. **Address:** 1152 Lodi Ln 94574

WHERE TO EAT

BRASSWOOD BAR + KITCHEN   707/302-5101   14
👑👑👑 California. Casual Dining. **Address:** 3111 St. Helena Hwy N 94574

THE CHARTER OAK   707/302-6996   23
👑👑👑 California. Casual Dining. **Address:** 1050 Charter Oak Ave 94574

FARMSTEAD AT LONG MEADOW RANCH   707/963-4555   24
👑👑👑 Pacific Northwest. Casual Dining. **Address:** 738 Main St 94574

GATEHOUSE RESTAURANT   707/967-2300   15
👑👑👑 California. Fine Dining. **Address:** 2555 Main St 94574

GOOSE & GANDER   707/967-8779   21
👑👑👑 American. Gastropub. **Address:** 1245 Spring St 94574

GOTT'S ROADSIDE   707/963-3486   22
👑 American. Quick Serve. **Address:** 933 Main St 94574

(See map & index p. 412.)

THE GRILL AT MEADOWOOD
707/968-3144

▼▼▼
**California
Casual Dining
$24-$48**

AAA Inspector Notes: Awaken your taste buds while enjoying views of the wooded hillsides from this spot's relaxed, seasonal deck. Many ingredients used in the kitchen are sourced on premises, including their very own honey. The freshest and most flavorful produce is used here and many healthy options await including king salmon, day boat scallops with garden greens and quinoa spaghetti. Sink your teeth into a dry-aged New York steak or Wagyu burger. **Features:** full bar, patio dining, Sunday brunch. **Reservations:** suggested. **Address:** 900 Meadowood Napa Valley. **Location:** From SR 29, 0.8 mi e on Pope St, 0.4 mi n on Silverado Tr, then just e; in Meadowood Napa Valley. **Parking:** onsite and valet. B L D

HIMALAYAN SHERPA KITCHEN
707/963-4439 20

▼▼ Indian. Casual Dining. **Address:** 1148 Main St 94574

MARKET
707/963-3799 19

▼▼▼
**American
Casual Dining
$15-$36**

AAA Inspector Notes: This cozy elegant eatery in the heart of town prepares American fare with a flair. Selections include succulent rack of lamb, organic fried chicken, wild king salmon and macaroni and cheese with a gourmet twist. I particularly enjoyed the ahi tartare with soy truffle vinaigrette paired with wonton chips from the small plates menu. **Features:** full bar, Sunday brunch. **Reservations:** suggested. **Address:** 1347 Main St 94574 **Location:** On SR 29; center. **Parking:** street only. L D CALL ♿

THE MODEL BAKERY
707/963-8192 18

▼ Breads/Pastries Sandwiches. Quick Serve. **Address:** 1357 Main St 94574

THE RESTAURANT AT MEADOWOOD
707/967-1205 17

▼▼▼▼▼ New American. Fine Dining. **Address:** 900 Meadowood Ln 94574

SALIDA pop. 13,722

FAIRFIELD INN & SUITES BY MARRIOTT
209/543-7800

▼▼▼ SAVE Hotel. **Address:** 4342 Salida Blvd 95368

AAA Benefit: Members save 5% or more!

HAMPTON INN & SUITES
209/543-3650

▼▼▼ SAVE Hotel. **Address:** 4921 Sisk Rd 95368

AAA Benefit: Members save up to 15%!

LA QUINTA INN & SUITES BY WYNDHAM MODESTO SALIDA
209/579-8723

▼▼▼
Hotel

Address: 4909 Sisk Rd 95368 **Location:** SR 99 exit 233 (SR 219), just e. **Facility:** 67 units. 3 stories, interior corridors. **Pool:** outdoor. **Activities:** hot tub, exercise room. **Guest Services:** coin laundry. **Featured Amenity:** full hot breakfast.

SAVE 🛗 CALL ♿ 🛎 ⚕ BIZ
📶 ✕ 🐾 🔌 🖥 💻
/ SOME UNITS 🐾

BAMBOO HOUSE
209/545-8888

▼▼ Chinese. Casual Dining. **Address:** 4525 Broadway Ave 95368

SALINAS (G-3) pop. 150,441, elev. 55'
• Restaurants p. 240

Salinas was the birthplace of Nobel and Pulitzer prize-winning author John Steinbeck and the setting for many of his novels. A statue of the man who wrote such classics as "The Grapes of Wrath" and "East of Eden" stands on the lawn of the John Steinbeck Library, 350 Lincoln Ave.; phone (831) 758-7311. Steinbeck is buried in Garden of Memories Memorial Park, 850 Abbott St.; phone (831) 422-6417.

The vast quantities and varieties of vegetables and fruits grown in the Salinas Valley are responsible for the nickname "Salad Bowl of the World."

Salinas Valley Chamber of Commerce: 119 E. Alisal St., Salinas, CA 93901. **Phone:** (831) 751-7725.

Shopping: The anchor stores at Northridge Mall, US 101 at Boronda Road and N. Main Street, are JCPenney, Macy's and Sears.

 NATIONAL STEINBECK CENTER is at One Main St. The John Steinbeck Exhibition Hall's several themed galleries feature interactive exhibits about Steinbeck's life and literature. Stage settings and film clips help bring this Nobel prize-winning author's works to life; other displays allow you to explore "Cannery Row" and "Of Mice and Men." Visitors also can see the camper that transported the author and his poodle Charley across America, an experience that was the basis for the episodic travelogue "Travels with Charley."

Time: Allow 2 hours minimum. **Hours:** Daily 10-5. Closed Jan. 1, Thanksgiving and Christmas. **Cost:** $12.95; $9.95 (ages 62+ and students, teachers, military and Monterey County residents with ID); $6.95 (ages 6-17). **Phone:** (831) 775-4721.

VISION QUEST RANCH is 4 mi. e. off the SR 68 River Rd./Reservation Rd. exit, following signs to 400 River Rd. The property includes Monterey Zoo, home to more than 100 animals ranging from African elephants to lions, tigers, bears, monkeys, birds, reptiles and more. In addition to daily guided public tours, Vision Quest offers many other animal experiences, with some lasting several hours and some lasting several days. Private and hands-on tours also are available.

Time: Allow 1 hour, 30 minutes minimum. **Hours:** Guided tours are given daily at 1 (also at 3, June-Aug.). Private and hands-on tours are available by reservation; phone ahead for details. Closed major holidays. **Cost:** $16; $14 (ages 0-14). **Phone:** (831) 455-1901.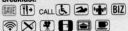

BEST WESTERN PLUS SALINAS VALLEY INN & SUITES
831/751-6411

Hotel

 Best Western PLUS. AAA Benefit: Members save up to 15% and earn bonus points!

Address: 187 Kern St 93905 **Location:** US 101 exit 328, just ne. **Facility:** 61 units. 3 stories, interior corridors. **Pool:** heated outdoor. **Activities:** hot tub, exercise room. **Guest Services:** coin laundry. **Featured Amenity:** full hot breakfast.

 CALL / SOME UNITS

BEST WESTERN SALINAS MONTEREY HOTEL
831/784-0176

Hotel

Best Western. AAA Benefit: Members save up to 15% and earn bonus points!

Address: 175 Kern St 93905 **Location:** US 101 exit 328, just ne. **Facility:** 58 units. 3 stories, interior corridors. **Pool:** outdoor. **Activities:** hot tub, exercise room. **Guest Services:** coin laundry. **Featured Amenity:** continental breakfast.

COMFORT INN & SUITES 831/770-1400
Hotel. **Address:** 181 Kern St 93905

COURTYARD BY MARRIOTT SALINAS MONTEREY
831/775-0491
Hotel. **Address:** 17225 El Rancho Way 93907

AAA Benefit: Members save 5% or more!

HAMPTON INN & SUITES BY HILTON SALINAS 831/754-4700
Hotel. **Address:** 523 Work St 93901

AAA Benefit: Members save up to 15%!

HOLIDAY INN EXPRESS & SUITES-SALINAS
831/737-1160

Hotel

Address: 195 Kern St 93905 **Location:** US 101 exit Market St, just e. **Facility:** 74 units. 3 stories, interior corridors. **Amenities:** safes. **Pool:** heated indoor. **Activities:** hot tub, exercise room. **Guest Services:** coin laundry. **Featured Amenity:** full hot breakfast.

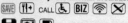

HOWARD JOHNSON BY WYNDHAM SALINAS
831/757-1020

Motel

Address: 131 John St 93901 **Location:** US 101 exit 327, 0.5 mi w. **Facility:** 38 units. 3 stories, exterior corridors. **Featured Amenity:** continental breakfast.

 CALL

LAUREL INN AND CONFERENCE CENTER
831/449-2474

Hotel

Address: 801 W Laurel Dr 93906 **Location:** US 101 exit 330, just e. **Facility:** 140 units. 2 stories (no elevator), exterior corridors. **Pool:** heated outdoor. **Activities:** hot tub. **Featured Amenity:** breakfast buffet.

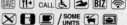
 / SOME UNITS

RESIDENCE INN BY MARRIOTT SALINAS MONTEREY
831/775-0410
Extended Stay Hotel. **Address:** 17215 El Rancho Way 93907

AAA Benefit: Members save 5% or more!

Make the Connection

Find this symbol for places to look, book and save on AAA.com.

WHERE TO EAT

DIM SUM INN   831/998-8690
▼▼ Chinese Dim Sum. Casual Dining. **Address:** 1938 N Main St 93906

FIRST AWAKENINGS   831/784-1125
▼▼ Breakfast. Casual Dining. **Address:** 171 S Main St 93901

GINO'S FINE ITALIAN FOOD   831/422-1814
▼▼ Italian. Casual Dining. **Address:** 1410 S Main St 93908

MONTEREY COAST BREWING   831/758-2337
▼▼ American. Brewpub. **Address:** 165 Main St 93901

SALINAS CITY BARBEQUE   831/758-2227
▼▼ Barbecue. Casual Dining. **Address:** 700 W Market St 93901

SAN BRUNO (D-8) pop. 41,114, elev. 20'
• **Hotels & Restaurants map & index p. 316**
• **Part of San Francisco area — see map p. 243**

San Bruno lies practically in the shadow of its much larger neighbor occupying the northern tip of the San Francisco Peninsula. It also shares San Francisco's multicultural heritage. Nurture your spiritual side at the Sanatan Mandir Hindu temple, 205 Angus Ave. W., which serves San Bruno's Fiji-Indian community. If it's your first visit, go on a Tuesday evening, when you can not only meditate but join others at mahaprasad (dinner).

Golden Gate National Cemetery, 1300 Sneath Ln., honors those who gave their lives during the Spanish-American War, World War II, the Korean War and other conflicts. Among the war heroes buried here is Admiral Chester W. Nimitz, commander of the Pacific fleet during World War II. The cemetery is open daily 8-5; phone (650) 589-7737.

COMFORT INN & SUITES SAN FRANCISCO AIRPORT WEST
                                   650/589-5089 **25**
▼▼ Hotel. **Address:** 611 San Bruno Ave E 94066

COURTYARD BY MARRIOTT SAN FRANCISCO AIRPORT   650/952-3333 **24**

▼▼▼ **Hotel**

COURTYARD **AAA Benefit:** Members save 5% or more!

Address: 1050 Bayhill Dr 94066 **Location:** I-380 exit El Camino Real S, 0.3 mi s, then just w. San Bruno, 52. **Facility:** 147 units. 2-3 stories, interior corridors. **Activities:** exercise room. **Guest Services:** valet and coin laundry, boarding pass kiosk, area transportation.

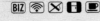

HOTEL AURA SAN BRUNO   650/588-0800 **27**
▼▼ Hotel. **Address:** 190 El Camino Real 94066

STAYBRIDGE SUITES - SAN FRANCISCO AIRPORT
                                   650/588-0770 **23**
▼▼▼ **Extended Stay Hotel**

Address: 1350 Huntington Ave 94066 **Location:** I-380 exit El Camino Real N, e on Sneath Ln, then just n. San Bruno, 52. **Facility:** 92 efficiencies, some two bedrooms. 3 stories (no elevator), exterior corridors. **Pool:** heated outdoor. **Activities:** hot tub, trails, exercise room. **Guest Services:** complimentary and valet laundry, area transportation. **Featured Amenity: breakfast buffet.**

SUPER 8 - SAN BRUNO   650/624-0999 **26**
▼▼ Hotel. **Address:** 421 El Camino Real 94066

WHERE TO EAT

THAI NAKORN   650/583-7555 **16**
▼▼ Thai. Casual Dining. **Address:** 464 San Mateo Ave 94066

SAN CARLOS (D-8) pop. 28,406, elev. 76'
• **Hotels & Restaurants map & index p. 316**
• **Part of San Francisco area — see map p. 243**

HILLER AVIATION MUSEUM is at 601 Skyway Rd. at the San Carlos Airport. The museum chronicles Northern California's contributions to aviation history. Hanging and ground displays of restored aircraft, full-size replicas and models range from an unmanned 1869 aeroplane to a 21st-century robotic flying wing. Youngsters can climb into the cockpit of a Navy jet and a Boeing 747. Other features include interactive displays, multimedia presentations and a glass-fronted restoration workshop. **Hours:** Daily 10-5. Closed Easter, Thanksgiving and Christmas. **Cost:** $16; $11 (ages 5-17 and 65+). **Phone:** (650) 654-0200.

COUNTRY INN & SUITES BY RADISSON   650/508-1800 **72**
▼▼▼ Hotel. **Address:** 251 El Camino Real 94070

FAIRFIELD INN & SUITES BY MARRIOTT SAN FRANCISCO/ SAN CARLOS   650/631-0777 **73**
▼▼▼ Hotel. **Address:** 555 Skyway Rd 94070

AAA Benefit: Members save 5% or more!

HOTEL SAN CARLOS   650/591-5771 **71**
▼▼ Motel. **Address:** 26 El Camino Real 94070

RESIDENCE INN BY MARRIOTT REDWOOD CITY SAN CARLOS   650/637-5500 **74**
▼▼▼ Extended Stay Hotel. **Address:** 800 E San Carlos Ave 94070

AAA Benefit: Members save 5% or more!

WHERE TO EAT

3 PIGS BBQ   650/592-4227 **69**
▼ Barbecue. Quick Serve. **Address:** 1754 Laurel St 94070

(See map & index p. 316.)

JERSEY JOE'S HOAGIES & CHEESESTEAKS
650/592-7317 (65)

Sandwiches. Quick Serve. **Address:** 21 El Camino Real 94070

KAYA TOFU & BBQ
650/595-9292 (66)

Korean Barbecue. Casual Dining. **Address:** 39 El Camino Real 94070

PIACERE RISTORANTE
650/592-3536 (68)

Italian. Casual Dining. **Address:** 727 Laurel St 94070

SNEAKERS PUB & GRILL
650/802-0177 (67)

American. Casual Dining. **Address:** 1163 San Carlos Ave 94070

Love the
Great Outdoors?

iStockphoto.com_pixelfit

San Francisco

Then & Now

In the shadow of a needle-pointed, 853-foot-tall skyscraper that signifies corporate America, an elderly vendor wearing silk slippers sells unfamiliar-looking vegetables piled in wooden crates under signs hand-lettered in Chinese characters.

A disheveled man sits cross-legged on a busy sidewalk in the Financial District, holding out a battered cup and soliciting spare change from wheeler-dealers dressed in expensive suits as they hurry by while perusing their smartphones.

A young woman with pierced ears, pierced eyebrows, a pierced nose and a bright green buzz cut walks along Haight Street gulping down a strong cappuccino and holding a bag containing a gluten-free, vegan banana muffin as she heads to work at a boutique that sells vintage hippie clothing. Meanwhile, in a fashionable home accessories store on Valencia Street two young men check out tables for the dining room of a renovated Victorian they've just purchased.

Droplets of dew still gleam on the grass as an early-morning jogger runs past a stand of eucalyptus trees; the scent of their leaves permeates the cool air. Meanwhile, the sun peeks above the horizon as fog rolls off the Pacific, billowing around the base of the Golden Gate Bridge as the sky turns from pink to pale blue.

AAA.com/travelguides—
more ways to look, book and save

Haight Street

This is San Francisco. Everywhere you turn there's an intriguing juxtaposition. The idealized image is of a worldly, sophisticated metropolis whose residents are blessed with the finer things in life—fantastic food, fine arts, handsome homes, picture-postcard views. And many do live this good life.

Then there's the other side of the coin: overcrowding, gentrifying neighborhoods and the impossibility of finding a parking space. The economic hardship extends to those free-spirited souls who by choice live in parks or on the street rather than under a traditional roof, and who have long given San Francisco its reputation for embracing both creative and alternative lifestyles.

And lurking in the background is an unpleasant thought that most residents manage to suppress but few can forget about completely, namely the threat of rattling dishes, wall cracks—or worse. Blame the San Andreas Fault.

(Continued on p. 244.)

Destination San Francisco

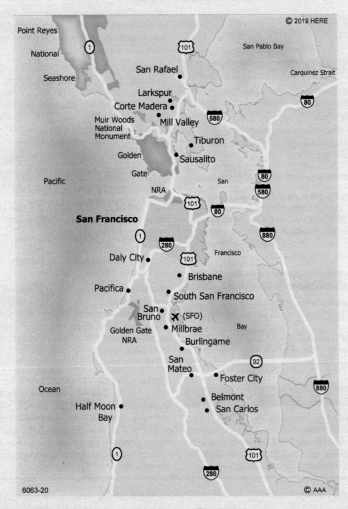

© 2019 HERE

Point Reyes
National
Seashore

San Pablo Bay

Carquinez Strait

San Rafael

Larkspur
Corte Madera

Muir Woods
National
Monument

Mill Valley

Tiburon

Golden
Gate

Sausalito

Pacific

San
Francisco

NRA

San Francisco

Daly City

Francisco

Brisbane

Pacifica

South San Francisco

San
Bruno

(SFO)

Millbrae

Golden Gate
NRA

Burlingame

Bay

San
Mateo

Foster City

Ocean

Belmont

Half Moon
Bay

San Carlos

6063-20

© AAA

This map shows cities in the San Francisco vicinity where you will find attractions, hotels and restaurants. Cities are listed alphabetically in this book on the following pages.

Fast Facts

ABOUT THE CITY

POP: 805,235 ■ **ELEV:** 63 ft.

MONEY

SALES TAX: State and county sales taxes total 8.5 percent in San Francisco. A hotel room tax of 15 to 15.5 percent also is levied.

WHOM TO CALL

EMERGENCY: 911

POLICE (non-emergency): (415) 553-0123

HOSPITALS: California Pacific Medical Center, (415) 600-6000 ■ Saint Francis Memorial Hospital, (415) 353-6000 ■ St. Mary's Medical Center, (415) 668-1000 ■ Zuckerberg San Francisco General Hospital, (415) 206-8000 ■ University of California San Francisco Medical Center, (415) 476-1000.

VISITOR INFORMATION

San Francisco Visitor Information Center: 749 Howard St., San Francisco, CA 94103. **Phone:** (415) 391-2000.

The center is open Mon.-Fri. 9-5, Sat.-Sun. and holidays 9-3 (also open Sat.-Sun. 4-5, when convention is in progress). Closed Jan. 1, Thanksgiving and Christmas.

TRANSPORTATION

AIR TRAVEL: San Francisco International Airport (SFO) is about 13 miles south near San Bruno off US 101 (Bayshore Freeway); it receives flights from some 50 airlines as well as private charters. Norman Y. Mineta San Jose International Airport (SJC) is about 3 miles northwest of downtown San Jose. Oakland International Airport (OAK) is off I-880 about 10 miles south of downtown Oakland. *For additional information, see Arriving, Air Travel.*

RENTAL CARS: Hertz, with locations at the San Francisco, Oakland and San Jose airports, offers discounts to AAA members. Phone (650) 624-6600 for the San Francisco airport location, (415) 771-2200 for the outlet at 325 Mason St., (510) 633-4300 for the Oakland airport location, (408) 938-6000 for the San Jose airport location, or (800) 654-3080.

 Book and save at **AAA.com/hertz**

RAIL SERVICE: For schedule and fare information phone Amtrak at (800) 872-7245. *For additional information see Arriving, Rail Service.*

BUSES: Greyhound Lines Inc., (800) 231-2222, departs from Bus Deck Level Three of the Salesforce Transit Center, 425 Mission St.

TAXIS: Taxis in San Francisco are metered, with fares averaging about $3.50 for the first one-fifth mile and 55c for each additional one-fifth mile or minute of waiting time. Either phone for a cab or wait at a hotel taxi stand (hailing one on the street often takes time and persistence). Limousine service ranges from $60-$80 per hour.

PUBLIC TRANSPORTATION: San Francisco Municipal Railway (Muni) provides public transportation consisting of buses, streetcars, light rail, trolley buses and cable cars. BART (Bay Area Rapid Transit) connects San Francisco with East Bay cities, and passenger ferries link the city with the northern Bay Area. *For additional information see Getting Around, Public Transportation.*

(Continued from p. 242.)

But the City by the Bay remains a seductive, one-of-a-kind destination for visitors. It's all about location, location, location. Varying in elevation from sea level to 939 feet, the city rests on some 40 hills at the northern end of a narrow peninsula, bounded on three sides by water—the Pacific Ocean, San Francisco Bay and the Golden Gate Strait. The urban cityscape almost seems to bob up and down on its rolling terrain, like a boat riding a wave. For the record, there are seven major hills: Nob Hill, Rincon Hill, Russian Hill, Telegraph Hill, Mount Davidson, Mount Sutro and Twin Peaks.

And San Francisco neighborhoods are true communities, not idealized versions of reality designed to appeal to tourists. Chinatown has bustled since the 1850s. Vibrant murals cover buildings and gritty back-alley walls in the Mission. Fillmore Street pulses to the beat of rock and jazz music as it did in the 1960s. North Beach's nonconformist beat and Haight-Ashbury flower power paved the way for the prominent and politically active LGBTQ community centered in the Castro.

So what should you do? For one thing, eat out at the local restaurants—San Francisco is home to some of the best restaurants in the world. Take a nice long walk in Golden Gate Park. Ride a ferry. Hang out in Union Square. Go to a farmers market. Enjoy the views of San Francisco Bay from a cable car climbing Nob Hill. See a film at the Castro Theatre. These are just a few of our suggestions; you'll no doubt come up with many more fun things to do on your vacation.

Must Do: AAA Editor's Picks

- Start your San Francisco vacation by spending the day in ⚜ **Golden Gate Park** (between Fulton Street, Lincoln Way, Stanyan Street and the Great Highway). Observe multicolored tropical fish and other marine creatures at ⚜ **The California Academy of Sciences** (55 Music Concourse Dr.), contemplate great art at the ⚜ **de Young Museum** (50 Hagiwara Tea Garden Dr.) or stroll through plantings from around the world at the **San Francisco Botanical Garden at Strybing Arboretum** (9th Avenue and Lincoln Way).

- If you're looking for things for couples to do, you can walk or bike across the ⚜ **Golden Gate Bridge** (across Golden Gate Strait via US 101). Dress in layers for the 1.7-mile trek, and remember that you'll have to turn around and walk back. Parking is extremely limited in the north- and south-side parking lots, so take public transportation to the bridge.

- Explore the **Sutro Baths** (1004 Point Lobos Ave.), the oceanside ruins (due to a fire) of what once was a lavish bathing spa complex with the world's largest indoor swimming pool. If you're wondering what to do to cap off your day, nothing beats watching the sun set from the nearby **Cliff House** (1090 Point Lobos Ave.).

- Yes, **Fisherman's Wharf** (along The Embarcadero from Pier 39 to Ghirardelli Square) is touristy, but who can resist restaurants where you can nibble Dungeness crab or scarf down clam chowder from a sourdough bread bowl; it is one of those things you just have to do. Stop by the flagship location of Boudin Bakery, watch the team of bakers do their thing from an observation window and don't forget to pick up a fresh loaf or two to take home.

- At Fisherman's Wharf, adventure travel awaits in the form of the sightseeing ferry cruise from Pier 33 to ⚜ **Alcatraz Island** (in San Francisco Bay), site of the infamous federal penitentiary where the likes of Al Capone and George "Machine Gun" Kelly did time. Purchase tickets in advance to get the departure time you want.

- There are many fun things to do in San Francisco like riding a cable car (just don't call it a trolley). The Powell-Hyde line begins at Powell and Market streets and ascends up and over steep Nob Hill before ending at Beach and Hyde streets. If you're interested in learning more about the massive engines and wheels that power this manually operated system, visit the **Cable Car Museum and Powerhouse Viewing Gallery** (1201 Mason St.).

- Climb the **Filbert Steps** (Filbert and Sansome streets) ascending the east side of **Telegraph Hill** (near the east end of Lombard Street) and then take the elevator to the observation deck at the top of 210-foot **Coit Tower** (1 Telegraph Hill) for panoramic views of San Francisco Bay and the Golden Gate and Bay bridges.

- The block of **Lombard Street** (between Hyde and Leavenworth streets) is often called "the crookedest street in the world." The serpentine brick street, with its sculpted hedges and seasonal displays of pink and blue hydrangeas, is a prime photo op.

- Walk through the ornamental gate and explore bustling ⚜ **Chinatown** (Bush Street and Grant Avenue). Plan a day trip where you can duck into Grant Avenue's souvenir shops and bakeries, then cross over to parallel Stockton Street for the sensory overload of produce and meat markets.

- Grab a sidewalk seat and sip a cappuccino in **North Beach** (along Columbus Avenue), this town's Little Italy. Browse the tomes at City Lights bookstore, a Beat generation hangout, then have dinner at the **North Beach Restaurant** (1512 Stockton St.), an old-school Italian experience all the way.

- No trip to San Francisco is complete without experiencing the smell of incense that still wafts along **Haight Street** (between Stanyan and Divisadero streets), which remains resolutely groovy nearly 50 years after the Summer of Love.

Sutro Baths

San Francisco 1-day Itinerary

AAA editors suggest these activities for a great short vacation experience. Those staying in the area for a longer visit can access a 3-day itinerary at AAA.com/TravelGuides.

Morning

- Begin your San Francisco day with a brisk walk along The Embarcadero, the street that runs along the city's northeastern perimeter, as seagulls swoop and streams of ferry commuters from Sausalito and Tiburon disembark at the Ferry Building—all against the panoramic backdrop of the mighty Bay Bridge.

- Take a spin through the **Ferry Building Marketplace** (on the waterfront at the foot of Market Street). Browse the specialty food markets, pick up a baguette at the Acme Bread Company and check out the North Arcade Shops, complete with heated patio seating. Make a pit stop at Blue Bottle Coffee, where every drink is drip-brewed individually.

- On Saturday mornings (and also Tuesdays and Thursdays in scaled-back versions) the Ferry Building is the scene of the Ferry Plaza Farmers Market. Expect fruits, veggies and herbs, homemade jams and gorgeous bunches of cut flowers to be among the market's many delights, and much of the emphasis is on organic and California grown.

- From the Ferry Building, walk up Market Street to Grant Avenue, turn right and continue to the arched gate (at Bush Street) marking the symbolic entryway into ▽ **Chinatown**. You could take a guided walking tour, but it isn't really necessary to appreciate this densely packed enclave; wander up and down Grant and parallel Stockton Street, and check out the narrow alleyways running in between both.

- In Portsmouth Square (between Grant and Kearny streets), kids play and elderly men engage in *xiangqi* (Chinese chess) matches. Stockton Street shoppers pass rows of skinned ducks hanging in meat market windows, rainbow-colored cakes and overflowing produce bins stacked on the sidewalk. Try an egg tart at the Golden Gate Bakery (1029 Grant Ave.). You'll smell the scent of vanilla at the Golden Gate Fortune Cookie Factory (56 Ross Alley), which has been assembling them since 1962.

Afternoon

- There's no way you can take on all of ▽ **Golden Gate Park** in an afternoon, or even an entire day—the verdant expanse is 174 acres larger than New York's Central Park. Just focus on your particular area of interest. There are orchids and other exotic plants at **The Conservatory of Flowers** (100 John F. Kennedy Dr.), an impressive collection of art at the ▽ **de Young Museum** (50 Hagiwara Tea Garden Dr.) and way-cool aquarium exhibits at

Chinatown

▽ **The California Academy of Sciences** (55 Music Concourse Dr.). Take a stroll through the precisely manicured **Japanese Tea Garden** (75 Hagiwara Tea Garden Dr.) or the National AIDS Memorial Grove. For exercise with a scenic backdrop, walk the 3-mile length of this rectangular green space from east to west; you can either walk back or hop on a Muni bus.

- For lunch, **Park Chow** (1240 9th Ave.) is just half a block south of the park. The comfort food (salads, tuna melts) is good, and for dessert the pumpkin cake is awesome. If it's sunny, try to get a table on the rooftop patio.

Evening

- No San Francisco visit is complete without riding a cable car. Get on the Powell-Hyde Street line at Beach and Market streets in Fisherman's Wharf. The route includes a look at the famous "crookedest" block of **Lombard Street** (between Hyde and Leavenworth streets) from the top of Russian Hill.

- Choosing just the right restaurant for dinner in **North Beach**, San Francisco's definitively Italian neighborhood, poses a delightful dilemma, but **Calzone's** (430 Columbus Ave.) fills the bill as far as atmosphere goes. Try and snag a sidewalk table for great people-watching.

- Order the house drink named after Beat Generation icon Jack Kerouac (rum, tequila, orange and cranberry juice served in a bucket glass with a lime) at **Vesuvio Cafe** (255 Columbus Ave.). Artists, poets and hipsters have hung out at this funky bar since the "On the Road" author frequented it in the early '60s.

Top Picks for Kids

Under 13

- Cutting-edge technology takes center stage at the **Children's Creativity Museum** (221 Fourth St.), whether it's crafting clay characters and learning the basics of stop-motion animation or testing new apps and high-tech games in the Innovation Lab. This is an absolute must for your list of "things to do today."

- What kid wouldn't be mesmerized at the sight of a giant thorny phasmid (more commonly known as a walking stick) or delight in feeding baby farm animals? The emphasis is on personal animal encounters at the San Francisco Zoo's **Fisher Family Children's Zoo** (Sloat Boulevard and Great Highway).

- Another popular destination is the top of the hill in **Grandview Park** (14th Avenue and Noriega Street) where the panoramic view is one of the city's best, offering not only visual "Wow!" but an opportunity for an impromptu geography lesson pointing out various city landmarks. The climb up—via five steep flights of stairs—is strenuous, so be watchful if you have younger kids.

Teens

- The roundup of interactive exhibits at the ⬚ **Exploratorium** (Pier 15 on The Embarcadero) will pique the curiosity of inquiring and non-inquiring minds alike. The scientific principles at work when you cook an egg and an optical-illusion experiment involving a very famous painting by Leonardo da Vinci are two of the intellectually stimulating offerings.

Stow Lake

- **Haight Street** (between Stanyan and Divisadero streets) is one of many fun things to do with friends as it still channels 1967 and the Summer of Love. **Amoeba Music** (1855 Haight St.) has a huge selection of vintage albums and rock posters. For hippie-style jewelry and all things tie-dye, **Love on Haight** (corner of Haight and Masonic) is the place to go. The aroma of incense fills **The Love of Ganesha** (1573 Haight St.), a cool shop that sells clothes, crystals, rings, necklaces and groovy trinkets.

All Ages

- No San Francisco vacation is complete without a visit to **Fisherman's Wharf** (along The Embarcadero from Pier 39 to Ghirardelli Square). This is the place for families to spend a fun-filled day. And if they're around, the antics of sea lions atop the floating pilings at Pier 39 will keep everyone entertained.

- How do you get kids interested in history? One way is to take a ferry to ⬚ **Alcatraz Island** (in San Francisco Bay), the notorious former federal penitentiary that is one of the city's top tourist attractions, and with good reason: The crumbling building's fascinating, and the ferry ride to get there is always fun. Exploring the cell blocks on a night tour increases the spook factor and makes for a great adventure travel experience!

- There are tons of things to see and do on your trip to ⬚ **Golden Gate Park,** but put ⬚ **The California Academy of Sciences** (55 Music Concourse Dr.) at the top of the list. The tanks full of multicolored tropical fish and other sea creatures are awesome, and the planetarium is spectacularly state of the art. The domed, four-story Osher Rainforest is a re-created environment right down to the steamy humidity, while the undulating living roof is a cool-looking lesson in green sustainability.

- **Stow Lake** (middle of Golden Gate Park) is an idyllic refuge. Rent a paddleboat and putt along in a lush green setting complete with quacking ducks and turtles sunning on logs. Or bring a picnic lunch, hike to the top of 430-foot Strawberry Hill and enjoy the views.

- If you're looking for relaxing things to do this weekend, **Crissy Field** (along the northern bayfront past Fisherman's Wharf) is a great place to take kids and let them run off steam while you enjoy up-close views of the ⬚ **Golden Gate Bridge.** At this wide-open green space you can throw a Frisbee, fly a kite, stick your toes in San Francisco Bay or take a nice long walk.

- In February, the ⬚ **Southwest Airlines Chinese New Year Festival & Parade** (throughout Chinatown) is an eye-popping spectacle, complete with floats, costumes and the serpentine Gum Lung (Golden Dragon). But on any day the neighborhood is a fascinating, educational immersion in Asian culture.

Arriving
By Car

Scenic north-south routes passing directly through San Francisco are US 101 and SR 1. They enter the city separately from the south, merge on the San Francisco approach to the Golden Gate Bridge and continue together through a few miles of southern Marin County. Because SR 1, the curvy coastal route, is subject to dense fog and the possibility of landslides, you should check weather and road conditions before driving it.

The fast north-south route, I-5, is east of San Francisco; connections to the San Francisco-Oakland Bay Bridge are via I-505 and I-80 from the north and I-580 from the south. Another route, SR 99, closely parallels I-5 and also has connections into the city.

The primary route from the east is I-80 across the Sierras. I-80 skirts the Sacramento metropolitan area to the north before approaching the Greater Bay Area via Vallejo and then merging with I-580; access into the city is via the San Francisco-Oakland Bay Bridge.

Air Travel

The San Francisco Bay Area is served by three major airports. San Francisco International Airport (SFO) is about 13 miles south near San Bruno off US 101 (Bayshore Freeway). Norman Y. Mineta San Jose International Airport (SJC) is about 3 miles northwest of downtown San Jose. Oakland International Airport (OAK), off I-880 about 10 miles south of downtown Oakland, is more convenient than SFO if your destination is the East Bay.

San Francisco International Airport

In keeping with the city's progressive reputation, San Francisco International offers travelers a yoga room and rotating museum exhibits. The popular "You Are Hear" concert series offers everything from jazz and classical to R & B and world music served up by Bay Area musicians. Live music takes place on Fridays in July and August between 11 and 2 and also during the Thanksgiving and Christmas holidays.

To reach downtown from SFO, exit from the north terminal area and take US 101 north. At the US 101/I-80 junction, choose I-80 and then take the 4th Street exit. Follow 4th Street north past Moscone Center to Market Street; Union Square's hotels and the Financial District are just a few blocks to the north and east.

SuperShuttle travels from San Francisco International to major downtown hotels every 30 minutes, 5 a.m.-4 p.m. One-way fare for the 30-minute ride is $17. For reservations phone (800) 258-3826.

Door-to-door minivan shuttle service between the airport and hotels, businesses and residences is offered by several companies, including SuperShuttle and Airport Express, (415) 775-5121. The vans make frequent pickups from the blue zones on pedestrian islands on the airport's upper level. One-way fare is $15-$17 per person.

Airport shuttle buses pick up passengers on the arrivals level. Taxi fares between downtown and San Francisco International Airport average $35-$50; limousine service costs $50-$75.

AirTrain, an automated light rail system with nine stops throughout the airport, links the International Terminal with other terminals, parking garages, the rental car center and the airport BART station.

Bay Area Rapid Transit's (BART) Pittsburg/Baypoint line provides direct service to the airport. Transfer at the San Bruno station to a Millbrae train to connect with Caltrain rail service down the peninsula to San Jose. Other BART lines can be accessed via the Balboa Park transfer station. Fare for the approximately 30-minute ride from the airport to the downtown Powell Street station is $8.95. For BART schedule and fare information phone (415) 989-2278.

Norman Y. Mineta San Jose International Airport is conveniently located just off US 101. When leaving Terminal C (which receives most domestic airline flights) or Terminal A (which receives American Airlines and United as well as JetBlue and Delta), follow signs to US 101 and head north. On the way to downtown San Francisco US 101 bypasses Palo Alto and San Mateo.

To reach downtown San Francisco from Oakland International Airport, exit the terminal building and take Airport Drive east toward downtown Oakland. Exit north onto I-880 (Nimitz Freeway), which connects with I-80. Continue west across the San Francisco-Oakland Bay Bridge. For automobiles the toll is $4-$6, depending on the time of day and the day of the week. Take exit 2A (5th Street) north to

Market Street to reach the Union Square/Financial District area.

Hertz, with locations at the San Francisco, Oakland and San Jose airports, offers discounts to AAA members. Phone (650) 624-6600 for the San Francisco airport location, (415) 771-2200 for the location at 325 Mason St., (510) 639-0200 for the Oakland airport location, (408) 437-5700 for the San Jose airport location, or (800) 654-3080.

Rail Service

Most Amtrak rail service terminates in Oakland at Jack London Square (Alice Street and the Embarcadero) or at Emeryville. From Jack London Square, passengers are transported via shuttle bus to the following San Francisco stops: the Ferry Building, downtown at the foot of Market Street; Fisherman's Wharf at Pier 39; the Westfield San Francisco Centre mall at 4th and Market streets; in front of Macy's at Union Square; outside the Hyatt Regency San Francisco at California and Drumm streets; and at the Caltrain depot, 4th and King streets. For schedule, fare and additional information phone (800) 872-7245.

Getting Around
Street System

Two main thoroughfares are Market Street, which runs diagonally from 17th and Castro streets to The Embarcadero, and north-south Van Ness Avenue. Major east-west streets downtown are Bush and Pine, both one-way streets with synchronized traffic signals. Bush goes toward downtown, while Pine heads out. Numbered avenues run north-south in the residential neighborhoods north and south of Golden Gate Park, and the streets form a grid pattern. Streets also form a grid in much of the downtown area.

The Financial District is anchored by north-south Montgomery Street. Union Square is bordered north-south by Post and Geary streets and east-west by Stockton and Powell streets. **Note:** Ongoing construction associated with an extension of Muni's T Third Line from Bayshore to SoMa to Chinatown may cause occasional traffic delays, especially in the vicinity of Union Square.

Government buildings cluster around Civic Center, between Van Ness Avenue and Leavenworth Street and Golden Gate Avenue and Market Street. Civic Center, Union Square and the Financial District are all north of Market Street; south of Market north-south streets are numbered.

Although the street layout looks straightforward on a map, keep the extremely variable topography in mind when traveling, as the steep hills can be difficult to negotiate. If you're visiting, it may be more advantageous to use public transportation or walk rather than drive. If you'll be driving your own car, you might want to have your brakes checked before departing.

San Francisco intersections are subject to strict enforcement of the Anti-Gridlock Act. The fine for blocking an intersection with your vehicle is $106;

Golden Gate Bridge

the fine for blocking an intersection while turning is $110.

"The Boot" (also known as "The Denver Boot") is a metal clamp that immobilizes a car when attached to its wheel. This device is applied when five or more parking tickets have accumulated or if registration is not current; it is removed only when all outstanding fines and/or registration fees and a $445 de-booting fee have been paid. If the fines are not paid, the car may be towed within 72 hours.

Visitors should also be aware that municipal buses are equipped with a video camera used to ticket motorists who drive in designated public transit-only lanes (a $79 fine) or park in designated bus zones (a $288 fine).

The downtown speed limit, unless otherwise posted, is 25 mph (15 mph at blind intersections). Right turns on red are legal unless otherwise posted. Traffic is heavy throughout the day in the downtown area and on major thoroughfares. Avoid the San Francisco-Oakland Bay Bridge during rush hours, about 7-9 a.m. and 4-6:30 p.m.

Pedestrians using designated crosswalks always have the right of way. Many major intersections downtown and throughout the Bay Area have visual countdown displays indicating the number of seconds remaining before the light changes for pedestrians.

The latest highway improvement is the Presidio Parkway, which took 15 years to plan and build and opened to traffic in 2015. It replaced Doyle Drive (US 101) as the main south access route to the Golden Gate Bridge from downtown. The 1.6-mile parkway features two sets of tunnels and a viaduct that climbs above the rolling green hills of the Presidio en route to the bridge.

Parking

San Francisco is not a parking-friendly city. There is a shortage of on-street spaces and a plethora of parking regulations, which are strictly enforced. On-street metered parking is permitted in some areas, but much neighborhood parking is reserved for local residents and is by permit only.

There are parking garages at Fisherman's Wharf, 655 Beach St. at Hyde Street, (415) 673-1735; downtown at 833 Mission St. (at 5th Street), (415) 982-8522; at the Moscone Center, 255 3rd St., (415) 777-2782; and in Chinatown at 733 Kearny St., (415) 982-6353. Fees range from $1.50-$7 per hour and $15-$34 per day. The only public parking available for recreational vehicles is at Candlestick RV Park, south of the city limits off US 101 on Gilman Avenue; phone (415) 822-2299.

On-street parking is strictly regulated. In addition to posted tow-away zones, pay particular attention to curb colors, which determine parking availability. Red means no stopping, standing or parking whatsoever; yellow curbs indicate commercial loading and unloading (7 a.m.-6 p.m.). Passenger cars left unattended in downtown loading zones are subject to heavy fines and towing.

White curbs allow a 5-minute limit to pick up or discharge passengers during the hours the adjacent public building is open. White curbs marked with a taxi sign are within a taxi zone. Green curbs indicate 10-minute parking 9 a.m.-6 p.m. Blue marks spaces for use by the disabled; the fine for illegally parking

Cable car

in designated spaces for the disabled is a hefty $875, while the fine for parking in bus zone spaces is $288. In several areas of the city local residents have priority parking rights; be sure to read carefully all posted regulations wherever you park.

How you park also is subject to regulation. It is illegal to park a vehicle on any grade exceeding 3 percent without effectively setting the brakes and blocking the wheels by turning them against the curb or by other means. When parking uphill, the front wheels must be "heeled," or turned out, so that a tire is resting securely against the curb. When parking downhill, they must be "toed," or turned in. If there is no curb you must use a block. The emergency brake must always be firmly set.

If your car is towed, expect to pay plenty to get it back. Parking violations start at $52 for blocking a private entranceway, plus a hefty fine for towing and additional daily storage fees. Fines for illegally parking in disabled-designated spaces, in bus zones or in an area blocking access to a wheelchair ramp range from $288-$875.

In most cases, towed vehicles can be retrieved from Auto Return at 450 7th St. (between Harrison and Bryant streets). For additional information contact the City of San Francisco Parking and Traffic Department; phone (415) 553-1200.

Public Transportation

San Francisco Municipal Railway (Muni) provides bus, streetcar, light rail, trolley bus and cable car transportation. The cash fare for buses, streetcars, light rail and trolley buses is $2.75; $1.35 (ages 5-17 and 65+ and the physically impaired). Exact change is required. Single-trip fares paid with a Clipper card or via MuniMobile on buses and trains cost 25c less than fares paid with cash.

Cash fare includes a free transfer good for use on any other Muni vehicle (except cable cars). A bus transfer can be used within a 30-minute period; the driver will give you one when you pay the fare. A light rail single-ride fare card purchased at a Muni station can be used one additional time within a 90-minute period.

The Clipper card is an all-purpose electronic transit card that can be used on Muni, BART, Caltrain and Golden Gate Transit and Ferry transportation. Clipper card readers on buses and at Muni and BART entrance stations tag the card and then display the remaining cash balance or pass expiration date. Transfers are automatically calculated, eliminating the need for a paper transfer. A variety of different passes and cash value options can be added. For more information phone (877) 878-8883.

The MuniMobile ticketing app can be downloaded to an Android or iPhone to purchase, save and use tickets for bus, rail and cable car travel. The app allows you to buy tickets and passes in advance or on the go and pay with a credit/debit card or PayPal account. For more information dial 311 (within San Francisco) or phone (415) 701-2311 (outside San Francisco).

The Muni Passport, valid on all Muni transportation, offers unlimited all-day usage and is worth purchasing if you're a visitor and plan on using the system multiple times. A 1-day pass costs $21; a 3-day pass, $32; a 7-day pass, $42. The 3- and 7-day passports are valid for consecutive days only. A pass valid for 1 month costs $75 (Muni only); $94 (Muni and BART); $38 (ages 5-17, ages 65+ and the physically impaired; Muni pass only). Monthly passes are only available on a Clipper card.

Passes and Clipper cards can be purchased at San Francisco International Airport; at the San Francisco Visitor Information Center, Hallidie Plaza (lower level) at Market and Powell streets; at TIX Bay Area, inside the Union Square Garage at the Geary Street entrance; and at Walgreens stores, Whole Foods markets and other businesses. For schedules, routing and other information phone (415) 673-6864.

Note: You must be prepared to show proof of payment (Muni pass, Clipper card, single-ride ticket or transfer) for the duration of your trip on all forms of Muni transportation. Random checks of passengers exiting the turnstiles at Muni stations are frequently conducted, and a citation of up to $120 may be issued if you cannot show proof of payment.

Muni buses are numbered and destinations are marked on the front of the vehicle above the windshield. During the day most buses make stops every 10 to 15 minutes; stops are more frequent on major streets. Routes along busy thoroughfares like Van Ness Avenue provide 24-hour service, although stops are less frequent at night. Many covered bus stops have an automated timetable that displays the number of minutes until the next bus arrives.

Muni light rail cars run underground along Market Street downtown and above ground in outlying neighborhoods. There are eight lines: F (Market & Wharves), J (Church), K (Ingleside), L (Taraval), M (Ocean View), N (Judah), S (Castro-Embarcadero shuttle) and T (Third Street). Color-coded maps of the system are posted on the wall at each underground station.

The Muni's F Line (also called the Market Street Railway) carries passengers on vintage streetcars. The route begins at Market and Castro streets, runs down Market to The Embarcadero, then runs up The Embarcadero to Fisherman's Wharf, ending at Jones and Beach streets. Don't board a streetcar if you're in a hurry; they're much slower and make more stops than the light rail lines.

A 1.7-mile extension of Muni's T Third Line, currently under construction, will extend the line from the 4th Street Caltrain Station north to Chinatown. Four new stations are being built: a street-level station at 4th and Brannan streets, and underground subway stations at 4th and Folsom streets, Stockton Street at Union Square, and Stockton and Washington streets.

Construction of the subway tunnel and stations is scheduled to last through 2017, with the new line opening sometime in 2019. Until then both motorists

and pedestrians can expect occasional disruptions, especially in the vicinity of Union Square.

Although there are frequent stops and the trip is slow (travel speed is 9.5 mph), riding a cable car is an essential San Francisco experience. Preserved as national historic landmarks—the only ones on wheels—they began operating back in 1873. Maroon with cream and blue trim, cable cars are an integral part of the urban landscape.

There are three routes. The Powell-Hyde line begins at Powell and Market streets and ends at Victorian Park, at Beach and Hyde streets. The Powell-Mason line also begins at Powell and Market streets but ends at Bay and Taylor streets near Fisherman's Wharf. The California Street line travels between Market Street and Van Ness Avenue.

Cable cars run daily from 6 a.m.-1 a.m. One-way fare is $7. A Clipper card loaded with a Muni monthly pass or cash value is also accepted. No transfers are issued or accepted. If you're just riding for fun, the California Street line is likely to be the least crowded.

BART (Bay Area Rapid Transit) connects San Francisco with East Bay cities, terminating at Richmond (north), Pittsburg/Bay Point (east), Dublin/Pleasanton (southeast) and Fremont (south). On the San Francisco side of the bay the terminus is Millbrae, approximately 30 minutes south of downtown.

BART operates Mon.-Fri. 4 a.m.-midnight, Sat. 6 a.m.-midnight, Sun. and holidays 8 a.m.-midnight. Color-keyed wall maps at the stations list destinations and fares; tickets are dispensed from machines at each station. The one-way fare between downtown San Francisco stations is $1.95; 70c (ages 5-12, ages 65+, the physically impaired and if paying with a Clipper card). All fares are posted at the ticket machines. Phone (415) 989-2278 for schedule and other information. *(For more information see the San Francisco Metrorail System map p. 270.)*

AC Transit is a bus service that runs from the Transbay Terminal to various destinations in the East Bay area (Alameda and Contra Costa counties). Bus service via the Golden Gate Bridge connects San Francisco to Sausalito, Mill Valley and Tiburon in Marin County and to Santa Rosa in Sonoma County. Phone (415) 455-2000 for schedule, fare and other information.

Passenger ferries link San Francisco with northern Bay Area destinations and also crisscross San Francisco Bay, providing both commuter service and sightseeing pleasure. The Blue & Gold Fleet, (415) 705-8200, operates daily commuter service to Tiburon and Sausalito. Golden Gate Ferry, (415) 455-2000, has daily service to Larkspur and Sausalito; no service is available Jan. 1, Thanksgiving or Christmas. One-way rates to Sausalito are $12; $6 (ages 6-18, ages 65+ and the physically impaired). Rates to Larkspur are $11.50; $5.75 (ages 6-18, ages 65+ and the physically impaired).

The San Francisco Bay Ferry operates weekday ferries from Alameda to the San Francisco Ferry Building. One-way fares are $6.80 (cash) or $5.10 (Clipper card); $3.40 (ages 5-18, ages 65+ and the physically impaired). The Alameda/Oakland Ferry provides service to and from Alameda, Angel Island, Oakland and San Francisco. The Alameda/Oakland/San Francisco one-way fare is $6.80; $5.10 (Clipper card), $3.40 (ages 5-18, ages 65+ and the physically impaired). Phone (415) 705-8291.

Shopping

Whether it's malls, farmers markets, retail complexes, souvenir shops, stylish boutiques, secondhand stores or designer showrooms, a San Francisco vacation offers cosmopolitan, funky, kitschy and trendy choices guaranteed to keep committed shopaholics blissfully happy.

Antiques

When it comes to things to do in San Francisco, the handsome brick and cast-iron commercial buildings in historic **Jackson Square** are a must. They are among the city's oldest, dating from the gold rush era, and most survived the 1906 earthquake. In the 1870s this was a rough-and-tumble part of town known as the Barbary Coast. Wedged between the Financial District, Chinatown and North Beach, it's the best place in the city to browse for high-quality art and antiques.

Within a two-block radius along Jackson, Washington and Montgomery streets you can find dealers specializing in fine and decorative arts, 17th- and 18th-century English and European furniture, 19th-century French impressionist paintings, fine rugs,

antique posters and maps, early California art and cutting-edge contemporary design. **Arader Galleries** (432 Jackson St.), paintings, watercolors and prints.

Malls

Within easy walking distance of Jackson Square is **Embarcadero Center,** near The Embarcadero and the waterfront between Sacramento, Clay, Battery and Drumm streets. This mixed-use office and retail development consists of four separate buildings (conveniently called One, Two, Three and Four) that cover a five-block area, each with three levels of semi-open-air shopping and landscaped plazas at the promenade level where you can relax in a green setting above busy downtown streets.

In addition to service businesses and an assortment of casual eateries there's a handful of chains (think Banana Republic, Gap and Sephora), plus the Embarcadero Center Cinema. The Villancourt Fountain in adjacent Justin Herman Plaza (between Four Embarcadero Center and The Embarcadero), an assemblage of massive concrete blocks and shooting sprays of water, is a refreshing sight when the water's running (which seems to be about half the time).

Max out your credit cards at **Westfield San Francisco Centre,** two blocks from Union Square on Market Street (between 4th and 5th streets). Bloomingdale's and Nordstrom anchor this sleek, nine-story vertical mall and set the upscale tone. In addition to more than 170 specialty retailers—among them American Eagle Outfitters, H&M, J. Crew and Michael Kors—there's a food court with eateries a cut above most mall fast-food choices and a plush nine-screen multiplex.

Farmers Markets

Ferry Building Marketplace *(see attraction listing at the end of this section)* is thronged with tourists and locals every day of the week but especially so on Saturday mornings when the **Ferry Plaza Farmers Market** sets up behind and in front of the building. As farmers markets go this one is fantastic—basically everything is organic, and the seasonal selection of fruits and vegetables, mostly from farms in nearby counties, is dazzling. Flowers, baked goods, jams, jellies and specialty foods are sold as well. Ditch the traditional restaurants and graze your way through the stalls, nibbling on free samples and marveling at the sheer bounty of it all.

You can get your breakfast here, too, courtesy of the food vendors offering omelets, quesadillas, fried oyster po'boys and much more. The people-watching is fun, the street musicians are cool and the view of the Bay Bridge simply can't be beat.

There's more browsing potential just across The Embarcadero from the Ferry Building, where souvenir vendors set up their merchandise every day of the week, although Saturday is the big day. Sure, you'll see jewelry, sunglasses and tie-dye T-shirts, but also interesting art and knickknacks.

Embarcadero Center

The market, at the foot of (appropriately enough) Market Street, is open Saturday 8-2 and, in smaller versions, on Tuesday and Thursday mornings. After making the rounds—if you aren't loaded down with purchases and especially if it's a sunny day—one of the fun things for couples to do is take a walk along The Embarcadero.

The **Noe Valley Farmers Market** is held Saturdays 8-1 on 24th Street between Sanchez and Vicksburg streets (across from Martha and Bros. Coffee). In addition to a bounty of organic fruits and veggies sold by local farmers, there's usually live music. Shop for heirloom tomatoes and other seasonal organic produce, plus baked goods, olive oil, honey and granola, at the **Castro Farmers Market.** It sets up on Noe Street (between Market and Beaver streets) Wednesdays from 4-8 p.m., mid-March to mid-December.

The **Alemany Farmers Market,** at 100 Alemany Blvd. in Bernal Heights, is a bit more ramshackle (some of the produce is sold out of the back of trucks). There are lots of prepared ethnic foods, along with spices, nuts, hummus and Thai chiles, and food trucks dish up yummy Mexican, Filipino and Afghan dishes. It's open Saturdays 6-2:30. Parking can be problematic, especially before noon, but the market is within walking distance of Muni's #67 bus, which you can board near BART's 24th Street station.

The Inner Richmond's **Clement Street Farmers Market** is held year-round on Sunday from 9 to 2 on Clement (between 2nd and 4th avenues). Organic fruits, veggies and eggs, honey, nuts, cheeses, olive oil, gluten-free baked goods, juices and fresh-cut flowers are some of the goodies you'll find. Street parking is problematic, but if you're lucky enough to find a space you won't have to pay the meter.

Neighborhoods

Although many tourists tend to think of **Chinatown** as a place to go for dim sum and souvenirs, this bustling city within a city offers a lot more. Shoppers will want to focus on the many establishments lining Grant Avenue, where the merchandise ranges from cheap (back scratchers, plastic Buddhas) to pricey (fine antiques, jade jewelry), and sidewalk displays are meant to lure you inside.

Peking Bazaar (826-832 Grant Ave.) has everything from kimonos and Chinese lanterns to plush panda dolls for the kids. On a more global scale is **Michael Fine Art and Antique** (400 Grant Ave.). Three floors offer a selection of expensive items like marble statues, decorative glass, bronze mermaids, candelabras and solid gold chess sets. It's nice eye candy even if you don't purchase anything.

Herb shops are located primarily along Washington and Jackson streets and are fun places to go. Even if you're feeling perfectly healthy, step inside a couple just to inhale the aroma of ginseng and tea leaves.

The **Golden Gate Bakery** (1029 Grant Ave.) is a nearby restaurant known for egg tarts—flaky pastry

Dim sum in Chinatown

surrounding a smooth custard filling. Loyal customers swear by them. They also sell almond cookies (get a pink box to go) and moon cakes (the sweetness comes from lotus seed paste). Expect to wait in line, and bring cash.

Shopping in Japantown (also known as Nihonmachi) focuses on the **Japan Center** complex bounded by Post, Geary, Laguna and Fillmore streets; look for kimonos, wind chimes, teapots and bonsai trees. **Daiso** (22 Peace Plaza) is the Japanese equivalent of a Dollar Store and therefore a boon in this expensive city; it carries everything from bento boxes to cosmetics to flip-flops. **Kinokuniya Bookstore,** 1581 Webster St., has a wide assortment of manga comics in both Japanese and English, Japanese movies and music, toys and electronics. There's a large children's section in the back of the store.

From Japantown it's a short walk up Fillmore Street to fashionable **Pacific Heights,** where shopping for women's clothes is chic, trendy and fun—as long as you bring plenty of money. A good place to start is the five-block stretch of Fillmore from California Street north to Pacific Avenue. Smartly dressed fashionistas peruse clothes from top European designers like Ann Demeulemeester and Dries Van Noten at **Cielo** (2225 Fillmore St.), a high-end boutique. **Eileen Fisher** (2216 Fillmore St.) is beloved by those who are fashion-conscious but not skinny; the established brand specializes in high-quality, figure-flattering basics like maxi skirts, cardigans and wool trousers.

Edgy apparel by hip designers (think Nanette Lepore and Trina Turk) is displayed in the window at **Heidi Says Collections** (2426 Fillmore St.). Be forewarned; the goods are definitely on the pricey side. **Gallery of Jewels** (2115 Fillmore St.) sells lots of items by California designers; prices for rings, necklaces, bracelets and cuff links range from pretty reasonable to stratospheric.

Hop on the #22 Muni bus heading north on Fillmore toward the bay to reach the six-block **Union Street** shopping district, full of art galleries, jewelry stores and boutiques. **Fog City Leather** (2060 Union St.) has a large selection of men's and women's leather jackets, pants, belts and motorcycle vests. They also custom make everything from wallets to murses (men's purses) and do repair work on damaged garments.

Four blocks north of Union, **Chestnut Street** (the blocks from Fillmore west to Divisadero) is another neighborhood shopping area where the emphasis is on local businesses and specialty boutiques. Well-to-do Marina homeowners frequent the likes of Williams-Sonoma and Pottery Barn. If you're on vacation and looking for places to eat, pop into **Lucca Delicatessen** (2120 Chestnut St.), an old-school Italian deli all the way. Narrow and cramped but packed to the gills with meats, cheeses, breads and specialty foods, it's a great one-stop choice for *delizioso* sandwiches to go or fixings for a picnic on the grass at nearby Marina Green.

If you remember—or want to relive—the counter-culture days of the Summer of Love, then a trip to **Haight Street** is a must. Parts of the Haight still look like they're stuck in 1967, even though the neighborhood as a whole has been gentrifying for years and isn't nearly as gritty as it used to be. Head shops,

The Love of Ganesha

funky boutiques and vintage clothing stores offer oodles of browsing potential.

You'll find clothes (Grateful Dead T-shirts plus some contemporary additions like tie-dye catsuits and tank tops), rings and gifts at **Love on Haight** (corner of Haight and Masonic). Formerly Positively Haight Street, this shop's exterior artwork isn't as groovy as it used to be.

Exotic jewelry, clothing, scarves, trinkets and a great selection of incense can be found at **The Love of Ganesha**, on Haight near Clayton Street. This shop overflows with good vibes, from the welcoming proprietor to a complimentary cup of lemonade at the door.

With "creepy little things" like doll baby heads and dried puffer fish, **Loved to Death** (1681 and 1685 Haight St.) appeals to the macabre side. The merchandise ranges from books, art, jewelry, old photographs and home décor to skulls, framed butterflies, dead creatures displayed in shadowbox frames and cool-but-weird wall art.

Haight head shops always have awesome window displays—usually featuring '60s music icons Jerry Garcia, Janis Joplin and Jim Morrison as well as reggae superstar Bob Marley—and **Land of the Sun** (1715 Haight St.) is no exception. Inside you'll find Dead posters, tie-dye T-shirts, peace necklaces, smoking paraphernalia, candles and other reminders of the Summer of Love.

No Haight visit is complete without a stop at **Amoeba Music** (at the foot of Haight near Stanyan Street). The selection of albums and CDs in this cavernous space is encyclopedic, plenty of signs identify the different music genres and store staff will knowledgeably steer you in the right direction. The murals that practically cover the building are classic examples of Haight Street graffiti art.

Cliff's Variety (479 Castro St.) is a **Castro** institution. It's a hardware store and carries all the things you'd expect to find in a hardware store—plus toys, games, gag gifts, crafts and fabrics, bar accessories and kitchen items (everything from cast-iron skillets to teapots).

These days the **Mission** is gentrifying at an alarming rate, but so far **24th Street** has remained pretty immune. The dozen or so tree-lined blocks between Guerrero and York streets are chock-full of craft and gift shops, green grocers, panaderías (bakeries) and taquerías, where the tantalizing aroma of grilling meat wafts out of open doorways. Murals and graffiti art cover practically every flat surface. It's one of the city's most rewarding streets to wander.

Valencia Street once had plenty of Mission grit, but now it's crowded with pricey condos. The blocks between 16th and 24th draw hordes of hipsters who congregate at restaurants and clubs, but for the non-hip there are plenty of offbeat shops. One of our favorites is **Paxton Gate** (824 Valencia St.), filled with all manner of bizarre things (mobiles of tiny bird skeletons instead of alphabet blocks and baby toys, giant insects displayed in glass frames, mounted bat heads). But it's not all bones and taxidermy; there's also a selection of hand-crafted garden tools and unusual plants, primarily succulents and orchids.

The **Community Thrift Store** (623 Valencia St.) harkens back to the halcyon hippie days of yore with its hodgepodge of funky furniture, vintage clothing, old-fashioned knickknacks, teacups and china, used books and old records. They also donate a portion of their proceeds to local charities.

If you're in need of a chocolate fix, do not pass up **Dandelion Chocolate** (740 Valencia St.). For one thing, as soon as you walk in the door you'll smell the earthy aroma of rich chocolate. There's an array of chocolate bars and treats like caramel chocolate tarts, plus hot and cold drinks (the Mission hot chocolate is yummy). Or relax for a spell at **Borderlands Cafe** (870 Valencia St. near 20th Street). This cozy, plant-filled space has quiet nooks with couches and easy chairs, plus a nice selection of coffees and loose-leaf teas.

Specialty Districts

Union Square, bordered north and south by Post and Geary streets and east and west by Powell and Stockton streets, was built in 1850 and named for the pro-Union rallies held here during the Civil War. Framed by date palms and attractively landscaped with exotic plants and flowers, it's the heart of the downtown hangout and shopping scene.

Bordering the square and lining the surrounding streets are major department stores and ultra-chic, ultra-expensive boutiques. A huge Macy's towers above Union Square. Saks Fifth Avenue and Tiffany & Co. rub elbows on Post Street. Neiman Marcus boasts a six-story rotunda topped with an elaborate stained glass dome. In this heady company the likes of Williams-Sonoma and Victoria's Secret are rather small potatoes.

Facing the square on Post Street, at the corner of Stockton, is **Apple Union Square**. The tech giant's brand-new West Coast flagship, which replaced the former location at Stockton and Market, is fronted by spiffy sliding glass doors that double as huge two-story windows. The customer service section boasts a lineup of living trees, bringing the outdoors inside, while a "forum" area behind the building is open 24/7 and features a 50-foot green wall, free Wi-Fi and a refurbished, landmark 1970 fountain created by San Francisco artist Ruth Asawa.

Maiden Lane was once lined with bordellos; today this small side alley between Stockton Street and Grant Avenue is the location of several fancy-schmancy boutiques. Bring plastic if you plan on hitting Chanel or Hermès. Nearby Burberry and Cartier are on Post Street between Stockton and Grant Avenue; Giorgio Armani is at Post and Grant.

About a block farther at 135 Post St. is **Gump's**, a San Francisco institution known for distinctive gift items, home and garden accessories, furnishings and Asian-inspired jewelry. The emphasis at the three-level **Crocker Galleria** (50 Post St. between Kearny and Montgomery streets) is on casual eateries, sweet shops (cupcakes, chocolates) and local

The Mission

businesses (hair and nail salons, florists). There's also a rooftop seating area. It's closed on Sunday. A small farmers market sets up on the first floor Thurs. 10-2.

FERRY BUILDING MARKETPLACE is on the waterfront along The Embarcadero at the foot of Market St. Until the opening of the San Francisco Bay Bridge in 1936 and the Golden Gate Bridge a year later, this was the transportation focal point for anyone arriving by ferry from points east and north. The Ferry Building, which celebrated its 100th anniversary in 2015, was restored to its former grandeur when the Embarcadero Freeway was torn down after being heavily damaged by the 1989 Loma Prieta earthquake.

The terminal's clock tower remains a San Francisco landmark, and the building hums with commuters and tourists traveling to and from Alameda, Oakland, Larkspur, Sausalito, Vallejo, Tiburon and Angel Island. It also houses two dozen or so specialty food retailers and several restaurants. Pick up fresh-made sourdough baguettes or a crusty loaf of levain walnut bread at the Acme Bread Company. Next door, Cowgirl Creamery offers an array of aromatic cheeses. For carnivores there's Boccalone Salumeria and the Prather Ranch Meat Co. Grocers, a Sur La Table cookware store and local favorites Peet's Coffee & Tea, Blue Bottle Coffee and ice cream maker Humphry Slocombe are here, too.

This is *the* place to be on Saturday morning, when the Ferry Plaza Farmers Market sets up; smaller versions operate on Tuesday and Thursday mornings.

Hours: Building open daily 7 a.m.-10 p.m. Hours for individual businesses vary but are normally Mon.-Fri. 10-7, Sat. 8-6, Sun. 11-5. Free guided walking tours are offered Tues. at noon and Sat. at 10 a.m. Closed Jan. 1, Thanksgiving and Christmas. **Phone:** (415) 983-8030. 🚇 Embarcadero, 40

FISHERMAN'S WHARF is part of the northern waterfront. This is a working wharf that also has enough picturesque sights and pungent smells to attract millions of visitors annually. The area is packed with restaurants, hotels, souvenir shops and attractions. On sunny weekends and throughout the summer season it can be extremely busy. But there are several good reasons to spend some time here. First and foremost, the nearby piers are departure points for scenic bay cruises and ferries to Sausalito, Angel and Alcatraz islands, and other destinations.

Sidewalk vendors sell fresh crab, one of the wharf's original attractions. You also have to try clam chowder in a sourdough bread bowl, which is offered at practically every restaurant. And all kinds of street performers—artists, musicians, mimes—are on hand to entertain the crowds.

Note: Street parking is very hard to come by, especially during the summer high season. There are public garages and parking lots along Beach and North Point streets. The Powell-Hyde cable car line beginning at Market Street lets off passengers in Victorian Park at Beach and Hyde streets, while the Powell-Mason cable car line lets passengers off at Taylor and Bay streets, both within easy walking distance. Muni's F Line streetcar and the #19, #30 and

#47 Muni buses also stop near Fisherman's Wharf. **Phone:** (415) 674-7503 Mon.-Fri. 10-6 for general information.

GHIRARDELLI SQUARE, between Beach, Polk, North Point and Larkin sts., is within walking distance of Fisherman's Wharf and the cable car turn-around. This complex of brick buildings is the site of the former Ghirardelli Chocolate Factory. They now house a handful of specialty retailers, and yes—you can still get your chocolate fix at the Ghirardelli Ice Cream and Chocolate Shop. Take a look at original chocolate manufacturing equipment and then indulge in one of their signature chocolate squares or have a dish of ice cream in the café.

There's certainly no shortage of gift shops at Fisherman's Wharf, but Jackson & Polk is one worth checking out. The out-of-the-ordinary items include seahorse necklaces, octopus rings, scarves, handbags, candles, art and books. The little gnome figurines are delightful. **Phone:** (415) 775-5500.

PIER 39 is at Beach St. at the northern end of The Embarcadero. This waterfront shopping and dining complex is touristy with a capital "T." And that's definitely not a bad thing if you're looking for souvenirs, mementos, keepsakes or kitsch. "I Escaped From Alcatraz" T-shirts? "I ♥ San Francisco" sweatshirts? Snow globes? Fridge magnets? They're all here, and much more.

Shops are primarily of the gift variety, selling collectibles, candy and casual clothing. Along with waffle cones, mini doughnuts and hot pretzels, the food options include favorites like clam chowder in a sourdough bread bowl and freshly caught seafood. Jugglers, musicians and acrobats provide free entertainment at the rear end of the pier, and musicians also perform daily at the entrance plaza.

Sea lions have been one of The PIER's chief attractions since 1989, when they began showing up just after the Loma Prieta earthquake. Lolling on floating docks built especially for them, uttering their distinctive bark, engaging in mock shoving matches or lazily rolling over like a dog playing dead, the whiskered marine mammals almost seem to pose for camera-toting tourists who position themselves for that one special shot.

In late 2009 almost all of the sea lions mysteriously disappeared. No one really knows what was behind the defection, although biologists suspect that changes in the food supply drove them elsewhere. Since then they've made something of a comeback, their numbers fluctuating depending on the time of year (you'll see fewer pinnipeds during the summer months). Learn more about them at the Sea Lion Center just above K-Dock. **Phone:** (415) 705-5500. 🚇 Chinatown, 126

Nightlife

Diversity is what this city is all about. The raucous forty-niners knew how to live it up way back when, and that good-time tradition continues. Cool blues, chill jazz, frenetic rock, classy cocktail lounges, bars

Ferry Building

with history, views with your booze (or some combination thereof)—San Francisco won't disappoint.

Bars

The perfect spot on a cool San Francisco night might just be the **Buena Vista Cafe,** near Ghirardelli Square and the cable car turnaround at 2765 Hyde St., where you can warm up with an Irish coffee. Legend has it that this is the birthplace of that whiskey-infused cup of joe, but in actuality it's the first place the drink was served in the United States. (in 1952, to be exact). Grab a seat and warm the cockles of your heart after a busy day of sightseeing. Phone (415) 474-5044.

The **Gold Dust Lounge** (165 Jefferson St.), a longtime Union Square bar, relocated to Fisherman's Wharf in 2013. This space is much larger but retains such signature features as the massive chandeliers and a pressed-tin ceiling complete with cherubs. It's one of San Francisco's fun places to go at happy hour. Phone (415) 397-1695.

In addition to being known as San Francisco's "Little Italy," **North Beach** is also where you'll find some of the city's most popular late-night hangouts. This is where the beat generation poets caroused in the 1950s, and two bars still recall that era.

Lawrence Ferlinghetti (former owner of the famed City Lights Bookstore), Allen Ginsberg and Jack Kerouac were regulars at **Vesuvio Cafe** (255 Columbus Ave., just off tiny Jack Kerouac Alley). From the San Fran memorabilia (loads of historic photos) to absinthe on the drinks menu, this place oozes hipster cred. It's cramped and can get crowded; try and snag one of the tiny tables on the second floor.

In an alley just across Columbus at 12 Saroyan Pl. is **Spec's Twelve Adler Museum Cafe** (Spec's for short), where irreverent cartoons and bizarre antiques cover the walls, and the beers come with crackers and a hunk of cheese to nibble on. Both bars attract a mixed clientele that enjoys reliving a bit of the past. Phone (415) 362-3370 for Vesuvio or (415) 421-4112 for Spec's.

At the **Tosca Café** (242 Columbus Ave.) an espresso machine still stands by the bar and the jukebox is still heavy on operatic standards, but the red booths were upgraded to real leather a couple of years ago. Tosca became one of the city's great places to eat with the addition of an open kitchen. Phone (415) 986-9651.

Hipsters love Chinatown's **Li Po Cocktail Lounge** (916 Grant Ave.)—but don't let that stop you from taking a look around. There's more than a little bit of David Lynch atmosphere going on in this dive bar's dark, red back room, with its parade of interesting characters. The signature drink here is a mai tai; if you want something more potent, the Chinese whiskey packs a wallop. Phone (415) 982-0072.

Another no-frills Chinatown joint is **Red's Place** (672 Jackson St.). It's got friendly bartenders, draws a mix of locals and out-of-towners, and features a wide selection of bottled beers plus Chinese pop tunes on the jukebox. Regulars engage in fervent

Vesuvio Cafe

dice games; ask the bartender to teach you how to play liar's dice. Phone (415) 956-4490.

Climb to the top of ritzy Nob Hill and The Fairmont San Francisco, then take the elevator downstairs to the **Tonga Room & Hurricane Bar.** It's tiki kitsch elevated to an art form, from the palm trees, thatched huts and a lagoon with a floating ship (doubling as a bandstand) to the thunderstorm that arrives on cue every 20 minutes. They make a mean mai tai—and yes, your drink comes in a coconut complete with paper umbrella. There's an Asian-inspired buffet on select weekdays during happy hour, and dancing begins at 8 p.m. Phone (415) 772-5278.

If you find yourself in Pacific Heights following an afternoon of shopping and are wondering what to do next—or you're looking for a place to kick-start the evening—sidle on in to **Harry's Bar** (2020 Fillmore St.). The ambience is casual but not grungy, and the crowd is mostly local residents and young professionals unwinding after a tough day at the office. Phone (415) 921-1000.

The **Marina Lounge** (2138 Chestnut St.) has been around for decades. There's no pretense here—decent beers on tap, a jukebox heavy on classic rock and '80s hits, a pool table, a couple of old-school video games and a distinct absence of yuppie types. In the Lower Haight, **Toronado** (547 Haight St.) has plenty of space for locals and tourists to hang while watching playoff games or knocking back brews. Their craft beer selection is notable. Phone (415) 922-1475 for the Marina Lounge, (415) 863-2276 for Toronado.

If you're looking for fun things to do with friends, the **Castro** is full of casual, friendly hangouts. Although it's a restaurant, **Cafe Flore** also has a full-service bar. The location—at the high-visibility corner of Market and Noe streets—makes this a prime spot to see and be seen. Go for one of the happy hour drink specials and sit outside for the best view of the always-entertaining street parade. The place is packed on warm evenings (or at least what passes for a warm evening in San Francisco), but even if the weather's chilly there are heat lamps and twinkling lights to keep the mood festive. Phone (415) 621-8579.

You won't encounter a lot of attitude at **Midnight Sun** (4067 18th St.). Convivial crowds gather at this small, laid-back bar for the 2-for-1 drink specials while watching music videos and "RuPaul's Drag Race" on big TV screens. **Twin Peaks Tavern** (across from the Castro Muni station), referred to as the "Glass Coffin" for its big windows and more mature clientele, is more amenable to conversation than most other Castro bars. Next door is Hot Cookie, highly regarded for fresh-baked treats. Phone (415) 861-4186 for Midnight Sun or (415) 864-9470 for Twin Peaks Tavern.

Cocktail Lounges

Among the many things for couples to do, a popular choice is indulging yourselves with cocktails at **Top of the Mark,** the classy lounge at the top of the InterContinental Mark Hopkins San Francisco that has been a Nob Hill landmark since 1939. The room isn't small but still feels intimate and cozy. Live music (mostly jazz) often enhances the mood, and movie screenings are offered on Tuesday nights in

Redwood Room

summer. Request a seat along the wall of windows for breathtaking views. Arrive with someone special at twilight, then watch the sun set and city lights come twinkling on for a truly magical experience. Phone (415) 392-3434.

Cool, sleek and fashionable defines the **Redwood Room** in the Clift Hotel at Union Square (495 Geary St.). This modern lounge exudes panache, from its redwood paneling to the changing display of digital artwork. Phone (415) 929-2372.

The Starlight Room is a throwback to when a night on the town meant dressing up for an evening at a swanky hotel's top-floor lounge—in this case Union Square's Sir Francis Drake Hotel (450 Powell St.). Cocktails and hors d'oeuvres are served in an opulent setting complete with red velvet booths, silk draperies and imported chandeliers. The dance floor can get crowded on weekend evenings. Sunday afternoon shifts gears with the very popular "Sunday's a Drag" hosted by local celebrity and drag performer Donna Sachet; in addition to the show there's an all-you-can-eat buffet brunch. Phone (415) 395-8595.

Dance Clubs

Locals and tourists looking for things to do this weekend can start at **SoMa** (South of Market Street) where the city's hippest clubs are concentrated. Two standbys are the **DNA Lounge** (375 11th St.) and **1015 Folsom** (the name is the address). Both are invariably packed and loud. Depending on the night, DNA might feature DJ sets, name bands or the Hubba Hubba Revue, a burlesque and variety show. At Folsom, DJs whip the crowds into a frenzy with hip-hop and electronic jams. Phone (415) 626-1409 for DNA, (415) 991-1015 for Folsom.

111 Minna Gallery (Minna Street at 2nd Street) leads a double life—art gallery by day, special event/dance club at night. It's a large space with high ceilings, and there's edgy, thought-provoking art everywhere—on the walls, on the bar, on the DJ platforms. Monthly dance party events include "Back to the '90s vs. 2000s." Phone (415) 974-1719.

Mezzanine (444 Jessie St. at Mint Street) is a cavernous, brick-walled space with a booming sound system that showcases live and electronic music—everything from salsa to hip-hop to electro-funk disco. When bands aren't playing, hot DJs take over. Multimedia art and fashion shows are regularly scheduled; purchasing advance tickets for these events is strongly recommended. Phone (415) 625-8880.

Temple Nightclub (540 Howard St.) has two dance floors. The floor on the main level is more spacious than at many other clubs; the music is mostly house. Downstairs it's crowded and sweaty and the music is mostly hip-hop. Phone (415) 312-3668. **Butter** (354 11th St.) calls itself a "white trash bistro," a theme borne out by Miller High Life served in paper bags and trailers (including a vintage Winnebago) that are part of the décor. DJs favor songs from the '90s and early '00s. Phone (415) 863-5964.

Note: Parts of SoMa can be sketchy, particularly after dark. If you're going to hit the clubs, go with a group. And neither Union Square nor SoMa is parking friendly; take a cab or use public transportation.

Rock and Blues Clubs

Complete your San Francisco vacation by visiting one of the cities many rock and blues clubs starting in the swanky and retro main room of **Bimbo's 365 Club** (1025 Columbus Ave.), a North Beach institution that's been in business since 1931. Tables and chairs in the red-accented room are arranged in a U-shape around a stand-or-dance area in front of the stage. The concert schedule is varied—rock bands, jazz artists, world music, stand-up comics—and plenty of big names appear. Arrive early if you want to snag a good table seat; phone (415) 474-0365.

Another San Francisco mainstay is the **Boom Boom Room** (1601 Fillmore St. at Geary). This was a blues spot in the 1930s, although nowadays you'll hear R&B, funk and soul as well. Check out the assemblage of old photos from past gigs on the club's walls. Legendary blues artist John Lee Hooker was affiliated with the Boom Boom Room in the late 1990s. Phone (415) 673-8000.

Former Steve Miller Band member Boz Scaggs opened **Slim's** (333 11th St.) back in the '80s, and it's one of the better places in town to see a rock band. Drink prices are reasonable and the sound system is decent. There's also a fair amount of street parking available in the vicinity, always a plus in this city. Phone (415) 255-0333.

Bottom of the Hill (1233 17th St.) is at the bottom of Potrero Hill. Pop, punk and noise bands, many local, play to young, enthusiastic crowds seven nights a week. The back patio is good for taking a break and chilling with friends. Go with a group, since the neighborhood tends to get a little sketchy late at night. Phone (415) 626-4455.

The **Great American Music Hall** (859 O'Farrell St.) started out in 1907 as a bordello; Sally Rand entranced audiences with fan dances during the 1930s, and it was a Moose Lodge in the '50s. Graced with marble columns and a frescoed ceiling, GAMH books a variety of rock and indie acts. You can pay general admission and stand in front of the stage or pay more to sit at a balcony table and have dinner. Phone (415) 885-0750.

The **Fillmore** (1805 Geary Blvd. at Fillmore) was a big name in the '60s San Francisco music scene: Promoter Bill Graham brought local rock bands like the Grateful Dead, Jefferson Airplane and Quicksilver Messenger Service as well as visionaries like Jimi Hendrix to his ballroom for concert "happenings" complete with psychedelic light shows. It's still the venue of choice for many performers today. Phone (415) 346-6000.

Another longtime rock palace is **The Warfield** (982 Market St.), a former vaudeville theater. The cozy ambience—complete with a beautifully detailed gold-leaf ceiling—is perfect for watching acts old

The Fillmore

and new do their thing. **Note:** Parking in the vicinity is practically nonexistent, but the theater is a short walk from the Powell Street Muni station. Phone (415) 345-0900.

The Chapel (777 Valencia St.) has rustic/industrial décor and a concert schedule featuring the usual buzzed-about names. Be forewarned that the venue sells out quickly depending on who's playing. If you can't make the show, hang out on the patio. Phone (415) 551-5157.

The Independent (628 Divisadero St., a block west of Alamo Square) is another popular joint with a good sound system and surprisingly non-funky bathrooms. The room is small enough that you have no trouble seeing the stage but big enough that it doesn't feel claustrophobic. Get tickets well in advance for shows by up-and-coming bands; they usually sell out quickly. Phone (415) 771-1421.

Big Events

San Francisco's packed events calendar kicks off with the **Sea Lions' Arrival at Pier 39,** a celebration welcoming the crowd-pleasing pinnipeds back to **Pier 39's K-Dock.** The sea lions, mostly young males, spend the winter in San Francisco Bay, feeding on herring, maneuvering for prime basking spots on the floating platforms—and seeming to mug for tourists' iPhone cameras. They first showed up at Pier 39 after the 1989 Loma Prieta earthquake, disappeared almost completely in 2009 (a vanishing act thought to be related to a reduced herring population) and have since made a partial comeback.

It's followed by an explosion of color—the ⬥ **Southwest Airlines Chinese New Year Festival & Parade.** Held in January or February in ⬥ **Chinatown,** the annual procession of stilt walkers, acrobats, lion dancers and ornate floats draws up to 500,000 spectators. The finale features a 250-foot-long golden dragon and a massive explosion of firecrackers.

Springtime in San Francisco is welcomed with a bevy of events. It arrives early at **Fisherman's Wharf** (around mid-February) courtesy of the **Tulipmania Festival,** when thousands of jewel-colored tulips—along with other spring flowers like daffodils, English primroses and Iceland poppies—burst forth from barrel planters in the vicinity of Pier 39. Sponsored by the San Francisco Orchid Society, the **Pacific Orchid and Garden Exposition** at The Hall of Flowers in Golden Gate Park features thousands of exotic varieties from around the world. The three-day event takes place in late February.

For fun things to do with friends, the **St. Patrick's Day Parade & Festival** takes place the Saturday before March 17 and includes religious services at St. Patrick's Church. The parade begins at 2nd and Market streets and proceeds up Market Street to Civic Center Plaza.

Another springtime celebration is the ⬥ **San Francisco Flower & Garden Show,** held at the **San Mateo County Event Center** in early April. The 5-day celebration of all things green not only spotlights beautiful gardens but offers practical tips for the home gardener, courtesy of guest speakers at some 100 seminars and workshops.

Sea lions at Pier 39's K-Dock

Among other things, you'll find out how to successfully garden in small spaces and nurture a healthy edible garden. The event also includes a roundup of well-known Bay Area chefs and wine producers.

Presented by a charitable organization whose members cross-dress as nuns and wear Kabuki-inspired makeup to call attention to gender and religious issues, the **Sisters of Perpetual Indulgence Easter Celebration** is campy fun, San Francisco style. There's an Easter egg hunt for kids on Easter Sunday morning, but the real entertainment commences afterward, with a bonnet contest, musical performances and various adult-oriented shenanigans. It usually takes place in ⬥ **Golden Gate Park**.

Two consecutive weekends in mid-April bring the **Northern California Cherry Blossom Festival,** an elaborate display of Asian culture and customs. Most events take place at the Japan Center complex at Post and Buchanan streets and the adjacent blocks of **Japantown.** The festival's Grand Parade begins at the Civic Center, proceeds up Polk to Post Street and ends at Post and Fillmore streets. If you're looking for fun places to go, this festival offers numerous opportunities to discover new places and immerse yourself in Asian cultures.

The 2-week **San Francisco International Film Festival,** which begins in early April, has been held nearly every spring since 1957. The works of adventurous filmmakers are screened at a handful of theaters, including the Victoria Theatre and the Alamo Drafthouse New Mission.

Mid-May brings the **Bay to Breakers 12K** race. The name Bay to Breakers was adopted in 1965, and it also describes the course—from a starting point a block east of The Embarcadero (and San Francisco Bay) to the finish line at the Great Highway at the western end of Golden Gate Park (and the ocean's crashing waves). The east-west route across the city officially measures 7.46 miles.

By the 1980s running boom the number of race participants had swelled to more than 100,000, and these days tens of thousands of people join in the trek along downtown streets and across the length of Golden Gate Park. Over the years different traditions also have emerged, from Batman and Wonder Woman costumes to occasional displays of public nudity. Today the party vibe is such that serious runners usually get an early start before the route becomes crowded with revelers.

Carnaval San Francisco, a multicultural, Mardi Gras-inspired street festival with a Latin American/Caribbean vibe, takes place in the **Mission District** over Memorial Day weekend. The main event is the Grand Parade, which begins at Bryant and 24th streets, proceeds west to Mission Street and then up Mission to 17th Street and the festival area. The parade is followed by a masquerade ball. Expect plenty of wildly colorful costumes, exuberant dancing and hip-shaking music.

For the **Union Street Festival,** which takes place the first weekend in June, six blocks of Union Street are transformed into "worlds" focusing on such topics as fashion, technology and health. Craft beer and wine-tasting pavilions offer gourmet culinary pairings, and food and craft vendors are also on hand if you're looking for places to eat or to try out samples of your newest fave restaurants.

The **Haight-Ashbury Street Fair,** the second weekend in June, celebrates the cultural history, diversity and overall grooviness of one of San Francisco's best-known neighborhoods. In addition to arts and crafts, food booths and a family-oriented area, live music takes place on two stages. In keeping with the Haight's long tradition of street art, each year a poster contest is held, and many of the creative posters advertising the event have become collector's items.

A trio of events takes place in early to mid-June. The **San Francisco Jazz Festival** brings the biggest names in jazz to the San Francisco Jazz Center and other venues around the city for a program of more than 30 concerts. The lineup of talent includes established names as well as up-and-coming talent and features artists from around the world who are creating traditional as well as adventurous new jazz sounds.

The **Juneteenth Festival** commemorates the end of slavery in the United States with a day of festivities that includes a parade along Fillmore Street between Eddy and Geary streets, a health fair, a classic car show and a petting zoo. The **North Beach Festival** is a lively street fair that includes a juried arts and crafts show, a pizza-tossing contest, a play area for kids and live entertainment.

The 3-day **Outside Lands Music and Arts Festival** in 🌲 **Golden Gate Park,** held in early August, is a huge event that has upped the ante when it comes to music festivals. The lineup of acts and DJs includes not only established big-name superstars but the newest buzzed-about bands and artists. Along with the performances there's food, wine, beer and exhibits of cutting-edge art. This festival is also noteworthy for emphasizing going green for everything from purified water stations to waste disposal. Parking is basically nonexistent; festivalgoers are strongly encouraged to use public transportation.

June is also Gay Pride Month, when visitors from all over the world come to San Francisco for a packed schedule of parties, dances, and film and arts festivals. The 2-day highlight in late June is the Lesbian, Gay, Bisexual and Transgender **SF Pride** parade up Market Street. With entertainment on more than 20 stages and venues—including the Main Stage in **Civic Center Plaza,** next to City Hall—this is the largest LGBT gathering in the country.

Held in conjunction with Pride and presented by Frameline, the **San Francisco International LGBTQ Film Festival** showcases the work of filmmakers from around the world. The 11-day schedule of gay, lesbian, bisexual and transgender-themed films includes features, documentaries, short films

and web series. Most showings take place at the Castro Theatre; other venues include the Roxie Theater and the Victoria Theatre.

All the world's a stage for the **San Francisco Shakespeare Festival,** which presents free weekend in-the-park productions of the Bard's plays throughout the month of September. Performances take place at the Presidio's Main Post Parade Ground Lawn (between Graham Street and Keyes Avenue) and at the Jerry Garcia Amphitheater in McLaren Park (40 John F. Shelley Dr.).

If experimental theater is more your style, the 2-week **San Francisco Fringe Festival** in mid-September spotlights local, national and international companies starring in some 200 low-priced performances—everything from comedy and drama to magic shows and free-wheeling experimental fare. Shows take place at the EXIT Theatre, 156 Eddy St. (two blocks from the Powell Street BART station). Tickets can be purchased online in advance or on the day of the show on a first-come, first-served basis.

Calling all chocoholics! The **Ghirardelli Chocolate Festival** the second weekend in September is a celebration that will appeal to the sweet tooth in everyone. More than 50 vendors showcase yummy products like chocolate-covered almond biscotti and a mini version of the Ghirardelli ice cream sundae, and dessert experts offer culinary demonstrations. A Chocolate & Wine Pavilion is especially popular. The event takes place at—naturally—**Ghirardelli Square.**

Thousands of people congregate in **North Beach** for the **Italian Heritage Parade** on the Sunday nearest Columbus Day. The festivities begin at Fisherman's Wharf with the customary blessing of the fishing fleet, followed by a parade of handcrafted floats winding its way to the "fisherman's church," the Church of Saints Peter and Paul at Washington Square. For a true celebration of Italian heritage, dine al fresco at one of the restaurants on Columbus Avenue along the parade route.

Over two weekends in mid- and late October the **Cow Palace** is the scene of the **Grand National Rodeo, Horse and Livestock Show,** which features rodeo events, prize-winning horse and livestock exhibits and the coronation of Miss Grand National Rodeo. Cheer on professional cowboys as they compete in bronc-busting, barrel-racing, bull-riding and steer-wrestling contests.

The **San Francisco International Auto Show** revs up in late November at the **Moscone Center.** In addition to showcasing new model year vehicles, attendees can get a look at classic cars, exotic sports cars from the world's major manufacturers, and a lineup of electric, hybrid and alternative fuel vehicles.

The **Macy's Union Square Tree Lighting Ceremony** ushers in the holiday season on the Friday after Thanksgiving. Macy's 83-foot-tall Great Tree, decorated with twinkling, energy-efficient LED lights and some 1,500 ornaments, is erected in the middle of the square. Live performances accompany the lighting ceremony. The illumination festivities bring hordes of onlookers, so taking public transportation is definitely advised. Union Square's seasonal ice-skating rink opens to the public at the beginning of November.

Rounding out the year in late December is the ▽▽ **Redbox Bowl,** which brings top college football teams from the Pac-12 and Big 10 conferences to **Levi's Stadium.**

Sports & Rec

Bay Area fans vigorously support their hometown teams, and San Francisco's and Oakland's professional and college lineup—the Giants, Oakland A's, 49ers, Golden State Warriors and Sharks—offer plenty to cheer for. In addition to the spectator sports venues listed below, the **Cow Palace,** 2600 Geneva Ave. at Santos Street in nearby Daly City, is a venue for rodeos, ice shows and other events; phone (415) 404-4100.

San Francisco's wilder side is within the 76,500-acre **Golden Gate National Recreation Area** *(see place listing p. 97).* The city's northern and western shorelines offer scenic views and miles of walking trails, a peaceful vacation getaway for bird-watchers, beachcombers, hikers, bicyclists, surfers and nature lovers.

Baseball Led by young pitching ace Madison Bumgarner, the **San Francisco Giants** won the 2014 World Series. The Giants play at **Oracle Park.** The stadium is right off The Embarcadero at 24 Willie Mays Plaza, seven blocks south of Market Street and just south of Pier 40. Phone (415)

Golden Gate National Recreation Area

972-2000 for ticket information. The rival **Oakland A's** play at the **Oakland-Alameda County Coliseum,** I-880 at the 66th Avenue exit in Oakland; phone (877) 493-2255.

Basketball Led by Stephen Curry, the Bay Area's **Golden State Warriors** achieved the seemingly impossible during the final game of the 2016 NBA season, defeating the Memphis Grizzlies to notch their 73rd win and break the Chicago Bulls' wins record set in 1996. The Warriors play at **Oracle Arena** in Oakland, off I-880 at either the 66th Avenue or Hegenberger Road exits. Phone (510) 569-2121 for ticket information.

Area universities whet hoop appetites as well. In San Jose, the **San Jose State University Spartans** play their home games at the **Event Center at San Jose State University,** 7th and E. San Carlos streets; phone (408) 924-6360. The **University of California Golden Bears** play at **Haas Pavilion** in Berkeley; phone (800) 462-3275. And fans of the **University of San Francisco Dons** head to **War Memorial Gymnasium**, 2335 Golden Gate Ave.; phone (415) 422-2873.

Football Bay Area football fans divide their attention between two NFL teams. The **San Francisco 49ers** have won the Super Bowl five times. From 1971 to 2013 they played home games at Candlestick Park, built in the late 1950s for baseball's San Francisco Giants. This city landmark near the San Francisco Bay shoreline is being disassembled manually by construction crews (local residents opposed an implosion) to make way for new housing, a mall and a hotel.

The 49ers play at **Levi's Stadium,** in Santa Clara at 4900 Marie P. DeBartolo Way and Tasman Avenue. Convenient access to the stadium is off major highways US 101, I-880, the Lawrence Expressway and the San Tomas Expressway. The venue has stadium-wide Wi-Fi capability and enormous HD video screens, features a green roof atop the suite tower on the west side and has three solar bridges that connect to the main parking area. For ticket information phone (415) 464-9377.

On game days, Caltrain provides service from San Francisco that connects with Valley Transportation Authority (VTA) light rail trains and buses at the Mountain View Transit Center, Evelyn Avenue and Castro Street. Caltrain passengers must purchase a separate ticket to ride VTA light rail; adult day passes can be purchased at Caltrain station ticket machines. For schedules and more information check the Caltrain or VTA websites or phone VTA at (408) 321-2300. 49ers games are always fun things to do with friends.

Hockey South of San Francisco Bay, the **San Jose Sharks** players circle their prey. The Bay Area's NHL representatives take to the ice at the **SAP Center at San Jose,** 525 W. Santa Clara St. at Autumn Street. For schedule and ticket information phone (408) 999-5757.

Bicycling Many San Franciscans avoid the city's formidable traffic congestion by riding a bike, and for visitors it's a great way to get some exercise on their trip while getting from point A to point B or seeing the sights. The steep hills do present a logistical challenge unless you're in great shape. Two of the flattest—and safest—areas to ride a bike are parallel to the Great Highway that runs along the ocean and in **Golden Gate Park.**

Bay City Bike provides rentals, maps, tours and recommended itineraries for those who want to pedal their way around the Bay Area. Two routes are especially popular: north across the Golden Gate Bridge to Sausalito, then returning by ferry; and through the Presidio into Golden Gate Park. Bikes can be rented at four locations in the Fisherman's Wharf area—2800 Leavenworth St., 2661 Taylor St., 2830 Jones St. and 501 Bay St. A fifth location is at 1669 Haight St. For more information phone (415) 346-2453.

Bike rentals are located along Stanyan Street and Geary Boulevard near Golden Gate Park. **Golden Gate Park Bike and Skate**, 3038 Fulton St. at 6th Avenue, is another convenient rental outlet for a ride through Golden Gate Park, the Presidio or across the Golden Gate Bridge. Rollerblades and roller skates also can be rented; phone (415) 668-1117. Several area touring companies organize longer jaunts to the Sonoma wine country and other scenic spots outside the Greater Bay Area.

Blazing Saddles offers bike rentals as well as tours. One of the fun things for couples to do is biking the popular route along the San Francisco Bay Trail over the Golden Gate Bridge to Sausalito; the return trip by ferry. This 9-mile-long route, which can be done as either a self-guiding or guided excursion, is quite scenic, stays close to the bay and covers mostly flat terrain, with the last 3 miles to Sausalito going downhill. Bikes can be rented at six Fisherman's Wharf locations, (2715 Hyde St., 2555 Powell St., 465 Jefferson St., 550 North Point St., 757 Beach St. and Pier 41) as well as at 433 Mason St. in Union Square. For more information phone (415) 202-8888.

Ford GoBike enables you to rent a bike from a solar-powered electronic kiosk, ride to your destination and return it at the closest kiosk. You can take a single ride or buy a day pass or annual membership. Single 30-minute ride $3 (available only through the app); $10 for a day pass or $124 per year with unlimited 45-minute trips.

Most kiosks are located in the Financial District, along Market Street and in the vicinity of Civic Center, with a planned expansion to other city neighborhoods, including the Mission, the Castro, Upper Market and Hayes Valley. The program is especially popular with commuters due to the emphasis on short trips. For more information phone (855) 480-2453.

Fishing At **Lake Merced**, south of the San Francisco Zoo, anglers can fish for largemouth bass, trout and catfish. Fly-casting pools are south of the bison paddock in Golden Gate Park, next to the Angler's Lodge; bring your own equipment. There's a

Sail on San Francisco Bay

municipal fishing pier in **Aquatic Park,** at the northern end of Van Ness Avenue. You can also cast a line from Pier 7 on The Embarcadero, a short walk north of the Ferry Building.

For a different kind of adventure travel, guided sport-fishing excursions ply the waters of San Francisco Bay for striped bass and giant sturgeon; outfitters are concentrated along Jefferson Street in the vicinity of Fisherman's Wharf.

Golf Rain may dampen fairways during winter and temperatures can also be on the nippy side, but otherwise San Francisco's year-round mild weather is nearly ideal for golf. With space at such a premium, however, there are only a few public courses within the city limits.

Two municipal courses are open to the public at **TCP Harding Park,** at Harding Road off Skyline Boulevard. The championship Harding Park Course has a backdrop of cypress-lined Lake Merced; the Fleming 9 Course features six par-3 and three par-4 holes. Phone (415) 664-4690.

The **Lincoln Park Golf Course** is at 34th Avenue and Clement Street in Lincoln Park. The layout includes glimpses of the ocean; phone (415) 221-9911. The **Presidio Golf Course** is on Finley Road at Arguello Boulevard; phone (415) 561-4661. There's also a nine-hole course at the western end of **Golden Gate Park** at 47th Avenue and John F. Kennedy Drive; phone (415) 751-8987.

Hiking A 4-mile stretch of sandy coastline, **Ocean Beach** parallels the Great Highway that runs along San Francisco's Pacific back door. It offers few frills, but the flat terrain is ideal for an extended hike.

One of the most delightful getaways in San Francisco is the **Coastal Trail,** which runs above the rocky shoreline at **Lands End** from 32nd Avenue west to the Sutro Baths site. At the signed detour to Mile Rock Beach (at the trail's approximate midpoint), descend a set of steep steps down to a rock-strewn beach with crashing waves and a view of the Golden Gate Bridge. It's hard to believe this serene, spectacularly scenic trail is in a densely packed urban area.

Mount Tamalpais State Park and the **Marin Headlands,** just across the Golden Gate Bridge in Marin County, offer hiking routes ranging from gentle to strenuous. Trails at higher elevations have the added bonus of sweeping San Francisco views. Miles of hiking trails run through the **Presidio** as well.

Also in neighboring Marin, **Muir Woods National Monument** has paved walkways threading through a reserve of towering redwoods. There's no more majestic place in the Bay Area to commune with nature.

The top of **Bernal Heights Park,** off Bernal Heights Boulevard in the Bernal Heights neighborhood, offers fantastic 360-degree views of the downtown skyline, San Francisco Bay and the hills of the East Bay. This is one of the sunniest areas in the city, and the windswept slopes of Bernal Hill often escape the afternoon fog that can roll in elsewhere. A network of dirt trails winds around the hill's flanks and up to the summit.

For a good workout, hike to the top of **Buena Vista Park** (access off Haight Street, Buena Vista Avenue E. or Buena Vista Avenue W.). A crisscrossing network of paved walking paths and wooden steps offers various ways to get there. Although you'll be huffing and puffing, the trails are shady. At the summit is a flat oval space where you can catch your breath and admire the tree-framed views. Despite being a popular place for city dwellers to walk their dogs, it's seldom crowded.

Nearby **Corona Heights Park** is also a hill, bare and rocky rather than cloaked in trees. A trail winds around the hill to the top, where the 360-degree views of downtown San Francisco, the Bay Bridge, Twin Peaks, the Potrero Hills and the Castro, Noe Valley and Haight-Ashbury neighborhoods are spectacular on clear days. To get there, take Castro Street north to 16th Street, then 16th Street west to Museum Way.

Jogging and Walking Stroll the foot trails in **Golden Gate Park** from the eastern boundary to the ocean, admiring the gardens and verdant parklands along the way; just remember that the distance is 3 miles and you'll have to walk back (or hop on a Muni bus).

If you don't mind whipping winds, the pedestrian walkway along the east side of the **Golden Gate Bridge** offers breathtaking views. It's 1.7 miles across, so unless you're up for the trek back, arrange to have someone pick you up at the north end.

One of the city's most popular jogging areas is the paved **Golden Gate Promenade,** part of the regional Bay Trail. It runs the length of Crissy Field to Fort Point and up to the southern end of the Golden Gate Bridge (via a stairway). There's beach access, a salt marsh habitat frequented by many types of birds and great views of the bridge. This level stretch is used by cyclists and in-line skaters as well as walkers and joggers.

The Embarcadero is a wonderful place to take a brisk early morning walk. From Pier 39 at Fisherman's Wharf south to the Ferry Building the sidewalk is wide and the views of the bay, the Bay Bridge and Alcatraz Island are terrific. Two blocks south of the Ferry Building is **Rincon Park,** a narrow strip of green bordering The Embarcadero where you can ponder "Cupid's Span," a giant sculpture of a bow and arrow created by Claes Oldenburg and Coosje van Bruggen.

If it's plain old exercise you're looking for, simply step outside your hotel room door. The city's seven principal hills provide both a good workout and scenic vistas galore, and some of the steepest sidewalks have built-in stairways. For starters, puff your way up **Lombard Street** from Leavenworth to Hyde—the famous block dubbed "the crookedest street in the world"—then turn around and take the much easier way back down, stopping at one of the wonderful nearby restaurants to renew your energy.

Tennis There are courts in Golden Gate Park off John F. Kennedy Drive opposite The Conservatory of Flowers. A fee is charged and reservations are recommended on weekends; phone (415) 753-7001. The **San Francisco Recreation and Parks Department** maintains some 150 public courts available on a first-come, first-served basis, as well as eight indoor swimming pools and an outdoor pool; for more information phone (415) 831-2700.

Water Sports Sailing the blue waters of **San Francisco Bay** offers year-round enjoyment and a close-up look at the San Francisco waterfront, Alcatraz and Angel islands, the Golden Gate Bridge and the San Francisco-Oakland Bay Bridge. Currents are tricky, however, so unless you're an accomplished skipper it's best to leave the sailing to experienced hands. Boat rentals and charters are available throughout the greater Bay Area.

Row, paddle and electric boats can be rented at **Stow Lake** in Golden Gate Park—perfect for a lazy afternoon sojourn around Strawberry Hill, which rises from the middle of this man-made body of water. Phone (415) 386-2531 for rates and information.

Another perfect afternoon on the water is a ferry ride to Sausalito or Tiburon. The **Blue & Gold Fleet,** departing from Pier 41 at Fisherman's Wharf, offers daily service to both of these picturesque waterfront communities, along with bay sightseeing cruises.

Performing Arts

San Francisco's tempestuous 19th-century adolescence was more attuned to drinking and gambling than refined pleasures. Even so, 15 legitimate theaters operated amid the saloons of the Barbary Coast. But today residents and visitors on vacation take advantage of a world-class symphony, opera and ballet companies, and theatrical fare from touring Broadway blockbusters to a full house of off-beat experimental productions.

Two major performing arts facilities are just west of the Civic Center. A bronze Henry Moore sculpture squats in front of **Louise M. Davies Symphony Hall**. The building's wraparound design places seating around and even behind the orchestra. Opera, dance and performing arts troupes perform at the **War Memorial Opera House**, opposite the Davies. This venerable structure looks just like it did in 1931.

When planning your trip, be sure to check the *San Francisco Chronicle's* Datebook section, published in the newspaper's Sunday edition, which carries complete listings of area theaters and nightspots as well as information about upcoming events. TIX Bay Area offers cash-only, half-price tickets for selected theater, dance and music events on the day of the performance, and also serves as a Ticketmaster ticket outlet (for credit card purchases). It is located inside the Union Square Garage, accessible through the Geary Street entrance; phone (415) 433-7827.

Dance Ballets are fun things to do with friends, especially the innovative new productions performed by the **San Francisco Ballet** at the War Memorial Opera House. The company's repertory season lasts from late January into early May, although the Nutcracker Suite is performed in December. For the box office, phone (415) 865-2000 Mon.-Fri. 10-4.

Across the bay, the **Oakland Ballet** has been presenting its own revivals and contemporary productions since 1965. The season begins in fall; performances take place at the **Paramount Theatre of the Arts**, 2025 Broadway near the 19th Street BART station. Phone (510) 465-6400 for information.

Film The Bay Area is a mecca for film lovers. Independent film-making tradition thrives here: Documentaries and experimental features are produced on cut-rate budgets throughout the city. Many movie theaters in San Francisco show primarily art house or foreign films, and film showings at several colleges and universities also ensure a wide variety of fare.

Travel to San Francisco almost requires a visit to the **Castro Theatre** (429 Castro St.). It doesn't matter what's playing ; buy a ticket, because it's worth the price of admission just to see the lavish interior of this Moorish/Art Deco-style jewel and behold the Wurlitzer organ rising from beneath the stage for a brief musical performance before the movie begins. In addition to a varied schedule of films (lost classics, repertory series, cult cinema,

Castro Theatre

Hollywood blockbusters, you name it), the theater is the site of frequent special events. It's also dark on occasional evenings; check the website or phone (415) 621-6120 to find out what's happening.

Film buffs should ask their travel advisor about local cinema offerings. The following theaters show a mix of foreign and independent films in addition to repertory programs and revivals of old classics. The **Embarcadero Center Cinema** is on the promenade level at One Embarcadero Center, at the corner of Battery and Clay streets; phone (415) 352-0835. The **Opera Plaza Cinema** is at 601 Van Ness Ave.; phone (415) 771-0183. The **Clay Theatre** is at 2261 Fillmore St.; phone (415) 561-9921. The **Roxie Theater** is at 3117 16th St.; phone (415) 863-1087. The **Yerba Buena Center for the Arts** is at 701 Mission St.; phone (415) 978-2787.

Music Under the direction of Michael Tilson Thomas, the **San Francisco Symphony** performs in Louise M. Davies Symphony Hall from September through June and is one of the most popular things for couples to do in the city. Guest conductors and internationally known soloists round out the repertoire of standards. The box office is open Mon.-Fri. 10-6, Sat. noon-6 and two hours before concerts on Sun.; phone (415) 864-6000.

As a free alternative to the often sold-out symphony productions, orchestral and band concerts take place summer Sundays in the natural amphitheater of **Sigmund Stern Recreational Grove**, Sloat Boulevard and 19th Avenue; phone (415) 252-6252 for concert information. **Golden Gate**

Park also is the scene of concerts throughout the year.

During the academic year both students and faculty perform at the **San Francisco Conservatory of Music** at 50 Oak St. Phone (415) 502-6275 for 24-hour schedule and price information, or (415) 864-7326 Mon.-Fri. 10-12:30 and 1:30-4 for tickets. Occasional classical music concerts take place at the **Nob Hill Masonic Center**, 1111 California St.; phone (415) 776-7457, or (800) 653-8000 (Live Nation) for tickets.

Jazz lovers have no need to wonder what to do in San Francisco as the **SFJAZZ Center**, 201 Franklin St. (at Fell Street) in Hayes Valley, functions as a hub for music, art and culture, encouraging interactions between audiences and musicians. The season, which runs from January to early June, features extended residencies by a wide spectrum of noted jazz artists. Summer sessions also are presented. Performances take place at the state-of-the-art Robert N. Miner Auditorium, which can be adjusted from 350 to 700 seats. Phone (866) 920-5299 for the box office.

A performance space at the former High School of Commerce was reborn as the **Sydney Goldstein Theater** (275 Hayes St., between Van Ness and Franklin streets). It was closed for more than 30 years before a restoration project in 2012 refurbished the 1,600-seat hall, preserving original architectural details while installing state-of-the-art lighting and sound. The theater is the home of City Arts & Lectures, a series of onstage conversations

Golden Gate Park

with leading figures in science, literature and the performing arts. For ticket information phone (415) 392-4400.

Opera The **San Francisco Opera**, founded in 1923, is the resident company at the War Memorial Opera House. International names frequently appear during the season, which begins in early September and lasts into December, with two additional months of performances in June and July. Many performances are sold out long in advance, but standing-room tickets are always made available the day of the performance; they go on sale (cash only and one per person) at the box office, 301 Van Ness Ave., beginning at 10 a.m. For performance and additional ticket information, phone (415) 864-3330 Mon. 10-5, Tues.-Sat. 10-6.

Theater Major touring plays and productions of Broadway shows are presented at the **Curran Theatre** (445 Geary St.) and the **Orpheum Theater** (1192 Market St.). Musicals run at the **Golden Gate Theater** (1 Taylor St.) and at the Curran. Phone (415) 358-1220 for the Curran; (888) 746-1799 for the Orpheum and Golden Gate theaters.

The **American Conservatory Theater** (ACT) is San Francisco's major repertory group and presents plays at the 1910, Edwardian-style **Geary Theater** (405 Geary St.) and the more intimate Strand Theater (1127 Market St.); phone (415) 749-2228.

Lamplighters Music Theatre, another repertory company, specializes in operettas and musical spoofs, with an emphasis on Gilbert & Sullivan musicals. Performances take place at various venues, including the **Yerba Buena Center for the Arts** (700 Howard St. at 3rd Street) and the Herbst Theater, 401 Van Ness Ave. Phone (415) 227-4797 for schedule and ticket information.

One of the most fun places to go in the city for a uniquely San Francisco theater experience is "**Beach Blanket Babylon**" at **Club Fugazi** at 678 Beach Blanket Babylon Blvd. (formerly Green Street). This feel-good show, which has been running since 1974, features cabaret-style entertainment, outlandish costumes and a constantly updated parade of pop culture characters. These days theatergoers will encounter everyone from Bernie Sanders and Sia to characters from "Game of Thrones" and "Orange is the New Black." Phone (415) 421-4222 for reservations.

The **Lorraine Hansberry Theatre** (762 Fulton St.) showcases the works of African-American writers; phone (415) 345-3980. The **Magic Theatre** in Building D at Fort Mason, Marina Boulevard and Buchanan Street in the Marina District, presents West Coast premieres and occasional solo shows; phone (415) 441-8822. And Fort Mason's **Cowell Theater**, Marina Boulevard at Buchanan Street (at the end of Pier 2), features one-man shows and other performances; phone (415) 345-7575.

INSIDER INFO:
CityPASS and Go San Francisco Card

If you're looking for fun things to do with friends, check out San Francisco's top sights and save money by buying combination passes that cover admission to multiple attractions.

San Francisco CityPASS offers a 42 percent savings off the normal cost of individual tickets for several San Francisco attractions. These attractions include a Muni & Cable Car 3-Day Passport (good for three days of unlimited rides on all Muni buses, light rail, streetcars and cable cars); The California Academy of Sciences in Golden Gate Park; the Blue & Gold Fleet Bay Cruise Adventure; the Aquarium of the Bay; and an option ticket for either the Exploratorium **or** the San Francisco Museum of Modern Art.

The validity period for each San Francisco CityPASS ticket booklet is 9 consecutive days, beginning with the first day of use. CityPASS is available online at CityPASS.com, at the San Francisco Travel Visitor Information centers at Macy's Union Square (cellar level) and at Moscone Center (749 Howard St.). Booklets can also be purchased at Powell and Market Public Transit Kiosk or from the participating attractions. Phone (888) 330-5008. Note: attraction options may change throughout the year.

Hop-on hop-off bus tour

A Day in the Mission

Perhaps no neighborhood more vividly reflects the current ideological divide between "the way San Francisco used to be" and the kind of city it is becoming today than the Mission. In some ways this enclave rich in Latino history and culture—the city's oldest neighborhood—is a battleground where decades-old traditions are butting up against an influx (some would say invasion) of gentrification brought on by the latest tech boom.

Of course skyrocketing rents and evictions are very real and serious issues to residents. Visitors, on the other hand, will find the Mission a feast for the senses, an intoxicating commingling of sights and sounds known for its nearby restaurants. And the fact that it's one of San Francisco's sunniest and least foggy neighborhoods is a definite plus when it comes to day tripping.

Generally speaking, the Mission is bounded north and south by 16th and 26th streets and east and west by Potrero Avenue and Guerrero Street. It's a neighborhood that's particularly rich when it comes to art and food, and any exploration should include one or both.

You won't find a more vibrant and varied display of street art created by and for the people anywhere else in the city (although Haight-Ashbury runs a close second). Start by checking out Balmy Alley (*see attraction listing*). This narrow alleyway's walls,

fences and garage doors are used as canvases. The subject matter is varied—everything from rainbow-hued, ethnically diverse family scenes to sharp critiques of well-heeled San Franciscans' hipster pretensions. What's especially cool is that vegetation, whether it's a pot of succulents or a flowering vine exuberantly hanging from the roofline of a building, is an integral part of the overall artistic composition.

If you didn't live in the neighborhood you'd probably never know about Lilac Alley (from 24th south to 26th Street between Mission and Capp streets), since its primary purpose is to provide access to private garages and the back doors of businesses. But it's jam-packed with street art. Garage doors are covered with intricate geometric patterns, beastly faces, Mayan gods, scantily clad women, cartoon characters and the occasional anti-gentrification screed. Lilac Alley also has lots of crazy graffiti scrawled everywhere.

Last but not least, Clarion Alley (from Valencia to Mission Street, just south of 17th Street) boasts an inspired mishmash of psychedelic designs, space aliens, free-form graffiti and pointed political messages. Although you're apt to see other tourists taking photos during the day, this is an alleyway in every sense, from the odd wandering panhandler to the occasional sharp smell of urine. But hey, it's the city.

Since street artists are constantly flexing their creative muscles, the mural art in all three of these alleys changes now and then, especially in response to topical events. You may even encounter an artist working on a new creation. It makes repeat visits rewarding.

As far as food goes, many aficionados of Mexican cuisine maintain that the best taquerias in the city are in the Mission. A number of Mission joints turn up regularly on various best-of lists, primarily because they're real-deal authentic. Take a walk along 24th Street from late morning on and you'll almost certainly encounter the intoxicating aroma of grilling meat wafting out of open doorways, making the area one of the most enticing places to eat in the city.

The best burritos, quesadillas, salsas and other taqueria staples are hotly debated, but all things considered you can't go wrong at La Taqueria (2889 Mission St.), Taqueria San Francisco (2794 24th Street) or Taqueria Cancun (2288 Mission St.). Even in the midst of the trendy, pricey eateries along hipper-then-hip Valencia Street stands El Toro Taqueria (598 Valencia St.), where an efficient assembly line of workers whip up carne asada burritos, fajita combo plates and other tasty, no-frills grub.

Tartine Bakery & Cafe (600 Guerrero St.) is another place foodies favor, but for morning buns and chocolate croissants rather than tacos. The baked goods, cakes, scones, cookies and tarts at this very popular bakery earn raves, and the cappuccino is

pretty darn good, too. To avoid the line that often extends out the door, go early and/or on a weekday, especially if you're intent on snagging a table inside this small, bustling space.

ATTRACTIONS

 For a complete list of attractions, visit AAA.com/travelguides/attractions

ALCATRAZ ISLAND, in San Francisco Bay, can be reached via Alcatraz Cruises ferries that depart from Pier 33 on The Embarcadero. Known as "The Rock," Alcatraz was a maximum security federal penitentiary for almost 30 years before closing in 1963 due to high operating costs and deteriorating facilities. Among the notorious criminals who did time on The Rock were Al Capone, Machine Gun Kelly and Robert Stroud, the "Birdman of Alcatraz."

One of the city's biggest tourist attractions is a fascinating piece of history. The buildings, including a guard tower, water tower, power plant, warden's house and four cellblocks, are in various states of disrepair. The recreation yard is a dismal-looking, fenced-in concrete rectangle. The prison cells—each furnished with a toilet, tiny sink and single bunk—are depressingly small and grim. Alcatraz was never filled to capacity; the average number of inmates was around 260.

The gardens add splashes of color and a great deal of beauty to the stark surroundings. Because it has no natural predators, the island also is a bird sanctuary. In addition to a large population of Western gulls, visitors will see such species as cormorants, black-crowned night herons and snowy egrets.

The ferry cruise takes about 15 minutes and offers a view of the San Francisco skyline and the Golden Gate Bridge. A 45-minute, self-guiding audio tour of the main prison building, narrated by inmates, correctional officers and their families, provides insight into what life was like on The Rock. A 17-minute orientation video, "Alcatraz: Stories from the Rock," offers an informative overview.

Ranger- and volunteer-led outdoor interpretive walks focus on the island's military history, famous inmates, escape attempts, historic gardens and 19-month occupation by the Indians of All Tribes. Visitors also can explore on their own; self-guiding tour brochures are available at the dock for a small fee. Building 64 contains historical exhibits.

The Alcatraz Night Tour features a boat cruise around the island, a guided tour from the dock to the cell house, special programs and dramatic evening views of the city.

Note: Visitors are advised to buy tickets in advance year-round and especially from May through

The Gardens of Alcatraz

San Francisco Bay Area
Metrorail System Map

Legend

Bay Area Rapid Transit (BART)

① Transfer Station ① Station

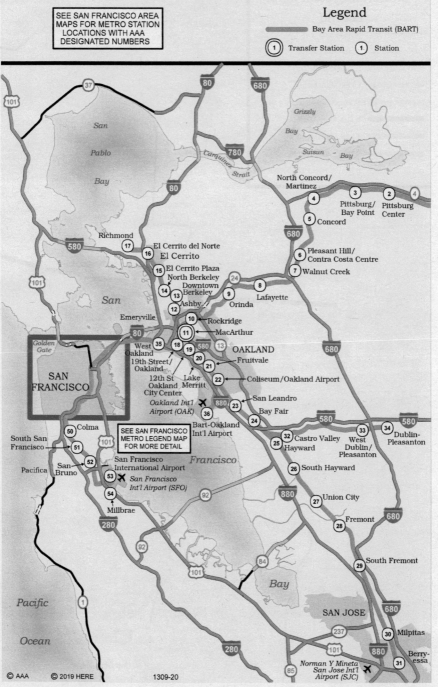

© AAA   © 2019 HERE   1309-20

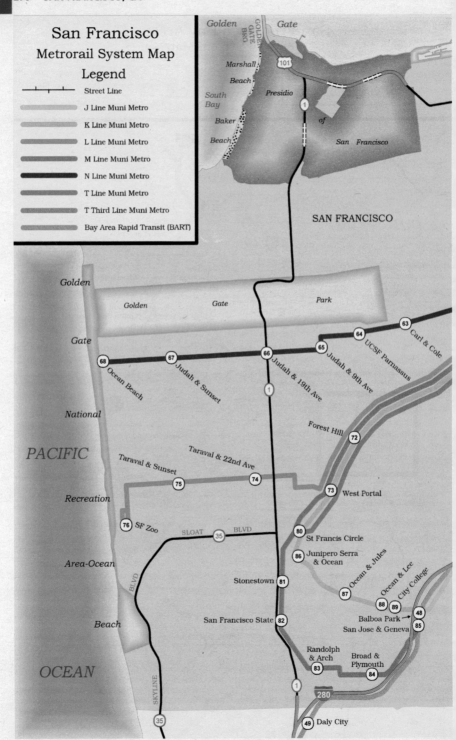

San Francisco
Metrorail System Map
Legend

┤──┤──├─	Street Line
▬▬▬	J Line Muni Metro
▬▬▬	K Line Muni Metro
▬▬▬	L Line Muni Metro
▬▬▬	M Line Muni Metro
▬▬▬	N Line Muni Metro
▬▬▬	T Line Muni Metro
▬▬▬	T Third Line Muni Metro
▬▬▬	Bay Area Rapid Transit (BART)

Golden Gate

Marshall Beach

South Bay

Presidio

Baker Beach

of

San Francisco

SAN FRANCISCO

Golden Gate Park

63 Carl & Cole

64 UCSF Parnassus

65 Judah & 9th Ave

66 Judah & 19th Ave

67 Judah & Sunset

68 Ocean Beach

Golden

Gate

National

PACIFIC

Recreation

Area-Ocean

Beach

OCEAN

Forest Hill 72

Taraval & 22nd Ave

Taraval & Sunset

75 74

73 West Portal

76 SF Zoo

SLOAT 35 BLVD

80 St Francis Circle

86 Junipero Serra & Ocean

Ocean & Jules

Ocean & Lee

City College

Stonestown 81

87

88 89

48

San Francisco State 82

Balboa Park → 85

San Jose & Geneva

Randolph & Arch

Broad & Plymouth

83 84

1

280

35

49 Daly City

SKYLINE

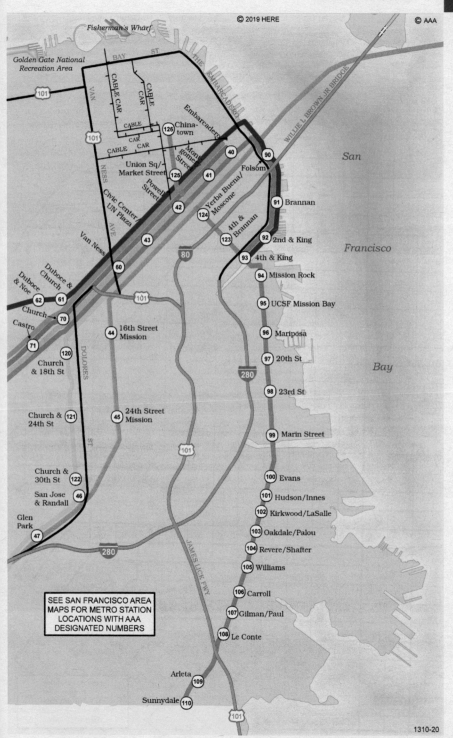

© 2019 HERE

© AAA

Fisherman's Wharf

Golden Gate National
Recreation Area

BAY ST

THE EMBARCADERO

WILLIE L BROWN JR BRIDGE

101

VAN NESS

CABLE CAR

CABLE CAR

CABLE CAR

CABLE

CAR

CABLE CAR

101

Embarcadero

126 China-
town

Montgomery Street

40

90

Folsom

San

Union Sq/-
Market Street

125

41

Powell Street

Civic Center
UN Plaza

42

124

Yerba Buena/
Moscone

91 Brannan

Francisco

Van Ness AVE

43

123

4th & Brannan

92 2nd & King

Bay

80

93 4th & King

Duboce &
Church

60

94 Mission Rock

Duboce
& Noe

62 61

Church

95 UCSF Mission Bay

70

DOLORES ST

96 Mariposa

Castro

71

44 16th Street
Mission

97 20th St

120

280

Church
& 18th St

98 23rd St

Church &
24th St

121

45 24th Street
Mission

99 Marin Street

101

Church &
30th St

122

100 Evans

San Jose
& Randall

46

101 Hudson/Innes

Glen
Park

102 Kirkwood/LaSalle

47

103 Oakdale/Palou

104 Revere/Shafter

280

105 Williams

JAMES LICK FWY

106 Carroll

107 Gilman/Paul

SEE SAN FRANCISCO AREA
MAPS FOR METRO STATION
LOCATIONS WITH AAA
DESIGNATED NUMBERS

108 Le Conte

Arleta

109

Sunnydale

110

101

1310-20

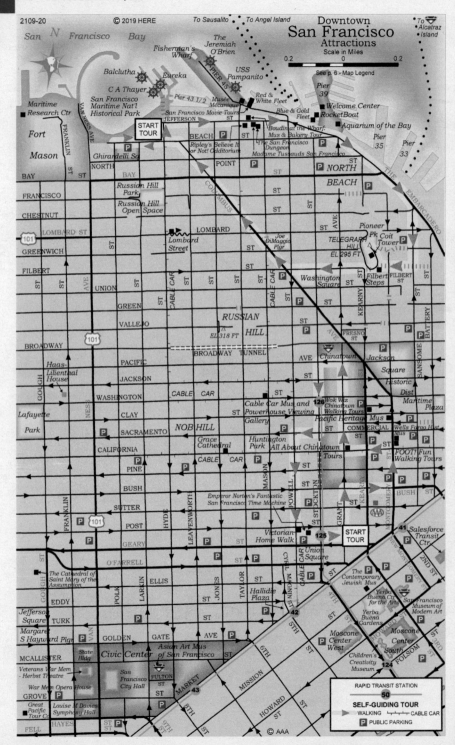

2109-20   © 2019 HERE

To Sausalito   To Angel Island   To Alcatraz Island

**Downtown
San Francisco
Attractions**
Scale in Miles
0.2   0   0.2
See p. 6 - Map Legend

San N *Francisco Bay*

Fisherman's Wharf
The Jeremiah O'Brien

Balclutha
Eureka
C A Thayer
San Francisco Maritime Nat'l Historical Park

USS Pampanito
PIER 45

Pier 43 1/2
Musée Mécanique

Red & White Fleet
Blue & Gold Fleet

Pier 39
Welcome Center
RocketBoat
Aquarium of the Bay
Pier 35
Pier 33

Maritime Research Ctr

START TOUR

San Francisco Movie Tours
JEFFERSON   ST

BEACH
Ripley's Believe It or Not! Odditorium

Boudin at the Wharf: Mus & Bakery Tour
The San Francisco Dungeon
Madame Tussauds San Francisco

Fort Mason

Ghirardelli Sq
NORTH   BAY
POINT   ST

NORTH BEACH

BAY   ST

FRANCISCO

Russian Hill Park

CHESTNUT

Russian Hill Open Space

LOMBARD ST

Pioneer Pk
Coit Tower

TELEGRAPH HILL
EL 295 FT

GREENWICH

Lombard Street

Joe DiMaggio Plgr

FILBERT

Washington Square

Filbert Steps
FILBERT ST

UNION

GREEN

CABLE CAR

CABLE CAR

VALLEJO

RUSSIAN   HILL
EL 318 FT

BROADWAY

BROADWAY TUNNEL

FRESNO ST

PACIFIC

Chinatown
Jackson Square
Historic Dist
Maritime Plaza

Haas-Lilienthal House

JACKSON

Lafayette Park

WASHINGTON

CABLE CAR

Cable Car Mus and Powerhouse Viewing Gallery

126 Wok Wiz Chinatown Walking Tours
Pacific Heritage Mus
Wells Fargo Hist Mus

CLAY

SACRAMENTO

NOB HILL

Grace Cathedral

Huntington Park
All About Chinatown Tours

COMMERCIAL ST
FOOT! Fun Walking Tours

CALIFORNIA

CABLE   CAR

PINE

BUSH

Emperor Norton's Fantastic San Francisco Time Machine

BUSH

SUTTER

POST

Victorian Home Walk
125

START TOUR

Union Square

41 Salesforce Transit Ctr

GEARY

2ND ST

O'FARRELL

The Contemporary Jewish Mus

The Cathedral of Saint Mary of the Assumption

ELLIS

JONES

TAYLOR

Hallidie Plaza

42

Yerba Buena Ctr for the Arts
San Francisco Museum of Modern Art

EDDY

Jefferson Square

TURK

Yerba Buena Gardens

Margaret S Hayward Plgr

GOLDEN   GATE   AVE

Moscone Center West

Moscone Center South

MCALLISTER

State Bldg
Civic Center

Asian Art Mus of San Francisco

Children's Creativity Museum
124

Veterans War Mem - Herbst Theatre
War Mem Opera House

San Francisco City Hall

FULTON ST

GROVE

43

MISSION

HOWARD

Great Pacific Tour Co

Louise M Davies Symphony Hall

RAPID TRANSIT STATION
50
SELF-GUIDING TOUR
WALKING   CABLE CAR
P PUBLIC PARKING

FELL

HAYES

© AAA

September, when they should be purchased at least 3 months ahead. Wear comfortable shoes and layered clothing to accommodate the unpredictable weather. **Hours:** Ferries depart daily beginning at 8:45 and run at 30- to 40-minute intervals throughout the day. The Alcatraz Night Tour departs Pier 33, Alcatraz Landing, Thurs.-Mon. at 5:55 and 6:30, Mar.-Oct.; at 3:50, rest of year. Phone ahead to confirm schedule. Last ferry departs Alcatraz around 6:30 p.m. during the summer months; around 4:30, rest of year. Closed Jan. 1, Thanksgiving and Christmas.

Cost: $39.90 (includes audio tour and round-trip ferry transportation); $37.65 (ages 62+); $24.40 (ages 5-11); $120.25 (family, two adults and two children ages 5-11). Alcatraz Night Tour $47.30; $46.25 (ages 12-17); $44 (ages 62+); $28 (ages 5-11). Alcatraz Behind the Scenes Tour $92.30; $88.25 (ages 12-17); $86 (ages 62+). Alcatraz and Angel Island Combo Tour $78.65; $76.40 (ages 62+); $52.40 (ages 5-11). Rates may vary; phone ahead. **Phone:** (415) 981-7625. GT

The Gardens of Alcatraz are on Alcatraz Island. Created by the families of correctional officers and the inmates themselves, they made maximum use of limited space and added touches of beauty to the otherwise forbidding atmosphere of "The Rock."

The natural environment—rocky ground, poor soil, a scarcity of fresh water and chilly, salt-laden winds—was not conducive to horticulture, but Alcatraz's early gardeners chose hardy, sustainable plants from places like South Africa and the Mediterranean, where weather conditions are similar to those in the San Francisco Bay Area. When the prison closed in 1963 the cultivated landscape became overgrown and wild, but since 2003 a crew of volunteers has worked to restore and maintain these historic gardens.

Fuchsias, geraniums and nasturtiums flourish in carefully tended flower beds. Creamy white calla lilies accent stone walls. Fig trees, fragrant roses and aeoniums, succulents with fleshy leaves in the shape of a rosette, provide a colorful contrast to the crumbling buildings. Unusual plants include *Gordonia axillaris,* more commonly known as the fried egg plant due to the appearance of its blooms.

Hours: Gardens open during regular visiting hours. Closed Jan. 1, Thanksgiving and Christmas. **Cost:** Included in Alcatraz Island admission. **Phone:** (415) 981-7625, or (415) 441-4300 for the San Francisco office of The Garden Conservancy.

ASIAN ART MUSEUM OF SAN FRANCISCO at 200 Larkin St. at Civic Center Plaza, is home to a world-renowned collection of more than 18,000 art treasures spanning some 6,000 years of history—including dynamic contemporary installations—all housed in galleries, an expansive exhibition pavilion and outdoor art terrace.

Masterpieces on view range from the oldest dated Chinese Buddha and an ancient bronze rhinoceros to a gilded Burmese devotional throne. Indonesian puppets and bejeweled krises (daggers)

share the story of cross-cultural pollination, and a glowing treasury of imperial jades is an eternal highlight. Bamboo baskets are featured alongside Japanese screens and scroll paintings, while nearby is an excellently preserved collection of rare Korean celadons from a millennium ago. An extravagant 19th-century silver elephant saddle, or howdah, from India once functioned as a ceremonial conveyance for royalty is also on display.

On Thursday evenings in spring and summer, the museum is open late and offers reduced admission. During these evenings, visitors can peruse the galleries, meet artists, listen to talks and enjoy special entertainment.

Time: Allow 2 hours minimum. **Hours:** Tues.-Sun. 10-5 (also Thurs.-Fri. 5-9, mid-Feb. to late Sept.). Closed Jan. 1, Thanksgiving and Christmas. **Cost:** $15; $10 (ages 13-17, ages 65+, college students with ID and Thurs. after 5); free (ages 0-12, SFUSD students, active military and up to five family members, and to all on the first Sun. of the month). An additional charge of $10 may apply for special exhibitions. **Phone:** (415) 581-3500. GT ⑪ ⑨ Civic Center/UN Plaza, 43

BALMY ALLEY runs from 24th St. s. to 25th St. between Treat and Harrison sts. In the heart of the Mission, this is one of the best places in San Francisco to see a concentrated collection of murals at a leisurely pace. Local artists began using the alley's walls, fences and garage doors as a canvas in the mid-1980s as a means to protest political and human rights abuses then taking place in Central America.

Since then the range of subject matter has broadened; a lot of the art is still explicitly political, but you'll also see pride-filled expressions of Latin American culture, tributes to victims of AIDS and Hurricane Katrina, and psychedelically inspired designs. The images are a mix of saintly and secular. An Indian goddess graces a wall between two windows with iron grilles, while nearby is Michael Jackson in classic crotch-grab pose, complete with black fedora and one dangling jheri curl.

Strong, matriarchal women and a rainbow coalition of children are well represented. And since the alley is lined with residences rather than businesses, it's conducive to strolling and stopping for a closer look. If you want to learn more about the history behind the art, Precita Eyes Mural Arts & Visitors Center *(see attraction listing p. 286)* offers guided walking tours.

Note: Parking is problematic, especially on weekends, so take advantage of public transportation; Muni bus #48 runs along 24th Street. The area around 25th Street can get somewhat iffy after dark. **Time:** Allow 30 minutes minimum. **Cost:** Free. **Phone:** (415) 285-2287. ⑨ 24th Street Mission, 45

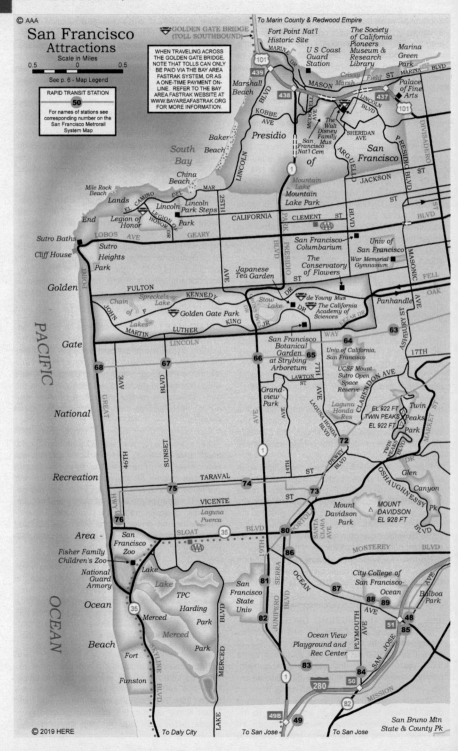

© AAA

San Francisco
Attractions

Scale in Miles
0.5   0.5

See p. 6 - Map Legend

RAPID TRANSIT STATION

50

For names of stations see
corresponding number on the
San Francisco Metrorail
System Map

WHEN TRAVELING ACROSS
THE GOLDEN GATE BRIDGE,
NOTE THAT TOLLS CAN ONLY
BE PAID VIA THE BAY AREA
FASTRAK SYSTEM, OR AS
A ONE-TIME PAYMENT ON-
LINE. REFER TO THE BAY
AREA FASTRAK WEBSITE AT
WWW.BAYAREAFASTRAK.ORG
FOR MORE INFORMATION.

GOLDEN GATE BRIDGE
(TOLL SOUTHBOUND)

To Marin County & Redwood Empire

Fort Point Nat'l
Historic Site

The Society
of California
Pioneers
Museum &
Research
Library

U S Coast
Guard
Station

Marina
Green
Park

Palace
of Fine
Arts

Crissy Field

Marshall
Beach

South
Bay

Baker
Beach

Presidio

The
Walt
Disney
Family
Mus

San
Francisco
Nat'l Cem

SHERIDAN
AVE

San
Francisco

China
Beach

Mile Rock
Beach

Lands

Lincoln
Park Steps

Legion of
Honor

Lincoln
Park

Mountain
Lake Park

Mountain
Lake

San Francisco
Columbarium

Univ of
San Francisco

End

Sutro Baths

Cliff House

Sutro
Heights
Park

Japanese
Tea Garden

The Conservatory
of Flowers

War Memorial
Gymnasium

Golden

Chain
of
F
Lakes

Spreckels
Lake

Golden Gate Park

Stow
Lake

de Young Mus

Panhandle

Gate

The California
Academy of
Sciences

San Francisco
Botanical
Garden
at Strybing
Arboretum

Univ of California,
San Francisco

National

Grand-
view
Park

UCSF Mount
Sutro Open
Space
Reserve

Laguna
Honda
Res

EL 922 FT
TWIN PEAKS
EL 922 FT

Twin
Peaks
Park

Recreation

TARAVAL

VICENTE

Mount
Davidson
Park

MOUNT
DAVIDSON
EL 928 FT

Glen
Canyon
Pk

Area -

San
Francisco
Zoo

Laguna
Puerca

Fisher Family
Children's Zoo

National
Guard
Armory

Lake
Lake

TPC
Harding
Park

San
Francisco
State
Univ

City College of
San Francisco -
Ocean

Balboa
Park

Ocean

Merced

Merced
Park

Ocean View
Playground and
Rec Center

Beach

Fort
Funston

San Bruno Mtn
State & County Pk

To Daly City

To San Jose

To San Jose

© 2019 HERE

PACIFIC

OCEAN

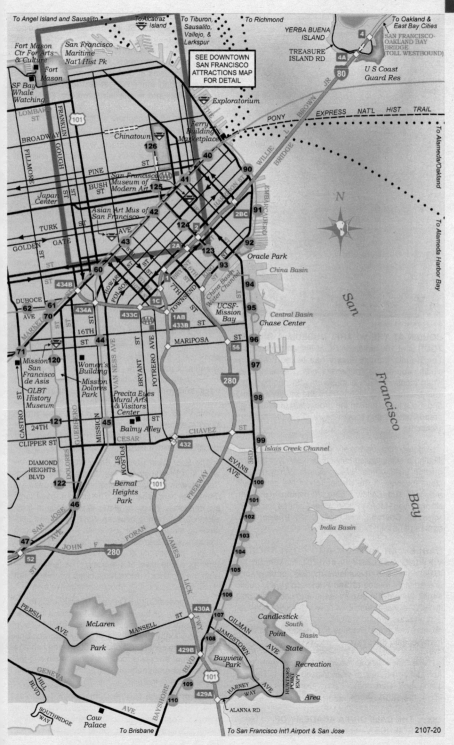

To Angel Island and Sausalito
To Alcatraz Island
To Tiburon, Sausalito, Vallejo, & Larkspur
To Richmond
To Oakland & East Bay Cities

YERBA BUENA ISLAND
TREASURE ISLAND RD
TREASURE ISLAND RD
SAN FRANCISCO-OAKLAND BAY BRIDGE (TOLL WESTBOUND)

U S Coast Guard Res

Fort Mason Ctr For Arts & Culture
Fort Mason
San Francisco Maritime Nat'l Hist Pk

SEE DOWNTOWN SAN FRANCISCO ATTRACTIONS MAP FOR DETAIL

SF Bay Whale Watching

Exploratorium

PONY
EXPRESS
NAT'L
HIST
TRAIL

To Alameda/Oakland
To Alameda Harbor Bay

LOMBARD ST
FRANKLIN
GOUGH
101
BROADWAY
FILLMORE
Chinatown
Ferry Building Marketplace

PINE
ST
126
ST
40
BUSH
ST
San Francisco Museum of Modern Art
41
125
90

Japan Center
Asian Art Mus of San Francisco
42
124
91
2BC

TURK
ST
VAN NESS
AVE
43
2A
123
92

GOLDEN
GATE
ST
Oracle Park
China Basin

60
434B
HOWARD
FOLSOM
1
7TH
China Basin Water Channel
93
94

DUBOCE
61
434A
433C
1C
Brannan
UCSF-Mission Bay
95
Central Basin
Chase Center

62
70
16TH
ST
1AB
433B
ST
MARIPOSA
96

71
44
97

Mission San Francisco de Asis
120
Women's Building
Mission Dolores Park
VAN NESS AVE
BRYANT
POTRERO AVE
280
98

GLBT History Museum
CASTRO
121
24TH
Precita Eyes Mural Arts & Visitors Center
ST
99
Islais Creek Channel

CLIPPER ST
45
CESAR
CHAVEZ
432
EVANS
AVE
100

DIAMOND HEIGHTS BLVD
122
FOLSOM
Bernal Heights Park
101
U.S 101
101
102
India Basin

46
JAMES
103
104

47
JOHN
F
280
LICK
FWY
105

52
FORAN
106
Candlestick Point State Recreation Area
South Basin

PERSIA
AVE
McLaren Park
MANSELL
ST
430A
107
GILMAN
JAMESTOWN
AVE

GENEVA
429B
108
Bayview Park
HARNEY WAY

SOUTHRIDGE WAY
429A
109
HARNEY
WAY
ALANNA RD
110
Cow Palace
BAYSHORE
AVE
101

To Brisbane
To San Francisco Int'l Airport & San Jose

San Francisco City Hall

BOUDIN AT THE WHARF: MUSEUM & BAKERY TOUR

is at 160 Jefferson St. at Fisherman's Wharf. The Boudin French Bakery has baked bread, including sourdough, for generations. The company's wharf location offers a museum with photographs, artifacts and exhibits that trace the bakery's history and the science behind the production of sourdough bread, one of this foodie city's signature culinary creations.

A demonstration bakery provides viewpoints, including a glass-walled catwalk directly over the production facility, from which visitors can watch the steps involved in the production of the company's products. **Time:** Allow 1 hour, 30 minutes minimum. **Hours:** Wed.-Mon. 11:30-6. Phone ahead to confirm schedule. **Cost:** $3; free (ages 0-12). **Phone:** (415) 928-1849. GT ▥

CABLE CAR MUSEUM AND POWERHOUSE VIEWING GALLERY

is at 1201 Mason St. (at Washington St.). It contains models, photographs and artifacts related to San Francisco's early public transit system. On display is the first cable car, built in 1873. A video describes how cable cars operate, and an underground viewing room allows visitors to observe the huge sheaves that guide the vehicles from beneath the street.

Time: Allow 1 hour minimum. **Hours:** Daily 10-6, Apr.-Oct.; 10-5, rest of year. Closed Jan. 1, Thanksgiving and Christmas. **Cost:** Donations. **Phone:** (415) 474-1887. ▥ Chinatown, 126

THE CALIFORNIA ACADEMY OF SCIENCES

—see Golden Gate Park p. 279.

CHINATOWN is symbolically entered via the gate at Bush St. and Grant Ave. The neighborhood is bounded roughly north and south by Vallejo and Bush streets and east and west by Kearny and Powell streets. Although there are other Chinese enclaves in San Francisco, notably in the Richmond and Inner Sunset districts, Chinatown was the first and is still the foremost. Part time-honored tourist destination, part workaday neighborhood, it has an atmosphere all its own.

The first Chinese immigrants arrived in San Francisco in 1848. They came to work for companies seeking cheap labor, and many ended up toiling at back-breaking menial jobs. Anti-immigration sentiment during the 1870s targeted these industrious new arrivals and reached a peak with the passage of the Chinese Exclusion Act of 1882. Today's Chinatown began taking shape in the 1880s as a safe haven for Chinese workers and their families.

The green-tiled ornamental gate that arches over Grant Avenue was dedicated in 1970. Grant is tourist central, with shops selling everything from cheap plastic Buddhas to fine jewelry and more restaurants than you can shake a chopstick at. Ornate tiled roofs cap apartment buildings, intertwined dragons coil around old-fashioned lampposts, red and yellow banners flutter in the breeze, and storefront signs are a mix of Chinese and English.

The vibe is a bit different along Stockton Street, a block west. Muni buses lurch to a stop, disgorging streams of passengers. Boxes of produce are unloaded from double-parked trucks. Grocers hustle back and forth arranging the merchandise in wooden bins while matriarchs inspect it with a discerning eye. Rows of roasted ducks, their brown skins glistening, are on display in the windows of meat markets, along with whole fish and sundry unidentifiable animal parts.

The East West Bank at the corner of Grant Avenue and Washington Street, formerly the Bank of Canton, was built in 1909 and originally housed the Chinatown telephone office. The tiered pagoda roofs are especially intriguing along Waverly Place (parallel to Grant Avenue between Washington and Sacramento streets). There are several temples along this narrow little street. Every floor of the Tien Hau Temple (on Waverly at Clay Street) has a different look; it's a little jewel of a building. The temple itself is on the top floor (visitors must climb three flights of stairs) and has exhibits about Chinatown's history.

The Chinese Culture Center of San Francisco, on the third floor of the Hilton San Francisco hotel at 750 Kearny St., provides information about Chinatown and features displays of contemporary Chinese art. The center also offers a 90-minute heritage walking tour that visits food markets, herbal and tea shops, and architectural and art-related and historical points of interest.

Hours: Chinese Culture Center open Tues.-Sat. 10-4. Phone for walking tour schedule. Closed major holidays. **Cost:** Chinese Culture Center by donation. Heritage walking tour $30. Other tours are offered;

phone for details. Advance reservations are required. **Phone:** (415) 986-1822 for heritage walking tour reservations. 🏛 Union Sq/Market St, 125

CIVIC CENTER is bordered n. and s. by Golden Gate Ave. and Market St. and e. and w. by Hyde and Franklin sts. Federal, state and city governmental buildings and cultural institutions are grouped around two expansive, open plazas, Civic Center Plaza and United Nations Plaza. Foremost among these architecturally impressive structures is the Beaux Arts-style San Francisco City Hall, capped by a striking dome. Also flanking Civic Center Plaza are the Supreme Court of California, the San Francisco Public Library and Bill Graham Civic Auditorium.

The United Nations Conference on International Organization, culminating in the signing of the Charter of the United Nations, was held at the Civic Center in 1945. 🏛 Civic Center/UN Plaza, 43

San Francisco City Hall is between Polk, Grove and McAllister sts. and Van Ness Ave. at 1 Dr. Carlton B. Goodlett Pl. Opened in 1915, this expansive building covers two full city blocks and is topped by one of the largest domes in the world. Two "light courts" featuring skylights and marble walls display changing art exhibits; the building's original marble staircase separates the two courts. Docents conduct 45-minute guided tours. **Time:** Allow 1 hour minimum. **Hours:** Guided tours are given Mon.-Fri. at 10, noon and 2. Closed major holidays. **Cost:** Donations. **Phone:** (415) 554-6139 for tour information. 🏛 Van Ness, 60

San Francisco War Memorial & Performing Arts Center (SFWMPAC) is across Van Ness Ave. from City Hall. This complex of buildings includes the War Memorial Opera House, Louise M. Davies Symphony Hall and the adjacent Harold L. Zellerbach Rehearsal Hall, and the Veterans Building, which houses the Herbst Theatre and The Green Room. Resident companies at SFWMPAC are the San Francisco Ballet, the San Francisco Opera and the San Francisco Symphony.

The stately War Memorial Opera House, built in 1932, is one of the last Beaux Arts buildings constructed in the United States. Along with ornate decorative accents, the main lobby features a 38-foot-tall ceiling. In contrast, Louise M. Davies Symphony Hall has a contemporary look, reinforced by the abstract bronze Henry Moore sculpture at the corner of Grove Street and Van Ness Avenue. The Herbst Theatre is a jewel of a facility, graced with a series of elegant murals by Frank Brangwyn that were originally created for the 1915 Panama-Pacific International Exposition.

Guided tours of the SFWMPAC complex leave from the symphony hall's Grove Street entrance. **Hours:** Tours are given on the hour Mon. 10-2, except on holidays. **Cost:** Tours $7; $5 (ages 65+ and students with ID). **Phone:** (415) 621-6600 for general information, or (415) 552-8338 for guided tour reservations. 🏛 Van Ness, 60

THE CONTEMPORARY JEWISH MUSEUM is at 736 Mission St. between 3rd and 4th sts., in the Yerba Buena cultural district. Designed by noted architect Daniel Libeskind, the museum is in the 1907 former Jessie Street Power Station. The contemporary design is reminiscent of the Hebrew letters that form the word *l'chaim,* which means "to life." Its traveling and permanent exhibits examine and celebrate Jewish culture, history, art and ideas.

Hours: Thurs.-Tues. 11-5 (also Thurs. 5-8). Guided tours are given Fri.-Tues. at 11:30 and 1:30, Thurs. at 11:30, 1:30 and 5:30. ASL and Verbal Description tours also are available; phone for details. Closed Jan. 1-2, the first day of Passover, July 4, the first day of Rosh Hashanah, Yom Kippur and Thanksgiving. **Cost:** $14; $12 (ages 65+ and students with ID); $5 (Thurs. after 5); free (ages 0-18). An additional fee may be charged for special exhibitions. **Phone:** (415) 655-7800.
GT 🍴 🏛 Union Sq/Market St, 125

EXPLORATORIUM is at Pier 15, at the foot of Green St. and The Embarcadero. The building has a contemporary industrial look, with six galleries displaying some 650 exhibits, most of them interactive. The Microscope Imaging Station in Gallery 4 produces high-resolution images of minuscule organisms like plankton and blood cells.

In Gallery 2 visitors can design their own Marble Machine, a contraption created from materials available at any local hardware store that sends a marble rolling along a circuitous path. A sure-fire crowd pleaser is "Rolling Through the Bay," a collection of city landmarks made entirely of toothpicks that took creator Scott Weaver nearly 40 years to complete. Visitors also can observe while museum staff create exhibits in the Exhibit Development Shop.

Check out a world without color in the Bechtel Gallery 3's Monochromatic Room. The Fisher Bay Observatory Gallery 6 gives visitors a look at San Francisco Bay's geography and ecology. Bring a jacket to enjoy the view of the Bay Bridge from the observatory's terrace or to stroll around the walkway outside the museum.

Gallery 5: Outdoor Exhibits features a 27-foot-tall Aeolian harp "played" by the wind. Experience upside-down views of The Embarcadero courtesy of the Rickshaw Obscura, a variation of the classic Camera Obscura; this one is mounted on a three-wheeled bike that is mobile.

The Tactile Dome (ages 7+) offers an interactive experience in total darkness; you feel your way through its chambers and mazes by crawling and sliding, relying only on your sense of touch and most likely gaining a renewed appreciation of your sense of sight when it's over.

Guests who are afraid of the dark, claustrophobic or who have back, neck or knee injuries should not participate in a Tactile Dome session, and those wearing casts are prohibited. Comfortable clothes are recommended.

Time: Allow 2 hours minimum. **Hours:** Daily 10-5 (also Thurs. 6-10 p.m. for ages 18+), in summer; Tues.-Sun. and some Mon. holidays 10-5 (also Thurs. 6-10 p.m. for ages 18+), rest of year. Tactile Dome sessions are at 10:15, 11:30, 12:45, 2:15, 3:30 and 4:45 on days the museum is open; each session lasts about an hour. The Tactile Dome also is available on a drop-in basis Thurs. 6-10 p.m. (ages 18+), some Thurs. and Fri. at 6:15 p.m. and 7:30 p.m.; phone ahead. Closed Thanksgiving and Christmas.

Cost: $29.95; $24.95 (ages 13-17, ages 65+, students with ID, teachers and persons with disabilities); $19.95 (ages 4-12). "Pay what you wish" community days are offered several times a year; check the website for specific dates. Admission Thurs. 6-10 p.m. (ages 18+ only) $19.95; $14.95 (daytime Exploratorium members); free (After Dark members). Separate Tactile Dome admission $15; $12 (Exploratorium members); advance reservations are strongly recommended. Thurs. night Tactile Dome drop-in session $10 (reservations not accepted). Phone ahead to confirm all prices. **Phone:** (415) 528-4444, or (415) 528-4444, option 5 for Tactile Dome reservations. 🍴 🚇 Embarcadero, 40

DE YOUNG MUSEUM—see Golden Gate Park p. 280.

FISHERMAN'S WHARF—see Shopping p. 256.

FORT POINT NATIONAL HISTORIC SITE—see Golden Gate National Recreation Area p. 98.

GHIRARDELLI SQUARE—see Shopping p. 256.

GLBT HISTORY MUSEUM is at 4127 18th St. (between Castro and Collingwood sts.). This small but very well-curated museum focuses on the San Francisco Bay Area's gay, lesbian, bisexual and transgender history from the late 19th century to the present. Exhibits, artifacts and multimedia presentations explore such deeply human themes as the search for companionship, the value of individual expression and the struggle for respect and equality in an often-hostile society. **Note:** Some displays include sexually themed material. **Time:** Allow 30 minutes minimum. **Hours:** Mon.-Sat. 11-6, Sun. noon-5. Phone ahead to confirm schedule. **Cost:** $5; $3 (California students with ID); free (first Wed. of the month). An audio tour is included; visitors also can call in on their cell or smartphones. **Phone:** (415) 621-1107. 🚇 Castro, 71

GOLDEN GATE BRIDGE crosses Golden Gate Strait, the entrance to San Francisco Bay, via US 101. The mighty span connecting the city with neighboring Marin County is not only a vital transportation link but a landmark recognized the world over, thanks to its appearance in countless dramatic photographs.

With a total length of 8,981 feet and a main span of 4,200 feet, this is one of the longest single-span suspension bridges ever built. And at 746 feet above

the water, its two massive towers are the world's highest bridge towers. A crew of painters works full time to maintain the distinctive international orange color that protects the bridge's steel components from the surrounding air's high salt content.

Walking or cycling across the bridge (a 1.7-mile trek one way) is a popular activity for both residents and visitors, and with good reason—on clear days the views of the city, the bay and the Marin Headlands are amazing (in summer afternoon fog often partially obscures both the bridge and the view). Pedestrians are allowed to use the east sidewalk; cyclists can access both the east and west sidewalks and must yield to pedestrians where the sidewalk is shared. In-line skates, roller skates and skateboards are not permitted on the east sidewalk.

Vista Point, at the north end, has restrooms and is a vantage point for photos of the bridge and the city skyline across the bay. The southeast plaza offers more up-close views from different perspectives. In conjunction with the bridge's 75th anniversary in 2012 the plaza was remodeled and landscaped, creating bench-lined strolling space and new bridge overlooks. Other visitor facilities include restrooms, the Golden Gate Bridge Pavilion information center and the Round House café.

Parking is limited at Vista Point and almost nonexistent in the vicinity of the southeast plaza, so taking public transportation (Golden Gate Transit or San Francisco Muni bus) or bicycling is recommended. There's free public parking in the vicinity of Fort Point National Historic Site, off Long Avenue at the end of Marine Drive; climb the hillside steps off Marine Drive to get to the southeast plaza.

Note: The electronic toll can be paid by setting up a FasTrak account (that can also be used to pay tolls on other Bay Area bridges); by one of three pay-by-plate options (license plate account, one-time payment or toll invoice); or by paying cash at an authorized merchant (gas stations, convenience stores or check cashing stores) at various locations in San Francisco and Bay Area cities. The one-time payment can be paid by credit card; a toll invoice is mailed to the registered owner of the vehicle.

Hours: Pedestrians can use the bridge's east sidewalk daily during daylight hours. **Cost:** Toll for cars and motorcycles $8.20 (southbound from Marin County to San Francisco); FasTrak fee $7.35; bicyclists and pedestrians free. Northbound free. **Phone:** (415) 486-8655 (Bay Area FasTrak Customer Service Center), or (877) 229-8655 (in Calif.).

GOLDEN GATE NATIONAL RECREATION AREA—see place listing p. 97.

GOLDEN GATE PARK is bordered by the Great Hwy. on the w., Lincoln Way on the s., Stanyan St. on the e. and Fulton St. on the n., extending 3 mi. from Fell and Stanyan sts. to the ocean. You can thank Scottish landscape gardener John McLaren for one of San Francisco's great treasures. A park superintendent for 60 years, he was largely responsible for transforming a windswept site consisting mostly of sand dunes and scrub oaks—a tract of land once beyond the city's western outskirts—into a verdant oasis of trees and plants speckled with man-made lakes.

Golden Gate Park is a wonderfully serene haven in the middle of a bustling city, a place to relax, stroll and forget life's cares (if only for an hour). Miles of roads and walking paths wind through this almost perfectly rectangular, 1,017-acre green space.

Gardens are chief among the park's many attractions. Seasonal blooms enhance the Rose Garden, between John F. Kennedy and Park Presidio drives (at its peak in summer); the Dahlia Dell, next to The Conservatory of Flowers (July through September); and the Queen Wilhelmina Tulip Garden, surrounding the Dutch Windmill in the park's northwest corner (mid-March to mid-April). The windmill (one of two in the park) once was part of an irrigation system, but today its function is purely scenic.

The Tree Fern Dell, across John F. Kennedy Drive from The Conservatory of Flowers, has an appropriately primeval look. It's lush with Australian tree ferns, bear's breeches (an ornamental plant that sends up spires of white flowers emerging from purple bracts) and giant rhubarb, a South American native with huge, exotic-looking leaves.

The Music Concourse, between the de Young Museum and The California Academy of Sciences, is a place to relax on a bench in the shade of chestnut trees or enjoy Sunday concerts performed at the band shell. The children's playground at Bowling Green, in the southeast corner of the park, features a lovingly restored Herschel Spillman carousel. At the corner of Bowling Green Drive and Middle Drive East is the National AIDS Memorial Grove, a quiet, contemplative retreat planted with redwoods. Stow Lake—actually a moat—encircles Strawberry Hill. Its summit is the park's highest point; climb to the breezy, tree-crowned top for views of the surrounding neighborhoods, and relax for a few minutes using a fallen log as a perch.

Numerous recreational facilities include archery, baseball, soccer and polo fields, basketball, tennis and handball courts, a nine-hole golf course, fly-casting pools, horseshoe pits and a boathouse at Stow Lake. The park visitor center, in the Beach Chalet on Great Highway, has Works Progress Administration (WPA) murals depicting scenes of the city during the Great Depression. You can also get a bite to eat or sip a micro-brewed beer while watching Pacific breakers crash against the shore.

Hours: Park open to visitors on foot daily 5 a.m.-midnight. Visitor center open daily 9-6. John F. Kennedy Dr. between Stanyan St. and Park Presidio Dr. is closed to vehicle traffic Sun. Concerts by the Golden Gate Park Band take place at the Music Concourse band shell most Sundays at 1, late Apr.-early Oct. **Cost:** Park free. **Phone:** (415) 831-2700 for general information.
🍴 🎿 🏕 🏛 Judah & 9th Ave, 65

The California Academy of Sciences is in Golden Gate Park at 55 Music Concourse Dr. Parking is available but limited; use public transportation. Muni's 44 bus line (O'Shaughnessy) stops at the Music Concourse on Tea Garden Drive (southbound) and in front of the academy on Music Concourse Drive (northbound). The 5 (Fulton) and 21 (Hayes) buses stop at 8th Avenue and Fulton Street just outside the park; from there it's a short walk to the museum.

Leading the way in sustainable architectural concepts, the building makes use of such recycled material as blue jeans for wall insulation. And the "living roof" is just that: a 2.5-acre carpet of native plants that include dozens of native wildflower species. Seven green hillocks provide a distinctive undulating profile, which visitors can view up close from the rooftop observation deck.

Visitors ages 21+ can enjoy music, cocktails and special presentations at NightLife on Thursday evenings.

Dioramas in the Kimball Natural History Museum's African Hall showcase mounted lions, zebras, baboons and other animals; and African penguins are among the living residents. The Foucault Pendulum, suspended from the ceiling next to the planetarium, proves irrefutable proof of planet Earth's rotation.

The Steinhart Aquarium's twin highlights are the Philippine Coral Reef, a 212,000-gallon tank populated with a spectacular assemblage of tropical fish that gleam like multicolored jewels, and the 100,000-gallon Northern California Coast tank, inhabited by such indigenous marine life as sea anemones, sardines, rockfish and grouper.

The all-digital Morrison Planetarium's state-of-the-art projector and software technologies present programs onto a 75-foot screen tilted at a 30-degree angle, seemingly immersing the viewer in space. Traditional star shows are augmented by special programming such as live NASA feeds.

In the Osher Rainforest, a four-story domed enclosure, visitors follow a spiraling path upward through an exhibit lush with orchids, bromeliads and mahogany trees and filled with free-flying birds and butterflies, reptiles and amphibians.

Time: Allow 4 hours minimum. **Hours:** Mon.-Sat. 9:30-5 (also Thurs. 6-10 for ages 21+), Sun. 11-5. Last admission 1 hour before closing. The schedule for the planetarium varies; phone ahead. The planetarium show is not recommended for children under 7. Phone ahead to confirm schedule. **Cost:** $35.95; $30.95 (ages 12-17, ages 65+ and students with ID); $25.95 (ages 4-11). Peak pricing may apply in summer and during holiday periods. Admission is discounted $3 for those arriving on foot, by bicycle or by public transportation. Admission is free to all on Community Free Days and on two weekends a year for San Francisco residents; early arrival is recommended on these days. **Phone:** (415) 379-8000.
GT 🍴 🏛 Judah & 9th Ave, 65

de Young Museum

The Conservatory of Flowers is at 100 John F. Kennedy Dr. at the eastern end of Golden Gate Park. This Victorian greenhouse, capped with an ornate dome, encapsulates the original intent of a plant conservatory: to transplant a bit of wonder and beauty from faraway jungles to a climate-controlled environment for the enjoyment of the masses.

The Lowland Tropics room, which sits beneath the conservatory's upper dome, contains a tangled assortment of exotic plants and trees, while the damp, humid environment in the Aquatic Plants room nurtures pitcher plants, bromeliads and Amazon water lilies. The name is actually a misnomer, as there are more than just flowers inside with a collection of close to 1,800 species of plants. Lovely orchids can be found in the Highland Tropics room. This is the perfect place to try out your new high-tech camera.

Time: Allow 30 minutes minimum. **Hours:** Tues.-Sun. (also Memorial Day and Labor Day) 10-6:30; 10-4:30, rest of year. Closes at 1:30 on Christmas Eve. Last admission 30 minutes before closing. Guided tours are given at 11, 12:30 and 2:30, subject to docent availability. Closed Jan. 1, Thanksgiving and Christmas. **Cost:** $9; $6 (ages 12-17, ages 65+, and college students and San Francisco residents with ID); $3 (ages 12-17, ages 65+ and college students with San Francisco ID) $3 (ages 5-11); free (ages 0-4). **Phone:** (415) 831-2090. 🚇 UCSF Parnassus, 64

de Young Museum is in Golden Gate Park at 50 Hagiwara Tea Garden Dr. at jct. John F. Kennedy Dr., following signs. It houses an outstanding collection of art from the Americas, Africa,

New Guinea and Oceania. Art in America to the 20th Century, on the upper level, displays paintings, sculpture, furniture and decorative arts in spacious, high-ceilinged galleries. Among the masterpieces here are Albert Bierstadt's "California Spring," which portrays a peacefully bucolic scene of cows grazing in a field contrasted with the fury of an approaching thunderstorm, and George Caleb Bingham's idyllic "Boatmen on the Missouri."

The Art of New Guinea features beautifully displayed shields, ceremonial masks and carved wooden figures. Also among the de Young's more than 2,000 works are displays of 20th-century and contemporary art; Native American, Central American and South American art; Maori sculptures; textiles and costumes; photography; and murals. Major special exhibitions are presented regularly.

A highlight is the indoor observation deck at the top of the Hamon Tower. The floor-to-ceiling glass walls from this ninth-floor perspective offer great views, including San Francisco Bay, the Golden Gate Bridge and downtown. The observation deck is free. Docent-led tours generally meet in Wilsey Court on the concourse level; rentals for self-paced audio tours are available near the main entrance.

Hours: Tues.-Sun. 9:30-5:15 (also some Fri. 5:15-8:15; phone for schedule). Last admission 1 hour before closing. Tower closes 45 minutes before museum. Closed Thanksgiving and Christmas. **Cost:** $15; $12 (ages 65+); $6 (college students with ID); free (ages 0-17 and to all first Tues. of the month; special exhibition fees still apply). An additional fee is charged for some special exhibitions. **Parking:** $4.50 per hour (Mon.-Fri.), $5 per hour (Sat.-Sun.) in the Music Concourse Garage. **Phone:** (415) 750-3600. GT 🚇 Judah & 9th Ave, 65

Japanese Tea Garden, 8th Ave. and John F. Kennedy Dr. in Golden Gate Park, was originally built as a Japanese village for the 1894 California Midwinter International Exposition. Japanese immigrant Makoto Hagiwara designed the bulk of this elegantly landscaped 5-acre site and was its official caretaker for a number of years.

The shaded stone walkways and footbridges are meant to be strolled at a leisurely pace. Among the sculpted trees and hedges are many plants native to Japan and China. Ponds, miniature waterfalls, a big bronze Buddha, stone lanterns, statuary and a couple of pagodas all contribute to the beauty of this tranquil little spot. Spring, when the cherry trees bloom, is a spectacular time to visit. Green teas and Japanese confections are served in the garden's teahouse.

Hours: Daily 9-6, Mar.-Oct.; 9-4:45, rest of year. **Cost:** $8; $6 (ages 12-17, ages 65+ and San Francisco residents); $3 (San Francisco residents ages 12-17 and 65+); $2 (ages 5-11); free (ages 0-4 and to all Mon., Wed. and Fri. if entering before 10 a.m.). **Phone:** (415) 752-1171. 🚇 Judah & 9th Ave, 65

San Francisco Botanical Garden at Strybing Arboretum main entrance is near 9th Ave. and Lincoln Way in Golden Gate Park. This outstanding botanical garden, which celebrated its 75th anniversary in 2015, features more than 8,500 species of plants from around the world. The Bay Area's Mediterranean climate—year-round mild temperatures, wet winters, dry summers and frequent fog—is shared by locations in such far-flung countries as New Zealand, South Africa and Chile.

Themed plantings include a cloud forest, a fragrance garden, a primitive plant garden, the Japanese Moonviewing Garden and gardens devoted to camellias, rhododendrons and California native plants. The sheer botanical variety ensures seasonal highlights throughout the year: camellias and giant magnolia blossoms from January to March, wildflowers and rhododendrons in April and May, flowering perennials in summer, fuchsias and the enormous leaves of giant rhubarb, a South American native, in fall.

A century-old redwood grove provides a cool, moist environment for ferns and other shade-loving plants as well as an enchanting retreat for humans. Bench-lined walking paths and expansive lawns throughout the garden's 55 acres offer plenty of opportunities to stop, relax and contemplate nature's beautiful and remarkable diversity.

Time: Allow 2 hours minimum. **Hours:** Opens daily at 7:30 a.m. and closes 1 hour after last entry. Last entry at 6 p.m., second Sun. in Mar.-Sept. 30; at 4, first Sun. in Nov.-Jan. 31; at 5, rest of year. Free 45-minute guided tours departing from the Main Gate are given daily at 1:30; also Sat.-Sun. at 2, spring-early fall, departing from the North Gate. Free bird walks are offered the first Sun. of the month beginning at 8 a.m. **Cost:** $8; $6 (ages 12-17 and 65+); $2 (ages 5-11); $18 (family, two adults and all children under 17 residing in the same residence); free (botanical garden members and San Francisco city and county residents with ID, and to all daily 7:30-9 a.m., all day the second Tues. of the month, and on Jan. 1, Thanksgiving and Christmas). **Phone:** (415) 661-1316.
GT 🅰 🅿 Judah & 9th Ave, 65

GRACE CATHEDRAL is atop Nob Hill at 1100 California St. at jct. Taylor St. After two of their homes were destroyed by fire following the 1906 earthquake, the wealthy Crocker family offered the site for construction of a cathedral. Nearby Grace Church was also devastated; The Ritz-Carlton, San Francisco luxury hotel was later built where that church stood.

Inside the French Gothic-style Episcopal cathedral, completed in 1964, are replicas of the bronze doors of the Baptistery in Florence, Italy ("The Gates of Paradise") by Lorenzo Ghiberti, "The Life of Christ" triptych altarpiece by Keith Haring, two labyrinths, stained glass, and medieval and contemporary furnishings. **Hours:** Fri.-Wed. 8-6, Thurs. 7-6, holidays 8-4. Docent-led tours are given Mon. and Thurs.-Fri. 1-3, Sat. 11:30-1:30, Sun. after 11 a.m.

service. A Grand Tour for ages 10+ is offered on select dates at 10 a.m.; reservations are required. Phone ahead to confirm schedule. **Cost:** Docent tours by donation. Grand Tour $25. **Phone:** (415) 749-6300. 🅿 Chinatown, 126

GRANDVIEW PARK is off Moraga St. between 14th and 15th aves. What this aptly named park lacks in size it more than makes up for in the spectacular 360-degree views that encompass downtown, Golden Gate Park, the Golden Gate Bridge, San Francisco Bay, the Marin Headlands and the Pacific. This hilltop in the Sunset neighborhood, crowned with several Monterey cypresses and one graceful eucalyptus tree, is not only one of the most delightfully secluded spots in San Francisco, but—to those in the know—also an unsurpassed vantage point for sunset watching.

Longtime residents call the 665-foot-tall outcrop of Franciscan chert rock Turtle Hill. Not all that many years ago the Sunset was nothing but shifting sand dunes, but residential development cut off the supply of ocean sand, and as a result the underlying rock is becoming more and more exposed. Native dune plants like beach strawberry, bush monkey flower and the endangered Franciscan wallflower and dune tansy grow on the hill; all must contend with a harsh, windswept environment and ground that retains little moisture.

Note: Reaching the summit involves climbing two steep sets of stairs. The first set, off Moraga and 14th, zigzags up to the base of the hill. The second set—five flights of 22 steps each—climbs to the top of the hill. A wood fence surrounds the summit, part

Grace Cathedral

of an ongoing restoration program to help protect the fragile plant community; stay on the dirt paths to help minimize the effects of erosion. **Hours:** Daily 5 a.m.-midnight. **Cost:** Free. **Phone:** (415) 831-2700. Judah & 19th Ave, 66

Hidden Garden Steps begin at Kirkham St. and 16th Ave. and climb up to Lawton St. Unveiled at the end of 2013, the undertaking was a community labor of love, transforming this 16th Avenue staircase from a site blemished by graffiti and litter to a beautiful public art space and a showcase for the neighborhood.

The artistic vision takes into account native flora and fauna and the steep hillside topography. Each of the 148 step risers is decorated with tiles that collectively form designs ranging from flowers to a salamander that extends up 26 steps. Native plants that include cuttings from neighborhood gardens beautify the stairway and provide a habitat for the endangered green hairstreak butterfly.

The steps look completely different depending on where you're standing. At the base looking up, the vibrantly colorful designs are on full display. At the top of the steps looking down, you can't see the mosaic tiles on the risers, only the top of each step—but the panoramic view of the Outer Sunset looking out toward the ocean is impressive. Judah & 19th Ave, 66

JAPANESE TEA GARDEN—see Golden Gate Park p. 280.

THE *JEREMIAH O'BRIEN* is berthed at Pier 45 at Fisherman's Wharf. This restored World War II Liberty ship is one of only two in operating condition out of 2,710 built during that war.

During "steaming" weekends, usually the third weekend of the month, the ship's engine is in operation. Special cruises take place seasonally.

Time: Allow 1 hour minimum. **Hours:** Daily 9-5. Last admission 1 hour before closing. Tours are not available when the ship is cruising on selected days May-Oct. Closed Jan. 1, Easter, Thanksgiving and Christmas. Phone ahead to confirm schedule. **Cost:** $20; $12 (ages 62+ and students with ID); $10 (ages 5-16 and active military with ID); $45 (family, two adults and two children). **Phone:** (415) 544-0100. GT

LANDS END is accessible from Point Lobos Ave. and Merrie Way. This little patch of wilderness at the outer western edge of urban San Francisco, overlooking the Pacific Ocean, is part of Golden Gate National Recreation Area *(see place listing p. 97)*. It's a great place for a quiet, relaxing hike, taking in a plethora of scenic views and otherwise escaping the city's bustle for an afternoon.

The California Coastal Trail runs the length of Lands End. The western end is near the Sutro Baths. You can access the eastern end from 32nd Avenue and El Camino del Mar, at the western edge of the Sea Cliff neighborhood. From here it's just a

few steps to Eagle's Point, an overlook with a great view of the Golden Gate Bridge, particularly on sunny days.

From Eagle's Point the Coastal Trail winds west through a forest of tall conifers and a lush tangle of undergrowth that includes seasonal wildflowers. Closer to the Sutro Baths the trail widens and runs along the edge of tall cliffs. There are frequent views of offshore rocks and the Marin Headlands across the water (this is the geographic point where bay and ocean merge). A couple of steep sections have steps built into the trail.

Toward the western end is a memorial to the men who died on the USS *San Francisco* during the Battle of Guadalcanal on Nov. 12-13, 1942. The memorial, a piece of the ship's bridge, stands above the Coastal Trail along the parallel El Camino del Mar Trail.

Note: There are free parking lots off Point Lobos Avenue in Sutro Heights Park. The #1 and #38 Muni bus lines stop a block away from the entrance to Lincoln Park at 34th Avenue and Clement Street. Walk up Legion of Honor Drive to the Legion of Honor parking lot, then follow the walking path that skirts the Lincoln Park Municipal Golf Course and runs into the Coastal Trail. You can also get off the #1 bus at California Street and 32nd Avenue and walk north two blocks on 32nd to El Camino del Mar at the trail's eastern end. **Hours:** Daily during daylight hours. **Cost:** Free. **Phone:** (415) 561-3000.

Cliff House is at 1090 Point Lobos Ave. (at Great Hwy.). The first Cliff House opened in 1863, a modest building frequented by such prominent San Francisco families as the Hearsts and the Stanfords, who would arrive at Ocean Beach in horse-drawn carriages. Destroyed by a chimney fire in 1894, it reopened 2 years later as an elegant destination for dining, dancing and entertainment—only to burn to the ground again in 1907.

The third and present Cliff House opened in 1909. Renovations restored the original neoclassic architecture, and the recent addition of the Sutro Wing added a two-story dining room with a stunning view of the ocean. More than 200 autographed photos of various dignitaries and movie stars offer a glimpse back at the landmark's nearly 150-plus-year history.

The building overlooks Seal Rocks; the guano-covered formations just offshore are the site of occasional sea lion sightings from May through October. The sidewalk approach along Great Highway and a walkway around the property are good vantage points to take in the coastline views. Window tables are popular at The Bistro, a casual walk-in restaurant; reservations are strongly recommended at the more upscale Sutro's at the Cliff House.

Hours: Lower observation deck open daily 24 hours. **Cost:** Free. **Phone:** (415) 386-3330.

Lands End Lookout is at Merrie Way and Point Lobos Ave., just e. of the Cliff House. Part of an ongoing project to restore the habitat at Lands End and improve visitor amenities, it has exhibits about the history and natural features of San Francisco's northwestern corner and information about Golden Gate National Recreation Area, as well as lots of handsome coffee table books and gift items for sale. The small building also incorporates a number of "green" features. **Hours:** Mon.-Fri. 9-5, Sat.-Sun. 9-7, early May-early Sept.; Mon.-Fri. 9-5, Sat.-Sun. 9-6, early Sept.-early Nov.; daily 9-5, rest of year. **Cost:** Free. **Parking:** There is free parking on either side of Point Lobos Avenue; the lots fill up on sunny weekends. **Phone:** (415) 426-5240. ⊞

Mile Rock Beach is reached via a stairway off the Coastal Trail that descends to the beach; the detour at the trail's approximate midway point is signed. At the bottom of the steps you can walk farther down to a pebble and boulder-strewn cove where waves crash impressively against the rocky shoreline and there's a view of the Golden Gate Bridge in the distance.

You'll sometimes see impromptu rock sculptures—several smooth, flat stones carefully balanced on top of a larger rock and looking somewhat like a stack of pancakes—assembled by an unknown artist indulging his or her creative side. The weather is often overcast or foggy, but on a sunny day the beach is a wonderful spot to sit on a log and contemplate your surroundings. To the right a dirt trail winds up a steep hill to a vantage point offering spectacular views, both of the beach below and looking out over the water to the Marin Headlands.

On a small plateau atop the hill is the Lands End Labyrinth. An assemblage of rocks placed in concentric circles, it was created by local artist Eduardo Aguilera in 2004 and added a bit of mystery to a tucked-away corner of the city. Sadly, this intriguing work of art has been destroyed and then rebuilt many times over the years due to vandalism, most recently in 2015. **Hours:** Daily during daylight hours. **Cost:** Free.

Sutro Baths site is off Point Lobos Ave. in Sutro Heights Park. These ruins are the only evidence of a lavish playground developed by wealthy former mayor Adolph Sutro that opened to the public in 1896. Standing literally at the ocean's edge, it boasted seven swimming pools (six saltwater and one freshwater), more than 500 private dressing rooms, an amphitheater, grand staircases and landscaped promenades, all looking out over the Pacific.

The extravagant structure was prohibitively expensive to operate, which led to its eventual closing. Fire destroyed the Sutro Baths in 1966 as it was in the process of being demolished. Nothing remains but a destroyed foundation, rusted pipes jutting out from vestiges of walls and long-abandoned stairways—and every inch of it can be explored. One interesting feature is a short tunnel that leads to a small opening with a view of waves crashing against the rocks.

Among the tangle of vegetation carpeting the hillside above the ruins is the bright green, fleshy-leaved ice plant, a low-growing succulent that

Lands End Lookout

blankets the sand dunes at many northern California beaches. Ice plants produce pretty pink and yellow flowers at various times of the year. Adding to the scenic quotient are expansive views of the ocean and the Marin Headlands. Stairways, paved walking paths and dirt paths descend from Point Lobos Avenue and the Coastal Trail.

Note: There are no guards on duty, and no guardrails or other protective aids; poke around at your leisure but also at your own risk. Watch for slippery spots near the water, and heed all warning signs. **Hours:** Site accessible daily during daylight hours. **Cost:** Free.

LINCOLN PARK, at 34th Ave. and Clement St., contains American artist George Segal's memorial to the victims of the World War II Holocaust. The park is an attractive starting point for hikes along El Camino del Mar and the Coastal Trail; both trails run the length of Lands End. **Cost:** Free.

Legion of Honor is in Lincoln Park near the jct. of 34th Ave. and Clement St. This world-class art museum owes its existence to Alma Spreckels, wife of wealthy sugar magnate Adolph B. Spreckels. An avid art collector, Mrs. Spreckels persuaded her husband to fund construction of a three-quarter-scale version of the 18th-century Palais de la Légion d'Honneur in Paris. Dedicated to California soldiers who died in France during World War I, the museum opened on Armistice Day in 1924.

The permanent collection spans more than 4,000 years of art. "The Thinker," a cast bronze and one of more than 70 sculptures by Auguste Rodin, dominates the outdoor Court of Honor; other noteworthy

Lyon Street Steps

sculptures in the Rodin Gallery include "The Three Shades" and "Bust of Victor Hugo."

European art features paintings by Fra Angelico, El Greco, Pablo Picasso, Rembrandt van Rijn and Peter Paul Rubens. Anthony van Dyck's "Marie Claire de Croy" is one of the artist's larger-than-life works of portraiture, while "Portrait of a Gentleman" by Nicolas de la Largillière depicts a member of Parisian royalty swaddled in expensive brocade and sporting a massive powdered wig. Don't miss "The Russian Bride's Attire" by Konstantin Makovsky; this enormous painting is full of lovely details and has a luminous quality.

Among the major gifts from Mrs. Spreckels' personal collection are French furniture, ceramics and decorative silver objects. Ancient works of art include antiquities from the Mediterranean and the Near East. Also on display are tapestries, porcelains, a group of illustrated books and an extensive collection of prints, drawings and photographs.

On the front lawn stands the equestrian statue "El Cid." The 11th-century Castilian military leader holds a spear aloft while his steed looks toward a panoramic view of San Francisco Bay, with the Golden Gate Bridge in the distance.

Time: Allow 2 hours minimum. **Hours:** Tues.-Sun. 9:30-5:15. Last admission is at 4:30. Free docent-led tours are given daily; consult the museum's online events calendar for details and times. Closed Thanksgiving and Christmas. **Cost:** $15; $12 (ages 65+); $6 (students with ID); free (ages 0-17 and to all on the first Tues. of the month). An additional fee is charged for some special exhibitions. **Phone:** (415) 750-3600, (415) 750-7645 for

sign language tour requests or TTY (415) 750-3509.
GT ⑪

Lincoln Park Steps are at the w. end of California St. off 32nd St. The city's newest mosaic tile stairway opened to the public in June 2015. The refurbished, 52-step staircase, a colorful assemblage of botanical and Beaux Arts-style designs, is the work of local artist Aileen Barr. The wide stairway is the official entry into Lincoln Park. Relax on one of the benches at the top of the steps and enjoy the fine view looking east toward Pacific Heights. **Hours:** Daily 24 hours. **Cost:** Free.

LYON STREET STEPS run up Lyon St. from Green St. to Broadway, near the southeast corner of the Presidio. Many San Francisco stairways are also necessary transportation routes, and these steps connect Cow Hollow to Pacific Heights. The fact that they also offer spectacular views is a bonus.

The first block begins at the point where Green dead-ends and is the steeper of the two sections, two narrow flights of 62 steps each heading up to Vallejo Street. The daunting stretch is a favorite workout for runners and fitness enthusiasts.

Across Vallejo an elaborate stone balustrade announces "Lyon Street," and a meticulously maintained flower bed features a Heart in San Francisco sculpture, one of several of these public installations located around the city. The stairway from Vallejo up to Broadway—eight flights of 15 steps—is landscaped, wider and less steep, offering more opportunities to stop, catch your breath and admire the handsome (and pricey) homes flanking the east side of the stairs. From Broadway the view encompasses the Palace of Fine Arts dome, the rooftops of the Marina District and San Francisco Bay.

Note: Street parking in this residential area is limited. The closest Muni bus stops are the #43 at Jackson Street and Presidio Boulevard (3 blocks from the top of the steps at Broadway) and the #41 at Lyon and Union streets (a block from the foot of the stairway beginning at Green Street). **Time:** Allow 30 minutes minimum.

MISSION DOLORES PARK is bordered n. and s. by 18th and 20th sts. and e. and w. by Dolores and Church sts. The rectangular swath of Dolores Park, San Francisco's "front yard," is one of the city's best-loved green spaces as well as the heart of the culturally diverse Mission District. Named for the Mission Dolores, which stands across 18th Street, the park occupies land that was once a Jewish cemetery and later served as a refugee camp for residents made homeless as a result of the 1906 earthquake and fire.

The park features expansive green lawns shaded by stately date palms. Recreational facilities include two soccer fields, six tennis courts, a basketball court, a clubhouse and the Helen Diller Playground. From the park's southwest corner at 20th and Church streets there's a great view of the downtown skyline.

Although dwarfed in size by Golden Gate Park, this is one of the most popular spots in the city to chill, picnic or just stretch out on the grass on a sunny afternoon. It's also the site of numerous weekend festivals, performances and cultural events. Following major renovations in 2015 and early 2016, the park has updated landscaping and lights, new restrooms and picnic areas, resurfaced tennis and basketball courts, a "bike polo" court and an off-leash dog play area.

Hours: Daily dawn-dusk. **Cost:** Free. **Phone:** (415) 831-2700. 🅿 ♿ Church & 18th St, 120

MISSION SAN FRANCISCO DE ASIS (Misión San Francisco de Asís, or Mission Dolores) is at 3321 16th St. at Dolores St.; street parking is limited. The oldest standing structure in San Francisco, the mission was founded by Father Francisco Palou under the direction of Father Junípero Serra on June 29, 1776, and dedicated on Oct. 9.

Daily mass still takes place in this venerable building, which has adobe walls 4 feet thick and retains the original redwood logs, still lashed together with rawhide, that support the roof. The *reredos* (altar screen), one of the most ornate examples of Baroque art among the California missions, was brought from San Blas, Mexico in 1797. The two side altars also came from Mexico in 1810 and feature wood columns that imitate marble.

While the mission withstood the 1906 earthquake, the adjacent brick parish church did not. The present concrete building was completed in 1918 and offers a striking contrast to the mission's simple appearance. The 1918 church was declared a basilica in 1952 by Pope Pius XII. It has an extravagantly decorative interior and beautiful stained-glass windows depicting St. Francis of Assisi, the mission's patron saint. A one-room museum displays religious artifacts and has exhibits about daily life at the mission, Father Serra and the Ohlone Indians who built the mission church.

More than 11,000 burials took place in the mission cemetery between 1782 and 1898; most of the markers designate individuals who died in the decades following the California gold rush, when San Francisco was a rapidly growing settlement that experienced a great deal of illness and many early deaths. A wooden grave marker acknowledges two Indians who were baptized, married and buried at the mission. The tall statue in the center of the garden is a likeness of Father Serra. Kim Novak and Jimmy Stewart walked through the cemetery in a scene from Alfred Hitchcock's "Vertigo." Cool, leafy and quiet, it's a lovely spot for quiet reflection.

Hours: Sun.-Fri. 9:30-4, Sat. 9-4. Closed Jan. 1, Easter, Thanksgiving and Christmas. **Cost:** $7; $5 (ages 65+ and students with ID). **Phone:** (415) 621-8203. ♿ Church & 18th St, 120

MUSÉE MÉCANIQUE is at Pier 45 at Fisherman's Wharf, at the end of Taylor St. This "mechanical museum" is a treasure trove of working antique mechanical games housed in a large, warehouse-like structure. The collection includes more than 200 coin-operated musical instruments and arcade machines such as player pianos, a boxing match, pinball machines, an arm-wrestling game and gypsy fortune tellers.

Near the front entrance is Laffing Sal, who formerly held court at the now-defunct Playland at the Beach amusement park. The towering, red-haired figure stands in a glass case, and her boisterous, vaguely menacing laugh gave many children nightmares when Laffing Sals were a standard feature in American fun houses of the 1930s and '40s. Bring plenty of coins if you want to play the games (change machines are also available).

Time: Allow 30 minutes minimum. **Hours:** Daily 10-8. Hours may be extended in summer. Phone ahead to confirm schedule. **Cost:** Free. Games 1c-$1. **Phone:** (415) 346-2000.

NORTH BEACH spreads w. and s. from Telegraph Hill to Columbus Ave. It's located in one of the hilliest sections of a hilly city (stairways rather than sidewalks line some of the steeper streets). Compact, crowded and vibrant, San Francisco's version of "Little Italy" is full of delis, bakeries, cafés and restaurants.

City Lights Bookstore on Columbus Avenue, founded by San Francisco poet laureate Lawrence Ferlinghetti, was once a hangout for Beat Generation poets and literary figures like Jack Kerouac. Check out the murals and wall quotations from the author of "On the Road" along tiny Jack Kerouac Alley, between Grant and Columbus avenues. You've also got seedy appeal in a smattering of strip joints that include the Condor Club, where topless go-go dancer Carol Doda gyrated her way to 15 minutes of fame in the swinging '60s.

And of course you've got food. Just walking around North Beach tends to make most people start salivating. Molinari (373 Columbus Ave.) is a deli and market chock-full of specialty items—dried pastas, marinated artichokes, robust house-cured salamis hanging above the counter. The Liguria Bakery (1700 Stockton St.) turns out freshly baked focaccia bread—rosemary, raisin and pizza are popular flavors—and invariably sells out before noon (get there early).

A fave hangout is Vesuvio, just up from City Lights. It's a classic bar in every sense, from the ambience (all kinds of cool stuff on the walls) to the wide drink selection and the jovial crowd of regulars. Another North Beach institution is Tosca Café (242 Columbus Ave.); it has a jukebox heavy on operatic selections, red leather booths and an open kitchen that serves dinner late. Washington Square, at Columbus Avenue and Union Street, is a tree-shaded patch of lawn sprinkled with park benches and frequented by pigeons, dog walkers, scrambling kids

Palace of Fine Arts

and early-morning practitioners of tai chi. 🚇 Chinatown, 126

PALACE OF FINE ARTS is at Palace Dr. and Lyon St., at the w. end of the Marina District. It is the last remaining structure associated with the 1915 Panama-Pacific Exposition, and the only one located at its original site. The design of this classically elegant building took its inspiration from ancient Greek and Roman architecture. After the exposition ended the palace functioned as a World War II storage facility for trucks and jeeps, a city Parks Department warehouse and a temporary fire department headquarters. The crumbling structure was demolished in 1964 and reconstructed right down to the original sculptures, ornamental urns, friezes and carved decorations that collectively symbolize Greek culture.

Built around an artificial lagoon, the palace complex is made up of a domed, colonnaded pergola flanked by rows of Corinthian columns. Walkways wind beneath the dome and around the lagoon, which not only provides a mirrored surface to reflect the grand architecture but offers a home for ducks, swans and migrating waterfowl. Inside is the 962-seat Palace of Fine Arts Theatre. **Time:** Allow 30 minutes minimum. **Hours:** Daily dawn-dusk. **Cost:** Free. **Phone:** (415) 563-6504 for theater events and information.

PIER 39—see Shopping p. 256.

PRECITA EYES MURAL ARTS & VISITORS CENTER is at 2981 24th St. This organization is committed to promoting San Francisco's rich tradition of street art and bringing attention to the city's gifted muralists, many of whom live in the Mission District. Rotating exhibits spotlight the work of such noted artists as Susan Cervantes and Juana Alicia. The center also offers a varied schedule of art classes and workshops.

The most enjoyable way to learn more about the history and cultural context of Mission murals is to take one of the center's guided walking tours. They visit such locations as nearby Balmy Alley, which is filled with outstanding examples of "the people's art," and 24th Street.

Hours: Visitors center open Mon.-Fri. 10-5, Sat. 10-4, Sun. noon-4. Classic Mission Mural Walk tours depart Sat.-Sun. at 1:30. Bicycle and bus tours are available by appointment. Tour tickets may be purchased online. Closed Easter. Phone ahead to confirm schedule. **Cost:** Tour fees $20; $10 (ages 65+ and college students with ID); $6 (ages 12-17); $3 (ages 0-11). **Phone:** (415) 285-2287. GT 🚇 24th Street Mission, 45

PRESIDIO OF SAN FRANCISCO—see Golden Gate National Recreation Area p. 98.

RIPLEY'S BELIEVE IT OR NOT! ODDITORIUM is at 175 Jefferson St. at Fisherman's Wharf. Like other Ripley's museums, it displays bizarre, oddball and unusual artifacts from around the world that will appeal to just about everyone, including a couple of gross-out exhibits for kids and some historically interesting ones for adults. Beneath the oddities and exotica—and some frightening practices like head shrinking—is a joyful celebration of life and the world around us, and the realization that people the world over follow traditions and ways of living taught to them by their elders.

There's the usual mind-boggling stuff, like a replica of the Golden Gate Bridge made entirely of toothpicks, as well as pop culture nods (artwork depicting Lady Gaga in all her over-the-top glory). Among the interactive elements are a shooting gallery, a "mystery gate" and a human-sized kaleidoscope. The Mirror Maze is summed up by its name; it's like being dropped into the opening credits of a James Bond movie. The Impossible LaseRace is another maze to navigate, but this one's comprised of a web of green lasers.

Hours: Sun.-Thurs. 10-10, Fri.-Sat. 10 a.m.-11 p.m.; hours may be extended in summer. Closing hours are subject to change; phone ahead to confirm. **Cost:** Museum $23; $18 (ages 5-12). Mirror Maze $10; $8 (ages 5-12) without museum admission. Combination ticket with Mirror Maze and Impossible LaseRace $25; $20 (ages 5-12). **Phone:** (415) 202-9850.

SAN FRANCISCO BOTANICAL GARDEN AT STRYBING ARBORETUM—see Golden Gate Park p. 281.

SAN FRANCISCO MARITIME NATIONAL HISTORICAL PARK is at the w. end of Fisherman's Wharf. In addition to a fleet of historic ships, a maritime museum and a maritime research center, the site also includes the bayside Aquatic Park's beach and cove.

The visitor center, in a restored 1907 warehouse, has interactive displays that relate the city's maritime history. Highlights include a first-order Fresnel lighthouse lens and an exhibit that allows visitors to walk through time along San Francisco's historic waterfront. **Hours:** Visitor center daily 9:30-5. Closed Jan. 1, Thanksgiving and Christmas. **Cost:** Historic ships boarding pass $15; free (ages 0-15). **Phone:** (415) 447-5000.

Aquatic Park Bathhouse Building/Maritime Museum is at 900 Beach St. Built in 1939, its Art Deco-inspired exterior mimics an ocean liner. Displayed in the lobby are fanciful and colorful murals, several miniature model ships encased in glass, a large chunk of the vessel *Niantic*. You'll also see the 19-foot sloop *Mermaid*, which 23-year-old Kenichi Horie used to sail solo across the Pacific in 1962. The veranda is open to the public. Changing exhibits are presented as well. **Hours:** Daily 10-4. Closed Jan. 1, Thanksgiving and Christmas. **Cost:** Free. **Phone:** (415) 447-5000.

Hyde Street Pier Historic Ships, at the foot of Hyde St., displays ships dating from the late 19th century. Visitors can board four ships. The *Balclutha* is a three-masted, square-rigged sailing vessel containing the immersive-environment exhibit "Cargo Is King!" that traces the ship's three careers through films, panels, and stacks of cargo ship relics and photographs. The *C.A. Thayer* is a coastal lumber schooner. The *Eureka* was the largest ferry operating on San Francisco Bay in its time; the *Hercules* is a steam-powered tugboat. The scow schooner *Alma*, which offers sailing tours in summer, and the tugboat *Eppleton Hall* are anchored nearby. Programs and demonstrations are offered.

Hours: Daily 9:30-5. Last admission 30 minutes before closing. Closed Jan. 1, Thanksgiving and Christmas. **Cost:** $15; free (ages 0-15 and National Park pass holders). **Phone:** (415) 447-5000.

Maritime Research Center, at Fort Mason, Building E, provides access to maritime books, achives and collections. **Hours:** Open by appointment only, Mon.-Fri. 1-4. **Cost:** Free. **Phone:** (415) 561-7030.

SAN FRANCISCO MUSEUM OF MODERN ART (SFMOMA) is at 151 Third St. (between Mission and Howard sts.); there are entrances on Third and Howard sts. BART and Muni public transportation and pay parking garages are close by. The museum reopened in May 2016 following a 3-year expansion and renovation project that nearly tripled the available gallery space.

The 10-story building, designed by architectural firm Snøhetta, features an exterior of rippling white fiberglass-reinforced polymer that evokes fog rolling in off the ocean, an iconic by-product of the Bay Area's topography and marine climate. It also incorporates elements of the original brick, granite and glass structure designed by Swiss architect Mario Botta.

Inside, seven floors of galleries showcase a noteworthy collection of modern and contemporary art, including paintings, sculpture, media arts, photography, architecture and design objects. The 19 inaugural exhibitions included a curated selection from the Doris and Donald Fisher Collection, new to the museum's permanent holdings, and a floor devoted to the Pritzker Center for Photography. Temporary exhibitions also are offered.

Artists represented range from Diego Rivera, Marcel Duchamp and Alfred Stieglitz to Richard Serra, Agnes Martin and Chuck Close. The Fisher Collection focuses on American pop and abstract art as well as post-1960 German art, with works by such notables as Ellsworth Kelly, Gerhard Richter and Andy Warhol.

Another feature is the 45,000 square feet of public space on the first and second floors that is free to visitors. Art installations in this free space include Julie Mehretu's "HOWL, eon (I, II)," two monumental abstract paintings exploring the American West in the first-floor atrium.

Special exhibitions are presented regularly. Flash photography and the use of a camera tripod or selfie sticks is not permitted. Backpacks must be hand-carried or worn in front. **Hours:** Galleries open Thurs.-Tues. 10-5 (also Thurs. 5-9). A timed ticket is required for special surcharged exhibitions. Closed Thanksgiving and Christmas. **Cost:** $25; $22 (ages 65+); $19 (ages 19-24 with ID). Public spaces free. Advance online ticket purchase is strongly recommended. **Phone:** (415) 357-4000.
🍴 🚇 Montgomery Street, 41

SAN FRANCISCO ZOO, on Great Hwy. between Skyline and Sloat blvds. at 1 Zoo Rd., is home to a variety of exotic animals. Orphaned grizzly bear sisters Kachina and Kiona (the names mean "sacred dancer" and "brown hills," respectively) reside at Hearst Grizzly Gulch; the grizzly is the California state mammal and its image appears on the state flag. Observe marsupials like red kangaroos and wallaroos from an overlook at the Australian Walkabout, which features plants and animals native to the island continent.

Giraffes, zebras, ostriches, crowned cranes and other wildlife coexist peacefully at the 3-acre Leanne B. Roberts African Savanna, an open-landscaped setting where you can watch animals interact from up-close vantage points. Gorillas call the Jones Family Gorilla Reserve home, while lemurs leap from tree to tree at the Lipman Family Lemur Forest. Other highlights include an antique Dentzel carousel and a miniature steam train.

Hours: Daily 10-5, mid-Mar. to early Nov.; 10-4, rest of year. Last admission 1 hour before closing. **Cost:** $23; $19 (ages 65+); $17 (ages 4-14). Reduced admission for San Francisco residents. Train rides $7; carousel rides $4. **Parking:** $11-$13. **Phone:** (415) 753-7080. 🚇 SF Zoo, 76

USS *Pampanito*

Fisher Family Children's Zoo, within the San Francisco Zoo, includes nature trails, a barnyard, an insect zoo and animals that may be petted and fed. **Hours:** Daily 10-5, mid-Mar. to early Nov.; 10-4, rest of year. Phone ahead to confirm schedule. **Cost:** Included in San Francisco Zoo admission.
SF Zoo, 76

TELEGRAPH HILL rises near the e. end of Lombard St. Called Loma Alta by the Spanish and Goat Hill by early city residents, Telegraph Hill's current name was adopted in 1849 from a structure similar to a windmill on the top of the hill that used a semaphore-like system to signal merchants of the imminent arrival of ships. Telegraph Hill is now crowned by Coit Tower, the monument to San Francisco firefighters that is a distinctive North Beach landmark.

One of the most visually rewarding ways to ascend Telegraph Hill is via the Filbert Steps, which rise in three sections up the east side. The steps end at Telegraph Hill Boulevard, the road that encircles the base of Coit Tower. The tower grounds are lovely, and from this elevated perspective there are fine views of the bay. Chinatown, 126

Coit Tower stands atop Telegraph Hill. This 210-foot-tall, Art Deco-style tower was built in 1933 with money provided by eccentric philanthropist Lillie Hitchcock Coit, who had an interest in blazes and was thus a longtime friend of the city's firefighters. Despite its appearance and a persistent urban legend, the tower's resemblance to a fire hose nozzle was not intentional.

One of the noteworthy features is a series of fresco murals in the lobby, painted in 1934 as part of

the New Deal Public Works of Art Project. Inspired by Mexican muralist Diego Rivera and created by 25 artists who worked for an hourly wage of $1, they depict the lives of the state's Depression-era working class.

A vintage elevator zips visitors to the observation deck at the top in 66 seconds for panoramic views (unless it's foggy) of North Beach, Lombard Street, the Golden Gate and Bay bridges, and Alcatraz Island. Depending on the time of year there may be a wait for the elevator.

Time and weather have taken their toll, and the tower closed in late 2013 to repair a leaky roof and some water damage to the murals. It reopened in 2014 with refurbished art and a new concession stand for visitors, but Coit Tower has always been less tourist attraction than local landmark beloved by longtime residents.

Note: Parking in the tower lot is very limited, and at peak times the line of cars waiting to park can be long. Muni's #39 bus runs between the base of the tower and Fisherman's Wharf. **Time:** Allow 1 hour minimum. **Hours:** Daily 10-6, Apr.-Oct.; 10-5, rest of year. Closed Jan. 1, Thanksgiving and Christmas. **Cost:** First floor murals free. Guided mural tour of first and second floors $8. Guided mural tour of second floor $5. Elevator to observation level $9; $6 (ages 12-17 and 65+); $2 (ages 5-11). San Francisco residents $6, $4 (ages 12-17 and 65+); $2 (ages 5-11). **Phone:** (415) 249-0995.
Chinatown, 126

Filbert Steps ascend the e. side of Telegraph Hill. The stairs begin at the foot of Filbert Street (at Sansome Street); look for the sign that says "Steps to Coit Tower." They rise in three sections and are wood as far up as Montgomery Street; the higher you climb, the better the views of San Francisco Bay, the Bay Bridge and Alcatraz Island, although the vista is always partially obscured by the luxuriant vegetation filling the backyard gardens of houses perched on either side of the steps. This lush, leafy enclave is a lovely retreat removed from the bustle of the city below.

The steps end at Telegraph Hill Boulevard, the road that encircles the base of Coit Tower. For a different perspective, take the parallel Greenwich Steps back down the hill (a sign in the Coit Tower parking area points the way to the head of the steps). There are more gardens and exotic flowering plants along these steps, and less huffing and puffing is involved. **Hours:** Daily during daylight hours. **Cost:** Free. Chinatown, 126

USS *PAMPANITO,* docked at Pier 45 on The Embarcadero near Taylor St., is a restored World War II submarine that saw action in the Pacific theater. A self-guiding audio tour features the voices of actual crew members telling their stories about life aboard the submarine during the war. Historic artifacts can be seen throughout the boat.

Note: The tours require climbing stairs and stooping through low bulkheads. **Hours:** Opens daily at 9. Closing times vary; phone to confirm. **Cost:** Guided tour $20; $12 (ages 62+ and students with ID); $10 (ages 6-12); $9 (active military with ID); $45 (family, two adults and two children); free (ages 0-5 and active military in uniform). **Phone:** (415) 775-1943. GT

WOMEN'S BUILDING is at 3543 18th St. (at Lapidge St.). This community center in the Mission District, founded in 1971, is owned and operated by women, provides community social services and programs, and has event space for rent. Its multiethnic and multicultural purpose is embodied by MaestraPeace, the stunning mural that completely covers two of the four-story building's exterior walls. The work of seven female artists, this mural is as educational and inspirational as it is visually striking, embracing the historical contributions of women as well as their healing power and wisdom.

Among the well-known real-life figures depicted are painter Georgia O'Keeffe and Caribbean-American writer and poet Audre Lorde, along with feminine archetypes like East Asian devotional figure Quan Yin. Particularly noteworthy is the way the art is seamlessly integrated with structural elements like windows and doors. You can pick up an informational key inside and also support the building's mission by purchasing a T-shirt or some note cards. **Hours:** Open Mon.-Fri. Hours vary; phone for schedule. **Cost:** Free. **Phone:** (415) 431-1180. 16th Street Mission, 44

YERBA BUENA GARDENS covers 2 blks. between Third and Fourth sts. and Mission and Folsom sts. This is one of downtown San Francisco's loveliest green retreats. The 5-acre Esplanade is graced with a grassy lawn, shade trees and bench-lined walkways landscaped with ornamental plants and flowers, while the Upper Terrace Garden, planted with evergreen shrubs, features a large reflecting pool with a view of lofty office buildings as a backdrop. The setting is perfect for strolling, relaxing or grabbing a bite to eat from one of the adjacent casual eateries (this is a fave spot for office workers to have lunch and enjoy a bit of fresh air).

The design of the Martin Luther King, Jr. Memorial incorporates a 10-foot-high, 50-foot-wide waterfall. It cascades in front of glass panels that are set in granite and inscribed with quotations from King's speeches and poems. Artist Terry Allen's whimsical "Shaking Man" greets passers-by on the Esplanade's terrace level with three sets of hands and feet that give this sculpture a multidimensional appearance.

On select days from May to October, the Yerba Buena Gardens Festival presents free outdoor programs on three different stages. The schedule includes music, theater and dance performances, children's programs and cultural events. **Hours:** Grounds open daily 6 a.m.-10 p.m. **Cost:** Free.

Phone: (415) 820-3550, or (415) 543-1718 for festival events and information. Yerba Buena/Moscone, 124

Yerba Buena Center for the Arts is on Third St. between Mission and Howard sts., adjacent to Yerba Buena Gardens. YBCA, a venue for contemporary visual art, performances and film/video, houses galleries, a screening room, two theaters and a sculpture court. Year-round performances, exhibitions and screenings feature artists from the Bay Area and around the world. Lectures and workshops are offered.

Hours: Galleries open Tues.-Sun. 11-6 (also Thurs. 6-8 p.m.). Closed Jan. 1 and Christmas. **Cost:** Galleries $10; $8 (ages 65+, students with ID, library card holders and teachers); free (ages 0-5, active military with ID and to all first Tues. of the month). **Phone:** (415) 978-2787. Montgomery Street, 41

Sightseeing

Sightseeing tours of San Francisco are available by land, sea and air; if your time is limited, we highly recommend the bus tours that touch upon city highlights.

Boat Tours

If you're not sure what to do to start your day, tours of the harbor operate from Fisherman's Wharf. In addition to 1-hour bay cruises, The Red and White Fleet *(see attraction listing)* also schedules combination boat and bus tours.

If you're interested in seeing what life on Alcatraz Island *(see attraction listing p. 268)* was like, be sure and buy your tickets ahead of time, as the tours frequently sell out. Ferries operated by Alcatraz Cruises depart for "The Rock" from Pier 33 on The Embarcadero. Reservations 2 weeks or more in advance are recommended during the summer months and around holidays; phone (415) 981-7625.

The Angel Island-Tiburon Ferry runs daily. The schedule varies with the season; phone (415) 435-2131 for information. Angel Island State Park *(see attraction listing in Tiburon p. 393, and the Recreation Areas Chart)* offers picnic facilities, beaches and hiking trails. The park includes the Angel Island Immigration Station *(see attraction listing in Tiburon p. 394).*

The Blue and Gold Fleet offers 60-minute bay cruises that depart Pier 39 daily at frequent intervals. The company also offers San Francisco, Muir Woods, Sausalito, Tiburon, Alcatraz and Angel Island tours by boat; phone (415) 705-8200.

Hornblower Cruises and Events, Pier 3 on The Embarcadero, offers daily dinner and lunch cruises and weekend brunch cruises aboard the motor yacht *California Hornblower*. Live music is provided with dinner and brunch, and there are dance floors on two decks. Other cruises are offered. Reservations are required; phone (415) 788-8866.

BLUE & GOLD FLEET departs from Pier 39 on The Embarcadero at Beach St. The fleet's 1-hour Bay Cruise Adventure gives passengers a scenic waterfront view of San Francisco as it sails past Pier 39 and its resident sea lions, under the Golden Gate Bridge, past Sausalito and Angel Island and around Alcatraz. A historical narration, available in nine languages, is provided along the way. Other cruises and ferry services also are offered, as are combination tours.

Time: Allow 1 hour minimum. **Hours:** Bay Cruise Adventure has frequent daily, year-round departures. Schedule varies; phone ahead. **Cost:** Bay Cruise Adventure $31; $25 (ages 12-18 and 65+); $21 (ages 5-11). **Phone:** (415) 773-1188. ⒤ 🐱 Chinatown, 126

RED AND WHITE FLEET departs from Pier 43 1/2 at the foot of Taylor St. at Fisherman's Wharf. The 1-hour Golden Gate Bay Cruise takes passengers sightseeing along the San Francisco waterfront, around Alcatraz and under the Golden Gate Bridge. Headphone narration is offered in 16 languages. Sunset cruises, a 90-minute cruise that takes passengers under the Bay Bridge as well as the Golden Gate Bridge, and combination tours also are available.

Time: Allow 1 hour minimum. **Hours:** Golden Gate Bay Cruise departs 8-12 times daily beginning at 10 a.m. (9:15 in summer). Trips generally depart every 30-45 minutes. Phone ahead to confirm schedule. **Cost:** Golden Gate Bay Cruise $32; $22 (ages 5-17); phone for information about family discounts. **Phone:** (415) 673-2900. ⒤

ROCKETBOAT departs from Pier 39 at Fisherman's Wharf. This high-speed, twisting and turning, 30-minute sightseeing tour offers amazing views of the bay, bridges, the San Francisco skyline and Alcatraz Island. The boat captain provides entertaining narration in between a soundtrack of classic rock tunes. There's also a very good possibility you'll get wet; if you actually *do* want to get splashed, sit toward the back.

Riders should be in good health and free from high blood pressure; heart, back or neck problems; osteoporosis; motion sickness; or other similar conditions. Expectant mothers should not participate. **Note:** RocketBoat is closed and is scheduled to reopen May 2020. **Phone:** (415) 705-8200. Ⓖ⒯ 🐱 Chinatown, 126

Bus and Van Tours

Numerous companies offer limousine tours of San Francisco, the Bay Area and Wine Country. The Blue & Gold Fleet offers motorcoach tours to destinations like the Napa and Sonoma valleys, Monterey, Carmel-by-the-Sea and Yosemite National Park; phone (415) 705-8200. When it comes to things couples to do in San Francisco, a limousine tour couldn't be more romantic.

GREAT PACIFIC TOUR CO. offers pickup service at local hotels. The half-day City Tour gives passengers a comprehensive overview of San Francisco, including Fisherman's Wharf, Nob Hill and the city's famous Victorians. Stops are made at Twin Peaks and at the Marin Headlands across the Golden Gate Bridge (weather and traffic permitting). Tours are conducted in 13-passenger minivans. Other tours are available.

Note: Children 0-4 require a car seat. **Time:** Allow 3 hours, 30 minutes minimum. **Hours:** City Tour departs daily at 9, 11 and 2. **Cost:** City Tour $72; $69 (ages 62+); $59 (ages 0-11). Reservations are required. **Phone:** (415) 626-4499. Ⓖ⒯ 🐱 Van Ness, 60

SAN FRANCISCO COMPREHENSIVE SHUTTLE TOURS depart from the front of the Ferry Building on The Embarcadero (across from the end of Market St.). The 5-hour Premium City Tour visits such landmarks as Chinatown, Lombard Street (both of these stops include a guided walk), the Palace of Fine Arts and the Golden Gate Bridge, plus an hour of shopping in Sausalito. The half-day Muir Woods Tour also schedules stops at the Marin Headlands and Muir Beach Overlook.

The two tours can be combined into one all-day experience. All-day Wine Country tours visit Napa Valley or Sonoma wineries. All itineraries include a ferry cruise across San Francisco Bay. Yosemite and Alcatraz trips also are available; phone for details.

Hours: Premium City Tour departs Mon.-Fri. at 9 and 11:15, Sat.-Sun. at 9 and 11:45. Muir Woods Tour departs daily at 9:30 and 12:45. Muir Woods/City Tour combination departs daily at 9. **Cost:** Premium City Tour $79; $74 (ages 65+); $65 (ages 0-12). Muir Woods Tour $79; $76 (ages 65+); $71 (ages 0-12). Muir Woods/City Tour combination $130; $125 (ages 65+); $107 (ages 0-12). Reservations are required. **Phone:** (415) 513-5400. Ⓖ⒯ 🐱 Embarcadero, 40

SAN FRANCISCO MOVIE TOURS depart from Pier 43 1/2 at Fisherman's Wharf. Three-hour city tours take passengers to San Francisco sites made famous by Hollywood movies, including locations from "Mrs. Doubtfire," "Bullitt," "Dirty Harry" and "The Princess Diaries." Scenes from each movie are shown on a big-screen TV while the van passes by that location.

The guide provides information about San Francisco and movie history and trivia about films, actors and directors. There are also photo and rest stops along the way. A movie-themed walking tour of North Beach and Chinatown, a Golden Gate Bridge tour and a "Dirty Harry"-themed van tour also are offered. **Time:** Allow 3 hours minimum. **Hours:** Van tours depart daily at 10 and 2, July-Aug.; at 10, rest of year. Phone for walking tour information. **Cost:** $49; $44 (ages 65+); $35 (ages 5-17 and students ages 18-22 with ID). Reservations are required. **Phone:** (415) 624-4949. Ⓖ⒯

Driving Tours

Skyline Boulevard (SR 35) follows the peninsula divide south of the city into the Santa Cruz Mountains, offering simultaneous scenic views of the bay and ocean.

Upon presentation of your AAA membership card, AAA Northern California, Nevada & Utah can furnish a map with a suggested tour covering much of San Francisco. The 49-Mile Scenic Drive map also is available from the San Francisco Convention & Visitors Bureau Visitor Information Center on the lower level of Hallidie Plaza at Market and Powell streets (near the cable car turnaround).

Segway Tours

Looking for fun things to do with friends? Zip around on a Segway tour.

Guided Walking Tours

Refer to the Downtown San Francisco map. This self-guiding tour takes about 2 hours, depending on your pace and the number of stops you make along the way. *Those in bold type have separate attraction listings.*

Let's face it—San Francisco is known for its treacherous hills, which can tax even the fittest walkers. This tour, however, takes advantage of flat stretches, although you'll still want to wear a pair of comfortable shoes. If you're unwilling or unable to navigate the steeper sections of certain streets, you can always hop on a Muni bus or cable car.

Union Square is the starting point. The Powell-Hyde cable car stops on the south (Geary Street) side. Garage parking is pricey, but if you must drive the underground Union Square Garage can be accessed from Geary Street (one-way westbound). Rates are cheaper at the Sutter-Stockton garage at 444 Stockton St. (between Sutter and Bush streets).

Note: Ongoing construction of Muni's T Third Line in the vicinity of Geary and Stockton streets creates occasional traffic and pedestrian disruptions; follow marked detours where necessary.

Built in 1850, this paved plaza was named for the demonstrations held in support of Union troops at the start of the Civil War. Standing at the center is the 97-foot-tall Dewey Monument, erected in 1903 to honor Commodore George Dewey's 1898 Manila Bay victory over the Spanish. A Goddess of Victory statue tops this needle-shaped column.

Union Square is the heart of the downtown hangout scene. Sidewalk vendors sell flowers, streetcar bells clang and car horns ceaselessly honk. People relax on benches, nap on grassy areas and fill umbrella-shaded tables at the Emporio Rulli café.

The historic Westin St. Francis (335 Powell St.) not only survived the 1906 earthquake but served breakfast on the morning of the disaster. The hotel's spectacular lobby features an antique grandfather clock and long served as a local meeting place, thereby coining the well-known request "Meet me at the St. Francis" (the catchphrase also appears on the city's cable cars).

A huge Macy's faces Union Square's south side. Saks Fifth Avenue rubs elbows with Tiffany & Co. Neiman Marcus, at Geary and Stockton streets, boasts a six-story rotunda topped with an elaborate stained-glass dome. An arched ceiling features a mural of a sailing ship and crowns The Rotunda, a fancy-schmancy restaurant where the well-heeled convene for afternoon tea.

Apple Union Square, at the corner of Post and Stockton, is up-to-the-minute cool, with giant windows providing a view of the square and all the latest technological gadgetry on display.

From Union Square, walk along Maiden Lane east to Grant Avenue. This short, narrow side street was lined with bordellos during the raucous Barbary Coast era more than 150 years ago. At Grant turn left and head to Post Street. Here die-hard shoppers will want to detour temporarily left and/or right and check out the high-end clothing retailers.

Past Post Street, continue on Grant to the corner of Bush Street and the symbolic entryway into **Chinatown,** a green-tiled gate bedecked with golden dragons. Dedicated in 1970, it was a gift to the city from the Republic of China. The carved stone guard dogs standing guard at each side are supposed to ward off evil.

You'll explore Chinatown later, but for now turn right on Bush, walk two blocks to Montgomery Street and turn left. You've entered the concrete canyons of "Wall Street West," the Financial District. Deals have been made here since the 1850s, when prospectors returned from gold mines flush with treasure that needed to be protected, thereby creating a demand for banks.

San Francisco's skyscrapers are architecturally varied. Lean and seemingly striped, 44 Montgomery (just north of Post) was built to house Wells Fargo's world headquarters. The concrete and steel structure stands 561 feet tall. The Mills Building, 220 Montgomery St. (at Bush), was built in 1892 (the tower was added in 1907). It occupies most of the block; various artworks are on display in the large lobby.

At 435 feet, the 1928 Russ Building (235 Montgomery St., just north of Bush) was the city's tallest until the 1960s, when construction of the Transamerica Pyramid began. Back then it was referred to simply as "the skyscraper." The Gothic design was modeled after the Chicago Tribune tower.

Speaking of "the pyramid," San Francisco's tallest building can be seen looking north. Standing at 600 Montgomery St. where Columbus Avenue meets Washington Street, this 48-story skyscraper has nearly 6,000 windows and is topped by a 212-foot-tall spire.

In its shadow is the Jackson Square Historical District, which dates from the gold rush era. The brick buildings with iron shutters that line Gold and Balance streets contain antique shops and restaurants. Victorian-style lampposts accentuate the old-timey feel.

Continue on Montgomery to California Street and turn left. Carved concrete, marble, brown stone and red brick decorate the facades of banks and office buildings, and extravagant chandeliers hang from lobby ceilings. The 52-story skyscraper at 555 California St., formerly known as the Bank of America Center, has an accordion-like exterior that features carnelian marble.

It's a short but relatively steep two-block climb up California back to Grant Avenue. Old St. Mary's Cathedral stands on the right, sandwiched between sleek high-rises and contrasting Chinese-style architecture. Built in 1854, this Catholic church is believed to be the first cathedral in California. It survived the 1906 earthquake and subsequent fires; following renovation, it was rededicated in 1909. Across the street in St. Mary's Square is a 12-foot-tall metal and granite statue of Dr. Sun Yat-sen, founder of the Republic of China.

Turn right onto Grant Avenue. Originally called Calle de Fundacion, this is Chinatown's main drag. Red and yellow flag pennants flutter above the narrow street, entwined dragons decorate lampposts, and store window and market signs are predominantly in Chinese. Apartment buildings, some with laundry-draped balconies, stand above the shops and businesses.

Numerous restaurants advertise dim sum specials, their employees handing out menus to passers-by. Stores sell fine antiques and jade sculpture. Sidewalk bins are filled with Chinese Barbie dolls, plastic Buddha statues, tea sets, embroidered slippers, postcards, bamboo flutes, three-for-$10 T-shirts, mah-jongg games and cricket toys that produce an ear-splitting shriek.

Do a little browsing. The Canton Bazaar (616 Grant Ave.) is a popular import shop. The Chinatown Kite Shop (717 Grant Ave.) sells fish kites and hand-painted paper kites, while the Wok Shop (718 Grant Ave.) peddles all sorts of housewares. Then check out the dragons adorning the columns and guarding the front doors at the Bank of America branch (at the corner of Grant and Sacramento).

Continue up Grant five blocks to Pacific Avenue, turn left and walk a block to Stockton Street, then turn left again and walk down Stockton. Instead of souvenir shops, Stockton has mostly produce markets, bakeries and delicatessens, the latter often featuring a row of skinned ducks (with the heads still attached) hanging upside down in the window.

Saturday mornings on Stockton explode with activity. Residents pack the sidewalks, grocery shopping and socializing. Elderly women inspect the fresh water chestnuts and giant jackfruit with a keen eye, and street vendors hawk Chinese newspapers.

At Sacramento Street turn right and walk a block to Powell Street. This is the one uphill slog along the route (just keep telling yourself it's good exercise). Once you reach Powell the reward is a vista looking east toward downtown. That's one of the *good* things about San Francisco's hills; they offer elevated vantage points from which to view the cityscape.

Turn left onto Powell. Among the tony hotels you'll pass is the Sir Francis Drake (450 Powell St.). Take a peek inside this historic 1928 hotel; the public spaces have a swanky, old-school grandeur.

If you're feeling hungry, stop at Sears Fine Foods (439 Powell St.), another historic spot that's been in business since 1938. The house specialty is Swedish pancakes—18 of the crepe-like morsels, served with whipped butter and warm maple syrup—and you can order them until 3 p.m.

Continue down Powell to Post Street and you're back at Union Square, where the tour began.

Self-guiding Walking Tours

A classic postcard image—and one making an appearance in many a tourist photo—is the row of Victorians along Steiner Street at Alamo Square. If you stand in the right spot you can capture these elegant facades backed by the downtown skyline. Bordered by Steiner, Scott, Fulton and Hayes streets, the square is actually a grassy hilltop park, and a pleasant spot for an afternoon bench break or an early evening stroll.

San Francisco is filled with awesome street art, which is on particularly vibrant display in the Mission. Artistic expression is represented in almost equal measure by graffiti and murals. Graffiti can be seen practically everywhere there's a surface to scrawl on, while murals adorn walls, churches, the sides of buildings, garage doors and alleyways. You could spend all day hitting Mission streets and checking out the art.

MaestraPeace, the stunning mural that covers two exterior walls of the four-story Women's Building (on 18th Street a block west of Valencia Street), is the work of seven female artists. The sheer vibrancy of the colors is remarkable; these walls practically sing. Note how the fabric patterns, human figures and historical scenes blend right into the building's structural elements.

La Llorona's Sacred Waters, the large wall mural at the corner of 24th and York streets, is the work of California muralist, printmaker, painter, educator and activist Juana Alicia. It's also known as the Blue Mural for obvious reasons; except for a bright red stripe at the roofline and a couple of well-placed red accents this mesmerizing work is executed entirely in shades of blue.

It's along Mission alleys where art and graffiti often mix to striking creative effect. One example: narrow Osage Alley, off 24th Street between Mission and Bartlett streets. The weathered brick walls are covered with a blizzard of graffiti, but look down at the sidewalk and you'll see a row of identical images of singer-songwriter Lou Reed from the cover of Reed's 1972 album "Transformer."

Long-term public art installations are mounted regularly at Pier 14 on The Embarcadero (just south of the Ferry Building). In recent years they've included a giant spider sculpture by Louise Bourgeois; the Raygun Gothic Rocketship, a metallic, 40-foot-tall retro-futuristic artwork; and SOMA, a free-form metal sculpture equipped with LED lights that could be interactively manipulated to produce a range of colors, mimicking neuron patterns in the brain.

For fun places to go, you can't miss out on San Francisco's amazing sights. A sightseeing tour is a cost-effective way to get the most out of your vacation, discover new restaurants and enjoy what makes San Francisco such a compelling destination.

AAA Walking Tours
Union Square/Chinatown

Refer to the Downtown San Francisco map. This self-guiding tour takes about 2 hours, depending on your pace and the number of stops you make along the way. *Those in bold type have separate attraction listings.*

Let's face it—San Francisco is known for its treacherous hills, which can tax even the fittest walkers. This tour, however, takes advantage of flat stretches, although you'll still want to wear a pair of comfortable shoes. If you're unwilling or unable to navigate the steeper sections of certain streets, you can always hop on a Muni bus or cable car.

Union Square is the starting point. The Powell-Hyde cable car stops on the south (Geary Street) side. Garage parking is pricey, but if you must drive the underground Union Square Garage can be accessed from Geary Street (one-way westbound). Rates are cheaper at the Sutter-Stockton garage at 444 Stockton St. (between Sutter and Bush streets).

Note: Ongoing construction of Muni's T Third Line in the vicinity of Geary and Stockton streets creates occasional traffic and pedestrian disruptions; follow marked detours where necessary.

Built in 1850, this paved plaza was named for the demonstrations held in support of Union troops at the start of the Civil War. Standing at the center is the 97-foot-tall Dewey Monument, erected in 1903 to honor Commodore George Dewey's 1898 Manila Bay victory over the Spanish. A Goddess of Victory statue tops this needle-shaped column.

Union Square is the heart of the downtown hangout scene. Sidewalk vendors sell flowers, streetcar bells clang and car horns ceaselessly honk. People relax on benches, nap on grassy areas and fill umbrella-shaded tables at the Emporio Rulli café.

The historic Westin St. Francis (335 Powell St.) not only survived the 1906 earthquake but served breakfast on the morning of the disaster. The hotel's spectacular lobby features an antique grandfather clock and long served as a local meeting place, thereby coining the well-known request "Meet me at the St. Francis" (the catchphrase also appears on the city's cable cars).

A huge Macy's faces Union Square's south side. Saks Fifth Avenue rubs elbows with Tiffany & Co. Neiman Marcus, at Geary and Stockton streets, boasts a six-story rotunda topped with an elaborate stained-glass dome. An arched ceiling features a mural of a sailing ship and crowns The Rotunda, a fancy-schmancy restaurant where the well-heeled convene for afternoon tea.

Apple Union Square, at the corner of Post and Stockton, is up-to-the-minute cool, with giant windows providing a view of the square and all the latest technological gadgetry on display.

From Union Square, walk along Maiden Lane east to Grant Avenue. This short, narrow side street was lined with bordellos during the raucous Barbary Coast era more than 150 years ago. At Grant turn left and head to Post Street. Here die-hard shoppers will want to detour temporarily left and/or right and check out the high-end clothing retailers.

Past Post Street, continue on Grant to the corner of Bush Street and the symbolic entryway into **Chinatown,** a green-tiled gate bedecked with golden dragons. Dedicated in 1970, it was a gift to the city from the Republic of China. The carved stone guard dogs standing guard at each side are supposed to ward off evil.

You'll explore Chinatown later, but for now turn right on Bush, walk two blocks to Montgomery Street and turn left. You've entered the concrete canyons of "Wall Street West," the Financial District. Deals have been made here since the 1850s, when prospectors returned from gold mines flush with treasure that needed to be protected, thereby creating a demand for banks.

San Francisco's skyscrapers are architecturally varied. Lean and seemingly striped, 44 Montgomery

iStockphoto.com_LeoPatrizi

For travel and everyday activities, insight from those you trust can make a good experience great!

AAA inspectors and travel writers spend their days evaluating hotels, sampling menus and exploring new sights so you don't have to. Use their recommended picks and itineraries to find the best places to go, stay, dine and play.

Photo source iStockphoto.com

Get AAA travel information at club offices and on AAA.com for experiences you'll remember for a lifetime.

(just north of Post) was built to house Wells Fargo's world headquarters. The concrete and steel structure stands 561 feet tall. The Mills Building, 220 Montgomery St. (at Bush), was built in 1892 (the tower was added in 1907). It occupies most of the block; various artworks are on display in the large lobby.

At 435 feet, the 1928 Russ Building (235 Montgomery St., just north of Bush) was the city's tallest until the 1960s, when construction of the Transamerica Pyramid began. Back then it was referred to simply as "the skyscraper." The Gothic design was modeled after the Chicago Tribune tower.

Speaking of "the pyramid," San Francisco's tallest building can be seen looking north. Standing at 600 Montgomery St. where Columbus Avenue meets Washington Street, this 48-story skyscraper has nearly 6,000 windows and is topped by a 212-foot-tall spire.

In its shadow is the Jackson Square Historical District, which dates from the gold rush era. The brick buildings with iron shutters that line Gold and Balance streets contain antique shops and restaurants. Victorian-style lampposts accentuate the old-timey feel.

Continue on Montgomery to California Street and turn left. Carved concrete, marble, brown stone and red brick decorate the facades of banks and office buildings, and extravagant chandeliers hang from lobby ceilings. The 52-story skyscraper at 555 California St., formerly known as the Bank of America Center, has an accordion-like exterior that features carnelian marble.

It's a short but relatively steep two-block climb up California back to Grant Avenue. Old St. Mary's Cathedral stands on the right, sandwiched between sleek high-rises and contrasting Chinese-style architecture. Built in 1854, this Catholic church is believed to be the first cathedral in California. It survived the 1906 earthquake and subsequent fires; following renovation, it was rededicated in 1909. Across the street in St. Mary's Square is a 12-foot-tall metal and granite statue of Dr. Sun Yat-sen, founder of the Republic of China.

Turn right onto Grant Avenue. Originally called Calle de Fundacion, this is Chinatown's main drag. Red and yellow flag pennants flutter above the narrow street, entwined dragons decorate lampposts, and store window and market signs are predominantly in Chinese. Apartment buildings, some with laundry-draped balconies, stand above the shops and businesses.

Numerous restaurants advertise dim sum specials, their employees handing out menus to passers-by. Stores sell fine antiques and jade sculpture. Sidewalk bins are filled with Chinese Barbie dolls, plastic Buddha statues, tea sets, embroidered slippers, postcards, bamboo flutes, three-for-$10 T-shirts, mah-jongg games and cricket toys that produce an ear-splitting shriek.

Do a little browsing. The Canton Bazaar (616 Grant Ave.) is a popular import shop. The Chinatown Kite Shop (717 Grant Ave.) sells fish kites and hand-painted paper kites, while the Wok Shop (718 Grant Ave.) peddles all sorts of housewares. Then check out the dragons adorning the columns and guarding the front doors at the Bank of America branch (at the corner of Grant and Sacramento).

Continue up Grant five blocks to Pacific Avenue, turn left and walk a block to Stockton Street, then turn left again and walk down Stockton. Instead of souvenir shops, Stockton has mostly produce markets, bakeries and delicatessens, the latter often featuring a row of skinned ducks (with the heads still attached) hanging upside down in the window.

Saturday mornings on Stockton explode with activity. Residents pack the sidewalks, grocery shopping and socializing. Elderly women inspect the fresh water chestnuts and giant jackfruit with a keen eye, and street vendors hawk Chinese newspapers.

At Sacramento Street turn right and walk a block to Powell Street. This is the one uphill slog along the route (just keep telling yourself it's good exercise). Once you reach Powell the reward was a vista looking east toward downtown. That's one of the *good* things about San Francisco's hills; they offer elevated vantage points from which to view the cityscape.

Turn left onto Powell. Among the tony hotels you'll pass is the Sir Francis Drake (450 Powell St.). Take a peek inside this historic 1928 hotel; the public spaces have a swanky, old-school grandeur.

If you're feeling hungry, stop at Sears Fine Foods (439 Powell St.), another historic spot that's been in business since 1938. The house specialty is Swedish pancakes—18 of the crepe-like morsels, served with whipped butter and warm maple syrup—and you can order them until 3 p.m.

Continue down Powell to Post Street and you're back at Union Square, where the tour began.

Fisherman's Wharf

Refer to the Downtown San Francisco map. This self-guiding tour takes about 3 hours, depending on your pace and the number of stops you make along the way. *Those in bold type have separate attraction listings.*

When it comes to **Fisherman's Wharf,** you're likely to hear many San Franciscans sniff, "You won't catch me there—that's for tourists." And it's true—the stretch of San Francisco Bay waterfront from Pier 39 west to Fort Mason is the city's most unabashedly touristy area. Although the souvenir-heavy atmosphere may not be to everyone's taste, most visitors do make the pilgrimage, and it's an obvious destination if you've got kids in tow.

The seafaring character that gave this area its name is still evident in the docked boats and squawking seagulls swooping over the water. If you threw on a sweatshirt and headed to the piers at the crack of dawn, you might spot fishermen preparing to head out for the day's catch. While the local fishing industry is a shadow of its former importance, boats still range as far north as Bodega and as far south as Monterey bays in search of sole, flounder, cod and king salmon. Most visitors, however, are content to sleep in a bit later and hit Fisherman's Wharf when the attractions and restaurants start opening.

This tour begins at Hyde and Jefferson streets. First take a stroll along the Hyde Street Pier, part of **San Francisco Maritime National Historical Park,** and snap some photos. Four berthed vessels dating from the late 19th century comprise the **Hyde Street Pier Historic Ships.** You can board each one and learn about what sailors of yore did and how they lived (the crewmen's quarters, for one thing, were really tiny). National Park Service rangers also conduct regularly scheduled free programs and tours.

Walk east on Jefferson Street toward The Embarcadero. Every couple of doorways is a souvenir emporium, all of them featuring the same mishmash of T-shirts, San Francisco Giants pennants and postcard stands.

A bit farther along you'll find a trio of tourist attractions: **Madame Tussauds San Francisco,** The San Francisco Dungeon and **Ripley's Believe it or Not! Odditorium.** If you're interested in seeing any or all of them you might want to budget time for a visit later, although it won't take long to duck into Madame Tussauds for obligatory photo ops with the likes of Abraham Lincoln, Al Capone, Jerry Garcia, Lady Gaga and other notables both famous and infamous.

At Jefferson and Al Scoma Way there's a gaggle of seafood restaurants, including well-known favorites like Scoma's Restaurant and Alioto's. The famous Fisherman's Wharf sign at the intersection turns up in many a vacation photo. Along "Fish Alley" are several stands where you can purchase lobster rolls or a seafood cocktail to go, assembled on the spot by vendors who constantly call out to passers-by.

At Jefferson and Taylor streets take a short detour on Pier 45 to the **Musée Mécanique.** This large, warehouse-like building contains a bunch of vintage arcade games as well as Laffing Sal, a red-haired figure with a creepy laugh who gave nightmares to impressionable young kids coming face to face with her in carnival fun houses during the 1930s and '40s. Also docked at Pier 45 are two more historic ships, the **USS Pampanito** and **The Jeremiah O'Brien.**

At **Boudin at the Wharf: Museum and Bakery Tour** you can see how one of San Francisco's signature culinary specialties is created. And if you want to get an early start on a day of culinary indulgence, check out the various products for sale at the Boudin store or have some clam chowder served in an edible vessel: a sourdough bread bowl.

Jefferson ends at The Embarcadero. After passing the **Blue & Gold Fleet** docks at Pier 41 you'll come to one of the most popular destinations at Fisherman's Wharf, **Pier 39.** You can't miss the flags fluttering in the breeze atop tall poles. For an elevated perspective, take the stairway up to the pedestrian bridge that arches over The Embarcadero.

Pier 39 is mostly about shopping, shopping and more shopping. You can also feast on funnel cakes, mini doughnuts, hot pretzels and other carb-loaded goodies. Kids will love the old-fashioned carousel, and of course there are souvenirs galore, from fog in a can to the ubiquitous "I Escaped From Alcatraz" T-shirts. The upper level offers better opportunities for photos of the surrounding waterfront and Alcatraz and Angel islands.

Ever since they began hanging out on the floating docks (built especially for them) at the end of the 1980s, sea lions have been one of Pier 39's biggest draws. Loud, gregarious and playful, their antics were guaranteed to draw a crowd. They almost totally disappeared in 2009, an event thought to be related to a shifting supply of food fish. Summer months, when females travel south to breed at offshore island rookeries, see the fewest sea lions; their presence at the pier begins to increase in the fall once breeding season is over.

From Pier 39, continue on The Embarcadero past Pier 33, embarkation point for ferries to **Alcatraz Island.** Cross The Embarcadero at Pier 29 (the foot of Chestnut Street), then cross Chestnut to Sansome Street. Walk three blocks on Sansome to Filbert Street; the **Filbert Steps** are to your right (look for the sign that says "Steps to Coit Tower").

Climbing the east side of Telegraph Hill, the stairway rises in three sections to Telegraph Hill Boulevard, encircling the base of Coit Tower. Pause along the way both to catch your breath and to admire the views of San Francisco Bay and the San Francisco-Oakland Bay Bridge. The flowering plants and backyard gardens of the houses perched on either side of the steps are at their most luxuriant in the winter and early spring, the rainy season.

When you reach the top of the steps, take another breather before following Telegraph Hill Boulevard to the Coit Tower parking area, where there are great views of the bay, Alcatraz Island and, in the distance, the Golden Gate Bridge. **Coit Tower,** 210 feet tall, was built in 1933 with help from a financial donation by wealthy San Franciscan Lillie Hitchcock Coit. Take the elevator to the top of the tower for a more spectacular view.

Backtrack to Filbert Street and continue five blocks to Columbus Avenue. Fortunately you'll be walking downhill, not uphill, and the street is so steep steps are built into the sidewalk at certain points.

At the intersection of Filbert and Columbus Avenue is Washington Square, the focal point of **North Beach,** San Francisco's "Little Italy." Just as North Beach isn't a beach, Washington Square is not a true square but a pentagon. On sunny days kids play, people catch rays on park benches or feed the pigeons, and devotees of tai chi do their thing on the lawn.

The twin white towers of the Romanesque-style Church of Saints Peter and Paul overlook the square's north side. Known as the "fisherman's church," it offers mass in English, Italian and Cantonese. The annual Blessing of the Fleet celebration, an old Sicilian tradition held in early October, begins at the church and proceeds to Fisherman's Wharf for a fishing boat parade and memorial ceremony at sea.

The restaurants and cafés lining Columbus Avenue are very popular for alfresco noshing, especially on sunny days. For some of the best coffee in North Beach—and that's saying something in a city where excellent coffee is basically taken for granted—stop by Caffe Trieste (just east of Columbus at 601 Vallejo St., two blocks south of Washington Square). You can grab a sandwich there, too.

From Washington Square, walk up Columbus Avenue seven blocks to Beach Street, turn left and walk a block to Hyde Street. At the corner of Beach and Hyde is the Buena Vista Cafe, a San Francisco institution where you can fortify yourself with more caffeine—in this case, an Irish coffee.

A block west of Hyde along Beach Street (between Polk and Larkin streets) is **Ghirardelli Square.** When Italian-born candy maker Domingo Ghirardelli purchased a city block back in the 19th century to build a factory to produce his product, he probably had no idea it would become the historical landmark it is today. In addition to the namesake ice cream and chocolate shop, this complex of brick buildings houses specialty stores and restaurants. If you don't mind braving the crowds, get your high-quality chocolate fix here.

The corner of Beach and Hyde marks the end of this walking tour and is also the northern end of the Powell & Hyde cable car line. Hop on the cable car (fare $7) and hold on tight as the car is pulled up very steep Russian Hill to Lombard Street. If you disembark to take photos of the famous block known as "the crookedest street in the world," remember that you'll have to pay again to board another car, unless you have a passport offering unlimited usage of Muni transportation for the duration of its validity period.

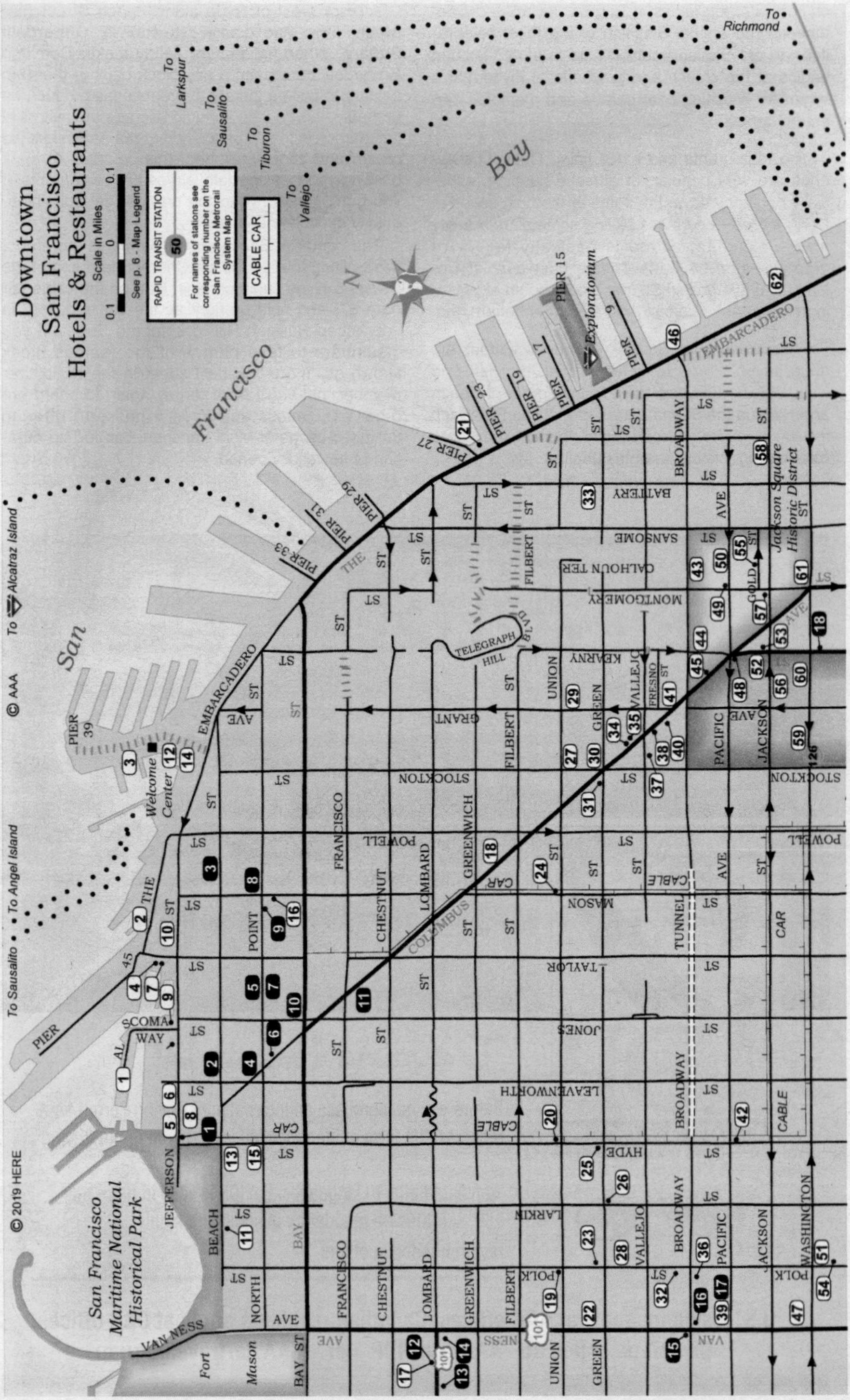

Downtown San Francisco Hotels & Restaurants

Scale in Miles

See p. 6 - Map Legend

50 RAPID TRANSIT STATION

For names of stations see corresponding number on the San Francisco Metrorail System Map

CABLE CAR

© 2019 HERE

© AAA

San Francisco Bay

To Richmond
To Larkspur
To Sausalito
To Tiburon
To Vallejo
To Alcatraz Island
To Sausalito • To Angel Island

San Francisco Maritime National Historical Park

Fort Mason

Exploratorium

Telegraph Hill

Jackson Square Historic District

Welcome Center

PIER 39

PIER 45
PIER 41
PIER 35
PIER 33
PIER 31
PIER 29
PIER 27
PIER 23
PIER 19
PIER 17
PIER 15
PIER 9

THE EMBARCADERO

Street names:
JEFFERSON ST, BEACH ST, NORTH POINT ST, BAY ST, FRANCISCO ST, CHESTNUT ST, LOMBARD ST, GREENWICH ST, FILBERT ST, UNION ST, GREEN ST, VALLEJO ST, BROADWAY, PACIFIC AVE, JACKSON ST, WASHINGTON ST

VAN NESS AVE, POLK ST, LARKIN ST, HYDE ST, LEAVENWORTH ST, JONES ST, TAYLOR ST, MASON ST, POWELL ST, STOCKTON ST, GRANT AVE, COLUMBUS AVE, KEARNY ST, MONTGOMERY ST, SANSOME ST, BATTERY ST, FRONT ST, DAVIS ST, CALHOUN TER, FRESNO ST

CABLE CAR, TUNNEL

US 101

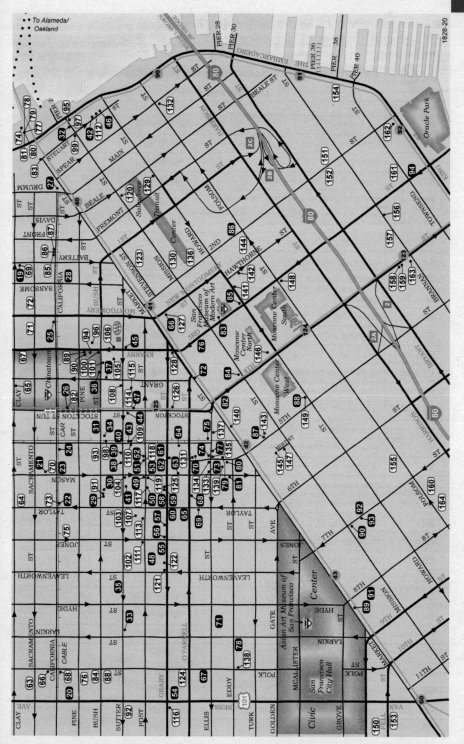

Downtown San Francisco

This index helps you "spot" where approved hotels and restaurants are located on the corresponding detailed maps. Restaurant price range is a combination of lunch and/or dinner. Turn to the listing page for more information and consult display ads for special promotions.

 For more details, rates and reservations: AAA.com/travelguides/hotels

SAN FRANCISCO

Map Page	Hotels	Diamond Rated	Member Savings	Page
1 p. 298	**The Argonaut**	◆◆◆◆	✔	324
2 p. 298	Courtyard by Marriott at Fisherman's Wharf	◆◆◆	✔	324
3 p. 298	Hotel Zephyr	◆◆◆		328
4 p. 298	**Holiday Inn at Fisherman's Wharf**	◆◆◆	✔	326
5 p. 298	**Holiday Inn Express & Suites at Fisherman's Wharf**	◆◆◆	✔	327
6 p. 298	San Francisco Marriott Fisherman's Wharf	◆◆◆	✔	331
7 p. 298	**Hyatt Centric Fisherman's Wharf**	◆◆◆	✔	328
8 p. 298	**Sheraton Fisherman's Wharf**	◆◆◆	✔	332
9 p. 298	**Hotel Zoe Fisherman's Wharf**	◆◆◆	✔	328
10 p. 298	Marriott Vacation Club Pulse, San Francisco	◆◆◆	✔	330
11 p. 298	Columbus Inn	◆◆		324
12 p. 298	**Travelodge By The Bay**	◆◆	✔	332
13 p. 298	Lombard Inn	◆◆		330
14 p. 298	**Comfort Inn by the Bay** *(See ad p. 325.)*	◆◆	✔	324
15 p. 298	Inn on Broadway	◆◆		329
16 p. 298	Castle Inn	◆◆		324
17 p. 298	Nob Hill Motor Inn	◆◆		330
18 p. 298	**Hilton San Francisco Financial District**	◆◆◆	✔	326
19 p. 298	Le Meridien San Francisco	◆◆◆	✔	330
20 p. 298	Holiday Inn Golden Gateway	◆◆◆		327
21 p. 298	**The Fairmont San Francisco**	◆◆◆◆	✔	325
22 p. 298	**Huntington Hotel**	◆◆◆◆	✔	328
23 p. 298	**InterContinental Mark Hopkins San Francisco**	◆◆◆	✔	329
24 p. 298	**Stanford Court Hotel**	◆◆◆	✔	332
25 p. 298	**Omni San Francisco Hotel**	◆◆◆◆	✔	331
26 p. 298	The Ritz-Carlton, San Francisco	◆◆◆◆◆	✔	331
27 p. 298	**Hyatt Regency San Francisco**	◆◆◆	✔	329
28 p. 298	**Loews Regency San Francisco**	◆◆◆◆	✔	330
29 p. 298	Petite Auberge	◆◆		331
30 p. 298	White Swan Inn	◆◆◆		332
31 p. 298	Executive Hotel Vintage Court	◆◆◆		325
32 p. 298	**Hotel Vitale, a Joie de Vivre hotel**	◆◆◆◆	✔	328
33 p. 298	**Hotel Carlton, a Joie de Vivre hotel**	◆◆◆	✔	327

SAN FRANCISCO (cont'd)

Map Page	Hotels (cont'd)	Diamond Rated	Member Savings	Page
34 p. 298	The Orchard Hotel	◆◆◆		331
35 p. 298	Hotel Vertigo	◆◆◆		328
36 p. 298	**The Orchard Garden Hotel**	◆◆◆	✔	331
37 p. 298	**Hotel Triton**	◆◆◆	✔	328
38 p. 298	Hotel Rex, a Joie de Vivre hotel	[fyi]		328
39 p. 298	**The Cartwright Hotel-Union Square, BW Premier Collection**	◆◆◆	✔	324
40 p. 298	**San Francisco Marriott Union Square**	◆◆◆	✔	331
41 p. 298	**Beresford Hotel**	◆◆	✔	324
42 p. 298	**Hotel Griffon**	◆◆◆	✔	327
43 p. 298	**Kimpton Sir Francis Drake Hotel**	◆◆◆	✔	330
44 p. 298	**Grand Hyatt San Francisco**	◆◆◆◆	✔	326
45 p. 298	**Galleria Park Hotel, a Joie de Vivre hotel**	◆◆◆	✔	326
46 p. 298	**Harbor Court Hotel**	◆◆◆	✔	326
47 p. 298	**Taj Campton Place**	◆◆◆◆	✔	332
48 p. 298	Courtyard by Marriott San Francisco Union Square	◆◆◆	✔	325
49 p. 298	**JW Marriott San Francisco**	◆◆◆◆	✔	329
50 p. 298	Hotel Zeppelin San Francisco	◆◆◆		328
51 p. 298	**Kensington Park Hotel**	◆◆◆	✔	329
52 p. 298	**The Inn At Union Square**	◆◆◆	✔	329
53 p. 298	**The Donatello**	◆◆◆	✔	325
54 p. 298	Courtyard by Marriott San Francisco Downtown/ Van Ness Ave	◆◆◆	✔	325
55 p. 298	**Adante Hotel**	◆◆	✔	324
56 p. 298	Staypineapple, An Elegant Hotel, Union Square, San Francisco	◆◆◆		332
57 p. 298	**Hotel Adagio, Autograph Collection**	◆◆◆	✔	327
58 p. 298	**Warwick San Francisco Hotel**	◆◆◆	✔	332
59 p. 298	**Hotel Diva**	◆◆◆	✔	327
60 p. 298	The Marker San Francisco	◆◆◆		330
61 p. 298	**The Westin St. Francis San Francisco on Union Square**	◆◆◆◆	✔	332
62 p. 298	**The Handlery Union Square Hotel**	◆◆◆	✔	326
63 p. 298	**King George Hotel**	◆◆	✔	330
64 p. 298	**Villa Florence**	◆◆◆	✔	332
65 p. 298	Hotel Spero	◆◆◆		328
66 p. 298	Palace Hotel, A Luxury Collection	◆◆◆◆	✔	331
67 p. 298	Alexis Park-San Francisco	◆◆		324
68 p. 298	**Hilton San Francisco Union Square**	◆◆◆	✔	326
69 p. 298	**Tilden Hotel**	◆◆	✔	332

SAN FRANCISCO (cont'd)

Map Page	Hotels (cont'd)	Diamond Rated	Member Savings	Page
70 p. 298	Holiday Inn Express San Francisco-Union Square	♦♦♦		327
71 p. 298	Cova Hotel	♦♦		325
72 p. 298	**Four Seasons Hotel San Francisco**	♦♦♦♦	✔	325
73 p. 298	**Hotel Nikko San Francisco**	♦♦♦♦	✔	327
74 p. 298	**Hotel Fusion**	♦♦♦	✔	327
75 p. 298	**Hotel Union Square**	♦♦	✔	328
76 p. 298	**Park Central Hotel San Francisco**	♦♦♦	✔	331
77 p. 298	Hotel Abri	♦♦♦		327
78 p. 298	Phoenix Hotel	♦♦		331
79 p. 298	**Axiom Hotel**	♦♦♦	✔	324
80 p. 298	**Parc 55 - a Hilton Hotel**	♦♦♦	✔	331
81 p. 298	Hotel Bijou	♦♦		327
82 p. 298	**HOTEL ZELOS**	♦♦♦	✔	328
83 p. 298	**The St. Regis San Francisco**	♦♦♦♦	✔	331
84 p. 298	**Marriott Marquis San Francisco**	♦♦♦	✔	330
85 p. 298	**W San Francisco**	♦♦♦	✔	333
86 p. 298	Courtyard by Marriott San Francisco Downtown	♦♦♦	✔	324
87 p. 298	Hotel Zetta	♦♦♦		328
88 p. 298	**InterContinental San Francisco**	♦♦♦♦	✔	329
89 p. 298	**Hotel Whitcomb San Francisco**	♦♦	✔	328
90 p. 298	Good Hotel	♦♦		326
91 p. 298	**BEI San Francisco**	[fyi]	✔	324
92 p. 298	**Americania Hotel**	♦♦♦	✔	324
93 p. 298	Carriage Inn	♦♦♦		324
94 p. 298	**Hyatt Place**	♦♦♦	✔	329

Map Page	Restaurants	Diamond Rated	Cuisine	Price Range	Page
1 p. 298	**Scoma's Restaurant**	♦♦	Seafood	$10-$61	340
2 p. 298	Franciscan Crab Restaurant	♦♦	Seafood	$10-$55	335
3 p. 298	Pier Market Seafood Restaurant	♦♦	Seafood	$12-$41	339
4 p. 298	Alioto's	♦♦♦	Seafood	$15-$63	333
5 p. 298	Capurro's Restaurant & Bar	♦♦	Italian	$13-$35	334
6 p. 298	Cioppino's on the Wharf	♦♦	Italian Seafood	$14-$40	335
7 p. 298	**Nick's Lighthouse**	♦♦	Seafood	$10-$50	338
8 p. 298	Blue Mermaid Chowder House & Bar	♦♦♦	Seafood	$14-$29	334
9 p. 298	**Castagnola's**	♦♦	Italian Seafood	$12-$40	334
10 p. 298	Bistro Boudin At The Wharf	♦♦	Seafood	$15-$59	334

Map Page	Restaurants (cont'd)	Diamond Rated	Cuisine	Price Range	Page
⑪ p. 298	McCormick & Kuleto's Seafood Restaurant	♦♦♦	Seafood	$13-$63	337
⑫ p. 298	Fog Harbor Fish House	♦♦	Seafood	$14-$49	335
⑬ p. 298	The Buena Vista Cafe	♦♦	American	$13-$24	334
⑭ p. 298	Crab House at Pier 39	♦♦	Seafood	$16-$70	335
⑮ p. 298	**Gary Danko**	♦♦♦♦♦	Continental	$98-$139	336
⑯ p. 298	Cafe Pescatore	♦♦	Italian	$13-$34	334
⑰ p. 298	Boboquivaris	♦♦♦	Steak Seafood	$23-$70	334
⑱ p. 298	The Italian Homemade Company	♦	Italian	$11-$16	336
⑲ p. 298	Leopold's	♦♦	German	$20-$27	337
⑳ p. 298	Zarzuela	♦♦	Spanish Small Plates	$7-$24	341
㉑ p. 298	Pier 23 Cafe	♦♦	American	$15-$28	339
㉒ p. 298	The Helmand Palace	♦♦	Afghan	$7-$23	336
㉓ p. 298	La Folie	♦♦♦♦	French	$100-$150	337
㉔ p. 298	Trattoria Contadina	♦♦♦	Italian	$11-$39	340
㉕ p. 298	Frascati	♦♦♦	Continental	$26-$38	336
㉖ p. 298	Amarena	♦♦	Italian	$12-$33	333
㉗ p. 298	Tony's Pizza Napoletana	♦♦	Pizza	$11-$41	340
㉘ p. 298	Gioia Pizzeria	♦	Italian Pizza	$10-$23	336
㉙ p. 298	Cafe Jacqueline	♦♦♦	French	$33-$60	334
㉚ p. 298	**North Beach Restaurant**	♦♦♦	Italian	$20-$42	338
㉛ p. 298	Chief Sullivan's	♦♦	Irish	$10-$19	334
㉜ p. 298	Street Restaurant	♦♦	Northern California	$13-$25	340
㉝ p. 298	Piperade	♦♦♦	French	$16-$32	339
㉞ p. 298	Calzone's	♦♦	Italian	$14-$40	334
㉟ p. 298	Original U.S. Restaurant	♦♦	Italian	$15-$32	338
㊱ p. 298	Lord Stanley	♦♦♦♦	California	$24-$97	337
㊲ p. 298	Capo's Chicago Pizza & Fine Italian Dinners	♦♦	Italian Pizza	$12-$38	334
㊳ p. 298	Ristorante Mona Lisa	♦♦	Italian	$12-$41	339
㊴ p. 298	Harris'	♦♦♦	Steak	$32-$58	336
㊵ p. 298	The Stinking Rose	♦♦	Italian	$17-$60	340
㊶ p. 298	The House	♦♦♦	Asian	$12-$32	336
㊷ p. 298	Seven Hills	♦♦♦	Italian	$16-$35	340
㊸ p. 298	Coi	♦♦♦♦	California	$250	335
㊹ p. 298	Tommaso's Restaurant	♦♦	Italian	$15-$30	340
㊺ p. 298	Tosca Cafe	♦♦♦	Italian	$18-$48	340
㊻ p. 298	The Waterfront Restaurant	♦♦♦	California Seafood	$22-$95	341

Map Page	Restaurants (cont'd)	Diamond Rated	Cuisine	Price Range	Page
47 p. 298	House of Prime Rib	♦♦♦	American	$42-$65	336
48 p. 298	Comstock Saloon	♦♦	American	$13-$26	335
49 p. 298	Cotogna	♦♦♦	Italian	$14-$30	335
50 p. 298	Quince	♦♦♦♦	New American	$165-$220	339
51 p. 298	1760	♦♦♦	California Small Plates	$10-$42	333
52 p. 298	House of Nanking	♦♦	Chinese	$7-$15	336
53 p. 298	Cafe Zoetrope	♦♦	Southern Italian	$12-$27	334
54 p. 298	Thai Spice	♦♦	Thai	$8-$16	340
55 p. 298	Bix	♦♦♦	Continental	$14-$40	334
56 p. 298	Great Eastern Restaurant	♦♦	Chinese Dim Sum	$10-$48	336
57 p. 298	Roka Akor	♦♦♦	Japanese	$22-$48	339
58 p. 298	Kokkari Estiatorio	♦♦♦	Greek	$14-$45	337
59 p. 298	Lucky Creation Vegetarian Restaurant	♦♦	Chinese Vegetarian	$7-$21	337
60 p. 298	Penang Garden Restaurant	♦♦	Thai	$8-$27	339
61 p. 298	Kusakabe	♦♦♦♦	Sushi	$98-$165	337
62 p. 298	La Mar Cebicheria Peruana	♦♦♦	Peruvian	$15-$34	337
63 p. 298	Acquerello	♦♦♦♦	Italian	$95-$225	333
64 p. 298	Nob Hill Cafe	♦♦	Italian	$11-$21	338
65 p. 298	New Chef Hung's Restaurant	♦♦	Chinese	$7-$22	338
66 p. 298	Swan Oyster Depot	♦♦	Seafood	$12-$45	340
67 p. 298	R & G Lounge	♦♦	Chinese	$14-$65	339
68 p. 298	Crustacean Restaurant	♦♦	Asian	$15-$39	335
69 p. 298	Park Grill	♦♦♦	California	$15-$29	339
70 p. 298	The Laurel Court Restaurant & Bar	♦♦♦	California	$16-$48	337
71 p. 298	Palio D'Asti	♦♦♦	Italian	$12-$30	338
72 p. 298	Wayfare Tavern	♦♦♦	American	$19-$39	341
73 p. 298	Big 4 Restaurant	♦♦♦♦	California	$29-$46	334
74 p. 298	Mijita Cocina Mexicana	♦	Mexican	$4-$10	337
75 p. 298	Osso Steakhouse	♦♦♦	American Steak	$15-$130	338
76 p. 298	Grubstake	♦♦	American	$10-$20	336
77 p. 298	Boulettes Larder	♦♦	California	$10-$26	334
78 p. 298	Hog Island Oyster Co.	♦♦	Seafood	$13-$23	336
79 p. 298	DELICA rf-1	♦	Japanese	$13-$16	335
80 p. 298	The Slanted Door	♦♦♦	Vietnamese	$12-$48	340
81 p. 298	Gott's Roadside	♦	American	$10-$17	336
82 p. 298	Parallel 37	♦♦♦♦	New American	$24-$135	338
83 p. 298	One Market Restaurant	♦♦♦	American	$16-$36	338

Map Page	Restaurants (cont'd)	Diamond Rated	Cuisine	Price Range	Page
84 p. 298	Aicha Moroccan Cuisine	◈◈◈	Moroccan	$10-$17	333
85 p. 298	Michael Mina	◈◈◈◈	New American	$22-$170	337
86 p. 298	Tadich Grill	◈◈◈	Seafood	$15-$50	340
87 p. 298	Perbacco Ristorante + Bar	◈◈◈	Italian	$18-$32	339
88 p. 298	Modern Thai	◈◈	Thai	$7-$17	338
89 p. 298	Ramen Underground	◈◈	Japanese Noodles	$10-$12	339
90 p. 298	Onigilly	◈	Japanese	$3-$12	338
91 p. 298	Del Popolo	◈◈	Pizza	$12-$19	335
92 p. 298	Alborz	◈◈	Middle Eastern	$7-$25	333
93 p. 298	Sons & Daughters	◈◈◈◈	New American	$175	340
94 p. 298	Sababa Hot Pita Bar	◈	Middle Eastern	$10-$12	339
95 p. 298	Boulevard	◈◈◈◈	American	$17-$52	334
96 p. 298	Cafe Tiramisu	◈◈◈	Italian	$18-$42	334
97 p. 298	Americano Restaurant & Bar	◈◈◈	Northern Italian	$9-$30	333
98 p. 298	Roxanne Cafe	◈◈	Italian	$10-$21	339
99 p. 298	Rosa Mexicano	◈◈	Mexican	$15-$28	339
100 p. 298	Muracci's Japanese Curry & Grill	◈	Japanese	$8-$13	338
101 p. 298	Akiko's Restaurant	◈◈◈	Japanese Sushi	$10-$40	333
102 p. 298	Liholiho Yacht Club	◈◈◈	New Hawaiian	$16-$67	337
103 p. 298	Sanraku Restaurant	◈◈	Japanese	$11-$48	339
104 p. 298	Cesario's Fine Food	◈◈	Northern Italian	$11-$25	334
105 p. 298	Cafe Claude	◈◈◈	French	$12-$29	334
106 p. 298	Sushirrito	◈	Japanese Sushi	$9-$13	340
107 p. 298	Le Colonial	◈◈◈	Vietnamese	$22-$37	337
108 p. 298	E & O Asian Kitchen	◈◈◈	Asian	$13-$28	335
109 p. 298	Scala's Bistro	◈◈◈	Italian	$13-$60	340
110 p. 298	Sears Fine Foods	◈◈	American	$12-$31	340
111 p. 298	Borobudur Restaurant	◈◈	Indonesian	$7-$32	334
112 p. 298	Ozumo	◈◈◈	Japanese	$12-$100	338
113 p. 298	Fino Bar & Ristorante	◈◈◈	Italian	$17-$34	335
114 p. 298	**Campton Place Restaurant**	◈◈◈◈	California Fusion	$39-$155	334
115 p. 298	hops & hominy	◈◈	Southern	$14-$38	336
116 p. 298	Tommy's Joynt	◈	American	$9-$13	340
117 p. 298	Rambler	◈◈	American	$16-$36	339
118 p. 298	Farallon	◈◈◈	Seafood	$12-$49	335
119 p. 298	Zingari Ristorante	◈◈◈	Italian	$15-$38	341
120 p. 298	RN74	◈◈◈	New French	$17-$39	339

Map Page	Restaurants (cont'd)	Diamond Rated	Cuisine	Price Range	Page
121 p. 298	Osha Thai Noodle Cafe	◆◆	Thai	$12-$20	338
122 p. 298	Mensho Tokyo	◆◆	Japanese Noodles	$9-$18	337
123 p. 298	Yank Sing	◆◆	Chinese Dim Sum	$12-$25	341
124 p. 298	Ike's Place	◆	Sandwiches	$12-$52	336
125 p. 298	colibri Mexican-Bistro	◆◆	Mexican	$13-$26	335
126 p. 298	Neiman Marcus-The Rotunda Restaurant	◆◆◆	California	$9-$38	338
127 p. 298	The Garden Court	◆◆◆	American	$25-$35	336
128 p. 298	Hakkasan San Francisco	◆◆◆	Cantonese	$17-$88	336
129 p. 298	Town Hall	◆◆◆	Southern American	$14-$24	340
130 p. 298	Roy's	◆◆◆	Pacific Rim Fusion	$18-$60	339
131 p. 298	Johnny Foley's	◆◆	Irish	$12-$30	336
132 p. 298	Prospect	◆◆◆	California	$14-$47	339
133 p. 298	Anzu Restaurant	◆◆◆	Pacific Rim	$15-$41	333
134 p. 298	New Delhi	◆◆	Indian	$13-$27	338
135 p. 298	Puccini & Pinetti	◆◆	Italian	$11-$28	339
136 p. 298	Lao Table	◆◆◆	Thai	$10-$20	337
137 p. 298	**John's Grill**	◆◆	American	$11-$40	336
138 p. 298	Brenda's French Soul Food	◆◆	Creole	$10-$17	334
139 p. 298	Kin Khao Thai Eatery	◆◆◆	Thai	$14-$50	337
140 p. 298	M.Y. China	◆◆◆	Chinese	$10-$45	338
141 p. 298	Thirsty Bear Brewing Co.	◆◆	Spanish Small Plates	$10-$32	340
142 p. 298	Benu	◆◆◆◆◆	New American	$310	333
143 p. 298	The Cavalier	◆◆◆	British	$15-$38	334
144 p. 298	The Fly Trap	◆◆	American	$12-$26	335
145 p. 298	54 Mint	◆◆◆	Italian	$14-$31	333
146 p. 298	Samovar Tea Lounge	◆◆	International	$9-$24	339
147 p. 298	Blue Bottle Cafe	◆	American	$8-$12	334
148 p. 298	Cha-am Thai Restaurant Bar & Grill	◆◆	Thai	$10-$16	334
149 p. 298	Luce	◆◆◆	American	$24-$42	337
150 p. 298	Nojo Ramen Tavern	◆◆	Japanese Small Plates Noodles	$4-$19	338
151 p. 298	21st Amendment	◆◆	American	$11-$17	333
152 p. 298	The American Grilled Cheese Kitchen	◆	American	$7-$12	333
153 p. 298	CALA	◆◆◆	Mexican Small Plates Seafood	$12-$32	334
154 p. 298	Town's End Restaurant & Bakery	◆◆	California	$9-$17	340
155 p. 298	Deli Board	◆	Sandwiches	$13-$19	335

Map Page	Restaurants (cont'd)	Diamond Rated	Cuisine	Price Range	Page
156 p. 298	Koh Samui and the Monkey	◈◈	Thai	$10-$24	337
157 p. 298	**Alexander's Steakhouse**	◈◈◈◈	Steak	$52-$165	333
158 p. 298	Cockscomb	◈◈◈	New American	$16-$125	335
159 p. 298	Fringale	◈◈	French	$12-$36	336
160 p. 298	Rocco's Cafe	◈◈	Italian	$11-$29	339
161 p. 298	**Saison**	◈◈◈◈◈	New American	$298	339
162 p. 298	MoMo's Restaurant	◈◈	American	$10-$28	338
163 p. 298	Marlowe	◈◈◈	American	$13-$30	337
164 p. 298	Basil Thai Restaurant & Bar	◈◈	Thai	$12-$18	333

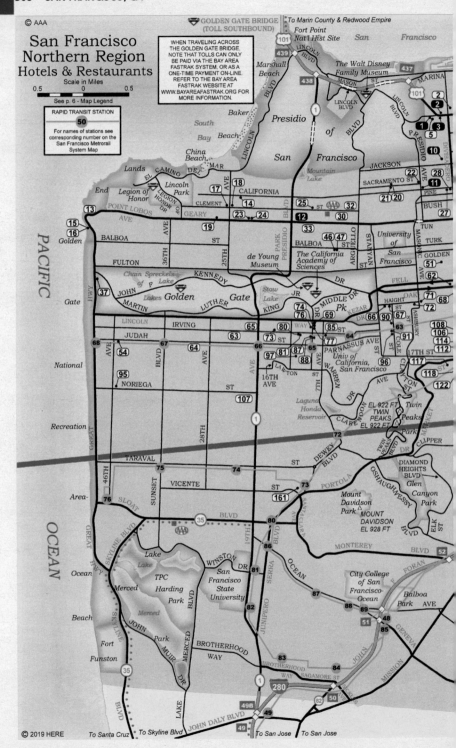

© AAA

San Francisco
Northern Region
Hotels & Restaurants

Scale in Miles
0.5   0   0.5

See p. 6 - Map Legend

RAPID TRANSIT STATION
50
For names of stations see
corresponding number on the
San Francisco Metrorail
System Map

GOLDEN GATE BRIDGE
(TOLL SOUTHBOUND)

To Marin County & Redwood Empire

WHEN TRAVELING ACROSS
THE GOLDEN GATE BRIDGE,
NOTE THAT TOLLS CAN ONLY
BE PAID VIA THE BAY AREA
FASTRAK SYSTEM, OR AS A
ONE-TIME PAYMENT ON-LINE.
REFER TO THE BAY AREA
FASTRAK WEBSITE AT
WWW.BAYAREAFASTRAK.ORG FOR
MORE INFORMATION.

© 2019 HERE

To Santa Cruz   To Skyline Blvd   To San Jose   To San Jose

San Francisco Northern Region

This index helps you "spot" where approved hotels and restaurants are located on the corresponding detailed maps. Restaurant price range is a combination of lunch and/or dinner. Turn to the listing page for more information and consult display ads for special promotions.

 For more details, rates and reservations: AAA.com/travelguides/hotels

SAN FRANCISCO

Map Page	Hotels	Diamond Rated	Member Savings	Page
1 p. 308	Inn at Golden Gate	◈◈	✔	329
2 p. 308	Marina Motel	◈◈		330
3 p. 308	La Luna Inn	◈◈	✔	330
4 p. 308	Lombard Plaza Motel	◈◈	✔	330
5 p. 308	Cow Hollow Inn & Suites	◈◈		325
6 p. 308	Chelsea Inn	◈◈		324
7 p. 308	Coventry Inn	◈◈		325
8 p. 308	Redwood Inn	◈◈	✔	331
9 p. 308	Hotel Del Sol	◈◈	✔	327
10 p. 308	Hotel Drisco	◈◈◈◈		327
11 p. 308	The Laurel Inn	◈◈◈	✔	330
12 p. 308	Geary Parkway Motel	◈◈	✔	326
13 p. 308	Kimpton Buchanan Hotel	◈◈◈	✔	330
14 p. 308	Hotel Kabuki, a Joie de Vivre Hotel	◈◈◈	✔	327
15 p. 308	Inn at the Opera	◈◈◈		329
16 p. 308	Civic Center Motor Inn	◈◈		324

Map Page	Restaurants	Diamond Rated	Cuisine	Price Range	Page
① p. 308	Greens Restaurant	◈◈◈	Vegetarian	$15-$25	336
② p. 308	A 16	◈◈◈	Italian	$13-$36	333
③ p. 308	Blackwood	◈◈	Thai Fusion	$12-$22	334
④ p. 308	Maybeck's	◈◈◈	Italian	$14-$38	337
⑤ p. 308	Baker Street Bistro	◈◈	French	$10-$26	333
⑥ p. 308	Viva Goa Indian Cuisine	◈◈	Indian	$8-$19	341
⑦ p. 308	Isa	◈◈	French	$12-$16	336
⑧ p. 308	Balboa Cafe	◈◈	American	$14-$32	333
⑨ p. 308	Atelier Crenn	◈◈◈◈	New French	$298	333
⑩ p. 308	Rose's Cafe	◈◈	Italian	$13-$30	339
⑪ p. 308	Belga	◈◈◈	Belgian	$6-$23	333
⑫ p. 308	Roam Artisan Burgers	◈◈	Burgers Natural/ Organic	$7-$8	339
⑬ p. 308	Louis'	◈◈	American	$9-$18	337
⑭ p. 308	Pizzetta 211	◈◈	Pizza	$14-$18	339
⑮ p. 308	Cliff House - Sutro's	◈◈◈	American	$23-$48	335
⑯ p. 308	Cliff House-The Bistro	◈◈	American	$13-$40	335

Map Page	Restaurants (cont'd)	Diamond Rated	Cuisine	Price Range	Page
⑰ p. 308	Hard Knox Cafe	◆◆	Soul Food	$6-$16	336
⑱ p. 308	PPQ Dungeness Island	◆◆	Vietnamese	$7-$21	339
⑲ p. 308	Jang Soo BBQ	◆◆	Korean Barbecue	$8-$34	336
⑳ p. 308	Spruce	◆◆◆◆	California	$17-$55	340
㉑ p. 308	Sociale	◆◆◆	Italian	$15-$36	340
㉒ p. 308	Garibaldi's on Presidio	◆◆◆	American	$12-$37	336
㉓ p. 308	Turtle Tower Restaurant	◆◆	Northern Vietnamese	$9-$15	341
㉔ p. 308	Dragon Beaux	◆◆	Chinese Dim Sum	$6-$78	335
㉕ p. 308	Grindz Restaurant	◆◆	Hawaiian	$7-$16	336
㉖ p. 308	La Mediterranee	◆◆	Mediterranean	$12-$17	337
㉗ p. 308	Eliza's	◆◆	Mandarin	$9-$17	335
㉘ p. 308	b. patisserie	◆	Breads/Pastries Desserts	$4-$11	334
㉙ p. 308	Troya Mediterranean Kitchen	◆◆	Turkish	$12-$26	341
㉚ p. 308	Burma Superstar	◆◆	Burmese	$11-$18	334
㉛ p. 308	Pizzeria Delfina	◆◆	Pizza	$14-$19	339
㉜ p. 308	Eats	◆◆	American	$8-$14	335
㉝ p. 308	My Tofu House	◆◆	Korean	$13-$27	338
㉞ p. 308	Roam Artisan Burgers	◆◆	Burgers Natural/ Organic	$7-$9	339
㉟ p. 308	Florio Cafe and Bar	◆◆	Continental	$16-$32	335
㊱ p. 308	SPQR	◆◆◆	Italian	$26-$70	340
㊲ p. 308	Beach Chalet Brewery and Restaurant	◆◆	American	$8-$35	333
㊳ p. 308	Hinodeya Ramen Bar	◆◆	Japanese Noodles	$8-$15	336
㊴ p. 308	Shabusen Restaurant	◆◆	Japanese Specialty	$12-$40	340
㊵ p. 308	Marufuku Ramen	◆◆	Japanese Noodles	$11-$16	337
㊶ p. 308	Izumiya	◆◆	Japanese	$6-$21	336
㊷ p. 308	On the Bridge	◆◆	Japanese	$10-$14	338
㊸ p. 308	Udon Mugizo	◆◆	Japanese Noodles	$10-$17	341
㊹ p. 308	Seoul Garden	◆◆	Korean	$11-$39	340
㊺ p. 308	Suzu Noodle House	◆◆	Japanese Noodles	$5-$12	340
㊻ p. 308	Mugu Boka Korean BBQ Restaurant	◆◆	Korean	$11-$41	338
㊼ p. 308	Katia's	◆◆	Russian	$14-$24	336
㊽ p. 308	State Bird Provisions	◆◆◆	New Small Plates	$5-$24	340
㊾ p. 308	1300 on Fillmore	◆◆◆	Soul Food	$15-$29	333
㊿ p. 308	Little Star Pizza	◆◆	Pizza	$9-$29	337
(51) p. 308	Chile Pies & Ice Cream	◆	American	$9-$12	334

Map Page	Restaurants (cont'd)	Diamond Rated	Cuisine	Price Range	Page
52 p. 308	4505 Burgers & BBQ	◆	American	$7-$29	333
53 p. 308	Bar Crudo	◆◆	Seafood	$14-$42	333
54 p. 308	Outerlands	◆◆◆	California	$8-$27	338
55 p. 308	NOPA	◆◆◆	California	$17-$29	338
56 p. 308	a Mano	◆◆	Italian	$12-$23	333
57 p. 308	Souvla	◆◆	Greek	$11-$21	340
58 p. 308	Suppenkuche	◆◆	Traditional German	$11-$23	340
59 p. 308	Hayes Street Grill	◆◆◆	Seafood	$17-$35	336
60 p. 308	Absinthe Brasserie and Bar	◆◆◆	French	$16-$30	333
61 p. 308	Lers Ros Thai	◆◆	Thai	$9-$18	337
62 p. 308	Nopalito	◆◆	Mexican	$11-$25	338
63 p. 308	Marnee Thai	◆◆	Thai	$8-$14	337
64 p. 308	Terra Cotta Warrior	◆◆	Chinese	$7-$18	340
65 p. 308	The Taco Shop at Underdogs	◆	Mexican	$6-$15	340
66 p. 308	Parada 22	◆◆	Puerto Rican	$11-$17	338
67 p. 308	The Alembic	◆◆◆	California Small Plates	$9-$14	333
68 p. 308	Ragazza	◆◆	Italian	$15-$24	339
69 p. 308	Pacific Catch Westcoast Fish House	◆◆	Pacific Rim	$10-$23	338
70 p. 308	The Little Chihuahua	◆	Mexican	$5-$13	337
71 p. 308	Magnolia Pub & Brewery	◆◆	American	$16-$28	337
72 p. 308	Pork Store Cafe	◆◆	American	$8-$13	339
73 p. 308	Izakaya Sozai	◆◆	Japanese Small Plates	$6-$12	336
74 p. 308	Nopalito on 9th	◆◆	Mexican	$8-$24	338
75 p. 308	Rich Table	◆◆◆	California	$16-$33	339
76 p. 308	Marnee Thai	◆◆	Thai	$8-$14	337
77 p. 308	Park Chow	◆◆	American	$11-$21	338
78 p. 308	RT- Rotisserie	◆◆	Chicken Sandwiches	$12-$19	339
79 p. 308	Straw	◆◆	American	$12-$17	340
80 p. 308	San Tung Chinese Restaurant	◆◆	Chinese	$7-$24	340
81 p. 308	Yummy Yummy Restaurant	◆◆	Vietnamese	$12-$29	341
82 p. 308	Memphis Minnie's	◆	Barbecue	$12-$24	337
83 p. 308	Uva Enoteca	◆◆	Italian	$15-$21	341
84 p. 308	Zuni Cafe	◆◆◆	California	$15-$28	341
85 p. 308	Poki Time	◆	Hawaiian	$11-$15	339
86 p. 308	Espetus Churrascaria	◆◆	Brazilian Barbecue	$55	335
87 p. 308	Nabe	◆◆	Japanese Specialty	$21-$29	338

Map Page	Restaurants (cont'd)	Diamond Rated	Cuisine	Price Range	Page
88 p. 308	Craw Station	◆◆	Seafood	$10-$36	335
89 p. 308	Thep Phanom	◆◆	Thai	$10-$18	340
90 p. 308	The Ice Cream Bar	◆	Specialty	$10-$12	336
91 p. 308	Padrecito	◆◆	Mexican Small Plates	$10-$16	338
92 p. 308	Izakaya Roku	◆◆	Japanese Small Plates	$5-$21	336
93 p. 308	It's Tops Coffee Shop	◆◆	American	$8-$21	336
94 p. 308	Destino	◆◆	New Latin American Small Plates	$14-$32	335
95 p. 308	Toyose	◆◆	Korean	$10-$33	340
96 p. 308	Zazie	◆◆	French	$11-$37	341
97 p. 308	Enjoy Vegetarian Restaurant	◆◆	Chinese Vegetarian Kosher	$10-$16	335
98 p. 308	Orenchi Beyond	◆◆	Japanese Noodles	$14-$17	338
99 p. 308	1601 Bar & Kitchen	◆◆◆	New Asian Small Plates	$11-$34	333
100 p. 308	Bar Agricole	◆◆◆	California	$12-$35	333
101 p. 308	Woodhouse Fish Company	◆◆	Seafood	$14-$37	341
102 p. 308	Chow	◆◆	American	$12-$20	334
103 p. 308	Mission Beach Cafe	◆◆	California	$5-$28	337
104 p. 308	Bellota	◆◆◆	Spanish Small Plates	$10-$50	333
105 p. 308	Rintaro	◆◆◆	Japanese	$10-$43	339
106 p. 308	Super Duper Burgers	◆	American	$6-$9	340
107 p. 308	Cafe Bakery & Restaurant	◆◆	International Comfort Food	$11-$23	334
108 p. 308	Starbelly	◆◆	California	$11-$29	340
109 p. 308	Pica Pica Arepa Kitchen	◆	Latin American	$10-$16	339
110 p. 308	Walzwerk	◆◆	Eastern German	$9-$19	341
111 p. 308	Restaurant Eiji	◆◆	Japanese Small Plates Sushi	$5-$30	339
112 p. 308	Catch	◆◆◆	Mediterranean	$12-$25	334
113 p. 308	Picaro	◆◆	Spanish Small Plates	$6-$12	339
114 p. 308	Frances	◆◆◆	California	$12-$30	335
115 p. 308	The Monk's Kettle	◆◆	American	$12-$28	338
116 p. 308	Pancho Villa Taqueria	◆	Mexican	$9-$17	338
117 p. 308	MaMa Ji's	◆◆	Szechuan Dim Sum	$6-$18	337
118 p. 308	Firewood Cafe	◆	Italian	$12-$18	335
119 p. 308	Maruya	◆◆◆	Japanese Sushi	$95-$150	337
120 p. 308	West of Pecos	◆◆	Southwestern	$10-$21	341
121 p. 308	Locanda	◆◆◆	Italian	$16-$35	337

Map Page	Restaurants (cont'd)	Diamond Rated	Cuisine	Price Range	Page
122 p. 308	Lark Bistro	◈◈◈	Mediterranean	$14-$34	337
123 p. 308	El Toro Taqueria	◈	Mexican	$5-$14	335
124 p. 308	Namu Gaji	◈◈	New Korean Small Plates	$11-$24	338
125 p. 308	Delfina	◈◈◈	Italian	$16-$32	335
126 p. 308	Pizzeria Delfina	◈◈	Pizza	$7-$22	339
127 p. 308	Hawker Fare	◈◈	Northern Thai	$13-$18	336
128 p. 308	Tartine Bakery & Cafe	◈	Breads/Pastries	$6-$23	340
129 p. 308	Mission Cheese	◈	Specialty Small Plates	$10-$13	337
130 p. 308	Gracias Madre	◈◈	Mexican Vegan	$9-$15	336
131 p. 308	Tacolicious	◈◈	Mexican Small Plates	$11-$16	340
132 p. 308	Craftsman and Wolves	◈	Breads/Pastries	$7-$9	335
133 p. 308	Commonwealth	◈◈◈	California	$11-$21	335
134 p. 308	Cha-Ya Vegetarian Japanese Restaurant	◈◈	Japanese Vegetarian	$10-$22	334
135 p. 308	Mission Chinese Food	◈◈	New Chinese	$11-$24	337
136 p. 308	Lazy Bear	◈◈◈◈	New American	$155-$185	337
137 p. 308	Tartine Manufactory	◈◈◈	California	$11-$37	340
138 p. 308	Universal Cafe	◈◈	California	$9-$28	341
139 p. 308	Mission Rock Resort	◈◈	Seafood	$8-$29	338
140 p. 308	Trick Dog	◈◈	International	$8-$19	340
141 p. 308	Dosa on Valencia	◈◈	Southern Indian	$10-$25	335
142 p. 308	Flour + Water	◈◈◈	Italian	$16-$32	335
143 p. 308	Central Kitchen	◈◈◈	California	$28-$29	334
144 p. 308	Plow	◈◈	American	$10-$18	339
145 p. 308	Aslam's Rasoi	◈◈	Indian	$12-$22	333
146 p. 308	Limon Rotisserie	◈◈	Peruvian	$10-$31	337
147 p. 308	Foreign Cinema	◈◈◈	California	$26-$33	335
148 p. 308	Heirloom Cafe	◈◈◈	French	$16-$28	336
149 p. 308	Aster	◈◈◈	California	$58-$98	333
150 p. 308	Lolo	◈◈	New Mexican Small Plates	$7-$28	337
151 p. 308	Los Shucos Latin Hot Dogs	◈	Guatemalan Hot Dogs	$6-$8	337
152 p. 308	Beretta	◈◈	Italian	$12-$22	334
153 p. 308	Papalote Mexican Grill	◈	Mexican	$6-$18	338
154 p. 308	Phat Philly	◈	American	$11-$17	339
155 p. 308	The Spice Jar	◈◈	Asian Fusion	$9-$19	340
156 p. 308	Wise Sons Deli	◈	Jewish Deli	$9-$16	341
157 p. 308	'āina	◈◈◈	Hawaiian	$8-$19	333

Map Page	Restaurants (cont'd)	Diamond Rated	Cuisine	Price Range	Page
(158) p. 308	Rosamunde Sausage Grill	💎	Hot Dogs	$7-$14	339
(159) p. 308	Piccino	💎💎💎	Italian	$12-$25	339
(160) p. 308	Serpentine	💎💎	California	$13-$27	340
(161) p. 308	Bursa Mediterranean Cuisine	💎💎	Mediterranean	$11-$28	334
(162) p. 308	Hard Knox Cafe	💎💎	Soul Food	$7-$17	336
(163) p. 308	La Taqueria	💎	Mexican	$4-$10	337
(164) p. 308	Taqueria San Francisco	💎	Mexican	$3-$14	340
(165) p. 308	Mission Pie	💎	American	$6-$12	337
(166) p. 308	Clay Oven Indian Cuisine	💎💎	Indian	$10-$21	335
(167) p. 308	La Ciccia	💎💎💎	Italian	$19-$29	337
(168) p. 308	The Old Clam House	💎💎	Seafood	$14-$45	338
(169) p. 308	Gialina	💎💎	Pizza	$11-$24	336

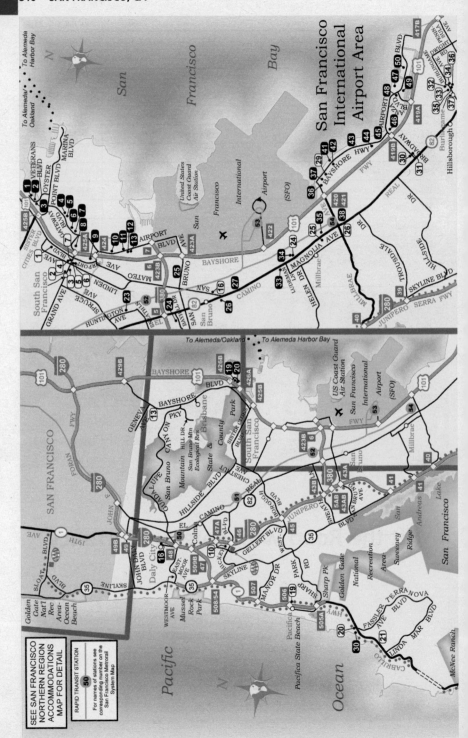

San Francisco International Airport Area

SEE SAN FRANCISCO NORTHERN REGION ACCOMMODATIONS MAP FOR DETAIL

RAPID TRANSIT STATION

50

For names of stations see corresponding number on the San Francisco Metrorail System Map

San Francisco
Southern Region
Hotels & Restaurants

Scale in Miles

See p. 6 - Map Legend

1829-20

To Hayward

San Mateo Bridge (TOLL WESTBOUND)

San Francisco Bay

To San Jose

SEAPORT BLVD

Menlo Park

Palo Alto

SEE PALO ALTO
AREA
ACCOMMODATIONS
MAP FOR DETAIL

Redwood City

MIDDLEFIELD

Atherton

PULGAS

Bair Island RD

San Francisco Bay National Wildlife Refuge

Don Edwards

Foster City

BEACH PARK BLVD

EDGEWATER BLVD

MARINERS ISLAND BLVD

TWIN DOLPHIN DR

San Carlos Airport (SQL)

VETERANS

JEFFERSON AVE

SELBY

WOODSIDE

To San Jose

BAYSHORE

EL CAMINO

San Mateo

HART

3RD AVE

CLINTON

HILLSDALE

20TH AVE

Belmont

Notre Dame de Namur Univ

Welcome Center

PULGAS

San Carlos

ALAMEDA

CANADA

Canada College

Woodside

San Mateo

CALIFORNIA

Burlingame

BROADWAY

SANTA INEZ AVE

J ARTHUR YOUNGER

RALSTON

Pulgas Ridge Open Space Pres

EDGEWOOD

EGGEWOOD

RD

RD

CRYSTAL SPRINGS RD

POLHEMUS

CANADA

Upper Crystal Springs Reservoir

Game

Refuge

BLVD

HALF MOON BAY RD

SKYLINE BLVD

SERRA

SKYLINE

Lower Crystal Springs Reservoir

Pilarcitos Lake

Peninsula

Watershed State

Fish

Springs Reservoir

HANNA RD

CRYSTAL SPRINGS RD

HALF MOON BAY RD

Miramontes Ridge Open Space Preserve

Burleigh H Murray Ranch State Park

SAN MATEO

SKYLINE

Purisima Creek Redwoods Open Space

SEE INSET MAP
FOR DETAIL

Gray Whale Cove St Beach

Montara St Beach

Montara

Moss Beach

CYPRESS AVE

Half Moon Bay Airport (HAF)

Princeton by the Sea

HARVARD AVE

AIRPORT ST

El Granada

Miramar

CABRILLO

Half Moon Bay State Beach

Half Moon Bay

MAIN ST

HIGGINS

CANYON

MIRAMONTES POINT RD

To Santa Cruz

Pacific

Ocean

HWY

© 2019 HERE

© AAA

1.5   0   1.5

✈ Airport Hotels

SAN FRANCISCO INTERNATIONAL
(Maximum driving distance from airport: 5.2 mi)

Map Page		Diamond Rated	Member Savings	Page
43 p. 316	Bay Landing Hotel, 4.0 mi	◆◆◆		48
46 p. 316	**Crowne Plaza San Francisco Airport, 3.4 mi**	◆◆◆	✔	48
48 p. 316	DoubleTree by Hilton Hotel San Francisco Airport, 4.1 mi	◆◆◆	✔	48
47 p. 316	Embassy Suites San Francisco Airport - Waterfront, 4.2 mi	◆◆◆	✔	48
42 p. 316	**Hampton Inn & Suites San Francisco Airport-Burlingame, 2.7 mi**	◆◆◆	✔	48
49 p. 316	Hilton Garden Inn San Francisco Airport/Burlingame, 4.2 mi	◆◆◆	✔	49
50 p. 316	**Hilton San Francisco Airport Bayfront, 4.7 mi**	◆◆◆	✔	49
45 p. 316	**Holiday Inn Express San Francisco Airport South, 3.6 mi**	◆◆◆	✔	49
44 p. 316	**Hyatt Regency San Francisco Airport, 3.8 mi**	◆◆◆	✔	49
41 p. 316	**San Francisco Airport Marriott Waterfront, 2.8 mi**	◆◆◆	✔	49
36 p. 316	**Aloft San Francisco Airport, 2.3 mi**	◆◆◆	✔	135
38 p. 316	The Dylan at SFO, 2.6 mi	◆◆◆		135
34 p. 316	**El Rancho Inn, BW Signature Collection, 3.2 mi**	◆◆◆	✔	136
35 p. 316	Fairfield Inn & Suites by Marriott San Francisco Airport/Millbrae, 2.6 mi	◆◆◆	✔	136
33 p. 316	**Millwood Inn & Suites, 3.5 mi**	◆◆◆	✔	136
37 p. 316	**The Westin San Francisco Airport, 2.4 mi**	◆◆◆	✔	136
25 p. 316	Comfort Inn & Suites San Francisco Airport West, 2.5 mi	◆◆		240
24 p. 316	**Courtyard by Marriott San Francisco Airport, 3.5 mi**	◆◆◆	✔	240
27 p. 316	Hotel Aura San Bruno, 4.1 mi	◆◆		240
23 p. 316	**Staybridge Suites - San Francisco Airport, 3.7 mi**	◆◆◆	✔	240
26 p. 316	Super 8 - San Bruno, 4.1 mi	◆◆		240
3 p. 316	AC Hotel by Marriott San Francisco Airport/Oyster Point Waterfront, 5.1 mi	◆◆◆	✔	386
12 p. 316	**Best Western Plus Grosvenor Airport Hotel, 3.4 mi**	◆◆◆	✔	386
8 p. 316	Comfort Inn & Suites SFO Airport North, 3.7 mi	◆◆		386
2 p. 316	**Courtyard by Marriott San Francisco Airport/Oyster Point Waterfront, 5.1 mi**	◆◆◆	✔	386
7 p. 316	**Embassy Suites by Hilton San Francisco Airport-South San Francisco, 3.9 mi**	◆◆◆	✔	386
6 p. 316	Hampton Inn San Francisco-Airport, 4.0 mi	◆◆◆	✔	387
5 p. 316	**Hilton Garden Inn San Francisco Airport North, 4.2 mi**	◆◆◆	✔	387
11 p. 316	Holiday Inn Express San Francisco Airport North, 3.3 mi	◆◆◆		387
10 p. 316	Holiday Inn San Francisco International Airport North, 3.2 mi	◆◆◆		387
13 p. 316	Hotel Nova SFO, 3.4 mi	◆◆		387
9 p. 316	La Quinta Inn & Suites by Wyndham San Francisco Airport North, 3.6 mi	◆◆◆		387
4 p. 316	**Larkspur Landing South San Francisco, 4.4 mi**	◆◆	✔	387
1 p. 316	**Residence Inn by Marriott at Oyster Point, 5.2 mi**	◆◆◆	✔	387

San Francisco Southern Region

This index helps you "spot" where approved hotels and restaurants are located on the corresponding detailed maps. Restaurant price range is a combination of lunch and/or dinner. Turn to the listing page for more information and consult display ads for special promotions.

 For more details, rates and reservations: AAA.com/travelguides/hotels

SOUTH SAN FRANCISCO

Map Page	Hotels	Diamond Rated	Member Savings	Page
1 p. 316	**Residence Inn by Marriott at Oyster Point**	◈◈◈	✔	387
2 p. 316	**Courtyard by Marriott San Francisco Airport/ Oyster Point Waterfront**	◈◈◈	✔	386
3 p. 316	AC Hotel by Marriott San Francisco Airport/Oyster Point Waterfront	◈◈◈	✔	386
4 p. 316	**Larkspur Landing South San Francisco**	◈◈	✔	387
5 p. 316	**Hilton Garden Inn San Francisco Airport North**	◈◈◈	✔	387
6 p. 316	Hampton Inn San Francisco-Airport	◈◈◈	✔	387
7 p. 316	**Embassy Suites by Hilton San Francisco Airport-South San Francisco**	◈◈◈	✔	386
8 p. 316	Comfort Inn & Suites SFO Airport North	◈◈		386
9 p. 316	La Quinta Inn & Suites by Wyndham San Francisco Airport North	◈◈◈		387
10 p. 316	Holiday Inn San Francisco International Airport North	◈◈◈		387
11 p. 316	Holiday Inn Express San Francisco Airport North	◈◈◈		387
12 p. 316	**Best Western Plus Grosvenor Airport Hotel**	◈◈◈	✔	386
13 p. 316	Hotel Nova SFO	◈◈		387

Map Page	Restaurants	Diamond Rated	Cuisine	Price Range	Page
① p. 316	Darby Dan's Sandwich Company	◈	Sandwiches	$8-$15	387
② p. 316	Ben Tre Restaurant	◈◈	Vietnamese	$10-$29	387
③ p. 316	Grand Palace Seafood Restaurant	◈◈	Cantonese Dim Sum	$8-$38	387
④ p. 316	Flavas Jamaican Grill	◈◈	Jamaican	$10-$16	387
⑤ p. 316	Thai Satay Restaurant & Bar	◈◈	Thai	$9-$16	387
⑥ p. 316	Izanami	◈◈	Japanese Sushi	$8-$26	387
⑦ p. 316	Buon Gusto Ristorante	◈◈	Italian	$13-$28	387

DALY CITY

Map Page	Hotel	Diamond Rated	Member Savings	Page
16 p. 316	Hampton Inn by Hilton San Francisco/Daly City	◈◈◈	✔	68

Map Page	Restaurant	Diamond Rated	Cuisine	Price Range	Page
⑩ p. 316	Koi Palace Restaurant	◈◈	Chinese Dim Sum	$8-$88	69

BRISBANE

Map Page	Hotels	Diamond Rated	Member Savings	Page
19 p. 316	**DoubleTree by Hilton San Francisco Airport North**	◈◈◈	✔	48
20 p. 316	Homewood Suites By Hilton San Francisco Airport-North	◈◈◈	✔	48

Map Page	Restaurant	Diamond Rated	Cuisine	Price Range	Page
⑬ p. 316	7 Mile House	◈◈	American	$7-$19	48

SAN BRUNO

Map Page	Hotels	Diamond Rated	Member Savings	Page
23 p. 316	**Staybridge Suites - San Francisco Airport**	◈◈◈	✔	240

SAN BRUNO (cont'd)

Map Page	Hotels (cont'd)	Diamond Rated	Member Savings	Page
24 p. 316	**Courtyard by Marriott San Francisco Airport**	◈◈◈	✔	240
25 p. 316	Comfort Inn & Suites San Francisco Airport West	◈◈		240
26 p. 316	Super 8 - San Bruno	◈◈		240
27 p. 316	Hotel Aura San Bruno	◈◈		240

Map Page	Restaurant	Diamond Rated	Cuisine	Price Range	Page
16 p. 316	Thai Nakorn	◈◈	Thai	$9-$18	240

PACIFICA

Map Page	Hotel	Diamond Rated	Member Savings	Page
30 p. 316	**Holiday Inn Express Hotel & Suites**	◈◈◈	✔	186

Map Page	Restaurants	Diamond Rated	Cuisine	Price Range	Page
19 p. 316	Salada Beach Cafe	◈	American	$5-$10	186
20 p. 316	Lovey's Tea Shoppe	◈◈	Specialty	$15-$27	186
21 p. 316	Puerto 27 Peruvian Kitchen & Pisco Bar	◈◈	Peruvian	$12-$32	186

MILLBRAE

Map Page	Hotels	Diamond Rated	Member Savings	Page
33 p. 316	**Millwood Inn & Suites**	◈◈◈	✔	136
34 p. 316	**El Rancho Inn, BW Signature Collection**	◈◈◈	✔	136
35 p. 316	**Fairfield Inn & Suites by Marriott San Francisco Airport/Millbrae**	◈◈◈	✔	136
36 p. 316	**Aloft San Francisco Airport**	◈◈◈	✔	135
37 p. 316	**The Westin San Francisco Airport**	◈◈◈	✔	136
38 p. 316	The Dylan at SFO	◈◈◈		135

Map Page	Restaurants	Diamond Rated	Cuisine	Price Range	Page
24 p. 316	Terrace Cafe	◈◈	American	$6-$17	136
25 p. 316	La Collina Ristorante	◈◈	Italian	$13-$28	136
26 p. 316	Hong Kong Flower Lounge Restaurant	◈◈	Chinese Dim Sum	$7-$45	136

BURLINGAME

Map Page	Hotels	Diamond Rated	Member Savings	Page
41 p. 316	**San Francisco Airport Marriott Waterfront**	◈◈◈	✔	49
42 p. 316	**Hampton Inn & Suites San Francisco Airport-Burlingame**	◈◈◈	✔	48
43 p. 316	Bay Landing Hotel	◈◈◈		48
44 p. 316	**Hyatt Regency San Francisco Airport**	◈◈◈	✔	49
45 p. 316	**Holiday Inn Express San Francisco Airport South**	◈◈◈	✔	49
46 p. 316	**Crowne Plaza San Francisco Airport**	◈◈◈	✔	48
47 p. 316	Embassy Suites San Francisco Airport - Waterfront	◈◈◈	✔	48
48 p. 316	DoubleTree by Hilton Hotel San Francisco Airport	◈◈◈	✔	48
49 p. 316	Hilton Garden Inn San Francisco Airport/Burlingame	◈◈◈	✔	49
50 p. 316	**Hilton San Francisco Airport Bayfront**	◈◈◈	✔	49

Map Page	Restaurants	Diamond Rated	Cuisine	Price Range	Page
29 p. 316	New England Lobster Market & Eatery	◈	Seafood	$14-$95	49
30 p. 316	Cafe Figaro	◈◈	Italian	$10-$25	49

Map Page	Restaurants (cont'd)	Diamond Rated	Cuisine	Price Range	Page
31 p. 316	Sesame Korean Cuisine	♦♦	Korean	$8-$40	49
32 p. 316	Steelhead Brewing Co.	♦♦	American	$8-$20	49
33 p. 316	Saltyard Restaurant and Bar	♦♦	American	$15-$40	49
34 p. 316	Limon Rotisserie	♦♦	Peruvian Small Plates	$9-$32	49
35 p. 316	Mingalaba Restaurant	♦♦	Burmese	$12-$28	49
36 p. 316	Trapeze	♦♦	Continental	$12-$22	49
37 p. 316	Pizzeria Delfina	♦♦	Italian Pizza	$10-$20	49
38 p. 316	Sapore Italiano	♦♦	Italian	$10-$27	49

FOSTER CITY

Map Page	Hotels	Diamond Rated	Member Savings	Page
53 p. 316	Crowne Plaza Hotel Foster City-San Mateo	♦♦♦		85
54 p. 316	TownePlace Suites by Marriott San Mateo - Foster City	♦♦♦	✔	85
55 p. 316	**Courtyard by Marriott San Mateo Foster City**	♦♦♦	✔	85

Map Page	Restaurant	Diamond Rated	Cuisine	Price Range	Page
41 p. 316	ABC Seafood Restaurant	♦♦	Cantonese Dim Sum	$5-$42	85

SAN MATEO

Map Page	Hotels	Diamond Rated	Member Savings	Page
58 p. 316	**Best Western Coyote Point Inn**	♦♦	✔	358
59 p. 316	Holiday Inn & Suites San Mateo-SFO	♦♦		358
60 p. 316	Hilton Garden Inn San Mateo	♦♦♦	✔	358
61 p. 316	**San Mateo Marriott San Francisco Airport**	♦♦♦	✔	358
62 p. 316	Residence Inn by Marriott	♦♦♦	✔	358
63 p. 316	Los Prados Hotel	♦♦		358

Map Page	Restaurants	Diamond Rated	Cuisine	Price Range	Page
44 p. 316	Fusion Peruvian Grill	♦♦	Peruvian	$9-$22	358
45 p. 316	Curry Up Now	♦	Indian	$9-$13	358
46 p. 316	Izakaya Mai	♦♦	Japanese	$8-$30	358
47 p. 316	Himawari-Tei Ramen Restaurant	♦♦	Japanese Noodles	$5-$12	358
48 p. 316	Little Sheep Mongolian Hot Pot	♦♦	Mongolian	$11-$30	358
49 p. 316	San Mateo Prime	♦♦	Steak	$22-$40	358
50 p. 316	Clay Oven	♦♦	Indian	$12-$20	358
51 p. 316	Viognier	♦♦♦	French	$60-$109	358
52 p. 316	Central Park Bistro	♦♦♦	American	$13-$36	358
53 p. 316	Espetus Churrascaria	♦♦♦	Brazilian Steak	$28-$55	358
54 p. 316	Ramen Dojo	♦♦	Japanese Noodles	$10-$15	358
55 p. 316	The Fish Market Seafood Market Restaurant	♦♦	Seafood	$10-$44	358
56 p. 316	Santa Ramen	♦♦	Japanese Noodles	$10-$12	358
57 p. 316	Little Shanghai Restaurant	♦♦	Chinese	$8-$35	358
58 p. 316	Jack's Prime Burgers	♦♦	Burgers	$12-$17	358

BELMONT

Map Page	Hotels	Diamond Rated	Member Savings	Page
66 p. 316	**Hyatt House Belmont/Redwood Shores**	◈◈◈	✔	37
67 p. 316	Hotel Belmont	◈◈		37
68 p. 316	Holiday Inn Express Hotel & Suites	◈◈◈		37

Map Page	Restaurants	Diamond Rated	Cuisine	Price Range	Page
61 p. 316	Vivace Ristorante	◈◈◈	Italian	$9-$26	37
62 p. 316	Godfather's Burger Lounge	◈◈	Burgers	$11-$14	37

SAN CARLOS

Map Page	Hotels	Diamond Rated	Member Savings	Page
71 p. 316	Hotel San Carlos	◈◈		240
72 p. 316	Country Inn & Suites by Radisson	◈◈◈		240
73 p. 316	Fairfield Inn & Suites by Marriott San Francisco/San Carlos	◈◈◈	✔	240
74 p. 316	Residence Inn by Marriott Redwood City San Carlos	◈◈◈	✔	240

Map Page	Restaurants	Diamond Rated	Cuisine	Price Range	Page
65 p. 316	Jersey Joe's Hoagies & Cheesesteaks	◈	Sandwiches	$7-$16	241
66 p. 316	Kaya Tofu & BBQ	◈◈	Korean Barbecue	$10-$25	241
67 p. 316	Sneakers Pub & Grill	◈◈	American	$7-$17	241
68 p. 316	Piacere Ristorante	◈◈◈	Italian	$13-$36	241
69 p. 316	3 Pigs BBQ	◈	Barbecue	$9-$34	240

REDWOOD CITY

Map Page	Hotels	Diamond Rated	Member Savings	Page
77 p. 316	**Pullman San Francisco Bay Hotel**	◈◈◈◈	✔	209
78 p. 316	TownePlace Suites by Marriott Redwood City/Redwood Shores	◈◈◈	✔	209
79 p. 316	Good Nite Inn Redwood City	◈◈		209
80 p. 316	Courtyard by Marriott Redwood City	◈◈◈	✔	209
81 p. 316	**Best Western Inn**	◈◈	✔	209
82 p. 316	Redwood Creek Inn	◈◈		209
83 p. 316	**Comfort Inn by Choice Hotels**	◈◈	✔	209
84 p. 316	Holiday Inn Express Redwood City Central	◈◈◈		209
85 p. 316	Pacific Inn Redwood City	◈◈		209
86 p. 316	Atherton Park Inn & Suites	◈◈◈		208
87 p. 316	**Best Western Plus Executive Suites**	◈◈◈	✔	209

Map Page	Restaurants	Diamond Rated	Cuisine	Price Range	Page
72 p. 316	Vesta	◈◈◈	Pizza Small Plates	$10-$23	209
73 p. 316	Portobello Grill	◈◈◈	New American	$9-$26	209
74 p. 316	CRU Wine Bar & Merchant Cafe	◈◈	American	$7-$18	209
75 p. 316	Donato Enoteca	◈◈◈	Italian	$10-$34	209
76 p. 316	Milagros Cantina Restaurant	◈◈	Mexican	$6-$26	209
77 p. 316	Harry's Hofbrau	◈	American	$9-$19	209

HALF MOON BAY

Map Page	Hotels	Diamond Rated	Member Savings	Page
90 p. 316	**Harbor View Inn**	◈◈	✔	101
91 p. 316	Beach House Hotel	◈◈◈		101
92 p. 316	The Oceanfront Hotel	◈◈◈		101
93 p. 316	Cypress Inn on Miramar Beach	◈◈◈		101
94 p. 316	Quality Inn	◈◈		101
95 p. 316	Coastside Inn Half Moon Bay	◈◈		101
96 p. 316	Mill Rose Inn	◈◈◈◈		101
97 p. 316	Nantucket Whale Inn	◈◈◈		101
98 p. 316	**Best Western Plus-Cameron's Inn**	◈◈◈	✔	101
99 p. 316	**The Ritz-Carlton, Half Moon Bay**	◈◈◈◈	✔	101
100 p. 316	Half Moon Bay Lodge	◈◈◈		101

Map Page	Restaurants	Diamond Rated	Cuisine	Price Range	Page
80 p. 316	Mezzaluna Italian Restaurant	◈◈	Italian	$9-$30	101
81 p. 316	Caffe Mezzaluna	◈	Italian Sandwiches Desserts	$6-$14	101
82 p. 316	Half Moon Bay Brewing Company	◈◈	American	$9-$27	101
83 p. 316	**Sam's Chowder House**	◈◈	Seafood	$13-$33	102
84 p. 316	**Miramar Beach Restaurant**	◈◈	California Seafood	$17-$39	101
85 p. 316	Asian Kings Kitchen	◈◈	Chinese	$8-$16	101
86 p. 316	Via Uno Cucina Italiana Bar	◈◈◈	Italian	$6-$19	102
87 p. 316	Mavericks Creperie	◈	American	$7-$15	101
88 p. 316	Jersey Joe's Coastside	◈	Sandwiches	$7-$21	101
89 p. 316	**Pasta Moon Ristorante**	◈◈◈	Italian	$14-$40	102
90 p. 316	Sushi Main Street	◈◈	Japanese Sushi	$12-$23	102
91 p. 316	It's Italia	◈◈◈	Italian	$19-$46	101
92 p. 316	Spice Me Thai Cuisine	◈◈	Thai	$8-$19	102
93 p. 316	Navio	◈◈◈◈	Northern California	$38-$65	102
94 p. 316	Half Moon Bay Joe's	◈◈	American	$7-$31	101

WOODSIDE

Map Page	Restaurant	Diamond Rated	Cuisine	Price Range	Page
97 p. 316	The Village Pub	◈◈◈◈	New American	$18-$52	419

SAN FRANCISCO
- Restaurants p. 333
- Hotels & Restaurants map & index p. 298, 308

ADANTE HOTEL
415/673-9221 **55**

Hotel

Address: 610 Geary St 94102 **Location:** Between Jones and Leavenworth sts. Powell Street, 42. **Facility:** 92 units. 7 stories, interior corridors. **Parking:** valet and street only. **Amenities:** safes. **Guest Services:** valet laundry. **Featured Amenity:** continental breakfast.

ALEXIS PARK-SAN FRANCISCO
415/673-0411 **67**

Motel. **Address:** 825 Polk St 94109

AMERICANIA HOTEL
415/626-0200 **92**

Contemporary Hotel

Address: 121 7th St 94103 **Location:** Just s of Market St; between Mission and Howard sts. Civic Center/UN Plaza, 43. **Facility:** 143 units. 4 stories, exterior corridors. **Parking:** valet only. **Amenities:** safes. **Pool:** heated outdoor. **Activities:** exercise room. **Guest Services:** valet and coin laundry.

THE ARGONAUT
415/563-0800 **1**

Hotel

Address: 495 Jefferson St 94109 **Location:** Fisherman's Wharf; adjacent to The Cannery. **Facility:** The nautical design of this hotel complements this uniquely renovated Cannery building of Fisherman's Wharf. The seafaring décor is repeated in the guest rooms, which feature original artwork. 252 units. 4 stories, interior corridors. **Parking:** valet only. **Amenities:** safes. **Dining:** Blue Mermaid Chowder House & Bar, see separate listing. **Activities:** bicycles, exercise room. **Guest Services:** valet laundry.

AXIOM HOTEL
415/392-9466 **79**

Hotel

Address: 28 Cyril Magnin St 94102 **Location:** At Powell St cable car turnaround. Powell Street, 42. **Facility:** 152 units. 5 stories, interior corridors. *Bath:* shower only. **Parking:** valet only. **Amenities:** safes. **Activities:** game room, exercise room. **Guest Services:** valet laundry.

BEI SAN FRANCISCO
415/626-6103 **91**

[fyi]
Hotel

Under major renovation, call for details. **Last Rated:** **Address:** 50 8th St 94103 **Location:** Between Market and Mission sts. Civic Center/UN Plaza, 43. **Facility:** 388 units. 14 stories, interior corridors. **Parking:** on-site (fee). **Amenities:** safes. **Pool:** heated outdoor. **Activities:** exercise room. **Guest Services:** valet and coin laundry.

BERESFORD HOTEL
415/673-9900 **41**

Historic Hotel

Address: 635 Sutter St 94102 **Location:** 1 blk nw of Union Square at Mason St. Union Sq/Market St, 125. **Facility:** This hotel offers petite, yet comfortably furnished, accommodations and the convenience of a Union Square location. 114 units. 7 stories, interior corridors. **Parking:** valet only. **Activities:** exercise room. **Guest Services:** valet laundry. **Featured Amenity:** continental breakfast.

CARRIAGE INN
415/552-8600 **93**

Boutique Hotel. **Address:** 140 7th St 94103

THE CARTWRIGHT HOTEL-UNION SQUARE, BW PREMIER COLLECTION
415/421-2865 **39**

Hotel. **Address:** 524 Sutter St 94102

AAA Benefit: Members save up to 15% and earn bonus points!

CASTLE INN
415/441-1155 **16**

Motel. **Address:** 1565 Broadway St 94109

CHELSEA INN
415/563-5600 **6**

Hotel. **Address:** 2095 Lombard St 94123

CIVIC CENTER MOTOR INN
415/621-2826 **16**

Motel. **Address:** 364 9th St 94103

COLUMBUS INN
415/885-1492 **11**

Hotel. **Address:** 1075 Columbus Ave 94133

COMFORT INN BY THE BAY
415/928-5000 **14**

Hotel

Address: 2775 Van Ness Ave 94109 **Location:** On US 101 (Van Ness Ave) at Lombard St. Chinatown, 126. **Facility:** 138 units. 11 stories, interior corridors. **Terms:** check-in 4 pm. **Amenities:** safes. **Guest Services:** valet laundry. **Featured Amenity:** full hot breakfast. *(See ad p. 325.)*

COURTYARD BY MARRIOTT AT FISHERMAN'S WHARF
415/775-3800 **2**

Hotel. **Address:** 580 Beach St 94133

AAA Benefit: Members save 5% or more!

COURTYARD BY MARRIOTT SAN FRANCISCO DOWNTOWN
415/947-0700 **86**

Hotel. **Address:** 299 2nd St 94105

AAA Benefit: Members save 5% or more!

(See maps & indexes p. 298, 308.)

COURTYARD BY MARRIOTT SAN FRANCISCO DOWNTOWN/
VAN NESS AVE   415/673-4711 **54**
▼▼▼ SAVE Historic Hotel. **Address:**
1050 Van Ness Ave 94109

> **AAA Benefit:**
> Members save 5%
> or more!

COURTYARD BY MARRIOTT SAN FRANCISCO UNION
SQUARE   415/346-3800 **48**
▼▼▼ SAVE Hotel. **Address:** 761
Post St 94109

> **AAA Benefit:**
> Members save 5%
> or more!

COVA HOTEL   415/771-3000 **71**
▼▼ Hotel. **Address:** 655 Ellis St 94109

COVENTRY INN   415/567-1200 **7**
▼▼ Hotel. **Address:** 1901 Lombard St 94123

COW HOLLOW INN & SUITES   415/921-5800 **5**
▼▼ Hotel. **Address:** 2190 Lombard St 94123

THE DONATELLO   415/441-7100 **53**

▼▼▼
Hotel

Address: 501 Post St 94102 **Location:**
Just w of Union Square at Mason St.
⊞ Union Sq/Market St, 125. **Facility:**
94 units. 15 stories, interior corridors.
Parking: valet only. **Amenities:** safes.
Dining: Zingari Ristorante, see separate
listing. **Activities:** sauna, hot tub, exercise room, massage. **Guest Services:**
valet laundry.

SAVE 🍴 📶 ♨ Ⓣ CALL ♿ 🛅

BIZ 📶 ✖ 🛄 📷 🖥 🚐

EXECUTIVE HOTEL VINTAGE COURT 415/392-4666 **31**
▼▼▼ Boutique Hotel. **Address:** 650 Bush St 94108

THE FAIRMONT SAN FRANCISCO   415/772-5000 **21**

▼◇▼ ▼◇▼
Historic Hotel

Address: 950 Mason St (atop Nob Hill)
94108 **Location:** Atop Nob Hill at California St. ⊞ Chinatown, 126. **Facility:**
This historic hotel atop Nob Hill features
an impressive lobby and selection of fine
shops and restaurants. Not to be missed
is The Tonga Room, a much-beloved
spot for tiki drinks and live music. 606
units, some two and three bedrooms.
7-22 stories, interior corridors. **Parking:**
valet only. **Terms:** check-in 4 pm. **Amenities:** safes. **Dining:** 2 restaurants,
also, The Laurel Court Restaurant & Bar,
see separate listing, entertainment. **Ac-
tivities:** bicycles, trails, health club, spa. **Guest Services:** valet
laundry, boarding pass kiosk, rental car service, area
transportation.

SAVE ECO 🍴 ♨ Ⓣ 🏋 CALL ♿ 🛅 BIZ
SHS 📶 ✖ 🛄 📷 🖥 / SOME UNITS 🐾 📷 🚐

FOUR SEASONS HOTEL SAN FRANCISCO
                                           415/633-3000 **72**

▼◇▼ ▼◇▼
Hotel

Address: 757 Market St 94103 **Location:** Between 3rd and 4th sts. ⊞ Union
Sq/Market St, 125. **Facility:** This is an
elegant downtown hotel located between Union Square and the Yerba
Buena cultural district. An upscale full
service health club is located inside the
building and available for guests' use.
277 units. 17 stories, interior corridors.
Parking: valet only. **Amenities:** safes.
Pool: heated indoor. **Activities:** sauna,
steamroom, health club, spa. **Guest
Services:** valet laundry, area
transportation.

SAVE 🛫 🍴 ♨ Ⓣ CALL ♿ 🛏 🛅 BIZ HS
📶 ✖ 🛄 📷 🖥 / SOME UNITS 🐾 📷 🚐

🔗 **For exclusive AAA member
savings and benefits:**

AAA.com/hertz

▼ See AAA listing p. 324 ▼

(See maps & indexes p. 298, 308.)

GALLERIA PARK HOTEL, A JOIE DE VIVRE HOTEL
415/781-3060 45

Hotel

Address: 191 Sutter St 94104 **Location:** 2 blks ne of Union Square; between Kearny and Trinity sts. Montgomery Street, 41. **Facility:** 177 units. 8 stories, interior corridors. **Parking:** valet only. **Amenities:** safes. **Activities:** trails, exercise room. **Guest Services:** valet laundry.

GEARY PARKWAY MOTEL
415/752-4406 12

Motel

Address: 4750 Geary Blvd 94118 **Location:** Between 11th and 12th aves. **Facility:** 20 units. 2 stories (no elevator), exterior corridors. *Bath:* shower only. **Amenities:** safes. **Featured Amenity:** continental breakfast.

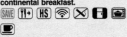

GOOD HOTEL   415/621-7001 90
Contemporary Hotel. **Address:** 112 7th St 94103

GRAND HYATT SAN FRANCISCO
415/398-1234 44

Contemporary Hotel

AAA Benefit: Members save up to 10%!

Address: 345 Stockton St 94108 **Location:** At Sutter St. Union Sq/Market St, 125. **Facility:** This contemporary hotel is in an excellent area for shopping and dining. Rooms feature enhanced technology including remote controlled window shades. 662 units. 30 stories, interior corridors. **Parking:** on-site (fee) and valet. **Terms:** check-in 4 pm. **Amenities:** safes. **Activities:** exercise room, massage. **Guest Services:** valet laundry.

THE HANDLERY UNION SQUARE HOTEL
415/781-7800 62

Hotel

Address: 351 Geary St 94102 **Location:** Between Powell and Mason sts; just sw of Union Square. Union Sq/Market St, 125. **Facility:** 377 units. 8 stories, interior/exterior corridors. **Parking:** valet only. **Amenities:** safes. **Dining:** Daily Grill, see separate listing. **Pool:** heated outdoor. **Activities:** sauna, exercise room. **Guest Services:** valet laundry.

HARBOR COURT HOTEL
415/882-1300 46

Hotel

Address: 165 Steuart St 94105 **Location:** On Embarcadero; between Howard and Mission sts. Folsom, 90. **Facility:** 131 units. 8 stories, interior corridors. **Parking:** valet only. **Amenities:** safes. **Pool:** heated indoor. **Activities:** sauna, hot tub, bicycles, trails, health club. **Guest Services:** valet laundry.

HILTON SAN FRANCISCO FINANCIAL DISTRICT
415/433-6600 18

Hotel

Hilton
HOTELS & RESORTS

AAA Benefit: Members save up to 15%!

Address: 750 Kearny St 94108 **Location:** Between Clay and Washington sts. Chinatown, 126. **Facility:** 544 units. 27 stories, interior corridors. **Parking:** on-site (fee) and valet. **Amenities:** safes. **Activities:** exercise room. **Guest Services:** valet laundry.

HILTON SAN FRANCISCO UNION SQUARE
415/771-1400 68

Hotel

Hilton
HOTELS & RESORTS

AAA Benefit: Members save up to 15%!

Address: 333 O'Farrell St 94102 **Location:** Just w of Mason and O'Farrell sts. Powell Street, 42. **Facility:** 1921 units. 19-44 stories, interior corridors. **Parking:** on-site (fee) and valet. **Amenities:** safes. **Dining:** 3 restaurants. **Pool:** heated outdoor. **Activities:** hot tub, exercise room. **Guest Services:** valet laundry.

HOLIDAY INN AT FISHERMAN'S WHARF
415/771-9000 4

Hotel

Address: 495 Beach St 94133 **Location:** Jct North Point St. Chinatown, 126. **Facility:** 243 units. 5 stories, interior corridors. **Parking:** on-site (fee). **Amenities:** video games, safes. **Guest Services:** valet and coin laundry, boarding pass kiosk.

For complete hotel, dining and attraction listings: AAA.com/travelguides

(See maps & indexes p. 298, 308.)

HOLIDAY INN EXPRESS & SUITES AT FISHERMAN'S WHARF   415/409-4600   5

Hotel

Address: 550 N Point St 94133 **Location:** Jct Columbus Ave. Chinatown, 126. **Facility:** 252 units. 4 stories, interior corridors. **Parking:** valet only. **Amenities:** safes. **Activities:** exercise room. **Guest Services:** valet laundry, boarding pass kiosk. **Featured Amenity: breakfast buffet.**

HOLIDAY INN EXPRESS SAN FRANCISCO-UNION SQUARE
415/951-1500   70
Hotel. **Address:** 235 O'Farrell St 94102

HOLIDAY INN GOLDEN GATEWAY   415/441-4000   20
Hotel. **Address:** 1500 Van Ness Ave 94109

HOTEL ABRI   415/392-8800   77
Hotel. **Address:** 127 Ellis St 94102

HOTEL ADAGIO, AUTOGRAPH COLLECTION
415/775-5000   57

Hotel

AUTOGRAPH COLLECTION HOTELS **AAA Benefit:** Members save 5% or more!

Address: 550 Geary St 94102 **Location:** 2 blks w of Union Square; between Jones and Taylor sts. Powell Street, 42. **Facility:** 171 units. 15 stories, interior corridors. **Parking:** valet only. **Amenities:** safes. **Activities:** exercise room. **Guest Services:** valet laundry.

HOTEL BIJOU   415/771-1200   81
Hotel. **Address:** 111 Mason St 94102

HOTEL CARLTON, A JOIE DE VIVRE HOTEL
415/673-0242   33

Boutique Hotel

Address: 1075 Sutter St 94109 **Location:** 0.5 mi w of Union Square; between Hyde and Larkin sts. Powell Street, 42. **Facility:** The theme at this boutique hotel is travel. The lobby is decorated with paraphernalia from all over the world and the elevator is adorned with a world map. 161 units. 9 stories, interior corridors. **Amenities:** safes. **Guest Services:** valet laundry.

HOTEL DEL SOL   415/921-5520   9

Motel

Address: 3100 Webster St 94123 **Location:** Just s of Lombard St at Greenwich St. **Facility:** 57 units. 3 stories, exterior corridors. **Parking:** on-site (fee). **Amenities:** safes. **Pool:** heated outdoor. **Guest Services:** valet laundry. Affiliated with Joie de Vivre Hotels & Resorts.

HOTEL DIVA   415/885-0200   59

Contemporary Hotel

Address: 440 Geary St 94102 **Location:** Between Taylor and Mason sts; on Theater Row. Union Sq/Market St, 125. **Facility:** 130 units. 6 stories, interior corridors. **Parking:** valet only. **Amenities:** safes. **Dining:** colibri Mexican-Bistro, see separate listing. **Activities:** exercise room. **Guest Services:** valet laundry.

HOTEL DRISCO   415/346-2880   10
Historic Boutique Hotel. **Address:** 2901 Pacific Ave 94115

HOTEL FUSION   415/568-2525   74

Hotel

Address: 140 Ellis St 94102 **Location:** Jct Powell St, just w; in Union Square area. Powell Street, 42. **Facility:** 120 units. 5 stories, interior corridors. **Parking:** valet only. **Amenities:** safes. **Activities:** exercise room. **Guest Services:** valet laundry.

HOTEL GRIFFON   415/495-2100   42

Hotel

Address: 155 Steuart St 94105 **Location:** Waterfront. On Embarcadero; between Howard and Mission sts. Folsom, 90. **Facility:** 62 units. 5 stories, interior corridors. **Parking:** valet only. **Amenities:** safes. **Guest Services:** valet laundry.

HOTEL KABUKI, A JOIE DE VIVRE HOTEL
415/922-3200   14

Hotel

Address: 1625 Post St 94115 **Location:** Jct Laguna St; in Japan Center. Van Ness, 60. **Facility:** 225 units. 5-16 stories, interior corridors. **Parking:** on-site (fee) and valet. **Amenities:** safes. **Activities:** bicycles, exercise room, massage. **Guest Services:** valet laundry.

HOTEL NIKKO SAN FRANCISCO   415/394-1111   73

Hotel

Address: 222 Mason St 94102 **Location:** At O'Farrell St. Powell Street, 42. **Facility:** This hotel showcases an elegant décor throughout. Guest rooms feature plush bedding, ample seating and plenty of storage space. A wonderful pet run is located on the roof. 533 units. 25 stories, interior corridors. **Parking:** valet only. **Amenities:** safes. **Dining:** Anzu Restaurant, see separate listing, nightclub, entertainment. **Pool:** heated indoor. **Activities:** sauna, hot tub, steamroom, health club. **Guest Services:** valet laundry.

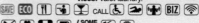

(See maps & indexes p. 298, 308.)

HOTEL REX, A JOIE DE VIVRE HOTEL   415/433-4434 **38**
[fyl] Hotel. Under major renovation, call for details. **Last Rated:** ♦♦♦ **Address:** 562 Sutter St 94102

HOTEL SPERO   415/885-2500 **65**
♦♦♦ Boutique Hotel. **Address:** 405 Taylor St 94102

HOTEL TRITON   415/394-0500 **37**

♦♦♦
Boutique Hotel

Address: 342 Grant Ave 94108 **Location:** Near Union Square at Bush St. 🚇 Union Sq/Market St, 125. **Facility:** A hip, vibrant hotel located just steps from Chinatown, this property is known for its suites that are designed by celebrities, such as Jerry Garcia and Kathy Griffin. 140 units. 7 stories, interior corridors. **Parking:** valet only. **Amenities:** *Some:* safes. **Activities:** bicycles, exercise room, massage. **Guest Services:** valet laundry.

HOTEL UNION SQUARE   415/397-3000 **75**

♦♦♦
Historic Boutique Hotel

Address: 114 Powell St 94102 **Location:** At Ellis St; just n of cable car turnaround. 🚇 Powell Street, 42. **Facility:** Conveniently located right on the cable car line and bustling Union Square. This hotel has sleek decor and amenities that maximize the use of space in rooms of varying sizes. 131 units. 5 stories, interior corridors. **Parking:** valet only. **Amenities:** *Some:* safes. **Guest Services:** valet laundry, boarding pass kiosk.

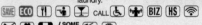

HOTEL VERTIGO   415/885-6800 **35**
♦♦♦ Boutique Hotel. **Address:** 940 Sutter St 94109

HOTEL VITALE, A JOIE DE VIVRE HOTEL
415/278-3700 **32**

♦♦♦
Boutique Hotel

Address: 8 Mission St 94105 **Location:** Waterfront. At The Embarcadero and Mission St. 🚇 Embarcadero, 40. **Facility:** Located across from the Ferry Building, this hotel has a modern urban feel and features multiple rooftop terraces with incredible views, plus an array of beautifully appointed guest rooms. 200 units. 8 stories, interior corridors. **Parking:** valet only. **Amenities:** safes. **Dining:** Americano Restaurant & Bar, see separate listing. **Activities:** exercise room, spa. **Guest Services:** valet laundry.

HOTEL WHITCOMB SAN FRANCISCO
415/626-8000 **89**

♦♦♦
Historic Hotel

Address: 1231 Market St 94103 **Location:** Between 7th and 8th sts. 🚇 Civic Center/UN Plaza, 43. **Facility:** After the 1906 earthquake, this San Francisco classic once served as City Hall from 1912-1915. Ask for a tour of the old jail cells in the basement. 459 units. 8 stories, interior corridors. **Parking:** valet only. **Amenities:** safes. **Activities:** exercise room. **Guest Services:** valet laundry.

HOTEL ZELOS   415/348-1111 **82**

♦♦♦
Hotel

Address: 12 4th St 94103 **Location:** At Market St. 🚇 Powell Street, 42. **Facility:** 202 units. 5 stories, interior corridors. **Parking:** valet only. **Amenities:** safes. **Activities:** exercise room, massage. **Guest Services:** valet laundry.

HOTEL ZEPHYR   415/617-6565 **3**
♦♦♦ Hotel. **Address:** 250 Beach St 94133

HOTEL ZEPPELIN SAN FRANCISCO   415/563-0303 **50**
♦♦♦ Historic Boutique Hotel. **Address:** 545 Post St 94102

HOTEL ZETTA   415/543-8555 **87**
♦♦♦ Boutique Contemporary Hotel. **Address:** 55 5th St 94103

HOTEL ZOE FISHERMAN'S WHARF   415/561-1100 **9**

♦♦♦
Hotel

Address: 425 North Point St 94133 **Location:** Just s of Fisherman's Wharf at Mason St. 🚇 Chinatown, 126. **Facility:** 221 units. 4 stories, interior corridors. **Parking:** valet only. **Amenities:** safes. **Dining:** Cafe Pescatore, see separate listing. **Guest Services:** valet laundry.

HUNTINGTON HOTEL   415/474-5400 **22**

♦♦♦
Hotel

Address: 1075 California St 94108 **Location:** Atop Nob Hill; corner of California and Taylor sts. 🚇 Chinatown, 126. **Facility:** This hotel was gorgeously renovated in 2014 with decor befitting its unforgettable name. A variety of room types and styles is available; all have lots of space, ample seating and upscale furnishing. 134 units. 12 stories, interior corridors. **Parking:** valet only. **Amenities:** safes. **Dining:** Big 4 Restaurant, see separate listing. **Pool:** heated indoor. **Activities:** sauna, hot tub, steamroom, trails, exercise room, spa. **Guest Services:** valet laundry, area transportation. Affiliated with Preferred Hotels & Resorts.

HYATT CENTRIC FISHERMAN'S WHARF
415/563-1234 **7**

♦♦♦
Hotel

HYATT CENTRIC

AAA Benefit: Members save up to 10%!

Address: 555 North Point St 94133 **Location:** Just s of Fisherman's Wharf at Taylor St. 🚇 Chinatown, 126. **Facility:** 316 units. 5 stories, interior corridors. **Parking:** valet only. **Amenities:** safes. **Pool:** heated outdoor. **Activities:** hot tub, exercise room. **Guest Services:** valet and coin laundry.

(See maps & indexes p. 298, 308.)

HYATT PLACE
415/767-2000 **94**

Hotel

AAA Benefit: Members save up to 10%!

Address: 701 3rd St 94107 **Location:** Corner of 3rd St. 2nd & King, 92. **Facility:** 230 units. 11 stories, interior corridors. **Parking:** valet only. **Terms:** off-site registration. **Amenities:** safes. **Activities:** exercise room. **Guest Services:** valet laundry.

HYATT REGENCY SAN FRANCISCO
415/788-1234 **27**

Hotel

HYATT REGENCY
AAA Benefit: Members save up to 10%!

Address: 5 Embarcadero Center 94111 **Location:** Foot of California and Market sts; in Financial District. Embarcadero, 40. **Facility:** 806 units. 17 stories, interior corridors. **Parking:** valet only. **Terms:** check-in 4 pm. **Amenities:** safes. **Activities:** trails, exercise room. **Guest Services:** valet laundry, boarding pass kiosk, rental car service.

INN AT GOLDEN GATE
415/567-2425 **1**

Motel

Address: 2707 Lombard St 94123 **Location:** Between Lyon and Baker sts. **Facility:** 23 units. 2 stories (no elevator), exterior corridors. **Parking:** on-site and street. **Amenities:** safes. **Featured Amenity: continental breakfast.**

INN AT THE OPERA
415/863-8400 **15**

Hotel. **Address:** 333 Fulton St 94102

THE INN AT UNION SQUARE
415/397-3510 **52**

Boutique Hotel

Address: 440 Post St 94102 **Location:** Between Powell and Mason sts; just w of Union Square. Union Sq/Market St, 125. **Facility:** This petite, charming European-style hotel offers such personalized services as an evening wine and cheese hour, fresh-baked cookies and milk and dinner room service from Morton's Steakhouse. 30 units. 6 stories, interior corridors. *Bath:* shower only. **Parking:** valet only. **Amenities:** safes. **Guest Services:** valet laundry. **Featured Amenity: continental breakfast.**

INN ON BROADWAY
415/776-7900 **15**

Motel. **Address:** 2201 Van Ness Ave 94109

INTERCONTINENTAL MARK HOPKINS SAN FRANCISCO
415/392-3434 **23**

Historic Hotel

Address: One Nob Hill 94108 **Location:** Corner of California and Mason sts. Chinatown, 126. **Facility:** This historic Nob Hill hotel is notable for its panoramic views and upscale, elegantly furnished rooms, which feature a unique décor, excellent bedding and large workstations. 383 units, some two bedrooms. 17 stories, interior corridors. **Parking:** valet only. **Amenities:** safes. **Dining:** entertainment. **Activities:** trails, exercise room, massage. **Guest Services:** valet laundry, area transportation.

INTERCONTINENTAL SAN FRANCISCO
415/616-6500 **88**

Contemporary Hotel

Address: 888 Howard St 94103 **Location:** Between 4th and 5th sts; in SoMa District. Adjacent to Moscone West Convention Center. Yerba Buena/Moscone, 124. **Facility:** Natural light showcases this contemporary hotel's upscale, residential-style décor. Floor-to-ceiling windows afford most guest rooms a beautiful view. 556 units. 32 stories, interior corridors. **Parking:** valet only. **Amenities:** safes. **Dining:** Luce, see separate listing. **Pool:** heated indoor. **Activities:** hot tub, exercise room. **Guest Services:** valet laundry, boarding pass kiosk, area transportation.

JW MARRIOTT SAN FRANCISCO
415/771-8600 **49**

Hotel

JW MARRIOTT
AAA Benefit: Members save 5% or more!

Address: 515 Mason St 94102 **Location:** Just w of Union Square at Mason St. Union Sq/Market St, 125. **Facility:** Designed by John Portman, this landmark property is situated in an excellent location for exploring the city. Rooms are spacious, comfortable and most have excellent city views. 344 units. 21 stories, interior corridors. **Parking:** valet only. **Terms:** check-in 4 pm. **Amenities:** safes. **Activities:** exercise room, massage. **Guest Services:** valet laundry, boarding pass kiosk.

KENSINGTON PARK HOTEL
415/788-6400 **51**

Hotel

Address: 450 Post St 94102 **Location:** Just w of Union Square. Union Sq/Market St, 125. **Facility:** 93 units. 8 stories, interior corridors. **Parking:** valet only. **Amenities:** safes. **Dining:** Farallon, see separate listing. **Guest Services:** valet laundry.

(See maps & indexes p. 298, 308.)

KIMPTON BUCHANAN HOTEL 415/921-4000 🔟🔟

Hotel

Address: 1800 Sutter St 94115 **Location:** At Sutter and Buchanan sts; 1 blk from Japan Center. 🚇 Van Ness, 60. **Facility:** 131 units. 8 stories, interior corridors. **Parking:** on-site (fee). **Amenities:** safes. **Activities:** bicycles, exercise room. **Guest Services:** valet laundry. Affiliated with Kimpton Hotels.

SAVE 🍴 CALL 🚻 📶
✖ 🎦 🛏 💻 / SOME UNITS 🐾 🚌

KIMPTON SIR FRANCIS DRAKE HOTEL 415/392-7755 🔟🔟

Historic Hotel

Address: 450 Powell St 94102 **Location:** Just n of Union Square at Sutter St. 🚇 Union Sq/Market St, 125. **Facility:** In a historic building offering the charm of a bygone era, this property is centrally located at Union Square. Rooms feature upscale bedding and attractive custom furnishings. 416 units. 21 stories, interior corridors. **Parking:** valet only. **Amenities:** safes. **Dining:** Scala's Bistro, see separate listing, nightclub, entertainment. **Activities:** bicycles, exercise room, massage. **Guest Services:** valet laundry.

SAVE ECO 🍴 🛎 🍸 CALL 🚻 📶 BIZ 📶 ✖
🎦 / SOME UNITS 🐾 🛏 🚌

KING GEORGE HOTEL 415/781-5050 🔟🔟

Hotel

Address: 334 Mason St 94102 **Location:** Just w of Union Square. 🚇 Union Sq/Market St, 125. **Facility:** 153 units. 9 stories, interior corridors. **Parking:** valet only. **Amenities:** safes. **Guest Services:** valet laundry.

SAVE ECO 🍴 🛎 🍸 CALL 🚻
BIZ 📶 ✖ 💻
/ SOME UNITS 🐾 🎦 🛏 💻 🚌

LA LUNA INN 415/346-4664 🔟

Motel

Address: 2599 Lombard St 94123 **Location:** US 101 at Broderick St. **Facility:** 62 units. 2-3 stories, exterior corridors. **Featured Amenity:** continental breakfast.

SAVE 🍴 CALL 🚻 BIZ 📶 ✖
💻 / SOME UNITS 🛏

THE LAUREL INN 415/567-8467 🔟🔟

Hotel

Address: 444 Presidio Ave 94115 **Location:** At California St. **Facility:** 49 units. 4 stories, interior corridors. **Parking:** on-site (fee). **Amenities:** safes. **Activities:** bicycles. **Guest Services:** valet laundry. Affiliated with Joie de Vivre Hotels & Resorts.

SAVE 🍴 🍸 CALL 🚻 BIZ 📶
✖ 🛏 / SOME UNITS 🐾 🎦 💻

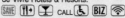
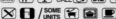

LE MERIDIEN SAN FRANCISCO 415/296-2900 🔟🔟

 SAVE Hotel. **Address:** 333 Battery St 94111

AAA Benefit:
Members save 5% or more!

LOEWS REGENCY SAN FRANCISCO 415/276-9888 🔟🔟

Hotel

Address: 222 Sansome St 94104 **Location:** Between Pine and California sts; in Financial District. 🚇 Embarcadero, 40. **Facility:** Guests will enjoy spectacular views of the city, the bridges, Alcatraz and the bay from this elegant and sophisticated hotel. Guest rooms start on the 38th floor, all affording great views. 155 units. 38-48 stories, interior corridors. **Parking:** on-site (fee) and valet. **Amenities:** safes. **Activities:** exercise room, spa. **Guest Services:** valet laundry, area transportation.

SAVE 🍴 🍸 🏋
CALL 🚻 📶 BIZ HS 📶 ✖ 🎦 🛏
/ SOME UNITS 🐾 🚌

LOMBARD INN 415/441-6000 🔟🔟

 Hotel. **Address:** 1475 Lombard St 94123

LOMBARD PLAZA MOTEL 415/921-2444 🔟

Motel

Address: 2026 Lombard St 94123 **Location:** On US 101 (Van Ness Ave). **Facility:** 29 units. 2-3 stories (no elevator), exterior corridors.

SAVE 🍴 📶 ✖ 🛏 💻 💻

MARINA MOTEL 415/921-9406 🔟

Motel. **Address:** 2576 Lombard St 94123

THE MARKER SAN FRANCISCO 415/292-0100 🔟🔟

Hotel. **Address:** 501 Geary St 94102

MARRIOTT MARQUIS SAN FRANCISCO 415/896-1600 🔟🔟

Contemporary Hotel

MARRIOTT

AAA Benefit:
Members save 5% or more!

Address: 780 Mission St 94103 **Location:** Corner of Mission and 4th sts. 🚇 Powell Street, 42. **Facility:** 1500 units. 39 stories, interior corridors. **Parking:** valet only. **Terms:** check-in 4 pm. **Amenities:** safes. **Dining:** 2 restaurants. **Activities:** steamroom, health club, massage. **Guest Services:** valet laundry, boarding pass kiosk.

SAVE ECO 🍴 🍸 CALL 🚻
📶 BIZ sHS 📶 ✖ 🎦 🛏 💻 💻 🚌

MARRIOTT VACATION CLUB PULSE, SAN FRANCISCO 415/885-4700 🔟

 SAVE Hotel. **Address:** 2620 Jones St 94133

AAA Benefit:
Members save 5% or more!

NOB HILL MOTOR INN 415/775-8160 🔟

 Motel. **Address:** 1630 Pacific Ave 94109

(See maps & indexes p. 298, 308.)

OMNI SAN FRANCISCO HOTEL 415/677-9494 25

Hotel

Address: 500 California St 94104 **Location:** At Montgomery St; in Financial District. Montgomery Street, 41. **Facility:** Located in the heart of the Financial District, but walkable to Chinatown and North Beach, this hotel offers spacious, elegantly appointed guest rooms and public areas. 362 units. 17 stories, interior corridors. **Parking:** valet only. **Amenities:** safes. **Activities:** exercise room. **Guest Services:** valet laundry, area transportation.

THE ORCHARD GARDEN HOTEL 415/399-9807 36

Hotel

Address: 466 Bush St 94108 **Location:** At Grant Ave. Union Sq/Market St, 125. **Facility:** 86 units. 10 stories, interior corridors. **Parking:** valet only. **Amenities:** safes. **Activities:** exercise room. **Guest Services:** valet laundry, area transportation.

THE ORCHARD HOTEL 415/362-8878 34
Hotel. **Address:** 665 Bush St 94108

PALACE HOTEL, A LUXURY COLLECTION 415/512-1111 66
Historic Hotel. **Address:** 2 New Montgomery St 94105
AAA Benefit: Members save 5% or more!

PARC 55 - A HILTON HOTEL 415/392-8000 80

Hotel

AAA Benefit: Members save up to 15%!

Address: 55 Cyril Magnin St 94102 **Location:** Corner of Cyril Magnin and Eddy sts; just sw of Union Square. Powell Street, 42. **Facility:** 1024 units. 32 stories, interior corridors. **Parking:** valet only. **Amenities:** safes. **Dining:** Kin Khao Thai Eatery, see separate listing. **Activities:** exercise room, massage. **Guest Services:** valet laundry, boarding pass kiosk.

PARK CENTRAL HOTEL SAN FRANCISCO 415/974-6400 76

Hotel

Address: 50 3rd St 94103 **Location:** Just n of Moscone Convention Center; between Jessie and Stevenson sts. Montgomery Street, 41. **Facility:** 681 units. 36 stories, interior corridors. **Parking:** valet only. **Terms:** off-site registration. **Amenities:** safes. **Activities:** bicycles, exercise room. **Guest Services:** valet laundry, boarding pass kiosk.

PETITE AUBERGE 415/928-6000 29
Historic Hotel. **Address:** 863 Bush St 94108

PHOENIX HOTEL 415/776-1380 78
Boutique Hotel. **Address:** 601 Eddy St 94109

REDWOOD INN 415/776-3800 8

Motel

Address: 1530 Lombard St 94123 **Location:** US 101 (Lombard St); between Franklin and Gough sts. **Facility:** 33 units. 2-4 stories, exterior corridors. **Guest Services:** coin laundry.

THE RITZ-CARLTON, SAN FRANCISCO 415/296-7465 26
Classic Hotel. **Address:** 600 Stockton St 94108
AAA Benefit: Unequaled service at special member savings!

THE ST. REGIS SAN FRANCISCO 415/284-4000 83

Hotel

ST REGIS
HOTELS & RESORTS

AAA Benefit: Members save 5% or more!

Address: 125 3rd St 94103 **Location:** At Mission St. Montgomery Street, 41. **Facility:** This handsome, sophisticated hotel has a warm and inviting lobby fireplace. Rooms feature superb bedding, outstanding marble baths with rain shower heads and deep soaking tubs. 260 units. 20 stories, interior corridors. **Parking:** valet only. **Amenities:** safes. **Pool:** heated indoor. **Activities:** sauna, hot tub, steamroom, exercise room, spa. **Guest Services:** valet laundry, area transportation.

SAN FRANCISCO MARRIOTT FISHERMAN'S WHARF 415/775-7555 6
Hotel. **Address:** 1250 Columbus Ave 94133
AAA Benefit: Members save 5% or more!

SAN FRANCISCO MARRIOTT UNION SQUARE 415/398-8900 40

Hotel

MARRIOTT

AAA Benefit: Members save 5% or more!

Address: 480 Sutter St 94108 **Location:** Just n of Union Square; corner of Powell St. Union Sq/Market St, 125. **Facility:** 400 units. 30 stories, interior corridors. **Parking:** valet only. **Terms:** check-in 4 pm. **Amenities:** Some: safes. **Activities:** exercise room. **Guest Services:** valet laundry, boarding pass kiosk.

(See maps & indexes p. 298, 308.)

SHERATON FISHERMAN'S WHARF   415/362-5500   8

Contemporary Hotel

AAA Benefit: Members save 5% or more!

SHERATON

Address: 2500 Mason St 94133 **Location:** Just se of Fisherman's Wharf at Beach St. Chinatown, 126. **Facility:** 531 units. 4 stories, interior corridors. **Parking:** on-site (fee) and valet. **Amenities:** safes. **Pool:** heated outdoor. **Activities:** trails, exercise room. **Guest Services:** valet laundry, boarding pass kiosk, rental car service.

STANFORD COURT HOTEL   415/989-3500   24

Hotel

Address: 905 California St 94108 **Location:** Atop Nob Hill; corner of California and Powell sts. Chinatown, 126. **Facility:** This service-oriented hotel caters to the tech-savvy crowd, and offers sweeping views of the city's famous skyline from some guest rooms. Rooms are decorative with an abundance of space and seating. 393 units. 8 stories, interior corridors. **Parking:** valet only. **Terms:** check-in 4 pm. **Amenities:** safes. **Activities:** bicycles, exercise room, massage. **Guest Services:** valet laundry, boarding pass kiosk, area transportation.

STAYPINEAPPLE, AN ELEGANT HOTEL, UNION SQUARE, SAN FRANCISCO   415/441-2700   56

Hotel. **Address:** 580 Geary St 94102

TAJ CAMPTON PLACE   415/781-5555   47

Classic Hotel

Address: 340 Stockton St 94108 **Location:** Just n of Union Square; jct Sutter St. Union Sq/Market St, 125. **Facility:** Located in the 1907 Haslett Warehouse, this stylish hotel showcases its historic architecture. There are a variety of room types; all include upscale decor with excellent beds and unique furnishings. 110 units. 15 stories, interior corridors. **Parking:** valet only. **Amenities:** safes. **Dining:** Campton Place Restaurant, see separate listing. **Activities:** exercise room, massage. **Guest Services:** valet laundry, area transportation.

TILDEN HOTEL   415/673-2332   69

Hotel

Address: 345 Taylor St 94102 **Location:** Just w of Union Square. Powell Street, 42. **Facility:** 118 units. 8 stories, interior corridors. **Parking:** valet only. **Amenities:** safes. **Dining:** 2 restaurants. **Activities:** lawn sports, limited exercise equipment. **Guest Services:** valet laundry. **Featured Amenity:** continental breakfast.

TRAVELODGE BY THE BAY   415/673-0691   12

Motel

Address: 1450 Lombard St 94123 **Location:** On US 101 (Lombard St); between Van Ness Ave and Franklin St. **Facility:** 70 units, some two bedrooms, efficiencies and kitchens. 2-3 stories, interior/exterior corridors. **Parking:** on-site (fee). **Amenities:** safes. **Guest Services:** coin laundry. **Featured Amenity:** continental breakfast.

VILLA FLORENCE   415/397-7700   64

Hotel

Address: 225 Powell St 94102 **Location:** Just s of Union Square; between O'Farrell and Geary sts. Union Sq/Market St, 125. **Facility:** 189 units. 7 stories, interior corridors. **Parking:** valet only. **Amenities:** safes. **Activities:** exercise room. **Guest Services:** valet laundry.

WARWICK SAN FRANCISCO HOTEL   415/928-7900   58

Hotel

Address: 490 Geary St 94102 **Location:** Between Taylor and Mason sts. Union Sq/Market St, 125. **Facility:** 74 units. 8 stories, interior corridors. **Parking:** valet only. **Amenities:** safes. **Guest Services:** valet laundry.

THE WESTIN ST. FRANCIS SAN FRANCISCO ON UNION SQUARE   415/397-7000   61

Hotel

WESTIN
HOTELS & RESORTS

AAA Benefit: Members save 5% or more!

Address: 335 Powell St 94102 **Location:** Across from Union Square. Union Sq/Market St, 125. **Facility:** With a commanding location fronting Union Square, this upscale, historic hotel is noted for its comfortable beds and high-standards of service. 1195 units. 32 stories, interior corridors. **Parking:** valet only. **Terms:** check-in 4 pm. **Amenities:** safes. **Dining:** 2 restaurants. **Activities:** exercise room, spa. **Guest Services:** valet laundry.

WHITE SWAN INN   415/775-1755   30
Historic Hotel. **Address:** 845 Bush St 94108

AAA.com/maps—

Dream, plan, go with

AAA travel planning tools

(See maps & indexes p. 298, 308.)

W SAN FRANCISCO 415/777-5300 (85)

Contemporary Hotel

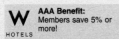

AAA Benefit: Members save 5% or more!

Address: 181 3rd St 94103 **Location:** At Howard St. 🚇 Yerba Buena/Moscone, 124. **Facility:** This ultra-contemporary facility offers "cool" luxury in all respects. The guest units are housed in a 31-story modern high-rise located near the Museum of Modern Art and Moscone Convention Center. 404 units. 31 stories, interior corridors. **Parking:** valet only. **Amenities:** safes. **Activities:** bicycles, health club. **Guest Services:** valet laundry, area transportation. **Featured Amenity:** full hot breakfast.

🆂🅰🆅🅴 ⓔⓒⓞ 🍴 🎣 🍸 CALL 🦽 ♨ 🅱🅸🆉 🆂🅷🆂 📶
✕ 🎦 🛗 💻 /SOME UNITS 🐾 🍽 🖨

WHERE TO EAT

1300 ON FILLMORE 415/771-7100 (49)
🔻🔻 Soul Food. Fine Dining. **Address:** 1300 Fillmore St 94115

1601 BAR & KITCHEN 415/552-1601 (99)
🔻🔻🔻 New Asian Small Plates. Gastropub. **Address:** 1601 Howard St 94103

1760 415/359-1212 (51)
🔻🔻🔻 California Small Plates. Casual Dining. **Address:** 1760 Polk St 94109

21ST AMENDMENT 415/369-0900 (151)
🔻🔻 American. Casual Dining. **Address:** 563 2nd St 94107

4505 BURGERS & BBQ 415/231-6993 (52)
🔻 American. Quick Serve. **Address:** 705 Divisadero St 94112

54 MINT 415/543-5100 (145)
🔻🔻🔻 Italian. Casual Dining. **Address:** 16 Mint Plaza 94103

A 16 415/771-2216 (2)
🔻🔻🔻 Italian. Casual Dining. **Address:** 2355 Chestnut St 94123

ABSINTHE BRASSERIE AND BAR 415/551-1590 (60)
🔻🔻🔻 French. Casual Dining. **Address:** 398 Hayes St 94102

ACQUERELLO 415/567-5432 (63)
🔻🔻🔻🔻 Italian. Fine Dining. **Address:** 1722 Sacramento St 94109

AICHA MOROCCAN CUISINE 415/345-9947 (84)
🔻🔻 Moroccan. Casual Dining. **Address:** 1303 Polk St 94109

'ĀINA 415/814-3815 (157)
🔻🔻🔻 Hawaiian. Casual Dining. **Address:** 900 22nd St 94107

AKIKO'S RESTAURANT 415/397-3218 (101)
🔻🔻🔻 Japanese Sushi. Casual Dining. **Address:** 431 Bush St 94108

ALBORZ 415/440-4321 (92)
🔻🔻🔻 Middle Eastern. Casual Dining. **Address:** 1245 Van Ness Ave 94109

THE ALEMBIC 415/666-0822 (67)
🔻🔻🔻 California Small Plates. Gastropub. **Address:** 1725 Haight St 94117

ALEXANDER'S STEAKHOUSE 415/495-1111 (157)
🔻🔻🔻🔻 ◆◆

Steak Fine Dining $52-$165

AAA Inspector Notes: Offering an array of the highest quality meats and produce are the key elements in delivering the memorable culinary delights here. Beef is sourced from small farms from the US, Australia and Japan, notably serving authentic Kobe beef. The Chef's table makes for a unique dining experience. **Features:** full bar. **Reservations:** suggested. **Address:** 448 Brannan St 94107 **Location:** Between 3rd and 4th sts. 🚇 4th & Brannan, 123. **Parking:** valet and street only. Ⓓ CALL 🦽 🖨

ALIOTO'S 415/673-0183 (4)
🔻🔻🔻 Seafood. Casual Dining. **Address:** 8 Fisherman's Wharf 94133

A MANO 415/506-7401 (56)
🔻🔻 Italian. Casual Dining. **Address:** 450 Hayes St 94102

AMARENA 415/447-0441 (26)
🔻🔻 Italian. Casual Dining. **Address:** 2162 Larkin St 94109

THE AMERICAN GRILLED CHEESE KITCHEN 415/243-0107 (152)
🔻 American. Quick Serve. **Address:** 1 S Park Ave 94107

AMERICANO RESTAURANT & BAR 415/278-3777 (97)
🔻🔻🔻 Northern Italian. Casual Dining. **Address:** 8 Mission St 94105

ANZU RESTAURANT 415/394-1100 (133)
🔻🔻🔻 Pacific Rim. Fine Dining. **Address:** 222 Mason St 94102

ASLAM'S RASOI 415/695-0599 (145)
🔻🔻 Indian. Casual Dining. **Address:** 1037 Valencia St 94110

ASTER 415/875-9810 (149)
🔻🔻🔻 California. Casual Dining. **Address:** 1001 Guerrero St 94110

ATELIER CRENN 415/440-0460 (9)
🔻🔻🔻🔻 New French. Fine Dining. **Address:** 3127 Filmore St 94123

BAKER STREET BISTRO 415/931-1475 (5)
🔻🔻 French. Casual Dining. **Address:** 2953 Baker St 94123

BALBOA CAFE 415/921-3944 (8)
🔻🔻🔻 American. Casual Dining. **Address:** 3199 Fillmore St 94123

BAR AGRICOLE 415/355-9400 (100)
🔻🔻🔻 California. Gastropub. **Address:** 355 11th St 94103

BAR CRUDO 415/409-0679 (53)
🔻🔻🔻 Seafood. Casual Dining. **Address:** 655 Divisadero St 94117

BASIL THAI RESTAURANT & BAR 415/552-8999 (164)
🔻🔻 Thai. Fine Dining. **Address:** 1175 Folsom St 94103

BEACH CHALET BREWERY AND RESTAURANT 415/386-8439 (37)
🔻🔻🔻 American. Casual Dining. **Address:** 1000 Great Hwy 94121

BELGA 415/872-7350 (11)
🔻🔻🔻 Belgian. Casual Dining. **Address:** 2000 Union St 94123

BELLOTA 415/430-6580 (104)
🔻🔻🔻 Spanish Small Plates. Casual Dining. **Address:** 888 Brannan St 94103

BENU 415/685-4860 (142)
🔻🔻🔻🔻🔻 New American. Fine Dining. **Address:** 22 Hawthorne St 94105

(See maps & indexes p. 298, 308.)

BERETTA   415/695-1199 (152)
♥♥♥ Italian. Gastropub. **Address:** 1199 Valencia St 94110

BIG 4 RESTAURANT   415/771-1140 (73)
♥♥♥♥ California. Fine Dining. **Address:** 1075 California St 94108

BISTRO BOUDIN AT THE WHARF   415/351-5561 (10)
♥♥♥ Seafood. Casual Dining. **Address:** 160 Jefferson St 94133

BIX   415/433-6300 (55)
♥♥♥ Continental. Fine Dining. **Address:** 56 Gold St 94133

BLACKWOOD   415/931-9663 (3)
♥♥ Thai Fusion. Casual Dining. **Address:** 2150 Chestnut St 94123

BLUE BOTTLE CAFE   415/495-3394 (147)
♥ American. Quick Serve. **Address:** 66 Mint St 94103

BLUE MERMAID CHOWDER HOUSE & BAR
                                       415/771-2222 (8)
♥♥♥ Seafood. Casual Dining. **Address:** 471 Jefferson St 94109

BOBOQUIVARIS   415/441-8880 (17)
♥♥♥ Steak Seafood. Casual Dining. **Address:** 1450 Lombard St 94123

BOROBUDUR RESTAURANT   415/775-1512 (111)
♥♥ Indonesian. Casual Dining. **Address:** 700 Post St 94109

BOUDIN BAKERY & CAFE   415/928-1849
♥ Soup Sandwiches. Quick Serve. **Address:** 160 Jefferson St 94133

BOULETTES LARDER   415/399-1155 (77)
♥♥ California. Casual Dining. **Address:** 1 Ferry Building Marketplace 94111

BOULEVARD   415/543-6084 (95)
♥♥♥♥ American. Fine Dining. **Address:** 1 Mission St 94105

B. PATISSERIE   415/440-1700 (28)
♥ Breads/Pastries Desserts. Quick Serve. **Address:** 2821 California St 94115

BRENDA'S FRENCH SOUL FOOD   415/345-8100 (138)
♥♥ Creole. Casual Dining. **Address:** 652 Polk St 94102

THE BUENA VISTA CAFE   415/474-5044 (13)
♥♥ American. Casual Dining. **Address:** 2765 Hyde St 94109

BURMA SUPERSTAR   415/387-2147 (30)
♥♥ Burmese. Casual Dining. **Address:** 309 Clement St 94118

BURSA MEDITERRANEAN CUISINE   415/564-4006 (161)
♥♥ Mediterranean. Casual Dining. **Address:** 60 W Portal Ave 94127

CAFE BAKERY & RESTAURANT   415/661-6136 (107)
♥♥ International Comfort Food. Casual Dining. **Address:** 1345 Noriega St 94122

CAFE CLAUDE   415/392-3505 (105)
♥♥♥ French. Casual Dining. **Address:** 7 Claude Ln 94108

CAFE JACQUELINE   415/981-5565 (29)
♥♥♥ French. Fine Dining. **Address:** 1454 Grant Ave 94133

CAFE PESCATORE   415/561-1111 (16)
♥♥ Italian. Casual Dining. **Address:** 2455 Mason St 94133

CAFE TIRAMISU   415/421-7044 (96)
♥♥♥ Italian. Casual Dining. **Address:** 28 Belden Pl 94104

CAFE ZOETROPE   415/291-1700 (53)
♥♥ Southern Italian. Casual Dining. **Address:** 916 Kearny St 94133

CALA   415/660-7701 (153)
♥♥♥ Mexican Small Plates Seafood. Casual Dining. **Address:** 149 Fell St 94102

CALZONE'S   415/397-3600 (34)
♥♥ Italian. Casual Dining. **Address:** 430 Columbus Ave 94133

CAMPTON PLACE RESTAURANT   415/938-3821 (114)

◆◆ ◆◆◆
California
Fusion
Fine Dining
$39-$155

AAA Inspector Notes: Inventive, eclectic Californian dishes showcase Indian influences with unforgettable flavors. Artful presentations distinguish each selection in an intimate, elegant atmosphere. Four- and seven-course tasting menus are offered at dinner. Don't miss the shrikhand dessert, if offered, when you are there. **Features:** full bar, Sunday brunch. **Reservations:** suggested. **Address:** 340 Stockton St 94108 **Location:** Just n of Union Square; jct Sutter St; in Taj Campton Place. 🅿 Union Sq/Market St, 125. **Parking:** valet only.

[B] [L] [D] [🅿]

CAPO'S CHICAGO PIZZA & FINE ITALIAN DINNERS
                                       415/986-8998 (37)
♥♥ Italian Pizza. Casual Dining. **Address:** 641 Vallejo St 94133

CAPURRO'S RESTAURANT & BAR   415/771-9371 (5)
♥♥ Italian. Casual Dining. **Address:** 498 Jefferson St 94109

CASTAGNOLA'S   415/776-5015 (9)

◆◆
Italian
Seafood
Casual Dining
$12-$40

AAA Inspector Notes: Classic. Since 1916, this established eatery has prepared Italian specialties, along with many seafood selections. The view overlooks the boat marina. **Features:** full bar, patio dining, happy hour. **Address:** 286 Jefferson St 94133 **Location:** 1 blk w of Fisherman's Wharf; at Jones St. **Parking:** on-site (fee). [L] [D]

CATCH   415/431-5000 (112)
♥♥♥ Mediterranean. Casual Dining. **Address:** 2362 Market St 94114

THE CAVALIER   415/321-6000 (143)
♥♥♥ British. Gastropub. **Address:** 360 Jessie St 94103

CENTRAL KITCHEN   415/826-7004 (143)
♥♥♥ California. Casual Dining. **Address:** 3000 20th St 94110

CESARIO'S FINE FOOD   415/441-9898 (104)
♥♥ Northern Italian. Casual Dining. **Address:** 601 Sutter St 94102

CHA-AM THAI RESTAURANT BAR & GRILL
                                       415/546-9711 (148)
♥♥ Thai. Casual Dining. **Address:** 701 Folsom St 94107

CHA-YA VEGETARIAN JAPANESE RESTAURANT
                                       415/252-7825 (134)
♥♥ Japanese Vegetarian. Casual Dining. **Address:** 762 Valencia St 94110

CHIEF SULLIVAN'S   415/722-9109 (31)
♥♥ Irish. Casual Dining. **Address:** 622 Green St 94133

CHILE PIES & ICE CREAM   415/614-9411 (51)
♥ American. Quick Serve. **Address:** 601 Baker St 94117

CHOW   415/552-2469 (102)
♥♥ American. Casual Dining. **Address:** 215 Church St 94114

(See maps & indexes p. 298, 308.)

CIOPPINO'S ON THE WHARF   415/775-9311   6
♥♥ Italian Seafood. Casual Dining. **Address:** 400 Jefferson St 94109

CLAY OVEN INDIAN CUISINE   415/826-2400   166
♥♥ Indian. Casual Dining. **Address:** 1689 Church St 94131

CLIFF HOUSE - SUTRO'S   415/386-3330   15

♥♥♥
American Fine Dining $23-$48

AAA Inspector Notes: In the Sutro wing of the historic Cliff House, this restaurant is perched above Ocean Beach. Take the elevator down to the restaurant. As the door opens guests enter the waiting area showcasing the open kitchen. The contemporary dining room features ceiling-to-floor panoramic views of the Pacific. The most memorable dining experience is at sunset with the orange sun setting, the sky changing from blue to pink to purple, and finally, twinkling stars appearing in the sky. **Features:** full bar, Sunday brunch. **Reservations:** suggested. **Address:** 1090 Point Lobos Ave 94121 **Location:** At Ocean Beach. **Parking:** valet and street only.   L   D

CLIFF HOUSE-THE BISTRO   415/386-3330   16

♥♥
American Casual Dining $13-$40

AAA Inspector Notes: On the upper level of the historic Cliff House, this restaurant is perched above Seal Rock and the ocean. The casual restaurant features a menu of classics such as omelets, soups, sandwiches and full entrées. The complimentary popovers are addictive. **Features:** full bar, Sunday brunch. **Address:** 1090 Point Lobos Ave 94121 **Location:** At Ocean Beach. **Parking:** street only.

B   L   D

COCKSCOMB   415/974-0700   158
♥♥♥ New American. Fine Dining. **Address:** 564 4th St 94107

COI   415/393-9000   43
♥♥♥♥ California. Fine Dining. **Address:** 373 Broadway St 94133

COLIBRI MEXICAN-BISTRO   415/440-2737   125
♥♥ Mexican. Casual Dining. **Address:** 438 Geary St 94102

COMMONWEALTH   415/355-1500   133
♥♥♥ California. Casual Dining. **Address:** 2224 Mission St 94110

COMSTOCK SALOON   415/617-0071   48
♥♥ American. Gastropub. **Address:** 155 Columbus Ave 94133

COTOGNA   415/775-8508   49
♥♥♥ Italian. Casual Dining. **Address:** 490 Pacific Ave 94133

CRAB HOUSE AT PIER 39   415/434-2722   14
♥♥ Seafood. Casual Dining. **Address:** 203 C Pier 39 94133

CRAFTSMAN AND WOLVES   415/913-7713   132
♥ Breads/Pastries. Quick Serve. **Address:** 746 Valencia St 94110

CRAW STATION   415/682-9980   88
♥♥ Seafood. Casual Dining. **Address:** 1336 9th Ave 94122

CRUSTACEAN RESTAURANT   415/776-2722   68
♥♥ Asian. Fine Dining. **Address:** 1475 Polk St 94109

DAILY GRILL   415/616-5000
♥♥ American. Casual Dining. **Address:** 347 Geary St 94102

DELFINA   415/552-4055   125
♥♥♥ Italian. Casual Dining. **Address:** 3621 18th St 94110

DELI BOARD   415/552-7687   155
♥ Sandwiches. Quick Serve. **Address:** 1058 Folsom St 94103

DELICA RF-1   415/834-0344   79
♥ Japanese. Quick Serve. **Address:** 1 Ferry Bldg, Suite 45 94111

DEL POPOLO   415/589-7940   91
♥♥ Pizza. Casual Dining. **Address:** 855 Bush St 94108

DESTINO   415/552-4451   94
♥♥ New Latin American Small Plates. Casual Dining. **Address:** 1815 Market St 94103

DOSA ON VALENCIA   415/642-3672   141
♥♥ Southern Indian. Casual Dining. **Address:** 995 Valencia St 94110

DRAGON BEAUX   415/333-8899   24
♥♥ Chinese Dim Sum. Casual Dining. **Address:** 5700 Geary Blvd 94121

E & O ASIAN KITCHEN   415/693-0303   108
♥♥ Asian. Casual Dining. **Address:** 314 Sutter St 94108

EATS   415/751-8000   32
♥♥ American. Casual Dining. **Address:** 50 Clement St 94118

ELIZA'S   415/621-4819   27
♥♥ Mandarin. Casual Dining. **Address:** 2877 California St 94115

EL TORO TAQUERIA   415/431-3351   123
♥ Mexican. Quick Serve. **Address:** 598 Valencia St 94110

ENJOY VEGETARIAN RESTAURANT   415/682-0826   97
♥♥ Chinese Vegetarian Kosher. Casual Dining. **Address:** 754 Kirkham St 94122

ESPETUS CHURRASCARIA   415/552-8792   86
♥♥ Brazilian Barbecue. Casual Dining. **Address:** 1686 Market St 94102

EXTREME PIZZA   415/929-8234
♥ Pizza. Quick Serve. **Address:** 1980 Union St 94123

FARALLON   415/956-6969   118
♥♥♥ Seafood. Fine Dining. **Address:** 450 Post St 94102

FINO BAR & RISTORANTE   415/928-2080   113
♥♥♥ Italian. Fine Dining. **Address:** 624 Post St 94109

FIREWOOD CAFE   415/252-0999   118
♥ Italian. Quick Serve. **Address:** 4248 18th St 94114

FLORIO CAFE AND BAR   415/775-4300   35
♥♥ Continental. Casual Dining. **Address:** 1915 Fillmore St 94115

FLOUR + WATER   415/826-7000   142
♥♥♥ Italian. Casual Dining. **Address:** 2401 Harrison St 94110

THE FLY TRAP   415/243-0580   144
♥♥ American. Casual Dining. **Address:** 606 Folsom St 94107

FOG HARBOR FISH HOUSE   415/421-2442   12
♥♥ Seafood. Casual Dining. **Address:** Pier 39, Suite A202 94133

FOREIGN CINEMA   415/648-7600   147
♥♥♥ California. Fine Dining. **Address:** 2534 Mission St 94110

FRANCES   415/621-3870   114
♥♥♥ California. Casual Dining. **Address:** 3870 17th St 94114

FRANCISCAN CRAB RESTAURANT   415/362-7733   2
♥♥ Seafood. Casual Dining. **Address:** Pier 43 1/2 Embarcadero 94133

(See maps & indexes p. 298, 308.)

FRASCATI 415/928-1406 (25)
🍷🍷 Continental. Fine Dining. **Address:** 1901 Hyde St 94109

FRINGALE 415/543-0573 (159)
🍷🍷 French. Casual Dining. **Address:** 570 4th St 94107

THE GARDEN COURT 415/546-5089 (127)
🍷🍷🍷 American. Fine Dining. **Address:** 2 New Montgomery St 94105

GARIBALDI'S ON PRESIDIO 415/563-8841 (22)
🍷🍷🍷 American. Casual Dining. **Address:** 347 Presidio Ave 94115

GARY DANKO 415/749-2060 (15)

🍷🍷🍷🍷🍷 **AAA Inspector Notes:** This world-renowned restaurant provides a pleasurable culinary adventure that incorporates the cosmopolitan atmosphere of the dining room, the sophistication of the service and the culinary prowess of the namesake chef. **Features:** full bar. **Reservations:** required. Semiformal attire. **Address:** 800 North Point St 94109 **Location:** Just e of Ghirardelli Square at Hyde St. **Parking:** valet only. 〔D〕 CALL 〔♿〕

Continental Fine Dining $98-$139

GIALINA 415/239-8500 (169)
🍷🍷 Pizza. Casual Dining. **Address:** 2842 Diamond St 94131

GIOIA PIZZERIA 415/359-0971 (28)
🍷 Italian Pizza. Casual Dining. **Address:** 2240 Polk St 94109

GOTT'S ROADSIDE 415/318-3423 (81)
🍷 American. Quick Serve. **Address:** 1 Ferry Bldg, Suite 6 94111

GRACIAS MADRE 415/683-1346 (130)
🍷🍷 Mexican Vegan. Casual Dining. **Address:** 2211 Mission St 94110

GREAT EASTERN RESTAURANT 415/986-2500 (56)
🍷 Chinese Dim Sum. Casual Dining. **Address:** 649 Jackson St 94133

GREENS RESTAURANT 415/771-6222 (1)
🍷🍷🍷 Vegetarian. Casual Dining. **Address:** Fort Mason Center, Bldg A 94123

GRINDZ RESTAURANT 415/221-4746 (25)
🍷🍷 Hawaiian. Casual Dining. **Address:** 832 Clement St 94118

GRUBSTAKE 415/673-8268 (76)
🍷🍷 American. Casual Dining. **Address:** 1525 Pine St 94109

HAKKASAN SAN FRANCISCO 415/829-8148 (128)
🍷🍷🍷🍷 Cantonese. Fine Dining. **Address:** 1 Kearny St 94108

HARD KNOX CAFE 415/648-3770 (162)
🍷🍷 Soul Food. Casual Dining. **Address:** 2526 3rd St 94107

HARD KNOX CAFE 415/752-3770 (17)
🍷🍷 Soul Food. Casual Dining. **Address:** 2448 Clement St 94121

HARRIS' 415/673-1888 (39)
🍷🍷🍷 Steak. Fine Dining. **Address:** 2100 Van Ness Ave 94109

HAWKER FARE 415/400-5699 (127)
🍷🍷 Northern Thai. Casual Dining. **Address:** 680 Valencia St 94110

HAYES STREET GRILL 415/863-5545 (59)
🍷🍷🍷 Seafood. Casual Dining. **Address:** 320 Hayes St 94102

HEIRLOOM CAFE 415/821-2500 (148)
🍷🍷🍷 French. Casual Dining. **Address:** 2500 Folsom St 94110

THE HELMAND PALACE 415/345-0072 (22)
🍷🍷 Afghan. Casual Dining. **Address:** 2424 Van Ness Ave 94109

HINODEYA RAMEN BAR 415/757-0552 (38)
🍷🍷 Japanese Noodles. Casual Dining. **Address:** 1737 Buchanan St 94115

HOG ISLAND OYSTER CO. 415/391-7117 (78)
🍷🍷 Seafood. Casual Dining. **Address:** One Ferry Bldg, Suite 11A 94111

HOPS & HOMINY 415/373-6341 (115)
🍷🍷 Southern. Casual Dining. **Address:** 1 Tillman Pl 94108

THE HOUSE 415/986-8612 (41)
🍷🍷🍷 Asian. Casual Dining. **Address:** 1230 Grant Ave 94133

HOUSE OF NANKING 415/421-1429 (52)
🍷🍷 Chinese. Casual Dining. **Address:** 919 Kearny St 94133

HOUSE OF PRIME RIB 415/885-4605 (47)
🍷🍷🍷 American. Casual Dining. **Address:** 1906 Van Ness Ave 94109

THE ICE CREAM BAR 415/742-4932 (90)
🍷 Specialty. Quick Serve. **Address:** 815 Cole St 94117

IKE'S PLACE 415/351-1972 (124)
🍷 Sandwiches. Quick Serve. **Address:** 901 Polk St 94109

ISA 415/567-9588 (7)
🍷🍷 French. Casual Dining. **Address:** 3324 Steiner St 94123

THE ITALIAN HOMEMADE COMPANY 415/712-8874 (18)
🍷 Italian. Quick Serve. **Address:** 716 Columbus Ave 94133

IT'S TOPS COFFEE SHOP 415/431-6395 (93)
🍷🍷 American. Casual Dining. **Address:** 1801 Market St 94103

IZAKAYA ROKU 415/861-6500 (92)
🍷🍷 Japanese Small Plates. Casual Dining. **Address:** 1819 Market St 94103

IZAKAYA SOZAI 415/742-5122 (73)
🍷🍷 Japanese Small Plates. Casual Dining. **Address:** 1500 Irving St 94122

IZUMIYA 415/441-6867 (41)
🍷🍷 Japanese. Casual Dining. **Address:** 1581 Webster St, Suite 270 94115

JANG SOO BBQ 415/221-8282 (19)
🍷🍷 Korean Barbecue. Casual Dining. **Address:** 6314 Geary St 94121

JOHNNY FOLEY'S 415/954-0777 (131)
🍷🍷 Irish. Casual Dining. **Address:** 243 O'Farrell St 94102

JOHN'S GRILL 415/986-3274 (137)

🍷🍷🍷 **AAA Inspector Notes:** *Classic Historic.* Established in 1908, this relaxed restaurant is furnished in turn-of-the-20th-century decor. This place was a setting in "The Maltese Falcon" by author Dashiell Hammett. You can't go wrong ordering the juicy rib-eye steak that comes with a baked potato and seasonal vegetables. **Features:** full bar. **Reservations:** suggested. **Address:** 63 Ellis St 94102 **Location:** Between Powell and Stockton sts. 🚇 Powell Street, 42. **Parking:** no self-parking. 〔L〕 〔D〕 🚊

American Casual Dining $11-$40

KATIA'S 415/668-9292 (47)
🍷🍷 Russian. Casual Dining. **Address:** 600 5th Ave 94118

(See maps & indexes p. 298, 308.)

KIN KHAO THAI EATERY   415/362-7456   (139)
🍷🍷🍷 Thai. Casual Dining. **Address:** 55 Cyril Magnin St 94102

KOH SAMUI AND THE MONKEY   415/369-0007   (156)
🍷🍷 Thai. Casual Dining. **Address:** 415 Brannan St 94107

KOKKARI ESTIATORIO   415/981-0983   (58)
🍷🍷🍷 Greek. Fine Dining. **Address:** 200 Jackson St 94111

KUSAKABE   415/757-0155   (61)
🍷🍷🍷🍷 Sushi. Fine Dining. **Address:** 584 Washington St 94111

LA CICCIA   415/550-8114   (167)
🍷🍷🍷 Italian. Casual Dining. **Address:** 291 30th St 94131

LA FOLIE   415/776-5577   (23)
🍷🍷🍷🍷 French. Fine Dining. **Address:** 2316 Polk St 94109

LA MAR CEBICHERIA PERUANA   415/397-8880   (62)
🍷🍷🍷 Peruvian. Casual Dining. **Address:** Pier 1.5 94111

LA MEDITERRANEE   415/921-2956   (26)
🍷 Mediterranean. Casual Dining. **Address:** 2210 Fillmore St 94115

LAO TABLE   415/278-9991   (136)
🍷🍷🍷 Thai. Casual Dining. **Address:** 149 2nd St 94105

LARK BISTRO   415/400-4623   (122)
🍷🍷🍷 Mediterranean. Casual Dining. **Address:** 4068 18th St 94114

LA TAQUERIA   415/285-7117   (163)
🍷 Mexican. Quick Serve. **Address:** 2889 Mission St 94110

THE LAUREL COURT RESTAURANT & BAR
415/772-5260   (70)
🍷🍷🍷 California. Fine Dining. **Address:** 950 Mason St 94108

LAZY BEAR   415/874-9921   (136)
🍷🍷🍷🍷 New American. Fine Dining. **Address:** 3416 19th St 94110

LE COLONIAL   415/931-3600   (107)
🍷🍷🍷 Vietnamese. Fine Dining. **Address:** 20 Cosmo Pl 94109

LEOPOLD'S   415/474-2000   (19)
🍷🍷 German. Casual Dining. **Address:** 2400 Polk St 94109

LERS ROS THAI   415/874-9661   (61)
🍷🍷 Thai. Casual Dining. **Address:** 307 Hayes St 94102

LIHOLIHO YACHT CLUB   415/440-5446   (102)
🍷🍷🍷 New Hawaiian. Casual Dining. **Address:** 871 Sutter St 94109

LIMON ROTISSERIE   415/821-2134   (146)
🍷 Peruvian. Casual Dining. **Address:** 1001 S Van Ness Ave 94110

THE LITTLE CHIHUAHUA   415/255-8225   (70)
🍷 Mexican. Quick Serve. **Address:** 292 Divisadero St 94117

LITTLE STAR PIZZA   415/441-1118   (50)
🍷🍷 Pizza. Casual Dining. **Address:** 846 Divisadero St 94117

LOCANDA   415/863-6800   (121)
🍷🍷🍷 Italian. Casual Dining. **Address:** 557 Valencia St 94110

LOLO   415/244-9798   (150)
🍷🍷 New Mexican Small Plates. Casual Dining. **Address:** 3230 22nd St 94110

LORD STANLEY   415/872-5512   (36)
🍷🍷🍷 California. Fine Dining. **Address:** 2065 Polk St 94109

LOS SHUCOS LATIN HOT DOGS   415/366-3868   (151)
🍷 Guatemalan Hot Dogs. Quick Serve. **Address:** 3224 1/2 22nd St 94110

LOUIS'   415/387-6330   (13)
🍷 American. Casual Dining. **Address:** 902 Point Lobos Ave 94121

LUCE   415/616-6566   (149)
🍷🍷🍷 American. Fine Dining. **Address:** 888 Howard St 94163

LUCKY CREATION VEGETARIAN RESTAURANT
415/989-0818   (59)
🍷🍷 Chinese Vegetarian. Casual Dining. **Address:** 854 Washington St 94108

MAGNOLIA PUB & BREWERY   415/864-7468   (71)
🍷 American. Brewpub. **Address:** 1398 Haight St 94117

MAMA JI'S   415/626-4416   (117)
🍷🍷 Szechuan Dim Sum. Casual Dining. **Address:** 4416 18th 94114

MARLOWE   415/777-1413   (163)
🍷🍷🍷 American. Casual Dining. **Address:** 500 Brannan St 94107

MARNEE THAI   415/731-9999   (76)
🍷🍷 Thai. Casual Dining. **Address:** 1243 9th Ave 94122

MARNEE THAI   415/665-9500   (63)
🍷🍷 Thai. Casual Dining. **Address:** 2225 Irving St 94122

MARUFUKU RAMEN   415/872-9786   (40)
🍷🍷 Japanese Noodles. Casual Dining. **Address:** 1581 Webster, Ste 235 St 94115

MARUYA   415/503-0702   (119)
🍷🍷🍷 Japanese Sushi. Casual Dining. **Address:** 2931 16th St 94103

MAYBECK'S   415/400-8500   (4)
🍷🍷🍷 Italian. Fine Dining. **Address:** 3213 Scott St 94123

MCCORMICK & KULETO'S SEAFOOD RESTAURANT
415/929-1730   (11)
🍷🍷🍷 Seafood. Fine Dining. **Address:** 900 N Point St, Suite H301 94109

MEMPHIS MINNIE'S   415/864-7675   (82)
🍷 Barbecue. Quick Serve. **Address:** 576 Haight St 94117

MENSHO TOKYO   415/800-8345   (122)
🍷 Japanese Noodles. Casual Dining. **Address:** 672 Geary St 94102

MICHAEL MINA   415/397-9222   (85)
🍷🍷🍷🍷 New American. Fine Dining. **Address:** 252 California St 94111

MIJITA COCINA MEXICANA   415/399-0814   (74)
🍷 Mexican. Quick Serve. **Address:** 1 Ferry Bldg, Space 44 94111

MISSION BEACH CAFE   415/861-0198   (103)
🍷🍷 California. Casual Dining. **Address:** 198 Guerrero St 94103

MISSION CHEESE   415/553-8667   (129)
🍷 Specialty Small Plates. Quick Serve. **Address:** 736 Valencia St 94110

MISSION CHINESE FOOD   415/863-2800   (135)
🍷🍷 New Chinese. Casual Dining. **Address:** 2234 Mission St 94110

MISSION PIE   415/282-1500   (165)
🍷 American. Quick Serve. **Address:** 2901 Mission St 94110

(See maps & indexes p. 298, 308.)

MISSION ROCK RESORT   415/701-7625 (139)
♦♦ Seafood. Casual Dining. **Address:** 817 Terry Francois Blvd 94158

MODERN THAI   415/922-8424 (88)
♦♦ Thai. Casual Dining. **Address:** 1247 Polk St 94109

MOMO'S RESTAURANT   415/227-8660 (162)
♦♦ American. Casual Dining. **Address:** 760 2nd St 94107

THE MONK'S KETTLE   415/865-9523 (115)
♦♦ American. Gastropub. **Address:** 3141 16th St 94103

MUGU BOKA KOREAN BBQ RESTAURANT
                                    415/668-6007 (46)
♦♦ Korean. Casual Dining. **Address:** 401 Balboa St 94118

MURACCI'S JAPANESE CURRY & GRILL 415/773-1101 (100)
♦ Japanese. Quick Serve. **Address:** 307 Kearny St 94108

M.Y. CHINA   415/580-3001 (140)
♦♦♦ Chinese. Casual Dining. **Address:** 845 Market St, 4th Floor 94103

MY TOFU HOUSE   415/750-1818 (33)
♦♦ Korean. Casual Dining. **Address:** 4627 Geary Blvd 94118

NABE   415/731-2658 (87)
♦♦ Japanese Specialty. Casual Dining. **Address:** 1325 9th Ave 94122

NAMU GAJI   415/431-6268 (124)
♦♦ New Korean Small Plates. Casual Dining. **Address:** 499 Dolores St 94110

NEIMAN MARCUS-THE ROTUNDA RESTAURANT
                                    415/362-4777 (126)
♦♦♦ California. Casual Dining. **Address:** 150 Stockton St 94108

NEW CHEF HUNG'S RESTAURANT   415/398-6883 (65)
♦♦ Chinese. Casual Dining. **Address:** 823 Clay St 94108

NEW DELHI   415/397-8470 (134)
♦♦ Indian. Casual Dining. **Address:** 160 Ellis St 94102

NICK'S LIGHTHOUSE   415/929-1300 (7)
♦♦
Seafood
Casual Dining
$10-$50
AAA Inspector Notes: Patrons can stop at a take-out stand with steaming kettles of crustaceans out front or dine in the restaurant for fresh shellfish and fish. Dungeness crab and California lobster merit top billing at this busy spot. Views look out to the wharf's fishing boats. **Features:** full bar, patio dining. **Address:** 2815 Taylor St 94133 **Location:** At Jefferson St, on Fisherman's Wharf. **Parking:** street only. [L] [D] [⚡]

NOB HILL CAFE   415/776-6500 (64)
♦♦ Italian. Casual Dining. **Address:** 1152 Taylor St 94108

NOJO RAMEN TAVERN   415/896-4587 (150)
♦♦ Japanese Small Plates Noodles. Casual Dining. **Address:** 231 Franklin St 94102

NOPA   415/864-8643 (55)
♦♦♦ California. Casual Dining. **Address:** 560 Divisadero St 94117

NOPALITO   415/437-0303 (62)
♦♦ Mexican. Casual Dining. **Address:** 306 Broderick St 94117

NOPALITO ON 9TH   415/233-9966 (74)
♦♦ Mexican. Casual Dining. **Address:** 1224 9th Ave 94122

NORTH BEACH RESTAURANT   415/392-1700 (30)
♦♦♦♦
Italian
Fine Dining
$20-$42
AAA Inspector Notes: Servers in tuxedos circulate through this Old World Italian restaurant, where Tuscan entrées lead up to luscious New York cheesecake for dessert. Classic, well-prepared dishes such as veal cannelloni, imported fresh burrata and house made zabaglione with berries are some of the offerings. **Features:** full bar, patio dining. **Reservations:** suggested. **Address:** 1512 Stockton St 94133 **Location:** At Columbus Ave. [⚡] Chinatown, 126. **Parking:** valet and street only. [L] [D] [⚡]

THE OLD CLAM HOUSE   415/826-4880 (168)
♦♦ Seafood. Casual Dining. **Address:** 299 Bayshore Blvd 94124

ONE MARKET RESTAURANT   415/777-5577 (83)
♦♦♦ American. Fine Dining. **Address:** 1 Market St 94105

ONIGILLY   415/671-4706 (90)
♦ Japanese. Quick Serve. **Address:** 343 Kearny St 94108

ON THE BRIDGE   415/922-7765 (42)
♦♦ Japanese. Casual Dining. **Address:** 1581 Webster St, Suite 205 94115

ORENCHI BEYOND   415/431-3971 (98)
♦♦ Japanese Noodles. Casual Dining. **Address:** 174 Valencia St 94103

ORIGINAL U.S. RESTAURANT   415/398-1300 (35)
♦♦ Italian. Casual Dining. **Address:** 414 Columbus Ave 94133

OSHA THAI NOODLE CAFE   415/673-2368 (121)
♦♦ Thai. Casual Dining. **Address:** 696 Geary St 94102

OSSO STEAKHOUSE   415/771-6776 (75)
♦♦♦ American Steak. Casual Dining. **Address:** 1177 California St 94108

OUTERLANDS   415/661-6140 (54)
♦♦♦ California. Casual Dining. **Address:** 4001 Judah St 94122

OZUMO   415/882-1333 (112)
♦♦♦ Japanese. Casual Dining. **Address:** 161 Steuart St 94105

PACIFIC CATCH WESTCOAST FISH HOUSE
                                    415/504-6905 (69)
♦♦ Pacific Rim. Casual Dining. **Address:** 1200 9th Ave 94122

PADRECITO   415/742-5505 (91)
♦♦ Mexican Small Plates. Casual Dining. **Address:** 901 Cole St 94117

PALIO D'ASTI   415/395-9800 (71)
♦♦♦ Italian. Casual Dining. **Address:** 640 Sacramento St 94111

PANCHO VILLA TAQUERIA   415/864-8840 (116)
♦ Mexican. Quick Serve. **Address:** 3071 16th St 94103

PAPALOTE MEXICAN GRILL   415/970-8815 (153)
♦ Mexican. Quick Serve. **Address:** 3409 24th St 94110

PARADA 22   415/750-1111 (66)
♦♦ Puerto Rican. Casual Dining. **Address:** 1805 Haight St 94117

PARALLEL 37   415/773-6168 (82)
♦♦♦♦ New American. Fine Dining. **Address:** 600 Stockton St 94108

PARK CHOW   415/665-9912 (77)
♦♦ American. Casual Dining. **Address:** 1240 9th Ave 94122

(See maps & indexes p. 298, 308.)

PARK GRILL   415/296-2933   69
▼▼ California. Casual Dining. **Address:** 333 Battery St 94111

PENANG GARDEN RESTAURANT   415/296-7878   60
▼▼ Thai. Casual Dining. **Address:** 728 Washington St 94108

PERBACCO RISTORANTE + BAR   415/955-0663   87
▼▼▼ Italian. Fine Dining. **Address:** 230 California St 94111

PHAT PHILLY   415/550-7428   154
▼ American. Quick Serve. **Address:** 3388 24th St 94110

PICA PICA AREPA KITCHEN   415/400-5453   109
▼ Latin American. Quick Serve. **Address:** 401 Valencia St 94103

PICARO   415/431-4089   113
▼▼ Spanish Small Plates. Casual Dining. **Address:** 3120 Valencia St 94103

PICCINO   415/824-4224   159
▼▼▼ Italian. Casual Dining. **Address:** 1001 Minnesota St 94107

PIER 23 CAFE   415/362-5125   21
▼▼ American. Casual Dining. **Address:** On The Embarcadero 94111

PIER MARKET SEAFOOD RESTAURANT   415/989-7437   3
▼▼ Seafood. Casual Dining. **Address:** Pier 39, Suite 103 94133

PIPERADE   415/391-2555   33
▼▼▼ French. Fine Dining. **Address:** 1015 Battery St 94111

PIZZERIA DELFINA   415/437-6800   126
▼▼ Pizza. Casual Dining. **Address:** 3611 18th St 94110

PIZZERIA DELFINA   415/440-1189   31
▼▼ Pizza. Casual Dining. **Address:** 2406 California St 94115

PIZZETTA 211   415/379-9880   14
▼▼ Pizza. Casual Dining. **Address:** 211 23rd Ave 94121

PLOW   415/821-7569   144
▼▼ American. Casual Dining. **Address:** 1299 18th St 94107

POKI TIME   415/702-6333   85
▼ Hawaiian. Quick Serve. **Address:** 549 Irving St 94122

PORK STORE CAFE   415/864-6981   72
▼▼ American. Casual Dining. **Address:** 1451 Haight St 94117

PPQ DUNGENESS ISLAND   415/386-8266   18
▼▼ Vietnamese. Casual Dining. **Address:** 2332 Clement St 94121

PROSPECT   415/247-7770   132
▼▼▼ California. Fine Dining. **Address:** 300 Spear St 94105

PUCCINI & PINETTI   415/392-5500   135
▼▼ Italian. Casual Dining. **Address:** 129 Ellis St 94102

QUINCE   415/775-8500   50
▼▼▼▼ New American. Fine Dining. **Address:** 470 Pacific Ave 94133

RAGAZZA   415/255-1133   68
▼▼ Italian. Casual Dining. **Address:** 311 Divisadero St 94117

RAMBLER   415/549-8008   117
▼▼ American. Casual Dining. **Address:** 545 Post St 94102

RAMEN UNDERGROUND   415/999-2503   89
▼▼ Japanese Noodles. Casual Dining. **Address:** 356 Kearny St 94108

R & G LOUNGE   415/982-7877   67
▼▼ Chinese. Casual Dining. **Address:** 631 Kearny St 94108

RESTAURANT EIJI   415/558-8149   111
▼▼ Japanese Small Plates Sushi. Casual Dining. **Address:** 317 Sanchez St 94114

RICH TABLE   415/355-9085   75
▼▼▼ California. Casual Dining. **Address:** 199 Gough St 94102

RINTARO   415/589-7022   105
▼▼▼ Japanese. Casual Dining. **Address:** 82 14th St 94103

RISTORANTE MONA LISA   415/989-4917   38
▼▼ Italian. Casual Dining. **Address:** 353 Columbus Ave 94133

RN74   415/543-7474   120
▼▼▼ New French. Casual Dining. **Address:** 301 Mission St 94199

ROAM ARTISAN BURGERS   415/440-7626   12
▼▼ Burgers Natural/Organic. Quick Serve. **Address:** 1785 Union St 94123

ROAM ARTISAN BURGERS   415/800-7801   34
▼▼ Burgers Natural/Organic. Quick Serve. **Address:** 1923 Fillmore St 94115

ROCCO'S CAFE   415/554-0522   160
▼▼ Italian. Casual Dining. **Address:** 1131 Folsom St 94103

ROKA AKOR   415/362-8887   57
▼▼▼ Japanese. Fine Dining. **Address:** 801 Montgomery St 94133

ROSA MEXICANO   415/874-4300   99
▼▼ Mexican. Casual Dining. **Address:** 30 Mission St 94105

ROSAMUNDE SAUSAGE GRILL   415/970-9015   158
▼ Hot Dogs. Quick Serve. **Address:** 2832 Mission St 94110

ROSE'S CAFE   415/775-2200   10
▼▼ Italian. Casual Dining. **Address:** 2298 Union St 94123

ROXANNE CAFE   415/989-5555   98
▼▼ Italian. Casual Dining. **Address:** 570 Powell St 94108

ROY'S   415/777-0277   130
▼▼▼ Pacific Rim Fusion. Fine Dining. **Address:** 575 Mission St 94109

RT- ROTISSERIE   415/355-9085   78
▼▼ Chicken Sandwiches. Quick Serve. **Address:** 101 Oak St 94102

SABABA HOT PITA BAR   415/800-6853   94
▼ Middle Eastern. Quick Serve. **Address:** 329 Kearny St 94108

SAISON   415/828-7990   161
▼▼▼▼▼ New American Fine Dining $298 — **AAA Inspector Notes:** Diners enjoy an exquisite tasting menu which is set depending on the finest quality ingredients available each day. Outstanding wine pairings are available and recommended for the full culinary experience. Ask for a table closer to the open kitchen to watch the chefs in action. The lighting is fantastic for taking photos of each gorgeous dish. **Features:** full bar. **Reservations:** required. **Address:** 178 Townsend St 94107 **Location:** Between 2nd and 3rd sts. 2nd & King, 92. **Parking:** valet and street only. D CALL 🅿

SAMOVAR TEA LOUNGE   415/227-9400   146
▼▼ International. Casual Dining. **Address:** 730 Howard St 94103

SANRAKU RESTAURANT   415/771-0803   103
▼▼ Japanese. Casual Dining. **Address:** 704 Sutter St 94109

(See maps & indexes p. 298, 308.)

SAN TUNG CHINESE RESTAURANT   415/242-0828 (80)
♥♥ Chinese. Casual Dining. **Address:** 1031 Irving St 94122

SCALA'S BISTRO   415/395-8555 (109)
♥♥♥ Italian. Casual Dining. **Address:** 432 Powell St 94102

SCOMA'S RESTAURANT   415/771-4383 (1)

♥♥♥
Seafood
Casual Dining
$10-$61

AAA Inspector Notes: A casual mood pervades this landmark restaurant. Picturesque views of the harbor invite wistful daydreaming. **Features:** full bar. **Reservations:** suggested. **Address:** Fisherman's Wharf, Pier 47 94133 **Location:** On Fisherman's Wharf.
Parking: street only. (L) (D)

SEARS FINE FOODS   415/986-0700 (110)
♥♥ American. Casual Dining. **Address:** 439 Powell St 94102

SEOUL GARDEN   415/563-7664 (44)
♥♥ Korean. Casual Dining. **Address:** 1655 Post St 94115

SERPENTINE   415/252-2000 (160)
♥♥ California. Casual Dining. **Address:** 2495 3rd St 94107

SEVEN HILLS   415/775-1550 (42)
♥♥♥ Italian. Fine Dining. **Address:** 1550 Hyde St 94109

SHABUSEN RESTAURANT   415/440-0466 (39)
♥♥ Japanese Specialty. Casual Dining. **Address:** 1726 Buchanan St 94115

THE SLANTED DOOR   415/861-8032 (80)
♥♥♥ Vietnamese. Casual Dining. **Address:** 1 Ferry Building, Suite 3 94111

SOCIALE   415/921-3200 (21)
♥♥♥ Italian. Casual Dining. **Address:** 3665 Sacramento St 94118

SONS & DAUGHTERS   415/391-8311 (93)
♥♥♥♥ New American. Casual Dining. **Address:** 708 Bush St 94108

SOUVLA   415/400-5458 (57)
♥♥ Greek. Quick Serve. **Address:** 517 Hayes St 94102

THE SPICE JAR   415/829-3668 (155)
♥♥ Asian Fusion. Casual Dining. **Address:** 2500 Bryant St 94110

SPQR   415/771-7779 (36)
♥♥♥ Italian. Fine Dining. **Address:** 1911 Fillmore St 94115

SPRUCE   415/931-5100 (20)
♥♥♥♥ California. Fine Dining. **Address:** 3640 Sacramento St 94118

STARBELLY   415/252-7500 (108)
♥♥ California. Casual Dining. **Address:** 3583 16th St 94114

STATE BIRD PROVISIONS   415/795-1272 (48)
♥♥♥ New Small Plates. Casual Dining. **Address:** 1529 Fillmore St 94115

THE STINKING ROSE   415/781-7673 (40)
♥♥ Italian. Casual Dining. **Address:** 325 Columbus Ave 94133

STRAW   415/431-3663 (79)
♥♥ American. Casual Dining. **Address:** 203 Octavia Blvd 94102

STREET RESTAURANT   415/775-1055 (32)
♥♥ Northern California. Casual Dining. **Address:** 2141 Polk St 94109

SUPER DUPER BURGERS   415/558-8123 (106)
♥ American. Quick Serve. **Address:** 2304 Market St 94114

SUPPENKUCHE   415/252-9289 (58)
♥ Traditional German. Casual Dining. **Address:** 525 Laguna St 94102

SUSHIRRITO   415/544-9868 (106)
♥ Japanese Sushi. Quick Serve. **Address:** 226 Kearny St 94108

SUZU NOODLE HOUSE   415/346-5083 (45)
♥♥ Japanese Noodles. Casual Dining. **Address:** 1825 Post St 94115

SWAN OYSTER DEPOT   415/673-1101 (66)
♥♥ Seafood. Casual Dining. **Address:** 1517 Polk St 94109

TACOLICIOUS   415/626-1344 (131)
♥♥ Mexican Small Plates. Casual Dining. **Address:** 741 Valencia St 94110

THE TACO SHOP AT UNDERDOGS   415/566-8700 (65)
♥ Mexican. Casual Dining. **Address:** 1824 Irving St 94122

TADICH GRILL   415/391-1849 (86)
♥♥ Seafood. Casual Dining. **Address:** 240 California St 94111

TAQUERIA SAN FRANCISCO   415/641-1770 (164)
♥ Mexican. Quick Serve. **Address:** 2794 24th St 94110

TARTINE BAKERY & CAFE   415/487-2600 (128)
♥ Breads/Pastries. Quick Serve. **Address:** 600 Guerrero St 94110

TARTINE MANUFACTORY   415/757-0007 (137)
♥♥ California. Casual Dining. **Address:** 595 Alabama St 94110

TERRA COTTA WARRIOR   415/681-3288 (64)
♥♥ Chinese. Casual Dining. **Address:** 2555 Judah St 94122

THAI SPICE   415/775-4777 (54)
♥♥ Thai. Casual Dining. **Address:** 1730 Polk St 94109

THEP PHANOM   415/431-2526 (89)
♥♥ Thai. Casual Dining. **Address:** 400 Waller St 94117

THIRSTY BEAR BREWING CO.   415/974-0905 (141)
♥♥ Spanish Small Plates. Brewpub. **Address:** 661 Howard St 94105

TOMMASO'S RESTAURANT   415/398-9696 (44)
♥♥ Italian. Casual Dining. **Address:** 1042 Kearny St 94133

TOMMY'S JOYNT   415/775-4216 (116)
♥ American. Quick Serve. **Address:** 1101 Geary Blvd 94109

TONY'S PIZZA NAPOLETANA   415/835-9888 (27)
♥♥ Pizza. Casual Dining. **Address:** 1570 Stockton St 94133

TOSCA CAFE   415/986-9651 (45)
♥♥♥ Italian. Gastropub. **Address:** 242 Columbus Ave 94133

TOWN HALL   415/908-3900 (129)
♥♥♥ Southern American. Casual Dining. **Address:** 342 Howard St 94105

TOWN'S END RESTAURANT & BAKERY   415/512-0749 (154)
♥♥ California. Casual Dining. **Address:** 2 Townsend St 94107

TOYOSE   415/731-0232 (95)
♥♥ Korean. Casual Dining. **Address:** 3814 Noriega St 94122

TRATTORIA CONTADINA   415/982-5728 (24)
♥♥♥ Italian. Casual Dining. **Address:** 1800 Mason St 94133

TRICK DOG   415/471-2999 (140)
♥♥ International. Gastropub. **Address:** 3010 20th St 94110

(See maps & indexes p. 298, 308.)

TROYA MEDITERRANEAN KITCHEN   415/563-1000 (29)
♥♥ Turkish. Casual Dining. **Address:** 2125 Fillmore St 94115

TURTLE TOWER RESTAURANT   415/221-9890 (23)
♥♥ Northern Vietnamese. Casual Dining. **Address:** 5716 Geary Blvd 94121

UDON MUGIZO   415/931-3118 (43)
♥♥ Japanese Noodles. Casual Dining. **Address:** 1581 Webster St, Suite 217 94115

UNIVERSAL CAFE   415/821-4608 (138)
♥♥ California. Casual Dining. **Address:** 2814 19th St 94110

UVA ENOTECA   415/829-2024 (83)
♥♥ Italian. Casual Dining. **Address:** 568 Haight St 94117

VIVA GOA INDIAN CUISINE   415/440-2600 (6)
♥♥ Indian. Casual Dining. **Address:** 2420 Lombard St 94123

WALZWERK   415/551-7181 (110)
♥♥ Eastern German. Casual Dining. **Address:** 381 S Van Ness Ave 94103

THE WATERFRONT RESTAURANT   415/391-2696 (46)
♥♥♥ California Seafood. Fine Dining. **Address:** Pier 7 94111

WAYFARE TAVERN   415/772-9060 (72)
♥♥♥ American. Gastropub. **Address:** 558 Sacramento St 94111

WEST OF PECOS   415/252-7000 (120)
♥♥ Southwestern. Casual Dining. **Address:** 550 Valencia St 94110

WISE SONS DELI   415/787-3354 (156)
♥ Jewish Deli. Casual Dining. **Address:** 3150 24th St 94110

WOODHOUSE FISH COMPANY   415/437-2722 (101)
♥ Seafood. Casual Dining. **Address:** 2073 Market St 94114

YANK SING   415/541-4949 (123)
♥♥ Chinese Dim Sum. Casual Dining. **Address:** 49 Stevenson St 94105

YUMMY YUMMY RESTAURANT   415/566-4722 (81)
♥♥ Vietnamese. Casual Dining. **Address:** 1015 Irving St 94122

ZARZUELA   415/346-0800 (20)
♥♥ Spanish Small Plates. Casual Dining. **Address:** 2000 Hyde St 94109

ZAZIE   415/564-5332 (96)
♥♥ French. Casual Dining. **Address:** 941 Cole St 94117

ZINGARI RISTORANTE   415/885-8850 (119)
♥♥♥ Italian. Casual Dining. **Address:** 501 Post St 94102

ZUNI CAFE   415/552-2522 (84)
♥♥♥ California. Casual Dining. **Address:** 1658 Market St 94102

SAN JOSE (F-3) pop. 945,942, elev. 94'
- Hotels p. 354 • Restaurants p. 355
- Attractions map p. 343
- Hotels & Restaurants map & index p. 346, 348

Sprawling across the Santa Clara Valley between the Mount Hamilton and Santa Cruz ranges, San Jose anchors the southern end of the San Francisco Peninsula. This major city's beginnings date to 1777, when the small settlement of Pueblo de San José de Guadalupe was established to raise crops and cattle for the nearby presidios of San Francisco and Monterey.

In 1849 San Jose became the state's first capital, a distinction that lasted only until 1851. But flash forward to the last half of the 1990s and California's third most populous city gained a nickname, "Capital of the Silicon Valley," thanks to a central role in the technological innovations that fueled the dot.com revolution.

The Japanese-American Internment Memorial, downtown in front of the Robert Peckham Federal Building at 280 S. First St., remembers those citizens confined in the U.S. during World War II. Narrative panels relate the experiences of those detained during this period.

One of the city's historic things to see is the Moorish-style California Theatre, downtown at 345 S. First St., which opened in 1927 as an ornate movie palace. Opulently restored, it is home to both Opera San Jose and Symphony Silicon Valley. For schedule and ticket information phone the opera company at (408) 437-4450 or the symphony at (408) 286-2600.

At the junction of I-280, I-680 and US 101, just off King Road—in the middle of bustling, high-tech San Jose—is Emma Prusch Farm Park, a reminder of the city's agricultural past and one of San Jose's fun things to do with kids. A barn, vintage farm equipment and fruit orchards are still at the site of this former dairy farm, as well as resident sheep, pigs, cows, geese and rabbits. It's a reminder of what life was like before the Santa Clara Valley hopped on the technological bandwagon; phone (408) 794-6262.

SAP Center at San Jose, at W. Santa Clara and Autumn streets, is home to the city's NHL hockey team, the San Jose Sharks. Other college and professional sporting events, concerts and live performances take place at the arena; phone (408) (408) 999-5757 for ticket information.

The Major League Soccer (MLS) San Jose Earthquakes play at Avaya Stadium, 1123 Coleman Ave.; from San Francisco, take the De La Cruz Boulevard exit off southbound US 101, following signs for San Jose and the stadium. Phone the box office at (408) 556-7700 for ticket and schedule information. The San Jose State University Spartans play basketball at the Event Center at San Jose State University, 7th and E. San Carlos streets; phone (408) 924-7589.

There are more than 50 wineries in the San Jose area, ranging from family-run establishments to large corporate ventures. Throughout the year festivals, concerts and other events celebrate viticulture. Santa Clara Valley Transportation Authority provides transportation to regional wineries; phone (408) 321-2300 for additional information.

Team San Jose: 408 Almaden Blvd., San Jose, CA 95110. **Phone:** (408) 295-9600 or (800) 726-5673.

Self-guiding tours: Walking tour maps are available from the San Jose Visitor Information and Business Center, located in the lobby of the San Jose

(See maps & indexes p. 346, 348.)
McEnery Convention Center at 150 W. San Carlos St.

Shopping: For a shopping experience that's anything but run of the mill, visit San Jose's Santana Row (355 Santana Row), a tree-lined avenue designed to look like a shopping district in a quaint European village. This residential-commercial development was completed in 2002 and quickly became a San Jose tourist destination thanks to its lovely architectural details, manicured landscaping, upscale boutiques and a wide selection of places to eat.

One highlight that shows up a lot on Instagram is the Gothic chapel façade imported from France that now serves as the entrance to a popular wine bar. The long list of Santana Row retailers includes Anthropologie, Boutique Harajuku, Chico's, Crate & Barrel, Gucci and Ted Baker London.

San Jose's Antique Row (1881 West San Carlos St.) occupies a compact three blocks but includes several stores such as Briarwood Antiques & Collectibles, Burbank Antiques and Memory Lane Antiques, as well as a host of nearby vintage clothing and consignment shops. Dozens of dealers display high-quality merchandise from yesteryear at Antiques Colony, the largest store in the district.

Another destination for antique hunters is The San Jose Flea Market (1590 Berryessa Rd.), a local institution since 1960 that offers more than 1,500 booths selling everything from books to jewelry to electronics. An entire row is dedicated to selling some of California's best produce, and if you get hungry while perusing the seemingly endless aisles of merchandise, there are several eating places serving pizza, corn dogs, barbecue beef sandwiches, tacos and ice cream.

Downtown's San Pedro Square is one of San Jose's oldest neighborhoods and where you'll find the 1797 Peralta Adobe, the city's oldest building. It's also one of the best places to go to sample fare from local restaurants. Bustling San Pedro Square Market (87 N. San Pedro St.) is crowded with food vendors selling a dizzying variety of cuisines as well as breweries pouring craft beer to suit every thirst. Check out San Pedro Square on summer Fridays from 10-2 for the Downtown Farmers' Market, which offers fresh produce from more than 30 Golden State growers.

Several shopping malls in San Jose and surrounding communities serve the area's retail needs including Eastridge Center (2200 Eastridge Loop), which has more than a million square feet of space dedicated to stores, local restaurants and entertainment, offering a variety of fun things to do with friends. The anchor stores here are JCPenney, Macy's and Sears. What sets Eastridge Center apart from other malls: pets are welcomed as long as they are on a leash or in a pet carrier.

Westfield Oakridge (925 Blossom Hill Rd.) has Macy's, Target and Nordstrom Rack along with smaller chain stores recognizable from shopping centers across the country. The Oakridge light rail station is across Winfield Boulevard from the mall, making public transportation to the mall a convenient option.

On the site of a former Ford Motor Co. plant in nearby Milpitas, Great Mall of the Bay Area (447 Great Mall Dr.) is also near a light rail station (Great Mall/Main) and is scheduled to have a new BART station connecting it to San Francisco in late 2019. More than 170 outlet stores offer deals here including Calvin Klein, Last Call by Neiman Marcus and Saks Fifth Avenue OFF 5th.

ALUM ROCK PARK is e. of US 101 on Alum Rock Ave.; use Penitencia Creek Rd. for vehicle access to the park. A 730-acre site in the foothills, the park offers scenic views of the Santa Clara Valley, picnic facilities, mineral springs, marked trails and the Youth Science Institute. The institute's science and nature center features animal exhibits such as birds of prey that have been injured and cannot be released back into the wild.

Landslides sometimes close the road through the park. Dogs are not permitted. **Hours:** Park open daily 8 a.m.-half-hour after sunset. Institute open Tues.-Fri. noon-4, Sat. noon-4:30 (also Sun. noon-4:30, Easter-Labor Day, and on Memorial Day, July 4 and Labor Day). The park may be closed at times June-Oct. if brush fires are present; phone ahead for updates. **Cost:** Free. Institute $1; 50c (ages 0-17). **Parking:** $6-$10 per private vehicle. **Phone:** (408) 259-5477, or (408) 258-4322 for the institute.

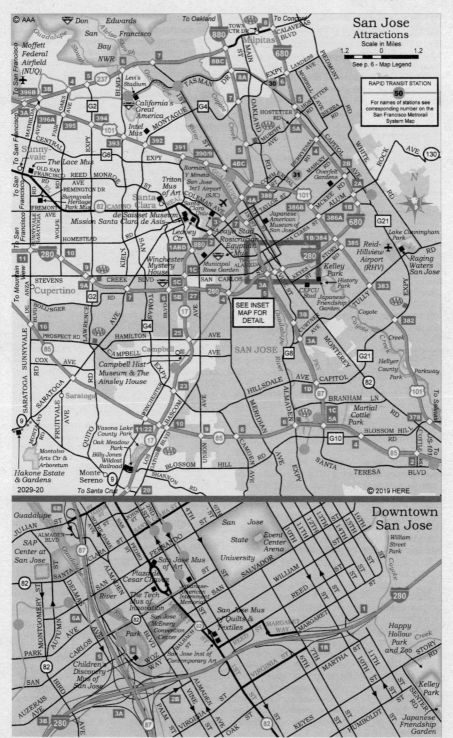

(See maps & indexes p. 346, 348.)

JAPANESE AMERICAN MUSEUM OF SAN JOSE is at 535 N. Fifth St., between Jackson and Empire sts. It focuses on the Japanese American experience in the Greater Bay Area from immigration during the early 1900s to the present. Photographs and memorabilia chronicle economic and social adaptations to life in the Santa Clara Valley as well as a forced removal during World War II.

In addition to an authentic replica of a barracks room that served as living quarters for Japanese Americans incarcerated during the war, exhibits include vintage vehicles and farm equipment. Knowledgeable docents can answer questions and provide background information.

Street parking in the vicinity is limited; public parking lots are within walking distance. **Time:** Allow 1 hour, 30 minutes minimum. **Hours:** Thurs.-Sun. noon-4. Closed Jan. 1, July 4, Thanksgiving, Christmas Eve, Christmas and Dec. 31. Phone ahead to confirm schedule. **Cost:** $5; $3 (ages 65+ and students with ID); free (ages 0-4). **Phone:** (408) 294-3138. GT

KELLEY PARK, at Senter and Story rds., is actually two parks—one geared toward children's activities, the other to area history and culture—as well as a Japanese-themed garden. **Hours:** Daily 8 a.m.-30 minutes after dusk. **Cost:** Free. **Parking:** $6-$10 per private vehicle. **Phone:** (408) 794-7275.

Happy Hollow Park and Zoo, 1300 Senter Rd., is a family park with more than 150 animals, seven rides, giant play structures and a puppet theater. Camps, sleepovers and year-round events also are offered. **Hours:** Park opens daily at 10 a.m. Closing hours vary by season; phone ahead for daily schedule information. **Cost:** $14.25 (includes playground, rides and zoo); $11.25 (ages 60+); free (ages 0-1). **Parking:** $10. **Phone:** (408) 794-6400.

History Park is at 1650 Senter Rd. at Phelan Ave. On the grounds are 27 historic structures that help tell the story of San Jose and the Santa Clara Valley and are representative of area life at the turn of the 20th century. Visitors can see a Chinese temple and a Portuguese *império* (church), observe letterpress printing and hop aboard a vintage trolley.

Time: Allow 2 hours minimum. **Hours:** Park grounds open Mon.-Fri. noon-5, Sat.-Sun. 11-5. Selected historic buildings and exhibits open Sat.-Sun. 11-5. Trolley rides Sat.-Sun. 11-4. Last admission is at 4:30. Park closed Jan. 1, Martin Luther King, Jr. Day, Presidents Day, Easter, Memorial Day, July 4, Labor Day, Thanksgiving, day after Thanksgiving, Christmas Eve and Christmas. **Cost:** Park admission free, except during special events. Admission $5 on Hands-on History Days and during special events; free (ages 0-3). Phone ahead for Hands-on History Days and special events schedule. **Parking:** $6. **Phone:** (408) 287-2290.

Japanese Friendship Garden is at Senter and Story rds. It features landscaping elements and lanterns that reflect Japanese culture. The garden is patterned after a park in Okayama, Japan, San Jose's sister city. **Hours:** Daily 10 a.m.-dusk. **Cost:** Free. **Parking:** $6. **Phone:** (408) 794-7275.

LICK OBSERVATORY is e. via Alum Rock Rd., then 19 mi. on narrow, winding Mount Hamilton Rd. (SR 130). The observatory, at the 4,209-foot summit of Mount Hamilton, was built in 1888 and is the center of observational astronomy for the University of California.

A visitor center in the Main Building contains exhibits, high-definition video displays and the original 36-inch refracting telescope. Talks, given in the dome of the 36-inch refractor, relate the history of the observatory and provide information about current research utilizing the nine telescopes at the mountaintop. A short walk leads to the Shane Dome, where the 120-inch reflector can be seen from a visitors gallery; the gallery also offers an audiovisual presentation and interpretive displays.

Note: Mount Hamilton Rd. is closed during heavy snowfalls. Automotive services are not available. **Time:** Allow 2 hours minimum. **Hours:** Visitor center open Thurs.-Sun. noon-5. Talks at the 36-inch Great Lick Refractor are given every hour on the half-hour 12:30-4:30. Visitor gallery at the 120-inch telescope open daily 10-5. Closed Thanksgiving, Christmas Eve and Christmas. **Cost:** Free. **Phone:** (408) 274-5061 for recorded information.

OVERFELT GARDENS, Educational Park Dr. and McKee Rd., has a self-guiding arboreal trail, wildflower path, fragrance garden and three small lakes. The 5-acre Chinese Cultural Garden contains statues, memorials and displays devoted to ancient Chinese architecture and culture. **Time:** Allow 1 hour, 30 minutes minimum. **Hours:** Daily 10 a.m.-dusk. Closed Jan. 1, Thanksgiving, day after Thanksgiving, Christmas Eve, Christmas and Dec. 31. **Cost:** Free. **Phone:** (408) 794-7275.

ROSICRUCIAN EGYPTIAN MUSEUM is at 1660 Park Ave. (between Naglee and Randol aves.) in the city's historic Rose Garden neighborhood. The museum building, modeled after the Temple of Amon in Karnak, Egypt, houses the largest collection of authentic ancient Egyptian artifacts in western North America.

The collection includes mummies, ancient ritual objects, textiles, musical instruments, toys, jewelry and objects from daily and temple life. Other highlights include an underground tomb and Babylonian, Sumerian and Assyrian artifacts, including seals and tablets with examples of early writing.

Rosicrucian Park is also home to the Rosicrucian Peace Garden, an educational garden authentic to the 18th dynasty of ancient Egypt. It features an outdoor temple, arbor, plants and a reflection pond, as well as the a research library containing rare books

(See maps & indexes p. 346, 348.)

on esoteric and mystical subjects, the Rosicrucian Labyrinth and the Alchemy Garden. **Time:** Allow 2 hours minimum. **Hours:** Museum open Wed.-Fri. 9-5, Sat.-Sun. 10-6. Last admission 1 hour before closing. Rosicrucian Peace Garden open daily 8 a.m.-dusk. Closed major holidays. **Cost:** Museum admission $9; $7 (ages 55+ and students with ID); $5 (ages 5-10). Rosicrucian Peace Gardens and research library free. **Phone:** (408) 947-3636.

THE TECH MUSEUM OF INNOVATION is at 201 S. Market St. The museum is a must-do Silicon Valley experience for all ages, with hundreds of hands-on interactive exhibits and activities. Visitors can measure their brain activity, build a robot, create with the latest in virtual reality and use lab equipment to change the color of bacteria. Educational films are shown on an 8-story, 270-degree screen in the Hackworth IMAX Dome Theater.

Time: Allow 1 hour, 30 minutes minimum. **Hours:** Daily 10-5. Closed Thanksgiving and Christmas. Phone ahead to confirm schedule. **Cost:** Museum galleries only $24; $19 (ages 3-17, ages 65+ and college students with ID). Combination ticket with educational IMAX film $29; $23 (ages 3-17, ages 65+ and college students with ID). **Phone:** (408) 294-8324. 🍽

WINCHESTER MYSTERY HOUSE is at 525 S. Winchester Blvd. (between I-280 and Stevens Creek Blvd.) This Victorian mansion's labyrinthine layout was designed to baffle the spirits that allegedly haunted Sarah Winchester, heiress to the Winchester Arms fortune and mistress of the house.

Bristling with a multitude of gables and cupolas, the wooden structure was under continuous construction for 38 years until Winchester passed away in 1922. The design was so complex—160 rooms, 2,000 doors, 13 bathrooms, 10,000 windows, 47 fireplaces, blind closets, secret passageways and 40 staircases—that the heiress and her servants needed maps to navigate their way around.

The Mansion Tour includes a 65-minute guided walk through the interior, a self-guiding tour of the Victorian gardens and access to two museums displaying collections of Winchester rifles and other products made by the arms manufacturing company. The 2.25-hour Explore More Tour starts with the Mansion tour, then goes deeper into the dark hideaways, attics and other spaces that are rarely open to the public. Halloween Candlelight and Friday the 13th Flashlight tours also are offered.

Time: Allow 2 hours minimum. **Hours:** Daily 9-7, Memorial Day weekend-Labor Day; 9-5, rest of year. Tour times vary; phone for schedule. Closed Christmas. **Cost:** Mansion Tour $39; $32 (ages 65+, military and first responders with ID); $20 (ages 6-12); free (ages 0-5 with paying adult). Explore More Tour $39; $32 (ages 65+, military and first responders with ID); $20 (ages 6-12). Under 6 not permitted on the Explore More Tour. **Phone:** (408) 247-2000.

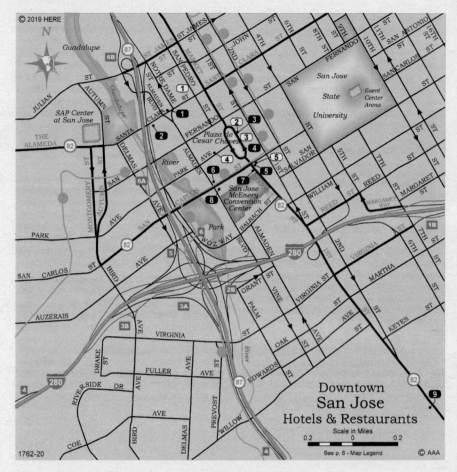

© 2019 HERE

N

Guadalupe

SAP Center at San Jose

THE ALAMEDA

San Jose State University

Event Center Arena

Plaza de Cesar Chavez

San Jose McEnery Convention Center

Downtown
San Jose
Hotels & Restaurants

Scale in Miles
0.2   0   0.2

See p. 6 - Map Legend

© AAA

1762-20

Downtown San Jose

This index helps you "spot" where approved hotels and restaurants are located on the corresponding detailed maps. Restaurant price range is a combination of lunch and/or dinner. Turn to the listing page for more information and consult display ads for special promotions.

 For more details, rates and reservations: AAA.com/travelguides/hotels

DOWNTOWN SAN JOSE

Map Page	Hotels	Diamond Rated	Member Savings	Page
❶ this page	**Hotel De Anza**	◈◈◈	✔	354
❷ this page	AC Hotel by Marriott San Jose Downtown	◈◈◈	✔	354
❸ this page	**The Fairmont San Jose**	◈◈◈◈	✔	354
❹ this page	Four Points by Sheraton San Jose Downtown	◈◈◈	✔	354
❺ this page	**The Westin San Jose**	◈◈◈	✔	354
❻ this page	**Hyatt Place San Jose Downtown**	◈◈◈	✔	354
❼ this page	San Jose Marriott	◈◈◈	✔	354
❽ this page	Hilton San Jose	◈◈◈	✔	354
❾ this page	**Americas Best Value Inn San Jose Convention Center**	◈◈	✔	354

Map Page	Restaurants	Diamond Rated	Cuisine	Price Range	Page
① p. 346	Peggy Sue's	◈	American	$6-$10	355
② p. 346	McCormick & Schmick's	◈◈◈	Seafood	$11-$50	355
③ p. 346	The Grill on the Alley	◈◈◈	Steak	$15-$65	355
④ p. 346	Morton's The Steakhouse	◈◈◈	Steak	$32-$62	355
⑤ p. 346	Il Fornaio	◈◈◈	Italian	$16-$35	355

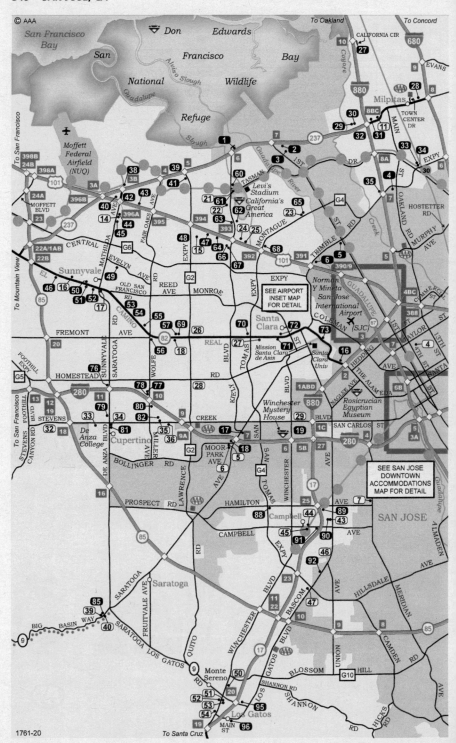

© AAA

1761-20

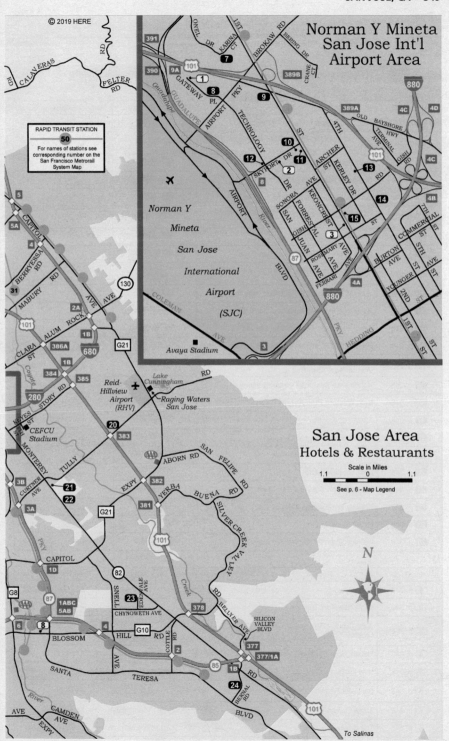

© 2019 HERE

Norman Y Mineta
San Jose Int'l
Airport Area

RAPID TRANSIT STATION
50
For names of stations see
corresponding number on the
San Francisco Metrorail
System Map

Norman Y
Mineta
San Jose
International
Airport
(SJC)

Avaya Stadium

Reid-
Hillview
Airport
(RHV)

Lake
Cunningham

Raging Waters
San Jose

CEFCU
Stadium

San Jose Area
Hotels & Restaurants
Scale in Miles
1.1   0   1.1
See p. 6 - Map Legend

N

To Salinas

San Jose Area

This index helps you "spot" where approved hotels and restaurants are located on the corresponding detailed maps. Restaurant price range is a combination of lunch and/or dinner. Turn to the listing page for more information and consult display ads for special promotions.

 For more details, rates and reservations: AAA.com/travelguides/hotels

SAN JOSE

Map Page	Hotels	Diamond Rated	Member Savings	Page
❶ p. 348	Aloft Santa Clara	◈◈◈	✔	355
❷ p. 348	Courtyard by Marriott San Jose North/Silicon Valley	◈◈◈	✔	355
❸ p. 348	**Hyatt House San Jose/Silicon Valley**	◈◈◈	✔	356
❹ p. 348	**Quality Inn San Jose Airport**	◈◈	✔	356
❺ p. 348	Homewood Suites by Hilton	◈◈◈	✔	356
❻ p. 348	La Quinta Inn & Suites by Wyndham San Jose Airport	◈◈		356
❼ p. 348	**Hyatt Place San Jose Airport**	◈◈◈	✔	356
❽ p. 348	**DoubleTree by Hilton Hotel San Jose**	◈◈◈	✔	355
❾ p. 348	**Fairfield Inn & Suites by Marriott San Jose Airport**	◈◈	✔	355
❿ p. 348	SpringHill Suites by Marriott San Jose Airport	◈◈◈	✔	357
⓫ p. 348	Residence Inn by Marriott San Jose Airport	◈◈◈	✔	356
⓬ p. 348	San Jose Airport Courtyard by Marriott	◈◈◈	✔	356
⓭ p. 348	Four Points by Sheraton San Jose Airport	◈◈◈	✔	355
⓮ p. 348	**Country Inn & Suites by Radisson, San Jose International Airport**	◈◈◈	✔	355
⓯ p. 348	**Holiday Inn San Jose - Silicon Valley**	◈◈◈	✔	356
⓰ p. 348	**Best Western Plus Airport Plaza**	◈◈	✔	355
⓱ p. 348	TownePlace Suites by Marriott San Jose/Cupertino	◈◈◈	✔	357
⓲ p. 348	Aloft San Jose Cupertino	◈◈◈	✔	355
⓳ p. 348	**Hotel Valencia Santana Row**	◈◈◈◈	✔	356
⓴ p. 348	**Best Western Lanai Garden Inn & Suites**	◈◈◈	✔	355
㉑ p. 348	**Hampton Inn & Suites San Jose**	◈◈◈	✔	356
㉒ p. 348	**Holiday Inn Express Central City**	◈◈	✔	356
㉓ p. 348	Hayes Mansion	◈◈◈		356
㉔ p. 348	Residence Inn by Marriott San Jose South	◈◈◈	✔	356

Map Page	Restaurants	Diamond Rated	Cuisine	Price Range	Page
① p. 348	Spencer's	◈◈◈	Steak	$15-$60	357
② p. 348	Vito's New York Trattoria	◈◈	Italian	$14-$29	357
③ p. 348	Jade Cathay Chinese Seafood Cuisine	◈◈	Chinese Seafood Dim Sum	$7-$27	357
④ p. 348	Minato Japanese Restaurant	◈◈	Japanese	$11-$23	357
⑤ p. 348	Koja Kitchen	◈	Asian	$8-$13	357
⑥ p. 348	Santouka Ramen	◈	Japanese Noodles	$10-$14	357
⑦ p. 348	Three Flames Restaurant	◈◈	Continental	$15-$30	357
⑧ p. 348	The Cheesecake Factory	◈◈◈	International	$10-$23	357

MILPITAS

Map Page	Hotels	Diamond Rated	Member Savings	Page
27 p. 348	Residence Inn by Marriott Milpitas Silicon Valley	◈◈◈	✔	137
28 p. 348	**Embassy Suites by Hilton Milpitas Silicon Valley**	◈◈◈	✔	137
29 p. 348	Hilton Garden Inn-San Jose/Milpitas	◈◈◈	✔	137
30 p. 348	**Larkspur Landing Milpitas**	◈◈	✔	137
31 p. 348	**Best Western Plus Brookside Inn**	◈◈◈	✔	137
32 p. 348	**Crowne Plaza San Jose-Silicon Valley**	◈◈◈	✔	137
33 p. 348	TownePlace Suites by Marriott Milpitas	◈◈◈	✔	137
34 p. 348	Milpitas Courtyard by Marriott	◈◈◈	✔	137
35 p. 348	**Sheraton San Jose Hotel**	◈◈◈	✔	137

Map Page	Restaurant	Diamond Rated	Cuisine	Price Range	Page
11 p. 348	Jang Su Jang	◈◈	Korean Barbecue	$11-$38	138

SUNNYVALE

Map Page	Hotels	Diamond Rated	Member Savings	Page
38 p. 348	**Sheraton Sunnyvale**	◈◈◈	✔	390
39 p. 348	**Radisson Hotel Sunnyvale**	◈◈◈	✔	390
40 p. 348	Staybridge Suites Sunnyvale	◈◈◈		390
41 p. 348	Quality Inn Santa Clara Convention Center	◈◈◈		390
42 p. 348	**Comfort Inn Sunnyvale - Silicon Valley**	◈◈	✔	389
43 p. 348	Americas Best Value Inn	◈◈		389
44 p. 348	**Larkspur Landing Sunnyvale**	◈◈◈	✔	390
45 p. 348	**Best Western Silicon Valley Inn**	◈◈◈	✔	389
46 p. 348	**TownePlace Suites by Marriott Sunnyvale/ Mountain View**	◈◈	✔	390
47 p. 348	Residence Inn by Marriott Silicon Valley I	◈◈◈	✔	390
48 p. 348	Residence Inn by Marriott Sunnyvale Silicon Valley II	◈◈◈	✔	390
49 p. 348	Aloft Sunnyvale	◈◈◈	✔	389
50 p. 348	**Grand Hotel**	◈◈◈	✔	389
51 p. 348	Holiday Inn Express Sunnyvale-Silicon Valley	◈◈◈		389
52 p. 348	**Courtyard by Marriott Sunnyvale Mountain View**	◈◈◈	✔	389
53 p. 348	AC Hotel Sunnyvale Cupertino	◈◈◈	✔	389
54 p. 348	**Maple Tree Inn**	◈◈◈	✔	390
55 p. 348	Corporate Inn Sunnyvale	◈◈◈		389
56 p. 348	**Wild Palms Hotel**	◈◈◈	✔	390
57 p. 348	**The Domain Hotel**	◈◈◈	✔	389

Map Page	Restaurants	Diamond Rated	Cuisine	Price Range	Page
14 p. 348	Dish N Dash	◈	Middle Eastern	$9-$19	390
15 p. 348	Faultline Brewing Company	◈◈	American	$16-$38	390
16 p. 348	Pezzella's Villa Napoli	◈◈◈	Italian	$12-$28	390
17 p. 348	P.F. Chang's China Bistro	◈◈◈	Chinese	$9-$25	390
18 p. 348	Vons Chicken	◈◈	Korean Chicken	$12-$27	391

SANTA CLARA

Map Page	Hotels	Diamond Rated	Member Savings	Page
60 p. 348	Hyatt Regency Santa Clara	◈◈◈	✔	362
61 p. 348	Hilton Santa Clara	◈◈◈	✔	362
62 p. 348	Santa Clara Marriott Hotel	◈◈◈	✔	362
63 p. 348	Avatar Hotel	◈◈	✔	361
64 p. 348	The Plaza Suites Silicon Valley@Santa Clara	◈◈◈	✔	362
65 p. 348	Hyatt House Santa Clara	◈◈◈	✔	362
66 p. 348	Embassy Suites by Hilton Santa Clara Silicon Valley	◈◈◈	✔	361
67 p. 348	TownePlace Suites by Marriott San Jose Santa Clara	◈◈◈	✔	362
68 p. 348	Biltmore Hotel & Suites/Silicon Valley	◈◈◈	✔	361
69 p. 348	Best Western Inn Santa Clara	◈◈	✔	361
70 p. 348	Holiday Inn Express & Suites Santa Clara-Silicon Valley	◈◈◈		362
71 p. 348	Holiday Inn Express & Suites Santa Clara	◈◈◈		362
72 p. 348	Best Western University Inn Santa Clara	◈◈◈	✔	361
73 p. 348	Candlewood Suites-Silicon Valley/San Jose	◈◈		361

Map Page	Restaurants	Diamond Rated	Cuisine	Price Range	Page
21 p. 348	La Fontana	◈◈◈	California	$10-$44	362
22 p. 348	Old Ironsides Cafe	◈	Mediterranean Deli	$6-$10	362
23 p. 348	Piatti Ristorante & Bar	◈◈◈	Italian	$14-$28	363
24 p. 348	Birk's Restaurant	◈◈◈	Steak	$13-$42	362
25 p. 348	Pedro's Restaurant & Cantina	◈◈	Mexican	$10-$36	362
26 p. 348	Jang Su Jang	◈◈	Korean Barbecue	$12-$42	362
27 p. 348	La Paloma Restaurante	◈◈	Mexican	$10-$24	362
28 p. 348	Orenchi Ramen	◈◈	Japanese Noodles Small Plates	$11-$15	362
29 p. 348	The Cheesecake Factory	◈◈◈	International	$11-$30	362

CUPERTINO

Map Page	Hotels	Diamond Rated	Member Savings	Page
76 p. 348	Cupertino Hotel	◈◈◈	✔	68
77 p. 348	Hilton Garden Inn Cupertino	◈◈◈	✔	68
78 p. 348	Courtyard by Marriott San Jose Cupertino	◈◈◈	✔	68
79 p. 348	Aloft Cupertino	◈◈◈	✔	68
80 p. 348	Hyatt House San Jose Cupertino	◈◈◈	✔	68
81 p. 348	Juniper Hotel Cupertino, Curio Collection by Hilton	◈◈◈◈	✔	68
82 p. 348	Residence Inn by Marriott San Jose Cupertino	◈◈◈	✔	68

Map Page	Restaurants	Diamond Rated	Cuisine	Price Range	Page
32 p. 348	The Blue Pheasant Restaurant	◈◈	American	$8-$56	68
33 p. 348	Fontana's Italian Restaurant	◈◈	Italian	$15-$40	68
34 p. 348	Parkview	◈◈	American	$10-$30	68
35 p. 348	Alexander's Steakhouse	◈◈◈◈	Steak	$12-$165	68

Map Page	Restaurants (cont'd)	Diamond Rated	Cuisine	Price Range	Page
㊱ p. 348	Little Sheep Mongolian Hot Pot	◆◆	Mongolian	$11-$30	68

SARATOGA

Map Page	Hotel	Diamond Rated	Member Savings	Page
(85) p. 348	The Inn at Saratoga	◆◆◆		372

Map Page	Restaurants	Diamond Rated	Cuisine	Price Range	Page
㊴ p. 348	The Plumed Horse	◆◆◆◆	California	$36-$54	372
㊵ p. 348	La Fondue	◆◆◆	Fondue	$49-$165	372

CAMPBELL

Map Page	Hotels	Diamond Rated	Member Savings	Page
(88) p. 348	**Larkspur Landing Campbell**	◆◆	✔	53
(89) p. 348	Courtyard by Marriott San Jose/Campbell	◆◆◆	✔	53
(90) p. 348	DoubleTree by Hilton-Campbell Pruneyard Plaza	◆◆◆	✔	53
(91) p. 348	TownePlace Suites by Marriott-San Jose/Campbell	◆◆◆	✔	53
(92) p. 348	Residence Inn by Marriott-San Jose/Campbell	◆◆◆	✔	53

Map Page	Restaurants	Diamond Rated	Cuisine	Price Range	Page
㊸ p. 348	Pacific Catch	◆◆◆	Seafood	$12-$27	53
㊹ p. 348	Blue Line Pizza	◆◆	Pizza	$8-$25	53
㊺ p. 348	Naschmarkt Restaurant	◆◆◆	Austrian	$26-$38	53
㊻ p. 348	Grill 'Em Steakhouse	◆◆	Steak	$9-$26	53
㊼ p. 348	Al Castello Ristorante	◆◆	Italian	$10-$25	53

LOS GATOS

Map Page	Hotels	Diamond Rated	Member Savings	Page
(95) p. 348	**Best Western the Inn of Los Gatos**	◆◆◆	✔	127
(96) p. 348	Hotel Los Gatos	◆◆◆		127

Map Page	Restaurants	Diamond Rated	Cuisine	Price Range	Page
㊿ p. 348	The Bywater	◆◆	Cajun Seafood	$12-$28	127
(51) p. 348	Pedro's Restaurant & Cantina	◆◆	Mexican	$13-$30	127
(52) p. 348	Oak & Rye	◆◆	Pizza	$8-$21	127
(53) p. 348	Manresa	◆◆◆◆◆	New American	$295	127
(54) p. 348	Opa! Authentic Greek Cuisine	◆◆	Greek	$11-$25	127

DOWNTOWN SAN JOSE
• Hotels & Restaurants map & index p. 346

AC HOTEL BY MARRIOTT SAN JOSE DOWNTOWN
408/924-0900 **2**

◈◈◈ SAVE Hotel. **Address:** 350 W Santa Clara St 95113

AAA Benefit: Members save 5% or more!

AMERICAS BEST VALUE INN SAN JOSE CONVENTION CENTER
408/993-1711 **9**

◈◈
Motel

Address: 1415 Monterey Rd 95110 **Location:** 1 mi s of I-280 and SR 82 via S 1st St. **Facility:** 26 units. 2 stories (no elevator), exterior corridors. **Amenities:** safes.

THE FAIRMONT SAN JOSE
408/998-1900 **3**

◈◈◈◈
Hotel

Address: 170 S Market St 95113 **Location:** At Fairmont Plaza. **Facility:** Walking distance to downtown attractions, the hotel offers an elegant ambience and is beautifully appointed. Guest rooms are spacious and offer views of Fairmont Square and the surrounding mountains. 805 units. 20 stories, interior corridors. **Parking:** valet only. **Amenities:** safes. **Dining:** 2 restaurants, also, The Grill on the Alley, McCormick & Schmick's, see separate listings. **Pool:** heated outdoor. **Activities:** sauna, steamroom, health club, spa. **Guest Services:** valet laundry.

FOUR POINTS BY SHERATON SAN JOSE DOWNTOWN
408/282-8800 **4**

◈◈◈ SAVE Hotel. **Address:** 211 S 1st St 95113

AAA Benefit: Members save 5% or more!

HILTON SAN JOSE
408/287-2100 **8**

◈◈◈ SAVE Hotel. **Address:** 300 Almaden Blvd 95110

AAA Benefit: Members save up to 15%!

🔗 **Love the great outdoors?**

Find places to camp

at AAA.com/campgrounds

HOTEL DE ANZA
408/286-1000 **1**

◈◈◈
Hotel

Address: 233 W Santa Clara St 95113 **Location:** SR 87 exit Santa Clara St, just e. **Facility:** 100 units. 10 stories, interior corridors. **Parking:** on-site (fee) and valet. **Dining:** entertainment. **Activities:** exercise room. **Guest Services:** valet laundry. Affiliated with Destination Hotels.

HYATT PLACE SAN JOSE DOWNTOWN
408/998-0400 **6**

◈◈◈
Hotel

 HYATT PLACE

AAA Benefit: Members save up to 10%!

Address: 282 Almaden Blvd 95113 **Location:** I-280 exit Almaden-Vine, 6 blks n. Opposite convention center. **Facility:** 236 units. 9 stories, interior corridors. **Parking:** on-site (fee). **Amenities:** safes, exercise room. **Guest Services:** valet laundry. **Featured Amenity:** breakfast buffet.

SAN JOSE MARRIOTT
408/280-1300 **7**

◈◈◈
Hotel

 MARRIOTT

AAA Benefit: Members save 5% or more!

Address: 301 S Market St 95113 **Location:** SR 87 exit Santa Clara St E, s on Almaden Blvd, then just e on San Carlos St. Adjacent to Fairmont Square. **Facility:** 510 units. 26 stories, interior corridors. **Parking:** valet only. **Terms:** check-in 4 pm. **Amenities:** safes. **Dining:** 2 restaurants. **Pool:** heated outdoor. **Activities:** hot tub, exercise room. **Guest Services:** valet and coin laundry.

THE WESTIN SAN JOSE
408/295-2000 **5**

◈◈◈
Historic Hotel

 WESTIN HOTELS & RESORTS

AAA Benefit: Members save 5% or more!

Address: 302 S Market St 95113 **Location:** SR 87 exit Santa Clara St E, s on Almaden Blvd, just e on San Carlos St. **Facility:** This beautifully restored 1926 hotel features public spaces that are impressive and photo worthy. Guest room décor is a beautiful blend of classic and modern design. 171 units, some two bedrooms. 6 stories, interior corridors. **Parking:** valet only. **Amenities:** safes. **Dining:** Il Fornaio, see separate listing. **Activities:** trails, exercise room. **Guest Services:** valet laundry.

(See map & index p. 346.)

WHERE TO EAT

THE GRILL ON THE ALLEY 408/294-2244 (3)
♦♦♦ Steak. Fine Dining. **Address:** 172 S Market St 95113

IL FORNAIO 408/271-3366 (5)
♦♦♦ Italian. Fine Dining. **Address:** 302 S Market St 95113

MCCORMICK & SCHMICK'S 408/283-7200 (2)
♦♦♦ Seafood. Fine Dining. **Address:** 170 S Market St 95113

MORTON'S THE STEAKHOUSE 408/947-7000 (4)
♦♦♦ Steak. Fine Dining. **Address:** 177 Park Ave 95113

PEGGY SUE'S 408/298-6750 (1)
♦ American. Quick Serve. **Address:** 29 N San Pedro St 95110

SAN JOSE
- Restaurants p. 357
- Hotels & Restaurants map & index p. 348

ALOFT SAN JOSE CUPERTINO 408/864-0300 (18)
♦♦♦ SAVE Hotel. **Address:** 4241 Moorpark Ave 95129
AAA Benefit: Members save 5% or more!

ALOFT SANTA CLARA 408/263-3900 (1)
♦♦♦ SAVE Hotel. **Address:** 510 America Center Ct 95002
AAA Benefit: Members save 5% or more!

BEST WESTERN LANAI GARDEN INN & SUITES
408/929-8100 (20)

♦♦♦ Hotel

BW Best Western. **AAA Benefit:** Members save up to 15% and earn bonus points!

Address: 1575 Tully Rd 95122 **Location:** US 101 exit Tully Rd, just e. **Facility:** 52 units. 2 stories, interior corridors. **Pool:** outdoor. **Featured Amenity:** continental breakfast.

SAVE ♦♦ CALL ♦ ♦ BIZ ♦
♦ ♦ ♦ ♦

BEST WESTERN PLUS AIRPORT PLAZA
408/243-2400 (16)

♦♦♦ Hotel

BW Best Western PLUS. **AAA Benefit:** Members save up to 15% and earn bonus points!

Address: 2118 The Alameda 95126 **Location:** I-880 exit The Alameda, just w. **Facility:** 40 units. 2 stories, interior corridors. **Pool:** outdoor. **Activities:** hot tub, exercise room. **Guest Services:** valet laundry. **Featured Amenity:** breakfast buffet.

SAVE ♦♦ CALL ♦ ♦ ♦ BIZ
HS ♦ ♦ ♦ ♦ ♦

COUNTRY INN & SUITES BY RADISSON, SAN JOSE INTERNATIONAL AIRPORT 408/467-1789 (14)

♦♦ Hotel

Address: 1350 N 4th St 95112 **Location:** US 101 exit N 1st St, 0.5 mi s to Rosemary St E. **Facility:** 126 units, some efficiencies. 3 stories, interior corridors. **Pool:** outdoor. **Activities:** hot tub, exercise room. **Guest Services:** valet and coin laundry. **Featured Amenity:** continental breakfast.

SAVE ♦ ♦♦ CALL ♦ ♦ ♦
BIZ ♦ ♦ ♦ ♦ ♦ ♦

COURTYARD BY MARRIOTT SAN JOSE NORTH/SILICON VALLEY 408/383-3700 (2)
♦♦♦ SAVE Hotel. **Address:** 111 Holger Way 95134
AAA Benefit: Members save 5% or more!

DOUBLETREE BY HILTON HOTEL SAN JOSE
408/453-4000 (8)

♦♦♦ Hotel
DOUBLETREE BY HILTON

AAA Benefit: Members save up to 15%!

Address: 2050 Gateway Pl 95110 **Location:** 0.3 mi e of Norman Y. Mineta San Jose International Airport via Airport Blvd; w of US 101 exit N 1st St; US 101 exit Brokaw Rd northbound. **Facility:** 505 units. 10 stories, interior corridors. **Parking:** on-site (fee) and valet. **Dining:** 2 restaurants, also, Spencer's, see separate listing. **Pool:** heated outdoor. **Activities:** hot tub, trails, exercise room. **Guest Services:** valet laundry.

SAVE ECO ♦ ♦♦ ♦ ♦ CALL ♦ ♦ ♦ BIZ
$HS ♦ ♦ ♦ /SOME UNITS ♦ ♦ ♦

FAIRFIELD INN & SUITES BY MARRIOTT SAN JOSE AIRPORT 408/453-3133 (9)

♦♦♦ Hotel
Fairfield
AAA Benefit: Members save 5% or more!

Address: 1755 N 1st St 95112 **Location:** US 101 exit N 1st St, just w. **Facility:** 186 units. 3 stories, interior corridors. **Amenities:** safes. **Pool:** heated outdoor. **Activities:** hot tub, exercise room. **Guest Services:** valet and coin laundry, area transportation. **Featured Amenity:** breakfast buffet.

SAVE ♦ ♦♦ CALL ♦ ♦ ♦
BIZ ♦ ♦ ♦ ♦ ♦
/SOME UNITS HS

FOUR POINTS BY SHERATON SAN JOSE AIRPORT
408/452-0200 (13)
♦♦♦ SAVE Hotel. **Address:** 1471 N 4th St 95112
AAA Benefit: Members save 5% or more!

(See map & index p. 348.)

HAMPTON INN & SUITES SAN JOSE
408/298-7373

Hotel

AAA Benefit: Members save up to 15%!

Address: 55 Old Tully Rd 95111 **Location:** US 101 exit Tully Rd, 1 mi w, then just s. **Facility:** 80 units. 3 stories, interior corridors. **Pool:** heated outdoor. **Activities:** exercise room. **Guest Services:** valet laundry. **Featured Amenity:** breakfast buffet.

HAYES MANSION   408/226-3200
Hotel. **Address:** 200 Edenvale Ave 95136

HOLIDAY INN EXPRESS CENTRAL CITY
408/279-6600

Hotel

Address: 2660 Monterey Hwy 95111 **Location:** US 101 exit Tully Rd, 1 mi w, then 0.8 mi s. **Facility:** 57 units. 2 stories, exterior corridors. **Amenities:** safes. **Pool:** heated outdoor. **Activities:** sauna, hot tub, exercise room. **Guest Services:** valet and coin laundry. **Featured Amenity:** breakfast buffet.

HOLIDAY INN SAN JOSE - SILICON VALLEY
408/453-6200

Hotel

Address: 1350 N 1st St 95112 **Location:** I-880 exit N 1st St, just w. **Facility:** 354 units. 9 stories, interior corridors. **Parking:** on-site (fee). **Pool:** heated outdoor. **Activities:** exercise room. **Guest Services:** valet and coin laundry.

HOMEWOOD SUITES BY HILTON   408/428-9900
SAVE Extended Stay Hotel. **Address:** 10 W Trimble Rd 95131

AAA Benefit: Members save up to 15%!

HOTEL VALENCIA SANTANA ROW   408/551-0010

Hotel

Address: 355 Santana Row 95128 **Location:** I-880 exit Stevens Creek Blvd, just w; in Santana Row shopping area. **Facility:** Located in the heart of Santana Row (an upscale shopping center), shops and restaurants are just steps outside the front door. This hotel is attractively appointed with Italian and Spanish elements. 215 units. 7 stories, interior corridors. **Parking:** on-site and valet. **Amenities:** safes. **Pool:** heated outdoor. **Activities:** hot tub, exercise room. **Guest Services:** valet laundry. **Featured Amenity:** continental breakfast.

HYATT HOUSE SAN JOSE/SILICON VALLEY
408/324-1155

Extended Stay Hotel

AAA Benefit: Members save up to 10%!

Address: 75 Headquarters Dr 95134 **Location:** SR 237 exit N 1st St, just s, then just e. **Facility:** 164 units, some two bedrooms and efficiencies. 7 stories, interior corridors. **Amenities:** safes. **Pool:** heated outdoor. **Activities:** exercise room. **Guest Services:** valet and coin laundry. **Featured Amenity:** breakfast buffet.

HYATT PLACE SAN JOSE AIRPORT   669/342-0007

Hotel

AAA Benefit: Members save up to 10%!

Address: 82 Karina Cir 95131 **Location:** US 101 exit Brokaw Rd, just nw; 0.5 mi ne of Norman Y. Mineta San Jose International Airport. **Facility:** 190 units. 7 stories, interior corridors. **Parking:** on-site (fee). **Pool:** heated outdoor. **Activities:** exercise room. **Guest Services:** complimentary and valet laundry.

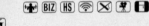

LA QUINTA INN & SUITES BY WYNDHAM SAN JOSE AIRPORT
408/435-8800
Hotel. **Address:** 2585 Seaboard Ave 95131

QUALITY INN SAN JOSE AIRPORT   408/434-9330

Hotel

Address: 2390 Harris Way 95131 **Location:** I-880 exit Montague Expwy, just e. Milpitas, 30. **Facility:** 49 units. 3 stories, interior corridors. **Activities:** exercise room. **Guest Services:** coin laundry. **Featured Amenity:** full hot breakfast.

RESIDENCE INN BY MARRIOTT SAN JOSE AIRPORT
408/650-0580
SAVE Extended Stay Contemporary Hotel. **Address:** 10 Skyport Dr 95110

AAA Benefit: Members save 5% or more!

RESIDENCE INN BY MARRIOTT SAN JOSE SOUTH
408/226-7676
SAVE Extended Stay Hotel. **Address:** 6111 San Ignacio Ave 95119

AAA Benefit: Members save 5% or more!

SAN JOSE AIRPORT COURTYARD BY MARRIOTT
408/441-6111
SAVE Hotel. **Address:** 1727 Technology Dr 95110

AAA Benefit: Members save 5% or more!

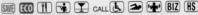

(See map & index p. 348.)

SPRINGHILL SUITES BY MARRIOTT SAN JOSE AIRPORT
408/650-0590 **10**
▼▼▼ SAVE Contemporary Hotel. **Address:** 10 Skyport Dr 95110

| **AAA Benefit:** Members save 5% or more! |

TOWNEPLACE SUITES BY MARRIOTT SAN JOSE/CUPERTINO
408/984-5903 **17**
▼▼▼ SAVE Extended Stay Hotel. **Address:** 440 Saratoga Ave 95129

| **AAA Benefit:** Members save 5% or more! |

WHERE TO EAT

ARMADILLO WILLY'S BAR-B-QUE
408/224-7427
▼ Barbecue. Quick Serve. **Address:** 878 Blossom Hill Rd 95123

THE CHEESECAKE FACTORY
408/225-6948 **8**
▼▼▼ International. Casual Dining. **Address:** 925 Blossom Hill Rd 95123

JADE CATHAY CHINESE SEAFOOD CUISINE
408/392-9388 **3**
▼▼ Chinese Seafood Dim Sum. Casual Dining. **Address:** 1339 N 1st St 95112

KOJA KITCHEN
408/418-5211 **5**
▼ Asian. Quick Serve. **Address:** 4342 Moorpark Ave, Suite B 95129

MINATO JAPANESE RESTAURANT
408/998-9711 **4**
▼▼ Japanese. Casual Dining. **Address:** 617 N 6th St 95112

SANTOUKA RAMEN
408/446-1101 **6**
▼ Japanese Noodles. Quick Serve. **Address:** 675 Saratoga Ave 95129

SPENCER'S
408/437-2170 **1**
▼▼▼ Steak. Fine Dining. **Address:** 2050 Gateway Pl 95110

THREE FLAMES RESTAURANT
408/269-3133 **7**
▼▼ Continental. Casual Dining. **Address:** 1547 Meridian Ave 95125

VITO'S NEW YORK TRATTORIA
408/453-1000 **2**
▼▼ Italian. Casual Dining. **Address:** 90 Skyport Dr, Suite 170 95110

SAN JUAN BAUTISTA (G-3) pop. 1,862, elev. 200'

MISSION SAN JUAN BAUTISTA is at 2nd and Mariposa sts. Founded June 24, 1797, the mission was named for St. John the Baptist. With a three-aisle entrance to the altar, it was the widest of the mission churches. In recognition of its importance, a set of nine bells once graced the chapel area; only three remain. The mission has period furnishings, and the convent wing contains relics.

Original artifacts include altar statues, wall decorations and a baptismal font as well as an 1816 altar screen. It is still an active Catholic church. **Hours:** Daily 9:30-4. Closed Jan. 1, Good Friday, day before Thanksgiving, Thanksgiving, Christmas Eve and Dec. 31. **Cost:** $4; $3 (ages 60+); $2 (ages 5-16). **Phone:** (831) 623-4528.

SAN JUAN BAUTISTA STATE HISTORIC PARK, on the plaza, includes the Plaza Hotel, built in 1858 on the site of the old Spanish soldiers' barracks, and the 1840 Castro-Breen Adobe, headquarters of the Mexican government and later home of the Patrick Breen family, survivors of the ill-fated Donner party.

Other attractions are the 1868 Zanetta House, a blacksmith shop, a jail, gardens, a Spanish orchard, a livery stable with old carriages and a slide show about the history of San Juan Bautista. **Time:** Allow 1 hour minimum. **Hours:** Daily 10-4:30. Closed Jan. 1, Thanksgiving and Christmas. **Cost:** $3; free (ages 0-16). **Phone:** (831) 623-4881. GT 🏕

SAN LEANDRO pop. 84,950, elev. 59'
• Hotels & Restaurants map & index p. 176

BUDGET INN
510/276-6290 **46**
▼▼▼
Hotel

Address: 16500 Foothill Blvd 94578 **Location:** I-580 exit 33 (164th Ave), just se. **Facility:** 45 units. 3 stories, interior corridors.

SAVE CALL 🚻 📶 🛗 🖥

HILTON GARDEN INN OAKLAND/SAN LEANDRO
510/346-5533 **49**
▼▼▼ SAVE Hotel. **Address:** 510 Lewelling Blvd 94579

| **AAA Benefit:** Members save up to 15%! |

THE MARINA INN ON SAN FRANCISCO BAY
510/895-1311 **47**
▼▼▼ Hotel. **Address:** 68 Monarch Bay Dr 94577

WHERE TO EAT

EL TORITO
510/351-8825
▼▼ Mexican. Casual Dining. **Address:** 5 Monarch Bay Dr 94577

HORATIO'S
510/351-5556 **48**
▼▼▼ American. Fine Dining. **Address:** 60 Monarch Bay Dr 94577

SAN MATEO (D-8) pop. 97,207, elev. 29'
• Hotels p. 358 • Restaurants p. 358
• Hotels & Restaurants map & index p. 316
• Part of San Francisco area — see map p. 243

This San Francisco residential suburb is connected to the East Bay via the 7-mile-long San Mateo-Hayward Bridge. Comprising five steel spans, it is one of the longest highway bridges in the country.

San Mateo Area Chamber of Commerce: 1700 S. El Camino Real, Suite 108, San Mateo, CA 94402. **Phone:** (650) 401-2440.

CURIODYSSEY is on Coyote Point Dr. in Coyote Point Park. The science museum and zoo lets kids

(See map & index p. 316.)

observe wild animals, experiment with scientific phenomena and allow the natural world to answer their questions.

Hours: Tues.-Sun. 10-5. Closed Jan. 1, July 4, Thanksgiving, Christmas Eve and Christmas. **Cost:** (includes museum and wildlife habitats) $11; $8 (ages 2-12); $7 (ages 13-17 and 62+); free (ages 0-1 and educators with ID). Park admission $6 per private vehicle (cash only). **Phone:** (650) 342-7755.

BEST WESTERN COYOTE POINT INN
650/347-9990 58

Hotel

Best Western. AAA Benefit: Members save up to 15% and earn bonus points!

Address: 480 N Bayshore Blvd 94401 **Location:** US 101 exit Dore Ave northbound; exit 3rd Ave E southbound, re-enter US 101 exit Dore Ave. **Facility:** 99 units. 4 stories, interior corridors. **Amenities:** safes. **Activities:** sauna, hot tub, exercise room. **Guest Services:** complimentary laundry. **Featured Amenity:** continental breakfast.

SAVE ¶↑ CALL 🚹 👭 BIZ HS
🛜 ✕ 🛏 💻 💻

HILTON GARDEN INN SAN MATEO
650/522-9000 60
👑👑👑 SAVE Hotel. **Address:** 2000 Bridgepointe Cir 94404

AAA Benefit: Members save up to 15%!

HOLIDAY INN & SUITES SAN MATEO-SFO
650/344-3219 59
👑👑 Hotel. **Address:** 330 N Bayshore Blvd 94401

LOS PRADOS HOTEL
650/341-3300 63
👑👑 Hotel. **Address:** 2940 S Norfolk St 94403

RESIDENCE INN BY MARRIOTT
650/574-4700 62
👑👑👑 SAVE Extended Stay Hotel. **Address:** 2000 Winward Way 94404

AAA Benefit: Members save 5% or more!

SAN MATEO MARRIOTT SAN FRANCISCO AIRPORT
650/653-6000 61

Hotel

MARRIOTT. AAA Benefit: Members save 5% or more!

Address: 1770 S Amphlett Blvd 94402 **Location:** Northwest of jct US 101 and SR 92; SR 92 exit Delaware St, e on Concar Dr. **Facility:** 476 units. 3-6 stories, interior corridors. **Parking:** on-site (fee) and valet. **Amenities:** Some: safes. **Pool:** heated outdoor. **Activities:** hot tub, exercise room, massage. **Guest Services:** valet laundry, boarding pass kiosk.

SAVE ECO ✈ ¶↑ 👭 🍸 CALL 🚹 🚐 👭 BIZ
sHS 🛜 ✕ 🎥 🛏 💻 / SOME UNITS 💻

WHERE TO EAT

ARMADILLO WILLY'S BAR-B-QUE 650/571-7427
👑 Barbecue. Quick Serve. **Address:** 2260 Bridgepointe Pkwy 94404

CENTRAL PARK BISTRO 650/558-8401 52
👑👑👑 American. Casual Dining. **Address:** 181 E 4th Ave 94401

CLAY OVEN 650/342-9194 50
👑👑 Indian. Casual Dining. **Address:** 78 E 3rd Ave 94401

CURRY UP NOW 650/316-8648 45
👑 Indian. Quick Serve. **Address:** 129 S B St 94401

ESPETUS CHURRASCARIA 650/342-8700 53
👑👑👑 Brazilian Steak. Casual Dining. **Address:** 710 S B St 94401

THE FISH MARKET SEAFOOD MARKET RESTAURANT 650/349-3474 55
👑👑 Seafood. Casual Dining. **Address:** 1855 S Norfolk St 94403

FUSION PERUVIAN GRILL 650/292-0788 44
👑👑 Peruvian. Casual Dining. **Address:** 45 N B St 94401

HIMAWARI-TEI RAMEN RESTAURANT 650/375-1005 47
👑👑 Japanese Noodles. Casual Dining. **Address:** 202 2nd Ave 94401

IZAKAYA MAI 650/347-2511 46
👑👑 Japanese. Casual Dining. **Address:** 212 2nd Ave 94401

JACK'S PRIME BURGERS 650/638-1479 58
👑👑 Burgers. Casual Dining. **Address:** 3723 S El Camino Real 94403

LITTLE SHANGHAI RESTAURANT 650/573-7161 57
👑👑 Chinese. Casual Dining. **Address:** 17 E 25th Ave 94403

LITTLE SHEEP MONGOLIAN HOT POT 650/343-2566 48
👑👑 Mongolian. Casual Dining. **Address:** 215 S Ellsworth Ave 94401

RAMEN DOJO 650/401-6568 54
👑👑 Japanese Noodles. Casual Dining. **Address:** 805 S B St 94401

SAN MATEO PRIME 650/558-8918 49
👑👑 Steak. Casual Dining. **Address:** 174 3rd Ave 94401

SANTA RAMEN 650/344-5918 56
👑👑 Japanese Noodles. Casual Dining. **Address:** 1944 S El Camino Real 94403

VIOGNIER 650/685-3727 51
👑👑👑 French. Fine Dining. **Address:** 222 E 4th Ave 94401

SAN RAFAEL (C-7) pop. 57,713, elev. 34'
• Part of San Francisco area — see map p. 243

This bustling Marin County residential city traces its beginnings to the early 19th-century founding of Mission San Rafael. The Downtown San Rafael Farmers Market sets up along Fourth Street (between B and Cijos streets) Thursday evenings from 6 to 9 p.m., April through September. In addition to seasonal produce from area farmers, the market offers healthy, yummy prepared foods from vendors and local businesses. Street musicians, art and craft booths and activities for kids add to the family-friendly atmosphere.

The Marin Shakespeare Company presents plays by the Bard at Forest Meadows Amphitheatre, on the campus of the Dominican University of California; take the US 101 Central San Rafael exit and follow signs to the university. Visitor parking is available in the lot on Belle Avenue (across from the Marin Tennis Club). The season runs from late June through September, with performances on Friday, Saturday and Sunday evenings, plus a Sunday matinee; phone (415) 499-4488 for the box office.

Marin Convention & Visitors Bureau: 1 Mitchell Blvd., Suite B, San Rafael, CA 94903. **Phone:** (415) 925-2060 or (866) 925-2060.

GUIDE DOGS FOR THE BLIND is w. off US 101 Freitas Pkwy. exit (southbound) or N. San Pedro Rd. exit (northbound), then w. to 350 Los Ranchitos Rd. The organization, which provides guide dogs and training for the visually impaired, offers guided walking tours of its facility.

Visitors see Labrador, Golden Retriever and Golden Retriever/Labrador-cross pups and learn about the guide dog training process. The tour also may include visits to the veterinary clinic, puppy socialization area and the state-of-the-art student residence.

Time: Allow 1 hour minimum. **Hours:** Guided tours are given Mon.-Sat. at 10:30 and 2. Phone to confirm holiday and graduation schedules. **Cost:** Free. Tours are not recommended for under age 5. **Phone:** (415) 499-4000 or (800) 295-4050.

MARIN COUNTY CIVIC CENTER, just n. of San Rafael off US 101, was the last major project of renowned architect Frank Lloyd Wright. The 140 landscaped acres include fairgrounds, theaters, exhibit halls and a lagoon. The civic center itself is divided into two wings—the administrative offices and the Hall of Justice—joined by an 80-foot dome. Both are included on a 1.5-hour, docent-led guided tour.

Time: Allow 1 hour, 30 minutes minimum. **Hours:** Self-guiding tours Mon.-Fri. 9-4. Guided tour offered Wed. at 10:30. Closed major holidays. **Cost:** Building free. Self-guiding tour booklet available for a small fee. Guided tour $10; $5 (ages 62+ and students with ID). **Phone:** (415) 473-3762. 🍴

EMBASSY SUITES BY HILTON SAN RAFAEL MARIN COUNTY 415/499-9222

▼▼▼▼ SAVE Hotel. **Address:** 101 McInnis Pkwy 94903

AAA Benefit: Members save up to 15%!

FOUR POINTS BY SHERATON SAN RAFAEL 415/479-8800

▼▼▼ SAVE Hotel. **Address:** 1010 Northgate Dr 94903

AAA Benefit: Members save 5% or more!

MARIN LODGE 415/578-2827

▼▼ Motel. **Address:** 1735 Lincoln Ave 94901

TRAVELODGE SAN RAFAEL 415/454-9470

▼▼ Motel. **Address:** 865 Francisco Blvd E 94901

WHERE TO EAT

IL DAVIDE RESTAURANT 415/454-8080

▼▼▼ Italian. Fine Dining. **Address:** 901 A St 94901

LE CHALET BASQUE RESTAURANT 415/479-1070

▼▼ Basque. Casual Dining. **Address:** 405 N San Pedro Rd 94903

LOTUS CUISINE OF INDIA 415/456-5808

▼▼ Indian. Casual Dining. **Address:** 704 4th St 94901

SOL FOOD PUERTO RICAN CUISINE 415/256-8900

▼ Puerto Rican. Quick Serve. **Address:** 901 Lincoln Ave 94901

UCHIWA RAMEN 415/991-3693

▼▼ Japanese Noodles. Casual Dining. **Address:** 821 B St 94901

WEST BROOKLYN PIZZA 415/453-7914

▼▼ Pizza. Casual Dining. **Address:** 900 B Anderson Dr 94901

YET WAH 415/460-9883

▼▼ Chinese. Casual Dining. **Address:** 1238 4th St 94901

SAN RAMON pop. 72,148
• Restaurants p. 360
• Hotels & Restaurants map & index p. 176

COURTYARD BY MARRIOTT SAN RAMON
925/866-2900 🔢44

▼▼▼ Hotel

COURTYARD **AAA Benefit:** Members save 5% or more!

Address: 18090 San Ramon Valley Blvd 94583 **Location:** I-680 exit 34 (Bollinger Canyon Rd), just w, then just s; jct Bollinger Crossing. **Facility:** 136 units. 4 stories, interior corridors. **Parking:** on-site (fee). **Pool:** heated outdoor. **Activities:** exercise room. **Guest Services:** valet and coin laundry, boarding pass kiosk, area transportation.

(See map & index p. 176.)

HYATT HOUSE SAN RAMON   925/743-1882 ④①

Extended Stay Contemporary Hotel

AAA Benefit: Members save up to 10%!

Address: 2323 San Ramon Valley Blvd 94583 **Location:** I-680 exit 36 (Crow Canyon Rd), just w, then just n. **Facility:** 142 efficiencies. 4 stories, interior corridors. **Amenities:** safes. **Pool:** heated outdoor. **Activities:** hot tub, exercise room. **Featured Amenity: breakfast buffet.**

/SOME UNITS

RESIDENCE INN BY MARRIOTT   925/277-9292 ④③

Extended Stay Hotel. **Address:** 1071 Market Pl 94583

AAA Benefit: Members save 5% or more!

SAN RAMON MARRIOTT   925/867-9200 ④②

Hotel

AAA Benefit: Members save 5% or more!

Address: 2600 Bishop Dr 94583 **Location:** I-680 exit 34 (Bollinger Canyon Rd), just e, n on Sunset Dr, then just w. **Facility:** 368 units. 6 stories, interior corridors. **Parking:** on-site (fee) and valet. **Dining:** Bishop Grill, see separate listing. **Pool:** heated outdoor. **Activities:** sauna, exercise room. **Guest Services:** valet and coin laundry, boarding pass kiosk, area transportation.

WHERE TO EAT

BISHOP GRILL   925/244-6114 ④④
American. Casual Dining. **Address:** 2600 Bishop Dr 94583

THE HOPYARD AMERICAN ALEHOUSE & GRILL   925/277-9600 ④⑤
American. Casual Dining. **Address:** 470 Market Pl 94583

ZACHARY'S CHICAGO PIZZA   925/244-1222 ④③
Pizza. Casual Dining. **Address:** 3110 Crow Canyon Pl 94583

SANTA CLARA (E-9) pop. 116,468, elev. 88'
• Restaurants p. 362
• Hotels & Restaurants map & index p. 348

Santa Clara was once an agricultural community renowned for its orchards. Today the Intel Corporation is among the high-tech giants headquartered in the city. In 2014 the Silicon Valley powerhouse welcomed the NFL's San Francisco 49ers, who play at Levi's Stadium.

Located at 4900 Marie P. DeBartolo Way and Tasman Avenue and accessible via US 101, I-880,

the Lawrence Expressway and the San Tomas Expressway, the venue—appropriately—is state of the art when it comes to technological innovation, featuring a green roof, stadium-wide Wi-Fi capability and huge HD video screens. On game days, Caltrain provides service from San Francisco that connects with Valley Transportation Authority (VTA) light-rail trains and buses. For schedules and fares check the Caltrain or VTA websites or phone VTA at (408) 321-2300. For 49ers ticket information phone (415) 464-9377.

Guided and self-guiding campus tours are available at Santa Clara University, founded in 1851. From US 101, take the De La Cruz Boulevard/Santa Clara exit to El Camino Real and follow signs to the university. Visitors are welcome at the free Music at Noon series, which takes place every Wednesday during the academic year at the Music Recital Hall and frequently features high-profile Bay Area performers. Pick up a campus map at the Admission & Enrollment Services Building (#406); for additional campus information phone (408) 554-4000.

Santa Clara Convention and Visitors Bureau: 1850 Warburton Ave., Santa Clara, CA 95050. **Phone:** (408) 244-9660 or (408) 244-8244.

Shopping: Westfield Valley Fair, off I-880 at Stevens Creek Boulevard, features Macy's, Nordstrom and more than 250 upscale specialty stores.

CALIFORNIA'S GREAT AMERICA, , at 4701 Great America Pkwy. between US 101 and SR 237, is a 100-acre family theme park combining movie magic with theme park thrills and excitement. Among more than 50 rides and attractions are the Great Barrier Reef wave pool; a double-decker carousel; Drop Tower, a 20-story free-fall ride; and Delirium, a spinning pendulum-like ride. Among the nine roller coasters is Patriot, a floorless coaster that reaches 45 mph.

Other highlights include the Australian-themed Boomerang Bay water park with waterslides and lazy river.

Planet Snoopy has rides, shows and opportunities to meet the Peanuts gang. Theaters present stage shows, and concerts are held in an outdoor amphitheater. Children can climb and play at the Construction Zone.

Hours: Park open daily at 10, June 1-Labor Day; schedule varies, Apr.-May and day after Labor Day-late Oct. Phone for hours during WinterFest in Dec. Water park open daily at 11, early June to mid-Aug.; schedule varies, mid-May to early June and mid-Aug. through Labor Day. Closing times vary for both parks. Closed Easter. Phone ahead to confirm schedule. **Cost:** $69 (includes water park); $48 (ages 62+ and under 48 inches tall); free (ages 0-2). Admission after 4 p.m. $35. Admission and parking is discounted for advance online purchases. **Parking:** $20. **Phone:** (408) 988-1776.

DE SAISSET MUSEUM, on the Santa Clara University campus, is both an art and history museum. The

(See map & index p. 348.)

permanent collection includes paintings by Renaissance, baroque and rococo artists; 19th-century, modernist and contemporary prints; and photographs. California historical items range from Native American baskets and hand tools to such Mission-period artifacts as devotional objects and decorative arts.

Time: Allow 1 hour minimum. Hours: Tues.-Sun. 11-4, mid-Sept. to mid-June. Closed major holidays and between exhibitions. Phone ahead to confirm schedule. Cost: Free. Phone: (408) 554-4528.

INTEL MUSEUM is .5 mi. n. off US 101 Montague Expwy. exit, then .4 mi. w. to 2200 Mission College Blvd., in the Intel Corp.'s Robert Noyce Building. Exhibits focus on the manufacture and use of computer chips. Visitors can communicate in binary code and learn how a computer performs simple calculations using a giant talking microprocessor. A section about clean rooms ("fabs") details 47 steps workers perform before entering a chip-making factory. A "bunny suit" also is on display.

A time line details the progress of computers and Intel history. Time: Allow 1 hour minimum. Hours: Mon.-Fri. 9-6, Sat. 10-5. Closed major holidays. Phone ahead to confirm schedule. Cost: Free. Phone: (408) 765-5050.

MISSION SANTA CLARA DE ASIS is on the Santa Clara University campus, off the US 101 De La Cruz exit to 500 El Camino Real. It was founded in 1777, the eighth of 21 missions built in California in the 1700s. It has the distinction of being the first mission named for a woman, Saint Clare of Assisi, the founder of the Poor Clares order. Established to help protect early settlers in the San Francisco Bay Area, it is the only mission associated with a university.

The building is a replica of the third mission, which was built in 1825. Artifacts on display include three bells given to the mission by the king of Spain. The original mission garden is intact; the months of peak bloom are April and May. Time: Allow 30 minutes minimum. Hours: Mission church open daily 7 a.m.-dusk. Office open Mon.-Fri. 1-5. Cost: Free. Phone: (408) 554-4023, or (408) 554-4528 for guided tours.

Love the Great Outdoors?

Visit AAA.com/campgrounds

AVATAR HOTEL

Hotel
408/235-8900 63

Address: 4200 Great America Pkwy 95054 Location: 0.5 mi n off US 101 exit 393 (Great America Pkwy); 0.8 mi s of California's Great America theme park. Facility: 168 units. 4 stories, exterior corridors. Pool: heated outdoor. Activities: hot tub, exercise room. Guest Services: valet laundry. Affiliated with Joie de Vivre Hotels & Resorts.

BEST WESTERN INN SANTA CLARA
408/244-3366 69

Motel

Best Western. AAA Benefit: Members save up to 15% and earn bonus points!

Address: 4341 El Camino Real 95051 Location: SR 82, 2 blks w of Lawrence Expwy. Facility: 52 units. 2 stories (no elevator), exterior corridors. Guest Services: valet and coin laundry. Featured Amenity: continental breakfast.

BEST WESTERN UNIVERSITY INN SANTA CLARA
408/244-8313 72

Hotel

Best Western. AAA Benefit: Members save up to 15% and earn bonus points!

Address: 1655 El Camino Real 95050 Location: I-880 exit The Alameda, 2 mi w. Facility: 70 units. 2 stories, exterior corridors. Pool: heated outdoor. Activities: exercise room. Guest Services: valet and coin laundry. Featured Amenity: continental breakfast.

BILTMORE HOTEL & SUITES/SILICON VALLEY
408/988-8411 68

Hotel

Address: 2151 Laurelwood Rd 95054 Location: US 101 exit Montague Expwy, just ne. Facility: 263 units. 2-9 stories, interior/exterior corridors. Pool: heated outdoor. Activities: hot tub, exercise room. Guest Services: valet laundry.

CANDLEWOOD SUITES-SILICON VALLEY/SAN JOSE
408/241-9305 73
Extended Stay Hotel. Address: 481 El Camino Real 95050

EMBASSY SUITES BY HILTON SANTA CLARA SILICON VALLEY
408/496-6400 66
Hotel. Address: 2885 Lakeside Dr 95054

AAA Benefit: Members save up to 15%!

(See map & index p. 348.)

HILTON SANTA CLARA 408/330-0001

 Hotel   Hilton HOTELS & RESORTS

AAA Benefit: Members save up to 15%!

 Address: 4949 Great America Pkwy 95054 **Location:** US 101 exit Great America Pkwy, 0.5 mi n. **Facility:** 280 units. 8 stories, interior corridors. **Amenities:** safes. **Dining:** La Fontana, see separate listing. **Pool:** heated outdoor. **Activities:** hot tub, trails, exercise room. **Guest Services:** valet laundry.

 / SOME UNITS

HOLIDAY INN EXPRESS & SUITES SANTA CLARA
408/554-9200
 Hotel. **Address:** 1700 El Camino Real 95050

HOLIDAY INN EXPRESS & SUITES SANTA CLARA-SILICON VALLEY 408/241-0100
Hotel. **Address:** 2455 El Camino Real 95051

HYATT HOUSE SANTA CLARA 408/486-0800

Extended Stay Hotel H HYATT house™

AAA Benefit: Members save up to 10%!

 **Address:** 3915 Rivermark Plaza 95054 **Location:** US 101 exit Montague Expwy, 1 mi e. **Facility:** 150 efficiencies. 7 stories, interior corridors. **Amenities:** safes. **Pool:** heated outdoor. **Activities:** hot tub, picnic facilities, trails, exercise room. **Guest Services:** valet and coin laundry, area transportation. **Featured Amenity:** breakfast buffet.

BIZ HS / SOME UNITS

HYATT REGENCY SANTA CLARA 408/200-1234

 Hotel HYATT REGENCY·

AAA Benefit: Members save up to 10%!

Address: 5101 Great America Pkwy 95054 **Location:** US 101 exit 393 (Great America Pkwy), 0.8 mi n. **Facility:** 505 units. 14 stories, interior corridors. **Parking:** on-site and valet. **Amenities:** safes. **Dining:** 2 restaurants. **Pool:** heated outdoor. **Activities:** hot tub, trails, exercise room. **Guest Services:** valet laundry.

BIZ / SOME UNITS

 Save on travel, shopping and more: AAA.com/discounts

THE PLAZA SUITES SILICON VALLEY@SANTA CLARA
408/748-9800

 Hotel

Address: 3100 Lakeside Dr 95054 **Location:** W of US 101 exit Lawrence Expwy, s on Oakmead Pkwy at Peterson Way. **Facility:** 219 units. 7 stories, interior corridors. **Amenities:** safes. **Dining:** 2 restaurants. **Pool:** heated outdoor. **Activities:** hot tub, game room, exercise room. **Guest Services:** valet and coin laundry. **Featured Amenity:** full hot breakfast.

SAVE CALL
BIZ HS

SANTA CLARA MARRIOTT HOTEL 408/988-1500

 Hotel MARRIOTT

AAA Benefit: Members save 5% or more!

 Address: 2700 Mission College Blvd 95054 **Location:** 0.5 mi n off US 101 exit 393 (Great America Pkwy); 0.8 mi s of California's Great America theme park. **Facility:** 759 units. 2-15 stories, interior corridors. **Parking:** on-site (fee) and valet. **Terms:** check-in 4 pm. **Amenities:** *Some:* safes. **Pool:** heated outdoor. **Activities:** sauna, hot tub, tennis, bicycles, exercise room. **Guest Services:** valet and coin laundry, boarding pass kiosk, rental car service.

SAVE ECO CALL BIZ
HS / SOME UNITS

TOWNEPLACE SUITES BY MARRIOTT SAN JOSE SANTA CLARA 408/969-9900
SAVE Extended Stay Hotel.
Address: 2877 Lakeside Dr 95054

AAA Benefit: Members save 5% or more!

WHERE TO EAT

BIRK'S RESTAURANT 408/980-6400 (24)
Steak. Fine Dining. **Address:** 3955 Freedom Cir 95054

THE CHEESECAKE FACTORY 408/246-0092 (29)
International. Casual Dining. **Address:** 3041 Stevens Creek Blvd, Space L1 95050

JANG SU JANG 408/246-1212 (26)
Korean Barbecue. Casual Dining. **Address:** 3561 El Camino Real, Suite 10 95051

LA FONTANA 408/330-0001 (21)
California. Fine Dining. **Address:** 4949 Great America Pkwy 95054

LA PALOMA RESTAURANTE 408/247-0990 (27)
Mexican. Casual Dining. **Address:** 2280 El Camino Real 95050

OLD IRONSIDES CAFE 408/727-5147 (22)
Mediterranean Deli. Quick Serve. **Address:** 4655 Old Ironsides Dr, Suite 150 95054

ORENCHI RAMEN 408/246-2955 (28)
Japanese Noodles Small Plates. Casual Dining. **Address:** 3540 Homestead Rd 95051

PEDRO'S RESTAURANT & CANTINA 408/496-6777 (25)
Mexican. Casual Dining. **Address:** 3935 Freedom Cir 95054

(See map & index p. 348.)

PIATTI RISTORANTE & BAR   408/330-9212   (23)
♥♥♥ Italian. Casual Dining. **Address:** 3905 Rivermark Plaza 95054

SANTA CRUZ (F-9) pop. 59,946, elev. 20'

- Hotels p. 368 • Restaurants p. 368
- Hotels & Restaurants map & index p. 365

This beautiful city on the Pacific coast off scenic SR 1 is a quintessential beach town. Surfing became popular in the 1930s, and Steamer Lane is an internationally renowned surfing site. The Santa Cruz Surfing Museum, inside the Mark Abbott Memorial Lighthouse on West Cliff Drive, displays a collection of surfboards and surfing photographs from the 1930s to the present; phone (831) 420-6289.

The northern end of Monterey Bay was first explored in 1769 by Spaniard Gaspar de Portolá; the name Santa Cruz means "holy cross." One of Father Junípero Serra's 21 California missions was built at the site. A half-scale replica of the original mission is on the grounds of Holy Cross Church at 126 High St. (facing the downtown plaza). All that remains of the original mission, built in 1791 and destroyed by an earthquake in 1857, are the ruins of soldiers' barracks and part of a stone foundation. The chapel is open to visitors; phone (831) 423-4182.

A summer highlight is ⚡ Santa Cruz Shakespeare. The University of California Santa Cruz's resident repertory company presents two of Shakespeare's works and a fringe show from late June through August at The Grove at DeLaVega Park. For schedule and ticket information, phone (831) 459-2159.

Visit Santa Cruz County: 303 Water St. Suite 100, Santa Cruz, CA 95060. **Phone:** (831) 425-1234 or (800) 833-3494.

THE MUSEUM OF ART AND HISTORY is at 705 Front St. at jct. Cooper St. (in the McPherson Center). It promotes interest in contemporary art and Santa Cruz County history through traveling exhibits and a collection of artifacts and memorabilia. Historical exhibits trace the area's history from Ohlone Indians and the mission era to the lumber industry and the 1989 Loma Prieta earthquake. Installed in the outdoor sculpture garden are works from the museum's permanent collection. Community events take place on the first and third Friday evenings of the month.

Time: Allow 1 hour minimum. **Hours:** Tues.-Sun. 11-5 (also Fri. 5-9). Closed Thanksgiving and Christmas. **Cost:** $10; $8 (students with ID); free (ages 0-4 and to all first Fri. of the month). **Phone:** (831) 429-1964.

MYSTERY SPOT is 2.5 mi. n. on Market St. (which becomes Branciforte Dr.) to the jct. with Mystery Spot Rd., then n. to 465 Mystery Spot Rd. Sir Isaac Newton's law of universal gravitation seemingly does not apply to this circular area of redwood forest approximately 150 feet in diameter, where visitors will experience puzzling variations in perspective. Theories run the gamut from a hole in the ozone layer to an underground guidance system for alien spacecraft, but the reason remains a mystery. There's nothing mysterious, however, about the scenic hiking trail that winds through the redwoods.

Hours: Guided 45-minute tours are given daily every 12 minutes Mon.-Fri. 10-6, Sat.-Sun. 9-7, Memorial Day-Labor Day; every 15 minutes Mon.-Fri. 10-4, Sat.-Sun. 10-5, rest of year. Last tour begins at closing. Advance ticket purchase is recommended in summer. **Cost:** $8; free (ages 0-3 and active military with ID). Cash or check only for tickets purchased at gate; debit cards include $2 fee. **Parking:** $5. **Phone:** (831) 423-8897 for information and to purchase tickets.

NATURAL BRIDGES STATE BEACH is off West Cliff Dr. It offers many tide pools for exploring. From about mid-October through February it's possible to observe monarch butterflies, which pass through on their annual migration; a boardwalk leads to the grove of trees where they can be spotted. A visitor center offers exhibits about area ecology and wildlife. *See Recreation Areas Chart.*

Time: Allow 2 hours minimum. **Hours:** Beach open daily dawn-dusk. Visitor center open daily 10-4, mid-Oct through Jan. 31; Fri.-Mon. 10-4, rest of year. Phone ahead to confirm visitor center hours. **Cost:** Day use $10 per private vehicle; $9 (ages 62+ per private vehicle). **Phone:** (831) 423-4609. ⊠ ⛱

SANTA CRUZ BEACH BOARDWALK is off SR 1 following signs to the municipal wharf. This beachside amusement park has been entertaining young and old alike for more than a century. In addition to more than three dozen rides, there are attractions like miniature golf, laser tag, a bowling alley and the nautically themed Neptune's Kingdom entertainment center. The Casino Arcade has pinball machines, air hockey, skee-ball and a variety of video games.

A highlight is a hand-carved Looff carousel, which dates from 1911 and features a rare brass ring machine and an original 342-pipe organ. Both the carousel and the Giant Dipper wooden roller coaster, built in 1924, are National Historic Landmarks. Logger's Revenge offers panoramic ocean views from a vantage point high above the park, and it's a certainty that you'll get splashed during the final drop. Little kids can pilot Kiddie Cruzers that are designed to resemble classic cars from the 1940s.

Thrill rides include the Double Shot, which propels brave souls 125 feet skyward for a spectacular bird's-eye view of the coast before shooting them back down to Earth. Nerves of steel are also required for a spin on Undertow, a roller coaster equipped with a dizzying assortment of sharp turns, sudden drops and speedy downhill lunges.

(See map & index p. 365.)

It wouldn't be an amusement park without a tasty array of munchies, and the caloric delights here include corn dogs, deep-fried artichoke hearts and Italian sausage sandwiches. On Friday nights during the summer months free band concerts take place at the beach bandstand.

Hours: Amusement park facilities open daily; hours vary. Rides operate daily, April 1-Labor Day and during spring break and Christmas vacation; weekends only, rest of year. Neptune's Kingdom and Mini-Golf, Casino Arcade and Laser Tag open daily year-round. Phone ahead to confirm schedule. **Cost:** Boardwalk admission free. Individual rides $4-$7; all-day ride wristband $39.95-$44.95. Individual attractions $7; all-day rides plus attractions $64.95-$69.95. **Parking:** $10-$20. **Phone:** (831) 423-5590. ⓣ

SEYMOUR MARINE DISCOVERY CENTER AT LONG MARINE LABORATORY is w. off SR 1 (Mission St.) on Swift St., then n. on Delaware Ave. to the end of the road. The center, part of the Joseph M. Long Marine Laboratory, is a research and educational facility of the University of California, Santa Cruz. The lab serves as a base for field research in Monterey Bay and the ocean beyond. Visitors can see an aquarium and a blue whale skeleton, check out the interactive displays in the exhibit hall, and touch sea stars and other marine animals.

Hours: Daily 10-5, July-Aug.; Tues.-Sun. 10-5, rest of year. Guided 45-minute lab tours are given on a first-come, first-served basis at 1, 2 and 3. Family tours are given at 11. Closed Jan. 1, Easter, July 4, Veterans Day, Thanksgiving, Christmas Eve, Christmas and Dec. 31. **Cost:** $8; $6 (ages 3-16, ages 65+ and students with ID). **Phone:** (831) 459-3800.

UNIVERSITY OF CALIFORNIA SANTA CRUZ (UCSC), corner of Bay and High sts., was founded in 1965 on a 2,000-acre portion of Cowell Ranch, overlooking Monterey Bay. Roads and walkways situated amid redwood groves and meadows connect nine residential colleges. Barn Theater, just inside the main entrance, is a former horse barn turned 158-seat theater. Self-guiding tour maps are available at the main entrance information booth.

Hours: Ninety-minute, student-led walking tours are given Mon.-Fri.; phone ahead for tour times. **Cost:** Tours free. Reservations must be made at least 2 to 4 weeks in advance. **Parking:** Permits $8; metered spaces are limited. Free lot parking is available during tour times; phone for instructions. **Phone:** (831) 459-4008.

Center for Agroecology & Sustainable Food Systems, reached by a footpath from Coolidge Dr., is a 33-acre teaching and research facility. Vegetables, flowers, herbs and fruit trees are grown on this organic farm. **Hours:** Daily 8-6. **Cost:** Free. **Phone:** (831) 459-3240.

Cook House, 1156 High St., is now the college's admissions office. Built in 1860, the building is the former Cowell Ranch cookhouse. The well-preserved structure also has served as the chancellor's office and headquarters for the campus police. **Phone:** (831) 459-4008.

Theater Arts Center is on Meyer Drive (off Heller) on the UCSC campus. The complex contains the 526-seat UCSC Mainstage Theater, a 231-seat second stage, a 400-seat music and recital hall, outdoor seating at the Sinsheimer-Stanley Festival Glen and specialized visual arts facilities. **Phone:** (831) 459-2159.

The UC Santa Cruz Arboretum is off High St. at Arboretum Rd., .5 mi. w. of the main campus entrance. The conservation garden includes rare, endangered and extraordinary plants from around the world. Sections of the arboretum are devoted to plants from Australia, South Africa and New Zealand in addition to California—all regions that share a similar Mediterranean climate. The flowering plants attract many hummingbirds and butterflies. **Hours:** Daily 9-5. Gift and garden shop 10-4. Check the website for holiday hours. **Cost:** $5; $2 (ages 6-17); free (ages 0-5, UCSC students and to all first Tues. of the month). **Phone:** (831) 502-2998.

WILDER RANCH STATE PARK, 1401 Old Coast Rd., is a 6,000-acre site with some 33 miles of trails open to mountain bikers, horseback riders and hikers. An interpretive center includes exhibits about plant and animal life on the ranch. The main house and outbuildings once utilized by ranchers and workers can be explored and include a barn, stables, a water-powered machine shop and a blacksmith shop. **Time:** Allow 1 hour minimum. **Hours:** Park open daily 8 a.m.-dusk. Interpretive center open Thurs.-Sun. 10-4. Phone ahead to confirm schedule. **Cost:** $10 per private vehicle; $9 (ages 62+ per private vehicle). **Phone:** (831) 423-9703, or (831) 426-0505 for the interpretive center.

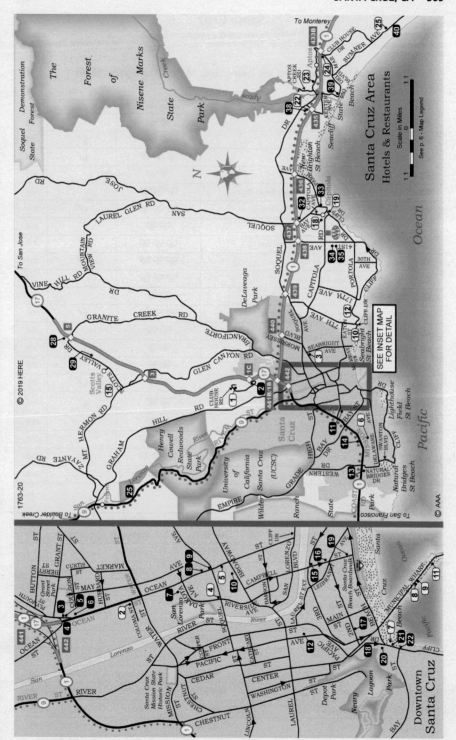

Santa Cruz Area
Hotels & Restaurants

See p. 6 - Map Legend

Scale in Miles

Downtown
Santa Cruz

© 2019 HERE

© AAA

Santa Cruz

This index helps you "spot" where approved hotels and restaurants are located on the corresponding detailed maps. Restaurant price range is a combination of lunch and/or dinner. Turn to the listing page for more information and consult display ads for special promotions.

 For more details, rates and reservations: AAA.com/travelguides/hotels

SANTA CRUZ

Map Page	Hotels	Diamond Rated	Member Savings	Page
2 p. 365	The Inn at Pasatiempo	◆◆		368
3 p. 365	**Best Western Inn**	◆◆	✔	368
4 p. 365	Hampton Inn Santa Cruz	◆◆◆	✔	368
5 p. 365	Comfort Inn-Santa Cruz	◆◆		368
6 p. 365	Holiday Inn Express & Suites Santa Cruz	◆◆◆		368
7 p. 365	Hotel Paradox, Autograph Collection	◆◆◆	✔	368
8 p. 365	The Islander Motel	◆◆		368
9 p. 365	**Best Western Plus All Suites Inn**	◆◆◆	✔	368
10 p. 365	**Hyatt Place Santa Cruz**	◆◆◆	✔	368
11 p. 365	The Babbling Brook Inn	◆◆◆		368
12 p. 365	Pacific Blue Inn	◆◆		368
13 p. 365	Fairfield Inn & Suites by Marriott Santa Cruz	◆◆◆	✔	368
14 p. 365	Mission Inn	◆◆		368
15 p. 365	Super 8 - Santa Cruz - East	◆◆		368
16 p. 365	Comfort Inn Beach Boardwalk	◆◆		368
17 p. 365	**Edgewater Beach Inn & Suites**	◆◆	✔	368
18 p. 365	**Howard Johnson Inn Santa Cruz Beach Boardwalk**	◆◆	✔	368
19 p. 365	Carousel Beach Inn	◆◆		368
20 p. 365	West Cliff Inn	◆◆◆		368
21 p. 365	Dream Inn Santa Cruz	◆◆◆ ·		368
22 p. 365	Sea & Sand Inn	◆◆		368

Map Page	Restaurants	Diamond Rated	Cuisine	Price Range	Page
① p. 365	Hollins House at Pasatiempo	◆◆◆	Continental	$15-$35	369
② p. 365	Santa Cruz Diner	◆◆	American	$6-$10	369
③ p. 365	Lillian's Italian Kitchen	◆◆	Italian	$9-$35	369
④ p. 365	Hindquarter Bar & Grille	◆◆◆	Steak	$15-$52	369
⑤ p. 365	Golden Palace	◆◆	Chinese	$8-$17	369
⑥ p. 365	Bantam	◆◆◆	Italian Pizza	$11-$23	368
⑦ p. 365	Jack O'Neill Restaurant	◆◆◆	Seafood	$10-$42	369
⑧ p. 365	Woodies Cafe	◆	Seafood	$10-$17	369
⑨ p. 365	Gilbert's Firefish Grill	◆◆	Seafood	$13-$30	369
⑩ p. 365	**Crow's Nest**	◆◆◆	Seafood	$19-$52	369
⑪ p. 365	Olitas Cantina & Grille	◆◆	Mexican	$10-$26	369
⑫ p. 365	Star Bene	◆◆	Italian	$16-$27	369

FELTON

Map Page	Hotel	Diamond Rated	Member Savings	Page
25 p. 365	Fern River Resort	◈◈		78

SCOTTS VALLEY

Map Page	Hotels	Diamond Rated	Member Savings	Page
28 p. 365	**Best Western Plus Inn Scotts Valley**	◈◈◈	✔	374
29 p. 365	Four Points by Sheraton Santa Cruz Scotts Valley	◈◈◈	✔	374

Map Page	Restaurant	Diamond Rated	Cuisine	Price Range	Page
15 p. 365	Bruno's Bar and Grill	◈◈	Barbecue	$8-$25	374

CAPITOLA

Map Page	Hotels	Diamond Rated	Member Savings	Page
32 p. 365	**Quality Inn & Suites**	◈◈	✔	54
33 p. 365	The Inn at Depot Hill	◈◈◈◈		54
34 p. 365	**Best Western Plus Capitola By-the-Sea Inn & Suites**	◈◈◈	✔	54
35 p. 365	Fairfield Inn & Suites by Marriott Santa Cruz-Capitola	◈◈◈	✔	54

Map Page	Restaurants	Diamond Rated	Cuisine	Price Range	Page
18 p. 365	Shadowbrook Restaurant	◈◈◈	Regional American	$22-$34	54
19 p. 365	Paradise Beach Grille	◈◈◈	Island Fusion	$12-$34	54

APTOS

Map Page	Hotels	Diamond Rated	Member Savings	Page
38 p. 365	**Best Western Seacliff Inn**	◈◈◈	✔	35
39 p. 365	**Rio Sands Hotel**	◈◈	✔	35
40 p. 365	**Seascape Beach Resort**	◈◈◈	✔	35

Map Page	Restaurants	Diamond Rated	Cuisine	Price Range	Page
22 p. 365	Severino's Grill	◈◈◈	American	$10-$19	35
23 p. 365	Aptos St. BBQ	◈	American	$10-$32	35
24 p. 365	Cafe Bittersweet	◈◈	American	$12-$18	35
25 p. 365	Palapas Restaurant & Cantina	◈◈	Mexican	$14-$33	35

(See map & index p. 365.)

THE BABBLING BROOK INN   831/427-2437   **11**
♥♥♥ Bed & Breakfast. **Address:** 1025 Laurel St 95060

BEST WESTERN INN   831/425-4717   **3**

♥♥♥◆
Hotel

Best Western. **AAA Benefit:** Members save up to 15% and earn bonus points!

Address: 126 Plymouth St 95060 **Location:** Jct SR 1 and 17 exit Ocean St; east side of Ocean St. N. **Facility:** 29 units. 2 stories (no elevator), exterior corridors. **Activities:** sauna, hot tub, exercise room. **Featured Amenity:** continental breakfast.

SAVE 〈T|↑〉 CALL 〈&〉 〈↦↤〉 BIZ 〈⌃〉 〈✕〉 〈❚〉 〈☐〉 〈▣〉

BEST WESTERN PLUS ALL SUITES INN
831/458-9898   **9**

♥♥♥◆
Hotel

Best Western PLUS. **AAA Benefit:** Members save up to 15% and earn bonus points!

Address: 500 Ocean St 95060 **Location:** Jct SR 1 and 17 exit Ocean St; at Soquel Ave. **Facility:** 77 units. 3 stories, interior corridors. **Terms:** check-in 4 pm. **Activities:** sauna, hot tub, exercise room. **Guest Services:** valet and coin laundry. **Featured Amenity:** breakfast buffet.

SAVE 〈T|↑〉 CALL 〈&〉 〈↦↤〉 BIZ 〈⌃〉 〈✕〉 〈❚〉 〈▣〉 〈☐〉 / SOME UNITS 〈HS〉

CAROUSEL BEACH INN   831/425-7090   **19**
♥♥ Motel. **Address:** 110 Riverside Ave 95060

COMFORT INN BEACH BOARDWALK   831/471-9999   **16**
♥♥ Hotel. **Address:** 314 Riverside Ave 95060

COMFORT INN-SANTA CRUZ   831/426-2664   **5**
♥♥ Hotel. **Address:** 110 Plymouth St 95060

DREAM INN SANTA CRUZ   831/426-4330   **21**
♥♥♥ Hotel. **Address:** 175 W Cliff Dr 95060

EDGEWATER BEACH INN & SUITES   831/423-0440   **17**

♥♥♥
Motel

Address: 525 Second St 95060 **Location:** Across from beach and boardwalk. **Facility:** 17 units, some kitchens. 1 story, exterior corridors. **Pool:** heated outdoor. **Activities:** beach access, trails. **Guest Services:** coin laundry.

SAVE 〈T|↑〉 〈⊷〉 〈↦↤〉 〈✕〉 〈✕〉 〈❚〉 〈▣〉 〈☐〉 / SOME UNITS 〈🐾〉

FAIRFIELD INN & SUITES BY MARRIOTT SANTA CRUZ
831/420-0777   **13**
♥♥♥ SAVE Hotel. **Address:** 2956 Mission St 95060

AAA Benefit: Members save 5% or more!

HAMPTON INN SANTA CRUZ   831/457-8000   **4**
♥♥♥ SAVE Hotel. **Address:** 1505 Ocean St 95060

AAA Benefit: Members save up to 15%!

HOLIDAY INN EXPRESS & SUITES SANTA CRUZ
831/466-9100   **6**
♥♥♥ Hotel. **Address:** 1410 Ocean St 95060

HOTEL PARADOX, AUTOGRAPH COLLECTION
831/425-7100   **7**
♥♥♥ SAVE Boutique Hotel. **Address:** 611 Ocean St 95060

AAA Benefit: Members save 5% or more!

HOWARD JOHNSON INN SANTA CRUZ BEACH BOARDWALK   831/423-7737   **18**

♥♥
Hotel

Address: 130 W Cliff Dr 95060 **Location:** 2 blks from beach. **Facility:** 30 units, some efficiencies and kitchens. 2 stories (no elevator), exterior corridors. **Amenities:** safes. **Activities:** hot tub. **Guest Services:** coin laundry. **Featured Amenity:** continental breakfast.

SAVE 〈T|↑〉 BIZ 〈⌃〉 〈✕〉 〈❚〉 〈☐〉 〈▣〉

HYATT PLACE SANTA CRUZ   831/226-2300   **10**

♥♥♥
Hotel

HYATT PLACE **AAA Benefit:** Members save up to 10%!

Address: 407 Broadway Ave 95060 **Location:** Jct SR 1 and 17 exit Ocean St, just s, then just e. **Facility:** 106 units. 4 stories, interior corridors. **Parking:** valet only. **Amenities:** safes. **Pool:** heated outdoor. **Activities:** hot tub, exercise room. **Guest Services:** valet laundry.

SAVE 〈T|↑〉 〈⊷〉 〈↦↤〉 BIZ 〈⌃〉 〈✕〉 〈❚〉 〈☐〉

THE INN AT PASATIEMPO   831/423-5000   **2**
♥♥ Hotel. **Address:** 555 Hwy 17 95060

THE ISLANDER MOTEL   831/426-7766   **8**
♥♥ Motel. **Address:** 522 Ocean St 95060

MISSION INN   831/425-5455   **14**
♥♥ Hotel. **Address:** 2250 Mission St 95060

PACIFIC BLUE INN   831/600-8880   **12**
♥♥ Boutique Hotel. **Address:** 636 Pacific Ave 95060

SEA & SAND INN   831/427-3400   **22**
♥♥ Hotel. **Address:** 201 W Cliff Dr 95060

SUPER 8 - SANTA CRUZ - EAST   831/426-3707   **15**
♥♥ Hotel. **Address:** 338 Riverside Ave 95060

WEST CLIFF INN   831/457-2200   **20**
♥♥♥ Bed & Breakfast. **Address:** 174 W Cliff Dr 95060

WHERE TO EAT

BANTAM   831/420-0101   **6**
♥♥♥ Italian Pizza. Casual Dining. **Address:** 1010 Fair Ave, Suite J 95060

(See map & index p. 365.)

CROW'S NEST　831/476-4560　 10

◈◈◈

Seafood
Casual Dining
$19-$52

AAA Inspector Notes: Diners are treated to picturesque views of the bay and Pacific Ocean, as well as well-prepared selections of fresh local seafood. The lively atmosphere makes this place popular with locals. **Features:** full bar. **Reservations:** suggested. **Address:** 2218 E Cliff Dr 95062 **Location:** 1.3 mi e; at South Shore Santa Cruz Small Crafts Harbor via Murray St Bridge. **Parking:** on-site (fee). B L D CALL ♿ Ⓧ

GILBERT'S FIREFISH GRILL　831/423-5200　9
◈◈ Seafood. Casual Dining. **Address:** 25 Municipal Wharf 95060

GOLDEN PALACE　831/427-9275　5
◈◈ Chinese. Casual Dining. **Address:** 415 Ocean St 95060

HINDQUARTER BAR & GRILLE　831/426-7770　4
◈◈◈ Steak. Casual Dining. **Address:** 303 Soquel Ave 95060

HOLLINS HOUSE AT PASATIEMPO　831/459-9177　1
◈◈◈ Continental. Fine Dining. **Address:** 20 Club House Rd 95060

JACK O'NEILL RESTAURANT　831/740-8069　7
◈◈◈ Seafood. Casual Dining. **Address:** 175 W Cliff Dr 95060

LILLIAN'S ITALIAN KITCHEN　831/425-2288　3
◈◈ Italian. Casual Dining. **Address:** 1148 Soquel Ave 95062

OLITAS CANTINA & GRILLE　831/458-9393　11
◈◈ Mexican. Casual Dining. **Address:** 49B Municipal Wharf 95060

SANTA CRUZ DINER　831/426-7151　2
◈◈ American. Casual Dining. **Address:** 909 Ocean St 95060

STAR BENE　831/479-4307　12
◈◈ Italian. Casual Dining. **Address:** 2-1245 E Cliff Dr 95062

WOODIES CAFE　831/421-9410　8
◈ Seafood. Quick Serve. **Address:** 25 Municipal Wharf 95060

SANTA NELLA pop. 1,380, elev. 78'

BEST WESTERN ANDERSEN'S INN　209/826-5534

◈◈
Hotel

BW Best Western. **AAA Benefit:** Members save up to 15% and earn bonus points!

Address: 12367 Hwy 33 S 95322 **Location:** I-5 exit 407 (SR 33), just e. **Facility:** 94 units. 2 stories (no elevator), exterior corridors. **Pool:** heated outdoor. **Guest Services:** coin laundry. **Featured Amenity:** continental breakfast.

SAVE 📶 CALL ♿ 🛏 BIZ 📶
🔲 🔲 🔲 /SOME UNITS

QUALITY INN　209/826-8282
◈◈ Hotel. **Address:** 28976 Plaza Dr 95322

WHERE TO EAT

PEA SOUP ANDERSEN'S RESTAURANT　209/826-1685
◈◈ Soup. Casual Dining. **Address:** 12411 S State Hwy 33 95322

SANTA ROSA (A-7) pop. 167,815, elev. 164'
• Hotels p. 370 • Restaurants p. 371
• Part of Wine Country area — see map p. 405

Three entrepreneurial businessmen joined forces in the early 1850s, plotted the town of Santa Rosa and sold lots for $25 apiece. After they promised to donate land for a courthouse, the county seat was moved to the fledgling town from Sonoma. The railroad arrived in 1870, and within 7 years the population of Santa Rosa grew tenfold.

The largest city in Sonoma County is closely associated with two of its most famous citizens. Horticulturist Luther Burbank, a resident for 50 years, called the town "the chosen spot of all the earth"; his home and gardens can be seen on guided tours. And cartoonist Charles Schulz, creator of the beloved "Peanuts" cartoon gang, lived and worked here for 3 decades.

Those interested in post-World War II aviation will enjoy a visit to the Pacific Coast Air Museum at Charles M. Schulz-Sonoma County Airport. In addition to aviation-related displays indoors, visitors also can see an outdoor collection of vintage aircraft; phone (707) 575-7900.

Visit Santa Rosa: 9 Fourth St., Santa Rosa, CA 95401. **Phone:** (707) 577-8674 or (800) 404-7673.

CHARLES M. SCHULZ MUSEUM is at 2301 Hardies Ln. (at W. Steele Ln.). It relates the life of the creator of the "Peanuts" comic strip and the development of its lovable gang of characters—Charlie Brown, his sister Sally, his faithful dog Snoopy, Lucy and Linus Van Pelt, Peppermint Patty, Marcie and Schroeder. A replica of Schulz's studio, a collection of his pencil sketches and doodles, a Snoopy labyrinth in an outdoor garden and a morphing Snoopy sculpture are highlights. Original "Peanuts" strips and other art by Schulz can be viewed.

Time: Allow 1 hour, 30 minutes minimum. **Hours:** Mon.-Fri. 11-5, Sat.-Sun. 10-5, Memorial Day-Labor Day; Mon. and Wed.-Fri. 11-5, Sat.-Sun. 10-5, rest of year. Closed Jan. 1, Easter, July 4, Thanksgiving, Christmas Eve and Christmas. **Cost:** $12; $8 (ages 62+); $5 (ages 4-18 and college students with ID). **Phone:** (707) 579-4452. ▣

LUTHER BURBANK HOME & GARDENS is at the corner of Santa Rosa and Sonoma aves. Docent-led tours describe the life and work of the horticulturist who introduced more than 800 varieties of fruits, vegetables, nuts, grains and ornamental flowers, including the Santa Rosa plum and the Shasta daisy. Examples of roses, fruit trees and other plants developed by Burbank are featured on the grounds. The 19th-century house, greenhouse and carriage house museum contain original furnishings and changing exhibits.

One star-studded photograph shows Burbank with Henry Ford, Thomas Alva Edison and other famous visitors following appearances at the 1915 Panama-Pacific International Exposition in San Francisco.

Hours: Gardens open daily 8-dusk. Guided house tours are offered Tues.-Sat. 10–3:30, Sun. 11-2:30, Apr.-Oct. Cell phone tours are offered. **Cost:** Gardens free. Guided tours $10; $8.50 (ages 12-18, ages 65+ and college students with ID). **Phone:** (707) 524-5445.

 SAFARI WEST is at 3115 Porter Creek Rd. Guided tours of the 400-acre wildlife preserve, home to more than 900 exotic animals and birds, are conducted by a naturalist in open-air safari vehicles. The preserve's residents include giraffes, zebras, antelopes, wildebeests, Cape buffalo, gazelles and elands. You'll also visit an open-air aviary and walk through an animal compound for up-close meetings with cheetahs and primates.

Children under 4 are not permitted on the classic safari tour. Pets are not permitted. **Time:** Allow 3 hours minimum. **Hours:** Tours given daily (weather permitting) at 9, 10, 1 and 4, Apr.-Aug.; daily at 9, 10, 1, 2 (also select weekends at 4), in Mar. and Sept.-Oct.; daily at 9, 10, 1 and 2, Nov.-Dec.; Fri.-Sun. and holidays at 10 and 2, rest of year. Closed Christmas. Phone ahead to confirm schedule. **Cost:** Mon.-Fri. admission June-Aug. starts at $98; $94 (ages 13-17 and 62+); $45 (ages 4-12). Sat.-Sun. admission June-Aug. starts at $115; $100 (ages 13-17 and 62+); $50 (ages 4-12). Admission rest of year starts at $83; $80 (ages 13-17 and 62+); $45 (ages 4-12). Admission is reduced for an overnight stay. Reservations are required. **Phone:** (707) 579-2551 or (800) 616-2695.

WINERIES

- **Matanzas Creek Winery** is 6 mi. s.e. at 6097 Bennett Valley Rd. **Hours:** Daily 10-4:30. Tours are given daily by appointment. **Phone:** (707) 528-6464.

AMERICAS BEST VALUE INN   707/523-3480
♥♥ Motel. **Address:** 1800 Santa Rosa Ave 95407

THE ASTRO   707/200-4655
♥♥ Vintage Motel. **Address:** 323 Santa Rosa Ave 95404

▼ *See AAA listing this page* ▼

BEST WESTERN PLUS WINE COUNTRY INN & SUITES
707/545-9000

Hotel

 AAA Benefit: Members save up to 15% and earn bonus points!

Address: 870 Hopper Ave 95403 **Location:** US 101 northbound exit Mendocino Ave/Old Redwood Hwy, just s to Mendocino Overcross to Cleveland Ave, just n to Hopper Ave, then just w; southbound exit Hopper Ave, then just w. **Facility:** 85 units. 2 stories (no elevator), exterior corridors. **Pool:** heated outdoor. **Activities:** exercise room. **Guest Services:** valet laundry. **Featured Amenity:** breakfast buffet.

COURTYARD BY MARRIOTT SANTA ROSA   707/573-9000
Hotel. **Address:** 175 Railroad St 95401

AAA Benefit: Members save 5% or more!

FLAMINGO CONFERENCE RESORT AND SPA   707/545-8530
Historic Hotel. **Address:** 2777 4th St 95405

THE GABLES WINE COUNTRY INN   707/585-7777
Historic Bed & Breakfast. **Address:** 4257 Petaluma Hill Rd 95404

HILLSIDE INN   707/546-9353
Motel. **Address:** 2901 4th St 95409

HILTON GARDEN INN SONOMA COUNTY AIRPORT
707/545-0444
Hotel. **Address:** 417 Aviation Blvd 95403

AAA Benefit: Members save up to 15%!

HOTEL AZURA   707/544-4141
Hotel. **Address:** 635 Healdsburg Ave 95401

HOTEL LA ROSE   707/579-3200
Historic Hotel. **Address:** 308 Wilson St 95401

HYATT REGENCY SONOMA WINE COUNTRY
707/284-1234

Hotel

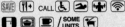 **AAA Benefit:** Members save up to 10%!

Address: 170 Railroad St 95401 **Location:** US 101 exit downtown, just w; jct 3rd St. Adjacent to Railroad Square and Old Town. **Facility:** 253 units. 3 stories, interior corridors. **Parking:** on-site (fee) and valet. **Amenities:** safes. **Pool:** heated outdoor. **Activities:** hot tub, bicycles, exercise room. **Guest Services:** valet laundry.

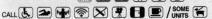

QUALITY INN & SUITES SANTA ROSA   707/521-2100
Hotel. **Address:** 3000 Santa Rosa Ave 95407

SANDMAN HOTEL   707/293-2100

Hotel

Address: 3421 Cleveland Ave 95403 **Location:** US 101 northbound exit Mendocino Ave/Old Redwood Hwy, just s to Mendocino Overcross to Cleveland Ave, then just s; southbound exit Hopper Ave, then just e. **Facility:** 135 units. 2 stories (no elevator), exterior corridors. **Terms:** check-in 4 pm. **Amenities:** safes. **Pool:** heated outdoor. **Activities:** hot tub, picnic facilities, exercise room. **Guest Services:** coin laundry. **Featured Amenity:** continental breakfast.

VINTNERS RESORT   707/575-7350

Hotel

Address: 4350 Barnes Rd 95403 **Location:** US 101 exit River Rd/Mark West Springs Rd, just w, then just s. **Facility:** There is a peaceful feel as you walk the path around the shaded courtyard to one of the intimate buildings holding spacious guest rooms. Inside you'll find feather beds and, in some rooms, fireplaces. 78 units. 2 stories (no elevator), interior corridors. **Parking:** on-site and valet. **Terms:** check-in 4 pm. **Amenities:** safes. **Dining:** John Ash & Co, see separate listing. **Pool:** heated outdoor. **Activities:** hot tub, steamroom, trails, exercise room, spa. **Guest Services:** valet laundry.

 WHERE TO EAT

BIRD AND THE BOTTLE   707/568-4000
Pacific Northwest Small Plates. Gastropub. **Address:** 1055 4th St 95404

JEFFREY'S HILLSIDE CAFE   707/564-6317
American. Casual Dining. **Address:** 2901 4th St 95409

JOHN ASH & CO   707/527-7687

California Fine Dining
$19-$48

AAA Inspector Notes: Sun-drenched outdoor patios are enclosed without sacrificing the outdoor feel at this fine dining spot. The lounge nurtures a relaxed, library-like mood. Menu items might include pan seared cod, Liberty duck breast or a Zinfandel braised lamb shank. Accompanying each of these dishes is a variety of unique sides like purple mashed potatoes, duck confit potato cake or delicious king trumpet mushrooms. **Features:** full bar, patio dining, happy hour. **Reservations:** suggested. **Address:** 4330 Barnes Rd 95403 **Location:** US 101 exit River Rd/Mark West Springs Rd, just w, then just s; in Vintners Resort. [D]

LA GARE FRENCH RESTAURANT   707/528-4355

French Fine Dining
$26-$38

AAA Inspector Notes: A popular dining spot since 1979, this restaurant will transport you to the French Swiss Alps with its cozy alpine décor and Old World ambience as you dine on a variety of traditional country-style French cuisine. Soup and salad are included with every entrée. **Features:** beer & wine. **Reservations:** suggested. **Address:** 208 Wilson St 95401 **Location:** US 101 exit downtown Santa Rosa, just w; just s of Railroad Square. [D]

LA ROSA TEQUILERIA AND GRILLE   707/523-3663
Mexican. Casual Dining. **Address:** 500 4th St 95401

LA VERA PIZZA   707/575-1113
Pizza. Casual Dining. **Address:** 629 4th St 95404

MONTI'S   707/568-4404
Mediterranean. Casual Dining. **Address:** 714 Village St 95405

ROSSO PIZZERIA AND WINE BAR   707/544-3221
♦♦ Italian Pizza. Casual Dining. **Address:** 53 Montgomery Dr 95404

RUSSIAN RIVER BREWING COMPANY   707/545-2337
♦♦ American. Brewpub. **Address:** 725 4th St 95404

SAZON AUTHENTIC PERUVIAN CUISINE   707/523-4346
♦♦ Peruvian. Casual Dining. **Address:** 1129 Sebastopol Rd 95407

SIMPLY VIETNAM EXPRESS   707/544-4585
♦ Vietnamese. Quick Serve. **Address:** 3381 Cleveland Ave 95403

THE SPINSTER SISTERS   707/528-7100
♦♦ California. Casual Dining. **Address:** 401 S A St 95401

THIRD STREET ALEWORKS   707/523-3060
♦♦ American. Casual Dining. **Address:** 610 3rd St 95404

WALTER HANSEL WINE AND BISTRO   707/546-6462
♦♦♦ French. Fine Dining. **Address:** 3535 Guerneville Rd 95401

WILLIE BIRD'S RESTAURANT   707/542-0861
♦♦ American. Casual Dining. **Address:** 1150 Santa Rosa Ave 95404

SARATOGA (E-9) pop. 29,926, elev. 480'
• **Hotels & Restaurants map & index p. 348**

Saratoga is at the northern end of a scenic 38-mile stretch of SR 9.

Saratoga Chamber of Commerce: 14460 Big Basin Way, Saratoga, CA 95070. **Phone:** (408) 867-0753.

MONTALVO ARTS CENTER AND ARBORETUM is .5 mi. s.e. on SR 9, then 1 mi. s.w. on Montalvo Rd. Formerly the summer home of U.S. senator and San Francisco mayor James D. Phelan, the estate now serves as a center for fine arts. The 1912 Mediterranean-style villa has a formal garden and trails to lookout points on the surrounding hills. A 10-studio artist residency complex, two performing arts venues and the Project Space Gallery are on the grounds. Two-hour walking tours of the villa and Montalvo's trails are offered. One-hour tours of the villa are offered July-August.

Time: Allow 1 hour minimum. **Hours:** Mon.-Thurs. 8-7, Fri.-Sun. and holidays 9-5, Apr.-Sept.; Mon.-Thurs. 8-5, Fri.-Sun. and holidays 9-5, rest of year. Project Space Gallery hours vary; phone for schedule. The garden is occasionally closed for private events. Closed Jan. 1 and Christmas. Phone ahead to confirm schedule. **Cost:** Free. Walking tour fee $20. Summer villa tour $10. Reservations are required for tours. **Phone:** (408) 961-5800 for recorded information, or (408) 961-5858 for the ticket office.

RECREATIONAL ACTIVITIES
Horseback Riding

• **Garrod Farms Riding Stables** is at 22647 Garrod Rd. **Hours:** One-hour guided trail rides are available by reservation Mon.-Fri. after 4:30 p.m., Sat.-Sun. 8:30-4:30, mid-June through

Labor Day; schedule varies, rest of year. Wine-tasting rides are offered on the last Sun. of the month. Under age 8 are not permitted on horses; pony walks are available for children under 8. Closed Thanksgiving and Christmas. Phone ahead to confirm schedule. **Phone:** (408) 867-9527.

THE INN AT SARATOGA   408/867-5020 (85)
♦♦♦ Boutique Hotel. **Address:** 20645 4th St 95070

WHERE TO EAT

LA FONDUE   408/867-3332 (40)
♦♦♦ Fondue. Casual Dining. **Address:** 14550 Big Basin Way 95070

THE PLUMED HORSE   408/867-4711 (39)
♦♦♦♦ California. Fine Dining. **Address:** 14555 Big Basin Way 95070

SAUSALITO (C-7) pop. 7,061, elev. 14'
• **Part of San Francisco area — see map p. 243**

Sausalito, Spanish for "little willow," is an impossibly charming Marin County town, just across the Golden Gate Bridge from San Francisco. Upscale boutiques, art galleries, gift shops and open-air cafés line Bridgeway, the main street, encouraging visitors to linger, shop and stop for lunch or a glass of wine. All the necessary scenic ingredients are present and accounted for: lovely, boat-dotted views of San Francisco Bay, houses picturesquely perched on the hillsides that rise behind Bridgeway, and Mount Tamalpais as a backdrop.

Sausalito's nautical history dates back to the early 1800s, when the area was settled by shipbuilders and sailors. The arrival of the railroad in the 1870s boosted development; ferries soon began plying the waters of the bay, transporting train passengers to San Francisco.

The opening of the Golden Gate Bridge in 1937 brought a decline in ferry service, but Sausalito's population took a leap when a huge shipyard that produced cargo vessels called Liberty ships for the U.S. Navy was established during the World War II years. After the war, the waterfront became home to a flotilla of houseboats occupied primarily by a bohemian crew of painters, writers and hippies—the beginning of Sausalito's artist colony. Today the houseboat community is concentrated north of the city, and you can take a guided walking tour of these funky floating residences.

The ♦ Sausalito Art Festival, held Labor Day weekend in Marinship Park, is not only one of the Bay Area's most popular outdoor art gatherings but is considered to be one of the finest juried art festivals in the nation. Many regional artists have been exhibiting at the festival for decades. This isn't a craft fair; the art for sale ranges from classic to modern to very quirky, and from affordable to seriously expensive. A convenient—and scenic—way to attend is by ferry; the Blue & Gold Fleet, based at San Francisco's Pier 41, offers a package deal that includes round-trip transportation to the festival site as well as the entrance fee. Phone (415) 332-3555 for festival information, or (415) 705-8200 for the Blue & Gold Fleet.

Passenger ferries link Sausalito with San Francisco. Regularly scheduled service by the Blue & Gold Fleet connects the two cities. Golden Gate Ferry also provides service; phone (415) 455-2000. *See Public Transportation in San Francisco p. 250.*

In addition to its hillside-hugging houses, Sausalito is known for views of the San Francisco skyline across the bay. Two good vantage points are aptly named Vista Point, at the north end of the Golden Gate Bridge, and the downtown marina.

Sausalito Chamber of Commerce: 1913 Bridgeway, Sausalito, CA 94965. **Phone:** (415) 331-7262.

Shopping: Bridgeway, the main drag, is lined with shops and boutiques; follow the crowds of sidewalk strollers and pop into any doorway that looks inviting. The menfolk might need to be sent on an expedition of some sort while ladies spend time browsing in Jewelry by the Bay (660 Bridgeway), which offers a variety of styles in different price ranges. The store also features cute gift items like miniature shoes and beaded animals (starfish, pelicans, geckos).

Gene Hiller for Men (729 Bridgeway) is an elegant store that sells conservative but stylish menswear, including beautifully tailored suits by European makers Canali and Eton. Sport coats, dress shirts, shoes, ties, pocket squares—everything a sharp-dressed man needs is here. And the customer service is exceptional. Soxalito (771 Bridgeway) is devoted entirely to socks—dinosaur socks, monkey socks, rainbow flag socks, Golden Gate Bridge socks and many more practical and offbeat designs to warm your toes.

The Scrimshaw Gallery (19 Princess St.) has all sorts of nautically themed artwork, sculptures and collectibles. A collection of reasonably priced prints includes vintage 19th-century San Francisco scenes as well as images of U.S. and Canadian lighthouses. And the scrimshaw designs—engravings and carvings done in bone or ivory—are expensive but exquisite.

Nightlife: Smack in the middle of touristy Bridgeway, the No Name Bar is a true local watering hole. Salty old geezers hold court at the bar, and the worn old wooden tables probably would have lots of stories to tell if they could talk. There's live music most nights, mostly mellow jazz as well as the occasional blues band.

Dive bar aficionados should also check out Smitty's (214 Caledonia St.), a real hole in the wall that nevertheless has its own peculiar charm; it's a good place to chat up the locals. There are plenty of beers on tap, four pool tables, a dart board and shuffleboard, all free. Karaoke nights are on the first and third Monday of the month at 8 p.m. It's packed on game days, and the people-watching is always interesting.

BAY MODEL VISITOR CENTER is at 2100 Bridgeway at the foot of Spring St.; use the Marinship Way access road. This environmental education facility, operated by the U.S. Army Corps of Engineers, shows a 9-minute introductory video and has a 1.5-acre hydraulic model simulating the tidal action and currents of San Francisco Bay and the Sacramento-San Joaquin Delta region.

Interactive exhibits provide an interesting view of the estuary. Visitors also can see an exhibit about Marinship, the World War II shipyard previously at this site. Audio tours are available in several languages.

Hours: Mon.-Fri. 9-4, Sat. 10-5, Memorial Day-Labor Day; Tues.-Sat. 9-4, rest of year. Phone ahead to confirm model operation. Closed Jan. 1, July 4, Thanksgiving and Christmas. **Cost:** Free. **Phone:** (415) 332-3871 or (415) 289-3007.

THE MARINE MAMMAL CENTER is in the Marin Headlands at 2000 Bunker Rd., within Fort Cronkhite. The center is an animal hospital that rescues and rehabilitates sick, injured and distressed marine animals from the California coast. Said to be the largest marine mammal facility in the world to combine rehabilitation with an on-site research lab, the center treats 600 to 800 animals a year.

Seals, sea lions, dolphins, porpoises and sea otters are frequent residents; visitors can see the animals in different "pens" being cared for by staff members. Exhibits provide information about marine mammals, ocean conservation and the center's work. **Time:** Allow 30 minutes minimum. **Hours:** Daily 10-4. Closed Jan. 1, Thanksgiving and Christmas. **Cost:** Donations. **Phone:** (415) 289-7325. **GT**

THE GABLES INN-SAUSALITO   415/289-1100
▼▼▼ Bed & Breakfast. **Address:** 62 Princess St 94965

THE INN ABOVE TIDE   415/332-9535
▼▼▼ Hotel. **Address:** 30 El Portal 94965

WHERE TO EAT

COPITA TEQUILERIA Y COMIDA   415/331-7400
▼▼ Mexican. Casual Dining. **Address:** 739 Bridgeway 94965

FISH   415/331-3474
▼▼ Seafood. Quick Serve. **Address:** 350 Harbor Dr 94965

MURRAY CIRCLE   415/339-4750
▼▼▼▼
California
Fine Dining
$25-$33

AAA Inspector Notes: A bronze tin-tiled ceiling adds a touch of historic ambience to this elegant dining room. For the perfect dining experience, request a table with a stunning view of the Golden Gate Bridge. Menu offerings include items like fresh ocean stew, wild king salmon, Prather Ranch pork tenderloin and roasted chicken for two. Definitely be sure to save room for dessert! **Features:** full bar, patio dining, Sunday brunch. **Reservations:** suggested. **Address:** 601 Murray Cir 94965 **Location:** US 101 exit Alexander Ave, just e on Sausalito Lateral Rd, 1 mi s on Bunker Rd, then 0.3 mi n; in Cavallo Point-The Lodge at the Golden Gate. **Parking:** on-site and valet. **B** **L** **D** CALL **&** **✗**

POGGIO   415/332-7771

▼▼▼ Italian. Casual Dining. **Address:** 777 Bridgeway 94965

SALITO'S CRABHOUSE & PRIMERIB   415/331-3226

▼▼ American. Casual Dining. **Address:** 1200 Bridgeway 94965

THE SPINNAKER   415/332-1500

▼▼	AAA Inspector Notes: This dining room over water offers panoramic views of the San Francisco Bay, nearby Tiburon and Sausalito and the tips of the Golden Gate Bridge. The menu offers guests diverse selections from simple sandwiches to grilled seafood and paella.
Seafood Casual Dining $31-$50	

Features: full bar, Sunday brunch. **Address:** 100 Spinnaker Dr 94965 **Location:** Center; adjacent to yacht harbor. **Parking:** valet and street only. L D

SCOTTS VALLEY pop. 11,580
• Hotels & Restaurants map & index p. 365

BEST WESTERN PLUS INN SCOTTS VALLEY
    831/438-6666   28

▼▼▼ Hotel	Best Western PLUS.	AAA Benefit: Members save up to 15% and earn bonus points!

Address: 6020 Scotts Valley Dr 95066 **Location:** SR 17 exit Granite Creek, just w. **Facility:** 58 units. 2 stories (no elevator), interior/exterior corridors. **Pool:** heated outdoor. **Activities:** hot tub, exercise room. **Guest Services:** valet and coin laundry. **Featured Amenity:** continental breakfast.

SAVE ❄ CALL ♿ ⟲ 🛁 BIZ
🛜 ✉ 🛗 🖥 / SOME UNITS 🐾

FOUR POINTS BY SHERATON SANTA CRUZ SCOTTS VALLEY
    831/438-1500   29

▼▼▼ SAVE Hotel. **Address:** 5030 Scotts Valley Dr 95066   **AAA Benefit:** Members save 5% or more!

WHERE TO EAT

BRUNO'S BAR AND GRILL   831/438-2227   15

▼▼ Barbecue. Casual Dining. **Address:** 230-G Mt. Herman Rd 95066

SEASIDE (G-3) pop. 33,025, elev. 33'
• Hotels & Restaurants map & index p. 144
• Part of Monterey Peninsula area — see map p. 141

You'll probably breeze right through Seaside without even realizing it if you're en route to Monterey on busy SR 1. But if you've got an hour or so to kill, Frog Pond Wetland Preserve is an under-the-radar detour where you can commune with nature in a quiet setting. A loop trail shaded by coast live oaks and Monterey pines traverses this wetlands habitat, which provides a home for frogs, hummingbirds, deer and ducks. It's a favorite spot for nature lovers and bird-watching enthusiasts. Access is off Canyon Del Rey Road between Gen. Jim Moore Boulevard and Highland Street; parking is limited to the Canyon Del Rey Road shoulder.

The site of a former U.S. Army post was designated Fort Ord National Monument in 2012, protecting some of the last remaining undeveloped land on the Monterey Peninsula. More than 80 miles of paved roads and narrow dirt trails are used by hikers, mountain bikers and horseback riders. The scenic central California coast environment varies from open, grass-covered hills and oak forests to maritime chaparral, a coastal habitat unique to California. There are beautiful fields of wildflowers in the spring. Several signed exits off SR 1 provide access to this 14,000-acre refuge.

EMBASSY SUITES BY HILTON MONTEREY BAY
    831/393-1115   42

▼▼▼ SAVE Hotel. **Address:** 1441 Canyon Del Rey 93955   **AAA Benefit:** Members save up to 15%!

HOLIDAY INN EXPRESS AT MONTEREY BAY SEASIDE
    831/394-5335   41

▼▼▼ Hotel. **Address:** 1400 Del Monte Blvd 93955

SANDCASTLE INN   831/394-6556   40

▼▼ Hotel. **Address:** 1011 La Salle Ave 93955

SEASIDE INN   831/394-4041   39

▼▼ Motel. **Address:** 1986 Del Monte Blvd 93955

WHERE TO EAT

SILVER TIDE BAR AND GRILL   831/393-1115   26

▼▼ American. Casual Dining. **Address:** 1441 Canyon Del Rey 93955

STAMMTISCH RESTAURANT   831/899-3070   25

▼▼ German. Casual Dining. **Address:** 1204 Echo Ave 93955

SEBASTOPOL (B-7) pop. 7,379, elev. 78'
• Part of Wine Country area — see map p. 405

Named after Sevastopol, the Russian seaport on the Crimean Peninsula, Sebastopol became a center of canned applesauce production in the late 19th century. That industry is still economically important today, as are the Gravenstein apple orchards and vineyards that blanket the surrounding rolling hills.

The Sebastopol Farmers Market is the perfect place to sample Sonoma County's agricultural bounty. Local farmers sell seasonal organic produce—including hard-to-find specialties like stone fruit and Amagaki persimmons—locally produced cheeses, honey, jams and hummus, and flowers and baked goods. Food vendors dish up Indian and Mediterranean treats, and you can grab the requisite to-go coffee at the Run Around Brew truck. A separate crafts section is always interesting to browse for jewelry, African handwoven baskets and pottery. There's also live music. This small but lively market has a quintessential NorCal hippie vibe. It sets up at the downtown plaza on Weeks Way (across from Whole Foods) Sundays from 10-1:30, year-round.

Sebastopol Area Chamber of Commerce and Visitor Center: 265 S. Main St., Sebastopol, CA 95472. **Phone:** (707) 823-3032.

FAIRFIELD INN & SUITES BY MARRIOTT SANTA ROSA SEBASTOPOL
707-829-6677

Hotel

 Fairfield **AAA Benefit:** Members save 5% or more!

Address: 1101 Gravenstein Hwy S 95472 **Location:** US 101 exit SR 116 W northbound, 8 mi w; exit SR 12 W southbound, 7 mi w to Main St. **Facility:** 82 units. 3 stories, interior corridors. **Terms:** check-in 4 pm. **Amenities:** safes. **Pool:** heated outdoor. **Activities:** hot tub, exercise room. **Guest Services:** valet and coin laundry.

SEBASTOPOL INN
707/829-2500

Hotel

Address: 6751 Sebastopol Ave 95472 **Location:** US 101 exit SR 12, 7 mi w. **Facility:** 31 units. 2 stories (no elevator), exterior corridors. **Pool:** heated outdoor. **Activities:** hot tub.

WHERE TO EAT

HANDLINE
707/827-3744
California. Quick Serve. **Address:** 935 Gravenstein Hwy S 95472

K & L BISTRO
707/823-6614
French. Casual Dining. **Address:** 119 S Main St 95472

KATHMANDU CAFE AND GRILL
707/861-9398
Nepali. Casual Dining. **Address:** 6761 Sebastopol Ave 95472

RAMEN GAIJIN
707/827-3609
Japanese. Casual Dining. **Address:** 6948 Sebastopol Ave 95472

SELMA pop. 23,219

BEST WESTERN COLONIAL INN
559/891-0300

Hotel

 Best Western. **AAA Benefit:** Members save up to 15% and earn bonus points!

Address: 2799 Floral Ave 93662 **Location:** SR 99 exit Floral Ave, just e. **Facility:** 56 units. 3 stories, interior corridors. **Pool:** outdoor. **Activities:** exercise room. **Guest Services:** coin laundry. **Featured Amenity:** breakfast buffet.

HOLIDAY INN SWAN COURT
559/891-8000
Hotel. **Address:** 2950 Pea Soup Anderson Blvd 93662

WHERE TO EAT

SAL'S MEXICAN RESTAURANT
559/896-7257
Mexican. Casual Dining. **Address:** 2163 Park St 93662

SPIKE 'N RAIL STEAK HOUSE
559/891-7000
American. Casual Dining. **Address:** 2910 Pea Soup Anderson Blvd 93662

SEQUOIA AND KINGS CANYON NATIONAL PARKS (G-5)
• Hotels p. 378 • Restaurants p. 378

Elevations in the parks range from 500 ft. in the foothills region to 14,494 ft. at the summit of Mount Whitney. Refer to AAA maps for additional elevation information.

In central California, stretching northward from 35 miles east of Visalia to 55 miles east of Fresno, and from the foothills of the San Joaquin Valley to the crest of the High Sierra, these two parks abut one another and are managed together. Sequoia is the second-oldest national park, behind Yellowstone National Park.

One way to turn back the clock some 3,000 years is to take a trip through Sequoia and Kings Canyon National Parks. The landscape is studded with the largest of trees, the giant sequoia *(Sequoiadendron giganteum)*. Many of the trees are more than 200 feet high and some have trunks more than 30 feet in diameter. Mount Whitney, at 14,505 feet the highest point in the contiguous United States, is on the eastern edge of Sequoia National Park.

Although the sequoias sparked the formation of these parks, magnificent forests of sugar and ponderosa pine, white and red fir and incense-cedar also exist here. Sugar pines have been known to grow to a base diameter of 11 feet.

Its variable climate has endowed this region with a significant variety of plants. About 1,530 species of trees, shrubs, plants and flowers have been identified, including 22 deciduous tree and 26 evergreen tree species.

Mule deer, marmots, chipmunks and squirrels are common. Because American black bears frequently are seen in campgrounds, proper food storage is strictly enforced. Raccoons, gray foxes and bobcats can be seen occasionally at night. Rarely seen, however, are Sierra bighorns and mountain lions. About 216 species of birds, including the golden eagle, have been spotted, and the streams along with some high-country lakes support rainbow, brook, brown and golden trout.

Only trails penetrate the alpine wilderness of both parks; therefore, the beauties of the High Sierra and backcountry are available only to hikers and those on horse, mule, burro or llama. Park trails are off-limits to bicyclists. *See Recreation Areas Chart.*

General Information and Activities

Sequoia and Kings Canyon National Parks are open all year, although the more remote areas are inaccessible in winter. High mountain passes are seldom open to travel before July 1. The roads to Giant Forest, Lodgepole and the Big Stump entrance are open all year; however, the Generals Highway between Lodgepole in Sequoia National Park and Grant Grove in Kings Canyon may be closed by heavy snow for periods during winter. Tire chains may be required at any time.

Connecting the two national parks is the Generals Highway, a 46-mile-long scenic road that extends from SR 198 at Ash Mountain in Sequoia National Park through Giant Sequoia National Monument to SR 180. The highway reaches 7,600 feet at Big Baldy Saddle. **Note:** From Ash Mountain to Giant Forest, the road is particularly difficult for motor homes and large trailers. The road is not recommended for vehicles longer than 22 feet. An alternate route for longer vehicles is SR 180 from Fresno through Kings Canyon National Park, a straighter, less steep and wider road. Vehicle combinations over 40 feet are prohibited between Hospital Rock and Giant Forest.

Sequoia Shuttle offers transportation to the Giant Forest Museum within Sequoia National Park from Visalia, Exeter and Three Rivers. The shuttle operates Memorial Day weekend through Labor Day; reservations are required. Phone (877) 287-4453.

Accommodations generally are open all year. While most campgrounds usually operate from Memorial Day through Labor Day, several campgrounds are open all year.

Lodgepole and Grant Grove/Kings Canyon visitor centers, in Sequoia and Kings Canyon National Parks, respectively, are hubs for activities. Naturalists give illustrated talks or campfire programs in summer at Cedar Grove, Grant Grove, Lodgepole and Potwisha amphitheaters. Schedules of programs and daily guided walks are posted on park bulletin boards. The parks' free newspaper contains seasonal information. It is available at park entrance stations and visitor centers.

A state fishing license is required for all persons 16 years and over. The $49.94 fee is good for a year for residents but only 10 days for non-residents. A 2-day resident or non-resident license costs $25.10. A second-pole license is $15.69. Hunting is permitted in season.

Trips over the hundreds of miles of backpacking trails are popular by horse, mule, burro and llama. Current information is available at the park visitor centers and in the park newspaper. Guided trail rides and pack trips or rental saddle stock are available from Grant Grove and Cedar Grove. Pack trips also can be arranged from the Owens Valley area on the east side of the Sierra. Cross-country ski and snowshoe rentals are available at Grant Grove and Wuksachi Lodge.

Headquarters for both parks, which are administered jointly, is at Ash Mountain, on the Generals Hwy. in Three Rivers via SR 198. The Foothills Visitor Center includes a photographic exhibit depicting life in the foothills.

ADMISSION to the parks is $35 per private vehicle, good for 7 days, or $20 per person arriving by other means.

PETS are permitted only if they are on a leash, crated or otherwise restricted at all times. They are prohibited on all trails and in buildings and may not be left unattended at any time.

ADDRESS inquiries to the Superintendent, Sequoia and Kings Canyon National Parks, 47050 Generals Hwy., Three Rivers, CA 93271-9700; phone (559) 565-3341.

ALTA PEAK (Sequoia), about 7 mi. from the Wolverton parking area, is 11,204 feet high; it can be reached on foot by a strenuous hike. **Phone:** (559) 565-3341.

BOYDEN CAVERN is 22 mi. n.e. of Grant Grove, off SR 180 at 74101 E. Kings Canyon Rd. within Sequoia National Forest. Guided 45-minute tours wind through underground chambers filled with a variety of sparkling, crystalline formations. The temperature inside is a cool 55 F; a sweater or light jacket is advised.

    Time: Allow 1 hour minimum. **Hours:** Tours depart daily on the hour 10-5, late May-Aug.; Wed.-Sun. 11-4, Sept. to mid-Nov. **Cost:** Tour $16; $8 (ages 4-12); $5 (ages 0-4). **Phone:** (888) 965-8243. GT 🏕

CEDAR GROVE (Kings Canyon) is within the canyon of the South Fork of the Kings River. Peaks rise more than a mile above the river, and spectacular views are available from road and trail. The level valley floor is especially well suited to leisurely bicycling. Cedar Grove also is a popular base point for longer trips into the high country. The area is inaccessible during winter. **Phone:** (559) 565-3341.

CRYSTAL CAVE (Sequoia) is 14 mi. from Lodgepole Visitor Center and accessible via a narrow, winding road that descends 2,000 feet to the Marble Fork Kaweah River bridge, and then from the parking area proceed down a steep half-mile trail to the cave entrance. **Note:** Vehicles longer than 22 feet are prohibited on the road to the cave entrance. This is the only one of the more than 275 caves within these national parks that is open to the public. The temperature inside the cave is a constant 50 degrees Fahrenheit, so visitors should bring warm clothing.

    Note: Persons with pre-existing heart or pulmonary conditions should not attempt this excursion. Strollers, baby backpacks, walking sticks and tripods are prohibited. Tickets must be purchased in advance. **Hours:** Fifty-minute guided tours are given every half-hour Mon.-Fri. 10-4:30, Sat. 10-6, Sun.

10-5, early June-Labor Day; on the hour Mon.-Fri. 10-3, Sat.-Sun. 10-4, late May-early June and day after Labor Day-early Oct. (weather and conditions permitting). Ages 0-12 are not permitted on tours at 10, 12:30 and 3:30, early June-Labor Day. Other tours are offered; phone for schedule and prices. **Cost:** Tours $17; $16 (ages 65+); $9 (ages 5-12); $6 (ages 0-4). **Phone:** (559) 565-3759 or (559) 565-4251. GT

GENERAL GRANT AND REDWOOD MOUNTAIN GROVES are in Kings Canyon. The General Grant Tree, one of the largest of known sequoias, stands in Grant Grove. It is more than 268 feet high and has a base circumference of approximately 107.5 feet. Big Stump Basin, the result of early logging operations, is nearby. Hart Tree, another large sequoia, stands in Redwood Mountain Grove. **Cost:** Free. **Phone:** (559) 565-3341.

Kings Canyon Visitor Center (Kings Canyon) is 3 mi. e. of Big Stump entrance station on SR 180. Visitor center exhibits highlight the three major features of the park: the canyon, the giant sequoias, and the High Sierra. **Hours:** Daily 9-5, Memorial Day-Labor Day; otherwise varies, rest of year. Phone ahead to confirm schedule. **Cost:** Free. **Phone:** (559) 565-3341 or (559) 565-4307.

GIANT FOREST (Sequoia) is 16 mi. from the park entrance station via the steep and winding Generals Hwy. It was named in 1875 by conservationist John Muir. The General Sherman Tree is thought to be the largest living tree in the world; standing about 275 feet tall and about 103 feet in circumference. The Giant Forest Museum has exhibits focused on giant sequoia ecology and the forest's natural and human history. From the museum several hiking trails lead to the Round Meadow and Hazelwood areas. **Hours:** Museum daily 9-4:30. **Phone:** (559) 565-3341, or (559) 565-4480 for museum.

HEATHER LAKE (Sequoia), 5 mi. by trail from Wolverton, is the first of a chain of alpine lakes accessible by the Lakes Trail. Two miles beyond is Pear Lake, in a barren granite basin. **Note:** The Lakes Trail is a very steep and difficult hike. **Phone:** (559) 565-3341.

THE HIGH COUNTRY extends from Coyote Peaks at the s. border of Sequoia to the n. boundary of Kings Canyon at Pavilion Dome. Trail trips are the only way to become acquainted with this rugged country. Mount Whitney is 72 miles from Giant Forest along the High Sierra Trail. A wilderness permit is required for overnight visitors. **Phone:** (559) 565-3341, or (559) 565-3766 for wilderness permits.

HOSPITAL ROCK (Sequoia) is 5 mi. beyond Ash Mountain entrance station on the road to the Giant Forest. Native American pictographs on the boulder mark an old village site once occupied by the Potwisha tribe of the Western Mono Indians. Also at the site are mortar-and-pestle holes used by the women to grind acorns into flour. Exhibits are on the site of an ancient village. **Phone:** (559) 565-3341.

LODGEPOLE VISITOR CENTER (Sequoia) is 4 mi. n.e. of the Giant Forest on Generals Hwy. The center has displays about the sequoias, geologic history and plant life. **Hours:** Daily 7-5, mid-May to early Oct. Phone to confirm schedule for ranger programs. **Cost:** Free. **Phone:** (559) 565-3341, (559) 565-4436 June-Sept., or (877) 444-6777 for camping reservations for Lodgepole and Dorst (in summer only).

MINERAL KING (Sequoia) is 25 mi. e. of Three Rivers via Mineral King Rd. and a steep, narrow, winding and partially paved road. Once a silver-mining area, this remote and peaceful valley retreat starts at an altitude of 7,500 feet, lying in the shadow of the Great Western Divide's towering peaks. Picnic tables and grills are available near the ranger's station. **Note:** The area is unsuitable for RVs (trailers and vehicles longer than 22 feet are not permitted) and is inaccessible in winter. **Hours:** Road open late May-late Oct. (weather permitting). **Phone:** (559) 565-3341. 🏕

MORO ROCK (Sequoia), 3 mi. by narrow road or hiking trail from Giant Forest, is 6,725 feet above sea level and more than 6,000 feet above the San Joaquin Valley floor. Scenic views of the Great Western Divide, especially at sunset, are the reward for reaching the top. A steep stairway with approximately 400 steps, inaccessible in winter, leads to the summit. **Note:** Lightning storms may be a hazard in summer months. **Phone:** (559) 565-3341.

PANORAMIC POINT (Kings Canyon) at the e. boundary of General Grant Grove is accessible via a 2.3-mi. road and then a quarter-mile walk from the parking lot. **Note:** The road is narrow and winding; trailers or motor homes are not permitted.

The point offers views of the High Sierra to the east and the San Joaquin Valley and Coast Range to the west. Within walking distance is another observation point at Park Ridge. **Hours:** Road closed to vehicular traffic in the winter, when it becomes a cross-country ski trail. **Phone:** (559) 565-3341.

THARP'S LOG (Sequoia) is at the end of Log Meadow, 1 mi. by trail from Crescent Meadow; or reached from the Circle Meadow and Congress trails. An old pioneer cabin was built within this fallen fire-hollowed sequoia log. **Cost:** Free. **Phone:** (559) 565-3341.

 Rest assured:

AAA.com/travelguides/hotels

CEDAR GROVE LODGE   801/559-4714

▽ Hotel. **Address:** Sequoia & Kings Canyon National Parks 93633

JOHN MUIR LODGE AT GRANT GROVE VILLAGE
                                          559/335-5500

▽▽ Motel. **Address:** 86728 Hwy 180 93633

WUKSACHI VILLAGE & LODGE   559/565-4070

◆◆◆◆
Hotel

Address: 64740 Wuksachi Way 93262 **Location:** 6 mi n of Giant Forest on General's Hwy. **Facility:** 102 units. 3 stories (no elevator), interior corridors. **Terms:** check-in 4 pm. **Dining:** The Peaks Restaurant, see separate listing. **Activities:** fishing, cross country skiing, trails.

SAVE ▮▮ ▽ CALL ⬤ HS 📶
✕ 🎿 🔲 🖳

WHERE TO EAT

THE PEAKS RESTAURANT   559/565-4070

◆◆◆ American. Casual Dining. **Address:** 64740 Wuksachi Way 93262

SEQUOIA NATIONAL FOREST (G-5)

Elevations in the forest range from 1,000 ft. at the Kings and Kern rivers along the forest's western edge to 12,432 ft. at Florence Peak in the Golden Trout Wilderness. Refer to AAA maps for additional elevation information.

Sequoia National Forest lies in Central California at the southern end of the Sierra Nevadas, extending from Kings River southward to the Kern River and Piute Mountains, and westward from the Sierra Nevada summit to the brush-covered foothills of the San Joaquin Valley.

Groves of giant sequoias, the Kern Plateau and the Golden Trout, Monarch, Jennie Lakes, South Sierra, Dome Land and Kiavah wildernesses are among the more popular attractions. The South Fork Kings Wild and Scenic River, Kings River Special Management Area, North Fork Kern Wild and Scenic River and South Fork Kern Wild and Scenic River also draw outdoor recreation enthusiasts to this spectacularly scenic wilderness area, which covers approximately 1,193,500 acres.

To permanently protect most of the nation's remaining giant sequoia trees, the Giant Sequoia National Monument was created in 2000. The monument's 353,000 acres, all within Sequoia National Forest, encompass 33 groves of these soaring specimens. The largest trees on Earth by volume, they can grow to nearly 300 feet in height and live more than 3,000 years. The monument is separated into two sections, divided by Sequoia National Park; the northern portion is in Fresno and Tulare counties, the southern entirely within Tulare County. The Trail of 100 Giants, a one-mile interpretive trail, can be reached mid-May through mid-November (weather permitting). Hiking and horseback riding are permitted, and motorcycles, all-terrain vehicles and snowmobiles may be used, although restrictions

apply. For additional information phone the national forest office.

More than 50 campgrounds and picnic areas provide bases for activities that include fishing, swimming, boating, hiking, horseback riding, rock climbing and hunting. White-water rafting is popular on the Kern and Kings rivers. Swimming along the shoreline is permitted on 87-acre Hume Lake. Fall-foliage color is particularly spectacular at Quaking Aspen, Indian Basin and the Kern Plateau. Snowmobiling and cross-country and downhill skiing take over in winter. A fire lookout tower and ranger cabins can be rented.

For information contact the Forest Supervisor, Sequoia National Forest, 1839 S. Newcomb St., Porterville, CA 93257-2035; phone (559) 784-1500. *See Recreation Areas Chart.*

SEQUOIA NATIONAL PARK—See Sequoia and Kings Canyon National Parks p. 375

SHASTA (C-2) pop. 1,771, elev. 1,026'

◣GEM **SHASTA STATE HISTORIC PARK** is on SR 299. Formerly a robust mining town with a population of 2,500, Shasta was the gateway to a large area of riches and a rendezvous for gamblers; it is now an interesting gold rush relic. The old courthouse has been converted to a museum that contains historical exhibits as well as the Boggs Collection—100 Years of California Art. A restored barn and stagecoach can be seen. Also in the park are unrestored buildings that stand as reminders of Shasta's mining heyday.

Hours: Park and museum open Thurs.-Sun. 10-5. Closed Jan. 1, Thanksgiving and Christmas. Phone ahead to confirm schedule. **Cost:** Historic park free. Museum $3; $2 (ages 6-17). **Phone:** (530) 243-8194. 🎟

SHASTA LAKE (C-2) pop. 10,164, elev. 790'

SHASTA DAM is 6 mi. w. on SR 151 (Shasta Dam Blvd.), following signs. Shasta Dam is reputedly the world's highest center-overflow spillway. A 30-minute videotape depicting water usage in California is shown at the visitor center upon request. Guided walking tours provide information about visitor center displays and the dam.

Hours: Visitor center open daily 8-5. A 1-hour tour of the dam departs daily at 9, 10:15, 11:30, 1, 2:15 and 3:30, Memorial Day-Labor Day; 9, 11, 1 and 3, rest of year. Visitors are advised to arrive 1 hour before tour time. Closed winter federal holidays. Phone ahead to confirm schedule. **Cost:** Free. **Phone:** (530) 275-4463. 🎟

⊘ **Use the free travel planning tools at AAA.com/maps**

SHASTA-TRINITY NATIONAL FORESTS (B-3)

Elevations in the forests range from 620 ft. at Lake Shasta to 14,162 ft. at Mount Shasta. Refer to AAA maps for additional elevation information.

In northern California, the Shasta-Trinity National Forests cover more than 2,100,000 acres and include portions of the Yolla Bolly-Middle Eel Wilderness Area and the Trinity Alps Wilderness. Mount Shasta, a dormant volcano capped with five glaciers, is 14,162 feet tall.

Three impounded lakes—Whiskeytown, Shasta and Clair Engle—are within the Whiskeytown-Shasta-Trinity National Recreation Area *(see place listing p. 402)*. Almost 1,200 miles of hiking trails wind through this vast wilderness area, including 154 miles of the Pacific Crest Trail. There are numerous opportunities for lake and stream fishing as well as hunting for waterfowl, upland birds, deer, bear and small game. Phone (877) 444-6777 or TTY (877) 833-6777 for reservations made through the National Recreation Reservation System.

For more information contact the Forest Supervisor, Shasta-Trinity National Forests, 3644 Avtech Pkwy., Redding, CA 96002; phone (530) 226-2500 or TTY (530) 226-2490. *See Recreation Areas Chart.*

SHELTER COVE (C-1) pop. 693, elev. 138'

Rising just offshore from the mountainous headland of Cape Mendocino—the westernmost point in California—is Sugar Loaf, a 326-foot-tall sea stack. Several other large rocks protrude from the shallow waters just off this stretch of northern California coast, and they posed hidden dangers for 19th-century sailing ships.

The Cape Mendocino Lighthouse began operations in 1868. The first tower had 16 sides and a double balcony and was bolted to a concrete foundation 422 feet above the ocean. The lighthouse remained active until the 1940s, when it was automated and the Fresnel lens removed. By the 1960s it had not only been abandoned but was inching down a hillside and succumbing to the debilitating effects of rust; in the late 1990s it was relocated 35 miles south to Shelter Cove and reassembled.

The reassembled and refurbished structure stands at the tip of Point Delgada in tiny Mal Coombs Park, 23 miles west of US 101 exit 642 (Redwood Drive). It is usually open to the public daily 11-3, Memorial Day-Labor Day. From the park there is access to a beach where you can explore tide pools.

THE TIDES INN   707/986-7900

Motel

Address: 59 Surf Point 95589 **Location:** Oceanfront. US 101 exit Shelter Cove, 1.7 mi s on Redwood Dr, 20.2 mi w on Briceland Rd/Shelter Cove Rd, then 0.6 mi sw on Machi Rd/Lower Pacific Dr. **Facility:** 8 units, some kitchens. 3 stories (no elevator), exterior corridors.

SIERRA CITY (D-4) pop. 221, elev. 4,187'

KENTUCKY MINE PARK AND MUSEUM, .5 mi. e. via SR 49 in Sierra County Historical Park, is on the site of a hard-rock gold mine. Guided 1-hour walking tours go from the mine portal through an operable ten stamp mill. Tools, photographs, documents and mineral samples displayed in the museum depict mining-camp life during California's gold rush era. Other exhibits include Native American and Chinese artifacts. Concerts take place Saturday evenings early July through August in an outdoor amphitheater; phone for concert information.

Hours: Open Wed.-Sun. 10-4, Memorial Day weekend-Labor Day weekend. Guided stamp mill and mine tours are given at 11 and 2. **Cost:** $7 (includes museum and tours); $3.50 (ages 7-17); $1 (museum only). Cash only. **Phone:** (530) 862-1310.
🅰

HERRINGTON'S SIERRA PINES RESORT   530/862-1151
♥♥ Motel. **Address:** 104 Main St 96125

WHERE TO EAT

HERRINGTON'S SIERRA PINES RESTAURANT   530/862-1151
♥♥ American. Casual Dining. **Address:** 104 Main St 96125

SIERRA NATIONAL FOREST (F-5)

Elevations in the forest range from 990 ft. at the Merced River to 13,157 ft. at the summit of Mount Ritter. Refer to AAA maps for additional elevation information.

Located between two of California's scenic crown jewels, Kings Canyon and Yosemite national parks *(see place listings p. 375 and p. 420)*, Sierra National Forest is a gem in its own right. This 1,300,000-acre wilderness area embraces almost all the land between these national parks—from the gently rolling foothills bordering the San Joaquin Valley to the jagged Sierra crest. Within the forest's boundaries lies much of what naturalist and Sierra Club founder John Muir described as the "Range of Light." More commonly called the High Sierra, it's a spectacular landscape dominated by craggy peaks, giant glacial stairways and mountainside natural amphitheaters filled with lakes and open meadows.

How this rugged landscape came to be was debated by many 19th-century scientists. Yet it was Muir's remark that "tender snow-flowers noiselessly falling through unnumbered centuries" came closest to the truth. Glacial ice gave these peaks their distinctive shape, further refined by the many swift streams and rivers fed by melting of the yearly snowpack. Such major rivers as the San Joaquin, the Merced, the Kings and their tributaries all carved deep canyons and gorges within the forest.

Hidden deep within these watersheds are clusters of sequoias. One stand of these majestic trees is the Nelder Grove, south of Yosemite National Park near Bass Lake; the McKinley Grove is farther south near Dinkey Creek.

Two highways offering access to the forest are SRs 41 and 168; the most accessible recreation areas are along or just off these routes. Shaver Lake and Bass Lake are two popular destinations, offering camping, fishing and boating. Other recreation areas, such as Florence Lake, Edison Lake, Redinger Lake and Pine Flat Reservoir, are accessible from forest roads branching off SR 168. During the winter months the focus switches to downhill skiing.

The John Muir and Ansel Adams wilderness areas straddle the forest's eastern border and the Sierra crest. The former, with its snowcapped peaks, dense forests and numerous lakes, is one of California's largest wilderness areas. Highlights of this untamed area include the John Muir Trail—a segment of the Pacific Crest Trail—and Humphreys Basin, with its countless lakes and views of Mount Humphreys, a favorite challenge for experienced climbers.

Within the Ansel Adams Wilderness Area are the jagged peaks of Ritter Range. Smaller in size are the Monarch, Dinkey Lakes and Kaiser wilderness areas. The John Muir and Kaiser wilderness areas, as well as portions of the Ansel Adams, are so popular that there is a quota system for visitors; making reservations at least 3 weeks in advance is recommended. More than a thousand miles of hiking trails and over 400 lakes are waiting to be explored in these areas.

Indigenous wildlife includes deer, bears, quail, bobcats, foxes, beavers and coyotes. Lakes and streams teem with rainbow, golden, brown and eastern brook trout, along with large- and smallmouth bass, crappie and bluegill.

There is no central visitor center, but information about campgrounds and recreational opportunities is available at district ranger stations and the forest headquarters in Clovis. Campground reservations, usually required for the months of June through August at Shaver Lake, Huntington Lake, Dinkey Creek and Bass Lake, can be made through the National Recreation Reservation System; phone (877) 444-6777 or TTY (877) 833-6777.

For more information contact the Forest Headquarters, Sierra National Forest, 1600 Tollhouse Rd., Clovis, CA 93611-0532; phone (559) 297-0706. *See Recreation Areas Chart.*

SIX RIVERS NATIONAL FOREST (B-1)

Elevations in the forest range from 350 ft. at Adams Station to 6,957 ft. at the summit of Salmon Mountain. Refer to AAA maps for additional elevation information.

Extending 135 miles south from the Oregon border along the west slope of the Coast Range, Six Rivers National Forest covers almost 990,000 acres;

it is named for the Smith, Klamath, Trinity, Mad, Van Duzen and Eel rivers.

Various roads access the forest, including SR 96 along the Trinity and Klamath rivers northward from Willow Creek through the Hoopa Valley Indian Reservation. Much of this region, however, is accessible only on foot or by horseback.

Many recreational opportunities center around water. Rafting and kayaking are especially popular on the Klamath, Trinity and Smith rivers. Trout, steelhead and salmon fishing and deer hunting are other activities.

Within the national forest is Smith River National Recreation Area. More than 65 miles of trails are used by horseback riders, mountain bikers and hikers, and wildlife observers can spot such rare and endangered species as bald eagles and peregrine falcons. For information contact the Forest Supervisor, Six Rivers National Forest, 1330 Bayshore Way, Eureka, CA 95501; phone (707) 442-1721. *See Recreation Areas Chart.*

SOLEDAD pop. 25,738, elev. 190'

VALLEY HARVEST INN   831/678-3833

Hotel

Address: 1155 Front St 93960 **Location:** US 101 exit Soledad, just e. **Facility:** 57 units. 2 stories (no elevator), interior/exterior corridors. **Dining:** Windmill Restaurant, see separate listing. **Pool:** outdoor. **Activities:** hot tub, exercise room. **Guest Services:** coin laundry. **Featured Amenity:** continental breakfast.

SAVE ◫ CALL ⬇ ⟲ ⊞ BIZ
🛜 ◫ ⊟ ⟲ /SOME UNITS ⊞

WHERE TO EAT

WINDMILL RESTAURANT   831/678-1775
⬖⬖ American. Casual Dining. **Address:** 1167 Front St 93960

SONOMA (B-7) pop. 10,648, elev. 84'
• Hotels p. 382 • Restaurants p. 383
• Hotels & Restaurants map & index p. 412
• Part of Wine Country area — see map p. 405

This Wine Country town is a big tourist destination, but it also left a prominent footprint on early California history. After overthrowing the Spanish government in 1823, the Mexican government issued a decree that all church properties be secularized. This included the Mission San Francisco Solano de Sonoma, recently established by Spanish priest Jose Altimira. Gen. Mariano Guadalupe Vallejo was sent from Monterey to confiscate the property, which he did; during his post he also founded the town of Sonoma around a central plaza, the Spanish model for cities in Mexico.

Settlers, lured to the area by the promise of free land, later were denied the opportunity to own property. Faced with the threat of deportation, their dissatisfaction came to a climax on June 14, 1846, when the group, calling themselves Osos (bears), arrested Vallejo at his home. They proclaimed California a republic and Sonoma its capital.

The Bear Flag—fashioned from unbleached muslin, a red petticoat and a crude berry-stained picture of a bear—was raised in Sonoma Plaza. The revolt was short-lived, however; on July 9 the flag was replaced by the Stars and Stripes. In 1911 the State Legislature adopted the Bear Flag as the state flag.

Depot Park Museum, in the original town depot on 1st Street W., preserves the history of the California Republic through displays of 19th-century clothing, railroad artifacts and furniture; phone (707) 938-1762.

Sonoma Valley Visitors Bureau: 453 1st St. E., Sonoma, CA 95476. **Phone:** (707) 996-1090 or (866) 996-1090.

CORNERSTONE SONOMA is 3 mi. s. at 23570 Arnold Dr. (SR 121). The wine country marketplace features a collection of boutique wineries and tasting rooms, artisanal foods, shops, art-inspired gardens and live music and is home to Sunset's Gardens and Outdoor Test Kitchen. The Cornerstone Gardens are an ever-changing series of gardens, showcasing innovative designs from international and local landscape architects and designers. The five Sunset Gardens highlight food production, the Sunset plant line, bee habitat, cut flowers and composting. **Time:** Allow 45 minutes minimum. **Hours:** Gardens daily 10-4. Tasting room, shops and café daily 10-5. Parts of the gardens may close early on weekends for special events; phone ahead to confirm schedule. **Cost:** Free. **Phone:** (707) 933-3010. ⊞

 SONOMA STATE HISTORIC PARK is centered around Sonoma Plaza. More than a dozen buildings important to early California history can be explored. The Toscano Hotel and Sonoma Barracks are on the plaza. The hotel, built during the 1850s, resembles its turn-of-the-20th-century appearance. The two-story, partially restored adobe barracks once housed Mexican general Mariano Vallejo's troops. Following the raising of the Bear Flag in 1846, the building was used by U.S. troops.

The 1823 Mission San Francisco Solano de Sonoma was the last of the California missions, which were located a day's journey apart along the coast. Destroyed and rebuilt several times, it contains exhibits about mission life as well as the Jorgensen watercolors of the Missions of California. Gen. Vallejo's former home, Lachryma Montis, contains family furnishings, and there are gardens on the grounds. Near the house is the Chalet, a building originally used to store wine and produce; it is now the park's visitor center. The mission can be seen on a self-guiding tour.

Several guided tours are available. **Time:** Allow 1 hour minimum. **Hours:** Park open daily 10-5. Tours of the mission are offered Fri.-Sun. 11-3. Vallejo home tours are offered Sat.-Sun. 1-4. Toscana Hotel and kitchen tours are offered Sat.-Sun. at 1 and 4. All tours are dependent on staff availability. Closed

(See map & index p. 412.)

Jan. 1, Thanksgiving and Christmas. **Cost:** $3 (includes mission, barracks and house); $2 (ages 6-17). **Phone:** (707) 938-9560.

SONOMA TRAINTOWN, 1 mi. s. on SR 12, offers a 20-minute miniature train ride through a forested railroad park past scaled-down reproductions of buildings and waterfalls. A diesel engine makes the trip Monday through Saturday; a steam engine is used Sundays and holidays. A petting zoo, Ferris wheel, merry-go-round and other rides are on the grounds.

Time: Allow 30 minutes minimum. **Hours:** Trips daily 10-5, mid-June to mid-Aug.; Fri.-Sun. and some holidays 10-5, rest of year. On Fridays from mid-Aug. to mid-June the train, carousel and airplane ride are the only activities available. Closed Thanksgiving and Christmas. **Cost:** Park admission free. Train rides $6.75 (12 months and older). Merry-go-round, Ferris wheel and other rides $2.75 each, or six rides for $14.75. **Phone:** (707) 938-3912.

SONOMA VALLEY MUSEUM OF ART is at 551 Broadway, just s. of Sonoma Plaza. Changing exhibits feature paintings, drawings, sculpture, photography, ceramics, film, crafts, architecture, print-making and video by local, national and international artists. **Time:** Allow 1 hour, 30 minutes minimum. **Hours:** Wed.-Sun. 11-5. **Cost:** $10; $7 (ages 62+, Sonoma Valley residents and college students with ID); $5 (ages 13-17); free (ages 0-12 and to all on Wed.); $15 (family). **Phone:** (707) 939-7862. 🍴

WINERIES

- **Buena Vista Winery** is 2 mi. n.e. at 18000 Old Winery Rd. **Hours:** Daily 10-5. Closed major holidays. **Phone:** (800) 926-1266. GT

- **Cline Cellars** is at 24737 Arnold Dr. **Hours:** Daily 10-6. Guided tours are given daily at 11, 1 and 3. Closed Christmas. **Phone:** (707) 940-4030 or (800) 546-2070. GT

- **Gloria Ferrer Caves & Vineyards** is at 23555 Arnold Dr. (SR 121). **Hours:** Daily 10-4:45. Guided tours are given daily at 11, 1 and 3; phone ahead after 9:30 on day of visit to confirm tour schedule. **Phone:** (707) 996-7256, or (707) 933-1917 to confirm the day's tour schedule. GT

- **Gundlach Bundschu Winery** is e. off SR 12 onto E. Napa St., s. onto 8th St. E., then e. to 2000 Denmark St. **Hours:** Daily 11-5:30, May-Oct.; 11-4:30, rest of year. Two different guided tours are available by appointment; phone ahead for tour schedule. Reservations are recommended for tastings. Closed Jan. 1, Thanksgiving, Christmas Eve and Christmas. **Phone:** (707) 938-5277 or (707) 939-3015. GT

- **Sebastiani Vineyards & Winery** is at 389 4th St. E. **Hours:** Tasting room open daily 10-5. Tours are given daily; phone for schedule. Musical performances take place Fri. evenings from 6-9 p.m., May-Sept. Closed major holidays. **Phone:** (707) 933-3200. GT

BEST WESTERN SONOMA VALLEY INN & KRUG EVENT CENTER 707/938-9200 72

Hotel

 Best Western. **AAA Benefit:** Members save up to 15% and earn bonus points!

Address: 550 2nd St W 95476 **Location:** 1 blk w of town plaza. **Facility:** 82 units. 2 stories (no elevator), exterior corridors. **Terms:** check-in 4 pm. **Amenities:** safes. **Pool:** heated outdoor. **Activities:** hot tub, steamroom, bicycles. **Guest Services:** complimentary and valet laundry. **Featured Amenity:** breakfast buffet.

EL PUEBLO INN 707/996-3651 70

Motel

Address: 896 W Napa St 95476 **Location:** SR 12, 1 mi w of town plaza. **Facility:** 53 units. 2 stories (no elevator), exterior corridors. **Amenities:** safes. **Pool:** heated outdoor. **Activities:** hot tub, bicycles, exercise room. **Guest Services:** valet laundry. **Featured Amenity:** continental breakfast.

THE FAIRMONT SONOMA MISSION INN & SPA 707/938-9000 69

Resort Hotel

Address: 100 Boyes Blvd 95476 **Location:** 2.5 mi n on SR 12. **Facility:** A mixture of Mediterranean and Spanish-Californian architecture distinguishes this historic inn set on 14 acres of spacious and well-manicured landscaped grounds. Expansive spa services are available. 226 units. 3 stories, interior/exterior corridors. **Parking:** on-site and valet. **Terms:** check-in 4 pm. **Amenities:** safes. **Dining:** 2 restaurants, also, Santé, see separate listing. **Pool:** heated outdoor. **Activities:** sauna, hot tub, steamroom, regulation golf, recreation programs, bicycles, lawn sports, trails, exercise room, spa. **Guest Services:** valet laundry, area transportation.

INN AT SONOMA 707/939-1340 73

🦃🦃🦃 Bed & Breakfast. **Address:** 630 Broadway 95476

(See map & index p. 412.)

THE LODGE AT SONOMA, A RENAISSANCE RESORT & SPA
707/935-6600 **75**

Hotel

R
RENAISSANCE®
HOTELS

AAA Benefit: Members save 5% or more!

Address: 1325 Broadway 95476 **Location:** On SR 12, 1 mi s of Sonoma Plaza. **Facility:** 182 units. 2 stories, interior/exterior corridors. **Parking:** on-site (fee) and valet. **Terms:** check-in 4 pm. **Amenities:** safes. **Dining:** Carneros Bistro & Wine Bar, see separate listing. **Pool:** heated outdoor. **Activities:** hot tub, bicycles, lawn sports, exercise room, spa. **Guest Services:** valet laundry, area transportation. **Featured Amenity: full hot breakfast.**

MACARTHUR PLACE
707/938-2929 **74**
Country Inn. **Address:** 29 E MacArthur St 95476

SONOMA CREEK INN
707/939-9463 **68**
Motel. **Address:** 239 Boyes Blvd 95476

SONOMA HOTEL
707/996-2996 **71**
Historic Country Inn. **Address:** 110 W Spain St 95476

WHERE TO EAT

CAFE LA HAYE
707/935-5994 **85**
California. Casual Dining. **Address:** 140 E Napa St 95476

CARNEROS BISTRO & WINE BAR
707/931-2042 **89**

California Casual Dining $10-$38

AAA Inspector Notes: Wine country cuisine makes up the menu in this relaxed and casually elegant bistro, where service is crisp and attentive. This place brings in many foods from local artisan farms and the salad ingredients are freshly picked from gardens on the premises. Many items are cooked in the rotisserie and wood-burning ovens. Outdoor seating is an option when the weather permits. **Features:** full bar, patio dining, Sunday brunch. **Reservations:** suggested. **Address:** 1325 Broadway 95476 **Location:** On SR 12, 1 mi s of Sonoma Plaza; in The Lodge at Sonoma, A Renaissance Resort & Spa. B L D

DELLA SANTINA'S
707/935-0576 **86**
Italian. Casual Dining. **Address:** 133 E Napa St 95476

EL DORADO KITCHEN
707/996-3030 **80**
California. Casual Dining. **Address:** 405 1st St W 95476

THE GIRL & THE FIG
707/938-3634 **79**
French. Casual Dining. **Address:** 110 W Spain St 95476

HOPMONK TAVERN SONOMA
707/935-9100 **87**
American. Casual Dining. **Address:** 691 Broadway St 95476

LA CASA RESTAURANT & BAR
707/996-3406 **83**
Mexican. Casual Dining. **Address:** 121 E Spain St 95476

LASALETTE RESTAURANT
707/938-1927 **84**
Portuguese. Casual Dining. **Address:** 452-H 1st St E 95476

LAYLA RESTAURANT
707/938-2929 **88**
Mediterranean. Fine Dining. **Address:** 29 E MacArthur St 95476

SANTÉ
707/939-2415 **78**

California Fine Dining $34-$55

AAA Inspector Notes: This elegant restaurant serves wine country cuisine using the freshest local ingredients with many organically grown. For a memorable dining experience, go with the seven course chef's tasting menu—it features Wagyu beef and a delightful cheese course. **Features:** full bar, patio dining. **Reservations:** suggested. **Address:** 100 Boyes Blvd 95476 **Location:** 2.5 mi n on SR 12; in The Fairmont Sonoma Mission Inn & Spa. **Parking:** on-site and valet. B D

SUNFLOWER CAFFE ESPRESSO & WINE BAR
707/996-6645 **82**
American. Quick Serve. **Address:** 421 1st St W 95476

SWISS HOTEL RESTAURANT
707/938-2884 **81**
Swiss. Casual Dining. **Address:** 18 W Spain St 95476

SONORA (F-4) pop. 4,903, elev. 1,796'

Sonora was initially settled by miners from Sonora, Mexico, in 1848 and became one of the largest and wealthiest towns in the Mother Lode country. Tourism, lumbering and agriculture provide the income today. Handsome Victorian houses are a legacy of the town's gold rush days.

Tuolumne County Visitors Bureau: 193 S. Washington St., P.O. Box 4020, Sonora, CA 95370. **Phone:** (209) 533-4420 or (800) 446-1333.

ALADDIN MOTOR INN
209/533-4971
Hotel. **Address:** 14260 Mono Way (Hwy 108) 95370

BARRETTA GARDENS INN
209/532-6039
Bed & Breakfast. **Address:** 700 S Barretta St 95370

BEST WESTERN PLUS SONORA OAKS HOTEL & CONFERENCE CENTER
209/533-4400

Hotel

Best Western PLUS

AAA Benefit: Members save up to 15% and earn bonus points!

Address: 19551 Hess Ave 95370 **Location:** SR 108 exit Phoenix Lake Rd westbound, just e to Hess Ave, then just s; exit Hess Ave eastbound, just s; jct Mono Way. **Facility:** 100 units, some two bedrooms. 2 stories (no elevator), interior/exterior corridors. **Pool:** outdoor. **Activities:** hot tub, exercise room. **Guest Services:** valet laundry. **Featured Amenity:** breakfast buffet.

WHERE TO EAT

THE DIAMONDBACK GRILL
209/532-6661
American. Casual Dining. **Address:** 93 S Washington St 95370

EMBERZ WOOD-FIRED FOODZ
209/532-2272
American. Casual Dining. **Address:** 177 S Washington St 95370

MANDY'S BREAKFAST HOUSE
209/588-8020
American. Casual Dining. **Address:** 22267 Parrots Ferry Rd 95370

THE PEPPERY   209/533-9033
♥♥ American. Casual Dining. **Address:** 13494 Mono Way 95370

SONORA THAI CUISINE   209/532-2355
♥♥ Thai. Casual Dining. **Address:** 51 S Washington St 95370

SOUTH LAKE TAHOE (E-4) pop. 21,403, elev. 6,254'
• Hotels & Restaurants map & index p. 114, 117
• Part of Lake Tahoe Area — see map p. 111

This popular tourist mecca dominates the southern tip of Lake Tahoe. The lake and nearby mountains offer a wealth of recreational activities, making South Lake Tahoe a year-round destination.

BLEU WAVE CRUISES departs from Tahoe Keys Marina and Yacht Club 2435 Venice Dr. Two-hour sightseeing lunch cruises to Emerald Bay on Lake Tahoe's east shore offer stunning views of the lake, 3,000-foot-high mountains and Vikingsholm castle. While aboard the classic 70-foot, 49-passenger yacht you might spot wildlife, including ospreys nesting around Emerald Bay. A sunset cruise also is available.

Time: Allow 2 hours minimum. **Hours:** Lunch cruise departs daily at 11. Sunset cruise departs daily at 6:30. **Cost:** Lunch cruise $90; $45 (ages 4-12). Sunset cruise $90; $45 (ages 4-12). Reservations are recommended. **Phone:** (775) 588-9283 or (866) 413-0985. GT

GONDOLA SIGHTSEEING & ADVENTURE PEAK is at 4080 Lake Tahoe Blvd. Eight-passenger gondola cabins transport riders on a 15-minute ride 2.4 miles up Heavenly Mountain, offering spectacular views of Lake Tahoe and the Sierras. The first stop is the observation deck (the gondola doesn't stop here on the way back down, so be sure to disembark on the way up). Wrapped around a granite outcropping at an elevation of 9,123 feet, the deck has Adirondack chairs for taking in the amazing vistas, and you also can look through binoculars. On the ride down passengers experience a dizzying 3,500-foot vertical drop.

At the top of the gondola is Adventure Peak, with three ropes courses; the 3,300-foot-long Blue Streak Zipline, a 1,000-foot-long, four-line zipline; tubing hill; climbing zones; and a children's play structure. There are hiking trails of varying lengths and difficulty levels as well as Tamarack Lodge, offering a full-service bar as well as cafeteria-style dining and an ice cream sundae bar.

Wear sunscreen; water is provided at gondola stations to aid in acclimating to the high-altitude environment. **Note:** Parking in the lot behind Heavenly Village is $25 per day and there is no validation; those who park in the shopping center lot across the street will be towed. The least expensive option is to walk from your hotel. **Time:** Allow 2 hours minimum. **Hours:** Gondola operates daily starting at 9 with the last ride up at 4:45 and the last ride down at 5:15, mid-June through Labor Day; schedule varies, day

after Labor Day-late Sept.; and mid-Nov. to mid-Apr. Phone ahead to confirm schedule. **Cost:** Gondola ride $48; $39 (ages 13-17 and 65+); $24 (ages 5-12). Prices are subject to change; phone to confirm. **Phone:** (775) 586-7000 or (800) 432-8365. 🍴 🎢

TALLAC HISTORIC SITE is on SR 89 n. of Camp Richardson. These elaborate summer estates were built along the shore of Lake Tahoe by three socially prominent San Francisco families during the late 19th and early 20th centuries.

The 1921 Baldwin Estate serves as both a house museum and as the site's visitor center. The 1894 Pope Estate, one of the most elaborate homes, can be seen on tours led by costumed docents. The 1924 Heller Estate, also known as Valhalla, functions as an events center. Highlights include an art gallery where resident artists work and a schedule of concerts, plays and classic films presented during the summer.

Hours: Grounds daily dawn-dusk. Museum and visitor center open daily 10-4, Memorial Day weekend to mid-Sept. **Cost:** House museum and visitor center free. **Phone:** (530) 541-5227 from 10-4 for historic site information, or (530) 544-7383 year-round to verify schedule. GT 🎢

The Pope Estate is part of Tallac Historic Site, on SR 89 n. of Camp Richardson. Guided 60-minute tours are given of the historic 1894 Pope House, the oldest and largest of the three mansions at Tallac Historic Site. The house also serves as the site's interpretive center. Participants get a chance to see how the Popes and their servants lived as they tour the two-story house and various outbuildings, including the laundry, dairy, barn, gardener's quarters and boat house. An arboretum has a waterfall, a pond and a gazebo.

Tickets can be purchased at the Baldwin Museum. **Time:** Allow 2 hours minimum. **Hours:** Grounds daily dawn-dusk. Pope House guided tours are given daily at 11, 12:30, 1:30 and 2:30, mid-June-late August; at 11 and 2:30, Memorial Day weekend-mid-June and late August to mid-Sept. Phone ahead to confirm schedule. **Cost:** Historic site free. Pope House guided tour $10; $5 (ages 6-12). **Phone:** (530) 541-5227 or (530) 544-7383. GT

TAYLOR CREEK VISITOR CENTER is 3 mi. n. on SR 89. The visitor center, operated by the U.S. Forest Service, offers naturalist-led interpretive programs; the Stream Profile Chamber, a diverted section of Taylor Creek and its stream environment that can be seen through floor-to-ceiling windows; and four short nature trails with educational signs.

Time: Allow 2 hours minimum. **Hours:** Visitor center daily 8-4:30, Memorial Day weekend-Oct. 30. The Stream Profile Chamber is open 9-4. Phone

(See maps & indexes p. 114, 117.)

ahead to confirm schedule. **Cost:** Free. **Phone:** (530) 543-2674. 🎫

ALPENROSE INN   530/544-2985   **4**
◈◈ Motel. **Address:** 4074 Pine Blvd 96150

AMERICANA VILLAGE   530/541-8022   **11**
◈◈ Vacation Rental Condominium. **Address:** 3845 Pioneer Tr 96150

BASECAMP HOTEL   530/208-0180   **2**

Hotel

Address: 4143 Cedar Ave 96150 **Location:** Just s of casino area to Stateline Ave, just w. **Facility:** 73 units. 2 stories (no elevator), interior/exterior corridors. **Terms:** check-in 4 pm. **Featured Amenity: continental breakfast.**

SAVE ▭ 🍴 📶 ✖ 🛗 ▭
/ SOME UNITS 🐾 ✂ ▭

BEACH RETREAT & LODGE AT TAHOE   530/541-6722   **14**
◈◈ Hotel. **Address:** 3411 Lake Tahoe Blvd 96150

STATION HOUSE INN   530/542-1101   **5**
◈◈ Hotel. **Address:** 901 Park Ave 96150

THE COACHMAN HOTEL   530/545-6460   **3**
◈◈ Hotel. **Address:** 4100 Pine Blvd 96150

HEAVENLY VALLEY LODGE   530/564-1500   **15**
◈◈ Motel. **Address:** 1261 Ski Run Blvd 96150

HOLIDAY INN EXPRESS   530/544-5900   **9**

◈◈◈ Motel

Address: 3961 Lake Tahoe Blvd 96150 **Location:** 0.5 mi s of casino area; at US 50 and Pioneer Tr. **Facility:** 89 units. 2-3 stories (no elevator), exterior corridors. **Terms:** check-in 4 pm. **Pool:** heated outdoor. **Activities:** sauna, hot tub. **Guest Services:** valet and coin laundry. **Featured Amenity: full hot breakfast.**

SAVE 🍴 CALL 🚹 ⭑ BIZ 📶
✖ 🛗 ▭ ▭

HOTEL BECKET TRADEMARK COLLECTION BY WYNDHAM
                                       530/544-6000   **8**
◈◈ Motel. **Address:** 4003 Lake Tahoe Blvd 96150

LAKE TAHOE RESORT HOTEL   530/544-5400   **6**

◈◈◈ Hotel

Address: 4130 Lake Tahoe Blvd 96150 **Location:** At casino area. **Facility:** 400 units, some two bedrooms. 9 stories, interior corridors. **Parking:** valet only. **Terms:** check-in 4 pm. **Dining:** Echo Restaurant & Lounge, see separate listing. **Pool:** heated indoor. **Activities:** hot tub, exercise room, massage. **Guest Services:** valet and coin laundry, rental car service. **Featured Amenity: breakfast buffet.**

SAVE ECO 🍴 ⭑ ⛖ CALL 🚹
⭑ ⭑ BIZ 📶 ✖ 🛗 ▭
▭

LAKE TAHOE VACATION RESORT - A DIAMOND RESORT
                                       530/541-6122   **10**
◈◈◈ Vacation Rental Condominium. **Address:** 901 Ski Run Blvd 96150

THE LANDING   530/541-5263   **1**
◈◈◈◈ Boutique Resort Hotel. **Address:** 4104 Lakeshore Blvd 96150

THE LODGE AT LAKE TAHOE   530/541-6226   **13**
◈◈ Condominium. **Address:** 3840 Pioneer Tr 96150

STARDUST LODGE   530/544-5211   **7**
◈◈ Condominium. **Address:** 4061 Lake Tahoe Blvd 96150

TAHOE BEACH & SKI CLUB   530/541-6220   **12**
◈◈ Vacation Rental Condominium. **Address:** 3601 Lake Tahoe Blvd 96150

TAHOE KEYS RESORT   530/544-5397   **16**

◈◈
Vacation Rental Condominium

Address: 599 Tahoe Keys Blvd 96150 **Location:** 0.5 mi e of jct US 50 and SR 89, 1 mi n. **Facility:** This property features some waterfront condos adjacent to shops and vacation homes in surrounding residential neighborhoods. Many units have a private dock and hot tub; some with a fireplace. 129 units, some houses, cabins and condominiums. 1-3 stories (no elevator), exterior corridors. **Pool:** heated outdoor, heated indoor. **Activities:** hot tub, marina, fishing, tennis, bicycles, playground, health club. **Guest Services:** complimentary laundry.

SAVE 🍴 ⭑ ⛖ 📶 ✖ 🛗 ▭ ▭
/ SOME UNITS 🐾 HS ✂

TAHOE SEASONS RESORT   530/541-6700   **17**
◈◈ Vacation Rental Condominium. **Address:** 3901 Saddle Rd 96150

TAHOE VALLEY LODGE   530/541-0353   **18**
◈◈ Motel. **Address:** 2241 Lake Tahoe Blvd 96150

WHERE TO EAT

A CUP OF CHERRIES   530/600-2350   **9**
◈◈ American. Casual Dining. **Address:** 3434 Lake Tahoe Blvd 96150

ARTEMIS MEDITERRANEAN GRILL   530/542-2500   **15**
◈◈ Mediterranean. Casual Dining. **Address:** 2229 Lake Tahoe Blvd, Suite A 96150

BASE CAMP PIZZA CO.   530/544-2273   **3**
◈◈ Pizza. Casual Dining. **Address:** 1001 Heavenly Village Way 96150

THE BREWERY AT LAKE TAHOE   530/544-2739   **7**
◈◈ American. Gastropub. **Address:** 3542 Lake Tahoe Blvd 96150

CAFE FIORE RISTORANTE ITALIANO   530/541-2908   **12**
◈◈◈ Italian. Fine Dining. **Address:** 1169 Ski Run Blvd 96151

ECHO RESTAURANT & LOUNGE   530/543-2140   **2**
◈◈ American. Casual Dining. **Address:** 4130 Lake Tahoe Blvd 96150

EVANS AMERICAN GOURMET CAFE   530/542-1990   **13**
◈◈◈ American. Fine Dining. **Address:** 536 Emerald Bay Rd 96150

FRESHIES RESTAURANT & BAR   530/542-3630   **5**
◈◈ Hawaiian. Casual Dining. **Address:** 3330 Lake Tahoe Blvd, Suite 3 96150

HEIDI'S PANCAKE HOUSE   530/544-8113   **6**
◈◈ American. Casual Dining. **Address:** 3485 Lake Tahoe Blvd 96150

(See maps & indexes p. 114, 117.)

KALANI'S   530/544-6100   (4)

♥♥♥ Hawaiian. Fine Dining. **Address:** 1001 Heavenly Village Way, Suite 26 96150

LAKE TAHOE PIZZA COMPANY   530/544-1919   (16)

♥♥ Pizza. Casual Dining. **Address:** 1168 Emerald Bay Rd 96150

MCP'S TAPHOUSE GRILL   530/542-4435   (1)

♥♥ Irish. Casual Dining. **Address:** 4125 Lake Tahoe Blvd, Suite A 96150

NEPHELES   530/544-8130   (11)

♥♥♥ California. Fine Dining. **Address:** 1169 Ski Run Blvd 96150

OFF THE HOOK SUSHI   530/544-5599   (14)

♥♥ Sushi. Casual Dining. **Address:** 2660 Lake Tahoe Blvd 96150

SPROUTS NATURAL FOODS CAFE   530/541-6969   (10)

♥ Natural/Organic. Quick Serve. **Address:** 3123 Harrison Ave 96150

TEP'S VILLA ROMA   530/541-8227   (8)

♥♥♥
**Italian
Casual Dining
$13-$22**

AAA Inspector Notes: *Classic.* Serving the area since 1975, patrons of this relaxing restaurant can order from an array of fresh seafood specialties as well as pizza, pasta, chicken and veal dishes. The antipasto salad bar lines up a nice variety of choices and is included with each entrée. **Features:** full bar. **Address:** 3450 Lake Tahoe Blvd 96150 **Location:** 1.5 mi w of casino area. (D)

SOUTH SAN FRANCISCO (D-8)

pop. 63,632, elev. 16'
• Hotels & Restaurants map & index p. 316
• Part of San Francisco area — see map p. 243

If you're a visitor, you might not even realize you're in South San Francisco; this bedroom community spreads out just south of the San Francisco city limits. It's also the location of busy San Francisco International Airport. Whether you're arriving or departing, arrange your schedule so you have a little extra time to peruse the exhibits at the SFO Museum (SFOM), in the International Terminal's Main Hall (pre-security) and designed to resemble SFO's 1930s-era passenger lobby. Permanent and rotating exhibits focus on commercial aviation history. Most gallery sites are located before security checkpoints, so you can visit them without a boarding pass. The airport also has a very cool collection of public art; most pieces are in Terminal 2 and the International Terminal.

The Bay Area abounds in outdoor recreational opportunities, and one of them is San Bruno Mountain State Park. Within the park is the northernmost reach of the Santa Cruz range. Hiking trails traverse hilly slopes, offering outstanding views of San Francisco and San Francisco Bay. From US 101, take the Bayshore Boulevard/Brisbane exit to Guadalupe Canyon Parkway, then continue west on the parkway to the park entrance.

AC HOTEL BY MARRIOTT SAN FRANCISCO AIRPORT/
OYSTER POINT WATERFRONT   650/742-9211   (3)

♥♥♥ SAVE Contemporary Hotel. **AAA Benefit:**
Address: 1333 Veterans Blvd 94080   Members save 5% or more!

BEST WESTERN PLUS GROSVENOR AIRPORT HOTEL
    650/873-3200   (12)

♥♥♥
Hotel

 Best Western PLUS   **AAA Benefit:** Members save up to 15% and earn bonus points!

Address: 380 S Airport Blvd 94080 **Location:** US 101 exit S Airport Blvd, 0.5 mi s. San Bruno, 52. **Facility:** 206 units. 8 stories, interior corridors. **Parking:** on-site (fee). **Pool:** heated outdoor. **Activities:** exercise room. **Guest Services:** valet and coin laundry, boarding pass kiosk. **Featured Amenity: breakfast buffet.**

SAVE ✈ 🍴 🍽 CALL ♿ ➔
/SOME UNITS (HS) 📷 🎦

COMFORT INN & SUITES SFO AIRPORT NORTH
    650/589-7100   (8)

♥♥ Hotel. **Address:** 121 E Grand Ave 94080

COURTYARD BY MARRIOTT SAN FRANCISCO AIRPORT/OYSTER POINT WATERFRONT
    650/871-4100   (2)

♥♥♥
Hotel

COURTYARD®   **AAA Benefit:** Members save 5% or more!

Address: 1300 Veterans Blvd 94080 **Location:** Waterfront. US 101 exit 425B (Oyster Point Blvd E), 0.3 mi n. **Facility:** 198 units. 4 stories, interior corridors. **Pool:** heated indoor. **Activities:** hot tub, trails, exercise room. **Guest Services:** valet and coin laundry, area transportation.

SAVE ECO ✈ 🍴 🍽 CALL ♿
➔ 🛄 BIZ 📶 ✕ 🛎 🖨
/SOME UNITS 📷

EMBASSY SUITES BY HILTON SAN FRANCISCO AIRPORT-SOUTH SAN FRANCISCO   650/589-3400   (7)

♥♥♥
Hotel

EMBASSY SUITES by HILTON   **AAA Benefit:** Members save up to 15%!

Address: 250 Gateway Blvd 94080 **Location:** US 101 exit 425A (Grand Ave), just e. **Facility:** 312 units. 10 stories, interior corridors. **Parking:** on-site (fee). **Pool:** heated indoor. **Activities:** hot tub, exercise room. **Guest Services:** valet and coin laundry, area transportation. **Featured Amenity: full hot breakfast.**

SAVE ECO ✈ 🍴 🍽
CALL ♿ ➔ 🛄 BIZ 📶 ✕

🎦 🛎 📷 🖨

(See map & index p. 316.)

HAMPTON INN SAN FRANCISCO-AIRPORT
650/876-0200

▽▽▽ [SAVE] Hotel. **Address:** 300 **AAA Benefit:**
Gateway Blvd 94080 Members save up to 15%!

HILTON GARDEN INN SAN FRANCISCO AIRPORT
NORTH 650/872-1515

▽▽▽▽ **Hilton Garden Inn** **AAA Benefit:** Members save up to 15%!
Hotel

Address: 670 Gateway Blvd 94080 **Location:** US 101 exit 425A (Grand Ave), 0.4 mi e, then 0.4 mi n. **Facility:** 169 units. 7 stories, interior corridors. **Parking:** on-site (fee). **Activities:** exercise room. **Guest Services:** valet and coin laundry.

[SAVE] [icons] CALL [icons]
[BIZ] [HS] [icons]

HOLIDAY INN EXPRESS SAN FRANCISCO AIRPORT NORTH
650/589-0600

▽▽▽ Contemporary Hotel. **Address:** 373 S Airport Blvd 94080

HOLIDAY INN SAN FRANCISCO INTERNATIONAL AIRPORT
NORTH 650/873-3550

▽▽▽ Hotel. **Address:** 275 S Airport Blvd 94080

HOTEL NOVA SFO 650/875-7878 [13]

▽▽ Hotel. **Address:** 410 S Airport Blvd 94080

LA QUINTA INN & SUITES BY WYNDHAM SAN FRANCISCO
AIRPORT NORTH 650/583-2223

▽▽▽ Hotel. **Address:** 20 Airport Blvd 94080

LARKSPUR LANDING SOUTH SAN FRANCISCO
650/827-1515

▽▽▽ **Address:** 690 Gateway Blvd 94080 **Location:** US 101 exit 425A (Grand Ave), 0.4 mi e, then 0.4 mi n. **Facility:** 111 efficiencies. 4 stories, interior corridors. **Activities:** hot tub, exercise room. **Guest Services:** complimentary and valet laundry. **Featured Amenity:** continental breakfast.
Hotel

[SAVE] [ECO] [icons] CALL [icons]
[BIZ] [HS] [icons]
/SOME UNITS [icon]

RESIDENCE INN BY MARRIOTT AT OYSTER POINT
650/837-9000 [1]

▽▽▽ **Residence INN.** **AAA Benefit:** Members save 5% or more!
Extended Stay Hotel

Address: 1350 Veterans Blvd 94080 **Location:** Waterfront. US 101 exit 425B (Oyster Point Blvd), just ne. **Facility:** 152 units, some two bedrooms, efficiencies and kitchens. 4 stories, interior corridors. **Pool:** heated outdoor. **Activities:** hot tub, trails, exercise room. **Guest Services:** valet and coin laundry, area transportation.

[SAVE] [ECO] [icons] CALL [icons]
[icons] [BIZ] [icons] /SOME UNITS [icon]

WHERE TO EAT

BEN TRE RESTAURANT 650/952-2243
▽▽ Vietnamese. Casual Dining. **Address:** 398 Grand Ave 94080

BUON GUSTO RISTORANTE 650/742-9776 [7]
▽▽ Italian. Casual Dining. **Address:** 224 Grand Ave 94080

DARBY DAN'S SANDWICH COMPANY 650/876-0122 [1]
▽ Sandwiches. Quick Serve. **Address:** 733 Airport Blvd 94080

FLAVAS JAMAICAN GRILL 650/244-9785 [4]
▽▽ Jamaican. Casual Dining. **Address:** 314 Linden Ave 94080

GRAND PALACE SEAFOOD RESTAURANT
650/872-1000 [3]
▽▽ Cantonese Dim Sum. Casual Dining. **Address:** 359 Grand Ave 94080

IZANAMI 650/636-2267 [6]
▽▽ Japanese Sushi. Casual Dining. **Address:** 257 Grand Ave 94080

THAI SATAY RESTAURANT & BAR 650/952-3439 [5]
▽▽ Thai. Casual Dining. **Address:** 265 Grand Ave 94080

STANISLAUS NATIONAL FOREST (E-4)

Elevations in the forest range from 1,200 ft. in the Lumsden area to 11,462 ft. at Sonora Peak. Refer to AAA maps for additional elevation information.

On the western slope of the Sierra Nevada Range, Stanislaus National Forest covers nearly 900,000 acres, forming the northwestern boundary of Yosemite National Park *(see place listing p. 420)*. The Merced, Mokelumne, Clavey, Stanislaus and Tuolumne rivers cut deep canyons through this wilderness region.

Popular summer activities include swimming, camping, picnicking, boating, rafting, canoeing and hunting. More than 800 miles of rivers and streams offer myriad opportunities for fishing. Numerous trails are suitable for hiking, horseback riding, backpacking, off-roading and mountain biking. There are skiing facilities at Dodge Ridge off SR 108 and at Mount Reba off SR 4. Snowmobiling and cross-country skiing also are popular during the winter.

Reservations for Pinecrest campground can be made through the National Recreation Reservation System; phone (877) 444-6777 or TTY (877) 833-6777.

Visitor tours and programs are offered June through August at Pinecrest. The Emigrant and Carson-Iceberg wildernesses are at the eastern end of the forest. Permits can be obtained at any Stanislaus National Forest office. For general forest information contact the Supervisor's Office, Stanislaus National Forest, 19777 Greenley Rd., Sonora, CA 95370; phone (209) 532-3671. *See Recreation Areas Chart.*

STOCKTON (F-3) pop. 291,707, elev. 14'
• Hotels p. 388 • Restaurants p. 388

Like other northern California cities, Stockton—named after a distinguished naval officer in the Mexican War—experienced a population boom during the gold rush. The city later became an agricultural center, and this heritage is celebrated in April during the 3-day ▽ San Joaquin Asparagus

Festival, held at the San Joaquin County Fairgrounds. The county's main crop is featured in cooking demonstrations, exhibits, food tastings in Asparagus Alley and the Deep-Fried Asparagus-Eating Championship.

The first of California's two inland seaports, Stockton is connected with San Francisco Bay by a channel 60 miles long and 37 feet deep. The San Joaquin waterways, 1,000 miles of navigable inland waters, offer plenty of boating and fishing opportunities. The city also is the home of the University of the Pacific, which in 1852 became the first chartered university in California.

Visit Stockton: 125 Bridge Pl., Stockton, CA 95202.
Phone: (209) 938-1555 or (877) 778-6258.

THE HAGGIN MUSEUM is .3 mi. n. of I-5 exit 473 (Pershing Ave.) to 1201 N. Pershing Ave. at Rose St., following signs. It contains 19th-century American and European paintings as well as local historical artifacts. Works by Albert Bierstadt, George Inness, "Golden Age" illustrator J.C. Leyendecker and Pierre Auguste Renoir are exhibited. Native American baskets; a Holt tractor and combine harvester, both developed locally; and reconstructed interiors of several turn-of-the-20th-century businesses are highlights. Touring exhibitions also are presented.

Tours are available by appointment. **Time:** Allow 1 hour, 30 minutes minimum. **Hours:** Wed.-Fri. 1:30-5, Sat.-Sun noon-5 (also first and third Thurs. of the month 5-9). Closed major holidays. **Cost:** $8; $7 (ages 65+); $5 (ages 10-17 and students with ID); free (ages 0-9 and to all on the first Sat. of the month). **Phone:** (209) 940-6300.

BEST WESTERN PLUS HERITAGE INN   209/474-3301

Hotel

AAA Benefit:
Best Western PLUS. Members save up to 15% and earn bonus points!

Address: 111 E March Ln 95207 **Location:** I-5 exit 476 (March Ln), 2.5 mi e; corner of El Dorado St. **Facility:** 203 units. 3 stories, interior corridors. **Pool:** outdoor. **Activities:** hot tub, exercise room. **Guest Services:** valet and coin laundry. **Featured Amenity: breakfast buffet.**

/SOME UNITS

COURTYARD BY MARRIOTT   209/472-9700
Hotel. **Address:** 3252 W March Ln 95219
AAA Benefit:
Members save 5% or more!

HILTON STOCKTON   209/957-9090
Hotel. **Address:** 2323 Grand Canal Blvd 95207
AAA Benefit:
Members save up to 15%!

HOLIDAY INN EXPRESS HOTEL STOCKTON SOUTHEAST
209/946-1234
Hotel. **Address:** 5045 S Kingsley Rd 95215

RESIDENCE INN BY MARRIOTT   209/472-9800
Extended Stay Hotel.
Address: 3240 W March Ln 95219
AAA Benefit:
Members save 5% or more!

WHERE TO EAT

BOUDIN SF   209/952-2000
Breads/Pastries Sandwiches. Quick Serve. **Address:** 5615 Pacific Ave 95207

BUD'S SEAFOOD GRILLE   209/956-0270
Seafood. Casual Dining. **Address:** 314 Lincoln Center 95207

DAVE WONG'S CHINESE CUISINE   209/951-4152
Chinese. Casual Dining. **Address:** 2828 W March Ln 95219

DE VEGA BROTHERS ITALIAN CUISINE   209/957-3839
Italian. Casual Dining. **Address:** 5757 Pacific Ave, Suite A140 95207

EL TORITO   209/957-6891
Mexican. Casual Dining. **Address:** 2593 W March Ln 95207

MARKET TAVERN   209/932-8001
New American. Casual Dining. **Address:** 236 Lincoln Center 95207

SUISUN CITY (B-8) pop. 28,111, elev. 7'

WESTERN RAILWAY MUSEUM is e. on SR 12 to 5848 SR 12. The museum, which is on the National Register of Historic Places, preserves the region's electric railway heritage. Vintage streetcars, including Key System trains and California's last 5-cent streetcar, are operated. In addition to railway exhibits, visitors can see more than 50 historic rail cars and take a 15-minute streetcar ride around the grounds. Fifty-minute interurban car rides also are offered.

Hours: Wed.-Sun. 10:30-5, mid-June to mid-Aug.; Sat.-Sun. 10:30-5, rest of year. Streetcar rides operate Sat.-Sun.; interurban cars operate daily. Last train departs at 3:30. Closed Jan. 1, Thanksgiving, Christmas Eve, Christmas and Dec. 31. Closed major holidays. **Cost:** $10 (includes rides on streetcars and interurban cars); $9 (ages 65+); $7 (ages 2-14). **Phone:** (707) 374-2978.

HAMPTON INN & SUITES SUISUN CITY WATERFRONT
707/429-0900
Hotel. **Address:** 2 Harbor Center Dr 94585
AAA Benefit:
Members save up to 15%!

WHERE TO EAT

ATHENIAN GRILL   707/425-0500
Greek. Casual Dining. **Address:** 750 Kellogg St 94585

CHIANTI OSTERIA   707/426-4887
Italian. Fine Dining. **Address:** 314 Spring St 94585

SUNNYVALE (E-8) pop. 140,081, elev. 105'
- Restaurants p. 390
- Hotels & Restaurants map & index p. 348

Although Silicon Valley doesn't appear on maps, it's a name known the world over. Sunnyvale is headquarters for hundreds of computer-related manufacturers turning out software and hardware products based on silicon chip technology.

Local inventors and entrepreneurs make good use of the Sunnyvale Public Library at 665 W. Olive Ave. The library, designated as a U.S. Patent and Trademark Depository Library (PTDL), has facilities for patent and trademark research as well as online access to the full patent database used by the Patent and Trademark Office in Washington, D.C. A research library features patents from 1790 to the present as well as trademark/logo information. Phone (408) 730-7300.

Sunnyvale Chamber of Commerce: 260 S. Sunnyvale Ave., Suite 4, Sunnyvale, CA 94086. **Phone:** (408) 736-4971.

THE LACE MUSEUM is at 552 S. Murphy Ave. It displays a comprehensive collection of lace, lace tools, books and other lace-related items. Changing exhibits feature many fine, detailed handmade lace pieces. **Hours:** Tues.-Sat. 11-4 (also third Fri. of the month 7-9) and by appointment. Phone for holiday season schedule. Closed Thanksgiving and Christmas. **Cost:** Free. **Phone:** (408) 730-4695.

AC HOTEL SUNNYVALE CUPERTINO   408/733-7950   **53**
  Hotel. **Address:** 597 E El Camino Real 94087

| | **AAA Benefit:** Members save 5% or more! |

ALOFT SUNNYVALE   408/736-0300   **49**

Contemporary Hotel. **Address:** 170 S Sunnyvale Ave 94086

| | **AAA Benefit:** Members save 5% or more! |

AMERICAS BEST VALUE INN   408/734-0555   **43**
Hotel. **Address:** 331 E Weddell Dr 94089

BEST WESTERN SILICON VALLEY INN
408/735-7800   **45**

Hotel

| Best Western. | **AAA Benefit:** Members save up to 15% and earn bonus points! |

Address: 600 N Mathilda Ave 94085 **Location:** US 101 exit Mathilda Ave, just s. **Facility:** 100 units. 2 stories (no elevator), interior corridors. **Activities:** exercise room. **Guest Services:** valet and coin laundry. **Featured Amenity:** breakfast buffet.

COMFORT INN SUNNYVALE - SILICON VALLEY
408/734-3742   **42**

Hotel

Address: 940 W Weddell Dr 94089 **Location:** N of and adjacent to US 101 exit Mathilda Ave, just e on Ross Dr, then just s. **Facility:** 92 units, some efficiencies. 3 stories, interior corridors. **Pool:** heated outdoor. **Activities:** exercise room. **Guest Services:** complimentary and valet laundry. **Featured Amenity:** breakfast buffet.

CORPORATE INN SUNNYVALE   408/220-1000   **55**
Extended Stay Hotel. **Address:** 805 E El Camino Real 94087

COURTYARD BY MARRIOTT SUNNYVALE MOUNTAIN VIEW
408/737-7377   **52**

Hotel

| COURTYARD | **AAA Benefit:** Members save 5% or more! |

Address: 660 W El Camino Real 94087 **Location:** SR 82 (El Camino Real); between Hollenbeck Ave/S Pastoria Ave and S Matilda Ave. **Facility:** 145 units. 4 stories, interior corridors. *Bath:* shower only. **Parking:** on-site (fee). **Pool:** heated outdoor. **Activities:** hot tub, exercise room. **Guest Services:** valet and coin laundry, boarding pass kiosk.

THE DOMAIN HOTEL
408/247-0800   **57**

Hotel

Address: 1085 E El Camino Real 94087 **Location:** On SR 82, 0.3 mi w of Lawrence Expwy. **Facility:** 136 units. 3 stories, interior corridors. **Amenities:** safes. **Pool:** heated outdoor. **Activities:** hot tub, recreation programs, exercise room. **Guest Services:** valet laundry, area transportation.

GRAND HOTEL
408/720-8500   **50**

Hotel

Address: 865 W El Camino Real 94087 **Location:** SR 82 (El Camino Real); between S Mary and S Pastoria aves. **Facility:** 104 units, some two bedrooms, efficiencies and condominiums. 2-3 stories, interior/exterior corridors. **Terms:** check-in 4 pm. **Pool:** heated outdoor. **Activities:** hot tub. **Guest Services:** valet laundry, area transportation. **Featured Amenity:** breakfast buffet.

HOLIDAY INN EXPRESS SUNNYVALE-SILICON VALLEY
408/773-1234   **51**
Hotel. **Address:** 852 W El Camino Real 94087

(See map & index p. 348.)

LARKSPUR LANDING SUNNYVALE 408/733-1212 44

Extended Stay Contemporary Hotel

Address: 748 N Mathilda Ave 94085 **Location:** US 101 exit Mathilda Ave, just s. **Facility:** 126 efficiencies. 4 stories, interior corridors. **Activities:** exercise room. **Guest Services:** valet and coin laundry, area transportation. **Featured Amenity: continental breakfast.**

MAPLE TREE INN 408/720-9700 54

Hotel

Address: 711 E El Camino Real 94087 **Location:** US 101 exit 394 (Lawrence Expwy), 2.9 mi w to El Camino Real exit, then 1.8 mi n. **Facility:** 178 units. 3 stories, interior corridors. **Amenities:** safes. **Pool:** heated outdoor. **Activities:** hot tub, picnic facilities, exercise room. **Guest Services:** valet and coin laundry.

QUALITY INN SANTA CLARA CONVENTION CENTER
408/744-1100 41
Hotel. **Address:** 1280 Persian Dr 94089

RADISSON HOTEL SUNNYVALE 408/747-0999 39

Hotel

Address: 1300 Chesapeake Terrace 94089 **Location:** SR 237 exit Lawrence Expwy N, just w. **Facility:** 180 units. 5 stories, interior corridors. **Pool:** heated outdoor. **Activities:** exercise room. **Guest Services:** valet and coin laundry, area transportation. **Featured Amenity: breakfast buffet.**

RESIDENCE INN BY MARRIOTT SILICON VALLEY I
408/720-1000 47
Extended Stay Hotel. **Address:** 750 Lakeway Dr 94085

AAA Benefit: Members save 5% or more!

RESIDENCE INN BY MARRIOTT SUNNYVALE SILICON VALLEY II
408/720-8893 48
Extended Stay Hotel. **Address:** 1080 Stewart Dr 94086

AAA Benefit: Members save 5% or more!

SHERATON SUNNYVALE 408/745-6000 38

Hotel

SHERATON

AAA Benefit: Members save 5% or more!

Address: 1100 N Mathilda Ave 94089 **Location:** SR 237 exit Mathilda Ave, just n. **Facility:** 173 units. 2 stories (no elevator), interior corridors. **Pool:** heated outdoor. **Activities:** hot tub, trails, exercise room. **Guest Services:** valet laundry, area transportation.

STAYBRIDGE SUITES SUNNYVALE 408/745-1515 40
Extended Stay Hotel. **Address:** 900 Hamlin Ct 94089

TOWNEPLACE SUITES BY MARRIOTT SUNNYVALE/MOUNTAIN VIEW 408/733-4200 46

Extended Stay Hotel

TOWNEPLACE SUITES MARRIOTT

AAA Benefit: Members save 5% or more!

Address: 606 S Bernardo Ave 94087 **Location:** SR 85 exit SR 82, 0.5 mi s. **Facility:** 94 units, some two bedrooms, efficiencies and kitchens. 4 stories, interior corridors. **Activities:** picnic facilities, limited exercise equipment. **Guest Services:** valet and coin laundry. **Featured Amenity: continental breakfast.**

WILD PALMS HOTEL 408/738-0500 56

Boutique Hotel

Address: 910 E Fremont Ave 94087 **Location:** US 101 exit Lawrence Expwy S, 1.5 mi s, 0.9 mi n on E El Camino Real, just w on S Wolfe Rd, then just s. **Facility:** Bright, bold colors, palm trees and assorted tropical plants transport you to the tropics. Guest rooms have comfortable rattan chairs and contemporary furniture, along with some 1950's accents. 205 units. 2 stories (no elevator), interior/exterior corridors. **Amenities:** safes. **Pool:** heated outdoor. **Activities:** hot tub, exercise room. **Guest Services:** valet laundry. Affiliated with Joie de Vivre Hotels & Resorts.

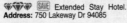

WHERE TO EAT

DISH N DASH 408/530-9200 14
Middle Eastern. Quick Serve. **Address:** 736 N Matilda Ave 94085

FAULTLINE BREWING COMPANY 408/736-2739 15
American. Casual Dining. **Address:** 1235 Oakmead Pkwy 94085

PEZZELLA'S VILLA NAPOLI 408/738-2400 16
Italian. Casual Dining. **Address:** 1025 W El Camino Real 94087

P.F. CHANG'S CHINA BISTRO 408/991-9078 17
Chinese. Fine Dining. **Address:** 390 W El Camino Real 94087

(See map & index p. 348.)

VONS CHICKEN   408/677-2111 (18)
🍷🍷 Korean Chicken. Casual Dining. **Address:** 1082 E El Camino Real, Suite 2 94087

SUSANVILLE (C-4) pop. 17,947, elev. 4,258'

Founded by pioneer Isaac Roop in 1854 and named for his daughter, the town of Susanville lies at the head of the Honey Lake Valley and is flanked by the cliffs of the Susan River Canyon. In the 19th century Susanville served as a stopping point on the Nobles Emigrant Trail, a popular alternate route to the Donner Pass Overland Trail.

The Bizz Johnson Trail follows an old branch line of the Southern Pacific Railroad for approximately 26 miles between Susanville and Westwood. Administered by the Bureau of Land Management and Lassen National Forest, the trail is popular with hikers, railroad history buffs and cross-country skiers. The Susanville Depot & Museum, 601 Richmond Rd. at the beginning of the trail, houses historic photographs and railroad memorabilia in a restored 1920s train station.

The Susanville murals, eight on outdoor walls and one indoors, are within a five-block area downtown. Begin a mural tour at the corner of Main and Union streets. Continue west on Main to Roop Street and then turn south; when you reach Cottage Street turn east. The last mural is at the corner of Cottage and Gay streets. The indoor mural is at the corner of Main and S. Lassen streets.

Lassen County Chamber of Commerce: 75 N. Weatherlow St., P.O. Box 338, Susanville, CA 96130. **Phone:** (530) 257-4323.

EAGLE LAKE, 16 mi. n.w. on Eagle Lake Rd., is the second largest natural lake in California. In summer campfire programs and slide presentations are held; phone ahead for schedule. *See Recreation Areas Chart.* **Hours:** Ranger office open Mon.-Fri. 8-4:30. **Cost:** Free. **Phone:** (530) 257-4188 or (530) 825-3454.

APPLE INN MOTEL   530/257-4726
🍷 Motel. **Address:** 2720 Main St 96130

DIAMOND MOUNTAIN CASINO & HOTEL   530/252-1100

Hotel

Address: 900 Skyline Dr 96130 **Location:** 1 mi ne on SR 139 from jct SR 36, then 1 mi w, follow signs to rancheria. **Facility:** In a mountain setting, this property offers attractive and spacious guest rooms with contemporary furniture. There is also a 24-hour casino attached. 70 units. 4 stories, interior corridors. **Amenities:** safes. **Pool:** heated indoor. **Activities:** hot tub, game room, exercise room. **Guest Services:** coin laundry. **Featured Amenity:** full hot breakfast.

SAVE ECO 🐾 🍴 📶 CALL &
🏊 🚡 BIZ HS 📶 ✕ 🖥
/SOME UNITS 🐕 🛗 🖨

RED LION INN & SUITES SUSANVILLE   530/257-3450

Hotel

Address: 3015 E Riverside Dr 96130 **Location:** 1.3 mi e on SR 36 from jct SR 139, then just ne. **Facility:** 66 units, some two bedrooms. 2 stories (no elevator), interior corridors. **Pool:** heated outdoor. **Activities:** hot tub, exercise room. **Guest Services:** coin laundry. **Featured Amenity:** breakfast buffet.

SAVE 🍴 CALL & 🚡 🛗 BIZ
📶 ✕ 🛗 🖨 /SOME UNITS 🐕

THE ROSEBERRY HOUSE BED & BREAKFAST 530/257-5675
🍷🍷🍷 Bed & Breakfast. **Address:** 609 North St 96130

SUPER 8   530/257-2782
🍷🍷 Motel. **Address:** 2975 Johnstonville Rd 96130

SURESTAY PLUS HOTEL BY BEST WESTERN SUSANVILLE
                                      530/257-4123
🍷🍷 Motel. **Address:** 2785 Main St 96130

WHERE TO EAT

HAPPY GARDEN CHINESE RESTAURANT   530/257-5553
🍷🍷 Chinese. Casual Dining. **Address:** 1960 Main St 96130

LASSEN ALE WORKS AT THE PIONEER SALOON
                                      530/257-7666
🍷🍷 American. Brewpub. **Address:** 724 Main St 96130

MAZATLAN GRILL   530/257-1800
🍷🍷 Mexican. Casual Dining. **Address:** 1535 Main St 96130

WHITE HOUSE RESTAURANT   530/257-6666
🍷🍷 Thai. Casual Dining. **Address:** 3085 Johnstonville Rd 96130

SUTTER CREEK (E-4) pop. 2,501, elev. 1,198'
• Restaurants p. 392

Sutter Creek, in the Sierra foothills, has a restored Main Street with stone, brick and weathered wood-frame buildings serving as reminders of the town's 19th-century gold rush heritage. The antique shops and B&Bs that line SR 49 attract lots of weekend visitors.

The Monteverde Store Museum at 11 Randolph St., at one time an old-fashioned country store, was owned and operated by the same family for more than 70 years. It was closed for more than 20 years before reopening as a museum. Such items as miner's supplies, dry goods, groceries, hardware, long underwear, penny candy and the store's original ledgers all recall its turn-of-the-20th-century heyday. Guided tours can be arranged with advance notice; phone the visitor center for information.

Sutter Creek Visitor Center: 71A Main St., Sutter Creek, CA 95685. **Phone:** (209) 267-1344.

Self-guiding tours: A brochure describing a walking tour past Sutter Creek's historic buildings is available from the visitor center.

THE FOXES INN OF SUTTER CREEK BED & BREAKFAST
                                      209/267-5882
🍷🍷🍷 Bed & Breakfast. **Address:** 77 Main St 95685

GREY GABLES BED & BREAKFAST INN   209/267-1039
◈◈◈ Bed & Breakfast. **Address:** 161 Hanford (Old SR 49) St 95685

SUTTER CREEK INN   209/267-5606
◈◈ Historic Bed & Breakfast. **Address:** 75 Main St 95685

WHERE TO EAT

GOLD DUST PIZZA SUTTER CREEK   209/267-1900
◈ Pizza. Casual Dining. **Address:** 20 Eureka St 95685

THE SUTTER   209/267-5211
◈◈ Regional American. Casual Dining. **Address:** 53 Main St 95685

TAHOE CITY (D-4) elev. 6,302'

• Hotels & Restaurants map & index p. 114
• Part of Lake Tahoe Area — see map p. 111

All the glory of winter at Lake Tahoe is celebrated in early March during ❄ North Lake Tahoe Snow-Fest! Events take place both on and off the mountain during the 10 days of festivities held each year at nearby resorts and towns throughout the North Lake Tahoe area. The cold-weather season is celebrated with parades, fireworks, concerts, ski races, ice-carving demonstrations and a polar bear swim.

TAHOE MARITIME MUSEUM is at 401 W. Lake Blvd. at jct. Granlibakken Rd. The boating history of Lake Tahoe is presented at this museum, which showcases watercraft and maritime artifacts from the lake's past. The museum features several vessels in its featured exhibit and many more in a museum annex that can be viewed once a month during summer open houses; some vessels and motors date to the late 19th century. The museum also has a children's area and an art exhibit. Boat rides aboard a 22-foot wooden runabout are available in summer months.

Time: Allow 30 minutes minimum. **Hours:** Thurs.-Tues. 10-4:30, Memorial Day weekend-Sept. 30; Fri.-Sun. 10-4:30, Oct. 1-day before Memorial Day weekend. Closes early on July 4. Phone ahead to confirm schedule for other holidays. **Cost:** $5; free (ages 0-12 and active-duty military and their families). Summer boat rides $25; $15 (ages 0-12). **Phone:** (530) 583-9283.

AMERICAS BEST VALUE INN LAKE TAHOE/TAHOE CITY   530/583-3766   **4**

◈ Motel

Address: 455 N Lake Blvd 96145 **Location:** SR 28 (N Lake Blvd), 0.3 mi e of jct SR 89. **Facility:** 46 units. 2 stories (no elevator), interior/exterior corridors. **Pool:** heated outdoor. **Activities:** hot tub. **Featured Amenity:** continental breakfast.

BASECAMP TAHOE CITY   530/580-8430   **7**
◈◈ Motel. **Address:** 955 N Lake Boulevard 96145

COTTAGE INN AT LAKE TAHOE   530/581-4073   **5**
◈◈◈ Cottage. **Address:** 1690 W Lake Blvd 96145

MOTHER NATURE'S INN   530/581-4278   **3**
◈◈ Motel. **Address:** 551 N Lake Blvd 96145

PEPPER TREE INN   530/583-3711   **2**

◈◈◈ Motel

Address: 645 N Lake Blvd 96145 **Location:** SR 28 (N Lake Blvd), 0.5 mi e of jct SR 89. **Facility:** 44 units. 2-7 stories, exterior corridors. **Pool:** heated outdoor. **Activities:** beach access. **Guest Services:** coin laundry. **Featured Amenity:** continental breakfast.

RIVER RANCH LODGE   530/583-4264   **1**
◈◈ Motel. **Address:** 2285 River Rd 96145

SUNNYSIDE RESTAURANT & LODGE   530/583-7200   **6**
◈◈◈ Hotel. **Address:** 1850 W Lake Blvd 96145

(See map & index p. 114.)

WHERE TO EAT

THE BLUE AGAVE MEXICAN RESTAURANT & CANTINA
530/583-8113 6
♥♥ Mexican. Casual Dining. **Address:** 425 N Lake Blvd 96145

BRIDGETENDER TAVERN & GRILL   530/583-3342 7
♥♥ American. Casual Dining. **Address:** 65 W Lake Blvd 96145

CHRISTY HILL RESTAURANT   530/583-8551 5
♥♥♥ American. Fine Dining. **Address:** 115 Grove St 96145

JAKE'S ON THE LAKE   530/583-0188 4
♥♥ Seafood. Casual Dining. **Address:** 780 N Lake Blvd 96145

RIVER RANCH LODGE RESTAURANT   530/583-4264 1
♥♥ American. Casual Dining. **Address:** 2286 River Rd 96145

ROSIE'S CAFE   530/583-8504 3
♥♥ American. Casual Dining. **Address:** 571 N Lake Blvd 96145

WOLFDALE'S   530/583-5700 2
♥♥♥ Fusion. Fine Dining. **Address:** 640 N Lake Blvd 96145

TAHOE NATIONAL FOREST (D-4)

Elevations in the forest range from 1,300 ft. on the Middle Fork of the American River to 9,143 ft. at the summit of Mount Lola. Refer to AAA maps for additional elevation information.

Covering land north and west of Lake Tahoe, Tahoe National Forest—despite its name—has little to do with the lake. Much of this 797,205-acre national forest lies in the Yuba River drainage. Here miners employed the placer pan, pick and hydraulic cannon, which utilized tons of pressurized water to blast away the hillsides, in their frantic pursuit of gold. The lake and its immediate environs are part of the Lake Tahoe Basin Management Unit.

Where pack trains and stagecoaches once traveled, SR 49 winds past remnants of former mining camps reclaimed by forest. Steep-walled canyons line the twisting course of the North Yuba River. The dramatic Sierra Buttes are riddled with old quartz mines.

The 170-mile-long Yuba Donner Scenic Byway, named for the unlucky 19th-century exploration party, is a loop route through alternating mountain and valley terrain. It incorporates portions of I-80 and SRs 20, 49 and 89 as it winds through the national forest and the Sierra Nevada mountains.

Miners weren't the only ones to leave their mark on the landscape. Touring the region as an entertainer in 1853, famed *femme fatale* Lola Montez christened Independence Lake during a Fourth of July picnic. Just north of the site is Mount Lola, named for the adventuress.

Independence Lake is but one of many lakes within the forest boundaries. Popular recreational areas include French Meadows Reservoir, in the upper reaches of the American River watershed; a cluster of glacial lakes north of Sierra City; and Bullards Bar Reservoir, on the edge of the Sacramento Valley.

Alpine and Nordic skiing and snowmobiling are popular winter diversions, while hiking, camping, boating, horseback riding and fishing take over the rest of the year. Hikers can explore 400 miles of trails. Water recreation includes sailing, water skiing, swimming, rafting, kayaking and canoeing. Reservations for Logger Campground can be made through the National Recreation Reservation System; phone (877) 444-6777 or TTY (877) 833-6777.

Publications about recreational opportunities and maps are available at most forest service stations and the forest headquarters in Nevada City. For more information contact the Forest Supervisor, Tahoe National Forest, 631 Coyote St., Nevada City, CA 95959; phone (530) 265-4531. *See Recreation Areas Chart.*

TAHOE VISTA pop. 1,433
• **Hotels & Restaurants map & index p. 114**
• **Part of Lake Tahoe Area — see map p. 111**

MOURELATOS LAKESHORE RESORT   530/546-9500 9
♥♥ Motel. **Address:** 6834 N Lake Blvd 96148

TIBURON (C-7) pop. 8,962, elev. 577'
• **Hotels p. 394**
• **Part of San Francisco area — see map p. 243**

Arguably as scenic as Sausalito, Tiburon is a quiet retreat for well-heeled residents who meet for lunch at the Corinthian Yacht Club or take an afternoon stroll along one of the community's quiet streets. From exceptionally picturesque Tiburon Boulevard, lined with expensive beach bungalows that have immaculately kept yards, there are lovely views of Belvedere Lagoon and Angel Island in the distance. Waterfront Main Street has a handful of specialty shops and restaurants with water views perfect for alfresco dining.

Regular ferry service between the Tiburon ferry dock at 21 Main St. and Angel Island, including seasonal sunset sightseeing cruises, is provided by the Angel Island-Tiburon Ferry. For schedule and fare information phone (415) 435-2131. The Blue & Gold Fleet, departing from Pier 41 in San Francisco, provides commuter service as well as sightseeing excursions; for schedule and fare information, phone (415) 705-8200.

Tiburon Peninsula Chamber of Commerce: 96B Main St., P.O. Box 563, Tiburon, CA 94920. **Phone:** (415) 435-5633.

ANGEL ISLAND STATE PARK is on Angel Island; access to the island is by public ferry from Tiburon or San Francisco, or by private boat. Angel Island, scenically situated in the middle of San Francisco Bay, is famous for being a vantage point that offers splendid views of the San Francisco skyline, Mount Tamalpais, the Marin Headlands, Sausalito and the Golden Gate Bridge.

Initially inhabited by Coastal Miwok Indians, the hilly island also served as a U.S. Army post, and was a processing point for immigrants from 1910-40. POWs were detained on the island during World War II; it later functioned as a missile base and currently is home to two Coast Guard stations.

A 1-hour, open-air audio tram tour provides information about the island's history. Tours of many historic sites, including the Angel Island Immigration Station, are conducted seasonally. Segway tours are offered twice daily. Outdoor activities include biking, hiking, fishing, beachcombing, boating, picnicking and camping. Food and bike rentals are available seasonally. *See Recreation Areas Chart.*

Note: Ferry service also is available from San Francisco and, seasonally, from Oakland and Alameda. **Hours:** Park open daily 8 a.m.-dusk. Tram tours available several times daily, Apr.-Sept.; Sat.-Sun. in Mar. and Oct.-Nov. Phone ahead to confirm tour schedules. **Cost:** Park admission included in ferry fare. Round-trip ferry from Tiburon $15; $14 (ages 65+); $13 (ages 6-12); $5 (ages 3-5); $1 (bicycles); free (one child ages 0-2 per paying adult). Tram tour $16.50; $15 (ages 65+); $10.50 (children ages 12 and under); free (child ages 0-2 on lap). Segway tours $68. **Phone:** (415) 435-5390 for the state park, (415) 435-2131 for ferry information from Tiburon, (415) 705-8200 for ferry information from San Francisco, or (415) 435-3392 for tram and Segway tour information. 🅰 🍴 ⌧ 🈁

Angel Island Immigration Station is within Angel Island State Park; access to the island is by public ferry from Tiburon or San Francisco, or by private boat. Angel Island Immigration Station was a processing center often called "the Ellis Island of the West." But unlike at Ellis Island, the immigrants—mostly from China—who sought entrance into the United States at this point of entry were frequently detained in overcrowded wooden barracks, endured embarrassing medical exams and lengthy interrogations, and were made to wait weeks (and sometimes months or years) to learn the outcome of their application. This was due to the Chinese Exclusion Acts, which were in effect from 1882 to 1943, and other anti-Asian legislation passed in 1917 and 1924. Immigrants from 80 countries were processed by the Immigration Station.

Many of these immigrants carved poetry into the walls of the barracks to convey their plight. The carvings were considered graffiti and were covered over with coats of paint. Visitors can see photographs, artifacts, a re-creation of the living quarters and hundreds of poems that were etched into the walls.

From the ferry dock the immigration station is a 1-mile walk (including a climb of 140 stairs) that takes 30 to 45 minutes. A 1-hour guided tour provides a first-hand look at those who were detained here and relates their strength and resiliency. Tour tickets can be purchased at the café at Ayala Cove.

Note: The hike and steep stair climb to the immigration station will be strenuous for visitors who are not in reasonably good physical shape. Shuttle service is available on a limited basis from the ferry landing to the immigration station; phone ahead for schedule and rates. Ferry service to Angel Island also is available from San Francisco, and seasonally from Oakland and Alameda.

Hours: Museum open Wed.-Sun. 11-3. Guided tours are given Wed.-Sun. at 11 and 12:30 (also Sat.-Sun. at 1:45), May-Sept.; schedule varies rest of year. Phone ahead to confirm schedule and tour availability. **Cost:** Museum admission $5; $3 (ages 6-17). Guided tour fee $7; $5 (ages 5-11). **Phone:** (415) 435-5390 for the immigration station, (415) 435-2131 for ferry information from Tiburon, (415) 435-3392 for shuttle and tour ticket information, or (415) 773-1188 for ferry information from San Francisco.

THE LODGE AT TIBURON   415/435-3133
▼▼▼ Hotel. **Address:** 1651 Tiburon Blvd 94920

TOMALES pop. 204

THE CONTINENTAL INN   707/878-2396

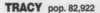

▼▼▼
Hotel

Address: 26985 Hwy One 94971 **Location:** On SR 1; at Dillon Beach Rd. **Facility:** 9 units. 2 stories (no elevator), interior corridors. **Terms:** check-in 4 pm.

SAVE 🍴 CALL ♿ 📶 ⌧ 🐾
📞 🅱 / SOME UNITS 🖥

TRACY pop. 82,922

BEST WESTERN LUXURY INN   209/832-0271

▼▼
Hotel

BW Best Western. **AAA Benefit:** Members save up to 15% and earn bonus points!

Address: 811 W Clover Rd 95376 **Location:** I-205 exit 8 (Central Tracy/Tracy Blvd), just s, then just w. **Facility:** 57 units. 3 stories, interior corridors. **Pool:** outdoor. **Activities:** hot tub, exercise room. **Guest Services:** coin laundry. **Featured Amenity:** full hot breakfast.

SAVE CALL ♿ 🛏 ♿ BIZ 📶
⌧ 🅱 🖼 🖥 / SOME UNITS 🐾

FAIRFIELD BY MARRIOTT   209/833-0135
▼▼ SAVE Hotel. **Address:** 2410 Naglee Rd 95376

AAA Benefit: Members save 5% or more!

HAMPTON INN BY HILTON   209/833-0483
▼▼▼ SAVE Hotel. **Address:** 2400 Naglee Rd 95304

AAA Benefit: Members save up to 15%!

HOLIDAY INN EXPRESS & SUITES   209/830-8500

Hotel

Address: 3751 N Tracy Blvd 95304 **Location:** I-205 exit 8 (Central Tracy/Tracy Blvd), just n. **Facility:** 102 units. 3 stories, interior corridors. **Pool:** outdoor. **Activities:** sauna, hot tub, exercise room. **Guest Services:** valet and coin laundry. **Featured Amenity:** breakfast buffet.

WHERE TO EAT

M & J BISTRO   209/832-2727
California. Casual Dining. **Address:** 2503 N Tracy Blvd 95376

MAZAA KABOB HOUSE   209/830-4402
Afghan. Casual Dining. **Address:** 2745 Naglee Rd 95391

TRINIDAD (B-1) pop. 367, elev. 175'

Spanish explorers, who came ashore near the site of present-day Trinidad on Trinity Sunday in 1775, named the area *La Santisima Trinidad,* "the most holy Trinity." Capt. George Vancouver arrived in 1793, and was followed in the early 19th century by a succession of fur traders.

Trinidad became a boomtown during gold rush days, as prospectors in search of instant wealth along nearby rivers loaded up with supplies before heading to the mines. Later a mill town and whaling port, this Pacific coast village today welcomes visitors in search of secluded beaches, hiking, fishing and opportunities for whale watching. A working lighthouse is near the edge of the promontory.

Greater Trinidad Chamber of Commerce: P.O. Box 356, Trinidad, CA 95570. **Phone:** (707) 677-1610.

PATRICK'S POINT STATE PARK is 5 mi. n. via US 101. Noted for its stunning coastal scenery, the heavily wooded state park features 6 miles of trails that thread through lush vegetation, along the tops of tall bluffs and down to sandy beaches. One path leads to Wedding Rock, a dramatic vantage point jutting out into the Pacific's pounding surf. A Yurok Indian village has been reconstructed in the park, and in spring a profusion of wildflowers bloom. *See Recreation Areas Chart.*

Note: Except for service animals, pets are not allowed on hiking trails. Dogs must be on a leash no more than 6 feet long during the day and must be confined to tents or vehicles at night. **Hours:** Daily dawn-dusk. **Cost:** Day use $8 per private vehicle; $7 (ages 62+ per private vehicle). **Phone:** (707) 677-3570.

TRINIDAD INN   707/677-3349
Motel. **Address:** 1170 Patrick's Point Dr 95570

TURTLE ROCKS OCEANFRONT INN   707/677-3707
Bed & Breakfast. **Address:** 3392 Patrick's Point Dr 95570

VIEW CREST LODGE   707/677-3393
Cottage. **Address:** 3415 Patrick's Point Dr 95570

WHERE TO EAT

THE LIGHTHOUSE GRILL   707/677-0077
American. Casual Dining. **Address:** 355 Main St 95570

MOONSTONE GRILL   707/677-1616
Regional American. Fine Dining. **Address:** 100 Moonstone Beach Rd 95570

SEASCAPE RESTAURANT   707/677-3762
Seafood. Casual Dining. **Address:** 1 Bay St 95570

SUNSET RESTAURANT AT CHER-AE HEIGHTS CASINO   707/825-2760
American. Casual Dining. **Address:** 27 Scenic Dr 95570

TRUCKEE (D-4) pop. 16,180, elev. 5,820'
- **Hotels p. 396 • Restaurants p. 396**
- **Hotels & Restaurants map & index p. 114**
- **Part of Lake Tahoe Area — see map p. 111**

Truckee, named for Washoe Indian Chief Trokay, was at one time a lawless lumber and railroad town, and some of that Old West charm still survives in restored 19th-century buildings and a train that runs through the middle of town. Winter sports enthusiasts take advantage of nearby skiing and snowboarding as well as the cross-country ski and snowshoe trails at Donner Memorial State Park.

Truckee Donner Chamber of Commerce: 10065 Donner Pass Rd., Truckee, CA 96161. **Phone:** (530) 587-8808.

Self-guiding tours: Maps outlining a self-guiding walking tour of the historic downtown district are available from the California Welcome Center, in the train depot at 10065 Donner Pass Rd.

DONNER MEMORIAL STATE PARK, 2 mi. w. on Donner Pass Rd., is near the site where the ill-fated Donner party was stranded trying to cross the Sierra Nevada Mountains during the severe winter of 1846-47. As members of the 89-person party died, some of those remaining resorted to cannibalism; only 47 were rescued.

The park visitor center has exhibits about the Chinese emigrant experience, construction of the railroad and early motoring adventures over Donner Pass. The Pioneer Monument is near the museum. One- to 2-hour guided hikes are offered in summer; phone ahead to confirm availability.

Hours: Park open daily dawn-dusk. Visitor center open daily 10-5. Closed Jan. 1, Thanksgiving and Christmas. **Cost:** Fee for day use $8 (per private vehicle); $7 (ages 62+ per private vehicle). **Phone:** (530) 582-7892.

(See map & index p. 114.)

BEST WESTERN PLUS TRUCKEE TAHOE HOTEL
530/587-4525

Hotel

 Best Western PLUS

AAA Benefit: Members save up to 15% and earn bonus points!

Address: 11331 Brockway Rd 96161 **Location:** I-80 exit 188 (SR 267) westbound; exit 188B eastbound, 1.5 mi se, then just w. **Facility:** 99 units. 2 stories, interior corridors. **Pool:** heated outdoor. **Activities:** hot tub, exercise room. **Guest Services:** coin laundry. **Featured Amenity:** breakfast buffet.

THE CEDAR HOUSE SPORT HOTEL   530/582-5655
Hotel. **Address:** 10918 Brockway Rd 96161

DONNER LAKE VILLAGE   530/587-6081
Vacation Rental Condominium. **Address:** 15695 Donner Pass Rd 96161

HAMPTON INN & SUITES TAHOE-TRUCKEE
530/587-1197
Hotel. **Address:** 11951 SR 267 96161

AAA Benefit: Members save up to 15%!

THE RITZ-CARLTON, LAKE TAHOE   530/562-3000

Contemporary Resort Hotel

THE RITZ-CARLTON

AAA Benefit: Unequaled service at special member savings!

Address: 13031 Ritz-Carlton Highlands Ct 96161 **Location:** I-80 exit 188 (SR 267) westbound; exit 188B eastbound, 5.6 mi se, then 2.5 mi sw on Highlands View Rd. **Facility:** This luxurious hotel features a jaw-dropping five-story fireplace as the centerpiece in the grand octagonal lobby. A gondola connects guests to The Village at Northstar. 170 units. 5 stories, interior corridors. **Parking:** valet only. **Terms:** check-in 4 pm. **Amenities:** safes. **Dining:** Manzanita, see separate listing. **Pool:** heated outdoor. **Activities:** sauna, hot tub, steamroom, downhill & cross country skiing, snowmobiling, snowboarding, recreation programs, kids club, game room, lawn sports, trails, health club, spa. **Guest Services:** valet laundry, boarding pass kiosk, rental car service, area transportation.

TAHOE MOUNTAIN LODGING   530/550-3300
Vacation Rental House.

TRUCKEE DONNER LODGE   530/582-9999

Hotel

Address: 10527 Cold Stream Rd 96161 **Location:** I-80 exit 184 (Donner Pass Rd), just s. Adjacent to Donner Memorial State Park. **Facility:** 64 units. 3 stories, interior corridors. **Pool:** heated outdoor. **Activities:** hot tub. **Guest Services:** coin laundry. **Featured Amenity:** continental breakfast.

BAR OF AMERICA   530/587-2626

American Casual Dining $18-$47

AAA Inspector Notes: Wood-fired pizza and items featuring organic and local produce are offered. Entrees include salmon roulade with Myer's Rum pineapple chutney, wild Alaskan halibut with roasted parsnips and rib-eye steak with peppercorn sauce and truffle mashed potatoes. The sweet endings include campfire s'mores and bananas Foster with a twist. **Features:** full bar, Sunday brunch. **Address:** 10040 Donner Pass Rd 96161 **Location:** Jct Brockway Rd; center. **Parking:** street only. L D

COTTONWOOD RESTAURANT & BAR   530/587-5711
American. Casual Dining. **Address:** 10142 Rue Hilltop Rd 96161

FIFTY FIFTY BREWING CO.   530/587-2337
American. Brewpub. **Address:** 11197 Brockway Rd, Suite 1 96161

JAX AT THE TRACKS   530/550-7450
American. Casual Dining. **Address:** 10144 W River St 96161

MANZANITA   530/562-3050
California. Fine Dining. **Address:** 13031 Ritz-Carlton Highlands Ct 96161

RUBICON PIZZA COMPANY   530/562-2199
Italian Pizza. Casual Dining. **Address:** 6001 Northstar Dr 96161

THAI DELICACY   350/550-1269
Thai. Casual Dining. **Address:** 11253 Brockway Rd 96161

TRUCKEE TAVERN AND GRILL   530/587-3766
California. Fine Dining. **Address:** 10118 Donner Pass Rd 96161

TULELAKE (A-3) pop. 1,010, elev. 4,035'

About 10 miles south of Tulelake, past Newell on SR 139, a steel cross and a basalt rock and concrete monument commemorate the Tule Lake Segregation Center, a World War II internment camp for Japanese-Americans. The Tule Lake Unit is part of the WWII Valor in the Pacific National Monument.

The center operated from 1942 to 1946 and at its height housed more than 18,000 detainees. Tule Lake became known for residents' resistance to their internment and the protests and demonstrations that resulted from overcrowded living conditions. Over time much of the camp's acreage was sold, and buildings were demolished or removed from the site. For tour information, phone (530) 260-0537.

The Tulelake-Butte Valley Fair & Museum of Local History, 800 S. Main St. in the Tulelake-Butte Valley Fairgrounds complex, features an exhibit about the internment camp, an original guard tower, part of a barracks, camp artifacts and a mural. There's also a visitor center and other exhibits pertaining to area history; phone (530) 667-5312.

TURLOCK pop. 68,549

BEST WESTERN ORCHARD INN 209/667-2827

Hotel

Best Western. **AAA Benefit:** Members save up to 15% and earn bonus points!

Address: 5025 N Golden State Blvd 95382 **Location:** SR 99 exit 217 (Taylor Rd), just e, then just n. **Facility:** 72 units. 2 stories (no elevator), exterior corridors. **Pool:** outdoor. **Activities:** hot tub. **Featured Amenity: continental breakfast.**

CANDLEWOOD SUITES 209/250-1501

Extended Stay Hotel

Address: 1000 Powers Ct 95380 **Location:** SR 99 exit 215 (Monte Vista Ave), just w, just s on N Tegner Rd, then just e. **Facility:** 89 efficiencies. 3 stories, interior corridors. **Activities:** exercise room. **Guest Services:** complimentary laundry.

FAIRFIELD INN & SUITES BY MARRIOTT 209/668-3800
Hotel. **Address:** 3301 Countryside Dr 95380

AAA Benefit: Members save 5% or more!

HAMPTON INN BY HILTON 209/664-9729
Hotel. **Address:** 1821 Lander Ave 95380

AAA Benefit: Members save up to 15%!

HOLIDAY INN EXPRESS & SUITES TURLOCK 209/664-9999
Hotel. **Address:** 3001 Hotel Dr 95380

WHERE TO EAT

ANGELINI'S ITALIAN RESTAURANT 209/667-6644
Italian. Casual Dining. **Address:** 2251 Geer Rd 95382

BISTRO 234 209/668-4234
American. Casual Dining. **Address:** 234 E Main St 95380

CHONG'S CUISINE 209/656-9189
Asian. Casual Dining. **Address:** 1801 Countryside Dr 95380

DUST BOWL BREWERY TAPROOM 209/250-2043
American. Brewpub. **Address:** 3000 Fulkerth Rd 95380

DUST BOWL BREWING CO. DOWNTOWN TAPROOM 209/250-2042
American. Brewpub. **Address:** 200 W Main St 95380

EL JARDIN 209/632-0932
Mexican. Casual Dining. **Address:** 409 E Olive Ave 95380

JU JU THAI CUISINE 209/815-8424
Thai. Casual Dining. **Address:** 235 W Main St 95380

VILLA NAPOLI 209/667-1800
Italian. Casual Dining. **Address:** 1102 Geer Rd 95380

UKIAH (D-1) pop. 16,075, elev. 635'
- **Hotels p. 398 • Restaurants p. 398**
- **Part of Wine Country area — see map p. 405**

The center of a flourishing wine region, Ukiah's name derives from a Pomo Indian word meaning "deep valley." Two popular annual events take place at the Redwood Empire Fair & Event Center, 1055 N. State St. The Redwood Empire Spring Fair in early June offers craft, gardening and home improvement vendors, carnival rides and a barbecue grilling competition. It's followed in early August by the 4-day Redwood Empire Fair, a summer celebration with a circus, jugglers, nightly concerts, food booths, farm animals, tractor races and other activities. For information about either event, phone (707) 462-3884.

Visit Ukiah: 200 S. School St., Ukiah, CA 95482. **Phone:** (707) 467-5766.

MONTGOMERY WOODS STATE NATURAL RESERVE is about 13.5 mi. w. via Orr Springs Rd. or about 30 mi. e. of Mendocino via Comptche-Ukiah Rd. (the jct. with SR 1 is just s. of the bridge crossing the Big River). The journey alone to reach Montgomery Woods—along a narrow, two-lane paved road that dips, bends and winds through a thickly forested section of Mendocino County's Coast Range—makes it a truly off-the-beaten-path destination for those who appreciate the primeval beauty of a redwood forest.

Less extensive than better-known and easier-to-get-to Muir Woods and Armstrong Woods, Montgomery Woods is what is known as a climax forest, where trees and plants like laurel, tan oak, ferns and wild iris grow beneath towering coast redwoods and giant sequoias. The Montgomery Woods Trail, a 2-mile loop, follows Montgomery Creek and links five redwood groves featuring impressively large trees in an area that was never logged.

From December 2000 until August 2006 the Mendocino Tree, a coast redwood, was the tallest known tree in the world at 367.5 feet (a lightning strike lopped off the top). More sunlight pierces the dense tree canopy here than at Muir Woods, enabling a lusher and more riotous understory of vegetation to thrive. The lack of crowds makes a very rewarding hike for those who relish solitude.

Note: The road to the reserve is well maintained but rough in spots. The small parking area is signed but easy to miss and has space for about seven vehicles; make sure your car is locked and don't leave valuables in sight. There is a very basic restroom at the lot and a wood gazebo with picnic tables at the trailhead. During the winter and spring months parts of the loop trail may be covered by water. **Time:** Allow 2 hours minimum. **Hours:** Daily dawn-dusk. **Cost:** Free. **Phone:** (707) 937-5804.

BEST WESTERN ORCHARD INN
707/462-1514

Hotel

 Best Western.
AAA Benefit: Members save up to 15%. and earn bonus points!

Address: 555 S Orchard Ave 95482 **Location:** US 101 exit Gobbi St, just w, then just n. **Facility:** 54 units. 2 stories (no elevator), interior corridors. **Pool:** outdoor. **Activities:** hot tub, exercise room. **Guest Services:** coin laundry. **Featured Amenity: continental breakfast.**

/ SOME UNITS

COMFORT INN & SUITES
707/462-3442
Hotel. **Address:** 1220 Airport Park Blvd 95482

DAYS INN
707/462-7584
Motel. **Address:** 950 N State St 95482

FAIRFIELD INN & SUITES BY MARRIOTT UKIAH/MENDOCINO
707/463-3600
Hotel. **Address:** 1140 Airport Park Blvd 95482

AAA Benefit: Members save 5% or more!

HAMPTON INN UKIAH
707/462-6555
Hotel. **Address:** 1160 Airport Park Blvd 95482

AAA Benefit: Members save up to 15%!

QUALITY INN
707/462-2906
Motel

Address: 1050 S State St 95482 **Location:** US 101 exit Talmage Rd, 0.4 mi w, then just n. **Facility:** 38 units. 2 stories (no elevator), exterior corridors. **Pool:** outdoor. **Featured Amenity: full hot breakfast.**

/ SOME UNITS

SUPER 8 UKIAH
707/468-8181
Motel. **Address:** 693 S Orchard Ave 95482

TRAVELODGE UKIAH
707/462-5745
Hotel

Address: 1720 N State St 95482 **Location:** US 101 exit N State St, then just n. **Facility:** 55 units. 2 stories (no elevator), exterior corridors. **Pool:** outdoor. **Activities:** hot tub. **Guest Services:** coin laundry. **Featured Amenity: full hot breakfast.**

/ SOME UNITS

VICHY HOT SPRINGS RESORT AND INN
707/462-9515
Historic Bed & Breakfast. **Address:** 2605 Vichy Springs Rd 95482

WHERE TO EAT

BE-BOPS DINER
707/462-1750
Burgers. Casual Dining. **Address:** 1200 S State St 95482

CRUSH ITALIAN STEAKHOUSE
707/463-0700
Italian. Casual Dining. **Address:** 1180 Airport Park Blvd 95482

CULTIVO
707/462-7007
Pizza. Casual Dining. **Address:** 108 W Standley St 95482

ELLIE'S MUTT HUT & VEGETARIAN CAFE
707/468-5376
American. Quick Serve. **Address:** 732 S State St 95482

SCHAT'S COURTHOUSE BAKERY AND CAFE
707/462-1670
Breads/Pastries Sandwiches. Quick Serve. **Address:** 113 W Perkins St 95482

STARS RESTAURANT
707/462-1622
American. Casual Dining. **Address:** 115 S Orchard Plaza 95482

UNION CITY pop. 69,516, elev. 92'

CROWNE PLAZA SILICON VALLEY NORTH-UNION CITY
510/489-2200

Hotel

Address: 32083 Alvarado-Niles Rd 94587 **Location:** I-880 exit 23 (Alvarado-Niles Rd), just se. **Facility:** 268 units. 3-6 stories, interior corridors. **Pool:** heated outdoor. **Activities:** exercise room. **Guest Services:** valet and coin laundry, rental car service.

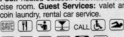

HAMPTON INN BY HILTON UNION CITY
510/475-5600
Hotel. **Address:** 31040 Alvarado-Niles Rd 94587

AAA Benefit: Members save up to 15%!

HOLIDAY INN EXPRESS UNION CITY
510/475-0600
Hotel. **Address:** 31140 Alvarado-Niles Rd 94587

WHERE TO EAT

BACKYARD BAYOU
510/657-0095
Cajun. Casual Dining. **Address:** 32280 Dyer St 94587

GERRY'S GRILL
510/441-9900
Philippine. Casual Dining. **Address:** 31005 Courthouse Dr 94587

PACIFIC POURHOUSE
510/768-7333
American. Casual Dining. **Address:** 32216 Dyer St 94587

UPPER LAKE pop. 1,052
• Part of Wine Country area — see map p. 405

SUPER 8
707/275-0888
Motel

Address: 450 E Hwy 20 95485 **Location:** Jct SR 29, 0.5 mi e. **Facility:** 34 units. 2 stories (no elevator), exterior corridors. **Pool:** outdoor. **Guest Services:** coin laundry. **Featured Amenity: continental breakfast.**

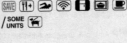
/ SOME UNITS

TALLMAN HOTEL
707/275-2244
Country Inn. **Address:** 9550 Main St 95485

WHERE TO EAT

BLUE WING SALOON RESTAURANT   707/275-2233
◆◆ American. Gastropub. **Address:** 9520 Main St 95485

VACAVILLE pop. 92,428, elev. 179'

BEST WESTERN HERITAGE INN   707/448-8453

◆◆
Motel

(BW) Best Western.

AAA Benefit: Members save up to 15% and earn bonus points!

Address: 1420 E Monte Vista Ave 95688 **Location:** I-80 exit 55 (Monte Vista Ave) westbound, just w; exit eastbound, just n on Allison Dr, then just e. **Facility:** 41 units. 2 stories (no elevator), exterior corridors. **Pool:** outdoor.

[SAVE] [ⓘ] CALL [♿] [🛥] [BIZ] [📶]
[🛎] [🖥] [🖵] / SOME UNITS [🐾]

FAIRFIELD BY MARRIOTT   707/469-0800
◆◆◆ [SAVE] Hotel. **Address:** 370 Orange Dr 95687

AAA Benefit: Members save 5% or more!

HAMPTON INN & SUITES VACAVILLE/NAPA VALLEY AREA   707/469-6200

◆◆◆
Hotel

(Hampton by HILTON)

AAA Benefit: Members save up to 15%!

Address: 800 Mason St 95688 **Location:** I-80 exit Davis St eastbound, 0.4 mi n, then just e; exit Mason St westbound, just w. **Facility:** 83 units. 3 stories, interior corridors. **Pool:** heated outdoor. **Activities:** hot tub, exercise room. **Guest Services:** valet and coin laundry. **Featured Amenity:** breakfast buffet.

[⊗] [🛎] [🖥] [🖵] / SOME UNITS [🐾]
[SAVE] CALL [♿] [🛥] [♿] [BIZ] [📶]

HOLIDAY INN EXPRESS HOTEL & SUITES VACAVILLE   707/451-3500
◆◆◆ Hotel. **Address:** 151 Lawrence Dr 95687

RESIDENCE INN BY MARRIOTT   707/469-0300
◆◆◆ [SAVE] Extended Stay Hotel. **Address:** 360 Orange Dr 95687

AAA Benefit: Members save 5% or more!

VACAVILLE COURTYARD BY MARRIOTT   707/451-9000
◆◆◆ [SAVE] Hotel. **Address:** 120 Nut Tree Pkwy 95687

AAA Benefit: Members save 5% or more!

WHERE TO EAT

BLACK OAK RESTAURANT   707/448-1311
◆◆ American. Casual Dining. **Address:** 320 Orange Dr 95687

BOUDIN BAKERY & CAFE   707/471-7240
◆ Breads/Pastries Sandwiches. Quick Serve. **Address:** 1620 E Monte Vista Ave 95688

FENTONS CREAMERY & RESTAURANT   707/469-7200
◆◆ American. Casual Dining. **Address:** 1669 E Monte Vista Ave 95688

LOS REYES RESTAURANTE Y CANTINA   707/448-2113
◆◆ Mexican. Casual Dining. **Address:** 21 Town Square Pl 95688

PURE GRAIN BAKERY & CAFE   707/447-4121
◆ Breads/Pastries. Quick Serve. **Address:** 11 Town Square 95687

TAHOE JOE'S   707/455-1326
◆◆ Steak. Casual Dining. **Address:** 1040 Helen Power Dr 95687

VALLEJO (B-8) pop. 115,942, elev. 40'
• Hotels p. 400 • Restaurants p. 400

In 1851 Gen. Mariano Guadalupe Vallejo (val-LEH-hoh) founded the settlement that bears his name where the Carquinez Straits meet the Napa River. The new town immediately gained prominence when it was designated the state capital on two separate occasions between 1851 and 1853.

Vallejo's Mare Island Naval Shipyard served as a vital defense installation; during World War I the destroyer USS *Ward* was built there in less than 18 days. Of particular interest is St. Peter's Chapel, which dates from 1901 and is believed to be the oldest military chapel in the country. Phone (707) 280-5742 for a tour reservation to view the chapel's 29 Tiffany windows.

San Francisco Bay Ferry provides service from the Vallejo Ferry Terminal at 289 Mare Island Way to the Ferry Building and then Pier 41 in San Francisco. Seasonal service is also available to and from San Francisco Giants baseball games at AT&T Park. For schedule information phone (877) 643-3779.

Vallejo Convention & Visitors Bureau: Vallejo Ferry Terminal, 289 Mare Island Way, Suite A, Vallejo, CA 94590. **Phone:** (707) 642-3653 or (800) 482-5535.

MARE ISLAND HISTORIC PARK FOUNDATION is on Mare Island at 1100 Railroad Ave.; from I-80, take the Tennessee Street/Mare Island exit, proceed w. approximately 3 mi. on Mare Island Cswy. across the Mare Island Causeway Lift Bridge and continue to Railroad Ave. Based in Vallejo for the entirety of its 142-year history (1854-1996), the Mare Island Navy Yard played a significant role in the nation's defense.

Several historic ships are docked at the Mare Island Naval Shipyard (at Nimitz Avenue and A Street), including the SSBN 658 *Mariano G. Vallejo* and the USS LCS 102 (aka the "Yankee Dollar"), a gunboat that served during World War II. Nicknamed "mighty midgets," the LCS vessels—outfitted with an array of guns and rocket launchers—provided vital support to landing craft and destroyers on picket duty during the invasion of Iwo Jima and, most crucially, in the Okinawa campaign.

The LCS 102 was decommissioned in 1946 and today is the sole survivor of a fleet that numbered 130 ships. Following cleanup and restoration work, it was dedicated in 2007. A guided tour includes the wardroom, enlisted compartments, officers' quarters, galley, the crew's mess hall, radio and navigation room, the engine room and the bridge. **Time:** Allow 1 hour minimum. **Hours:** Tours are given by appointment; phone for details. Closed Jan. 1 and Christmas. **Cost:** Donations. **Phone:** (707) 557-4646.

Mare Island Historic Park Foundation Artifacts Museum is at Railroad Ave. and 8th St. in Building 46, within Mare Island Historic Park. The museum, in a building that served as a pipe shop from 1855 to 1984, is easy to find—a 35-foot patrol boat with shark's teeth is parked in front. On display are artifacts from the Mare Island Naval Shipyard, including tools, historic radios, uniforms and photographs that underscore the shipyard's significance during World War II. **Hours:** Mon.-Fri. 10-2, Sat. 10-4. Closed Jan. 1 and Christmas. **Cost:** Donations. **Phone:** (707) 557-4646.

SIX FLAGS DISCOVERY KINGDOM is at 1001 Fairgrounds Dr. This 135-acre wildlife park, oceanarium and theme park features rides, shows, play areas and educational encounters with wildlife for the entire family. Dolphins, sea lions, birds, tigers and more appear in daily shows.

Highlights include Odin's Temple of the Tiger, a tiger show and exhibit; Ocean Discovery, a 2-acre Caribbean-themed destination where families can see sea lions, penguins and stingrays; Shark Experience, where the creatures can be seen through an underwater tunnel; and Tava's Jungleland, a children's adventure area with family rides, interactive zones and up-close animal attractions.

Roller coasters include The Joker, a steel-wood hybrid coaster; SUPERMAN Ultimate Flight, a record-breaking loops coaster; HARLEY QUINN Crazy Coaster, a dual looping coaster; Medusa, a floorless, seven-loop mega coaster; Vertical Velocity, a spiraling coaster that propels riders up and down two 150-foot towers; Kong, a tangled track with five inversions; Boomerang, a trio of high-speed loops with a boomerang backward; WONDER WOMAN Lasso of Truth, a pendulum ride that propels at 70 miles per hour; and SkyScreamer swing ride, which spins visitors around a tower at speeds up to 43 mph.

Allow a full day. **Hours:** Park open daily, Memorial Day weekend to mid-Aug.; Sat.-Sun., holidays and select Fri., Jan.-May and Sept.-Dec.; otherwise varies. Phone ahead to confirm schedule. **Cost:** $68.99; $48.99 (under 48 inches tall); free (ages 0-2). See AAA location for members discount. **Parking:** $25. **Phone:** (707) 556-5216 to verify hours of operation and prices.

🎟 **Booth or table?**

AAA.com/travelguides/restaurants

COURTYARD BY MARRIOTT VALLEJO NAPA VALLEY
707/644-1200

🎗🎗🎗 [SAVE] Hotel. **Address:** 1000 Fairgrounds Dr 94589

AAA Benefit: Members save 5% or more!

HAMPTON INN DISCOVERY KINGDOM NAPA GATEWAY
707/554-9655

🎗🎗🎗 [SAVE] Hotel. **Address:** 1596 Fairgrounds Dr 94589

AAA Benefit: Members save up to 15%!

WHERE TO EAT

BUTTERCUP DINER & BAR
707/643-9030

🎗🎗 Comfort Food. Casual Dining. **Address:** 3288 Sonoma Blvd 94590

MICHAEL WARRING
707/655-4808

🎗🎗🎗 New American. Fine Dining. **Address:** 8300 Bennington Dr 94591

WALNUT CREEK pop. 64,173, elev. 135'
• Hotels & Restaurants map & index p. 176

MOUNT DIABLO STATE PARK—see Danville p. 69.

EMBASSY SUITES BY HILTON WALNUT CREEK
925/934-2500

🎗🎗🎗 [SAVE] Hotel. **Address:** 1345 Treat Blvd 94597

AAA Benefit: Members save up to 15%!

HOLIDAY INN EXPRESS WALNUT CREEK 925/932-3332

Hotel

Address: 2730 N Main St 94597 **Location:** I-680 exit 48, just s. Ⓜ Pleasant Hill/Contra Costa Centre, 6. **Facility:** 164 units. 2 stories, interior corridors. **Parking:** on-site (fee). **Amenities:** safes. **Pool:** heated outdoor. **Activities:** hot tub, exercise room. **Guest Services:** valet and coin laundry, area transportation.

RENAISSANCE WALNUT CREEK HOTEL AND BAY CLUB 925/938-8700

Hotel

RENAISSANCE®
HOTELS

AAA Benefit: Members save 5% or more!

Address: 2805 Jones Rd 94597 **Location:** I-680 exit 48, just e on Treat Blvd, then just s. Ⓜ Pleasant Hill/Contra Costa Centre, 6. **Facility:** 175 units. 6 stories, interior corridors. **Parking:** valet only. **Dining:** Citrus Fresh Market, see separate listing. **Pool:** heated outdoor. **Activities:** sauna, hot tub, steamroom, kids club, bicycles, health club, spa. **Guest Services:** valet laundry, area transportation.

(See map & index p. 176.)

WALNUT CREEK MARRIOTT   925/934-2000   56
▼▼▼ SAVE Hotel. **Address:** 2355 N Main St 94596

AAA Benefit:
Members save 5% or more!

WHERE TO EAT

ATRIO   925/934-2000   55
▼▼▼ American. Casual Dining. **Address:** 2355 N Main St 94596

BRODERICK ROADHOUSE   925/945-6960   57
▼▼ American. Casual Dining. **Address:** 1548 Bonanza St 94596

BUTTERCUP DINER & BAR   925/932-2763
▼▼ Comfort Food. Casual Dining. **Address:** 660 Ygnacio Valley Rd 94596

CITRUS FRESH MARKET   925/942-6360
▼▼ American. Casual Dining. **Address:** 2805 Jones Rd 94597

EMBASSY GRILL   925/934-2500
▼▼ American. Casual Dining. **Address:** 1345 Treat Blvd 94597

IL FORNAIO   925/296-0100   59
▼▼▼ Italian. Fine Dining. **Address:** 1430 Mt. Diablo Blvd 94596

MASSIMO RISTORANTE   925/932-1474   56
▼▼▼ Northern Italian. Fine Dining. **Address:** 1604 Locust St 94596

TELEFÈRIC BARCELONA   925/300-3826   58
▼▼▼ Spanish. Casual Dining. **Address:** 1500 Mt Diablo Blvd 94596

VA DE VI BISTRO & WINE BAR   925/979-0100   60
▼▼▼ International Small Plates. Casual Dining. **Address:** 1511 Mt. Diablo Blvd 94596

WATSONVILLE (F-9) pop. 51,199, elev. 23'

Watsonville is located in the Pajaro Valley, where apples, strawberries and flowers are grown. Apples are harvested in late September and early October.

Pajaro Valley Chamber of Commerce: 44 Brennan St., P.O. Box 1748, Watsonville, CA 95077. **Phone:** (831) 724-3900.

Self-guiding tours: Maps for walking and driving tours of Watsonville and the Pajaro Valley are available from the chamber of commerce.

ELKHORN SLOUGH NATIONAL ESTUARINE RESEARCH RESERVE is 3.5 mi. e. of SR 1 on Dolan Rd., then 1.9 mi. n. to 1700 Elkhorn Rd. This 1,700-acre coastal area protects the habitat of hundreds of species of birds, fish and invertebrates. It is an important feeding and nesting ground for many waterfowl and migratory shorebirds. Walking trails wind beneath a canopy of coastal live oak trees and along fingers of salt marsh. The reserve's visitor center has educational displays.

Picnicking is permitted near the visitor center; smoking is prohibited. Dogs and bicycles are not permitted. **Hours:** Reserve and visitor center open Wed.-Sun. 9-5. Guided nature walks departing from the visitor center are given Sat.-Sun. at 10 and 1. A birding tour is offered on the first Sat. of the month at 8:30 a.m. **Cost:** Visitor center free. Fee to walk trails $4 (payable by credit card only); free (ages 0-15). **Phone:** (831) 728-2822.

BEST WESTERN ROSE GARDEN INN   831/724-3367
▼▼▼ Hotel

 Best Western. **AAA Benefit:** Members save up to 15% and earn bonus points!

Address: 740 Freedom Blvd 95076 **Location:** On SR 152; jct Main St. **Facility:** 46 units, some two bedrooms and efficiencies. 2 stories (no elevator), exterior corridors. **Pool:** heated outdoor. **Activities:** hot tub, exercise room. **Guest Services:** coin laundry. **Featured Amenity:** continental breakfast.

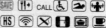
/ SOME UNITS

HOLIDAY INN EXPRESS HOTEL & SUITES   831/728-3600
▼▼▼ Hotel

Address: 1855 Main St 95076 **Location:** SR 1 exit SR 152 southbound; exit S Green Valley Rd northbound. **Facility:** 65 units. 3 stories, interior corridors. **Pool:** heated indoor. **Activities:** trails, exercise room. **Guest Services:** coin laundry. **Featured Amenity:** full hot breakfast.

WEOTT (C-1) pop. 288, elev. 338'

HUMBOLDT REDWOODS STATE PARK, along the Redwood Hwy. (US 101) between Miranda and Redcrest, covers more than 53,000 acres, including some 17,000 acres of old-growth coast redwoods. Created in 1921 to protect these magnificent trees, the park is part of a diverse coast redwood ecosystem that includes the Rockefeller Forest, the largest remaining old-growth redwood forest in the world, and the Bull Creek watershed.

Within the park are more than 250 campsites and 100 miles of hiking, biking and horseback riding trails. Among the many breathtaking specimens in the park's memorial redwood groves is the famous Dyerville Giant Tree, a 362-foot redwood considered to be the world's tallest tree until it was felled by another tree in 1991. Popular day use areas are Dyerville Overlook, which offers expansive views of the south fork of the Eel River, and Williams Grove.

The Humboldt Redwoods Visitor Center, on SR 254 (Avenue of the Giants) between Weott and Myers Flat, has a theater, educational and wildlife displays and a brochure outlining the Avenue of the Giants driving tour route. Naturalist-led interpretive activities during the summer months include nature walks and Junior Ranger programs. *See Recreation Areas Chart.*

Note: Except for service animals, dogs are restricted from trails. **Hours:** Park open daily 8 a.m.-11:30 p.m. Visitor center open daily 9-5, Apr.-Oct.; 10-4, rest of year. Visitor center closed Thanksgiving and Christmas. **Cost:** Day use fee (Apr.-Oct.) $8 per private vehicle; $7 (ages 62+ per private vehicle). Visitor center free. **Phone:** (707) 946-2409 for the park, or (707) 946-2263 for the visitor center.

Avenue of the Giants parallels US 101 between Phillipsville and Pepperwood. Winding along the course of the Eel River, this 32-mile section of pre-freeway US 101 passes through a wilderness that is awe-inspiring in its natural majesty. While the surrounding hills are lush with oak, maple and madrone trees, it is the magnificent redwoods along this route that tower above everything.

The two-lane highway has plenty of turnouts where you can park, get out, take photos and in general be awed by the sheer enormity of these trees. A shadowed solitude prevails in the redwood groves. Exuberant growths of ferns (one of the few plants that thrive in the damp, low-light conditions) carpet the ground beneath them. Signed trailheads for hikes (most of them short and level) are at the parking areas.

Numerous hiking trails traverse the Rockefeller Forest Redwood Grove. At Founders Grove is the Founders Tree, a redwood 346 feet tall and almost 13 feet in diameter at its base. There are a number of large redwoods in this grove, including a few fallen trees—you'll really get a sense of just how big they are when you encounter one lying on the ground. An oddity is the Eternal Tree, which survives despite being hit by lightning, flooded and cut by an ax; a fifth-generation redwood grows next to it. **Note:** Bring food and water if you plan on spending the day hiking.

WEST SACRAMENTO pop. 48,744
• Hotels & Restaurants map & index p. 224

HAMPTON INN & SUITES BY HILTON-WEST SACRAMENTO
916/374-1909 **63**

WWW SAVE Hotel. **Address:** 800 Stillwater Rd 95605

AAA Benefit:
Members save up to 15%!

RODEWAY INN CAPITOL 916/371-6983 **64**
WW Motel. **Address:** 817 W Capitol Ave 95691

WHISKEYTOWN-SHASTA-TRINITY NATIONAL RECREATION AREA (B-2)

At the head of the Sacramento Valley and Upper Trinity River country, north and west of Redding, Whiskeytown-Shasta-Trinity National Recreation Area's three components embrace 246,087 acres and four major dam-created lakes: Whiskeytown, about 8 miles west of Redding via SR 299; Trinity and Lewiston, northeast of Weaverville; and Shasta, north of Redding. Shasta, California's largest manmade lake, has 370 miles of shoreline.

The recreation area's three units are managed by two different federal agencies: Whiskeytown is part of the National Park Service, while the Shasta and Trinity units are under the jurisdiction of the Forest Service.

The visitor center for the Whiskeytown recreation area is at SR 299 and Kennedy Memorial Drive in Whiskeytown; phone (530) 246-1225. It is open daily 10-4; hours may be extended in summer. Closed Jan. 1, Thanksgiving and Christmas. The Shasta Lake Visitor Information Center is at 14225 Holiday Rd. in Mountain Lake, outside Redding; phone (530) 275-1589. It is open Thurs.-Mon. 9-5, Memorial Day-Labor Day. Information is available at the ranger station across the street the rest of the year. The Trinity unit's visitor center, 360 Main St. in Weaverville, is open Mon.-Sat. 8-4:30, Memorial Day-Labor Day; Mon.-Fri. 8-4:30, rest of year. Phone (530) 623-2121.

Recreational activities include hiking, swimming, boating, sailing, water skiing, camping, fishing, backpacking, horseback riding, wildlife viewing and mountain biking. Ranger-guided activities such as kayaking and hiking to waterfalls are available in summer. One hike includes a 1.7-mile trail that leads to recently discovered Whiskeytown Falls, a 220-foot cascade.

Recreational gold panning using a metal or plastic gold pan is permitted in the Whiskeytown unit only; day permits are required and are available at the park for $1. A pass valid for 7 consecutive days is $10 (per private vehicle). An additional fee is charged for camping. Phone (530) 242-3400 for park information, or (877) 444-6777 for camping reservations through the National Recreation Reservation System. *See Recreation Areas Chart.*

WILLIAMS pop. 5,123, elev. 80'

GRANZELLA'S INN 530/473-3310

WWW Hotel

Address: 391 6th St 95987 **Location:** I-5 exit 577 (Williams), 0.5 mi w, then just n. **Facility:** 43 units. 2 stories (no elevator), interior corridors. **Terms:** check-in 3:30 pm. **Dining:** Granzella's Restaurant & Deli, see separate listing. **Pool:** outdoor. **Activities:** hot tub, limited exercise equipment. **Guest Services:** coin laundry. **Featured Amenity:** continental breakfast.

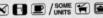

TRAVELER'S INN
530/473-5387

◈◈◈ **Motel**

Address: 215 N 7th St 95987 **Location:** I-5 exit 577 (Williams), just w on E St (SR 20 business route), then 0.3 mi n. **Facility:** 20 units. 1 story, exterior corridors. **Pool:** outdoor. **Activities:** exercise room. **Guest Services:** coin laundry. **Featured Amenity:** continental breakfast.

WHERE TO EAT

GRANZELLA'S RESTAURANT & DELI
530/473-5583

◈◈◈ **American Casual Dining** **$13-$27**

AAA Inspector Notes: Sandwiches, pizza, charbroiled burgers, steaks, seafood, pasta and prime rib (available on Saturday night) are all served among comfortable décor. The adjoining specialty shop and deli are hard to pass through without picking up something for the road. Most notable are the pastry and gelato cases with the made-in-house baked goods and gelato. **Features:** full bar, happy hour. **Address:** 451 6th St 95987 **Location:** I-5 exit 577 (Williams), 0.5 mi w, then just n; adjacent to Granzella's Inn.

B L D CALL&

LA FORTUNA
530/473-2023

Mexican Breads/Pastries. Quick Serve. **Address:** 669 F St 95987

LOUIS CAIRO'S RESTAURANT
530/473-5927

◈◈ Steak. Casual Dining. **Address:** 558 7th St 95987

WILLITS (D-1) pop. 4,888, elev. 1,364'
• Part of Wine Country area — see map p. 405

Settled by a group of pioneer ranchers in the 1850s and originally called Willitsville, this serene Mendocino County community benefits from a location that offers varied outdoor recreation, from hiking and bicycling to lake, river and ocean fishing. Willits also is the eastern terminus of the Skunk Train, based in Fort Bragg *(see place listing p. 81)*.

Willits Chamber of Commerce: 299 E. Commercial St., Willits, CA 95490-3105. **Phone:** (707) 459-7910.

SKUNK TRAIN-WILLITS departs from the Willits Depot, 3 blks. e. of Main St. at 299 E. Commercial St. The scenic 2-hour round-trip will take you from the Willits valley floor to the highest point on our rail line. You will pass through Tunnel #2 to the California redwoods of Noyo River Canyon. Skunk Train also operates out of Fort Bragg. **Hours:** Wolf Tree Turn trip departs at 10:30 a.m. year round with seasonal adjustments; phone for scheduled departure days. **Cost:** Wolf Tree Turn fare $49.95; $29.95 (ages 2-12); $10.95 (ages 0-2). An additional $10.95 fee is charged for dogs. Reservations are recommended. **Phone:** (707) 964-6371.

BAECHTEL CREEK INN, AN ASCEND HOTEL COLLECTION MEMBER
707/459-9063

◈◈◈ Hotel. **Address:** 101 Gregory Ln 95490

BEST WESTERN WILLITS INN
707/459-5800

◈◈◈ **Hotel**

 Best Western.

AAA Benefit: Members save up to 15% and earn bonus points!

Address: 1777 S Main St 95490 **Location:** US 101, 1.3 mi s of jct SR 20. **Facility:** 44 units. 3 stories (no elevator), exterior corridors. **Pool:** outdoor. **Activities:** hot tub. **Guest Services:** coin laundry. **Featured Amenity:** continental breakfast.

SUPER 8 WILLITS
707/459-3388

◈◈ Hotel. **Address:** 1119 S Main St 95490

WILLOW CREEK (B-1) pop. 1,710, elev. 610'

Situated along the Trinity River, Willow Creek is at the junction of two scenic byways, SR 299 and SR 96. The town's former name, China Flat, is a reference to Chinese laborers who once worked in mines and lumber mills. Outdoor recreation rules today; surrounded by the rugged wilderness of Six Rivers National Forest, this area offers numerous opportunities for backpacking, mountain biking, fishing and white-water rafting.

The primeval wilderness setting surrounding Willow Creek has been the scene of many alleged "Bigfoot" sightings. Also known as Sasquatch, Bigfoot—most often described as a large, hairy, apelike humanoid—is thought by some to inhabit forests in the Pacific Northwest, although the great majority of scientists attribute documented incidents to a combination of folklore, mistaken identification and hoax.

One of the most publicized sightings occurred back in 1967, when Roger Patterson and Robert Gimlin used a hand-held 16 mm Kodak camera to film a large hominid walking across a sandbar on Bluff Creek, about 25 miles north of Willow Creek. *Argosy*, a men's adventure magazine, published an article that included photo stills; many years later, however, an acquaintance of the two Bigfoot investigators claimed he had donned a gorilla suit for the making of the film. It's no wonder, then, that Willow Creek bills itself the "Bigfoot Capital of the World" with tongue planted somewhat firmly in cheek.

COHO COTTAGES
530/629-4000

◈◈◈ Cottage. **Address:** 76 Willow Rd 95573

🌐 **For highways, byways and more: AAA.com/maps**

WILLOWS pop. 6,166, elev. 135'

BEST WESTERN WILLOWS INN
530/934-4444

Motel

 Best Western.

AAA Benefit: Members save up to 15% and earn bonus points!

Address: 475 N Humboldt Ave 95988 **Location:** I-5 exit 603 (SR 162/Willows/Oroville), just e, then just n. **Facility:** 49 units. 2 stories, exterior corridors. **Pool:** outdoor. **Activities:** exercise room. **Guest Services:** coin laundry. **Featured Amenity:** breakfast buffet.

SAVE ⬆ CALL 🦽 🛏 💺 BIZ
📶 ✕ 🔒 🍽 💻

/SOME UNITS 🐾

HOLIDAY INN EXPRESS WILLOWS
530/934-8900

fyi Hotel. Under major renovation, call for details. **Last Rated:** 🔸🔸🔸 **Address:** 545 N Humboldt Ave 95988

SUPER 8 BY WYNDHAM WILLOWS
530/934-2871

🔸🔸 Hotel. **Address:** 457 N Humboldt Ave 95988

WHERE TO EAT

CASA RAMOS
530/934-0600

🔸🔸 Mexican. Casual Dining. **Address:** 247 N Humboldt Ave 95988

THE LAST STAND BAR & GRILL
530/934-7246

🔸 American. Quick Serve. **Address:** 414 N Tehama St 95988

WINDSOR pop. 26,801

• Part of Wine Country area — see map p. 405

HAMPTON INN & SUITES-WINDSOR-SONOMA WINE COUNTRY
707/837-9355

🔸🔸🔸
Hotel

 Hampton

AAA Benefit: Members save up to 15%!

Address: 8937 Brooks Rd S 95492 **Location:** US 101 exit Central Windsor, just ne on Lakewood Dr, then just n. **Facility:** 116 units. 3 stories, interior corridors. **Amenities:** safes. **Pool:** heated outdoor. **Activities:** hot tub, exercise room. **Guest Services:** valet and coin laundry. **Featured Amenity:** breakfast buffet.

SAVE 🍴 ⬆ CALL 🦽 🛏 💺
BIZ HS 📶 ✕ 🔒 🍽 💻

HOLIDAY INN EXPRESS WINDSOR-SONOMA WINE COUNTRY
707/837-0808

🔸🔸🔸 Hotel. **Address:** 8865 Conde Ln 95492

HOLIDAY INN WINDSOR WINE COUNTRY
707/838-8800

🔸🔸🔸 Hotel. **Address:** 8755 Old Redwood Hwy 95492

WHERE TO EAT

KC'S DOWNTOWN GRILL
707/838-7800

🔸🔸 American. Casual Dining. **Address:** 9501 Duvander Ln 95492

KIN WINDSOR
707/837-7546

🔸🔸 California. Casual Dining. **Address:** 740 McClelland Dr 95492

MARY'S PIZZA SHACK
707/836-0900

🔸🔸 Italian. Casual Dining. **Address:** 9010 Brooks Rd 95492

RUSSIAN RIVER BREWING COMPANY
707/545-2338

🔸🔸 American. Brewpub. **Address:** 700 Mitchell Ln 95492

WINE COUNTRY

You're in a basket beneath a hot air balloon, soaring over a two-lane country road cradled in a lush valley. Acre upon acre is planted with neat rows of leafy grapevines, forming pale green pinstripes against the fertile soil. Rose bushes awash in red blooms mark the beginnings of some rows, which extend from the road and seem to disappear into rolling, forested hills. Beyond these hills are dark stands of redwoods, their feathery branches sheltering a damp, fern-carpeted ground, and beyond them rocky cliffs bordering the Pacific. The ride is quiet and seemingly still, following the whim of the wind with only the roar of the burners to break the silence.

"Heaven?" you ask. Close. You're in Wine Country. And while the views in Napa, Sonoma, Lake and Mendocino counties are enough to make you dizzy with delight, the extravagantly verdant countryside isn't for shutterbugs alone.

There's a business growing here, and a fruitful one at that. Every year some 400 wineries produce nearly 2 billion bottles of wine thanks to an ideal, varied climate—balmy days with cool mornings and evenings interspersed with floating blankets of Pacific fog. Add relatively cheap labor and mineral-rich soil, and the bottled result has caught the eyes, noses and palates of wine lovers around the globe.

With all its many fun things to do—hot air ballooning, shopping in elite boutiques, hiking, bicycling, touring historical sites, kayaking, gorging on sinfully delicious gourmet food, horseback riding, relaxing with a massage or sinking into a mud or mineral bath—it still comes as no surprise that most visitors are here for one thing: fermented grape juice. Yes, the sweet nectar of the gods.

It's All About the Wine

Napa Valley's main drag, SR 29—as well as its parallel counterpart, the Silverado Trail—is a north-south valley bisector with stunning mountain views to the east and west. The rural route leads from the town of Napa north through St. Helena's picturesque Main Street to the hot springs and mud bath mecca of Calistoga. Farmers in pickup trucks along with locals in Land Rovers pack the lanes, making way for bicyclists. Small wooden signs facing the road denote grapes grown here: Cabernet Sauvignon, Chardonnay, Chenin Blanc, Merlot, Pinot Noir, Riesling, Sauvignon Blanc or the precious, California-grown Zinfandel.

Large signs proclaim grape owners, names no doubt you've seen adorning labels on wine bottles in your local grocery store—Beringer, Robert Mondavi, Sutter Home and hundreds of others sharing the soil in this world-famous viticultural region.

Peppering the valley floor are magnificent winery estates: orange-hued, postmodern Clos Pegase; Sterling Vineyards' white, Greek island-style stucco building; Oscar-winning director Francis Ford Coppola's giant, gray stone château; the gabled Victorian Rhine House (complete with Art Nouveau-style stained-glass windows) at Beringer Winery; and the simple, California mission-style Robert Mondavi Winery.

Choose a winery—perhaps St. Supéry, Inglenook or Beaulieu—and follow the driveway to a majestic mansion. You'll pass workers tending expansive rows of vines. Among the fun things to do with friends is to take a tour to learn about the delicate art of winemaking, from the plucking of sweet, plump grapes to the long-awaited popping of the cork.

This map shows cities in the Wine Country where you will find attractions, hotels and restaurants. Cities are listed alphabetically in this book on the following pages.

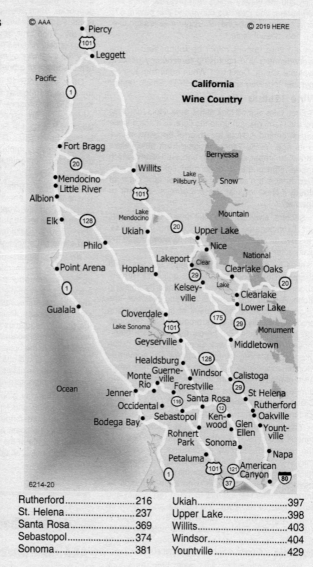

You may be surprised to find how scientific the process is; long gone are the days when ladies tied up their skirts, removed their shoes and stomped on juicy grapes until their toes turned purple. Winemaking is a complicated, subjective blend of technology, nature and experience. Biologists, chemists and winemakers each have a hand in the steps from grape to glass.

After you've walked through a vineyard, felt the cold steel of a giant, shiny fermentation tank, smelled the scent of grapes fermenting, watched bottles clattering along an assembly line and glimpsed the winery's high-tech presses, filters and computers, you might be convinced that paying $75 for a bottle of Cabernet Sauvignon is reasonable. But how does it *taste?*

First-time tasters might be intimidated by the overwhelming and confusing terminology used to evaluate wines. Don't fret! When sampling, just remember four little words: Look. Swirl. Smell. Taste.

Wine Tasting 101

First, take a good look at the wine. Hold the glass (by the stem, please) up to the light, or place a white napkin behind it. Note the *color* of the wine, a clue to its age. White wines, ranging from pale yellow (straw) to amber, darken with age. Red wines, which appear light purple to deep ruby, lighten with age. Also notice the *clarity* of the wine. Is it clear or cloudy? Next look at the *brightness*—brilliant or opaque?

Second, swirl the wine. Not only is this quite fun, but it oxygenates the wine, releasing its aromas. Observe its *legs,* little drops running down inside the glass after it's swirled.

Now hold the glass under your nose and sniff sharply. (Don't worry, everyone's doing it.) Remark about its *nose*—the scent determined by smelling alone. A good nose reveals a strong *bouquet*—the fragrance acquired as a result of the wine's aging process. Usually, the more prominent the bouquet, the older the wine. But here's the best part: determining the wine's *aroma.* Scents recall the grape used to make the wine, and there are numerous aromas associated with each varietal. They range from grapefruit to cream to butterscotch for a Chardonnay, mint to grass to apricot for a Sauvignon Blanc, and blackberry to cloves to olives for a Zinfandel.

Take a big drink of the wine. Let it flow over your tongue and chew it like pasta, allowing it to reach all the taste buds. Identify its *taste*—a Chenin Blanc may suggest red apple, while a Cabernet Sauvignon might hint of cedar. Determine the *balance* (how the flavors combine): A good wine evenly blends its sugar, tannins (astringents found in red wines) and fruit. Observe the *body,* the way the liquid feels on your tongue. This may range from thin and light to full and heavy. Finally, swallow and note the *length* or *finish,* the aftertaste: How long does it last, and how does the taste differ from the initial flavor?

Sound confusing? It just takes time, as it took time for this region to become famous for its wine.

Missionary Padre José Altimira brought vine cuttings to the Sonoma Valley in 1823 to make wine for Catholic mass, but it was Hungarian nobleman "Count" Agoston Haraszthy who created the California wine industry as we know it. In 1857 he planted European varieties and established Buena Vista, the state's oldest winery. You'll find the original, ivy-clad stone buildings tucked away near the town of Sonoma, where this winery shares a quiet, rustic road alongside homes, farms and vineyards.

Take a relaxed bike ride along Sonoma's streets and you may catch a glimpse of one of the resident peacocks, often seen parading along Lovall Valley Road. Pedal to Sebastiani Vineyards & Winery for a sample. Then tour Sonoma State Historic Park, a group of historic sites near Sonoma Plaza. Together they tell the story of early "Alta" California and the establishment of a brief, 26-day California Republic.

Drive along SR 12, Sonoma Valley's main drag, for more tastings at Benziger Family Winery or Kunde Family Winery. The vintners at these two establishments are especially friendly and easygoing. West of SR 12, the Russian River Wine Road traverses the Russian River Valley, where vineyards and Gravenstein apple orchards cover hillsides, redwoods form magnificent groves and a lazy river flows.

Take a break from wine and head to Petaluma, where there are enough brightly colored Victorians to make your jaw drop; to Santa Rosa for gorgeous gardens; or to Healdsburg for scads of antique shops and art galleries. Or pack your fishing pole and stake out a spot at giant Clear Lake.

And by all means do not pass up the chance to explore the spectacular Pacific coast, which offers so many wonderful things to see. Mendocino, an artsy, laid-back hamlet with adorable New England-style architecture, rests on bluffs overlooking the steel blue ocean. Rainbow-colored wildflowers dot the grassy headlands in spring, and eruptive white water crashes against jagged ocean rocks. Daytrippers have the option of hiking, kayaking or horseback riding, and a coastal drive along winding SR 1 is sure to elicit gasps and awestruck grins on the faces of photographers, artists and nature buffs.

To end the day, stop by a deli, bakery or roadside produce stand and fill a picnic basket with homegrown and homemade delicacies. Find a quiet spot to relax on the coast and watch the sunset. Pull the cork on a bottle of the area's claim to fame, make a toast and drink it all up.

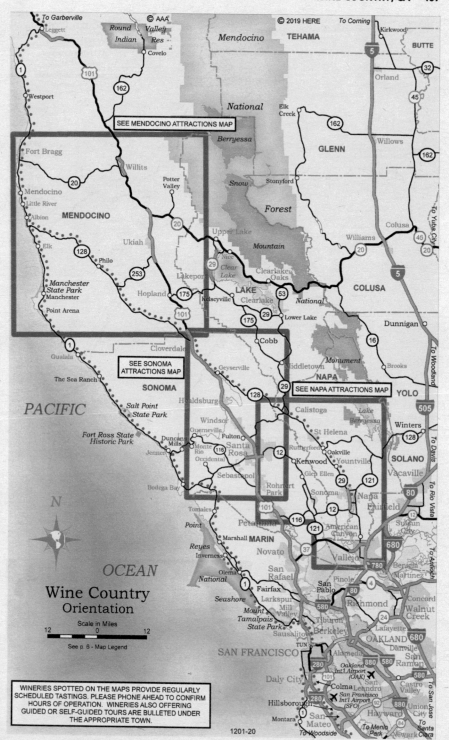

SEE MENDOCINO ATTRACTIONS MAP

SEE SONOMA ATTRACTIONS MAP

SEE NAPA ATTRACTIONS MAP

PACIFIC

OCEAN

Wine Country
Orientation

Scale in Miles

12   0   12

See p. 6 - Map Legend

N

WINERIES SPOTTED ON THE MAPS PROVIDE REGULARLY
SCHEDULED TASTINGS. PLEASE PHONE AHEAD TO CONFIRM
HOURS OF OPERATION. WINERIES ALSO OFFERING
GUIDED OR SELF-GUIDED TOURS ARE BULLETED UNDER
THE APPROPRIATE TOWN.

1201-20

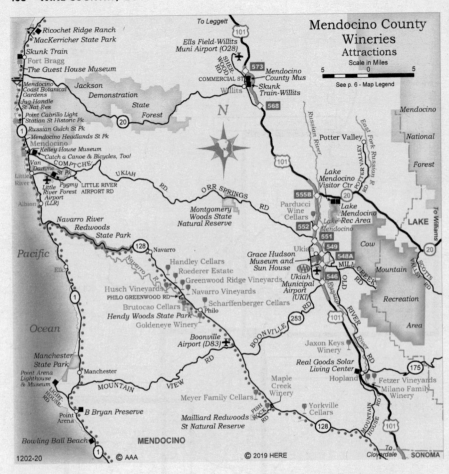

Mendocino County Wineries
Attractions

Scale in Miles

See p. 6 - Map Legend

Share the security and savings with those you love

Add drivers in your household as Associate members and give them the same great benefits you trust and enjoy.

Add an Associate membership today:
- Online at AAA.com/membership
- Visit your local club office
- Call 800-Join-AAA (564-6222)

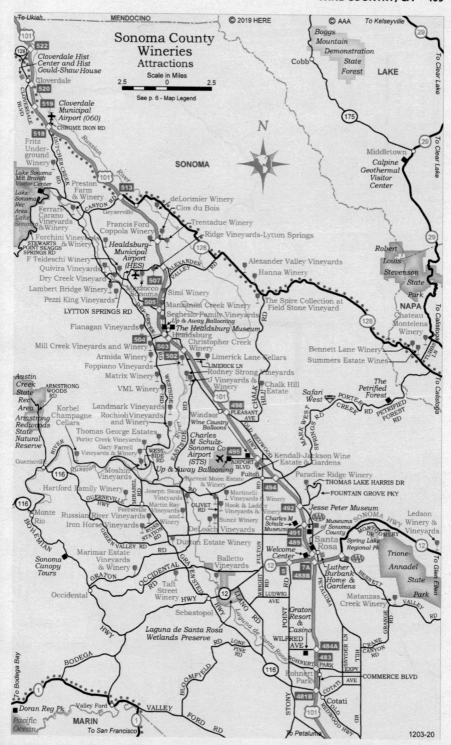

Sonoma County
Wineries
Attractions

Scale in Miles

2.5   0   2.5

See p. 6 - Map Legend

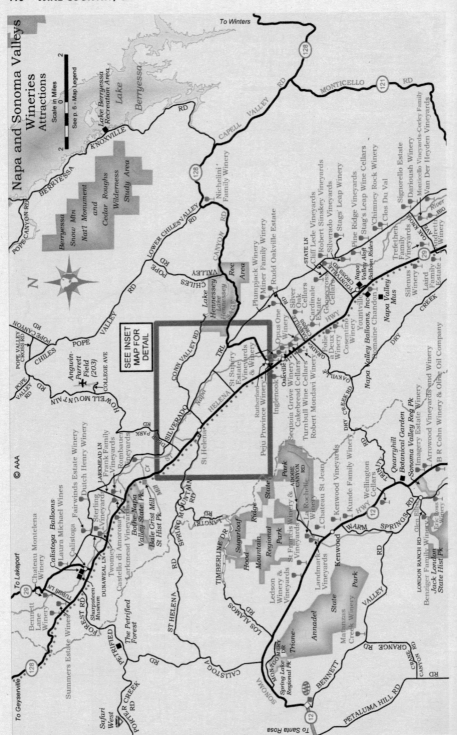

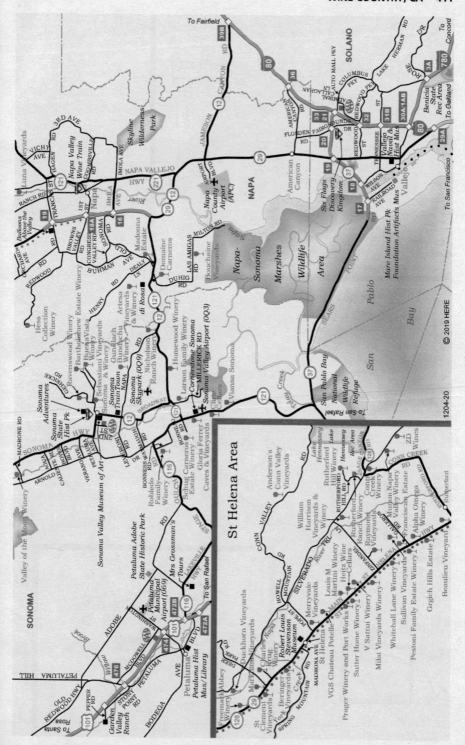

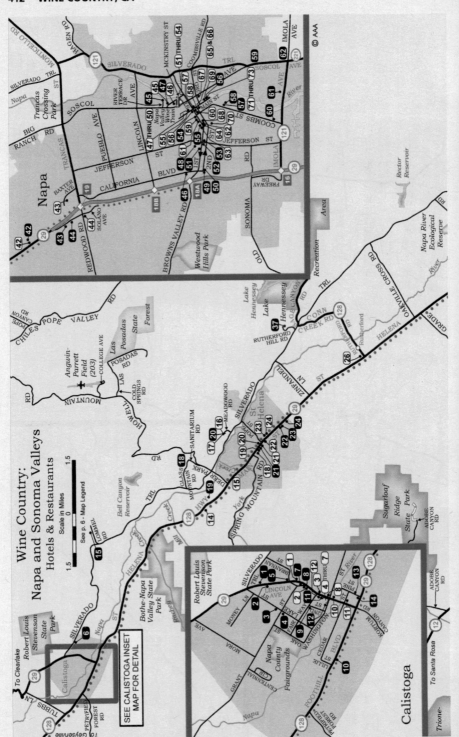

Wine Country:
Napa and Sonoma Valleys
Hotels & Restaurants

See p. 6 · Map Legend

Scale in Miles

1.5   0   1.5

SEE CALISTOGA INSET
MAP FOR DETAIL

Napa

Calistoga

© AAA

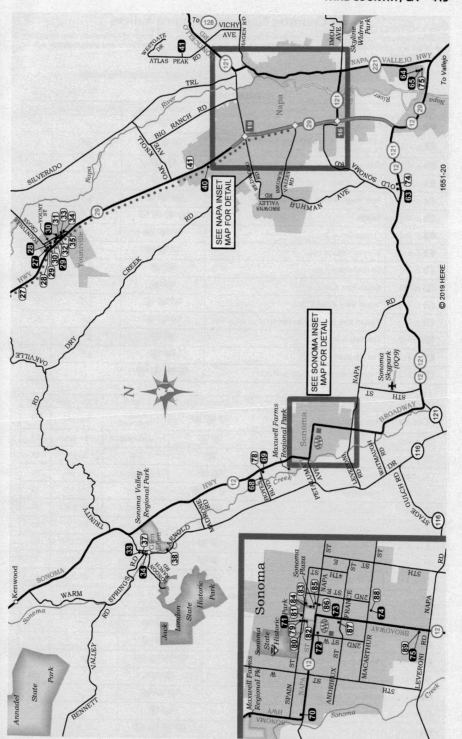

1651-20

Wine Country: Napa and Sonoma Valleys

This index helps you "spot" where approved hotels and restaurants are located on the corresponding detailed maps. Restaurant price range is a combination of lunch and/or dinner. Turn to the listing page for more information and consult display ads for special promotions.

 For more details, rates and reservations: AAA.com/travelguides/hotels

CALISTOGA

Map Page	Hotels	Diamond Rated	Member Savings	Page
1 p. 412	**Calistoga Motor Lodge and Spa**	♦♦♦	✔	51
2 p. 412	**UpValley Inn & Hot Springs, an Ascend Hotel Collection Member**	♦♦♦	✔	52
3 p. 412	Golden Haven Hot Springs	♦♦		51
4 p. 412	Carlin's Cottage Court	♦♦		51
5 p. 412	**Best Western Plus Stevenson Manor**	♦♦♦	✔	51
6 p. 412	**Solage**	♦♦♦♦	✔	52
7 p. 412	Cottage Grove Inn	♦♦♦		51
8 p. 412	Brannan Cottage Inn	♦♦♦		51
9 p. 412	Chelsea Garden Inn	♦♦		51
10 p. 412	Aurora Park Cottages	♦♦		51
11 p. 412	**Mount View Hotel & Spa**	♦♦♦	✔	52
12 p. 412	**Roman Spa Hot Springs Resort** (See ad p. 52.)	♦♦♦	✔	52
13 p. 412	**EuroSpa & Inn**	♦♦	✔	51
14 p. 412	**The Bergson**	♦♦	✔	51
15 p. 412	Calistoga Ranch, an Auberge Resort	♦♦♦♦		51

Map Page	Restaurants	Diamond Rated	Cuisine	Price Range	Page
1 p. 412	Sam's Social Club	♦♦♦	Pacific Northwest	$20-$42	53
2 p. 412	Sushi Mambo	♦♦	Japanese	$4-$24	53
3 p. 412	Palisades Deli Cafe	♦	Deli	$6-$11	53
4 p. 412	Johnny's	♦♦	California	$12-$44	53
5 p. 412	Evangeline	♦♦♦	French	$19-$34	53
6 p. 412	Cafe Sarafornia	♦♦	Breakfast	$7-$16	53
7 p. 412	Hydro Bar & Grill	♦♦	American	$8-$20	53
8 p. 412	All Seasons Bistro	♦♦	American	$10-$29	52
11 p. 412	Lovina	♦♦	American	$16-$38	53
12 p. 412	Lincoln Avenue Brewery Calistoga	♦♦	American	$9-$12	53

ST. HELENA

Map Page	Hotels	Diamond Rated	Member Savings	Page
18 p. 412	Spanish Villa Inn	♦♦♦		237
19 p. 412	Wine Country Inn	♦♦♦		237
20 p. 412	**Meadowood Napa Valley**	♦♦♦♦	✔	237
21 p. 412	Hotel St. Helena	♦♦		237
22 p. 412	Vineyard Country Inn	♦♦♦		237
23 p. 412	El Bonita Motel	♦♦		237
24 p. 412	Harvest Inn	♦♦♦♦		237

Map Page	Restaurants	Diamond Rated	Cuisine	Price Range	Page
(14) p. 412	Brasswood Bar + Kitchen	◆◆◆	California	$20-$42	237
(15) p. 412	Gatehouse Restaurant	◆◆◆	California	$35-$55	237
(16) p. 412	**The Grill at Meadowood**	◆◆◆	California	$24-$48	238
(17) p. 412	The Restaurant at Meadowood	◆◆◆◆◆	New American	$285-$500	238
(18) p. 412	The Model Bakery	◆	Breads/Pastries Sandwiches	$4-$11	238
(19) p. 412	**Market**	◆◆◆	American	$15-$36	238
(20) p. 412	Himalayan Sherpa Kitchen	◆◆	Indian	$12-$26	238
(21) p. 412	Goose & Gander	◆◆◆	American	$13-$52	237
(22) p. 412	Gott's Roadside	◆	American	$8-$17	237
(23) p. 412	The Charter Oak	◆◆◆	California	$20-$55	237
(24) p. 412	Farmstead at Long Meadow Ranch	◆◆◆	Pacific Northwest	$19-$29	237

YOUNTVILLE

Map Page	Hotels	Diamond Rated	Member Savings	Page
(27) p. 412	Napa Valley Lodge	◆◆◆◆		429
(28) p. 412	Lavender	◆◆◆		429
(29) p. 412	Maison Fleurie	◆◆		429
(30) p. 412	Bardessono Hotel & Spa	◆◆◆◆		429

Map Page	Restaurants	Diamond Rated	Cuisine	Price Range	Page
(27) p. 412	Mustards Grill	◆◆◆	American	$13-$38	429
(28) p. 412	R+D Kitchen	◆◆◆	California	$14-$32	429
(29) p. 412	**The French Laundry**	◆◆◆◆◆	American	$310	429
(30) p. 412	Bouchon	◆◆◆	French	$19-$60	429
(31) p. 412	La Calenda	◆◆◆	Mexican	$7-$29	429
(32) p. 412	Bottega Napa Valley	◆◆◆	Italian	$17-$36	429
(33) p. 412	Bistro Jeanty	◆◆◆	French	$14-$41	429
(34) p. 412	Ad Hoc	◆◆◆	American	$33-$55	429
(35) p. 412	Coqueta Napa Valley	◆◆◆	Spanish	$10-$48	429

GLEN ELLEN

Map Page	Hotels	Diamond Rated	Member Savings	Page
(33) p. 412	Gaige House + Ryokan	◆◆◆		97
(34) p. 412	Jack London Lodge	◆◆		97

Map Page	Restaurants	Diamond Rated	Cuisine	Price Range	Page
(37) p. 412	Glen Ellen Star	◆◆◆	American	$11-$30	97
(38) p. 412	Yeti Restaurant	◆◆	Indian	$14-$36	97

RUTHERFORD

Map Page	Hotel	Diamond Rated	Member Savings	Page
(37) p. 412	Auberge du Soleil	◆◆◆◆		216

Map Page	Restaurant	Diamond Rated	Cuisine	Price Range	Page
(26) p. 412	Rutherford Grill	◆◆◆	American	$15-$48	216

NAPA

Map Page	Hotels	Diamond Rated	Member Savings	Page
(40) p. 412	Hotel Indigo - Napa Valley	◆◆◆		166

NAPA (cont'd)

Map Page	Hotels (cont'd)	Diamond Rated	Member Savings	Page
41 p. 412	**Silverado Resort and Spa**	◆◆◆◆	✔	166
42 p. 412	**Napa Winery Inn**	◆◆◆	✔	166
43 p. 412	Hilton Garden Inn-NAPA	◆◆◆	✔	166
44 p. 412	Napa Valley Marriott Hotel & Spa	◆◆◆	✔	166
45 p. 412	**River Terrace Inn**	◆◆◆	✔	166
46 p. 412	**Embassy Suites by Hilton Napa Valley**	◆◆◆	✔	165
47 p. 412	**The Westin Verasa Napa**	◆◆◆◆	✔	167
48 p. 412	The Napa Inn	◆◆◆		166
49 p. 412	**Bel Abri**	◆◆◆	✔	165
50 p. 412	**Best Western Plus Elm House Inn**	◆◆◆	✔	165
51 p. 412	**The Inn on First**	◆◆◆	✔	166
52 p. 412	1801 First Inn	◆◆◆		165
53 p. 412	Blackbird Inn	◆◆◆		165
54 p. 412	**Archer Hotel Napa**	◆◆◆◆	✔	165
55 p. 412	**Andaz Napa**	◆◆◆	✔	165
56 p. 412	Napa River Inn	◆◆◆		166
57 p. 412	Cedar Gables Inn	◆◆◆		165
58 p. 412	Churchill Manor	◆◆◆		165
59 p. 412	**Hawthorn Suites by Wyndham**	◆◆	✔	166
60 p. 412	Wine Valley Lodge	◆◆		167
61 p. 412	Hampton Inn & Suites Napa	◆◆◆	✔	166
62 p. 412	**Best Western Plus Inn at the Vines**	◆◆◆	✔	165
63 p. 412	Carneros Resort and Spa	◆◆◆◆		165
64 p. 412	**Vista Collina Resort**	◆◆◆◆	✔	167
65 p. 412	**The Meritage Resort and Spa**	◆◆◆◆	✔	166

Map Page	Restaurants	Diamond Rated	Cuisine	Price Range	Page
41 p. 412	Bistro Don Giovanni	◆◆◆	Italian	$19-$45	167
42 p. 412	Galpao Gaucho Brazilian Steakhouse	◆◆	Brazilian Steak	$39-$60	167
43 p. 412	Heritage Eats	◆	International Sandwiches	$10-$12	167
44 p. 412	La Taquiza Fish Tacos	◆	Mexican	$4-$15	167
45 p. 412	La Toque	◆◆◆◆	New French	$110-$220	167
46 p. 412	**Napa Valley Wine Train** *(See ad p. 164.)*	◆◆◆	Continental	$141-$161	167
47 p. 412	Napa Valley Bistro	◆◆◆	New American	$14-$33	167
48 p. 412	Azzurro Pizzeria E Enoteca	◆◆	Italian Pizza	$18-$22	167
49 p. 412	Mango on Main	◆◆	Thai	$9-$17	167
50 p. 412	TORC	◆◆◆	California	$21-$51	168
51 p. 412	Hog Island Oyster Bar Napa	◆◆	Seafood	$12-$56	167
52 p. 412	C Casa	◆	New Mexican	$6-$23	167

Map Page	Restaurants (cont'd)	Diamond Rated	Cuisine	Price Range	Page
53 p. 412	Kitchen Door	◈◈◈	New American	$16-$25	167
54 p. 412	Gott's Roadside	◈	Burgers	$10-$17	167
55 p. 412	Cole's Chop House	◈◈◈	Steak	$34-$65	167
56 p. 412	Ristorante Allegria	◈◈◈	Italian	$16-$38	168
57 p. 412	Bounty Hunter	◈◈◈	Barbecue	$14-$38	167
58 p. 412	Ca' Momi Osteria	◈◈◈	Italian	$16-$32	167
59 p. 412	Charlie Palmer Steak Napa	◈◈◈	Steak	$27-$75	167
60 p. 412	Small World Cafe & Restaurant	◈	Middle Eastern	$8-$14	168
61 p. 412	Eiko's	◈◈	Japanese Sushi	$16-$42	167
62 p. 412	Norman Rose Tavern	◈◈	Comfort Food	$10-$28	167
63 p. 412	Tarla Mediterranean Bar and Grill	◈◈	Mediterranean	$16-$39	168
64 p. 412	Oenotri	◈◈◈	Italian	$13-$38	168
65 p. 412	Napkins Bar & Grill	◈◈	American	$12-$39	167
66 p. 412	Zuzu	◈◈	Spanish	$8-$36	168
67 p. 412	Stone Brewing - Napa	◈◈	California	$13-$28	168
68 p. 412	Grace's Table	◈◈	California Comfort Food	$11-$31	167
69 p. 412	Morimoto Napa	◈◈◈	Japanese	$18-$90	167
70 p. 412	Alexis Baking Company and Cafe	◈◈	Breakfast	$7-$17	167
71 p. 412	Celadon	◈◈◈	American	$17-$46	167
72 p. 412	Napa General Store	◈◈	American	$12-$18	167
73 p. 412	Angele	◈◈◈	French	$12-$39	167
74 p. 412	Boon Fly Cafe	◈◈	California	$14-$28	167
75 p. 412	Siena	◈◈◈	American	$12-$55	168

SONOMA

Map Page	Hotels	Diamond Rated	Member Savings	Page
68 p. 412	Sonoma Creek Inn	◈◈		383
69 p. 412	**The Fairmont Sonoma Mission Inn & Spa**	◈◈◈◈	✔	382
70 p. 412	**El Pueblo Inn**	◈◈◈	✔	382
71 p. 412	Sonoma Hotel	◈◈◈		383
72 p. 412	**Best Western Sonoma Valley Inn & Krug Event Center**	◈◈◈	✔	382
73 p. 412	Inn at Sonoma	◈◈◈		382
74 p. 412	MacArthur Place	◈◈◈◈		383
75 p. 412	**The Lodge at Sonoma, A Renaissance Resort & Spa**	◈◈◈	✔	383

Map Page	Restaurants	Diamond Rated	Cuisine	Price Range	Page
78 p. 412	**Santé**	◈◈◈◈	California	$34-$55	383
79 p. 412	the girl & the fig	◈◈◈	French	$14-$37	383
80 p. 412	El Dorado Kitchen	◈◈◈	California	$15-$32	383

Map Page	Restaurants (cont'd)	Diamond Rated	Cuisine	Price Range	Page
🟤81 p. 412	Swiss Hotel Restaurant	❤️❤️❤️	Swiss	$11-$34	383
🟤82 p. 412	Sunflower Caffe Espresso & Wine Bar	❤️❤️	American	$9-$16	383
🟤83 p. 412	La Casa Restaurant & Bar	❤️❤️	Mexican	$10-$22	383
🟤84 p. 412	LaSalette Restaurant	❤️❤️❤️	Portuguese	$11-$28	383
🟤85 p. 412	Cafe La Haye	❤️❤️❤️	California	$19-$39	383
🟤86 p. 412	Della Santina's	❤️❤️❤️	Italian	$16-$33	383
🟤87 p. 412	HopMonk Tavern Sonoma	❤️❤️❤️	American	$13-$25	383
🟤88 p. 412	Layla Restaurant	❤️❤️❤️	Mediterranean	$21-$68	383
🟤89 p. 412	**Carneros Bistro & Wine Bar**	❤️❤️❤️	California	$10-$38	383

WOODLAND (A-9) pop. 55,468, elev. 65'

First known as Yolo City, Woodland was a gold rush town established in 1861. Downtown at Main and Second streets is the Woodland Opera House. The original building, built in 1885, burned down in 1892 when a major fire destroyed much of the downtown area. The opera house was rebuilt and was the site of theatrical productions until 1913, after which the building remained boarded up for almost 60 years. Saved from the wrecking ball by the county historical society, the restored brick opera house presents live entertainment throughout the year; phone (530) 666-9617 for event information.

Gibson House Yolo County Historical Museum, 512 Gibson Rd., occupies a Classical Revival-style mansion. Three outbuildings and a barn with historical exhibits also are on the grounds; phone (530) 666-1045. At the Woodland Museum of Biblical Archaeology, 240 N. West St., guided tours provide information about more than 200 excavated artifacts and antiquities dating from 4000 B.C. to 200 A.D. and how the items relate to stories in the Bible; phone (530) 662-1675.

Reiff's Retro Automobile Gas Station Museum is rather hard to miss, courtesy of the car crashed into the garage and a Cessna that appears to have landed on the roof. Gas station memorabilia, antique gas pumps and more than 200 vintage gas station signs are displayed indoors and out, and there are re-creations of a gas station, a general store, a diner and a vintage movie theater. Guided tours are given by appointment only and reservations are required; phone (530) 666-1758.

The Woodland Farmer's Market offers a summer bonanza of locally grown fruits and vegetables, fresh eggs and artisan breads. There are two locations: at Woodland Healthcare, 1325 Cottonwood St. (Tues. 4:30-7 p.m., June through August), and across from the public library at First and Court streets (Sat. 9-noon, mid-May to mid-October).

Woodland Chamber of Commerce: 307 First St., Woodland, CA 95695. **Phone:** (530) 662-7327.

BEST WESTERN SHADOW INN   530/666-1251

Hotel

AAA Benefit: Members save up to 15% and earn bonus points!

Address: 584 N East St 95776 **Location:** I-5 exit 538, just w. Located behind Chevron station. **Facility:** 119 units. 2 stories, exterior corridors. **Pool:** heated outdoor. **Activities:** hot tub. **Guest Services:** coin laundry. **Featured Amenity:** continental breakfast.

COMFORT SUITES WOODLAND SACRAMENTO AIRPORT   530/723-5900

❤️❤️❤️ Hotel. **Address:** 2080 Freeway Dr 95776

DAYS INN   530/666-3800

❤️❤️ Hotel. **Address:** 1524 E Main St 95776

FAIRFIELD INN & SUITES BY MARRIOTT SACRAMENTO AIRPORT WOODLAND   530/723-5067

❤️❤️❤️ [SAVE] Hotel. **Address:** 2100 Freeway Dr 95776

AAA Benefit: Members save 5% or more!

HAMPTON INN & SUITES WOODLAND/SACRAMENTO AREA   530/662-9100

Hotel

AAA Benefit: Members save up to 15%!

Address: 2060 Freeway Dr 95776 **Location:** I-5 exit 536 (CR 102), just n, just e on E Main St, then just s. **Facility:** 71 units. 3 stories, interior corridors. **Pool:** outdoor. **Activities:** hot tub, limited exercise equipment. **Guest Services:** valet and coin laundry. **Featured Amenity:** full hot breakfast.

HOLIDAY INN EXPRESS HOTEL & SUITES   530/662-7750

❤️❤️❤️ Hotel. **Address:** 2070 Freeway Dr 95776

WHERE TO EAT

THE BURGER SALOON   530/668-2747
♦♦ Burgers. Casual Dining. **Address:** 601 Main St 95695

EL CHARRO MEXICAN RESTAURANT   530/661-3166
♦♦ Mexican. Casual Dining. **Address:** 415-417 Main St 95695

KITCHEN 428   530/661-0428
♦♦ New American. Casual Dining. **Address:** 428 1st St 95695

MORGAN'S ON MAIN   530/402-1275
♦♦ New American. Casual Dining. **Address:** 614 Main St 95695

WOODSIDE (E-8) pop. 5,287, elev. 382'
• Hotels & Restaurants map & index p. 316

Woodside was founded in 1849, when the gold rush drastically increased the size and population of San Francisco. The wood needed for wharves, houses and commercial buildings was harvested from virgin redwood forests in this part of San Mateo County, and at one time there were 14 lumber mills in the vicinity.

FILOLI is off I-280 via Edgewood Rd. to Cañada Rd. This country estate was built over a 2-year period beginning in 1915 for prominent San Franciscans Mr. and Mrs. William B. Bourn II. The property includes a beautiful, 16-acre formal English Renaissance garden. The elegant, Georgian-style house is decorated with a large collection of 17th- and 18th-century English antiques. Docent-led nature hikes and orchard walks are offered.

Time: Allow 2 hours minimum. **Hours:** Grounds open Tues.-Sun. 10-5 (also 5-8 in summer), mid-Feb. to late Oct. Guided, 2-hour house and garden tours are given Tues.-Sat. at 10:30 and 1. Last admission 30 minutes before closing. Other tours are offered; phone for details. Nature hikes depart Sat. at 10, mid-May to mid-Nov. with select days off in summer; Orchard walks offered on select days June-Oct. Closed major holidays. Phone ahead to confirm schedule. **Cost:** $20; $17 (ages 65+); $10 (ages 5-17 and students with ID). An additional fee may be charged during special events. House and garden tour $10; reservations are required. **Phone:** (650) 364-8300, ext. 507. [¶]

THE VILLAGE PUB   650/851-9888   (97)
♦♦ ♦♦ New American. Fine Dining. **Address:** 2967 Woodside Rd 94062

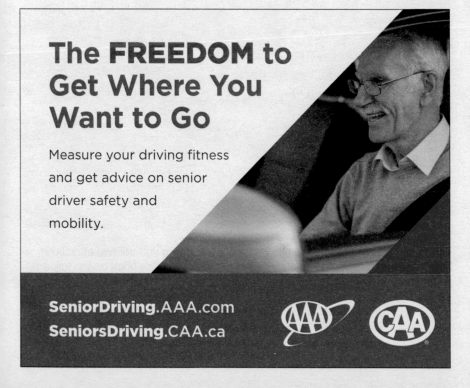

YOSEMITE NATIONAL PARK (F-4)

- Hotels p. 429 • Restaurants p. 429
- Attractions map p. 423
- Hotels & Restaurants map & index p. 426

Elevations in the park range from 2,000 ft. at the park boundary at El Portal on SR 140 to 13,014 ft. at the summit of Mount Lyell. Refer to AAA maps for additional elevation information.

Reached by SR 140 (El Portal Road) from Merced, SR 41 (Wawona Road) from Fresno, and SR 120 (Big Oak Flat Road) from Stockton, Yosemite National Park lies in central California on the western slope of the Sierra Nevada in a region of unusual beauty.

Glaciers transformed the rolling hills and meandering streams of pre-Pleistocene Yosemite into the colossal landscape of the present. And although Indian tribes lived in the Yosemite area for thousands of years, the first non-Indian visit was probably made by the Joseph Walker expedition in 1833.

It was not until 1851, however, before the existence of the magnificent valley became well known. The Mariposa Battalion was sent to the area that year to extinguish an ongoing conflict between gold miners seeking their fortune and the resident American Indians. The battalion entered Yosemite Valley at Inspiration Point, and word of the land's beauty quickly spread.

To preserve it for posterity, Abraham Lincoln set aside the Mariposa grove of giant sequoias in the Yosemite Valley as the nation's first state park on June 30, 1864. John Muir, one of America's earliest and foremost naturalists and conservationists, tirelessly advocated federal park status for Yosemite Valley and its surroundings, and 26 years later, in 1890, Yosemite became a national park.

The park is much greater both in area and beauty than most people generally realize; Yosemite Valley actually comprises only a very small portion of park land. The territory above the rim of the valley is less celebrated principally because it is less well-known. However, 196 miles of primary roads and more than 800 miles of trails now make much of this mountain region easily accessible to both motorist and hiker.

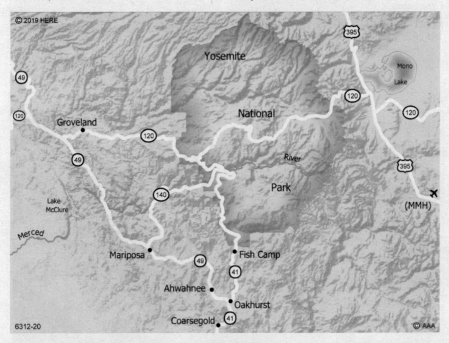

This map shows cities in Yosemite National Park where you will find attractions, hotels and restaurants. Cities are listed alphabetically in this book on the following pages.

(See map & index p. 426.)

The crest of the Sierra Nevada is the park's eastern boundary, and the two rivers that flow through the park—the Merced and Tuolumne—originate among the snowy peaks. The Merced River flows through Yosemite Valley, and the Tuolumne River carves a magnificent gorge through the northern half of the park. Though spectacular through most of the year, many of the park's famous waterfalls are often dry during the late summer months.

With the exception of the Tioga Pass Road portion of SR 120, the Glacier Point Road and the Mariposa Grove Road, all of which are closed late fall through early summer, all roads are open year-round; chains may be required at any time during winter months.

The road to Mirror Lake and Happy Isles, at the eastern end of Yosemite Valley, is closed to most cars but is served by a free shuttle bus. Southside Drive is one-way eastbound from Bridalveil Fall to Half Dome Village; Northside Drive is one-way westbound from the Yosemite Valley Lodge; and the road between Half Dome Village and Yosemite Village also is one-way westbound.

General Information and Activities

Yosemite National Park is open daily all year. Many roads in Yosemite Valley are one-way, and traffic can be heavy, especially in summer. Maps and information are available at the park's four visitor centers, and schedules of events are provided at park entrances and posted throughout the valley. A free shuttle bus operates in the east end of the valley daily 7 a.m.-10 p.m., in summer; hours vary rest of year. In the winter a shuttle runs from Yosemite Valley Lodge to the Yosemite Ski & Snowboard Area.

Wilderness permits, required of all overnight backpackers, are free at the Yosemite Valley Visitor Center or at any other wilderness permit station. Some stations are open seasonally; phone ahead to confirm locations and hours. Reservations also are available for a fee of $5 per reservation plus $5 per person if obtained by phone or mail; phone (209) 372-0740. To make reservations by mail write Wilderness Association, P.O. Box 545, Yosemite, CA 95389. For information about wilderness permits phone (209) 372-0200.

A California fishing license is required for all park waters; an annual permit costs $49.94 for residents. A 10-day non-resident pass also is $49.94. A 2-day resident or non-resident license costs $25.10. Information about bicycle rentals is available at Half Dome Village and the Yosemite Valley Lodge; tour bus information also is given at these spots as well as at all lodging facilities.

Ranger-naturalists conduct year-round nature walks that last from a half-hour to 2 hours; snowshoe walks are available in the winter. Evening programs are presented all year at the Yosemite Valley Lodge, and in summer at Half Dome Village, Lower Pines, Glacier Point, Tuolumne Meadows, Crane Flat, Wawona and White Wolf campgrounds.

An open-air tram offers frequent 2-hour tours of the valley during summer and occasional trips after Labor Day; reservations can be made at The Majestic Yosemite Hotel, Half Dome Village and the Yosemite Valley Lodge. Other tours depart daily in summer to Glacier Point and Mariposa Grove. Guided horseback tours of Wawona, Tuolumne Meadows and the valley also are available, as are multiday saddle and pack trips. A hiker shuttle goes to Glacier Point and Tuolumne Meadows.

Self-guiding tours of a re-created Ahwahneechee Indian village as well as a historic cemetery are available at Yosemite Village in Yosemite Valley. A museum houses photographs and historic books, while the artifacts in the Indian Cultural Exhibit depict the history of the Miwok and Paiute. A visitor center, a theater and an art center also are found in the village.

Skiing and skating can be enjoyed in winter. Half Dome Village has an outdoor skating rink; Yosemite Ski & Snowboard Area has downhill and cross-country skiing. Cross-country ski trails lead from the Yosemite Ski & Snowboard and Crane Flat areas. Snowshoe tours are offered.

Child care is available in winter at Yosemite Ski & Snowboard Area. During summer the Junior Ranger Program of nature walks and classes welcomes students in grades 3 through 6; phone (209) 372-0200.

Campground reservations are available through the National Recreation Reservation System; phone (877) 444-6777, or TTY (877) 833-6777. See Recreation Areas Chart.

The main visitor center in Yosemite Valley is open year-round. Additional visitor information can be obtained at Big Oak Flat, Tuolumne Meadows and Wawona centers that usually are open June through September; for recorded information about camping, roads, weather conditions and recreation, phone (209) 372-0200.

ADMISSION to the park is by $35 private vehicle fee ($25, Nov.-Mar.), $30 per motorcycle or $20 per person arriving by other means, and is good for 7 days.

PETS are not allowed on the trails or in public buildings and accommodations and must be leashed at all times. Pets are permitted in Upper Pines in Yosemite Valley, the west end of the campground at Tuolumne Meadows, and at White Wolf (Section C), Bridalveil (Section A), Crane Flat (Section A), Wawona, Hodgdon Meadows and Yosemite Creek campgrounds. Dogs can be boarded in Yosemite Valley from late May to mid-October.

ADDRESS inquiries concerning the park to the Superintendent, Yosemite National Park, P.O. Box 577, Yosemite National Park, CA 95389. Phone (209) 372-0200.

INSIDER INFO:
High-Altitude Health

Temples throbbing, gasping for breath and nauseated, you barely notice the scudding clouds or the spectacular view.

(See map & index p. 426.)

You might be suffering from Acute Mountain Sickness (AMS). Usually striking at around 8,000 feet (2,450 meters) in altitude, AMS is your body's way of coping with the reduced oxygen and humidity of high altitudes. Among the symptoms are headaches, shortness of breath, loss of appetite, insomnia and lethargy. Some people complain of temporary weight gain or swelling in the face, hands and feet.

You can reduce the effect of high altitude by being in top condition. If you smoke or suffer from heart or lung ailments, consult your physician before your trip. Certain drugs will intensify the symptoms. To avoid Acute Mountain Sickness, adjust to elevations slowly; a gradual ascent with a couple days of acclimatization is best if you have time. For example, if you are planning a trip to the Rocky Mountains of Colorado, you might want to spend the first night in a lower altitude city such as Denver as opposed to heading directly to an environment with extreme elevations.

On the way up, eat light, nutritious meals and stay hydrated by drinking a large amount of water and taking care to avoid caffeine, alcohol and salt. In addition, your doctor may be able to prescribe medication that can offset the effects at high altitude.

If you develop AMS, you should stop ascending; you will recover in a few days. If the AMS is mild, a quick descent will end the suffering immediately.

Other high-altitude health problems include sunburn and hypothermia. Dress in layers to protect yourself from the intense sun and wide fluctuations in temperature.

Finally, after you lounge in the sauna or whirlpool bath at your lodgings, remember to stand up carefully, for the heat has relaxed your blood vessels and lowered your blood pressure.

GLACIER POINT is 30 mi. from Yosemite Valley via Wawona Rd. to Chinquapin, then continuing on Glacier Point Rd. to the lookout point. The spectacularly scenic panorama embraces domes, pinnacles, waterfalls and—dominating all—the granite monolith Half Dome. From the stone lookout you can study the detail of the distant High Sierra and its flanking ranges. On the valley floor 3,214 feet below, automobiles appear as moving specks, and the Merced River resembles a silver thread.

The paved road to the point winds through pine and fir forests. In summer, bus tours and hiker shuttles to the point are available and ranger-naturalists are on duty. A 1.5-mile walk from the parking area leads to 8,122-foot Sentinel Dome. **Hours:** The road to Glacier Point normally is open late May through October; it is closed in winter past Badger Pass.

THE GRAND CANYON OF THE TUOLUMNE can be traversed only on foot; Waterwheel Falls is accessible by a trail 6 mi. from Tioga Rd. along the Tuolumne River Gorge to Glen Aulin High Sierra Camp, then 3 mi. down the river. At Waterwheel Falls the rushing river hits shelves of projecting rock with terrific force, throwing enormous arcs of water into the air; this spectacle is best viewed mid-June to mid-July.

Below the falls the river descends abruptly, plunging through a mile-deep gorge. Trails lead to Pate Valley, where only ancient mortar holes remain as a reminder of the Native Americans who once lived in this region. North of the Tuolumne River is a vast expanse of lakes and valleys. Although crisscrossed by numerous trails, this area is not often visited and offers a true wilderness experience. Hikers should inquire in advance about trail conditions.

HETCH HETCHY RESERVOIR is accessed from SR 120, just w. of the Big Oak Flat entrance; visitors can follow Evergreen Rd. to re-enter the park at Hetch Hetchy. The 38-mile drive from the valley can be covered easily in 2 hours. A paved road leads 7 miles from Mather to the 312-foot dam, which impounds San Francisco's water supply.

Before the dam was built in the 1920s, the Hetch Hetchy Valley rivaled Yosemite Valley in beauty. The Hetch Hetchy Valley floor is now under 300 feet of water. You should carry tire chains in the fall, winter and spring.

MARIPOSA GROVE, reached via Wawona Rd. (SR 41), is in the extreme s. end of the park; the easy 36-mi. paved drive from Yosemite Valley is closed to vehicles during winter and spring.

This giant sequoia grove is one of the finest in the Sierras. The oldest sequoia, Grizzly Giant, has a base diameter of 30.7 feet, a girth of 96.5 feet and is 210 feet high; the 232-foot California Tree is a walk-through tunnel tree. The other tunnel tree in the park, the 40-foot stump Dead Giant, is in Tuolumne Grove.

Mariposa Grove Welcome Center has exhibits about giant sequoias. Guided walks and ranger-led programs are offered. Nearby is the fallen Massachusetts Tree, 280 feet long and 28 feet in diameter; several broken sections provide opportunities to study the wood. Guided bus tours run from the valley to the grove, with a stop in Wawona. An overlook at the 4,233-foot Wawona tunnel offers a view of the entire valley. Hiking trails in the grove vary in intensity and range from 0.3 mile to 7 miles.

Hours: Shuttle service from Mariposa Grove Welcome Plaza runs approximately every 10 minutes daily 8-8, May 15-Oct. 14; 8-5, Oct. 15-Nov. 30 and Mar. 15-May 14. **Cost:** Free. **Phone:** (209) 372-0200.

TIOGA PASS ROAD begins at SR 120 and US 395, just s. of Lee Vining. Also designated SR 120, this paved, two-lane road traverses the park and provides the only entrance from the east.

The first 12 miles ascend nearly a mile in elevation and overlook a vast canyon. The route traverses

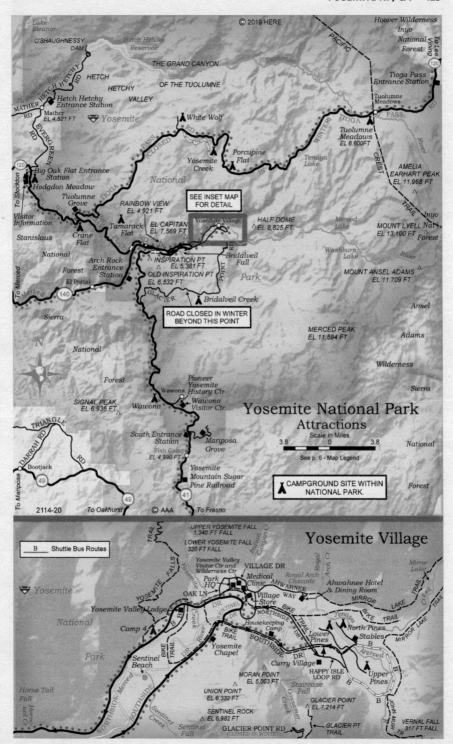

© 2019 HERE

Hoover Wilderness
Inyo
National
Forest

To Lee Vining

Lake
Eleanor

O'Shaughnessy
DAM

HETCH
HETCHY

RD

THE GRAND CANYON

Tuolumne

OF THE TUOLUMNE

PACIFIC

Tioga Pass
Entrance Station

120

Tuolumne
Meadows

Hetch Hetchy
Reservoir

HETCHY VALLEY

Hetch Hetchy
Entrance Station

Mather
EL 4,521 FT

Yosemite

White Wolf

Porcupine
Flat

TIOGA

PASS

Tuolumne
Meadows
EL 8,600 FT

WINTER

Tenaya
Lake

AMELIA
EARHART PEAK
EL 11,968 FT

120

To Stockton

Big Oak Flat Entrance
Station

Hodgdon Meadow

Tuolumne
Grove

Visitor
Information

Stanislaus

National

Yosemite
Creek

RD

(CLOSED)

National

RAINBOW VIEW
EL 4,921 FT

Tamarack
Flat

EL CAPITAN
EL 7,569 FT

SEE INSET MAP
FOR DETAIL

Yosemite Village

Merced
Lake

Inyo

MOUNT LYELL Natl
EL 13,100 FT

Forest

HALF DOME
EL 8,825 FT

Washburn
Lake

River

CREST

TRAIL

MOUNT ANSEL ADAMS
EL 11,709 FT

Ansel

Crane
Flat

Forest

Arch Rock
Entrance
Station

El Portal

National

INSPIRATION PT
EL 5,381 FT

OLD INSPIRATION PT
EL 6,532 FT

GLACIER

Bridalveil
Fall

POINT

Park

Bridalveil Creek

ROAD CLOSED IN WINTER
BEYOND THIS POINT

MERCED PEAK
EL 11,594 FT

Adams

To Merced

140

Sierra

N

National

Forest

Pioneer
Yosemite
History Ctr

Wawona

Wawona
Visitor Ctr

Wilderness

Sierra

National

Wawona

SIGNAL PEAK
EL 6,936 FT

TRIANGLE

DARRAH RD

RD

Bootjack

49

South Entrance
Station

Fish Camp
EL 4,990 FT

Mariposa
Grove

Yosemite National Park
Attractions

Scale in Miles

3.8   0   3.8

See p. 6 - Map Legend

National

Yosemite
Mountain Sugar
Pine Railroad

CAMPGROUND SITE WITHIN
NATIONAL PARK.

Forest

2114-20

To Mariposa   To Oakhurst

49

© AAA

41

To Fresno

Yosemite Village

UPPER YOSEMITE FALL
1,340 FT FALL

LOWER YOSEMITE FALL
320 FT FALL

Royal Arch Cr

Mirror
Lake

B   Shuttle Bus Routes

Yosemite

Yosemite Valley
Visitor Ctr and
Wilderness Ctr

VILLAGE DR

Park
HQ

Medical
Clinic

Royal Arch
Cascade

AHWAHNEE

Ahwahnee Hotel
& Dining Room

MIRROR

OAK LN

Village
Store

WAY

BIKE

LAKE

BIKE TRAIL

TRAIL

National

Yosemite Valley Lodge

Camp 4

DR

SENTINEL

NORTHSIDE

Housekeeping
Camp

BIKE
TRAIL

Tenaya

Lower
Pines

North Pines

Stables

MIRROR LAKE

Park

BIKE

TRAIL

Sentinel
Beach

SOUTHSIDE

DR

Yosemite
Chapel

Curry Village

Upper
Pines

Horse Tail
Fall

NORTHSIDE

Merced

SOUTHSIDE

Sentinel
Creek

MORAN POINT
EL 5,003 FT

UNION POINT
EL 6,332 FT

SENTINEL ROCK
EL 6,982 FT

Sentinel
Fall

GLACIER POINT RD
(CLOSED IN WINTER)

HAPPY ISLE
LOOP RD

Staircase
Fall

Gossamer Creek

GLACIER POINT
EL 7,214 FT

GLACIER PT
TRAIL

JOHN MUIR

VERNAL FALL
317 FT FALL

GLACIER POINT RD

(See map & index p. 426.)

Tuolumne Meadows, descends to Tenaya Lake and continues west to Big Oak Flat Road, offering a scenic trip with frequent overlooks to stop and admire the views. Although portions of the drive are more demanding than relaxing for motorists, the magnificent scenery makes up for it, and Tioga Pass Road is a very popular park destination. Motorists should carry tire chains, since weather and road conditions can change quickly. **Hours:** The road is usually open late May-early Nov. (weather permitting). **Cost:** Free. **Phone:** (209) 372-0200 for road conditions.

TUOLUMNE GROVE, on old Big Oak Flat Rd., 17 mi. from Yosemite Valley, contains 20 giant sequoia trees, including the Dead Giant stump. Automobiles are no longer permitted on the section of Big Oak Flat Road adjacent to the grove. Visitors may park their cars near the Crane Flat Junction at a lot off of Tioga Road and walk to Tuolumne Grove; however, the mile-long route descends approximately 700 feet and the return ascent to the parking lot is a moderately strenuous climb.

TUOLUMNE MEADOWS is in the High Sierra, about 56 mi. from Yosemite Valley over Big Oak Flat and Tioga rds. At 8,600 feet in elevation and surrounded by lofty peaks, the area is ideal for camping and fishing, hiking and mountain-climbing.

Trips can be taken on foot or horseback to Waterwheel Falls, Mount Lyell, Lyell Glacier, Lembert Dome, Glen Aulin, Muir Gorge, Soda Springs and Tenaya Lake. Nature walks, hikes and evening campfire programs are conducted seasonally. Saddle horses, gas station, store and post office services and a mountaineering school and guide service also are available.

Hours: Tuolumne Meadows is accessible by car from about early June-Oct. 31. Daily bus service from Yosemite Valley is available early June to mid-Sept. (weather permitting), as are walks, hikes and campfire programs.

WASHBURN AND MERCED LAKES, accessible by trail only from Yosemite Valley, are typical of the many lakes bordering the western slopes of the Sierras. One of six High Sierra camps is at the head of Merced Lake and can be reached by trail from Yosemite Valley, Tenaya Lake or Tuolumne Meadows.

WAWONA is about 27 mi. s. of Yosemite Valley off Wawona Rd. (SR 41). Native Americans originally dubbed the area *Pallahchun,* meaning "a good place to stop." In the 1800s Wawona became an important pioneer stage stop and later evolved into a popular mountain resort. Its meadows, nearby river, and surrounding pine and oak trees create an idyllic recreation area that offers camping, riding, golf, swimming and tennis facilities.

Pioneer Yosemite History Center, 10 mi. n.w. of the South Entrance Station in Wawona, has historic cabins and buildings as well as outdoor, self-guiding exhibits about stagecoach days in Yosemite. The buildings are open and living-history demonstrations are offered in summer; the buildings can be seen from the outside the rest of the year. **Hours:** Center open daily. Buildings open and living-history demonstrations presented early Apr. to mid-Oct.; check at the visitor center to confirm schedule. **Phone:** (209) 375-9531.

YOSEMITE VALLEY is 27 mi. n. on SR 41 and is also accessible from SRs 120 and 140. The canyon walls on either side of the valley, which is 7 miles long and averages about three-quarters of a mile in width, rise to 3,200 feet. Immense precipices and lofty waterfalls (some seasonal) are impressive natural features.

Upper Yosemite Fall drops 1,430 feet in one fall, a height equal to nine Niagaras. Lower Yosemite Fall drops 320 feet. Illilouette Fall drops 370 feet; Nevada Fall, 594 feet; and Ribbon Fall, 1,612 feet. The falls are at their fullest in May and June while winter snows melt. Fairly abundant up to mid-July, many practically disappear for the balance of the summer, then reappear with the first autumn storm and run lightly during winter.

The valley's geological landmarks—Three Brothers, El Capitan, Cathedral Spires, North Dome and Half Dome—are as celebrated as the falls. **Hours:** Open all year.

Bridalveil Fall is accessed via the Bridalveil Fall parking area, .5 mi. e. of the start of Wawona Rd. (SR 41) in Yosemite Valley. Flowing all year, the 620-foot-tall waterfall is often the first seen by entering park visitors. Because the fall doesn't always reach the ground due to its light, swaying flow summer through winter, the Ahwahneechee Indians named it *Pohono,* meaning "spirit of the puffing wind." A quarter-mile-long paved trail leads to a viewing area. **Note:** The trail's final 50 feet is a very steep stretch that will be challenging for those without full mobility.

El Capitan is about 4 mi. s.w. of Yosemite Village, reached via Yosemite Valley hiking trails. Rising nearly 3,000 feet above the valley floor, the world's largest granite monolith is a popular challenge for experienced rock climbers. El Capitan was first conquered in 1958 over a period of 17 months; in 1975, a trio of climbers ascended to the top in 1 day. Bridalveil Fall offers a particularly good vantage point for a view of this landmark. El Capitan Meadow, off Northside Drive, is another good viewpoint.

Half Dome is about 3.3 mi. e. of Yosemite Village, reached via Yosemite Valley hiking trails. The granite dome, a familiar landmark, rises more than 4,000 feet above the valley floor; it can be seen throughout eastern Yosemite Valley and Glacier Point.

A very strenuous 8.5-mile hike to the top typically takes 5-6 hours one way, with metal cables assisting hikers up the last 900 feet. Permits are required

(See map & index p. 426.)

above the subdome and can be reserved in a pre-season lottery held in March. A limited number of permits also are available in a daily lottery; the winning applicants on a particular day can hike the dome on the second day following the drawing.

Note: Hikers are advised not to ascend Half Dome when cables are not erected or if thunderclouds are visible. **Hours:** Daily 24 hours (weather permitting); cables available late May-early Oct. **Cost:** $10 for permits to ascend above the subdome.

Vernal Fall is accessible via the 1.5-mi. Mist Trail from Happy Isles in Yosemite Valley. Visitors climb the uphill trail through the mist of the fall, which flows year-round. By mid- to late summer, the 317-foot-tall waterfall often splits into separate falls as water flows decrease. A footbridge along Mist Trail offers great views of Vernal Fall, as does Glacier Point. The top of Vernal Fall is accessible via the Mist Trail, May through October; access is via the John Muir Trail the rest of the year.

Note: The steep hike to the top of the fall requires climbing 600 granite steps. In spring and early summer, hikers should expect to get wet. **Hours:** Daily 24 hours (weather permitting).

Yosemite Falls is .5 mi. e. of Yosemite Village, accessed via Yosemite Valley hiking trails. Towering at 2,425 feet, the highest North American waterfall is actually made up of three separate falls: Upper Yosemite Fall, the middle cascades and Lower Yosemite Fall. Starting at the Lower Yosemite Fall shuttle bus stop, a .25-mile paved trail leads to the bottom of the lower fall. A strenuous 3.6-mile hike to the top of the upper fall typically takes about 3-4 hours one way. **Note:** Hiking to the top of the upper fall requires full mobility.

YOSEMITE VALLEY VISITOR CENTER AND WILDERNESS CENTER is in Yosemite Village; take El Portal Rd. (SR 140) e. 3.3 mi. to Southside Dr./Tecoya Rd., then .3 mi. to Village Dr. The center provides detailed trip-planning information about the park, offering maps, books, exhibits and audiovisual programs. An orientation film called "Spirit of Yosemite" is shown in the Valley Visitor Center Theater.

Also featuring information about the park's backcountry and wilderness areas, it contains a variety of displays for hikers and climbers. Interactive exhibits for children include a bear cave and a simulated sequoia tree and glacier. **Hours:** Visitor center daily 9-6, year-round. Wilderness center daily 8-5, May-Oct. The film is shown Mon.-Sat. every 30 minutes 9:30-5:30, Sun. every 30 minutes noon-5:30. **Cost:** Free. **Phone:** (209) 372-0200.

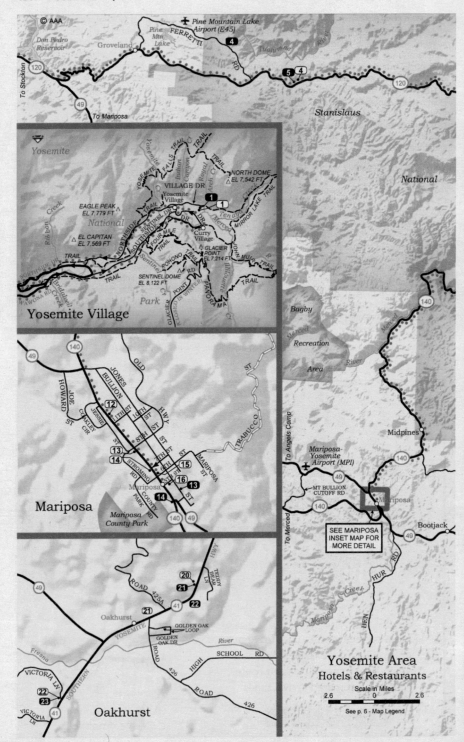

© AAA

Pine Mountain Lake
Airport (E45)

FERRETTI

Don Pedro
Reservoir

Groveland

Pine
Mtn.
Lake

4

Tuolumne

River

120

To Stockton

120

49

To Mariposa

5 4

RD

Stanislaus

National

Yosemite Village

Yosemite

Yosemite

FALLS TRAIL

TRAIL

TRAIL

TRAIL

Indian
Canyon

Royal
Arch

NORTH DOME
EL 7,542 FT

VILLAGE DR

1 1

Yosemite
Village

EAGLE PEAK
EL 7,779 FT

YOSEMITE

TRAIL

NORTHSIDE

SENTINEL DR

DR

Tenaya

Merced

MIRROR LAKE TRAIL

National

EL CAPITAN
EL 7,569 FT

Ribbon

Creek

Curry
Village

FOUR
MILE

SOUTHSIDE

GLACIER
POINT
EL 7,214 FT

JOHN MUIR TRAIL

R

NORTHSIDE DR

TRAIL

Sentinel

POHONO

TRAIL

SENTINEL DOME
EL 8,122 FT

RD

TRAIL

BRIDALVEIL CREEK

WAWONA RD

TRAIL

Park

GLACIER

POINT

ILLILOUETTE WINTER

PANORAMA

TRAIL

Bagby

Merced

Recreation

River

Area

140

Mariposa

49

140

JONES

OLD

ST

HOWARD

JOE
CRANLEY
CIR

BULLION

11TH

JESSIE

HWY

12

10TH
ST

ST

9TH
ST

8TH
ST

ST

7TH
ST

6TH

5TH

ST

ST

ST

TRABUCCO

13

14

STROMING
RD

Mariposa

15

16

13

Mariposa
COUNTY
PARK

14

ST

Mariposa
County Park

140

49

To Angels Camp

Mariposa-
Yosemite
Airport (MPI)

49

MT BULLION
CUTOFF RD

140

SEE MARIPOSA
INSET MAP FOR
MORE DETAIL

Midpines

140

Mariposa

Bootjack

49

Oakhurst

49

ROAD 425A

41

20

21

TEDDY
BEAR
LN

22

21

Oakhurst

GOLDEN OAK
LOOP

GOLDEN
OAK DR

YOSEMITE

Fresno

River

SCHOOL RD

426

HIGH

ROAD

VICTORIA LN

SOUTHERN

22

23

VICTORIA
LN

41

426

ROAD

HEN

HUR

RD

Mariposa

Creek

Yosemite Area
Hotels & Restaurants

Scale in Miles

2.6   0   2.6

See p. 6 - Map Legend

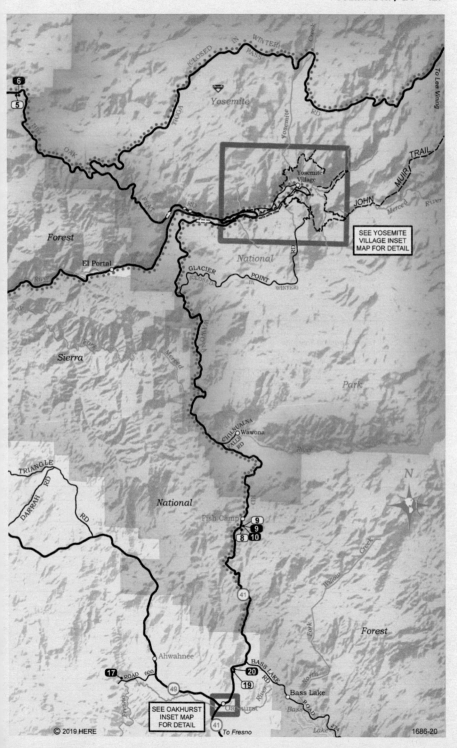

SEE YOSEMITE VILLAGE INSET MAP FOR DETAIL

SEE OAKHURST INSET MAP FOR DETAIL

© 2019 HERE

1686-20

Yosemite Area

This index helps you "spot" where approved hotels and restaurants are located on the corresponding detailed maps. Restaurant price range is a combination of lunch and/or dinner. Turn to the listing page for more information and consult display ads for special promotions.

 For more details, rates and reservations: AAA.com/travelguides/hotels

YOSEMITE NATIONAL PARK

Map Page	Hotel	Diamond Rated	Member Savings	Page
❶ p. 426	The Ahwahnee	♦♦♦	✔	429

Map Page	Restaurant	Diamond Rated	Cuisine	Price Range	Page
① p. 426	The Majestic Yosemite Dining Room	♦♦♦	Continental	$18-$50	429

GROVELAND

Map Page	Hotels	Diamond Rated	Member Savings	Page
❹ p. 426	Yosemite Rose Bed & Breakfast	♦♦♦		100
❺ p. 426	Yosemite Westgate Lodge	♦		100
❻ p. 426	Rush Creek Lodge at Yosemite	♦♦♦		100

Map Page	Restaurants	Diamond Rated	Cuisine	Price Range	Page
④ p. 426	Buck Meadows Restaurant	♦♦	American	$10-$26	100
⑤ p. 426	Tavern at Rush Creek Lodge	♦♦	American	$12-$30	100

FISH CAMP

Map Page	Hotels	Diamond Rated	Member Savings	Page
❾ p. 426	Tenaya Lodge at Yosemite	♦♦♦♦	✔	79
❿ p. 426	The Cottages at Tenaya Lodge	♦♦♦	✔	79

Map Page	Restaurants	Diamond Rated	Cuisine	Price Range	Page
⑧ p. 426	Timberloft Pizzeria	♦	Pizza	$17-$26	79
⑨ p. 426	Jackalope's Bar & Grill	♦♦	American	$16-$37	79

MARIPOSA

Map Page	Hotels	Diamond Rated	Member Savings	Page
⓭ p. 426	Quality Inn Yosemite Valley Gateway (See ad p. 130.)	♦♦	✔	129
⓮ p. 426	Best Western Plus Yosemite Way Station Motel	♦♦♦	✔	129

Map Page	Restaurants	Diamond Rated	Cuisine	Price Range	Page
⑫ p. 426	1850 Restaurant	♦♦	Traditional American	$11-$38	129
⑬ p. 426	Jantz Bakery	♦	Breads/Pastries	$6-$11	129
⑭ p. 426	Charles Street Dinner House	♦♦	American	$11-$38	129
⑮ p. 426	Savoury's	♦♦♦	American	$17-$39	129
⑯ p. 426	Castillo's Mexican Restaurant	♦♦	Mexican	$8-$16	129

AHWAHNEE

Map Page	Hotel	Diamond Rated	Member Savings	Page
⓱ p. 426	Homestead Cottages	♦♦		33

OAKHURST

Map Page	Hotels	Diamond Rated	Member Savings	Page
⓴ p. 426	Hounds Tooth Inn	♦♦		171
㉑ p. 426	Best Western Plus Yosemite Gateway Inn	♦♦	✔	170
㉒ p. 426	Comfort Inn Yosemite Area	♦♦		170
㉓ p. 426	Château du Sureau	♦♦♦♦♦	✔	170

Map Page	Restaurants	Diamond Rated	Cuisine	Price Range	Page
⑲ p. 426	El Cid	◆◆	Mexican	$10-$24	171
⑳ p. 426	Oakhurst Grill	◆◆	American	$13-$36	171
㉑ p. 426	DiCicco's Italian Restaurant	◆◆	Italian	$10-$23	171
㉒ p. 426	**Erna's Elderberry House Restaurant**	◆◆◆◆◆	French	$145	171

THE AHWAHNEE
209/372-1407 **1**

◆◆◆
Historic Hotel

Address: 1 Ahwahnee Dr 95389 **Location:** 0.8 mi e; beyond park headquarters. **Facility:** Along with gorgeous park views, this hotel has impressive public areas. A vast great room fills up in the evenings with those wanting to socialize or just take in the hotel's workmanship and artistry. 121 units, some cottages. 1-7 stories, interior/exterior corridors. **Parking:** on-site and valet. **Terms:** check-in 4 pm. **Amenities:** safes. **Dining:** The Majestic Yosemite Dining Room, see separate listing. **Pool:** heated outdoor. **Activities:** recreation programs, bicycles, trails, massage. **Guest Services:** valet laundry, area transportation.

SAVE 🍴 ✦ 🍸 CALL ♿ 🛏 BIZ 📶 ✕ 🖥
/ SOME
/ UNITS 📠

WHERE TO EAT

THE MAJESTIC YOSEMITE DINING ROOM
209/372-1489 **1**
◆◆◆ Continental. Fine Dining. **Address:** 1 Ahwahnee Dr 95389

YOUNTVILLE (B-8) pop. 2,933, elev. 100'
• Hotels & Restaurants map & index p. 412
• Part of Wine Country area — see map p. 405

Yountville, on a scenic stretch of SR 29 extending from Calistoga to Napa, was founded by George Yount, a fur trader from North Carolina, in 1835. Yount is said to have planted the first grapevines in the Napa Valley.

Yountville Chamber of Commerce: 6484 Washington St., Suite F, Yountville, CA 94599. **Phone:** (707) 944-0904.

Shopping: V Marketplace 1870, 6525 Washington St., offers specialty shops, art galleries and upscale dining choices in a restored 19th-century winery.

BARDESSONO HOTEL & SPA   707/204-6000 **30**
◆◆◆ ◆◆◆ Contemporary Hotel. **Address:** 6526 Yount St 94599

LAVENDER   707/944-1388 **28**
◆◆◆ Bed & Breakfast. **Address:** 2020 Webber Ave 94599

MAISON FLEURIE   707/944-2056 **29**
◆◆ Bed & Breakfast. **Address:** 6529 Yount St 94599

NAPA VALLEY LODGE   707/944-2468 **27**
◆◆◆ ◆◆◆ Hotel. **Address:** 2230 Madison St 94599

WHERE TO EAT

AD HOC   707/944-2487 **34**
◆◆◆ American. Casual Dining. **Address:** 6476 Washington St 94599

BISTRO JEANTY   707/944-0103 **33**
◆◆◆ French. Casual Dining. **Address:** 6510 Washington St 94599

BOTTEGA NAPA VALLEY   707/945-1050 **32**
◆◆◆ Italian. Fine Dining. **Address:** 6525 Washington St, Suite A-9 94599

BOUCHON   707/944-8037 **30**
◆◆◆ French. Casual Dining. **Address:** 6534 Washington St 94599

COQUETA NAPA VALLEY   707/244-4350 **35**
◆◆◆ Spanish. Casual Dining. **Address:** 6525 Washington St 94599

THE FRENCH LAUNDRY   707/944-2380 **29**
◆◆◆◆◆

American Fine Dining $310

AAA Inspector Notes: Chef Thomas Keller has created a distinctive dining experience in the midst of Napa Valley wine country. The old stone farm house has been delightfully outfitted for an intimate outing with just a few more than a dozen tables. The meal might include delectable morsels such as sesame cornets with smoked salmon, Elysian Fields Farm lamb chops with Belgian endive gratin and Hen-of-the-Woods mushrooms. **Features:** beer & wine, patio dining. **Reservations:** required. Semiformal attire. **Address:** 6640 Washington St 94599 **Location:** From SR 29, e on Madison St, then just s. **Parking:** street only. **D**

LA CALENDA   833/682-8226 **31**
◆◆◆ Mexican. Casual Dining. **Address:** 6518 Washington St 94599

MUSTARDS GRILL   707/944-2424 **27**
◆◆◆ American. Fine Dining. **Address:** 7399 St. Helena Hwy 94558

R+D KITCHEN   707/945-0920 **28**
◆◆◆ California. Fine Dining. **Address:** 6795 Washington St 94599

YREKA (A-2) pop. 7,765, elev. 2,625'
• Hotels p. 430 • Restaurants p. 430

Yreka (pronounced Why-REEK-uh), 22 miles south of the Oregon border, was incorporated in 1857, 6 years after Abraham Thompson discovered gold flecks on the roots of the grass his mules were eating. Miners soon swarmed into this lush valley, which had long been home to the Karuk and Shasta Indians. The boom fizzled out about 1885, after more than $60 million worth of valuable ore had been extracted from the earth. I-5 is a scenic route to and through Yreka.

The historic downtown district—including the appropriately named main thoroughfare, Miner Street—contains a number of beautifully restored, late 19th- and early 20th-century buildings housing shops and restaurants. Information markers throughout the district describe the original purpose of many of the structures. Such residential areas as

Third Street are rich with Gothic Revival and Victorian houses that date back to the 1800s.

The headquarters office of Klamath National Forest *(see place listing p. 109)*, 1711 S. Main St., has information about recreational activities, which include hiking, fishing, snowmobiling and biking; phone (530) 842-6131. *See Recreation Areas Chart.*

Yreka Chamber of Commerce: 310 S. Broadway St., Yreka, CA 96097. **Phone:** (530) 842-1649.

Self-guiding tours: Stop by the chamber of commerce office for walking and driving tour maps of the historic district and historic homes area.

SISKIYOU COUNTY MUSEUM, 910 S. Main St., contains exhibits of the region dating from the 19th and 20th centuries. Featured are displays about Native Americans, fur trappers, gold mining, logging and lumbering, and the military. The outdoor museum displays equipment and restored buildings in a mid-1800s mining and pioneer settlement. **Time:** Allow 2 hours minimum. **Hours:** Museum open Tues.-Sat. 9-3 (outdoor exhibits open 10-2, May-Oct.). Phone ahead to confirm schedule, as it may vary due to staff availability. Closed major holidays. **Cost:** $3; $1 (ages 6-12). **Phone:** (530) 842-3836.

BEST WESTERN MINER'S INN   530/842-4355

Motel

Best Western	**AAA Benefit:** Members save up to 15% and earn bonus points!

Address: 122 E Miner St 96097 **Location:** I-5 exit 775, just w. **Facility:** 130 units, some two bedrooms and efficiencies. 2 stories (no elevator), exterior corridors. **Pool:** heated outdoor. **Activities:** playground. **Featured Amenity:** continental breakfast.

COMFORT INN   530/842-1612
Hotel. **Address:** 1804-B Fort Jones Rd 96097

HOLIDAY INN EXPRESS & SUITES YREKA-SHASTA
530/842-1600

Hotel

Address: 707 Montague Rd 96097 **Location:** I-5 exit 776, just e. **Facility:** 68 units. 3 stories, interior corridors. **Pool:** heated indoor. **Activities:** exercise room. **Guest Services:** coin laundry. **Featured Amenity:** breakfast buffet.

KLAMATH MOTOR LODGE   530/842-2751

Motel

Address: 1111 S Main St 96097 **Location:** I-5 exit 775, just w to Main St, then 0.9 mi s. **Facility:** 28 units. 2 stories (no elevator), exterior corridors. **Pool:** outdoor. **Featured Amenity:** continental breakfast.

RODEWAY INN   530/842-4412
Motel. **Address:** 1235 S Main St 96097

SUPER 8 BY WYNDHAM YREKA   530/842-5781

Motel

Address: 136 Montague Rd 96097 **Location:** I-5 exit 776, just w. **Facility:** 61 units. 2 stories (no elevator), exterior corridors. **Amenities:** safes. **Pool:** outdoor. **Activities:** exercise room. **Guest Services:** coin laundry. **Featured Amenity:** continental breakfast.

WHERE TO EAT

CASA RAMOS   530/842-7172
Mexican. Casual Dining. **Address:** 145 Montague Rd 96097

JEFFERSON'S ROADHOUSE   530/842-9866
American. Casual Dining. **Address:** 1281 S Main St 96097

NATURE'S KITCHEN CAFE   530/842-1136
Sandwiches Natural/Organic. Casual Dining. **Address:** 412 S Main St 96097

STRINGS ITALIAN CAFE   530/842-7704
Italian. Casual Dining. **Address:** 322 W Miner St 96097

YUBA CITY (D-3) pop. 64,925, elev. 60'
• Hotels p. 430 • Restaurants p. 431

Yuba City was founded in 1849 as a gold rush development; it is now a marketing center for the surrounding agricultural area. The 1899 county courthouse and the 1891 county hall of records are both part of the Second Street historic district. Surrounding blocks contain a collection of Victorian residences that reflect Italianate, Classical and Eastlake characteristics.

Yuba-Sutter Chamber of Commerce: 1300 Franklin Rd., Yuba City, CA 95993. **Phone:** (530) 743-6501.

BEST WESTERN YUBA CITY INN   530/674-1650

Motel

Best Western	**AAA Benefit:** Members save up to 15% and earn bonus points!

Address: 894 W Onstott Rd 95991 **Location:** Just s of jct SR 99 and 20. **Facility:** 91 units. 2 stories (no elevator), exterior corridors. **Pool:** outdoor. **Activities:** hot tub, exercise room. **Guest Services:** coin laundry. **Featured Amenity:** breakfast buffet.

HAMPTON INN & SUITES   530/751-1714

Hotel

AAA Benefit: Members save up to 15%!

Address: 1375 Sunsweet Blvd 95991 **Location:** Just s of jct SR 99 and 20, just w. **Facility:** 88 units. 3 stories, interior corridors. **Pool:** heated outdoor. **Activities:** hot tub, exercise room. **Guest Services:** valet and coin laundry. **Featured Amenity: continental breakfast.**

WHERE TO EAT

THE CITY CAFE   530/671-1501
American. Casual Dining. **Address:** 667 Plumas St 95991

COSTA VIDA FRESH MEXICAN GRILL   530/673-9283
Mexican. Quick Serve. **Address:** 1074 Harter Rd, Suite 101B 95993

DANCING TOMATO CAFFE   530/790-0300
Italian. Casual Dining. **Address:** 990 N Walton Ave 95993

MARCELLO'S ITALIAN RESTAURANT   530/674-2171
Italian. Casual Dining. **Address:** 1235 Bridge St 95991

SOPA THAI CUISINE   530/790-7672
Thai. Casual Dining. **Address:** 720 Plumas St 95991

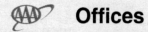

Offices

Main office listings are shown in **BOLD TYPE** and toll-free member service numbers appear in *ITALIC TYPE*.
All are closed Saturdays, Sundays and holidays unless otherwise indicated.
The addresses, phone numbers and hours for any AAA/CAA office are subject to change.
The type of service provided is designated below the name of the city where the office is located:

✛ Auto travel services, including books and maps, and on-demand TripTik® routings.
● Auto travel services, including selected books and maps, and on-demand TripTik® routings.
■ Books/maps only, no marked maps or on-demand TripTik® routings.
▲ Travel Agency Services, cruise, tour, air, car and rail reservations; domestic and international hotel reservations; passport photo services; international and domestic travel guides and maps; travel money products; and International Driving Permits. In addition, assistance with travel related insurance products including trip cancellation, travel accident, lost luggage, trip delay and assistance products.
✪ Insurance services provided. If only this icon appears, only insurance services are provided at that office.
⊂ Car Care Plus Facility provides car care services.
⊡ Electric vehicle charging station on premises.

AAA NATIONAL OFFICE: 1000 AAA DRIVE, HEATHROW, FLORIDA 32746-5063, (407) 444-7000

NORTHERN CALIFORNIA

ALAMEDA—AAA NORTHERN CALIFORNIA NEVADA & UTAH, 2650 5TH STR BLG-F STE H, 94501. WEEKDAYS (M-F) 9:00-6:00, SAT 9:00-5:00. (510) 336-7100 ✛▲✪

ANTIOCH—AAA NORTHERN CALIFORNIA NEVADA & UTAH, 5799 LONE TREE WAY, 94531. WEEKDAYS (M-F) 9:00-6:00, SAT 9:00-5:00. (925) 522-7920 ✛▲✪

AUBURN—AAA NORTHERN CALIFORNIA NEVADA & UTAH, 2480 GRASS VALLEY HWY, 95603. WEEKDAYS (M-F) 9:00-6:00, SAT 9:00-5:00. (530) 886-2500 ✛▲✪

BERKELEY—AAA NORTHERN CALIFORNIA NEVADA & UTAH, 1775 UNIVERSITY AVE, 94703. WEEKDAYS (M-F) 9:00-6:00 (SAT: SALES BY APPT ONLY). (510) 898-7600 ✛✪

CAPITOLA—AAA NORTHERN CALIFORNIA NEVADA & UTAH, 4400 CAPITOLA RD STE 100, 95010. WEEKDAYS (M-F) 9:00-6:00, SAT 9:00-5:00. (831) 824-9128 ✛▲✪

CHICO—AAA NORTHERN CALIFORNIA NEVADA & UTAH, 2221 FOREST AVE, 95928. WEEKDAYS (M-F) 9:00-6:00 (SAT: SALES BY APPT ONLY). (530) 332-2600 ✛▲✪

CITRUS HEIGHTS—AAA NORTHERN CALIFORNIA NEVADA & UTAH, 6109 SUNRISE BLVD, 95610. WEEKDAYS (M-F) 9:00-6:00 (SAT: SALES BY APPT ONLY). (916) 560-0501 ✛▲✪

CLOVIS—AAA NORTHERN CALIFORNIA NEVADA & UTAH, 1595 SHAW AVE, 93611. WEEKDAYS (M-F) 9:00-6:00 (SAT: SALES BY APPT ONLY). (559) 323-3000 ✛▲✪

CLOVIS—AAA NORTHERN CALIFORNIA NEVADA & UTAH, 900 HERNDON, 93612. WEEKDAYS (M-F) 9:00-6:00, SAT 9:00-5:00. (559) 323-5400 ✛▲✪⊡

CONCORD—AAA NORTHERN CALIFORNIA NEVADA & UTAH, 2095 DIAMOND BLVD B-135, 94520. WEEKDAYS (M-F) 9:00-6:00, SAT 9:00-5:00. (925) 808-6201 ✛▲✪

DALY CITY—AAA NORTHERN CALIFORNIA NEVADA & UTAH, 455 HICKEY BLVD 3RD FL, 94015. WEEKDAYS (M-F) 9:00-6:00, SAT 9:00-5:00. (650) 301-1400 ✛▲✪

DUBLIN—AAA NORTHERN CALIFORNIA NEVADA & UTAH, 4460 TASSAJARA RD STE B, 94568. WEEKDAYS (M-F) 9:00-6:00, SAT 9:00-5:00. (925) 479-7840 ✛▲✪

EL DORADO HILLS—AAA NORTHERN CALIFORNIA NEVADA & UTAH, 4630 POST STREET, 95762. WEEKDAYS (M-F) 8:00-6:00. (916) 933-4002 ⊂

ELK GROVE—AAA NORTHERN CALIFORNIA NEVADA & UTAH, 8225 LAGUNA BLVD STE 120, 95758. WEEKDAYS (M-F) 9:00-6:00, SAT 9:00-5:00. (916) 478-7500 ✛▲✪

EUREKA—AAA NORTHERN CALIFORNIA NEVADA & UTAH, 1470 BROADWAY ST, 95501. WEEKDAYS (M-F) 9:00-6:00 (SAT: SALES BY APPT ONLY). (707) 444-1000 ✛✪

FAIRFIELD—AAA NORTHERN CALIFORNIA NEVADA & UTAH, 1495 GATEWAY BLVD, 94533. WEEKDAYS (M-F) 7:30-5:30, SAT 8:00-5:00. (707) 425-4880 ⊂

FAIRFIELD—AAA NORTHERN CALIFORNIA NEVADA & UTAH, 1495 GATEWAY BLVD, 94533. WEEKDAYS (M-F) 8:30-5:30. (707) 426-4790, *(800) 922-8228.* ✛▲✪

FOLSOM—AAA NORTHERN CALIFORNIA NEVADA & UTAH, 2796 E BIDWELL ST, 95630. WEEKDAYS (M-F) 9:00-6:00, SAT 9:00-5:00. (916) 351-2600 ✛▲✪

FRESNO—AAA NORTHERN CALIFORNIA NEVADA & UTAH, 632 WEST SHAW AVE STE 60, 93704. WEEKDAYS (M-F) 9:00-6:00. (559) 241-6800 ✛▲✪

FRESNO—AAA NORTHERN CALIFORNIA NEVADA & UTAH, 6717 N RIVERSIDE DR # 102, 93722. WEEKDAYS (M-F) 9:00-6:00, SAT 9:00-5:00. (559) 276-7100 ✛✪

FRESNO—AAA NORTHERN CALIFORNIA NEVADA & UTAH, 8380 N FRESNO ST STE 101, 93720. WEEKDAYS (M-F) 9:00-6:00, SAT 9:00-5:00. (559) 433-6780 ✛▲✪

GILROY—AAA NORTHERN CALIFORNIA NEVADA & UTAH, 7210 CAMINO ARROYO # 103, 95020. WEEKDAYS (M-F) 9:00-6:00, SAT 9:00-5:00. (408) 847-9220 ✛✪

GRASS VALLEY—AAA NORTHERN CALIFORNIA NEVADA & UTAH, 113 DORSEY DR, 95945. WEEKDAYS (M-F) 9:00-6:00 (SAT: SALES BY APPT ONLY). (530) 271-2600 ✛✪

HANFORD—AAA NORTHERN CALIFORNIA NEVADA & UTAH, 780 N IRWIN ST, 93230. WEEKDAYS (M-F) 9:00-6:00 (SAT: SALES BY APPT ONLY). (559) 587-4600 ✛✪

HAYWARD—AAA NORTHERN CALIFORNIA NEVADA & UTAH, 1580 CHABOT CT, 94545. WEEKDAYS (M-F) 9:00-6:00, SAT 9:00-5:00. (510) 670-4380 ✛▲✪

HOLLISTER—AAA NORTHERN CALIFORNIA NEVADA & UTAH, 351 TRES PINOS RD STE D, 95023. WEEKDAYS (M-F) 9:00-6:00 (SAT: SALES BY APPT ONLY). (831) 635-3900 ✛✪

JACKSON—AAA NORTHERN CALIFORNIA NEVADA & UTAH, 11992 ST HWY 88 STE 2048, 95642. WEEKDAYS (M-F) 9:00-6:00 (SAT: SALES BY APPT ONLY). (209) 223-6900 ✛▲✪

LAKEPORT—AAA NORTHERN CALIFORNIA NEVADA & UTAH, 1464 PARALLEL DR, 95453. WEEKDAYS (M-F) 9:00-6:00 (SAT: SALES BY APPT ONLY). (707) 262-5900 ✛✪

LODI—AAA NORTHERN CALIFORNIA NEVADA & UTAH, 2715 W KETTLEMAN LN #201, 95242. WEEKDAYS (M-F) 9:00-6:00 (SAT: SALES BY APPT ONLY). (209) 366-6900 ✛✪

LOS BANOS—AAA NORTHERN CALIFORNIA NEVADA & UTAH, 1451 W PACHECO BLVD #H, 93635. WEEKDAYS (M-F) 9:00-6:00, SAT 9:00-5:00. (209) 827-5000 ✛✪

LOS GATOS—AAA NORTHERN CALIFORNIA NEVADA & UTAH, 15450 LOS GATOS BLVD #300, 95032. WEEKDAYS (M-F) 9:00-6:00 (SAT: SALES BY APPT ONLY). (408) 399-8400 ✚ ▲ ○

MADERA—AAA NORTHERN CALIFORNIA NEVADA & UTAH, 221 N G ST, 93637. WEEKDAYS (M-F) 9:00-6:00 (SAT: SALES BY APPT ONLY). (559) 662-4700 ✚ ○

MANTECA—AAA NORTHERN CALIFORNIA NEVADA & UTAH, 190 COMMERCE AVE #101, 95336. WEEKDAYS (M-F) 9:00-6:00. (209) 824-6100 ✚ ○ ▣

MENLO PARK—AAA NORTHERN CALIFORNIA NEVADA & UTAH, 65 EL CAMINO REAL, 94025. WEEKDAYS (M-F) 9:00-6:00, SAT 9:00-5:00. (650) 798-3200 ✚ ▲ ○

MERCED—AAA NORTHERN CALIFORNIA NEVADA & UTAH, 3065 M ST, 95348. WEEKDAYS (M-F) 9:00-6:00 (SAT: SALES BY APPT ONLY). (209) 726-7440 ✚ ○

MILL VALLEY—AAA NORTHERN CALIFORNIA NEVADA & UTAH, 750 REDWOOD HWY STE 1210, 94941. WEEKDAYS (M-F) 9:00-6:00 (SAT: SALES BY APPT ONLY). (415) 380-6000 ✚ ▲ ○

MILPITAS—AAA NORTHERN CALIFORNIA NEVADA & UTAH, 607 E CALAVERAS BLVD #607, 95035. WEEKDAYS (M-F) 9:00-6:00, SAT 9:00-5:00. (408) 635-0100 ✚ ▲ ○

MODESTO—AAA NORTHERN CALIFORNIA NEVADA & UTAH, 3525 COFFEE RD, 95355. WEEKDAYS (M-F) 9:00-6:00 (SAT: SALES BY APPT ONLY). (209) 530-2600 ✚ ▲ ○

MONTEREY—AAA NORTHERN CALIFORNIA NEVADA & UTAH, 53 SOLEDAD DR, 93940. WEEKDAYS (M-F) 9:00-6:00 (SAT: SALES BY APPT ONLY). (831) 645-1900 ✚ ▲ ○

MOUNTAIN VIEW—AAA NORTHERN CALIFORNIA NEVADA & UTAH, 900 MIRAMONTE AVE, 94040. WEEKDAYS (M-F) 9:00-6:00, SAT 9:00-5:00. (650) 623-3200 ✚ ▲ ○

NEWARK—AAA NORTHERN CALIFORNIA NEVADA & UTAH, 39600 BALENTINE DR, 94560. WEEKDAYS (M-F) 9:00-6:00, SAT 9:00-5:00. (510) 360-3300 ✚ ▲ ○

OAKLAND—AAA NORTHERN CALIFORNIA NEVADA & UTAH, 1982 PLEASANT VALLEY AV#A, 94611. WEEKDAYS (M-F) 9:00-6:00, SAT 9:00-5:00. (510) 350-2042 ✚ ▲ ○

OROVILLE—AAA NORTHERN CALIFORNIA NEVADA & UTAH, 2024-A ORO DAM BLVD E, 95966. WEEKDAYS (M-F) 9:00-6:00, SAT 9:00-5:00. (530) 538-8900 ✚ ○

PETALUMA—AAA NORTHERN CALIFORNIA NEVADA & UTAH, 111 LYNCH CREEK WAY, 94954. WEEKDAYS (M-F) 9:00-6:00 (SAT: SALES BY APPT ONLY). (707) 781-6700 ✚ ▲ ○

PINOLE—AAA NORTHERN CALIFORNIA NEVADA & UTAH, 1202 FITZGERALD DR, 94564. WEEKDAYS (M-F) 9:00-6:00, SAT 9:00-5:00. (510) 262-4900 ✚ ▲ ○

PLACERVILLE—AAA NORTHERN CALIFORNIA NEVADA & UTAH, 3979 MISSOURI FLAT RD#120, 95667. WEEKDAYS (M-F) 9:00-6:00 (SAT: SALES BY APPT ONLY). (530) 295-6600 ✚ ▲ ○

PLEASANT HILL—AAA NORTHERN CALIFORNIA NEVADA & UTAH, 2390 MONUMENT BLVD STE A, 94523. WEEKDAYS (M-F) 9:00-6:00, SAT 9:00-5:00. (925) 288-3700 ✚ ○

REDDING—AAA NORTHERN CALIFORNIA NEVADA & UTAH, 943 MISSION DE ORO DR, 96003. WEEKDAYS (M-F) 9:00-6:00 (SAT: SALES BY APPT ONLY). (530) 722-1600 ✚ ▲ ○

REDWOOD CITY—AAA NORTHERN CALIFORNIA NEVADA & UTAH, 510 VETERANS BLVD STE A, 94063. WEEKDAYS (M-F) 9:00-6:00, SAT 9:00-5:00. (650) 216-3100 ✚ ▲ ○

ROSEVILLE—AAA NORTHERN CALIFORNIA NEVADA & UTAH, 1161 GALLERIA BLVD, 95678. WEEKDAYS (M-F) 8:30-5:30, SAT 9:00-5:00. (916) 724-0200 ✚ ▲ ○

ROSEVILLE—AAA NORTHERN CALIFORNIA NEVADA & UTAH, 1161 GALLERIA CIRCLE, 95678. WEEKDAYS (M-F) 7:30-5:30, SAT 8:00-5:00. (916) 724-1020 ◖

ROSEVILLE—AAA NORTHERN CALIFORNIA NEVADA & UTAH, 1850 DOUGLAS BLVD STE 406, 95661. WEEKDAYS (M-F) 9:00-6:00 (SAT: SALES BY APPT ONLY). (916) 724-0320 ✚ ▲ ○

SACRAMENTO—AAA NORTHERN CALIFORNIA NEVADA & UTAH, 1056 FLORIN RD, 95831. WEEKDAYS (M-F) 9:00-6:00, SAT 9:00-5:00. (916) 288-2000 ✚ ▲ ○

SACRAMENTO—AAA NORTHERN CALIFORNIA NEVADA & UTAH, 2216 FAIR OAKS BLVD, 95825. WEEKDAYS (M-F) 9:00-6:00, SAT 9:00-5:00. (916) 379-1300 ✚ ▲ ○

SACRAMENTO—AAA NORTHERN CALIFORNIA NEVADA & UTAH, 2701 DEL PASO RD STE 100, 95835. WEEKDAYS (M-F) 9:00-6:00, SAT 9:00-5:00. (916) 574-8700 ✚ ○

SACRAMENTO—AAA NORTHERN CALIFORNIA NEVADA & UTAH, 621 CAPITOL MALL, STE 118, 95814. WEEKDAYS (M-F) 8:00-5:00 (SAT: SALES BY APPT ONLY). (916) 658-4900 ✚ ○

SALINAS—AAA NORTHERN CALIFORNIA NEVADA & UTAH, 1019 POST DR, 93907. WEEKDAYS (M-F) 9:00-6:00, SAT 9:00-5:00. (831) 771-4000 ✚ ○

SAN FRANCISCO—AAA NORTHERN CALIFORNIA NEVADA & UTAH, 1585 SLOAT BLVD, 94132. WEEKDAYS (M-F) 9:00-6:00, SAT 9:00-5:00. (415) 682-3400 ✚ ▲ ○

SAN FRANCISCO—AAA NORTHERN CALIFORNIA NEVADA & UTAH, 160 SUTTER ST, 94104. WEEKDAYS (M-F) 9:00-6:00 (SAT: SALES BY APPT ONLY). (415) 773-1900 ✚ ○

SAN FRANCISCO—AAA NORTHERN CALIFORNIA NEVADA & UTAH, 2300 16TH ST STE 280, 94103. WEEKDAYS (M-F) 9:00-6:00, SAT 9:00-5:00. (415) 553-7200 ✚ ▲ ○ ▣

SAN FRANCISCO—AAA NORTHERN CALIFORNIA NEVADA & UTAH, 599 CLEMENT ST, 94118. WEEKDAYS (M-F) 9:00-6:00 (SAT: SALES BY APPT ONLY). (415) 750-7800 ▮ ▲ ○

SAN JOSE—AAA NORTHERN CALIFORNIA NEVADA & UTAH, 1035 E BROKAW RD STE 10, 95131. WEEKDAYS (M-F) 8:30-5:30, SAT 8:00-5:00. (408) 436-7373 ◖

SAN JOSE—AAA NORTHERN CALIFORNIA NEVADA & UTAH, 1035 E BROKAW RD STE 10, 95131. WEEKDAYS (M-F) 8:30-5:30, SAT 8:00-5:00. (408) 436-7300 ✚ ▲ ○

SAN JOSE—AAA NORTHERN CALIFORNIA NEVADA & UTAH, 1779 EAST CAPITOL EXY D0A, 95121. WEEKDAYS (M-F) 9:00-6:00, SAT 9:00-5:00. (408) 574-2300 ✚ ○

SAN JOSE—AAA NORTHERN CALIFORNIA NEVADA & UTAH, 5026 ALMADEN EXPWY #10, 95118. WEEKDAYS (M-F) 9:00-6:00, SAT 9:00-5:00. (408) 448-5900 ✚ ▲ ○

SAN JOSE—AAA NORTHERN CALIFORNIA NEVADA & UTAH, 5120 STEVENS CREEK BLVD, 95129. WEEKDAYS (M-F) 9:00-6:00, SAT 9:00-5:00. (408) 551-4900 ✚ ▲ ○

SAN JOSE—AAA NORTHERN CALIFORNIA NEVADA & UTAH, 5291 PROSPECT RD, 95129. WEEKDAYS (M-F) 9:00-6:00 (SAT: SALES BY APPT ONLY). (408) 725-4300 ✚ ▲ ○

SAN RAFAEL—AAA NORTHERN CALIFORNIA NEVADA & UTAH, 99 SMITH RANCH RD, 94903. WEEKDAYS (M-F) 9:00-6:00 (SAT: SALES BY APPT ONLY). (415) 488-2900 ✚ ▲ ○

SAN RAMON—AAA NORTHERN CALIFORNIA NEVADA & UTAH, 2435 SAN RAMON VLY BLVD#5, 94583. WEEKDAYS (M-F) 9:00-6:00 (SAT: SALES BY APPT ONLY). (925) 314-2600 ✚ ▲ ○

SANTA ROSA—AAA NORTHERN CALIFORNIA NEVADA & UTAH, 1501 FARMERS LN, 95405. WEEKDAYS (M-F) 9:00-6:00, SAT 9:00-5:00. (707) 566-4000 ✚ ▲ ○

SANTA ROSA—AAA NORTHERN CALIFORNIA NEVADA & UTAH, 2180 MENDOCINO AVE, 95401. WEEKDAYS (M-F) 9:00-6:00, SAT 9:00-5:00. (707) 543-5300 ✚ ▲ ○

SONOMA—AAA NORTHERN CALIFORNIA NEVADA & UTAH, 650 2ND ST W, 95476. WEEKDAYS (M-F) 9:00-6:00 (SAT: SALES BY APPT ONLY). (707) 528-5900 ✚ ▲ ○

SONORA—AAA NORTHERN CALIFORNIA NEVADA & UTAH, 1071 SANGUINETTI RD, 95370. WEEKDAYS (M-F) 9:00-6:00 (SAT: SALES BY APPT ONLY). (209) 536-2540 ✚ ○

STOCKTON—AAA NORTHERN CALIFORNIA NEVADA & UTAH, 10916 TRINITY PKWY STE A, 95219. WEEKDAYS (M-F) 9:00-6:00, SAT 9:00-5:00. (209) 475-3400 ✚ ▲ ○

TRACY—AAA NORTHERN CALIFORNIA NEVADA & UTAH, 2102 W GRANT LINE RD, 95377. WEEKDAYS (M-F) 9:00-6:00 (SAT: SALES BY APPT ONLY). (209) 833-5900 ✛ ▲ ✺

TRUCKEE—AAA NORTHERN CALIFORNIA NEVADA & UTAH, 11200 DONNER PASS RD #E3, 96161. WEEKDAYS (M-F) 9:00-6:00 (SAT: SALES BY APPT ONLY). (530) 550-2060 ✛ ✺

TURLOCK—AAA NORTHERN CALIFORNIA NEVADA & UTAH, 3180 HOTEL DR, 95380. WEEKDAYS (M-F) 9:00-6:00 (SAT: SALES BY APPT ONLY). (209) 656-3060 ✛ ▲ ✺

UKIAH—AAA NORTHERN CALIFORNIA NEVADA & UTAH, 601 KINGS CT, 95482. WEEKDAYS (M-F) 9:00-6:00 (SAT: SALES BY APPT ONLY). (707) 463-3000 ✛ ▲ ✺

VACAVILLE—AAA NORTHERN CALIFORNIA NEVADA & UTAH, 1633 E MONTE VISTA AVE, 95688. WEEKDAYS (M-F) 9:00-6:00, SAT 9:00-5:00. (707) 451-7150 ✛ ▲ ✺

VALLEJO—AAA NORTHERN CALIFORNIA NEVADA & UTAH, 1183 ADMIRAL CALLAGHAN LN, 94591. WEEKDAYS (M-F) 9:00-6:00, SAT 9:00-5:00. (707) 551-3500 ✛ ▲ ✺

WALNUT CREEK—AAA NORTHERN CALIFORNIA NEVADA & UTAH, 1276 S CALIFORNIA BLVD, 94596. WEEKDAYS (M-F) 9:00-6:00 (SAT: SALES BY APPT ONLY). (925) 287-7600 ✛ ▲ ✺ ▣

WALNUT CREEK—AAA NORTHERN CALIFORNIA NEVADA & UTAH, 1277 TREAT BLVD STE 1000, 94597. WEEKDAYS (M-F) 8:00-5:30. (925) 274-8400 ✺

WATSONVILLE—AAA NORTHERN CALIFORNIA NEVADA & UTAH, 1195 S GREEN VALLEY RD, 95076. WEEKDAYS (M-F) 9:00-6:00 (SAT: SALES BY APPT ONLY). (831) 768-4540 ✛ ✺

WOODLAND—AAA NORTHERN CALIFORNIA NEVADA & UTAH, 95 W LINCOLN AVE, 95695. WEEKDAYS (M-F) 9:00-6:00 (SAT: SALES BY APPT ONLY). (530) 406-3500 ✛ ✺

YREKA—AAA NORTHERN CALIFORNIA NEVADA & UTAH, 1876 FORT JONES RD, 96097. WEEKDAYS (M-F) 9:00-6:00 (SAT: SALES BY APPT ONLY). (530) 841-6340 ✛ ✺

YUBA CITY—AAA NORTHERN CALIFORNIA NEVADA & UTAH, 1290 STABLER LN STE 800, 95993. WEEKDAYS (M-F) 9:00-6:00, SAT 9:00-5:00. (530) 634-7800 ✛ ✺

Photo Credits

Page numbers are in bold type. Picture credit abbreviations are as follows:
- (i) numeric sequence from top to bottom, left to right ■ (AAA) AAA Travel library.

- **(Cover)** Lake Tahoe / © iStockphoto.com / MariuszBlach
- **2** (i) © iStockphoto.com / YinYang
- **2** (ii) © iStockphoto.com / gregobagel
- **2** (iii) © iStockphoto.com / nelik
- **2** (iv) © Dave Wilson / Grace Cathedral
- **8** (i) © iStockphoto.com / LeoPatrizi
- **8** (ii) © iStockphoto.com / YinYang
- **9** © iStockphoto.com / nelik
- **10** (i) North Wind Picture Archives / Alamy Stock Photo
- **10** (ii) © AAA / Inspector 511
- **13** (i) © iStockphoto.com / Srongkrod
- **13** (ii) © iStockphoto.com / NickLustPhotography
- **13** (iii) © AAA / Thuyvi Gates
- **13** (iv) © iStockphoto.com / zrfphoto
- **13** (v) © iStockphoto.com / Lucila10
- **14** (i) © iStockphoto.com / gregobagel
- **14** (ii) © iStockphoto.com / zrfphoto
- **14** (iii) © iStockphoto.com / robandrew
- **14** (iv) © iStockphoto.com / Csondy
- **242** © AAA / Thuyvi Gates
- **245** © iStockphoto.com / gypsyslice
- **246** © AAA/ Thuyvi Gates
- **247** © iStockphoto.com / jmoor17
- **248** © AAA / Thuyvi Gates

- **249** © AAA / Thuyvi Gates
- **250** © AAA / Thuyvi Gates
- **252** © AAA / Thuyvi Gates
- **253** © AAA / Thuyvi Gates
- **254** © AAA / Thuyvi Gates
- **255** © AAA / Thuyvi Gates
- **256** © AAA / Thuyvi Gates
- **257** © AAA / Thuyvi Gates
- **258** Courtesy of Wikimedia Commons / CC0
- **259** © Dianne Yee / flickr / CC BY ND
- **260** © iStockphoto.com / coleong
- **262** © iStockphoto.com / aimintang
- **263** © iStockphoto.com / LUNAMARINA
- **265** © AAA / Greg Weekes
- **266** © AAA / Thuyvi Gates
- **267** © AAA / Thuyvi Gates
- **268** © iStockphoto.com / Eric Broder Van Dyke
- **276** © iStockphoto.com / atosan
- **280** © AAA / Thuyvi Gates
- **281** © Dave Wilson / Grace Cathedral
- **283** © iStockphoto.com / amedved
- **284** © iStockphoto.com / noeliaSF
- **286** © AAA / Thuyvi Gates
- **288** © iStockphoto.com / NNehring

Use the free travel planning tools
at AAA.com/maps

Sit. Stay. Play.

Before you travel with pets, visit
AAA.com/PetTravel for information and ideas
to minimize the unexpected. Discover thousands of
pet friendly AAA-listed places to stay, play and dine.
Get practical tips to guide your decisions. And after
your trip, enter your favorite photo in the next
AAA Pet Travel Photo Contest.

Visit AAA.com/PetTravel

Contest entry open to U.S. residents only.

Make the Connction

For trip planning and local activities, AAA guidebooks are just the beginning.

Open the door to a whole lot more on **AAA.com**. Get extra travel insight, more information and online booking.

Find this symbol for places to look, book and save on AAA.com.